W9-AKU-895

Warman's
AMERICANA
& COLLECTIBLES

Volumes in the Encyclopedia of Antiques and Collectibles

Harry L. Rinker, Series Editor

Warman's Americana & Collectibles, 7th Edition,
edited by Harry L. Rinker

Warman's American Pottery & Porcelain,
by Susan and Al Bagdale

Warman's Coins & Currency,
by Allen G. Berman and Alex G. Malloy

Warman's Country Antiques & Collectibles, 2nd Edition,
by Dana Gehman Morykan and Harry L. Rinker

Warman's English & Continental Pottery & Porcelain, 2nd Edition,
by Susan and Al Bagdale

Warman's Furniture,
edited by Harry L. Rinker

Warman's Glass, 2nd Edition,
by Ellen Tischbein Schroy

Warman's Jewelry,
by Christie Romero

Warman's Oriental Antiques,
by Gloria and Robert Mascarelli

Warman's Paper,
by Norman E. Martinus and Harry L. Rinker

Warman's
AMERICANA
& COLLECTIBLES

7th EDITION

Edited by
HARRY L. RINKER

Wallace-Homestead Book Company
Radnor, Pennsylvania

EDITORIAL STAFF

HARRY L. RINKER
Editor

ELLEN T. SCHROY
Senior Editor

TERESE J. OSWALD
Associate Editor

DANA N. MORYKAN
Associate Editor

NANCY M. BUTT
Research Librarian

HARRY L. RINKER, JR.
Art Director

JOCELYN C. MOUSLEY, RICHARD SCHMELTZLE
Support Staff

BOARD OF ADVISORS

Franklin Arnall
The Collector
PO Box 253
Claremont, CA 91711
(909) 621-2461
Padlocks

Jeff Bartheld
14018 NE 85th St.
Elk River, MN 55330
(612) 441-7059
Spark Plugs

Dick Bitterman
1701 West Chase Ave.
Chicago, IL 60626
(312) 743-3330
*Flag Collectibles, Pens
and Pencils, Pin-Up Art*

Bob Block
PO Box 51
Milford, CT 06460
(203) 926-8448
Marbles

Stanley A. Block
PO Box 51
Trumball, CT 06611
(203) 261-0057
Marbles

Rick Botts
2545 SE 60th Ct.
Des Moines, IA 50317
(515) 265-8324
Jukeboxes

Lorie Cairns
Cairns Antiques
PO Box 44026
Lemoncove, CA 93244
(209) 564-2158
Labels

Tina M. Carter
882 S. Mollison Ave.
El Cajon, CA 92020
(619) 440-5043
Teapots

Kathie Diehl
PO Box 5672
Baltimore, MD 21210
(301) 243-3747
Little Golden Books

Craig Dinner
PO Box 4399
Sunnyside, NY 11104
(718) 729-3850
Figural, Bottle Openers

Marilyn Dipboye
33161 Wendy Dr.
Sterling Hts., MI 48315
(313) 264-0285
Cat Collectibles

Bruce Flamm
10445 Victoria Ave.
Riverside, CA 92503
Calculators

M. D. Fountain
201 Alvena
Wichita, KS 67203
(316) 943-1925
Swankyswigs

Roselyn Gerson
PO Box Letter 40
Lynbrook, NY 11563
Compacts

Ted Hake
Hake's Americana &
Collectibles
PO Box 1444
York, PA 17405
(717) 848-1333
*Disneyana, Political
Items*

v

Doris & Burdell Hall
B & B Antiques
PO Box 1501
Fairfield Bay, AR 72088
(501) 884-6571
Morton Potteries

Mrs. Mary Hamburg
20 Cedar St.
Danville, IL 61832
(217) 446-2323
Pig Collectibles

Tim Hughes
PO Box 3636
Williamsport, PA 17701
(717) 326-1045
Newspapers, Headline Editions

Joan Hull
1376 Nevada
Huron, SD 57350
(605) 352-1685
Hull Pottery

David and Sue Irons
Irons Antiques
223 Covered Bridge Rd.
Northampton, PA 18067
(610) 262-9335
Irons

Shad John Kvetko
3821 W. San Miguel
Phoeniz AZ 85019
(602) 589-0151
Funeral Memorabilia

Bob Levy
The Unique One
2802 Centre St.
Pennsauken NJ 08109
(609) 663-2554
Pinball Machines, Slot Machines, Vending Machines

Ron Lieberman
The Family Album
RD #1, Box 42
Glen Rock, PA 17327
(717) 235-2134
Books

Richard W. Massiglia
380 Medford St.
Somerville, MA 02145
(617) 625-4067
Elephant Collectibles

Patricia McDaniel
Old Storefront Antiques
PO Box 357
Dublin, IN 47335
(317) 478-4809
Drugstore Collectibles

Nancy McMichael
PO Box 53132
Washington, DC, 20009
Snowdomes

Jocelyn C. Mousley
137 South Main St.
Quakertown, PA 18951
(215) 536-9211
Dog Collectibles

Joan Collett Oates
685 S. Washington
Constantine, MI 49042
(616) 435-8353
Phoenix Bird Pattern

Clark Phelps
Amusement Sales
127 North Main
Midvale, UT 84047
(801) 255-4731
Punchboards

Ferill J. Rice
302 Pheasant Run
Kaukauna, WI 54130
Fenton

Harry L. Rinker
5093 Vera Cruz Rd.
Emmaus PA 18049
(610) 965-1122
Canal Collectibles

Harry L. Rinker, Jr.
5093 Vera Cruz Rd.
Emmaus PA 18049
(610) 965-1122
World War II

Christie Romero
PO Box 424
Anaheim, CA 92815-0424
Jewelry, Costume

Jim and Nancy Schaut
Box 10781
Glendale, AZ 85318
(602) 878-4293
Horse Collectibles

Virginia R. Scott
275 Milledge Terrace
Athens, GA 30606
(404) 548-5966
Candlewick

Richard Shields
The Carolina Trader
PO Box 769
Monroe, NC 28112
(704) 289-1604
Scouting

George Theofiles
Miscellaneous Man
Box 1776
New Freedom, PA 17349
(717) 235-4766
Posters

Dixie Trainer
25 Falls Rd.
Roxbury, CT 06783
(203) 355-1575
Souvenir Buildings

Bill Utley
PO Box 4095
Tustin CA 92681
(714) 730-1250
Flashlights

Lewis S. Walters
2640 Washington St.
Allentown, PA 18104
(215) 820-5088
Radios

Maret Webb
4118 E. Vernon Ave.
Phoenix, AZ 85008-2333
(602) 957-6294
Swarovski Crystal

Kathy Wojciechowski
PO Box 230
Peotone, IL 60468
Nippon

Estelle Zalkin
7524 West Treasure Dr.
Miami Beach, FL 33141
(305) 864-3012
Thimbles

INTRODUCTION

Welcome to *Warman's Americana & Collectibles*, the cornerstone of the Warman's Encyclopedia of Antiques and Collectibles. In 1984 the first edition of *Warman's Americana & Collectibles* introduced the collecting community to category introductions featuring collecting hints, history, references, periodicals, and reproduction and copycat information complemented by detailed, accurate listings and values. As a result of the enthusiastic acceptance to this format, it was extended to *Warman's Antiques and Collectibles Price Guide* and ultimately to volumes in the Warman's Encyclopedia of Antiques and Collectibles.

Warman's Americana and Collectibles was a pioneering work, the first general price guide to mass–produced, twentieth–century objects. It helped define and solidify the modern collectibles market. As the collectibles market has matured, so has *Warman's Americana and Collectibles*. If you have a copy of the first edition, compare the categories listed in it to those found in this seventh edition. Times *have* changed. Perhaps this is why so many individuals find the collectibles market so exciting.

Collectibles are the things with which your parents, you, and your children have played and lived. The things that belonged to your grandparents are now *antiques*. The evolution of an object from new to desirable to collectible to antique within one's lifetime, i.e., an approximately fifty-year span, is difficult for some to accept. However, it is reality.

Warman's Americana & Collectibles takes you on a nostalgic trip down memory lane. Do not get angry about the things you or your parents discarded. Be thrilled by the value of the things that were saved. Do not hesitate to buy back the things from your childhood that evoke pleasant memories. As you do, you will find that the real value of objects is not monetary, but the joy that comes from collecting, owning, and, most importantly, playing and living with them once again.

Finally, do not ever be embarrassed by what you collect. *Warman's Americana & Collectibles* is based on the premise that it is acceptable to collect anything you wish. Remember one simple fact: All of today's antiques were collectibles in the past.

WHAT IS A COLLECTIBLE?

As the twentieth century nears its end, the definition of what constitutes an antique is becoming clearer and what is a collectible more confusing. Part of the confusion rests within myself. I am not yet ready to admit that I am an antique.

An antique is anything made before 1945. A great many individuals in the antiques and collectibles field disagree with this definition, but with each passing year it becomes harder and harder to deny that it is fact. The key is the war years of 1942–1945. During this period, production switched from domestic to wartime products. When the war ended, things were different. American life and expectations were very different in 1948 than in 1938. New war technology turned to civilian use was partially responsible. However, the most telling fact of all is that well over half the population living in America today was born after 1945 and approximately two–thirds grew up in the post–1945 era.

Keeping this in mind and seeking technical definitions, a collectible then becomes an object made between 1945 and 1962 and a desirable an object made after 1962. The difference between a collectible and a desirable is that a collectible has a clearly established secondary market while desirables exist in a market rampant with speculation.

Actually the post–1945 era is breaking down into three distinct collecting periods: 1945–1962; 1962–1980; and post–1980. Goods in the 1962 to 1980 period are moving out of their speculative mode to one of price stability.

As a pre–baby boomer, I am not ready to admit that I am antique. As a writer in the trade, I am still trying to get the majority of antiques dealers to admit the twentieth century exists; a number are now willing to mumble "1915" under their breath.

Within the Warman's Encyclopedia of Antiques and Collectibles, *Warman's Americana & Collectibles* is the volume designed to deal with objects from the twentieth century. Three criteria help define what objects appear: (1) mass produced; (2) made in the twentieth century, preferably after 1945; and (3) the majority of the items in each category must sell between a few pennies and two hundred dollars. The ideal collectible fits all three qualifications.

There is a fourth factor: attitude. I collect things relating to the American canal movement. As a result, I own a number of pieces of dark blue English Staffordshire which were made when the Erie Canal was completed in the mid–1820s. Staffordshire of this type is considered a blue chip antique, but I collect it primarily for its "canal–related" value. Does this make it a collectible rather than an antique? In my eyes and mind it does.

Since collecting antiques became fashionable in the early twentieth century, there have been attempts to define certain groups of objects as "true" antiques, worthy of sophisticated collectors, and to ignore the remaining items. Most museums clearly demonstrate this attitude. Where do early twentieth century tin toys, toy soldiers, or dolls fit? Those made before 1915 are antique. No one argues this any longer. Those made between 1920 and 1940 are in transition. We designate them "prestige" collectibles, objects changing in people's minds from collectible to antique.

In reality these divisions are artificial and deserve to be broken down. Today's Star Wars items, if properly preserved, will someday be over one hundred years old. They may be a much better key to interpreting life in the twentieth century than the Knoll furniture now found on pedestals in leading museums in the United States.

In summary, collectibles are the objects with which you and your children have played and lived. As mentioned previously, your grandparents' things are antiques. Your parents' objects are in transition—a few already in the antiques category, about one–third classified as prestige collectibles, and the remainder still collectibles.

INTERNATIONAL MARKET

Collectibles began to draw worldwide interest at the end of the 1980s. All of a sudden American buyers found themselves competing with buyers from Europe and Japan on their home turf. In head to head competition, the American buyers frequently lost. How can this be explained?

The most dominant portion of the 1990s collectibles market is post–World War II material. During this period, the youth of the world fell under three dominant influences: American movies, music, and television. As the generations of the 1950s, 1960s, and even 1970s reached adulthood and started buying back their childhood, many of the things they remember and want have American associations.

America is the great motherlode of post–war collectibles. At the moment it is packages and boxes of American collectibles that are being sent abroad. It will not be too much longer before the volume reaches container loads.

American collectors also are expanding their horizons. They recognize that many objects within their favorite collectible category were licensed abroad. They view their collections as incomplete without such examples. Objects are obtained by either traveling abroad or by purchasing through mail or auction from foreign sources.

PRICE NOTES

Prices in the collectibles field are not as firmly established as in the antiques area. Nevertheless, we do not use ranges unless we feel they are absolutely necessary.

Our pricing is based on an object being in very good condition. If otherwise, we note this in our description. It would be ideal to suggest that mint, or unused, examples of all objects do exist. Objects from the past were used, whether they be glass, china, dolls, or toys. Because of this use, some normal wear must be expected. Furthermore, if the original box is important in establishing a price, it is assumed that the box is present with the article.

The biggest problem in the collectibles field is that an object may have more than one price. A George Eastman bubble gum card may be worth one dollar to a bubble gum card collector, but thirty–five dollars to a collector of photographic memorabilia. I saw the same card marked both ways. In preparing prices for this guide we have looked at the object within the category being considered. Hence, a "girly" matchcover sells for twenty–five to fifty cents to a matchcover collector and two to five dollars to a pin–up art collector. However, if all you can find are matchcover collectors, take the quarter and move on.

Some collectibles do have regional interest. However, a national price consensus has formed as a result of the publication of specialized price guides, collectors' club newsletters, and magazines and newspapers. This guide also has contributed to breaking down regional pricing.

ORGANIZATION OF THE BOOK

Listings: We have attempted to make the listings descriptive enough so the specific object can be identified. Most guides limit their descriptions to one line, but not *Warman's*. We have placed emphasis on those items which are actively being sold in the marketplace. Nevertheless, some harder–to–find objects are included in order to demonstrate the market spread. A few categories in this book also appear in *Warman's Antiques and Collectibles Price Guide*. The individual listings, however, seldom overlap except for a few minor instances. It is our intention to show the low to middle price range of a category in *Warman's Americana & Collectibles* and the middle to upper range in our main antiques guide, *Warman's Antiques and Collectibles Price Guide*, thus creating two true companion lists for the general dealer or collector.

Collecting Hints: This section calls attention to specific hints as they relate to the category. We note where cross–category collecting and nostalgia are critical in pricing. Clues are given to spotting reproductions. In most cases, we just scratch the surface. We encourage collectors to consult specialized publications.

History: Here we discuss the category, describe how the object was made, who are or were the leading manufacturers, and the variations of form and style. In many instances a chronology for the object is established. Finally, we place the object in a social context—how it was used, for what purpose, etc.

References: A few general references are listed to encourage collectors to learn more about their objects. Included are author, title, most recent edition, publisher (if published by a small firm or individual, we have indicated "published by author"), and a date of publication.

Finding these books may present a problem. The antiques and collectibles field is blessed with a dedicated core of book dealers who stock these specialized publications. You may find them at flea markets, antiques shows, and through their advertisements in leading publications in the field. Many dealers publish annual or semi–annual catalogs. Ask to be put on their mailing lists. Books go out–of–print quickly, yet many books printed over twenty–five years ago remain the standard work in a field. Also, haunt used book dealers for collectible reference material.

Collectors' Clubs: The large number of collectors' clubs adds vitality to the collectibles field. Their publications and conventions produce knowledge which often cannot be found anywhere else. Many of these clubs are short lived; others are so strong that they have regional and local chapters.

Periodicals: In respect to the collectibles field, there are certain general monthly periodicals to which the general collector should subscribe:

Antiques & Collecting Hobbies, 1006 South Michigan Avenue, Chicago, IL 60605.

Collectors' Showcase, 7130 South Lewis, Suite 210, Tulsa, OK 74136.

The Inside Collector, PO Box 98, Elmont, NY 11003.

There are also a number of specialized collectible periodicals, e.g., *Antique Toy World* (PO Box 34509, Chicago, IL 60634). Special attention is directed toward the publications of Krause Publications, Inc., (700 East State Street, Iola, WI 54945), especially *Toy Shop.*

Although no weekly publication is devoted exclusively to collectibles, *The Antique Trader Weekly* (Box 1050, Dubuque, IA 52001) and *Antique Week* (PO Box 90, Knightstown, IN 46148) extensively cover the range of items listed in this book. Specialized auctions of prestige collectibles are regularly reported in depth in the *Maine Antique Digest* (Box 358, Waldoboro, ME 04572).

Museums: The best way to study a specific field is to see as many documented examples as possible. For this reason, we have listed museums where significant collections of collectibles are on display. Special attention must be directed to the Margaret Woodbury Strong Museum in Rochester, New York, and the Smithsonian Institution's Museum of American History in Washington, D.C.

Reproductions: Reproductions are a major concern, especially with any item related to advertising. Most reproductions are unmarked; the newness of their appearance is often the best clue to uncovering them. Where "Reproduction Alert" appears, a watchful eye should be kept within the entire category.

Reproductions are only one aspect of the problem; outright fakes are another. Unscrupulous manufacturers make fantasy items which never existed, e.g., a Hopalong Cassidy guitar from the non–existent Jefferson Musical Toys.

RESEARCH

Collectors of the categories found in this book deserve credit for their attention to scholarship and the skill by which they have assembled their collections. This book attests to how strong and encompassing the collectibles market has become through their efforts.

We obtain our prices from many key sources—dealers, publications, auctions, collectors, and field work. The generosity with which dealers have given advice is a credit to the field. Everyone recognizes the need for a guide that is specific and has accurate prices. We study newspapers, magazines, newsletters, and other publications in the collectibles and antiques field. All of them are critical in understanding what is available in the market. Special recognition must be given to those collectors' club newsletters and magazines which discuss prices.

Our staff is constantly in the field—from Massachusetts to Florida, Pennsylvania to California. Our Board of Advisors provides regional as well as specialized information. Over one hundred specialized auctions are held annually, and their results provided to our office. Finally, private collectors have worked closely with us, sharing their knowledge of price trends and developments unique to their specialties.

BUYER'S GUIDE, NOT SELLER'S GUIDE

Warman's Americana and Collectibles is designed to be a buyer's guide, a guide to what you would have to pay to purchase an object on the open market from a dealer or collector. **It is not a seller's guide to prices.** People frequently make this mistake and are deceiving themselves by doing so.

If you have an object in this book and wish to sell it, you should expect to receive approximately 35 to 40% of the values listed. If the object cannot be resold quickly, expect to receive even less. The truth is simple. Knowing to whom to sell an object is worth 50% or more of its value. Buyers are very specialized; dealers work for years to assemble a list of collectors who will pay top dollar for an item.

Examine your piece as objectively as possible. If it is something from your childhood, try to step back from the personal memories in evaluating its condition. As an antiques appraiser, I spend a great deal of my time telling people their treasures are not "gold," but items readily available in the marketplace.

In respect to buying and selling, a simple philosophy is that a good purchase occurs when both the buyer and seller are happy with the price. Don't look back. Hindsight has little value in the collectibles field. Given time, things tend to balance out.

WHERE TO BUY COLLECTIBLES

The collectible has become standard auction house fare in the 1990s. Christie's East (219 East 67th Street, New York, NY 10021) and Sotheby's (1334 York Avenue, New York, NY 10021) conduct collectibles sales several times each year. Specialized auction firms, e.g., Lloyd Ralston Toys (447 Stratfield Road, Fairfield, CT 06432) in toys and James Julia, Inc., (PO Box 830, Fairfield, MA, 04937) in advertising, toys, and a host of other categories, have proven the viability of the collectible as a focal point.

The major collectibles marketing thrust continues to be the mail auction, either with material on consignment or directly owned. Hake's Americana & Collectibles (PO Box 1444, York, PA 17405) is the leading mail auction. Hake's is being challenged by Debby and Marty Krim's New England Auction Gallery (PO Box 2273, Peabody, MA 01960), Smith House Toy Sales (PO Box 336, Eliot, ME 03903), and a host of others. A recent development is the mail auction conducted through classified and display advertising in trade periodicals.

Direct sale catalogs abound. Most major categories have one or more. These dealers and many more advertise in periodicals and collectors' clubs' newsletters. Most require an annual fee to receive their catalogs.

Of course, there is an unlimited number of flea markets, estate and country auctions, church bazaars, and garage sales. However, if you are a specialized collector, you may spend days looking for something to add to your collection. If you add in your time to the cost of the object, its real cost will be much higher than the purchase price.

All of which brings us to the final source, the specialized dealer. The collectibles field is so broad that dealers do specialize. Find the dealers who handle your material and work with them to build your collection.

BOARD OF ADVISORS

Our Board of Advisors are dealers, authors, collectors and leaders of collectors' clubs from throughout the United States. All are dedicated to accuracy in description and pricing. If you wish to buy or sell an object in their field of expertise, drop them a note. Please include a stamped, self–addressed envelope with all correspondence. If time or interest permits, they will respond.

We now list the names of our advisors at the end of their respective categories. Their full mailing addresses and often their phone numbers are in the front of this book.

COMMENTS INVITED

Warman's Americana & Collectibles is a major effort to deal with a complex field. Our readers are encouraged to send their comments and suggestions to Rinker Enterprises, 5093 Vera Cruz Road, Emmaus, PA 18049.

ACKNOWLEDGMENTS

After twelve years, *Warman's Americana & Collectibles* continues to enjoy the unique distinction of being the only general price devoted exclusively to things made in the 20th century. It is one of the few general price guides that has gone without formal opposition for over a decade.

There are two principal reasons—you, the users, and the skilled staff of Rinker Enterprises, Inc., that assembles the introductory information and price descriptions and listings that constitute this book. Let me begin by thanking those of who have supported *Warman's Americana & Collectibles* through six editions. Your loyalty is deeply appreciated by the Rinkettes and myself. Your sharing of information, cooperation when asked to allow us to photograph your objects, and willingness to share praise and criticism has made *Warman's Americana & Collectibles* as much your book as it is mine.

I also want to extend my thanks to the auctioneers, auction houses, trade papers, collectors' clubs, collectors, and dealers who provided the data for the listing descriptions and prices. None of these individuals received any compensation for their contributions. They provided the information because of their commitment to the trade and desire to see that the most accurate information possible is made available to the users of this book. The names and addresses of some of these individuals and organizations appear in the front of the book and in the category heads. Many receive no acknowledgment, nor do they demand it. A general thanks to all. You know who you are and so do we at Rinker Enterprises, Inc. You represent the best and finest in the trade. We look forward to working with you in the future.

The two years that have transpired between the preparation of the sixth and seventh editions of this work have been busy years for the Rinkettes. The manuscript for *Warman's Country, 2nd Edition*, *Warman's Paper*, and the twenty-eight and twenty-ninth editions of *Warman's Antiques and Collectibles Price Guide* were completed. The Rinkettes expanded their editorial activities by providing monthly copy for *Collector News* and *Collector*. The Rinkettes held the fort as I entered into several television and radio ventures.

Rinker Enterprises, Inc., operates on a team concept. Although my name is on the cover of this book as editor, every Rinkette played a major role in its preparation. Ellen Schroy served as clerk of the works. Dana Morykan and Terese Oswald handled the responsibility of doing the listings. Harry Rinker, Junior, is responsible for most of the photography and artwork. Nancy Butt reviewed and updated the reference and collectors' club listings.

I appreciate the patience that the employees of Chilton Books, parent company of the Wallace-Homestead and Warman titles, especially Edna Jones and Troy Vozzella, showed in allowing us the necessary time to prepare a manuscript of which we all can be proud. Good things simply cannot be rushed.

It is hard to believe that we are halfway through the 1990s. The twenty-first century is five years away. Things are changing. Within the next two years look for antiques and collectibles data to become more and more linked to the information superhighway and CD-ROM technology. Rinker Enterprises, Inc., is taking a pioneering role in several projects in both sectors.

In the back of my mind, there is a weak voice saying this seventh edition of *Warman's Americana & Collectibles* will be the last edition in the traditional format that has marked the book through its formulative years. The eight edition will be very different. Perhaps this is as it should be. *Warman's Americana and Collectibles* is now a teenager. It is time for a major growth spurt.

Enjoy this seventh edition and look forward to the eighth. I promise you that it will be far different from the book you now hold in your hand. No, I am not going to tell you in advance what is coming. A little mystery in life is a good thing.

5093 Vera Cruz Road   Harry L. Rinker
Emmaus, PA 18049   Editor
                                                   October 1995

AUCTION HOUSES

The following auction houses cooperate with Rinker Enterprises, Inc., by providing catalogues of their auctions and price lists. This information is used to prepare *Warman's Antiques and Collectibles Price Guide*, volumes in the Warman's Encyclopedia of Antiques and Collectibles, and Wallace-Homestead Book Company publications. This support is most appreciated.

Sanford Alderfer Auction
Company
501 Fairgrounds Rd.
Hatfield, PA 19440
(215) 368-5477

Andre Ammelounx
PO Box 136
Palatine, IL 60078
(708) 991-5927

Al Anderson
PO Box 644
Troy, OH 45373
(513) 339-0850

Ark Antiques
Box 3133
New Haven, CT 06515
(203) 387-3754

Arthur Auctioneering
RD 2
Hughesville, PA 17737
(717) 584-3697

Noel Barrett Antiques and
Auctions Ltd.
PO Box 1001
Carversville, PA 18913
(215) 297-5109

Robert F. Batchelder
1 West Butler Ave.
Ambler, PA 19002
(215) 643-1430

Biders Antiques, Inc.
241 South Union St.
Lawrence, MA 01843
(508) 688-4347

The Bottle Mine
Western Glass Auctions
PO Box 28
New Brighton, PA 15066
(412) 843-0622

Butterfield & Butterfield
7601 Sunset Blvd.
Los Angeles, CA 90046
(213) 850-7500

Butterfield & Butterfield
220 San Bruno Ave.
San Francisco, CA 94103
(415) 861-7500

W. E. Channing & Co.
53 Old Santa Fe Trail
Santa Fe, New Mexico 87501
(505) 988-1078

Christie's
502 Park Ave.
New York, NY 10022
(212) 546-1000

Christie's East
219 E. 67th St.
New York, NY 10021
(212) 606-0400

Christmas Morning
1850 Crown Rd. Suite 1111
Dallas, TX 75234
(817) 236-1155

Cincinnati Art Galleries
635 Main St.
Cincinnati, OH 45202
(513) 381-2128

Clinton-Ivankovich Auction
Co. Inc.
PO Box 29
Ottisville, PA 18942
(215) 847-5432

Cobb's Doll Auctions
1909 Harrison Rd. N.
Johnstown, OH 43031
(614) 964-0444

Cohasco, Inc.
Postal 821
Yonkers, NY 10702
(914) 476-8500

Marvin Cohen Auctions
Box 425, Routes 20 & 22
New Lebanon, NY 12125
(518) 794-9333

Collector's Auction Services
PO Box 13732
Seneca, PA 16346
(814) 677-6070

Marlin G. Denlinger
RR 3, Box 3775
Morrisville, VT 05661
(802) 888-2774

William Doyle Galleries, Inc.
175 E. 87th St.
New York, NY 10128
(212) 427-2730

Dunbars Gallery
76 Haven St.
Milford, MA 01757
(508) 634-8697

Early Auction Co.
123 Main St.
Milford, OH 45150
(513) 831-4833

Ken Farmer Realty & Auction
Co.
1122 Norwood St.
Radford, VA 24141
(703) 639-0939

Steve Finer Rare Books
PO Box 758
Greenfield, MA 01302
(413) 773-5811

Fink's Off The Wall Auctions
108 E. 7th St.
Lansdale, PA 19446
(215) 855-9732

William A. Fox Auctions, Inc.
676 Morris Ave
Springfield, NJ 07081
(201)467-2366

Freeman/Fine Arts Co. of
Philadelphia, Inc.
1808 Chestnut St.
Philadelphia, PA 19103
(215) 563-9275

Garth's Auction, Inc.
2690 Stratford Rd.
PO Box 369
Delaware, OH 43015
(614) 362-4771 or 369-5085

Glass-Works Auctions
PO Box 187-102 Jefferson St.
East Greenville, PA 18041
(215) 679-5849

Morton M. Goldberg Auction
Galleries
547 Baronne St.
New Orleans, LA 70113
(504) 592-2300

Grandma's Trunk
The Millards
PO Box 404
Northport, MI 49670
(616) 386-5351

Guerney's
136 East 73rd St.
New York, NY 10021
(212) 794-2280

Hake's Americana and
Collectibles
PO Box 1444
York, PA 17405
(717) 848-1333

Harmer Rooke Numismatists,
Inc.
3 East 57th St.
New York, NY 10022
(212) 751-4122

Gene Harris Antique Auction
Center, Inc.
203 S. 18th Ave.
Marshalltown, IA 50158
(515) 752-0600

Norman C. Heckler &
Company
Bradford Corner Rd.
Woodstock Valley, CT 06282
(203) 974-1634

Leslie Hindman, Inc.
215 West Ohio St.
Chicago, IL 60610
(312) 670-0010

Jackson Auction Co.
2227 Lincoln St.
Cedar Falls, IA 50613
(319) 277-2256

James D. Julia, Inc.
PO Box 830
Fairfield, ME 04937
(207) 453-7904

Charles E. Kirtley
PO Box 2273
Elizabeth City, NC 27906
(919) 335-1262

Kurt Krueger
106 N. Washington St.
Iola, WI 54945
(715) 445-3845

Henry Kurtz, Ltd.
163 Amsterdam Ave
Suite 136
New York, NY 10023
(212) 642-5904

Howard Lowery
3818 W. Magnolia Blvd.
Burbank, CA 91505
(818) 972-9080

Majolica Auctions
Michael G. Strawser
200 North Main
PO Box 332
Wolcottville, IN 46795
(219) 854-2859

Alex G. Malloy, Inc.
PO Box 38
South Salem, NY 10590
(203) 438-0396

Manion's International Auction
House, Inc.
PO Box 12214
Kansas City, KS 66112
(913) 299-6692

Martin Auctioneers, Inc.
Larry L. Martin
PO Box 477
Intercourse, PA 17534
(717) 768-8108

Robert Merry Auction
Company
5501 Milburn Rd.
St. Louis, MO 63129
(314) 487-3992

Mid-Hudson Auction Galleries
One Idlewild Ave.
Cornwall-On-Hudson, NY
12520
(214) 534-7828

Milwaukee Auction Galleries
318 N. Water
Milwaukee, WI 53202
(414) 271-1105

Neal Auction Company
4038 Magazine St.
New Orleans, LA 70115
(504) 899-5329

New England Auction Gallery
Box 2273
W. Peabody, MA 01960
(508) 535-3140

New Hampshire Book
   Auctions
Woodbury Rd.
Weare, NH 03281
(603) 529-1700

Nostalgia Publications, Inc.
21 South Lake Dr.
Hackensack, NJ 07601
(201) 488-4536

Pam & Dick Oestreicher
4025 Saline St.
Pittsburgh, PA 15217
(412) 421-5230

Richard Opfer Auctioneers Inc.
1919 Greenspring Dr.
Timonium, MD 21093
(410) 252-5035

Pacific Book Auction Galleries
139 Townsend St.
Suite 305
San Francisco, CA 94107
(415) 896-2665

Pettigrew Auction Company
1645 South Tejon St.
Colorado Springs, CO 80906
(719) 633-7963

Phillips Ltd.
406 East 79th St.
New York, NY 10021
(212) 570-4830

Postcards International
PO Box 2930
New Haven, CT 06515-0030
(203) 865-0814

David Rago Arts & Crafts
PO Box 3592 Station E
Trenton, NJ 08629
(609) 585-2546

Lloyd Ralston Toys
173 Post Road
Fairfield, CT 06432
(203) 255-1233 or 366-3399

Renzel's Auction Service
PO Box 222
Emigsville, PA 17318
(717) 764-6412

R. Niel & Elaine Reynolds
Box 133
Waterford, VA 22190
(703) 882-3574

Roan Bros. Auction Gallery
RD 3, Box 118
Cogan Station, PA 17728
(717) 494-0170

Selkirk Gallery
4166 Olive Street
Saint Louis, MO 63108
(314) 533-1700

L. H. Selman Ltd.
761 Chestnut Street
Santa Cruz, CA 95060
(408) 427-1177

Robert W. Skinner Inc.
Bolton Gallery
357 Main St.
Bolton, MA 01740
(508) 779-6241

C. G. Sloan & Company, Inc.
4920 Wyaconda Rd.
North Bethesda, MD 20852
(301) 468-4911

Smith House Toy Sales
26 Adlington Rd.
Eliot, ME 03903
(207) 439-4614

Sotheby's
1334 York Avenue
New York, NY 10021
(212) 606-7000

Rex Stark
49 Wethersfield Rd.
Bellingham, MA 02019
(508) 966-0994

Swann Galleries, Inc.
104 E. 25th St.
New York, NY 10010
(212) 254-4710

Theriault's
PO Box 151
Annapolis, MD 21401
(301) 224-3655

Victorian Images
PO Box 284
Marlton, NJ 08053
(609) 985-7711

Vintage Cover Story
PO Box 975
Burlington, NC 27215
(919) 584-6990

Winter Associates
21 Cooke St., Box 823
Plainville, CT 06062
(203) 793-0288

Tom Witte's Antiques
PO Box 399
Front St West
Mattawan, MI 49071
(616) 668-4161

Wolf's Auction Gallery
13015 Larchmere Blvd.
Shaker Heights, OH 44120
(216) 231-3888

Woody Auction
Douglass, KS 67039
(316) 746-2694

ABBREVIATIONS

The following are standard abbreviations which we have used throughout this edition of **Warman's**.

3D	= three dimensional	lb	= pound
4to	= 8 x 10″	litho	= lithograph or lithographed
8vo	= 5 x 7″	LS	= letter signed
12mo	= 3 x 5″	MBP	= mint in bubble pack
ADS	= autograph document signed	mfg	= manufactured
adv	= advertising	MIB	= mint in box
ALS	= autograph letter signed	MIP	= mint in package
AQS	= autograph quotation signed	MOC	= mint on card
C	= century	MOP	= mother of pearl
c	= circa	n.d.	= no date
cov	= cover or covered	No.	= number
CS	= card signed	opal	= opalescent
d	= diameter or depth	orig	= original
dec	= decorated	oz	= ounce or ounces
dj	= dust jacket	pat	= patent
DQ	= Diamond Quilted	pc	= piece
DS	= document signed	pcs	= pieces
ed	= edition	pgs	= pages
emb	= embossed	pkg	= package
ext.	= exterior	pr	= pair
Folio	= 12 x 16″	PS	= photograph signed
ftd	= footed	pt	= pint
gal	= gallon	qt	= quart
ground	= background	rect	= rectangular
h	= height or high	sgd	= signed
hp	= hand painted	SP	= silver plated
illus	= illustrated, illustration, or illustrations	SS	= sterling silver
		sq	= square
imp	= impressed	TLS	= typed letter signed
int.	= interior	unp	= unpaginated
irid	= iridescent	vol	= volume
IVT	= Inverted Thumbprint	w	= width or wide
j	= jewels	yg	= yellow gold
K	= karat	#	= numbered
l	= length or long		

ABINGDON POTTERY

Collecting Hints: Like many contemporary potteries, Abingdon pottery is readily available in the market. The company produced over 1,000 shapes and used over 150 colors to decorate its wares. Because of this tremendous variety, collectors are advised to specialize in a select number of forms and/or colors from the beginning.

Abingdon art pottery, with its vitreous body and semi–gloss and high–gloss glazes, is found at all levels of the market from garage sales to antiques shows. For this reason, price fluctuation on identical pieces is quite common. Study the market carefully before buying. Learn to shop around.

While there is no price guide devoted exclusively to Abingdon pottery, price listings can now be found in all the general antiques and collectibles price guides along with several of the specialized ceramic and pottery guides. Pieces regularly appear for sale in classified advertisements in most trade papers, thus allowing one to obtain a strong sense of the Abingdon market.

Collectors and dealers are still in the process of defining the market relative to the most desirable shapes and colors. At the moment black (gunmetal black), a semi–gloss dark blue, a metallic copper brown, and several shades of red are the favored colors. Decorated pieces command a premium of 15% to 20%.

History: The Abingdon Sanitary Manufacturing Company, Abingdon, Illinois, was founded in 1908 for the purpose of manufacturing plumbing fixtures. Sometime during 1933–34 Abingdon introduced a line of art pottery ranging from decorative pieces to vases. In 1945 the company changed its name to Abingdon Potteries, Inc. Production of the art pottery line continued until 1950 when fire destroyed the art pottery kiln.

After the fire, the company placed its emphasis once again on plumbing fixtures. Eventually, Abingdon Potteries became Briggs Manufacturing Company, a firm noted for its sanitary fixtures.

Reference: Susan and Al Bagdade, *Warman's American Pottery and Porcelain*, Wallace-Homestead, 1994.

Collectors' Club: Abingdon Pottery Club, 212 South Fourth, Monmouth, IL 61462.

Bookends, pr	
Horse Head, black, #441	50.00
Seagull, 6" h	40.00
Bowl	
Blue, floral decals, low, #518, 12" d	25.00
White, oval, 13" d	10.00
Candleholders, pr, pink, double lites, #575	25.00
Conch Shell, pink, 9" l	25.00

Cookie Jar	
Daisy, 7" h	30.00
Granny	
Black	450.00
White	225.00
Hobby Horse	250.00
Jack O' Lantern, #674	265.00
Little Bo Peep	375.00
Little Miss Muffet, #622	200.00
Pineapple, 10½" h	75.00
Pumpkin	425.00
Sunflower	40.00
Train, #651	100.00
Windmill, #678	225.00
Cornucopia	
#449, 4½" h	25.00
#474, pink	20.00
#565, pink, dec, 7" l	30.00
#643, cool blue, low, 9½" l, label	35.00
Double Cornucopia, green, #482	22.00
Drip Jar, daisy dec, #679	40.00
Figure, peacock, pink, 7" h, price for pair	20.00
Flowerpot, Cattails, #150	30.00
Geranium Bowl, #543	45.00
Planter	
Daffodil, #668D	30.00
Donkey, blue, #669	35.00
Scroll and Leaf pattern, yellow, 9 x 3½"	7.50
Scroll Bowl, #532, 14½" l	
Chartreuse	38.00
Cool Blue	27.00
Pink	20.00
White	20.00
String Holder, mouse, 8½" d	80.00
Vase	
Acanthus, pink, #486, 10⅞" h, 7⅛" d	30.00
Alpha, white, leaf handles, #105, 8" h, 9½" w	20.00
Barrel, blue, #522, 9" h	27.00
Embossed scroll top, ribbed base, blue, handles, #125, 10" h	30.00
Ship, pink, #494, 7" h, 6½" w	35.00
Swirl, blue, #512, 7" h	25.00
Wall Pocket	
Butterfly, #601	65.00
Calla Lily	30.00
Cookbook, #676D	45.00
Morning Glory, #377, pink	40.00
Window Box	
Pink, #476, 10" l, 3⅛" w, 3" h	20.00
White, #576, 11¾" l, 4½" w, 4¼" h	25.00

ACTION FIGURES

Collecting Hints: This is one of the hot, trendy collecting categories of the 1990s. While there is no question that action figure material is selling and selling well, much of the pricing is highly speculative. Trends change from month to month as one figure or group of figures becomes hot and another cools off.

The safest approach is to buy only objects in fine or better condition and, if possible, with or in their original packaging. Any figure that has been played with to any extent will never have long–term value. This is a category of off–the–rack expectations.

Be extremely cautious about paying premium prices for figures less than ten years old. For the past ten years dealers have made a regular practice of buying action figures in quantity, warehousing them, and releasing their stash slowly into the market once production ceases.

Also examine packaging very closely. A premium is placed on having a figure in the packaging in which he, she, or it was introduced into the market. Later packaging means a lower price.

History: An action figure is a die–cast metal or plastic posable model with flexible joints that portrays a real or fictional character. In addition to the figures themselves, great emphasis is placed on the collecting of clothing, personal equipment, vehicles, and other types of accessories.

Collectors need to be aware of the following practices: (1) limited production—a deliberate act on the part of manufacturers to hold back on production of one or more figures in a series; (2) variations—minor changes in figures made by manufacturers to increase sales (previously believed to be mistakes, but now viewed as a deliberate sales gimmick), and (3) prototypes—artist models used during the planning process. Any prototype should be investigated thoroughly since there are many examples in the market made by individuals solely for the purpose of deceiving collectors.

The earliest action figures were the hard plastic Hartland figures of popular television Western heroes of the 1950s. Louis Marx also utilized action figures in a number of its playsets of the late 1950s. Although Barbie, who made her appearance in 1959, is posable, she is not considered an action figure by collectors.

G. I. Joe, introduced by Hassenfield Bros. in 1964, triggered the modern action figure craze. In 1965 Gilbert introduced action figures for James Bond 007, The Man From U.N.C.L.E., and Honey West. Bonanza figures arrived in 1966.

The year 1966 also marked the arrival of Ideal Toy Corporation's Captain Action. By changing heads and costumes, the figure's personality and role were altered. Captain Action and his accessories were the hot collectible of the late 1980s.

In 1972 Mego introduced the first six super-heroes in what would become a series of thirty–four different characters. Mego also established the link between action figures and the movies with its issue of Planet of the Apes and

Star Trek: The Motion Picture series. Mego's television series figures included CHiPs, Dukes of Hazzard, and Star Trek. When Mego filed for Chapter 11 bankruptcy protection in 1982, the days of eight– and twelve–inch cloth–clothed action figures ceased.

The introduction of Kenner's Star Wars figure set in 1977 opened a floodgate. Action figures enjoyed enormous popularity. Manufacturers rushed into the action figure market. Mattel followed quickly on Kenner's heels. Before long, the market was flooded, not only by a large selection, but also by production runs in the hundreds of thousands.

Not all series were successful; just ask companies such as Colorform, Matchbox, and TYCO. Some sets were never produced when initial sales did not justify the costs of manufacture. These sets have limited collector value. Scarcity does not necessarily equate to high value in the action figure market.

References: Paris and Sue Manos, *Collectible Male Action Figures: Including G.I. Joe Figures, Captain Action Figures, and Ken Dolls,* Collector Books, 1990, 1992 value update; Carol Markowski and Bill Sikora, *Tomart's Price Guide To Action Figure Collectibles, Revised Edition,* Tomart Publications, 1992.

Collectors' Clubs: Captain Action Collectors Club, PO Box 2095, Halesite, NY 11743; Captain Action Society of Pittsburgh, 516 Cubbage St., Carnegie, PA 15106.

Periodicals: *Action Figure News & Review,* 556 Monroe Turnpike, Monroe, CT 06468; *Tomart's Action Figure Digest,* Tomart Publications, 3300 Encrete Lane, Dayton, OH 45439.

DC Powers, Kenner, 5" h
Cyborg, 1986	**175.00**
Joker, minicomic, 1984	**30.00**
Kalibak, #99950, 1985	**15.00**
Steppenwolf, 1985	**80.00**

Major Matt Mason, Mattel
Captain Lazer, #6330, 1967	**320.00**
Major Matt Mason, Cat Trac, #6318	**125.00**
Scorpio, villain, 7" h, #6359, 1969	**1,800.00**

Man From U.N.C.L.E., Gilbert
Illya Kuryakin	**200.00**
Napoleon Solo	**225.00**

Marvel Secret Wars, Mattel, 4¼" h
Baron Zemo, #0139, 1984	**30.00**
Doctor Octopus, #7213, 1984	**18.00**
Hobgoblin, flying bat, #9138, 1984	**50.00**
Wolverine, silver claws, #7208, 1984	**60.00**

Marvel Superheroes, Toy Biz, 1990–91 5" h
Daredevil, Extending Billy Club, #4808	**35.00**
Dr Doom, Power Driven Weapons, #4803	**13.00**

Human Torch, Fireball Flinging
Action, #4837, 1993 . . . . 15.00
Incredible Hulk, Crushing Arm,
#4809 . . . . 10.00
Silver Surfer with Action Surfboard,
#4807 . . . . 30.00
15" h
The Punisher, 1991 . . . . 60.00
Venom, electronic talking figure,
#4897, 1991 . . . . 20.00
M.A.S.H., Tri–Star
Hawkeye
Large 35.00
Small 12.00
Hot Lips
Large 50.00
Small 15.00
Klinger, wearing dress 35.00
Masters of the Universe, Mattel, 5¾" h
Battle Armor He–Man, #7302, 1984   6.00
Clamp Champ, #3073 . . . . 8.00
Dragon Blaster Skeletor, #9017, 1986 10.00
Kutsu, #4924, 1984 . . . . 7.00
Terror Claws Skeletor, 5th anniversary
collector's edition, #9696, 1986 . . 10.00
Mighty Crusaders, Archie Comics,
Secret Sonic Signaling Shields and
Mighty Punch Action, Remco, The
Brain Emperor, 1974 . . . . 16.00
Mike Hazard, Marx, with accessories,
1967 . . . . 400.00
Moon McDare, Gilbert 95.00
The Noble Knights, Marx, 1968
Sir Gordon, The Gold Knight 175.00
The Black Knight 225.00
Outer Space Men, Colorforms
Alpha 7, Man from Mars 600.00
Colossus Rex, Man from Jupiter 750.00
Phantom, Phantom Bendie, Lakeside . . 120.00
Pocket Super Heroes, Mego, 1979
3¾" h
Aquaman 90.00
Batman 40.00
Captain Marvel 40.00
General Zod 15.00
Green Goblin 90.00
Police Academy, Kenner, 1990
Captain Harris, mail–in figure 40.00
Carey Mahoney 7.00
Sky Glidin' Zed 22.00
S.W.A.T. Eugene Tackleberry 15.00
Punisher Marvel Super Heroes Bend–em,
Just Toys, #12059, 1991 . . . . 6.00
Robin Hood Prince of Thieves, Kenner,
1991
Dark Warrior, Pike Scythe, #05880   18.00
Friar Tuck, Battle Staff, #05860 . . . . 30.00
Long Bow Robin Hood, #05810 . . . 5.00
Robocop and the Ultra Police, Kenner
Ultra Police
Birdman Barnes, 1989 . . . . 10.00
Gatlin' Blaster Robocop, 1990 . . . 25.00

Night Fighter Robocop, #64430,
1990 . . . . 18.00
Officer Ann Lewis, #64370, 1989   12.00
Vandals
ED–260 Droid, boxed, 1989 . . . . 18.00
Headhunter, #64220, 1989 . . . . . 10.00
Shazam Superhero Bendable, Mego,
1970s 125.00
Six Million Dollar Man, Kenner
Bionic Bigfoot, Sasquatch Beast, 15"
h, #65170, 1976 . . . . 80.00
Maskatron, 13" h, #65600, 1976 . . . 50.00
The Bionic Man, engine block, 13" h,
#65000, 1975 . . . . 40.00
Space: 1999, Mattel
Commander John Koenig 60.00
Zython 150.00
Spider–Man, Amazing
Spider–Man, Marx, 6" h, 1966 . . . . . 20.00
Web Spinning Spider–Man, Mego,
12½" h 150.00
Star Trek, Mego, 1974, 8" h
Cheron 160.00
Kirk 45.00
McCoy 80.00
Mugato 450.00
Romulan 675.00
Scotty 100.00
Talos 400.00
Uhura 70.00
Star Trek: The Motion Picture, Mego,
1979
3¾" h
Arcturian 160.00
McCoy 25.00
12" h
Arcturian 75.00
Decker 145.00
Kirk 60.00
Star Trek III
Kirk 25.00
Spock 25.00
Star Trek: The Next Generation
Galoob, 1988, 3¾" h
Captain Jean–Luc Picard 10.00
Data
Blue Face 125.00
Speckled Face 45.00
Ferengi Leader 75.00
Playmates, 1992
Commander William Riker, #6014   10.00
Counselor Deanna Troi 25.00
Gowron the Klingon, #6010 . . . . . 15.00
Superman
Mego
Supergirl Superhero Bendable, 1970s 175.00
Superman, 12½" h, 1976 . . . . 100.00
Remco, 12" h, energized 65.00
Tarzan, Mego, Tarzan Superhero
Bendable, 5" h, 1970s 75.00
Teenage Mutant Ninja Turtles, Play-
mates, 1988, 4½" h

April O'Neil, no stripe, Turtle Force fan club flyer	40.00
Baxter Stockman, #5057, type B pack, 1988	10.00
Donatello, Turtle Force fan club flyer	20.00
Genghis Frog, #5051, type B pack, 1989	6.00
Panda Khan, #5108, 1989	15.00
Ray Filet, Awesome Mutant Color Change, purple torso, red V, #5110, 1990	20.00
Splinter, #5006, type A pack, 1988	6.00
Terminator T2, Kenner Blaster T–1000, Rapid Deploy Missiles, 1992	8.00
White Hot T–100, Arrow Blaster, 1993	15.00
Thor, Marx, 6" h, 1966	15.00
Wonder Woman, Ideal, Justice League, 3" h, 1966–67	75.00

ADVERTISING

Collecting Hints: Many factors affect the price of an advertising collectible—the product and its manufacturer, the objects or persons used in the advertisement, the period and aesthetics of design, the designer and illustrator of the piece, and the form the advertisement takes. Add to this the continued use of advertising material as decorative elements in bars, restaurants, and other public places. The interior decorator purchases at a very different price level than the collector.

In truth, almost every advertising item is sought by a specialized collector in one or more collectible areas. The result is a divergence in pricing, with the price quoted to an advertising collector usually lower than that quoted to a specialized collector.

Most collectors seem to concentrate on the period prior to 1940, with special emphasis on the decades from 1880 to 1910. New collectors should examine the advertising material from the post–1940 period. Much of this material still is very inexpensive and likely to rise in value as the decorator trends associated with the 1950s through the 1970s gain in importance.

History: The earliest advertising in America is found in colonial newspapers and printed broadsides. By the mid–19th century manufacturers began to examine how a product was packaged. The box could convey a message and help identify and sell more of the product. The advent of the high–speed, lithograph printing press led to regional and national magazines, resulting in new advertising markets. The lithograph press also brought the element of vivid colors into the advertising spectrum.

Simultaneously, the general store branched out into specialized departments or individual stores.

By 1880 advertising premiums such as mirrors, paperweights, trade cards, etc., arrived on the scene. Premiums remained popular through the early 1960s, especially with children.

Advertising continues to respond to changing opportunities and times. The advertising character developed in the early 1900s. By the 1950s the star endorser was established firmly as an advertising vehicle. Advertising became a big business as specialized firms, many headquartered in New York City, developed to meet manufacturers' needs.

References: Bob Alexander and Mike Bruner, *A Collectors Guide To Telephone, Telegraph, & Express Co. Advertising*, Guard Frog Books, 1992; Kit Barry, *The Advertising Trade Card: Information And Prices, Book I*, published by author, 1981; Miles Beller and Jerry Leibowitz, *Hey Skinny: Great Advertisements from the Golden Age of Comic Books*, Chronicle Books, 1995; Al Bergevin, *Drugstore Tins And Their Prices*, Wallace–Homestead, 1990; Al Bergevin, *Food And Drink Containers And Their Prices*, Wallace–Homestead, 1988; Al Bergevin, *Tobacco Tins and Their Prices*, Wallace–Homestead, 1987; A. Walker Bingham, *The Snake–Oil Syndrome: Patent Medicine Advertising*, Christopher Publishing House, 1994; Michael Bruner, *Encyclopedia of Porcelain Enamel Advertising*, Schiffer Publishing, 1994; Leslie and Marcie Cabarga, *Trademark Designs of the Twenties*, Dover Publications, 1991; Douglas Collins, *America's Favorite Food: The Story of Campbell Soup Company*, Harry N. Abrams, 1994; Douglas Congdon–Martin, *America For Sale: A Collector's Guide to Antique Advertising*, Schiffer Publishing, 1991; Douglas Congdon–Martin, *Tobacco Tins: A Collector's Guide*, Schiffer Publishing, 1992; Douglas Congdon–Martin and Robert Biondi, *Country Store Antiques: From Cradles to Caskets*, Schiffer Publishing, 1991; Douglas Congdon–Martin and Robert Biondi, *Country Store Collectibles*, Schiffer Publishing, 1990; Fred Dodge, *Antique Tins: Identification & Values*, Collector Books, 1995; Ted Hake, *Hake's Guide to Advertising Collectibles*, Wallace–Homestead, 1992; Ted Hake and Russ King, *Collectible Pin–Back Buttons, 1896–1986, An Illustrated Price Guide*, Wallace–Homestead, 1986; Sharon and Bob Huxford, *Huxford's Collectible Advertising: An Illustrated Value Guide*, Collector Books, 1993; Sharon and Bob Huxford, *Huxford's Collectible Advertising, Second Edition*, Collector Books, 1995; Jerry Jankowski, *Shelf Life: Modern Package Design 1920–1945*, Chronicle Books, 1992; Jim and Vivian Karsnitz, *Oyster Cans*, Schiffer Publishing, 1993; Ray Klug, *Antique Advertising Encyclopedia*, Vol. 1, (1978, 1993 value update) and Vol. 2 (1985), L–W Promotions; John Margolies and Emily Gwathmey, *Signs Of Our Time*, Abbeville

Press, 1993; Norman E. Martinus and Harry L. Rinker, *Warman's Paper*, Wallace–Homestead, 1994; Tom Morrison, *Root Beer: Advertising and Collectibles*, Schiffer Publishing, 1992; Dana Gehman Morykan and Harry L. Rinker, *Warman's Country Antiques & Collectibles, Second Edition*, Wallace–Homestead, 1994; Alice L. Muncaster and Ellen Sawyer, *The Black Cat Made Me Buy It!*, Crown Publishers, 1988; Alice L. Muncaster and Ellen Sawyer, *The Dog Made Me Buy It!*, Crown Publishers, 1990; Alice L. Muncaster, Ellen Sawyer, and Ken Kapson, *The Baby Made Me Buy It!*, Crown Publishers, 1991; Murray Cards (International) Ltd. (comp.), *1992 Catalog of Cigarette & Other Trade Cards*, Murray Cards (International) Ltd., 1992; Dawn E. Reno, *Advertising: Identification and Price Guide*, Avon Books, 1993; Joleen Robison and Kay Sellers, *Advertising Dolls: Identification and Value Guide*, Collector Books, 1980, 1994 value update; B. J. Summers, *Value Guide To Advertising Memorabilia*, Collector Books, 1994; Robert Sloan and Steven Guarnaccia, *A Stiff Drink and A Close Shave: The Lost Art of Manliness*, Chronicle Books, 1995; Wescott *Price Guide To Advertising Water Jugs*, Globe Press, 1991; David L. Wilson, *General Store Collectibles: An Identification and Value Guide*, Collector Books, 1994; Neil Wood, *Smoking Collectibles: A Price Guide*, L–W Book Sales, 1994; David Zimmerman, *The Encyclopedia of Advertising Tins: Smalls and Samples*, published by author, 1994.

Collectors' Clubs: Antique Advertising Assoc. of America, PO Box 1121, Morton Grove, IL 60053; Inner Seal Collectors Club, 6609 Billtown Rd., Louisville, KY 40299; The Ephemera Society of America, PO Box 37, Schoharie, NY 12157; Tin Container Collectors Assoc., PO Box 440101, Aurora, CO 80044; Trade Card Collector's Assoc., Box 284, Marlton, NJ 08053.

Periodicals: *The Advertising Collectors Express*, PO Box 221, Mayview, MO 64071; National Assoc. of Paper and Advertising Collectors, *P.A.C.*, PO Box 500, Mt. Joy, PA 17552; *Paper Collectors' Marketplace* (PCM), PO Box 128, Scandinavia, WI 54977; *The Trade Card Journal*, 143 Main St., Brattleboro, VT 05301.

REPRODUCTION ALERT

ASHTRAY

Chrysler Corp, 7½", brass, metal figure center, inscribed "Master Technician Service Conference/Awarded by Chrysler Corp/9 Year Award," engraved recipient's name, 1940–50 .. **75.00**
Cliff House, San Francisco, shell, litho ... **15.00**
Firestone Tire **20.00**
Ford, 1950 style, stainless steel, die cut **70.00**

Ashtray, Ernest A. Brey, Quality Meats, Spinnerstown, PA, 1955, round Bakelite base, $5.00.

Gallagers Honey Dew Tobacco **22.00**
General Electric Motor **15.00**
Goodyear Tire **20.00**
Howard Iron Works, metal **15.00**
Kentucky Colonel **8.00**
Luchow's Restaurant Since 1882, blue
  and white, stein in center **20.00**
Napril Laboratory, Kansas City, MO ... **5.00**
Old Judge Coffee, tin **90.00**
Quorum Club of Texas, 9" d **8.00**
Richland Snack Bar, tin **5.00**
Seiberling Tire, Market St, Williamsport,
  PA **18.00**
Smith's General Store, Birdseye, IN, tin **4.00**
Winston Cigarettes, tin **4.00**

BOOKLET

Adirondack Rest Camp, c1930 ...... **10.00**
Franco–American Soup, color, 1908 .. **22.00**
Yellow Cab, New Orleans, c1930 .... **10.00**

Brochure, Quaker Oats, "Travels of a Rolled Oat," 1933 Chicago World's Fair souvenir, 12 pgs, black and white illus, Aunt Jemima and other recipes, $18.00.

BOX

Bee Soap, wood, paper label	65.00
Brookfield Cheese, wood, red clover dec	10.00
Bulldog Tobacco, wood, hinged lid, dog on front and back	70.00
Castoria, 5¼" x 1" x 2", colorful baby head, 2 oz bottle, Purepac Corp, NY	6.00
Cupples "Topseal" Jar Rings, full	3.00

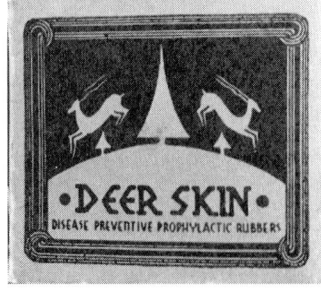

Box, Deer Skin Prophylactic Rubbers, silver and black, 2¼ x 2 x¾", $5.00.

DeLong Hair Pins, 3½" x 2½" x ⅝", red flowers, blue ground, includes hair pins	4.00
Dr Hobson's Ox Marrow Pomade, 3½" x 2" x 2", 1923, includes jar dated 1921, picture of lady on label and box	15.00
El Vampiro Bellow, 3¾" x 2¾" x ¾", bug killer, Allaire Woodard & Co, Peoria, IL, dated June 15, 1918	12.00
Fairbanks Santa Claus Soap, wood, paper label one end	150.00

Box, Fairy Soap, Gold Dust Corp., 2⅜ x 3⅞ x 1", $7.50.

Ferry Seed	95.00
Fine Shoes, lithographed	50.00
Gay Times Soft Drink, children scene	20.00
Hungerford's Dark Cocoa, wood	15.00
Jackson Fly Killer, display, wood	24.00

La Florita Face Powder, blue with basket of flower dec, logo, unopened, 1920s	15.00
Log Cabin Syrup, shipping crate, wooden, dovetail, rope handles, cabin graphics both ends	145.00
Lyon Tobacco, women sorting tobacco, 1870s	95.00
Melbaline Face Powder, 3⅜" x 3⅜" x 1", lavender, gold, and purple	8.00
Nabisco, tin hinged lid	30.00
Parker Snuff, broken cannon on front	100.00
Quaker Oats, 26" x 18" x 11", wood ..	65.00
Shuwhite Cream, wood	35.00
Swift Co, Heliotrope Soap, fancy Art Nouveau graphics	25.00
Union Biscuit	20.00

BROCHURE

Butternut Bread, sailor boy illus	10.00
Champion Harvesting Machine, 6 x 9", 12 pgs, black and white illus, c1882	35.00
Cottolene, The Evolution of an Apple Pie, 1898	28.00
Cushman Scooter Co, 6" x 3⅜", multicolored, Truckster, 24 pgs, 1955 ...	5.00
Gentleman Beer, hunting and trapping manual, 1947	28.00
Independent Motor Truck, Davenport, IA, c1920	8.00
Jell–O Girl Entertains, nine O'Neill illustrations	38.00
Merry–Go–Round, Health Co, 1906, 50 pgs	75.00
Metropolitan Life Insurance, The Metropolitan Mother Goose, color illustrations, c1920s	25.00
None Such Mincemeat, Little Rhymes for Little People	25.00
Pantasote, leather substitute, National Export Expo, Philadelphia, 1899 ...	40.00
Quaker Oats Nursery Rhymes	10.00
Smith and Wesson, seven shooter description, mid 19th C	15.00
Wallpapers for Home Decor, c1930 ..	8.00
White Mountain Ice Cream, woman making ice cream	25.00

MIRROR

Aetna Life Insurance, black and white, black, white, and red symbol, early 1900s	40.00
Angelus Marshmallows, angels image, multicolored	60.00
Arnold's Bakery, black and white, 25th Anniversary, 1923	60.00
Ball Optical Co, Guild Opticians, office photo	68.00
Benj Harris Novelty Co, multicolored birthstone rim, black and white inscription	55.00

Boston Herald, multicolored, running newsboy holding newspaper, early 1900s **75.00**
Brooklyn Dress Shields, blue and white, early 1900s **35.00**
Ceresota Flour, Prize Bread Flour of the World, boy cutting loaf of bread, multicolored **28.00**
Columbia Tool Steel Co, It Pays To Use Good Tool Steel, red, white, and blue   **22.00**
Copper–Clad Range, elongated oval, blue and orange **28.00**

Mirror, Horlick's Malted Milk, 2" d, gold rim, blue lettering, brown cow, blue dress, white apron, $55.00.

Mirror, Dingman Soap, 1⅞" d, red ground, white letters, printed, embossed, $35.00.

Drink Puck Rye, round, multicolored   **75.00**
Duffy's Malt Whiskey, round **70.00**
E H Berlin Photography, When You Do Think Of Photos, Give Us A Call, multicolored, portrait illus, early 1900s **50.00**
Ford Dealers, pocket **25.00**
Garland Stoves and Ranges, The World's Best, white and red **20.00**
Geo F Murray Fine Cigars, multicolored   **40.00**
Gitche Aamee Shoes, Duluth, MN . . .   **75.00**
Green's Infallible Liniment For Scratches, Wounds, Burns, Galls & Chilblains, black and white **25.00**
Hofbrau Haus Restaurant, black and white, image of restaurant, red, blue, and black accents **55.00**
Hood Rubbers, We Sell Hood Rubbers, Hood's Kickoff Heel, You Should Wear Them, Gives Extra Wear, Just Where It Is Needed, red and white   **14.00**
Horlick's, pocket **55.00**
Ideal Or Progress Cooking Oil, multicolored, family seated at table, 1911 copyright, Louisville Cotton Oil Co   **400.00**
Kentucky Wagon Mfg Co, tin rim, blue and white, emb paper image of wagon line, early 1900s **75.00**
Kingan's Hams, Bacon, Sausage–Lard, Always The Best, yellow and blue . .   **35.00**

Litholin Collars, red, white, and blue, early 1900s **50.00**
Maccabees Insurance, green, black, white, and red, 1920s **50.00**
Mackie–Clemens Fuel Co, Jay Hawk Coal, red, white, and blue **45.00**
Maryland Casualty Company, red, black, and white **22.00**
Mascot Curshe Cut Tobacco, dog image, red and white **30.00**
Menominee Saw Company, beige, orange, and black **35.00**
Old Reliable Coffee, image of seated man leaning on product, multicolored **95.00**
Omar Pearls, None Better Made, Every String Perfect, Guaranteed Indestructible, image of woman wearing triple strand, multicolored **38.00**
Oxford Chocolates, Hazen Confectionery Co, Boston, MA, image of woman with yellow rose in hair, multicolored **75.00**
Pacific Mutual Life Insurance Co, mother and children image, multicolored **72.00**
Persia Shoe Store, red, white border with blue lettering, early 1900s **35.00**
Revelation Tooth Powder, blue and gray, 1920s **25.00**
Sears, Roebuck and Co, black lettering, red company name **50.00**
Singer Sewing Machines, green and red   **75.00**
Sky Riders Shoes For Boys, airplane image, beige **30.00**
Snyder's Shoe Store, Rochester, NY, rect, black and white **10.00**
Standard Remington Typewriter, red, black and white image of typewriter, white lettering **40.00**
Starrett Tools, tool image, red and gold   **55.00**
St Paul Foundry Co, St Paul, MN, foundry image, red and white **35.00**

Superior Drill Co, multicolored, image
of farm lady, early 1900s **400.00**
W J White Chewing Gums, red, white,
and blue **75.00**

MISCELLANEOUS

Baby Rattle, Heinz **10.00**
Banner, Federal Tires, 28 x 11", felt,
early 1900s **40.00**
Beach Bag, Maxwell House Coffee, fig-
ural, coffee can **25.00**
Bill Holder, Walker's Austex Products,
wall mount **30.00**
Blotter, Sunoco, bride and groom
Mickey and Minnie in convertible . .   **25.00**
Broom Rack, Blu–Jay, holds twelve
brooms **375.00**
Brush, John W Henney & Company,
Designers and Builders, Motor
Vehicles, Freeport, IL, red, black, and
white **22.00**
Bucket, Heinz, wood, mincemeat, lid   **110.00**

**Pinback Button, Infallible Smokeless
Shotgun, celluloid, blue-and-white flag,
1¼" d, $25.00.**

Cabinet, Fairy Dye **125.00**
Cake Pan, Swansdown, angel food . . .   **20.00**
Can Opener, Pet Milk **10.00**
Change Apron, Chicago Daily Times . .   **18.00**
Chart, handwriting analysis, Folger's
Coffee **10.00**
Clamp, Trubyte Teeth, brass **28.00**
Clipboard, Liverpool, London & Globe
Insurance Co, 1936 100th Anniver-
sary, bronze, adjustable, 9 x 6" **35.00**
Clock
Blatz man, 1960 . . . .   **100.00**
Premier Vacuum Cleaner, 1930s . . .   **160.00**
Sylvania TV, Halolight, lighted **175.00**
Winston Cigarette, clock and counter
display, lighted **60.00**
Clothing Bag, 28½" x 60", wood grain
color, metal hanger, pictures woman
spraying clothes, giveaway from Flit
moth spray **4.00**

Coffee Cup, Mobilgas, Flying Red Horse   **20.00**
Coloring Book Set, Bird's Eye, includes
crayons, General Foods premium
mailer **25.00**
Cookie Jar
Alpo Dog **55.00**
Case Engine **125.00**
Sak's Fifth Avenue, Santa **150.00**
Corkscrew
Listerine **15.00**
Rawleigh **15.00**
Counter Card, National Oats, diecut,
girl carrying basket with product,
c1900 . . . .   **40.00**
Cuff Links, pr, oval, sepia tone image of
Lydia Pinkham **58.00**
Cup
National Oats, collapsible **25.00**
Patton's Sun–proof Paints, aluminum,
collapsible **20.00**
Worcester Salt **7.00**
Demitasse Spoon, Heinz, engraved
building in bowl, pickle on handle . .   **20.00**
Dispenser, T–Lax, 19½" x 1⅝" x 1¼",
tin, "10¢", black and yellow **40.00**
Display
Beech–Nut/Beechies, rack, metal,
two shelf **20.00**
Campbell's Soup, rack, metal, 18 x
22 x 5", 1930–40 . . . .   **75.00**
Cosmic Diamond Rings, Santa on
mica, 8 x 11" platform **40.00**
Oscar Mayer Weiner Mobile, friction,
Little Oscar bobs up **155.00**
Red Wing Grape Juice, cardboard,
bottles, two children drinking
through straws **90.00**
Shelby Razor Blade, card, 9" x 12½",
20 pkgs, 1940s **18.00**
Doll
Cream of Wheat, 18" h, cloth, 1920   **148.00**
Uneeda Biscuit, boy, Ideal, 1914 . . .   **350.00**
Door Push
Cresent Flour, tin, bag of flour **85.00**
Duke's Mixture, porcelain **115.00**
Egg Cup, NJ Bell Telephone, Lenox China   **65.00**
Fan, Nature's Remedy **12.00**
Flyswatter, wire, 1900s **16.00**
Fork, Wesson Veg–eat–eer **18.00**
Handkerchief, Buster Brown, child's . .   **85.00**
Hat, Ehler's Grade 'A' Ceylon Tea, red,
white, and blue **20.00**
Humidor, La Palina, brass **22.00**
Jacket, Lee Jeans, rooster dec **85.00**
Jar
DeWitt's Vaporizing Balm, 1½ oz, EC
DeWitt & Co, Chicago, IL, 2⅜" x
2¼" x 2¼" orig box **8.00**
Horlicks, 104 oz **18.00**
National Biscuit Co, store, 1900s . . .   **135.00**
Wan–eta Cocoa, qt, amber **35.00**
Vaseline Pomade Hair Dressing, 1¾

oz, color label, flowers, orig box, Chesebrough Mfg Co, Cons'd, NY, NY 8.00
Wrigley's Gum 130.00
Jigsaw Puzzle, Sun Drop Golden Cola, 9" x 12", lady with shopping cart loaded with Sun Colas, baby boy and girl drinking, orig envelope, 1965 . .   6.00
Knife, "Apply Antiphlogistine Warm & Thick", aluminum 12.00
Knife Board, Oakey's Knife Polish 48.00
Lapel Pin, Life Boy Soap, diecut sailor   10.00
Letter Opener
  Fuller Brushman 6.50
  Lincoln, Nebraska Telephone/Telegraph, Silver Anniversary, phone logo on handle 75.00
  Pacific Mutual 25.00
Lunch Pail, Pedro Tobacco 50.00
Magazine Ad, Cream of Wheat, heavy paper, Old King Cole with Rastus, color, 1902 . . . .   30.00
Marble Bag, Weather–Bird Shoes, includes marbles 20.00
Match Holder
  Brown Shoe Co 165.00
  Winged Horse Flour, tin 85.00
Match Safe
  Bradley's Excel Phosphate, cast iron, orig paint 65.00
  Old Judson Whiskey 120.00
  Rochester Composite Brick Co, 1½ x 2¾", silvered brass, name and ad text on gray brick, early 1900s . . .   35.00
  Vacuum Oil Co, celluloid, barrel illus   175.00
Measuring Spoon, Monibak Ground Coffee, tin 12.00
Menu
  Hotel Astor, NYC watercolor scenes, 1945 . . . .   7.00
  Mickey Mantle's Holiday Inn Menu, c1950 . . . .   75.00
  RH Macy's, large, 1937 . . . .   25.00
Mug
  Buckeye Root Beer, pottery 45.00
  Dad's Root Beer, glass, barrel 30.00
  Ovaltine, Little Orphan Annie, beetleware 40.00
Pancake Turner, Halligan Coffee, tin . .   12.00
Paper Doll, McLaughlin's Coffee, early 1900s 6.50
Paperweight, Babbitt Paint, Dutch boy with brush 45.00
Pencil Clip
  Keen Kutter 20.00
  Sterling Motor Oil, logo design, red, yellow, black, and white 10.00
Pencil Sharpener, Baker's Chocolate, figural, lady 45.00
Pin Cushion, Bunny Bread, felt 12.00
Pitcher, Meredith's Diamond Club Whiskey 45.00

Playing Cards, Hearn's Dept store, sailboat back 22.00
Pocket Knife
  Champion Spark Plug 25.00
  Purina, 3" l, red and white checkerboard design on plastic sides, black lettering, two steel blades, Kutmaster, c1950s 25.00
Pocket Watch, Ford, premium 85.00
Pot Scraper, Babitts Cleanser 225.00
Print, Swan Soap 80.00
Puppet, Dutch Boy Paint 30.00
Radio
  Atlas Battery 30.00
  Coca–Cola Cooler, MIB 45.00
  Tropicana Orange, with straw 25.00
Rolling Pin
  Columbus Flour, milk glass, faded red symbol and logo, wood turned handles, 17½" l 250.00
  Kelvinator, porcelain 85.00
Sample or Promotional Item
  De Laval, oil bottle, emb, orig box, 1913 . . . .   100.00
  Ford
    Mustang, 1964 . . . .   45.00
    T–Bird, 1957, MIB 125.00
  Royal Super Ware, aluminum cooking pan, 1½" d, 3" l, information inside about waterless cooking 110.00
  Wienermobile, Little Oscar, first issue, metal bottom, MIB 250.00
Scissors, 7" l, Star Brand Shoes Are Better 25.00
Shoe Horn
  A S Beck Shoes, metal, 1940s 5.00
  Normal Shoe Co 11.00
Shuffle Board Picks, Heywood Wakefield 30.00
Spinner, Poll Parrot Shoes 28.00
Spoon
  Armour's Extract of Beef 25.00
  Grand Union Tea Co 20.00
  Tums for the Tummy, long handle . .   15.00
Statue, Jockey Mensware, jockey, chrome, wood base 65.00

Stirrers, plastic, various hotels and restaurants, price each, $.50.

Straight Razor, Red Devil Tobacco, adv
on blade **18.00**
String Holder
Post Toasties, round, tin front **50.00**
Red Goose Shoes **950.00**
Tape Measure, Feeney Grocery Stores,
celluloid **25.00**
Torch, hanging, gasoline, "A. Shure Co.
Novelties & Streetmans Supply,
Chicago" on tank **235.00**
Yo–Yo
GE, wood **10.00**
Spaulding Luxury Bread, tin **40.00**
Wristwatch, Spam **10.00**

PAPERWEIGHT

Artistic Woven Labels, Pompton Lakes,
NJ, cloth under celluloid **25.00**
Bell Telephone, bell shape, cobalt blue
glass **45.00**
Canadian National **85.00**
Crane Co, 50th Anniversary, bronze
medal, 1930 . . . .   **10.00**
E W Wagner, Commission merchant,
celluloid **50.00**
Fageol Safety Coach, 7/8 x 7/8 x 2¾", lead
replica of c1920s bus, inscription on
both sides **20.00**
Hamilton Felt, Miami Woolen Mills,
Hamilton, OH, factory scene **10.00**
John Lovell Arms Co, Boston, glass, bust
of founder **125.00**
National, figural, cash register, cast iron,
orig paint **50.00**
Parker Vices, figural, teddy bear, cast
iron **85.00**
Reeves Stove Co **40.00**
Rogers Carriage Goods, celluloid and
iron, turtle shape **35.00**
Superior Stove & Range Co, cast iron   **35.00**
Transo Envelope Co, Chicago, IL, mirror **18.00**
White Mountain Refrigerator **55.00**

PINBACK BUTTON

Baby Bear Bread, red, black, and white,
Nip, Tuck, and Tige **28.00**
Ball Brand Trade Mark All Knit, red,
black, and white **10.00**
Bartles & Jaymes, Thank You For Your
Support, multicolored, photo **8.00**
Big Chief White Bread, red and white,
blue accent, 1930s **20.00**
Black Cat Club Hosiery, black, red, yel-
low, and blue, cat illus **24.00**
Buck Brand Coffee, multicolored, One
Pound Free For Every Ten Wrappers
Returned, c1900s **22.00**
Cameo Baking Powder, Purest Best, red,
yellow, black, and white, product il-
lus **8.00**

Cascarets, Don't Kick! Take Cascarets
Candy Cathartic, blue and white . . .   **14.00**
Ceresota Flour, multicolored **30.00**
Cherry Smash, multicolored, George
Washington Portrait **50.00**
Cooper Huddleston Company, Boys'
Suits, Two Pair Pants, red, black, and
white **6.00**
Dead Shot Smokeless Powder, Mallard
duck image, multicolored **55.00**
Delco Battery, Save A Battery, Service
Twice A Month, orange, black, and
white **5.00**
Diamond Edge Tools and Cutlery, Buy
Diamond Edge Tools and Cutlery,
Diamond Edge is a Quality Pledge,
red, black, and white **12.00**
Dold Quality Food Products, oval, yel-
low, red, white, and blue **10.00**
Dutch Java Blend Coffee, It's Good,
multicolored **25.00**
Favorite Stoves and Ranges, We
Guarantee, Best In The World, multi-
colored **8.00**
Gold Medal Flour, Washburn Crosby
Co, blue, white, and gold **12.00**
Hudson, Ride The Green Lane Of Safety
In A New 1939 Hudson, green, blue,
black, and white **15.00**
Hummer Plow, Hummer Will Plow
Anything Anywhere, multicolored . .   **25.00**
International Harvester, Whetstone Bark
River Culvert & Equipment Co, Our
50th Year, red and gold **12.00**
Karl's Bread, green, gold, and white,
cloverleaf illus **6.00**
Koveralls, Look For the Label, red,
black, and white **8.00**
Lekko Scouring Powder, Best Made
Cleanser, multicolored **12.00**
Majestic Ranges, multicolored **24.00**
National Hotel Cafe, Minneapolis, red,
black, and white **8.00**
National Lead Co, Pure White Lead,
Old Dutch Process, multicolored,
Dutch Boy illus **18.00**
Overland, multicolored, shaped, car
image **15.00**
Patton's Sun–Roof Paints, yellow and
brown **12.00**
Peters Superior Cartridges, brown,
black, and white **35.00**
Pilgrim Bread and Cakes, blue, white,
and orange, 1920–30 . . . .   **15.00**
Pulver's Gum, red and white, Get A
Collection Of Buttons, early 1900s   **20.00**
Rex Pepsin Gum, red, white, and blue,
Cudahy Pharmaceutical Co, c1896   **18.00**
Standard Safe & Lock Co Manufac-
turers, brown, black, and white **12.00**
Studebaker, red, white, blue, and yel-
low, spoked wheel image **22.00**

Thorola Radio, tin, black and orange, radio illus 20.00
Toblers Swiss Milk Chocolate, multicolored 24.00
Uncle Jerry's New Enlgand Pan Cake Flour, multicolored 35.00
Van Camp Hard Ware, elongated oval, blue, white, and gold 6.00
Velvet Molasses Candy, yellow, black lettering, c1900 . . . .   15.00
Wessel Brothers Cough Drops, blue and white 22.00
White Lead–Linseed Oil, John T Lewis & Bros Co, multicolored, Dutch Boy illus 8.00

POSTER

Booster Cigar, 27 x 30", black man, lady adjusting garter, framed 175.00
Chesapeake Steamship Co, 31 x 40", litho, 1915 . . . .   250.00
Florida Blossoms Minstrels, 9¼ x 42", stamped on bottom Sept 13, 1922 . .   25.00
Granger Tobacco, 30 x 42", sea captain, 1931 . . . .   60.00
Hill Bros Fur Co, price list on back, 1928 . . . .   15.00
Mandeville & Co, 17 x 20", litho, girl in flower garden 70.00
Mission Orange Soda, 20 x 26¼", paper, white Everybody's Choice slogan, late 1940s, early 1950s 50.00
Peerless Rubber Co, 23 x 17", litho, two scenes, framed 2000.00
Red Goose Shoes, Red Goose and children outside schoolhouse, 1920 . . .   275.00
Royal Baking Powder, 25 x 20", 1920s   30.00
Stoctonia Flour, 19 x 14", litho, 1905   50.00

United States Fur Co, 20 x 14", stone litho, 1920 . . . .   225.00

SIGN

AAA Service 100.00
Aetna Fire & Marine Ins 25.00
Arrow Shirt, man and woman in boat, sgd illus 375.00
Auto Strop Razor, tin, hand sharpening razor 375.00
Baker Boy, Butternut Bread, 10 x 14", cardboard, 1930s 23.00
Barker Powder, woman chased by bull, 1890 . . . .   450.00
Be Cozy Under Balsam Wool, 40 x 30", tin, snow laden house, 1920s 75.00
Blackberry Punch, 14" x 5½", cardboard, barefoot boy, bottle of punch, bucket of blackberries 45.00
Borden, tin, red 55.00
Brown Shoes, Baby's First Shoes, 1901   375.00
Burma Shave, wood 110.00
Busch Ginger Ale, 12 x 26", porcelain, c1920 . . . .   125.00
Camels, Don't Get Your Wind, 11 x 24", cardboard, c1920 . . . .   35.00
Cleo Cola, 13 x 29", tin, Cleopatra, 1930s 225.00
Dental Snuff, man and woman, 1930s   85.00
Double Orange, 24 x 25", cardboard, c1940 . . . .   125.00
Dr. Bell's Pine Tar Honey Cures Coughs, 13 x 14", cardboard, large blue bell, white ground, printed by Globe Co, Akron, OH 75.00
Duck Head Overalls, man wearing overalls, diecut 375.00

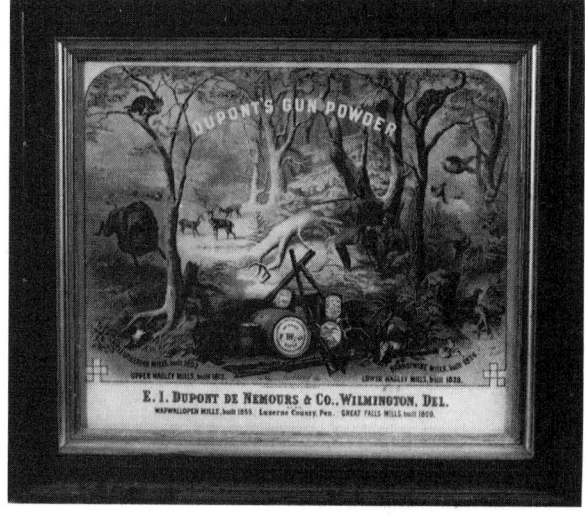

Sign, Dupont's Gun Powder, paper, chromolithograph, Major & Knapp, 1869, $20,900.00. Photo courtesy of James D. Julia.

Duplex Corset, woman in corset, 1880	375.00
Durham Tobacco, drunk man on horse, 1890s	275.00
Dutch Boy Marine	200.00
Edsel Shock Absorbers	200.00
Emerson Fans, articulated	175.00
Fidelity Underwriters, New York Fire Insurance, 12 x 15″, porcelain	45.00
Flame Proof Wax, women ironing clothes, 1890s	875.00
Francisco Auto Heater, 20 x 38″, tin, family in 1930 Packard scene, 1930s	875.00
Golden Girl Cola, 33″, metal, bottle cap shape	125.00
Granger Tobacco, diecut Frank Kelly Olympic shooter with guns	95.00
Green's Seed Corn	60.00
Heinz Soup, tin, diecut, 15¢ Bowl of Soup	150.00
Helmar Tobacco, porcelain	125.00
Homelite Chain Saws	100.00
Hood's Tire, policeman with flag, tin	650.00
Howel's Root Beer, tin, emb, boy with tray	65.00
Illinois Surgical Appliance, man bound in trusses	275.00
Iron Clad Hosiery, 10¼ x 13″, cardboard, flapper girl, off–image foxing, 1920s	15.00
Kemp's Balsam for Cough, Girl with bottle, diecut	125.00
Kerns Bread, 1½ x 10″	15.00
Kirk's Flake Soap, 15 x 41″, porcelain, red, white, and black, bar of soap image	475.00
Kitchen Kleanzer, cardboard	45.00
Korn Krisp, doll and boxes, 1905	650.00
Laddies Short Smoker, two men facing night club and fancy car scene	575.00
Lee Tires, tire scene, metal, flange	450.00
Lincoln Seed, metal, picture of Abe	75.00
Mascaro Tonique for Hair, woman with bottle	185.00
Min–Lax Tonic, 16 x 20″, tin, c1930	35.00
Mogul Timing Gears for Cars, magician holding giant gear	75.00
Myers Pump, tin, flange, double sided, milk maid squirts farm boy, c1900	115.00
North Carolina Tobacco, Our Next President's head obscured by smoke, 1880s	550.00
Nu–Grape, tin, rect, green ground, bottle in foreground	95.00
Old Bradbury, sewing	60.00
Oldsmobile Service, 18 x 12″, porcelain, c1920	225.00
Peak Chocolates, hand holding bar, tin	475.00
Perfection Overalls, father and sons wearing overalls working and playing	125.00
Peters Powder, retriever puppies and wood ammunition box, diecut	875.00

Pittsburgh Paints, 7¼″ x 9¼″, cardboard, Just Painted and Pittsburgh Plate Glass Co, multicolored, 1953	4.00
Polly Stamp, 13″ w, 27″ h, electric, colorful parrot, orig box, unused	85.00
Richardson Root Beer, 10 x 14″	32.00
Royal Typewriter, Santa Claus taking orders on typewriter, peeking family, 1920	375.00
Salvation Army	100.00
Sinclair Credit Card	75.00
Smoke El Baton, Follow The Leader, 6½ x 7″, diecut, cardboard, easel back, band leader holding baton	85.00
Snow King Baking Powder, 12 x 26″, cardboard, c1930	40.00
Society Brand Clothes, chic man and woman	110.00
South Bend Fishing Tackle, man catching fish	950.00
Speidel, celluloid, watch, cowboy, mountains, fence post frame	45.00
Star Shoe, farmer, carpenter, and shoes, litho	375.00
Star Soap, girl on tricycle mailing letter, 1896	1,450.00
Studebaker, 1961, 18½ x 11¾″, cardboard, color photo	15.00
Sun Crest, 25 x 39″, cardboard, multicolored, image of girl, bottle, and logo, six silhouettes of sports scenes, 1940s	175.00
Toledo Motoring School, Learn To Be Salesman or Repairman, Model T scene	90.00
Triangle Shirt Collar, collar inside heart	125.00
Tydol Flying A, porcelain, pump, round, five color	125.00
Uncle John's Syrup, 12 x 18″, cardboard, stone litho, 1915	26.00
Valu Orange Drink, 2 Drinks For 5¢, metal, 1930s	145.00
Venus Pencil, wood	325.00
Washington Crisps, box with Washington on front	175.00
WDC Pipes, tin	95.00
We Use Genuine Chevrolet Parts, 18 x 19″, metal, flanged, painted, multicolored	300.00
White Rock, metal, nymph illus, framed	35.00
Whiz Car Polish, Maxfield Parrish character	85.00
Wrigley's Chewing Gum, woman selling gum to girl	375.00

THERMOMETER

Amphora Pipe Tobacco	100.00
Anheuser–Busch, Dr. Stork, tin, 1915	75.00
Arbuckles Coffee, tin, package shape	175.00
C. D. Kinney, oval, litho of rabbits and tea party	150.00

Cobbs Creek Blended Whiskey, Drink–O–Meter, 38 x 8", c1936 .... 40.00
Doan's Pills, 6 x 24", wood, c1923 ... 115.00
Dr Pepper, round 80.00
Dr. Scholls, foot illus 40.00
Dr. Wells Soda 60.00
Ex–Lax
  Porcelain, circular dial 170.00
  Tin, 39" l 40.00
Folger's Coffee, 9" 75.00
Frosty Rootbeer, pictures Frosty 75.00
Gaines Dog Meal, tin 75.00
GE Radio/TV 50.00
Hires Root Beer, bottle shape 65.00
Jordan's Ready–To–Eat Meats, 15", wood, yellow enamel paint, black trim, stamped red text and markings, c1930 .... 40.00
Kentucky Club Pipe Tobacco, tin 35.00
Lincoln Laundry, 12 x 3", wood, early 1900s 25.00
Little Debbie, illus of Debbie 48.00
Major Anti–Freeze, 7 x 36", wood, drum majorette, yellow, red, and black ... 150.00
Mapco Pipeline Systems 40.00
Morton Salt 60.00
Nu–Grape, tin, bottle shape 55.00
Orange Crush, Crushie, wood 135.00
Packard Automobiles 65.00
Quaker State, round 90.00
Red Seal Battery, porcelain 75.00
Rolling Rock, horse illus 45.00
Roseberg Oregon Timber 40.00
Royal Crown Cola, 25" 60.00
Scott Seed 30.00
Standard Home Heating Oils, tin, torch logo 35.00
Texaco, men fishing 28.00
Universal Batteries 125.00
Whistle Soda 70.00

TIN

A–1 Marshmallows 35.00
A Bonnie Holland, 1885 .... 30.00
Allens Sodium Bicarbonate, Tampa Drug 10.00
Ann Page Cream of Tartar 7.00
B & B Baby Talc 35.00
Beaver, typewriter ribbon 10.00
Blue Bird Coffee 45.00
Breakfast Delight Coffee 32.50
Brownie Salted Peanuts, litho, Brownie on both sides 125.00
Butternut Coffee 15.00
Byerlys Coffee 42.00
Cain's Cloves 10.00
Campfire Marshmallows, campfire scene 35.00
Capstan Navy Cut Tobacco, round ... 18.00
Choisa Ceylon Tea, 1906 .... 20.00
Clarion Cream of Tartar 4.50

Colgate Eclat Talc 10.00
Davis Baking Powder, 3 oz, unopened 45.00
DeLaval Cream Separator Oil 55.00
Dr David Roberts Veterinary Worm Powder 22.00
Dream Girl Talc 40.00
Droste's Cocoa, ¼ oz, sample 50.00
Elmers New Orleans Chee–Whee, 1 lb, key wind 25.00
Flemings Coffee, 1 lb, key wind 25.00
Forest & Stream, tobacco, fisherman, pocket 75.00
Frank's Cinnamon 8.50
Gardenia Bouquet Talc 18.00
Giant Brand Coffee 65.00
Godfrey Phillips tobacco 20.00
Golden Harvest Coffee, lid missing ... 20.00
Gold Label Baking Powder 12.00
Gold Leaf Honeydew Tobacco 18.00

Tin, Good Cheer Cigar, mug form, strap handle, marked on bottom "Fact No. 215/25/Dist Kas," $40.00.

Half & Half Tobacco 5.00
Harvest Moon Candy 35.00
Hills Bros Coffee, 2 lb, 1952 .... 24.00
Hollingshead Neatsfoot 8.00
Hoosier Maid Mustard 8.00
Ivin's Saltines, 1 lb, round 18.00
Jolly Time Popcorn, red 18.00
Judd's Pickling Spice 7.00
Keen's Mustard, Lord Nelson, six scenes 185.00
Kemps Chocolate Table Fingers, snuff box shape 20.00
Kentucky Club Tobacco 5.00
King Cole Coffee, pictures king, key lid 18.00
Kraft Malted Milk 8.00
Kroger Bay Leaves 6.25
Len Wright's Chocolate Biscuits, Art Deco, paper label 30.00
Little Elf Spice 6.00
Loft's Candy, ½ lb 10.00
Luzianne Coffee, can, red, black mammy, pry lid 50.00
MacMillan Ground Mustard 6.75
Make Klean, waterless cleaner, pail shape 20.00

McCormick Bee Brand Pepper, large . .	10.00
McKessons Seidlitz Powder	10.00
McNess Baking Powder, biscuits image, 1 lb	55.00
Mennen Shave Talc	6.00
Merkels Tooth Powder	10.00
Mexene Chili Powder, image of devil stirring cauldron, 30 oz	75.00
Monarch Whole Mustard Seed	8.00
Mr. Potato Chip	75.00
Mrs. Kline's Potato Chips	25.00
Mule Kick Pipe Cleaner, mule scene . .	12.00
Nash's Coffee	15.00
Nestles Egyptian Henna Talc	17.00
Nutrine Candy, blue	55.00
Old Reliable Typewriter, beavers chewing trees	25.00
Old Southern Coffee	100.00
O'Neill's Vegetable Remedy	20.00
Packard Bulb Kit	15.00
Panama, typewriter ribbon	10.00
Pat Hand Tobacco, pocket size	110.00
Petrocarbo Salve, Watkins Co, Boston, MA, round, red and black	20.00
Planters Cashews, 4oz, 1944	38.00
Presto Stove Polish	6.00
Quaker Oats	15.00
Rawleighs Cocoa	16.00
Red Owl Harvest Queen Coffee	20.00
Red Robin Ogden, blue and yellow . . .	10.00
Red Rose Coffee, key lid	16.00
Regent Coffee, red checkered design, key lid	10.00
Royal Baking Powder, 2¾" h	45.00
Royal Chef Celery Seed	5.50
Rumford Baking Powder, sample	34.00
Sanfords Ink	20.00
Seacrest Oyster, boat, colorful	20.00
Shedds Peanut Butter, 5 lb	15.00
Skat Cleanser	6.00
Southern Rose Shortening, pail, red rose, bail handle	15.00
Sultana Peanut Butter, 1 lb pail, orange	95.00
Sunshine Biscuit, US Capitol, cherry blossoms	65.00
Tannette Powder, Walgreen	8.00
Texide Water Cured Prophylactics, ¼ x 1½ x 2", litho, multicolor illus, native	

workers extracting latex from rubber trees, two of three prophylactics enclosed, copyright 1931	35.00
Thomas Webb Steel–Cut Coffee	12.00
Unicy Marshmallows, 4½", tin, litho, red and black design, Brandle & Smith Co, Philadelphia, 1920–30 . . .	15.00
Velvet Night Talc	24.00
Walnut Plug Tobacco	15.00
Watkin's Baking Powder, 1930s	12.00
White Cap Baking Powder,¼ lb, unopened	18.00
Wizard of Oz, peanut butter pail, 2 lb	45.00
Yacht Club Coffee	15.00

TRADE CARD

Collecting Hints: Most advertising trade cards sell in the range from $1.00 to $10.00. A few command higher prices because of subject matter, artist, or scarcity. The advertised product being shown is among the most desirable features of a card. Many were made in sets, and collectors still seek to complete them today.

Cards taken from old albums should be handled with care, as there is often valuable information on the reverse side. Kit Barry's *The Advertising Trade Card* (privately printed, 1981) contains excellent information for the removal of cards from album pages.

History: These cards are small, thin cardboard pieces extolling the merits of a product and bearing the name and address of a merchant.

With the invention of lithograpy, colorful trade cards became a popular advertising medium in the late 19th and early 20th centuries. They were made to appeal to children, especially. Young and old alike collected and treasured them in albums and scrapbooks. Very few are dated; 1880 to 1893 were the prime years for trade cards; 1810 to 1850 cards can be found, but rarely. By 1900 trade cards were rapidly losing their popularity, perhaps due to the influx of the household magazine. By 1910 they had vanished from the American scene, except in rare instances.

Notes: The listing for trade cards is as follows: product name, description of card, copyright

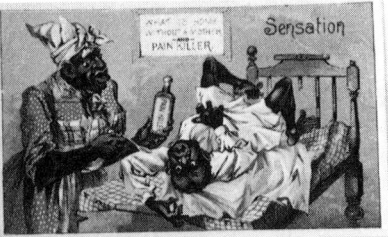

Trade Card, Perry Davis Pain Killer, three panel (two shown), Achert Krebs Litho Co., Cincinnati, OH, $18.00.

date if known, printer if known, and size. We have tried to focus on cards which show the product. All cards are in full color unless otherwise specified. There are thousands of cards in several hundred categories. We have tried to give a sampling to show the market range.

Bitters, Drugs, and Medicines

Burdock Blood Bitters, boy with bottle	**6.00**
Congress Bitters, Washington DC buildings	**7.00**
Dr Niemeyer's Vital Tonic, little girl, colorful	**10.00**
Kidds Cough Syrup, girl and pug dog	**5.00**
Lutted's Cough Drops	**8.00**
Take Schencks Mandrake Pills	**6.00**

Clothing

Clothier & Hatter, mechanical, 19C . . .	**45.00**
My Lady's Gloves, lady removing gloves	**4.00**
Todtman Clothier, diecut, youngster in wash tub	**10.00**
Venus Self Closing Bustle, lady attaching bustle	**4.00**

Cosmetics and Perfumes

Chinese Cologne, Hartford Soldier's Memorial, brown litho on white . . .	**6.00**
Espey's Fragrant Cream, lady holding fan	**6.00**
Hind's Honey and Cream, girl holding bottle, boy on either side, c1891 . . .	**7.00**
Howards Lotus Flower Cologne, lady sniffing flowers	**4.00**
Mennen's Borated Talcum Toilet Powder, boy popping out of can holding flag	**6.00**
Pompeia Perfume, 1929 calendar	**17.00**
Stoddart's Peerless Liquid, lady profile	**5.00**

Food

Beeman's Pepsi Gum, hold to light type	**18.00**
Eagle Condensed Milk	**18.00**
Falstaff–Lemp, 6 x 4″, double sided, brewery, white sand pouring out of beer barrel on front	**95.00**
Hecker's Buckwheat, hold to light, man in moon appears eating buckwheats, 1890s	**20.00**
Heinz, pickle shape, 1890s	**24.00**
Hood's Sarsaparilla, 1889	**45.00**
Huylers Chocolates, rooster and baby chicks waking sleeping girl	**10.00**
Millbourne Flour, diecut, flour sack, triple fold out, color, 1894	**50.00**
Newton Brothers Pepsin Chewing Gum, figural, emb, 1887	**85.00**
Ridges Food, baby with bottle	**7.00**

Household

Burger & Co Fine Furniture, gold gilt dec	**25.00**
Davol Rubber Co, celluloid, anti–colic nipple for baby bottle	**15.00**
Empire Wringer Co, printed color illus	**5.00**
Hartshorn Shade Rollers, baby pulls down shade, mother napping in chair	**4.00**
Lepages Glue, printed color illus	**15.00**
Lustro Silver Polish, printed color illus	**10.00**
Mundells Solar Tip Shoes for Children, printed color illus	**20.00**
Smith's Sprinkler and Force Pump, girl, lawn, and garden scene	**5.00**

Sewing

Clarks O.N.T. Spool Cotton, children with toys	**8.00**
Household Sewing Machine Co, little girl talking on telephone	**5.00**
Merrick Thread Co, stars and stripes . .	**10.00**
Royal St. John Sewing Machines	**8.00**
Standard Sewing Machine Co, Spirit of '76 scene, dated 1885	**6.00**

Soap

Acme Soap, printed color illus	**6.00**
Fairy Soap, Theodore Roosevelt photo	**25.00**
Larkin, Ottumwa Starch	**3.00**
R. P. Halls Complexion Soap, girl illus	**8.00**
Wool Soap	**3.00**

Stoves and Ranges

Acorn Stoves and Ranges, printed color illus of woman	**10.00**
Buckwater Stove Co, celluloid with cardboard insert	**15.00**
Gold Coin Stoves & Ranges, children by pond	**25.00**
Noble Cook Stoves, early wood stove, happy chef	**10.00**
Richmond Stove Co, sepia	**8.00**

Tobacco

Bull Durham, Simmons & Co, 1882 . .	**20.00**
Horsehead Tobacco, horse's head, plug in mouth	**8.50**
Lang's Plug, barometer card	**8.00**
Newsboy Plug, five puppies	**5.00**
Prince Albert Cigarettes	**10.00**

TRAY

Billy Baxter Ginger Ale, tin	**35.00**
Braumeister, man holding bottle and glass	**45.00**
Chero–Cola	**65.00**

Tray, Cottolene Shortening, multicolor, black ground, N. K. Fairbanks Co., 4¼" d, $75.00.

Cottolene, 4¼", litho tin, full color illus, black lady and youngster picking cotton, black rim, yellow lettering, c1920   75.00
Crown Baking Powder, 10", litho 175.00
Dawson's Diamond Ale, porcelain, playing card 125.00
Deys Dry Goods, store building 30.00
Dr. Pepper, King of Beverage 35.00
Evervess Sparkling Water, 10½ x 14" . .   35.00
Fairy Soap, tip, tin 38.00
Falls City Ice and Beverage 45.00
Ferris Brick Co, beautiful lady wearing hat, 1903 . . . .   25.00
Franks' Pale Dry Ginger Ale, soda bottle illustration, 1930s 65.00
Globe Wernecke, change 85.00
Gypsy Hosiery, Henry & Gott Dry Goods, image of lady, 8" l 85.00
Hyroller Whiskey, change 25.00
Jersey Cream, round 150.00
Kenny's Tea and Coffee, lady picking flowers 40.00
Lemon–Kola, tip 90.00
Lord Calvert Whiskey, 23" 48.00
Martha Washington Wine, Texas 95.00
Mascot Crushed Cut Tobacco 30.00
Nafruco Flavors, girl with horse 95.00
Old Elkhorn Rye, change 35.00
Orange Julep, bathing beauty under parasol 125.00
Parsely Salmon, change, salmon steak   40.00
Prudential Insurance, change, oval . . .   18.00
Round Oak Stove, change 18.00
Sheboygan Mineral Water, two black waiters 100.00
Sparks Kidney and Liver tonic, porcelain 275.00
Success Manure Spreader, rect, horses pulling wagon 1,000.00
Taka Cola, tip, litho tin 75.00
Ubero Coffee, Boston, change 60.00
West End Brewing, Utica, NY, rect, two dogs at table 290.00
Wrigleys' Soap, 3½" d, change 65.00

Whistle, Baby Ruth, Curtiss Candy Co., red ground, white lettering, $15.00.

WHISTLE

Bostock's Fighting Tiger/Goldie, black and white, early 1900s 50.00
Haines Shoe, trapezoid shape, plastic, black top with "Blow And Talk Of Haines The Shoe Wizard/Shoes For All," underside orange, late 1940s . .   20.00
Jack & Jill Gelatin, tin, litho 30.00
Millbrook Bread 10.00
New York Evening Telegraph, brass, chain 40.00
Oscar Meyer Weiner mobile 10.00
Peters Weatherbird Shoes, yellow litho tin, 1930s 20.00
Royal Luncheon, tin litho, Made in Germany 12.00

ADVERTISING CHARACTERS

Collecting Hints: Concentrate on one advertising character. Three–dimensional objects are more eagerly sought than two–dimensional objects. Some local dairies, restaurants and other businesses developed advertising characters. This area has received little focus from collectors.

History: Advertising characters represent a sampling of those characters used in advertising from the early 20th century to the present.

Americans learned to recognize specific products by their particular advertising characters. During the first half of the 1900s, many immigrants could not read but could identify with the colorful characters. The advertising character helped to sell the product.

Some manufacturers developed similar names for products of lesser quality, like Fairee Soap versus the popular Fairy Soap. Later, when trade laws were enacted, this practice was stopped. Use of trademarks had become popular by this time. The advertising character often was part of the trademark.

Trademarks and advertising characters are found on product labels, in magazines, as premiums, and on other types of advertising. Popular cartoon characters also were used to advertise products.

Some advertising characters were designed especially to promote a specific product like Mr. Peanut and the Campbell Kids. The popular Campbell Kids first appeared on streetcar advertising in 1906. The illustrations of Grace G. Drayton were aimed at housewives. The Campbell Kids were gradually dropped from Campbell's advertising until the television industry expanded the advertising market. In 1951, Campbell redesigned the kids and successfully reissued them. The kids were redesigned again in 1966. Other advertising characters also have enjoyed a long life, e.g., Aunt Jemima. Others, like Kayo and the Yellow Kid, have disappeared from modern advertising.

References: Douglas Collins, *America's Favorite Food: The Story of Campbell Soup Company*, Harry N. Abrams, 1994; Warren Dotz, *Advertising Character Collectibles: An Identification and Value Guide*, Collector Books, 1993; Mary Jane Lamphier, *Zany Characters of the Ad World*, Collector Books, 1995; David Longest, *Character Toys and Collectibles*, Collector Books, 1984, 1992 value update; David Longest, *Character Toys and Collectibles, Second Series*, Collector Books, 1987, 1990 value update; Norman E. Martinus and Harry L. Rinker, *Warman's Paper*, Wallace–Homestead, 1994; Richard D. and Barbara Reddock, *Planters Peanuts, Advertising & Collectibles*, Wallace–Homestead, 1978; Joleen Robison and Kay Sellers, *Advertising Dolls, Identification and Value Guide*, Collector Books, 1980, 1994 value update; Dave Stivers, *The Nabisco Brands Collection of Cream of Wheat Advertising Art*, Collectors' Showcase, 1986.

Collectors' Clubs: Campbell Kids Collectors, 649 Bayview Drive, Akron, OH 44319; R. F. Outcault Society, 103 Doubloon Drive, Slidell, LA 70461.

REPRODUCTION ALERT

See: All advertising categories; Black Memorabilia; Cartoon Characters; Fast Food; Planter's Peanuts.

Aunt Jemima
  Cinnamon Shaker **18.00**
  Glass, Mammy's Shanty **15.00**
  Pinback Button, Aunt Jemima
    Breakfast Club, litho tin, diecut,
    portrait, red and white lettering . .   **15.00**
  Syrup **25.00**

Buster Brown
  Box, stockings, graphics **40.00**
  Clicker, 1¼" l, multicolored, c1900   **40.00**
  Coat Hook **28.00**
  Jacks, orig ball, c1920 . . . .   **10.00**
  Periscope, Secret Agent **20.00**
  Pinback Button, 1" d, sepia, portrait
    illus, logo and inscription for
    Brown Shoe Co, St Louis on back
    paper, late 1890s–early 1900s . . .   **38.00**
  Plate, Buster Brown and Tige, china   **55.00**
  Post Card, Buster and Tige, colorful,
    Tuck, 1906 . . . .   **25.00**
  Shoehorn **40.00**
Campbell Kids
  Baseball Bat, wood **85.00**
  Case, vinyl, red **18.00**
  Doll, Bicentennial, MIB **60.00**
  Pennant, 17½" l, felt, burnt–orange,
    white inscription, c1930 . . . .   **30.00**
  Plate, 7" d, Homer Laughlin, 1935 . .   **25.00**
  Pot Holders, chalkware **95.00**
  Salt and Pepper Shakers, pr, F&F
    Mold & Die Works **35.00**
  Spoon, 6" l, SP, boy on handle, c1950   **12.00**
  Wristwatch, full color image on dial,
    gold luster metal bezel, black vinyl
    straps, plastic display case and orig
    papers, 1970–80 . . . .   **75.00**
Charlie Tuna
  Doll, 7" h, vinyl, squeeze, painted
    black glasses, orange cap with
    raised "Charlie" letters, 1973 copy-
    right **20.00**
  Lamp **50.00**
  Patch, embroidered **15.00**
  Pinback Button, 1½" d, litho tin,
    Charlie for President, red, white,
    and blue, 1960s **25.00**
  Scale, 10½ x 13", oval, vinyl over
    metal, Charlie image, 1972 copy-
    right **75.00**
  Wristwatch **40.00**
Chiquita Banana, doll pattern, uncut
  cotton fabric sheet, orig mailing en-
  velope, Kellogg's Corn Flakes pre-
  mium, late 1940s **100.00**
Dino the Dinosaur, Sinclair Oil
  Toy, inflatable, vinyl, green, brown
    lettering, sealed packet, c1970 . . .   **15.00**
  Tumbler, 5" h, green illus, "Drive with
    Care and Buy Sinclair," c1930 . . .   **20.00**
Dutch Boy
  Keychain, 2¼" h, plastic, dayglow,
    figural, holding brushes behind
    back, c1940s **30.00**
  Paperweight, lead **18.00**
Elsie the Cow
  Badge, brass, raised relief image,
    wearing daisy collar **75.00**
  Charm, white plastic, diecut, head
    portrait, 1950s **15.00**

Esso Tiger, paper cocktail napkins, printed color logo, 5 x 5" sq (folded size), 1960s, pkg of 10, $18.00.

Coloring Book, 1957	15.00
Creamer and Sugar, plastic, missing cov	75.00
Doll, plush, c1986	80.00
Game, Elsie and Her Family, 1941 Selchow & Righter Co, orig box, complete	75.00
Ice Cream Sundae Dish, 4" d	17.50
Lamp, ceramic, Elsie holding baby	235.00

Milk Bottle

1/2 Pint, short, Elsie on red ground, square	9.00

Quart

Elsie in Daisy, red ground	15.00
"Borden's" in red, round	17.00
Borden's Deposit bottle, orange ring on neck, square	20.00
1½ gal, Elsie dec around top, "Let your grocer be your milkman"	22.00
Pail, 5½" h, tin, silvered, litho full color portrait, wire and wood bail, Ohio Art Co logo symbol on reverse side, 1930–40	40.00
Tab Button	15.00

Gerber Baby

Child's Cup, emb illus	5.00
Doll, orig box, 1972	15.00

Gold Dust Twins Washing Powder

Pinback Button, multicolored	60.00
Sign, 20 x 13", "Do Your Work," orange and black	100.00
Hawaiian Punch, game, 17½" sq playing board, cardboard spinner, plastic spinner, mold, model clay packets, and instruction sheet, Mattel, 1978 copyright	40.00

Hush Puppy

Bank, figural, dog	20.00
Frisbee, 9¼" d, plastic, white dayglow, blue dog, red lettering, 1960s–1970s	12.00
Joe Camel, ice bucket and four glasses	35.00

Keebler Elf

Doll, 6½" h, soft vinyl, movable head, stamped "1974 copyright by Keebler Co"	20.00
Telephone	85.00
Wristwatch	125.00
Kool Aid Man, bank, 5½" h, plastic, figural, mechanical, red, yellow base, orig instruction tag, copyright of General Foods, 1970–80	20.00
Marky Maypo, doll	60.00
Morris the Cat, Nine Lives Cat Food, pinback button, 2¼" d, litho tin, Morris For President, red, white, and blue border	10.00

Mr. Peanut

Container, papier mache	175.00
Jar, 10" h, glass, emb, peanut finial	100.00
Nut Tray, 6" l, figural, plastic, green, matching serving spoon with figure on handle	30.00

Nipper, RCA Victor

Bank, cast iron	275.00
Figure, 4" h, chalk, marked "Victor Windsor–Poling Co, Akron, OH" on base	95.00
Key Case, emb gold letters	60.00
Salt and Pepper Shakers, pr, Lenox	35.00
Sign, cardboard, framed	20.00

Pillsbury Doughboy

Cookie Jar	33.00
Doll, 7" h, white vinyl, movable head, painted blue dot eyes, 1971 copyright	25.00

Poll Parrot Shoes

Figure, chalk	125.00
Spinner Top, metal, diecut, yellow, red, and green, c1940s	25.00
Whistle, litho tin, oval trademark, 1930s	25.00

Red Goose Shoes

Child's Shoes, pr, boy's, orig box	20.00
Egg Dispenser, 33" h, figural, plastic, straw nest, c1950	135.00
Pinback Button	7.00
Token, brass	8.00

Reddy Kilowatt

Coaster, 3½" d, set of 20, paper, black, white, and red, each with image, wax paper backing, unused	15.00
Cuff Links, ¾" d, brass, clear glass dome over multicolored face, Reddy Kilowatt copyright	80.00
Figure, 5¼" h, plastic, diecut, white dayglow head, hands, and feet, clear red body, black base, copyright 1961	85.00
Lapel Pin	20.00
Pin, 1" h, brass, diecut, figural, red enamel accents, 1950s	20.00
Plate, 6¼" d, metal, enamel, color illus, light green background, in-	

scription "Reddy Kilowatt/Servant
Of The Century" sticker marked
"Bovano," 1950s 35.00
Playing Cards, double deck 35.00
Pot Holder, magnetic, MIP 30.00
Poster, 11 x 13½", paper, peel–off,
red, white, and blue, unused,
1960s 40.00
Smokey Bear
Bowl, plastic, Arrowhead 9.00
Doll, cloth, Ideal, 1950s 60.00
Figure, Aim Toothpaste premium,
1960s 18.00
Salt and Pepper Shakers, pr, figural   65.00
Snap, Crackle, Pop, Kellogg's Rice
Krispies
Doll, 15" h, Crackle, cloth, 1930s . .   78.00
Figure, 4" h, set of 3, MIB 95.00
Puppet, Kellogg's premium 25.00
Song Book, 1937 . . . .   5.00
Speedy, Alka Seltzer
Bank, 5½" h, vinyl, slight discol-
oration, 1950s 350.00
Cup, expandable 12.00
Figure, 8" h, vinyl, bright color 500.00
Lapel pin, ⅝" h, brass, enameled,
diecut, figural, 1950s–1960s 70.00
Post Card 12.00
Spuds Mackenzie
Stuffed Toy 10.00
Wristwatch 20.00
Sugar Bear, wristwatch, chrome luster
case, black leather straps, Sugar Bear
image on dial, Made in Israel, 1970s   75.00
Tony The Tiger, Kellogg's Frosted Flakes
Cereal Bowl, 5" d, figural, hard plas-
tic, white, orange plastic feet shape
base, Kellogg's, copyright 1981 . .   15.00
Cookie Jar, hard plastic, figural head,
orange, white, and black, dark
green and red accents, orig brown
cardboard mailing box, 1968
Kellogg's copyright 125.00
Cup, glass 12.00

AKRO AGATE GLASS

Collecting Hints: Akro Agate is marked "Made in
USA" and often includes a mold number. Some
pieces also include a small crow in the mark. It is
a thick type of glass; therefore, collectors should
buy only mint pieces. The marbleized types of
Akro Agate were made in many color combinations. The serious collector should be looking for
unusual combinations.

History: The Akro Agate Co. was formed in 1911.
Their major product was marbles. In 1914 the
owners moved from near Akron, Ohio, to
Clarksburg, West Virginia, where they opened a
large factory. They continued to produce marbles
profitably until after the Depression. In 1930, the
competition in the marble business became too
great, and Akro Agate Co. decided to diversify
into other products.

Two of their most successful products were the
floral ware lines and children's dishes, first made
in 1935. The children's dishes were very popular
until after World War II, when metal dishes captured the market.

The Akro Agate Co. also made special containers for cosmetics firms—including the
Mexicali cigarette jar, which was originally filled
with Pick Wick bath salts, and a special line
made for the Jean Vivaudou Co., Inc. Operations
continued successfully until 1948. The factory, a
victim of imports, metals, and increased use of
plastics, was sold to the Clarksburg Glass Co. in
1951.

References: Gene Florence, *The Collectors
Encyclopedia of Akro Agate Glassware*, Revised
Edition, Collector Books, 1975, 1992 value up-
date; Roger and Claudia Hardy, *The Complete
Line of The Akro Agate*, published by author,
1992; Ellen Tischbein Schroy, *Warman's Glass*,
Second Edition, Wallace–Homestead, 1995.

Collectors' Clubs: Akro Agate Art Association,
PO Box 758, Salem, NH 03079; Akro Agate
Collector's Club, 10 Bailey St., Clarksburg, WV
26301.

REPRODUCTION ALERT: Pieces currently reproduced are not marked "Made In USA" and are
missing the mold number and crow.

Ashtray, Goodrich Tire, blue and black
marbleized 40.00
Basket, two handles, orange and white   30.00
Bell, white 50.00
Bowl, 7½" d, tab handle, cream and red   30.00
Children's Dishes, small size unless oth-
erwise noted
Bowl, Int Panel, green and white,
large 22.50
Cereal Bowl, J Pressman, fired on red   7.00
Creamer
Chiquita, green 4.00
Int Panel, green and white, large   30.00
Octagonal, blue, large 20.00
Stippled Band, light amber, large   30.00
Cup
Chiquita, green 3.50
Concentric Ring, green opaque . .   9.00
Int Panel, green and white, large   20.00
J Press, green opaque 4.50
Octagonal
Green, large 5.00
Pumpkin, small, closed handle   25.00
Stippled Band
Amber, large 18.00
Light amber, small 9.00

Pitcher
  Int Panel, transparent green, 2⅞" h   **12.00**
  Stippled Band, green **17.00**
Plate
  Chiquita, green **2.00**
  Concentric Rib, blue opaque, 3¼" d   **6.00**
  Int Panel, yellow, 4¼" d **10.00**
  Octagonal
    Lime Green, large **7.00**
    Lime Green, small **7.00**
    White **4.00**
  Stippled Band, light amber, large   **15.00**
Saucer
  Chiquita, transparent cobalt blue   **4.00**
  Int Panel, green and white, large   **18.00**
  J Press, green opaque **3.50**
  Octagonal
    Lemonade and oxblood, large . .   **14.00**
    White, small **5.00**
  Raised Daisy, blue **16.00**
  Stippled Band
    Amber, large **15.00**
    Green, small **4.00**
Set
  J Pressman, Tea Set for Six, boxed   **165.00**
  Octagonal, orig box, 17 pc set,
    larger size **175.00**
  Stacked Disc, 16 pc set **150.00**
  Stippled Band, topaz, 17 pc set,
    larger size **250.00**
Sugar
  Int Panel, green and white, large   **20.00**
  Stippled Band, light amber, cov,
    large **50.00**
Teapot, cov
  Chiquita, green **12.00**
  Int Panel, topaz, larger size **65.00**
  J Pressman, fired on cobalt **20.00**
  Octagonal, blue teapot, white lid,
    large **20.00**
  Stippled Band, transparent green   **18.00**
Tumbler
  Stacked Disc Int Panel, transparent
    green **12.50**
  Stippled Band, green **11.00**
Demitasse Cup and Saucer, blue and
  white **17.50**
Electric Fan, small **75.00**

**Tumblers, Stacked Disk & Panel, cobalt
blue, set of four, $50.00.**

Flower Pot
  Graduated Dart, orange and white,
    2" h **15.00**
  Ribbed Top, green and white, 2¼" h   **2.50**
  Stacked Disk, blue and white, 2½" h   **9.50**
Game, Tiddley Winks, J Pressman,
  boxed set **25.00**
Ivy Bowl, brown and white, Westite . .   **25.00**
Jardiniere, Graduated Dart, bell shape,
  tab handle, green and white **30.00**
Lamp
  Table, blue pineapple body **95.00**
  Wall, sq base, orange marble **55.00**
Mexicali Jar, orange and white **35.00**
Mortar and Pestle, black **35.00**
Planter, Graduated Dart, No. 651, oval,
  scalloped top, green and white **45.00**
Powder Jar, cov
  Colonial Lady, white **85.00**
  Scottie
    Turquoise **65.00**
    White **85.00**
Shell, 246, green and white **6.00**
Urn, ftd, sq, brown and white **7.50**
Vase, Graduated Dart, No. 316, scal-
  loped top, dark green, 6¼" h **55.00**

ALUMINUM, HAND WROUGHT

Collecting Hints: Some manufacturers' marks are synonymous with quality, e.g., Continental Hand Wrought Silverlook. However, some quality pieces are not marked and should not be overlooked. Check carefully for pitting, deep scratches, and missing pieces of glassware.

History: During the late 1920s the use of aluminum for purely utilitarian purposes resulted in a variety of decorative household accessories. Although manufactured by a variety of methods, the hammered aluminum with repousse patterns appears to have been the most popular and certainly was more demanding of the skill of the craftsman producing the articles.

At one time many companies were competing for the aluminum giftware market with numerous silver companies adding aluminum articles as promotional items or as a more competitive and affordable product during the depression years. Many well–known and highly esteemed metal–smiths contributed their skills to the production of hammered aluminum. With the advent of mass production methods and the accompanying wider distribution of aluminum giftware, the demand began to decline, leaving only a few producers who have continued to turn out quality work by the age–old and time–tested methods of metal crafting.

References: Everett Grist, *Collectible Aluminum: An Identification and Value Guide,* Collector Books, 1994; Dannie Woodard and Billie Wood, *Hammered Aluminum: Hand Wrought Collectibles,* published by authors, 1983; Dannie A. Woodard, *Revised 1990 Price List for Hammered Aluminum: Hand Wrought Collectibles,* Aluminum Collectors' Books, 1990; Dannie A. Woodard, *Hammered Aluminum Hand Wrought Collectibles, Book Two,* Aluminum Collectors' Books, 1993.

Collectors' Club: Aluminum Collectors, PO Box 1346, Weatherford, TX 76086.

Periodical: *The Aluminist,* PO Box 1346, Weatherford, TX 76086.

Ashtray, 3½", triangular shape, apple blossoms, Town/Hand Made Aluminum **3.50**
Basket
  11", fluted edge, double handle with square knot, sailing ship, Hand Wrought by Federal S Co **10.00**
  12", flared sides, Harvest pattern, scalloped handle, Hand Forged . . **8.00**
Beverage Set, pitcher, eight 20 oz tumblers, applied flowers, sq knot handle on pitcher, World Hand Forged **45.00**
Bowl
  7¼", cov, wooden knob, applied leaves, Shup Laird/Argental **12.00**
  10", tulip, flower ribbon handles, Rodney Kent #450 . . . . **20.00**
  11", iris, handles, World Hand Forged **12.00**
  11¼", Chrysanthemum pattern, Continental Silverlook **14.00**
Butter, cov, Buenilum **18.00**
Candleholder
  2½" sq base, arrow shape, corners form feet, handle, #1020, Everlast Forged Aluminum **3.50**
  6" h, beaded edge base, aluminum stem with wooden ball, Buenilum **5.00**
Candy Dish
  Double, opposing rose pattern in dish, center handle with leaf pattern, Farberware **28.00**
  Thick glass dish, three sections, aluminum cov, fruit pattern, pear knob, unmarked **25.00**
Casserole Holder, cov
  7½", rose, beaded knob, Everlast Forged Metal **12.00**
  8", twisted handles, looped finial, Buenilum **10.00**
  10", footed ring, wheat and vegetables, fan shape handles and knob, baking dish, unmarked **15.00**
Cheese, cov **18.00**
Coaster
  5", turtle, Wendell August Forge . . . **3.00**

Set of 8, caddy, beaded edge, double loop finial, Buenilum **10.00**
Cocktail Shaker, straight sides, grooved Art Deco top, clear plastic knob lid, Buenilum **12.00**
Coffee Urn, stand, and warmer **60.00**
Compote, 5" h, Continental Hand Wrought Silverlook, wild rose **12.00**
Creamer and Sugar, World Hand Forged, cupped shape **8.00**
Crumb Tray, 12" with well, stamped leaf pattern, Wrought Farberware **12.00**
Desk Set, three pc, graduated sizes, Bali bamboo pattern, B 24, Forged Everlast **20.00**
Gravy Boat, 7" l, Hand Forged/Everlast Metal **10.00**
Ice Bucket, cov, 11½" h, double twisted handles, plastic knob on lid, Lehman **12.00**
Ladle, 14½" l, Argental Cellini Craft . . **18.00**
Lazy Susan, 18", leaf and acorns, Continental Silverlook **15.00**
Match Box Holder, Wendell August Forge **8.00**
Pitcher, Buenilum, ovoid, twisted handle **24.00**
Platter, ftd, grape leaves, tree and well **25.00**
Salad Utensils, wooden, teardrop shape aluminum dec, dogwood pattern . . . **10.00**
Samovar, one gallon container with spigot, double loop finial cov, stand and cov candle holder, unmarked, Buenilum style **35.00**
Server, 11", fluted flange, stamped flowers, removable divider, cov, handles, #5010 Everlast Forged Metal **12.00**
Silent Butler, 6 x 8", oval, floral bouquet, Henry & Miller **8.00**
Tray
  7½ x 14½", zinnia panel, spiral handle, Farber & Shlevin **18.00**

Sandwich Tray, carved primroses, Everlast, 12" sq, $25.00.

10 x 16", gold anodized, chessmen,
Authur Armour **15.00**
11 x 16", bird on flowering limb, N S
Co (National Silver Co) **15.00**
12 x 18", leaf and flower, fluted edge,
Buenilum **17.00**
14 x 20", tulip, handles, #425,
Rodney Kent **25.00**

AMERICAN BISQUE

Collecting Hint: When searching for American Bisque products, look for a mark consisting of three stacked baby blocks with the letters "A," "B," and "C." This common mark is readily found.

History: The American Bisque Company was founded in Williamstown, West Virginia, in 1919. Although the pottery's original product was china head dolls, it quickly expanded its inventory to include serving dishes, cookie jars, ashtrays, and various other decorative ceramic pieces. B. E. Allen, founder of the Sterling China Company, invested heavily in the company and eventually purchased the remaining stock. Sequoia Ware and Berkeley are two trademarks used by American Bisque, the former used on items sold in gift shops, and the latter found on products sold through chain stores. Cookie jars marked with the letters ABC in blocks were also produced by this company. In 1982 the plant was sold and operated briefly under the name American China Company. The plant closed in 1983.

References: Susan and Al Bagdade, *Warman's American Pottery and Porcelain*, Wallace–Homestead, 1994; Mary Jane Giacomini, *American Bisque: A Collector's Guide With Prices*, Schiffer Publishing, 1994; Lois Lehner, *Lehner's Encyclopedia of U.S. Marks on Pottery, Porcelain & Clay*, Collector Books, 1988.

Periodical: *The Pottery Collectors Express*, PO Box 221, Mayview, MO 64071-0221.

Bank
Fred and Wilma Flintstone **275.00**
Little Audrey **550.00**
Popeye **400.00**
Cookie Jar
Albert Apple, marked ABC **90.00**
Baby Elephant **195.00**
Bear with Cookie **50.00**
Blackboard Girl, marked ABC **295.00**
Churn Boy **200.00**
Davy Crockett **425.00**
Lady Pig **110.00**
Pearl Bear, airbrushed, marked ABC **125.00**
Rabbit with Hat **100.00**
Sailor Elephant **50.00**
Spaceship, marked ABC **325.00**

Umbrella Kids, marked ABC **350.00**
Dinnerware, Ballerina Mist, painted
Cereal Bowl **4.00**
Plate
Dinner **5.00**
Lunch **3.00**
Lamp, Billy the Kid **175.00**
Planter
Brown Bear Cubs, tree stump **10.00**
Duck, 24K gold, wearing flower hat **24.00**
Kitten, wailing **20.00**
Parrot, burgundy and green **12.00**
Puppy, 24K gold **35.00**
Rooster, 5" h **16.00**
Salt and Pepper Shakers, pr, churn . . . **65.00**

ANIMATION ART

Collecting Hints: The vocabulary involving animation cels is very specific. The difference between a Courvoisier, Disneyland, master, key production, printed or publication, production, and studio background can mean thousands of dollars in value. Sotheby's and Christie's East, the two major auction houses selling animation art, do not agree on terminology. Read the glossary section of any catalog carefully.

A second of film requires over twenty animation cels. If you multiply the length of a cartoon in minutes times sixty times twenty–four, you will derive the approximate number of cels used to make that cartoon. The question that no one seems to be asking as prices reach the ten– and hundred–thousand dollar level for some cels is what happened to all the other animation cels. Cels exist in storage in vast quantities.

There is no doubt that Walt Disney animation cels are king. Buying is being driven more by nostalgia, legend, and hype than historical importance or workmanship. The real bargains in the field lie outside the Disney material.

Although animation art has a clearly established track record, it also is an area that has proven itself subject to manipulation, representational abuse, and shifting nostalgia trends. It is not the place for the casual collector.

Avoid limited edition serigraphs. A serigraph is a color print made by the silk screen process. Although they appear to be animation cels, they are not.

History: Film historians credit Winsor McCay's 1909 "Gertie the Dinosaur" as the first animated cartoon. Early animated films were largely the work of comic strip artists. The invention of the celluloid process (a "cel" is an animation drawing on celluloid) is attributed to Earl Hurd. Although the technique reached perfection under animation giants such as Walt Disney and Max Fleischer, individuals such as Ub Iwerks, Walter Lantz, and Paul Terry along with studios

such as Columbia, Charles Mints and Screen
Gems, MGM, Paramount/Famous Studios, UPA,
and Warner Brothers did pioneering work.

Leonard Maltin's *Of Mice and Magic: A
History of American Animated Cartoons* (A
Plume Book/New American Library, revised and
upated edition 1987) is excellent for historical
background.

References: Jeff Lofman, *Animation Art: The
Early Years 1911–1954*, Schiffer Publishing,
1995; Jerry Weist, *Original Comic Art:
Identification and Price Guide*, Avon Books,
1992.

Collectors' Club: Greater Washington Animation
Collectors Club, 12423 Hedges Run Drive #184,
Lake Ridge, VA 22192.

Periodicals: *Animation Film Art*, PO Box 25547,
Los Angeles, CA 90025; *Animation Magazine*,
Suite 210, 4676 Admiralty Way, Marina Del Ray,
CA 90292; *Animato!*, PO Box 1240, Cambridge,
MA 02238; *In Toon!*, PO Box 217, Gracie
Station, New York, NY, 10028; *Storyboard/The
Art of Laughter*, 80 Main St., Nashua, NH 03060.

Museums: International Museum of Cartoon Art,
Boca Raton, FL; Museum of Cartoon Art, Rye
Brook, NY; The Baltimore Museum of Art,
Baltimore, MD; The Museum of Modern Art,
New York, NY; Walt Disney Archives, Burbank,
CA.

**Animation Cel, Ursula, *The Little
Mermaid,* Walt Disney, gouache on celluloid, $2,000.00.**

Don Bluth Studio, 7 x 13", An American Tail, Fievel, framed	**825.00**
Filmation Studios, 1970s, Fat Albert and the Cosby Kids, tempera background sheet, framed	**880.00**
Hanna–Barbera Studio, 1960s, 8 x 10", Augie Doggie and Doggie Daddy, tempera background sheet, framed, price for pair	**1,870.00**
King Features, Heinz Edelman, Yellow Submarine, 1968, 7½ x 9" gouache on celluloid, John Lennon and Ringo Starr	**2,200.00**
MGM Studio, Chuck Jones	
Chip and Dale, 1960s, 4 x 8½" gouache on celluloid, chipmunks carrying hobo packs, Disney TV show, untrimmed, framed	**1,045.00**
Horton Hears a Who, 1970, 9 x 12" gouache on celluloid, tempera on background sheet, Horton portrait, studio notes on background	**1,650.00**
Walt Disney Studio	
Donald Duck, 1950s, 7 x 9½" gouache on celluloid, portrait, cel trimmed to 10½ x 12", framed	**990.00**
Dumbo, 1941, 6 x 7", portrait, label on back "prepared by Courvoisier"	**2,650.00**
Melody Time, 1948, 6 x 6½" gouache on celluloid, couple in horse-	

drawn sleigh, Once Upon A
Wintertime, cel trimmed to outline
of figure, framed **715.00**
Mickey's Christmas Carol, 1983, 9 x
14" gouache on celluloid, Willie
the Giant as the Ghost of Christmas
Present, laminated, Disney seal,
untrimmed, framed **475.00**
Mother Goose Goes Hollywood,
1938, 7½ x 7½" gouache on celluloid, Oliver Hardy as the Pieman,
Silly Symphony, untrimmed,
framed **1,650.00**
Peter Pan, 1953, 7 x 3" gouache on
celluloid, full figure portrait of
Michael as Indian, carrying teddy
bear **800.00**
Sleeping Beauty, 1959, 10 x 9"
gouache on celluloid, full figure
Aurora in field, two birds fluttering
overhead, color print background,
Disneyland label on back, cel
trimmed to 12 x 10", framed ... **2,310.00**
Test Pilot Donald, 1951, 5½ x 4"
gouache on celluloid, full figure
Donald Duck wearing mechanic's
cap and aviator jacket, untrimmed,
framed **935.00**
The Jungle Book, 1967, 6½ x 4"
gouache on celluloid, full figure
Baloo, cel trimmed to 10 x 12", unframed **880.00**
The Rescuers, 1977, 7½ x 10½"
gouache on celluloid, Madame
Medusa staring into Devil's Eye diamond, laminated, Disney seal,
untrimmed, framed **825.00**
Who Framed Roger Rabbit?, 1988,
8½ x 11½" gouache on celluloid,
Roger cel mounted on color frame
enlargement of live action film, cel
trimmed to outline of figure, unframed **1,760.00**
Walter Lantz Studio, Woody Woodpecker, late 1940s–early 1950s, 8½ x
11½" gouache on celluloid, colored

pencil on animation sheet, Woody carving name from cartoon title opening, matching animation drawing of Woody, mat insets with recent Woody drawing and Lantz autograph, untrimmed, slit in cel paint **1,650.00**
Warner Brothers Studio
Bugs Bunny, 7 x 3", holding carrot in hand **2,310.00**
Foghorn Leghorn, 1950s, 6 x 4½", full figure, framed **880.00**

AUTOGRAPHS

Collecting Hints: The condition and content of letters and documents bears significantly on value. Signatures should be crisp, clear, and located so that they do not detract from the rest of the item. Whenever possible, obtain a notarized statement of authenticity, especially for pieces over $100.

Forgeries abound. Copying machines compound the problem. Further, many signatures of political figures, especially presidents, movie stars, and sports heroes are machine or secretary signed rather than by the individual themselves. Photographic reproduction can produce a signature resembling an original. Check all signatures using a good magnifying glass or microscope.

Presentation material, something marked "To _____," is of less value than a non–presentation item. The presentation personalizes the piece and often restricts interest, except to someone with the same name.

There are autograph mills throughout the country run by people who write to noteworthy individuals requesting their signatures on large groups of material. They in turn sell this material on the autograph market. Buy an autograph of a living person only after the most careful consideration and examination.

Autograph items are sold using standard abbreviations denoting type and size. They are:

ADS	Autograph Document Signed
ALS	Autograph Letter Signed
AQS	Autograph Quotation Signed
CS	Card Signed
DS	Document (printed) Signed
LS	Letter Signed
PS	Photograph Signed
TLS	Typed Letter Signed
Folio	12 x 16"
4to	8 x 10"
8vo	5 x 7"
12mo	3 x 5"

History: Autograph collecting is an old established tradition, perhaps dating back to the first signed documents and letters. Early letters were few and hence are treasured by individuals in private archives. Municipalities, churches, and other institutions maintained extensive archives to document past actions.

Autograph collecting became fashionable during the 19th century. However, early collectors focused on the signatures alone, clipping off the signed portion of a letter or document. Eventually collectors realized that the entire document was valuable.

The advent of movie stars, followed by sports, rock 'n roll, and television personalities, brought autograph collecting to the popular level. Fans pursued these individuals with autograph books, programs and photographs. Everything imaginable was offered for signatures. Realizing the value of their signatures and the speculation that occurs, modern stars and heroes are less willing to sign material than in the past.

References: Mark Allen Baker, *All Sport Autograph Guide,* Krause Publications, 1994; Mary A. Benjamin, *Autographs: A Key To Collecting,* Dover Publications, 1986; Charles Hamilton, *American Autographs,* University of Oklahoma Press, 1983; George S. Lowry, *Autographs: Identification and Price Guide,* Avon Books, 1994; Norman E. Martinus and Harry L. Rinker, *Warman's Paper,* Wallace–Homestead, 1994; Susan and Steve Raab, *Movie Star Autographs of the Golden Era: 1930–1960,* published by authors, 1994; George Sanders, Helen Sanders, and Ralph Roberts, *The Sanders Price Guide to Sports Autographs, 1994 Edition,* Scott Publishing, 1993; George Sanders, Helen Sanders, and Ralph Roberts, *The 1994 Sanders Price Guide to Autographs, Number 3,* Alexander Books, 1994.

Collectors' Clubs: The Manuscript Society, 350 N. Niagara Street, Burbank, CA 91505; Universal Autograph Collectors Club, PO Box 6181, Washington, DC 20044.

Periodicals: *All–Star Celebrity Address Book,* PO Box 1566, Apple Valley, CA 92307; *Autograph Collector,* 510–A. S. Corona Mall, Corona, CA 91720; *Autograph Dealer's Price Guide,* PO Box 63, Umpqua, CA 97486; *Autograph Quarterly & Buyers Guide,* PO Box 55328, Stockton, CA 95205; *Autograph Times,* 2302 N. 44th St., #225, Phoenix, AZ 85008; *Autographs & Memorabilia,* PO Box 24, Coffeyville, KS 67337; *Celebrity Access Directory,* 20 Sunnyside Ave., Suite #A241, Mill Valley, CA 94921; *John L. Raybin's Baseball Autograph News,* 527 Third Ave., #294–A, New York, NY, 10016; *The Autograph Review,* 305 Carlton Rd., Syracuse, NY 13207; *The Collector,* PO Box 225, Hunter, NY 12442.

Libraries: The New York Public Library, New York, NY; The Pairpoint Morgan Library, New York, NY.

Album Page Signed (AP)
Andrews, Dana 15.00
Baxter, Anne 15.00
Calhern, Louis 15.00
Chevalier, Maurice 35.00
Colman, Ronald 45.00
Cooper, Jackie 15.00
Erksine, John 30.00
Ford, Glenn 25.00
Gaynor, Janet 25.00
Gillette, William, 1936, 3 x 2" 65.00
Grey, Zane 55.00
Hall, John 25.00
Hayworth, Rita 145.00
Knight, Ted 20.00
Laughton, Charles 55.00
Mack, Connie 150.00
Moses, Grandma, 4 x 3" 160.00
Penner, Joe 15.00
Powell, Dick 25.00
Renaldo, Duncan, signed as "Cisco
Kid" 45.00
Ritchard, Cyril 15.00
Weismuller, Johnny, inscribed, Tarzan   75.00
Autograph Letters Signed (ALS)
Bush, George, 41st president, 6 x 5"
blue bordered personalized card,
"8–14–80 Dear Bill—Just a note to
thank you for your loyal support
and to wish you well. During the
War I was a carrier based Navy
Pilot in the Pacific. Shot Down Sept
2 1944, I was rescued by a U.S.
Submarine. Hope all's well with
you–George Bush," inscribed black
white glossy 8 x 10" signed photo
that was sent with the above ALS,
penned across top area with blue
ink To Bill Dooley—a fellow vet
with warm best wishes, George
Bush," 6 x 5" 3,000.00
Fromme, Lynette, member of Manson
Family, attempted to kill President
Ford, holograph address on back of
picture post card, 1986, thanks for
book, full signature 85.00
Gluck, Alma, 6 x 4" personal card,
mounted on gray 12 x 16" board,
book plate photo, and obituary . .   75.00
Hayes, Rutherford B, 19th President,
8 x 5" lined paper 875.00
Izzi, Basil, WWII seaman, plain 5 x 7"
paper 25.00
Knobloch, WWII co–pilot, 8 x 4"
plain white paper 45.00
Melba, Nellie, personal stationery,
photo, and news article about her
death, 5 x 7", 3 pgs 85.00
Potter, Hank, WWII navigator, 8 x 4"
yellow plain paper 20.00
Autograph Quotations Signed (AQS)
Dickinson, Anna E., 4 x 3" 25.00

Pitney, Gene, 4 line quotation, per-
sonal blue stationery, 4 line mes-
sage, 4to 55.00
Stedman, Edmund Clarence, Civil
War correspondent, plain paper,
Dec, 1901, five lines, 4 x 6" 45.00
Suyin, Han, 6 x 5" New Year greeting
card, inscribed 45.00
Thaxter, Cilia, 30 line poem, plain pa-
per, 5 x 7" 60.00
Cards Signed (CS)
Abel, Sid, 5 x 3" unlined card 4.00
Albee, Edward, 5 x 3" 10.00
Andretti, Mario, 5 x 3" 5.00
Austin, Tracey, 5 x 3" 5.00
Bench, Johnny, 5 x 3" unlined card .   7.00
Beecher, Henry Ward, 3 x 2" 45.00
Boyer, Charles, 5 x 3" 30.00
Byrnes, Ed, 8 x 10" black and white
photo, 4 x 2" opening with signa-
ture, 11 x 14" black mat 15.00
Campbell, Malcolm, 4 x 2" 65.00
Chaplin, Charlie, blue ink signature on
white card, matted with magazine
photo, "The Little Tramp," 11 x 16" 250.00
Davis, Bette, 8 x 10" color photo, 4 x
2" opening with signature, 11 x 14"
black mat 20.00
Diddley, Bo, 5 x 3" plain white card   10.00
Dorsett, Tony, 5 x 3" 7.00
Ford, Whitey, 5 x 3" 5.00
Foss, Joe, aviator, 5 x 3" 15.00
Horning, Paul, 5 x 3" 5.00
Hubbell, Carl, 5 x 3" 10.00
Hughes, Sarah T., administered oath
of office to LBJ, Christmas card . . .   45.00
John, Olivia Newton, 5 x 3" plain
white card 10.00
Jones, George, 5 x 3" plain white card   5.00
Kesey, Ken, 5 x 3" 15.00
Kiel, Richard, 9 x 7 color close–up
photo as "Jaws," white card signed
"Richard "Jaws" Kiel," rust colored
mat, 12 x 13" 25.00
Leonard, Buck, 5 x 3" 8.00
Mays, Willie, 4 x 3" 10.00
Mellon, A. W., 3 x 1" 15.00
Perot, Ross, 5 x 3" 15.00
Rehnquist, William, Supreme Court
card 45.00
Retton, Mary Lou, 5 x 3" 5.00
Riggs, Bobby, 5 x 3" 5.00
Roosevelt, Eleanor, White House card 250.00
Salk, Jonas, 5 x 3" plain white card   10.00
Schwab, C. M., imprinted thank you
card, 4 x 4" 35.00
Staubach, Roger, 5 x 3" 10.00
Susann, Jacqueline, 6 x 4", inscribed   75.00
Trudeau, Gary, 5 x 3", inscribed 20.00
Turner, Tina, 4 x 3" plain white card   15.00
Walker, Hershel, 5 x 3" 5.00
Zorn, Jim, 5 x 3" unlined card 4.00

Baltimore Orioles Official Scorebook, 1970, back cover, autographed by Milwaukee Brewers' Brabender, Hegen, Smith, Baldwin, and Ermer, 8½ x 11", $18.00.

Document Signed (DS)

Caldwell, Erskine, typescript, Chapter 1, Tobacco Road, 8 x 10", 1 pg .. 60.00

Capote, Truman, news article, photo at top, black ink signature across photo, 3 x 7" 75.00

Edison, Charles, son of Thomas Edison, National State Bank of Newark check, 1965 . . . . 25.00

Fish, Hamilton, Governor NY, Bank of NY check, 1855 . . . . 40.00

Garland, Judy, bank check, filled in and signed, Jan 22, 1965, check included in black mat to right of close up color photo, random glittering stars and music notes, black metallic plate with name in gold letters beneath photo, under glass, black frame, 28 x 16" 950.00

Thurston, Howard, membership card for Society of American Magicians, 1929 . . . . 95.00

Van Buren, Martin(1782–1862), 8th President, partly printed, 1840, as president, consul appointment to New Granada, co–signed by John Forsyth as Secretary of State, white paper wafer seal intact, left edge discoloration due to long gone frame, wrinkled left side, normal aging, 17 x 12" 800.00

First Day Covers (FDC)

Adams, Ansel and Jousuf Karsh, honoring photography 75.00

Allen, Brooke 20.00

Dickerson, Eric, canceled Dec 9, 1984, day he broke Simpson's sin-

gle season record, color photo cachet of scoring 30.00

Duke, Charlie, Ed Mitchell, Harrison Schmidt, astronauts 125.00

Eisenhower, Mamie Doud, honoring Dwight Eisenhower, canceled, Washington, DC, May 21, 1971 .. 20.00

Fisher, Anna Lee 20.00

Hayes, Anna Mae 20.00

Ivanov, George & Nikolai Rukavish-nikov, Russian cosmonauts 75.00

Merrill, Dick 60.00

Seeger, Pete 15.00

Taylor, Maxwell 95.00

Thomas, Clarence 20.00

Townsend, Peter 50.00

Truman, Harry S, President, honoring 150th Anniversary of Missouri statehood 125.00

Letters Signed (LS)

Hale, John P., lined paper, Washington, DC, 1863, 8vo 30.00

Nutting, Wallace, personal stationery, imprinted vignette of one of his works on upper center of 1st page, 1941, orig holograph envelope, 2 pgs 275.00

Seward, William H., Secretary of State, plain stationery, 1861, 12mo 35.00

Photograph Signed (PS)

Ashford, Evelyn, color, 4to 12.00

Brubeck, Dave, black and white glossy, 8 x 10" 10.00

Carey, Harry, sepia, 5 x 7" 150.00

Charo, Cuchi–Cuchi, black and white glossy, 8 x 10" 50.00

Crosby, Bing, black and white matte portrait, 8 x 10" 50.00

Denver, Bob, black and white glossy, "Gilligan," 8 x 10" 15.00

Dern, Bruce, black and white glossy, 8 x 10" 10.00

Elway, John, color, 4to 15.00

Funicello, Annette and Frankie Avalon, black and white glossy, beach scene from "Where The Boys Are," 8 x 10" 40.00

Ishkabibble, sepia, bust pose, wearing funny hat, 4 x 5" 20.00

Jackson, Jesse, bust pose, smiling, color, 8 x 10" 55.00

Joel, Billy, color, 8 x 10" 40.00

LaBelle, Patti, black and white glossy, 8 x 10" 15.00

Lawford, Peter, sepia, 8 x 10" 60.00

Lombardo, Victor, sepia portrait, 4to 20.00

McIntyre, Joe, New Kids On The Block, color, 8 x 10" 60.00

Meeker, Bobby, publicity, 8 x 10" .. 10.00

Montana, Joe, 4to 15.00

Motley Crue, four signatures, color performance, 8 x 10" 95.00

Nelson, Cindy, color, 4to	**12.00**
O'Connor, Sinead, close–up, signed first name only, color, 8 x 10" . . .	**75.00**
Righteous Brothers, color, 8 x 10" . .	**55.00**
Spillane, Mickey, color publicity photo, Lite Beer, 5 x 7"	**15.00**
Walker, Hershel, color, 4to	**15.00**

Typed Letters Signed (TLS)

Ferber, Edna, personal stationery, 1962, 4to	**50.00**
Fosdick, Harry Emerson, Baptist minister and author, Union Theological Seminary stationery, 1925, 8 x 8"	**25.00**
Galli–Curci, Amelita, plain paper, 1922, 4to	**75.00**
Hoover, J. Edgar, FBI stationery, 1936, blue ink signature, 7 x 9"	**60.00**
Hubbard, Elbert, Roycroft Shop stationery, 1900, 12mo	**48.00**
Hughes, Charles E., Chief Justice, Supreme Court, Governor of NY, Executive Chamber stationery, gold emb seal, 1910	**50.00**
Hull, Cordell, secretary of state, Dept of State stationery, 1937, 4to	**50.00**
Humphrey, Hubert, Senate stationery, 1971	**25.00**
MacDonald, Betty, personal stationery, 8vo	**20.00**
McCool, Harry C., WWII navigator, plain white paper, 8 x 8"	**20.00**
Mencken, H. L., personal stationery, 1946, 8 x 5"	**125.00**
Porter, Katherine Anne, plain stationery, 1958, 8 x 6"	**85.00**
Rogers, Richard, personal stationery, 1973, 7 x 9"	**40.00**
Turner, Ted, business stationery, 4to	**15.00**

AVIATION COLLECTIBLES

Collecting Hints: This field developed in the 1980s and is now firmly established. The majority of collectors focused on personalities, especially Charles Lindbergh and Amelia Earhart. New collectors are urged to look to the products of airlines, especially those items related to the pre–jet era.

History: The first airlines in the United States depended on subsidies from the government for carrying mail for most of their income. The first non–Post Office Department flight for mail carrying was in 1926 between Detroit and Chicago. By 1930 there were 38 domestic and 5 international airlines operating in the United States. A typical passenger load was ten. After World War II, four–engine planes with a capacity of 100 or more passengers were introduced.

The jet age was launched in the 1950s. In 1955 Capitol Airlines used British–made turbo-prop airliners in domestic service. In 1958 National Airlines began domestic jet passenger service. The giant Boeing 747 went into operation in 1970 as part of the Pan American fleet. The Civil Aeronautics Board, which regulates the airline industry, ended control of routes in 1982 and fares in 1983.

Major American airlines include American Airlines, Delta Air Lines, Northwest Airlines, Pan American World Airways, Trans World Airlines, and United Airlines. There are many regional lines as well; new airlines are forming as a result of deregulation.

References: Aeronautica & Air Label Collectors Club of Aerophilatelic Federation of America, *Air Transport Label Catalog*, published by club; Stan Baumwald, *Junior Crew Member Wings*, published by author; Trev Davis and Fred Chan, *Airline Playing Cards: Illustrated Reference Guide, 2nd Edition*, published by authors, 1987; Lynn Johnson and Michael O'Leary, *En Route: Label Art from the Golden Age of Air Travel*, Chronicle Books, 1993; Norman E. Martinus and Harry L. Rinker, *Warman's Paper*, Wallace–Homestead, 1994; Richard R. Wallin, *Commercial Aviation Collectibles: An Illustrated Price Guide*, Wallace–Homestead, 1990.

Collectors' Clubs: Aeronautica & Air Label Collectors Club, PO Box 1239, Elgin, IL 60121; C.A.L.'s;N–X–211 Collectors Society, 226 Tioga Ave., Bensenville, IL 60106; The World Airline Historical Society, 3381 Apple Tree Lane, Erlanger, KY 41018.

Periodical: *Airliners*, PO Box 52–1238, Miami, FL 33152.

COMMERCIAL

Brochure, Pan Am Jet Clippers Are Here, 8½ x 11½", full color, Pan American World Airways copyright 1958	**25.00**
Calendar	
Scandinavian Air Lines, 1950	**8.00**
United Airlines, 13 scenes, 1943 . . .	**20.00**
Chopsticks, TWA, clear package, unopened	**15.00**
Figure, 27" h, United Airlines, three dimensional, Good Luck Man	**100.00**
Flatware	
Teaspoon, 6½" l, National on handle	**7.50**
Fork, 6½" l, Pan Am in globe on handle	**6.50**
Game, Pan Am World Jet Flight Game, Hasbro, playing board, plastic aircraft playing pcs, die, shaker cup, and 40 cards, orig box, 1956 Pan American World Airways copyright	**65.00**

Glass, Eastern Airlines	10.00
Map, Air France, world routes, early 1940s	30.00
Matchbook Cover, 3 x 4½", Piedmont	.50
Mirror, KLM Airlines, illus of plane, brown and white	50.00
Paperweight, Trans World Airlines, Framed Milestones, Man in Flight, six medallions	65.00
Pin, United Airlines, 1" w, metal, logo, 1930–1940s	15.00
Pinback Button, United Airlines Boeing 747–D, ¹³⁄₁₆" d, litho, black and white illus, yellow ground	10.00
Plate, American Airlines, china, marked Hall	10.00
Playing Cards, Delta Air Lines, San Francisco on back	8.00
Poster, TWA to Las Vegas, 28 x 40", 1953	20.00
Punchboard, Benrus Watches, "Official Watch of Famous Airlines," small, 1940	10.00
Service Pin, Pan Am	70.00
System Map, American Airlines	15.00
Timetable	
Pan–Am, c1936	30.00
United Airlines, 1935	30.00

GENERAL

Ashtray, brass, made from shell casings	45.00
Banner, "Welcome Trans–Atlantic Heroes," 9 x 13", felt, illus of mono-plane "Bremen" and aviators von Huenefeld, Fitzmaurice, and Coehl, orange and tan illus, yellow accents, white lettering, dark blue ground, April 1928 flight	85.00
Blotter, 3½ x 6¼", cardboard, illus and description of P51 North American Mustang pursuit plane, Bond Bread adv, early 1940s	12.00
Book	
Aeroplane Cut–outs, 9¾ x 14¾", Whitman, #W933, stiff paper pun-chout pgs, 1930	75.00
Heroes of Aviation, Laurence LaTourette Driggs, dj, 1927	20.00
Calendar Plate, 6½" d, biplane, 1912 .	35.00
Clock, figural airplane, wood and metal, Sessions	40.00
Coloring Book, Planes and Jets, Whitman, 11 x 15", 1952, half neatly colored	18.00
Comic Book, Aviation Cadets, Street & Smith, 1943	12.00
Employee Identification Badge, St Paul Airport Official, 1¾" d, yellow and black, c1930	12.00
Game, Aviation Air Mail, Parker Brothers, c1930s	18.00

Helmet, leather, pilot, 1930s	35.00
Jigsaw Puzzle, Night Bombing Over Germany, 14½ x 21", Victory Series, #315, full color, JS Publishing Corp, New York City, 1943 copyright	18.00
Magazine, Popular Aviation, Dec 1932, 68 pgs, 8½ x 11¼"	8.00
Model, Grumman F–14, 10¼" l, plastic and metal, gray, clear plastic teardrop base	100.00

Needle Case, Trans-Atlantic Aeroplane Needle Book, multicolored litho, $5.00.

Pennant, 28½" l, felt, airship Akron, Goodyear hangar structure and air-ship illus, early 1930s	75.00
Pinback Button	
Howie Wing Aviation Corps/Cadet, ⅞" d, dark blue on gold ground, club member button, 1930s	25.00
Parachute Jumps, 2¼" d, light blue photo, orange and blue inscription, c1930	18.00
The Sky Climbers, brown, blue, black, and white	28.00

Plaque, 100,000 Mile Club, United Airlines, 1955, 6½ x 8½", $20.00.

Promotional Photograph, Eagle Squadron, movie lobby contest, real airplane illus **28.00**

Ribbon

Goodyear Zeppelin Trip, winner of newsboy contest, July 7, 1931, white, blue letters **50.00**

National Air Races, News–Bee Pilot, Toledo, Sept 4, 1931, pale blue, black lettering **50.00**

Sheet Music, *Come Josephine in My Flying Machine (Up She Goes!)*, 10½ x 13½", red, white, and blue cov illus, young couple in early biplane, orig loose center page, 1910 copyright **30.00**

Stamp Album, 5½ x 8", soft cov, 20 pgs, premium, issued by Tydol–Veedol service stations, copyright 1940 .... **30.00**

Tin, Aero Eastern Oil Can, 2 gallon size, DC3 airplane illus **95.00**

Toy

Boeing 707, tin, Japan, MIB **65.00**

Boeing Stratocruiser, four motors, 13" wingspan, metal **125.00**

Capital Airlines, four motors, 17" wingspan, tin, Japan **95.00**

FW–189 ID, MIB **95.00**

Jenny, bi–wing, 15" wingspan, tin, Japan **150.00**

Jet, folding wings

Red and blue, 11½" wingspan, landing gear, Hubley, MIB **125.00**

Red and silver, 6" wingspan **45.00**

Yellow and green, 8" wingspan, landing gear, Hubley, MIB **75.00**

P–40, Hubley, diecast

Orange, red, and silver **65.00**

Yellow and green camouflage ... **65.00**

Red Baron, tri–wing, 9" l **95.00**

Super Sonic Jet Liner, tin, battery operated, Japan, 24" l **95.00**

Twin Engine, retractable wheels, Hubley, MIB **75.00**

USA Defense Bomber, two motors, 13" wingspan **75.00**

US Army, tin, Japan, MIB **55.00**

Voo Doo Jet, US Air Force, friction and battery, 19" l, Japan **250.00**

PERSONALITIES

Byrd, Richard E.

Commemorative Coin, 1¾" d, nickel, portrait, "First Over South Pole, Byrd Ant. Exp. 1928–1930" **18.00**

Pinback Button, 1³⁄₁₆" d, Yank Junior Airplane Series, litho, multicolored, plane, "Fokker F32/Admiral Byrd's North Pole Plane," 1930s .. **20.00**

Pocket Watch, 2" d, silvered case,

black and white dial face illus of Byrd's plane over Antarctic camp, etched image inscription "Trail Blazer/Commemorating Byrd's Antarctic Expedition" on reverse, 1929–30 .... **300.00**

Earhart, Amelia

Photograph, 7½ x 9½", black and white, supplement of *Philadelphia Record*, Sunday, July 11, 1937 ... **15.00**

Pinback Button, Bond Bread, #4, "Amelia Earhart's Friendship," black, white, and red **20.00**

Lindbergh, Charles

Blotter and Card, Lindbergh and *Spirit of St Louis* illus, 1927 .... **45.00**

Bread Wrapper, 12 x 21½", Lindy Bread, waxed paper, repeated Lindbergh illus **75.00**

Commemorative Item

Telephone Pad, 3 x 4", blue and white celluloid cov depicts Lindy, his plane, Statue of Liberty, and Eiffel Tower, attaches to candlestick phone, unused, 1928–29 calendar **115.00**

Tray, 3¼ x 5", white china, hp, Lindy's plane, US and French flags on continents, Moisy & LeRoi, dated May 21, 1927 ... **69.00**

Label, cigar, 6½ x 7¾", *Spirit of St Louis*, New York and Paris skylines, plane flying overhead, American Lithograph Co **15.00**

Model, Air Force Rescue Boat, motorized, orig box, unassembled **48.00**

Noise Maker, 7" h, horn, souvenir, cardboard, wood mouth tip, oval sepia portrait sticker, 1927 ...... **100.00**

Pencil Case, litho tin, black and white photos, black "WE" inscription, Wallace Pencil Co, late 1920s ... **60.00**

Pennant, 25¾" l, blue felt, white portrait and "Welcome Home" inscription **50.00**

Photograph, 9½ x 7½", Lindbergh standing beside *Spirit of St Louis*, just prior to flight, at inspection of oil or fuel line **125.00**

Pinback Button, photo with plane silhouette background, black and white **20.00**

Pocket Watch, 2" d, silvered brass, illus of Lindy's plane above "New York to Paris Airplane Model" inscription, New York and Paris skyline illus on reverse **300.00**

Post Card, 3¼ x 5¼", Lindbergh, 1927 Trans–Atlantic Flight, monotone photos, set of 4 .... **45.00**

Puzzle, picture on both sides, complete **25.00**

Sheet Music, *Lindbergh (The Eagle of the USA)*, 9 x 12", 6 pgs, sepia photos, 1927 .... **20.00**
Tablet, 8 x 10", lined paper, black and white cov photos, Lindy and his plane, flight statistics, 1927–28 .. **32.00**
Tapestry, 19 x 56", soft colors, woven, Lindy and plane over skylines of New York and Mexico City, 1" wide fringe, blue ground **75.00**
Rickenbacker, Eddie
    Advertising Booklet, "Flying News," published by the American Society for Promotion of Aviation, 5 x 8", soft cov, 32 pgs, black and white photos, 1930 .... **15.00**
    Autograph, 3 x 4" book plate, bust pose, casual attire **60.00**
    Game, Rickenbacker Ace Game—Keep Em Flying, Milton Bradley, 1945 .... **20.00**
Trout, Bobbie, pinback button, 13⁄16" d, litho, black and white, "Bobbie Trout/Woman Transport Pilot," #67 in series, 1930s **22.00**
Wright Brothers
    Calendar Plate, 8½" d, 1912 ...... **30.00**
    Pinback Button, Wright Brothers Home Celebration, ⅞" d, 1909 Dayton, OH, event, full color portraits, green shaded ground, white text **75.00**

AVON

Collecting Hints: Avon collectibles cover a wide range of objects, including California Perfume Company bottles, decanters, soaps, children's items, jewelry, plates, catalogs, etc. Another phase of collecting focuses on Avon representatives' and managers' awards.

Avon products are well marked. Four main marks exist. The name of the California Perfume Company appeared from 1930 to 1936. The words "Avon Products, Inc." have been used since 1937 on the trademark.

Due to the vast number of Avon collectibles, a collector should buy only items of interest. Do not ignore foreign Avon material, although it is hard to find. New items take longer to increase in value than older items. Do not change the object in any way. This destroys the value.

History: David H. McConnell founded the California Perfume Co. in 1886. He hired saleswomen, a radical concept for that time. They used a door-to-door technique to sell their first product, "Little Dot," a set of five perfumes; thus was born the "Avon Lady." By 1979 there were more than one million Avon ladies.

In 1929, California Perfume Co. became the Avon Company. The tiny perfume company grew into a giant corporation. Avon bottles attracted collector interest in the 1960s.

References: Bud Hastin, *Bud Hastin's Avon Collectible Price Guide*, published by author, 1991; Bud Hastin, *Bud Hastin's Avon Products & California Perfume Co. Collector's Encyclopedia*, 13th Edition, published by author, 1994; Joe Weiss, *Avon 8—Western World Handbook & Price Guide to Avon Bottles*, Western World Publishers, 1987.

Collectors' Clubs: National Assoc. of Avon Collectors, Inc., PO Box 7006, Kansas City, MO 64113; Shawnee Avon Bottle Collectors Club, 1418 32nd NE, Canton, OH 44714; Sooner Avon Bottle Collectors Club, 6119 S. Hudson, Tulsa, OK 74136; Western World Avon Collectors Club, PO Box 23785, Pleasant Hills, CA 94523.

Periodical: *Avon Times*, PO Box 9868, Kansas City, MO 64134.

Museum: Nicholas Avon Museum, Clifton, VA.

REPRODUCTION ALERT

Note: Prices quoted are for empty, mint and boxed condition.

Awards and Representative's Gifts
    Bracelet, silver, bell, ringing, 1961 .. **22.00**
    Clock, travel alarm, gold label, 1977 **16.00**
    Corsage, green and gold, red holly, Avon seven dollar bill, 1960 .... **20.00**
    Cup, 6½", pewter, 4A Design, 1977 **42.00**
    Jewelry Box, 10 x 5", brocade and brass, musical, 1968 **55.00**
    Key Chain, gold horseshoe, blue box, 1971 .... **18.00**
    Money Clip, 10K gold filled, 4A Design, initials, 1963 .... **70.00**
    Pin, red circle, gold feather, 50th Anniversary, 1936 .... **50.00**
California Perfume Company
    Atomizer, glass, green paint, gold plated top, 1928 .... **85.00**
    Bay Rum, 8 oz, glass, green and black label, 1930 .... **42.00**
    Christmas Perfume, 2 oz, glass stopper, 1905 .... **145.00**
    Cold Cream, 2 oz, glass, white, aluminum lid, 1926 .... **48.00**
    Elite Foot Powder, paper, round, 1919 **85.00**
    Rouge, powder can, 1908 .... **50.00**
    Sachet, powder, envelopes, 1908 ... **35.00**
    Shaving Stick, nickel, 3 pcs, 1923 .. **44.00**
    Tooth Powder, glass bottle, white, 1908 .... **105.00**
    Violet Perfume, 1 oz, gift box, 1915 **95.00**
Children's Toys
    Batman Brush, plastic, 1977 ...... **6.50**
    Bumbley Bee Pin, yellow, black stripes, 1973 .... **5.00**

Crayola Lip Gloss, plastic, crayon shape, 3 pcs, 1981 . . . . **4.00**

First Mate Sailor Shampoo, 8 oz, plastic, 1964 . . . . **14.00**

Funny Bunny Pin, perfume glace, 1973 . . . . **4.50**

Globe Bank, bubble bath, 10 oz, plastic, 1967 . . . . **15.00**

Jumpin' Jimminy, bubble bath, 8 oz, 6", 1970 . . . . **4.00**

Looney Lather, bubble bath, 6 oz, 1971 . . . . **4.00**

Six Shooter, no tears shampoo, 6 oz, plastic, 1962 . . . . **15.00**

Snoopy Comb and Brush, 5½", 1972 **4.00**

Spinning Top, bubble bath, 4 oz, 1966 . . . . **8.00**

Toofie the Clown, toothbrush holder, plastic, blue and pink brushes, 1978 . . . . **2.00**

Men's Items

Deodorant, ½ oz, sample bottle, 1950 **24.00**

Figural

Alaskan Moose, after shave, 8 oz, glass, amber, 1974 . . . . **6.00**

Barber Shop Brush, cologne, 1½" oz, glass, brown, 1976 . . . . **4.00**

Blood Hound Pipe, after shave, 5 oz, glass, tan paint, 1976 . . . . . **5.00**

Bugatti '27, after shave, 6½ oz, glass, black, 1975 . . . . **9.00**

Calculator, black, 1979 . . . . **5.00**

Classic Lion, after shave, 8 oz, glass, green, 1973 . . . . **5.00**

Dutch Pipe, cologne, 2 oz, glass, white, 1973 . . . . **6.00**

Ferrari '53, after shave, 2 oz, glass, amber, 1974 . . . . **2.00**

Fire Fighter, after shave, 6 oz, glass, red paint, 1975 . . . . **6.00**

Golf Cart, green, 1973 . . . . **4.50**

Liberty Bell, after shave, 5 oz, sprayed bronze, 1976 . . . . **4.00**

Pheasant, brown, green plastic head, 1972 . . . . **7.50**

Piano, after shave, 4 oz, 4", glass, amber, 1972 . . . . **3.00**

Rainbow Trout, 1973 . . . . **5.00**

Smooth Going Oil Can, after shave, 1½ oz, glass, SP, 1978 . . **3.50**

Snowmobile, after shave, 4 oz, glass, blue, 1974 . . . . **4.50**

Spark Plug, after shave, 1½ oz, glass, white, 1975 . . . . **3.00**

Spirit of St Louis, silver paint, 1970 **12.00**

Stage Coach, brown **7.50**

Stein, 6 oz, glass, silver paint, 1968 **5.00**

Wild Mustang Pipe, cologne, 3 oz, glass, white paint, 1976 . . . . . . **4.00**

Hair Tonic, 6 oz, glass, 1938 . . . . . **28.00**

Spicy Soap Set, brown, five bars, 1965 . . . . **20.00**

Talc, black and white can, 1959 . . . **10.00**

Traveler Set, 4 oz, shaving lotion, cream, toothpaste, 1941 . . . . **65.00**

Windjammer Towelettes, blue and white box, 1968 . . . . **2.00**

Miscellaneous

Candle, turtle, glass, white and green, 1972 . . . . **4.00**

Christmas Plate, 1975 through 1980, each **12.00**

Nail Clipper, 1960 . . . . **6.00**

National Association of Avon Collectors Bottle, Avon lady club bottle, porcelain, blue, 1975 . . . . **35.00**

Mirror, convention banquet, white and red, St Louis, MO, June 1979 **9.00**

Plate, 6th in series, 1936 Avon lady, 1982 . . . . **30.00**

President's Set, antique brush gold, six busts, 1980 . . . . **125.00**

Ribbon, convention banquet, blue, 1973 . . . . **12.00**

Women's Items

Attention, toilet water, 2 oz, purple cap, 1942 . . . . **45.00**

Bath Salts, ribbed glass, blue cap, 1933 . . . . **65.00**

Bird of Paradise, bath oil, 6 oz, plastic, blue, 1974 . . . . **3.00**

Cameo Brooch, gold, pink and white lady's face, 1965 . . . . **20.00**

Charisma Foaming Bath Oil, clock, white, 5 oz, $5.00.

Cotillion Hairspray, 7 oz, pink can, 1966 . . . . **5.00**

Deluxe Lipstick, carved ivory, 1970 **4.00**

Empress Compact, green, 1971 . . . . **4.00**

Face Powder, paper box, silver and blue, 1936 . . . . **20.00**

Figural

Angel Song, cologne, 1 oz, frosted glass, 1979 . . . . **3.00**

Betsy Ross, white, 1976 . . . . **12.00**

Church Mouse Bride, milk glass base, 1978 . . . . **5.00**

Golden Thimble, cologne, 2 oz, clear glass, 1972	**4.00**
Good Fairy, cologne, 3 oz, glass, blue paint, 1978	**6.00**
Looking Glass, hand mirror shape, 1970	**3.00**
Magic Pumpkin Coach, cologne, 1 oz, glass, 1976	**4.00**
Planter, hanging, glass, green, bath crystals and rope, 1977	**8.00**
Regal Peacock, cologne, 4 oz, glass, blue, gold cap, 1974	**12.00**
Sea Treasure, bath oil, 5 oz, glass, gold cap, 1971	**10.00**
Skater's Waltz, cologne, 4 oz, glass, 1979	**10.00**
Sweet Tooth Terrier, cologne, 1 oz, glass, white, 1979	**4.00**
Venetian Pitcher, cologne, 3 oz, plastic, blue, 1973	**6.00**
Floral Talc Trio, 3½ oz, 1965	**15.00**
French Ribbon Sachet Pillows, satin, blue, 1978	**8.00**
Lavender Soap, 3 pcs, 1946	**45.00**
Mascara, paper box, blue and white feather design, 1945	**15.00**
Nail Beauty, 1 oz, white jar and lid, 1955	**3.00**
Pomander	
American Tradition, 5 x 7", wood look frame, 1982	**12.00**
Pampered Piglet, ceramic, 1979 . .	**10.00**
Parasol, wax chips, lavender, 1975	**5.00**
Pretty Peach Soap, two peach halves, seed center, 1965	**25.00**
Rapture Perfumed Oil, ½ oz, glass, green, 1964	**10.00**
Vanity Tray, 10 x 12", metal, 1980 . .	**10.00**

BANKS, STILL

Collecting Hints: The rarity of a still bank has much to do with determining its value. Common banks, such as tin advertising banks, have limited value. The Statue of Liberty cast iron bank by A. C. Williams sells for hundreds of dollars. See Long and Pitman's book for a rarity scale for banks.

Banks are collected by maker, material, or subject. Subject is the most prominent, focusing on categories such as animals, food, mailboxes, safes, transportation, world's fair, etc. There is a heavy crossover in buyers from other collectible fields.

Banks are graded by condition. They should be in very good to mint condition and retain all original paint or decorative motif. Few banks are truly rare; hence, the collector should wait until he finds a bank in the condition he seeks.

History: Banks with no mechanical action are known as still banks. The first banks were made of wood, pottery, or from gourds. Redware and stoneware banks, made by America's early potters, are prized possessions of today's collectors.

Still banks reached a "golden age" with the arrival of the cast iron bank. Leading manufacturing companies include Arcade Mfg. Co., J. Chein & Co., Hubley, J. & E. Stevens, and A. C. Williams. The banks often were ornately painted to enhance their appeal. During the cast iron era, some banks and other businesses used the still bank as a form of advertising.

The tin lithograph advertising bank reached its zenith between 1930 and 1955. The tin bank was an important premium, whether it be a Pabst Blue Ribbon beer can bank or a Gerber's Orange Juice bank. Most tin advertising banks resembled the packaging shape of the product.

Almost every substance has been used to make a still bank—die cast white metal, aluminum, brass, plastic, glass, etc. Many of the early glass candy containers also converted to banks once the candy was eaten. Thousands of varieties of still banks were made and hundreds of new varieties appear on the market each year.

References: Savi Arbola and Marco Onesti, *Piggy Banks*, Chronicle Books, 1992; Don Cranmer, *Collectors Encyclopedia: Toys–Banks*, L–W Book Sales, 1986, 1994–95 value update; Don Duer, *A Penny Saved: Still and Mechanical Banks*, Schiffer Publishing, 1993; Dick Heuser, *Heuser's Quarterly Price Guide To Official Collectible Banks*, Heuser Enterprises, 1992; Earnest and Ida Long and Jane Pitman, *Dictionary of Still Banks*, Long's Americana, 1980; Andy and Susan Moore, *Penny Bank Book: Collecting Still Banks*, Schiffer Publishing, 1984, 1994 value update; Hubert B. Whiting, *Old Iron Still Banks*, Forward's Color Productions, Inc., 1968, out of print.

Periodical: *Heuser's Quarterly Collectible Bank Newsletter,* 508 Clapson Road, PO Box 300, West Winfield, NY 13491.

Collectors' Club: Still Bank Collectors Club of America, 1456 Carson Ct., Homewood, IL 60430.

REPRODUCTION ALERT

Advertising	
Amoco 586 Oil	**15.00**
Bob's Big Boy, figural	**24.00**
Hershey Bar	**35.00**
Howard Johnson's Restaurants, 3½" h, plastic, restaurant replica, late 1950s	**25.00**
McDonald's, 5¼" h, plastic, wastebasket shape, yellow lid, white bin, McDonald's logos, 1975 copyright	**15.00**
Pig, adv, cast iron	**70.00**

Red Goose Shoes, 4½" h **198.00**
Rival Dog Food **10.00**
Wolf's Head Oil, can shape **16.00**
Arabian Safe, cast iron **130.00**
Astronaut Daily Dime, 2½ x 2½ x ¾"
   thick, tin, multicolored, c1960 . . . . .   **25.00**
Bank Building, 3½" h, cast iron, turret
   top **95.00**
Baseball, Chein **25.00**
Baseball Player, child, 6¼" h, composi-
   tion, painted, "Pittsburgh" on uniform
   shirt, c1960 . . . .   **18.00**
Beaky, metal, Warner Bros **45.00**
Bear, celluloid, nightlight and bank . . .   **38.00**
Big Al, Treasure Craft **20.00**
Book, *My Penny Bank*, cardboard, emb
   image of teen-age Penny character
   created by Harry Haenigsen, early
   1940s **30.00**
Boy Scout, cast iron, orig paint **95.00**
Camel, cast iron, painted red **90.00**
Chevy Coupe, 7½" l, 2½" h, metal, sil-
   ver accents, black ground, black rubber tires, marked "Maryland Black,"
   late 1940s **130.00**
Chicago World's Fair, Sears Building,
   4½" h, cast iron, painted, white, blue
   accents made by Arcade, 1934 . . . .   **400.00**
Coronation Throne, 3½" h, metal, sil-
   vered, replica English throne, profile
   portrait of Queen Elizabeth on back-
   rest, inscribed "Coronation 1953,"
   marked "Sixpenny Piece Bank" **25.00**
Darth Vader, ceramic, Roman Ceramics   **95.00**
Donald Duck, china, standing **350.00**
Drum, Chein **50.00**
Elephant
   Cast Iron
      On Tub, circus blanket, orig paint   **139.00**
      Standing, howdah **70.00**
   Glass, Lucky Jumbo, excellent paint   **98.00**
ET, 6" h, ceramic, glazed, figural, yel-
   low, orange, and brown, early 1980s   **25.00**
Flower the Skunk, *Bambi*, 7" h, plaster,
   red, blue, and green airbrushed ac-
   cents on black and white ground,
   c1940 . . . .   **50.00**
Fred Flintstone, 9" h, vinyl, brown base,
   Homecraft Products, 1973 Hanna–
   Barbera copyright **25.00**
Galen, 11" h, plastic, Planet of the Apes
   character, figural, brown base, Play
   Pal Plastics, copyright 1974 Apjac
   Productions **30.00**
Globe
   Cast Iron, combination, planetary
      globe on claw foot **100.00**
   Chein **10.00**
Gulliver's Travels, 1 x 3 x 4¼", book
   shape, metal, key–open, simulated
   white leather cov, emb depiction of
   Twinkletoes and Gabby's horse, "The

Atlas Fruit Jar, glass, 3¾" h, $7.50.

   First Step" and "Zell" inscribed on
   spine, copyright Paramount Pictures,
   1939 . . . .   **50.00**
Hopalong Cassidy, 4½" h, plastic, por-
   trait bust image, bronze color, red
   and olive green accents, Texas bank
   premium, early 1950s **60.00**
Howdy Doody on Pig, 7" h, china, early
   1950s **280.00**
Humpty Dumpty, pot metal **28.00**
Liberty Bell, 4" h, cast iron, figural,
   bronze finish, 1776–1926 Sesqui–
   centennial inscriptions on each side   **75.00**
Lincoln, bust, metal **25.00**
Mary Had A Little Lamb, metal **28.00**
Mickey Mouse, 5" h, composition,
   alarm clock shape, "Time to Save,"
   yellow and gold, red, white, and
   black image of Mickey on dial, foil
   sticker reads "Enesco Imports/Japan,"
   c1960 . . . .   **70.00**
Middy Bank, cast iron **85.00**
Money Hungry, 6" h, plastic, spool
   shape, set of teeth mounted on top,
   inscribed "Lick Inflation/Money
   Talks/Put Your Money Where Your
   Mouth Is" around sides, Poynter
   Products, 1975 . . . .   **30.00**
Monkey, china, red jacket, Regal China   **150.00**
New Deal, Chein **90.00**
New York World's Fair, 6 x 6 x 4", glass,
   inscribed "Watch Your Savings Grow
   With Esso" and "New York World's
   Fair 1939," Trylon and Perisphere im-
   ages **50.00**
Penguin, 8" h, plastic, Batman charac-
   ter, figural from waist up, Mego,
   copyright National Periodical Publi-
   cations **65.00**
Pig
   Cast Iron, seated **60.00**
   China, ivory ground, pink clover and
      bow in relief on back **100.00**

Pinocchio, metal, no trap **25.00**
Popeye Daily Dime Register, litho tin, characters pictured on sides, copyright 1956 . . . . **68.00**
Porky Pig, pink **35.00**
Post Office Box, cast iron **40.00**
Prince Valiant, litho tin, full color illus of Prince Valiant on horse, castle, King Features Syndicate, copyright 1954 . . . . **65.00**
Raggedy Ann, 6" h, composition, painted, gold yarn hair, Japan, c1950 **60.00**
RCA Victor Dog, 6¼" h, metal, orig closure **250.00**
Roller Safe, cast iron **105.00**
Rosco Bear, glass, figural **10.00**
Roy Rogers and Trigger, 7½" h, china, glossy glaze, inscription on base front, c1950 . . . . **200.00**
Sailor, ceramic, Seaman's **40.00**
Santa, 5" h, pottery, golden brown glaze, skinny, standing with bag . . . **124.00**
Snowman, top hat, ABC **35.00**
Statue of Liberty, 6" h, cast iron **115.00**
Takasashi Cat **25.00**
Television, 1½ x 2 x 4" h, litho tin, brown wood design, black and white screen and accents, "Television Co of Baltimore" marked on top, c1950 . . **25.00**
Terrytoon character, 8½" h, plastic, gold with black and white accents, coins deposited in horn–like nose, Spec Toy, copyright Terrytoons, c1950 . . . **25.00**
Tin Can, 2¼" d, 3½" h, tin, souvenir, litho illus, exhibit buildings, skyride, and airship, inscribed "Made by the American Can Company at a Century of Progress, Chicago, 1934" **45.00**
Troll, 7" h, vinyl, blue hair, brown glass eyes, flannel outfit and hair bow, c1960 . . . . **50.00**
World Globe, 17" h, 5" h tin litho, rooster on top crows when cranked **95.00**

BARBER SHOP COLLECTIBLES

Collecting Hints: Many barber shop collectibles have a porcelain finish. If chipped or cracked, the porcelain is difficult, if not impossible, to repair. Buy barber poles and chairs in very good or better condition. A good display appearance is a key consideration.

Many old barber shops are still in business. Their back rooms often contain excellent display pieces.

History: The neighborhood barber shop was an important social and cultural institution in the 19th and first half of the 20th centuries. Men and boys gathered to gossip, exchange business news, and check current fashions. "Girlie" magazines and comic books, usually forbidden at home, were among the reading literature, as were adventure and police gazettes and magazines.

In the 1960s the number of barber shops dropped by half in the United States. "Unisex" shops broke the traditional men–only barriers. In the 1980s several chains ran barber and hair dressing shops on a regional and national basis.

References: Keith E. Estep, *The Shaving Mug and Barber Bottle Book*, Schiffer Publishing, 1995; Richard Holiner, *Collecting Barber Bottles*, Collector Books, 1986; Phillip L. Krumholz, *A History of Shaving and Razors*, Ad Libs Publishing, 1987; Phillip L. Krumholz, *Value Guide For Barberiana & Shaving Collectibles*, Ad Libs Publishing, 1988; Norman E. Martinus and Harry L. Rinker, *Warman's Paper*, Wallace–Homestead, 1994; Robert Sloan and Steven Guarnaccis, *A Stiff Drink And A Close Shave: The Lost Arts of Manliness*, Chronicle Books, 1995.

Collectors' Clubs: National Shaving Mug Collectors' Association, 320 S. Glenwood St., Allentown, PA 18104; Safety Razor Collectors' Guild, PO Box 885, Crescent City, CA 95531.

Advertising Trade Card, Barber Shop, hairstyle illus, black and pink **16.00**

Bottle, apple green, blown, enameled yellow, orange, and white dots, 8½" h, $85.00.

Barber Bottle
  Advertising
    Koken's Quinine Tonic for the Hair, clear, label under glass, 7½" h **195.00**
    Le Varn's Rose Hair Tonic, label under glass **50.00**
  Amethyst, enameled flowers, 7¾" h **160.00**
  Crystal, pewter top, sgd, pr **50.00**

Milk Glass, "Witch Hazel" in red letters, painted flowers, 9" h 110.00
Stephan's Y–5 Hair Groom, 16 oz, 9½" h, "Sold Only By Barbers," Stephen Co, Ft Lauderdale, FL . . . 15.00
Barber Pole, wall mount type, repainted 375.00
Bench, 48" w, oak, drawer 300.00
Blade Bank
   Barber, bust, 4¾" h, marked "Ceramic Arts Studio, Madison, Wis" 75.00
   Treasure Chest, "Insist on Genuine Ever–Ready Blades" 15.00
Book, *Once Over Lightly*, Charles DeZemler, c1939, 270 pages 35.00
Box, Jiffy Barber's Pride Horsehide Stropping Kit, colorful 6.00
Business Card, Dendy's Beauty Culture and Barber College 8.00
Catalog
   Clifford & Co. Manufacturing Perfumers, Boston, 1884–85, 62 pages, printed wrappers, illus, bottles, brushes, clippers, combs, colognes, mirrors, mugs, poles, razors, etc., 3 x 5" 175.00
   Hudson Beauty Shop Equipment, No. 1 Supplement, Los Angeles, CA, 1936, 8 pgs, 5¾ x 8¾" 26.00
   Koken Company, St Louis, MO, 1920s, The Standard of Excellence, Adjusto Automatic Beauty Shop Chairs, 16 pgs, 7¼ x 10¼" 44.00
   Noonan's Toilet Specialities, early 1900s 22.00
   T S Simms & Co, Maker of Better Brushes, 31 pgs 30.00
Chair
   Oak 35.00
   Walnut, carved swan head 1,100.00
Clock, Gem Safety Razors, brown 350.00
Counter Display, 11 x 13", standup, cardboard, Crescent Razor Blades, 24 pkgs of razors, quarter moon logo, Plexiglas sleeve 78.00
Dispenser, stand–up, metal, Opera double edge razor blades, 5 for 10¢, man in top hat, eleven pkgs of blades . . . 75.00
Display Case, revolving, four sided, drawers, compartments, fancy hardware, mirrors, golden oak finish, 1896 . . . . 2,700.00
Footstool, Koken 125.00
Hair Dying Comb, cov, metal 12.00
Hair Shaper, patent 1907 . . . . 12.00
Letterhead, Madison Barbers' Supplies, c1900 . . . . 10.00
Matchcover, Gillette Blue Blades adv, 1930s, unused 3.00
Mirror
   Hand, tin, wood handle, tilts 55.00
   Shaving, 15" h, beveled mirror, plated brass frame, marked "Apollo" . . . 22.00

Neck Duster, 10" l, turned cherry handle 24.00
Photograph, 5 x 7", barber shop int. . . 40.00
Playing Cards, Gillette adv, 1905, unused 150.00
Pole
   26" h, revolving, red, white, and blue stripes, orig case 125.00
   43" l, porcelain, wall mount, milk glass globe, orig spring power, electric lights 450.00
Post Card, barber shop ext., c1900 . . . 10.00
Receipt Book, Keen Kutter, 1920s 25.00
Safety Razor Set, cased
   Ever–ready, chrome razor, purple leather case, orig box and instructions 14.00
   Griffon, unused wedge blade, tin case with dark blue lettering, gold highlights 60.00
Sharpener, steel razor blades, mechanical, Kress Kross, folding crank handle, blade turns against rotating disc, flips over to sharpen other side, dated 1921 . . . . 45.00
Shaving Mug
   Kern Barber Supply 50.00
   Middletown Silverplate Co, soap container, brush holder, c1870 . . . . . 65.00
   Milk Glass, double compartment, molded flowers 74.00
   Occupational, carpenter tools, Limoges 150.00
Sign
   Bicklmore Shaving Cream, 1930s, 31" h 75.00
   Burma Shave, wood 110.00
   Damschinsky's Liquid Hair Dye, six dyed hair samples, c1910, 14 x 19" 175.00
   Gillette Safety Razor, diecut tin, two sided, 13½ x 15" 3,025.00
   Member United Master Barbers of Michigan, eagle on banner, "In You We Trust," metal 55.00
Sterilizer
   Barbicide 35.00
   DeWitt, porcelain, four sections 65.00
Strop, Peerless Automatic, Pat 1912 . . 12.00
Token, Gillette, King Gillette and slogan on front, razor and slogan on back 28.00
Tool Case, 9 x 6", oak, brass handle . . 15.00
Waste Bowl, 7½" h, cobalt blue glass, applied enamel and gold dec, push–up base 315.00

BARBIE

Collecting Hints: Never forget the quantities in which Barbie and related material were manufactured. Because of this, the real value rests only in material in excellent to mint condition and which has its original packaging in very good or better condition. If items show signs of heavy use, their value is probably minimal.

Collectors prefer items from the first decade of production. Learn how to distinguish a Barbie #1 doll from its successors. The Barbie market is one of subtleties. You must learn them.

Recently collectors have shifted their focus from the dolls themselves to the accessories. There have been rapid price increases in early clothing and accessories, with some of the prices bordering on speculation.

History: In 1945 Harold Matson (MATT) and Ruth and Elliott (EL) Handler founded Mattel. Initially the company made picture frames. The company became involved in the toy market when Elliott Handler began to make doll furniture from scrap material. When Harold Matson left the firm, Elliott Handler became chief designer and Ruth Handler principal marketer. In 1955 Mattel advertised its products on "The Mickey Mouse Club." The company prospered.

In 1958 Mattel patented a fashion doll. The doll was named "Barbie" and reached the toy shelves in 1959. By 1960 Barbie's popularity was assured.

Development of a boy friend for Barbie, named Ken after the Handler's son, began in 1960. Over the years many other dolls were added to the line. Clothing, vehicles, room settings, and other accessories became an integral part of the line.

From September 1961 through July 1972 Mattel published a Barbie magazine. At its peak the Barbie Fan Club was the second largest girls' organization, next to the Girl Scouts, in the United States.

Barbie is now a billion–dollar baby, the first toy in history to reach this prestigious mark. That's a billion dollars per year, just in case you are wondering. Barbie is one of the most successful dolls in history.

References: Sibyl DeWein and Joan Ashabraner, *The Collectors Encyclopedia Of Barbie Dolls and Collectibles,* Collector Books, 1977, 1994 value update; Sarah Sink Eames, *Barbie Fashion, Volume 1, 1959–1967,* Collector Books, 1990, 1995 value update; Laura Jacobs, *Barbie: What a Doll!,* Artabras, 1994; M. G. Lord, *Forever Barbie: The Unauthorized Biography of a Real Doll,* Avon Books, 1995; A. Glenn Mandeville, *Doll Fashion Anthology & Price Guide,* 4th Revised Edition, Hobby House Press, 1993; Paris and Susan Manos, *The Wonder Of Barbie: Dolls And Accessories 1976–1986,* Collector Books, 1987, 1994 value update; Paris and Susan Manos, *The World Of Barbie Dolls: An Illustrated Value Guide,* Collector Books, 1983, 1994 value update; Margo Rana, *Collector's Guide To Barbie Exclusives: Identification and Values,* Collector Books, 1995; Kitturah B. Westenhouser, *The*

Story of Barbie, Collector Books, 1994; Craig Yoe, *The Art of Barbie: Artists Celebrate the World's Favorite Doll,* Workman Publishing, 1994.

Periodicals: *Barbie Bazaar,* 5617 6th Ave., Kenosha, WI 53140; *Barbie Fashions,* 387 Park Ave. S., New York, NY 10016; *Barbie Talks Some More,* 19 Jamestown Dr., Cincinnati, OH 45241–1432; *Collector's Corner* 519 Fitzooth Dr., Miamisburg, OH 45342; *Miller's Price Guide & Collectors' Almanac,* West One Summer, #1, Spokane, WA 99204.

Videotapes: Joe Blitman, *Oh, You Beautiful Doll!,* published by author, 1994; Those Swell Doll Guys, *Swell Dolls, Volume 1,* TSDG Holdings, 1994.

Beach Bus, #7805, c1974	**30.00**
Beauty Kit, 1961, MIB	**25.00**
Book	
Barbie's Fashion Success, 5½ x 8¼", hard cov, Random House, sixteen chapters, copyright 1958 and 1962	**10.00**
Here's Barbie, 5½ x 8¼", hard cov, Random House, seven stories, copyright 1958 and 1962	**8.00**
Carrying Case, vinyl	
Barbie and Midge	
Black, 7 x 11 x 6½", zipper lid, "Barbie and Midge Travel Pals," copyright 1963	**25.00**
Light Blue, 14 x 18 x 4" deep, copyright 1963	**25.00**
Barbie Goes Travelin', 3 x 10 x 15½", multicolored, car and plane illus, black handle, copyright 1965	**30.00**
Ken, 11 x 13 x 4" deep, yellow/green, black handle, copyright 1962	**30.00**
Clothing and Accessories	
Barbie/Midge	
American Airlines Stewardess, #984, 1961	**27.50**
Ballerina, #989, 1961	**20.00**
Evening Gala, #1660, 1965	**45.00**
Picnic Set, denim peddle pushers, red and white check blouse, straw hat and bag, fishing line with plastic fish, packaged	**300.00**
Stormy Weather, yellow rain coat, hat, umbrella, and boots, packaged	**125.00**
Sweater and Skirt, knit, red plastic shoes, miniature "Mattel Daily" newspaper, Book 4 fashion catalog, 1964 Mattel copyright, unopened package	**10.00**
Ken/Allan	
Baseball Cap, ball, and mitt, plastic	**3.00**
Graduation, black gown and mortar board	**12.50**
Hunting Cap, red plastic	**2.00**

Rally Day, all weather coat and hat,
#795 . . . .   8.00
Roller Skates 2.50
Shirt, white, matching blue jacket
and pants, red necktie, black
plastic shoes and gloves, fashion
catalog, 1964 Mattel copyright,
unopened package 10.00
Shoes, plastic, eight pairs, copyright
Mattel, 1972, unopened 18.00
Coloring Book, 8 x 11", Watkins–
Strathmore, Mattel copyright, 1962
and 1963 . . . .   15.00
Cookin'Fun Kitchen 35.00
Diary, 1 x 4 x 5½", vinyl, glossy, One
Year Diary, copyright Mattel, 1961   30.00
Dictionary, *Webster's Dictionary*, 4 x
5½", glossy black vinyl cov, full color
Barbie illus, 380 pgs, Standard
Products copyright 1959, Mattel
copyright 1963 . . . .   35.00

Doll, Barbie, #1, brown ponytail, pearl earrings, orig stand, played-with condition, $500.00.

Doll
Allan, bendable leg 250.00
Barbie
Ballerina Barbie, MIB, 1976 . . . . .   45.00
Bendable Leg Barbie, wearing
swimsuit, 1965 . . . .   900.00
Fashion Queen Barbie, 1963 . . . .   300.00
Happy Holiday, red gown, MIB,
1988 . . . .   500.00
Malibu Barbie, twist and turn,
1971 . . . .   45.00
Pink Jubilee, 1987, Walmart 25th
year anniversary 85.00
Twist 'n Turn, wearing swimsuit,
1966 . . . .   300.00
Ken, #750, 12" h, flocked blonde
hair, wire pedestal stand, Sports
Shorts outfit #783, copyright 1961   130.00

Midge, #860, 12" h, jointed, hard
plastic, soft vinyl head, rooted
blonde hair, knit shirt and shorts,
high heels, wire pedestal stand,
copyright 1962, orig box 120.00
Skipper, #0950, 9" h, rooted red-
dish–blonde hair, painted eyes,
wearing red and white playsuit, red
plastic shoes, wire stand, copyright
1963 . . . .   100.00
Dream House, 1962 . . . .   75.00
Game, Queen of the Prom, 18" sq
board, orig box, Mattel copyright
1960 . . . .   30.00
Horse, Dallas, MIB 30.00
Ice Cream Shop, box 35.00
Jigsaw Puzzle, 100 pcs, Barbie and Ken
in King Arthur court type setting,
1964 . . . .   35.00
Lawn Swing and Planter, excellent con-
dition 200.00
Lunch Box, vinyl, glossy black, ther-
mos, King–Seely Thermos Co, copy-
right 1965 . . . .   80.00
Magazine, *Mattel Barbie Magazine*,
Jan–Feb 1969, 22 pgs 15.00
Manicure Set, Good Grooming
Manicure Set, polish, nail brush, and
emery boards, orig box 35.00
Paint 'n Dazzle Gift Set, 1993 . . . .   35.00
Paper Doll, Barbie and Ken, 9" h, card-
board, diecut, cardboard carrying
case, plastic bases, 40–piece
wardrobe, Whitman, Mattel copy-
right 1962 . . . .   50.00
Radio, earphones, battery operated . . .   35.00
Record Case, 1961, MIB 20.00
Sports Car, convertible, pink, Irwin
Corporation, 1963 . . . .   100.00
Suitcase, 1962 Ken and Barbie 17.00
Telephone, Barbie Mattel–A–Phone . . .   25.00
Wristwatch, orig box, 1963 . . . .   50.00

BASEBALL CARDS

Collecting Hints: Condition is a key factor. The list below is priced for cards in excellent condition, and collectors should strive only for cards in excellent to mint condition.

Concentrate on the superstars; these cards are most likely to increase in value. Buy full sets of modern cards. In this way you have the superstars of tomorrow on hand. When a player becomes a member of the Baseball Hall of Fame, his cards and other memorabilia will increase significantly.

The price of cards fluctuates rapidly; it changes on a weekly basis. Spend time studying the market before investing heavily. Finally, reproduced cards and sets have become a fact of life in this category. Novice collectors should not buy cards until they can tell the difference between the originals and reproductions.

The latest trend is the collecting of rookie cards, i.e., the first year of issue for a player. This is a highly speculative category at the moment.

History: Baseball cards date from the late 19th century. By 1900 the most common cards, known as "T" cards, were those produced by tobacco companies such as American Tobacco Co., with the majority of the tobacco–related cards being produced between 1909 and 1915. By far the most popular set was "T206" issued between 1909 and 1911. During the 1920s American Caramel, National Caramel, and York Caramel candy companies issued cards identified in lists as "E" cards.

From 1933 to 1941 Goudey Gum Co. of Boston and, in 1939, Gum, Inc., were the big producers of baseball cards. Following World War II, Bowman Gum of Philadelphia (B.G.H.L.I.), the successor to Gum, Inc., lead the way. Topps, Inc. (T.C.G.) of Brooklyn, New York, followed. Topps bought Bowman in 1956 and enjoyed almost a monopoly in card production until 1981.

In 1981 Topps was challenged by Fleer of Philadelphia and Donruss of Memphis. All three companies annually produce sets of cards numbering 600 cards or more.

References: James Beckett, *The Official 1996 Price Guide to Baseball Cards, Fifteenth Edition*, House of Collectibles, 1995; James Beckett, *Sport Americana Baseball Card Price Guide, No. 17*, Edgewater Books, 1995; James Beckett, *The Sport Americana Baseball Card Alphabetical Checklist No. 6*, Edgewater Books, 1994; Tol Broome, *From Ryan to Ruth: Unbeatable Card Buys*, Krause Publications, 1994; Gene Florence, *The Standard Baseball Card Price Guide, 6th Edition*, Collector Books, 1994; Jeff Fritsch, *The Sport Americana Team Baseball Card Checklist No. 7*, Edgewater Books, 1994; Allan Kaye and Michael McKeever, *Baseball Card Price Guide, 1996*, Avon Books, 1995; Troy Kirk, *Collector's Guide To Baseball Cards*, Wallace–Homestead, 1990; Krause Publications, *All Sport Alphabetical Price Guide*, Krause Publications, 1995; Mark Larson (ed.), *Baseball Cards Questions & Answers*, Krause Publications, 1992; Mark Larson, *Sports Collectors Digest Minor League Baseball Card Price Guide*, Krause Publications, 1993; Mark Larson (ed.), *Sports Collectors Digest: The Sports Card Explosion*, Krause Publications, 1993; Bob Lemke (ed.), *Sportscard Counterfeit Detector*, Krause Publications, 1992; Bob Lemke (ed.), *Sports Collectors Digest Baseball Card Price Guide, Ninth Edition*, Krause Publications, 1995; Bob Lemke (ed.), *Sports Collectors Digest Standard Catalog of Baseball Cards, Fourth Edition*, Krause Publications, 1994; Roderick A. Malloy, *Malloy's*

Guide To Sports Cards Values, Wallace–Homestead, 1995; Alan Rosen *True Mint: Mr. Mint's Price & Investment Guide To True Mint Baseball Cards*, Krause Publications, 1994; Sports Collectors Digest, *101 Sportscard Investments*, Krause Publications, 1993; Sports Collectors Digest, *Premium Insert Sports Cards*, Krause Publications, 1995; *The Charlton Standard Catalogue of Canadian Baseball & Football Cards, 4th Edition*, The Charlton Press, 1995.

Periodicals: The following appear on a monthly or semi–monthly basis: *Baseball Update*, Suite 284, 220 Sunrise Highway, Rockville Centre, NY 11570; *Beckett Baseball Card Monthly*, Suite 200, 4887 Alpha Rd., Dallas, TX 75244; *Beckett Focus on Future Stars*, Suite 200, 4887 Alpha Rd, Dallas, TX 75244; *Card Trade*, 700 E. State St., Iola, WI 54990; *Sports Cards*, 700 E. State St., Iola, WI 54990; *Sports Collectors Digest*, 700 E. State St., Iola, WI 54990; *The Diamond Angle*, PO Box 409, Kaunakakai, HI 96748; *The Old Judge*, PO Box 137, Centerbeach, NY 11720; *Your Season Ticket*, 106 Liberty Rd., Woodsburg, MD 21790.

Collectors' Clubs: There are many local card collecting clubs throughout the United States. However, there is no national organization at the present time.

REPRODUCTION ALERT: The 1952 Topps set, except for 5 cards, was reproduced in 1983 and clearly marked by Topps. In addition, a number of cards have been illegally reprinted including the following Topps cards:

1963 Peter Rose, rookie card, #537
1971 Pete Rose, #100
1971 Steve Garvey, #341
1972 Pete Rose, #559
1972 Steve Garvey, #686
1972 Rod Carew, #695
1973 Willie Mays, #100
1973 Hank Aaron, #305
1973 Mike Schmidt, rookie card, #615

Note: The listing for the cards beginning in 1948 shows the price for a complete set, common player, and superstars. The number of cards in each set is indicated in parentheses.

PRE–BOWMAN/TOPPS PERIOD

Tobacco Insert
   T–206, white border, color
      Complete set (523) **10,000.00**
      Major League players (1–389) . . . **15.00**
      Minor League players (390–475) **17.50**
      Southern League players (476–523) **37.00**
Candy Companies
   E–120, American Caramels, color,
    1922

Complete set (240) **1,350.00**	
Common player (1–240) **5.00**	

Goudey and Gum, Inc.
1933, Goudey Gum, color
Complete set (240) **7,200.00**
Common player (1–240) **15.00**

BOWMAN ERA

1948 Bowman (black and white)
Complete set (48) **525.00**
Common player (1–36) **5.00**
Common player (37–48) **7.50**
2 Ewell Blackwell **13.50**
9 Walker Cooper **7.00**
21 Ferris Fain **9.00**
29 Joe Page **16.00**
45 Hank Sauer **16.00**
1949 Bowman
Complete set (240) **2,975.00**
Common player (1–144) **5.00**
Common player (145–240) **20.00**
6 Phil Cavarretta **18.00**
31 Dick Kokos **14.00**
36 Pee Wee Reese **50.00**
100 Gil Hodges **80.00**
1950 Bowman
Complete set (252) **1,825.00**
Common player (1–72) **10.00**
Common player (72–252) **5.00**
4 Gus Zemial **22.50**
35 Enos Slaughter **40.00**
217 Casey Stengel **50.00**
248 Sam Jethroe **7.50**
1951 Bowman (color)
Complete set (324) **3,850.00**
Common player (1–252) **5.00**
Common player (253–324) **15.00**
26 Phil Rizzuto **32.50**
53 Bob Lemon **22.50**
122 Joe Garagiola **50.00**
233 Leo Durocher **20.00**
314 Johnny Sain **27.50**
1952 Bowman (color)
Complete set (252) **475.00**
Common player (1–216) **1.00**
Common player (217–252) **2.00**
1 Yogi Berra **30.00**
44 Roy Campanella **85.00**
101 Mickey Mantle **600.00**
196 Stan Musial **200.00**
218 Willie Mays **400.00**
1953 Bowman (black and white)
Complete set (64) **850.00**
Common player (1–64) **10.00**
15 Johnny Mize **50.00**
27 Bob Lemon **45.00**
28 Hoyt Wilhelm **50.50**
46 Bucky Harris **25.00**
1953 Bowman (color)
Complete set (160) **1,200.00**
Common player (1–112) **10.00**

Common player (113–128) **16.00**
Common player (129–160) **12.00**
44 Berra, Bauer, Mantle **175.00**
46 Roy Campanella **110.00**
59 Mickey Mantle **500.00**
93 Rizzuto and Martin **100.00**
117 Duke Snider **250.00**
121 Yogi Berra **250.00**
146 Early Wynn **55.00**
153 Whitey Ford **175.00**
1954 Bowman
Complete set (224) **450.00**
Common player (1–128) **2.00**
Common player (129–224) **2.40**
55 Jim Delsing **3.00**
90 Roy Campanella **55.00**
132 Bob Feller **32.50**
181 Les Moss **3.50**
224 Bill Bruton **5.00**
1955 Bowman (color)
Complete set (320) **1,150.00**
Common player (1–224) **2.50**
Common player (225–320) **4.00**
22 Roy Campanella **45.00**
23 Al Kaline **50.00**
179 Hank Aaron **90.00**
202 Mickey Mantle **200.00**
242 Ernie Banks **150.00**

TOPPS ERA

1951 Topps, blue backs
Complete set (52) **625.00**
Common player (1–52) **10.00**
3 Richie Ashburn **20.00**
30 Enos Slaughter **16.00**
50 Johnny Mize **20.00**
1951 Topps, red backs
Complete set (52) **250.00**
Common player (1–52) **3.00**
1 Yogi Berra **25.00**
31 Gil Hodges **10.00**
38 Duke Snider **20.00**
1952 Topps
Complete set (407) **3,800.00**
Common player (1–80) **11.00**
Common player (81–252) **6.00**
Common player (253–310) **12.00**
Common player (311–407) **25.00**
1 Andy Pafko **75.00**
26 Monte Irvin **50.00**
33 Warren Spahn **85.00**
48 Joe Page (correct) **32.50**
48 Joe Page (error) **150.00**
59 Robin Roberts **60.00**
65 Enos Slaughter **60.00**
88 Bob Feller **60.00**
175 Billy Martin **150.00**
191 Yogi Berra **175.00**
400 Bill Dickey **250.00**
407 Eddie Mathews **500.00**

1953 Topps
Complete set (280) 2,800.00
Common player (1–165) 4.50
Common player (166–200) 3.50
Common player (221–280) 16.00
37 Eddie Mathews 40.00
76 Pee Wee Reese 45.00
77 Johnny Mize 27.50
82 Mickey Mantle 600.00
86 Billy Martin 45.00
147 Warren Spahn 45.00
191 Ralph Kiner 22.50
220 Satchell Paige 175.00
258 Jim Gilliam 135.00
280 Milt Bolling 50.00
1954 Topps
Complete set (250) 1,675.00
Common player (1–50) 3.50
Common player (51–75) 3.00
Common player (76–250) 3.50
3 Monte Irvin 12.50
17 Phil Rizzuto 27.50
32 Duke Snider 50.00
94 Ernie Banks 300.00
102 Gil Hodges 32.50
132 Tom Lasorda 75.00
201 Al Kaline 300.00
250 Ted Williams 150.00
1955 Topps
Complete set (210) 1,225.00
Common player (1–160) 2.50
Common player (160–210) 4.00
1 Dusty Rhodes 5.00
28 Ernie Banks 55.00
100 Monte Irvin 10.50
123 Sandy Koufax 325.00
124 Harmon Killebrew 125.00
187 Gil Hodges 475.00
194 Willie Mays 200.00
198 Yogi Berra 100.00
210 Duke Snider 100.00
1956 Topps
Complete set (340) 1,260.00
Common player (1–180) 1.50
Common player (181–260) 2.50
Common player (261–340) 3.00
10 Warren Spahn 22.50
20 Al Kaline 32.50
30 Jackie Robinson 60.00

Topps, Jackie Robinson, #30, 1956, $60.00.

31 Hank Aaron 80.00
79 Sandy Koufax 110.00
109 Enos Slaughter 11.00
130 Willie Mays 110.00
166 Brooklyn Dodgers 75.00
292 Luis Aparicio 50.00
1957 Topps
Complete set (407) 1,575.00
Common player (1–264) 1.25
Common player (265–352) 5.00
Common player (353–407) 1.25
1 Ted Williams 100.00
10 Willie Mays 90.00
35 Frank Robinson 100.00
76 Roberto Clemente 80.00
95 Mickey Mantle 375.00
302 Sandy Koufax 125.00
328 Brooks Robinson 175.00
407 Yankee Power Hitters, Berra,
    Mantle 100.00
1958 Topps
Complete set (495) 975.00
Common player (1–110) 1.25
Common player (111–440) 1.00
Common player (441–495) 60
1 Ted Williams 100.00
5 Willie Mays 65.00
30A Hank Aaron 65.00
52A Roberto Clemente 45.00
70A Al Kaline 27.50
150 Mickey Mantle 250.00
187 Sandy Koufax 50.00
1959 Topps
Complete set (572) 975.00
Common player (1–506) 1.00
Common player (507–572) 2.50
10 Mickey Mantle 150.00
50 Willie Mays 55.00
163 Sandy Koufax 50.00
380 Hank Aaron 45.00
514 Bob Gibson 150.00
543 Corsair Trio 25.00
1960 Topps
Complete set (572) 875.00
Common player (1–506) 75
Common player (507–572) 2.25
50 Al Kaline 13.50
73 Bob Gibson 16.00
148 Carl Yastrzemski 175.00
200 Willie Mays 40.00
250 Stan Musial 40.00
300 Hank Aaron 40.00
316 Willie McCovey 65.00
350 Mickey Mantle 150.00
564 Willie Mays, AS 40.00
566 Hank Aaron, AS 40.00
1961 Topps
Complete set (589) 1,260.00
Common player (1–522) 50
Common player (523–589) 7.50
2 Roger Maris 50.00
10 Brooks Robinson 12.50

35 Ron Santo	6.00	500 Hank Aaron	7.50
120 Eddie Matthews	9.00	550 Willie McCovey	12.00
150 Willie Mays	40.00	598 Gaylord Perry	22.00
200 Warren Spahn	11.00	**1967 Topps**	
260 Don Drysdale	9.00	Complete set (609)	825.00
287 Carl Yastrzemski	75.00	Common player (1–533)	.50
290 Stan Musial	37.50	Common player (534–609)	2.00
417 Juan Marichal	40.00	150 Mickey Mantle	8.00
475 Roger Maris	15.00	200 Willie Mays	7.25
1963 Topps		250 Hank Aaron	7.25
Complete set (576)	950.00	355 Carl Yastrzemski	8.00
Common player (1–196)	30.00	400 Roberto Clemente	4.00
Common player (197–446)	.45	569 Rookies	15.00
Common player (447–506)	2.25	570 Maury Wills	22.00
Common player (507–576)	1.25	581 Rookies	36.00
25 Al Kaline	12.00	600 Brooks Robinson	35.00
54 Rookie Stars	3.75	**1968 Topps**	
108 Hoyt Wilhelm	37.50	Complete set (598)	450.00
115 Carl Yastrzemski	22.50	Common player (1–457)	.20
120 Roger Maris	22.50	Common player (458–598)	.40
125 Robin Roberts	4.50	45 Tom Seaver	60.00
242 Power Plus	9.00	50 Willie Mays	22.50
340 Yogi Berra	27.50	72 Tommy John	2.00
360 Don Drysdale	9.00	150 Bob Clemente	17.50
412 Dodger Big Three	12.50	247 Reds Rookies	175.00
490 Willie McCovey	40.00	257 Phil Niekro	2.50
544 Rookie Stars	13.50	363 Rod Carew, AS	4.50
1964 Topps		408 Steve Carlton	15.00
Complete set (587)	600.00	530 Bird Belters	3.00
Common player (1–370)	.25	**1969 Topps**	
Common player (371–522)	.40	Complete set (664)	425.00
Common player (523–587)	1.25	Common player (1–218)	.20
13 Hoyt Williams	1.25	Common player (219–327)	.30
21 Yogi Berra	5.00	Common player (328–512)	.20
29 Lou Brock	7.50	Common player (513–664)	.25
50 Mickey Mantle	18.50	50 Bob Clemente	15.00
146 Indians Rookies	8.00	75 Luis Aparicio	2.50
225 Roger Maris	3.50	95 Johnny Bench	60.00
260 Frank Robinson	4.00	100 Hank Aaron	17.50
280 Juan Marichal	3.50	260 Reggie Jackson	175.00
342 Willie Stargell	18.00	480 Tom Seaver	40.00
460 Bob Gibson	4.75	485 Gaylord Perry	30.00
468 Gaylord Perry	5.25	573 Jim Palmer	10.00
541 Braves Rookies	15.00	**1970 Topps**	
1965 Topps		Complete set (720)	325.00
Complete set (598)	700.00	Common player (1–132)	.15
Common player (1–506)	.45	Common player (133–459)	.15
Common player (507–598)	1.25	Common player (460–546)	.20
170 Hank Aaron	6.00	Common player (547–633)	.30
250 Willie Mays	7.25	Common player (634–720)	.60
300 Sandy Koufax	4.00	10 Carl Yastrzemski	12.50
350 Mickey Mantle	10.00	17 Hoyt Wilhelm	1.75
477 Rookies	25.00	140 Reggie Jackson	37.50
540 Lou Brock	4.50	150 Harmon Killebrew	2.50
1966 Topps		211 Ted Williams	3.00
Complete set (598)	750.00	453 Rod Carew, AS	2.50
Common player (1–506)	.50	464 Johnny Bench, AS	4.00
Common player (507–598)	3.00	470 Willie Stargell	3.25
1 Willie Mays	8.00	537 Joe Morgan	3.25
50 Mickey Mantle	8.25	539 Phillies Rookies	2.00
70 Carl Yastrzemski	7.50	**1971 Topps**	
126 Jim Palmer	10.00	Complete set (752)	350.00

Common player (1–523)	.20		599 Rookie Pitchers	5.00
Common player (524–643)	.35		1977 Topps	
Common player (644–752)	.70		Complete set (660)	110.00
5 Thurman Munson	10.50		Common player	.08
14 Dave Concepcion	3.00		10 Reggie Jackson	3.50
20 Reggie Jackson	16.00		110 Steve Carlton	2.00
30 Phil Niekro	1.75		140 Mike Schmidt	7.00
55 Steve Carlton	8.00		295 Gary Carter	2.50
117 Ted Simmons	4.00		390 Dave Winfield	2.00
264 Joe Morgan	3.00		400 Steve Garvey	1.75
341 Steve Garvey . . . . , .	37.50		476 Rookie Catchers	25.00
525 Ernie Banks	7.50		1978 Topps	
570 Jim Palmer	6.00		Complete set (726)	90.00
1972 Topps			Common player	.06
Complete set (787)	350.00		36 Eddie Murray	17.50
Common player (1–394)	.15		40 Carl Yastrzemski	1.85
Common player (395–525)	.15		100 George Brett	2.50
Common player (526–656)	.25		120 Gary Carter	1.50
Common player (657–787)	.65		200 Reggie Jackson	2.00
49 Willie Mays	9.00		350 Steve Garvey	1.50
79 Red Sox Rookies	30.00		360 Mike Schmidt	3.75
100 Frank Robinson	2.50		1979 Topps	
200 Lou Brock	2.25		Complete set (726)	60.00
300 Aaron in Action	3.50		Common player	.06
420 Steve Carlton	7.00		30 Dave Winfield	1.25
510 Ted Williams	3.00		50 Steve Garvey	.60
595 Nolan Ryan	30.00		116 Ozzie Smith	14.00
754 Frank Robinson Traded	11.00		586 Bob Horner	.75
1973 Topps			700 Reggie Jackson	.85
Complete set (660)	200.00		1980 Topps	
Common player (1–396)	.10		Complete set (726)	60.00
Common player (397–528)	.40		Common player	.06
Common player (529–660)	.45		160 Eddie Murray	1.75
1 Home Run Kings	3.75		230 Dave Winfield	1.00
31 Buddy Bell	2.00		270 Mike Schmidt	1.00
160 Jim Palmer	2.75		482 Rickey Henderson	22.00
170 Harmon Killebrew	1.75		580 Nolan Ryan	2.50
280 Al Kaline	2.50		1981 Topps	
350 Tom Seaver	6.50		Complete set (726)	60.00
380 Johnny Bench	7.50		Common player	.06
474 RBI Leaders	2.50		100 Rod Carew	.60
1974 Topps			210 Jim Palmer	.60
Complete set (660)	150.00		261 Rickey Henderson	3.25
Common player	.10		315 Kirk Gibson	3.50
1 Hank Aaron	5.00		347 Harold Baines	1.85
80 Tom Seaver	4.00		479 Expos Rookies	4.25
130 Reggie Jackson	5.50		643 Lloyd Moseby	.50
252 Dave Parker	12.50		1982 Topps	
283 Mike Schmidt	33.50		Complete set (792)	56.00
456 Dave Winfield	20.00		Common player	.05
1975 Topps			30 Tom Seaver	.35
Complete set (660)	225.00		70 Tim Raines	1.00
Common player	.50		100 Mike Schmidt	.85
70 Mike Schmidt	18.00		179 Steve Garvey	.40
228 George Brett	45.00		346 Tom Seaver, AS	.15
616 Rookie Outfielders	15.00		383A Pascual Perez ERR	15.00
1976 Topps			653 Angels Future Stars	1.00
Complete set (660)	110.00		668 Dale Murphy	1.00
Common player	.05		1983 Topps	
230 Carl Yastrzemski	3.75		Complete set (792)	60.00
480 Mike Schmidt	10.00		Common player	.05
500 Reggie Jackson	4.00		49 Willie McGee	.85

60 Johnny Bench	.35
70 Steve Carlton	.27
83 Ryne Sandberg	5.00
163 Cal Ripken	1.25
268 Storm Davis	.50
350 Robin Yount	.50
431 Gary Gaetti	2.25
482 Tony Gwynn	10.00
498 Wade Boggs	17.50
1984 Topps	
Complete set (792)	55.00
Common player	.05
8 Don Mattingly	10.00
182 Darryl Strawberry	7.50
206 Andy Van Slyke	1.25
470 Nolan Ryan	.85

BASEBALL COLLECTIBLES

Collecting Hints: Baseball memorabilia spans a wide range of items that have been produced since baseball became the national pastime over 100 years ago. This variety has made it more difficult to establish reliable values, leaving it to the collector himself to identify and determine what price to pay for any particular item he uncovers. This "value in the eye of the beholder" approach works well with the veteran collector. The novice collector should solicit the advice of a reliable dealer or advanced collector about values before investing heavily. This is compounded by the emerging interest in unique pieces, especially items associated with superstars such as Cobb, Ruth, and Mantle that now command inordinately high prices.

Because of the unlimited variety of items available, it is virtually impossible to collect everything. Develop a collecting strategy, concentrating on particular player(s), team(s), or type of collectibles, such as Hartland Statues or Perez–Steele autographed postcards. This special emphasis allows the collector to become more familiar with the key elements affecting pricing within their area of interest—such as condition and availability—and permits him to build his collection within a prescribed budget.

History: Baseball has its beginnings in the mid–19th century and by 1900 had become the national pastime. Whether sandlot or big league, baseball was part of almost every male's life until the 1950s, when leisure activities expanded in myriad directions.

The superstar has always been the key element in the game. Baseball greats were popular visitors at banquets, parades, and more recently at baseball autograph shows. They were subjects of extensive newspaper coverage and, with heightened radio and TV exposure, achieved true celebrity status. The impact of baseball on American life has been enormous.

References: Gwen Aldridge, *Baseball Archaelogy: Artifacts From The Great American Pastime,* Chronicle Books, 1993; Mark Allen Baker, *All Sport Autograph Guide,* Krause Publications, 1994; Mark Allen Baker, *Sports Collectors Digest Baseball Autograph Handbook,* Second Edition, Krause Publications, 1991; Mark Baker, *Team Baseballs: The Complete Guide to Autographed Team Baseballs,* Krause Publications, 1992; Don Bevans and Ron Menchine, *Baseball Team Collectibles,* Wallace–Homestead, 1994; David Bushing, *Guide To Spalding Bats 1908–1938,* published by author; David Bushing, *Sports Equipment Price Guide,* Krause Publications, 1995; David Bushing and Joe Phillips, *Vintage Baseball Bat 1994 Pocket Price Guide,* published by authors, 1994; David Bushing and Joe Phillips, *Vintage Baseball Glove Pocket Price Guide, No. 3,* published by authors, 1995; Bruce Chadwick, *Baseball's Hometown Teams: The Story of the Minor Leagues,* Abbeville Press, 1994; Bruce Chadwick, *When The Game Was Black and White: The Illustrated History of Baseball's Negro Leagues,* Abbeville Press, 1992; Bruce Chadwick and David Spindel, *The Boston Red Sox,* Abbeville Press, 1992; Bruce Chadwick and David Spindel, *The Bronx Bombers,* Abbeville Press, 1992; Bruce Chadwick and David Spindel, *The Chicago Cubs: Memories and Memorabilia of the Wrigley Wonders,* Abbeville Press, 1994; Bruce Chadwick and David Spindel, *The Cincinnati Reds: Memories and Memorabilia of the Big Red Machine,* Abbeville Press, 1994; Bruce Chadwick and David Spindel, *The Dodgers: Memories and Memorabilia From Brooklyn To L.A.,* Abbeville Press, 1993; Bruce Chadwick and David Spindel, *The Giants: Memories and Memorabilia From A Century of Baseball,* Abbeville Press, 1993; Douglas Congdon–Martin and John Kashmanian, *Baseball Treasures: Memorabilia from the National Pastime,* Schiffer Publishing, 1993; Mark Cooper, *Baseball Games: Home Versions of the National Pastime, 1860s–1960s,* Schiffer Publishing, 1995; Bruce Kronnick, *The Baseball Fan's Complete Guide to Collecting Autographs,* Betterway Publications, 1990; Mark Larson, *Sports Collectors Digest Complete Guide to Baseball Memorabilia,* Second Edition Krause Publications, 1994; Mark Larson, Rick Hines, and Dave Platta (eds.), *Mickey Mantle Memorabilia,* Krause Publications, 1993; Roderick A. Malloy, *Malloy's Sports Collectibles Value Guide,* Wallace–Homestead, 1993; Norman E. Martinus and Harry L. Rinker, *Warman's Paper,* Wallace–Homestead, 1994; Ron Menchine, *A Picture Postcard History of Baseball,* Almar Press Book Publishers, 1992; Joe Phillips and Dave Bushing, *Vintage Baseball*

Glove Price Guide: A Comprehensive Guide To Valuation of Vintage Baseball Gloves, published by authors, 1992; Don Raycraft, *Collecting Baseball Player Autographs,* Collector Books, 1991; M. Donald and R. Craig Raycraft, *Value Guide To Baseball Collectibles,* Collector Books, 1992.

Periodicals: *Baseball Hobby News,* 4540 Kearney Villa Rd., San Diego, CA 92123; *John L. Raybin's Baseball Autograph News,* 527 Third Ave., #294–A, New York, NY 10016; *Kovels on Sports Collectibles,* PO Box 22200, Beachwood, OH 44122; *Sports Collectors Digest,* 700 E. State St., Iola, WI 54990; *Tuff Stuff,* PO Box 1637, Glen Allen, VA 23060.

Collectors' Clubs: Society for American Baseball Research, PO Box 93183, Cleveland, OH 44101–5183, members receive *Baseball Research Journal, The SABR Bulletin* and *The National Pastime*; The Glove Collector, 14057 Rolling Hills Lane, Dallas, TX 75210.

Museum: National Baseball Hall of Fame and Museum, Cooperstown, NY.

REPRODUCTION ALERT: Autographs and equipment.

Ashtray, 4½" d, LA Dodgers, baseball glove shape, ceramic, brown stitched accent, attached bat and baseball   ..   **5.00**
Bat, Little Slugger
  Mantle, Mickey **25.00**
  Montgomery, Bob **15.00**
Beer Can, 1979 World Champion Pirates Commemorative, 5", litho aluminum, Iron City Beer **15.00**
Blotter, baseball game pictured on portable TV screen, 1930s **15.00**
Book
  Big–Time Baseball, 192 pgs, Ben Olan, 1958, history text **30.00**
  The Babe Ruth Story, 96 pgs, 8½ x 11", soft cov, first edition, 1948   ..   **40.00**
Box, tin, Baseball Legends, pictures on 4 sides, Ted Williams, Roberto Clemente, Babe Ruth, Willie Mays ..   **45.00**
Calendar Page, 1915, US Army team, sepia **125.00**
Cake Decoration, six painted glass figures, white uniforms with red accents, c1950s **25.00**
Catcher's mask, early **125.00**
Cigar Box Label, American League and National League, price for pr **25.00**
Cigarette Lighter, 4½" l, figural, china batter holding trophy, silvered metal lighter, orig box, copyright 1962 by Amico Import of Japan **50.00**
Coaster, 3½" d, plastic, brown, Philadelphia Phillies Trivia **7.50**

Counter Display, 11 x 14", cardboard, Yoo Hoo Chocolate Drink, Berra, Mantle, Skowron, Howard, Pepitone, Tresh, Richardson, Ford **1,250.00**
Dart Board, metallic, Major League Baseball, orig cardboard envelope, 1950s **44.00**
Decal, 1¾ x 2⅛", Mickey Mantle, peel–off full color picture, Topps Gum insert **25.00**
Doll, 12" h, stuffed cloth
  Detroit Tiger, blue and white cap and uniform, "Detroit" printed on back, 1960–70 ....   **20.00**
  New York Yankees, printed blue and white cap, black and white uniform, 1960–70 ....   **15.00**
Fan, Pete Rose, "Ty–Breaker/Cobb Buster," diecut, cardboard **15.00**
Game
  Hand Held, Home Run King **45.00**
  Play Ball, gambling tavern, counter top, 1930s **175.00**
Glass, 4½" h, Baltimore Orioles/World Champions 1966, clear, orange and black inscriptions and designs **25.00**
Glove, Catfish Hunter **20.00**
Gum Ball Machine, Play Ball, keys, 1950s **135.00**
Hartland Figure, 7" h
  Mickey Mantle, plastic, white uniform, blue cap, 1960s **100.00**
  Nellie Fox, red and black uniform, early 1960s **200.00**
  Yogi Berra, blue and white uniform, early 1960s **125.00**
Inkwell, tin, baseball mounted in center with hinged lid, white glass well, gold gilt finish, c1890 ....   **125.00**
Lamp, 4" h, Cubs, china, white, baseball shape, black wire tripod base, 12½" d parchment paper shade, c1940 ....   **80.00**
Magazine
  Babe Ruth Baseball Advice **85.00**
  Baseball Monthly, first issue, Vol 1 #1 March 1962, BRS Publishing Co, 64 pgs **30.00**
  Official Baseball Annual, No 3, Whitestone Publications, 1965 ...   **25.00**
Movie Handbill, *Kill the Umpire,* William Bendix **15.00**
Mug, 5" h, Boston "Pennant Is Ours," ceramic, white, glossy, newspaper print, gold trim on edge **25.00**
Nodder, composition
  Baltimore Orioles, 7" h, painted, gold rounded diamond shape base, 1967–1972 ....   **75.00**
  Chicago White Sox, 6½" h, white sq base, Chicago decal on base, 1961–62 ....   **125.00**

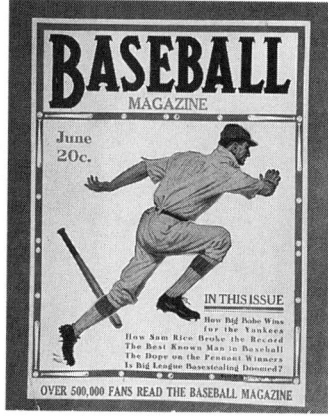

Magazine, *Baseball,* June, 1921, cover art by Gerrit A. Beneker, 1911, 9½ x 11½", $25.00.

Houston Colts, 6" h, painted, round green base, Made in Japan marking, orig box, 1962 copyright **75.00**
Kansas City Athletics, 4½" h, painted, white round base with decal, 1961–62 . . . . **100.00**
Oakland Athletics, 6½" h, yellow and green uniform, gold base with decal, copyright Sports Specialties . . **35.00**
Pass, Rochester Trolley, colorful baseball scene, 1935 . . . . **22.00**
Pencil, 5½" l
Baseball's 100th Anniversary, baseball bat shape, mechanical point, gold Hillerich & Bradsby Co logo **15.00**
Detroit Tigers/1940 Champions, bat shape, mechanical, brown inscription **30.00**
Pennant, felt
Baltimore Orioles, 26½" l, orange, white design accented with orange and dark gray, black lettering, c1950 . . . . **40.00**
Dodger Stadium Commemorative, 27" l, red and blue background, white lettering and design, grand opening of Dodger Stadium, April 9, 1962 **50.00**
Little League Baseball, 12" l, blue, white lettering and design, black inked player's shoes, 1950–60 . . . **15.00**
New York Mets, 12" l, black, white lettering and design, black inked player's shoes, c1962 . . . . **50.00**
Philadelphia Phillies, 29" l, red, white design with yellow accent, c1950s **30.00**
San Francisco Giants, 12" l, blue, white lettering and design, c1958 **45.00**
Washington Senators, 29" l, red, white design, blue, pink, and dark gray accents, white lettering **25.00**

Photo
Goose Goslin, 8 x 10", black and white, matte finish, black ink signature **75.00**
Philadelphia Phillies, 9 x 11", full color team, 1946 . . . . **25.00**
Pinback Button
Gil Hodges, black and white photo, late 1940s **55.00**
Jackie Robinson, 1¾" d, "I'm Rooting For Jackie Robinson" and "Dodgers," 1947 rookie year, red rim **250.00**
Jerome (Dizzy) Dean, black and white photo, late 1940s **50.00**
Poker Chip **25.00**
Poster
7¼ x 20", Bob Feller Popsicle, 1947 **425.00**
11 x 15½", Red Man Tobacco, 1952 **150.00**
Premium, patch, 3" d, Babe Ruth Champions, flannel, emblem, stitched, Quaker Cereal, c1935 . . . . **75.00**
Press Pass, 2½ x 3¾", 1939 Chicago Cubs, inked Western Union employee name, red symbol **35.00**

Press Pin, 1952 Yankee World Series, $300.00.

Program
Buffalo Bisons, 7 x 10", 16 pgs, Offermann Stadium, Bisons and Jersey City Giants, 1940 . . . . **18.00**
Decatur Athletic Club Dance, Brooklyn, 1913, 14 pages **18.00**
Hagerstown Owls, 7 x 10¼", four pgs, Owls and Wilmington, Delaware, 1945 . . . . **15.00**
Salute To Hank Aaron, 5½ x 8½", Sept 17, 1976 at Milwaukee Co Stadium, 1976 . . . . **15.00**
Punchboard, 7½ x 7½", 5¢ punch, framed **35.00**
Ring, Chicago Cubs, brass, glass top, team logo inset **125.00**
Schedule, folder, Princeton, 1913 . . . . **25.00**
Sign, Lou Gehrig Baseball Gloves **45.00**

Ticket, 3½ x 5¼", April 22 opening
game, New York Yankees and
Philadelphia, Polo Grounds **30.00**
Tin, chewing tobacco
Chicago Cubs **75.00**
Philadelphia Athletics, Bat Chewing
Tobacco **95.00**
Whiskey Bottle, 10½" h, Baseball's
100th Anniversary Commemorative,
china, Jim Beam Distilling Co, 1969   **40.00**
Yearbook, 8½ x 11", 1955 Milwaukee
Braves, 48 pgs **75.00**

BATTERY OPERATED AUTOMATA

Captain Blushwell, litho tin and cloth,
made by Yonezawa, Japan, orig box, 11"
h, $95.00.

Collecting Hints: Prices fluctuate greatly. Many
of the collectors are in Japan and dealers must allow enough margin for shipment of pieces overseas. Operating condition is a key factor. Many
pieces had accessory parts; these must be present
to have full value. The original box, especially if
it has a label, adds 10 to 20% to the price. Also,
the more elaborate the action, the higher the
value.

History: Battery operated automata began as
"cheap" Japanese import goods in the 1950s.
They were meant for amusement only, many
finding themselves located on the shelves of bars
in the recreation rooms of private homes. They
were marketed through 5 and 10 cent stores and
outlets.
    The subjects were animals—bears being fa-
vored—and humans. Quality of pieces varies
greatly, with Linemar being among the best
made.

References: Don Hultzman, "Battery Operated
Toys," in Richard O'Brien, *Collecting Toys: A
Collector's Identification & Value Guide*, 7th
Edition, Books Americana, 1995; Brian Moran,
Battery Toys, Schiffer Publishing, 1984.

Beethoven the Piano Playing Dog, TN,
Japan, plush dog, rubber hands, litho
tin base, plays litho tin piano, head
moves, 8½" h, orig box **265.00**
Blinky the Xylophone Clown, Amico,
Japan, remote control, cloth and tin
clown with paper hat, walks and
plays xylophone, eyes light, head
moves, 10" h, orig box **400.00**
Captain Blushwell, Yone, Japan, tin and
plastic, plush hair, fabric clothing,
plastic "Scotch Whiskey" bottle and
glass, man blushes, eyes spin, 11" h   **95.00**
Charlie the Drumming Clown, Alps,
Japan, litho tin, plastic, and cloth,
clown hits snare drums and small

cymbal with drum sticks, plays bass
drum and large cymbal with feet,
head moves, nose lights, 9" h, small
split below jaw, orig box **125.00**
Chef Cook, Yonezawa, Japan, vinyl,
cloth, and litho tin, swaying chef
chews, flips omelet, and seasons it,
stove lights, 10" h, orig box **230.00**
Cragstan Telly Bear, Cragstan, Japan,
plush and cloth bear, tin desk and
large phone, dial large phone to start
action, phone rings and lights, bear
picks up small phone, talks, and starts
writing, 9" h, orig box **325.00**
Fishing Polar Bear, Alps, Japan, plush
bear, litho tin base, lifts pole from
pond with fish on line, reaches down,
grabs fish, throws it in basket, and
laughs, one litho tin fish, 10½" h, orig
box **175.00**
Frankie the Rollerskating Monkey, Alps,
Japan, remote control, plush monkey
skates forward and backward, realistic head, arm, and leg movements,
12" h, orig box **145.00**
Happy the Clown Puppet Show,
Yonezawa, Japan, tin clown, cloth
costume, vinyl face, operates tin and
wood Pinocchio type marionette,
clown sways and changes facial ex-
pressions, 10½" h, orig box **275.00**
High Jinks at the Circus, Alps, Japan,
clown, cloth, tin, and plastic, nose
lights, moves head, kicks foot, blows
whistle, pushes cymbal playing monkey in air on extending ladder, 10" h,
orig box **185.00**
Hoopy the Fishing Duck, Alps, Japan,
plush and litho tin duck with rubber
feet, lifts pole from pond with fish on

line, reaches down, grabs fish, throws it in basket, quacks as eyes light, two litho tin fish, 10″ h, orig box **445.00**

Hungry Baby Bear, Yonezawa, Japan, plush, litho tin, and cloth, mother bear with moving head and eyes, feeding baby bear from milk bottle, baby kicks and cries when mother takes bottle away, 9″ h, orig box . . . **180.00**

Jolly Santa on Snow, Alps, Japan, vinyl face, cotton beard, plush outfit, cloth sack, silver bell, plastic boots with wheels, 12″ h, orig box **195.00**

Jumbo the Bubble Blowing Elephant, Yonezawa, Japan, plush elephant, litho tin base, raises and lowers head into cup, ears flap, bubble blowing action, does not work, 7″ l, orig box **90.00**

Jungle Jumbo, Teddy Roosevelt, BC, Japan, remote control, plush elephant walks with wagging tail and moving head, stops and howls while hunter swivels and shoots, 11″ l, 10″ h, orig box **315.00**

Kissing Couple, Ichida, Japan, litho tin car, man and woman with vinyl heads, celluloid bird on hood, car with bump–and–go action, bird spins and chirps, couple turn and kiss, man blushes, 10″ l, orig box **225.00**

Maxwell Coffee–Loving Bear, TN, Japan, plush bear, litho tin base, holds coffeepot that lights and smokes, pours and drinks coffee, smoking action not working, 11″ h, orig box **180.00**

Mickey the Magician, Linemar, Walt Disney Productions, litho tin Mickey, cloth outfit, rubber hands, makes squeaking sound while pointing to top hat, makes tin chick appear and disappear, 11″ h, orig box **2,050.00**

Miss Friday the Typist, Japan, litho tin, vinyl head and arms, girl types with moving hands, head, and typewriter carriage, bell rings, 7″ l, 6″ h, orig box **185.00**

Nutty Nibs, Linemar, Japan, litho tin native with large earrings, flips ball bearing "nuts" into mouth and swallows, eyes move, 11″ h, orig box . . **1,300.00**

Picnic Monkey, Alps, Japan, plush monkey, litho tin base, alternately eats banana and drinks from soda can, leans back as stomach bloats, squeaks and pats stomach as it deflates, 9″ h **225.00**

Pretty Peggy Parrot, Japan, plush bird on litho tin base, head turns as wings and tail flap, eyes light, squawks and moves mouth, 12″ h, orig box **220.00**

Teddy the Artist, Yonezawa, Japan, litho tin, plush bear wearing fabric shirt, sitting at desk, draws, comes with crayon and nine templates, 9″ h, orig box **315.00**

Telephone Bear, MT, Japan, plush bear, litho tin chair, holding stick phone, when phone rings, bear lifts phone and talks, mouth moves, 9½″ h, orig box **260.00**

Trick–Cycling Clown, Cragstan, Japan, tin clown with cloth costume and vinyl head, riding litho tin unicycle, pedals and turns, head and body move, holds blinking ball in each hand, 12″ h, orig box **470.00**

Walking Penguin, MT, Japan, remote control, plush and litho tin, wearing hat, walks, flaps wings, opens beak, makes penguin sounds, eyes light, 9″ h **140.00**

Whistling Spooky Kooky Tree, Summer Version, Marx, litho tin tree with vinyl arms and nose, rolls along with bump–and–go action, arms swing up and down, mouth and eyes open and close, loud whistling sound, 13″ h, orig box **1,900.00**

Windy the Juggling Elephant, TN, Japan, plush elephant, litho tin base, waves feet in air while spinning umbrella or blowing ball in air, 10½″ h, orig box **140.00**

BAUER POTTERY

Collecting Hints: The key is to focus on highly stylistic, designer forms. Bauer pieces range from Art Deco to Streamlined Modern. Interest in utilitarian redware and stoneware pieces is minimal.

Remember that jiggered and cast production was done in quantity. Hand–thrown pieces by Matt Carlton and Fred Johnson were done in limited quantity. Unfortunately, these pieces are not marked. Learn to identify them by studying photographs of known examples. Among the more desirable shapes are oil jars with prices increasing as the jar becomes taller.

In the dinnerware patterns some colors are more highly prized than others. Burgundy, orange–red, and white are premium colors in all patterns.

History: In 1885 John Bauer founded the Paducah Pottery, Paducah, Kentucky, to manufacture stoneware and earthenware utilitarian pieces such as crocks and jugs. Bauer died in 1898. John Andrew Bauer continued the business in Paducah until 1909 at which time the plant was moved to Los Angeles, California.

Bauer's initial California production consisted of redware flowerpots. Stoneware production did not resume immediately because of the difficulty of locating suitable stoneware clay. Utilitarian ware such as bean pots and mixing bowls remained a company staple.

In 1913 Matt Carlton, an Arkansas potter, and Louis Ipsen, a Danish designer, developed an artware line of glazed bowls, jardinieres, and vases. The company won a bronze medal at the Panama–California Exposition of 1915–1916. Within a short period, the firm's artware line was replaced by a line of molded stoneware vases.

In 1922 John Andrew Bauer died. Just prior to his death, he established a partnership with Watson E. Brockmon, his son–in–law. The firm prospered under Brockmon's leadership.

In the early 1930s Bauer introduced a line of popular dinnerware designed by Ipsen and covered with glazes developed by Victor Houser, a ceramic engineer. In 1931 "ring" ware was introduced to contrast with the plain ware of a year earlier. Over a hundred different shapes and sizes were manufactured in table and kitchen lines. Among the more successful tableware lines are: Brusche Contempo (1948–1961), La Linda (1939–1959), Monterey (1936–1945), and Monterey Moderne (1948–1961). Ipsen's Aladdin teapot design was part of the Glass Pastel Kitchenware series.

The company continued operations during World War II, reformulating the glazes to correspond to wartime restrictions on some materials. Wheel–thrown artware featuring the work of Carlton and Fred Johnson was made. Cast forms of the 1930s and 1940s were kept in production. Tracy Irwin, a designer, developed a modern line of floral containers.

Following the war, the company faced stiff competition both in the national and California markets. A bitter strike in 1961 signaled the end. In 1962 W. E. Brockmon's widow closed the plant.

References: Susan and Al Bagdade, *Warman's American Pottery and Porcelain,* Wallace-Homestead, 1994; Jack Chipman, *Collector's Encyclopedia of California Pottery,* Collector Books, 1992, 1995 value update; Lois Lehner, *Lehner's Encyclopedia of U. S. Marks on Pottery, Porcelain & Clay,* Collector Books, 1988.

LA LINDA. Dinnerware line produced from 1939 until 1959. Blue, Burgundy, Chartreuse, Dark Brown, Gray, Ivory, Light Brown, Olive Green, Pink, Turquoise, and Yellow were featured colors.

Carafe	
Black, no lid	**85.00**
Chartreuse, wood handle	**20.00**
Creamer	
Turquoise	**20.00**
Yellow	**20.00**
Cup and Saucer, Olive Green	**20.00**

Creamer, medium green, imp "Bauer USA" in bottom, 4¾" w, 3" h, $10.00.

Custard Cup	
Olive Green	**10.00**
Turquoise	**8.00**
Fruit Bowl	
Light Brown	**10.00**
Olive Green	**10.00**
Yellow	**10.00**
Jug, ball, ice lip, gray, plain	**95.00**
Plate	
6" d, bread and butter	
Ivory	**6.50**
Pink	**6.00**
7½" d, salad	
Dark Brown	**12.00**
Olive Green	**10.00**
9" d, dinner	
Chartreuse	**15.00**
Ivory	**12.00**
Platter, 12" l, Dark Brown	**15.00**
Shaker, large, Turquoise	**6.50**
Sugar, Olive Green	**20.00**
Vegetable	
8" l, oval, Dark Brown	**20.00**
9½" d, round, Pink	**25.00**

MISCELLANEOUS

Candlesticks, pr, Delph	**55.00**
Dinner Service, four place settings and serving pieces, pink speckleware . . .	**95.00**
Vase	
Gilt, Tracy Irwin	**55.00**
White, #504	**65.00**

MONTEREY. Line of dinnerware produced from 1936 until 1945. Burgundy, Green, Ivory, Monterey Blue, Orange–Red, Red–Brown, Turquoise Blue, White, and Yellow were featured colors.

Cake Plate, pedestal base, Orange–Red	**100.00**
Casserole, cov, Green, metal frame, crazed lid, 2 qt	**35.00**
Cereal Bowl, Ivory	**15.00**

Chop Plate, 13" d, Yellow 35.00
Creamer, Light Blue 20.00
Cup, Green 12.00
Custard Cup, White 20.00
Fruit Bowl, Burgundy 20.00
Gravy Boat, Red–Brown 35.00
Pitcher, Green 45.00
Plate
  6" d, bread and butter
    Turquoise Blue 10.00
    White 9.00
  7½" d, salad
    Burgundy 15.00
    Monterey Blue 15.00
  9½" d, luncheon
    Green 10.00
    Light Blue 12.00
  10½" d, dinner, Orange–Red 30.00
Saucer, Red–Brown 10.00
Soup Bowl, 7½" d, Monterey Blue . . .   27.50
Sugar, Light Blue 20.00
Teapot, cov, 6 cup, Yellow 65.00
Tumbler, Light Blue 17.50
Vegetable Bowl, oval, divided, Red–
Brown 40.00

RING. Introduced in 1931. Original colors consisted of Black, Burgundy, Dark Blue, Green, Ivory, Light Blue, Orange–Red, White, and Yellow. Due to government restrictions during World War II, some glazes were either reformulated or replaced with pastel colors.

Baking Dish, cov, 4" d, Orange–Red . .   25.00
Batter Jug, cov, Dark Blue 95.00
Beater Bowl
  Black 65.00
  Orange–Red 65.00
Butter Dish, Orange–Red 150.00
Casserole, cov
  4¾" d, individual size, Green 35.00
  7½" d, Ivory 50.00
Cereal Bowl, Light Blue 15.00
Chop Plate, 17" d, Orange–Red 225.00
Cookie Jar, cov, Orange–Red 125.00
Creamer and Sugar, midget, yellow . . .   55.00
Cup and Saucer
  Burgundy 45.00
  Dark Blue 45.00
  Green 30.00
  Orange–Red 45.00
  Yellow 30.00
Juice Tumbler
  Green 18.00
  Orange–Red 18.00
  Yellow 18.00
Mixing Bowl
  #3, Yellow 125.00
  #12, Green 27.00
  #24, Yellow 18.00
  #36, Ivory 65.00

Plate
  6" d, bread and butter
    Burgundy 9.00
    Yellow 8.50
  7½" d, salad
    Dark Blue 15.00
    White 15.00
  10" d, dinner
    Orange–Red 25.00
    White 20.00
  11" d, Orange–Red 75.00
Soup Bowl, 7½" d, Burgundy 25.00
Teapot, cov
  Black 100.00
  Orange–Red 145.00
Tumbler, Yellow 25.00

BEATLES

Collecting Hints: Beatles' collectibles date from 1964 to the present. The majority of memorabilia items were produced from 1964–1968. The most valuable items are marked "NEMS." Most collectors are interested in mint or near–mint items only. Some items in very good condition, especially if scarce, have considerable value as well.

Each year Sotheby's holds one or two auctions which include Beatles' memorabilia, primarily one–of–a–kind items such as guitars and stage costumes. These items command high prices. The "average" collector generally does not participate.

History: The fascination with the Beatles began in 1964. Soon the whole country was caught up in Beatlemania. The members of the group included John Lennon, Paul McCartney, George Harrison and Ringo Starr. The group broke up in 1970. After this date, the members pursued their individual musical careers. Beatlemania took on new life after the death of John Lennon.

References: Jeff Augsburger, Marty Eck, and Rick Rann, *The Beatles Memorabilia Price Guide, Second Edition,* Wallace–Homestead, 1993; Perry Cox and Joe Lindsay, *The Official Pride Guide To The Beatles,* House of Collectibles, 1995; Barbara Fenick, *Collecting The Beatles, An Introduction and Price Guide to Fab Four Collectibles, Records and Memorabilia, Volume 1* (1984) and *Volume 2* (1988), Pierian Press; Norman E. Martinus and Harry L. Rinker, *Warman's Paper,* Wallace–Homestead, 1994; Jerry Osborne, Perry Cox, and Joe Lindsay, *The Official Price Guide To Memorabilia of Elvis Presley And The Beatles,* House of Collectibles, 1988; Michael Stern, Barbara Crawford, and Hollis Lamon, *The Beatles,* Collector Books, 1994.

Periodicals: *Beatlefan,* PO Box 33515, Decatur, GA 30033; *Instant Karma,* PO Box 256, Sault Ste. Marie, MI 49783.

Collectors' Clubs: Beatles Connection, PO Box 1066, Pinellas Park, FL 34665; Beatles Fan Club, 397 Edgewood Ave., New Haven, CT 06511; Beatles Fan Club of Great Britain, Superstore Productions, 123 Marina, St. Leonards on Sea, East Sussex, England TN38 OBN; Working Class Hero Club, 3311 Niagara St., Pittsburgh, PA 15213.

REPRODUCTION ALERT: Records, picture sleeves, and album jackets have been counterfeited. Sound quality may be inferior. Printing on labels and picture jackets usually is inferior to the original. Many pieces of memorabilia also have been reproduced, often with some change in size, color, design, etc.

Bank, drum shape, 1964	10.00
Beach Towel, 34 x 56", white cloth, Beatles illus, facsimile signatures, "The Beatles" and "Yeh, Yeh, Yeh" in red and blue lettering, 1965 copyright by Nems	200.00
Book, *Yellow Submarine,* punch out, 9½ x 15", 8 pgs, glossy paper, copyright 1968 King Features	38.00
Bottle Stopper, 4½" h, composition, Ringo figural head, marked "Ringo," cork marked "Achatit," c1960	175.00
Cake Decoration, four figures	12.00
Change Purse, 1964	10.00
Charm, Twist & Shout record	5.00
Clothes Hanger, 16 x 17", stiff diecut cardboard attached to white plastic hanger, George Harrison, copyright Henderson/Hoggard Inc, King Features—Suba Films Ltd, 1968	60.00
Coloring Book, 8½ x 11", Saalfield Publishing Co, 124 pgs, copyright 1964 Nems Enterprises Ltd	40.00
Commemorative Coin, United States trip, 1964	10.00
Costume, Blue Meanie, orig box, no mask	175.00
Cup, 6½" h, plastic, transparent plastic, color photo of Beatles playing instruments and gold facsimile signatures on paper insert, four pink lips around rim, copyright Nems Enterprises, c1960	52.00
Curtains, pr, 46 x 57", fabric, black, white, and blue illus on brown ground, printed song titles, Beatles' names and logo, marked "The Beatles—World Copyright NV Stoomweveru Nuverheid," made in Holland, c1960	800.00
Doll	
Paul McCartney, 4½" h, molded hard plastic body, soft vinyl head, artifi-	

cial hair, Remco, copyright 1964 Nems **180.00**

Set of Four, 15", vinyl, inflatable, with musical instruments, Nems Ltd, 1966, orig pkg	125.00
Fan Club Kit, Beatlemaniac	35.00
Game, Flip Your Wig, Milton Bradley, copyright Nems Enterprises Ltd, 1964	100.00
Glass, 4¾" h, Ringo, portrait picture and name in black, remaining red design, marked "Nems Enterprises Ltd, Ldn," c1964	110.00
Guitar, 31" l, plastic, red back, orange and maroon front, Beatles decal, raised silver "New Beat" logo, facsimile autographs, orig box	500.00
Gum Cards, set of 50, #116–165, third series, Topps, 1964, black and white photo and facsimile signature on each 2½ x 3½" card	40.00
Gum Wrapper, 5 x 6", waxed paper, black and blue illus, yellow and red lettering, issued by Topps, c1960 . . .	15.00
Hairbrush, 3¾" l, soft plastic, blue, photos, facsimile signatures and "The Beatle Brush" in relief, Genco, c1960s, orig unopened pkg	90.00
Home Movie, "Ticket to Ride," 3½" d plastic reel, Super 8, unopened pkg	90.00
Key Chain, guitar shape, picture, 1964	15.00
Lunch Box, Yellow Submarine, metal, King–Seeley, copyright 1968 King Features Syndicate	175.00
Mug, 4" h, glazed white ceramic, black, white, and blue photos, facsimile signatures and "The Beatles" in black, imprinted "England" on bottom, c1960	150.00
Nodder, 8" h, set of 4, composition, issued by Car Mascots, Inc, 1964, price for set of 4	275.00
Pencil Case, 3½ x 8", vinyl, blue, browntone photos, black facsimile signatures, zippered pocket, copyright 1964 by Standard Plastic Products and Beatles	95.00
Photo Ring, plastic, price for set of 4 . .	35.00
Pin	
Beetle shape, 2" h, standing, gold metal, painted black jacket and shoes, red striped shirt, mink fur hair, movable head and legs, playing guitar, c1960, orig display card	60.00
Guitar shape, orig card, 1964	25.00
Yellow Submarine characters, set of 8, figural, 1" l, plastic metal clasps, hp, c1960	65.00
Plate, 7" d, glazed white ceramic, black, white, and blue photos, facsimile signatures, "the Beatles" in black, c1960	80.00
Pocket Disk, 4" black flexidisk record, "Hey Jude/Revolution," gray apple	

and Columbia logo on label, 1969, unused **200.00**
Poster, 18 x 18", pinktone photo, "The Beatles Bulletin" fan club addresses, 1969 summer issue, color band photo **24.00**
Program, concert, Sept 5, 1964, Chicago concert **64.00**
Puzzle, 19 x 19", "Beatles in Pepperland," Sgt Pepper Band color illus, people in background, copyright 1968 King Features Syndicate, orig box **75.00**
Ring, ceramic **45.00**
Record Case, 7½" d, 6¾" h, Disk–Go–Case, plastic, purple/pink, holds 45 rpm records, black illus and facsimile signatures, Charter Industries Inc, copyright 1966 Nems Enterprises Ltd **100.00**
Sheet Music, 9 x 12", *She Loves You*, 4 pgs, written by Lennon and McCartney, red and white cov design, copyright 1963 Northern Songs, London, and 1964 Gil Music Corp, US **20.00**
Stick–on Sheets, two 9 x 12" sheets, *Yellow Submarine*, vinyl stickers, full color, "Popstickles" line, Dal Mfg Corp **30.00**
Switchplate Cover, 6 x 12", stiff cardboard, "Yellow Submarine," day glow, Blue Meanie character, inscribed "Stamp Out Fun," copyright 1968 King Features Syndicate, sealed in orig pkg **32.00**
Thermometer, 7½" h, Beatles Fan Club **10.00**
Toy
  Chubops, complete set in store display **75.00**
  Ringo with Drum, Remco **55.00**

Wig, Lowell Toy Mfg. Co., black, one size fits all, orig display bag, c1960s, $50.00.

Yellow Submarine, 2 x 5 x 3", diecast metal, replica, four plastic revolving periscopes, spring operated hatches, Corgi, copyright King features and Subafilms Ltd, 1968 ... **160.00**
Wallet, 3½ x 4½", vinyl plastic, gray, folder, pinktone group photo on one side, black facsimile signatures on other side, Standard Plastic Products, copyright Rmat & Co, Ltd, London, c1964 .... **120.00**
Wig, black, Lowell Toy Mfg Co, c1960s, orig display bag **50.00**

BEER BOTTLES

Collecting Hints: Beer bottles often are found by digging in old dumps or wells. When found, these bottles may have discolored and flaked. However, the key is whether the bottle remains unbroken or not. Damage to the bottle is of greater concern in pricing than the discoloration.

Concentrate on the bottles from one brewery or area. When an example is brought back to an area of its origin, it is likely to command more money than when sold outside the local region. A brewery is likely to change its bottle style several times in the course of its history. This also is true for the paper label designs found on later bottles.

The early bottles had special closures. The bottle is worth more if the closure is intact. The metal caps are not critical to the value of later bottles. However, an active collecting interest in metal caps is growing, as witnessed by dealer displays at several recent beer collector shows.

History: Breweries began in America shortly after the arrival of the first settlers. By the mid–19th century most farmsteads had a small brewery on them. Local breweries dominated the market until the arrival of Prohibition. A few larger breweries were able to adjust, but the majority closed.

When Prohibition ended, a much smaller number of local breweries renewed production. The advertising, distribution, and production costs of the 1950s and 1960s led to the closing of most local breweries and the merger of many other breweries into a few nationally oriented companies.

In the 1960s imported beers from Europe entered the American market. Some companies signed licensing agreements to produce these foreign labels in the United States. The 1980s have witnessed the growing popularity of beers brewed in Canada and Mexico.

References: Ralph and Terry Kovel, *The Kovels' Bottles Price List, 9th Edition,* Crown Publishers, 1992; Byron and Vicky Martin, *Here's To Beers: Blob Top Beer Bottles, 1880–1910,* published by authors, 1973; Jim Megura, *The Official Price*

Guide to Bottles, Eleventh Edition, House of Collectibles, 1991; Michael Polak, *Bottles: Identification and Price Guide,* Avon Books, 1994; Carlo and Dorothy Sellari, *The Standard Old Bottle Price Guide,* Collector Books, 1989.

Collectors' Club: American Breweriana Assoc., Inc., PO Box 11157, Pueblo, CO 81001.

Embossed

Cumberland, MD Brew Co, amber . .	**7.50**
Foss–Schneider Brew Co, Cincinnati, amber	**10.00**
George W Hoxsie, Premium Beer, dark amber, early blob top	**75.00**
Hand Brew Co, Pawtucket, RI, aqua	**7.50**
Iroquois, Buffalo, Indian head, amber	**7.50**
Johann Hoff, olive green, blob top, 8" h	**10.00**
Kessler Malt Extract, amber, squat type, 8½" h	**10.00**
Lion Brewery Ltd, amber, crown top, 11¾" h	**5.00**
McCormick Brewery, Boston, clear, 1897	**10.00**
National Brewing Co, Baltimore, eagle, amber, blob top	**15.00**
Oakland Bottling Co, Oakland, CA, amber, blob top, 9" h	**10.00**
Pittsburgh Brewing Co, amber, crown top, 12" h	**5.00**
Schlitz, ruby red	**15.00**
Sidney O Wagner, amber, crown top, 11½" h	**5.00**
William Gerst, Nashville, aqua, 11½" h	**7.50**
William Mulligan, Philadelphia, aqua, blob top, 9½" h	**5.00**

Painted Label

Augusta Brewing Co, Augusta, GA, aqua, 7" h	**12.00**

Esquire Premium Pale Beer, Jones Brewing Co., Smithton, PA, painted label, brown bottle, 7 oz, $10.00.

Cock'N Bull Ginger Beer, brown and tan, crown top, 7" h	**5.00**
James Handley Brew Co, clear, blob top	**12.50**

Paper Label

Bohemian Lager Beer, Bodie Bottling Work, Bodie, CA, aqua, crown top	**7.00**
Grand Prize Beer, Gulf Brewing Co, clear, crown top, 9" h	**5.00**
Northern Brewing Co, Superior, WI	**4.00**
Pabst Blue Ribbon Beer, Souvenir Special, amber, metal lid, crown top, 4¼" h	**8.00**

Stoneware

Biscombe's, brown and tan, 8½" h . .	**9.00**
Dr Earl's Premium Beer, 9½" h	**32.00**

BEER CANS

Collecting Hints: Rusted and dented cans have little value unless they are rare. Most collectors remove the beer from the cans. Cans should be opened from the bottom to preserve the top unopened.

As beer can collecting became popular, companies issued special collectors' cans which never contained beer. Many were bought on speculation; value has been shaky.

History: Before Prohibition, beer was stored and shipped in kegs and dispensed in returnable bottles. When the Prohibition Act was repealed in 1933, only 700 of 1700 breweries resumed operation. Expanding distribution created the need for an inexpensive container that would permit beer to be stored longer and shipped safely. Cans were the answer.

The first patent for a lined can was issued to the American Can Co. on Sept. 25, 1934, for their "Keglined" process. Gotfried Kruger Brewing Co., Newark, New Jersey, was the first brewery to use the can. Pabst was the first major company to join the canned beer movement.

Continental Can Co. introduced the cone–top beer can in 1935. Schlitz was the first brewery to use this type of can. The next major change in beer can design was the aluminum pop–top in 1962.

References: Bill Mugrage, *The Official Price Guide To Beer Cans, Fifth Edition,* House of Collectibles, 1993; Thomas Toepfer, *Beer Cans: 1932–75,* L–W Book Sales, 1976, 1995 value update.

Collectors' Clubs: Beer Can Collectors of America, 747 Merus Court, Fenton, MO 63026; Capitol City Chapter of the Beer Can Collectors of America, PO Box 287, Brandywine, MD 20613; Gambrinus Chapter of the Beer Can Collectors of America, 985 Maebelle Way, Westerville, OH 43081.

Museum: The Museum of Beverage Containers and Advertising, Goddlettsville, TN.

Note: The listings include the name, type of beer, brewery location, top identification, price. The following abbreviations are used in the listings:
CR—Crowntainer type cone top
CT—cone type
FT—flat top
PT—pull top
ML—malt liquor.

7 oz.
Lucky Lager, Lucky Lager, San Francisco, CA, FT 8.00
Pabst, 5 cities, PT 2.00
Rheingold, Rheingold, 2 cities, PT . .   1.50
8 oz.
Bull Dog ML, Grace, Santa Rosa, CA, FT 15.00
Goebel Ale, Goebel, Detroit, MI, FT   30.00
National Bohemian, National, Baltimore, MD, PT 8.00
Neuweiler, Neuweiler's, Allentown, PA, FT 15.00
Pearl, Pearl, 2 cities, PT 2.50
Storz–ette, (1953), Storz, Omaha, NE, FT 40.00
University Club ML, Miller, Milwaukee, WI, FT 15.00
10 oz.
Budweiser, Anheuser–Busch, 7 cities, PT 5.00
Colt 45 ML, National, 4 cities, PT . .   4.00
Old Milwaukee (1973), Schlitz, 6 cities, PT 2.50
11 and 12 oz.
A–1 Premium, National, Phoenix, AZ, PT 15.00
Atlas Prager, Atlas, Chicago, IL, FT . .   55.00
Big Apple, Waukee, Hammonton, NJ, FT 100.00
Bohack Premium, Richards, Newark, NJ, PT 8.00
Brau Haus, General, Los Angeles, CA, PT 10.00
Brew 82, Brew 82, Cleveland, OH, FT 75.00
Buckhorn, Hamm, 2 cities, PT 1.00
Chippewa Pride, Leinenkugel, Chippewa Falls, WI, PT 2.00
Dixie, Dixie, New Orleans, LA, PT   1.00
El Rancho, Falstaff, San Francisco, CA, PT 3.00
Fitger's, Fitger, Duluth, MN, FT 5.00
Friars Ale, Drewrys, South Bend, IN, FT 25.00
Gettelman, Gettelman, Milwaukee, WI, FT 20.00
Gilt Edge, Bosch, Houghton, MI, PT .   15.00
Heidelberg, Carling, Tacoma, WA, PT   4.00
Horlacher, Pilsner, Horlacher, Allentown, PA, FT 8.00

International Frankenmuth Ale, International, Covington, KY, FT . .   25.00
Karl's, Grace, Santa Rosa, CA, FT . . .   75.00
Kold Brau, Schoen–Edelweiss, Chicago, IL, FT 35.00
Leisy's Light, Leisy, Cleveland, OH, FT 40.00
Lucky Lager, Falstaff, 6 cities, PT 75
Metbrew, Metropolis, Trenton, NJ, PT   .50
Monticello, Monticello, Norfolk, VA, PT 50.00
Near Beer, Goetz, St Joseph, MO, FT   5.00
Old Milwaukee Draft (1971), Schlitz, 8 cities, PT 1.50
Oyster House, Pittsburgh, Pittsburgh, PA, PT 1.00
Potosi, Potosi, Potosi, WI, FT 10.00
Progress, Progress, Oklahoma City, OK, FT 75.00
Queens Brau, Queen City, Cumberland, MD, FT 45.00
Reading, Reading, Reading, PA, PT   2.50
Rolling Rock, Latrobe, Latrobe, PA, FT 12.00
Salzburg, Schoen–Edelweiss, Chicago, IL, FT 50.00
Schlitz Light (1975), Schlitz, 6 cities, PT 1.00
Stoney's, Jones, Smithon, PA, PT . . .   1.00
Texas Pride, Pearl, San Antonio, TX, PT 1.50
Tuborg, Carling, Baltimore, MD, PT .   2.00
Van Merritt, Van Merritt, Oconto, WI, FT 7.00
Walter's Light, Walter, Pueblo, CO, PT 2.00
Western, Cold Spring, Cold Spring, MN, PT 1.00
Yusay, Pilsen, Chicago, IL, FT 20.00
12 oz., Cone Top
Blatz Old Heidelberg Castle, Blatz, Milwaukee, WI, CC 35.00

Irish Brand Cream Ale, green and white, $50.00.

Breunig's Lager, Rice Lake, Rice Lake, WI, CT	**50.00**
Champagne Velvet, Terre Haute, Terre Haute, IN, CT	**40.00**
Dawson's Pale Ale, Dawson, New Bedford, MA, CT	**40.00**
Fehr's, Fehr, Louisville, KY, CR	**25.00**
Ortlieb's Premium Lager, Ortlieb, Philadelphia, PA, CT	**55.00**
Stag Premium Dry, Griesedieck– Western, 2 cities, CT	**25.00**
15 and 16 oz.	
Budweiser, Anheuser–Busch, 6 cities, PT	**5.00**
Eastside Old Tap, Pabst, Los Angeles, CA, FT	**15.00**
Land of Lakes, Pilsen, Chicago, IL, FT	**20.00**
Mustang Malt Lager, Pittsburgh, Pittsburgh, PA, PT	**25.00**
Pabst, Pabst, Milwaukee, WI, FT . . .	**22.00**
Piels Light, Piels, Brooklyn, NY, FT	**20.00**
Stroh's, Stroh, Detroit, MI, PT	**2.50**

BICYCLES

Collecting Hints: Collectors divide bicycles into two groups—antique and classic. The antique category covers early high wheelers through safety bikes made into the 1920s and 1930s. Highly stylized bicycles from the 1930s and 1940s represent the transitional step to the classic period, beginning in the late 1940s and running through the end of the balloon tire era.

Unfortunately there are no reliable guide books for the beginning collector. A good rule is that any older bike in good condition is worth collecting.

Never pay much for a bicycle that is rusted, incomplete, or repaired with non–original parts. Replacement of leather seats or rubber handle bars does not affect value since these have a short lifetime.

Restoration is an accepted practice. Make certain to store an old bicycle high (hung by its frame to protect the tires) and dry (no more than 50% humidity).

Do not forget all the secondary material, e.g., advertising premiums, brochures, catalogs, posters, etc., that featured the bicycle. This material provides important historical data for research, especially for restoration.

Bicycle collectors and dealers gather each year on the last weekend in April at the Saline/Ann Arbor Swap Meet and Show.

History: In 1818 Baron Karl von Drais, a German, invented the Draisienne, a push scooter, that is viewed as the "first" bicycle. In 1839 Patrick MacMillan, a Scot, added a treadle system; a few years later Pierre Michaux, a Frenchman, revolutionized the design by adding a pedal system. The bicycle was introduced in America at the 1876 Centennial.

Early bicycles were high wheelers with a heavy iron frame and two disproportionately sized wheels with wooden rims and tires. The exaggerated front wheel was for speed, the small rear wheel for balance.

James Starley, an Englishman, is responsible for developing a bicycle with two wheels of equal size. Pedals drove the rear wheels by means of a chain and sprocket. By 1892 the wooden rim wheel was replaced by pneumatic air–filled tires to be followed by the standard rubber tire with inner tube.

The year 1898 witnessed the development of the coaster brake. This important milestone made cycling a true family sport. Bicycling became a cult among the urban middle class. As the new century dawned, over four million Americans owned bicycles.

The automobile challenged the popularity of bicycling beginning in the 1920s. Since that time, interest in bicycling has been cyclical. Technical advances continued. The 1970s was the decade of the ten speed.

The success of American Olympiads in cycling and cycle racing, especially the Tour d'France, have kept the public's attention focused on the bicycle. However, the tremendous resurgence enjoyed by bicycling in the 1970s appears to have ended. The next craze is probably some distance in the future.

References: Frederick Alderson, *Bicycling: A History*, Praeger, 1972; Fermo Galbiati and Nino Ciravegna, *The Bicycle*, Chronicle Books, 1994; Jim Hurd, *Introductory Guide to Collecting The Classics*, Antique/Classic Bicycle News, 1987; Jim Hurd, *1991 Bicycle Blue Book*, Antique/Classic Bicycle News, 1991; Neil S. Wood, *Evolution of the Bicycle*, Volume 1 (1991, 1994 value update), Volume 2 (1994) L–W Book Sales.

Periodicals: *Antique/Classic Bicycle News*, PO Box 1049, Ann Arbor, MI 48106; Bicycle Trader, PO Box 5600, Pittsburgh, PA 15207; *Classic Bicycle & Whizzer News*, PO Box 765, Huntington Beach, CA 92648; *National Antique & Classic Bicycle*, PO Box 5600, Pittsburgh, PA 15207.

Collectors' Clubs: Cascade Classic Cycle Club, 7935 SE Market St., Portland, OR 97215; Classic Bicycle and Whizzer Club, 35769 Simon, Clinton Twp, MI 48035; International Veteran Cycle Assoc., 248 Highland Dr., Findlay, OH 45840; National Pedal Vehicle Assoc, 1720 Rupert, NE, Grand Rapids, MI 49505; The Wheelmen, 55 Bucknell Ave., Trenton, NJ 08619.

Museum: Schwinn History Center, Chicago, IL.

Advertising

Brochure, Crescent Bicycles, 1899 . .   **20.00**

Clock, Columbia Built Bicycles Since 1877—America's First Bicycle, electric, 15" d, c1950 . . . .   **325.00**

Poster

Mentor Bicycles, young girls riding, c1890 . . . .   **750.00**

Presto, cyclist and monoplane illus, half sheet **775.00**

Rambler Cycles, lady riding, France, 48 x 35" **950.00**

Sign, Columbia Bicycle, cardboard, litho, MacDonald Bald, Sims and their Columbias, racers, Gies & Co Litho, Buffalo, NY **1,250.00**

Trade Card

Clark Bicycle Co, Christmas, Santa on high wheeler, c1880 . . . . . .   **20.00**

Pope Mfg Co, Columbia Bicycle, men riding bikes at night illus . .   **12.00**

Alarm

Butcher **25.00**

Perfection **15.00**

Badge, 1¼ x 2" link type, marked "Solid Silver" on back, enameled center front disk, hanger bar inscribed "Queens Co Course June 19 1898," pendant rim inscription "Century Medal/Survivor" and "Royal Arcanum Wheelman/New York City" **60.00**

Bicycle

Beckley–Ralston, Chicago, tricycle, push pull action, wood seat and handles, spoke wheels, orig paint   **700.00**

BF Goodrich, boy's, 26" tires, new paint, orig light, carrier, locking fork, bendix auto 2–speed **150.00**

Bowden

300 . . . .   **6,000.00**

Spacelander **7,000.00**

Colson

Firestone Cruiser, 1941 . . . .   **1,500.00**

Packard, 1936 . . . .   **1,750.00**

Columbia

Carnival, 1936 . . . .   **2,500.00**

Model 50, chainless pneumatic, 1898 . . . .   **900.00**

Ranger, 1936 . . . .   **2,000.00**

Super Deluxe, 1938 . . . .   **2,500.00**

Victory, 1939 . . . .   **1,750.00**

Comet, men's, worn orig paint, coaster brake, aluminum fenders   **85.00**

Dayton

Super Streamliner, 1936 . . . .   **3,250.00**

Twin Flex, 1939 . . . .   **2,000.00**

Elgin, Sears Roebuck

Blackhawk **3,000.00**

Dolly Bike, 1939 . . . .   **1,250.00**

Twin 30 . . . .   **750.00**

Firestone, Deluxe Speed Cruiser, 1959 . . . .   **500.00**

Hawthorne, Montgomery Ward, Comet Rollfast, 1936 . . . .   **1,000.00**

Higgins, lady's, worn orig paint, carrier, skirt guard, truss rod, rusty rims   **85.00**

Huffman (Huffy)

Coca Cola Classic, 1987 . . . .   **300.00**

Dial A Ride, 1952 . . . .   **1,750.00**

Radiobike, 1950s **2,500.00**

Iroquois, Iroquois Cycleworks, 1898   **1,000.00**

J C Higgins, Sears Roebuck, 1953 . .   **600.00**

Monark

Coupe De Ville, 1954 . . . .   **750.00**

Firestone Holiday, 1953 . . . .   **750.00**

Silver King, M237 . . . .   **1,000.00**

Murray, Flatline, 1956 . . . .   **800.00**

Pacemaker, Cleveland Welding Co, 1941 . . . .   **1,500.00**

Roadmaster, Cleveland Welding Co

Boy's, Flying Falcon, 1965 . . . . . .   **200.00**

Girl's, cream and blue, red pinstripe, horn tank, headlight, carrier, chrome rims, orig condition   **140.00**

Rollfast, DP Harris Co, Hopalong Cassidy, 20", 1951 . . . .   **2,500.00**

Schwinn

Corvette, 1955 . . . .   **350.00**

Deluxe Hornet **500.00**

Hollywood Special **500.00**

Orange Krate **400.00**

Pea Picker **350.00**

Phantom Deluxe, 1959 . . . .   **1,500.00**

Stingray **200.00**

Typhoon Deluxe, 1968 . . . .   **375.00**

Skyline, tricycle, 1930s **100.00**

Walton, tandem, wood rim, block chain fixed drive, rat trap pedals, new cork grips, new polymer tires   **450.00**

Western Flyer

Mercury, 1939 . . . .   **1,500.00**

Sonic Flyer, 1950s **350.00**

Catalog

Indian Motorcycles and Bicycles, 1915 . . . .   **50.00**

Iver Johnson Bicycle & Motorcycle Supplies, 1909 . . . .   **35.00**

Mead Cycle Co, Chicago, IL, Bargain List No. 24, 24 pages, 8¼ x 10", 1924 . . . .   **20.00**

Union Cycles, 1896, 8 x 5" **30.00**

Chain, Diamond **10.00**

Horn, Yoder, c1950 . . . .   **7.00**

Lapel Stud, Corbin Bells, The Best, metal, copper finish, handlebar bell, late 1890s **30.00**

Light, Schwinn Phantom, chrome, battery operated **60.00**

O'Hara Porcelain, oval porcelain disk made by O'Hara Watch Dial Co, Waltham, MA, pastel pink illus, black lettering

La Tour Bike, for Laclede Mfg Co, St Louis maker **30.00**

The Alvin Cycle Mfg Co, for Phila-
delphia bike maker 30.00
The Newton Bike, tiny hairline at top   25.00
Pedals, Schwinn, girl's, glass reflectors   50.00
Pinback Button
97 Tally–Ho Bike Lantern, purple and
white, illus of metal lantern, "Easily
Cleaned Can't Jar Out" 40.00
Champion Cyclist, 7/8" black and
white cello portrait, issued by
Whitehead   &   Hoag   Co,
c1896–1900
Eddie Bald, Cyclist, Champion
1896 . . . .   35.00
F. T. Titus, Cyclist 30.00
Thomas Cooper, Cyclist 30.00
Damascus Bicycle, 7/8" d, multicolored, green and yellow gold Sword
of Damascus, blue rim inscribed
"Terre Haute Mfg Co, Dixon, IL,"
c1896, small tear in orig back pa-
per 35.00
Topeka Wheelmen Track Association,
1¼" d, lightly tinted black and
white illus, four female cyclists approaching head on, light blue center ground blending to white edges,
blue rim inscription, red serial
number, c1890 . . . .   60.00
Tried and True Pierce, 1¼" d, black
and white logo, plum red ground,
logo border inscribed "The Geo H
Pierce   Co/Makers/Buffalo,   NY,
USA," 1890s 50.00
Saddle Pin, replica of bicycle seat, short
stickpin soldered on back, late 1890s
Mesinger, ¾ x 7/8", diecut tin 30.00
Richards Bicycle, 7/8 x 1½", silvered
brass,   inscription   at   top
"Richards/Buchanan, Mich" 40.00
Stickpin
Olympic Bike, ¾" cello, metal stick-
pin, green victory wreath border
around small red slogan "Good As
Gold," black title bar "Olympic
Cycle Mfg's Co. NY" 35.00
Syracuse Bicycles, brass, profile of bi-
cycle under title inscription and
above "Crimson Rims," reverse re-
peats name and inscription for
Chas J Stebbins, New York City ad-
dress 30.00
The Hoffman Bike, diecut brass, em-
blem title plate featuring letter "H"
at center over "Cleveland Ohio"   25.00
Stud, 7/8", celluloid, metal lapel stud fastener, c1896
Andrea Cycle, black and pale pink,
slogan "The Wheel That Never
Disappoints" 10.00
Business Bicycles Mean Business, orange, black inscription and illus,

bicycle profile on background of
tall masted sailing ship, oversized
bicycle wheels, front ring inscribed
"Business," rear inscribed "Bicy-
cles" 40.00
LAW, League of American Wheelman,
blue and white, silvered tin rim . .   30.00
Olympic Cycle Mfg Co, red and
white 15.00
Pierce Cycles, yellow, black logo and
inscription, slogan "Tried and True"   25.00
Superb Bicycles, purple, white inscription and illus, profile of cyclist
on bike 30.00
Union Crackajack II, orange lettering
on black 30.00
Wolff American High Art Cycle, pale
pink, inscription, illus of running
wolf 15.00
Zimmy, black, yellow symbol, in-
scription "Ask To See A Zimmy" . .   20.00
Tire, Schwinn, wide, white sidewalls,
knobbys 15.00
Tobacco Card, Honest Tobacco 20.00

BIG LITTLE BOOKS

Collecting Hints: As more research is done and published on Big Little Books, the factors deter-mining value shift. Condition always has been a key. Few examples are in pristine mint condition since the books were used heavily by the chil-dren who owned them. Each collector strives to obtain copies free from as many defects (bent edges on cover, missing spine, torn pages, muti-lation with crayon or pencil, missing pages, etc.) as possible.

The main character in a book will determine price since it is a collector from another field who will vie with the Big Little Book collector for the same work. Dick Tracy, Disney characters, Buck Rogers, Flash Gordon, Charlie Chan, The Green Hornet and Tom Mix are examples. Other cowboy heroes are experiencing renewed popu-larity.

Until recently little attention has been directed to the artists who produced the books. Now ex-amples by Alex Raymond and Henry Vallely command top dollar. Other desirable artists are Al Capp, Allen Dean, Alfred Andriola, and Will Gould. Personal taste still is a critical factor at this time.

Little is known as to how many copies of each book were printed. Scarcity charts have been prepared, but constantly are being revised. Books tend to hit the market in hoards, with prices fluc-tuating accordingly. However, the last decade has witnessed a stabilization of prices.

Larry Lowery, in the introduction to his book, has prepared an excellent section on the care and storage of Big Little Books. He also deserves credit for the detailed research which he has brought to each listing.

History: Big Little Books, although a trademark of the Whitman Publishing Co., is a term used to describe a wealth of children's books published during the 1930s and continuing to the present day. The origin of Big Little Books dates to a number of 1920s series by Whitman among which were Fairy Tales, Forest Friends and Boy Adventure.

The first Big Little Book appeared in 1933. Ten different page lengths and eight different sizes were tried by Whitman prior to the 1940s. Whitman and Saalfield Publishing Company dominated the field. However, other publishers did enter the market. Among them were Engel–Van Wiseman, Lynn Publishing Co., Goldsmith Publishing Co. and Dell Publishing Co.

Whitman also deserves attention for the various remarketing efforts it undertook with many of its titles. It contracted to provide Big Little Book premiums for Cocomalt, Kool Aid, Pan–Am Gas, Macy's, Lily–Tulip's Tarzan Ice Cream and others. Among its series names are Wee Little Books, Big Big Books, Nickel Books, Penny Books and Famous Comics.

In the 1950s television characters were introduced into Big Little Book format. Whitman Publishing became part of Western Publishing, owned by Mattel. Waldman and Son Publishing Co., under its subsidiary, Moby Books, issued their first Big Little Book–style book in 1977.

References: Larry Lowery, *Lowery's The Collector's Guide To Big Little Books and Similar Books*, privately printed, 1981; Norman E. Martinus and Harry L. Rinker, *Warman's Paper*, Wallace–Homestead, 1994.

Collectors' Club: Big Little Book Collector Club of America, PO Box 1242, Danville, CA 94526.

Note: Books are priced in very fine condition. Cover and spine are intact with only slight bending at the corners. All pages are present; only slightest discoloration of pages. Book has a crispness from cover color to inside.

No effort has been made to list the variations and premiums published by Whitman.

See: Cartoon Characters, Cowboy Heroes, Disneyana and Space Adventurers.

AERONAUTICS

Buzz Sawyer and Bomber 13, WBLB, 1415, 1946, Roy Crane, ss **24.00**
Men with Wings, WBELB, 1475, 1938, Eleanor Parker, Fred MacMurray, Paramount Pictures, ss, 240 pgs, hc   **12.00**
Pat Nelson, Ace of the Test Pilots, WBLB, 1445, 1937, Dougal Lee, ss   **15.00**

Saalfield Little Big Book, *Jackie Cooper in Peck's Bad Boy,* #1804, 1934, $80.00.

Tailspin Tommy, The Dirigible Flight to the North Pole, WBLB, 1124, 1934, Hal Forest, ss **25.00**
Thirteen Hours by Air, Lynn Publishing, L26, 1936, Wallace West, 128 pgs, 5 x 7″ **35.00**
Uncle Sam's Sky Defenders, WBLB, 1461, 1941, Erwin L Hess, artist, Peter A Wyckoff, author, ss, flip **15.00**
Windy Wayne and His Flying Wing, WBLB, 1433, 1942, Erwin L Darwin, artist, Russell R Winterbotham, author, ss, left handed flip **15.00**

CARTOON CHARACTERS, MOVIE

Andy Panda and the Mad Dog Mystery, WBELB, 1431, 1947, Walter Lantz Productions, ss, 288 pgs, hc **18.00**
Adventures of Krazy Kat and Ignatz Mouse in Koko Land, Saalfield, Little Big Book, 1056, 1934, George Herriman, horizontal **35.00**
Bugs Bunny in Risky Business, WBELB, 1440, 1948, Warner Bros Productions, ss, 288 pgs, hc **18.00**
Donald Duck, Such a Life!, WBELB, 1404, 1939, Al Taliaferro, ss, 432 pgs, hc **20.00**
Mickey Mouse in the Foreign Legion, WBELB, 1428, 1940, Floyd Gottfredson, ss, 432 pgs, hc **35.00**
Oswald Rabbit Plays G–Man, WBLB, 1403, 1937, Eleanor Parker, Universal Pictures, ss, 240 pgs, hc **15.00**

CARTOON CHARACTERS, NEWSPAPER

Alley Oop and Dinny, WBLB, 763, 1935, Vince T Hamlin, artist and author, ss, 384 pgs, sc **20.00**

Blondie, Count Cookie in Too!, WBLB, 1430, 1947, Chic Young, ss **20.00**
Just Kids and the Mysterious Stranger, Saalfield, Little Big Book, 1324, 1935, Ad Carter, sc, ss **20.00**
Little Orphan Annie in the Thieves' Den, WBELB, 1446, 1948, Harold Gray, artist, Helen Berke, author, ss, 288 pgs, hc **20.00**
Nancy and Sluggo, WBLB, 1400, 1946, Ernie Bushmiller, ss **26.00**
Popeye, Saalfield, Little Big Book, 1051, 1934, Elzie Crisler Segar, horizontal   **36.00**
Popeye and the Quest for the Rainbird, WBLB, 1459, 1943, Bud Sagandorf, ss **28.00**
Skeezix at the Military Academy, WBLB, 1408, 1938, Frank King, ss, 432 pgs, hc **12.00**
Smitty in Going Native, WBLB, 1477, 1938, Walter Berndt, ss **20.00**

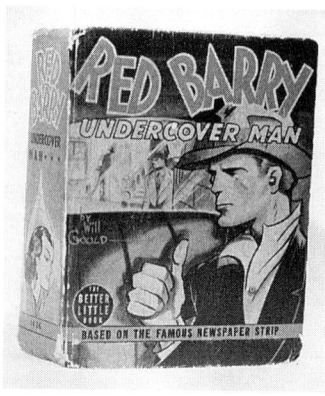

Whitman Better Little Book, Red Barry Undercover Man, #1426, 1937/1939, $18.00.

DETECTIVE

Apple Mary and Dennie Foil the Swindlers, WBLB, 1130, 1936, Martha Orr, reprints from first Mary Worth strips, ss **24.00**
Bob Stone, the Young Detective, 1432, 1937, Henry E Vallely cover, Peter K Maple, author, ss **18.00**
Brenda Starr and the Masked Impostor, WBLB, 1427, 1940, Dale Messick, ss **25.00**
Detective Higgins of the Racket Squad, WBELB, 1484, 1938, Herbert Anderson, Millard Thacksen, ss, hc, 432 pgs **15.00**

JUNGLE

Jungle Jim, WBLB, 1138, 1936, Alex Raymond, ss **22.00**
Tarzan and the Ant Men, WBLB, 1444, 1945, Rex Maxon, artist, John Coleman Burroughs, cover, Edgar Rice Burroughs, author, ss **20.00**
Tarzan Twins, WBLB, 770, 1934, Edgar Rice Burroughs, ss, 432 pgs, hc **24.00**
The Tiger Lady, Mabel Stark, Saalfield, Little Big Book, 1588, 1935, Gertrude Orr, sc **20.00**

LITERATURE

Adventures of Tom Sawyer, Saalfield, Little Big Book, 1308, 1934, Park Sumner, artist, Mark Twain, Charles T Clinton, author, sc **35.00**
Great Expectations, Engel–Van Wiseman, Inc, 8, 1934, adapted from Charles Dickens by A J Sharick, 158 pgs, 4 x 5½" **30.00**
Little Women, WBLB, 757, 1934, adapted from Louisa May Alcott, 160 pgs, hc, 4⅝ x 5¼ x ⅞", sc spine . . .   **18.00**
Robinson Crusoe, WBLB, 719, 1934, adapted from Daniel Defoe, 3½ x 2 x 1⅝", 360 pgs, sc **18.00**

MOVIE

Cowboy Millionaire, Saalfield, Little Big Book, 1106, 1935, George O'Brien, Atherton Pictures **15.00**
Jackie Cooper, Movie Star of Skippy and Sooky, WBLB, 714, 1933, Eleanor Packer, ss **24.00**
Laurel and Hardy, Saalfield, Little Big Book, 1086, 1934, Charles T Clinton, ss **28.00**
Mickey Rooney and Judy Garland and How They Got Into the Movies, WBELB, 1493, 1941, Henry E Vallely, artist, Edward I Gruskin, author, ss, 432 pgs, hc **30.00**
One Night of Love, Saalfield, Little Big Book, 1099, 1935, Charles Beahan and Dorothy Speare, ss **16.00**
Strawberry Roan, Saalfield, Little Big Book, 1090, 1934, Ken Maynard, Universal, Grace Mack, ss **15.00**
Union Pacific, Joel Macrae and Barbara Stanwyck, WBELB, 1411, 1939, Eleanor Parker, Paramount, ss **18.50**

RADIO

Calling W–1–X–Y–Z Jimmy Kean and the Radio Spies, WBLB, 1412, 1939, Sam Nisenson, artist, Thorp McClusky, author, ss **18.00**

Fire Chief Ed Wynn and His Old Fire Horse, Goldsmith Publishing, 1934, Henry E Vallely, artist, Harold Sherman, author 25.00

The Green Hornet Strikes!, WBELB, 1453, 1940, Robert R Weisman, artist, adapted from Fran Striker, ss, 432 pgs, hc 22.00

The Shadow and the Master of Evil, WBELB, 1443, 1941, Erwin L Hess, artist, Maxwell Grant, author, ss, 432 pgs, hc, flip 15.00

Uncle Don's Strange Adventures, WBLB, 1114, 1936, Uncle Don Carney, ss 15.00

SPORTS

Brick Barton and the Winning Eleven, Coach Bernie Bierman's, WBLB, 1480, 1938, R M Williamson, artist, Bernie Bierman, author, ss 15.00

Hockey Spare, Saalfield, Little Big Book, 1605, 1937, Robert A Graef, artist, Harold M Sherman, author, ss   15.00

Joe Palooka, The Heavyweight Boxing Champ, WBLB, 1123, 1934, Ham Fisher, ss 20.00

Stan Kent, Captain, Saalfield, Little Big Book, 1132, 1937, Louis G Schroeder, artist, William Heyliger, author, ss . .   15.00

WESTERN

Arizona Kid on the Bandit Trail, WBLB, 1192, 1936, Hal Arbo, artist, Peter Maple, author, ss 18.00

Big Chief Wahoo and the Magic Lamp, WBLB, 1942, Elmer Woggon, Allen Saunders, author, ss 18.00

Buck Jones and the Two Gun Kid, WBLB, 1404, 1937, Robert Weisman, artist, Gaylord DuBois, author, ss . . .   24.00

Buckskin and Bullets, Saalfield, Little Big Book, 1135, 1938, Luther Hittle, artist, Ward M Stevens, ss 15.00

Buffalo Bill Plays a Lone Hand, WBLB, 1194, 1936, Hal Arbo, artist, Buck Wilson, author, ss 15.00

Gene Autry and the Bandits of Silver Tip, WBELB, 1940 . . . .   15.00

Kit Carson and the Mystery Riders, Saalfield, Little Big Book, 1105, 1935, Charles T Clinton, ss 15.00

Lone Ranger and His Horse Silver, WBLB, 1935, Henry Vallely, artist, Fran Striker, author, ss 45.00

Prairie Bill and the Covered Wagon, WBLB, 758, 1934, Hal Arbo, artist, G A Alkire, ss 15.00

Red Ryder and the Circus Luck, WBLB, 1466, 1949, Fred Harman, ss 15.00

BLACK MEMORABILIA

Collecting Hints: Black memorabilia was produced in vast quantities and variations. As a result, collectors have a large field from which to choose and should concentrate on one or a combination of limited categories.

Outstanding examples or extremely derogatory designs in any given area of the field command higher prices. Certain categories, e.g., cookie jars, draw a higher concentration of collector interest resulting in higher prices. Regional pricing also is a factor.

New collectors frequently overpay for common items of little worth because they mistakenly assume all Black collectibles are rare or of great value. As in any other collecting field, misinformation and a lack of knowledge leads to these exaggerated values. The Black memorabilia collector is particularly vulnerable to this practice since so little documentation exists on the subject.

New collectors should familiarize themselves with the field by first studying the market, price trends, and existing reference material. Again, because of the limited reference material and the relative newness of the field, seeking out other collectors is especially valuable for the novice.

Black memorabilia has developed into an established collecting field primarily within the past few years and continues to grow with increased public attention and interest.

History: The term "Black memorabilia" refers to a broad range of collectibles that often overlap other collecting fields, e.g., toys, postcards, etc. It also encompasses African artifacts, items created by slaves or related to the slavery era, modern Black cultural contributions to literature, art, etc., and material associated with the Civil Rights Movement and the Black experience throughout history.

The earliest known examples of Black memorabilia include primitive African designs and tribal artifacts. Black memorabilia dates back to the arrival of African natives upon American shores.

The advent of the 1900s launched an incredible amount and variety of material depicting Blacks, most often in a derogatory and dehumanizing manner that clearly reflected the stereotypical attitude held toward the Black race during this period. The popularity of Black portrayals in this unflattering fashion flourished as the century wore on.

As the growth of the Civil Rights Movement escalated and aroused public awareness to the Black plight, attitudes changed. Public outrage and pressure eventually put a halt to the offensive practice during the early 1950s.

Black representations still are being produced today in many forms, but no longer in the demoralizing designs of the past. These modern objects, while not as historically significant as earlier examples, will become the Black memorabilia of tomorrow.

References: Douglas Congdon–Martin, *Images In Black: 150 Years of Black Collectibles*, Schiffer Publishing, 1990; Patiki Gibbs, *Black Collectibles Sold In America*, Collector Books, 1987, 1993 value update; Patiki Gibbs and Tyson Gibbs, *The Collector's Encyclopedia of Black Dolls*, Collector Books, 1987, 1989 value update, out–of–print; Kenneth Goings, *Mammy and Uncle Mose: Black Collectibles and American Stereotyping*, Indiana University Press, 1994; Dee Hockenberry, *Enchanting Friends: Collectible Poohs, Raggedies, Golliwoggs, & Roosevelt Bears*, Schiffer Publishing, 1995; Jan Lindenberger, *Black Memorabilia Around The House: A Handbook and Price Guide*, Schiffer Publishing, 1993; Jan Lindenberger, *Black Memorabilia For the Kitchen: A Handbook and Price Guide*, Schiffer Publishing, 1992; Jan Lindenberger, *More Black Memorabilia: A Handbook and Price Guide*, Schiffer Publishing, 1995; Norman E. Martinus and Harry L. Rinker, *Warman's Paper*, Wallace–Homestead, 1994; Myla Perkins, *Black Dolls: 1820–1991*, Collector Books, 1993, 1995 value update; Myla Perkins, *Black Dolls, Book II: An Identification And Value Guide*, Collector Books, 1995; Dawn Reno, *Collecting Black Americana*, Crown Publishing, 1986; Darrell A. Smith, *Black Americana: A Personal Collection*, Black Relics, 1988; Jean Williams Turner, *Collectible Aunt Jemima*, Schiffer Publishing, 1994; Jackie Young, *Black Collectibles: Mammy and Her Friends*, Schiffer Publishing, 1988.

Periodicals: *Black Ethnic Collectibles*, 1401 Asbury Court, Hyattsville, MD 20782; *Blackin'*, 559 22nd Ave., Rock Island, IL 61201; *Fabric of Life*, PO Box 1212, Bellevue, WA 98009.

Collectors' Club: Black Memorabilia Collector's Assoc., 2482 Devoe Terrace, Bronx, NY 10468.

Museums: Black American West Museum, Denver, CO; Black Archives Research Center and Museum, Florida A&M University, Tallahassee, FL; Museum of African American History, Detroit, MI; National Baseball Hall of Fame, Cooperstown, NY; Studio Museum, Harlem, NY; Center for African Art, New York, NY; The Jazz Hall of Fame, New York, NY; Schomburg Center for Research in Black Culture, New York, NY; John Brown Wax Museum, Harper's Ferry, WV; The Museum of African Art, Smithsonian Institution, Washington, D.C.; Robeson Archives, Howard University, Washington, D.C.

REPRODUCTION ALERT: Black memorabilia reproductions have grown during the 1980s. Many are made of easily reproducible materials which generally show signs of "newness." Collectors should beware of any given item offered in large or unlimited quantities.

Note: The following price listing is based upon items in excellent to mint condition. Major paint loss, chips, cracks, fading, tears, or other extreme signs of age warrant a considerable reduction in value, except in very rare or limited production items. Collectors should expect a certain amount of wear on susceptible surfaces.

Box, Gold Dust Washing Powder, Fairbank's, 6¼" h, $25.00.

Advertising	
Can, Gold Dust Cleanser, unopened	**85.00**
Sign, 12" d, H C F Koch & Son Dry Goods, black girl holding huge umbrella, litho on heavy board, round walnut frame	**950.00**
Apron, Mammy, pecan pralines recipe, 1976	**24.00**
Ashtray	
Boy eating watermelon slice	**30.00**
Mammy face	**25.00**
Ashtray Stand, figural, butler, cast iron, orig paint	**575.00**
Bag, Plantation Coffee, cloth, Negro illus, 1930s	**5.00**
Bank	
Lucky Joe	**15.00**
Mammy on commode	**40.00**
Bell, souvenir, Mammy, ceramic	**22.00**
Biscuit Jar, cov, Mammy, marked "Japan"	**695.00**
Book	
Golliwog At Sea Shore	**395.00**
Little Black Sambo, Whitman	**12.00**
Uncle Remus, His Songs & Sayings, Joel Chandler Harris, 1908	**65.00**
Bookends, pr, chalkware, boys with watermelon	**175.00**
Bottle Stopper, 3" h, Golliwog	**50.00**

Candleholder, Mammy 45.00
Cigar Box, Virginia Cheroots, 1883 . . .   48.00
Clock, Mammy, marked "Red Wing" . .   198.00
Comic Strip Art, orig, Joe & Asbestos,
  Ken Kline illus, horse racing content,
  c1930 . . . .   90.00
Cookbook, *Southern Cookbook*, wood
  cov, Mammy profile, 722 recipes . . .   60.00
Cookie Jar, cov
  Angel, pink dress, gold trim, marked
    "Brush" 525.00
  Aunt Jemima, soft plastic 325.00
  Chef, Pearl China 435.00
  Mammy
    F & F, brown face 325.00
    Japanese, plaid, marked "Japan" . .   895.00
    National Silver 275.00
    Pearl China 650.00
Creamer and Sugar, F & F 125.00
Cup Holder, wood, Folk Art, Mammy
  and gray hair man 75.00
Dart Board, Black Sambo 105.00
Doll
  Cloth
    Aunt Jemima, uncut oil cloth 60.00
    Chad Valley, Black King, orig
      clothes, foot tag, chest button,
      glass eyes, hand sewn 350.00
    Mammy, large embroidered face,
      all orig clothing, c1930 . . . . . .   175.00
  Composition, 1930s 125.00
  Rubber, Sun Rubber, 1956 . . . .   50.00
Doorstop, 12" h, Mammy, cast iron,
  black trim, Hubley 425.00
Feeding Dish, 10" d, hot water type, boy
  walking through woods with birds,
  rabbits, and dog illus 150.00
Figure
  Boy on cotton bale, bisque 85.00
  Outhouse with two boys, 2½" h,
    bisque, Germany 35.00
  Waiter, Fred Curtis 30.00
Glass, Coon Chicken Inn 27.00
Laundry Bag, Mammy washing clothes   38.00
Magazine Tear Sheet
  Jell-O, 1921 . . . .   35.00
  Whiskey adv, 1935 . . . .   30.00
Map, souvenir, Mammy Chicken Inn . .   35.00
Matchbook, Coon Chicken Inn 35.00
Match Holder, chalk, man with water-
  melon 25.00
Memo Board, Mammy 36.00
Mug, face, great expression, marked
  "Japan" 100.00
Mustard Jar, chef, marked "Occupied
  Japan" 88.00
Note Pad Holder, Aunt Jemima, red and
  yellow plastic 70.00
Palm Puzzle, 1⅞" d, tin frame, glass
  cov, emb caricature portrait of man
  with open red mouth, metal balls
  form man's teeth, inscribed "Try The

Humidor, chalkware, olive green jacket, mustard yellow hat and pants, 10½" h, $185.00.

Other Side," Sunshine Stoves,
  Furnace adv 60.00
Pancake Mold, Aunt Jemima 175.00
Pie Bird
  Chef
    Green suit 185.00
    Yellow suit 75.00
  Mammy, holding rolling pin 55.00
Pinback Button
  Aunt Jemima Breakfast Club, mint . .   10.00
  Gold Dust Washing Powder, ⅞" d,
    caricature of twins in washing tub,
    multicolored, white ground, black
    rim lettering 65.00
  Topsy Club 18.00
Pipe, ceramic, bone color, man's head   55.00
Place Mat, Aunt Jemima 20.00
Planter, 3 x 3 x 4", Mammy, white
  china, dark brown face and hands,
  orange bandanna, multicolored
  dress, brick wall illus on back, made
  in Japan, c1930 . . . .   30.00
Post Card, Mammy Chicken Inn 30.00
Pot Holder Plaque, 5 x 5", boy and girl
  eating watermelon slice, plaster,
  painted, metal hooks, 1930–40 . . . .   30.00
Print, framed
  Coon Chicken Inn, 8 x 10" 22.00
  Golliwog, "Washing Day," Vogue . .   110.00
Program
  Ladies Be Seated, 18 pgs, soft cov,
    Aunt Jemima illus, issued by
    Quaker Oats, 1944 . . . .   15.00
  Porgy and Bess, 1944 . . . .   45.00
Puppet, hand, Floyd Patterson 45.00
Puzzle
  Little Black Sambo Jigsaw Puzzle . . .   10.00
  Sambo Ball Puzzle, cast metal,
    Enardoe, MIB 30.00
Rag Doll, 15" h 30.00

Recipe Booklet, Aunt Jemima Cake Mix
Miracles **12.00**
Recipe Box, Mammy, plastic, red **85.00**
Recipe Card, Golliwog **8.00**
Salt and Pepper Shakers, pr
Butler and maid with flowers **265.00**
Chef and maid
Gold, wear **65.00**
White, black, and red **35.00**
Head wearing orange hat, other wa-
termelon slice **45.00**
Kids in basket **98.00**
Mammy and Butler, plaid **98.00**
Native eating watermelon slice **70.00**
Native playing banjo on alligator . . . **65.00**
Shaker
Aunt Jemima, plastic **10.00**
Mammy, Occupied Japan **35.00**
Sheet Music
A Zoot Suit (For My Sunday Gal), 9 x
12", caricature of woman on front
cov, browntone photo inset of Kay
Kyser, 1942 copyright **16.00**
Carry Me Back to Old Virginny, color
litho of family in front of house,
1906 . . . . **10.00**
Sign, embossed cardboard, diecut,
black children with watermelon,
c1920 . . . . **40.00**
Soap Holder, 5" h, Mammy **40.00**
Soda Bottle, 14" h, Mammy **185.00**
Spice Set, Aunt Jemima
Metal holder **850.00**
Steamboat rack, complete **750.00**

Spoon Rest
Chef's Hat, 8¼" h, ceramic, glazed
finish, Japan **80.00**
Mammy **75.00**
Statue, 11" h, wood, carved, bare footed
man, patched pants, wiping perspira-
tion from neck, holding primitive tool **75.00**
String Holder
Butler **450.00**
Maid **190.00**
Syrup, Aunt Jemima **95.00**
Tablecloth, 48" sq, Ole Man River
Theme, cotton and linen, green, yel-
low, red, and black illus, white
ground **90.00**
Tab Pin, Aunt Jemima Pancake Break-
fast Club, metal **15.00**
Teapot
Clown **35.00**
Native on elephant, wicker handle . **85.00**
Tea Set, 3 pcs, teapot, creamer, and
sugar, black face **365.00**
Thermometer, composition, child peek-
ing around thermometer **28.00**
Thermos, Sambo **35.00**
Toaster Cover, Mammy, red, yellow and
blue dots dec **30.00**
Valentine
4 x 5", stiff paper, diecut, late 1930s **10.00**
5½ x 6", cardboard, diecut, emb, disk
wheel, child eating Valentine
cards, dated 1924 . . . . **20.00**
Whiskey Pitcher, Canadian Club **55.00**

Target Game, Black Sambo, Wyandotte Toys, litho tin, cardboard back, wire stand, black metal pistol, 14 x 23", $140.00.

BLUE RIDGE POTTERY

Collecting Hints: Blue Ridge patterns are among the best established of the collectible American dinnerwares. Collectors pay a premium for artist–signed pieces. The Talisman Wallpaper dinnerware pattern, because of its failure to at- tract buyers, is the most difficult dinnerware pattern to find. Among the harder–to–find shapes are the China demi pot and the character jugs.

Among the most popular patterns and forms are those made in the 1940s. As in most dinner- ware patterns, hollow ware pieces command higher prices than flat pieces. Demi sets that still have their tray are considered a real find. Blue Ridge collectors must compete with children's dish collectors for miniature pieces.

Because they are hand decorated, identical pieces often contain minor variations. Develop a practiced eye in respect to identifying those hands whose work is more aesthetically pleasing than others. Minor color changes also can change a highly pleasing pattern into one that is ordinary.

History: In 1917 the Carolina Clinchfield and Ohio Railroad, in an effort to promote industry along its line, purchased land along its right-of-way and established a pottery in Erwin, Tennessee. Erwin was an ideal location because of the local availability of white kaolin clay and feldspar, two of the chief ingredients in pottery. Workers for the new plant were recruited from East Liverpool and Sebring, Ohio, and Chester, Virginia.

In 1920 J. E. Owens purchased the pottery and received a charter for Southern Potteries, Incorporated. Within a few years the pottery was sold to Charles W. Foreman. Foreman introduced hand painting under glaze and trained girls and women from the nearby hills to do the painting. By 1938 Southern Potteries, Incorporated, was producing Blue Ridge "Hand Painted Under The Glaze" dinnerware. The principal sales thrust was to contrast the Blue Ridge hand-painted ware with decal ware produced by most other manufacturers.

Blue Ridge maintained a large national sales organization with eleven showrooms scattered nationwide. Few catalogs were issued and trade advertising was limited. As a result, researching Blue Ridge is difficult.

Most of the patterns used on Blue Ridge originated at the plant. Lena Watts, an Erwin native, was chief designer. Eventually Watts left Blue Ridge and went to Stetson China Company. Blue Ridge also produced limited production patterns for a number of leading department stores.

As the 1930s came to a close, Southern Potteries was experiencing strong competition from cheap imports from the Far East. World War II intervened and changed the company's fortune. Southern Potteries' work force increased tenfold. The company experienced a golden age between the mid–1940s and early 1950s. Production averaged over 300,000 pieces per week.

By the mid–1950s imports and the arrival of plastic dinnerware once again threatened Southern Potteries' market position. The company tried half–time production. The end came on January 31, 1957, when the stockholders voted to close the plant.

References: Susan and Al Bagdade, *Warman's American Pottery and Porcelain,* Wallace-Homestead, 1994; Jo Cunningham, *The Collector's Encyclopedia of American Dinnerware,* Collector Books, 1982, 1995 value update; Lois Lehner, *Lehner's Encyclopedia of U. S. marks on Pottery, Porcelain & Clay,* Collector Books, 1988; Betty and Bill Newbound, *Collector's Encyclopedia of Blue Ridge Dinnerware: Identification and Value Guide,* Collector Books, 1994; Betty and Bill Newbound, *Southern Potteries, Inc.: Blue Ridge Dinnerware, Revised Third Edition,* Collector Books, 1989, 1995 value update.

Periodicals: *National Blue Ridge Newsletter,* 144 Highland Drive, Blountville, TN 37617; *The Daze,* PO Box 57, Otisville, MI 48463.

Collectors' Club: Blue Ridge Collectors Club, Rte. 3, Box 161, Erwin, TN 37650.

Museum: Unicoi Heritage Museum, Erwin, TN.

Common Backstamp, used after 1945.

Arlington Apple, Skyline shape	
Cup and Saucer, rope handle	**5.50**
Plate, 9½" d	**5.50**
Brittany, demitasse cup and saucer . . .	**40.00**
Calico, candy box	**175.00**
Celandine, Colonial shape, dinner service, 31 pcs	**250.00**
Champagne Pink, teapot	**95.00**
Cheers, plate, 6" sq	**28.00**
Cherry Bounce, dinner service, 45 pcs	**200.00**
Cherry Tree Glen	
Bowl	
5½" d	**6.00**
6¼" d	**7.50**
9½" d	**12.00**
Creamer	**7.50**
Plate	
6" d	**3.50**
7½" sq	**15.00**
9½" d	**9.00**
Vegetable Dish, oval, 9¼" l	**15.00**

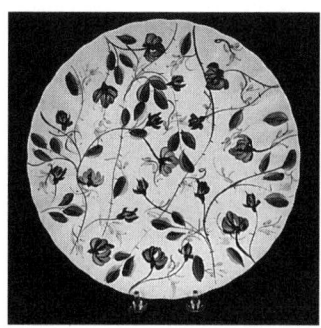

Plate, Briar Patch pattern, white ground, red, green, and rust dec, 10½" d, $12.00.

Chick, jug	95.00
Chintz	
Bonbon	38.00
Cake Plate, maple leaf shape	45.00
Celery	20.00
Children's Set, complete	250.00
Creamer, pedestal	25.00
Christmas Tree	
Cup and Saucer	55.00
Plate, 10" d	50.00
Corsage, soup bowl	17.50
Crab Apple	
Cereal Bowl, 6" d	5.00
Creamer and Sugar	45.00
Demitasse Cup and Saucer	28.00
Dinner Service, 6 dinner plates, 6 bread and butter plates, 6 berry bowls, 6 cups and saucers, creamer, sugar, platter, and round vegetable	395.00
Plate, 8½" d	8.00
Platter, oval, 13½" l	9.00
Vegetable Dish, oval	10.00
Fantasia, Skyline shape, teapot	65.00
French Peasant	
Cake Plate, maple leaf shape	85.00
Celery	100.00
Ramekin, red base, 5" d	10.00
Relish, leaf shape	95.00
Salad Bowl	125.00
Salt and Pepper Shakers, pr	150.00
Server, handled	95.00
Vase, handled	70.00
Gladys, vase, boot shape, 8" h	65.00
Jigsaw, child's feeding dish	90.00
Mallard, salt and pepper shakers, pr	395.00
Mardi Gras	
Creamer	2.50
Cup and Saucer	6.00
Fruit Bowl	3.50
Gravy Boat, matching underplate	18.00
Plate	
6½" d	1.25
9½" d	3.25
Vegetable Dish, oval, 9" l	8.00
Mood Indigo, vase	80.00
Nocturne, Colonial shape	
Cereal Bowl, 6" d	6.00
Creamer, wide	12.00
Cup and Saucer	10.00
Flat Soup, 8" d	12.00
Fruit Bowl, 5¼" d	5.00
Plate	
6" sq	38.00
9½" d, dinner	7.00
Platter, 11½" l	20.00
Sugar, open, wide	12.00
Vegetable Bowl, 9½" d	12.00
Nove Rose	
Bonbon, shell shape	65.00
Celery Tray, leaf shape	38.00
Relish, deep, shell shape	45.00

Panel, teapot	125.00
Petunia, hostess set, plate with cup	20.00
Poinsettia	
Creamer and Sugar	16.00
Cup and Saucer	9.00
Plate	
6¼" d	3.00
9¼" d	8.00
Quaker Apple, dinner service, service for four	150.00
Rooster	
Cigarette Set, cov box and four ashtrays	175.00
Platter	95.00
Salt and Pepper Shakers, pr, toe flake	85.00
Rustic Plaid	
Creamer	4.50
Cup and Saucer	4.50
Dinner Service, 26 pcs	80.00
Plate, 9" d	3.75
Sugar	5.00
Rutledge, Candlewick shape, dinner service, 22 pcs	225.00
Stanhome Ivy, Skyline shape, dinner service, 39 pcs	80.00
Sunfire, dinner service, 42 pcs	200.00
Sunflower, plate, 10" d	9.00
Wild Cherry #1, dinner service, 46 pcs	250.00

BOOKS—LIMITED EDITION CLUB

Collecting Hints: George and Helen Macy, founders of the Limited Editions Club, also owned the Heritage Press and issued popular inexpensive versions of the Limited Editions Club books under the Heritage Press imprint. These unsigned and unlimited editions usually have the same artwork and typography as the LEC books but were printed on cheaper paper and were less handsomely bound.

Heritage Press Books are available in the $12.00 to $25.00 range and represent an excellent value for readers and far-sighted collectors.

History: In 1931 George and Helen Macy founded The Limited Editions Club, dedicated to the production of beautiful books and the preservation of classic works. They selected standard texts of enduring value and had them illustrated, printed, and bound by fine artists and craftsmen. Initially, distribution was limited to 1,500 subscribers. The number of subscribers increased to 2,000 after 1972.

Most copies were signed by the illustrators (including Picasso and Matisse), authors, and/or printers.

Though the quality is uneven, they are all in demand by collectors. Condition is the key.

These books must be very crisp and clean with slipcases that show little wear to achieve best prices.

References: Allen Ahearn, *Book Collecting: A Comprehensive Guide*, G. P. Putnam's Sons, 1989; Allen and Patricia Ahearn, *Collected Books, The Guide To Values*, G. P. Putnam's Sons, 1991; *American Book Prices Current*, published annually; *Huxford's Old Book Value Guide, Seventh Edition*, Collector Books, 1995; Jean Peters (ed.), *Book Collecting: A Modern Guide*, R. R. Bowker Company, 1977; Jean Peters (ed.), *Collectible Books: Some New Paths*, R. R. Bowker Company, 1979; Marie Tedford and Pat Goudey, *The Official Price Guide To Old Books*, House of Collectibles, 1994; John Wade, *Tomart's Price Guide to 20th Century Books*, Tomart Publications, 1994; Nancy Wright, *Books: Identification and Price Guide*, Avon Books, 1993.

Periodical: *Book Source Monthly*, 2007 Syosett Dr., PO Box 567, Cazenovia, NY 13035.

Advisor: Ron Lieberman.

Aristophanes, *Lysistrata*, 1934, illus and sgd by Picasso **2,000.00**
Bacon, Sir Francis, *Essays, Or Councils Civill and Morall*, 1944 . . . . **100.00**
Balzac, Honore De, *Droll Stories*, Southworth Press, 1932, 3 vols, color headpieces and initials illus, octavo, deco paper boards, gilt cloth back, sgd by A. W. Dwiggins **75.00**
Baudelaire, *Flowers of Evil*, 1940, illus by Jacob Epstein **120.00**
Beckford, William, *Vathek: An Arabian Tale*, 1945 . . . . **50.00**
Bellamy, Edward, *Looking Backward*, 1941, illus by Elise **55.00**
Benet, Stephen, *John Brown's Body*, 1948, illus by Curry **50.00**
Bennett, Arnold, *The Old Wives' Tale*, 1941, 2 vols, illus by John Austen . . **100.00**
Boswell, James, *The Life of Samuel Johnson*, Curwen Press, 1934, 3 vols, octavo, brown cloth, leather labels **135.00**
Bourget, *La Vengeance De La Vie*, ... **35.00**
Brooks, Van Wyck, *The Flowering of New England*, 1941 . . . . **50.00**
Buck, Pearl S., *All Men Are Brothers*, 1948, 2 vols **110.00**
Bunyan, John, *Pilgrim's Progress*, 1941 **120.00**
Burton, Richard F., *The Book of the Thousand Nights and a Night*, William Edwin Rudge, 1934, 6 vols, line illus by Valenti Angelo, octavo, paper boards, pigskin backs, sgd by Angelo **200.00**
Butler, Samuel, *Erewhon*, Pynson Printers, 1934, XXI, 229P, colored il-

lus by Rockwell Kent, octavo, cloth, sgd by Rockwell Kent **150.00**
Canis, *Le Fils Des trois Mousquetaires* **35.00**
Carlyle, Thomas, *Sartor Resartus, The Life and Opinions of Herr Teufelsdrockh*, Oliver Simon, Curwen Press, 1931, XIX, 377P, octavo, blue gilt dec cloth, sgd by Oliver Simon **35.00**
Castillo, Diaz Del, *The Discovery and Conquest of Mexico*, 1942 . . . . **175.00**
Chaucer, Geoffrey, *The Canterbury Tales*, George W. Jones at the sign of the Dolphin, 1934, 2 vols, folio, dec paper boards, buckrum backed, sgd by Jones **125.00**
Chauveau, *Ramponnot*, ... **35.00**
Dana, Richard Henry, *Two Years Before the Mast*, 1947 . . . . **60.00**
Daudet, Alphonse, *Tartarin of Tarascon*, Richard W. Ellis, The Georgian Press, 1930, 2 vols, illus by W. A. Dwiggins, 24mo, paper boards, cloth spines, sgd by Dwiggins **50.00**
De Coster, Charles, *The Glorious Adventures of Tyl Ulenspeigl* Jon, Enschede En Zonen, 1934, illus by Richard Floethe, folio, gilt dec buckrum, sgd by Floethe **60.00**
Dickens, Charles, *Great Expectations*, R. & R. Clark Ltd, 1937, illus by Gordon Ross, octavo, green cloth, sgd by Gordon Ross **95.00**
Dickinson, Emily, *The Unpublished Poems of Emily Dickinson*, ... **100.00**
Dumas, Alexandre, *The Black Tulip*, 1951 . . . . **50.00**
Emerson, Ralph Waldo, *The Essays*, John Henry Nash, 1934, folio, paper boards, sgd by Nash **75.00**
Epicurus, *The Works of Epicurus*, 1947, sgd by the book's designer Bruce Rogers **100.00**
Flaubert, Gustave, *Madame Bovary*, Fretz Brothers Ltd, 1938, illus by Gunter Bohmer, octavo, yellow silk cloth, sgd by Bohmer **55.00**
France, Anatole
  At the Sign of the Queen Pedauque, 1933, illus and sgd by Sauvage . . **65.00**
  The Crime of Sylvestre Bonnard, Marchbanks Press, 1937, illus by Sylvain Sauvage, Quarto, green dec cloth, sgd by Sauvage **75.00**
Gay, John, *The Beggar's Opera*, G. Govone, 1937, illus by Mariette Lydis, folio, blue cloth emb in gilt, sgd by Mariette Lydis **75.00**
Hamilton, Alexander, et al, *The Federalist*, 1945, 2 vols **75.00**
Hawthorne, Nathaniel, *The House of the Seven Gables*, Edmund B. Thompson, 1935, illus by Valenti

Angelo, octavo, boards, leather back, sgd by Angelo **85.00**

Hughes, Richard, *The Innocent Voyage,* 1944, illus and sgd by Lynd Ward . . **75.00**

Kingston, *St. George and the Dragon,* **35.00**

Lesage, Alain-Rene, *The Adventures of Gil Blas of Santillane,* John Johnson, 1937, 2 vols, illus by John Austen, small folio, cloth, sgd by Austen . . . **125.00**

Longus, *The Pastoral Loves of Daphnis and Chloe,* Porter Garnett, 1934, illus by Ruth Reeves, tall octavo, full leather with gilt medallion, sgd by Ruth Reeves **75.00**

Maccurdy, *Notebooks of Leonardo Da Vinci,* 2 vols **80.00**

Millay, Edna St. Vincent, *Conversation at Midnight,* sgd by Edna St. Vincent Millay **200.00**

Milton, John, *Paradise Lost and Paradise Regain'd,* John Henry Nash, 1936, lithographs by Carlotta Petrina, folio, paper boards, sgd by Carlotta Petrina **100.00**

Moncrieff, Charles Scott, *The Song of Roland,* Edmund B. Thompson, Hawthorn House, 1938, XII, 138P, tall octavo, blue deco paper boards, gilt vellum back, sgd by Valenti Angelo **100.00**

Montaigne, *The Essays of Montaigne,* 4 vols, illus and sgd by T. M. Cleland **125.00**

Parkman, Francis, *The Oregon Trail,* 1945, illus by Thomas Hart Benton, sgd by T. H. Benton **250.00**

Peattie, Donald Culross, *An Almanac For Moderns,* Judd & Detweiler, 1938, Wood Engraved Vignettes by Asa Cheffetz, octavo, green dec cloth, sgd by Asa Cheffetz **65.00**

Pennell, *Adventures Of An Illustrator,* **200.00**

Plato, *The Republic,* 1944, 2 vols **100.00**

Polo, Marco, *The Travels of Marco Polo, 1271–1295,* Lester Douglas, Judd & Detweiler, Inc., 1934, 2 vols, illus by Nikolai Lapshin, octavo, sgd by N. Lapshin **75.00**

Pushkin, Alexander, *The Golden Cockerel,* 1949, illus and sgd by Edmund Dulac **140.00**

Rabelais, Francois, *Gargantua and Pantagruel,* Southworth–Anthoensen Press, 1936, 5 vols, illus and sgd by W. A. Dwiggins, octavo, green cloth **100.00**

Reade, Charles, *The Cloister and The Hearth,* A. Colish Press, 1932, 2 vols, illus by Lynd Ward, octavo, cloth, sgd by Lynd Ward **100.00**

Rostand, Edmond, *Cyrano de Bergerac,* 1936, illus and sgd by Brissaud **50.00**

Schiller, Friedrich Von, *William Tell,* 1951 . . . . **35.00**

Shaw, George Bernard, *Back to Methuselah,* 1939, illus and sgd by John Farleigh **75.00**

Shelly, Mary Wollstonecraft, *Frankenstein or the Modern Prometheus,* Walpole Press, 1934, illus by Everett Henry, tall octavo, backed in leather gilt, sgd by Everett Henry **100.00**

Sheridan, R. B., *The School For Scandal, A Comedy,* Oxford University Press, 1934, hand colored etchings by Rene Ben Sussan, tall octavo, dec paper over boards, sgd by Rene Ben Sussan **95.00**

Smollet, Tobias, *The Adventures of Peregrine Pickle,* John Johnson, 1936, 2 vols, illus by John Austen, folio, cloth, sgd by Austen **110.00**

Southey, Robert, *The Chronicle of The CID,* 1958, illus and sgd by Rene Ben Sussan **50.00**

Stendhal, *The Red and The Black,* illus and sgd by Rafaello Busoni **50.00**

Stephens, James, *The Crock of Gold,* 1942, illus by Robert Lawson, sgd by Robert Lawson **125.00**

Sterne, Laurence, *The Life & Opinions of Tristram Shandy, Gentleman,* A. Colish, 1935, 2 vols, illus by T. M. Cleland, blue boards, sgd by T. M. Cleland **100.00**

Tolstoy, Leo, *Anna Karenina,* 1933, 2 vols, illus and sgd by Nicholas Piskariov **100.00**

Turgenev, Ivan, *Fathers and Sons,* 1951, illus and sgd by Fritz Eichenberg . . . **60.00**

Virgil, *Aeneid,* 1944 . . . . **70.00**

Wilder, Thornton, *The Bridge of San Luis Rey,* 1962 . . . . **225.00**

Willke, Wendell, *One World,* 1944 . . . **55.00**

Wister, Owen, *The Virginian,* 1951 . . . **50.00**

BOTTLE OPENERS, FIGURAL

Collecting Hints: Condition is most important. Worn or missing paint and repainted surfaces lower value. Damaged or rusty pieces have greatly diminished value.

History: Figural bottle openers were produced expressly for removing a bottle cap from a bottle. They were made in a variety of metals, including cast iron, brass, bronze, and white metal. Cast iron, brass, and bronze openers are generally solid castings; white metal openers are usually cast in hollow blown molds.

The vast majority of figural bottle openers date from the 1950s and 1960s. Paint variation on a figure is very common.

References: Donald Bull, *A Price Guide to Beer Advertising, Openers and Corkscrews*, Donald Bull, 1981; Figural Bottle Openers Collectors, *Figural Bottle Openers: Identification Guide*, Figural Bottle Openers Collectors, 1992; Michael Jordan, *Figural Bottle Openers*, published by author, 1981.

Collectors' Clubs: Figural Bottle Opener Collectors Club, 117 Basin Hill Rd., Duncannon, PA 17020; Just For Openers, 6095 Windsong Lane, Durham, NC 27713.

Advisor: Craig Dinner.

REPRODUCTION ALERT

Drunk, leaning on palm tree, painted white metal, $30.00.

Amish Man, cast iron, wall mount, 4⅛" h, 3⅝" w, flesh face, black hat, red hair, Wilton Products	550.00
Bear, 3⅞ x 3¹⁄₁₆", cast iron, wall mount, head, black highlights, John Wright Co	85.00
Black Boy with green alligator	
2⅝" h, hands down, Wilton Products	125.00
3", hand in air, green base, John Wright Co	155.00
Black Man, 4⅜ x 3¾", wall mount, smiling, red bow tie, Wilton Products	135.00
Boy, winking, cast iron, wall mount, 3⅞ x 3⅝", flesh face, red lips and freckles, red hair, Wilton Products	400.00
Canada Goose, head extended to ground, brown and black markings on body, green base, black neck and face with tan markings, Wilton Products	45.00
Cathy Coed, 4⅛" h, cast iron, preppie girl holding stack of books, green base with white front, marked "L & L Favors"	385.00
Clown, 4⅛ x 4", brass, wall mount, white bow tie with red polka dots, bald head, marked "495", John Wright Co	65.00
Cocker Spaniel, 2¾" h, 3¾" l, cast iron, black patches on off white body, front right foot up, John Wright Co	55.00
Cowboy	
3⅞" h, drunk, holding green cactus, yellow hat, red bandanna, blue pants, black boots, brown jacket, John Wright Co	95.00
4³⁄₁₆" h, drunk, sign post, yellow hat, blue pants, red bandanna, yellow jacket, John Wright Co	80.00
4½" h, 2¾" w, cast iron, gray chaps, brown hat, black gun in right hand in air, red bandanna, black holster and boots, Wilton Products	240.00
Dinky Dan, 3¹³⁄₁₆" h, cast iron, preppie boy with hands in pockets, green base, marked "Gadzik Phila"	225.00
Do Do Bird, 2¾" h, cast iron, cream, black highlights, red beak	155.00

Drunk, Palm Tree	
4" h, bald head, orange and yellow tails, blue vest, white pants, yellow tree, green leaves, red flower on green base, Wilton Products	30.00
4¼" h, yellow hat, blue jacket vest, yellow pants, yellow tree, green leaves, green base, John Wright Co	30.00
Elephant	
2 x 3", cast iron, flat, pink, black base, sitting on hind legs, trunk up, open mouth	75.00
3 x 2³⁄₁₆", brass, flat, trunk up, standing, mouth is opener, dark brown	75.00
False Teeth, 2⅜" h, 3⅜" w, cast iron, wall mount, flesh gums, off white teeth	100.00
Fish, cast iron	
4¾" l, yellow and green body, tail raised, John Wright Co	110.00
5" l, trout, red, orange, and green body, Wilton Products	75.00
Fisherman, Old Salt, 4¼" h, 3" w, pot metal, hollow blow mold, yellow rain gear and hat, gray beard, flesh face and hands, black boots, John Wright Co	60.00
Foundry Man, 3⅛" h, cast iron, pouring melted iron, white pants, black belt, no shirt, black hair, John Wright Co	125.00
Four Eyes, two sets of eyes	
Bald Man, 3¼ x 3⅛", blue eyes, large black mustache, Wilton Products	30.00
Man, 4 x 3⅛", black hair and mustache, John Wright Co	30.00
Women, blue eyes, marked "Wilton Products" on back	30.00
Freddie Frosh, 4" h, cast iron, preppie boy standing with hands in pockets, legs crossed, green base with white front, marked "L & L Favors"	355.00
Goat, 4¼" h, tan body with gray highlights, sitting, yellow curved horn on top of head, green base, Wilton Products	40.00

Grass Skirt Greek, 5" h, cast iron, black native girl, white sign and post, green base, marked "Gadzik Phila" **335.00**

Mademoiselle, 4½" h, cast iron, street walker by lamp post, black, flesh face, hands, and legs, yellow light, John Wright Co **22.00**

Mallard Duck, 2⅝" h, greenish, tan back, red breast, green head, yellow bead, Wilton Products **40.00**

Mexican, 2¹³⁄₁₆" h, taking Siesta, seated leaning on cactus, head in hands on knees, light green hat, yellow cape, red shirt, green cactus, brown pants, yellow base, Wilton Products **230.00**

Monkey, 2½" h, holding branch at left side, black with tan chest and tan face markings, brown branch, John Wright Co **125.00**

Mr. Dry, cast iron, wall mount, 5½" h, 3½" w, man in black high top hat, reddish hair, blue bags under eyes, red lips, flesh face, Wilton Products **125.00**

Paddy the Pledgemaster, 4" h, cast iron, preppie boy, green base with white front, marked "Gadzik Phila" **220.00**

Patty Pep, 4" h, girl with hands behind head, yellow mini skirt, blue blouse, yellow hat, emb "Women's Weekend '55' marked "L & L Favors" **400.00**

Pelican, cast iron
  3⅛", red and black, yellow beak, orange feet, green base, Wilton Products **45.00**
  3¼" h, white, black and red highlights, yellow beach, orange feet, ruffled black comb, green base . . **145.00**
  3¾" h, cream, orange beak and feet, head up, green base, John Wright Co **140.00**

Pheasant, 2⅛" h, yellow crest, blue, red, yellow back, tail with black markings, red breast, green base, John Wright Co **140.00**

Rooster
  3³⁄₁₆" h, cast iron, yellow, orange, black, and white body, orange–yellow feet, green base, tall opener, Wilton Products **25.00**
  3⅞" h, metal, black body, red comb, orange–yellow beak and feet, green base, opener under tail, John Wright Co **45.00**

Sailor, 3¾" h, hitch hiking, white uniform, black tie and shoes, white sign with black trim, John Wright Co . . . **35.00**

Sea Gull, 3³⁄₁₆" h, cast iron, cream, black, and gray highlights, red beak, orange feet, gray and black stump, John Wright Co **30.00**

Seahorse, 4¼" h, brass, green, white highlights, green base with blue and black highlights **75.00**

Setter, 2½" h, front left paw up, tail extended out, green base, tan dog with black patches, John Wright Co **50.00**

Skull, 4¼" h, 3" w, wall mount, off white, black, eye sockets **500.00**

BOYD CRYSTAL ART GLASS

Collecting Hints: The Boyds have gone to great lengths to see that their production of pieces utilizing the Degenhart molds is not confused with pieces made during the Degenhart period. Look for the "B" in a diamond mark to identify a Boyd product.

Boyd can be collected in two distinct ways—color and shape. Most collectors find concentrating on just a few colors too confining. Shape is the collecting preference.

Because of its contemporary nature, a firm secondary resale market has not yet been established for Boyd. Prices remain modest with dealers charging a premium for their particular favorites. Pieces do appear for sale on a regular basis in trade papers.

A visit to the Boyd plant in Cambridge, Ohio, is strongly recommended. In addition to a buying opportunity, it also provides an excellent way to learn about new issues. When visiting Cambridge, take time to visit the Degenhart Museum, which houses the extensive glass collection of Elizabeth Degenhart.

History: The Boyd family has a long tradition associated with glass making. Zackary Thomas Boyd (1888–1968) worked for over twenty-one different glass companies including Cambridge, Imperial, and New Martinsville. Bernard C. Boyd (1907–1988) began working at Cambridge Glass as an apprentice in his early teens. By sixteen he was employed in the glass business full time.

While working at Lornetta Glass, near Point Marion, Pennsylvania, Bernard began working with a chemist on glass formulas. Most formulas were developed through trial and error. Bernard focused on identifying the glass characteristic produced by specific chemicals. Using this information, he was able to create a number of new formulas.

Zack Boyd developed a reputation as a maker of paperweights while working for Degenhart Glass. In addition, he gained experience in pressing novelty items. After a brief period of retirement, Elizabeth Degenhart asked Zack Boyd to assist her in the management of Degenhart Glass in 1964. When Zack Boyd died in 1968, Bernard Boyd, who was working full-time at the Cambridge State Hospital, was asked by

Elizabeth Degenhart to take over his father's responsibilities. Between 1968 and 1972 Bernard was assisted by Gus Therat. In 1976 Bernard gave up his job at the Cambridge State Hospital to become a full–time glassmaker.

Bernard F. Boyd, son of Bernard C., was discouraged from entering the glass business. Although working as a barber and beauty school instructor, Bernard F. could not hide his love of glass. When Elizabeth Degenhart died in 1978, Bernard C. and Bernard F. purchased the Degenhart factory.

Fifty Degenhart molds were included in the acquisition. The Degenhart "D" was replaced with the Boyd "B" in a diamond. The Boyds began production on October 10, 1978. Today the firm has available over two hundred different molds. A new color is produced about every six weeks. The firm's color list is rapidly approaching three hundred different colors.

John, son of Bernard F., joined the firm after graduating from the University of Wisconsin–Milwaukee. Among his special interests are pressing process.

The Boyds carefully document all production molds and colors. This information is made available to collectors through *Boyd's Crystal Art Glass*, published by the company.

References: Boyd's Crystal Art Glass, *Boyd's Crystal Art Glass: The Tradition Continues*, Boyd's Crystal Art Glass, n.d.; Todd Holmes, *Boyd Glass Workbook*, published by author, 1992.

Periodicals: *Boyd's Crystal Art Glass*, PO Box 127, 1203 Morton Ave., Cambridge, OH 43725; *Jody & Darrell's Glass Collectibles*, PO Box 180833, Arlington, TX 76096.

Collectors' Club: Boyd Art Glass Collectors Guild, PO Box 52, Hatboro, PA 19040.

Balloon Bear, figurine, Patrick, limited to 30 colors, 2" h, solid glass
Alexandrite	**6.00**
Country Red	**6.50**

Bernie, The Eagle, figurine, 2½" h, limited to thirty colors, first color:
Cardinal Red Carnival	**9.00**

Bingo Deer, figurine, retired 1987
Azure Blue	**8.00**
Custard	**8.00**
Heliotrope	**8.00**
Indian Orange	**8.00**
Milk White	**8.00**
Misty Vale	**8.00**
Skytop Blue	**9.00**

Boyd Airplane, figurine, 4" l, 3¼" w, 2" h, introduced in Nov, 1991, first color: Classic Black **15.00**

Bull Dog Head
Ice Green	**10.00**

Candy Dish, Dawn	**12.00**

Chick Salt, orig Degenhart mold, Degenhart logo replaced by Boyd diamond B trademark in 1978, produced in over 125 colors.
Alexandrite, #104, 1989	**7.00**
Butterscotch, #5, 1979	**25.00**
Cardinal Red, #126, 1992	**8.00**
Daffodil, #54, 1984	**8.00**
English Yew, #43, 1983	**6.00**
Flame, #32, 1981	**20.00**
Kumquat, #81, 1986	**9.50**
Mulberry Mist, #65, 1985	**11.00**
Peanut Butter, #30, 1980	**12.00**
Pippin Green, #39, 1982	**8.00**
Robin Egg Blue, #12, 1979	**20.00**
Royalty, #2, 1978	**10.00**
Vaseline Carnival, #93, 1988	**8.00**

Chuckles The Clown, figurine
Baby Blue	**7.00**
Confetti	**7.00**
Pistachio	**7.50**
Ritz Blue	**7.00**
Vaseline	**8.00**
White Opal	**8.00**

Colonial Doll, doll, introduced October 1984, limited to 26 different names and colors **14.00**

Debbie Duck, figurine, introduced July 21, 1981, trademark on all items "B" in a diamond
Mardi Gras	**6.00**
Snow	**5.00**

Ducklings, figurine, introduced Sept 15, 1981, trademark on all items "B" in a diamond
Golden Delight	**2.50**
Light Rose	**2.50**

Duck, salt
Buckeye	**6.00**
Cardinal Red	**6.00**
Classic Black	**6.00**
Crown Tuscan	**6.00**
Dove Blue	**6.00**
Lime Carnival	**6.00**
Orange Spice	**6.00**
Spinnaker Blue	**6.00**
Vaseline	**6.00**

Fuzzy Bear, figurine, retired 1989
Alexandrite	**10.00**
Autumn Beige	**12.00**
Country Red	**10.00**
Orange Calico	**12.00**
Oxford Gray	**10.00**
Pistachio	**10.00**
Rosewood	**10.00**
Sunflower Yellow	**10.00**
Thistlebloom	**10.00**

Grape, card holder
Buckeye	**6.00**
Cardinal Red	**7.00**
Classic Black Slag	**6.00**

Columbus Blue	6.00		Cobalt	15.00
Primrose	6.00		Olde Lyme	15.00

Columbus Blue 6.00
Primrose 6.00
Hobo Clown, figurine, Freddie, limited
to 30 colors, 3" h, solid glass
Alexandrite 8.00
Cobalt 8.50
Jeremy, introduced October, 1992, 2¼"
l, 1¼" h, vaseline 6.00
Joey, figurine, leaping pony, introduced
March, 1980, trademark on all items
"B" in a diamond
Candyland 40.00
Lavender 12.00
Lime Carnival 18.00
Persimmon 12.00
Ruby 25.00
Zack Boyd Slag 12.00
Kitten on Pillow, figurine 15.00
Louise, doll, introduced Sept 1979,
trademark on all items "B" in a dia-
mond
Apricot 20.00
Cornsilk 15.00
Firefly 15.00
Golden Delight 10.00
Lemon Ice 100.00
Pink Champagne 25.00
Sunburst 12.00
Violet Slate 15.00
Lucky Unicorn, figurine 12.00
Owl, figurine
Aggravation 15.00
Apricot Slag 50.00
Crown Tuscan 9.00
Dawn 9.00
Delphinium 9.00
Heather 9.00
Light Rose 9.00
Mardi Gras 9.00
Old Ivory 9.00
Peanut Butter 20.00
Redwood 50.00
Shasta White 15.00
Teal Swirl 15.00
Pooch, figurine
Confetti 20.00
Marigold 9.00
Tropical Green Slag 9.00
Walnut Green Slag 9.00
Winter Green Slag 9.00
Sammy The Squirrel, figurine
Alexandrite 5.00
Autumn Beige 5.00
Cashmere Pink 6.00
Classic Black Carnival 6.00
Dijon 5.00
Grape Parfait 5.00
Mulberry Carnival 6.00
Peach 5.00
Shasta White 5.00
Santa, bell
Cardinal Red Carnival 17.00

Cobalt 15.00
Olde Lyme 15.00
Rubina 16.00
Scottie Dog, JB, figurine, mold retired in
1988, marked with "R," vaseline car-
nival 10.00
Skippy, figurine, sitting dog, trademark
on all items "B" in a diamond
Cornsilk 8.00
Crown Tuscan 8.00
Golden Delight 8.00
Mint Green 8.00
Pippin Green Slag 8.00
Pocono 8.00
Violet Slate Carnival 8.00
Swan, 4½" h, master salt
Lemonade 12.00
Lilac 13.00
Milk White 12.00
Orange Spice 13.00
Spinnaker Blue 12.00
Willie The Mouse, figurine, 2" h, intro-
duced April, 1990
Christmas Willie, 1991 .... 12.00
Lime Carnival, 1990 .... 8.00
Woodchuck, (Ground Hog), figurine,
Bermuda Slag 10.00
Zack Elephant, figurine
Crystal 12.00
Lilac 14.00

BRAYTON LAGUNA

Collecting Hints: Brayton Laguna produced a
wide variety of hollow ware pieces including
lamps, cookie jars, figurines, planters, and salt
and pepper shakers, in addition to handcrafted
dinnerware. At present the shaker sets, figurines,
and planters are the most readily found, while
dinnerware remains more elusive. Cookie jars
are quite expensive.

History: Brayton Laguna Pottery operated in
South Laguna Beach from 1927 until 1963. The
pottery was founded by Durlin E. Brayton, who
started making pottery in his home. The company produced lamps, cookie jars, figurines,
tiles, and salt and pepper shakers, in addition to
handcrafted dinnerware. Following Durlin's
death in 1951, employees operated the company
until it closed in 1963, a victim of an abundance
of inexpensive Japanese imports.

References: Susan and Al Bagdade, *Warman's
American Pottery and Porcelain,* Wallace–
Homestead, 1994; Jack Chipman, *Collector's
Encyclopedia of California Pottery,* Collector
Books, 1992.

Periodical: *The Pottery Collectors Express,* PO
Box 221, Mayview, MO 64071-0221.

Bud Vase, male and female, pr 90.00
Bust, island man and woman, pr 125.00
Canister, Provincial 45.00
Cookie Jar
  Granny 325.00
  Matilda 475.00
  Provincial Lady pattern, sq 90.00
Figure
  Cow, bull, and calf, set of three 500.00
  Ellen, little girl 85.00
  Fighting Stallions, avocado, pr 140.00
  Gazelle, aqua and gold 100.00
  Girl and Doll 95.00
  Grouse, tall 65.00
  Little Joe Crap Shooter 75.00
  Peasant Man and Donkey, carrying
    straw, pr 175.00
  Penguin 75.00
  Pluto 100.00
  Purple Cow and Calf, pr 225.00
  Pushcart Vendor 65.00
  Zizi and Fifi Cat, pr 225.00
Planter
  Baby Cradle 30.00
  Blackamoor, gold trim 85.00
  Girl and Two Wolfhounds, 11" h . . .   125.00
  Girl with Bonnet and Basket 65.00
  Lady, tall, rose colored 85.00
  Maiden 40.00
  Sally 45.00
  Shoe 25.00
  Wheelbarrow 35.00
Salt and Pepper Shakers, pr
  Granny 65.00
  Mammy and Chef 125.00
  Mammy and Pappy 200.00

BREWERIANA

Collecting Hints: Many collectors concentrate on items from one specific brewery or region. An item will bring slightly more when it is sold in its locality. Regional collectors' clubs and shows abound.

History: Collecting material associated with the brewing industry developed in the 1960s when many local breweries ceased production. Three areas occupy the collectors' interest—pre–Prohibition material, advertising items for use in taverns, and premiums designed for individual use.

References: George J. Baley, *Back Bar Breweriana: A Guide To Advertising Beer Statues and Beer Shelf Signs,* L–W Book Sales, 1992; Donald Bull, *A Price Guide To Beer Advertising Openers And Corkscrews,* privately printed, 1981; Donald Bull, Manfred Friedrich, and Robert Gottschalk, *American Breweries,* Bullworks, 1984; Norman E. Martinus and Harry

L. Rinker, *Warman's Paper,* Wallace–Homestead, 1994; Jack McDougall and Steve Pawlowski, *United States Micro/Brew Pub Coaster Guide,* published by authors, 1995; Keith Osborne and Brian Pipe, *The International Book of Beer Labels, Mats, & Coasters,* Chartwell Books, 1979; Steve Pawlowski and Jack McDougall, *New Jersey Brewery Coasters,* published by authors, 1995; Robert Swinnich, *Contemporary Beer Neon Signs,* L–W, 1994; Dale P. Van Wieren (ed.), *American Breweries II,* East Coast Breweriana Assoc., 1995; *Westcott Price Guide To Advertising Water Jugs,* Globe Press, 1991.

Collectors' Clubs: American Breweriana Assoc. Inc., PO Box 11157, Pueblo, CO 81001; East Coast Breweriana Assoc., 3712 Sunningdale Way, Durham, NY 27707; National Assoc. of Breweriana Advertising, 2343 Met–To–Wee Lane, Wauwatosa, WI 53226.

Periodicals: *Barley Corn News,* PO Box 2328, Falls Church, VA 22042; *Suds 'n' Stuff,* 4765 Galacia Way, Oceanside, CA 92056.

Museum: The Museum of Beverage Containers & Advertising, Goodlettsville, TN.

REPRODUCTION ALERT Advertising trays have been heavily reproduced.

Bank, Falls City Beer, balloon shape,
  chalkware 75.00
Beer Can Opener, bar mounted, Jax . .   75.00
Beer Label, Iroquois with Indian 4.00
Belt Buckle
  Coors 10.00
  Stroh's Beer 5.00
Blotter, Schlitz 4.00
Bottle, Bills specialty Beer 22.00
Bottle Opener, Fehrs Beer, wood 45.00
Calendar
  Indianapolis Brewing Co, 1904 . . . .   125.00

Oriental Brewery Co., Weisbrod & Hess, Philadelphia, PA, 1898, full pad, $1,210.00. Photo courtesy of James D. Julia.

Pabst Extract, 1913, woman with
parasol **85.00**
Change Tray
Hannis Whiskey, tin, round, yellow,
black, and red, Philadelphia,
Baltimore, New York, Martinsburg
on rim **40.00**
Los Angeles Brewery **90.00**
Charm, Budweiser, commemorative,
wood, 1876–1976 . . . . **12.00**
Clock
Lowenbrau, lions hold clock **95.00**
Pabst, wood, electrified, early 1950s **100.00**
Piels **90.00**
Coaster, Ruppert Beer **5.00**
Corkscrew, Anheuser Busch **75.00**
Display
Falstaff Beer, cardboard and plastic,
emb figure **45.00**
Pabst Blue Ribbon, 15" h, figural, bar-
tender and bottle, bartender with
brass mugs on outstretched arm,
metal and composition, painted . . **150.00**
Door Push, Old Milwaukee **95.00**
Foam Scraper
Grand Prize, celluloid **12.50**
Piel's, metal, two dwarfs holding
keg **30.00**
Glass, etched
American Brew, Rochester, NY, eagle
in shield logo, flared, 4½" h **35.00**
Bohemian Brewing Co, St Louis, bar-
rel shape, 3¼" h **40.00**
Handkerchief, 20" sq, Coors **5.00**
Ice Bucket, Booths London Gin, double
decker bus **30.00**
Match Case, Bonte Bros Distillers **90.00**
Mug
Coors Golden Beer, pottery, yellow **25.00**
Minneapolis Brewing Co **65.00**
Pencil Clip, Krueger Beer Ales, red,
black, and white **22.00**
Pinback Button
Budweiser, 3" d, litho, color illus,
blue lettering, 1970s **12.00**
Miller High Life Beer, multicolored **25.00**
Pitcher, Tadcaster Brewery, York **25.00**
Plate
Grain Belt Beer, brass, emb **15.00**
Krug Beer, 50th anniversary, 1859–
1900 . . . . **175.00**
Poster
Miller Beer, Keep On Rocking,
Michigan **25.00**
Schlitz Beer, festival **20.00**
Recipe Book, Indianapolis Brewing Co,
1912 . . . . **22.00**
Salt and Pepper Shakers, pr, Piels Real
Draft Beer, 4" h, bottle shape, brown
glass, orig box, 1960–70 . . . . **35.00**
Shopping Bag, Iroquois Indian Head
Beer & Ale **5.00**

Sign
Ballantine Ale, emb **15.00**
Carlsburg Beer, celluloid **10.00**
E & O Beer, 9¼ x 11¼", metal **55.00**
Miller Lite Beer, counter type **50.00**
Pabst Beer, neon **75.00**
Piels Beer, 15½ x 20", cardboard,
diecut, full color, 1960s **40.00**
Pilsener, 9½" d, POC Extra Dry Beer,
gold, red, white, and blue **85.00**
Rolling Rock Beer, 34" h, neon, copy-
right 1939 . . . . **115.00**
Schaefer Beer
9½ x 12½", hard plastic, white, applied beer can, relief image of
gold swordfish, logo disk, and
disk with "Take Home" **35.00**
15½ x 17¼", litho tin over cardboard, full color, hand holding
glass, "Schaefer Beer, Real Beer,"
hanging cord **65.00**

**Beer Tap, Neuweiler Light Lager Beer,
yellow casing, black and red lettering,
$10.00.**

Tray, tin
Anheuser–Busch, lady in center, an-
gels holding bottles **60.00**
Ballantine Ale & Beer, 12" d, litho,
yellow and white lettering, red and
black three–ring logo, blue back-
ground with scattered yellow star
motifs **50.00**
Blitz Beer **25.00**
Ebling's Beer, lady image **45.00**
Ehret's Brewery **100.00**
Leinenkugel, 110th Anniversary,
1977 . . . . **50.00**
Miller, girl on moon **60.00**
Monroe Brewing Co, king raising
stein **225.00**
Peerless Beer, oval, yellow, black,
and red letters **125.00**
Rainier Beer, 13" d **110.00**
Ruppert Beer, Art Deco, Hans Flato . **95.00**
Stegmaier Beer **210.00**

BRITISH ROYALTY COMMEMORATIVES

Collecting Hints: Some collectors choose one monarch around whom to build their collections. Others choose only pieces for special occasions, such as coronations, jubilees, marriages, investitures, births, or memorials. Another approach is to specialize in only one form, e.g., thimbles, mugs, beakers, teapots, spoons, etc.

Since most early pieces were used in the home for eating and drinking, it is especially difficult to find older commemoratives in good condition. Wear from use and age often shows through fading and loss of colors and transfers. Porous pottery pieces lend themselves to crazing inside and out from age and shrinkage.

Serious collectors seek the older and rarer pieces, while keeping up–to–date with examples from the modern events. Crown–shaped teapots, etched and cut crystal, hand– and machine–woven tapestries, and jewelry are just a few of the things that link old and new collecting.

History: British commemorative china was first produced rather crudely in design and form. These were basically cheaper and more available pieces of Delft, stoneware, and slipware. With John Brook's invention of transfer printing in the mid–18th century, British commemorative wares bore a closer likeness to the reigning monarch.

King George IV's coronation was the first royal occasion for which children received municipal gifts. Some towns presented medals, while others gave plates with commemorative inscriptions. China commemorative pieces were produced by the thousands for Queen Victoria's 1887 and 1897 jubilees. It was not until 1902 that the presentation of municipal gifts became widespread; the practice is continued today. Thousands of children received mugs with the official coronation design of Queen Elizabeth II in celebration of her 1953 coronation.

Through the years, improved production techniques combined with finer artistic design enhanced the overall appearance of British Royalty commemoratives. Aynsley, Minton, Paragon, Royal Doulton, Shelley, Wedgwood, and other leading manufacturers have produced outstanding limited and unlimited edition items. Artists such as Clarice Cliff, Dame Laura Knight, and Professor Richard Guyatt have designed special pieces.

Some British Royalty commemoratives are easily recognized by the portraits of the monarchs they honor. Often these portraits are surrounded by decorations such as flags, the national flowers (roses, thistles, daffodils, and shamrocks), ribbons with commemorative messages or lions and unicorns. Cyphers and crowns also are popular decorations. Royal residences such as Windsor

Castle, Balmoral and Highgrove House may also appear. Town mottos or crests were added to individualize municipal gifts for earlier coronations. Advertisers often linked their products to royal events.

Other British Royalty commemoratives are not easy to recognize. Many do not have portraits of monarchs on them, although there might be a silhouette profile. Other characteristics include crowns, dragons, royal coats of arms, national flowers, swords, scepters, dates, messages and cyphers of the monarch. Earlier pieces sometimes bear crude likenesses of early monarchs. Timely verses or couplets may be inscribed, e.g., "God Save The King," "Long Live The Queen."

A listing of outstanding achievements or inventions during a monarch's reign may appear on jubilee or memorial pieces. Some newer items list the order of succession to the throne, previous holders of a title, and family trees.

References: Susan and Al Bagdade, *Warman's English & Continental Pottery & Porcelain,* Second Edition, Wallace–Homestead, 1991; Douglas H. Flynn and Alan H. Bolton, *British Royalty Commemoratives: 19th & 20th Century Royal Events In Britain Illustrated by Commemoratives, Value Guide With Photographs,* Schiffer Publishing, 1994; Lincoln Hallinan, *British Commemoratives: Royalty, Politics, War and Sport,* Antique Collectors' Club, 1993; Eric Knowles, *Miller's Royal Memorabilia,* Reed Consumer Books, 1994, distributed by Antique Collectors' Club; John May, *Victoria Remembered, A Royal History 1817–1861,* Heinemann, London, 1983; John and Jennifer May, *Commemorative Pottery 1780–1900, A Guide for Collectors,* Charles Scribner's Sons, 1972; Sussex Commemorative Ware Centre, *200 Commemoratives,* Metra Print Enterprises, 1979; Geoffrey Warren, *Royal Souvenirs,* Orbis, 1977.

Queen Elizabeth II, February 6, 1952, to present
Coronation, June 2, 1953

Beaker, 4″ h, sepia portrait color dec, Royal Doulton	**45.00**
Bowl, 9¾″ d, color portrait surrounded by emb gold, hp dec, wide gold border, gold overlay on cobalt blue outside, gold foot, Aynsley bone china	**900.00**
Box, cov, 5″ h, orb shape, purple and gold crown finial, hp color dec, Wedgwood & Co Ltd	**90.00**
Bust, 5½″ h, coronation and 1953 Bermuda visit, white, light blue glazed base with gold trim, Foley bone china	**90.00**
Cup and Saucer	
Multicolored flowers, pale green border with gold overlay, Paragon bone china	**55.00**

Sepia portrait, color dec, blue emb border, gold trim, Clarice Cliff design, Newport pottery   **35.00**

Jug, 4½" h, black on white dec and bust portrait, mask spout, wreathed cypher and crown on reverse, Royal Worcester bone china **100.00**

Mug

3" h, sepia portraits of Queen with young Charles and Anne, Salisbury bone china **70.00**

3½" h, sepia portrait, color and gold dec, "E" handle, Royal Doulton bone china **90.00**

4" h, color dec with lion, unicorn, crown, and cypher, Eric Ravilious, Wedgwood **160.00**

Plate

7" d, black and white portrait, color dec, gold overlay design around border, Victoria Pottery **30.00**

8¾" d, sepia portrait, color and gold dec, gold emb rim with gold overlay on deep red border, Coalport bone china **120.00**

9" d, sepia portrait, color dec with emb rim and gold trim, Weatherby **45.00**

10½" d, large color portrait framed in emb gold, gold overlay on deep red border with emb gold rim, Aynsley bone china **350.00**

Teapot

5½" h, profile white jasperware portraits on royal blue background, Wedgwood **250.00**

6" h, sepia portrait, color dec, gold bands and trim, cypher and crown, Rita **100.00**

Tin

5½" h, color portraits, cypher, arms, red background, Rowntree **20.00**

6" h, tea caddy with color portraits, gold dec on red background, Bilsland Brothers Bakery **35.00**

7" d, color portrait of Queen in State Coach, red and gold crowns **25.00**

Silver Jubilee, 1977

Box, cov, 4¾ x 3¼", heart shape, white profile portraits and dec on royal blue background, jasperware, Wedgwood, price for pair   **110.00**

Paperweight, 1¾" h, 3" d, millefiori crown inside, hexagonal, full lead crystal, Limited Edition of 1500, Whitefriars **395.00**

Plate

10½" d, profile portrait with silver and color dec, Limited Edition of 1500, Paragon bone china **100.00**

10¾" d, lion, unicorn, coat of arms, blue, beige, and maroon dec, Royal Tuscan bone china   **45.00**

40th Wedding Anniversary, November 20, 1987

Model, 1¼" h, 3¼" l, miniature Rolls Royce, ruby red, beige, and black, diecast by Lido (London) Ltd **40.00**

Mug, 3" h, color portrait and flowers, slightly waisted shape, Coalport bone china **45.00**

Prince Charles' Investiture as Prince of Wales, July 1, 1969

Plate

9¾" d, gold and bronze profile portrait, gold overlay on cobalt blue border, Falcon Ware Pottery . . .   **70.00**

10½" d, color Caernavon Castle scene with Prince of Wales' feathers, Royal Worcester bone china **150.00**

Spoon, 6" l, raised Prince of Wales' feathers in bowl, dragon atop handle holds shield of four lions, SS, J D Beardmore & Co, Ltd **195.00**

Prince Charles and Lady Diana Spencer, Royal Wedding, July 29, 1981

Bust, 4½" h, white glaze, gold lettering and trim, Limited Edition of 250, Coalport bone china **100.00**

Dish

3¾" d, raised portraits and Prince of Wales' feathers, names and dates around border, SS **115.00**

6" d, black and white profile portraits, color dec, Wedgwood Queensware **25.00**

Jardiniere, 5¾" h, 6½" d, sepia portraits, color dec, green band around top, pottery **50.00**

Jug, 6¼" h, milk jug shape, dark brown profiles, color and gold dec, A E Rodda, Cornwall **65.00**

Knife, 3¼" l, sepia portraits in gold frames, color flowers, mother of pearl on reverse, two blades **25.00**

Lamp Base, 8½" h, sepia portraits, color dec, molded Prince of Wales' feathers at top, Derek Fowler Studio Ltd **110.00**

Mug

3½" h, color portraits within heart, color dec **30.00**

3¾" h, sepia portraits, feathers, gold trim, Royal Overhouse Pottery **25.00**

Plate

8" d, black and white portraits, color dec, wedding bells around border, gold trim, bone china, England 30.00

9½" d, brown tone portraits and dec, emb floral border, English Ironstone Tableware Ltd 60.00

10¼" d, gold silhouette portraits on cobalt blue background, fretwork border, St Paul's Dome above portraits, Limited Edition of 2500, Bing & Grondahl 125.00

10¾" d, royal residences around border with doves, wedding bells, and crowns, coat of arms, Limited Edition of 5000, Caverswall bone china 75.00

Teapot, 5¼" h, sepia portraits, color dec, Prince of Wales' feathers, flowers, ribbons 65.00

Tray, 6 x 3¼", white applied profiles and dec on pale blue jasperware, Wedgwood 60.00

Prince William of Wales, born June 21, 1982

Bell, 3¼" h, color picture of Windsor Castle, flowers, gold ring handle, Aynsley bone china 25.00

Loving Cup, 3¼" h, color and gold dec, gold lion handles, Paragon bone china 110.00

Money Box, 4¼" h, book shape, colorful Bunnykins design, Royal Doulton 40.00

Mug

2⅞" h, gold on white dec, Richard Guyatt Design, Wedgwood bone china 55.00

3½" h, color design by children of Hornsea Primary School, Hornsea Pottery 35.00

Plate

8¼" d, color dec, cherubs, full name, gold trim, Limited Edition of 500, Royal Crown Derby . . . 190.00

10½" d, color portrait and dec, gold overlay on border, Limited Edition of 1500, Crown Staffordshire 110.00

Thimble, first birthday, color portrait, gold trim, Finsbury bone china . . . 10.00

Prince Henry of Wales, born September 15, 1984

Bootee, 1¾" h, 2¾" l, color portrait with Princess of Wales, Coronet bone china 20.00

Box, cov, 4" d, color picture of Balmoral Castle, Aynsley bone china 35.00

Miniature, loving cup, 1¼" h, 2¼" w, roses, color and gold dec, Royal

Crown Derby bone china 80.00

Mug, 3½" h, color dec, gold trim, Limited Edition of 1000, Caverswall bone china 50.00

Plate, 8½" d, color flowers and gold trim, Royal Albert bone china . . . 30.00

Prince Andrew and Miss Sarah Ferguson, Royal Wedding, July 23, 1986

Bell, 4" h, blue silhouettes with gold dec, Royal Worcester bone china 40.00

Jigsaw Puzzle, tin container, color portraits and dec, Waddingtons . . 45.00

Loving Cup, 2⅞" h, color portraits in wedding attire, gold trim, Fenton bone china 60.00

Mug

3½" h, Corgis in shades of gray and black, pink background, Kiln Craft Pottery 30.00

3¾" h, color portraits, gold trim, Colclough bone china 25.00

4" h, confirment of Dukedom of York, black silhouette portraits, black, gold, and blue dec, designed by Richard Guyatt, Limited Edition of 1000, Wedgwood 200.00

Plate

7" d, white profile portraits on light blue jasperware, Wedgwood . . 40.00

8" d, color portraits and dec, gold trim, Johnson Ceramics bone china 24.00

8¼" d, color portraits and dec, light blue emb border, Royal Albert bone china 45.00

Tray, 12" d, metal, large color portrait, blue printing and trim on white background 20.00

Princess Beatrice, born August 8, 1988

Decanter, 8" h, color and gold dec, white background, gold stopper, Wade Porcelain 115.00

Mug

2⅞" h, gold on white design by Richard Guyatt, Limited Edition of 2000, Wedgwood bone china 75.00

3" h, burnished gold profile portraits, gold on white dec, Limited Edition of 2500, Coalport bone china 70.00

King George VI and Queen Elizabeth, December 10, 1936 to February 6, 1952

Coronation, May 12, 1937

Card Receiver, 7¼ x 4", cypher and "1937" in well, crown handles, ftd, SS 165.00

Cuff Links, raised profile portraits, names and "1937" on each link, bronze 45.00

Cup and Saucer, sepia portraits, small portrait of Princess Elizabeth bone china 40.00

Loving Cup, 3¼" h, sepia portraits, color dec, gold handles and trim, cypher and crown, pottery 75.00

Mug

3" h, color dec, gold lion handle and trim, Paragon bone china 125.00

3¾" h, black and white portraits on light blue background, color dec, crown and flag, Royal Doulton bone china . .   65.00

4" h, sepia Marcus Adams family portrait, emb design around sides, Royal Albert bone china   80.00

Plaque, 4¾" d, brass mounted on wood, profile relief portraits and commemoration 50.00

Plate

9½" d, amber pressed glass with gold backed profile portraits and national flowers 55.00

9¾" d, hp dec by Charlotte Rhead, orange sq with black and gold highlights, Crown Ducal 80.00

Teapot, 5" h, sepia portraits, color dec, blue trim, Norbury Pottery   100.00

Queen Elizabeth, The Queen Mother, 80th Birthday, August 4, 1980

Mug

3½" h, sepia portrait, color and gold dec, Spode bone china . . .   75.00

3¾" h, color portrait, crown and flowers, Crown Staffordshire bone china 70.00

Plate, 10½" d, 85th birthday, 1985, color portrait and dec, gold rim, Limited Edition of 2000, Coalport bone china 100.00

Tin, 90th birthday, 1990, color portrait, Glamis Castle, coat of arms, Walkers 30.00

King Edward VIII, January 20, 1936, abdicated December 10, 1936. Coronation scheduled for May 12, 1937. Coronation items are not rare since most were in stores prior to the abdication.

Bowl, 9¾" d, pressed glass, profile portrait in well 70.00

Cookie Jar, 9" h, caravan shape, sepia portraits, color dec, rattan handle, Parrott and Co 200.00

Cup and Saucer, color portrait and dec, St George slaying dragon, cypher and "1937," Royal Doulton bone china 80.00

Door Knocker, 4¼ x 2", accession, crown at top, profile head and

shoulders of King, "Edward VIII" and "1936," brass 125.00

Fabric, 36 x 52", color portrait, coronation scene, procession, Buckingham Palace, Westminster Abbey, cotton chintz 45.00

Loving Cup, 4½" h, 7" w, brown tone portrait, color dec, color flowers inside and reverse, thick gold bands around top edge and base, Shelley bone china 600.00

Mug, 4" h, sepia portrait, color dec, empire shields, flowers on handle, gold rim, Aynsley bone china 75.00

Plate, 8¾" d, medium blue profile portrait and dec, blue rim, Copeland Spode 145.00

Tin, 9¼ x 7½", color portrait as Prince of Wales with gold feathers, war ships inside lid 50.00

King George V and Queen Mary, May 6, 1910 to January 20, 1936

Coronation, June 26, 1911

Plate, George V and Mary, 1911 coronation, multicolored coat of arms, crowns, partially hand painted, late Foley Shelley, $135.00.

Beaker, 3¾" h, black and white portraits with small portrait of Edward, Prince of Wales, color dec and rim gilding, bone china   70.00

Box, cov, heart shape, color dec, gilding flowers, coat of arms, Aynsley bone china 90.00

Egg Cup, color portrait of King on one, Queen on other, their names beneath portraits, bone china, price for pair 65.00

Mug, 3" h, enamel on tin, color portraits and dec, brown rim . .   80.00

Silver Jubilee, 1935

Mug, 4¼" h, color portraits and dec, King alone on reverse, gold trim 50.00

Mug, King George V, Silver Jubilee, white ground, 4⅛" h, $60.00.

Tea Strainer, 5¾" l, 2¼" d, "G 1935 M" formed by holes in bowl, crown at top of handle, SS **175.00**
Marriage, 1863
  Plate, 7¼" d, brown tone portraits and ribbons, marriage date, made for William Whiteley by Doultons, bone china **190.00**
King Edward VII and Queen Alexandra, January 22, 1901 to May 6, 1910. Coronation originally scheduled for June 26, 1902, but postponed because of the King's appendicitis attack. It took place on August 9, 1902. Items with the earlier date are far more common.
  Cup and Saucer, color portraits and floral dec, gold trim, "Irthington Parish" beneath portraits, Bisto bone china **85.00**
  Dish, 6¾ x 6", color dec partially hp, gold trim and emb design, Foley bone china **65.00**
  Figure, 12¼" h, pr, Staffordshire, names on front of base **700.00**
  Mug, 2¾" h, lithophane, King Edward VII's likeness seen in base when held to light, color cypher, crown date, bone china **90.00**
  Plate, 7" d, blue crown, initials and "MCMII," floral background, Royal Copenhagen bone china **190.00**
  Tape Measure, 1¼" d, brown sepia photo of young Edward, Prince of Wales, c1863 .... **75.00**
  Teapot, 5 x 7", color portrait and dec, emb floral band and swirl handle, bone china **160.00**
  Tin, color portraits on lid, Prince of Wales and Prince Edward of Wales on ends, Coronation and outside Westminster Abbey scenes on sides **60.00**
Queen Victoria and Prince Albert, June 20, 1837 to January 22, 1901

Coronation, June 28, 1838
  Plate 7" d, Swansea transfer portrait in blue, coronation, birth, and proclamation dates, emb floral border **1,200.00**
Diamond Jubilee, 1897
  Beaker, 4" h, white raised profile portrait on lime green background, beige trim, Copeland late Spode **170.00**
  Dish, 4" d, color crown and cypher, gold rim, W H Goss bone china **60.00**
  Plate 8" d, color portrait, dec, servicemen, ships, angels, bone china **180.00**
  Tin, 2 x 3¼ x 3", color portraits, young Queen on horseback on lid, young and mature portraits, ships, trains on sides **95.00**
Golden Jubilee, 1887
  Mug, 4" h, black portrait and dec on blue background, Foley **150.00**
  Plate, 10½" d, large blue profile portrait of young queen in center, decorative border, Royal Worcester **115.00**
In Memoriam, 1901
  Beaker, 3¾" h, color portrait, purple dec, birth, accession, coronation, death dates, gold rim, Royal Doulton bone china **295.00**
Marriage, February 10, 1840
  Plate, 7⅜" d, hexagonal, black and white portraits, color dec, emb border **350.00**
King William IV and Queen Adelaide, June 26, 1830 to June 20, 1837
Coronation, September 8, 1831
  Jug
    5" h, purple transfer of King on front, coronation scene on reverse, Staffordshire Ironstone . **800.00**
    7½" h, purple transfer of King and Queen, floral dec **700.00**
  Mug, 2½" h, "Her Most Gracious Majesty Queen Adelaide" above portrait on front, coronation scene on reverse, dark red dec **1,400.00**
King George IV and Queen Caroline, January 29, 1820 to January 26, 1830
Coronation, July 19, 1821
  Cup and Saucer, "Long Live Queen Caroline" below black profile portrait, coat of arms opposite handle, pink luster trim **300.00**
  Plate
    8½" d, color dec and emb, molded inscription "King George IV," below color profile portrait, attributed to the Portobello Factory at

Edinburgh **1,500.00**
8⅞" d, black crown and national flowers, commemoration on ribbons reads "George IV Crown'd July 19, 1821," made by Hartley Greens and Co, Leeds, for the Leeds Parish Church School Dinner **1,650.00**
In Memoriam, 1830
Jug
6¾" h, 7½" w, black portrait and floral dec, birth, accession, proclamation and death dates **1,000.00**
8¾" h, 8" w, angels and flowers in relief, profile portrait of King under spout, lion handle, light beige unglazed **1,300.00**
King George III and Queen Charlotte, October 25, 1760 to January 29, 1820
In Memoriam
Bowl, 9¾" d, full length portrait of king in robes with young child, "I hope the time will come when every poor child in my dominions will be able to read the Bible" appears under the transfer, blue and white flowers around wide border **1,200.00**
Wax bust profile portrait, 2¾ x 2", framed, colors include pink, white, gray, tan, and burgundy   **600.00**

BUBBLE GUM CARDS, NON–SPORT

Collecting Hints: Don't buy individual cards; buy full sets. The price of a set is below the sum of individual cards. By collecting sets you do lose some of the fun of trading cards, nevertheless, cards from this vintage are sold by sets. Any set should contain a sample of the wrapper plus any stickers that belong to the set.

Because of the availability of these cards, make certain the sets you buy are in mint condition. You can buy boxes of gum packages. With Topps you are 100% certain you will get at least one full set from a box. Donruss and Fleer average 85%.

Collectors should store cards in plastic sleeves. Place the wrapper first and then the cards in numerical order.

History: The birthplace of the modern bubble gum (trading) card is the tobacco insert cards of the late 19th century. From 1885 to 1894 there were over 500 sets issued, with only about 25 devoted to sports. Trading cards lost their popularity in the decade following World War I.

However, in 1933 "Indian Gum" issued a product containing a stick of bubble gum and a card in a waxed paper package. A revolution had begun.

Goudey Gum and National Chicle controlled the market until the arrival of Gum, Inc., in 1936. Gum, Inc., issued The Lone Ranger and Superman sets in 1940. From 1943 to 1947 the market in cards was again quiet. In 1948 Bowman entered the picture. A year later Topps Chewing Gum produced some non–sports cards. A war between Bowman and Topps ensued until 1956 when Topps bought Bowman.

Although Topps enjoyed a dominant position in the baseball card market, it had continual rivals in the non–sports field. Frank Fleer Company, Leaf Brands, and Philadelphia Chewing Gum provided competition in the 1960s. Fleer and Donruss Chewing Gum provide the modern–day assault.

References: Christopher Benjamin, *The Sport Americana Price Guide To Non–Sports Cards: 1930–1960, No. 2,* Edgewater Books, 1993; Christopher Benjamin, *The Sport Americana Price Guide To Non–Sports Cards: 1961–1992 No. 4,* Edgewater Books, 1992; Norman E. Martinus and Harry L. Rinker, *Warman's Paper,* Wallace–Homestead, 1994; John Neuner, *Checklist & Prices of U. S. Non–Sport Wrappers,* Wrapper King Inc., 1992; Robert Reed, *Collector's Guide To Trading Cards,* Collector Books, 1993; Stuart Wells III, *Comic Cards and Their Prices,* Wallace–Homestead, 1994.

Collectors' Club: United States Cartophilic Society, PO Box 4020, Saint Augustine, FL 32085.

Periodicals: *Non–Sports Illustrated,* PO Box 126, Lincoln, MA 01773; *Non–Sport Update,* 4019 Green St., PO Box 5858, Harrisburg PA 17110; *The Non–Sport Report* (catalog from The Card Coach, but loaded with articles), PO Box 128, Plover, WI 54467; *The Wrapper,* PO Box 227, Geneva, IL 60134.

DONRUSS

Addams Family, 66 cards, 1964	**250.00**
All–Pro Skateboard, 44 sticker cards, 1978	**8.00**
Awesome! All–Stars, 127 cards	**13.00**
Baseball Super Freaks, 1st Series, 42 cards	**20.00**
Bionic Woman, 44 cards, 1976	**9.00**
BMX Bikes, 59 cards	**3.00**
CB Convoy Code, 44 cards	**17.50**
Choppers & Hot Bikes, 66 cards	**27.50**
Combat, 132 cards, 1964	**300.00**
Disneyland, puzzle backs, 66 cards, 1965	**80.00**
Dukes of Hazzard, 44 cards, 1983 . . .	**13.00**

Elvis Presley, 66 cards, 1978 . . . .   **12.00**
Fiends and Machines, 66 cards **20.00**
Flying Nun, 66 cards, 1968 . . . .   **160.00**
Freddie & The Dreamers, 66 cards,
   1965 . . . .   **55.00**
Green Hornet, 44 cards **165.00**
Idiot Cards, 66 cards, 1961 . . . .   **60.00**
King Kong, 55 cards, 1965 . . . .   **155.00**
Kiss, 1978
   Series 1, 66 cards **22.50**
   Series 2, 66 cards **30.00**
Magnum P I, 66 cards, 1983 . . . .   **6.50**
Marvel Super Heroes, 66 cards, 1966   **145.00**
Monkees, 44 cards, 1966 . . . .   **100.00**
Osmonds, 66 cards, 1973 . . . .   **45.00**
Saturday Night Fever, 66 cards, 1978   **6.50**
Voyage To The Bottom Of The Sea, 66
   cards, 1964 . . . .   **190.00**

Batman, Flying Foes, No. 3 of 6 Penguin
Puzzle Cards, copyright 1966, National
Periodical Publications, $1.00.

FLEER

Believe It Or Not, 84 cards, 1970 . . . .   **50.00**
Drag Nationals, 70 cards, 1972 . . . . . .   **120.00**
Dune, 132 cards, 44 stickers **9.50**
Gomer Pyle, 66 cards, 1965 . . . .   **47.50**
Grossville High, 66 cards, 1987 . . . . .   **7.00**
Here's Bo, 72 cards, 12 stickers, 1981   **7.50**
McHale's Navy, 66 cards **47.50**
Pirates Bold, 66 cards **150.00**
Race USA, 74 cards, 1972 . . . .   **125.00**

LEAF

Garrison's Gorillas, 72 cards, 1967 . . .   **85.00**
Good Guys & Bad Guys, 72 cards, 1966   **87.50**
Munsters, 72 cards **315.00**
Spook Stories, Series 1, 1961 . . . .   **165.00**
What's My Job?, 72 cards, 1965 . . . . .   **85.00**

MISCELLANEOUS

Bubbles Inc, Outer Limits, 50 cards,
   1964 . . . .   **310.00**
Ellio's Pizza, Teenage Mutant Ninja
   Turtles, 17 cards, mail order set **9.00**
Nabisco
   Mickey Mouse and His Pals, 25 cards   **45.00**
   Water World Heroes, 50 cards, 1972   **30.00**
   Wildlife Card Collection, 50 cards . .   **25.00**
Nu–Cards, Monster Cards, 84 cards . .   **155.00**
Pacific Trading Cards
   Andy Griffith, 110 cards, 1990 . . . . .   **10.00**
   Leave It to Beaver, 60 cards **24.00**
   Total Recall, 110 cards, 1990 . . . . . .   **20.00**
   Wizard of Oz, 110 cards, 1990 . . . .   **7.50**
Performance Years Quality Card Co,
   Muscle Cards, 104 cards, 1992 . . . .   **10.00**
Wendy's, Kid Meal, Mighty Mouse—
   The New Adventures, 6 cards **3.50**

PHILADELPHIA CHEWING GUM CO

Daktari, 66 cards, 1966 . . . .   **75.00**
Dark Shadows, pink, 66 cards, 1968 . .   **325.00**
Happy Horoscopes, 72 cards, 1972 . .   **30.00**
Horrible Horoscopes, 72 cards **30.00**
James Bond, 66 cards, 1965 . . . .   **190.00**
Robert F. Kennedy, 55 cards, 1968 . . .   **95.00**
Tarzan, 66 cards, 1966 . . . .   **150.00**
War Bulletin, 88 cards, 1965 . . . .   **165.00**

TOPPS

Astronauts, 55 cards, 1963 . . . .   **200.00**
Baby, 66 cards, 11 stickers, 1984 . . . .   **6.00**
Batman, 55 cards, 1966 . . . .   **125.00**
Battle, 66 cards, 1965 . . . .   **350.00**
Battlestar Galactica, 132 cards, 22
   stickers, 1978 . . . .   **22.50**
Beatles, 1964
   A Hard Day's Night, 55 cards **135.00**
   Beatles Diary, 60 cards **145.00**
Beverly Hillbillies, 66 cards, 1963 . . . .   **330.00**
Black Hole, 88 cards and 22 stickers,
   1979 . . . .   **12.00**
Casey & Kildare, 110 cards, 1962 . . . .   **250.00**
Close Encounters, 66 cards and 11 stick-
   ers, 1978 . . . .   **9.00**
Comic Book Foldees, 44 cards, 1966 .   **165.00**
Creature Feature, You'll Die Laughing,
   128 cards, 1973 . . . .   **55.00**
Flag Midgee, 99 cards, 1963 . . . .   **40.00**
Flags Of The World, 1963
   Currency, 17 pcs **15.00**
   Dictionary Cards, 5 cards **7.50**
   Flags, 77 cards **67.50**
Gilligan's Island, 55 cards, 1965 . . . . .   **375.00**
Good Times, 55 cards and 21 stickers,
   1975 . . . .   **18.00**
Happy Days, Series A, 44 cards and 11
   stickers, 1976 . . . .   **9.50**

Incredible Hulk, 88 cards and 22 stickers, 1979	**15.00**
Kung Fu, 60 cards, 1973	**30.00**
Laugh–In, 1968	
Cards, 77 cards	**180.00**
Stickers, 24	**120.00**
Lost In Space, 55 cards, 1966	**265.00**
Man From UNCLE, 55 cards, 1966	**100.00**
Mars Attacks, 55 cards, 1962	**1,050.00**
Mod Squad, 55 cards, 1969	**95.00**
Rambo, 66 cards, 22 stickers, 1985	**10.00**
Rat Patrol, 66 cards, 1966	**75.00**
Return To Oz, 44 sticker cards, 1985	**9.00**
Smurf Supercards, 55 cards, 1982	**5.50**
Superman, 66 cards, 1966	**190.00**
Three's Company, 44 stickers, 16 puzzle cards	**10.00**
Welcome Back Kotter, 53 cards, 1976	**10.00**

BUSINESS AND OFFICE EQUIPMENT

Collecting Hints: The most important considerations are condition and function. Mechanical novelty and clearly identifiable period styles heighten desirability.

Calculators and adding machines are the most commonly collected items. However, other types of machines are becoming more collectible because of their inherent scarcity. Other types of office equipment include: accounting machines, account registers, check writers and punches, dictating machines (wax cylinder machines), pencil sharpeners, staplers, mimeograph duplicators, autographic and key–driven cash registers, time recorders, slide rules, stenographic machines, telephones, etc.

Collectibility of office and business equipment has less to do with age than with its novelty and/or functionality. Many individuals buy them to keep at their offices or places of business as conversation pieces. Collectors are few and not very well organized. Calculator and adding machine collectors, often linked to the typewriter collecting community, are the exception.

Generally speaking, the smaller an item is, the more collectible it is. An example of the reverse are accounting machines. They are very scarce and difficult to find, yet they usually cost very little. The major cost involved is in the shipping hassle and expense to get them home. Many of these mechanical monsters weigh over 200 pounds.

History: The enormous growth in large business enterprises in the latter half of the 19th century demanded increased efficiency in office operations. The old methods of record generation and organization were not sufficient to keep up with the explosion of industrial and commercial activity of the late 1800s and early 1900s. Combined with the tremendous mechanical inventiveness of many individuals, this resulted in a large number of sometimes unique mechanical devices which offered, to a greater or lesser degree, increased efficiency and profitability.

Most office machines fall within two categories—financial record keeping and communication.

The duplicator was one of the earliest types of office equipment. It took on a number of forms, the first recognizable one being the simple letter press. A recently penned letter, its ink still wet, would be sandwiched with a number of thin absorbent sheets of paper and pressed. Copies were poor but easier than the labor–intensive hand copying. Thomas Edison's invention of the Mimeograph in the 1870s coupled with skilled marketing by A. B. Dick made the Mimeograph a common sight in nearly every turn–of–the–century office.

Calculating machines have been a part of some offices since the 1830s through the use of Thomas Arithmometers or its variations. They were not particularly suitable for high–volume and high–speed addition. Truly practical and useful adding machines and calculators were not perfected until late in the 19th century. Early successful machines included Dorr E. Felt's Comptometer, Burrough's adding machines, and the numerous variations of the Baldwin–Ohdner type rotary calculators.

Checkpunches were the earliest mechanical attempts to limit the losses inflicted upon businesses through altered checks. The early machines actually punched figures in the paper check to show the true amount. They were quite slow and tedious to operate. Checkwriters in which the amount on the check was printed and the ink permanently imbedded into the paper fibers by the use of a perforating wheel or gear were the next natural evolutionary step. These machines became very popular after 1920. Next to the typewriter, the smaller checkwriters have more variations based on style than most other office equipment. Perhaps this had to do with the fact that these were generally kept on (or in) the boss's desk.

References: William Aspray, *Computing Before Computers*, Iowa State University Press, 1989; *The Business Machines and Equipment Digest 1927*, Chicago, 1927; Thomas F. Haddock, *A Collector's Guide To Personal Computers And Pocket Calculators*, Books Americana, 1993; Norman E. Martinus and Harry L. Rinker, *Warman's Paper*, Wallace–Homestead, 1994; NCR, *Celebrating the Future, 1884–1984*, published by company, 1984; Michael R. Williams, *A History of Computing Technology*, Prentice Hall, 1985.

Collectors' Clubs: Early Typewriter Collectors Assoc., 2591 Military Ave., Los Angeles, CA 90064; International Assoc. of Calculator Collectors, 14561 Livingston St., Tustin, CA 92680; Internationales Forum Historische Burowelt e.w. (IFHB), PO Box 50 11 68, D–5000 Koln 50, Germany.

Museums: The Computer Museum, Boston, MA; Henry Ford Museum, Dearborn, MI; National Office Equipment Historical Museum, Kansas City, KS; Smithsonian Institution, National Museum of American History, Division of Engineering & Industry, Washington, DC.

Advisor: Todd Holmes.

See: Telephones and Typewriters.

Charm, typewriter and desk, typewriter swings to top, silver plated, c1965, $10.00.

Accounting and Related Machines

Dalton bookkeeping machine	**100.00**
McCaskey account register	**40.00**
Moon Hopkins/Burroughs accounting machine	**350.00**
Remington Model 23 bookkeeping machine	**350.00**
Sundstrand bookkeeping machine	**20.00**
Underwood bookkeeping machine	**400.00**

Adding Machines

American	**25.00**
Burroughs	**15.00**
Fell & Tarrant, fine orig condition	**65.00**
Golden Gem	**80.00**
Star	**15.00**

Checkpunches and Checkwriters

F & E, International Detective Agency, check writer	**25.00**
Instant Checkwriter	**20.00**
Paymaster, check protector	**25.00**
SafeGuard Checkwriter	**20.00**

Dictating Machines, Wax Cylinder Machines

Dictaphone	
Type A, Model 10 dictating machine	**50.00**
Type B, Model 10, transcribing machine	**50.00**
Type S, Saving machine	**50.00**
Ediphone	
Dictating machine	**40.00**
Saving machine	**40.00**
Transcribing machine	**40.00**
Typease typewriter attachment	**15.00**

Duplicators and Mimeographs

A. B. Dick	
Edison Mimeoscope	**300.00**
Edison Model 1	**175.00**
Edison Model 75	**20.00**
Gem notecard duplicator	**10.00**
Rotary Neostyle 8–F duplicator	**45.00**

Office Related

Catalog	
A C McClurg & Co, Chicago, IL, Office Supplies & New Year Specials, 1925, 64 pages, 10¼ x 14¼"	**24.00**
Irwin Paper Co, Quincy, IL, Empire bond papers, 1931, 28 pages, 5¼ x 8"	**22.00**
Latsch Brothers, Lincoln, NE, Commercial Stationers' Complete Line of Office Supplies, 1931, 304 pages, 8¼ x 10¾"	**30.00**
L C Smith & Corona Typewriter Co, Syracuse, NY, "How To Use Corona Silent, The Portable Typewriter," 1935, 30 pages, 5½ x 8¾"	**10.00**
Stapler, Bostitch, black	**10.00**
Stock Ticker, Western Union, glass dome, matching walnut base, c1910	**3,750.00**

CALCULATORS

Collecting Hints: Mechanical calculators found in flea markets are often in very poor condition. Look for models in working order with no missing parts. Crank– or lever–operated machines are desirable but 110–volt electro–mechanical machines, perhaps because they are still so common, have not attracted collector interest.

Slide rules made of wood or metal are widely collected but plastic models are not. Most slide rules are six to twelve inches in length. Longer rules and circular models are less common and more valuable.

Electronic calculators have no moving parts. Battery–operated or "pocket" models are desirable while desktop printing machines generally are not. Like early transistor radios (1955–1965), the first pocket calculators (1970–1980) have become an exciting collectible. But unlike transistor radios, early pocket calculators are still easy to find at thrift stores and flea markets. Best of all, thrift stores often sell 1970s models for less than $5. Models with display numbers that light up (LED type) were made only during the 1970s and are thus obsolete and collectible. Since 1980 almost all pocket calculators have been made with liquid crystal (black) display numbers. With the exception of "novelty" types, these newer models are not currently collectible. A very easy way to identify the early (1970s) models is to look for a socket (hole) for an adaptor plug. Almost all early pocket calculators have an adaptor socket while newer pocket models do not. Collectors generally don't care if the adaptor and cord are missing as long as the calculator has a socket. Fortunately for the collector, almost every pocket calculator has both the manufacturer name and the model number printed clearly on the front or back of the case.

History: Although the abacus has been used for over a thousand years, the first mechanical calculating devices were not invented until the 1600s. Few of these early machines survived and those that did are now in museum collections. A very early hand–made brass calculating device recently sold for several million dollars.

Calculators were not manufactured on a commercial scale until the early to mid 1800s. By the late 1800s mechanical calculators were being produced by many companies and some models, such as Felt's comptometer, are still found in flea markets today. Electric motors were added at the turn of this century and these "electro–mechanical" calculators were still in common use in the 1960s. During the 1960s transistorized desktop calculators began to appear but initially cost thousands of dollars.

In the early 1970s, thanks to the invention of the integrated circuit, which packed thousands of transistors onto a microchip, the first "affordable" electronic calculators began to appear. The first pocket–sized electronic calculators came out in 1971–1972 for $200 to $400. This was the end of the line for mechanical calculator and slide rule companies. Competition to produce cheaper electronic calculators soon reached a frenzy and dozens of companies either went bankrupt or were quickly forced out of the calculator business. Bad news for calculator manufacturers but good news for collectors! By 1973 the price of a basic pocket calculator had fallen to the incredibly "low" price of $100 (about $300 in terms

of today's adjusted currency). Today a similar four–function calculator sells for about $5. Only two American companies, Texas Instruments and Hewlett–Packard, still produce pocket calculators. As the pocket calculator celebrates its 25th anniversary, the battle over whether to allow them into classrooms still rages on in some school districts. Note that some manufacturers, like Texas Instruments and Unisonic, made dozens of different models. The first models made by a given company are generally the most sought after.

References: David Baxandall, *Calculating Machines and Instruments,* Crown, 1975; Bruce Flamm and Guy Ball, *A Collector's Guide to Pocket Calculators,* IACC, 1995; Thomas F. Haddock, *A Collector's Guide to Personal Computers and Pocket Calculators,* Books Americana, 1993; Geoffrey Tweedale, *Calculating Machines and Computers,* Shire, 1990.

Collectors' Clubs: International Association of Calculator Collectors (IACC), 14561 Livingston St., Tustin, CA, 92680; The Oughtred Society (Slide Rules), 2160 Middlefield Road, Palo Alto, CA 94301.

Periodical: *The Calculator Collector,* 10445 Victoria Avenue, Riverside, CA, 92503.

Museums: Cambridge University Science Museum; The Smithsonian Institute's National Museum of American History, Washington, DC.

Advisor: Bruce L. Flamm.

Hand–Held
Arithma	**15.00**
Baby Calculator	**35.00**
Chadwick Brain	**15.00**
Ve–po–ad	**55.00**
Wizard Adder	**20.00**

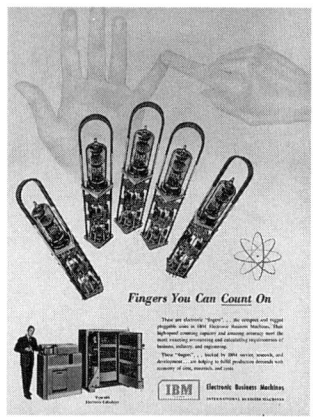

Magazine Tear Sheet, IBM, Fingers You Can Count On, #604 electronic calculator, 1950s, 10 x 13", $15.00.

Mechanical, desktop
Brunsviga 45.00
Burroughs 35.00
Felt's Comptometer 55.00
Monroe Adding Machine 20.00
Victor Adding Machine 25.00
Pocket, electronic
APF Mark 21 .... 20.00
Bohn Instant 20.00
Bohsei 3000 .... 30.00
Bowmar
901B 35.00
92001 .... 25.00
Brother
408 .... 30.00
807 .... 15.00
Busicom Handy LE 175.00
Calcupen 130.00
Canon Pocketronic 95.00
Commodore
887D 7.00
MM1 .... 50.00
MM2 .... 40.00
MM3 .... 8.00
S61 .... 65.00
Corvus 411 .... 8.00
Craig
4501 .... 30.00
4502 .... 35.00
4509 .... 7.00
Crown, CL130 .... 40.00
Facil, 1140 .... 25.00
Heathkit IC2008 .... 100.00
Hewlett–Packard
35 .... 35.00
55 .... 20.00
HP–01 Calculator and Watch 450.00
Keystone
390 .... 18.00
2030 .... 15.00
Kings Point
8412 .... 15.00
SC20 .... 12.00
Litronix, 2220 .... 20.00
Lloyds, 303 .... 15.00
Miida, 838 .... 15.00
National Semiconductor, 600 ..... 12.00
Omron 606 .... 30.00
Radio Shack EC425 .... 20.00
Rapid Data 800 .... 25.00
Rockwell 76 .... 15.00
Royal 90K 15.00
Royal Digital 3 .... 125.00
Sanyo ICC 804D 100.00
Sharp EL8 .... 45.00
Sinclair Sovereign 50.00
Sperry Remington 663 .... 20.00
Summit KO9V 45.00
Texas Instruments
30 .... 5.00
1000 .... 15.00
2500 Datamath 25.00

SR 52 .... **7.00**
Unisonic
740 .... **7.00**
940 .... **14.00**
Unitrex Mini–Handy **40.00**
Slide Rules
K & E **15.00**
Long Rule, 22″ **70.00**
Otis King, cylinder **125.00**
Pickett **15.00**
Thacher, cylinder **250.00**

CALENDARS

Collecting Hints: Value increases if all monthly pages are attached. Most calendars are bought by collectors interested in the subject on the calendar as opposed to the calendar itself.

History: Calendars were a popular advertising giveaway in the late 19th century and first five decades of the 20th. Recently, a calendar craze has swept bookstores throughout America. These topic–oriented calendars contain little or no advertising.

Reference: Norman E. Martinus and Harry L. Rinker, *Warman's Paper,* Wallace–Homestead, 1994.

Additional Listing: Pin–up Art.

REPRODUCTION ALERT

Prospect Brewing Company, Philadelphia, PA, 1898, $1,210.00. Photo courtesy of James D. Julia.

1901, Colgate, miniature, flower **15.00**
1902, Fertilizer Co, litho, scene **20.00**
1903
Franco American, miniature **15.00**
Grecian Maidens, Raphael Tuck ... **18.00**
1905
Christian Herald, diecut, four panel,
Victorian girls and birds **98.00**

Grand Union Tea Co, 29 x 10", diecut, color, litho, four sections for seasons	90.00
1906, Youths Companion Minutemen	65.00
1908 Antikamia Tablets	140.00
Metropolitan Life Insurance Co, mother and daughter in oval center	60.00
1909, Aubry Sisters Greaseless Cream	12.00
1910, Chinese Student Alliance, rope hanger	6.00
1913, 4½ x 12", plastic insert of Art Nouveau woman, metal frame	15.00
1915, Cosgroves Detective Agency, moose hunting scene	10.00
1916, University of Wisconsin, Madison, tinted Bascom Hall photo on cover, 6 x 8" university building photo on each month	100.00
1919, Woodrow Wilson	10.00
1924, Pompeian Co, beautiful lady and man	16.00
1926, Calgary Brewing	175.00
1927, Wrigley's Gum, desk style, elf in Mother Goose scene, three unopened samples of gum attached	40.00
1928, Bakers Cocoanut, recipes	20.00
1929, Absence Makes the Heart Grow Fonder, two Indian maidens, canoe, moonlight	45.00
1930, De Laval Separator Co, sgd Norman Price, Story of John & Mary, orig mailer	150.00
1933, Keen Kutter, different products each month	85.00
1935, Central's Gold Standard Footwear	15.00
1937, C & N W, 12 x 24"	18.00
1941, New York World's Fair, 6 x 8" wall plaque, Trylon and Perisphere illus, foil border, inscribed New York World's Fair 1940, thermometer	75.00
1942, Chesapeake & Ohio Railway, Peake, Chessie's Old Man, Joins the Service, complete pad with cover, 15¾ x 27"	90.00
1945, Double Cola	110.00
1948 Esquire, Ladies of the Harem, 12 sheet	15.00
Squirt, pin–up girls	37.00
1950, Wandering Brook Farm, outdoor scene, children and animals	9.00
1955 Marilyn Monroe, 8 x 14", cardboard, full color photo, Golden Dreams pose, red ground, Dec sheet	125.00
Miss Sylvania Electric, pin–up girl, no pad, Elvgren	48.00
1959 Paul Webb	35.00
Playboy	35.00
1962, horse racing	6.00
1965, Jayne Mansfield, 9 x 14", cardboard, full color glossy photo, wearing gold gown with white polka dots, 12 sheet	85.00
1969, Elvgren Curly Horse Ranch, cowgirl	46.00

CAMERAS

Collecting Hints: The camera market seems to fluctuate weekly. However, the long–range average price for any camera is steady. The Leica market no longer is in an upward movement, but interest in unusual cameras, e. g., subminiatures and stereo cameras, is growing.

Leather–covered cameras should have all the leather. Some wear does not detract from the value.

Folding cameras should have the bellows in good condition. Black bellows should be light–tight. Colored bellows matching colored cameras need not be light–tight. Having a matching bellow adds to the value of a colored camera.

History: A German monk, Johann Zahn, is credited with creating in the early 1800s the first fully portable wood box camera with a movable lens, an adjustable aperture, and a mirror to project the image. Zahn could view his image, but had no film on which to record it. In 1826 Joseph Nicephore Niepce produced the first photographic plate. Louise Jacques Mande Daguerre joined Niepce in his efforts. Peter Von Voigtlander of Vienna developed the quality lens needed. The photography industry was born.

The Germans were the initial leaders in camera manufacture. By the late 19th century the English and French had a strong market position. American strength would begin around 1900. America's strongest contributions have come in the development of films and the Polaroid camera, invented by Dr. Land and marketed in late 1948.

George Eastman revolutionized the photography industry in 1888 when his simple box camera was introduced. It was small, 3¼ x 3¾ x 6½", and was modeled after earlier European examples. The camera had a magazine and could take 100 pictures without being reloaded. The pictures were 2½" in diameter. Many later models built upon the success of Kodak No. 1. Kodak's first folding camera was Model No. 4; the Brownie arrived in 1900.

Prior to World War II Japan made the Konica and Minolta. After the war Japan made a strong commitment to the camera market. The Japanese have introduced many technical changes into the camera, including solar power.

References: Norman E. Martinus and Harry L. Rinker, *Warman's Paper,* Wallace–Homestead,

1994; Michael McBroom, *McBroom's Camera Blue Book 1993–1994*, Amherst Media, 1993; Jim and Joan McKeown (eds.), *Price Guide To Antique And Classic Cameras, 1994–1995, 9th Edition*, Centennial Photo Service, 1994; Douglas St. Denny, *The Hove International Blue Book Guide Prices for Classic and Collectable Cameras: 1922–1993*, Hove Foto Books, 1992.

Periodicals: *Camera Shopper Magazine*, 313 N. Quaker Lane, PO Box 37029, West Hartford, CT 06137; *Shutterbug*, PO Box F, Titusville, FL 32781.

Collectors' Clubs: American Society of Camera Collectors, 4918 Alcove Ave., North Hollywood, CA 91607; Leica Historical Society of America, 7611 Dornoch Lane, Dallas, TX 75248; National Stereoscopic Assoc., PO Box 14801, Columbus, OH 43214; Nikon Historical Society, PO Box 3213, Munster, IN 46321; Photographic Historical Society, PO Box 39563, Rochester, NY 14604; The Movie Machine Society, 50 Old Country Rd., Hudson, MA 01749; Zeiss Historical Society, PO Box 631, Clifton, NJ 07012.

Museum: International Museum of Photography at George Eastman House, Rochester, NY.

CAMERAS

Adams & Co (London, England), Idento, 3¼ x 4¼", folding, f5.3 lens, c1908	**175.00**
Aires Camera Industry Co (Japan), Air King Camera Radio, tube–type radio and plastic 120 roll film camera, brown lizard skin covering	**165.00**
Ansco (Binghamton, NY), merged with Agfa in 1928	
Billy, Igestar 105mm f8.8 lens	**15.00**
Karat, 35mm, folding, c1937	**30.00**
Official Boy Scout Memo Camera	**175.00**
Rediflex	**10.00**
Readyset Royal, No 1, folding, Antar lens, c1926	**90.00**
Bell & Howell Inc (Chicago, IL), Stereo Colorist, 35mm, Rodenstock Trinar f3.5 lens, c1952	**145.00**
Canon, Inc (Tokyo, Japan), Canonex, leaf shutter, fixed lens, c1963	**75.00**
Ciro Cameras Inc (Delaware, OH)	
35 rangefinder for 35 mm film, 1949	**15.00**
Ciroflex, Model A, twin lens reflex, 1940s	**20.00**
Eastman Kodak (Rochester, NY)	
Anniversary Box Camera, tan box, given away to mark the 50th anniversary of Eastman Kodak Co in 1930	**30.00**
Falcon, box, 101 roll film, rotary shutter, 1897–1899	**65.00**

Instamatic, 314, lever wind, light meter, uses flash cubes, 1968–71	**12.00**
Pony, 135, Kodak Anaston f4.5 lens, 1950–54	**10.00**
Retina, Stuttgart type No. 126, 35mm, viewfinder, Kodak Ektar 5cm f3.5 lens	**50.00**
Vest Pocket Series III, 127 roll film, 1926–1934	**40.00**
Graflex, The Folmer & Schwing Mfg. Co (NY)	
Graflex, No 1A, Kodak Anastigmat f4.5 lens, 116 roll film, 1909–1925	**175.00**
The Press Graflex, Bausch & Lomb Zeiss Tessar Series Ic No 16 f4.5 lens, c1908	**400.00**
Ihagee Kamerawerk (Dresden, Germany)	
Exakta VX, 35mm, Tessar 50mm f2.8 lens, c1955	**100.00**
Ultrix Auto, folding, Schneider Xenar 70mm f4.5 lens, c1934	**45.00**
Mick–A–Matic, 126 cartridge, shape of Mickey Mouse's head, meniscus lens in nose, 1969	**80.00**
Minolta (Chiyoda Kogaku Seiko Co, Ltd, Osaka, Japan), Minolta 35, Model II, 35mm, c1954	**90.00**
Nikon Inc. (Nippon Kogaku K.K., Tokyo, Japan)	
Nikon S, 35mm, Nikkor 50mm f2 coated lens, 1950–1954	**400.00**
Nikkorex Zoom–8, 8mm movie camera, f1.8 lens, zooms 8 to 32mm, manual zoom	**25.00**
Perry Mason & Co (Boston, MA), Harvard Camera, tin box, meniscus lens, c1890, premium giveaway	**150.00**
Scovill Mfg Co (American Optical Co, NY)	
American Optical Revolving Back Camera, front focus, Daisy dry plate holder, c1888	**200.00**

Prontor II, Photovit-Werk, Schneider lens, compact 35mm, 24 x 24 mm exp, $125.00.

American Optical View Camera, brass fittings and lens, c1883 .... **170.00**

Klondike, meniscus lens, rotary shutter, c1898 .... **50.00**

Universal Camera Corp (New York City, NY)

Minute 16, 16mm subminiature, meniscus lens, c1950 .... **85.00**

Roamer 63, folding **15.00**

Voigtlander & Son (Braunschweig, Germany)

Bessa, 75mm f3.5 lens, folding **40.00**

Vito, 35mm, folding, c1950 .... **30.00**

Wm. R. Whittaker Co, Ltd (Los Angeles, CA), Whittaker Micro–16, subminiature, meniscus lens, c1950 .... **80.00**

Zeiss, Carl, Optical Co (Dresden, Germany; merged with Contessa–Nettel, Ernemann, Goerz, Ica to form Zeiss–Ikon in 1926

Contar II, sonnar 50mm f2 lens, 1936–42 .... **125.00**

Maximar B, folding plate camera, 1940s **80.00**

CAMERA RELATED

Advertising Trade Card, Heywood's Mammoth Photograph, Ambrotype Gallery, Boston, MA, 2 x 2¼" **15.00**

Book, *Guide To Kodak Retina, Retina Reflex, Signet and Pony,* Kenneth S Tydings, 1952, 128 pgs, soft cov ... **8.50**

Booklet, Kodak & Kodak Supplies, 1916, 64 pages **15.00**

Box, Eastman Kodak Developing Powders, "For Use In Brownie Tank Developer," c1900 .... **8.50**

Brochure, Kodak Medallist II, 24 pages, c1949 .... **24.00**

Catalog

George Murphy Camera, 1917, 192 pages **25.00**

Hyatt's Catalog, c1900, 206 pgs, cameras, parts, equipment, and supplies **35.00**

Korona, 1926, 52 pages **25.00**

Poco Cameras, Rochester Camera and Supply Co, Rochester, NY, 1903, 44 pages **30.00**

Watson and Sons, Ltd, Camera Lenses and Accessories, 1937, 24 pages **20.00**

Magazine, *Kodakery–A Magazine for Amateur Photographers,* 1919–21 .. **35.00**

Manual

Eastman's No. 2, Eureka Camera, c1899, 18 pages **20.00**

Leica Reflex Housing, 1956, 8 pages **5.00**

Window Display Card, glossy, Kodak Color Experts, 1949, 8 x 10" **30.00**

CANAL COLLECTIBLES

Collecting Hints: Concentrate on one state or one specific canal. Look not only for canal material, but also for the canal motif on non–canal items.

Beware of people trying to pass off tools and lanterns as having a canal origin. Ship boatyards used exactly the same tools as the canal boatyards. Insist on a good provenance for any canal item and check out the family name in the canal records.

Canal buffs are extremely well organized. Try to make contact early in your collecting interest with individuals working on the same topics as you. Many collectors own more than one example of an item and will gladly sell the duplicate to a new collector.

History: The American canal era had its origins in the 18th century with projects in New England, along the Potomac, and Louisiana. George Washington was intensely interested in canals and was a shareholder in several canal companies.

The building of the Erie and Champlain canals in New York launched canal mania. From 1825 to 1840 hundreds of canal projects were begun. States such as Pennsylvania and Ohio actually had more miles of canals than New York.

While the railroads contributed to the demise of the canals, it was the high maintenance costs, repair due to floods, and economic depressions which finally closed many of the canals.

A number of canals continued into the twentieth century. Modern canals include the Chesapeake and Delaware Canal and the Erie Barge Canal.

References: James Lee, *Tales The Boatmen Told,* Canal Press, 1977; William J. McKelvey, *Champlain To Chesapeake: A Canal Era Pictorial Cruise,* Canal Press, 1978; Harry L. Rinker, "The Old Raging Erie . . . There Have Been Several Changes": A Postcard History Of The Erie And Other New York State Canals (1895 to 1915), Canal Captain's Press, 1984; Harry L. Rinker, *The Schuylkill Canal: A Photographic History,* Canal Captain's Press, 1991.

Collectors' Clubs: American Canal Society, 117 Main St., Freemansburg, PA 18017; Canal Society of Ohio, 550 Copley Rd., Akron, OH 44320; Pennsylvania Canal Society, c/o Canal Museum, PO Box 877, Easton, PA 18042.

Museums: Canal Museum, Hugh Moore Park, Easton, PA; Chesapeake and Delaware Canal Museum, Chesapeake City, DE; Erie Canal Museum, Syracuse, NY.

Advisor: Harry L. Rinker.

Ashtray, 5" d, Pennsbury Pottery, shows Lehigh Canal boat at dock, camelback bridge in background, advertising premium from "The Solebury National Bank of New Hope Pa.", green, gray, and brown, light brown ground **20.00**

Autograph, letter signed
Abner Lacock, Office of Western Division of Penna. Canal, February 11, 1828, to Alexander Mahon, Treasurer of the Board of Canal Commissioners, letter informing Mahon that Lacock has issued a check for $35,000 . . . .   **40.00**

R & G D Coleman, Lebanon Furnaces, May 31, 1849, to Eckert & Stone, concerning passage of boats on Susquehanna and Tidewater Canal near Safe Harbor, PA   **25.00**

Badge, 3⅛" x 2⅛", Canal Days, Manayunk, PA, May 17, 1980, blue ground, photo of canal passing under railroad bridge **4.00**

Bank Note, broken
Chemung Canal Bank, $10 note, No. 1896, September 1, 1846, Elmira, NY, vignette of Greek god reclining in front of flight of canal locks, engraved by Rawdon, Wright, Hatch & Co **30.00**

Tide Water Canal, $1 note, No. 10782C, May 1, 1840, issued in Baltimore, MD, two vignettes, first with oval showing mule pulling canalboat, second of New York scene, engraved by Draper, Toppan & Co **50.00**

Book
Doran, Edith M, *High–Water Cargo*, New Brunswick, NJ: Rutgers University Press: 1950 and 1965, 224 pgs, hardcover, orig dj, illus by Forrest Orr, novel about life along the Delaware and Raritan Canal in the 1850s **20.00**

Robert J McClellan, *The Delaware Canal: A Picture Story*, New Brunswick, NJ: Rutgers University Press: 1967, 112 pgs, hardcover, orig dj **15.00**

Whitford, Noble E, *History Of The Canal System Of New York Together With Brief Histories Of The Canals Of The United States and Canada, Volume 1 and Volume 2*, issued as a *Supplement To The Annual Report Of The State Engineer And Surveyor Of The State Of New York*, Albany: Brandow Printing Company: 1906,

hardcover, and foldout charts, price for set of two volumes **100.00**

Check, Albany City Bank, No. 82871, March 27, 1857, $10,116 deposited by H H Martin to the credit of The Treasurer of the State of New York, Canal Fund **15.00**

Document
Pay Order, Ohio Canal, No. 2007, April 5, 1828, $100 for work done under the contract of Wilcox & Dill for Section 115 of the Ohio Canal south of Portage Summit **10.00**

Towing receipt, "B." and "S." Towing Line, Bernard & Samsel, Steam Tug *William Cramp*, towing from Bristol to Bridesburg for Lehigh Coal and Navigation Co canalboat, Philadelphia, June 5, 1916 . . . . . .   **5.00**

Medal, commemorative, 100th Anniversary of Hamburg Savings And Trust Company, 1872–1972, bronze, obverse shows bank, reverse shows mules pulling canalboat, bronze, 1½" d, orig packaging **10.00**

Patent Model
#154,978, William Baxter and William Baxter, Jr, September 15, 1874, wooden boat model, introduction of steam propulsion, the Baxters won a special prize awarded by New York for the best method of introducing steam propulsion to canals **300.00**

#218,363, Bernard Bird, Buffalo, New York, August 12, 1879, coupling devices for lines, white metal working model, spring powered whiffletree that snaps open when a lever is thrown **150.00**

Photograph, Minetto Shade Cloth Co, Minetto, NY, black and white, 8⅞" x 6⅛", shows canal and lock in lower left quadrant, river through center, and town in background **20.00**

Post Card
Delaware Canal, photo post card of aqueduct at Point Pleasant, PA, sepia tone **7.50**

Erie Canal, American Locomotive Works, Schenectady, NY, full view, multicolored, shows factories, railroad lines, and canal **5.00**

James River and Kanawha Canal, Old Libby Prison, Richmond, VA, multicolored, made by Hugh C Leighton Co, Portland, ME, #25682, printed in Germany, c1910, shows canal horizontally across center, Libby Prison in background, sailing vessels to right **4.00**

Puzzle, wooden, jigsaw, Joseph K. Straus, No. P–201, "Great Falls Tavern" (Chesapeake and Ohio Canal), 9" x 12", 200 pieces, orig box 25.00

Staffordshire, American Historical
Jackson, Job and John, View of Canal, Little Falls, Mohawk River, soup plate, 10½" d, light pink transfer, long stem roses border 80.00
William Ridgway, Harper's Ferry From The Potomac Side, plate, 9" d, black transfer, shows Chesapeake and Ohio Canal at base of mountain in background 50.00
Wedgwood, plate, 9¼" d, Poe Lock, Sault Ste Marie, MI, shows boats exiting lock, dark blue, first quarter of 20th C, made for Rudell Drug Co in Sault Ste Marie 50.00
Enoch Wood & Sons, Erie Canal, View Of The Aqueduct Bridge At Little Falls, chamber pot lid, 8⅜" d, dark blue, oval handle held in place with support piece screwed into top 275.00

Stereograph
Chesapeake and Ohio Canal, No. 327 Harper's Ferry, photographed and published by Kilburn Brothers, Littleton, NH, shows railroad bridge across Potomac, C & O canal in foreground 7.50
Lehigh Canal, View in the Gap— Early Morning, Klechner's Stereoscopic Views of the Lehigh and Wyoming Valleys On The Line of the Central Railroad of New Jersey (L. & S. Div), shows canal aqueduct at Lehigh Gap, yellow ground ... 10.00

Stock Certificate or Mortgage Bond
Black River Canal, New York, No. 109, issued November 9, 1837, center vignette of goddesses flanking oval shield featuring sunrise scene with spread–winged eagle on top, three vignettes on left of which two are oval New York State Stock cuts, a small railroad and a small steamship vignette on right, signed by Robert White, canceled with large oval cuts, engraved by Rawdon, Wright & Hatch 75.00
Chesapeake & Delaware Canal, No. 2427, 15 shares, issued June 15, 1913, vignette of wooden summit bridge built in 1826, light yellow tone, canceled 15.00
New York State 5 per cent Stock on behalf of the Delaware and Hudson Canal, No. 70, March 16,

1827, side identification vignettes only, hand canceled, engraved by J H Hill 45.00
Pennsylvania Canal Company, Six Percent Mortgage Bond, Principal Payable July 1st, 1910, No. 4, center vignette of canalboat about to cross under stone arch railroad bridge, stamp canceled, coupons clipped, folded 50.00
Ticket, C M Reed's Passage Ticket, 10⅜" x 4¼", unissued, c1840, features a small vignette of a steamship and a small vignette of a canalboat at top   20.00

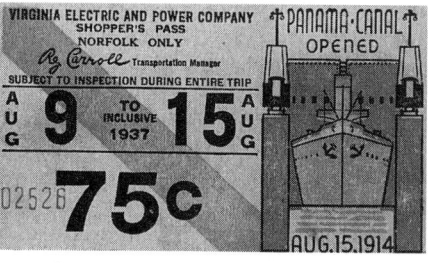

Trolley Ticket, commemorates Panama Canal opening, Aug 9–15, 1937, 3½ x 2", $8.00.

CANDLEWICK

Collecting Hints: Select pieces without chips, cracks, or scratches. Learn the characteristics, shapes, and types of Imperial pieces made. Many items have been made that are similar to Candlewick and are often mixed with or labeled Candlewick at shops and shows. Learn to identify "look alikes." Be wary and beware!

History: Candlewick, Imperial Glass Corp.'s No. 400 pattern, introduced in 1936, was made continuously until October 1982 when Imperial declared bankruptcy. In 1984 Imperial was sold to Lancaster–Colony Corp. and Consolidated Stores International, Inc. Imperial's assets, including inventory, molds, buildings, and equipment, were liquidated in 1985.

Imperial's Candlewick molds were bought by various groups, companies, and individuals. Approximately 200 molds were purchased by Mirror Images, Lansing, Michigan. Eighteen small molds were bought by Boyd Crystal Art Glass, Cambridge, Ohio. At present, the location of some Candlewick molds is unknown.

Anna Maroon Enterprises, Bridgeport, Ohio, purchased the building and lands belonging to the Imperial Glass Corporation in 1985. The planned tourist attraction never developed.

Candlewick is characterized by the crystal–drop beading used around the edge of many pieces; around the foot of tumblers, shakers, and other items; in the stems of glasses, compotes, cake and cheese stands; on the handles of cups, pitchers, bowls, and serving pieces; on stoppers and finials; and on the handles of ladles, forks, and spoons. The beading is small on some pieces, while on others it is larger and heavier.

A large variety of pieces were produced in the Candlewick pattern. Over 650 items and sets are known. Shapes include round, oval, oblong, heart, and square. Imperial added or discontinued items according to popularity and demand. The largest assortment of pieces and sets were made during the late 1940s and early 1950s.

Candlewick was produced mostly in crystal. Viennese Blue (pale blue, 1937–1938), Ritz Blue (cobalt, 1938–1941), and Ruby Red (red, 1937–1941) were made. Other colors that have been found include amber, black, emerald green, lavender, pink, and light yellow. From 1977 to 1980, four items of 3400 Candlewick stemware were made in solid color Ultra Blue, Nut Brown, Verde Green, and Sunshine Yellow. Solid black stemware was made on an experimental basis at the same time.

Other decorations on Candlewick include silver overlay, gold encrustations, cuttings, etchings, and hand–painted designs. Pieces have been found with fired–on gold, red, blue, and green beading. Other companies encased Candlewick pieces in silver, chrome, brass, and wood.

References: National Imperial Glass Collector's Society, *Imperial Glass Encyclopedia, Volume I: A–Cane,* Antique Publications, 1995; Ellen Tischbein Schroy, *Warman's Glass, Second Edition,* Wallace-Homestead, 1995; Virginia R. Scott, *The Collector's Guide to Imperial Candlewick, 2nd Edition,* privately printed, (available from the author), 1987; Mary M. Wetzel, *Candlewick: The Jewel of Imperial Price Guide II, Revised 2nd Edition,* published by author, 1993.

Collectors' Clubs: California Candlewick Collectors, 1360 Lomay Place, Pasadena, CA 91103; Michiana Assoc. of Candlewick Collectors, 17370 Battles Rd., South Bend, IN 46614; The National Candlewick Collector's Club, 275 Milledge Terrace, Athens, GA 30606.

Museum: Bellaire Museum, Bellaire, OH 43906.

Videos: National Imperial Glass Collector's Society, *Candlewick, At Home, In Any Home, Volume I, Imperial Beauty, Volume II, Virginia and Mary.*

Advisor: Virginia R. Scott.

REPRODUCTION ALERT: Six–inch baskets in pink and Alexandrite and a pink four–piece child's set (consisting of a demitasse cup and saucer, 6" plate, and 5" nappy) have been made by Viking Glass Co., New Martinsville, Ohio, for Mirror Images, Lansing, Michigan. In 1987 Viking made clear plates, bowls, cups, saucers, large and small flat–base sugars and creamers (400/30 and 400/122), and 6½" trays (400/29) for Mirror Images. These pieces have ground bottoms and are somewhat heavier than original Candlewick pieces. They are not marked.

Light green Candlewick items have recently appeared. The origin of these items is not presently known.

Boyd Crystal Art Glass, Cambridge, Ohio, has used Candlewick molds to make items in various slag and clear colors. All Boyd molds have been marked with a B in a diamond trademark.

In late 1990 Dalzell–Viking Corporation, New Martinsville, West Virginia, began making a five–piece place setting (6" plate, 8½" plate, 10" dinner plate, cup and saucer) in Crystal, Black, Cobalt, Evergreen, and Ruby Red. Retail price is $75 to $95 a place setting. The 1991 Dalzell–Viking Price List also includes a 5" and 6" two–handled bowl, 7" and 8" two–handled tray, and 10" five-part relish dish in Crystal. These new pieces are quite heavy when compared to period Candlewick, have ground bottoms, and etched "Dalzell" on the center base rim.

Ashtray	
4¼" oblong, large beads, 400/134/l	**6.00**
6" round, large beads, 400/150	
Caramel slag	**75.00**
Cobalt blue	**20.00**
Crystal	**7.00**
Pink	**12.00**
Ashtray Set, nested, 4", 5", 6", three piece	
Blue, yellow, and pink, 400/550 . . .	**26.50**
Crystal, 400/450	**17.50**
Red, white, and blue, patriotic, 400/550	**150.00**
Atomizer	
400/96 shaker with atomizer top made by De Vilbiss, amethyst, green, aqua, yellow, or amber . . .	**95.00**
400/167 shaker bottoms, aqua and amethyst	**95.00**
400/247 shaker bottoms, aqua and amethyst	**100.00**
Banana Stand, 11" plate, 2 sides turned up, 4–bead stem, 400/103E	**700.00**
Basket, applied handle	
6½", turned up sides, 400/40/0	**35.00**
11", 400/73/0	**150.00**
Bonbon, 6", beaded edge, heart shaped, curved over center handle, 400/51T	

Crystal 25.00
Light blue 75.00
Ruby red with crystal handle 200.00
Bowl, beaded edge
8½", two handles, 400/72B 25.00
9", square crimped, 4 ball toes,
400/72SC
Black 150.00
Crystal 40.00
Light blue 75.00
Red 150.00
10½", 400/75 . . . . 32.00
11", float, cupped edge, 400/92F . . . 35.00
14", belled, large beads on sides,
400/104B 65.00
Buffet Set
400/92D, 14" plate, 2 pc set 50.00
400/166B, 5½" cheese compote,
plain stem 50.00
400/9266B 50.00
Butter Dish, cov
California, 6¾ x 4", 400/276
Beaded top, c1960 . . . . 95.00
Plain top, c1951 . . . . 115.00
Rectangular, quarter lb, graduated
beads on cov, 400/161 . . . . 25.00
Round, 5½", 2–bead finial, 400/144 30.00
Cake Stand/Plate
10", domed foot, wedge marked
plate, 400/67D 65.00
11", 3–bead stem, 400/103D 50.00
14", round, birthday cake plate, 72
candle holes, 400/160 . . . . 295.00
Candleholder
3½"
Domed foot, small beads, round
handle, 400/81 . . . . 50.00
Rolled saucer, small beads,
400/79R 12.50
5", round bowl with beaded or fluted
insert vase, 400/40CV 75.00
5½", ftd, three sections, arched beads
on stem, 400/224 . . . . 75.00
6½", 3–bead stem
400/175 . . . . 70.00
400/1752, prisms 95.00
9", oval beaded base, three candle
cups, 400/115 . . . . 75.00
Candy Dish, cov
5½", box, 2–bead finial, 400/59 . . . . 30.00
6½", round bowl, sq cov, 2–bead
finial, 400/245 . . . . 110.00
7", 2–bead finial, three partitions,
400/110 . . . . 45.00
Celery Tray, 13½", oval, 2 curved open
handles, 400/105 . . . . 27.50
Cheese and Cracker Set, 400/151
cheese compote, 400/145D 11½"
handled plate, 2 pc set, 400/145 . . . 75.00
Cheese, Toast or Butter Plate, 7¾" with
cupped edge, domed cov, bubble
knob, 400/123 . . . . 115.00

Cigarette Set, frosted crystal, 6½"
1776/eagle ashtray, 3" cigarette jar,
small beads, 2 pc set 65.00
Clock, 4", beaded edge 125.00
Coaster, 3½" d, round, spoon rest,
400/226 . . . . 12.00
Cocktail Set, 6" plate, 2½" off–center indent, 400/39; 1–bead cocktail glass;
set, 400/97 . . . . 35.00
Compote, beaded edge, ftd
5", 3 sections, arched beads in stem,
400/220 . . . . 90.00
8", 4 bead stem, 400/48F 65.00
9"
Domed foot, large bead stem,
ribbed, 400/67B 75.00
Flat foot, plain or crimped beaded
edge, 400/67B 65.00
Condiment Set
Jam Set, two 400/89 cov marmalade
jars, 3–bead ladles, 400/159 oval
tray; 5 pc set, 400/1589 . . . . 95.00
Oil and Vinegar Set, two 400/164 and
400/166 cruets, beaded foot,
400/29 7" kidney shaped tray; 3 pc
set, 400/2946 . . . . 85.00
Console Set, bowl and pr candleholders
12" float bowl, 92F, cupped edge,
2–light candleholders, 400/100; set
400/920F 75.00
13" mushroom bowl, 400/92L on
400/127B 7½" base, 6" ftd urn candleholders, 400/129R; 4 pc set,
400/136 . . . . 120.00
Cordial Bottle, 15 oz, beaded foot, handle, 3–bead stopper, 400/82
Crystal 135.00
Crystal with red stopper and base . . 250.00
Creamer and Sugar Set
Flat base, beaded handles, 400/30, 7"
kidney shaped tray, 400/29, 3 pc
set 400/29/30 . . . . 25.00
Footed, beaded foot, plain handles,
c1937, 400/31
Crystal 40.00
Light blue 60.00
Footed, plain foot, question–mark
handles, 400/31 . . . . 30.00
Cup and Saucer
After Dinner, small, slender, 5½"
beaded saucer, set 400/77 . . . . . . 18.50
Coffee, slender, beaded handle,
400/37, saucer, 400/35, set 400/37 15.00
Tea, round, beaded handle, 400/35,
beaded saucer, 400/35, set 400/35 12.00
Decanter, beaded foot, round stopper,
26 oz, 400/163 . . . . 195.00
Deviled Egg Tray, 11½", twelve indenta-
tions, heart shaped center handle,
400/154 . . . . 85.00
Dresser Set, 4 pcs, round mirrored tray,
400/151, powder jar, beaded base,

3–bead cov; two round perfume bottles, beaded base, 4–bead stoppers,
made for I. Rice Co, 1940s **175.00**
Epergne Set, 9″ ftd crimped bowl,
1–bead stem, 400/196, 7¾″ 2–bead
peg vase, set 400/196 . . . . **160.00**
Jelly, 6″, divided, beaded edge, 400/52 **15.00**
Lamp, hurricane, 3½″ saucer candleholder, 400/79R, 9″ chimney
2 pc set
   Bohemian, cranberry flashed, cranberry and gold bird and leaves . **125.00**
   Crystal **65.00**
3 pc set, including 400/152 Candle-
wick adapter, 400/152R **90.00**
Lemon Tray, 5½″ plate, center handle of
3 sections of arched beads, large
bead on top, 400/221 . . . . **30.00**
Marmalade Jar, round, beaded edge
cover, 2–bead finial, 400/89 . . . . . . **30.00**

**Marmalade Jar, cov, spoon, 400/89,
$40.00.**

Marmalade Ladle, 4¾″, small bowl,
3–bead handle, 400/130 . . . . **12.00**
Marmalade Set, 400/19 old fashion
tumbler, beaded notched cov, 2–bead
finial, 400/130 ladle, set, 400/1989 **40.00**
Mayonnaise Set, 7″ beaded plate,
400/23D, 5″ heart shaped bowl,
400/49/1, 3–bead ladle, 400/165, set,
400/49 . . . . **30.00**
Mint Tray, 9″, heart shaped center han-
dle, 400/149 . . . . **25.00**
Mirror, domed beaded glass base, brass
holder and frame, two sided mirror
flips on hinges, maker unknown . . . **65.00**
Mustard Jar, beaded foot, notched
beaded cover, 2–bead finial, 3½″
glass spoon, shell bowl, fleur–de–lis
handle, 3 pc set, 400/156 . . . . **30.00**
Nappy, 6″, beaded edge, 400/3F **10.00**
Pastry Tray, 11½″, beaded plate, heart
shaped center handle, 400/68D **30.00**
Pitcher
   Manhattan, beaded foot, plain handle, 400/18
      40 oz **110.00**
      80 oz **145.00**
   Water, 80 oz, beaded question–mark
   handle, ice lip **95.00**

Plate, beaded edge
   6″, bread and butter, 400/1D **6.00**
   8½″, salad–dessert, 400/5D **8.00**
   9″, luncheon, 400/7D **12.00**
   10″, 2 handles, crimped, 400/72C . . **25.00**
   10½″, dinner, 400/10D **22.50**
   12″, 2 open handles, 400/145D **30.00**
Punch Set
   11 pcs, cov family punch jar, domed
   beaded foot, notched 2–bead cov,
   400/139, small 400/139 ladle,
   eight 400/77 demi–cups,
   400/139/77 set **225.00**
   15 pcs, 6 quart, 400/20 bowl,
   400/128B base, 400/91 ladle,
   twelve 400/37 cups, question–
   mark handle **250.00**
Relish and Dressing Set, 10½″ d, round
4 part relish, 400/112, 400/89 cov jar
fits center well, long ladle 3–beads,
c1941, 4 pcs **75.00**
Relish Dish, beaded edge
   6½″, 2 part, 2 tab handles, 400/54 . . **10.00**
   8½″, oval, pickle–celery, 400/57 . . . **15.00**
   10½″
      2 part, 2 tab handles, 400/256 . . . **22.00**
      3 part, 2 tab handles, also called
      "Butter 'n Jam", center holds
      stick of butter, 400/262 . . . . **45.00**
   12″, rect, 3 sections one side, long
   section on other, tab handle each
   end, 400/215 . . . . **50.00**
Salad Set, 10½″ beaded bowl, 400/75B,
13″ cupped edge plate, 400/75V, fork
and spoon set, 400/75, 400/75 set . . **65.00**
Salt and Pepper Shakers, pr, beaded foot
   Bulbous, 9 beads, plastic tops,
   c1941, 400/96 . . . . **15.00**
   Individual, chrome tops, 400/109 . . **10.00**
   Round
      400/96, 8 beads, chrome tops . . . **10.00**
      400/116, 1–bead stem, plastic or
      metal tops, c1941 . . . . **60.00**
      400/190, trumpet foot, chrome
      tops **32.50**
Sauce Boat Set, oval handled gravy
boat, 9″ oval plate with indent,
400/169 . . . . **85.00**
Stemware
   400/190 Line, bell shaped bowl, hollow trumpet shaped stems, beaded
   around foot, crystal
      Cocktail, 4 oz **16.50**
      Goblet, 10 oz **16.50**
      Seafood Icer **35.00**
      Sherbet, 5 oz **12.50**
      Wine, 5 oz **17.50**
   3400 Line, flared bell top
   Four graduated beads in stem, crystal
      Cordial, 1 oz **25.00**
      Goblet, 9 oz **15.00**

Sherbet–champagne, tall, 5 oz .	**12.50**
Wine, 4 oz	**20.00**
One bead stem, crystal	
Parfait	**30.00**
Sherbet, 5 oz, low	**10.50**
Tumbler, 12 oz, iced drink	**15.00**
Ruby red bowls, crystal foot, any	
3400 piece	**90.00**
Solid colors, verde green, ultra blue, sunshine yellow, nut brown, made 1977–90, goblet, iced tea, sherbet, wine, each ..	**35.00**
Tid–Bit Server, two tier, 7½" and 10½" plates joined with metal rod, round handle at top, 400/2701	
Crystal	**50.00**
Emerald green	**450.00**
Tid–Bit Set, nested, heart shaped, 4½", 5½", 6½", beaded edges, 400/750, 3 pc set	**30.00**
Torte Plate, 17", beaded edge, flat or cupped edge, 400/20V	**40.00**
Tumbler	
400/18, domed beaded foot, rounded top	
Dessert, 6 oz	**25.00**
Iced tea, 12 oz	**22.50**
Water, 9 oz	**20.00**
400/19, beaded base, straight sides	
Iced tea, 12 oz	**12.00**
Juice, 5 oz	**8.00**
Old fashion, 7 oz	**15.00**
Sherbet, 5 oz, low	**8.00**
Water, 10 oz	**10.00**
Vase	
3¾", bud, beaded foot, ball, crimped top, 400/25	**20.00**
5¾", bud, beaded foot, tapered large beads, crimped top, 400/107	**25.00**
7", rolled beaded top, solid glass arched handles with small bead edging, flat foot, 400/87R	**35.00**
8"	
Crimped beaded top, graduated beads down sides, 400/87C ...	**22.50**
Fan shape, beaded top, solid glass arched handles with small bead edging, flat foot, 400/87F	**25.00**
8½", bud, beaded foot, ball	
Narrowed top slants, applied handle, 400/227	**85.00**
Trumpet shape top, crimped, 400/28C	**35.00**

CANDY CONTAINERS

Collecting Hints: Candy containers with original paint, candy, and closures command a high premium, but be aware of reproduced parts and repainting. The closure is a critical part of each container; its loss detracts significantly from the value.

Small figural perfumes and other miniatures often are sold as candy containers. Study all reference books available and talk with other collectors before entering the market. Be aware of reproductions.

History: One of the first candy containers was manufactured in 1876 by Croft, Wilbur and Co., confectioneries. They filled a small glass Liberty Bell with candy and sold it at the 1876 Centennial Exposition in Philadelphia.

Jeannette, Pennsylvania, was a center for the packaging of candy in containers. Principal firms included Victory Glass, J. H. Millstein, T. H. Stough, and J. C. Crosetti. Earlier manufacturers were West Bros. of Grapeville, Pennsylvania, L. E. Smith of Mt. Pleasant, Pennsylvania, and Cambridge Glass of Cambridge, Ohio.

Containers were produced in shapes that would appeal to children and usually sold for ten cents. Candy containers remained popular until the 1960s when they became too expensive to mass produce.

References: Eikelberner and Agadjanian, *American Glass Candy Containers* (out–of–print); Jennie Long, *An Album of Candy Containers*, published by author, 1978; Robert Matthews, *Antiquers of Glass Candy Containers*, published by author, 1970; Mary Louise Stanley, *A Century of Glass Toys*, published by author, n.d.

Collectors' Club: Candy Container Collectors of America, PO Box 8707, Canton, OH 44711.

REPRODUCTION ALERT

Airplane, Spirit of St Louis, glass	**165.00**
Alarm Clock, glass	**180.00**
Apple, singing, 3¾" h, papier mache ..	**185.00**
Bank, litho tin, glass insert	**30.00**
Basket, hanging, glass	**30.00**
Bathtub, glass	**300.00**
Bear, papier mache, white, riding brown rabbit, wood, cloth, glass eyes, 8½" h	**175.00**
Bell, glass, Liberty Bell Candy Container	**85.00**
Bird, 4" h, plaster, wearing uniform, German	**40.00**
Bird Cage, glass	**90.00**
Black Cat, papier mache	
Face on Pumpkin, 2½" h	**75.00**
Sitting on Pumpkin, 4½" h, German .	**65.00**
Boat, glass, Model Cruiser	**15.00**
Boot	
Chenille, 4" h, Japan	**36.00**
Glass, 2" h	**10.00**
Bug, 8½", composition, sitting up, smiling, black top hat and glasses, red umbrella, German	**125.00**
Bureau, glass	**175.00**
Cannon, Rapid Fire Gun, glass	**225.00**

Cap, glass, military style	15.00
Charlie Chaplin, glass, Borgfeldt	125.00
Chicago Bus, glass	200.00
Chicken on Basket, glass	55.00
Chinaman, papier mache, sitting on log, 4″ h, German	245.00
Church, litho tin, glass insert	25.00
Clown, glass	10.00
Condiment Set, glass, 1906	60.00
Cornucopia, 6″ h, foil, celluloid Santa head	28.00
Dalmatian Pup, 11″ h, papier mache . .	30.00
Devil, 3¾″ h, papier mache	90.00
Dog, glass	
Little Doggie in the Window	15.00
Pup, tin top and hat	8.00
Scottie Dog, head up	20.00
With Umbrella	15.00
Donkey, 5″ h, papier mache, glass eyes, blanket, German	215.00
Duck	
Composition, 7″, female, pink bonnet, purple int., German	85.00
Glass, on basket	85.00
Papier Mache, dressed, German . . .	58.00
Egg, 4½ x 5″, composition, emerging chick, aqua, bead eyes, German . . .	135.00
Elephant, GOP, glass	150.00
Father Christmas, 11″ h, papier mache, white, glitter dec	85.00
Fire Engine, #11, glass	10.00
Fire Station, tin, 1914	40.00
Fire Wagon, glass	85.00
Fish, 5″ h, papier mache	90.00
Football, tin	15.00

Footballs, tin, brown, ribbon trim, 2″ l, price each, $15.00.

Gentleman, papier mache, top hat and tails, neck on spring, 8″ h, German	100.00
Girl, two geese, glass	20.00
Golf Club, glass	40.00
Gun, glass	
Cambridge Automatic	80.00
Indian Head Revolver	65.00
Square Butt Revolver	20.00
Hat	
China, Dresden, German	42.00

Glass	
Brim	60.00
Uncle Sam's	50.00
Heart Shape, 5″ d, tin, holly design . . .	15.00
Hen	
Composition, 3½″, white, sitting on box, two colored eggs, wood base, German	100.00
Papier Mache, German	125.00
House	
Cardboard, mica coated, Japan, c1940	18.00
Glass	150.00
Irish Hat, paper, painted, shamrock decal, 2″ h	35.00
Jack–O–Lantern	
Glass	155.00
Papier Mache	45.00
Jeep, glass	15.00
Kettle, glass, three ftd	45.00
Kewpie, by barrel, glass	90.00
Lantern, glass, pat 1904	25.00
Locomotive, glass, #999	95.00
Mail Box, glass	125.00
Milk Bottle, glass	30.00
Motor Boat, glass	8.00
Mug, drum shape, glass	40.00
Opera Glass, glass, plain panels	100.00
Owl, glass	125.00
Pear, papier mache, German	68.00
Phonograph, glass horn	250.00
Pig, papier mache, German	98.00
Pipe, glass, fancy bowl	50.00
Powder Horn, glass	40.00
Pumpkin Man	
Bisque, 3″ h	35.00
Crepe Paper, 10″ h, Schrafft's Candy	85.00
Rabbit	
Glass, seated	
Eating carrot	25.00
Painted, 4½″ h, green, orange accents, green tin base, early 1900s	125.00
Papier Mache	
Sitting, glass eyes, German	52.00
Walking, German	68.00
Reindeer, papier mache, glass eyes, metal antlers, 8″ h, German	185.00
Rolling Pin, glass	180.00
Santa Claus	
Composition, twist off arm	95.00
Cotton, body separates, Occupied Japan	89.00
Glass, with chimney	100.00
Santa Boot, glass	8.00
School House, litho tin, glass insert . . .	18.00
Skull 2¼″ h, papier mache, German . .	75.00
Sled, Santa, cardboard, mica coated, Japan, 1920s–30s	30.00
Snowman	
Cardboard, 9″ h, mica coated, wooden carrot nose, German	45.00
Glass	5.00

Station Wagon, glass 38.00
St Patrick's, papier mache, girl on box,
  German 88.00
Submarine, glass and tin 275.00
Suitcase, glass
  Milk Glass 50.00
  Tin Closure, wire handle 70.00
Tank, glass, man in turret 20.00
Telephone, glass, Victory Glass Co, sou-
  venir of Jeanette, PA 47.50
Terrier, frosted glass 15.00
Three Chicks and Mother Hen on lid,
  2½ x 3½", cotton 65.00
Top, glass, winder 85.00
Truck, glass, round top 75.00
Trumpet, glass 140.00
Turkey
  Composition, 4½" h, metal legs,
    black body, red and white tail
    feathers, c1930s 80.00
  Glass, dressed 90.00
  Papier Mache, German 68.00
  Plaster, 4" h, German 25.00
Valentine Heart, 5" h, papier mache,
  German 42.00
Village, glass, bungalow 95.00
Washington in Boat, papier mache,
  German 145.00
Watch, glass 350.00
Wheelbarrow, glass 75.00
Windmill, Dutch, glass 100.00
  Bisque, 5½" h, holding vegetables . .   40.00
  Papier Mache, 3" h, standing, holding
    broom, Japan 45.00
Witch's Hat, 3½" h, paper, painted,
  German 20.00
Yacht, glass 12.00

CANDY MOLDS

Collecting Hints: Insist on molds in very good or
mint condition. The candy shop had to carefully
clean molds to insure good impressions each
time. Molds with rust or signs of wear rapidly
lose value.

History: The chocolate or candy shops of Europe
and America used molds to make elaborate
chocolate candy items for holidays and other fes-
tive occasions. The heyday for these items was
1880 to 1940. Mass–production, competition,
and the high cost of labor and supplies brought
an end to local candy shops.

The makers of chocolate molds are often difficult to determine. Unlike pewter ice cream
molds, maker's marks were not always on the
mold or were covered by frames. Eppelsheimer &
Co. of New York marked many of their molds, either with their name or a design resembling a
child's toy shop with "Trade Mark" and "NY."

Many chocolate molds were imported from
Germany and Holland and are marked with the
country of origin and, in some cases, the mold
maker's name.

References: Ray Broekel, *The Chocolate
Chronicles*, Wallace-Homestead, 1985, out–of–
print; Eleanore Bunn, *Metal Molds*, Collector
Books, 1981, out of print; Judene Divone, *Anton
Reiche Chocolate Mould Reprint Catalog*,
Oakton Hills Publications, 1983.

Museum: Wilbur's Americana Candy Museum,
Lititz, PA.

REPRODUCTION ALERT

Candy, pewter, 2 pcs
  Horse and rider, #233, 2½" h 20.00
  Policeman, standing, #201, 3" h . . .   15.00
  Poodle, #94, 1¾" h 20.00
  Sailboat, #40, 1¾" h 85.00
  Steam Train Engine, #39, 1½" h 38.00
  Uncle Sam, #200, 8" h 110.00
  Woman Churning Butter, #30, 1" h   30.00
Chocolate, tin, clamp style
  Basket, stamped "6038, Made in
    U.S.A.," 9" l 16.00
  Chick, hatching from egg, #REI
    26112, 3" h 16.00
  Crocodile Egg, stamped "4750, Made
    in U.S.A., Eppisheimer & Co, New
    York," 2½" h 10.00
  Duck, wearing Tyrolean hat, #REI
    23011, 5¾" h 32.00
  Eagle, wings spread, shield at chest,
    "LIBERTY" above, #JAB 10, 4½" h   50.00

Four Easter eggs, $85.00.

Egg
  Man in the Moon, smoking pipe,
    #REI 4749, 3⅜" h 28.00
  Rabbits' 4th of July band design,
    #JAB 13, 6¾" h 38.00
  Elf, riding on running rabbit, egg bas-
    ket on his back, #REI 6526, 4¼" h   65.00
  Girl, hugging large rabbit, #21889S,
    7" h 90.00
  Kewpie Doll, finger at mouth, #REI
    17499, 11" h 170.00

Lovers, sitting on each side of basket, #EPP 5682, 7½" h, green spotting   82.00
Rabbit
Gang Mold, three dressed rabbits, stamped "26022, T.C. Wegandi Co., Made in Germany, New York, U.S.A.," 5½" h, very minor rust 75.00
Running through carrot patch, #JAB 22, 9½" h, minor rust 45.00
Sitting on fence, smoking pipe, #EPP 4808, 4¼" h 45.00
Walking upright, carrying basket with both paws, #6629, 12½" h   155.00
Rooster, stamped "Jaburg 20," 5¾" h   38.00
Santa, nickel–silver, Belsnickle type, #7, 5" h, minor tarnish 75.00

CAP GUNS

Collecting Hints: Condition is a critical pricing element. A broken spring that can be replaced is far less critical than a crack that cannot be repaired. Many older cast iron cap pistols rusted and suffered other ravages of time. While restoration is acceptable, an unrestored gun in fine condition is valued far higher than a restored example.

Beware of restrikes, reproductions, and new issues. Several of the molds for cast iron cap pistols have survived. Owners have authorized restrikes as a means of raising money. Often these restrikes are passed as period examples to the unknowing. Reproductions based on recasts often have a sandy or pebbled finish and lack the details found on period examples. New issues are frequently done with the intention of deceiving. Examples include the Liberty Bell cap bomb and the Deadshot powder keg cap bomb.

It is important to know the full history of any post–World War II cap pistol, especially if it is part of a pair. Toy guns associated with a character or personality sell better than their generic counterparts. Some of the price difference can be overcome when a leading manufacturer, e.g., Hubley, is a factor. The presence of the original box, holster, and/or other accessories can add as much as 100% to the value of the gun.

History: Although the first toy gun patents date from the 1850s, toy guns did not play an important part in the American toy market until after the Civil War. In the 1870s the toy cap gun was introduced.

The golden age of cast iron cap pistols is 1870 to 1900, with J. & E. Stevens and Ives among the leading manufacturers. Realism took second place to artistic imagination. Designs ranged from leaf and scroll to animal and human heads. The use of cast iron persisted until the advent of

World War II, although guns made of glass, lead, paper, rubber, steel, tin, wood, and zinc are known from the 1920 to 1940 period.

In the 1950s diecast metal and plastic became the principal material from which cap guns were manufactured. Leading manufacturers of diecast guns were Hubley, Kilgore, Mattel, and Nichols. Many of the guns were associated with television cowboys and detective heroes. Often the guns were part of larger sets that consisted of a holster and numerous other accessories.

Collecting cap and other toy guns began in the 1930s with the principal emphasis on early cast iron examples from the 1875 to 1915 period. In the mid–1980s the collecting emphasis shifted to the cap pistols of the post–World War II period.

Reference: Samuel H. Logan and Charles W. Best, *Cast Iron Toy Guns and Capshooters*, published by authors, 1990.

Periodical: *Toy Gun Collectors of America Newsletter*, 312 Starling Way, Anaheim, CA 92807.

Flyrite Products, Atom Water Gun, diecast, orig box, tear in flap, 1940s   75.00
Hubley
Cowboy, gold plated, black grips, 12 x 5¼", near mint 200.00
Mountie, automatic, engraving all over gun, mint 125.00
Rodeo Pistol, cowboy on bucking horse, red, white, and blue, 8¼ x 3½ x 1⅜" orig box, near mint . . .   125.00
Texan 38, engraved all over, turquoise grips, 10½ x 5¼", near mint 250.00
The Rifleman, Flip Special, rifle, 33¼ x 7¾ x 1⅞" orig box, MIB 600.00
Western Cap Pistol, white grips, black steer, 9½ x 4½" 45.00
Ideal, Yo Gun, red and yellow, plastic, 6½ x 7", 1950s, near mint 30.00
Kilgore
Buck, No. 407, red, navy, and white, black grips, 7¼ x 3⅝ x 1¼" orig box with illus of buck deer, near mint 100.00
Deputy, single holster, 2¼" wide fancy belt 195.00
Hawkeye, automatic, Indian head and eagle on barrel, 4¼ x 3⅛" . . .   40.00
Pal, 5½ x 3", mint 10.00
Ranger, cast iron, mint 75.00
Leslie Henry
Gene Autry Flying A Ranch, double leather holster set, two 44s, complete with bullets, tan and black, near mint 600.00
Wagon Train, #48, pistol, antique bronze, 16 x 9½ x 1⅞" shadow box with six bullets 400.00

Wild Bill Hickok, double leather holster set, two Marshall guns, bronze grips, tan leather, felt lining, near mint **500.00**

Mason, National Automatic, 45 cap, brown grips, 4½ x 6½", 1940s, near mint **60.00**

Mattel
Bandolier, Winchester, leather, thirty two all metal play bullets, belt, 1958, end flaps missing on box . .   **125.00**

Shootin Shell Remington Derringer, buckle gun, Matty's Funday Funnies, ABC TV, 1958–59, mint on card **100.00**

Winchester Saddle Gun, Official, stock no. 544, 33¾ x 6⅜ x 1½" orig box **500.00**

Nichols
Civil War Period Model 1861, revolver, shell firing, Model 61, orig 10½ x 16 x 2⅛" shadow box, six shells, eighteen bullets, mint gun, near mint box **600.00**

Dyna–Mite Derringer, #2782, presentation box, 3½ x 4⅞ x¾" orig box, jewel on top, "It's a Jewel," mint .   **40.00**

Stallion 38, two oak leaves on side, white grips, 10½ x 4½", six brass colored shells on lever on side . . .   **125.00**

Parris Mfg Co, Savannah, TN, Kadet Officer, target pistol, holster, shoots corks, 28 page Kadet handbook and ammo included, orig 5½ x 11" package   **50.00**

Remco
Okinawa Pistol, Monkey Division, 1964, 13" l, near mint **35.00**

Screaming Mee–Mee–E Rifle, 38¼ x 15¼ x 3½" box, never opened . . .   **300.00**

Unknown Maker
Automatic, 45, chrome steel, 4½ x 6½"   **45.00**

Big Scout, cast iron, white grips, 7½ x 3½", near mint **100.00**

Cowboy Pistol, tin, red, black, gold, and white, cowboy riding horse on grips, 11 x 4⅛", 1940s, near mint   **30.00**

G–Men Automatic, windup, black, G–Men illus, red, yellow, and green, steel, 1940s, near mint . . .   **75.00**

Hero, cast iron, 5¾ x 3", cowboy on cast iron grips, mint **40.00**

Pistol, metal, cork stopper, red, black, and silver, 9¾" l **30.00**

Police, automatic, steel, picture of policeman on both sides, 8" l, 1940s **40.00**

Scout, cast iron, metal grips with cowboy, 3 x 6½", near mint **90.00**

Smoky, gold plated, 2½ x 5½", mint   **10.00**

Wells Fargo, pistol, brown and white grips, horse head, designs on bar', 11½ x 4½", near mint **125.00**

CARNIVAL CHALKWARE

Collecting Hints: Most chalkware pieces appear worn, either because of age or inexpensive production techniques. These factors do not affect the value, provided the piece is whole and has no repairs. Some pieces are decorated with sparkling silver. This adds nothing to the authenticity of the piece or its value. Carnival chalkware in bank form is considered part of this category.

History: Carnival chalkware, cheerfully painted plaster–of–paris figures, was manufactured as a cheap decorative art form. Doll and novelty companies mass produced and sold chalkware for as little as a dollar a dozen. Many independents, mostly immigrants, molded chalkware figures in their garages. They sold directly to carnival booth owners.

Some pieces are marked and dated; most are not. The soft nature of chalkware means it is easily chipped or broken.

Carnival chalkware was marketed for a nominal price at dime stores. However, its prime popularity was as a prize at games of chance located along carnival midways. Concessionaires, e.g., breaking a balloon with a dart, awarded small prizes called a "build ups." As you won, you accumulated the smaller prizes and finally traded them for a larger prize, often a piece of chalkware.

Chalkware ranges in size from three to twenty-four inches. Most pieces were three dimensional. However, some had flat backs, ranging from a plaque format to a half–thick figure. Colors depended upon the taste of each individual decorator.

A wide variety of animal, character, and personality figures were made in chalkware. You can find Betty Boop, Sally Rand, Mae West, Shirley Temple, Charlie McCarthy, W. C. Fields, Mickey Mouse, etc. However, you will not find these names on the figures or in the advertising literature of the company who made them. Shirley Temple was the "Smile Doll"; Mae West was the "Mae Doll." Most character dolls were bootlegged, i.e., made without permission.

Although some carnival chalkware was made before the 1920s, its peak of popularity was in the 1930s and 1940s. The use of chalkware prizes declined in the late 1950s and ended in the 1960s.

References: Thomas G. Morris, *The Carnival Chalk Prize*, Prize Publishers, 1985; Ted Sroufer, *Midway Mania*, L–W, Inc., 1985.

Boxer Dog, 12" h **25.00**
Buddy Lee, 1920–30, 13½" h **65.00**

Buffalo	35.00
Bugs Bunny, flat back, c1940, 9¼" h	40.00
Cat, seated, gray and beige, 7½" h	45.00
Chipmunk, 1945–50, 5½" h	5.00
Circus Horse, c1930, 10" h	20.00
Clown, 1930=40, 8¾" h	25.00
Dopey, c1937, 6" h	45.00
Drum Majorette, 15" h	20.00
Felix the Cat, 12½" h	75.00
Ferdinand the Bull, c1940, 8½" h	20.00
Gigolo, string holder	30.00
Gorilla, c1940, 6¼" h	10.00
Horse, lamp, 1940–50, 13" h	80.00
Kewpie, 12" h	75.00
King Kong, 1930–40, 13¼" h	28.00
Lady and Dog, floral trim, c1935, 11¼" l	15.00
Lamb, flat back, marked "Rosemead Novelty Co," c1940, 7" h	5.00
Light House, lamp, 1935–45, 15½" h	50.00
Little Red Riding Hood, marked "Connie Mamat," 1930s, 14" h	30.00
Man, wearing derby hat, 1930–40, 10¼" h	40.00
Miss America, wearing bathing suit, c1940, 15" h	20.00
Mother Dog and two pups, seated, re-painted, bank, 6½" h	25.00
Pig, standing, carrying tray, marked "J Y Jenkins," 1937, 10" h	20.00
Pirate Girl, 1936, 10¾" h	50.00
Porky Pig, 1940–50, 11" h	32.00
Rabbit, holding carrot, 6⅜" h	50.00
Sailor Girl, c1940, 9" h	10.00
Ship, flat back, c1940, 10" h	5.00
Soldier Boy, c1940, 9" h	10.00
Spaniel, seated, 6¼" h	15.00
Superman, glitter dec, 16" h	30.00

Rosie, Maggie's daughter from Maggie & Jiggs comics, yellow hair, beige dress, green stockings, oxblood shoes, brown base stamped "Geo McManus, Manufactured by Yetown Gossip, San Francisco," 9¼" h, $45.00.

CARTOON CHARACTERS

Collecting Hints: A vast majority of collectible categories yield an object related to a cartoon character. Cartoon characters appeared in advertising, books, comics, movies, television, and as a theme in thousands of products designed for children.

Concentrate on one character or the characters from a single strip. Most collectors tend to focus on a cartoon character that was part of their childhood. Another method is to focus on the work of a single artist. Several artists produced more than one cartoon character.

The most popular cartoon characters of the early period are Barney Google, Betty Boop, Dick Tracy, Gasoline Alley, Li'l Abner, Little Orphan Annie, and Popeye. The movie cartoons produced Bugs Bunny, Felix the Cat, Mighty Mouse, Porky Pig, and a wealth of Disney characters. The popular modern cartoon characters include Garfield, Peanuts and Snoopy.

History: The first daily comic strip was Bud Fisher's "Mutt and Jeff," which appeared in 1907. By the 1920s the Sunday comics became an American institution. One of the leading syndicators was Captain Joseph Patterson of the News–Tribune. Patterson, who partially conceived and named "Moon Mullins" and "Little Orphan Annie," worked with Chester Gould to develop "Dick Tracy" in the early 1930s.

Walt Disney and others pioneered the movie cartoon, both in short and full–length form. Disney and Warner Brothers characters dominated the 1940 to 1960 period. With the advent of television the cartoon characters of Hanna–Barbera, e.g., the Flintstones, added a third major force. Independent studios produced cartoon characters for television, and characters multiplied rapidly. By the 1970s the trend was to produce strips with human characters, rather than the animated animals of the earlier period.

A successful cartoon character created many spin–offs. Comic books and paperback books and earlier Big Little Books followed quickly. Games, dolls, room furnishings, and other materials which appeal to children are marketed. The secondary market products may produce more income for the cartoonist than the drawings themselves.

References: Bill Blackbeard (ed.), *R. F. Outcault's Yellow Kid,* Kitchen Sink Press, 1995; Bill Blackbeard (ed.), *The Comic Strip Century: 1896–1985,* Kitchen Sink Press, 1995; Bill Bruegman, *Cartoon Friends Of The Baby Book Era: A Pictorial Price Guide,* Cap'n Penny Productions, 1993; Ted Hake, *Hake's Guide* *to Comic Character Collectibles,* Wallace–Homestead, 1993; Maurice Horn and Richard Marshall (eds.), *World Encyclopedia of Comics,* Chelsea House Publications, 1976; David Longest, *Character Toys and Collectibles, First Series,* (1984, 1992 value update) and *Second Series,* (1987, 1990 value update), Collector Books; L–W Book Sales, *Cartoon & Character Toys of the 50s, 60s, & 70s: Plastic & Vinyl,* L–W Book Sales, 1995; Alex G. Malloy and Stuart Wells III, *Comic Collectibles & Their Values,* Wallace–Homestead, 1995; Freddi Margolin and Andrea Podley, *The Official Price Guide To Peanuts Collectibles,* House of Collectibles, 1990; Norman E. Martinus and Harry L. Rinker, *Warman's Paper,* Wallace–Homestead, 1994; Robert M. Overstreet, *The Overstreet Premium Ring Price Guide,* Gemstone Publishing, 1994.

Collectors' Clubs: Peanuts Collector Club, 539 Sudden Valley, Bellingham, WA 98226; Pogo Fan Club, 6908 Wentworth Ave., S. Richfield, MN 55423; Popeye Fan Club, Suite 151, 5995 Stage Rd., Barlette, TN 38184; R. F. Outcault Society, 103 Doubloon Dr., Slidell, LA 70461; The Betty Boop Fan Club, 6025 Fullerton Ave., Apt. 2, Buena Park, CA 90621.

Periodical: *Frostbite Falls Far–Flung Flier* (Rocky & Bullwinkle), PO Box 39, Macedonia, OH 44056.

Museum: The Museum of Cartoon Art, Port Chester, NY.

See: Disneyana and index for specific character.

Archie, pinback button, 1½" d, blue, white, and orange, "Member Archie Club," 1950s **16.00**
Barney Google
  Book, *Barney Google and Spark Plug,* published by Cupples & Leon, 1925 copyright, #3 of series, black and white comic strip reprints, 10 x 10", cardboard cov, 48 pgs **75.00**
  Game, Barney Google an' Snuffy Smith, Milton Bradley, boxed board game, 16 x 16" playing board, complete, 1963 . . . . **38.00**
  Member Card, Brotherhood of Billy Goats, 2¾ x 4¼", buff color, black ink, text and "Bernard Google" facsimile signature on front, text, password, and image of billy goat in tuxedo and hooded mask on reverse, Chicago Herald and Examiner premium, c1920 . . . . **30.00**
  Sheet Music, Barney and Spark Plug on cov, 1923 . . . . **22.50**
  Toy, Spark Plug,¼" thick, 5" l, 4" h, jigsawed plywood, painted yellow, green, and black, red accents,

wooden wheels, sgd "DeBeck," 1925 copyright **165.00**
Beanie and Cecil
  Carrying Case, 8½ x 9", vinyl, red, zippered, red vinyl strap, color illus, Bob Clampett logo, 1961 . . . **50.00**
  Doll, 17" h, Beanie, talking, cloth, molded soft vinyl head, hands, and sneakers, red sweatshirt, aqua corduroy pants, pull string, orig Mattel tag, 1949 Bob Clampett copyright **100.00**
  Guitar, 14" h, animated, plastic, black, litho paper scene, music crank, Bob Clampett picture trademark, Mattel copyright, 1961 . . . . **80.00**
  Handbag, vinyl **100.00**
  Target Game, tin **60.00**
Betty Boop
  Charm, 1", celluloid, tinted colors, brass loop at top, 1930s **30.00**
  Figure
    3¼" h, musical, bisque, painted, holding accordion, "Fleischer Studios" and "Made In Japan" inscribed on back **130.00**
    3" h, celluloid, hollow, movable arms, holding white hoop, fleshtone, green dress, gold, black, and red accents, c1930 . . . . . . **130.00**
  Mask, 9½ x 9", stiff paper, diecut, full color, Bob–o–link Shoes, 1930s . . **125.00**
  Pin, figural, silvered brass, enameled, dark red dress, sq disk with oranges and "Florida" suspended from link at wrist, 1930s **80.00**
  Valentine, 3½ x 4½", mechanical, stiff diecut paper, movable feather in hair moves eyes and changes message from "Don't Keep Me Waiting For Your Love, Valentine," to "Or I'll Start Looking Around, Valentine," 1940 . . . . **30.00**
Blondie
  Birthday Card, 5 x 6", multicolored, Dagwood carrying large greeting card on front, int. Dagwood doing dishes, red ribbon dish towel attached, Hallmark, 1939 copyright **12.50**
  Book, *Blondie & Dagwood's Snapshot Clue,* text and cartoons, 1934 . . . . **45.00**
  Coloring Book, 8½ x 11", Whitman #1121–15, 92 pgs, art by Chic Young, 1950 . . . . **15.00**
  Cook Book, dj **35.00**
  Cookie Cutters, 1948, MIB **125.00**
  Jigsaw Puzzle, set of three, Jaymar, orig package **35.00**
  Paint Box, tin, 1946 . . . . **24.00**
  Pencil, Dagwood, 1929 . . . . **10.00**
  Valentine, 3 x 4", diecut stiff paper, Alexander and Daisy, c1940 . . . . **8.00**

Bringing Up Father
  Figure, 4" h, set of three, Jiggs, Maggie, and daughter, bisque, multicolored, figures inscribed "King Features copyright/Made in Japan" and mold number, orig box, 1934 copyright 175.00
  Pinback Button, ¾" d, red and black, white ground, Jiggs, Joplin Globe, c1930 .... 15.00
  Pocket Mirror, 2 x 3", black and white, paper covered illus of Jiggs leaning on fence, adv Casey's Tool Works factory, balloon caption reads "So Does Mine But I Don't Advertise It On Every Fence," c1930 .... 70.00
  Salt and Pepper Shakers, pr, 2½" h, china, multicolored Maggie and Jiggs, orange and black holder, marked "Made in Japan," c1930 70.00
Bugs Bunny
  Doll, 10" h, plush, molded soft rubber face, 1¾" d litho pinback button inscribed "What's Up Doc?" c1950 . 100.00
  Figure, 7¼" h, glazed china, hollow, light gray, white, and pink, brown base, name inscribed on front, Warner Bros copyright, c1940 ... 110.00
  Planter, 3 x 6 x 7½" h, china, glossy white, gray, and pink, figural, holding wheelbarrow, name and Warner Bros Cartoon copyright on back, late 1940s 80.00
Casper the Friendly Ghost
  Bank, plastic 35.00
  Doll, 15" h, talking, white terrycloth, stuffed, molded hard plastic face, pull cord at neck 75.00
  Game, Jumping Beans, orig box, 1959 .... 30.00
  Soaky Bottle, 10" h, Wendy, hard plastic, red and yellow, c1960 ... 15.00
Dick Tracy
  Badge, shield, brass, black and red accents, late 1930s
    Dick Tracy Crime Stoppers 35.00
    Dick Tracy Detective Club 30.00
  Big Little Book
    Dick Tracy And His G–Men, Whitman Better Little Book, #1439, 1936 .... 25.00
    Dick Tracy In Chains Of Crime, Whitman, #1185, 1935 ...... 25.00
  Camera 35.00
  Lunch Box 100.00
  Model, Aurora, MIB 125.00
  Pin, 2" l, Dick Tracy Air Detective, brass, wings, airplane center, 1938 65.00
  Pinback Button, 1¼" d, Dick Tracy Detective, illus of Tracy pointing gun, sgd "Chester Gould" 30.00

Puppet, hand
  Bonny Braids, 10" h, soft molded vinyl plastic head, hands, and feet, flannel pajama outfit, baby blanket, orig tag, c1953 ...... 60.00
  Dick Tracy, dated 1961 .... 45.00
Salt and Pepper Shakers, pr, Dick Tracy and Junior, 2½" h, plaster, painted, c1940 .... 30.00
Tab, brass, black and red accents, Dick Tracy Detective Club premium, 1942 .... 60.00
Trading Cards, set of 24, #121–144, 2½ x 2⅞", full color pictures, descriptions on back, Dick Tracy Caramels, issued by Walter H Johnson Candy Co, Chicago 60.00
Felix The Cat
  Brochure, 5¼ x 8¼", Eastman Kodak Co adv, Kodatoy film projector and theater, black, white, and red Felix, late 1920–30s 55.00
  Coloring Book, 8½ x 10¾", Saalfield, 96 pgs, unused, 1959 .... 25.00
  Figure, 3¾" h, wood, jointed, elastic stringing, black leather ears, 1924 Pat Sullivan copyright decal, 1930s 125.00
  Palm Puzzle, 3" d, silvered tin, German, 1930s 100.00
  Soaky Bottle, 10" h, hard vinyl, incised "Felix" on chest, Colgate Palmolive Co, 1960s 55.00
Flintstones
  Bank, 8¼" h, Dino, glazed china, white ground, blue, yellow, and black accents, brown golf bag, 1961 Hanna–Barbera copyright .. 115.00
  Costume, Fred, vinyl plastic molded mask, one pc cover–all costume, Ben Cooper, 1973 Hanna–Barbera copyright 25.00

Flintstones, banks, molded plastic, Homecraft Products, Vinyl Prod. Corp., 1971, left: Fred Flintstone, 12¼" h; center: Dino and Pebbles, 13" h; right: Barney Rubble and Bam–Bam, 12¼" h, price each, $45.00.

Game, Pebbles Flintstone, 19" sq playing board, eleven cardboard figures,
plastic stands, missing parts, orig
box, Transogram, 1962 copyright   **25.00**
Jewelry Display, 9 x 18", cardboard,
diecut, easel type, applied foam
chest holds 36 character rings,
1972 Hanna–Barbera copyright   ..   **225.00**
Jigsaw Puzzle, Whitman, 14 x 18",
Fred and Wilma on floating Dino,
1962 Hanna–Barbera copyright,
orig box **8.00**
Lamp, Fred, Flintstone characters
printed on shade, 1961 ....   **110.00**
Toy
    Ramp Walker, Fred and Barney,
    hard plastic, Marx, 1962
    Hanna–Barbera copyright **150.00**
    Wind–up, 8" l, Fred on Dino, litho
    tin, movable vinyl head, Marx,
    1962 Hanna–Barbera copyright   **250.00**
Waste Can, 13" h, oval, metal, litho,
twelve full color images, Harvell–
Kilgore Sales Corp, Hanna–Barbera
copyright, 1960s **75.00**
Happy Hooligan
Bank, pottery, dated 1920 ....   **175.00**
Charm, 1½" h, Alphonse, white
metal, blue metallic tint, flat back,
early 1900s **25.00**
Hector Heathcote
Book, *The Minute An A Half Man,*
Wonder Book, 20 pgs, 1960   ....   **35.00**
Game, 17" sq playing board, four fig-
ures, 64 cards, playing piece, mar-
ble cannon ball, and instruction
leaflet, Transogram, 1963 ....   **55.00**
Huckleberry Hound
Book, *Huckleberry Hound Giant
Storybook,* Whitman, 1961 copy-
right, 192 pgs, hard cov **25.00**
Camera, plastic, black, image on
right side, instructions, orig box   ..   **40.00**
Game, Huckleberry Hound Bumps
Game, 17" sq, playing board,
twelve plastic playing pieces, spinner, 22 cards, and instructions,
Transogram, 1961 Hanna–Barbera
copyright **55.00**
Pencil Sharpener, mint on card **35.00**
Jetsons
Colorforms, vinyl stick–ons, black
and white jet–age airport board, in-
struction leaflet, 1963 Colorforms
and Hanna–Barbera copyrights,
orig box, complete **35.00**
Doll, 12" h, orig tags, Applause **25.00**
Toy, ramp walker, Astro and George,
hard plastic, Marx, Hanna–Barbera
copyright, early 1960s **100.00**
Katzenjammer Kids
Mask, Fritz, molded **24.00**

Ring, The Captain, plastic, figural,
gold, white, and blue accents, late
1940s **30.00**
Li'l Abner
Bank
    Daisy May **145.00**
    Shmoo, 7" h, hard plastic, blue,
    black accents, inscribed "Li'l–
    Abner–Sez, Woo the Shmoo,
    with Lucky Money/Make Your
    Future Bright and Sunny!" on
    back, orig diecut money bag
    shape card, Gould & Co 1948
    copyright **65.00**
Clock, 4 x 6", Shmoo, wall type, plastic, diecut, key wind, metal mecha-
nism case and hanging plate, blue
hands and pendulum, red numer-
als, Lux Clock Mfg Co, late 1940s   **80.00**
Coloring Book, 8 x 11", Saalfield,
#209, 80 pgs, copyright 1941   ...   **30.00**
Figure, 7" h, Mammy Yokum, chalk-
ware, dated 1968 ....   **18.00**
Pinback Button, ¾" d, litho, red,
white, blue, and black, Sweet
Shmoo, late 1940s **20.00**
Ring, brass, adjustable, raised image
of Shmoo on top, two small
Shmoos on side bands, late 1940s   **35.00**
Toy, wind–up, Li'l Abner And His
Dogpatch Band, litho tin, multicol-
ored, Unique Art, orig 6 x 9 x 8½"
box **550.00**
Little Lulu
Book, *Little Lulu,* Curtis Publishing
Co, Rand McNally Co printer,
1937, hardcover, 64 pgs **55.00**
Clothespin Set, mint on card **85.00**
Greeting Card, set of 4, full color il-
lus, 1944 Marjory H Buell copy-
right series, Hallmark **75.00**
Magilla Gorilla
Bottle, 10½" h, figural, hard vinyl,
movable arms, Purex Corp,
Hanna–Barbera copyright, 1960s   .   **75.00**
Toy, 4" h, plastic, movable arms and
legs, jointed with elastic string,
Hanna–Barbera copyright sticker,
Kohner Bros, 1960s **25.00**
Mighty Mouse
Book, *Mighty Mouse/Kinky Learns To
Fly,* Wonder Book, 1953 Terrytoons
copyright, 20 pgs **18.00**
View Master Reel, set of 3,
D5261–63, story booklet, orig en-
velope **25.00**
Moon Mullins
Figure, 5" h, wood, jointed, Moon,
orig box **120.00**
Nodder, bisque, Mayo **60.00**
Salt and Pepper Shakers, pr, Moon
Mullins and Kayo **20.00**

Toothbrush Holder, 5" h, bisque, Uncle Willy and Emmy **118.00**

Mutt and Jeff, sheet music, 1916 . . . . . **17.50**

Peanuts

Candle Holder, 7½" h, Linus, composition, sucking thumb and holding blanket, brass insert cup, Hallmark Candles sticker, 1970s **25.00**

Clock, Snoopy chasing butterfly, 1958 . . . . **37.00**

Lunch Box, Snoopy's doghouse, American Thermos Co, copyright 1968 . . . . **30.00**

Nodder, Linus **30.00**

Pencil Holder, Snoopy, ceramic, doghouse shape, 1975 . . . . **25.00**

Soup Bowl, Snoopy Around the World **15.00**

Wristwatch, Snoopy, pilot on doghouse, 1965 . . . . **45.00**

Pogo

Book, Simon & Schuster, first edition *Positively Pogo*, 190 pgs, 1957 copyright **25.00**

The Incompleat Pogo, 96 pgs, 1955 copyright **35.00**

Figures, set of six, vinyl plastic, Pogo and swamp friends, movable heads and arms, 1969 Walt Kelly copyright inscribed with name on base **90.00**

Mug, 4⅛" h, set of six, plastic, full color character images, Walt Kelly copyright, 1950–60 . . . . **55.00**

View Master Reel, set of 3, story booklet, unopened package, 1980 copyright Possum Productions Inc **30.00**

Popeye

Ashtray, "Blow Me Down" **110.00**

Charm Bracelet **45.00**

Figure

Olive Oyl, ceramic **12.00**

Popeye the Thinker, 6" h, chalk, 1929 . . . . **95.00**

Handkerchief, 8½" sq, multicolored, Popeye giving bouquet to Olive in center, corner pictures of Popeye and Olive, mid 1930s **30.00**

Jack In The Box, spinach can, head pops up **95.00**

Lantern, Line Mar, MIB **350.00**

Paint Set, five 4 x 4¾" picture sheets, 18 water color tablets mounted on inset board, Milton Bradley, orig box, 1934 copyright **125.00**

Pen, 5" l, yellow, Popeye and Olive **95.00**

Pencil, 10½" l, mechanical, by Eagle, marked "King Features Syndicate" **35.00**

Pinback Button, Popeye center, rim inscribed "I Yam Strong for King Comics," late 1930s **30.00**

Plate, face image, Vandor **50.00**

Playing Cards, complete deck, 1938 **30.00**

Puppet, Popeye and Olive Oyl, push button, orig box, 1940s, price for pair **85.00**

Sand Pail, 8" h, tin litho, Popeye Under The Sea, continuous full color illus, copyright 1933 T Cohn Inc **40.00**

Tab, 2½" d, diecut cardboard, Popeye in white and blue sailor suit, red ground, white lettering "I Yam Strong For Sunshine Popeye Cookies" **65.00**

Toy

Pow'er Strength Test, 9 x 15" colorful cardboard diecut figure, strength test piece mounted in center, hitting plate, wooden mallet, wooden can of spinach, metal bell, plastic peg scorer, HG Toys, c1960, unopened . . . **65.00**

Squeak, Olive Oyl, King Features Syndicate **120.00**

Porky Pig

Bank, 4½" h, metal, painted, green base with red "Porky," Warner Bros copyright, 1940s **125.00**

Soaky Bottle, 9½" h, molded vinyl plastic body, hard plastic removable head, pink and blue, c1960 **18.00**

Road Runner

Figure, 9" h, plastic, painted, movable vinyl head, R Dakin & Co, Warner Bros copyright, early 1970s **45.00**

Toy, 3½" h, Super–Flex, bendable, unopened blister pack, Lakeside Industries, 1970 Warner Bros copyright **15.00**

Rocky and Bullwinkle

Coloring Book, Bullwinkle and Dudley Do–Right, Saalfield, 1971 Ward copyright, 160 pgs, unused **25.00**

Doll, plush body, molded soft vinyl plastic head

13" h, Rocky, green felt aviator's cap, Ideal tag, 1960s **65.00**

15½" h, Bullwinkle, felt hands, red and yellow fabric outfit, "B" on chest, 1961 Terry Toons copyright **65.00**

Jigsaw Puzzle, Rocky and His Friends, 63 pcs, Whitman, Ward copyright, 1960s **30.00**

Toy, Bullwinkle's Spelling and Counting Board, 7¼" d, plastic, red, unopened blister pack, 1969 Ward copyright, Made in Hong Kong, Larami Corp **35.00**

Skippy, pinback button, 1⅛" d, Skippy Blade, black on white ground, 1930s **40.00**

Underdog

Glass, 6¼" h, set of 2, one with Underdog image, other with Sweet

Polly image, Pepsi Collector Series, mid 1970s **25.00**

Thermos, 7½" h, steel, full color, white plastic cup, Universal Vacuum Products, 1974 . . . . **200.00**

Woody Woodpecker

Alarm Clock, 1½ x 4½", animated, wind–up, Woody's Cafe, metal, ivory enamel, color dial with tree cafe, Woody stands in opening of tree, rocks back and forth as clock runs, Columbia Time Products, c1959 . . . . **120.00**

Game, Travel with Woody Woodpecker, Cadaco–Ellis, 1956 Lantz copyright orig box **80.00**

Yellow Kid

Bookmark, 2½ x 6¼", diecut cardboard, issued by "A No. 1 Candy Company," full color, yellow ground, illus of Yellow Kid depicted as chocolate candy surrounded by other candies, late 1890s **60.00**

Pinback Button, "I hate to take medicine!" **28.00**

Post Card, Buster Brown, Tige, and Yellow Kid, "Over The Bounding Main," 1903 . . . . **45.00**

Yogi Bear

Camera, plastic, black, Yogi image, instruction sheet, orig box, Made in Hong Kong **40.00**

Lamp, Yogi, orig shade **75.00**

Record Set, 33 rpm LP record and storybook **20.00**

Toy, friction, hard plastic, running action, orig box, Graham Bros **110.00**

CATALINA POTTERY

Collecting Hints: Many dinnerware patterns were produced under the Catalina name, in addition to the wide variety of decorative pieces. From 1937 to 1947 production of many of the art ware lines was taken over by Gladding, McBean and Company. Although the island plant was closed, many pieces made during this period were still marked "Catalina Island." Collectors must learn the subtle differences in the various marks used in order to distinguish between pieces made before and after the Gladding, McBean takeover.

History: The Catalina Pottery began producing clay building products in 1927 at its original location on Santa Catalina Island. In 1930 the pottery expanded its inventory to include decorative and utilitarian pieces. Dinnerware was added in

1931. Gladding, McBean and Company bought the company in 1937, closed the Island plant and limited production to the mainland. Ownership of the trademark reverted to the Catalina Island Company in 1947.

References: Susan and Al Bagdade, *Warman's American Pottery and Porcelain,* Wallace–Homestead, 1994; Jack Chipman, *Collector's Encyclopedia of California Pottery,* Collector Books, 1992; Steve and Aisha Hoefs, *Catalina Island Pottery,* published by authors, 1993.

Periodical: *The Pottery Collectors Express,* PO Box 221, Mayview, MO 64071-0221.

Ashtray

Cowboy Hat, green **100.00**

Goat, white **500.00**

Bowl, sq, white **25.00**

Charger, 14" d **65.00**

Compote, turquoise, orig factory sticker **175.00**

Console Set, bowl and pr candlesticks, 10½" d bowl, price for set **350.00**

Dish, sq, #C253 . . . . **25.00**

Figure

Cowboy Hat, yellow **65.00**

Fish, #C641 . . . . **75.00**

Flower Frog, pelican **225.00**

Head Vase, woman, aqua **95.00**

Planter, square, green **15.00**

Teapot **20.00**

Vase

Aqua, #639 . . . . **75.00**

Green, handled, 8" h **250.00**

Oxblood, 5" h **75.00**

Polynesian

#378 . . . . **145.00**

#385, 6¾" h **250.00**

White and turquoise, 8" h **35.00**

Water Set, carafe and six tumblers, red **250.00**

Wine Carafe, turquoise, handle **125.00**

CATALOGS

Collecting Hints: The price of an old catalog is affected by the condition, data, type of material advertised, and location of advertiser.

History: Catalogs are used as excellent research sources. The complete manufacturing line of a given item is often described, along with prices, styles, colors, etc. Old catalogs provide a good way to date objects.

Many old catalogs are reprinted for use by collectors as an aid to identification of their specialties, such as Imperial and The Cambridge Glass Co.

References: Don Fredgant, *American Trade Catalogs,* Collector Books, 1984, out–of–print;

Norman E. Martinus and Harry L. Rinker, *Warman's Paper,* Wallace–Homestead, 1994; Lawrence B. Romaine, *A Guide to American Trade Catalogs,* Dover Publications, 1960, 1990 reprint.

How to Build and Fly Model Airplanes, Catalogue of Ideal Supplies for Model Airplane Builders, $20.00.

MAIL ORDER

Macy's, 1908, 448 pgs, 15 pgs toys . . .	**85.00**
Montgomery Ward	
1913, Men's, Women's, Children's Fashions, 224 pgs	**55.00**
1942, Christmas	**38.00**
1946, Spring & Summer, 994 pgs . . .	**30.00**
1969, Fall & Winter, 1436 pgs	**11.00**
Sears	
1951, Christmas	**23.00**
1961, Diamond Jubilee	**38.00**
Spiegel, 1944, Fall & Winter, 630 pgs	**32.00**

TRADE

American Chair Manufacturers, Tropique Rattan, 1940s, 16 pgs	**18.00**
Atlas Portland Cement, Concrete Country Residences, c1900, 168 pgs	**85.00**
Bazar Patterns, 1875, 16 pgs	**20.00**
Betz, Frank S, medical supplies, 1931, 298 pgs	**25.00**
Butterick, 1885, 31 pgs	**25.00**
Charles Broadway Rouss, NY, 1912, general wholesale	**50.00**
Collis Motor Co Instruction Book & Repair Parts	**35.00**
Colt, 1941	**20.00**
De Soto, 1937, 20 pgs, 7 x 10½"	**25.00**
Doll Catalogue, 1962, 62 pgs	**24.00**
Dorrect–Way Store Displays, 1938 . . .	**15.00**

Doyles, M. L., Fashion Guide	**45.00**
Edison & Music, 1920, phonograph cabinets	**38.00**
Elmira Arms Sporting Goods, 1931, 180 pgs	**30.00**
Ford V–8, 1935, 12 pgs, local dealer stamp on front cov, 5¾ x 7½"	**25.00**
Frost and Adams Catalog of Artists & Architects Supplies, 1914	**25.00**
Goerz Cameras, 1913	**15.00**
Greenlee Tools, Mortising, Boring, 1927, 68 pgs	**10.00**
Harris Homes, Chicago, 1923	**35.00**
Heany's Magic, early 1920s	**25.00**
Higgenbothen Perlstone Hardware, Dallas, TX, 1939	**35.00**
Homan Manufacturing, 1911, 55 pgs, 10¼ x 13½", electro–plated hollow ware, toilet ware, novelties, etc	**85.00**
Hovey & Co, 1858, 32 pgs, seeds	**75.00**
Hueg & Co Confections, c1900, 48 pgs	**45.00**
Ideal Toy, 1950s, 8 pgs, 5 x 7", full color	**15.00**
Indian Art Palace, 36 pgs	**15.00**
Jacobson Architectural Ornaments, hard cover, 1915, 183 pgs	**35.00**
Keuffel & Essex Co, NY, drawing materials, mathematical and surveying instruments, 1915	**38.00**
Leacock Sports Supply, 1925	**25.00**
Lipscomb Co, Hardware, 1913	**50.00**
Louden Machinery Barn Equipment, IA, 1915, 224 pgs	**55.00**
Lufkin Precision Tools, #7	**22.00**
Majestic Stove, 1913	**40.00**
Marshall Field Holiday Goods, Fancy Goods, Notions, 1888–89, 210 pgs, 9½ x 12½", hardcover, toiletry, cutlery, photo albums, etc	**165.00**
May–Stern's, Toy Sale, 1950s, 32 pgs, 8 x 10"	**25.00**
National Modern Welded Pipe, 1928, 87 pgs	**12.00**
Newcomb–Macklin Manufacturers, c1910, 55 pgs, 14¼ x 10¾", picture frames, moldings, mirrors	**50.00**
Northland Electrical and Radio Supplies, 1932, 136 pgs	**12.00**
Pep Boys, 1954, May, 88 pgs, 8 x 11" .	**50.00**
John Pritzlaff House Furnishings Goods, 1910, 202 pgs, 10¼ x 12", coffee mills, scales, refrigerators	**40.00**
Punwani Bro, 1940, 16 pgs, illus	**15.00**
Remington Fire Arms, 1908–09, 64 pgs, 9⅛ x 8", illus and prices	**200.00**
Reynold's Watch Makers' Supplies, 1933	**30.00**
Schwarz, FAO, 1949, 82 pgs, Christmas scene on cov, 9 x 12"	**50.00**
Scott's Standard Postage Stamp Catalog, 1938, 1,300 pgs	**10.00**
Shelly Seamless Tubes, 1920, 71 pgs . .	**10.00**
Shure Winner, 1907, 588 pgs, toys,	

dolls, novelties	**60.00**
Spalding Athletic Goods, 1911	**150.00**
Specialty Engineering Co Zephyr Bodies, 1930s, beverage trucks, pictures Coca–Cola and other soft drink trucks	**125.00**
Spencer Microscopes, 1930, 108 pgs .	**32.00**
Stanley Tool Guide, 1935	**25.00**
Starrett Tools	**20.00**
Strong Aluminum, Alloys, Allco, 1928, 60 pgs, hardcover	**10.00**
Studebaker Champion, 1941, 8 pgs, 10¼ x 15½"	**15.00**
Thresher and Tractor Supply, 1926 . . .	**7.50**
US Ammunition, 1929, pocket size . . .	**30.00**
US Leather Goods Co, Gifts of Leather, Fall 1922–23 Winter, Chicago, jewelry, toilet seats, etc	**20.00**
Waterford Irish Crystal, 1924	**20.00**

CAT COLLECTIBLES

Collecting Hints: Cat–related material can be found in almost all collecting categories. Advertising items, dolls, figurines, folk art, jewelry, needlework, plates, postcards, and stamps are just a few of them. Because of the popularity of cats, modern objets d'feline constantly are appearing on the market. However, as cat collectors becomes more experienced, their interests are more with antique rather than newer items.

The cat collector competes with collectors from other areas. Chessie, the C & O Railroad cat, is collected by railroad and advertising buffs. Felix is a favorite of toy and cartoon character enthusiasts.

Because cat collectors are attracted to all cat items, all breeds, and realistic or abstract depictions, they tend to buy too many items. It is best to specialize. Money and display space extend only so far; time for research is limited. Three of the most popular new areas of cat collecting are cat cards, calendars, and stickers.

Throughout the 1980s cats have grown in popularity as the pet of choice and along with this has grown the love of collecting cat items. The new and newer (secondary) market, tomorrow's collectibles, has grown by leaps and bounds. Some cat pieces bought ten years ago are showing considerable price increases. Examples are Lowell Davis porcelains, especially the limited editions and/or retired pieces; Kliban's cat in all categories; older books, especially ones illustrated by Louis Wain; cartoon cats are popular, but reproductions require caution if the collector is concentrating on antiques—Felix, Sylvester, Tom and Jerry, and Garfield, who continues on the new market. The next hot cat collectibles include First Day covers and Telephone Calling Cards. As true antique cats become rare and

costly, buy what you can, but also concentrate on quality, limited editions, and original pieces in the current market.

History: Cats always have been on a roller coaster ride between peaks of favoritism and valleys of superstition. In ancient Egypt cats were deified. Cats were feared by Europeans in the Middle Ages. Customs and rituals bore down brutally on felines. Cats became associated with witchcraft, resulting in tales and superstitions which linger to the present. This lack of popularity is why antique cat items are scarce.

References: Pauline Flick, *Cat Collectibles,* Wallace–Homestead, 1992; Marbena Jean Fyke, *Collectible Cats: An Identification & Value Guide,* Collector Books, 1993; Bruce Johnson, *American Catalogue: The Cat in American Folk Art,* Avon Books, 1976; J. L. Lynnlee, *Purrrfection: The Cat,* Schiffer Publishing, 1990; Norman E. Martinus and Harry L. Rinker, *Warman's Paper,* Wallace–Homestead, 1994; Alice L. Muncaster and Ellen Sawyer, *The Black Cat Made Me Buy It!,* Crown Publishers, 1988; Alice Muncaster and Ellen Yanow; *The Cat Made Me Buy It,* Crown Publishers, 1984; Alice L. Muncaster and Ellen Yanow Sawyer, *The Cat Sold It!,* Crown Publishers, 1986; Silvester and Mobbs, *The Cat Fancier: A Guide To Catland Postcards,* Longman Group, 1982.

Collectors' Club: Cat Collectors, 33161 Wendy Dr., Sterling Hts., MI 48310.

Museums: The Metropolitan Museum of Art, New York, NY; British Museum, London, England; The Cat Museum, Basel, Switzerland.

Advisor: Marilyn Dipboye.

REPRODUCTION ALERT

Advertising Trade Cards, set of six, A. B. Seeley, 1881, price for set, $45.00.

Bank, Kliban's Cat, four red tennis shoe
  feet **65.00**
Book
  Gift, The, Moscow Foreign Language
  Press, softcover **20.00**
  Goyder, Alice, *Christmas in Cat Land,*
  Thomas Y. Crowell, NY, hardcover,
  1978 . . . . **20.00**
  Newberry, Claire Turlay, *Drawing a
  Cat,* The Studio, NY and London,
  hardcover, jacket torn, 1940 . . . . **10.00**
  Wain, Louis, *The Lament of Billy
  Willy,* Raphael Tuck & Sons, 1895 **115.00**
Cane, carved ivory cat head, glass eyes,
  silver collar, rosewood shaft, horn fer-
  rule, English, c1890, head measures
  3½" h **1,980.00**
Cigarette Holder, ivory, cat with ball . . **125.00**
Cigarette Pack, Black Cat Cigarettes,
  soft pack, unopened, wax seal **22.00**
Cookie Jar, Kliban's Cat
  Cat on stool **125.00**
  Full figure **135.00**
Doorstop
  Black Cat, probably Albany Foundry
  Co, mid 1920s, 6¾" h **75.00**
  Persian Cat, Hubley, 8½" h **100.00**
  Three Cats, black and white, one atop
  the other, marked "Made in
  Canada Jean 91," 7¾" h **45.00**
  Three Cats in Basket, John Wright
  USA, reproduction **50.00**
Figurine
  Beatrix Potter
    Simpkins **75.00**
    Susan **85.00**
  Cybis, porcelain, Taffee, Toffee and
  Tiger, LE400, issued 1982 . . . . . . **740.00**
  Danbury Mint, Cats of Character, is-
  sued 1986, 4" h **14.00**
  English, ironstone, green glaze, late
  19th C, 12" h **2,990.00**
  Jackfield Pottery, black cats, pr, 7" h **1,100.00**
  Royal Copenhagen
    Siamese, model #3281, issued 1976 **275.00**
    Sleeping Cat, model #422 . . . . . . **145.00**
  Royal Doulton, Siamese cat, the
  Chatcull Collection, 1960 . . . . . . **130.00**
  Royal Worcester, black and white kit-
  ten, reclining **225.00**
  Sebring Pottery, Egyptian–style cat,
  allover small floral pattern, c1920s,
  6½" h **40.00**
  Shafford Ceramics, Himalayan, Japan
  label, c1960s, 6¼" h, 8" l **40.00**
Handkerchief, Christmas, 1967 . . . . . . **55.00**
Mug, Kliban's Cat, full face **25.00**
Pillow Cover, cotton, litho, smoking cat
  playing banjo, "Don't Forget the
  Kitty" **175.00**
Pin Tray, Limoges, porcelain, four kit-
  tens playing with spool, 6 x 4" **55.00**

Planter
  Royal Copley, brown cat, green bow,
  yellow yarn ball, 7" h **28.00**
  Uhl Pottery, blue cat **120.00**
Plate
  1973, Mother's Day, Kaiser, blue and
  white **45.00**
  1980, The Booted Cat, Meissen an-
  nual **175.00**
  1983, Chessie, set of twelve, 5" d . . **300.00**
  1988, Mother's Day, Berlin, blue and
  white **85.00**
Poster Art
  Magazine, color litho by Charles
  Verneau, Paris, France, design by
  Theophile–Alexandre   Steinlen,
  "Prochainement, la tres illustre
  Compagnie du Chat Noir. . . ," laid
  down on linen, small black mark
  top left, c1900, 14¼ x 24½" **2,185.00**
  1988 Olympic, Seoul, Korea, mascot
  Hodori the tiger, blue ground, 33 x
  23¼" **15.00**
Salt and Pepper Shakers, pr
  Black Cats
    4" h, Shafford, Japan paper label **18.00**
    4½" h, snow dome bellies, Japan
    paper label **245.00**
  Jazz Cat, striped, playing piano **15.00**
  Kittens of Knightsbridge, Fitz and
  Floyd **18.00**
  Kitty's Wedding Cake, stacking **15.00**
Nodders
  Black Cats, mother and baby,
  Japan, 4" h **240.00**
  Orange Cat, green cat in base, nod
  sideways, Japan paper label,
  3½" h **45.00**
Sheet Music
  Home Scenes **7.00**
  Just as a Cat Will Play With a Mouse **5.00**
  Sylvester the Cat Nine Lives **10.00**
  The Foxy Kitten **3.00**
  The Tom Cat **4.00**
Toy
  Automaton, Roullet and Decamps,
  key wind, cat, fur–covered card-
  board and papier mache, walks
  and meows, 10" h **1,200.00**
  Nodder, clockwork, Puss 'N' Boots,
  24" h **2,400.00**

CERAMICS, MISCELLANEOUS

Collecting Hints: The majority of ceramics covered here were made in vast quantities, with long
production runs. Condition is the key element.
Don't settle for anything less than perfect. When

collecting dinnerware, prices for individual pieces, especially hollow ware serving pieces, are higher than when sold as a set. This is a phenomenon common to all dinnerware, European or American. The reason is that many people have a basic set and are looking for filler pieces.

The 1980s was a period of discovery for collectors of the various wares from West Coast potteries. Part of the excitement comes from the fact that many of the pieces speak to the stylish trends of the 1940s through the 1960s. What California collectors have kept secret for over a decade is now drawing nationwide attention. Collecting California potteries is "in."

California pottery is currently experiencing a price run. Speculation is rampant. No one is quite certain how much is available. Prices vary regionally. Pieces are more scarce on the East Coast than on the West Coast. Collectors generally concentrate on items from a particular firm, pattern, or period.

References: Susan and Al Bagdade, *Warman's English & Continental Pottery & Porcelain, 2nd Edition,* Wallace–Homestead, 1991; Jack Chipman, *Collector's Encyclopedia of California Pottery,* Collector Books, 1992; Lois Lehner, *Lehner's Encyclopedia of U.S. Marks on Pottery, Porcelain & Clay,* Collector Books, 1988.

BESWICK

Since the 1890s the father and son team of James Wright Beswick and John Beswick have been well known for their ceramic figures of horses, cats, dogs, birds, and other wildlife. Animals from children's literature such as Winnie the Pooh and Beatrix Potter characters have also been modeled. Royal Doulton Tableware, Ltd. bought the company in 1969.

Beatrix Pottery, Peter Rabbit, 100th Anniversary, orig box	**48.00**
Display Stand	**150.00**
German Shepherd, G.S. Ulrica of Brittas	**75.00**
Hunca Munca #2	**250.00**
Jemima Puddleduck #2	**225.00**
Mr Benjamin Bunny #2	**600.00**
Mr Jeremy Fisher #2, chip	**250.00**
Vase, 8" h, blue/yellow dribble glaze, pinched sides	**50.00**

BRAD KEELER

Brad Keeler started a pottery in his garage in Glendale, California, in 1939. By World War II, Keeler employed 50 to 60 people and had moved operations to space leased from Evan K. Shaw's American Pottery plant. Keeler sculpted figures of birds, lobsters, etc., which were made

into figurines, and adorned decorative pieces such as bowls, planters, and candlesticks. The pottery also produced Disney figurines including Donald Duck and Jose Carioca. The business relocated to Los Angeles in 1946 after Shaw's pottery was destroyed by fire. The plant closed in 1953, shortly after Keeler's death in 1952.

Figure	
Flamingo, 7" h	**65.00**
Tropical Bird	**65.00**
Lobster Dish	
14" l	**65.00**
18" l	**85.00**
Smoking Set, 3 pcs	**40.00**
Tomato Dish, 2 part, spoon	**55.00**

BRUSH

Brush Pottery operated in Roseville, Ohio, from 1925 to 1982. The pottery was an outgrowth of the Brush–McCoy Pottery and produced a wide range of decorative kitchenware including highly collectible cookie jars.

Bank, brownie	**35.00**
Canister, earthenware, ivory	**25.00**
Cookie Jar	
Cinderella's Coach	**295.00**
Circus Horse, brown, green trim . . .	**950.00**
Clown Bust	**350.00**
Cow, purple	**1,100.00**
Owl, yellow	**225.00**
Panda Bear	**250.00**
Three Bears	**125.00**
Cruet, earthenware, ivory	**25.00**
Decanter Set, black, frosted rim	**30.00**
Eggcup, chicken	**14.00**
Figure	
Frog, reclining, 10" l	**75.00**
Turtle, 7" l	**65.00**
Garden Dish, mermaid	**55.00**
Jardiniere, Indian motif, high gloss rose, Kolorkraft	**150.00**
Jewelry Holder, wall mounted, mermaid	**75.00**
Lantern, cat, pink	**75.00**
Mug	
Little Boy Blue	**125.00**
Peter Pan	**95.00**
Planter, standing turtle, pink	**10.00**
Teapot, earthenware, ivory	**30.00**
TV Lamp, ship, metal sails	**50.00**
Wall Pocket	
Boxer	**85.00**
Fish	**75.00**
Flying Duck	**75.00**
Horse	
Bucking	**135.00**
Grazing	**100.00**

CAMARK

Samuel Jack Carnes founded the Camark Pottery in Camden, Arkansas, in 1926. The pottery employed well-known professional potters and artists to design and produce earthenware art pottery and decorative accessories. The plant was sold in 1966.

Figure
Lion	35.00
Pointer	35.00

Planter
Elephant, 11 x 8"	60.00
Rolling Pin, N1–51	8.00

CASTLETON Sunnyvale pattern

Introduced in 1940, Castleton China was marketed as fine dinnerware. Shenango Pottery had money invested in this company from the start, and in 1951 Shenango purchased all the stock and took over both the sales and manufacture of this china. The Castleton line was discontinued around 1970.

Cup and Saucer	24.00
Fruit Bowl	24.00
Plate, Dinner	24.00

Vegetable Dish
Covered, minimal wear on finial	165.00
Open, oval, 11" l	60.00

CERAMIC ARTS STUDIO

Lawrence Rabbitt and Reuben Sand founded Ceramic Arts Studio in Madison, Wisconsin, in 1941. In 1942 they hired Betty Harrington as chief designer. The pottery closed in 1955, following the huge influx of foreign imports and copies on the American market. Not all Ceramic Arts Studio pieces were marked—beware of copies.

Candleholder, Speak No Evil	48.00

Figure
Alligator	50.00
Cheese	15.00
Colonial Man	25.00
Columbine	65.00
Frisky Lamb	24.00
Little Blue Boy, reclining	28.00
Pepita	20.00
Skunk	25.00
Spaniel Puppy	18.00
Sung–Tu	15.00
Waterman and Woman, pr	180.00
Wing Sang	15.00
Planter, Chinese girl	15.00

Salt and Pepper Shakers, pr
Dutch Children	25.00
Mouse and Cheese	25.00

Mr and Mrs Penguin	25.00
Oriental Children	40.00

Wall Plaque
Cockatoo	50.00
Zor and Zorina, pr	60.00

CLAY SKETCHES

Clay Sketches, located in Pasadena, California, began producing detailed figures and figurines in 1943.

Cookie Jar
Humpty Dumpty	95.00
Jazz Singer	175.00
Figurine, cockatoo	20.00

HAEGER

In 1871 David H. Haeger bought an interest in the Dundee Brick Yard in Dundee, Illinois. Eventually, he expanded his interests to include two other brick and tile factories. In 1900 David's sons took over management of the company. In 1912 they began producing flowerpots. With the introduction of glazed pottery in 1914, Haeger Potteries, Inc. was founded.

Basket, brown, 8" h	10.00

Figure
Indian Girl with Basket	24.00

Mermaid
14"	95.00
22"	200.00
Panther, 12" l	18.00
Planter, Madonna and Child	15.00
Seashell	90.00
TV Lamp, tiger, green	30.00
Vase, 18" h	85.00

Double Leaf, dark green, #4104,
15" h	25.00
Gazelle, 15" h	25.00
Rebeccah Puddle–Duck	45.00
Squirrel Nutkin	45.00
Timmy Tiptoes	50.00
Timmy Willie	50.00

JOHNSON BROTHERS

Four Johnson brothers—Alfred, Henry, Robert, and Fred—founded a pottery in Staffordshire, England, in 1883. By 1914 the brothers owned five factories and their products were well-received on both sides of the Atlantic. In 1968 Johnson Brothers became part of the Wedgwood Group. Johnson Brothers dinnerware was often given away as premiums by local businesses.

Coaching Scenes, blue and white
Berry Bowl	5.00
Cereal Bowl	15.00
Cup and Saucer	8.00

Johnson Bros., platter, Coaching Scenes, marked "Johnson Bros., Coaching Scenes," 13¾" l, 10" w, $45.00.

Plate
6" d	3.50
Dinner	8.00
Pitcher 50.00
Platter 45.00
Saucer 1.50
Soup Bowl, rimmed 20.00
Soup Tureen 300.00
Teapot 125.00
Vegetable
Covered	110.00
Open, round	35.00
Dorchester, dinner service, 42 pcs 300.00
Friendly Village
Plate
Bread and Butter	5.00
Dessert, 8" sq	10.00
Dinner	15.00
Platter	40.00
Old London, 29 pcs 165.00
Rose Chintz, cup and saucer 12.00
Sheraton, 78 pcs 500.00

JOSEF ORIGINALS

In 1946 Muriel Josef George started production of her Birthday Girls figurines in Arcadia, California. Within a few years, companies in Japan, Korea, and Taiwan were marketing copies at cheaper prices. In order to compete, Mrs. George relocated to Japan in 1955 and expanded her line to include Christmas items, animals, and other utilitarian ceramics. Items produced in Arcadia between 1946 and 1955 are marked "California," those produced in Japan are marked "Josef Originals."

Figure
Angel, with cake 30.00
Birthstone Girl
December	20.00
February, amethyst	17.00
October, opal, 4" h	20.00

Bride, 7" h 95.00
Christmas Belle 30.00
England 35.00
Girl at Piano 65.00
Girl, wearing blue dress, holding birthday card 45.00
Ladybug 10.00
Little Jack Horner 25.00
Little Mouse, ladybug on head 10.00
Peaches & Cream 35.00
Sweden 35.00
Music Box
How Much Is That Doggie In The Window? 75.00
Little Green Apples 75.00
Planter, mouse, Christmas, large 45.00
Sprinkler Bottle, elephant 55.00

LOS ANGELES POTTERY

The Los Angeles Pottery operated in Lynwood, California, from before 1941 until after 1967. The company produced artware and several lines of dinnerware.

Chip and Dip Bowl 50.00
Leaf Dish, large 30.00

MADDUX

Maddux of California was founded in 1938. The pottery made and distributed a full line of novelties including figurines, planters, lamps, console sets, and decorative bowls. They ceased production in 1975.

Cookie Jar, bear 150.00
Figure
Double Cockatoos 100.00
Horse, #982 15.00
Siamese Cat, sgd 32.00
Planter, flamingo, sgd 38.00
TV Lamp
Horse, prancing, #810, 12" l 25.00
Mallards, in flight 45.00

PACIFIC CLAY

Pacific Clay Products Company originally produced commercial wares such as crocks and tile. The company began operating in 1881 in Los Angeles, and by the late 1800s had plants in several locations, including Elsinore, Alberhill, and Riverside. By 1937 the pottery was marketing a full line of dinnerware and accessory pieces. The company closed sometime after World War II.

Bowl, 11" d, raised floral pattern 140.00
Carafe
Cobalt 55.00

Red	55.00
Yellow	45.00

Chop Plate, 14" d
Chartreuse	45.00
Red	60.00
Cornucopia, 4" l, pr	40.00
Figure, nude, holding feather, 15½" h	50.00
Grill Plate, 11" d	10.00
Plate, dinner, set of four	45.00
Salt and Pepper Shakers, pr, yellow ...	18.00

Vase
Fan, #3401	25.00
Turquoise, #3060	20.00

ROSELANE

William "Doc" Fields and his wife, Georgia, established the Roselane Pottery in Pasadena in 1938. Their decorative accessory line included figures, ashtrays, candleholders, vases, etc. The pottery relocated to Baldwin Park in 1968. Following William's death in 1973, Georgia sold to Rod and Audrey Prathos and later relocated to Long Beach, Ca.

Bowl, #12, Pasadena, CA, modern pink with gray incised pattern, bizarre modern form	60.00
Dish, rect, yellow butterfly	26.00

Figure
Boy with dog, white and brown, 5½" h	8.00
Deer, head down	50.00
Giraffe, stylized, glossy gray, 5½" h	20.00
Owl, small	15.00
Vase, Chinese Modern, white ext., terra cotta int., 8" h	18.00

ROSEMEADE

The Wahpeton Pottery Company/Rosemeade Pottery operated in Wahpeton, North Dakota, from 1940 to 1961. Laura Hughes, the potter, incorporated a wildlife theme in the design of her novelty and utilitarian wares. The pottery's salesroom closed in 1964.

Bank, goldfish	495.00
Creamer and Sugar, blue petal	50.00

Figure
Fighting Cock	95.00
Swan, aqua, 5" h	38.00

Wolfhound
Black, pr	270.00
Sable	135.00
White, blue spots	135.00
Flower Bowl, black	38.00
Pitcher, blue, twist handle, 5" h	35.00
Planter, squirrel	30.00

Salt and Pepper Shakers, pr
Fox Terriers	35.00
Golden Pheasant Hens	50.00
Greyhounds	35.00
Pheasants, tail down	55.00
Scotties	35.00
Shoe, button type, tan	40.00

TV Lamp
Horse	695.00
Rooster Pheasant	495.00
Vase, doe	30.00

SORCHA BORU

Box, trolley car	95.00
Dish, calla lily, 6½" w	85.00

Figure
Blue Bird	100.00
Blue Jay, 6½" h	165.00
Mustard Jar, lady, figural	95.00
Planter, bird, 5" l	85.00
Shaker, bride	35.00
Vase, boy on side, no squirrel	35.00

WILL–GEORGE

Will–George is the trademark used by Claysmiths, located in San Gabriel, California, during the late 1940s to early 1950s. The pottery's line included vases, console sets, candy boxes, and figurines.

Dachshund, stamped mark, 9" l	50.00
Flamingos, male and female, sgd, pr ..	195.00

CEREAL BOXES

Collecting Hints: There are two keys to collecting cereal boxes. The first is graphics, i.e., the box features the picture of a major character or personality or a design that is extremely characteristic of its period. The second hinges on the premium advertised on the box.

Cereal boxes are divided into vintage boxes (those dating before 1970) and modern boxes. Hoarding of modern cereal boxes began in the mid–1980s. Hence, beware of paying premium prices for any boxes after this date.

There is no question that a small group of dealers and collectors is attempting to manipulate the cereal box market, much as was done to the lunch kit market in the early 1980s. While there is some collector resistance, prices keep rising. Before paying hundreds of dollars for a particular box, remember the lunch kit market collapse currently in process. What goes up, etc.

More desirable than cereal boxes themselves are large countertop and other cereal box display pieces. Cereal box collectors compete actively against advertising collectors for these items, thus driving up prices.

Many cereal box themes also cross over into other collecting categories. In many cases, these secondary collectors are responsible for maintaining a "high" price for some boxes. Once the outside demand is met, prices drop. Carefully study which market component is the principal price determinant.

History: Oatmeal and wheat cereals achieved popularity in the nineteenth century. They were available in quantity from any general store. The first packaged, ready–to–eat breakfast cereals appeared around 1900. Initially, the packaging pitch contained an appeal directed to mothers.

Everything changed in the late 1930s and early 1940s. Companies such as General Mills, Quaker, Post, and Ralston redirected the packaging appeal to children, using as a hook the lure of premiums for the submittal of one or more box lids or coupons. Many of these promotions were geared to the popular radio shows of the period. However, it was the arrival of television and its advertising that established a firm link between cereal manufacturers and children.

In the 1940s General Mills successfully used the premium approach to introduce Cheerios and Kix. In the 1950s sugar–coated cereals were the rage. By the 1960s and 1970s cereal manufacturers linked the sale of their brands to licensed characters. As the popularity of characters faded, the box was changed but not the cereal. Today an endless variety of cereal brands parade across supermarket shelves, some lasting less than a year.

References: Scott Bruce, *Cereal Box Bonanza: The 1950's,* Collector Books, 1995; Scott Bruce and Bill Crawford, *Cerealizing America: The Unsweetened Story of American Breakfast Cereals,* Faber and Faber, 1995; Norman E. Martinus and Harry L. Rinker, *Warman's Paper,* Wallace–Homestead, 1994; Tom Tumbusch, *Tomart's Price Guide to Radio Premiums and Cereal Box Collectibles,* Wallace–Homestead, 1991.

Collectors' Club: Sugar–Charged Cereal Collectors, 92B N. Bedford St., Arlington, VA 22201.

Periodical: *Flake,* PO Box 481, Cambridge, MA 02140.

Alpha Bits, Archie cutout record on
back, 1970, Post 150.00
Boo Berry, monster poster offer, 1970s,
General Mills 30.00
Cheerios, General Mills
American Airlines Game Kit offer,
1956 . . . .   20.00
Muppet Movie Trading Cards, 1980   15.00
Clover Farm Regular Cooking Rolled
Oats, 10" h, cylindrical, bee and
clover flower, 1930s 40.00
Cocoa Krispies
Choco–Cluster Recipe Box, 1965 . . .   50.00

Hot Wheels offer, 1988, Kellogg's . .   20.00
Corn Chex, Party Mix recipe on back,
1950s 65.00
Corn Flakes, Kellogg's
Frying pan set offer, 1952 . . . .   20.00
Vanessa Williams, 1984 . . . .   45.00
Donkey Kong Junior, baseball card
pack, 1984, Ralston 30.00
Fairway Oat Flakes, 10" h, cylindrical,
boy and girl, c1910 . . . .   90.00
Frosted Flakes, Kellogg's, Tony the Tiger
spoon offer on back, 1975 . . . .   40.00
George Washington Corn Flakes, un-
opened 60.00
Golden Grahams, roller blade offer,
1980s, General Mills 3.00
Honey Nut Cheerios, Winnie the Pooh
offer, 1988, General Mills 10.00
Jersey Corn Flakes, 1920s, unopened,
multicolored box, family eating ce-
real 40.00
Kellogg's, baseball games and graphics
int., 1910 . . . .   110.00

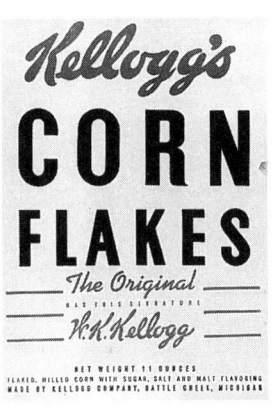

Kellogg's Corn Flakes, red and black lettering, white ground, c1945, 7½ x 10¼ x 2¾", $27.50

Kix, personalized pencil offer, 1987,
General Mills 10.00
Nabisco Shredded Wheat, 1942 . . . . .   65.00
Nutri Grain, 1989, Kellogg's 3.00
Post Super Sugar Crisp, 1974 . . . .   35.00
Quaker Puffed Wheat
No 8 Space Flight To Moon, 1953 . .   100.00
Sgt Preston, Yukon Trail No 2, 1949   100.00
Raisin Bran, Duck Tales duck track
stickers, 1987, Kellogg's 10.00
Red Owl Quick Cooking Oats, 10" h,
cylindrical, c1940 . . . .   35.00
Rice Chex, red check dec, 1950s 65.00
Rice Krispies, Pop A Ball offer, 1964,
Kellogg's 20.00
Sugar Crisp, Kool–Aid Wacky Ware-
house Bank on back, 1988, Post . . .   3.00

Sugar Smacks, Eager B Beaver, 1963,
  Kellogg's **50.00**
Wheaties, General Mills
  Bowling Champion contest, 1959 . .   **30.00**
  Minnesota Twins, 1987 . . . .   **7.00**
  Steve Largent Commemorative, 1988   **20.00**

CEREAL PREMIUMS

Collecting Hints: The rising collectibility of cereal premiums reflects the shift of emphasis in
collectibles from the 1920–1940 period to the
post–1945 era. The radio premium generation is
getting older. They have watched the price of
their childhood treasures rise to the point of un-
affordability for the scarcer pieces. Further, they
are reaching an age when selling, rather than
buying, dominates their mindset. It is time for a
new generation to enter the picture. Herald the
arrival of the cereal premium.

At the moment, collectors do not differentiate
between premiums that were found in the box
versus those that were obtained by sending in the
requisite number of box tops. As collectors become more sophisticated, look for this distinction
to occur.

The cereal premiums of most interest in the
current market are those associated with a fictional advertising, cartoon, or television character. As a result, much of the pricing in this category is being driven by the non–cereal premium
collector. This does not appear likely to change
in the decade ahead.

Collectors of cereal premiums narrow their
collecting by focusing on the premiums found in
a single brand or distributed by one manufacturer. These change depending on whether one
concentrates on the 1945–1962 or post–1962
period. The lack of a comprehensive list of manufacturers, brands, and premiums often makes at-
tribution a problem. When buying a cereal premium with which you are unfamiliar, insist that
the seller indicate the manufacturer, brand name,
and date on the sales receipt.

Unclear at the moment is the importance of
original packaging, much of which was nondescript. Current collectors tend to leave unopened
packages sealed when found. Most examples are
found with their packaging missing.

At the moment there is little enthusiasm for
generic pieces. However, anyone who compares
the history of Cracker Jack premium collecting
with that of cereal premiums will quickly see the
long–term potential for generic material.

History: Cereal premiums began in the 1930s
when manufacturers such as General Mills, Post,
Quaker, and Ralston offered premiums to individuals who sent in the requisite number of box

tops or coupons. Many of these premiums had a
radio show tie–in.

Although the use of in–the–box premiums and
on–pack promotions dates from the 1930s, this
approach achieved its greatest popularity in the
post–1945 period. Buildings, dolls, games,
masks, and puzzles were just a few of the many
items that a child could obtain by carefully following the cut–out directions on the back of a
cereal box. Many of these in–box and on–pack
promotional premiums related to a popular television program or movie.

When sugar–coated brands were introduced in
the mid–1950s, advertising characters were developed to assist in the merchandising effort.
Characters such as Captain Crunch, Sugar Bear,
Tony the Tiger, and Toucan Sam achieved widespread recognition. Often in–box and on–pack
promotions tied in directly with these characters.

In the 1970s shorter run tie–ins were developed. Cereals responded almost immediately to
the latest movie or television craze. Local and regional promotions became prominent. One result of this trend is that emphasis shifted from the
premium to the box itself as the important collectible unit. Cereal box collecting is now a separate category. The value of most boxes now exceeds any value for the premium associated with
it.

References: Scott Bruce, *Cereal Box Bonanza:
The 1950's,* Collector Books, 1995; Scott Bruce
and Bill Crawford, *Cerealizing America: The
Unsweetened Story of American Breakfast
Cereals,* Faber and Faber, 1995; Tom Tumbusch,
*Tomart's Price Guide to Radio Premiums and
Cereal Box Collectibles,* Wallace–Homestead,
1991.

Periodical: *Flake,* PO Box 481, Cambridge, MA
02140.

General Mills
  Cut–out, Rocket Firing Star Fighter
  Jet and Exploding Light Tank,
  Cheerios, 1950s, ...   **12.00**

**Jogometer, enameled metal, belt clip,
Wheaties, 2⅝" d, $18.50.**

Mug, plastic, black and white, three
different illus, Cheerios, 1950s . . .   30.00
Plate, 8" d, plastic, white, Bullwinkle
jumping off diving board with
Cheerios kid watching 25.00
Puppet, Trix Rabbit, 12" h, cloth and
vinyl, 1960s 30.00
Post Card
    Cheerios Kid and Donald Duck,
    Huey, Louie, and Disneyland,
    3½ x 6", black and white,
    Cheerios, 1957 . . . .   10.00
    Lone Ranger, 3 x 6", photo with sig-
    nature, Cheerios, 1956 . . . .   10.00
Kellogg's
    Cereal Bowl and Mug, Digger Frog il-
    lus on bowl, figural mug, Sugar
    Smacks, 1973 . . . .   20.00
    Cut–out, Decoder, 3" l, Toucan Sam,
    figural, plastic, Fruit Loops, 1970s   10.00
    Eraser, Yogi Bear, 2" h, 1960s 20.00
    Figure
        Caveman, Ogg, blonde hair, Cocoa
        Krispies, 1970 . . . .   28.00
        Crackle, jointed, Rice Krispies . . .   15.00
        Huckleberry Hound, plastic, re-
        movable head with secret stor-
        age space, 1960s 30.00
        Mr Jinx, plastic, 3 pc, 1960 . . . . . 100.00
    Party Kit, Singing Lady Party Kit,
    masks, uncut, 1936 . . . .   60.00
    Pinback Button, 3" d, Huck Hound
    For President, 1960 . . . .   15.00
    Punch–Out Card, 4 x 7", Train–O–
    Gram, Santa Fe Twin Unit Diesel,
    set of 3, unused, Shredded Wheat,
    1956 . . . .   30.00
    Puppet, Banana Splits, Bingo, plastic,
    1969 . . . .   10.00
    Radio, Tony the Tiger, 8" h, figural,
    plastic, 1970s 20.00
    Ring, Flasher, Yogi and Boo Boo,
    1960 . . . .   18.00
    Spoon, Dennis The Menace, silver
    plate 20.00
    Toy, Wacky Races Bi–Plane, Muttley,
    missing one wing support, 1969 . .   50.00
Nabisco
    Game, Rin Tin Tin Bead In Hole
    Game, circular casing, 1956 . . . .   12.00
    Ring, brass, portrait, 1950 . . . . 50.00
Post
    Comic Book, Baseball Facts & Fun,
    52 pgs, Sugar Crisp 30.00
    Pin, Roy Rogers, Grape Nut Flakes,
    1953 . . . .   5.00
    Record, 33⅓ rpm, Archies,
    Jingle–Jangle, 1968–70 . . . .   5.00
    Toy
        Car, Chitty Chitty Bang Bang, plas-
        tic, two–tone, cardboard wings,
        1968 . . . .   30.00

Mighty   Mouse   Merry–Pack,
punch–out sheets, Alpha Bits,
c1956 . . . .   60.00
Rickshaw, plastic, So–Hi figure
pulls cart, Rice Krinkles, 1965   85.00
Quaker
    Book, Dick Tracy, Quaker Oats,
    c1939 . . . .   25.00
    Doll, stuffed, 1960s 28.00
    Figure, Cap'n Crunch, 8" h, vinyl,
    1971 . . . .   35.00
    Game, Space Match Card Game,
    color illus box, Quisp, 1968 . . . .   25.00
    Puppet, Cap'n Crunch, plastic, 1960s   24.00
    Ring, Quisp Meteorite, 1960s 55.00
    Telescope, 12" l extended, plastic,
    emb illus of Quake, marked
    "Quake is Better," 1960s 40.00
    Toy
        Cap'n Crunch Sea Cycle, plastic,
        Cap'n Crunch and Seadog figure,
        rubber band powered, orig mail-
        ing box, unused, 1960s 60.00
        Satellite Launcher, 2" d, plastic,
        rubber band powered launcher
        with emb "Quake" on each side,
        unused, Quisp, 1960s 40.00
        Wall Plaque, 8 x 10", Oath of
        Allegiance, paper, color illus, un-
        used, Cap'n Crunch, 1960s 24.00

CHARACTER & PROMOTIONAL GLASSES

Collecting Hints: Contemporary character and
promotional glasses are usually produced in series. It is important to collect the full series, including any color variations. This is not as easy
as it sounds. Sports team glasses are frequently issued regionally, i.e., Philadelphia Eagles glasses
can appear just in the Philadelphia market while
San Diego Chargers glasses are available only in
the area around San Diego. Before paying a great
deal of money for a recent glass, ask yourself if
what may be rare in your area is common some-
where else. Any serious collector needs this
sense of perspective.

Some early examples were decorated with
lead–based paint. They should not be used for
drinking purposes.

Collectors place a premium on glasses with
out–of–the–box luster. The mere act of washing a
glass in a dishwasher or sink can lessen its value.
Avoid examples with any evidence of fading.

Because of their wide availability, character
and promotional drinking glasses should be collected only if they are in excellent to mint condi-

tion. Pay premium prices only for glasses that pre–date 1980. After that date, glasses were hoarded in quantity by distributors, dealers, and collectors.

History: Character and promotional drinking glasses date to the movie premiere of *Snow White and the Seven Dwarfs* in December of 1937. Libbey Glass and Walt Disney designed tumblers with a safety edge and sold the glasses through variety stores and local dairies. The glasses proved extremely popular. Today collector glasses can be found for almost every Disney character, cartoon, and movie theme.

In 1953 Welch's began to package their jelly in decorated tumblers that featured Howdy Doody and his friends. Once again, the public's response was overwhelming. Welch's soon introduced other cartoon characters, such as Mr. Magoo, in their tumbler series.

In the late 1960s, fast food restaurants and gasoline stations started to use drinking glasses as advertising premiums. Soft drink manufacturers like Coke and Pepsi saw the advertising potential and developed marketing plans focusing on licensed characters and movies. Sports team licensing also entered the picture. By the early 1980s hundreds of new glasses were being issued each year.

As the 1980s drew to a close, plastic drinking cups replaced glasses. The use of licensed images continued. While most collectors still prefer to collect glass, a few far–sighted individuals are stashing away pristine plastic examples.

References: Mark E. Chase and Michael Kelly, *Contemporary Fast Food and Drinking Glass Collectibles,* Wallace–Homestead, 1988, out–of–print; John Hervey, *Collector's Guide To Cartoon & Promotional Drinking Glasses,* L–W Book Sales, 1990, 1995 value update; Carol and Gene Markowski, *Tomart's Price Guide to Character & Promotional Glasses, Second Edition,* Tomart Publications, 1993.

Periodical: *Collector Glass News,* PO Box 308, Slippery Rock, PA 16057.

Animal Crackers, 1978
Dodo	**8.00**
Lyle	**8.50**
Annie and Sandy, Swenson's, 1982 . . .	**5.00**

Arby's
B C Ice Age, riding on wheel, 1981	**8.00**

Bicentennial, 1976
Bullwinkle, Crossing the Delaware, 11 oz	**8.00**
Rocky, In The Dawn's Early Light, 11 oz	**8.00**
Underdog, Never Fear, 16 oz	**9.00**
Movie Star Series, Charlie Chaplin . .	**6.00**
Thought Factory Series, First Flake, 1982	**7.00**

Wizard of Id, 1983
King	**12.00**
Knight	**10.00**
Wizard	**8.00**

Archies, 1971, 8 oz
Archie Takes The Gang For A Ride . .	**4.00**
Betty and Veronica Fashion Show . .	**4.00**
Hot Dog Goes To School	**3.50**

Battlestar Galactica, Universal Studios, 1979
Apollo	**7.50**
Commander Adama	**7.50**
Cyclon Warriors	**9.00**
Starbuck	**7.00**

Beatles, 6½" h, clear glass, black letters and illus, repeated illus of Beatles and Yea, Yea, Yea, 1960s	**45.00**

Big Top Peanut Butter, 1940–50
Girl I Left Behind, dark red	**5.00**
Good-By My Lover	**5.00**
K for Kangaroo, blue	**5.00**
Pop Goes the Weazel, blue	**5.00**
Yankee Doodle, red	**5.00**

Bugs Bunny, Happy Birthday Bugs . . .	**2.00**

Burger Chef
Endangered Series, Bengal Tiger, 1978	**6.00**
Frankenburger Scores A TD, 1977 . .	**8.00**
Jefferson, Thomas, Presidents Series	**5.00**
Washington, 1975 Bicentennial Series	**6.00**

Burger King
Burger King, 1979	**9.00**
Dallas Cowboys, Charlie Waters . . .	**5.00**
Denver Broncos, Moses	**7.50**
Empire Strikes Back	**2.50**
I've Got The Magic That It Takes, 1978	**10.00**
Jabba, Star Wars, 1983 . . ./. . . .	**2.00**
Luke Skywalker, 1977	**3.00**
Shake A Lot, 1979	**8.00**

Coca Cola
Betty, tray girl	**10.00**
Coke, German	**5.00**
Heritage Collector Series, Patrick Henry	**5.00**
Holly Hobbie, Good Friends Are Like Sunshine	**5.00**
Olympics, Sam the Eagle, boxing, 1980	**1.00**
Outdoor Scene, buttered corn	**5.00**

Santa
Elves	**5.00**
Reindeer flying over house, McCroy Stores	**10.00**

Crockett, Davy, 6½" h	**10.00**

DC Comics
Aquaman, 1978	**5.00**
Batman, 1966	**4.00**
Green Lantern	**8.00**
Shazam	**3.00**
Superman, 1975	**5.00**
Wonder Woman	**3.00**

Disney, Walt
  Donald Duck and Daisy, orange, 5" h **10.00**
  Fantasia, Canadian **10.00**
  Ferdinand The Bull, 1930s **12.00**
  Goofy, 1930s **15.00**
  Mickey, 1930s **18.00**
  Minnie, Mickey Mouse Club **9.00**
  Snow White and the Seven Dwarfs,
    4¾" h, 1939 . . . . **12.00**
  Winnie The Pooh, Winnie and
    friends, Sears **7.50**
Domino's Pizza, 1988
  Noid, beach chair **2.00**
  Noid, tennis **2.00**
Dr Pepper
  Hot Air Balloon **7.00**
  Mr Spock, Star Trek, 1976 . . . . **7.00**
  Tiffany type dec **3.00**
Good To The Last Drop, 5¼" h, clear
  glass, two black illus of cartoon type
  gas station attendants, orange ring
  bands, c1950 . . . . **10.00**
Harvey Cartoons
  Casper, blue **5.00**
  Ritchie Rich **3.00**
  Wendy **4.00**
Indy 500, 1954 . . . . **25.00**
Kellogg's, Tony **3.00**
Kentucky Derby
  1945, tall **375.00**
  1952, gold cup **125.00**
  1956 . . . . **50.00**
  1962 . . . . **50.00**
  1964 . . . . **40.00**
  1965 . . . . **50.00**
  1966 . . . . **38.00**
  1967 . . . . **38.00**
  1968 . . . . **38.00**
  1970 . . . . **38.00**
  1991 . . . . **4.00**
Lone Ranger, 1938 . . . . **50.00**
McDonalds
  Big Mac, McVote, 1986 . . . . **3.50**
  Camp Snoopy, Civilization is Over-
    rated **1.00**
  Garfield, mug **1.50**
  Hamburglar, 5⅝" h **2.00**
  Kermit the Frog, 1981 . . . . **3.00**
  Mac Tonight, microphone, 1988 . . . **4.00**
  Mayor McCheese Taking Pictures,
    1977 . . . . **2.00**
  Olympics, sailing, blue dec, mug . . . **1.50**
  Pittsburgh Steelers, Superbowl XIII,
    Bradshaw, Webster, and Green-
    wood **2.00**
  Ronald McDonald Saves The Falling
    Star, 1977 . . . . **3.50**
Marvel Comics
  Amazing Spiderman, 1977 . . . . **4.00**
  Fantastic Four, 1977 . . . . **2.00**
  Howard The Duck, 1977 . . . . **3.00**
  Hulk, 1978 . . . . **3.00**

MGM, Wizard of Oz **10.00**
Mobil, football, ten different logos,
  price for set **17.50**
National Periodical Publications
  Batman **8.00**
  Joker **8.00**
  Superman, Fighting the Dragon, clear
    glass, blue and pink text and illus,
    1965 copyright, 5¼" h **10.00**
  Wonder Woman **7.00**
Pan American Airlines, 5½" h, clear
  glass, weighted bottom, solid color il-
  lus of Holland, Portugal, France, or
  Italy, Pan Am logo, c1950, price for
  set of four **25.00**
Paramount Pictures, Inc, 1939
  Gulliver's Travels Sneak **35.00**
  Little King **35.00**
Pepsi
  Bambi **4.00**
  Caterpillar Tractor **3.00**
  Happy Birthday Goofy, 1978 . . . . . . **6.00**
  Jingle Bells, 1984 . . . . **5.00**
  Mickey, 1979 . . . . **5.00**
  Shere Kahn, 1977 . . . . **8.00**
Pizza Hut
  Bullwinkle, blue truck **7.50**
  Care Bears, Funshine Bear, 1983 . . . **8.00**
  Dudley Do–Right, helicopter **7.00**
  ET, Universal Studios, 1982 . . . . **5.00**
Schmoo, Al Capp, 1949 . . . . **35.00**
Warner Bros
  Beaky Buzzard, Cool Cat, kite, Action
    Series, 1976 . . . . **6.00**
  Cool Cat, 1973 . . . . **4.00**
  Daffy Duck, Bugs Bunny, hunting,
    Action Series, 1976 . . . . **6.00**
  Elmer Fudd, Bugs Bunny, Shotgun
    Sam, carrots, Action Series, 1976 **6.00**
  Foghorn Leghorn, 1973 . . . . **4.00**
  Pepe Le Pew, Canadian, 1978 . . . . . **7.50**
  Porky Pig, 1973 . . . . **3.00**

**Flintstones, Welch's Jelly, 8 oz, "The
Flintstones–Fred and Barney Play Golf,"
green image, white lettering, 1962, 4¼"
h, $6.00.**

Road Runner, catapult, tunnel, Action Series, 1976	6.00
Sylvester, 1973	4.00
Tasmanian Devil, 1973	6.00
Yosemite Sam, Speedy Gonzales, panning for gold, Action Series, 1976	6.00
Welch's, 8 oz	
Archies	3.50
Flintstones, 1963	15.00
Howdy Doody, 1953	45.00

CHILDREN'S BOOKS

Collecting Hints: Most collectors look for books by a certain author or illustrator. Others are interested in books from a certain time period such as the 19th century. Accumulating the complete run of a series such as Tom Swift, Nancy Drew, or the Hardy Boys is of interest to some collectors. Subject categories are popular too, and include ethnic books, mechanical books, first editions, award–winning books, certain kinds of animals, rag books, Big Little Books, and those with photographic illustrations.

A good way to learn about children's books is to go to libraries and museums where special children's collections have been developed. Books on various aspects of children's literature are a necessity. You also should read a general book on book collecting to provide you with background information. Significant bits of information can be found on the title page and verso of the title page of a book. This information is especially important in determining the edition of a book. You eventually will want to own a few reference books most closely associated with your collection.

Although children's books can be found at all the usual places where antiques and collectibles are for sale, also seek out book and paper shows. Get to know dealers who specialize in children's books; ask to receive their lists or catalogs. Some dealers offer to locate certain books for you. Most used and out–of–print book stores have a section with children's books. If your author or illustrator is still actively writing or illustrating, a regular book store may carry his most recent book.

Things to be considered when purchasing books are the presence of a dust jacket or box, condition of the book, the edition, quality of illustrations and binding, and the prominence of the author or illustrator. Books should be examined very carefully to make sure that all pages and illustrations are present. Missing pages will reduce the value of the book. Try to buy books in the best condition you can afford. Even if your budget is limited, you can still find very nice inexpensive children's books if you keep looking.

History: William Caxton, a printer in England, is considered to have been the first publisher of children's books. Among his early publications was *Aesop's Fables* printed in 1484. Other very early books include John Cotton's *Spiritual Milk for Boston Babes* in 1646, *Orbis Pictis* translated from the Latin about 1657, and *The New England Primer* in 1691.

Children's classics had their beginning with *Robinson Crusoe* in 1719, *Gulliver's Travels* in 1726, and Perrault's *Tales of Mother Goose* translated into English in 1729. The well–known *A Visit from St. Nicholas* by Clement C. Moore appeared in 1823. Some of the best–known children's works were published between 1840 and 1900, including Lear's *Book of Nonsense*, Andersen's and Grimm's Fairy Tales, *Alice in Wonderland*, *Hans Brinker*, *Little Women*, *Tom Sawyer*, *Treasure Island*, *Heidi*, *A Child's Garden of Verses*, and *Little Black Sambo*.

Series books for boys and girls began around the turn of the century. The Stratemeyer Syndicate, established about 1906, became especially well known for their series, such as Tom Swift, The Bobbsey Twins, Nancy Drew, Hardy Boys, and many others.

Following the turn of the century, informational books such as Van Loon's *The Story of Mankind* were published. This book received the first Newbery Medal in 1922. This award, given for the year's most distinguished literature for children, was established to honor John Newbery, an English publisher of children's books. Biographies and poetry also became popular.

The most extensive development, however, has been with picture books. Photography and new technologies for reproducing illustrations have made picture book publishing a major part of the children's book field. The Caldecott Medal, given for the most distinguished picture book published in the United States, was established in 1938. The award, which honors Randolph Caldecott, an English illustrator from the 1800s, was first given in 1938 to Dorothy Lathrop for *Animals of the Bible*.

During the late 1800s, novelty children's books appeared. Lothar Meggendorfer, Ernest Nister, and Raphael Tuck were the most well–known publishers of these fascinating pop–up and mechanical or movable books. The popularity of this type of book has continued to the present. Some of the early movable books are being reproduced, especially by Intervisual Communication, Inc., of California.

Books that tie in with children's television programs, e.g., Sesame Street, and toys, e.g., Cabbage Patch dolls, have become prominent. Modern merchandising methods include multimedia packaging of various combinations of books, toys, puzzles, cassette tapes, videos, etc. There are even books which unfold and become a costume to be worn by children.

References: Barbara Bader, *American Picture Books From Noah's Ark To The Beast Within*, Macmillan, 1976; E. Lee Baumgarten, *Price List for Children's and Illustrated Books for the Years 1880–1940, Sorted by Artist*, published by author, 1993; E. Lee Baumgarten, *Price List for Children's and Illustrated Books for the Years 1880–1940, Sorted by Author*, published by author, 1993; Margery Fisher, *Who's Who In Children's Books: A Treasury of the Familiar Characters of Childhood*, Holt, Rinehart and Winston, 1975; Virginia Haviland, *Children's Literature, A Guide To Reference Sources*, Library of Congress, 1966, first supplement 1972, second supplement 1977, third supplement 1982; Bettina Hurlimann, *Three Centuries Of Children's Books In Europe*, tr. and ed. by Brian W. Alderson, World, 1968; Norman E. Martinus and Harry L. Rinker, *Warman's Paper*, Wallace–Homestead, 1994; Jack Matthews, *Toys Go To War: World War II Military Toys, Games, Puzzles, & Books*, Pictorial Histories Publishing, 1994; Cornelia L. Meigs, ed., *A Critical History of Children's Literature*, 2nd ed, Macmillan, 1969.

Periodicals: *Book Source Monthly*, 2007 Syossett Dr., PO Box 567, Cazenovia, NY 13035; *Martha's KidLit Newsletter*, PO Box 1488, Ames, IA 50010; *Mystery & Adventure Series Review*, PO Box 3488, Tucson, AZ 85722; *Yellowback Library*, PO Box 36172, Des Moines, IA 50315.

Collectors' Clubs: Louisa May Alcott Memorial Assoc., PO Box 343, Concord, MA 01742; Horatio Alger Society, 4907 Allison Dr., Lansing, MI 48910; International Wizard of Oz Club (L. Frank Baum), 220 N. 11th St., Escanaba, MI 49829; Thorton W. Burgess Society, Inc., PO Box 45, East Sandwich, MA 02537; Burroughs Bibliophiles (Edgar Rice Burroughs), Burroughs Memorial Collection, Univ. of Louisville Library, Louisville, KY 40292; Randolph Caldecott Society, 112 Crooked Tree Trail, Moultrie Trails, RR #4, Saint Augustine, FL 32086; Lewis Carroll Society of North America, 617 Rockford Rd., Silver Spring, MD 20902; Dickens Society, 100 Institute Rd., Worcester Polytech, Dept. of Humanities, Worcester, MA 01609; Kate Greenaway Society, PO Box 8, Norwood, PA 19074; Happyhours Brotherhood, 87 School Street, Fall River, MA 02770; Kipling Society (Rudyard Kipling), c/o Dr. Enamul Karim, Dept. of English, Rockford College; Rockford, IL 61107; New York C. S. Lewis Society, c/o Jerry L. Daniel, 419 Springfield Ave., Westfield, NJ 07092; Melville Society (Herman Melville), c/o Donald Yannella, Dept. of English, Glassboro State College, Glassboro, NJ 08028; Mystery and Detective Series Review, PO Box 3488, Tucson, AZ 85722; Mythopoeic Society, PO Box 6707, Altadena, CA 91003; National Fantasy Fan Federation, 1920 Division St., Murphysboro, IL 62966; Series Book Collector Society, c/o Jack Brahce, 5270 Moceri Ln., Grand Blanc, MI 48439; Stowe–Day Foundation (Harriet Beecher Stowe), 77 Forest St., Hartford, CT 06105; American Hobbit Association (J. R. R. Tolkien), Rivendell–EA, 730 F Northland Rd., Forest Park, OH 45240; American Tolkien Society, PO Box 373, Highland, MI 48031; Tolkien Fellowships, c/o Bill Spicer, 329 N. Ave. 66, Los Angeles, CA 90042; Mark Twain Boyhood Home Assoc., 208 Hill Street, Hannibal, MO 63401; Mark Twain Memorial, 351 Farmington Ave., Hartford, CT 06105; Mark Twain Research Foundation, Perry, MO 63462.

Libraries and Museums: Many of the clubs maintain museums. *Subject Collections* by Lee Ash (ed.) contains a list of public and academic libraries which have children's book collections. Large collections can be found at: Florida State Univ., Tallahassee, FL; Free Library of Philadelphia, PA; Library of Congress, Washington, DC; Pierpont Morgan Library, New York, NY; Toronto Public Library, Toronto, Ontario, Canada; Uncle Remus Museum (Joel Chandler Harris), Eatonton, GA; Univ of Minnesota, Walter Library, Minneapolis, MN; Univ of South Florida, Tampa, FL.

Notes: Prices are based on first editions with a dust jacket (dj) and in very good condition. The absence of a dust jacket, later printings, and a condition less than "very good" are all factors that lessen the value of a book.

Autographs and special boxes are additional factors that will increase the value. Books that have been award winners, e.g., Newbery, Caldecott, etc., generally are higher in value.

Reprints: A number of replicas of antique originals are now appearing on the market, with most being done by Evergreen Press and Merrimack. A new "Children's Classics" series offers reprints of books illustrated by Jessie Willcox Smith, Edmund Dulac, Frederick Richardson, and possibly others.

Anderson, Hans Christian, *The Nightingale*, Nancy Ekholm Burkert, illus, Harper & Row, 1965, 33 pgs, 1st ed, dj	**25.00**
Anglund, Joan Walsh, *A Friend is Someone Who Likes You*, Harcourt, Brace & World, 1958, 1st ed	**12.00**
Appleton, Victor, *Tom Swift and His Great Searchlight*, Grosset & Dunlap, 1912, 214 pgs	**8.00**
Beard, Patten, *Twilight Tales*, Ruth Caroline Eger, illus, Rand McNally, 1929, 66 pgs	**14.00**
Blos, Joan W., *A Gathering of Days*, Scribners, 1979, 145 pgs, 1st ed, dj, 1980 Newbery Medal	**20.00**

Blyton, Enid, *Just Time for a Story*, Grace Lodge, illus, MacMillan, 1948, 144 pgs 10.00

Boston, Lucy M., *The Stones of Green Know*, Peter Boston, illus, Atheneum, 1976, 117 pgs, 1st ed, dj 16.00

Brooks, Walter, *Freddy the Cowboy*, Kurt Wiese, illus Knopf, 233 pgs, 1st ed, dj 20.00

Browning, Robert, *Pied Piper of Hamelin*, Roger Duroisin, illus, Grosset & Dunlap, 1936, 1st ed, dj   17.00

Burgess, Thornton W., *The Adventures of Grandfather Frog*, Harrison Cady, illus, Little, Brown, 1944, 96 pgs, dj   20.00

Thornton W. Burgess, *The Adventures Of Paddy The Beaver*, Little, Brown & Co., 1917, 4¾ x 7 x 4½", $10.00.

Calhoun, Frances Boyd, *Miss Minerva and William Green Hill*, Reilly & Britton, 1909, 212 pgs 11.00

Carroll, Lewis, *Alice's Adventures in Wonderland*, A. E. Jackson, illus, Garden City, 216 pgs 45.00

Chadwick, Lester, *Baseball Joe Club Owner*, Cupples & Leon, 1926, 244 pgs   12.00

Chapman, Allen, *Ralph and the Missing Mail Pouch*, Grosset & Dunlap, 1924, 242 pgs, dj 8.00

Clyne, Geraldine, *The Jolly Jump-ups Number Book*, McLoughlin, 1950, 6 pop ups 35.00

Collodi, C., *Pinocchio*, Maria L. Kirk, illus, Lippincott, 1914, 234 pgs, 1st ed   32.00

Dahl, Ronald, *Charlie and the Great Glass Elevator*, Knopf, 163 pgs, 1st ed, dj 16.00

Daniels, Leslie N, *Jack Armstrong the All–American Boy and the Ivory Tower Treasure*, Whitman, 1937, 424 pp, Big Little Book, illus, Henry E. Vallely, #1435 .... 16.00

De Angeli, Marguerite, *Ted and Nina Have a Happy Rainy Day*, Doubleday, 1936, 1st ed, dj 27.00

De Jong, Meindert, *The Wheel on the School*, Maurice Sendak, illus, Harper, 1954, 298 pgs, 1st ed, dj ... 30.00

Deming, Richard, *Dragnet*, Whitman, 1957, 282 pgs, (Whitman TV series)   3.00

Dickey, James, *Tucky the Hunter*, Marie Angel, illus, Crown, 1978, 48 pgs, dj 15.00

Disney, Walt, *Mickey Mouse Takes A Vacation*, Franklin Watts, 1976, puppet book 15.00

Dixon, Franklin W., *Following the Sun Shadow*, Grosset & Dunlap, 1932, 215 pgs, dj, (Ted Scott Series) 5.00

DuBois, William Pene, *The Forbidden Forest*, Harper & Row, 1978, 56 pgs, 1st ed, dj 17.00

Emberley, Ed, *London Bridge is Falling Down*, Little, Brown, 1967, 32 pgs, 1st ed, dj 20.00

Ernest, Edward, *The Animated Circus Book*, Julian Wehr, Animateons, Saalfield, 1943 .... 35.00

Farquharson, Martha, *Elsie Dinsmore*, Dodd, Mead, 1896, 342 pgs, 25 yr ed   4.00

Fitzhugh, Percy Keese, *Tom Slade in the North Woods*, Howard L. Hastings, illus, Grosset & Dunlap, 244 pgs, dj   6.00

Frees, Harry Whittier, *Circus Day at Catnip Center*, Manning, 1932, wraps   12.00

Garis, Howard R., *Uncle Wiggily's Fortune*, Elmer Rache, illus, Platt & Munic, 1942, 186 pgs 8.00

Graham, Lynda, *Pinky Marie*, Ann Kirn, illus, Saalfield, 1939, wraps 22.00

Gray, William, *Dick and Jane*, Scott, Foresman, 1930, 40 pgs, wraps 17.00

Johnny Gruelle, *Beloved Belinda*, 1926, $60.00.

Gruelle, Johnny
  Beloved Belindy 1926 . . . .   60.00
  Wooden Willie Donohue, Volland,
  1927 . . . .   50.00
Haviland, Virginia, *Favorite Fairy Tales
  Told in Italy,* Evaline Hess, illus, Little,
  Brown, 1965, 90 pgs, 1st ed, dj 15.00
Heisenfelt, Kathryn, *Jane Withers and
  the Swamp Wizard,* Whitman, 1944,
  242 pgs, dj 20.00
Hoban, Russell, *Emmet Otter's Jug–
  Band Christmas,* Lillian Hoban, illus,
  Parents Magazine Press, 1971, 41
  pgs, 1st ed 10.00
Hope, Laura Lee
  Six Little Bunkers, 1918 . . . .   12.00
  Two Bunny Brown, c1920, dj 8.00
Jenks, Tudor, *The Century World's Fair
  Book for Boys and Girls,* Century,
  1893, 245 pgs 15.00
Keene, Carolyn, *The Clue in the
  Crumbling Wall,* Grosset & Dunlap,
  1945, 217 pgs, dj, (Nancy Drew
  Series) 8.00
Kenny, Kathryn, *Trixie Belden and the
  Mystery at the Emerald,* Whitman,
  1965, 254 pgs 2.00
Lenski, Lois, *Coal Camp Girl,*
  Lippincott, 1959, 173 pgs, 1st ed, dj   25.00
Lindman, Maj., *Flicka, Ricka, Dicka
  and the Girl Next Door,* Whitman,
  1938, 1st ed, dj 25.00
Little Boy Blue, Dean's Rag Book, 1905
  Ragbook 22.00
Mack, Nila, *Let's Pretend,* Whitman,
  1948, 68 pgs 15.00
Maybee, Bette Lou, *Barbie's Fashion
  Success,* Random House, 1962, 188
  pgs 10.00
Mitchell, Lebbeus, *Bobby in Search of a
  Birthday,* Joseph Pierre Nuyttons, il-
  lus, Volland, 1916, 64 pgs, 1st ed   .   30.00
Montgomery, Frances Trego, *Billy
  Whiskers Stowaway,* David Jadwyn,
  illus, Saalfield, 1930, 146 pgs 12.00
Montgomery, L. M., *Anne of the Island,*
  Page, 1915, 326 pgs, 1st ed 15.00
Nelson, Faith, *Randolph the Bear Who
  Said No,* Nedda Walker, illus,
  Wonder Book, 1946 . . . .   2.00
Newman, Isidora, *The Legend of the
  Tulip and Other Fairy Flowers,* Willy
  Pogany, illus, Whitman, 1926 . . . . .   9.00
Norton, Mary, *The Borrowers Afield,*
  Beth and Joe Drush, illus, Harcourt,
  1955, 193 pgs, 1st ed, dj 35.00
O'Day, Dean, *Shirley Temple Story
  Book,* Corrine and Bill Bailey, illus,
  Saalfield, 1935, 106 pgs, dj 28.00
Pansy (Isabell Alden), *Four Girls at
  Chautauqua,* D. Lothrop, 1876, 474 pgs   21.00
Pease, Howard, *The Mystery on

Telegraph Hill, Doubleday, 1961,
  216 pgs, 1st ed, dj 12.00
Perkins, Lucy Fitch, *The French Twins,*
  Houghton, Mifflin, 1918, 201 pgs, 1st
  ed 12.00
Petersham, Maud & Miska, *The Story
  Book of Trains,* Winston, 1935, dj . .   8.00
Piper, Watty, *Children of Other Lands,*
  Lucille W. and H. C. Holling, illus,
  Platt & Munk, 1933 . . . .   18.00
Rae, John, *Grasshopper Green and the
  Meadow Mice,* Algonquin, 1922 . . .   18.00
Richards, Mel, *Peter Rabbit the Magi-
  cian,* manufactured for Jewel Tea Co,
  1942, spiral in box, contains six
  magic tricks with wand 35.00
Rip Van Winkle, McLoughlin, linen . . .   30.00
Seredy, Kate, *Lazy Tinka,* Viking, 1962,
  57 pgs, 1st ed, dj 22.00
Sidney, Margaret, *The Five Little Peppers
  at School,* Lothrop, 1903, 453 pgs . .   8.00
Sutton, Margaret, *The Secret of the
  Barred Window,* Pelagie Doane, illus,
  Grosset & Dunlap, 1943, 207 pgs, dj,
  (Judy Bolton) 6.00
Taylor, Elizabeth, *Nibbles & Me,* Duell,
  Sloan & Pearce, 1946, 77 pgs, dj . . .   20.00
Thorndyke, Helen Louise, *Honey
  Bunch: Her First Days on the Farm,*
  Grosset & Dunlap, 1923, 182 pgs . .   3.00
Tousey, Sanford, *Airplane Andy,*
  Doubleday, Doran, 1942, 43 pgs . . .   8.00
Upham, Elizabeth, *Little Brown Bear
  and His Friends,* Marjorie Hartwell,
  illus, Platt & Munk, 1952 . . . .   14.00
Vandegriff, Peggy, *Dy–Dee Dolls Days,*
  Rand McNally, 1937 . . . .   15.00
Webster, Frank V., *The Boy Scouts of
  Flenox,* Cupples & Leon, 1915, 212
  pgs 4.00
West, Jerry, *The Happy Hollisters and
  the Ice Carnival,* Doubleday, 1958,
  180 pgs, dj 3.00
Wilde, Oscar, *The Happy Prunie and
  Other Fairy Tales,* Spencer Baird
  Nichols, illus, Frederick A. Stoker,
  1913, 204 pgs, 1st ed 225.00
Winfield, Arthur M., *The Rover Boys on
  the River,* Grosset & Dunlap, 1905,
  254 pgs 9.00

CHILDREN'S DISHES

Collecting Hints: Children's dishes were played
with, so a bit of wear is to be expected. Avoid
rusty metal dishes. Also avoid broken glass
dishes.

History: Dishes for children to play with have
been popular from Victorian times to the present.

Many glass companies made small child–size sets in the same patterns as large table sets. Many young girls delighted in using a set just like mother's.

During the period when Depression glass was popular, the manufacturers also made child–size pieces to complement the full–size lines. These child–size dishes were used for tea parties, doll parties, and many other happy occasions.

Child–size dishes are found in aluminum, tin, china, and glass.

References: Doris Anderson Lechler, *Children's Glass Dishes, China and Furniture,* Collector Books, 1983, 1991 value update; Doris Anderson Lechler, *Children's Glass Dishes, China, Furniture, Volume II* Collector Books, 1986, 1993 value update; Doris Lechler, *English Toy China,* Antique Publications, 1989; Doris Lechler, *Toy Glass,* Antique Publications, 1989; Lorraine May Punchard, *Child's Play,* published by author, 1982; Lorraine May Punchard, *Playtime Kitchen Items and Table Accessories,* published by author, 1993; Noel Riley, *Gifts For Good Children: The History of Children's China, Part I, 1790–1890,* Richard Dennis Publications, 1991; Ellen Tischbein Schroy, *Warman's Glass, Second Edition,* Wallace–Homestead, 1995; Margaret and Kenn Whitmyer, *Collector's Encyclopedia of Children's Dishes: An Illustrated Value Guide,* Collector Books, 1993, 1995 value update.

Collectors' Club: Toy Dish Collectors, PO Box 351, Camillus, NY 13031.

See: Akro Agate

Akro Agate, small size unless noted
Bowl, Chiquita, fired–on red	**5.00**
Cereal Bowl, J Pressman, fired–on red	**7.00**
Creamer	
Chiquita	
Fired–on color, cobalt blue	**7.00**
Green	**4.00**
J Pressman, fired–on color, cobalt blue	**8.00**
Octagonal, white, closed handle, larger size	**8.00**
Cup	
Chiquita	
Fired–on, red	**5.00**
Green	**3.50**
Transparent Cobalt Blue	**12.00**
Concentric Ring	
Aqua	**20.00**
Green Opaque	**9.00**
Lavender	**35.00**
Interior Panel	
Green, large	**9.00**
Pink	**15.00**
J Pressman, fired–on color, red . . .	**6.00**
Octagonal, green opaque, closed handle, larger size	**4.00**

Raised Daisy, green	**32.50**
Stacked Disc	
Green	**8.00**
Pink	**8.00**
Stippled Band, transparent green	**11.00**
Pitcher, Interior Panel, transparent green, 2⅞" h	**12.00**
Plate, dinner	
Chiquita, green	**2.00**
Concentric Ring	
Blue	**8.00**
Medium Green	**14.00**
Opaque Green	**5.00**
Interior Panel, yellow, 4¼" d	**10.00**
J Pressman	
Fired–on Color, green	**4.00**
Transparent Cobalt Blue	**8.00**
Octagonal, green opaque, larger size	**4.00**
Stippled Band, transparent green	**5.00**
Saucer	
Chiquita	
Green	**1.50**
Transparent Cobalt Blue	**4.00**
Concentric Ring	
Aqua	**15.00**
Beige	**7.00**
Pink	**8.00**
White	**4.00**
Interior Panel	
Green, 2¾" d	**3.00**
Pink	**15.00**
J Pressman, fired–on color, yellow	**4.00**
Octagonal, lime, larger size	**4.00**
Raised Daisy, blue	**16.00**
Stippled Band, transparent green	**3.50**
Set	
Concentric Rib, Playtime #280, blue creamer, four green cups, blue pitcher, four green plates, four white saucers, blue sugar, blue teapot, white teapot lid, four white tumblers, 21 pcs, orig box	**175.00**
Interior Panel, lemonade and oxblood, 17 pcs, orig box	**600.00**
Stacked Disc, 16 pcs, white creamer, blue cup, green dinner plate, pink saucer, white sugar, blue teapot, pink teapot lid	**150.00**
Stippled Band, 17 pcs, topaz, larger size, no box	**250.00**
Sugar, Chiquita, transparent cobalt blue	**8.00**
Teapot, cov	
Chiquita, green	**12.00**
Concentric Ring	
Blue, white lid	**14.50**
White, white lid	**18.00**
Interior Panel, topaz, larger size . .	**65.00**
J Pressman, fired–on color, cobalt blue	**20.00**

Stacked Disc
Blue, white lid **12.00**
Pumpkin, pink lid, small chip . . **12.00**
Stippled Band, transparent green **18.00**
Teapot, open
Interior Panel
Green Luster, 2⅜" h **12.00**
Transparent Green, 2⅝" h **20.00**
J Pressman, transparent green **45.00**
Tumbler
Octagonal, ivory, larger size **10.00**
Stacked Disc, ivory **10.00**
Stacked Disc Interior Panel, trans-
parent green **12.50**
Aluminum, tea set, nursery rhyme dec,
15 pcs **22.00**
China
Cake Plate, Willow Ware, open han-
dles **20.00**
Casserole, cov, Willow Ware, 4¾" . . **25.00**
Cereal Bowl
Children with pumpkin **12.00**
Rabbit with basket and flowers,
Salem China **12.00**
Creamer
Phoenix Bird **20.00**
Willow Ware **9.00**
Cup and Saucer, Willow Ware **10.00**
Dinner Service, white, floral sprays,
six plates, two cov tureens, serving
plate, ftd compote **90.00**
Gravy Boat, Willow Ware **25.00**
Plate
American Modern, pink **95.00**
Children on rocking horse **10.00**
Girl with lamb and flowers **10.00**
Luray, pastel **4.00**
Willow Ware
3¼" **6.00**
4½" **8.50**
Platter, Willow Ware, 4¼" **14.00**
Soup Set, 6 x 3½" tureen, cov, under-
plate, ladle, six 4½" bowls, blue
acorn dec, Staffordshire marks . . . **130.00**
Tea Set
13 pcs, PA Dutch design, West
Germany, MIB **40.00**
15 pcs, dressed cats, Germany . . . **165.00**
16 pcs, Nippon, rabbits on sleds,
rising sun mark **150.00**
Cutlery, 2¼" l, knife, fork, spoon,
wooden handles, marked "Germany,"
MIB **12.00**
Depression Glass
Creamer, Cherry Blossom, pink **45.00**
Creamer and Sugar, Doric and Pansy,
Ultra **75.00**
Cup, Cherry, pink **35.00**
Cup and Saucer
Cherry Blossom, Delphite **40.00**
Diana, crystal **4.50**
Twentieth Century, decals **5.00**

Plate, Moderntone
Blue **10.00**
Gray **10.00**
Green **10.00**
Pink **10.00**
Yellow **10.00**
Saucer
Cherry Blossom, pink **6.50**
Moderntone
Green **7.75**
Pink **7.75**
Yellow **7.75**
Set
Server, Little Deb, Moderntone pat-
tern **95.00**
Tea
Cherry Blossom, delphite, 14 pcs **310.00**
Doric and Pansy, pink, 14 pcs,
no box **260.00**
Little Hostess, Moderntone, ma-
roon, gray, chartreuse, dark
green, maroon teapot and cov,
16 pcs, no box **225.00**
Sugar, Laurel, ivory, McKee **32.50**
Federal Glass Co, cup and saucer,
lavender flashed dec **35.00**
Graniteware
Bowl, blue and white swirls **40.00**
Coffeepot, white **60.00**
Cup and Saucer, blue **30.00**
Pie Plate, gray, 5" d **8.50**
Plate, green and white swirls, 2½" d **8.50**
Teacup and Saucer, white, gold bor-
der, green leaf dec, marked
"England" **18.00**

**Tea Set, porcelain, white ground, boy
with blue shirt, girl with orange dress, 17
pc set, box marked "Made in Japan,"
$40.00.**

Silver Plated, Little Mother's Service, 26
pcs, butter spreader, six forks, six knives,
six teaspoons, German, orig box . . . **95.00**
Tin
Cup, saucer, plate, and tray, Little Red
Riding Hood **24.00**

Dinner Set, white rabbit dec, light blue ground, 18 pcs	**30.00**
Play Set, cooking utensils, pots, pans, teapot, wooden knobs, 12 pcs, MIB	**18.00**

Tea Set

8 pcs, Ohio Art, Snow White, orig box	**125.00**
11 pcs, elephants	**35.00**
25 pcs, Raggedy Ann and Andy . .	**25.00**

CHRISTMAS ITEMS

Collecting Hints: Beware of reproduction ornaments. New reproductions are usually brighter in color and have shiny paint. Older ornaments should show some signs of handling. It is common to find tops replaced on ornaments.

History: Early Christmas decorations and ornaments were handmade. In 1865 the Pennsylvania Dutch brought the first glass ornaments to America. By 1870, glass ornaments were being sold in major cities. By the turn of the century, the demand created a cottage industry in European countries. Several towns in Germany and Czechoslovakia produced lovely ornaments, which were imported by F. W. Woolworth, Sears, etc., who found a ready market.

References: Ann Bahar, *Santa Dolls: Historical to Contemporary,* Hobby House Press, 1992; Robert Brenner, *Christmas Through the Decades: A Guide To Christmas Antiques,* Schiffer Publishing, 1993; Polly and Pam Judd, *Santa Dolls & Figurines Price Guide: Antique to Contemporary, Revised,* Hobby House Press, 1994; Chris Kirk, *The Joy of Christmas Collecting,* L–W Book Sales, 1994; Norman E. Martinus and Harry L. Rinker, *Warman's Paper,* Wallace–Homestead, 1994; Robert M. Merck, *Deck The Halls: Treasures of Christmases Past,* Abbeville Press, 1992; Mary Morrison, *Snow Babies, Santas and Elves: Collecting Christmas Bisque Figures,* Schiffer Publishing, 1993; Maggie Rogers and Peter Hallinan, *The Santa Claus Picture Book,* E. P. Dutton, 1984; Maggie Rogers and Judith Hawkins, *The Glass Christmas Ornament, Old & New,* Timber Press, 1977; Lissa and Dick Smith, *Christmas Collectibles: A Guide To Selecting, Collecting and Enjoying The Treasures of Christmas Past,* Chartwell Books, 1993; Margaret and Kenn Whitmyer, *Christmas Collectibles: Identification and Value Guide, Second Edition,* Collector Books, 1994.

Periodicals: *Golden Glow of Christmas Past,* 6401 Winsdale St., Golden Valley, MN 55427; *I Love Christmas,* PO Box 5708, Coralville, IA 52241; *Ornament Collector,* RR #1, Canton, IL 61520.

Museums: Many museums prepare special Christmas exhibits.

Additional Listings: Santa Claus.

REPRODUCTION ALERT

CHRISTMAS VILLAGE/GARDEN

Animals

Chicken, 1½" h, composition, metal feet	**6.50**
Cow, 3½" h, celluloid	**10.00**
Duck, celluloid, metal legs	**10.00**

Putz Animals, German, leather covered, wood legs, 2¾" h lion with wool mane, 4" h giraffe, price each, $35.00.

Goat, 3" h, celluloid	**8.00**
Horse, 4", composition, wooden legs, Germany	**38.00**
Lamb, 1½" h, standing in grass, plaster, Germany	**5.00**
Ram, 3½", celluloid	**7.50**
Sheep, 5", composition, wool covering, wooden legs, paper collar with bell, Germany	**55.00**
Stork, celluloid body and legs	**10.00**

Fence

Wire, green, four interlocking sections	**45.00**
Wooden, green and red, folding, 3"	**30.00**

Houses

Cardboard

Barn, faded red, tan trim	**40.00**
Church, 3½ x 6¼ x 10" h, grainy texture, white, red cellophane windows, gold trim	**50.00**
House, cellophane windows, bisque Santa on porch, 4", Japan	**10.00**
Paper, village, "Peaceful Valley Farm Set," Pan Confection Factory, Chicago, 1923	**48.00**

People

Couple, park bench, Barclay	**20.00**
Skater, Barclay	**10.00**
Sled rider, Barclay	**15.00**

NON TREE–RELATED ITEMS

Advertising Trade Card
Old Lion Coffee Trade Card, child and Christmas wreath around shoulders **7.00**
Santa Claus Soap, diecut, Santa with package on back **30.00**
Bank, chalkware, Santa climbing down chimney **55.00**
Book
Christmas Book, Christmas Cut Out Series, Charles Graham and Co .. **10.00**
Miracle on 34th St, Valentine Davies, Harcourt, Brace and Co, 1947 ... **10.00**
Night Before Christmas or A Visit from St Nicholas, McLaughlin Bros, 1896 .... **20.00**
Candleholder, figural, Santa **10.00**
Candy Box, cardboard, string handle, fireplace and stocking scene, 3 x 5", c1940–50 .... **5.00**
Candy Canes, chenille, 5 to 8" h, set of 5 .... **12.00**
Candy Container
Santa
On skis, 4¼" **18.00**
Wearing black stove pipe hat, papier mache **65.00**
Snowman, 7½", papier mache, red hat **12.00**
Church, wind–up, musical, mica cov wood, plays "Silent Night," 1930 ... **25.00**
Figure
Choir Boy, 3½" h, hard plastic **4.50**
Reindeer
3" h, celluloid, brown **7.50**
4", hard plastic **4.00**
Santa Claus riding on skis, bag of toys **15.00**

Light, glass, red outfit, yellow highlights on front, black on toys, dark green tones on tree, porcelain fixture, Japan, 9" h, $100.00.

Snowman, 8" h, hard plastic, electric light insert **7.00**
Greeting Cards
"At Christmas time may Peace o'er shadow you," sgd Prang, flowers, white fringe **15.00**
Children and dog playing in the snow, Tuck, Raphael, 4 x 2" **6.00**
"Merry Christmas and a Happy New Year," children playing in a toy room **5.00**
"Wishing you a Happy Christmas," child with sled and a doll, sgd Prang **12.00**
Jewelry, pin, 2" h, Christmas tree, multicolored rhinestones, Eisenberg **65.00**
Lamp, glass, metal, holder in base, wire handle
Four sided **25.00**
Six sided, collapsible **25.00**
Lantern, Snowman, glass, metal handle and base, 1950 .... **25.00**
Nativity Scene, cardboard
Boxed set, Dennison **10.00**
Fold out, standing emb, marked Germany, 4½ x 5½" **12.00**
Pinback Button
7/8" d, "Health to All," National Tuberculosis Assoc, Santa, Association symbol on his hat ... **7.00**
1¼" d, "Shop in Pottsville," Santa, white ground **15.00**
Postcard
A Merry Christmas, toy soldiers, cannons **3.00**
Christmas Wishes, children in sled pulled by two rabbits, Germany .. **4.00**
Reflector
Foil, bright colors, set of 6 .... **3.00**
Metal, jeweled, set of 6 .... **3.00**
Serving Tray, Coca–Cola, Santa, 1972 **35.00**
Stereograph Card, Keystone View Co, children, Santa peeping at each other through keyhole, 1899 .... **10.00**
Stocking
Red flannel, stenciled Santa and sleigh **5.00**
White flannel, red toe, bell trimmed top **7.00**
Toy, wind–up, reindeer, metal, rubber antlers, orig box, Japan **30.00**
Wreath, 10" d, chenille, candle **15.00**

TREE–RELATED ITEMS

Icicles, clear plastic, tree hooks, on orig card, set of 6 .... **2.00**
Light Bulb
Bubble, Noma **3.00**
Figural, milk glass
Baby, red stockings **20.00**
Birdcage **15.00**
Clown, red on white ball **25.00**

Dick Tracy	**40.00**
Dog, Sandy	**40.00**
Dog, yellow, polo player	**20.00**
Light Set, string, Noma, eight different	
figural bulbs, box	**100.00**
Ornament	
Beaded, double cross, Czechoslovakia	**15.00**
Cardboard, two sided, twelve letters	
of Alphabet, Germany, orig pkg ..	**10.00**
Chromolithograph, tinsel	
Bell, red and green	**10.00**
Little girl sleeping	**15.00**
Glass	
Pine Cone, 3½"	**12.00**
Santa, hp, Polish, orig box, set of 6	**18.00**
Zeppelin, US flag, spun glass tail,	
1920s	**85.00**
Tree	
Brush	
1½" h, green, red base	**1.25**
3" h, green, red base	**3.00**
5" h	
Green, decorated, red base	**10.00**
Green, red base	**5.00**
Red, decorated, red base	**10.00**
9" h, green, red base	**12.50**
Feather Tree	
9" h, white, sparse, sq base	**85.00**
12" h, green, candle clips, round	
base	**100.00**
Tree Stand, cast iron, three legs, black,	
bolted to hinged wood box	**30.00**
Tree Topper	
Angel, 4" h, hard plastic, white and	
silver	**4.50**
Star	
Krystal, lighted, orig box	**6.00**
Noma, metal, five candle bulbs ..	**24.00**
Tree Trim, foil rope, 72" l, red, silver,	
and green	**5.00**

CIGAR COLLECTIBLES

Collecting Hints: Concentrate on one geographic region or company. Cigar box labels usually are found in large concentrations. Check on availability before paying high prices.

History: Tobacco was one of the first export products of the American colonies. By 1750 smoking began to become socially acceptable for males. The cigar reached its zenith from 1880 to 1930 when it was the boardroom and after dinner symbol for the withdrawal of males to privacy and conversation.

Cigar companies were quick to recognize national political, sports and popular heroes. They encouraged them to use cigars and placed their faces on promotional material.

The lithograph printing press brought color and popularity to labels, seals and bands. Many have memories of a cigar band ring given by a grandfather or family friend. The popularity of the cigarette in the 1940s reduced the cigar to second place in the tobacco field. Today, cigar–related material is minimal due to the smaller number of companies making cigars.

References: Douglas Congdon–Martin, *Tobacco Tins: A Collector's Guide*, Schiffer Publishing, 1992; Joe Davidson, *The Art of the Cigar Label*, Wellfleet, 1989; Glyn V. Farber, *Hickey Brothers Cigar Store Tokens*, The Token and Medal Society, Inc., 1992; Tony Hyman, *Handbook of American Cigar Boxes*, Arnet Art Museum, 1979; Franklyn Kircher, *Tobacco Pocket Tin Guide*, published by author, 1984; Norman E. Martinus and Harry L. Rinker, *Warman's Paper*, Wallace–Homestead, 1994.

Collectors' Clubs: Cigar Label Collectors International, 14761 Pearl Rd. #154, Strongsville, OH 44136; International Seal, Label and Cigar Band Society, 8915 E. Bellevue St., Tucson, AZ 85715.

Periodical: *Tobacco Antiques and Collectibles Market*, Box 11652, Houston, TX 77293.

Museum: Arnet Collection, New York Public Library, New York, NY.

Advertising Trade Card, Dude Cigars,	
Simmons & Co, 1882	**20.00**
Binder, single, 5 Cents Cigar, 5½ x 8",	
color, 1910	**12.00**
Change Tray, Tom Moore Cigars	**20.00**
Cigar	
Buster Brown	**7.00**
Monogram, 5 Cents, 1910	**12.00**
Cigar Box Label, Big Bear, 4½" sq	**7.00**
Cigar Cutter	
Indian on motorcycle	**90.00**
Trick Lock Cigar Cutter, 1930s	**20.00**
Dish, 5¼" d, cigar band	**8.00**

Cigar Band Dish, 7⅛" d, $30.00.

Hatchet, Tom Moore Cigar	28.00
Humidor, Colt	150.00
Key Chain, Muriel Cigars	10.00

Label

Las Vegas Cigars, cigar crate	5.00
Rudolph Valentino, 2½ x 5", 1920s	8.00
Lighter, brass, counter model	65.00

Match Safe

Pierce's 9 Cigars	40.00
United Cigar, book shape	55.00
Mold, wood, 20 cavities, Miller, Dubrul & Peters	32.00

Note Pad, 2½ x 4½", celluloid cov, hinged

Civil Rights Havana Cigars, signing of Magna Carta illus, pencil holder and string, 1890s	20.00
Francie Wilson Havana Cigars, black and white portrait, cigar text inside cov, early 1900s	15.00
Pin, enameled, Tampa–Cuba Cigar Co	45.00

Pocket Mirror, 2⅛" d, Union Made Cigars, celluloid, light blue Union Cigar label facsimile, tan, black lettering, early 1900s 60.00

Sign

AK Walch's Cigar, 8 x 14", tin, red and white	65.00
Call Again, 5 Cents Cigar, red, white, and blue, cardboard, 7 x 16"	14.00
Dark Horse Cigar, 12 x 23", paper, two race horses trotting	65.00
Denby Cigar, tin, man with cigar	375.00
El Wadora Cigars, 24 x 36", tin, c1930	45.00
Eventual 5 Cent Cigar, red and green, cardboard, 7 x 20", 1920s	14.00
Pointers 5¢ Cigar, double sided	150.00
Pollocks Cigar, can with riverboats unloading and commercial buildings scene	175.00
Whip Handle Cigars, tin, buggy whip and lit cigar	375.00

Tin

Good Cheer Cigar, handled	60.00
Phillies	10.00
Sunset Trail Cigars	410.00
Tom Moore	25.00
Trimmer, pelican, figural	40.00

Watch Fob, 1¾", United Cigar Makers League, blue and white, metal strap loop, early 1900s 65.00

CIGARETTE ITEMS

Collecting Hints: Don't overlook the advertising which appeared in the national magazines of the 1940s to 1960s. The number of star and public heroes endorsing cigarettes is large. Modern promotional material for brands such as Marlboro and Salem has been issued in large numbers, and much

has been put aside by collectors. Most collectors tend to concentrate on the pre–1950 period.

History: Although the cigarette industry dates back to the late 19th century, it was the decades of the 1930s and 1940s that saw cigarettes become the dominant tobacco product. The cigarette industry launched massive advertising and promotional campaigns. Radio was one of the principal advertising vehicles. In the 1950s, television became the dominant advertising medium.

The Surgeon General's Report, which warned of the danger of cigarette smoking, led to restrictions on advertising and limited the places where cigarettes could be smoked. The industry reacted with a new advertising approach aimed at females and people in the 20– to 40–year age bracket. The need to continue the strong positive public image for cigarette smoking still leads to more and more cigarette–related items entering the collectibles marketplace.

References: Art Anderson, *Casinos and Their Ashtrays: A Collector's Guide with Values and Casino Histories*, published by author, 1994; Philip Collins, *Smokerama: Classic Tobacco Accoutrements*, Chronicle Books, 1992; Douglas Congdon–Martin, *Tobacco Tins: A Collector's Guide*, Schiffer Publishing, 1992; Urban K. Cummings *Ronson, World's Greatest Lighter*, Bird Dog Books, 1993; James Flanagan, *Collector's Guide To Cigarette Lighters: Identification & Values*, Collector Books, 1995; Franklyn Kircher, *Tobacco Pocket Tin Guide*, published by author, 1984; Murray Cards International, Ltd. (comp.), *Cigarette Card Values: 1992 Catalogue of Cigarette & Other Trade Cards*, Murray Cards International Ltd., 1992; Norman E. Martinus and Harry L. Rinker, *Warman's Paper*, Wallace–Homestead, 1994; A. M. W. van Weert, *The Legend of the Lighter*, Electa, 1995; Neil Wood, *Collecting Cigarette Lighters*, L–W Book Sales, 1994; Neil Wood, *Collecting Cigarette Lighters, Volume II*, L–W Book Sales, 1995; Neil Wood, *Smoking Collectibles: A Price Guide*, L–W Book Sales, 1994.

Periodical: *Tobacco Antiques and Collectibles Market*, Box 11652, Houston, TX 77283.

Collectors' Clubs: Ashtray Collectors Club, PO Box 11652, Houston, TX 77293; Cigarette Pack Collectors Assoc., 61 Searle St., Georgetown, MA 01833; International Lighter Collectors, Route 3, 136 Circle Dr., Quitman, TX 75783; International Seal, Label & Cigar Band Society, 8915 E. Bellevue St., Tucson, AZ 85715; Pocket Lighter Preservation Guild & Historical Society, 11220 W. Florissant, Suite 400, Florissant, MO 63033.

Ashtray, Griswold	38.00
Box, lead glass, hinged lid	35.00
Camera, Parliament	12.00

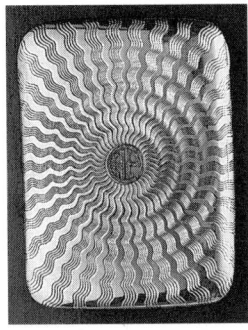

Cigarette Case, 14K yg, machine finish, lid set with monogram "HP" in rose diamonds, 80.5 dwts, $825.00.

Cigarette Card Album, German, 1950s, complete 50.00
Cigarette Case, 4 x 2", Ronson, unused   45.00
Cigarette Holder
   Amethyst, three compartments, silver dog dec 50.00
   Bone
      14K gold trim 28.00
      Trumpet shape, gold bowl 38.00
   Figural, sitting camel 75.00
   Gutta percha, gold band 28.00
Cigarette Lighter
   Advertising
      Chesterfield 15.00
      Hastings Piston Ring, 3" l, metal tube, removable black cap, red, yellow, and back trademark figure, yellow ground, 1940s 15.00
      Royal Crown Cola, brass, bottle shape 10.00
   Barcroft, PA state logo, MIB 125.00
   Evans, bone china 40.00
   Occupied Japan, china 40.00
   Ronson
      Crown 18.00
      Mayfair 35.00
   Zippo, truck logo 55.00
Cigarette Maker, V Master Deluxe, orig box 25.00
Cigarette Pack Holder, Camel, glass, figural, kneeling camel, painted 65.00
Counter Sign, Winston Cigarettes, lights up, clock 60.00
Lighter, Zippo, Phillips 66 .... 30.00
Matchbox
   Hunting scene, silver plated 35.00
   Lithophane 175.00
Matchbox Cover, sterling 9.00
Matchsafe
   Advertising, Red Top Dye, gutta percha, 2 pc 75.00
   Figural
      Book, stamps on side, matches on other 75.00

Dragon, ½ x 1½ x 3" h, brass, hinged head, c1890 .... 135.00
Package, unopened
   Lion 15.00
   Sunshine 15.00
   Wings 15.00
Poster, 12 x 18", paper, glossy, full color portrait
   Kool Cigarette, Willie the Penguin wearing military outfit 45.00
   Raleigh Cigarette, "Get War Stamps With Your B & W Coupons" inscription 20.00
Radio, Benson & Hedges, battery, MIB   20.00
Record, L & M Cigarettes, Christmas, Liggett & Meyers Tobacco Co giveaways, shows L & M TV quartet in Santa suits, orig carton holder 10.00
Sign
   Old Gold Cigarettes, 12 x 4", tin, emb, dancing box 25.00
   Piedmont Cigarettes, porcelain 125.00
   Viceroy, store hours 45.00
   Virginia Slims, metal 10.00
Thermometer
   Chesterfield, 13" l 40.00
   L & M 45.00
   Winston, round 60.00
Tin
   Camel 100's, round 45.00
   JBR Turkish Cigarette 12.50
   Lucky Strike 100's, round 44.00
   Phillip Morris 50's, round 38.00
   Players, Navy Cut 20.00
   Salem Cigarettes 20.00
   Sporting Cigarettes 18.00

CIRCUS ITEMS

Collecting Hints: Circus programs are one of the most popular items in this category. Individuals have collected them since the 1920s. Programs prior to the 1930s are hard to find; post–1930 material is readily available.

Model building plays an active part in collecting. Some kits are available. However, most collectors like·to build their models from scratch. Great attention is placed on accuracy of detail.

There are a wealth of books published about the circus. These are sought by collectors both for intrinsic as well as research value.

History: The 18th–century circus was a small traveling company of acrobats and jugglers, and the first record of an American troupe was at that time. Washington is known to have attended a circus performance.

By the mid–19th century the tent circus with accompanying side shows and menagerie became popular throughout America. P. T. Barnum was one of the early circus promoters. His American Museum in New York featured live animal acts in 1841. Other successful Barnum promotions included Jenny Lind in 1850, Tom Thumb from 1843 to 1883, and the purchase of Jumbo from the London Zoo in 1883.

The Ringlings and Barnum and Bailey brought a magical quality to the circus. The golden age of the tent circus was the 1920s to the 1940s, when a large circus would consist of over 100 railroad cars.

As television challenged live entertainment, the tent circus fell on hard times. Expenses for travel, food, staff, etc., mounted. A number of mergers took place, and many smaller companies simply went out of business. There are a few tent circuses remaining. However, most modern circuses now perform inside large convention centers.

Reference: Norman E. Martinus and Harry L. Rinker, *Warman's Paper,* Wallace–Homestead, 1994.

Periodical: *Circus Report,* 525 Oak Street, El Cerrito, CA 94530.

Collectors' Clubs: Circus Fans Assoc. of America, PO Box 59710, Potomac, MD 20859; The Circus Historical Society, 743 Beverly Park Place, Jackson, MI 49203; Circus Model Builders International, 347 Lonsdale Avenue, Dayton, OH 45419.

Museums: P.T. Barnum Museum, Bridgeport, CT; Circus World Museum Library–Research Center, Baraboo, WI; Ringling Circus Museum, Sarasota, FL.

Announcement, Ringling Bros and Barnum & Bailey Circus, "Due to the great number of requests for posters and lithographs, the management of Ringling Bros and Barnum & Bailey has been obliged to discontinue free distribution of such materials for private purposes," black and white, 4 x 6¼" 35.00
Book, *The Fabulous Showman. The Life and Times of P.T. Barnum,* Irving Wallace, 1959, 279 pgs, illus, hardbound, 5¾ x 8½" 3.00
Calendar, "Season's Greetings, Helen and Karl Wallenda," multicolor, 1977, 7¼ x 12¼" 10.00
Directory, The Great American Circus Directory, Informative Guide for Agents, Circus & Variety Artists, sample issue, 1976, 8 pgs, illus, 9 x 12" 15.00
Greeting Card, "1925–1926, Greetings From Ringling Bros. and Barnum & Bailey Combined Shows," multicolor, heavy paper 40.00
Letterhead, "The Original Arcaris, The Great and Only Knife Throwers, P.O.

Box 794, Brookfield, Ill (permanent address), Signoretta Rosina Tamborine Queen, Signor Gustaf Flagelette King, The Original Tamborine and Flagelette Solos In This Country," black and white images, 8½ x 14¼", creased 50.00
Magazine, *Cole Bros. Circus, America's Favorite Show,* 1942, multicolor cov, 34 pgs, 8¼ x 11" 30.00
Map, U.S., shows circus route, black and white, 7 x 5" 25.00
Mechanical Drawing, big top, Ringling Bros. and Barnum & Bailey Circus, 183 x 354', 59,372 sq ft, two plan views, 45 x 30" 65.00
Menu, "Fourth of July, Ringling Bros. and Barnum & Bailey Combined, The World's Largest Amusement Institution at Home on the Nation's Birthday, Bridgeport, CT, 1920," 6¼ x 9½" 22.00
Newspaper, *Sarasota Herald–Tribune,* circus edition, Sarasota, FL, Friday, March 24, 1944, "Circus comes to Town," 8 pgs 28.00
Pennant, Ringling Bros and Barnum & Bailey Circus, brown felt, white lettering and circus scenes, yellow trim and streamers, 1940s, 24" l 25.00
Photograph
Bird's–eye view of circus grounds including big top, black and white, 10¼ x 13", creased and torn 7.00
Ringling Brothers Barnum & Bailey Combined Circus group shot, sepia tone, 12 x 20", several creases ... 45.00
Pinback Button, "I Am a Lion Tamer in Mandel Brothers Circus," litho, black, white, red, and yellow, 1930–40, 1⅜" d 15.00
Post Card, Ringling Bros, fold–out, 1943 20.00
Poster
Clyde Beatty–Cole Bros Combined Circus, The World's Largest Circus, "Clyde Beatty in Person," Roland Butler, lion tamer, multicolor, 19 x 26" 90.00

Poster, Ringling Brothers and Barnum & Bailey, 20 x 28", $95.00.

Hoxie Bros Old Time Circus Land, One Mile West of Walt Disney World, multicolor view of circus grounds and big top, 20 x 27" ...   **60.00**
Print, pair of tigers, lady and elephant, lady and horse, clown, and Big Show entrance, black and white, 6½ x 7½"   **15.00**
Program, Ringling Bros and Barnum & Bailey Combined Shows, 1923 season, 14 pgs, illus, black and white, 6¾ x 10" **28.00**
Route Book, Ringling Bros and Barnum & Bailey, 1946 Route Book, The Greatest Show on Earth, red and black cov with clown sitting on elephant illus, 61 pgs, illus, black and white, 8¼ x 5" **15.00**
Route Card, Barnum & Bailey, Greatest Show on Earth, 1918 season, permanent address and winter quarters, Bridgeport, CT, lists date, town, state, R.R., and miles, multicolor, 9 x 15½"   **75.00**
Tickets, Clyde Beatty–Cole Bros Combined Circus, 1960 season, issued by F.F.R. Brown, black and red, 5½ x 2", price for pair **65.00**
Transfer, color, Ringling Bros World's Largest Menagerie, 9 x 11¼" **2.00**

CLEMINSON CLAY

Collecting Hints: Cleminson Clay produced novelty items such as pie birds, wall pockets, and spoon holders, as well as several dinnerware lines. Each piece was hand decorated with colored slip, which will account for slight variations from piece to piece. The Distlefink dinnerware line is currently finding favor with many collectors.

History: In 1941 Betty Cleminson established Cleminson Clay in the garage of her home in El Monte, California, with husband, George, handling the business affairs. In 1943 the company expanded to a new plant constructed in El Monte, and its name was changed to The California Cleminsons. The pottery produced hand–decorated artware and kitchen accessories including pie birds, lazy susans, spoon holders, and pitchers, in addition to a popular line of tableware called Distlefink.

Reference: Jack Chipman, *Collector's Encyclopedia of California Pottery*, Collector Books, 1992.

Periodical: *The Pottery Collectors Express*, PO Box 221, Mayview, MO 64071-0221.

Cookie Jar
   Candy House **95.00**
   Christmas House **150.00**

Creamer and Sugar
   Jumbo **25.00**
   Pop **20.00**
Egg Separator **20.00**
Hair Receiver, girl, 2 pcs **30.00**
Lazy Susan, brown distlefink **85.00**
Match Holder, wall mount **27.00**
Pie Bird, rooster **25.00**
Pitcher, Distelfink, 9½" h **22.00**
Plate, hillbilly **20.00**
Razor Bank, dome **20.00**
Ring Holder, bulldog **18.00**
Saki Set, Dragonware, orange **32.00**
Spoon Rest, leaf **12.00**
Wall Plaque
   "Home Sweet Home," rooster and smiling sun, minor damage **75.00**
   Pinocchio **65.00**
   Spray of Flowers **55.00**
Wall Pocket
   Clock **15.00**
   Kettle **25.00**

CLICKERS

Collecting Hints: Clickers with pictures are more desirable than clickers with just printing. Value is reduced by scratches in the paint and rust. Some companies issued several variations of a single design—be alert for them in your collecting.

History: Clickers were a popular advertising medium for people, products, and services ranging from plumbing supplies, political aspirants, soft drinks, and hotels to beer and whiskey. The most commonly found clickers are those which were given to children in shoe stores. Brands include Buster Brown, Poll Parrot, and Red Goose. Many shoe store clickers have advertising whistle mates.

Clickers were not confined to advertising. They were a popular holiday item, especially at Halloween. Impressed animal forms also provided a style for clickers.

The vast majority of clickers were made of tin. The older and rarer clickers were made of celluloid.

ADVERTISING

Buster Brown Hosiery, red, white, black, and blue **25.00**
Crackin' Good Cookies and Crackers ..   **6.00**
Endicott–Johnson Shoes, yellow and black **18.00**
Hasting's Bread, celluloid **8.00**
Humpty Dumpty Shoes, tin, litho, full color illus, c1930 ....   **30.00**
Nibroc, yellow, red, and black, dachshund and bone, 1940–50 ....   **20.00**

OK Bread, multicolored, baby chick emerging from egg, early 1900s **55.00**
Peters Weatherbird Shoes, ¾ x 1¾", tin, litho, multicolored, 1930s **25.00**
Phoenix Socks, tin, litho, red, white, and blue **8.00**
Quaker State Motor Oil, tin, litho, green design, white background, 1930s . . .   **15.00**
Reading Bone Fertilizer Co, celluloid .   **8.00**
Real Kill, white, orange, and black, "Mamma Get . . . Real Kill" **10.00**
Red Goose Shoes, ¾ x 1¾", tin, litho, red goose, yellow lettering and ground, 1930s **22.50**
Smith's Ice Cream **20.00**
Tastykake, Tastykake girl image, 1940–50 . . . .   **12.00**

NON–ADVERTISING

Bug Snapper, round, ladybug, green ground, 1946 . . . .   **7.00**
Christmas, tin, litho, Santa and fireplace scene **25.00**
Felix, 1¾", metal, black and white, brown ground, "Do You Really Mean All You Say Felix?" slogan **50.00**
Halloween, tin, orange, black, and white, 1930s **12.00**
Mickey Mouse, tin, litho, playing banjo, green background, 1930s **40.00**
Nixon, "Click with Dick," tin **25.00**
Rooster Weathervane, tin, litho **5.00**
Soldier, tin, litho, movable arms, 1930s, marked "Made in Germany" **50.00**

CLOCKS

Collecting Hints: Many clocks of the twentieth century were reproductions of earlier styles. Therefore, dating should be checked by patent dates on the mechanism, maker's label, and construction techniques.

The principal buyers for the advertising and figural clocks are not the clock collectors, but the specialists with whose area of interest the clock overlaps. For example, the Pluto alarm clock is of far greater importance to a Disneyana collector than to most clock collectors.

Condition is critical. Rust and non–working condition detract heavily from the price.

History: The clock always has served a dual function: decorative and utilitarian. Beginning in the late 19th century the clock became an important advertising vehicle, a tradition still continuing today. As character and personality became part of the American scene, the clock was a logical target, whether an alarm or wall model. The novelty clock, especially figural, was common in the 1930 to the 1960 period.

In the 1970s the popularity of digital wrist watches and clocks has led to less emphasis on the clock as a promotional item.

References: Robert W. D. Ball, *American Shelf and Wall Clocks: A Pictorial History*, Schiffer Publishing, 1992; Howard S. Brenner, *Identification and Value Guide To Collecting Comic Character Clocks and Watches*, Books Americana, 1987; Hy Brown, *Comic Character Timepieces: Seven Decades of Memories*, Schiffer Publishing, 1992; Philip Collins, *Pastime: Telling Time from 1920 to 1960*, Chronicle Books, 1993; Alan and Rita Shenton, *The Price Guide To Collectible Clocks, 1840–1940*, Antique Collectors' Club, 1985.

Periodical: *Watch & Clock Review*, 2403 Champa St., Denver, CO 80205.

Collectors' Club: National Assoc. of Watch and Clock Collectors, Inc., 514 Poplar St., Columbia, PA 17512.

Museums: American Clock & Watch Museum, Bristol, CT; Greensboro Clock Museum, Greensboro, NC; Museum of National Assoc. of Watch and Clock Collectors, Columbia, PA; Old Clock Museum, Pharr, TX; The Time Museum, Rockford, IL.

Additional Listings: See *Warman's Antiques and Their Prices*.

Advertising
B L Johnson & Co Mfg Confectioners, regulator **995.00**
Country Club Ice Cream, round, plastic, Dualite **175.00**
Diet Rite Cola, glass bubble dome cov, black, white, and blue **150.00**
G W Bishop Drugs & Jewelry, regulator   **995.00**
Hastings Piston Ring, round, light–up, dome glass, Dualite **225.00**
J Stern & Son Clothiers, Baird **2,900.00**
Merrick Spool Cotton **895.00**
Michelin Tires **65.00**
Mountain Dew **50.00**
Non Such Mincemeat **850.00**
Orange Crush, regulator **1,095.00**
Pepsi, round, light–up, glass dome, Telechron **275.00**
Premier Vacuum Cleaner, 1930s . . .   **160.00**
RC Cola, round, light–up, plastic dome, Ohio Advertising Display Co **200.00**
Reed's Tonic **1,395.00**
Sylvania TV, Halolight, lighted **175.00**
Vermont Household Remedies **1,095.00**
Winston Cigarette, clock and counter display, lighted **60.00**
Animated
Apollo XI, ivory case, red, white, and blue diecut, gold numerals, marked "Lux Clock Mfg Co" **115.00**

Felix the Cat, wall type, red, tail
moves 25.00
Home Sweet Home, Haddon, grand-
mother rocking in rocking chair . .   85.00
Huck Finn, boy fishing, pole moves
up and down, fish dart in and out,
white metal, 12 x 9" 225.00
Kit Kat 30.00
Mastercrafter's, swinging bird in cage   225.00
Remembrance, projector clock, time
shows on ceiling 45.00
Spinning Wheel, Lux 50.00
Water Wheel, Spartus 60.00
Character
Beatles, alarm, plastic, silver, silver
with black illus, silver metal bells
and feet, orig box, copyright 1988
Apple Corps Ltd 50.00
Donald Duck, electric, Phinney–
Walker, Germany 22.00
ET, head raised, finger & chest light
up when alarm sounds, battery op-
erated 120.00
Mickey Mouse, alarm, head moves to
tick off seconds, orig box, Bayard,
late 1960s 200.00
Peter Max, 9" d, cardboard, day–glo
hands, abstract lines, circles, and
shapes design, white painted metal
box on back, copyright Peter Max,
marked "General Electric," late
1960s 75.00
Popeye and Swee' Pea, alarm, ivory
enameled steel case, color illus on
dial, Smiths, c1968 . . . .   100.00
Roy Rogers, Ingraham 100.00
Sesame Street, Cookie Monster,
radio 15.00
Snow White, alarm, Bayard/Blanche
Niege, Made in France 75.00

**Shelf, Waterbury, Empire, painted tablet,
16" h, $250.00.**

Figural
Car, brass, Waltham 45.00
Ship, walnut hull, chrome plated sails
and riggings, lighted portholes,
United Clock Co, 1955 . . . .   90.00
Kitchen
Pottery, bluebirds on sides, ivory bor-
der 50.00
Tin, Dutch children on face, electric   24.00
Musical, drum, red 35.00

CLOTHING AND CLOTHING ACCESSORIES

Collecting Hints: Vintage clothing should be clean and in good repair. Designer labels and original boxes can add to the value.

Collecting vintage clothing appears to have reached a plateau. Although there are still dedicated collectors, the category is no longer attracting a rash of new collectors annually.

History: Clothing is collected and studied as a reference source in learning about fashion, construction and types of materials used.

References: Joanne Dubbs Ball and Dorothy Hehl Torem, *The Art of Fashion Accessories*, Schiffer Publishing, 1993; Adele Campione, *Women's Hats*, Chronicle Books, 1994; C. Willett and Phillis Cunnington, *The History of Underclothes*, Dover, 1992; Maryanne Dolan, *Vintage Clothing, 1880–1980, Third Edition*, Books Americana, 1995; Kate Dooner, *A Century of Handbags*, Schiffer Publishing, 1993; Kate E. Dooner, *Plastic Handbags: Sculpture to Wear*, Schiffer Publishing, 1993; Dover Publications, *Gimbel's Illustrated 1915 Fashion Catalog*, Gimbel Brothers, Dover, 1994; Dover Publications, *Women's Fashions of the Early 1900s: An Unabridged Republication of New York Fashions*, National Cloak & Suit Co., Dover, 1992; Rod Dyer and Ron Spark, *Fit To Be Tied: Vintage Ties of the Forties and Early Fifties*, Abbeville Press, 1987; Roseann Ettinger, *'50s Popular Fashions for Men, Women, Boys & Girls*, Schiffer Publishing, 1995; Roseann Ettinger, *Handbags*, Schiffer Publishing, 1991; Roselyn Gerson, *Vintage Vanity Bags and Purses: An Identification and Value Guide*, Collector Books, 1994; Evelyn Haertig, *Antique Combs & Purses*, Gallery Press, 1983; Richard Holiner, *Antique Purses, Second Edition*, Collector Books, 1987, 1994 value update; Jo Anne Olian (ed.), *Children's Fashions, 1860–1912: Costume Designs from "La Mode Illustree,"* Dover, 1994; Jo Anne Olian (ed.), *Everyday Fashions of The Forties As Pictured in Sears Catalogs*, Dover,

1992; Franklin Simon & Co, *Franklin Simon Fashion Catalog for 1923*, Dover, 1993; Sheila Steinberg and Kate E. Dooner, *Fabulous Fifties: Designs for Modern Living*, Schiffer Publishing, 1993; Mary Trasko, *Heavenly Soles: Extraordinary Twentieth Century Shoes*, Abbeville Press, 1989; Merideth Wright, *Everyday Dress of Rural America: 1783–1800*, Dover, 1992.

Periodicals: *Lady's Gallery*, PO Box 1761, Independence, MO 64055; *Lill's Vintage Clothing Newsletter*, 19 Jamestown Dr., Cincinnati, OH 45241; *The Glass Slipper*, 653 S. Orange Ave., Sarasota, FL 34236; *The Vintage Gazette*, 194 Amity St., Amherst, MA 01002; *Vintage Clothing Newsletter*, PO Box 1422, Corvallis, OR 97339.

Collectors' Clubs: Federation of Vintage Fashion, PO Box 412, Alamo, CA 94507; Living History Assoc., PO Box 578, Wilmington, VT 05363; Textile & Costume Guild, 301 N. Pomona Ave., Fullerton, CA 92632; The Costume Society of America, 55 Edgewater Dr., PO Box 73, Earleville, MD 21919.

Museums: Boston Museum of Fine Arts, Boston, MA; Chicago Historical Society, Chicago, IL; Detroit Historical Museum, Detroit, MI; Fashion Institute of Technology, New York, NY; Indianapolis Museum of Art, Indianapolis, IN; Metropolitan Museum of Art, New York, NY; Missouri Historical Society, Saint Louis, MO; Museum at Stony Brook, Stony Brook, NY; Museum of Art, Rhode Island School of Design, Providence, RI; Museum of Vintage Fashion, Lafayette, CA; National Museum of American History, Washington, DC; Philadelphia College of Textiles & Science, Philadelphia, PA; Philadelphia Museum of Art, Philadelphia, PA; The Arizona Costume Institute, Phoenix Art Museum, Phoenix, AZ; The Costume and Textile Dept. of the Los Angeles County Museum of Art, Los Angeles, CA; Valentine Museum, Richmond, VA; Wadsworth Atheneum, Hartford, CT; Western Reserve Historical Society, Cleveland, OH.

CLOTHING

Bed Jacket, taffeta, watered, aquamarine, bands of Valenciennes lace . . .	**125.00**
Blouse	
Cotton, white, c1940	**15.00**
Silk, beige, print, high neck, leg of mutton sleeves	**35.00**
Bush Jacket, cotton, white, bellow pockets, full belt, unused, 1940s . . .	**20.00**
Camisole	
Cotton, white, crocheted yoke	**40.00**
Silk, pink, lace trim	**24.00**
Cape	
Beaded, black lace, Victorian	**150.00**
Fur, blue fox	**65.00**

Opera, blue, 1920s	**95.00**
Wool, pearl gray, triangular shape, tassel hung hood, narrow steel gray braid trim, c1910	**55.00**
Coat	
Evening, silk and velvet, ermine trim	**125.00**
Fur	
Mink, full length	**200.00**
Raccoon, full length, c1930	**125.00**
Opera, full length, black, rabbit trim	**125.00**
Dress	
Baby, cotton, tucked, eyelet trimmed yoke, sleeves, skirt, 3½" open work, scalloped hem, 38" l	**20.00**
Child's, satin, black, white lace trim, early 1900s, size 10–12	**24.00**
Day	
Cotton, polished, black, miniature dots, ruffled bodice, leg of mutton sleeves	**95.00**
Lawn, white with print edge, Cluny lace bodice, net and ruffled sleeves	**75.00**
Linen, white, lace trim, c1912 . . .	**85.00**
Dinner, chiffon, cerise print on purple, black lace bodice, orig taffeta slip, bolero type jacket with matching lace trim, c1930	**475.00**
Work, cotton, gray, white stripe, high waist, buttons down front, long sleeves, black and white scallop trim, shell buttons	**35.00**
Evening Gown	
Chiffon, aquamarine over green, narrow silver braid trim, c1910	**75.00**
Crepe, black, beaded, c1920	**80.00**
Dotted Swiss, white, matching voile jacket, white and red chiffon flower center	**125.00**
Moire, purple scoop neck, gathered front, full hip ruffle, c1940	**85.00**
Organdy, peach, c1930	**45.00**
Satin, gold, beaded	**150.00**
Velvet, dark brown, draped, weighted neckline, short sleeves	**85.00**
Voile, salmon and white flowers, Hawaiian style, V neck, ¾ length sleeves, five foot train with ruffle	**60.00**
Jacket	
Brocade front, pleated, brown, large mother–of–pearl buckle	**50.00**
Crochet, lace, white, Irish, puffed sleeves	**225.00**
Sequins, net, gold, long sleeves, c1935	**275.00**
Velvet, black, crushed, white silk lining, c1920	**50.00**
Knickers, wool, black	**40.00**
Mourning Outfit, black, 5 pcs	**200.00**
Nightgown, cotton, white, leg of mutton sleeves, high collar, handmade eyelet lace trim	**285.00**

Petticoat
  Bustle back, lace trimmed ruffles, size
    8–10 . . . .   **50.00**
  Muslin, white, deep laced edge
    flounce, 24" waist **18.00**
  Skirt and top, homespun, black lace
    bodice and cuffs, high neck **125.00**
Slip, cotton
  Full, crocheted, tucked **35.00**
  Half, string waist, lace bottom **35.00**
Swimsuit, wool, orig tags and box,
  Jantzen, dated 1931 . . . .   **65.00**
Uniform, maid's, La Mode, white cotton
  pongee, ankle length, high starched
  collar, matching cap, c1916 . . . . . .   **300.00**

CLOTHING ACCESSORIES

Apron
  Cotton, dainty **5.00**
  Silk, white, lace dec, embroidered
    "Souvenir of France" **15.00**
Belt, 1" w, jet beads **40.00**
Bonnet, silk, hand crocheted lace,
  handmade **35.00**
Collar
  Lace, MIB **45.00**
  Satin, black, five panel, 1" jet beads .   **65.00**
Cuffs, pr, crochet, white **8.00**
Eyeglass case, mesh, silver **20.00**
Gloves, pr
  Cotton **4.00**
  Leather **5.00**
Handkerchief, lace trim, point de gaze,
  oak leaves, floral motif **40.00**
Hat
  Cloche, flapper type, brown velvet .   **15.00**
  Derby, black **18.00**
Head Band, flapper's, rhinestones **25.00**
Muff, black **25.00**
Necktie, silk, Sak's Fifth Ave **20.00**
Parasol
  Lace, white, handmade, c1900 . . . .   **300.00**

Handbag, Lucite, white, $18.00.

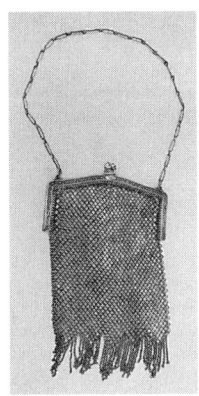

Handbag, mesh, emb frame, chain link strap, Whiting Davis, 6" l plus fringe, $50.00.

Satin, peach, crystal tip, wooden han-
  dles **175.00**
Purse
  Crocheted, Victorian **40.00**
  Enameled
    Art Deco, 6½ x 3½", black and
      blue, Whiting Davis **95.00**
    Mesh, Whiting Davis **50.00**
  Leather, hand tooled, suede lined,
    1920s **25.00**
  Marcasite, framed **35.00**
  Mesh
    Aqua/gold **58.00**
    Silver frame, blue mesh lining, blue
      metal inlay, silver chain, 4 x 5"   **60.00**
  Velvet, black, drawstring, beading,
    horsehair, chenille tassel on bottom   **185.00**
Scarf, silk, hand embroidered **45.00**
Shawl
  Lace, black, flowers, scalloped hem,
    112" w, 54" l, Victorian **36.00**
  Silk, paisley, 72" sq, knotted fringe . .   **65.00**
Shoes
  Alligator, pumps **35.00**
  Baby, leather, high top, 1930s **20.00**
  Spike heel, 1950s **9.00**
Spats, pr **18.00**
Stockings, silk, rhinestone design at an-
  kle, WWII **25.00**

COCA–COLA ITEMS

Collecting Hints: Most Coca–Cola items were produced in large quantity; the company was a leader in sales and promotional materials. Don't ignore the large amount of Coca–Cola material in languages other than English. Remember, "Coke" has a worldwide market.

History: The originator of Coca–Cola was John Pemberton, a pharmacist from Atlanta, Georgia. In 1886, Dr. Pemberton introduced a patent medicine to relieve headaches, stomach disorders, and other minor maladies. Unfortunately, his failing health and meager finances forced him to sell his interest.

In 1888, Asa G. Candler became the sole owner of Coca–Cola. Candler improved the formula, increased the advertising budget, and widened the distribution. Accidentally, a patient was given a dose of the syrup mixed with carbonated water instead of the usual still water. The result was a tastier, more refreshing drink.

As sales increased in the 1890s, Candler recognized that the product was more suitable for the soft drink market and began advertising it as such. From these beginnings a myriad of advertising items have been issued to invite all to "Drink Coca–Cola."

Dates of interest: "Coke" was first used in advertising in 1941. The distinctively shaped bottle was registered as a trademark on April 12, 1960.

References: Gael de Courtivron, *Collectible Coca–Cola Toy Trucks: An Identification and Value Guide,* Collector Books, 1995; Shelly and Helen Goldstein, *Coca–Cola Collectibles* (four volumes, plus index), published by author, 1970s; Deborah Goldstein Hill, Wallace–Homestead *Price Guide To Coca–Cola Collectibles,* Wallace–Homestead, 1984, 1991 value update; *Goldstein's Coca–Cola Collectibles: An Illustrated Value Guide,* Collector Books, 1991, 1993 value update; Norman E. Martinus and Harry L. Rinker, *Warman's Paper,* Wallace–Homestead, 1994; Allan Petretti, *Petretti's Coca–Cola Collectibles Price Guide, 9th Edition,* Nostalgia Publications, Wallace–Homestead, 1994; Al Wilson, *Collectors Guide To Coca–Cola Items,* Volume I (1985, 1992 value update) and Volume II (1987, 1993 value update), L–W Book Sales; Al and Helen Wilson, *Coca–Cola: The Real Price Guide,* Schiffer Publishing, 1994.

Collectors' Clubs: Coca–Cola Collectors Club International, PO Box 49166, Atlanta, GA 30359; Florida West Coast Chapter of the Coca–Cola Collectors Club International, 1007 Emerald Dr., Brandon, FL 33511.

Museums: Coca–Cola Memorabilia Museum of Elizabeth, Inc., Elizabethtown, KY; The World of Coca–Cola Pavilion, Atlanta, GA.

REPRODUCTION ALERT: Be especially careful in the area of Coca–Cola trays.

Badge, 1¾ x 2¾", flicker, full color, 1994 World Cup soccer competition	**10.00**
Bank, tin, vending machine	**100.00**
Banner, 18 x 54", 1941, mint	**175.00**
Beach Chair, child's, aluminum frame, cloth cover	**85.00**

Billhead	
1905, 3¾ x 8½", logo and Coke bottle, Waycross, GA	**48.00**
1923, 8½ x 7", logo, Augusta, GA	**30.00**
Blotter, with paper label bottle, 1913	**39.00**
Bottle Holder, 1950s	**8.00**
Bottle Opener, brass, 1910	**40.00**
Brochure, Pause For Living, 1957	**5.00**
Calendar	
1942, framed glass, pull down pad	**225.00**
1954, full pad	**100.00**
Carrier	
12½ x 16½", cardboard, diecut, panel with uncut Max Headroom face mask, unused	**15.00**
Ballpark vendor, holds twenty bottles	**135.00**
Change Tray	
1912	**325.00**
1914, Betty	**90.00**
Clock	
Fishtail, lighted	**135.00**
Schoolhouse, wood, 1970s, MIB	**275.00**
Cuff Links, figural, bottle, SS, price for pair	**85.00**
Display Bottle	
1930	**285.00**
1968	**100.00**
Game	
Chinese Checkers, wood board, marbles	**55.00**
Tic–Tac–Toe, MIB	**80.00**
Glass, 6 oz, orig box, set of 12	**125.00**
Hat, truck driver's, 1930s	**100.00**
Letterhead, red and green logo at top, 1903	**90.00**
Lunch Tote, vinyl, 1950s	**25.00**
Magazine Tear Sheet, 1906, couple toasting with Coca–Cola	**8.00**
Marbles, unopened pack	**27.00**
Matchbook, 1950	**2.50**
Menu Board, emb fishtail, 1960	**325.00**
Mirror, pocket, celluloid	**125.00**
Pencil Case, "Coca–Cola Pure Drink of Natural Flavors," two unused pencils, ruler, "School Size Blotter," used eraser, blotter, wood pen, all "Coca–Cola," complete	**55.00**
Pill Container, 2½" l, bottle shape, brass lined	**2.00**
Playing Cards, complete deck, Hund & Eger	**65.00**
Post Card, business reply, "Fashion Books," 1912	**15.00**
Radio, figural, cooler, MIB, c1984	**35.00**
Ruler, Coca–Cola	**5.00**
Sign	
Coca–Cola Sold Here, Christmas bottle	**145.00**
Drink Coca–Cola, porcelain, green and white, center red circle, 1950s	**650.00**
Ice Cold, Drink Coca–Cola, plastic, raised lettering and images	**75.00**

Tie Clip, All Star Dealer Campaign Award, metal and enamel, 1950s, $32.00.

Syrup, 1 gal	15.00
Tablet, "Drink Coca–Cola," orig pencil	8.00
Thermometer	
1939, girl silhouette	125.00
1950s, tin, flat bottle	95.00
1952, bottle shape	95.00
Toy	
Fountain Dispenser	25.00
Frisbee, plastic, MIB	20.00
Tray	
1937	435.00
1938, Summer Girl	95.00
1941, ice skater	50.00
1942, Roadster Girls	95.00
Vending Machine, Vendo 44, orig	2,000.00

COCKTAIL SHAKERS

Collecting Hints: Concentrate on cocktail shakers that are style statements for their era. Make aesthetics, line, form, and materials principal focus points. A collection numbering in the hundreds can be built around examples of the streamlined modern style.

When buying glass shakers run your fingers around the edge to check for chipping. A small chip reduces the price by a minimum of 30%. Shakers with brilliant, sharp colors are more desirable than those composed of clear glass.

Be on a constant alert for cracks and fractures. Most individuals want shakers that are fine or better in appearance and can be used if necessary.

Figural shakers are in a class of their own. Among the more common forms are bowling pins, dumbbells, golf bags, and penguins. Shakers based on the designs of Norman Bel Geddes often command in excess of $500.00.

History: The cocktail shaker traces its origins back to 7,000 B.C. and the South American jar gourd, a closed container used to mix liquids. The ancient Egyptians of 3,500 B.C. added spices to their grain fermentations before serving them, perhaps history's first cocktails. History records the use of alcoholic drinks through the modern era.

By the late 1800s, bartenders used a shaker as a standard tool of their craft. Passing the liquid back and forth between two containers created a much appreciated show.

The modern cocktail shaker arrived on the scene in the 1920s, when martinis were in vogue. Shapes tended to be stylish. Materials ranged from glass to sterling silver. Perhaps nothing symbolizes the Jazz Age more than the flapper dress and cocktail shaker. When Prohibition ended in 1933, the cocktail shaker enjoyed another surge of popularity.

Movies helped popularize the cocktail shaker. William Powell instructed a bartender how to mix a proper martini in *The Thin Man*, a tradition continued by James Bond 007. Tom Cruise's portrayal of a bartender in *Cocktail* helped solidify the collecting interest that was shown in cocktail shakers during the 1980s.

Following World War II, the home bar became a common fixture. Every home bar featured one or more cocktail shakers and/or cocktail shaker sets. Chrome–plated stainless steel shakers replaced the sterling silver shakers of the 1920s and 1930s. Major glass companies such as Cambridge, Heisey, and Imperial offered cocktail shakers.

Life in the fabulous fifties was filled with novelties. Cocktail shakers were no exception. Figural and other forms of novelty shakers appeared.

The electric blender and ready–mix cocktail packets ended the reign of the cocktail shaker. Showmanship was replaced by button–pushing. An era passed.

Cocktail Set, Art Deco style, glass shaker, six tall glasses, five shorter glasses, frosted stippled surface, gold and colored mid bands, 1950s **60.00**

Magazine Tear Sheet, Glenmore Distilleries Co., Louisville, KY, Christmas motif, 1941, 10½ x 13½", $7.00.

Cocktail Shaker
Aluminum, hand wrought, straight
sides, grooved Modernistic top,
clear plastic knob lid, Buenilum . .   **20.00**
Glass, Cambridge
Diane pattern, crystal, glass top . .   **125.00**
Wildflower pattern, crystal, chrome
top **75.00**
Cordial Set, Central Glass Co, Balda
Orchid pattern, decanter, six match-
ing cordial glasses **365.00**
Decanter, orig stopper
Cambridge, Cleo pattern, pink **225.00**
Imperial, Cape Cod pattern, crystal   **65.00**
Waterford, Irish, cut crystal, Balfray
pattern **150.00**
Ice Bucket
Aluminum, hand wrought
Buenilum, ridged band handles,
ring finial **15.00**
Lehman, double twisted handles,
plastic knob **15.00**
Glass
Cambridge
Decagon pattern, amethyst **35.00**
Mt Vernon pattern, red **75.00**
Fenton, Plymouth pattern, red . . .   **50.00**
Fostoria, green, polar bear dec . . .   **30.00**
Liquor Set, brass ring holds four gold
banded glasses, c1950 . . . .   **18.00**
Martini Pitcher, Cambridge, Diane pat-
tern, crystal **750.00**
Martini Set, glass, pheasants on pitcher
and glasses, brass stirrer **18.00**
Punch Bowl Set
Duncan Miller, Caribbean pattern,
crystal, 10″ d bowl, dozen punch
cups, matching ladle, price for
fourteen piece set **225.00**
Heisey, Lariat pattern, crystal, seven
quart punch bowl, ten cups, price
for eleven piece set **175.00**
Stemware, glass
Claret
Cambridge, Rose Point pattern,
crystal, 4½″ oz **45.00**
Fostoria, Hermitage pattern, amber   **15.00**
Tiffin, Flanders pattern, pink **95.00**
Cocktail
Heisey, Plantation pattern, crystal,
pressed **50.00**
Tiffin, Cadena pattern, yellow,
5¼″ h **25.00**
US Glass, Deerwood pattern,
green, 5″ h **30.00**
Cordial
Cambridge
Caprice pattern, blue, 1 oz **125.00**
Chantilly pattern, crystal, gold
dec, 1 oz **65.00**
Heisey, Plantation pattern, crystal,
blown **90.00**

Wine
Cambridge
Imperial Hunt Scene pattern,
emerald green, 2½ oz **55.00**
Valencia pattern, crystal, 2½ oz   **30.00**
Fostoria, Fairfax pattern, rose, 3 oz   **30.00**
Swizzle Stick, glass
Advertising, colored **3.00**
Amber **1.25**
Black **2.00**
Blue and Crystal, clear spoon **2.00**
Blue–green, clear spoon **2.25**
Christmas, set of six **20.00**
Cobalt Blue **1.25**
Colored Knob, clear stirrer **1.75**
Man, top hat **3.00**
Plain, crystal **1.00**
Red and Crystal, clear spoon **2.00**
Souvenir, Hotel Lexington, amethyst,
1939 World's Fair **15.00**
Spatter knob, clear stirrer . . . .   **.75**
Tom & Jerry, Skokie Green, McKee
Bowl **65.00**
Cup **9.00**
Mug **10.00**
Tumbler
Bar
Cambridge, Portia pattern, crystal,
2½ oz **30.00**
Heisey
Ridgeleigh pattern, crystal, 2½
oz **30.00**
Victorian pattern, crystal, 2 oz   **35.00**
Old Fashioned
Duncan Miller, Tear Drop pattern,
crystal, 7 oz **10.00**
Fostoria, Baroque pattern, blue, 6½
oz **75.00**
Heisey, Saturn pattern, 7 oz, crystal   **10.00**
Whiskey Glass
Duncan Miller, Tear Drop pattern,
crystal, 2 oz   **15.00**
Fostoria
American pattern, crystal, 2½″ h   **10.00**
Kasmir pattern, yellow, ftd, 2 oz . .   **25.00**
Heisey, Plantation pattern, crystal,
blown **50.00**

COMIC BOOKS

Collecting Hints: Remember, age does *not* determine value! Prices fluctuate according to supply and demand in the marketplace. Collectors
should always buy comic books in the best possible condition. While archival restoration is
available, it's frequently costly and may involve a
certain amount of risk.

Comic books should be stored in an upright
position away from sunlight, dampness, and insect infestations. Avoid stacking comic books be-

cause the weight of the uppermost books may cause acid and oils to migrate. This results in stains on the covers of books near the bottom of the stack which are difficult or impossible to remove.

Golden Age (1939–1950s), Marvel, and D.C. first issues and key appearances continue to gain in popularity as do more current favorites like Marvel's "X–Men" and D.C.'s "The New Teen Titans."

History: Who would ever believe that a cheap, disposable product sold in the 1890s would be responsible for the multi–million dollar industry composed of comic books and their spin–offs today? That 2¢ item was none other than the Sunday newspaper. Improved printing techniques helped 1890s newspaper publishers change from a weekly format to a daily one that included a full page of comics. The rotary printing press allowed the use of color in the "funnies." Comics were soon reprinted as advertising promotions by companies such as Procter & Gamble for products and by movie theatres.

It wasn't long until reprint books like these promotional giveaways were selling in candy and stationery stores for 10¢ each. They appeared in various formats and sizes, many with odd shapes and cardboard covers. Others were printed on newsprint and resembled comic books sold today.

Comics printed prior to 1938 have value today only as historical artifacts or intellectual curiosities.

From 1939 to 1950 comic book publishers regaled readers with humor, adventure, western, and mystery tales. Super–heroes such as "Batman," "Superman," and "Captain America" first appeared in books during this era. This was the Golden Age of comics, a time for expansion and growth.

Unfortunately, the bubble burst in the spring of 1954 when Fredric Wertham published his book, *Seduction of the Innocent.* That book pointed a guilt–laden finger at the comic industry for corrupting youth, causing juvenile delinquency, and undermining American values. This book forced many publishers out of business, while others fought to establish a "comics code" to assure parents that their comics were compliant with morality and decency standards upheld by the code authority.

Thus, the Silver Age of comics is marked by a declining number of publishers due to the public uproar surrounding Wertham's book and the increased production costs of an inflationary economy.

The period starting with 1960 and continuing to the present has been marked by a revitalized surge of interest in comic books. Starting with Marvel's introduction of "The Fantastic Four" and "The Amazing Spider–Man," the market has increased to the extent that many new publishers are now rubbing elbows with the giants and the competition is keen!

Part of the reason for this upswing must be credited to that same inflationary economy that spelled disaster for publishers in the 1950s. This time, however, people are buying valuable comics as a hedge against inflation. Even young people are aware of the market potential. Today's piggy bank investors may well be tomorrow's Wall Street tycoons.

References: Stephen Becker, *Comic Art In America,* Simon And Schuster, 1959; Mike Benton, *Crime Comics: The Illustrated History,* Taylor Publishing, 1993; Mike Benton, *Horror Comics: The Illustrated History,* Taylor Publishing, 1991; Mike Benton, *Science Fiction Comics: The Illustrated History,* Taylor Publishing, 1992; Mike Benton, *Superhero Comics of the Golden Age: The Illustrated History,* Taylor Publishing, 1992; Mike Benton, *Superhero Comics of the Silver Age: The Illustrated History,* Taylor Publishing, 1992; Mike Benton, *The Comic Book in America: An Illustrated History,* Taylor Publishing, 1993; Pierre Couperie and Maurice C. Horn, *A History of the Comic Strip,* Crown Publishers, 1968; Hubert H. Crawford, *Crawford's Encyclopedia of Comic Books,* Jonathan David Publishers, 1978; Les Daniels, *COMIX, A History of Comic Books in America,* Bonanza Books, 1971; Ernst and Mary Gerber (compilers), *Photo–Journal Guide To Comics, Volume One (A–J)* and *Volume 2 (K–Z),* Gerber Publishing, 1990; John Hegenberger, *Collector's Guide To Comic Books,* Wallace–Homestead, 1990; Maurice Horn (ed.), *World Encyclopedia of Comics,* Chelsea House; D. W. Howard, *Investing In Comics,* The World of Yesterday, 1988; Alex Malloy, *Comic Values Annual 1995 Edition,* Wallace–Homestead, 1994; Alex G. Malloy (ed.), *Comic Book Artists,* Attic Books, Wallace–Homestead, 1993; Robert M. Overstreet, *The Overstreet Comic Book Price Guide, 25th Edition,* Avon Books, 1995; Robert M. Overstreet and Gary M. Carter, *The Overstreet Comic Book Grading Guide,* Avon Books, 1992; Jerry Robinson, *The Comics, An Illustrated History of Comic Strip Art,* G. P. Putnam's Sons, 1974; Don and Maggie Thompson (eds.), *Comic Book Superstars: Who Is Who Among Comic Creators,* Krause Publications, 1993; Don and Maggie Thomson (eds.), *Marvel Comics Checklist & Price Guide: 1961–Present,* Krause Publications, 1993; Don and Maggie Thompson and Julie Stuemfig (eds.), *Comic Buyer's Guide 1995 Annual,* Krause Publications, 1994; Don and Maggie Thompson and Julie Stuemfig (eds.), *1995 Comic Book Checklist & Price Guide: 1961–Present,* Krause Publications, 1994; Jerry Weist, *Original Comic Art: Identification and Price Guide,* Avon Books, 1993.

Periodicals: *Comic Book Market Place,* PO Box 180900, Coronado, CA 92178; *Comic Buyers Guide,* 700 E. State Street, Iola, WI 54990; *Comics Values Monthly,* Attic Books, 15 Danbury Road, Ridgefield, CT 06877; *Duckburg Times,* 3010 Wilshire Blvd. #362, Los Angeles, CA 90010; *Overstreet Comic Book Marketplace,* 801 20th St. NW, Suite 3, Cleveland, TN 37311; *Overstreet's Advanced Collector,* 801 20th St., NW, Suite 3, Cleveland, TN 37311; *The Comic Scene,* 475 Park Ave., New York, NY 10016; *Western Comics Journal,* 143 Milton St., Brooklyn, NY 11222.

Collectors' Club: Fawcett Collectors of America & Magazine Enterprise, Too!, 301 East Buena Vista Ave., North Augusta, SC 29841.

Museum: Museum of Cartoon Art, Rye, NY.

Video: Overstreet Productions and Tom Barker Video, *The Overstreet World of Comic Books,* 1994.

REPRODUCTION ALERT: Publishers frequently reprint popular stories, even complete books, so the buyer must pay strict attention to the title, not just the portion printed in outsized letters on the front cover. If there's ever any doubt, look inside at the fine print on the bottom of the inside cover or first page. The correct title will be printed there in capital letters.

Buyers also should pay attention to the size of the comic they purchase. Recently many customers have been misled by unscrupulous dealers. The comics offered are exact replicas of expensive Golden Age D.C. titles, which would normally sell for thousands of dollars. The seller offers the large, 10 by 13", copy of Superman #1 in mint condition for $10 to $100. The novice collector jumps at the chance since he knows this book sells for thousands on the open market. When the buyer gets his "find" home and checks the value, he discovers that he's paid way too much for the treasury–sized "Famous First Edition" comic printed in the mid–seventies by D.C. These comics originally sold for $1 each and are exact reprints except for the size. Several came with outer covers which announced the fact that they were reprints, but it didn't take long for dishonest dealers to remove these and sell the remaining portion for greatly inflated prices.

Notes: Just like advertising, comic books affect and reflect the culture which nurtures them. Large letters, bright colors, and "pulse–pounding" action seem to hype this product. Many would say comics are as American as mom's apple pie since good almost always triumphs over evil. Yet there's truly something for every taste in the vast array of comics available today. There are underground (adult situation) comic foreign comics, educational comics, and comics intended to promote the sale of products or services.

The following listing concentrates on "mainstream" American comics published between 1938 and 1985. Prices may vary from region to region due to excessive demand in some areas. Prices given are for comic books in fine condition; that is, these comics are like new in most respects, but may show a little wear. Comics should be complete, with no pages or chunks cut out.

Classic Comics

Classics Illustrated started with #35. All first editions carry an advertisement for the next issue on the inside covers (except #168 and #169). All titles have been reprinted and reprints are worth only about 10–25% of first edition values. Prices listed here are for first edition titles only.

A Christmas Carol, #16	5.00
Arabian Nights, #8	15.00
Call of the Wild, #10	4.00
Don Quixote, #10	2.75
Frankenstein, #6	4.00
Hamlet, #2	1.00
Oliver Twist, #17	1.25
Robinson Crusoe, #10	2.50
Sherlock Holmes, #2	35.00
The Deerslayer, #12	2.00
The Last of the Mohicans, #4	12.00
The Spy, #51	15.00
Uncle Tom's Cabin, #15	36.00

Crime

All True Crime, #27	7.50
Crime and Punishment, #10	4.00
Crime Clinic, #11	10.00
Crime Fighters, #12	3.00
Crime Must Stop, #1	50.00
Crime Reporter, #2	65.00
Crime Smashers, #2	20.00
Criminals On The Run, #10	60.00
Detective Picture Stories, #5	250.00
Dick Tracy Monthly, #20	100.00
Gangsters Can't Win, #8	6.50
Thrilling Crime Cases, #47	6.50

Funny Animals

Billy Bunny's Christmas Frolics, #1	6.50
Bugs Bunny, #30	1.50
Cosmo Cat, #1	10.00
Felix the Cat, #6	5.00
Funny Stuff, #10	10.00
Howard the Duck, #2	1.00
Jing Pals, #2	4.00
Looney Tunes & Merrie Melodies Comics, #55	6.00
New Funnies, #85	18.00
Nutty Comics, #1	10.00
Peter Panda, #3	8.00
Porky Pig, #25	1.50
Super Rabbit, #6	12.00

Horror
Adventures Into Terror, #3	8.00
Alarming Tales, #5	7.50
Bernie Whiteson Master Of the	
Macabre, #3	4.00
Chamber of Chills, #9	8.00
Crypt of Terror, #18	900.00
Ghost Stories, #25	6.00
Haunt of Fear, #21	20.00
House of Mystery, #10	15.00
Spellbound, #32	9.25
Spook Suspense and Mystery, #26 . .	45.00
Tales of Suspense, #44	18.00
Tales of Terror, #1	1.50
Terror Illustrated, #1	18.00
The Thing, #5	17.50
The Vault Of Horror, #36	145.00
Unknown World, #1	20.00
Web of Evil, #17	32.00

Jungle
Jann of the Jungle, #17	12.00
Jumbo, #149	10.00
Jungle Adventures, #3	1.50
Jungle Girl, #1	90.00
Jungle Jo, #4	18.00
Jungle Thrills, #16	20.00
Korak, Son of Tarzan, #15	1.25
Sheena, Queen of the Jungle, #4 . . .	30.00
Tarzan, Lord of the Jungle, #1	4.00
Tegra Jungle Empress, 1948, #1	25.00
Terrors of the Jungle, #9	37.00
White Princess of the Jungle, #5 . . .	20.00
Zegra Jungle Empress, #3	20.00

Juvenile
Adventures for Boys, #1	2.50
Archie's Girls Betty & Veronica,	
#100	4.00
Barbie & Ken, #5	10.00
Bugs Bunny, #53	10.00
Bullwinkle, #22	8.00
Groo, The Wanderer, #12	6.00
Jughead's Fantasy, #3	10.00
Katy Keene, #45	12.00
Kiddie Kapers, #1	4.00
Little Lotta, #7	12.00
Little Lulu, #40	12.00
Mighty Atom, #6	4.00
New Funnies, #87	32.00
Raggedy Ann and Andy, #5	60.00
Teenage Mutant Ninja Turtles, #1,	
2nd printing	12.50
The Flintstones, #43	11.00

Newspaper Reprints
Beetle Bailey, #5	2.50
Brenda Starr, #14	50.00
Comics Revue, #4	5.00
Flash Gordon, #4	40.00
Peanuts, #4	5.00

Number 1's
Amazing Spiderman	350.00
Cerebus, #1	200.00
D.C. Special, #1	10.00

Fantastic Four	500.00
Justice League of America	170.00
Little Archie	60.00
Strange Adventures	150.00
Tales of the Unexpected	50.00
The Adventures Of Alan Ladd, #1 . .	300.00
Torchy	210.00
Warlord	8.00
What If?, #1	23.00

Radio/TV/Movie Related
Abbott and Costello, #1	24.00
Adventures of Jerry Lewis, #92	1.50
Bewitched, #8	3.50
Cheyenne, #25	4.25
Famous Stars, #5	15.00
Get Smart, #5	4.50
Gomer Pyle, #2	2.00
Jackie Gleason & the Honeymooners,	
#2	32.00
Jimmy Durante, #20	18.00
My Favorite Martian, #2	4.00
Star Trek, #2	15.00
Stoney Burke, #2	3.00

Romance
All Love, #26	3.00
Best Love, #35	5.00
Boy Meets Girl, #3	1.35
Brides Romances, #23	2.00
Broadway Romances, #13	12.00
Career Girl Romances, #32	2.25
Cinderella Love, #7	4.50
Cowgirl Romances, #11	20.00
Glamorous Romances, #90	2.00
Love Letters, #2	16.00
My Secret Story, #28	30.00
Secret Hearts, #40	3.50
True Confidences, #73	25.00
True Love Pictorial, #7	15.00
Untamed Love, #4	35.00
Young Love, #6–11	12.00

**Young Romance, feature pub., Oct. 1949,
Vol. 3, No. 14, $4.00.**

Science Fiction

Attack on Planet Mars, (1951)	**90.00**
Buck Jones, #8	**20.00**
Doctor Solar, Man of the Atom, #10	**1.50**
Earth Man on Venus, (1951)	**170.00**
Flash Gordon, #16	**12.00**
Incredible Science Fiction, #31	**50.00**
Strange Adventures, #60	**5.00**
Strange Planets, #16	**4.00**
Strange Worlds, #20	**10.00**
T.H.U.N.D.E.R. Agents, #9	**12.00**
Tom Corbett Space Cadet, #2	**10.00**
UFO & Outer Space, #14	**.50**
Unknown Worlds of Science Fiction, #3	**1.00**
Weird Science, #11	**35.00**

Sports

Baseball Heroes, (1952)	**40.00**
Baseball Thrills, #10	**20.00**
Famous Plays of Jackie Robinson, #6	**20.00**
Sport Thrills, #11	**10.00**
True Sports Picture Stories, #4–6 . . .	**55.00**

Super Heroes

Amazing–Man, #22	**75.00**
Amazing Spider-Man, #40	**72.00**
Aquaman, #3	**8.00**
Captain America, (1968), #100	**35.00**
Captain Flash, #1	**20.00**
Flash Gordon, #3	**30.00**
Human Torch (1954), #38	**35.00**
Iron Man, #68	**1.00**
Metamorpho, #10	**2.50**
Submariner Comics, #14	**85.00**
Super Heroes, #4	**2.00**
Tales of the Legion, #314	**.50**

Three Dimensional

Alien Worlds, #1	**2.00**
E C Classics, #1	**60.00**
Three Stooges (1953), #3	**35.00**
Tor (Oct, Nov 1953)	**25.00**
True 3–D, #1	**15.00**

Walt Disney

Chip 'n Dale, #6	**.50**
Disneyland Birthday Party, #1	**7.50**
Donald Duck, #57	**2.50**
Huey, Dewey, & Louie Back to School, #35	**80.00**
Mickey Mouse, #234	**2.00**
Peter Pan, #2	**3.00**
Picnic Party, #8	**15.00**
Pluto, #429	**3.25**
Silly Symphonies, #6	**12.00**
Sleeping Beauty, #1	**15.00**
Three Caballeros, #71	**145.00**
Walt Disney's Comics and Stories, #311	**6.00**
Walt Disney Showcase, #30	**1.00**
Zorro, #13	**4.50**

War

Air War Stories, #2	**1.50**
American Air Forces, #2	**4.50**
Battle Squadron, #1	**4.50**
Blazing Combat, #1	**12.00**
Fightin' Marines, #15	**4.75**
GI Joe, A Real American Hero, #2 . .	**4.25**
GI War Brides, #1	**3.00**
Military Comics, #32	**55.00**
Our Army at War, #5	**18.00**
Soldiers of Fortune, #11	**4.00**
Star Spangled War Stories, #101 . . .	**8.50**
Tell It to the Marines, #3	**8.00**
This is War, #8	**4.00**
U.S. Tank Commandos, #3	**20.00**
War at Sea, #22	**1.50**
War is Hell, #11	**4.00**
War Stories, #5	**11.50**
War Victory Adventures, #2	**20.00**
Wing Comics, #116	**41.00**

Western

All American Western, #111	**15.00**
Annie Oakley & Tagg, #7	**8.00**
Billy the Kid Adventure Magazine, #9	**6.00**
Black Rider Rides Again, #1	**12.00**
Bob Colt, #3	**15.00**
Bronco Bill, #5	**5.00**
Clay Cody, Gunslinger, #1	**3.00**
Desperado, #4	**20.00**
Gabby Hayes Western, #15	**8.00**
Ghost Rider, #7	**17.00**
Gunsmoke, #10	**6.00**
Hopalong Cassidy, #50	**12.00**
Kid Colt OutLaw, #45	**39.00**
Lobo, #2	**1.50**
Roy Rogers Comics, (1948), #10 . . .	**15.00**
Tom Mix Western, #35	**10.00**
Two Gun Western, #14	**5.00**
Wild Western, #48	**28.00**

COMPACTS

Collecting Hints: Only mirrors that are broken should be removed and replaced in a vintage compact. Do not replace a mirror that is discolored, flawed, or in need of resilvering. The original mirror enhances the value of the compact.

Never apply a sticker directly to the surface of a compact. The acids from the glue may discolor or irreparably damage the finish, especially an enamel finish.

If a compact comes in the original box or pouch, do not destroy or discard it. The value of the compact is increased if it has its original presentation box.

History: In the first quarter of the 20th century, attitudes regarding cosmetics changed drastically. The use of make–up during the day was no longer looked upon with disdain. As women became "liberated" and as more and more of them entered the business world, the use of cosmetics became a routine and necessary part of a woman's grooming. Portable containers for cosmetics became a necessity.

Compacts were made in myriad shapes, styles, combinations and motifs, all reflecting the mood of the times. Every conceivable natural or man–made medium was used in the manufacture of compacts. Commemorative, premium, souvenir, patriotic, figural, combination compacts, Art Deco, and enamel compacts are a few examples of the compacts that were made in the United States and abroad. Compacts combined with cigarette cases, music boxes, watches, hatpins, canes, lighters, etc., also were very popular.

Compacts were made and used until the late 1950s when women opted for the "au natural" look. Compacts manufactured prior to that time are considered vintage compacts.

Some vintage compacts were exquisitely crafted, often enameled or encrusted with precious or synthetic jewels. These compacts were considered a form of jewelry or fashion accessory. The intricate and exacting workmanship of some vintage compacts would be virtually impossible to duplicate today.

References: Juliette Edwards, *Compacts,* published by author, 1994; Roseann Ettinger, *Compacts and Smoking Accessories,* Schiffer Publishing, 1991; Roselyn Gerson, *Ladies' Compacts of the 19th and 20th Centuries,* Wallace–Homestead, 1989; Roselyn Gerson, *Vintage Vanity Bags and Purses: An Identification and Value Guide,* Collector Books, 1994; Laura M. Mueller, *Collector's Encyclopedia of Compacts, Carryalls & Face Boxes: Identification and Values,* Collector Books, 1994.

Collectors' Club: Compact Collectors Club, PO Box Letter 40, Lynbrook, NY 11563.

Advisor: Roselyn Gerson.

Coppertone, compact, lid with black enamel cat and blue stars, 2¾ x 2⅜″ **50.00**
Dorothy Gray, vanity, silvertone, enameled lid, four shades of blue, int. metal mirror separates powder and rouge/lipstick compartments, powder grinder under back lid, 1¾ x 2″ **50.00**
Elgin American, compact, round, goldtone, multicolored enamel Eastern Star emblem on lid, 3″ d **50.00**
Evans, presentation set, goldtone, matching compact and cigarette lighter dec with scenic transfers, tap–sift model compact, 2″ d, fitted tan suede box **80.00**
Fillkwik, Art Deco, silvertone, pyramid shaped, black and red stripes, int. metal mirror separates powder and rouge compartments, small triangular fraternal emblem on lid, 1½ x 1¾″ **85.00**

K & K
Compact, basket shaped, brass colored, engine tooled, satin finish lid, emb swinging handle, metal int., 2⅛″ d **100.00**
Compact/bracelet combination, polished satin finish, hinged bracelet, 2 x 1½″ **225.00**
La Mode, vanity/cigarette case combination, black enameled, white enamel design on lid, int. metal mirror and powder and rouge compartments, 3 x 7″ **160.00**
Richard Hudnut, Le Debut, tango chain vanity, octagonal, dark green and gold enameled lid and lipstick tube, int. mirror separates powder and rouge compartments, 2″ w **210.00**
Unknown Maker
Advertising, Buick Eight logo on lid, silvertone and maroon, 3″ d **80.00**
Art Deco
Compact, round, silvertone, orange, black, and silver design on lid, 2″ d **65.00**
Vanity, oblong, goldtone, blue and goldtone design on lid, int. mirror and side by side rouge and powder compartments, 2¾ x 1½″ **85.00**
Commemorative
Compact, US Navy hat, plastic, blue and black, goldtone navy insignia on lid, 3 x 1¼″ **85.00**
Vanity, US Marine, enameled white, insignia centered on lid, int. metal mirror separates powder and rouge compartments, 2¼ x 2¼″ **50.00**
Figural
Book, goldtone, mother–of–pearl dec, lipstick tube slides out from spine, int. beveled mirror, powder and rouge compartments, 2 x 2½ x ½″ **80.00**

14K Yellow Gold, ornate monogram design, 39 dwt, $245.00.

Hand Mirror, goldtone, petit point dec, filigree handle, Austria, 2¾" d, 4" l **70.00**

Lock Motif, polished goldtone, 2½" d **90.00**
Petit Point, compact/cigarette case combination, lip–lock lipstick, front lid dec with floral petit point reveals powder compartment, brushed goldtone back lid reveals cigarette compartment, patent #2060466, 3½ x 2½ x ¾" **150.00**

Photo Compact, lucite, picture behind removable mirror, 3¼ x 3¼" . **75.00**

Souvenir, Paris, black enameled, front lid with goldtone Paris scenes, made in France, 3½ x 2¾" **150.00**

Tango Chain, vanity, green enameled flowers on lid and lipstick holder, int. metal mirror separates powder and rouge compartments, lipstick holder suspended by two chains, opens to accept slim lipstick tube, 1½ x 2 x 4½" **140.00**

Wadsworth

Ball and Chain, compact, goldtone, lipstick tube attached by chain to round compact, plastic int., 2" d . . **165.00**

Hatbox, vanity, two sided, tan leather, polished goldtone lids both sides, powder/mirror compartment one side, rouge/locket compartment other side, leather finger carrying handle, 1½" d **60.00**

COOKBOOKS

Collecting Hints: Look for books in good, clean condition. Watch for special, interesting notes in margins.

History: Among the earliest Americana cookbooks are *The Frugal Housewife* or *Complete Woman Cook* by Susanna Carter, published in Philadelphia in 1796 and *American Cookery* by Amelia Simmons, published in Hartford, Connecticut, in 1796. Cookbooks of this era are crudely written, for most cooks could not read well and measuring devices were not yet refined.

Other types of collectible cookbooks include those used as premiums or advertisements. This type is much less expensive than the rare 18th century books.

References: Bob Allen, *A Guide To Collecting Cookbooks and Advertising Cookbooks*, Collector Books, 1990, 1995 value update; Mary Barile, *Cookbooks Worth Collecting*, Wallace–Homestead, 1994; Mary–Margaret Barile, *Just Cookbooks!*, published by author, 1990; Linda J. Dickinson, *A Price Guide to Cookbooks, and Recipe Leaflets*, Collector Books, 1990, 1995

value update; Norman E. Martinus and Harry L. Rinker, *Warman's Paper*, Wallace–Homestead, 1994; Dana Gehman Morykan and Harry L. Rinker, *Warman's Country Antiques & Collectibles, Second Edition*, Wallace–Homestead, 1994.

Collectors' Club: Cook Book Collectors Club of America, 231 E. James Blvd., PO Box 85, St. James, MO 65559.

Periodical: *Cookbook Collectors' Exchange*, PO Box 32369, San Jose, CA 95152.

American Woman's Home, Catharine E Beecher, Harriet Beecher Stowe, 1869 **75.00**

A Thousand Ways To Please a Husband, 1917 .... **60.00**

Austin's Domestic Science Book One, 1914 .... **15.00**

Baker's Chocolate, 1904 .... **20.00**

Best From Midwest Kitchens, 1946 ... **5.00**

Betty Crocker Cookbook for Boys & Girls, 1957, first edition **95.00**

Brides Book, 1934, soft cover **12.00**

Calendar of Dinners, 1925 .... **20.00**

Calumet, Kewpie cov, c1920 .... **15.00**

Campbell Soup Kids, 64 pgs **30.00**

Chicago Daily News, 1930s **9.00**

Confers Guide & Cook Book, Confer Medical Co, 1910, 32 pgs, 5¾ x 9" . **15.00**

Cookies & More Cookies, L Sumption, 1938 .... **5.00**

Dr Caldwells Home Cook Book, Pepsin Syrup Co, 32 pgs **10.00**

Dr. Fenners Cook Book, 1912, blue and white **15.00**

Durkee Foods, 1933 Chicago World's Fair **7.50**

Every Step In Canning, G Gray, 1920, wear to orig dust jacket **5.00**

General Foods, 1932, 1st edition **10.00**

Good Housekeeping Cook Book, Recipes and Methods For Every Day and Every Occasion, 264 pgs, 1st ed., 1933, green letters, $12.00.

Gourmet In Low Calorie Kitchen	**8.50**
Healthy Cooking, Mrs E Kellogg, Kellogg Food Co, soft brown cov . . .	**7.00**
Home Comfort Cook Book, Home Comfort Family Ranges, 211 pgs, 6 x 8½"	**20.00**
Household Searchlight Cookbook, 1943	**10.00**
Jell–O, Jell–O box image on train tracks	**10.00**
Lowney's Cook Book, M Howard, 1907, 1st edition	**25.00**
Midwestern Jr League, 1976, 1st edition, tear in dust jacket	**8.00**
Mother Hubbard Flour	**35.00**
Mrs Peterson Simplified Cook 1924 . . .	**14.00**
New Congregational Church Cook Book, LaGrange, IL, 1935	**9.00**
New Orleans Creole Recipes, 1957 . . .	**8.00**
Old Warsaw, 1958, worn dust jacket . .	**12.00**
Palm Springs Cookbook, 374 pgs	**15.00**
Pepperidge Farm, M Rudkin, 1st edition, orig dust jacket	**24.00**
Pillsbury Balanced Recipes, aluminum cov, 1933	**20.00**
Practical Housekeeping, 1884	**15.00**
Prudential, teddy bears seated at table, 1910, sgd "W Meyer"	**18.00**
Rector, 1928, ragged dust jacket	**9.00**
Reliable Recipes, Calumet Baking Powder Co, 80 pgs	**6.00**
Rumford Fruit Cook Book, 1927, 48 pgs	**6.00**
Savannah Cookbook, 1933	**12.50**
Sunset Kitchen Cabinet Recipes, 1944, dust jacket	**6.00**
Teddy Bear Baking School, Fleischmann, 1906	**25.00**
The New Cookery, autographed by author, 1922	**20.00**
Thousand Ways To Please A Husband, 1917	**25.00**
US Navy, 1944	**12.00**
Vincent Price Treasury Great Recipes, 1965, 1st edition, brown padded cov, ribbon markers	**35.00**
What Cooks At Stillmeadow, G Taber, 1st edition, dust jacket	**35.00**
White House Cookbook, 1894, white, silver cover, some wear and stains . .	**75.00**
Woman's Favorite Cookbook, 1907 . . .	**15.00**

COOKIE JARS

Collecting Hints: Cookie jars are subject to chips and paint flaking. Collectors should concentrate on jars which have their original lid and are in very good or better condition.

Learn to identify makers' marks and codes. Do not fail to include some of the contemporary manufacturers in your collection.

Above all, ignore the prices and hype associated with the cookie jars sold at the Andy Warhol sale in 1988. Neither is realistic.

History: Cookie jars, colorful and often whimsical, are one of the fastest growing categories in the collectibles field. Many cookie jars have been made by more than one company and as a result can be found with different marks. This resulted from mergers or splits by manufacturers, e.g., Brush–McCoy which is now Nelson McCoy. Molds also were traded and sold among companies.

Cookie jars often were redesigned to reflect newer tastes. Hence, the same jar may be found in several different style variations.

References: Mary Jane Giacomini, *American Bisque: A Collector's Guide with Prices*, Schiffer Publishing, 1994; John W. Humphries, *Humphries Price Guide To Cookie Jars*, published by author, 1992, 1994–95 value update, distributed by L–W Book Sales; Harold Nichols, *McCoy Cookie Jars: From The First To The Latest, Second Edition*, Nichols Publishing, 1991; *1995 Cookie Jar Express Pricing Guide To Cookie Jars*, Paradise Publications, 1995; Fred Roerig and Joyce Herndon Roerig, *Collector's Encyclopedia of Cookie Jars*, Collector Books, Book I (1990, 1995 value update), Book II (1994); Mike Schneider, *The Complete Cookie Jar Book*, Schiffer Publishing, 1991; Diane Stoneback, *Kitchen Collectibles: The Essential Buyer's Guide*, Wallace–Homestead, 1994; Mark and Ellen Supnick, *The Wonderful World of Cookie Jars*, L–W Book Sales, 1995; Ermagene Westfall, *An Illustrated Value Guide To Cookie Jars*, Collector Books (1983, 1995 value update), Book II (1993, 1995 value update), Collector Books.

Collectors' Club: The Cookie Jar Collector's Club, 595 Cross River Rd., Katonah, NY 10536.

Periodicals: *Cookie Jarrin'*, RR #2, Box 504, Walterboro, SC 29488; *Crazed Over Cookie Jars*, PO Box 254, Savanna, IL 61074; *The Cookie Jar Express*, PO Box 221, Mayview, MO 64071.

Abingdon	
Money Sack	**40.00**
Pumpkin	**375.00**
Train, yellow and black	**250.00**
Advertising	
Alpo Dog	**45.00**
Avon Bear	**45.00**
Century 21 House	**995.00**
Elsie in Barrel	**365.00**
Keebler Elf	**45.00**
Kraft T Bear	**165.00**
Marshall Fields, double decker bus, red	**675.00**
Spuds MacKenzie	**245.00**
American Bisque	
Baby Elephant	**195.00**
Bear with Hat	**75.00**

Casper	325.00	Donald Duck	45.00
Chalkboard Saddle	185.00	Mickey Mouse	75.00
Cheerleader, flasher	450.00	Hull	
Chick	35.00	Barefoot Boy	435.00
Clown, flasher	395.00	Train Depot	75.00
Collegiate Owl	85.00	Lefton	
Cookies Out Of This World	295.00	Cow	35.00
Cowboy Boots	150.00	French Girl	275.00
Davy Crockett	425.00	Girl, head	125.00
Dog in Basket	65.00	Lovebirds on house	165.00
Dog with Toothache	550.00	Scottish Girl	235.00
Dutch Girl	500.00	Maddux, Raggedy Andy	195.00
Elf, orange hat	35.00	Maurice	
Grandma	90.00	Clown	225.00
Indian Maiden	250.00	Koala Bear	75.00
Jack In The Box	175.00	McCoy	
Kitten with Yarn	40.00	Baseball Boy	195.00
Majorette	325.00	Boy on Football	215.00
Milk Wagon	125.00	Chilly Willy, MIB	35.00
Paddle Boat	395.00	Coffee Mug	35.00
Pig, female	75.00	Cookie Barrel, large	22.00
Spaceship	295.00	Covered Wagon	50.00
Spool of Thread	210.00	Grandfather Clock	85.00
APCO, clown	35.00	Indian Head	350.00
Applause		Keebler Tree House	35.00
Fairy Godmother	45.00	Owl, beige	30.00
57 Chevrolet Wheelie	95.00	Panda	45.00
Avon, Panda Bear	65.00	Pig	25.00
Brush		Pineapple	60.00
Covered Wagon	475.00	Raggedy Ann	70.00
Hippopotamus, sitting	275.00	Santa	125.00
Humpty Dumpty, peak top	295.00	Squirrel	90.00
Little Angel	750.00	Strawberry, white	45.00
Owl, gray	80.00	Teepee, slanted	295.00
Panda	195.00	Touring Car	125.00
California Originals		Winking Pig	175.00
Airplane, pilot	465.00	Wren House	210.00
Baseball Boy	55.00	Metlox	
Bear, brown	55.00	Barrel of Apples	45.00
Clown	60.00	Basset Hound	575.00
Fire Truck, red	375.00	Bear, blue sweater	40.00
Girl	225.00	Bear on Roller Skates	100.00
Octopus on Chest	325.00	Boy's Head, blond hair, hairline on	
Owl, #2728	15.00	lid	100.00
Pelican	30.00	Cat's Head	125.00
Scarecrow	175.00	Clown	130.00
Sesame Street, The Count	775.00	Ears of Corn	75.00
Sheriff	40.00	Fido Dog	275.00
Superman	425.00	Humpty Dumpty	250.00
Tigger	225.00	Hutula Tattletale	800.00
Turtle, sitting	35.00	Lion	450.00
Cardinal, Cookieville Bus	475.00	Orange	45.00
Deforest, monkey	125.00	Penguin	100.00
Disney		Piggy, chip on tail	60.00
Donald Duck, sitting	250.00	Porsche, coupe, convertible	125.00
Eeyore	750.00	Rabbit on Cabbage	165.00
Winnie the Pooh	110.00	Sierra Vista Train	80.00
Doranne		Sir Francis Drake	15.00
Pinocchio	295.00	Mosaic Tile, Mammy	475.00
World Globe, green	125.00	Napco, Woody Woodpecker on bar-	
Enesco, Here Comes Trouble	225.00	rel	250.00
Hoan		National Silver, Mammy	275.00

Potbelly Stove	75.00
Practical Pig	100.00
Twin Winton	
Cow	80.00
Dutch Girl	100.00
Mother Goose	175.00
Ranger Bear	55.00
Rooster	75.00
Sheriff Bear	50.00
Vandor	
Betty Boop	650.00
Fred Flintstone and Pebbles, sitting in chair	300.00

Clown, Morton Pottery, $25.00.

Pfaltzgraff, Derby Dan	195.00
Pottery Guild	
Dutch Boy	55.00
Dutch Girl	75.00
Puppy	65.00
Red Riding Hood	155.00
Regal	
Barn	275.00
Majorette, gold	400.00
Oriental Woman	600.00
Quaker Oats	100.00
Robinson–Ransbottom, Peter Pumpkin Eater	145.00
Shawnee	
Drummer Boy, gold	800.00
Dutch Boy, blue stripes	125.00
Fern, yellow	65.00
Little Chef	100.00
Mugsy	350.00
Puss 'n Boots	150.00
Queen Corn	75.00
Smiley, shamrocks	225.00
Snowflake, yellow	65.00
Winnie, blue collar	250.00
Sigma	
Dalmatian Fireman	425.00
Kermit on TV	525.00
Kliban Cat	
With kiss on cheek	175.00
With kitten	375.00
Mrs Tiggy Winkle	450.00
Peter Rabbit	495.00
Planetary Pals	275.00
Taylor, Robot	60.00
Treasure Craft	
Big Al, small nick	50.00
Coffeepot, blue spatter	25.00
Farmer Pig	50.00
Granny	
Blue	75.00
Yellow	75.00
Locomotive, smiling	30.00
Monk	48.00

COORS POTTERY

Collecting Hints: Cookie jars and the bright, solid–colored dinnerware lines, in the tradition of Bauer and Homer Laughlin's Fiesta, are the principal focuses of Coors Pottery collectors. Kitchen collectors focus on the company's utilitarian products.

Coors products were meant to be used, and they were. When collecting, concentrate on pieces whose decorative elements are still bright and complete. Add ten percent if a piece still has a period paper sales label attached.

History: J. J. Herold, a former designer and manager for companies such as J. B. Owens, Roseville Pottery, and Weller Pottery, moved to Golden, Colorado, late in the first decade of the twentieth century. His experiments in producing pottery from local clay attracted the attention of Adolph Coors, a local brewery owner. In 1910 Coors offered Herold the use of his abandoned Colorado Glass Works plant. Shortly thereafter Herold founded the Herold China and Pottery Company for the purpose of making ovenproof china cooking utensils.

Herold left in January 1912 to work for Western Pottery Company in Denver. Coors and other stockholders kept the plant open and expanded its product line to include spark plugs and scientific wares. Herold Pottery also was known as the Golden Pottery. By 1914 a line of chemical porcelain products was available. Herold returned for a one–year stint as manager in 1915. The company received an injunction against Herold's new employer, Guernsey Earthenware Company (Cambridge Art Pottery), to prevent it from using the formula knowledge Herold gained while in Golden.

In 1920 the company's name legally became Coors Porcelain Company. The company continued to concentrate on chemical, industrial, and scientific porcelain products. The household cooking line was trademarked "Thermo–Porcelain." A Thermo–Porcelain White Hotel Ware line was developed, one result of which was Coors' involvement in the manufacturer of dinnerware and other kitchen accessories.

In the 1930s Coors introduced six colored, decorated dinnerware lines: Coorado, Golden Ivory, Golden Rainbow, Mello–Tone, Rock–Mount, and Rosebud Cook–N–Serve. Dinnerware had a high–gloss, colored glaze while vases tended to be matte glazed. When Prohibition ended in 1933, Coors also began making accessories for the tavern trade.

Dinnerware production ended when the company switched to wartime production in 1941. When the war was over, the company did manufacture some ovenware, teapots, coffee makers, beer mugs, ashtrays, and novelty items, but no dinnerware. Coffee makers, ovenware, teapots, and vases were discontinued in the 1950s, mugs in the early 1960s, and ashtrays by the late 1970s.

Herman Coors, third son of Adolph Coors, founded the H. F. Coors Company at Inglewood, California, in 1925. It was an entirely separate company from Coors Porcelain Company. H. F. Coors Company made hotel and institutional commercial pottery, doll heads, plumbing fixtures, and wall tiles.

References: Carol and Jim Carlton, *Colorado Pottery,* Collector Books, 1994; Robert H. Schneider, *Coors Rosebud Pottery,* published by author, 1984.

Periodical: *Coors Pottery Newsletter,* 3808 Carr Place N., Seattle, WA 98103.

Cookie Jar, barrel shape, maroon	**125.00**
Mello–Tone, pastel colors, late 1930s, early 1940s	
Cereal Bowl, 6¼" d, spring green . . .	**6.50**
Cup and Saucer, azure blue	**15.00**
Gravy, attached underplate, spring green	**20.00**
Pitcher, 2 qt, canary yellow	**25.00**
Plate	
4" d, bread and butter, canary yellow	**8.00**
7" d, dinner, coral pink	**12.00**
Platter, 15" l, oval, spring green	**20.00**
Vegetable Bowl, 9" d, azure blue . . .	**20.00**
Rosebud, emb and hp rosebud and leaves, solid ground, introduced 1934	
Cake Plate, blue	**30.00**
Casserole	
French, orange	**50.00**
Triple Service, rose, small	**35.00**
Cream Soup, rose	**18.00**
Custard, blue	**15.00**
Fruit Bowl, orange	**12.00**
Mixing Bowl, handled, orange	**35.00**
Platter, ivory	**35.00**
Pudding, orange, large	**60.00**
Teapot, yellow, large	**175.00**

COWAN POTTERY

Collecting Hints: Cowan was primarily a modernistic designer. In addition to focusing on design, he also worked on developing glaze formulas that complemented his work. Several pieces were made in limited numbers.

Focus on pieces that have delicate decorative elements. Aesthetics is a major pricing factor. A slight difference in glaze or assembly can affect price.

In 1931 Cowan brought together a group of distinguished potters including Alexander Blazys, Paul Bogatay, Thelma Frazier, Waylande Gregory, A. D. Jacobson, and Margaret Postgate. Pieces made by these artists while at Cowan often command premium prices.

Several individuals are currently attempting to find publishers for books about Cowan pottery. The sudden appearance of several new books certainly will trigger renewed market interest in Cowan material. Be alert to the possibility of market price manipulation on the part of one or more authors.

History: R. Guy Cowan operated a pottery on Nicholson Avenue in Lakewood, Ohio, a suburb of Cleveland, between 1912 and 1917. Lakewood pieces have a red clay body. After a period of service during World War I, Cowan returned to Lakewood and reopened the pottery. Within a short period, Cowan's gas well ran dry, necessitating a move to Rocky River.

Upon arriving in Rocky River, Cowan switched from his red clay body to one of high–fired porcelain. By 1921 he had developed over 1,000 outlets for his wares. A commercial line was launched in the early 1920s. By 1925 Cowan was involved in the manufacture of dinnerware place settings, console sets, and figures. One of his clients was Wahl Pen Company, for whom he made ceramic desk sets. The 1930 product line included planters and ivy jars.

In addition to utilitarian products, Cowan also made art pottery. He exhibited regularly at the Cleveland Museum of Art, the Pennsylvania Academy of Art, and the Metropolitan Museum of Art, winning numerous awards for his work. In 1930 Cowan Potters, Inc., was organized as an artists' colony. The project lasted only one year, a period when many of the most desirable Cowan pieces were produced. Cowan ceased operations in December 1931.

Initially, the name Cowan Pottery was incised on pieces. Later a black stamp with "Cowan" or "Cowan Potteries" or a mark with the initials "R.G." and "Cowan" in a circle was used.

References: Susan and Al Bagdade, *Warman's American Pottery and Porcelain,* Wallace–Homestead, 1994; Ralph and Terry Kovel, *Kovels' American Art Pottery: The Collector's*

Guide To Makers, Marks, and Factory Histories, Crown Publishers, 1993; Leslie Pina, *Pottery: Modern Wares, 1920–60,* Schiffer Publishing, 1994; Tim and Jamie Saloff, *The Collector's Encyclopedia of Cowan Pottery: Identification & Values,* Collector Books, 1994.

Museums: Cowan Pottery Museum, Rocky River Public Library, Rocky River, OH; Everson Museum of Art, Syracuse, NY.

Candleholders, pr, #735	**45.00**
Centerpiece Bowl, 6½" h, figural nude flower frog	**175.00**
Cigarette Holder, figural, seahorse, ivory	**50.00**
Compote, 7" d, 2½" h, diamond shape	**25.00**
Cup and Saucer, melon dec, tan glaze .	**30.00**
Flower Frog 6½" h, nude dancer with scarf	**135.00**

Flower Frog, figural, c1920, marked "Lakewood, Ohio," 7" h, $125.00.

11¼" h, 6" d, flamingo, perforated base, white glaze, diestamped twice	**300.00**
Soap Dish, 4 x 7", white and pink matte, seahorses at base	**40.00**
Trivet, 6½" d, scalloped rim, bust of young girl framed by flowers, sgd . .	**275.00**
Vase, Logan, brown crystalline	**150.00**

COWBOY HEROES

Collecting Hints: Cowboy hero material was collected and saved in great numbers. Don't get fooled into thinking an object is rare until you have checked carefully. Tom Mix material remains the most desirable, followed closely by Hopalong Cassidy, Roy Rogers, and Gene Autry memorabilia. Material associated with the Western stars of the silent era and early talking films still has not achieved its full potential as a collectible.

History: The era when the cowboy and longhorn cattle dominated the Great Western Plains was short, lasting only from the end of the Civil War to the late 1880s. Dime novelists romanticized this period and created a love affair in America's heart for the Golden West.

Motion pictures saw the cowboy as a prime entertainment feature. William S. Hart developed the character of the cowboy hero—often in love with his horse more than the girl. He was followed by Tom Mix, Ken Maynard, Tim McCoy, and Buck Jones. The "B" movie, the second feature of a double bill, was often of the cowboy genre.

In 1935 William Boyd starred in the first of the Hopalong Cassidy films. Gene Autry, "a singing cowboy," gained popularity over the airwaves of the West and Midwest. By the late 1930s, Autry's Melody Ranch was a national institution on the air as well as the screen. Roy Rogers replaced Autry as the featured cowboy at Republic Pictures in the mid–1940s. Although the Lone Ranger first appeared on the airwaves in 1933, he did not enter the movie medium until 1938.

The early years of television enhanced the careers of the big three—Autry, Boyd, and Rogers. The appearance of the Lone Ranger in shows made specifically for television strengthened the key role held by the cowboy hero. "Gunsmoke," "Wagon Train," "Rawhide," "The Rifleman," "Paladin," and "Bonanza" were just a few of the shows that followed.

By the early 1970s the cowboy hero had fallen from grace, relegated to reruns or specials. In early 1983 The Library of Congress in Washington, D.C., conducted a major show on the "Cowboy Hero," perhaps a true indication that he is now a part of past history.

References: Joseph J. Caro, *Collector's Guide Hopalong Cassidy Memorabilia,* L–W Book Sales, 1992; Bernard A. Drew, *Hopalong Cassidy: The Clarence E. Mulford Story,* The Scarecrow Press, 1991; Lee J. Felbinger, *The Lone Ranger Pictorial Scrapbook,* published by author, 1988; Ted Hake, *Hake's Guide To Cowboy Character Collectibles: An Illustrated Price Guide Covering 50 Years of Movie & TV Cowboy Heroes,* Wallace–Homestead, 1994; Theodore L. Hake and Robert D. Cauler, *Six–Gun Heroes: A Price Guide To Movie Cowboy Collectibles,* Wallace–Homestead, 1976; Robert Heide and John Gilman, *Box–Office Buckaroos,* Abbeville Press, 1989; Norman E. Martinus and Harry L. Rinker, *Warman's Paper,* Wallace–Homestead, 1994; Harry L. Rinker, *Hopalong Cassidy: King of the Cowboy Merchandisers,* Schiffer Publishing, 1995; David Rothel, *The Gene Autry Book,* Empire Publishing, 1988; David Rothel, *The Roy Rogers Book,* Empire Publishing Company, 1987; Neil Summers, *The Official TV Western Book,* Vol. 1 (1987), Vol. 2 (1989), Vol. 3 (1991), and Vol. 4 (1992), The Old West Shop Publishing; Richard West, *Television*

Westerns: Major and Minor Series, 1946–1978, McFarland & Company, 1987.

Periodicals: *Collecting Hollywood,* American Collectors Exchange, 2401 Broad St., Chattanooga, TN 37408; *Favorite Westerns & Serial World,* Route One, Box 103, Vernon Center, MN 56090; *The Westerner,* Box 5232–32, Vienna, WV 26105.

Museums: Gene Autry Western Heritage Museum, Los Angeles, CA; National Cowboy Hall of Fame and Western Heroes, Oklahoma City, OK; Roy Rogers Museum, Victorville, CA.

Corporal Barlow, movie still, *Colt .45, The Escape,* Peter Miles and Wayde Preston, Warner Brothers, $12.00.

GENE AUTRY

Badge, 1¼" d, celluloid, "Official Gene Autry Club," portrait center, black, white, and bright orange, c1940 ...	**65.00**
Book, *Gene Autry Goes to the Circus,* 5½ x 6½", hard cov, Whitman, Tell–A–Tale series, 28 pgs, 1950 ...	**20.00**
Bread Label, 2¾" sq, diecut corners, full color photo scene, series #5, #6–8, early 1950s, set of three	**54.00**
Cap Gun, 7½" l, metal, silvered, ivory plastic grips, rearing horse, marked "BH," inscribed "Gene Autry"	**90.00**
Clothing, cowgirl outfit, orig box	**85.00**
Coloring Book, 11 x 15", Whitman, 48 pgs, unused, 1949	**30.00**

Comic Book, *Gene Autry Comics,* Vol 1, #20, Dell, Oct 1948	**18.00**
Guitar, Emenee	**145.00**
Frame Tray Puzzle, 11½ x 15", Whitman, copyright 1953	**25.00**
Lobby Card, 11 x 14", "Red River Valley," full color, action scene	**18.00**
Pinback Button, 1¼" d, black and white photo, dark blue ground, "Gene Autry's Brand/Sunbeam Bread," c1950	**35.00**
Poster, 24 x 30", stiff paper, sgd "Best Wishes, Gene Autry" at center, portraits and film scenes, Pat Buttram and Smiley Burnette, inscribed "America's Favorite Cowboy/GENE AUTRY" at bottom, #191 from limited edition series, certificate of authenticity from The Art Merchant, Hollywood, copyright 1982	**100.00**
Program, 8½ x 11", "The Gene Autry Show," 8 pgs, traveling show souvenir, c1950	**32.00**
Ring, Dell Comics	**95.00**
Rubber Boots, orig box	**155.00**
Sheet Music, 9 x 12", *No Letter Today,* blue and white cov photo, copyright 1943	**12.00**
Song Folio, 9 x 12", De Luxe Edition, soft cov, 96 pgs, 1938	**32.00**
Tablet, 8 x 10", lined paper, full color illus of Gene and Champion and facsimile signature on cov, inscribed "Gene Autry/Columbia Pictures," c1950, unused	**22.50**
Wristwatch, animated, silver metal case, color portrait on dial face, Autry holding sixgun, inscribed "Gene Autry Watch" on face and "Always Your Pal/Gene Autry" on face and back, tan tooled leather straps, New Haven Watch Co, c1951	**315.00**

HOPALONG CASSIDY

Belt, 30" l, leather, black, silver "Hopalong" between metal rivets and stars on center back, early 1950s	**35.00**
Bolo Tie, steer head	**10.00**
Bowl	**30.00**
Camera, 3 x 4 x 5", box type, metal, black, illus of Hoppy on Topper on title plate, Galter Products of Chicago, 1940 William Boyd copyright	**90.00**
Child's Play Outfit, shirt and pants ...	**145.00**
Coloring Book	**35.00**
Coloring Kit, color picture of Hoppy, orig box	**30.00**
Comic Book, Vol 5, #29, Fawcett, March 1949	**55.00**
Display, Butter–Nut Bread, bread loaf shape	**75.00**

Doll, 22" h, cloth, stuffed, molded vinyl child's face stitched to fabric head, removable black felt hat, yellow hat band inscribed "Hopalong Cassidy," plush hair and chaps, early 1950s .. **190.00**

Fan Card, 3½ x 5½", color portrait, facsimile signature, blank back, early 1950 .... **25.00**

Flashlight, Siren Lite, 7" l, metal, silvered siren cap, litho scene around side, red lettering, inscribed "Hong Kong British Empire" on cap, 1940–50s **80.00**

Game, MIB, 1950 .... **55.00**

Glass, 5" h, milk glass, illus of Hoppy and message in black, raised "Hoppy" on bottom, early 1950s ... **25.00**

Greeting Card, birthday, 4½ x 5½", paper, portrait, opens horizontally, "Official Hopalong Cassidy Cards" inscribed on back, Buzza Cardozo, Hollywood, orig envelope, early 1950s **27.50**

Hair Trainer **55.00**

Hanger, wood, jigsawed, "Hoppy's Bunkhouse Clothes Corral," three wood pegs, inscriptions stamped in black, Northland Milk, premium ... **100.00**

Ice Cream Container, quart **65.00**

Iron–On Transfer, 2½ x 10", tissue, brown, "Hopalong Cassidy/Deputy," early 1950s **10.00**

Jigsaw Puzzle, MIB, set of three ... **55.00**

Lunch Box, Thermos, cloud label, 1950s **110.00**

Milk Carton, waxed cardboard, 5½ x 11½", red, white, and blue **12.00**

Miniature Knife and Scabbard, ¾ x 5" l, black vinyl belt loop sheath, inscribed "Hopalong Cassidy," 4" l knife, single blade, white plastic handle, marked "USA," early 1950s ... **60.00**

Mug, 3" h, white china, color Hoppy illus, early 1950s **70.00**

Party Plates, cardboard, multicolored Hoppy on Topper, white ground, orig cellophane shrink wrap, unopened, set of six **20.00**

Pencil Sharpener, 1¾ x 2½", flat, image of Hoppy on Topper, black and white, dark blue ground, sharpener mounted on reverse **30.00**

Pillow Case, 16 x 17", satin, 2" gold brocade and fringe border, head and shoulder Hoppy portrait, six shooter, cactus, Bar–20 Ranch symbol, facsimile signature, unused **60.00**

Pin, Bulldogger Savings **22.00**

Plate, china **55.00**

Playing Cards, "Hopalong Canasta," Hoppy and Topper portraits on backs, Pacific Playing Card Co, copyright 1950 .... **85.00**

Pocket Knife **85.00**

Radio, red and silver, Arvin **125.00**

Record Album, Square Dance Hold Up, pictures, two records **75.00**

Scrapbook **125.00**

Snowdome **50.00**

Tab, litho tin, "Burry's Hopalong Cassidy Cookies" rope border, Hoppy portrait center, inscription and "Hoppy's Secret Code" on back, early 1950s **65.00**

Thermos **40.00**

Tin, 5" h, 2¾" d, popcorn can, litho, bright colors, portrait **30.00**

Trading Card, Wild West **12.00**

Utensils, 7½" l knife, 6" l fork and spoon, stainless steel, Hoppy on handle, vertical stem lettering, early 1950s **65.00**

Waste Can **95.00**

Wood Burning Set, orig box **195.00**

Wristwatch, 1" d chrome case, silver dial face, red numerals and hands, black and white depiction of Hoppy, black lettering, engraved "Good Luck From Hoppy" on back, US Time ... **140.00**

DAVY CROCKETT

Archery Set, 46" strung wood bow, seven feathered wood arrows, paper target sheet, orig box and sleeve with name and portrait illus, Rollin Wilson Co, mid 1950s **45.00**

Barlow Knife **65.00**

Belt Buckle, 1½ x 3", silvered metal, rounded, raised border, inscription, Old Betsy rifle, leather belt, brown, simulated alligator texture **32.00**

Box, 2 x 4½ x 8", Davy Crockett Cookies, cardboard, diecut, figural, covered wagon drawn by oxen, portrait illus, Dutch Maid, Federal Sweets & Biscuit Co, Clifton, NJ, 1952 .... **80.00**

Cereal Bowl, 5" d **25.00**

Clock, pendulum, MIB **125.00**

Clothing, complete outfit, orig box ... **95.00**

Coloring Book **10.00**

Cookie Jar, Brush **125.00**

Flashlight, ¼ x 1¼ x 3¼" h, metal case, painted, removable red cap, brown and red Crockett illus, cream color ground, fringed fabric carrying strap, Bantam Lite Inc, mid 1950s **45.00**

Glass, 5" h, frosted white, dark brown portrait illus both sides, Ritchey's Milk, mid 1950s **35.00**

Gun, 10½" l, plastic, flintlock, brown, silver accents, "Davy Crockett" in gold lettering on side, raised pirate and ship on handle, c1955 .... **30.00**

Hat, straw **26.00**
ID Bracelet, Davy Crockett Club, metal, silvered finish, expandable, raised gold color Crockett holding rifle illus on cov, hinged, photo frames inside, two black and white photos included, red, white, blue, and brown Crockett illus on inside lid, Drema Mfg Co, 22 West 19th St, NY, orig display case and charter member card, mid 1950s **85.00**
Lamp, figural, copper **85.00**
Lunch Box, steel, full color illus, silver gray ground, green trim, American Thermos, 1955–56 .... **90.00**
Mug, pottery, figural, young Davy, gun handle **15.00**
Pinback Button, 1¼" d, black lettering and Crockett illus, yellow ground, white metal horse head in horseshoe hanger, 1950s **15.00**
Plate, 9½" d, china, white, brown name and illus, Oxford China Co, mid 1950s **50.00**
Playset, compass, belt, powder horn, orig pkg, mint **85.00**
Puzzle, frame tray, 10 x 12½", aerial view of fort being attacked by Indians, black and white photo of Parker in upper left corner, c1955 .. **15.00**
Ring, plastic **20.00**
Sand Pail, 8" h, litho tin, colorful scenes on red ground, Ohio Art, copyright 1955 .... **60.00**
Sheet Music, *Ballad of Davy Crockett,* Fess Parker cov, Disney **20.00**
Souvenir Planter, 3½ x 6 x 5" h, china, figural, young Davy, bear, tree stump, "Davy Crockett Birthplace/Limestone, Tenn," inscribed in gold on back of stump, c1950 .... **25.00**
Stamp Book, 8½ x 11", Simon & Schuster, 32 pgs, 48 color photo stamps, 1955 .... **35.00**
Target, tin **5.00**
Thermos, 8½" h, steel, plastic cap, full color illus around sides, American Thermos, c1955–56 .... **40.00**
Tie, mounted on orig card **15.00**
Wallet, plastic, black western illus on red and cream ground, ID card, mid 1950s **20.00**
Wristwatch, play **15.00**

LONE RANGER

Badge, Silver's, lucky horseshoe **45.00**
Blotter, colorful, Bond Bread adv **10.00**
Book
  The Lone Ranger, Little Golden Book, 6½ x 8", stiff cov, Simon & Schuster, 24 pgs, copyright 1956 **11.00**

The Lone Ranger Rides North, 5½ x 7½", hard cov, dj, Grosset & Dunlap, 214 pgs, copyright 1946 **18.00**
Crayon Box, tin **35.00**
Flashlight, signal siren **65.00**
Game, Legend of the Lone Ranger ... **10.00**
Gun and Holster Set, Lone Ranger Official Outfit, two black enameled steel clicker pistols, black pebble grained stiff cardboard holster, silver accents on guns and holster, black, red, and white neckerchief, orig box, Feinberg–Henry Co, copyright 1938 **130.00**
Hairbrush, orig box **85.00**
Holster, 11" l, molded black rubber, textured design, silvered brass buckle, "Lone Ranger" inscription on holster, metal cap gun, glossy black, white pistol grips, "Fanner 50" and Mattel logo on each side, late 1950s **40.00**
Magazine, *Golden West,* Lone Ranger on cov **10.00**
Mask, 3½ x 6½", black fabric, molded, starched, elastic head string, 1950s **25.00**
Membership Card, Lone Ranger US Savings Bond Peace Patrol, picture of Moore, unused **20.00**
Model Kit, Tonto, #183, plastic, brown, eight page comic book, instructions, backdrop mural, Aurora Products Corp, copyright 1974, unopened ... **32.00**
Movie Viewer, films, orig box **125.00**
Paint Book, 1940 .... **40.00**
Palm Puzzle, ½ x 3½ x 5" w, litho tin frame, red and white checkerboard design, full color Lone Ranger scene with four small metal balls fit in holes, clear glass cov, #5, "Guarding Gold Panners" series, c1940 ...... **25.00**
Pedometer, 2¾" d, black, white, and red center dial, "Official Lone Ranger Pedometer," aluminum rim, black back, premium, 1948 .... **35.00**
Pen, Silver Bullet Secret Code Ball Point, MOC, 1950s **75.00**
Pencil Box **125.00**
Pinback Button, 2¼" d, "Lone Ranger Silver Bullet Award," celluloid, red, white, and blue, bullet in center, red inscription on silver ribbon, purple ribbon, issued by Lone Ranger Family Restaurants, c1970 .... **25.00**
Pistol, 9" l, brown marbleized grips ... **35.00**
Playset, Lone Ranger Old West Playset, plastic figures and fort, tepee, Multiple Toymakers, copyright 1974, orig sealed box **40.00**
Pocket Knife, 3" l, single blade, combination screw driver/opener, white illus and inscription on red plastic handle, late 1930s **70.00**
Record Set, boxed **75.00**

Ring
Flashlight 58.00
Six Shooter 125.00
Sheet Music, *Hi Yo Silver, The Lone Ranger's Song,* 1938 . . . . 80.00
Target Game, gun and stand, Morton Salt premium, copyright 1938, orig box 120.00
Token, 1¼" d, "The Lone Ranger Seventeenth Anniversary 1933–1950," silvered brass, Lone Ranger and Tonto on reverse, inscribed "The Lone Ranger Lucky Piece," premium 30.00
Toothbrush Holder, LR & Co, 1938 . . . 135.00
Toy, wind–up, Roy spinning lasso on rearing Silver, Marx, copyright 1938 300.00

TOM MIX

Bar Pin, red and white checkerboard fabric, white plastic dayglow horse-shoe hanger, "Tom Mix Sharpshooters Award," premium, c1945 . . . . 100.00
Belt, plastic, dayglow, checkerboard and western motifs, brass buckle with secret compartment, raised Tom image, Ralston premium, c1946 . . . . . 95.00
Belt Buckle, secret compartment 95.00
Book
The Fabulous Tom Mix, Olive Stokes Mix, Eric Heath assistant, 6 x 8½", hard cov, dj, Prentice–Hall, 178 pgs, copyright 1957 . . . . 15.00
The Range War, Big Little Book 30.00
Cereal Bowl, 5½" d, china, white, illus and inscription "Hot Ralston Cereal For Straight Shooters" repeated around rim, checkerboard and T–M Bar Ranch symbol int., Ralston Purina copyright 1982 . . . . 35.00
Comic Book, #3, Jan 1941, Ralston premium 60.00
Compass, Straight Shooter, Ralston . . . 65.00
Cowboy Boots, orig box, 1930s 350.00
Dixie Lid, 2¼" d, brown and white, photo, "Miracle Rider" rim inscription, 1935 . . . . 25.00
Film, 16 mm, used with toy projector 35.00
Folder, premiums, 1935 . . . . 28.00
Frame, 1½ x 3 x 4½", silvered brass, checkerboard design, name and ranch symbol on front, photo of Tom and Tony, Ralston premium, c1938 50.00
Gun, 9" l, wood, painted, black, opens at top, moving cylinder, facsimile signature, ranch brand symbol, and "Ralston Straight Shooters" on grip, premium, c1933 . . . . 150.00
ID Bracelet, silvered brass, pair of six-guns and initial "B" on oval disk, Ralston address and serial number on reverse, chain link, premium 35.00

Manual, *Life of Tom Mix,* 5 x 7", 24 pgs, revised first edition, Ralston premium, orig envelope, 1933 . . . . 75.00
Model Kit, Flying Model Airplane, biplane, balsa wood, pre–cut, paper stickers, premium, 1937 . . . . 120.00
Movie Viewer, 6½" h, cardboard, mechanical, diecut opening, axle rods at top and bottom for winding black and white paper films, "Rustler's Roundup" film included, Ralston premium, 1930–35 . . . . 200.00
Patch, 3" sq, cloth, red checkerboard design, T–M Bar Ranch symbol in blue at center, Ralston premium, 1933 . . . . 70.00
Periscope 75.00
Pinback Button, 1¾" d, "Tom Mix Circus," black and white portrait, black ground, white lettering, 1930s 60.00
Pocket Knife, 3" l, single blade, white pearlized handle, black and red checkerboard logo, 1939 . . . . 75.00
Post Card, 3½ x 5½", photo, brown, inscribed with name and film title "Desert Love," c1920 . . . . 19.00
Poster, safety 30.00
Record, Original Radio Broadcasts, Vol 1, 33⅓ rpm, commemorative, first two episodes of "The Mystery of the Vanishing Village," Ralston premium, orig album cov, c1982–83 . . . . 18.00
Ring, Straight Shooters 80.00
Rocket, 8½" l balsa and cardboard, red and white checkerboard design, paper parachute holds diecast metal figure, orig mailing box and instructions, c1933 . . . . 145.00
Sheet Music, *The Old Spinning Wheel,* Straight Shooters cov photo, copyright 1933 . . . . 30.00
Spinner, silvered brass, red lettering, "Ralston Wheat Cereal" on handle, "Good Luck–TM" message on spinning disk, premium, 1933 . . . . 65.00
Spurs, aluminum, glow in the dark rowel wheels, ranch brand symbol on fork, Ralston premium, c1947 . . . . . 145.00
Statue, Tony, plaster 35.00
Telephone Set, mailing box, instructions 80.00
Tobacco Card, 1½ x 2", cigarette pack insert, black and white photo, #350, series D, Orami Cigarettes, Germany, c1930 . . . . 10.00
Watch Fob 45.00
Wristwatch, 1⅜" d gold colored metal case, full color dial face illus, clear plastic crystal, figural arms holding pistols, marked "The Original/Registered Model," faux alligator leather bands, story book included, Ralston revival premium, 1982–83 . . . . 70.00

ROY ROGERS

Badge, star, tin, silver finish, "Roy
Rogers/Deputy," 1950s 35.00
Bank, figural
  Boot 25.00
  Horseshoe, metal and plastic, wall
    mount, Roy Rogers and Trigger
    Savings Bank 85.00
Bedspread, 77 x 102", chenille, tan, red
  and brown lettering, multicolor steer
  skull, branding iron, and rearing
  horse with cowboy throwing lasso il-
  lus, green piping, c1950 . . . .   100.00
Binoculars, MIB 60.00
Book, *Favorite Western Stories*, orig box   95.00

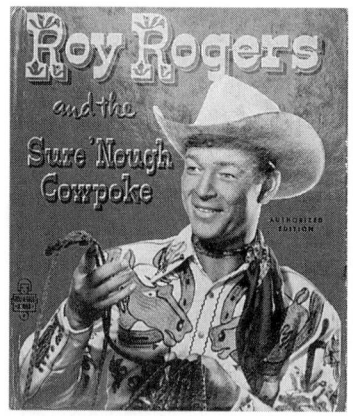

**Roy Rogers, children's book, *Roy Rogers
and the Sure 'Nough Cowpoke*, Whitman
Publishing, 1952, 6⅝" sq, $7.50.**

Calendar, Nestle's Co, 1959 . . . .   165.00
Camera, box type, Roy on Trigger illus   45.00
Cereal Premium, Post, Double Bar
  Ranch, unopened 85.00
Charm Bracelet, 6" l, silver link, four
  black and white photos in clear plastic disks, Roy in one disk, other stars
  in remaining disks, c1950 . . . .   60.00
Clock, 1½ x 4 x 4¼", windup, ani-
  mated, enameled metal case, ivory
  color, brass frame, clear plexiglas
  crystal, western desert scene illus on
  dial face, black and white rope design numerals, diecut Roy and Trigger
  figure rocks as clock runs, E Ingraham
  Co, c1951 . . . .   300.00
Coloring Book, Trigger and Bullet, 6½ x
  7½", Whitman, #2958, 1959 . . . . . .   24.00
Comic Book, Roy Rogers Comics, Vol 1,
  #17, Dell Publishing Co, file copy is-
  sue, May 1949 . . . .   80.00
Comic Book Holder 145.00
Curtains, price for pair 100.00

Flashlight, Signal Siren, Rogers and
  Trigger 35.00
Harmonica, 4½" l, Roy Rogers' Riders,
  white plastic and silvered metal,
  "Good Luck" and "King of the
  Cowboys" on engraved plates, 1950s   38.00
Hartland Figure
  Bullet, orig tags, MIB 125.00
  Roy and Trigger, mint on card 120.00
Holster, cartridge belt, rhinestone dec   65.00
Iron–on Transfer
  Cowgirl on rearing horse, desert
    scene in background, "Dale Evans"
    in rope script, mid 1950s 42.00
  Roy 3.00
  Trigger 3.00
Jigsaw Puzzle, 15 x 21", family picture,
  Roy, Dale, and Dusty, Whitman, orig
  box, mid 1950s 26.00
Lamp, 8" h, Roy and Trigger, plaster, fac-
  simile signatures 250.00
Lantern, 7½" h, litho metal, replica
  ranch lantern, red, blue, and yellow
  design, horseshoe handles, wire bail,
  hanging loop, clear plastic globe, bat-
  tery operated, mid 1950s 90.00
Lunch Box, eight scenes, green band . .   85.00
Membership Card, 2½ x 4⅛", Roy
  Rogers' Riders Club, stiff paper, buff
  color, black and white Roy and
  Trigger photo surrounded by red lasso
  design, facsimile signature, nine rules
  for club members on reverse,
  1948–50 . . . .   30.00
Mug, Roy's face 65.00
Neckerchief, 5½ x 35", gold synthetic,
  Roy portrait printed on ends, rope
  script name, 1950 . . . .   55.00
Outfit, child's
  Dale Evans, cowgirl, orig box 75.00
  Roy Rogers, shirt and vest, khaki long
    sleeved shirt, "Roy Rogers Frontier
    Wear" label, made by Rob Roy,
    stitched floral design, tan leather
    vest, red leather pockets and straps,
    silver metal rosettes, "Sheplers"
    tag, mid 1950s 40.00
Paint Book, 11 x 15", Whitman, #1158,
  48 pgs, copyright 1948, unused 60.00
Paint Set, orig box 65.00
Photograph, Sears Roebuck Christmas
  giveaway 25.00
Pinback Button, Trigger 15.00
Pistol, 2¾" l, miniature 22.50
Plate, china, Roy Rogers Rodeo, un-
  signed 25.00
Playset
  Roy Rogers Fix–It Chuckwagon and
    Jeep, plastic, Ideal Toys, orig box,
    mid 1950s 125.00
  Roy Rogers Rodeo Ranch 100.00
Playing Cards, complete deck 55.00

Pocket Knife, 3½" l, steel, two blade, plastic handle, black and white illus, c1950 .... 75.00

Poster, 27 x 41", "Spoilers of the Plains," full color, 1951 Republic Picture ... 80.00

Pup Tent, cloth, Hettrick Mfg Co 45.00

Raincoat, child's, knee length, vinyl, fabric lining, yellow, black trim and designs, fringe, mid 1950s 100.00

Record, 78 rpm, Golden Record, inspirational, Roy singing The Lord's Prayer one side, Dale singing Ave Maria on other, orig cov, mid 1950s 30.00

Record Player, litho 150.00

Slippers, boot style, black wool felt, white felt fringe, sole edges, and spur rowel, yellow, red, black, and white ink stamped Roy and Trigger illus on sides, "Pledge to Parent" sheet included, orig box, mid 1950s 175.00

Tee Shirt, Roy Rogers 35.00

Thermos, 8½" h, Double R Bar Ranch, litho metal, red plastic cap, mid 1950s 35.00

Tie, yellow 75.00

Tie Clip, 2¾" l, metal, gold color, six shooter, Double R Bar Ranch symbol on grips, fires caps, 3" l thin leather holster, c1950 .... 60.00

Token 17.50

Toothbrush, orig pkg 30.00

Toy
  Pull, musical, 20" l, 6" h, wood horse and wagon, litho paper sides, painted steel wheels, Roy, Bullet, and Trigger symbols, NN Hill Brass Co, c1950 .... 100.00
  Push, 34" l, wood figure of Bullet and head of Trigger at either end of wood rod joined at center by metal coupling, red steel wheels and bells at Bullet end, fabric strap reins, full color litho paper illus on both sides, Hill Toys and Bells, NN Hill Brass Co, mid 1950s 175.00
  Telephone 40.00
  Van, litho metal, 15½" l, cab and detachable trailer van, black rubber wheels, Marx, mid 1950s 60.00

View–Master Reel 15.00

Wristwatch
  Dale Evans 135.00
  Happy Trails, 1985, MIB 110.00
  Roy Rogers, green ground 175.00

CHARACTERS, OTHER

Cisco Kid
  Gun, 7¼" l, cardboard, folder, black, white, and blue illus both sides, metal "cricket" inside, inscribed

Jack Bentel, arcade card, greentone, $1.00.

"Listen to the Cisco Kid," early 1950s 30.00

Jigsaw Puzzle 25.00

Picture Card, 3½ x 5½", stiff paper, black and white photo, glossy, facsimile signature, red and white Wards Tip–Top Bread adv on reverse, early 1950s 18.00

Program, 8½ x 11", stiff paper folder, glossy, souvenir, "Cisco Kid Rodeo," dated mid July, Wrigley Field, Chicago, early 1950s 23.00

Tab, litho tin, red, white, and blue, Pancho in bright green hat, "Pancho/Weber's Bread/Cisco Kid," 1950s 20.00

Wyatt Earp
  Big Little Book, Hugh O'Brian TV's Wyatt Earp, Whitman, #1644, 276 pgs, from TV Series, 1958 ..... 14.00
  Color and Stencil Set, Hugh O'Brian, MIB 135.00
  Gun and Holster Set, cap gun, holster, and badge, orig card 125.00
  Hartland Statue 35.00

Red Ryder
  Belt Buckle, 2" sq, silvered brass, cowboy on bronco, name spelled twice in rope script, 1940s 35.00
  Decoder, 3" d, Rodeomatic Radio, paper, disk wheels, red, white, and blue, brass cotter pin, c1942 .... 55.00
  Flashlight, 7" l, metal, litho illus by Fred Harman, copyright 1949 ... 70.00
  Gloves, child's, black, white gauntlet, black title and illus, fringed, early 1940s 40.00
  Molding and Coloring Kit, four soft rubber molds, plaster, orig box with Fred Harman art, Bersted's Hobby Crafts, late 1940s 70.00
  Pop Gun, double barrel, Daisy, 1950s 75.00

Rin Tin Tin
Canteen, 7" h, "Official Rin Tin Tin 101st Cavalry," textured plastic, brown, black cap, brown vinyl carrying strap, raised inscription, Nabisco premium, orig box, copyright Screen Gems Inc, 1957 .... **70.00**
Game, The Adventures of Rin Tin Tin, Transogram, 1955 .... **20.00**
Paint By Number Kit, four 9¼ x 12" preprinted illus sheets, watercolor tablets, orig box, Transogram, 1956 **60.00**
Palm Puzzle, 1¼" d, tin disk, clear plastic cov, three small balls fit in holes, boy in cavalry uniform yelling "Go, Rinty/Rusty," Nabisco premium, c1956 .... **12.50**
Playset, Rin Tin Tin at Fort Apache, #3627, 2½" h plastic figures sealed in orig bags, blue cavalrymen, assorted colored Indians, cream colored Rip Masters, Rusty, and Rin Tin Tin, tin fort, Marx, 1950s, orig box, unused **450.00**
Punch Out Card, totem poles, plastic, emb, full color, Nabisco premium, late 1950s, set of three **30.00**
Ring, brass, raised portrait, hinged lid reveals two ink pads, c1930 ..... **85.00**
Stuffed Toy, 9" h, plush, gray and white, rubber face, inset brown glass eyes **62.00**
View–Master Reel, "Vanishing Guns," "Indian Ambush," and "High Danger," orig cov envelope, copyright 1955 .... **35.00**
Sgt Preston
Flashlight **50.00**
Gold Ore Detector, instructions, mailing box **225.00**
Sky King
Autographed Photograph, 7 x 9" glossy, black and white glossy photo, Kirby Grant, blue ink "For Cheryl/Sky King", c1950 .... **65.00**
Bolo Tie, brown cording with silver tips, silvered brass tie slide with longhorn steer illus, orig photo cover sheet and mailing envelope, Peter Pan Peanut Butter premium, c1950 .... **70.00**
Straight Arrow
Bandanna **75.00**
Finger Puppets, cardboard, 7½" sq sheet, unpunched, script card, "The Stage Raider," Nabisco Shredded Wheat premium, c1955 **40.00**
Wild Bill Hickok
Cavalry Game, 1950s **15.00**
Gun and Holster Set, orig box **150.00**
Pinback Button, ⅞" d, brown photo, light pink ground, "Wild Bill Hickok," 1950s **20.00**

PERSONALITIES

Benson, Bobby, pinback button, 1¼" d, blue lettering and rope design on yellow ground, "Bobby Benson/Special Captain," 1930s **30.00**
Cody, Buffalo Bill
Post Card, black and white photo, Cody wearing buckskins standing leaning on rifle, sgd in negative "Marh Gestner Allen" **85.00**
Figure, 6" h, composition and wood, "Buffalo Bill" and 1941 maker's copyright inscribed on base **65.00**
Pinback Button
1¼" d, sepia photo, gold finish white metal Rough Riders–style hat suspended from bar on back of button, back paper marked "Stacy Photographer, Brooklyn," early 1900s **40.00**
1⅜" d, litho, black, white, tan, and dark red, Cody on horse behind buffalo, #1 of Van Brode America Series, biography on back paper, c1950 .... **20.00**
Spill Holder, 5½" h, souvenir, figural, white metal, gold finish, late 1890s **100.00**
Gray, Gene, pinback button, 1¾" d, blue illus and lettering, white ground, Gray on horse, "Gene Gray/Silver King of Cowboys," 1930s **25.00**
Jones, Buck
Badge, "Buck Jones Club," brass, black and red, c1930 .... **30.00**
Book, *Buck Jones and the Night Riders,* 7½ x 9½", hard cov, Whitman Big Big Book, #4069, 316 pgs, Gaylord DuBois, Hal Arbo, illustrator, story by Gaylord DuBois, 1937 .... **90.00**
Guitar, 37" l, pressed wood, illus and "Good Luck/Buck Jones & Silver" on face, made by Gibson for Sears, Roebuck & Co, c1930 .... **130.00**
Manual, *Buck Jones Rangers–Cowboys Collection,* #1, 1932 ... **65.00**
Maynard, Ken
Cigar Band, 1 x 3", diecut, emb paper, red, gold, and black design, black and white photo, 1930s ... **20.00**
Lobby Card, 14 x 22", cardboard, red, white, blue, flesh, and brown design for 1933 Universal western film **50.00**
Pinback Button, ⅞" d, black portrait and lettering, white ground, "Ken Maynard Club/First National Pictures," 1930s **15.00**
McCoy, Tim
Big Little Book, *The Prescott Kid,* starring Tim McCoy, #1152, Columbia

Pictures, adapted by Eleanor
Packer, 1935, 4⅝ x 5¼", 160 pgs,
hard cov, soft spine **22.50**
Pinback Button,⅞" d, litho, blue por-
trait and lettering, white ground,
"Tim McCoy's Vigilantes," 1930s .   **25.00**
Wayne, John
Mug, 3¼" h, china, blue, gray, black,
and yellow design, black "Good
Luck" signature, stamped "Ketchum
Originals" on bottom, *McQ* movie
issue **30.00**
Tablet, 5½ x 9", color photo and fac-
simile signature on cov, c1950 . . .   **30.00**

COW COLLECTIBLES

Collecting Hints: Image is everything. It makes
no difference if the object was made yesterday or
one hundred years ago, just so it pictures the collector's favorite bovine. It goes without saying
that the representation must be a favorable one.

Cow collectors collect in quantity. Advertising
pieces and folk art are two groups of cow images
where secondary collectors frequently outbid
cow collectors.

Cow creamers, some dating as early as the
eighteenth century, are a favorite specialized collecting category. Antiques devotees focus on examples from the early period. Most cow collectors are perfectly willing to settle for twentieth
century examples.

In order for an object to be considered a true
cow collectible, it must either be in the shape of
a cow or have a picture of a cow on its surface.
Milk– and dairy–related material without a cow
image is not a cow collectible. T–shirts with cow
sayings fall into a gray area.

History: The domesticated cow has been around
for over 8,000 years. Cows are part of Greek
mythology. The Egyptians worshiped Hathor, the
cow–goddess. The Hindus venerate the cow as a
sacred being. From the beginning the cow has
been the focal point for artists and sculptors.

Some of the more famous nursery rhymes feature a cow, e.g. Hey, Diddle, Diddle and The
House That Jack Built. Poetry and literature are
rich with cow references.

It is impossible to divorce the cow from the
dairy industry. Cow motifs appear throughout a
wide range of dairy product advertising. The
three most popular images being the Guernsey,
Holstein, and Jersey.

There are a number of famous twentieth cen-
tury cows. Early Disney cartoons featured
Clarabelle. The dairy industry created Brooksie,
Bossie, *La Vache Qui Ri*, and, of course, Elsie.

When she was at her peak, only the president
of the United States had more public recognition

than Elsie the Borden Cow. In the late 1930s Elsie
made her initial appearances in a series of medical journal advertisements for Borden's Eagle
Brand condensed milk. Her popularity grew as a
result of Borden's 1939–1940 World's Fair exhibition. A 1940 Hollywood appearance further
enhanced her national reputation. In 1957 a
name–Elsie's–calf contest produced three million
entries. Borden briefly retired Elsie in the late
1960s. The public demanded her return. Today
she is once again found on labels, in animated
commercials, and at live appearances across the
country.

In this age of equality, alas, the fabled bull re-
ceives short shrift. With the exception of Walt
Disney's Ferdinand, the male of the species is
regulated to a conspicuous second place.

Reference: Emily Margolin Gwathmey, *Wholly
Cow!*, Abbeville Press, 1988.

Periodical: *Moosletter,* 240 Wahl Ave., Evans
City, PA 16033.

Activity Book, Elsie, 1950s **20.00**
Blotter, 4 x 9¼", Cow Brand Baking
Soda, product package with cow,
c1920 . . . .   **10.00**
Booklet, Elsie, *Trip To The Moon,* 1950s
. . . .   **15.00**
Butter Print, round
4½" d, standing cow, one piece
turned handle, dark finish **330.00**
5¼" d, cow, tree, and flower,
scrubbed white, one piece turned
handle **150.00**
Coloring Book, Elsie, 1950s **20.00**
Creamer, plastic **75.00**
Figure, Ferdinand, rubber, Seiberling,
Walt Disney Enterprises copyright,
c1930 . . . .   **75.00**
Keychain Charm, 1" d, Swift's
Brookfield, brass, emb cow on award
base, inscribed "June Dairy Month
Award," early 1900s **15.00**
Mug, 2½" h, china, white, full color
Elsie illus, blue accent stripe, Juvenile
Ware and Borden copyright, c1940   **75.00**
Pinback Button
Ayrshires, 1¼" d, standing cow, US
outline background, maroon and
white, 1940s **15.00**
Dairy Class '01, ⅞" d, black and
white cow and initials "KSAC" . . .   **15.00**
Guernsey's Rich Inheritance, cow il-
lus, yellow, brown, and white,
1930–40 . . . .   **18.00**
Livestock Steer, blue and white, bull
illus, 1901–12 . . . .   **12.00**
Poster, Evaporated Milk—Pure Cow's
Milk, black and white illus of cows,
green background, c1940 . . . .   **15.00**

Magazine Tear Sheet, auction sale of pure bred registered holsteins, 1921, 10 x 13¾", $10.00.

Sign, Elsie, Borden's, neon, red, white, and blue **450.00**
Sugar, Elmer, figural, china, 1930–40 . **40.00**
Toy
Pull, Cow Jumped Over The Moon, MIB **650.00**
Ramp Walker, 3½" l, plastic, brown and white, orig sealed cellophane bag, marked "Made In Hong Kong," 1950s **25.00**
Windup, Walking Cow, plush, built–in key, walks forward, head moves, mooing sound, orig box, T N, Japan, 1960s **75.00**
Weather Vane, 27" l, molded copper . **1,000.00**

CRACKER JACK

Collecting Hints: Most collectors concentrate on the pre–plastic era. Toys in the original packaging are very rare. One possibility for specializing is toys from a given decade, for example World War II soldiers, tanks, artillery pieces, and other war–related items.

Many prizes are marked "Cracker Jack" or carry a picture of the Sailor Boy and Bingo, his dog. Unmarked prizes can be confused with gumball machine novelties or prizes from Checkers, a rival firm.

History: F. W. Rueckheim, a popcorn store owner in Chicago, introduced a mixture of pop-corn, peanuts, and molasses at the World's Columbian Exposition in 1893. Three years later the name "Cracker Jack" was applied to it. It gained popularity quickly and by 1908 appeared in the lyrics of *Take Me Out To The Ball Game*.

In 1910 Rueckheim included coupons on the box which could be redeemed for prizes. In

1912 prizes appeared in the box itself. The early prizes were made of paper, tin, lead, wood, or porcelain. Plastic was introduced in 1948.

The Borden Company's Cracker Jack prize col-lection numbers over 10,000 examples; but this is not all of them. Knowledge continues to ex-pand as more examples are found in bottoms of drawers, old jewelry boxes, and attics.

Today's items are largely paper, the plastic magnifying glass being one exception. The com-pany buys toys in lots of 25 million and keeps hundreds of prizes in circulation at one time. Borden's annual production is about 400 million boxes.

Reference: Alex Jaramillo, *Cracker Jack Prizes,* Abbeville Press, 1989.

Collectors' Club: Cracker Jack Collectors Assoc., 72 Charles St., Rochester, NH 03867.

Museum: Columbus Science Museum, 280 E. Broad St., Columbus, OH 43215.

Prize, plastic, red elephant, blue parader, red cowgirl, price each, $5.00.

Baseball Card, 2½ x 3½", set of two, full color photo, #6 Mickey Mantle, #13 Willie Mays, Borden Inc and Topps Chewing Gum copyright, 1982 . . . . **20.00**
Bird, plastic, green, c1950 . . . . **7.00**
Boat, 1 x 2½", wood, orig 3 x 4" mailing box, c1930 . . . . **50.00**
Booklet, Cracker Jack Riddles, 2¾ x 5", paper, Rueckheim Bros & Eckstein, 40 pgs, black and white Jack and his dog illus **25.00**
Bookmark, 2¾" h, litho tin, brown ter-rier, c1930s **18.00**
Box, Jack and Bingo, 1919 . . . . **48.00**
Clicker, aluminum **15.00**
Cookbook, Angelus Recipes, 4 x 6", black and white, 14 pgs **15.00**
Corn Popper, 14" handle, c1930 . . . . . **60.00**
Decoder, Jack the Sailor **22.00**
Delivery Wagon, litho tin, red, white, and blue, Cracker Jack box image on one side, Angelus Marshmallows box on other, 1920s **75.00**

Doll, stuffed cloth, sailor's outfit, Vogue Dolls, copyright 1980, orig pkg, unopened 25.00
Figurine, stand–up, diecut, litho tin
  Moon Mullins 20.00
  Smitty, 1 1/3" h, 1930s 45.00
Fish, plastic, yellow, c1950 . . . .   5.00
Flasher, 1¼" d, cardboard, inscription on back, c1960 . . . .   5.00
Fortune Wheel, 1¾" d, litho tin, red, white, and blue, alphabet letters, diecut opening 35.00
Frog, 2 x 2¼", cardboard, diecut, "Spread Me Open and See Me Jump"   15.00
Game
  Checkers, premium, orig envelope . .   15.00
  Toy Surprise Game, Milton Bradley, 1976, complete 28.00
Hat, "Me For Cracker Jack," paper, red, white, and blue design, early 1900s   65.00
Lapel Stud, "CJ Air Corps," metal, white   40.00
Lunch Box 35.00
Mask, 8½ x 10", "Cracker Jack" on front, c1960 . . . .   15.00
Pencil, wood 15.00
Pinback Button, 1¼" d, lady, multicolored, black hair, pink ribbon, green ground, red and white "Cracker Jack 5¢/Candied Popcorn & Roasted Peanuts" on back paper, copyright 1910 . . . .   60.00
Plate, 1¾" d, tin, silvered, c1930s 35.00
Post Card, 3 x 5½", multicolored, bears on Statue of Liberty, Cracker Jack box replaces torch, Rueckheim Bros & Eckstein, copyright 1907 . . . .   35.00
Premium, baseball bat 95.00
Print Block, ¾ x 1 x 1¾", wood, engraved image, early 1900s 75.00
Puzzle, two–piece, wire nail, 1940s . .   20.00
Puzzle Book, 2½ x 4", four pgs, series one, color memory retention puzzles, Angelus Marshmallow adv on back cov, copyright 1917 . . . .   80.00
Rocker, ⅜" h, metal, litho, red, white, and blue 20.00
Rocket Ship, 1½" h, plastic, green, c1950 . . . .   10.00
Sign, 7 x 11", cardboard, c1930 . . . . .   45.00
Sled, 2" l, silvered tin, marked, c1930s   35.00
Spinner Top
  Litho Tin, red, white and blue, 1930s   50.00
  Plastic, marbled light brown, marked "Cracker Jack," 1950s 25.00
Squeaker, 2½ x 3½", cardboard, accordion shape 35.00
Stationery, envelope, red and blue box   6.00
Tape Measure, 1½" d, Angelus Marshmallow design, c1930 . . . . . .   40.00
Train Set, 2 pcs 22.00
Wheelbarrow, 2¼" l, silvered tin, marked 32.00

CREDIT COINS AND TOKENS

Collecting Hints: Specialization is the key to successful collecting. Plan a collection that can be completed. Completeness tends to increase a collection's value.

When collecting charge coins, stay away from rusted or damaged pieces. Inferior pieces attract little interest unless rare.

Metal charge plates have little collector interest. They should remain affordable for years, which means they'll probably not advance in value.

Most interest is in credit cards. Scarce and rare cards, when they can be located, are still affordable. National credit cards are eagerly sought. American Express is the most popular.

Paper and laminated paper credit cards are highly desirable. When it comes to collecting these, don't concern yourself with condition. Go ahead and acquire any you find. They're so difficult to locate that it could take years to find another specimen. Some are so rare that they might be unique!

Plastic credit cards issued before 1970 are scarce. Occasionally, you'll find a mint condition card. Generally, you'll have to settle for used. Plastic cards issued after 1980 should be collected in mint condition.

The best collecting hint is collect what you like. You'll provide yourself with years of enjoyment and that's the best investment you'll ever make!

History: Charge coins, the first credit pieces, were first issued in the 1890s. Charge coins are approximately the size of a quarter or half dollar. Because of their size, they were often carried with change. This is why they were commonly referred to as coins.

Charge coins come in various shapes, sizes and materials. Most are square, round or oval. Some are in the shapes of shirts, socks or hats. They're made from various materials such as fiber, German silver, celluloid, steel, or copper. The issuing store has its name, monogram, or initials on the coin. Each coin has a customer identification number. Charge coins were still in use as late as 1959.

Metal charge plates were in use from the 1930s to the 1950s. These plates look like military dog tags. The front of the plate contains the customer's name, address and account number. The back has a piece of cardboard that carries the store's name and customer's signature space.

Paper credit cards were in use in the early 1930s. They were easily damaged, so some companies began laminating them with clear plastic in the 1940s. Laminated cards were issued until the 1950s. The plastic cards we know today replaced the laminated cards in the late 1950s.

References: Stephen P. Albert and Lawrence E. Elman, *Tokens and Medals: A Guide to the Identification and Values of United States Exonumia,* published by authors, 1991; Glyn V. Farber, *Hickey Brothers Cigar Store Tokens,* The Token and Medal Society, Inc., 1992; Gerald E. Johnson, *Trade Tokens of Wisconsin,* Krause Publications, 1993; Russell Rulau, *Early American Tokens: 1700–1832,* 3rd Edition, Krause Publications, 1991; Russell Rulau, *Hard Times Tokens: 1832–1844,* 4th Edition Krause Publications, 1992; Russell Rulau, *Standard Catalog of U. S. Tokens: 1700–1900,* Krause Publications, 1994; Russell Rulau, *Tokens of the Gay Nineties,* Krause Publications, 1987; Russell Rulau, *U.S. Merchant Tokens: 1845–1860,* Krause Publications, 1990; Russell Rulau, *U.S. Trade Tokens: 1866–1889,* Second Edition, Krause Publications, 1988; Greg Tunks, *Credit Card Collecting Bonanza,* Second Edition, published by author, 1989.

Periodical: *Credit Card Collector,* 150 Hohldale, Houston, TX 77022.

Collectors' Clubs: Active Token Collectors Organization, PO Box 1573, Stone Falls, SD 57101; American Numismatic Assoc., 818 N. Cascade Ave., Colorado Springs, CO 80903; American Tax Token Society, PO Box 260170, Lakewood, CO 80226; American Vecturist Assoc., PO Box 1204, Boston, MA 02104; Indiana, Kentucky & Ohio Token & Medal Collectors, 1725 N. 650 W, Columbia City, IN 46725; New Jersey Exonumia Society, 112 Carlton Ave., Westmont, NJ 08108; Token & Medal Society, Inc., PO Box 366, Bryantown, MD 20617.

Museum: Museum of the American Numismatic Assoc., Colorado Springs, CO.

CARDS

American Airlines	5.00
American Express	
1958, red printing, purplish blue ground, paper	500.00
1968, violet, centurion on upper left	100.00
1970, green, "The Money Card"	25.00
1972, gold, "The Executive Money Card," card appears to change colors when rotated	50.00
ARCO, 1976, Atlantic Richfield Company	4.00
Bank Americard, account number in tan area	
Magnetic stripe	15.00
Without magnetic stripe	7.50
Bloomingdale's, brown on white, tan border	10.00
Carte Blanche	
1973, gold, blue on gold	40.00

1977, blue on white, gold border	7.50
Chevron National Credit Card, 1967, attendants servicing car	20.00
Choice, 1984	4.00
Diners Club	
Booklet, April 30, 1956, 126 pgs, Hertz ad in back with drawing of '55 Ford, blank memo pgs bound inside to record charge transactions	175.00
Colored blocks, 1967, blue top	45.00
Gray ground, Citicorp	12.50
Silver and blue logo, white ground	6.00
Eastern, October 1984	7.50
Esso, 1966, "Happy Motoring," waving attendant	15.00
Fina, early 1970s, large blue Fina	5.00
General Tire, December 31, 1953, paperboard, lightly soiled, calendar on back	25.00
Gimbels, black on brown, New York and all branch stores	4.00
Goodyear, blimp illus	7.50
Gulf Travel Card, land, sea, air, car, boat, and plane drawing	10.00
Hilton Hotels, paperboard, 1955	35.00
Hotel McLure, 1951–52, paperboard	25.00
Hotels Statler, 1952, paperboard	45.00
Illinois Bankcharge, red, white, and blue shield	15.00
International Credit Card, 1960, sailing ship logo	30.00
Jordan Marsh Co, blue on white, store drawing, good in Boston, Framingham, Malden, and Peabody	20.00
Korvettes, personal charge plate	3.00
Lit Brothers, blue and white stripes	10.00
Macy's, red star, "It's smart to be thrifty"	5.00
Marshall Field & Company, green and white	5.00
Mastercard	
Pre–hologram	3.00
Pre–hologram, cardholder photograph on back	6.00
Mastercharge	
Cardholder photograph on back, early 1970s	60.00
Magnetic stripe	7.50
Midwest Bank Card, Charge–It, Harris Bank, 05/67, blue top	22.50
Mobil, Pegasus on Mobil sign on front upper left	10.00
Montgomery Ward, yellow and white, national charge–all card	7.50
Neiman Marcus, commemorative credit card, 75th anniversary	15.00
Penneys, black on blue, "always first quality"	8.00
Phillips 66, non–expiring, "passport to everywhere"	12.00
Playboy Club International	
Gold, Jan 1979	6.00
Membership Card, Feb 1986	5.00

Credit Card, The Playboy Club, $5.00.

Saks Fifth Avenue, paper, charge account identification card 30.00
Shannon's Furniture, 1939, Tulsa, OK, black on blue, paper, store drawing 12.00
Sinclair, 1971, motoring credit, waving green dinosaur 6.00
Skelly, ladies credit card, two gloved hands holding Skelly symbol 20.00
Standard Oil, 1972, red and blue map of United States 15.00
Sunoco, custom blended gasoline pump drawing 7.50
Texaco Travel Card, car, boat, and plane drawings 5.00
The Texas Company (Texaco), 1957, tan and white, paper 60.00
TWA, 1974, getaway card, couple wearing swim suits holding hands .. 10.00
Uni–Card, 1970s 10.00
Vickers Refining Co, lifetime courtesy card, crown over V logo 17.50
Visa, pre–hologram 2.50
Wallachs, undated, high gloss paperboard 25.00
John Wanamaker, metal charge plate, carrying case 17.50
Woolco, orange on white 10.00

TOKENS

Boggs and Buhl, Pittsburgh, PA, oval, white metal, knight's helmet between backward and regular B 15.00
Conrad's, Boston, MA, irregular round, golden plating, picture of store 25.00
George B Evans, Philadelphia, PA, diamond shape, white metal, drugs and gifts 15.00
Gilchrist, Boston, MA, golden shield, G Co 17.50
Gimble Brothers
  Philadelphia, PA, rect, white metal, lion holding shield, GB initials, finder mailing instructions on back 14.00
  New York City, oval, white metal, GB in circle at top, New York at bottom 18.00
Lit Brothers, Philadelphia, PA, irregular oval, white metal, LB, date of issue 20.00
C F Massey, Rochester, MN, octagonal,

white metal, ornate interlocking C F M 15.00
Neill, Philadelphia, PA, sq, white metal, Neill script 12.50
Plotkin Brothers, Boston, MA, rect, white metal, lion head over shield containing PB 17.50
Pocohontas Pioneer Garage, Philadelphia, PA, oval, white metal, high relief Indian profile 17.50
R H Stearns, Boston, MA, oval, white metal, interlocking R H S Co 15.00
R H White, Boston, MA, pear shape, white metal, interlocking R H W Co script 20.00

DAIRY ITEMS

Collecting Hints: Concentrate on the material associated with one specific dairy, region, such as blotters, brochures, post cards, and trade cards, or national firm. Much of the material available, relates to advertising.

Collectors of dairy items compete with many other groups. Milk bottle collectors try to supplement their collection with these "go–withs." Farm item collectors concentrate on cream separator materials and other farm–related items. Ice cream collectors seek cartons and other material. Finally, home decorators like the milk cans and other large, showy objects.

History: There were hundreds of small dairies and creameries scattered throughout the United States during the late 19th to mid–20th centuries. Many issued a variety of material to promote their products.

Eventually regional cooperatives expanded the marketing regions, and many smaller dairies closed. Companies such as Borden distributed products on a national level. Borden created the advertising character of "Elsie, the Borden Cow" to help sell its products. Additional consolidation of firms has occurred, encouraged in part by state milk marketing boards and federal subsidies.

References: Dana Gehman Morykan and Harry L. Rinker, *Warman's Country Antiques & Collectibles, Second Edition* Wallace–Homestead, 1994; John Tutton, *Udder Delight*, published by author.

Collectors' Club: Cream Separator News, Rt. 3, Box 189, Arcadia, WI 54612.

Periodicals: *Creamers,* PO Box 11, Lake Villa, IL 60046; *The Milk Route,* 4 Ox Bow Road, Westport, CT 06880; *The Udder Collectibles,* HC 73, Box 1, Smithville Flats, NY 13841.

Museums: New York State Historical Assoc. and The Farmers Museum, Cooperstown, NY;

Southwest Dairy Museum, Arlington, TX; Billings Farm Museum, Woodstock, VT.

Advisors: Tom Gallagher and Tony Knipp.

Notes: A milk bottle cap refers to a plug–type cap placed on a bottle by the dairy in a bottling room. A milk bottle cover was made of either metal or glass and often contained dairy advertising. It was used to cover the bottle after the paper cap was removed. A milk bottle cap pick was used to remove the plug–type milk bottle caps. A milk bottle cap opener had the same function but was used to remove a different style cap found on more modern bottles, known as the DACRO type.

See: Milk Bottles.

Hot Pad, Kriebel's Dairies, Hereford, PA, muslin, hemp backing, 4¼" sq, $2.00.

Bank, Rutter Bros Dairy Products, dairy truck, plastic, white, red decal, c1960   **40.00**
Blotter, Universal Super Strength Milk Bottles, white and orange lettering, white ground **7.00**
Booklet
  Borden's, Streamline Your Figure, 5¼ x 7", 32 pgs, 1942 . . . .   **8.00**
  Jones Milk Co, color litho, giveaway, 1935 . . . .   **18.00**
Box, Bossie's Best Brand Butter, four color picture of a Jersey cow, Aberdeen Creamery Co., folded **5.00**
Bucket, Sunny Field Lard, 4 lbs **28.00**
Calendar
  1903, Melotte Cream Separators, framed **65.00**
  1908, De Laval Cream Separators, girl hugging cow, framed **350.00**
  1922, Sharples Tubular Cream Separators, January pad **110.00**
  1927, Broad View Farm, pure milk from our accredited herd, Rochester, NH **12.00**
Change Tray, De Laval **85.00**

Clock, Garst Bros Dairy, double globe   **125.00**
Cream Separator
  Dilution Gravity, tin, blue, three wood legs **35.00**
  Junior #33, table top type, royal blue   **145.00**
Cream Siphon, Marvel, aluminum, fits in bottle and siphons cream into a cream pitcher or other vessel **6.00**
Creamer
  Anthony's Cream **13.00**
  Freeman's Dairy, glass **20.00**
  Rosebud Dairy **9.00**
Doilies, Carver Ice Cream, linen–like, emb, Christmas, 1920s, pkg of 12 . .   **10.00**
Fan, "Compliments of Lebel's Dairy, 145 E. Hollis Street, Nashua, NH," girl in highchair **10.00**
Jigsaw Puzzle, 18 x 11", cardboard, Borden's milk wagon and milkman, middle piece shaped like milk bottle, 1928 . . . .   **100.00**
Measuring Cup, 8 oz., Lenkerbrook Farms, Inc., glass, red markings, Pyrex **5.00**
Milk Bottle
  Borden Weiland, emb, round, qt . . .   **20.00**
  Gail Borden, amber, 1½ gal **22.00**
  VM&I Co, emb, amber, qt **50.00**
Milk Bottle Cap
  Davol Anti Germ, rubber, fits over lip of milk bottle to keep out dirt, orig container **7.00**
  Deerfoot Farms, Southborough, MA   **5.00**
  Grade A Raw Milk, red and white . .   **.25**
  Heber Springs Dairy, Heber Springs, AR . . . .   **.10**
  Kents Dairy Farms, Vitamin D, Olean, NY . . . .   **.10**
  Parker Goat Dairy, Raw Milk, picture of goat **1.25**
Milk Bottle Cap Opener, Brock Hall Dairy Products, Purity Protected Dacro Sealed Milk on back **5.00**
Milk Bottle Cap Pick
  Borden Select Milk **5.00**
  Sheffield Farms Company, Inc **5.00**
Milk Box, wood, dairy name logo, holds 4 to 6 quarts **7.00**
Mug, Elsie in daisy on ext., Elsie head on int. bottom **35.00**
Pencil, Rutters Dairy, York and Hanover, PA, wood, unsharpened **3.00**
Playing Cards, Quality Dairy, Q motif on each card, complete deck **8.00**
Post Card
  De Laval Cream Separator, The World's Standard, full color image   **20.00**
  Ebert Ice Cream Company, factory pictured **5.00**
  Elsie, Elmer, and Beauregard, travel-ing representatives of Borden's

family of fine foods, shows charac-
ters in traveling bedroom, explana-
tion of bedroom furnishings on
back, color **3.00**
Poster, 12¼ x 17", US Cream Separator,
Vermont Farm Machine Co **35.00**
Ruler
    Breyer Ice Cream, colorful **15.00**
    Bryant & Chapman Dairy, Hartford,
    CT, wood, 6" l **4.00**
Sewing Kit, Borden's Mitchell Dairy,
picture of Elsie on cover, slogan
"Milk's Good Anytime, Better Still
Make It Borden's" **8.00**
Sign
    Borden, tin, red **55.00**
    Meiers Ice Cream, porcelain **65.00**
    Sharples Tubular Cream Separators,
    27 x 18", girl wearing bonnet . . . **1,100.00**
Songbook, 6 x 8½", Sharples Cream
Separator, man and woman on cov,
1920s **20.00**
Tape Measure, celluloid, "Cass Dairy
Farm, Inc., Jersey & Ayshire Milk, For
Service Call 820 W Athol, MA" on
front, "You Can Whip Our Cream But
You Can't Beat Our Milk, Try Our
Cream" on back **28.00**
Thermometer
    Primrose Dairy Products **60.00**
    Sealtest Milk, carton **75.00**

DEGENHART GLASS

Collecting Hints: Degenhart pressed glass novelties are collected by mold (Forget–Me–Not toothpick holders or all Degenhart toothpick holders),
by individual colors (Rubina or Bloody Mary), or
by group colors (opaque, iridescent, crystal, or
slag).

Correct color identification is the key to full enjoyment of collecting Degenhart glass. Because of
the slight variations in the hundreds of colors produced at the Degenhart Crystal Art Glass factory
from 1947 to 1978, it is important for beginning
collectors to acquire the eye for distinguishing
Degenhart colors, particularly the green and blue
variations. A knowledgeable collector or dealer
should be sought for guidance. Side by side color
comparison is extremely helpful.

Later glass produced by the factory can be distinguished by the trademark of a "D" in a heart or
only a "D" on certain molds where space pro-
hibited the full mark. Use of this mark began
around 1972 and by late 1977 most of the
molds had been marked. Prior to this time,
c1947–1972, no glass was marked, with the exception of the owl and occasionally other pieces

that were identified by hand stamping a block
letter "D" to the object as it came out of the
mold. This hand stamping was started and continued during the period 1967 to 1972.

Collecting unmarked Degenhart glass made
from 1947 to c1970 poses no problem once a
collector becomes familiar with molds and colors being worked during that period. Some of the
most sought after colors, such as Amethyst &
White Slag, Amethyst Carnival, and Custard Slag,
are unmarked, yet are the most desirable. Keep
in mind that some colors such as Custard
(opaque yellow), Heliotrope (opaque purple),
and Tomato (opaque orange red) were repeated
and can be found marked and unmarked depending on production date.

History: John (1884–1964) and Elizabeth
(1889–1978) Degenhart operated the Crystal Art
Glass factory of Cambridge, Ohio, from 1947 to
1978. The factory specialized in reproduction
pressed glass novelties and paperweights. Over
50 molds were worked by this factory including
ten toothpick holders, five salts, and six animal
covered dishes of various sizes.

When the factory ceased operation, many of
the molds were purchased by Boyd Crystal Art
Glass, Cambridge, OH. Boyd has issued pieces
in many new colors. All are marked with a "B" in
a diamond.

References: Gene Florence, *Degenhart Glass and
Paperweights: A Collector's Guide To Colors And
Values,* Degenhart Paperweight and Glass
Museum, 1982; Ellen Tischbein Schroy, *Warman's
Glass, Second Edition* Wallace–Homestead,
1995.

Collectors' Club: The Friends of Degenhart,
Degenhart Paperweight and Glass Museum, Inc.,
65323 Highland Hills Rd., PO Box 186,
Cambridge, OH 43725.

Museum: The Degenhart Paperweight and Glass
Museum, Inc., Cambridge, OH. The museum
covers all types of Ohio Valley glass.

REPRODUCTION ALERT: Although most of the
Degenhart molds were reproductions themselves, there are contemporary pieces that can be
confusing such as Kanawha's bird salt and bow
slipper; L. G. Wright's mini–slipper, daisy & button salt, and 5" robin covered dish; and many
other contemporary American pieces. The 3"
bird salt and mini–pitcher also are made by an
unknown glassmaker in Taiwan.

Animal Dish, covered
    Hen, 3", intro 1967, marked 1973,
    Mint Green **20.00**

Lamb, intro 1961, marked 1972,
Cobalt **40.00**
Robin, intro 1960, marked 1972,
Fawn **55.00**
Turkey, intro 1971, marked 1972
Amber **35.00**
Tomato **100.00**
Bicentennial Bell, intro 1974, marked
1974, Ivorene **12.00**
Boot
Daisy & Button, high, intro 1952,
marked 1972, Peach Blo **25.00**
Skate, intro 1961, marked 1972,
Sapphire Dark **30.00**
Texas, intro 1974, marked 1974
Baby Green **15.00**
Peach (clear) **12.00**
Candy Dish, cov, Wildflower pattern,
intro 1971, marked 1972, Twilight
Blue **25.00**
Child's Mug, Stork & Peacock pattern,
intro 1971, marked 1972
Baby Green **20.00**
Smokey Heather **25.00**
Coaster, intro 1974, marked 1975
Crystal **8.00**
Shamrock **6.00**
Creamer and Sugar
Daisy & Button, intro 1970, marked
1972, Cambridge Pink **75.00**
Texas, intro 1962, marked 1972, Pine
Green **45.00**
Cup Plate
Heart & Lyre, intro 1965, marked
c1977, Mulberry **15.00**
Seal Of Ohio, intro 1971, marked
c1977, Opalescent **15.00**
Hat, Daisy & Button pattern, intro 1974,
marked 1972, Milk Blue **12.00**
Jewel Box, Heart, intro 1964, marked
1972
Blue Jay **25.00**
Heliotrope **35.00**
Owl, intro 1967, marked 1967, over
200 colors made
Crown Tuscan **40.00**
Misty Green **40.00**
Nile Green Opal **45.00**
Paperweight
Crystal Art Glass, Zack & Bernard
Boyd, Rollin Braden, Gus Theret
and William Degenhart
Hand painted plate weight **75.00**
Marble **150.00**
Multicolored **75.00**
Red Flower **65.00**
Single–colored window weight . .   **200.00**
Paperweight by John or Charles
Degenhart
Morning Glories **80.00**
Name Weight **35.00**
Star Flower **70.00**

**Portrait Paperweight, designed by Jack
Choko, Millville, NJ, made by Imperial
Glass for Crystal Art Glass Co., intro-
duced 1977, $150.00.**

Pitcher, Mini, intro 1973, marked 1973,
Jade **20.00**
Pooch, intro 1976, marked 1976, ap-
proximately 110 colors made
Canary **15.00**
Heatherbloom **30.00**
Smokey Blue **12.00**
Portrait Plate, Degenhart, intro 1974,
marked 1974, Crystal **35.00**
Priscilla, intro 1976, marked 1976, only
40 colors made
Daffodil **100.00**
Periwinkle **75.00**
Salt
Bird, 1½", intro 1966, marked 1972
Amber **12.00**
Orchid **15.00**
Daisy & Button, intro 1970, marked
1972
Amberina **15.00**
Rose Marie **12.00**
Pottie, intro 1971, marked 1972, Milk
White **10.00**
Star & Dew Drop, intro 1952, marked
1972
Forest Green **12.00**
Lemon Opal **20.00**
Salt and Pepper Shakers, pr, Bird, intro
1958, marked 1973
Baby Green **35.00**
Ruby **50.00**
Slipper
Daisy & Button or Bow, Blue Marble
Slag **25.00**
Kat, intro 1947, marked 1972,
Sapphire **15.00**
Miniature, intro 1965, marked 1972
Emerald Green **12.00**
Vaseline **15.00**
Tomahawk, intro 1947, marked c1975,
Custard Maverick **55.00**

Toothpick Holder
 Baby or Tramp Shoe, intro 1962,
 marked 1972
  Gold 8.00
  Pigeon Blood 25.00
 Basket, intro 1963, marked c1974,
 Milk White 20.00
 Beaded Oval, intro 1967, marked
 1972, Bittersweet 30.00
 Bird, intro 1959, marked 1972,
 Persimmon 15.00
 Colonial Drape & Heart, intro 1961,
 marked 1972
  Amethyst, Light 12.00
  Ruby 20.00
 Daisy & Button, intro 1970, marked
 1972
  Apple Green 15.00
  Fawn 12.00
 Elephant Head, intro c1957, marked
 1972
  Amber 20.00
  Jade 50.00
 Forget–me–not, intro 1965, marked
 1972, made in over 150 colors
  April Green #1 . . . .   15.00
  Bloody Mary #2 . . . .   40.00
  Grape 15.00
 Gypsy Pot, intro 1962, marked 1972
  Bittersweet 30.00
  Elizabeth's Lime Ice 25.00
 Tray, Hand, intro 1949, marked c1975
  Bittersweet 15.00
  Taffeta 12.00
Wine
 Buzz Saw, intro 1967, marked 1973
  Honey Amber 15.00
  Pistachio 20.00
  Taffeta 40.00
 Daisy & Button, intro 1969, marked
 1972, Sunset 20.00

DEPRESSION GLASS

Collecting Hint: Many collectors specialize in one pattern; others collect by a particular color. Prices listed are for pieces in mint condition—no chips, scratches, etc.

History: Depression glass is glassware made during the period 1920–1940. It was an inexpensive machine–made glass, produced by several different glass companies.

The colors varied from company to company. The number of items made for each pattern also varied. Like pattern glass, depression glass pattern names are sometimes confusing; therefore, a collector should learn all names for their particular pattern.

References: Gene Florence, *Collectible Glassware from the 40's, 50's & 60's, Second Edition* Collector Books, 1994; Gene Florence, *Elegant Glassware of the Depression Era, Sixth Edition,* Collector Books, 1995; Gene Florence, *Kitchen Glassware of the Depression Years: Identification & Values, Fifth Edition,* Collector Books, 1995; Gene Florence, *The Collector's Encyclopedia of Depression Glass, Twelfth Edition,* Collector Books, 1995; Gene Florence, *Very Rare Glassware of the Depression Years, First Series* (1988, 1990 value update) and *Second Series* (1990), *Third Series* (1993, 1995 value update), *Fourth Series* (1995), Collector Books; Ralph and Terry Kovel, *Kovels' Depression Glass & American Dinnerware Price List, Fifth Edition,* Crown, 1995; Carl F. Luckey and Mary Burris, *An Identification & Value Guide To Depression Era Glassware, Third Edition,* Books Americana, 1994; Naomi L. Over, *Ruby Glass of the 20th Century,* Antique Publications, 1990, 1993–94 value update; Mark Schliesmann, *Price Survey, Second Edition,* Park Avenue Publications, 1984; Ellen Tischbein Schroy, *Warman's Glass, Second Edition* Wallace–Homestead, 1995; Kent G. Washburn, *Price Survey, 4th Edition,* published by author, 1994; Hazel Marie Weatherman, *Colored Glassware of the Depression Era, Book 2,* published by author, 1974, available in reprint; Hazel Marie Weatherman, *1984 Supplement & Price Trends for Colored Glassware of the Depression Era, Book 1,* published by author, 1984.

Periodical: *The Daze,* 10271 State Rd., Box 57, Otisville, MI 48463.

Collectors' Clubs: National Depression Glass Assoc., PO Box 69843, Odessa, TX 79769; 20–30–40 Society Inc., PO Box 856, La Grange, IL 60525; Western Reserve Depression Glass Club, 8669 Courtland Dr., Strongsville, OH 44136.

Videotape: Ro Cliff Communications, *Living Glass, Popular Patterns of the Depression Era,* Volume 1 and Volume II, 1993.

REPRODUCTION ALERT: Because of recent interest in collecting depression glass, many reproductions are surfacing. Most reproductions are made in colors not originally made. They are sometimes made in the original molds and often are marked. However, several patterns have been reproduced in original colors but the molds are slightly different. Thorough knowledge of patterns, colors and markings is very important.

Send a self–addressed stamped business envelope to *The Daze* and request a copy of their glass reproduction list. It is one of the best bargains in the collectibles field.

AMERICAN PIONEER

Liberty Works, 1931–1934. Made in amber, crystal, green, and pink.

	Amber	Crystal	Green	Pink
Bowl, 5" d, handle	29.00	17.00	17.00	14.50
Candlesticks, pr, 6½" h		60.00	80.00	65.00
Candy Dish, cov, 1 lb		75.00	96.00	78.00
Creamer, 3½" h	40.00	18.50	21.00	20.00
Cup and Saucer	30.00	15.00	18.50	15.00
Goblet, 6" h, 8 oz	—	40.00	42.00	—
Pitcher, 5" h, cov urn	250.00	125.00	200.00	125.00
Plate				
6" d, handle	24.00	12.50	15.00	12.00
8" d, luncheon	20.00	10.00	11.00	10.00
Sherbet, 4¾" h	—	30.00	35.00	32.00
Sugar, 3½" h	36.00	18.00	21.00	20.00
Tumbler, 4" h, 8 oz	—	25.00	45.00	25.00

AUNT POLLY

U. S. Glass Company, late 1920s. Made in blue, green, and iridescent.

	Blue	Green	Iridescent
Bowl, 4¾" d, berry	17.50	8.00	7.50
Butter Dish, cov	185.00	210.00	200.00
Candy Dish, cov, two handles	—	60.00	60.00
Creamer	42.00	26.00	25.00
Pitcher, 8" h, 48 oz	165.00	—	—
Plate			
6" d, sherbet	12.00	6.50	6.00
8" d, luncheon	18.00	—	—
Salt and Pepper Shakers, pr 195.00	—	—	
Sherbet	12.00	10.00	9.00
Sugar	30.00	23.00	23.00
Tumbler, 3⅝" h, 8 oz	26.00	—	—
Vase, 6½" h, ftd	37.50	27.50	27.50

AVOCADO

"No. 601," Indiana Glass Company, 1923–1933. Made in crystal, green, pink, and some white. Reproductions known in amber, amethyst, blue, frosted pink, green, orange–pink, and yellow.

	Crystal	Green	Pink
Bowl, two handles			
5¼" d	10.00	30.00	25.00
8" d	9.00	25.00	20.00
Cake Plate, 10¼" d	14.00	48.00	35.00
Creamer, ftd	12.00	35.00	30.00
Cup, ftd	—	35.00	30.00
Pitcher, 64 oz	3.50	900.00	700.00
Plate			
6⅜" d, sherbet	5.00	15.00	12.50
8¼" d, luncheon	6.50	18.00	17.00
Salad Bowl, 7½" d	9.00	45.00	30.00
Saucer, 6⅜" d	—	27.50	25.00
Sherbet	—	50.00	45.00
Sugar, ftd	12.00	32.00	30.00
Tumbler	25.00	225.00	150.00

CHINEX CLASSIC

MacBeth–Evans Division of Corning Glass Works, late 1930s–early 1940s. Made in ivory and ivory with decal decoration.

	Plain Ivory	Castle Decal Dec	Rose Decal Dec
Butter Dish, cov	50.00	40.00	75.00
Cereal Bowl, 5¾" d	5.50	15.00	8.50
Creamer	5.00	17.50	10.00
Cup and Saucer	7.00	20.00	12.00
Plate			
6¼" d, sherbet	2.50	7.00	3.50
9¾" d, dinner	4.00	15.00	8.00
Sandwich Plate, 11½" d	8.00	24.00	14.00
Sherbet, low, ftd	7.50	20.00	12.00
Soup Bowl, 7¾" d	12.00	30.00	18.00
Sugar, open	5.50	16.00	10.00
Vegetable Bowl, 7" d	13.50	30.00	20.00

COLONIAL

"Knife and Fork," Hocking Glass Company, 1934–1936. Made in crystal, green, and pink.

	Crystal	Green	Pink
Berry Bowl, 4½" d	6.50	15.00	14.50
Butter Dish, cov	40.00	55.00	575.00
Cereal Bowl, 5½" d	20.00	80.00	50.00
Cream Pitcher, 5" h, 16 oz	15.00	20.00	50.00
Cup	7.50	10.00	10.00
Goblet, water, 5¾" h	20.00	27.50	36.00
Iced Tea Tumbler, 12 oz	24.00	48.00	42.00
Juice Tumbler, 3" h	13.00	16.00	24.00
Mug, 4½" h, 12 oz	—	750.00	450.00
Pitcher, 7" h, 54 oz	27.50	50.00	45.00
Plate			
6" d, sherbet	4.00	7.50	6.00
8½" d, luncheon	4.50	9.00	9.50
10" d, dinner	25.00	50.00	45.00
10" d, grill	13.00	24.00	24.00
Platter, 12" l, oval	15.00	20.00	30.00
Salt and Pepper Shakers, pr	60.00	125.00	125.00

Colonial, wine, green, $25.00.

Coronation, bowl, royal ruby, 6½" w, $10.00.

	Crystal	Green	Pink
Saucer	4.00	6.00	6.00
Sherbet, 3⅜"	6.00	12.00	10.00
Sugar, 5"	10.00	15.00	25.00
Tumbler, 4" h, ftd	16.50	35.00	25.00
Vegetable Bowl, 10" l, oval	17.50	32.00	30.00
Whiskey, 2½" h	10.00	15.00	12.00
Wine, 4½" h	15.00	25.00	—

CORONATION

"Banded Rib, Saxon," Hocking Glass Company, 1936–1940. Made in green, pink, and royal ruby.

	Green	Pink	Royal Ruby
Berry Bowl			
Individual, 4¾" d	25.00	4.50	6.50
Master, 8" d, handles	—	8.50	15.00
Cup and Saucer	—	7.50	15.00
Nappy, 6½" d	—	6.00	12.00
Plate			
6" d, sherbet	—	2.00	—
8½" d, luncheon	35.00	4.50	8.00
Sherbet	50.00	5.00	—
Tumbler, 5" h, 10 oz, ftd	125.00	20.00	—

DORIC

Jeannette Glass Company, 1935–1938. Made in Delphite, green, and pink.

	Delphite	Green	Pink
Berry			
Individual, 4½" d.	35.00	8.00	7.50
Master, 8¼" d	110.00	17.00	14.50
Bowl, 9" d, handles.	—	15.00	15.00
Butter Dish.	—	80.00	65.00
Cake Plate, 10" d	—	21.00	24.00
Candy Dish, cov, 8" d	—	35.00	32.00
Cereal Bowl, 5½" d.	—	55.00	45.00
Coaster, 3" d.	—	15.00	15.00
Creamer, 4" h	—	12.00	10.00
Cup and Saucer	—	14.00	16.00
Pitcher, 5½" h, 32 oz, flat	900.00	40.00	35.00
Plate			
6" d, sherbet	—	5.00	4.00
7" d, salad.	—	16.50	15.50
9" d, dinner.	—	15.00	12.00
9" d, grill.	—	16.00	12.50
Platter, 12" l, oval	—	20.00	22.00
Relish Tray, 4 x 8".	—	15.00	12.00
Sherbet.	5.00	14.00	13.00
Sugar, cov	—	32.50	30.00
Tray, 8 x 8", serving.	—	20.00	18.00
Tumbler, 4" h, 10 oz, ftd	—	80.00	50.00
Vegetable Bowl, 9" l, oval	—	30.00	25.00

FORTUNE

Hocking Glass Company, 1937–1938. Made in crystal and pink.

	Crystal	Pink		Crystal	Pink
Berry Bowl			Juice Tumbler, 3½" h . . .	7.00	7.50
Individual, 4" d	3.50	3.50	Plate		
Master, 7¾" d	12.00	12.00	6" d, sherbet	3.00	3.50
Candy Dish, cov, flat . . .	20.00	22.00	8" d, luncheon	15.00	15.00
Cup and Saucer	7.00	7.50	Salad Bowl, 7¾" d	12.00	12.00
Dessert Bowl, 4½" d	4.50	5.00	Tumbler, 4" h	9.00	10.00

LORAIN

"Basket, No. 615," Indiana Glass Company, 1929–1932. Made in crystal, green, and yellow.

	Crystal	Green	Yellow
Cereal Bowl, 6" d	35.00	35.00	50.00
Creamer, ftd	15.00	15.00	20.00
Cup and Saucer	15.00	15.00	20.00
Plate			
5½" d, sherbet	6.50	7.50	12.00
7¾" d, salad	10.00	10.00	15.00
8⅜" d, luncheon	15.00	15.00	25.00
10¼" d, dinner	30.00	35.00	50.00
Relish, 8" d, 4 part	15.00	17.50	32.00
Salad Bowl, 7¼" d	36.00	36.00	55.00
Sherbet, ftd	17.50	20.00	30.00
Sugar, ftd	15.00	18.00	24.00
Tumbler, 4¾" h, ftd	17.50	19.00	25.00
Vegetable Bowl, 9¾" l, oval	36.00	36.50	47.00

MADRID

Federal Glass Company, 1932–1939. Indiana Glass Company, 1980s. Originally made in amber, blue, crystal, green, and pink. Reissued by Federal in 1976 in amber as "Recollections." Indiana Glass produced reproductions in crystal, blue, pink, and teal.

	Amber	Blue	Green	Pink
Bowl, 5" d, sauce	6.00	—	6.50	6.50
Butter Dish, cov	68.00	—	80.00	—
Console Bowl, 11" d	15.00	—	—	12.00
Cookie Jar, cov	45.00	—	—	30.00
Creamer, ftd	8.50	20.00	12.00	—
Cup and Saucer	11.00	27.00	14.00	12.50
Pitcher, 8" h, 60 oz, sq	45.00	150.00	135.00	35.00
Plate				
6" d, sherbet	4.00	8.00	4.00	4.00
8⅛" d, luncheon	8.00	18.00	9.00	7.50
10½" d, dinner	35.00	65.00	30.00	—
Salt and Pepper				
Shakers, pr, ftd	65.00	135.00	80.00	—
Sherbet	7.50	15.00	12.00	—
Soup Bowl, 7" d	15.00	30.00	16.00	—
Sugar, cov	45.50	170.00	50.00	—
Tumbler, 4¼" h, 9 oz	15.00	25.00	20.00	15.00

MISS AMERICA

"Diamond Pattern," Hocking Glass Company, 1935–1938. Made in crystal, green, and pink. Limited production in green, ice blue, jadeite, and royal ruby. Reproductions made in cobalt blue, crystal, green, ice blue, pink, and red amberina.

	Crystal	Green	Pink
Butter Dish, cov	200.00	—	500.00
Cake Plate, 12" d, ftd	26.00	—	42.00
Candy Jar, cov, 11½" h	55.00	—	135.00
Celery Dish, 10½" l	15.00	—	25.00
Cereal Bowl, 6¼" d	9.50	17.50	20.00
Coaster, 5¾" d	15.00	—	25.00
Compote, 5" d	15.00	—	25.00
Creamer, ftd	9.50	—	17.50
Cup and Saucer	14.50	17.50	28.00
Fruit Bowl, 8¾" d	30.00	—	50.00
Goblet, 5½" h	20.00	—	40.00
Iced Tea Tumbler, 5¾" h	25.00	—	70.00
Juice Tumbler, 4¾" h	25.00	—	75.00
Pitcher, 8½" h, ice lip	65.00	—	125.00
Plate			
5¾" d, sherbet	6.00	—	9.50
8½" d, salad	7.50	9.50	21.00
10¼" d, dinner	14.00	—	24.00
Relish, 8¾" d, 4 part	12.00	—	24.00
Salt and Pepper Shakers, pr	30.00	290.00	55.00
Sherbet	8.00	—	14.00
Sugar	8.50	—	16.00
Tumbler, 4½" h	15.00	18.00	28.00
Vegetable Bowl, 10" l, oval	15.00	—	27.50
Wine, 3¾" h	20.00	—	65.00

OLD CAFE

Hocking Glass Company, 1936–1940. Made in crystal, pink, and royal ruby.

	Crystal	Pink	Royal Ruby
Berry Bowl, 3¾" d	3.00	3.00	5.00
Bowl			
5" d	5.00	10.00	—
9" d	10.00	12.00	15.00
Candy Dish, 8" d, low	11.00	11.00	12.00
Cereal Bowl, 5½" d	6.00	6.50	10.00
Cup	5.00	5.00	10.00
Juice Tumbler, 3" h	10.00	10.00	9.00
Lamp	17.50	22.00	25.00
Olive Dish, 6" l, oblong	5.00	5.00	—
Pitcher			
36 oz	60.00	65.00	—
80 oz	75.00	175.00	—
Plate			
6" d, sherbet	2.00	2.50	8.00
10" d, dinner	25.00	27.50	30.00
Saucer	3.00	3.00	8.00
Sherbet	6.00	7.00	10.00
Tumbler, 4" h	10.00	10.00	17.50
Vase, 7¼" h	13.00	14.50	18.00

Miss America, candy jar, cov, pink, $135.00.

Patrician, sherbet, ftd, yellow, 3″ h, 3½″ d, $9.00.

PATRICIAN

"Spoke," Federal Glass Company, 1933–1937. Made in amber, crystal, green, and pink.

	Amber	Crystal	Green	Pink
Butter Dish, cov	85.00	80.00	100.00	200.00
Cereal Bowl, 6″ d	22.00	20.00	24.00	22.00
Creamer, ftd	9.00	9.00	10.00	11.50
Cream Soup, 4¾″ d	15.00	14.00	17.50	16.00
Cup and Saucer	16.50	15.00	20.00	18.00
Jam Dish	27.50	25.00	32.00	27.50
Pitcher, 8″ h, molded handle	100.00	100.00	125.00	115.00
Plate				
6″ d, sherbet	10.00	8.00	8.00	8.00
7½″ d, salad	15.00	10.00	17.00	15.00
9″ d, luncheon	12.00	10.00	11.00	12.00
10½″ d, dinner	7.50	6.50	35.00	30.00
10½″ d, grill	14.00	12.00	15.00	12.00
Salt and Pepper Shakers, pr	55.00	45.00	60.00	80.00
Sherbet	13.00	13.00	14.00	13.00
Sugar, cov	50.00	45.00	55.00	52.00
Tumbler, 4¼″ h, 9 oz	25.00	20.00	25.00	25.00

PRINCESS

Hocking Glass Company, 1931–1935. Made in apricot yellow, blue, green, pink, and topaz yellow.

	Apricot Yellow	Green	Pink	Topaz Yellow
Ashtray, 4½″ d	85.00	65.00	85.00	85.00
Bowl, 5″ d	28.00	22.00	24.00	28.00
Butter Dish, cov	600.00	85.00	85.00	600.00
Cake Plate, 10″ d	—	24.00	28.00	—
Coaster	85.00	32.00	64.00	85.00
Cookie Jar, cov	—	50.00	55.00	—
Creamer	14.00	14.00	15.00	14.00
Cup and Saucer	12.50	22.00	24.00	14.00

	Apricot Yellow	Green	Pink	Topaz Yellow
Plate				
6" d, sherbet	—	10.00	—	4.00
9½" d, dinner	14.50	24.00	22.00	15.00
Sherbet................	35.00	20.00	20.00	35.00
Sugar	8.50	10.00	12.00	9.00
Tumbler, 4" h, 9 oz	22.00	25.00	26.00	24.00

RAINDROPS

"Optic Design," Federal Glass Company, 1929–1933. Made in crystal and green.

	Green			Green
Berry Bowl, 7½ d	35.00	6" d, sherbet		2.50
Cereal Bowl, 6" d	7.50	8" d, luncheon		6.00
Creamer	8.00	Sherbet		6.50
Cup and Saucer	9.50	Sugar, cov		36.00
Fruit Bowl, 4½" d	5.00	Tumbler, 4⅛" h		10.00
Plate		Whiskey, 1⅞" h		7.50

SANDWICH

Indiana Glass Company, 1920s–1980s. Made in amber (late 1920s–1980s), crystal (late 1920s–present), green (1920s–early 1930s), milk white (mid 1950s), pink (1920s–early 1930s), red (1933, 1969–early 1970s), smokey blue (1976–1977), and teal blue (1950s–1980s).

	Amber/ Crystal	Green/ Pink	Red	Teal Blue
Ashtray	3.25	—	—	
Basket, 10" h	35.00	—	—	—
Berry Bowl, 4¼" d	3.50	—	—	—
Bowl				
6" d, hexagonal	5.00	—	—	14.00
8½" d	10.00	—	—	—
Butter Dish, dome cover	22.00	—	—	150.00
Candlesticks, pr, 3½" h	17.50	—	—	—
Console Bowl, 9" d	16.50	—	—	—
Creamer	10.00	—	—	—
Cup and Saucer	6.00	—	35.00	12.00
Decanter, stopper	22.00	110.00	80.00	—
Goblet	13.00	—	45.00	—
Pitcher, 68 oz	22.00	—	120.00	—
Plate				
6" d, sherbet	3.00	—	—	7.00
7" d, bread and butter	4.00	—	—	—
8¾" d, luncheon	4.75	—	18.00	—
10½" d, dinner	8.00	18.00	—	—
Sandwich Plate, 13" d	14.00	24.00	35.00	25.00
Sherbet, 3¼" h	5.50	—	—	12.00
Sugar	10.00	—	45.00	—
Tumbler, ftd, 8 oz	9.00	—	—	—
Wine, 3" h	6.50	22.00	14.00	—

Sharon, plate, amber, 9½" d, $10.00.

Swirl, sherbet, green, 2⅞" h, 4⅛" d, $4.00.

SHARON

"Cabbage Rose," Federal Glass Company, 1935–1939, amber, green, pink, and some crystal. Reproductions made in blue, burnt umber, cobalt blue, dark green, light green, and pink.

	Amber	Green	Pink
Berry Bowl			
Individual, 5" d	8.50	14.00	12.50
Master, 8½" d	6.50	25.00	27.50
Butter Dish, cov	23.00	80.00	47.50
Cake Plate, 11½" d, ftd	24.00	55.00	35.00
Candy Jar, cov	45.00	150.00	50.00
Cereal Bowl, 6" d	18.00	24.00	22.00
Cheese Dish, cov	180.00	—	—
Creamer, ftd	10.00	20.00	25.00
Cream Soup, 5" d	27.50	45.00	40.00
Cup	9.00	18.00	17.50
Fruit Bowl, 10½" d	21.00	35.00	35.00
Jam Dish, 7½" d	35.00	40.00	160.00
Pitcher, 80 oz			
Ice Lip	100.00	350.00	150.00
Plain	120.00	400.00	130.00
Plate			
6" d, bread and butter	4.00	8.00	7.50
7½" d, salad	15.00	20.00	24.00
9½" d, dinner	10.00	21.00	17.50
Platter, 12½" l, oval	18.00	27.50	27.50
Salt and Pepper Shakers, pr	40.00	65.00	45.00
Saucer	6.00	5.00	5.00
Sherbet, ftd	12.00	25.00	13.00
Soup Bowl, 7¾" d	45.00	—	40.00
Sugar, cov	30.00	45.00	28.00
Tumbler			
4⅛" h, 9 oz, thick	23.00	40.00	37.50
4⅛" h, 9 oz, thin	25.00	37.50	30.00
5¼" h, 12 oz, thick	25.00	37.50	37.50
5¼" h, 12 oz, thin	28.00	40.00	48.00
6½" h, 15 oz, ftd	90.00	—	50.00
Vegetable Bowl, 9½" l, oval	20.00	30.00	24.00

SPIRAL

Hocking Glass Company, 1928–1930. Made in crystal, green, and pink.

	Green		Green
Berry Bowl		6" d, sherbet	2.00
Individual, 4¾" d	5.00	8" d, luncheon	3.50
Master, 8" d	12.00	Platter, 12" l	25.00
Creamer	7.50	Preserve Jar, cov	30.00
Cup and Saucer	8.00	Salt and Pepper Shakers, pr	35.00
Ice Tub	25.00	Sandwich Server, center handle	24.00
Juice Tumbler	7.50	Sherbet	4.00
Mixing Bowl, 7" d	8.50	Sugar	7.50
Pitcher, 7⅝" h	30.00	Tumbler, 5" d	7.50
Plate			

TEA ROOM

Indiana Glass Company, 1926–1931. Made in amber, some crystal, green, and pink.

	Green	Pink
Banana Split, 7½"		
Flat	75.00	75.00
Footed	80.00	80.00
Bowl, 8¾" d	80.00	65.00
Candlesticks, pr	48.00	45.00
Celery Bowl, 8¼" d	30.00	25.00
Creamer		
3¼" h	25.00	27.00
4½" h, ftd	22.00	25.00
Rectangular	20.00	18.00
Cup and Saucer	75.00	75.00
Finger Bowl	45.00	35.00
Goblet	70.00	60.00
Ice Bucket	55.00	65.00
Lamp, 9" h	55.00	45.00
Marmalade, notched lid	175.00	150.00
Mustard, cov	135.00	120.00
Parfait	65.00	60.00
Pitcher, 64 oz	200.00	175.00
Plate		
6½" d, sherbet	25.00	25.00
8¼" d, luncheon	35.00	30.00
Relish, divided	24.00	20.00
Salad Bowl, 8¾" d	75.00	72.00
Salt and Pepper Shakers, pr	55.00	55.00
Sandwich Plate, 10½" d	50.00	48.00
Sherbet		
Low	30.00	28.00
Low, flared edge	35.00	32.00
Tall, ftd	45.00	40.00
Sugar, cov		
3" h	100.00	90.00
4½" h, ftd	28.00	26.00
Rectangular	20.00	18.00
Sundae, ftd, ruffled	85.00	75.00
Tray		
Center handle	185.00	195.00
Rectangular	50.00	45.00

	Green	Pink
Tumbler		
6 oz, ftd	35.00	35.00
8 oz, flat	30.00	28.00
8 oz, ftd	35.00	35.00
11 oz, ftd	65.00	65.00
12 oz, ftd	55.00	55.00
Vase		
6½" h, ruffled	145.00	85.00
9½" h, ruffled	140.00	80.00
9½" h, straight	65.00	60.00
11" h, ruffled	185.00	200.00
11" h, straight	90.00	85.00
Vegetable Bowl, 9½" l, oval	60.00	55.00

VICTORY

Diamond Glassware Company, 1929–1932. Made in amber, black, cobalt blue, green, and pink.

	Amber	Black	Cobalt Blue	Green	Pink
Bonbon, 7" d	11.00	20.00	20.00	12.00	11.00
Bowl, 11" d, rolled edge	28.00	50.00	50.00	28.00	28.00
Candlesticks, pr, 3" h	30.00	90.00	90.00	30.00	30.00
Cereal Bowl, 6½" d	11.00	26.00	26.00	12.00	12.00
Cheese and Cracker Set	40.00	—	—	45.00	45.00
Creamer	15.00	45.00	45.00	15.00	15.00
Cup and Saucer	13.00	44.00	44.00	14.00	15.00
Plate					
6" d, bread and butter	6.00	16.00	16.00	6.50	7.00
7" d, salad	7.50	18.00	18.00	7.00	7.50
8" d, luncheon	7.00	25.00	25.00	7.50	8.00
9" d, dinner	20.00	38.00	38.00	20.00	20.00
Sandwich Server, center handle	30.00	70.00	70.00	30.00	30.00
Sherbet	14.00	25.00	25.00	15.00	15.00
Sugar	15.00	45.00	45.00	15.00	15.00

DIONNE QUINTUPLETS

Collecting Hints: Almost all the doll companies in the 1930s released dolls resembling the Quints. The only "genuine" Dionne Quintuplet dolls are the Madame Alexander dolls dating from 1935 to 1939. They realize the highest prices.

History: The Dionne Quintuplets were born on May 28, 1934, on a small farm between Corbeil and Callander, Ontario, Canada. The five baby girls weighed a total of 10 lbs, 1¼ ozs. They were delivered by Dr. Dafoe and two midwives. They were named Yvonne, Annette, Cecile, Emilie, and Marie.

When they were just two days old, their father, Oliva Dionne, and the parish priest signed a contract to exhibit the babies at the Chicago World's Fair. The Canadian government passed "An Act For the Protection Of the Dionne Quintuplets" to prevent this. The girls became special wards of King George V.

A special house, the Dafoe Hospital, was built for them across the road from their place of birth. It had one-way glass through which visitors could view the children. People came by the thousands during the mid to late 1930s. In this nursery they were attended by Dr. Dafoe and a staff of professionals. Newspapers gave daily reports and photographs of their progress. Souvenirs of every type were sold including rocks, called "Fertility Stones," from the farm which brought between 50¢ and $1.00.

Emilie died in a convent in August 1954 and Marie died February 27, 1970. Yvonne, Annette, and Cecile remain alive today.

Reference: John Axe, *The Collectible Dionne Quintuplets*, Hobby House Press, 1977, out–of–print.

Collectors' Club: Dionne Quint Collectors, PO Box 2527, Woburn, MA 01888.

Blotter, unused	**10.00**
Book, *The Dionne Quintuplets Growing Up*, 8½ x 11", brown and white cov, 1935	**40.00**
Calendar	
1936, Watch Us Grow, photos and stories	**18.00**
1942	**30.00**
1955	**20.00**
Cereal Bowl	
China, Marie in high chair, c1935 . .	**18.00**
Silverplated	**38.00**
Coloring Book, 10 x 15", The Dionne Quintuplets Pictures To Paint, Merill, 1940	**20.00**
Doll, 7½" h, mohair wig, painted brown eyes, Madame Alexander, 1936	**225.00**
Fan, cardboard, wooden handle, picture of quints and ducks at stream, Howard M Davies Funeral Chapel adv on reverse	**25.00**
Game, Line Up The Quints	**30.00**
Handkerchief, 8½" sq, black, white, and blue portraits, red ground	**30.00**
Magazine Cover	
Look, Oct 11, 1938, Dr Dafoe	**5.00**
Woman's World, Feb, 1937	**10.00**
Paper Doll, book, Let's Play House with the Dionne Quints, uncut, #4	**49.00**
Photo, tinted, damaged frame, 1935 . .	**20.00**
Picture, titled "The Darling Dionnes," holding dolls, framed	**48.00**
Pin	**17.50**
Poster, 14 x 32", "Today The Dionne Quints Had Quaker Oats," 1935 . . .	**60.00**
Puzzle, ball, steel, glass top, place quints in buggy	**35.00**
Sign, 11 x 16", cardboard, Quints with tea set	**60.00**
Spoon, set of five	**125.00**
Thermometer, 3⅞ x 6", cardboard, multicolored, Cupp's Dairy adv	**25.00**

DIRIGIBLES

Collecting Hints: All areas of dirigible material remain stable. Focus on one specific topic, e.g., material about one airship, models and toys, post cards, etc. The field is very broad, and a collector might exhaust his funds trying to be compre-

hensive. The most common collecting focus is material relating to specific flights.

History: The terms *airship* and *dirigible* are synonymous. Dirigible (Latin for directable) means steerable and can apply to a bicycle. Dirigible evolved through usage into a word for *airship*.
There are three types of dirigibles: (1) *Rigid*—a zeppelin, e.g., HINDENBURG, GRAF, SHENANDOAH, (2) *Non–Rigid*—a blimp, e.g., GOODYEAR BLIMPS and Navy blimps, and (3) *Semi–Rigid*—non–rigid with a keel, e.g., NORGE and ITALIA. Note: Hot air balloons, barrage balloons, hydrogen balloons, etc., are not dirigibles. They are not directable. They go where the wind takes them.
Prior to 1900 only non–rigid and semi–rigid dirigibles existed.
Zeppelins date from 1900 to 1940, the last being the LZ130 sister ship to the HINDENBURG. The GRAF ZEPPELIN was the most successful zeppelin, flying between 1928 and 1940. The HINDENBURG was the most famous zeppelin, due to the spectacular fire that led to its demise in 1937. Its flying dates were 1936 to 1937.
America never used its four zeppelins for passenger travel. They were strictly military. The Naval Air Station at Lakehurst, New Jersey, where the well–known zeppelins docked, has remained open to this day. However, its name has been changed to the Naval Air Engineering Center. None of its present operations include lighter–than–air vehicles, except for an occasional blimp. The famous Hangar #1 has been refurbished, but the base is currently off limits to the general public. The last Navy blimp flew from Lakehurst in 1962.

References: Walter Curley, *The Graf Zeppelin's Flights to South America*, Spellman Museum, 1970; Arthur Falk, *Hindenburg Crash Mail*, Clear Color Litho, 1976; Sieger, *Zeppelin Post Katalog*, Wurttemberg, 1981, in German.

Collectors' Club: Zeppelin Collectors Club, c/o Aerophilatelic Federation, PO Box 1239, Elgin, IL 60121–1239.

Museum: Navy Lakehurst Historical Society, Cinnaminson, NJ.

REPRODUCTION ALERT

Badge, pilot's, German zeppelin, silver, hallmarked	**375.00**
Bank, Goodyear blimp, porcelain, pedestal base, 8½" l	**50.00**
Button, brass, airship, globe, and swastika	**35.00**
Cap, souvenir, leather, Airship *Akron* . .	**125.00**
Charm, binoculars, miniature, white celluloid, brass fittings, black and white views of Graf Zeppelin and	

Empire State Building inside, France, late 1920s **100.00**

Flight Cover, Century of Progress, 50¢ zeppelin stamp **65.00**

Key Chain Token, Airship *Akron*, Duralumin **45.00**

Launch Souvenir, aluminum disk, Goodyear Zeppelin ZRS–4, emb US Navy airship, Goodyear logo, "Akron, Ohio, U.S.A. Oct. 31, 1929," 3" d **50.00**

Needle Book, Air Fleet, Zeppelin, Statue of Liberty cov **22.50**

Palm Puzzle, silvered tin frame, glass cov, airship launching scene, black cardboard underside, Germany, mid 1930s, 4" d **200.00**

Photograph, black and white, Goodyear Zeppelin dock and Airship *Macon*, text sticker on cardboard back, dated April 23, 1933, Duralumin frame, 8 x 10" **90.00**

Picture Frame, commemorative, title inscription "Winner, Park Service Station, Third Annual Goodyear Dealers Zeppelin Race July–August 1931," tag at bottom center reads "Made of Duralumin Used in Girder Construction of the United States Airship *Akron* Built by the Goodyear Zeppelin Corporation," 20¼ x 26" .. **100.00**

Pin, figural airship
 Silver Plated Brass, Airship *D–LZ 130*, swastika symbols on upper and lower tail fins, mid 1930s, 1¾" l .. **75.00**
 Sterling Silver, 3½" l **85.00**

Pinback Button, Zeps, litho tin, Sunday school award, airship flying through clouds, red, white, and blue, 1930s, ⅝" d **15.00**

Plaque, Goodyear adv, cast iron, relief factory scene with blimp, buses, plane, trucks, and cars, painted gold, c1930, 12" w, 17" h **130.00**

Playing Cards, Airship No. 909, Standard Playing Card Co, Chicago, orig box, dated 1894 .... **40.00**

Poster, "12 Hours at Sebring, Florida," racetrack scene, Goodyear blimp flying overhead, 1963, 27½ x 36" matted and framed **240.00**

Sheet Music, *The Hindenburg* **18.00**

Soda Bottle, Zep, depicts airship **85.00**

Tin, Zeppelin Motor Oil, 2 gal, Zeppelin flying over ocean, red and white lettering, 1925–45, 11½" h **85.00**

Toy
 K & K, Japan, "Airship," windup, tin, string for hanging from ceiling, c1925, orig box and instructions, 7" l **575.00**
 Stasco, USA, celluloid, red, blue wooden wheels, raised "USA" on sides, 1930s, 5½" l **125.00**
 Strauss, "Flying Airship," windup, aluminum, brass rear props, string for hanging from ceiling, c1925, orig box, 10" l **650.00**

DISNEYANA

Collecting Hints: The products from the 1930s command the most attention. Animated celluloids range in value from $100 into the tens of thousands of dollars depending on subject and complexity of scene. Disneyana is a popular subject, and items tend to be priced on the high side.

Make condition a key element in your purchase. An incomplete toy or game should sell for 40 to 50% less than one in mint condition.

History: Walt Disney and the creations of the famous Disney studio hold a place of fondness and enchantment in the hearts of Americans and people throughout the world. The release of "Steamboat Willie" in 1928 heralded an entertainment empire.

Walt and his brother, Roy, showed shrewd business acumen. From the beginning they licensed the reproduction of Disney characters in products ranging from wrist watches to clothing.

The market in Disneyana has been established by a few determined dealers and auction houses. Hake's Americana and Collectibles has specialized in Disney material for over a decade. Sotheby's Collector Carousel auctions and Lloyd Ralston Toys auctions have continued the trend.

Walt Disney characters are popular throughout the world. Belgium is a leading producer of Disneyana along with England, France, and Japan. The Disney characters often take on the regional characteristics of the host country; don't be surprised to find a strange looking Mickey Mouse or Donald Duck. Disney has opened a

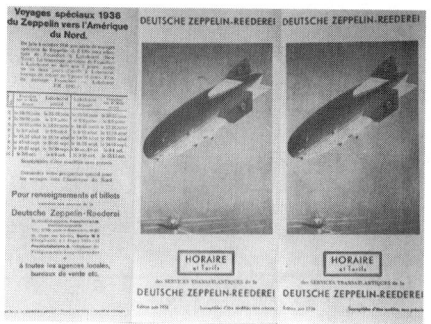

Timetable, *Hindenburg*, tri–fold, French, 3⅞ x 8⅜" folded size, $18.00.

new theme park in Japan; it will produce a wealth of new Disney collectibles.

References: Marcia Blitz, *Donald Duck,* Harmony Books, 1979; Robert Heide and John Gilman, *Cartoon Collectibles,* Doubleday & Co., 1984; Robert Heide and John Gilman, *Disneyana: Classic Collectibles 1928–1958,* Hyperion, 1994; Bevis Hillier, *Walt Disney's Mickey Mouse Memorabilia,* Harry N. Abrams, 1986; David Longest and Michael Stern, *The Collector's Encyclopedia of Disneyana,* Collector Books, 1992; Leonard Maltin, *The Disney Films,* Crown Publishers, 1973; Walton Rawls, *Disney Dons Dogtags: The Best of Disney Military Insignia From World War II,* Abbeville Press, 1992; Richard Schickel, *The Disney Version: The Life, Times, Art and Commerce of Walt Disney,* Avon Books, 1968; Michael Stern, *Stern's Guide to Disney Collectibles, First Series* (1989, 1992 value update), *Second Series* (1990, 1993 value update), *Third Series* (1995), Collector Books; Tom Tumbusch, *Tomart's Illustrated Disneyana Catalog and Price Guide, Volume 1* (1985), *Volume 2* (1985), *Volume 3* (1985), *Volume 4* (1987), Tomart Publications; Tom Tumbusch, *Tomart's Illustrated Disneyana Catalog and Price Guide, Condensed Edition,* Tomart Publications, 1989.

Periodicals: *Tomart's Disneyana Digest,* 3300 Encrete Ln., Dayton, OH 45439; *Tomart's Disneyana Update,* 3300 Encrete Ln., Dayton, OH 45439.

Collectors' Clubs: Mouse Club East, PO Box 3195, Wakefield, MA 01880; National Fantasy Club For Disneyana Collector & Enthusiasts, PO Box 19212, Irvine, CA 92713; The Mouse Club, 2056 Cirone Way, San Jose, CA 95124.

Archive: Walt Disney Archives, Burbank, CA.

Advisor: Ted Hake.

Alice in Wonderland
  Figurine, 6" h, china, 1960 signature
    style Disney copyright under base   **18.00**
  Sheet Music, *In A World Of My Own,*
    9 x 12", white, blue, yellow, and
    green cov, copyright 1949 . . . . . .   **20.00**
Bambi
  Lamp, 12" h, open upright storybook,
    paper label inscribed with text,
    plastic Bambi and Thumper figures
    in front, Dolly Toy Co, c1950 . . . .   **55.00**
  Pin, plastic, Bambi and pine trees
    above "Disneyland/Walt Disney
    Productions," red plastic heart sus-
    pended below, marked Germany,
    late 1950s **20.00**
  Planter, Thumper **45.00**
Cinderella
  Bank **30.00**

Little Golden Book, *Cinderella's
  Friends,* first edition, 1950 . . . . . .   **20.00**
Sheet Music, *So This Is Love,* 9 x 12",
  white and pink cov, copyright 1949   **20.00**
Soaky Bottle, 10½" h, light blue dress,
  swivel arms, mid 1960s **15.00**
Davy Crockett, Record, *Ballad of Davy
  Crockett,* Peter Pan Peanut Butter pre-
  mium, orig picture sleeve showing
  Fess Parker, 1950s **25.00**
Donald Duck
  Bank, 6" h
    Ceramic, white, raised hand,
      painted black, blue, yellow, and
      red, c1940s **50.00**
    Composition, painted, orig tag in-
      scribed "Walt Disney's Donald
      Duck," c1960s **35.00**
  Book
    Donald Duck in Disneyland, Little
      Golden Book, copyright 1955
      and 1960 . . . .   **12.50**
    Donald Duck Sees Stars, Better
      Little Book, #1422, Whitman . .   **40.00**
  Bookend, 7", chalkware, carrying
    school books **60.00**
  Bottle, soda, quart, 10" h, clear glass,
    two large and two small heads emb
    each side, inscribed "Donald
    Duck/Not To Be Refilled/Trademark
    Copyright/Walt Disney Produc-
    tions," bottom marked "One Pint 8
    Fl Oz," early 1960s **35.00**
  Cookie Jar, marked "Walt Disney Co
    by Hoan Ltd" **50.00**
  Doll, Dancing Donald, 16" h, hard
    plastic, white vinyl hands, fabric
    outfit, hinged legs, Hasbro, c1970   **10.00**
  Figure
    Bisque, 3¼" h, long–billed, holding
      small gold horn, 1930s **30.00**
    Celluloid, 3" h, movable feet and
      arms, red jacket, blue bow tie,
      green hat, Walt Disney around
      one side of body, "Japan"
      marked on foot, c1950s **65.00**
    Plywood, 4 x 6", diecut, painted,
      fits in groove on base, purple
      fabric bow tie, early 1950s **30.00**
  Greeting Card, Easter, 4 x 6", diecut,
    light brown flocked body, Hall-
    mark, 1942 . . . .   **25.00**
  Lamp, figural **45.00**
  Puppet, orig box, Gund **55.00**
  Roly–Poly, 6" d, 11" h, vinyl, figural,
    black, white, yellow, and blue,
    chimes, c1970 . . . .   **15.00**
  Salt and Pepper Shakers, pr, pottery,
    figural, "Souv Grand Island Neb,"
    1930s **33.00**
  Toy, pull, 9" h, wood, movable arms,
    clicking sound, colorful paper la-

bels, Fisher Price, c1950 . . . .   **85.00**
Wrist Watch, color illus, white
ground, figural arms and hands,
white flocked straps, Bradley,
c1960 . . . .   **50.00**
Dumbo
Figure, 5½" h, ceramic, seated, wear-
ing yellow bonnet, Shaw **60.00**
Novelty, ¾" l, plastic, dark green, fig-
ural Dumbo, copyright symbol in
ear, c1940s **12.50**
Pinback Button, 1¼", black, white,
and red, picture of Dumbo, gaso-
line company premium, "Walt
Disney's Dumbo D–X," c1941 . . .   **30.00**
Pitcher, 8" h, ceramic, pink and blue,
white ground, Leeds China, "Walt
Disney/Dumbo/2 Qt Jug" stamped
under base, 1947 . . . .   **40.00**
Goofy
Figure, 6" h, vinyl, day glow pink,
Disney and Marx copyrights, 1971   **12.50**
Flasher Button, 2⅜" d, I'm Goofy
About Disneyland, red and white
logo on back, c1960s **16.00**
Pin, 1", brass, enameled, multicolor,
1970s **10.00**
Valentine, 3 x 5", full color, movable
arm holding net, copyright 1939   **28.00**
Mickey Mouse
Ashtray, figural, Mickey and Minnie,
4 x 4 x 5", plaster, black, silver, red,
and green, carnival giveaway,
1930s **100.00**
Ball, 2¼" d, rubber, baseball design,
black Mickey illus, red ground,
Seiberling, c1930s **110.00**
Balloon, 5 x 3½", dark green rubber,
head and ear shape, face on one
side, figure on other, Oak Brand,
1930s **75.00**
Bank, 6" h, ceramic, white glaze,
painted, 1940s **45.00**
Belt Buckle, man's, Sun Rubber Co,
1937 . . . .   **45.00**
Book
*Mickey Mouse Flies the Christmas
Mail*, Mickey Mouse Club Book,
first edition, published by Simon
& Schuster, 1956 . . . .   **18.00**
Mickey Never Fails, 6 x 8½", hard-
cover, school reader, DC Heath,
Boston, 104 pgs, copyright 1939   **30.00**
Bottle Warmer **24.00**
Car, Mickey Mouse Fire Dept, 2½ x
6½ x 4", dark red, white wheels,
Mickey driving, Donald on back,
Sun Rubber Co, 1940s **50.00**
Card
Bubble Gum, #23, #24, #26, and
#29, lot of 4 . . . .   **30.00**
Recipe, 3¼ x 5", paper, multicolor,

**Big Little Book, *Mickey Mouse The Mail
Pilot*, Whitman, 1933, 320 pgs, $35.00.**

from Recipe Scrapbook, recipes
and Weber Baking co adv on
back, lot of 4 . . . .   **35.00**
Yarn Sewing, 4 x 6", stiff cardboard,
"Big Chief Mickey Mouse and
"Mickey Mouse Has a Party," is-
sued by Marks Brothers, Boston   **30.00**
Charm
Brass, Mickey Mouse Club, ¾", red,
white, and black, copyright on
reverse, c1960 . . . .   **12.00**
Celluloid, Mickey with guitar,
black and red, white ground,
Japan, 1930s **25.00**
Christmas Tree Lights, Noma, Walt
Disney Enterprises, MIB **295.00**
Colorform Theatre, Mickey and
Minnie puppet forms, Walt Disney
Productions, MIB **55.00**
Coloring Book, 1931 . . . .   **75.00**
Cookie Jar, turn–about, Mickey and
Minnie **110.00**
Figure, 2½" h, composition, spring
arms and legs, bouncing, hangs
from elastic thread **60.00**
Fire Truck, Sun Rubber **75.00**
Flag Holder, 3¼" h, cast iron, figural,
holding pole, red paint, John
Wright Foundry, c1970s **20.00**
Game
Coming Home, 16" sq gameboard,
Mickey in center, various characters on corners, paper label on
back, Marks Brothers, Boston . .   **100.00**
Spin–N–Win, 10 x 10 x 1½", metal,
black, white, red, and yellow,
various character illus, Northwestern Products, St Louis,
c1950 . . . .   **40.00**
3–D Rickety Bridge, 1972 . . . . . .   **15.00**

Mickey Mouse, figure, hard rubber, black, orig tail, marked "Made in Akron, Ohio," 3½" h, $95.00.

Kaleidoscope 68.00
Lamp, electric, 7" h, 5" d, round, metal, beige, three Mickey decals around sides, Soren–Manegold, Chicago 85.00
Lunch Box, Disney World On Ice, Mickey and Minnie, Thermos 20.00
Paint Set, tin, Mickey and Donald, 1950s 40.00
Pinback Button
   7/8", black and white, orange ground, Mickey illus, "Mickey Mouse Spingle–Bell–Chicko–K," 1930s 135.00
   1¼"
      Eat Freihofer's Perfect Loaf/Member/Mickey Mouse Globetrotters," celluloid, red, white, and black, orig back paper, late 1930s 30.00
      Mickey Mouse, red, white, and black, Mickey illus, mid 1930s   110.00
Plaque, 6 x 7½", set of 4, full color, Donald, Mickey, Bambi, and Pluto, tin hanger on back, late 1940s . . .   100.00
Puppet, punch out and put together, Donald Duck bread premium, unpunched, 1950s 25.00
Radio, Mickey Mouse Sing Along . .   45.00
Record, Mickey and the Beanstalk, 78 rpm 28.00
Riding Toy, Hoppity Sun Products, Tally Industries 100.00
Ring, silvered brass, adjustable, diecut, high relief, Mickey head, silver, black ears, red accents, late 1950s 30.00
Salt and Pepper Shakers, pr, pottery, figural, 1930s 31.00
Sand Pail, 6" h, litho tin, swivel handle, Mickey leading parade, build-

ings outline background, Ohio Art, marked "Walt Disney Enterprises"   100.00
Scissors, child's, 2 x 3", silver metal, red handles, litho tin diecut of Mickey mounted on one side, marked "WD Ent" 90.00
Shoe Brush 25.00
Spoon, 5½" l, SP, Mickey and name on handle, marked "William Rogers Mfg Co," Post Toasties premium 15.00
Toy, squeeze, rubber, Dell 50.00
Valentine, 2½ x 5½", diecut, movable arms, 1939 copyright 12.50
Wall Pocket, 3 x 5 x 2", china, color illus, Mickey playing horn and Minnie walking with umbrella, inscribed "Mickey Mouse Corp By Walt E Disney/Made in Japan" . . .   185.00
Wrist Watch, rect, black, white, red, and yellow illus on silver dial, red numbers, red plastic straps, Ingersoll, late 1940s 160.00
Minnie Mouse
   Doll, cloth, pie eyes, 20" h 45.00
   Figure, 5" h, frosted glass, pale pink, standing, holding pocketbook, marked "Walt Disney Productions" on base, c1960s 30.00
   Fork, 4¾" l, "My Minnie Mouse" inscribed on handle, imp Mickey on end, marked "AHB & Co Stainless Nickel" on back 25.00
   Puppet, 10" h, felt and fabric, soft rubber head, red bow on neck, orig tag, Gund, 1950s 35.00
Miscellaneous
Disneyland
   Locket, brass, heart shape, raised castle on front, pink and blue accents, late 1950s 24.00
   Map, 1970s 12.00
   Postcard, 1970s 8.00
Fantasia, salt and pepper shakers, pr, 3¼" h, ceramic, oriental mushrooms, tan, marked "Disney copyright 1941/Vernon Kilns USA" . . .   125.00
Ferdinand the Bull, hair bows, pr, pink fabric, brass centers and clips, orig card with full color illus, printed verse and 1938 copyright, unused 40.00
Jungle Book, doll, vulture, 5" h, felt and fabric, black yarn hair, 1966 copyright tag 40.00
Mickey Mouse Club
   Hat, Mouseketeer, Mickey ears . . .   35.00
   Pin, 3" 25.00
   View–Master Reel, Mouseketeers, three reels, #865 A, B, and C, copyright 1956 . . . .   25.00
101 Dalmatians, pencil case, 5 x 10 x

2", dark blue, full color paper label, copyright 1960 .... **12.50**

Pollyanna, golden record, 78 rpm, yellow, America the Beautiful, orig jacket shows Halley Mills, copyright 1960 .... **15.00**

Three Caballeros, figure, Jose Carioca, 3" h, ceramic, full color, stamped "Walt Disney/Mexico" and "30" under base, 1940s **90.00**

Three Little Pigs
Figure, wall type, wolf and pigs, plaster, painted, high relief, wire hook on back, 1930s **125.00**
Handkerchief, 8½" sq, black and white illus, red ground, early 1930s **30.00**
Puzzle, Three Little Pigs at Work and Play, orig box, 1940s **15.00**

Walt Disney, stamp book, *Animals of Africa*, 8½ x 11", Simon & Schuster, 32 pgs, 1956 .... **20.00**

Peter Pan
Book, *Walt Disney's Peter Pan and Wendy*, Little Golden Book, first edition, 1952 .... **20.00**
Figurine, Tinkerbell **50.00**

Pinocchio
Bank, ceramic **75.00**
Figure, 10½", jointed composition head, wood body, arms, and legs, brown felt hat, painted, Ideal **100.00**
Game, Walt Disney's Pinocchio— The Merry Puppet Game, Milton Bradley, orig box, complete, 1939 **40.00**
Glass, J Worthington Foulfellow, 4¾" h, clear, brown illus, four line verse on back **30.00**
Golden Record, 78 rpm, orange, orig jacket, copyright 1972 .... **10.00**
Hand Puppet, 9" h, composition head, red fabric body, white hands, marked "W Disney Ent" on back **100.00**
Marionette, 14", composition and wood, white felt collar, red bow tie, yellow shirt, purple vest and pants, plastic eyes, rubber nose grows from ½" to over 1", strings, cardboard, hand control, 1950s **200.00**
Paint Book, 11 x 15", Whitman, 48 pgs, c1939 .... **40.00**
Pinback Button, 1¼", blue, white ground, Walt Disney's Pinocchio/ Hi Diddle Dee Dee!," English, 1960s **20.00**
Toy, wind–up, Figaro the Cat, 2½" h, litho tin, black and white, color details, red, and yellow name on back, rubber ears, Marx **135.00**
Transfer, 5 x 6" clear cellophane bag, colorful diecut folder, set of characters, Tower Press, England, 1950s **35.00**

Valentine, Jiminy Cricket, 3 x 5", diecut, movable arms, copyright 1939 .... **25.00**

Pluto
Badge, 2½ x 3", molded plastic, multicolor illus, man beside circus tent, flasher picture of Pluto balancing on ball, mid 1960s **15.00**
Figure, 3 x 3 x 6½", glazed china, tan body, light blue collar, 1970s **20.00**
Toy, friction, 2 x 4½ x 2½" h, plastic, figural, yellow body, black and red details, Marx, early 1950s **40.00**

Robin Hood, toy, wind–up, Friar Tuck, 4" h, figure, soft rubber, turns in circle, c1973 .... **24.00**

Scrooge McDuck, key holder, wall mount, brass, sgd **8.00**

Snow White and the Seven Dwarfs
Charm, Grumpy, plastic, light green, copyright symbol, 1940s **10.00**
Cup, 2" d, 2½" h, SP, raised illus, engraved initials "FMU," hallmarks under base, c1939 .... **65.00**
Doll, 12", Dopey, cloth body, Gund **45.00**
Figurine Set, 6½" h Snow White, 4½" h dwarfs, bisque, dwarfs hold musical instruments, Japan **700.00**
Lamp, Dopey, figural **65.00**
Pin, Happy, wood, painted, 1940s .. **15.00**
Plaque, 5 x 5", ceramic, pastel green, tan, and blue background, gold trim, high relief figure of Happy, bird in upper right corner, imp "Ceramica/Cuernavaca/Mexico" on back, 1950s **65.00**
Puppet, Dopey, Gund **22.00**
Puzzle, 14 x 22", full color, Snow White, dwarfs, and forest animals, cottage background, Jaymar, orig box, 1940s **30.00**
Safety Blocks, set of 16, wood, alphabet letters and animals on four sides, raised character images and name on two sides, orig box, marked "by Special Permission of Walt Disney Enterprises," c1939 **75.00**
Salt and Pepper Shakers, pr, Doc, 2½" h, ceramic, figural, multicolor, marked "Foreign" on bottom, c1939 .... **25.00**
Soap, figural, Doc, 3½" h, tan, red accents, Kirk, c1939 .... **25.00**
Valentine, Grumpy, movable, 1930s **10.00**

Zorro
Comic Book, *Walt Disney Presents Zorro*, #7, Sept 1967 .... **10.00**
Costume, cape, belt, mask, orig box **69.00**
Dry Cleaning Bag, cut out costume, 23 x 36", white paper, black, white, red, and orange illus, dry cleaner adv and "Walt Disney Studios

Presents Zorro on ABC–TV" printed
  on bag, c1960 . . . .   **32.00**
Little Golden Book, 1958 . . . .   **15.00**
Magic slate and game **65.00**
Model, assembled, orig box, Aurora,
  1966 . . . .   **125.00**
Ring, plastic, silver finish, Zorro logo
  on black stone, 1960s **18.00**
Tie Slide, 1¼", silvered brass, black,
  white, and red plastic insert, c1960   **30.00**
TV Guide, Zorro on cov, 1958 . . . . .   **25.00**
Wrist Watch **65.00**

DOG COLLECTIBLES

Collecting Hints: A collection of dog related
items may be based on one particular breed.
Another way to collect dog items is by items picturing a dog or even dog–shaped objects. With
millions of dog owners in the United States, dog
collectibles are very popular.

History: Dogs, long recognized as "Man's Best
Friend," have been a part of human life since the
early cavemen. The first dogs probably were
used for hunting and protection against the
wilder animals. After man learned that dogs
could be trained to provide useful services, many
types of dogs were bred and trained for specific
purposes. Over 100 breeds of dogs have evolved
from the first dog which roamed the earth over
15 million years ago. Today, dogs are still
hunters, protectors, herders, and are trained to
see and hear for people.

Man has continued to domesticate the dog, developing today's popular breeds. The American
Kennel Club has divided the breeds into seven
classifications: herding, hounds, sporting,
non–sporting, terriers, toy breeds, and working
dogs.

In 1859 in Newcastle, England, the first modern dog show was held. People enjoyed this
show and many others were started. The breed-
ing of prize dogs became important. The blood-
lines of important dogs were established and
recorded. Today, the dogs with the largest pedi-
grees command the highest prices.

As the dog's popularity grew, so did the fre-
quency of its appearance on objects. They became popular in literature, in paintings and other
art forms.

References: Norman E. Martinus and Harry L.
Rinker, *Warman's Paper,* Wallace–Homestead,
1994; Alice L. Muncaster and Ellen Sawyer, *The
Dog Made Me Buy It!,* Crown Publishers, 1990;
William Secord, *Dog Painting: 1840–1940: A
Social History of the Dog in Art,* Antique
Collectors' Club, 1992.

Collectors' Clubs: Canine Collectibles Club of
America, Suite 314, 736 N. Western Ave., Lake
Forest, IL 60045; Wee Scots, Inc., PO Box 1512,
Columbus, IN 47202.

Museum: The Dog Museum of America, Jarville
House, St. Louis, MO.

Advisor: Jocelyn C. Mousley.

Advertising Sign, Old Vitality Dog Food,
  10 x 14" **85.00**
Ashtray
  Hunting Dog, round, Stangl **40.00**
  Pointer, brass, marked "United Brass,
    Brooklyn, NY" **50.00**
  Scottie, figural **10.00**
Bank
  Bulldog, Mack Trucks, vinyl, brown,
    figural, 1950–60, 7" h **75.00**
  Nipper, ceramic **25.00**
Bookends, pr
  Borzoi
    Brass **125.00**
    Rosemeade **50.00**
  German Shepherds, standing **60.00**
  Scotties, metal, c1929 . . . .   **85.00**
Bottle Opener, Setter, figural **75.00**
Brush Holder, Scottie **10.00**
Button, Scottie, Bakelite **12.00**

**Cane Handle, carved ivory, threaded
metal screw, 3¹⁄₁₆" l, $85.00.**

Cocktail Shaker, crystal, four black and
  white dogs **35.00**
Dish, portrait of poodle, marked "Bon
  Appetit" and "Limoges" **30.00**
Doorstop, Scottie, cast iron **175.00**
Dresser Box, blue, Akro Agate **175.00**
Egg Timer, figural, Germany **60.00**
Figure
  Airdale, wood, carved, two pups on
    chain **35.00**
  Beagle, 1984, Boehm **225.00**

Children's Book, *Animal Pictures,* Saalfield Publishing, color linenette cover, 1947, 7 x 9", $10.00.

Boxer
  Mortens Studio, reclining 55.00
  Royal Dux, brown 125.00
Bulldog
  Bisque, 5½" h 50.00
  Pottery, standing figure, Italian . . . 225.00
  Wood, carved
    Anri 12.00
    Unknown maker 22.00
Cocker Spaniel
  Group of three, Royal Worchester 150.00
  Mortens Studios, charcoal, 4½" l 50.00
  With pheasant, HN1028, Royal
    Doulton 150.00
Collie
  Hutschenreuther, standing, 4" h . . 145.00
  Mortens Studios, sitting 35.00
Dachshund, sitting up, begging,
  Rosenthal 475.00
Dalmatian, Penny, large, Enesco . . . 50.00

Dish, girl petting dog, transfer, white ground, gold trim, Buffalo Pottery, 6" d, $35.00.

Dog, recumbent, bronze, 5" l 150.00
English Setter
  Mortens Studio, 6½ x 10" 65.00
  Royal Doulton, HN1049, large . . . 375.00
Foxhound, K7, Royal Doulton 65.00
Fox Terrier, #1118, Dahl Jensen 95.00
German Shepherd, large, on base,
  Royal Dux 95.00
Great Dane, seated, minor damage,
  Morten Studios 65.00
Hunter with Dogs, Chicago World's
  Fair, 1933 . . . . 35.00
Labrador Retreiver
  Christmas decorated, Lenox, c1922 80.00
  Playful puppy, large, Goebel 65.00
Poodle
  Boehm, reclining, white, bisque . . 265.00
  Lladro, #1259 . . . . 300.00
  Staffordshire, gray, 6½" h 150.00
Scottie, wood, carved 28.00
Sealyham, HN1032, Royal Doulton 180.00
Setter, standing with duck in mouth,
  Royal Dux 475.00
Spaniel, #1145, Dahl Jensen 150.00
Wire Hair Terrier
  Mortens Studio, puppy, yawning . . 45.00
  Royal Doulton, HN1014 . . . . 110.00
Foot Scraper, Dachshund, cast iron,
  21⅞" l 240.00
Hood Ornament, Bulldog, Mack Trucks 25.00
Jewelry, pin, two Scotties, round 10.00
Lamp, rose color, Van Briggle 225.00
Napkin Ring, figural dog chained to
  doghouse, ftd base 250.00
Needlepoint, framed, St Bernard 60.00
Needle Tin, RCA Victor, Nipper, orig
  needles 35.00
Nodder
  Beagle, puppies 20.00
  Boston Terrier 12.00
  Red dog on back, bisque 50.00
Nut Cracker, Newfoundland, standing,
  black iron 85.00
Photo Album, dogs on celluloid cover 175.00
Pin Tray, Borzoi, bronze, 4½ x 6" 195.00
Pipe Holder
  Dog, figural, Syroco, 5¼" l 12.00
  Pointer 60.00
Pitcher
  Majolica, head and tail, white dog in
    stylized oak bucket, maroon inte-
    rior 350.00
  Wedgwood, hound, light green, 7" h 125.00
Planter
  Bird Dog, McCoy 40.00
  Poodle, Hull 95.00
  Scottie, Japan, 4 x 4" 18.00
Plaque
  Dog, #2608, c1930, Royal Copen-
    hagen 400.00
  Fox Terrier, Royal Copenhagen 45.00
  Pointer, full body, Mortens Studios . . 185.00

Plate, Scottie, D5386, Royal Doulton	**175.00**
Ring Holder, Bulldog, Cleminsons	**25.00**
Rug	
Hooked, German Shepherd, 42 x 28"	**195.00**
Wool, lap, St Bernard	**195.00**
Salt and Pepper Shakers, pr	
Blood Hound, heads, Rosemeade . .	**35.00**
Borzoi, gold trim	**15.00**
Dog on arm chair	**18.00**
Greyhounds, heads, Rosemeade . . .	**45.00**
Spaniels, adult, Ceramic Arts Studio	**20.00**
Stuffed Toy	
Dachshund, Steiff, c1950	**50.00**
Poodle, mohair, glass eyes and nose, movable legs	**20.00**
Tape Measure, Scottie, cloth body, concealed tape measure	**30.00**
Tie Rack, wood, carved, seated Scottie, glass eyes	**22.00**
Tray, Borzoi, tin, bronze	**195.00**
Ventriloquist Dummy, dog, sitting, mouth opens, head turns, c1890 . . .	**495.00**
Waste Basket, French Poodle, metal . .	**70.00**
Whistle, Hush Puppy Shoes, figural Basset Hound, molded plastic, stamped "Hush Puppy"	**5.00**

DOLL HOUSE FURNISHINGS

Collecting Hints: Doll house furnishings are children's toys. Some wear may be expected. It is possible to find entire room sets in original boxes. These sets will command higher prices.

History: Doll house furnishings are the tiny articles of furniture and accessories used to outfit a doll house. They may be made of many types of materials, from fine handmade wooden pieces to molded plastic. Furnishings were played with by children to decorate and redecorate their favorite doll house. Several toy manufacturers, such as Tootsietoy, Petite Princess, and Renwal, made doll house furnishings.

Doll houses and doll house furnishings have undergone a current craze and are highly collectible. Many artists and craftsmen devote hours to making scale furniture and accessories. This type of artist–oriented doll house furnishing is not included in this listing. It does, however, affect the market by offering the buyer a choice of an old piece versus a present–day handmade piece.

References: Flora Gill Jacobs, *Doll's Houses in America: Historic Preservation in Miniature,* Charles Scribner's Sons; Constance Eileen King, *Dolls and Doll's Houses,* Hamlyn; Margaret Towner, *Dollhouse Furniture: The Collector's Guide To Selecting and Enjoying Miniature Masterpieces,* Courage Books, Running Press,

1993; Dian Zillner, *American Dollhouses and Furniture From The 20th Century,* Schiffer Publishing, 1995.

Periodicals: *Doll Castle News,* PO Box 247, Washington, NJ 07882; *Miniature Collector,* PO Box 631, Boiling Springs, PA 17007; *Nutshell News* 21027 Crossroads Circle, PO Box 986, Waukesha, WI 53187.

Collectors' Clubs: Dollhouse & Miniature Collectors, 9451 Lee Hwy. #515, Fairfax, VA 22302; International Guild Miniature Artisans, PO Box 71, Bridgeport, NY 13030; National Assoc. of Miniature Enthusiasts, PO Box 69, Carmel, IN 46032.

Museums: Margaret Woodbury Strong Museum, Rochester, NY; Mildred Mahoney Jubilee Doll House Museum, Fort Erie, Ontario, Canada; Toy and Miniature Museum of Kansas City, Kansas City, MO; Toy Museum of Atlanta, Atlanta, GA; Washington Dolls' House and Toy Museum, Washington, DC.

Bathinette, pink, Renwal	**22.00**
Bath Tub, metal, Tootsie Toy	**12.00**
Bathroom Scale, Renwal	**3.00**
Bathroom Set, 3 pcs, bathtub, toilet, and sink, white, Plasco	**12.00**
Bed	
Petite Princess, plastic	**10.00**
Strombecker, wood, twin size	**5.00**
Superior, plastic, red, double	**3.00**
Tootsie Toy, twin, 1¼ x 3¼"	**8.00**
Bedroom Set	
3 pcs, 1" scale, Victorian, walnut, 5" highback bed, triple dresser, mirror, and washstand	**120.00**
4 pcs	
Plastic, bed, vanity, wardrobe, and mirror, c1930	**45.00**
Wooden, 1" scale, 6½" l bed, chest of drawers, nightstand, and lamp table	**100.00**
Card Table, gold, Renwal	**12.00**
Chair	
Arm, metal, Tootsie Toy	**15.00**
Hitchcock, reed seat	**25.00**
Ladderback	**25.00**
Occasional, Petite Princess, aqua velveteen	**8.00**
Straight	
German, wood, fabric seat, carved floral back	**10.00**
Plasco, ivory	**4.00**
Renwal, brown	**5.00**
Wing	
Needlepoint, flame stitch	**18.00**
Petite Princess, red brocade	**15.00**
Strombecker	**5.00**
Chest of Drawers	
Petite Princess	**15.00**

Renwal **6.00**
Strombecker, wood, painted white . .   **10.00**
China Cabinet, curved front, Isinglass
door, 4″ h **25.00**
Corner Cupboard, 8″ h, maple, Tynee
Toy **25.00**
Cradle
Plasco, pink **5.00**
Wood, blue, floral dec **10.00**
Desk, stenciled top, bentwood chair . .   **95.00**
Dining Room Set
4 pcs, mahogany, 3½ x 5″ table, 6″ h
hutch, sewing cabinet, and braided
rug, German **55.00**
5 pcs, plastic, table, four chairs,
c1945, MIB **8.00**
7 pcs, cardboard, handmade, table,
three chairs, corner cupboard, and
buffet **125.00**
8 pcs, Tootsie Toy, metal, 2½″ h
pedestal table, four matching fid-
dleback chairs, maroon radio, and
two floor lamps **60.00**
Dollhouse Doll
Baby
2″ h, bisque, blonde human hair,
orig organdy dress, matching
quilt, Angel Baby #58, Eunice
Tuttle **170.00**
3″ h, bisque, bent limbs, painted
features, made in Occupied
Japan **15.00**
Child, 3″ h, German, one pc, molded,
curly hair, painted facial features .   **50.00**
Father, brown, Renwal **25.00**
Flapper, 3″ h, bisque, molded hair,
orig costume, Germany, c1920 . .   **65.00**
Lady, 6″ h, bisque, solid domed
shoulderhead, blue eyes, orig
muslin body, mohair wig **175.00**
Mother, red, Renwal **25.00**
Young Girl, 6″ h, bisque, swivel head,
marked "Karen #9, Eunice P.
Tuttle," c1960 . . . .   **150.00**
Dust Mop, Renwal **17.00**
Fainting Couch, Petite Princess, green
brocade **18.00**
Fireplace, brown, Renwal **35.00**
High Chair, cast iron **25.00**
Hutch
Petite Princess **45.00**
Renwal, brown **5.00**
Ice Box, metal, glass block of ice **125.00**
Kitchen Set, 7 pcs, 1″ scale, chestnut
wood, colonial style, cupboard,
table, four chairs **50.00**
Kitchen Stove, 4″ h, silver plated gas,
two burners, gilded daisy on oven
door, signed "505 Champion" **30.00**
Lamp
Floor, Renwal **4.00**
Table, Petite Princess **4.00**

Little Homemaker Plastic Kitchen Furniture, 8 pieces, interior of box is kitchen
scene, Plastic Art Toy Corporation, Rutherford, NJ, $40.00.

Living Room Set, 5 pcs, Sheraton style,
5″ l striped sofa, wing chair, drop leaf
table, and stool **50.00**
Mirror, cheval, 4½″ h, oval, walnut
frame, pedestal base **40.00**
Phonograph, red, Renwal **20.00**
Piano, bench, and metronome, MIB,
Petite Princess **25.00**
Playpen, pink, blue accents, Renwal . .   **12.00**
Potty Chair, blue, Renwal **6.00**
Radio, floor model, Renwal **6.00**
Refrigerator, Superior, plastic, ivory . . .   **2.00**
Rocking Chair, decal, Renwal **22.00**
Rug
Braided, oval, shades of rose, red,
white **20.00**
Polar Bear, 10½ x 6½″, white fur,
open mouth, tiny teeth, royal pur-
ple velvet lining **25.00**
Tobacco Rug, cotton, Oriental rug
style, fringed **2.50**
Sewing Machine, blue, Renwal **30.00**
Sofa
Metal, Tootsie Toy **12.00**
Plastic, Superior, red, 3 molded cush-
ions **8.00**
Stove, white, red accents, Renwal **15.00**
Study Set, 7 pcs, wooden, grandfather
clock, console table, candlestand,
two lyre back side chairs, and two
brass candlesticks, Exacto **25.00**
Table
Cast iron, 3¾ x 6½″ top, 3″ h, red,
Arcade **10.00**

Maple, 4" d, pedestal base, removable marble top	**25.00**
Tea Cart, Tootsie Toy, metal	**15.00**
Telephone, yellow, red accents, Renwal	**25.00**
Tricycle, yellow, Renwal	**10.00**
Vacuum Cleaner, Renwal	**8.00**
Washstand, metal, Tootsie Toy	**8.00**
Woodburning Stove	**10.00**
Wringer Washer, Renwal	**12.00**

DOLLS

Collecting Hints: The most important criteria in buying dolls are sentiment and condition. The value of a particular doll increases if it is a childhood favorite or family heirloom.

When pricing a doll, condition is the most important aspect. Excellent condition means that the doll has all original parts.

The wig should not be soiled or restyled. The surface of the skin must be free of marks and blemishes. Original sleep eyes must be free–moving. All mechanical parts should be operational. Original clothing means original dress, underclothes, shoes, and socks in excellent and clean condition, preferably with original tags and labels.

A doll that is mint in the original box is listed as "MIB." Many modern collectible doll prices depend on the original box. Mattel's original Barbie doll, for example, is valued over $1,000 MIB. However, without the original box, the doll is worth much less. Another pricing consideration is appeal. Only a collector knows how important and valuable a particular doll is to her collection.

Modern and 20th century dolls are highly collectible. They offer many appealing features to collectors, one of which is price. A collector of modern dolls need not spend thousands of dollars. This type of doll collecting fits into the average person's budget.

Another feature is the sizes of dolls, which enables collectors to artfully display them. Many dolls are made of materials easily cleaned and maintained. An attractive appeal of modern dolls is that they are easily available at flea markets, garage sales, swap meets, etc.

History: The history of modern doll manufacturers is long and varied. While competitors, these companies used similar procedures, molds, and ideas. When Effanbee was successful with the Patsy dolls, Horsman soon followed with a Patsy look–alike named Dorothy. Vogue's Ginny doll was imitated by Cosmopolitan's Ginger. Some manufacturers reused molds and changed sizes and names to produce dolls which were similar for many years.

Dolls have always been popular with Americans. The early Patsy dolls with their own wardrobes were a success in the 1930s and 1940s. During the 1950s Vogue's Ginny Doll was very successful in generating the sales of dolls, clothes, and accessories. The next decade of children enjoyed Mattel's Barbie. Collectors will determine what the collectible dolls of the 1970s and 1980s will be. Doll collecting has become a major hobby.

References: John Axe, *The Encyclopedia of Celebrity Dolls,* Hobbie House Press, 1983; Joseph Bourgeois, *Collector's Guide To Dolls In Uniform,* Collector Books, 1995; Debra Clark, *Troll: Identification & Price Guide,* Hobby House Press, 1993; Julie Collier, *Official Identification and Price Guide to Antique and Modern Dolls, Fourth Edition,* House of Collectibles, 1989; Jan Foulke, *11th Blue Book Dolls & Values,* Hobby House Press, 1993; Dee Hackenberry, *Enchanting Friends: Collectible Poohs, Raggedies, Golliwoggs & Roosevelt Bears,* Schiffer Publishing, 1995; Patricia Hall, *Johnny Gruelle: Creator of Raggedy Ann and Andy,* Pelican Publishing, 1993; R. Lane Herron, *Herron's Price Guide to Dolls,* Wallace–Homestead, 1989; Judith Izen, *Collector's Guide To Ideal Dolls: Identification & Value Guide,* Collector Books, 1994; Polly Judd, *Cloth Dolls of the 1920s and 1930s,* Hobby House Press, 1990; Polly and Pam Judd, *Composition Dolls: 1909–1928, Volume II,* Hobby House Press, 1994; Polly and Pam Judd, *Composition Dolls: 1928–1955,* Hobby House Press, 1991; Polly and Pam Judd, *European Costumed Dolls,* Hobby House Press, 1994; Polly and Pam Judd, *Glamour Dolls of the 1950s & 1960s Identification and Values, Revised Edition,* Hobby House Press, 1993; Polly and Pam Judd, *Hard Plastic Dolls I, Third Revised Edition,* Hobby House Press, 1993; Polly and Pam Judd, *Hard Plastic Dolls II, Revised,* Hobby House Press, 1994; Kathy and Don Lewis, *Chatty Cathy Dolls: An Identification and Value Guide,* Collector Books, 1994; A. Glenn Mandeville, *Alexander Dolls Collector's Price Guide, 2nd Edition,* Hobby House Press, 1995; A. Glenn Mandeville, *Contemporary Doll Stars: Forty Years of the Best,* Hobby House Press, 1992; A. Glenn Mandeville, *Doll Fashion Anthology & Price Guide, 4th Revised Edition,* Hobby House Press, 1993; A. Glenn Mandeville, *Ginny: An American Toddler Doll, 2nd Revised Edition,* Hobby House Press, 1994; A. Glenn Mandeville, *Madame Alexander Dolls Value Guide,* Hobby House Press, 1994; Jeanne Du Chateau Niswonger, *That Doll, Ginny,* Cody Publications, 1978; Edward R. Pardella, *Shirley Temple Dolls and Fashion: A Collector's Guide To The World's Darling,* Schiffer Publishing, 1992; Myla Perkins, *Black Dolls: 1820–1991,* Collector Books, 1993, 1995 value update; Myla Perkins, *Black Dolls, Book II, An Identification and Value Guide,* Collector Books, 1995; Pat Peterson, *Collector's Guide To Trolls,*

Collector Books, 1995; Joleen Ashman Robison and Kay Sellers, *Advertising Dolls: Identification & Value Guide*, Collector Books, 1980, 1994 value update; Patricia N. Schoonmaker, *Patsy Doll Family, Vol. I*, Hobby House Press, 1992; Patricia R. Smith, *Collector's Encyclopedia of Madame Alexander Dolls, 1965–1990*, Collector Books, 1991, 1994 value update; Patricia R. Smith, *Madame Alexander Collector's Dolls*, Collector Books, 1978, 1995 value update; Patricia R. Smith, *Madame Alexander Collector's Doll Price Guide #20*, Collector Books, 1995; Patricia R. Smith, *Modern Collector's Dolls, Series 1, 2, 3, 4, 5, 6, 7* Collector Books, 1973, 1975, 1976, 1979, 1984, 1994, 1995: 1995 value update Vols. 1–6; Patricia R. Smith, *Patricia Smith's Doll Values: Antique to Modern, Eleventh Edition*, Collector Books, 1995; Florence Theriault, *More Dolls: The Early Years, 1780–1910*, Gold Horse Publishing, 1992.

Periodicals: *Celebrity Doll Journal*, 5 Court Place, Puyallup, WA 98372; *Costume Quarterly for Doll Collectors*, 118–01 Sutter Ave., Jamaica, NY 11420; *Doll Collector's Price Guide*, 306 E. Parr Rd., Berne IN 46711; *Doll Life*, 243 Newton–Sparta Rd., Newton, NJ 07860; *Doll Reader*, 6405 Flank Dr., Harrisburg, PA 17112; *Doll Times*, 218 West Woodin Blvd, Dallas, TX 75224; *Dolls—The Collector's Magazine*, 170 Fifth Ave., 12th Floor, New York, NY 10010; *Doll World*, 306 E. Parr Rd, Berne, IN 46711; *Rags*, PO Box 823, Atlanta, GA 30301; *The Cloth Doll Magazine*, PO Box 1089, Mt. Shasta, CA 96067.

Collectors' Clubs: Cabbage Patch Kids Collectors Club, PO Box 714, Cleveland, GA 30528; Chatty Cathy Collectors Club, 2610 Dover St., Piscataway, NJ 08854; Ginny Doll Club, 9628 Hidden Oaks Cir., Tampa, FL 33612; Ideal Doll Collector's Club, PO Box 623, Lexington, MA 02173; Madame Alexander Fan Club, PO Box 330, Mundeline, IL 60060; United Federation of Doll Clubs, 8B East St., PO Box 14146, Parkville, MO 64152.

Museums: Margaret Woodbury Strong Museum, Rochester, NY; Museum of Collectible Dolls, Lakeland, FL; The Doll Museum, Newport, RI; Yesteryears Museum, Sandwich, MA.

Videotapes: *Scarlett Dolls: An Alexander Tradition, 1937–1991*, Sirocco Productions, 1991; *The Coronation Story*, Sirocco Productions, 1993; *The Extraordinary World of Doll Collecting*, Cinebar Productions, 1994.

Note: All prices listed here are for dolls in excellent condition and original clothes, unless otherwise noted.

AMERICAN ARTISTS

Americans have been making dolls for children for centuries. During the past several decades, several artists began making dolls on a limited edition basis, emphasizing exquisite detailing and uniqueness. Today's doll artists offer a varied range of collectible dolls.

The listing below is a sampling of artists' dolls which have been sold during the past year. Many artists currently producing dolls are not included because their works have not yet begun to appear in the secondary market. Speculation runs high in this area of doll collecting.

Blakely, Halle, 18" h, Court Lady, 1953, bisque shoulderplate, cloth body . . **1,500.00**
Bruns, Nancy, 21" h, Rebecca, 1986, wood head, cloth body, curly wig . . **300.00**
Clear, Emma
   25" h , Young Victoria, 1945, china head, cloth body, long dress, orig corset, marked "C 45 L" **350.00**
   30" h, George and Martha Washington, 1947, orig clothes, price for pair **1,600.00**
Fisher, Ruth E, 10" h, Granddaughter, 1939, bisque, Oriental features, marked "REF" **150.00**
Motter, Jennifer Berry, 18" h, Mable, 1987, cloth, painted details, sgd on torso "Jennifer Berry Motter" and date **250.00**
Sorensen, Lewis, 26" h, Mother Goose, 1972, wax head and hands, blue glass eyes, label under skirt **1,800.00**
Wick, Faith, 12" h, Little Apple, 1979, bisque head, arms, and feet, cloth body, orig rabbit suit **200.00**
Zeller, Fawn, 15" h, Miami Miss, 1961, bisque head, arms, and legs, cloth body, marked "Fawn Zeller UFDC 1961" **210.00**

AMERICAN CHARACTER DOLL COMPANY

The American Character Doll Company was founded in 1918 and made high quality dolls. When the company was liquidated in 1968, many molds were purchased by the Ideal Toy Co. American Character Dolls are marked with the full company name, "Amer. Char." or "Amer. Char" in a circle. Early composition dolls were marked "Petite."

9½" h, Cricket, plastic, vinyl body, orig dress, marked "American Character" **35.00**
10½" h, Tiny Toodles, vinyl, molded, painted hair, 1958 . . . . **25.00**
12" h, Campbell Kid, composition, orig clothing, marked "A/Petite/Doll" . . . **700.00**
15" h
   Baby Tiny Tears, hard plastic head, rubber body, molded hair, orig clothes, marked "Pat. No. 2675644/

Amer. Character," 1950 . . . . **90.00**
Infant Toodles, heavy vinyl, car bed
and orig comic book, c1959 . . . . **225.00**
16" h, Sally, composition swivel head
and limbs, cloth body, orig plaid
dress, 1935 . . . . **100.00**
17" h, Margaret–Rose, vinyl head, arms,
and legs, plastic body, rooted blonde
hair **48.00**
18" h, Little Love, composition head
and limbs, cloth body, brown human
hair wig, 1942 . . . . **60.00**
20" h, Bottletot, cloth body, composi-
tion arms, holds bottle, marked
"Petite/America's Wonder Baby Doll" **325.00**
21" h

Graduate, one piece vinyl body, orig
cap and gown, 1960 . . . . **50.00**
Sally, composition head, arms, and
legs, cloth body, redressed, marked
"Horseshoe Sally" **375.00**

ARRANBEE

This company was founded in 1922. Arranbee's
finest dolls were made in hard plastic. Two of
Arranbee's most popular dolls were Nancy and,
later, Nanette. The company was sold to Vogue
Dolls, Inc., in 1959. Marks used by this company
include "Arranbee," "R7B," and "Made In USA."

7" h, Character Baby, composition,
molded hair **75.00**
9" h, My Dream Baby, bisque neck,
cloth body, rubber hands, wearing
baby dress, marked "AM German
351 4/" **275.00**
10" h
Miss Cody, vinyl head, hard plastic
body, rooted brown hair, walker,
1950 . . . . **30.00**
Oriental Baby, composition, multi-
colored taffeta outfit, braid trim . . **48.00**
11" h, Littlest Angel, vinyl head, hard
plastic body, jointed shoulders, hips
and knees, rooted dark brown hair,
marked "R & B, 1959" **36.00**
14" h
Bessie, black, composition, wearing
wool coat and matching hat, socks,
and shoes **115.00**
Nanette, vinyl, orig skating dress,
MIB, 1953 . . . . **40.00**
17" h, Baby Donna, hard plastic head,
cloth body, latex arms and legs,
molded hair, 1949 . . . . **45.00**
19" h, Rosie, composition swivel head
on shoulderplate, cloth body, molded
hair, 1935 . . . . **80.00**
21" h
Nancy, composition, blue glass eyes,
dress and orig cutout shoes **375.00**

So Big, composition head and limbs,
cloth body, 1936 . . . . **55.00**

CAMEO DOLL PRODUCTS COMPANY

The Cameo Doll Products Company was
founded in 1922. The original owner was Joseph
L. Kallus. The most well–known doll made by
this company was the Kewpie designed by Rose
O'Neill. The company was sold in 1970 to
Strombecker. However, Mr. Kallus retained some
company molds and is reissuing dolls like Miss
Peeps under the name of Cameo Exclusive
Products.

10" h, Margie, composition head, wood
body, molded hair, painted eyes, orig
dress and box, c1930 . . . . **275.00**
12" h, Scootles, composition head and
five piece chubby body, bold molded
and painted hair, pink flowered dress
and bonnet, c1930 . . . . **275.00**
17" h, Little Annie Rooney, composition
head and jointed body, pale blonde
hair, large painted brown eyes, water-
melon smile, 1926 . . . . **250.00**
19" h, Miss Peeps, vinyl, brown skin, inset eyes, marked "Cameo" on head,
"Cameo Doll Products/Strombecker
Corp" on tag, 1973 . . . . **32.00**

CLOTH, PRINTED

Cloth dolls were manufactured by several
companies and became quite popular after the
invention of the sewing machine. Dolls and animals were frequently sold by the yard. Uncut
early examples can still be found.

Advertising, stuffed
Cream of Wheat **75.00**
Kellogg's
Crackle, 1940s **40.00**
Mama Bear **75.00**
Foxy Grandpa, stuffed **130.00**
Hen and Chickens, uncut **65.00**
Indian Girl, stuffed, 1920s **40.00**
Papoose, 8" h, stuffed **25.00**

COSMOPOLITAN DOLL COMPANY

Little recorded history is available about this
company. Dolls dating from the late 1940s
through the 1960s are found with the mark of
CDC. It is believed that the company made many
unmarked dolls. One of their most popular dolls
was Ginger, made in 1955–1956, which was a
takeoff of Vogue Doll's Ginny. Many of these
Ginger dolls are found with original clothes
made by the Terri Lee Doll Company.

7½" h, Ginger, plastic body, arms, and legs, vinyl head, rooted medium blonde hair, closed mouth, 1956 . . . **35.00**

14" h, Merri, plastic, rooted blonde hair red gown, white fur trim, 1960 . . . . **20.00**

25" h, Emily, hard plastic head, cloth body, composition arms and legs, blonde wig, 1949 . . . . **60.00**

EEGEE DOLL MFG COMPANY

The owner and founder of this company was E. G. Goldberger. He began his company in 1917, marking his dolls "E. G." Other marks used by the company include E. Goldberger and Eegee.

10½" h, Schoolgirl, stuffed vinyl head, hard plastic body, jointed knees, walker, orig jumper and blouse, 1957 **18.00**

11" h, Tina, vinyl head, hard plastic body, rooted blonde hair, closed mouth, jointed knees, walker, marked "S" on head, 1959 . . . . **12.00**

14" h

Playpen Baby, vinyl head, plastic body, rooted blonde hair, nurser, marked "13/14AA/Eegee Co," 1968 **12.00**

Sleepy, vinyl head and limbs, plastic body, molded and painted hair, asleep, marked "Eegee/1967" **25.00**

15" h, Gemette, vinyl head and arms, plastic body, rooted brown hair, molded adult hands, closed mouth, marked "Eegee 1963/11" on back . . **15.00**

16" h

Newborn Baby Doll, vinyl head and limbs, cloth body, marked "Eegee Co/173," 1963 . . . . **20.00**

Rose Red Flowerkin, plastic and vinyl, marked "8/F2/Eegee" on head, "Goldberger Doll/Mfg Co, Inc/Pat Pend" on back, 1963 . . . . **25.00**

17" h, Buster, vinyl head and arms, plastic body and legs, molded hair, marked "1959/Eegee" **22.00**

EFFANBEE DOLL CORPORATION

The Effanbee Doll Corporation was founded in 1912 by Bernard E. Fleischaker and Hugo Baum. Its most successful line was the Patsy Doll and its many variations. Patsy was such a success that a whole wardrobe was designed and it also sold well. This was the first marketing of a doll and her wardrobe.

Effanbee experimented with materials as well as molds. Rubber was first used in 1930; the use of hard plastic began in 1949. Today vinyl has replaced composition. Effanbee is still making dolls and last year's catalog contained over 170 specimens.

7½" h, Baby Tinyette, composition, solid domed head, five piece body, molded, painted brown baby hair, orig checkered playsuit and bonnet, marked "Effanbee" on head, "Effanbee Baby Tinyette" on torso **132.00**

9" h, Patsyette, composition, five piece body, molded and painted brown bobbed hair, bangs, painted features, closed mouth, orig pink organdy dotted Swiss dress, marked "Effanbee Patsyette Doll" **125.00**

10" h, Patsy Baby, all composition, molded and painted hair, redressed, marked "FB20," c1932 . . . . **135.00**

11" h

Dy–Dee Baby, hard plastic head, rubber applied ears, molded hair, open mouth, nurser, 1950 . . . . **80.00**

Mickey, all vinyl, molded football helmet, painted features, marked "Effanbee/10" on head, "Effanbee/8" on back, 1956 . . . . **42.00**

12" h, Little Red Riding Hood, set of wolf, grandma, and Little Red Riding Hood, Patsy type, all composition, painted features **325.00**

12½" h, Candy Kid, composition, dressed, 1946 . . . . **165.00**

13" h, Skippy, composition swivel head, cloth body, composition hands and legs with molded socks and shoes, molded hair, painted side glancing eyes, orig military type suit, c1929 . . **245.00**

14½" h, Patricia, composition head and five piece body, light brown human hair wig in bangs and braids, brown sleep eyes, cotton flowered dress and pinafore, c1932 . . . . **100.00**

15" h, Twinkie, vinyl, molded hair, open mouth, nurser, marked "Effanbee 1959" **45.00**

16" h, Patsy Joan, composition head and five piece body, molded painted hair, green sleep eyes, red organdy dress, orig box **400.00**

18" h

Sugar Baby, composition head and limbs, cloth body, molded red hair, Effanbee gold heart bracelet **85.00**

Sweetie Pie, composition head and limbs, cloth body, brown flirty eyes **100.00**

19" h, Patsy–Ann, composition socket head and five piece body, molded and painted hair, blue sleep eyes, white flowered print dress, c1928 . . **75.00**

19½" h, Alyssia, vinyl head, plastic body, all fingers separate, rooted pigtails, closed mouth, walker, orig red velvet dress, white trim **150.00**

21" h, Dy–Dee Baby, plastic swivel head, jointed soft vinyl body, brown

synthetic wig, blue sleep eyes, MIB,
c1935 .... **200.00**
27" h, Lovums, composition swivel
head, cloth body, composition limbs,
painted hair, blue tin sleep eyes, redressed, c1930 .... **100.00**

HASBRO

Hasbro is primarily a toy manufacturer. Among
its most popular dolls were GI Joe and his
friends. The detailed accessories made for GI Joe
include military sets and numerous adventure
pieces (camping, mountain climbing, etc.).
Hasbro is also noted for its advertising and personality dolls.

4½" h, Mama Cass, Mamas And The
Papas, vinyl, 1967 .... **30.00**
7½" h, Junior Miss Sewing Kit, jointed
arms, orig box with doll patterns, material, dresses to sew, sewing implements, c1948 .... **25.00**
9" h, Choo Choo Charlie, soft vinyl
head, bean bag body, rooted hair,
painted eyes, marked "Copyright
1972 Quaker City Chocolate 7
Conf'y Co, Inc" **20.00**
12" h, GI Joe, vinyl, flocked hair, beard,
orig clothes, c1974 .... **20.00**

HORSMAN

The Horsman Dolls Company, Inc., was
founded in 1865 by E. I. Horsman, who began by
importing dolls. Soon after the founding,
Horsman produced bisque dolls. It was the first
company to produce the Campbell Kids. The
company invented Fairy Skin in 1946, Miracle
Hair in 1952, and Super Flex in 1954. The
Horsman process for synthetic rubber and early
vinyl has always been high quality.

9" h, Angie Dickinson, Sergeant Pepper,
MIB, 1976 .... **35.00**
11" h, Heebee Shebee, bride and groom **85.00**
11½" h, Mary Poppins, vinyl head and
arms, plastic body, 1964 .... **40.00**
17" h
Ella Cinders **65.00**
Ronald Reagan, vinyl, fully jointed **65.00**
19" h, Pram Baby, vinyl, jointed head,
glass sleep eyes, closed mouth, coos **65.00**
20" h, Baby Dimples, 125th Anniversary **75.00**
24" h, Emmett Kelly Jr, vinyl head, cloth
body, movable mouth, 1979 ...... **65.00**
27" h, Baby Rosebud, blue eyes, open
mouth with teeth, dress and matching
bonnet **125.00**

IDEAL TOY CORPORATION

The Ideal Toy Corp. was formed in 1902 by
Morris Michtom to produce his teddy bear. By
1915 the company had become a leader in the
industry by introducing the first sleep eyes. In
1939, Ideal developed magic skin. It was the first
company to use plastic. Some of their most popular lines include Shirley Temple, Betsy Wetsy,
and Toni dolls.

11¾" h, Mitzi, vinyl, jointed neck and
shoulders, rooted Saran hair, closed
mouth, painted eyes, 1965 .... **25.00**
12" h
Betsy Wetsy
Composition head, rubber body,
jointed at neck, shoulders, and
hips, drinks and wets, marked
"IDEAL" **65.00**
Hard plastic head, vinyl body ... **40.00**
Cinnamon, plastic, vinyl, rooted red
hair, marked "1971/Ideal Toy Corp
GH–12–H 183/Hong Kong" **35.00**
13" h, Shirley Temple, composition
socket head and five piece jointed
body, blonde mohair wig, hazel sleep
eyes, orig dress, c1935 .... **350.00**
13½" h, Baby Coos, hard plastic head,
rubber body, molded and painted
light brown hair, blue sleep eyes,
open/closed mouth, MIB, c1950 ... **150.00**
14" h
Judy Garland Teen Doll, all composition, dark auburn human hair wig,
open mouth, six teeth, 1941 .... **100.00**
Mary Hartline, P–90 line, blonde wig,
orig red outfit, white boots, baton **85.00**
15" h, Sparkle Plenty, hard plastic head,
one piece latex body, yellow yarn
hair, marked "Made in USA/Pat No
2252077," 1947 .... **55.00**
16" h
Baby Giggles, vinyl head, arms, and
legs, plastic body, rooted hair, blue
eyes, MIB, 1965 .... **45.00**
Betsy Wetsy, composition head, five
piece rubber jointed body, molded
hair, blue sleep eyes, redressed,
c1937 .... **50.00**
Velvet, vinyl head, plastic body and
legs, frosted blonde hair, hair grow
feature, marked "1969/Ideal Toy
Corp" **18.00**
17" h, Saucy Walker, hard plastic swivel
head and jointed walker body, orig
blonde synthetic wig, blue sleep
eyes, MIB, c1951 .... **150.00**
18" h
Flossie Flirt, composition, cloth body,
red wig **150.00**

Shirley Temple, composition, jointed at neck, arms, and legs, blonde mohair wig in deep ringlets, green sleep eyes, blue polka dot dress, orig blue satin wrist bows, c1930 **400.00**

Walking Sleeping Doll, composition head and limbs, cloth body, painted tin sleep eyes, orig clothes, c1915 . . . . **90.00**

19" h

Diana Ross, vinyl, fully jointed, 1969 **150.00**

Miss Revlon, vinyl head, hard plastic body, high heel feet, rooted light brown hair, blue sleep eyes, orig tagged clothing, c1955 . . . . **90.00**

21" h

Princess Mary, vinyl head, plastic body, orig ball gown and wrist tags, 1952 . . . . **150.00**

Shirley Temple Baby, composition swivel head on shoulderplate, cloth body, composition limbs, mohair curly wig, hazel sleep eyes, open mouth, five teeth, orig pink dress and bonnet, c1935 . . . . . . **625.00**

23" h, Tickletoes, hard plastic head, latex arms and legs, cloth body, open mouth, two upper teeth, felt tongue, dark brown wig, mama crier, marked "P200/Ideal Doll" on head, 1948 . . . **150.00**

26" h, Miss Ideal, vinyl, jointed, redressed **50.00**

27" h, Sister–Coos, composition head and shoulderplate, cloth stuffed body, composition arms and legs, brown mohair wig, brown sleep eyes, redressed, c1935 . . . . **175.00**

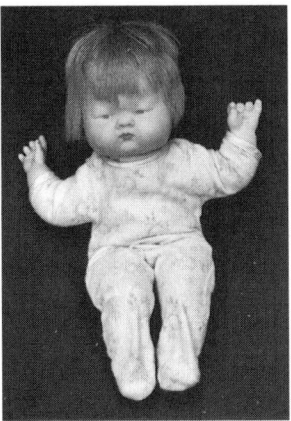

Jolly Toy, Thumbelina, 12" h, plastic head, forearms, and hands, cloth body, music box, rooted blonde hair, molded features, marked "1961 Jolly Toy," $12.00.

KNICKERBOCKER

This currently operating toy company has produced some dolls which collectors are beginning to recognize. One of the biggest doll lines centers around Holly Hobbie and her accessories.

7" h

Punjab, Annie, Geoffrey Holder, vinyl, fully jointed, 1982 . . . . **18.00**

Sunbonnet Doll, May, all vinyl, painted eyes, marked "K.T.C./Made in Taiwan/1975" **6.50**

12" h, Mickey Mouse, Mouse Club . . . **22.00**

15" h

Raggedy Andy, orig clothes and tags, 1970s **25.00**

Sleeping Beauty, composition, dark blonde wig, 1939 . . . . **85.00**

Snow White, composition, bent right arm, black wig, marked "Knickerbocker Toy Co/NY" on back, 1939 . . . . **95.00**

24" h, Hollie Hobbie **12.00**

MADAME ALEXANDER DOLL COMPANY

The Madame Alexander Doll Co. was started in 1923 by Bertha Alexander. The dolls made by this company are beautifully done with exquisite costumes. Hundreds of dolls have been made including several series such as the International Dolls and the Americana Dolls. Marks used include "Madame Alexander," "Alexander," and "Alex," and many are unmarked on the body but can be identified by clothing tags. Today, Madame Alexander continues to make dolls which are very collectible. Many dolls are made for a limited time period of one year. Others are offered for several years before being discontinued.

7" h

Amish Girl **350.00**

Gretel **135.00**

Spanish Boy **275.00**

Spanish Girl **120.00**

7½" h, Cousin Grace, hard plastic, blue sleep eyes, closed mouth, orig clothes, blonde synthetic wig, bent knee walker, straw picture hat, c1956 **675.00**

8" h

Beth, Little Women Series, 1951 . . . **325.00**

Betsy Ross, Americana Series, 1976 **175.00**

Billy, hard plastic, bending knee walker, brunette wig, one piece red and white suit, red tie, 1960 . . . . **400.00**

Little Genius, hard plastic swivel head, vinyl body, molded and painted hair, sleep eyes, open mouth, orig clothes, c1958 . . . . . **165.00**

Scarlett, green velvet dress **95.00**
Wendy, hard plastic, bending knee
walker, red wig, side ponytails,
1961 . . . . **175.00**
10" h
Cinderella, hard plastic, 1950 . . . . . **250.00**
Cissette, hard plastic, blonde bubble
cut wig, 1963 . . . . **100.00**
Cleopatra **55.00**
Little Shaver, brown string wavy hair,
black painted eyes, closed mouth,
cloth stockinet body, orig tagged
rose taffeta and pink organdy dress,
c1968 . . . . **250.00**
12" h, Lucinda, vinyl, auburn long
straight rooted hair, blue sleep eyes,
closed mouth, Janie face, orig blue
taffeta dress, straw hat, and parasol,
c1969 . . . . **425.00**
13" h, Little Colonel, composition head
and five piece body, Betty face, blue
tin sleep eyes, blonde mohair wig,
c1936 . . . . **225.00**
14" h
Dionne Quintuplets, Emilie, compo-
sition, wig, orig dress **350.00**
Muffin, pink flannel head and body,
yellow yarn wig, blue felt eyes,
tagged pink floral print cotton
dress, MIB, c1975 . . . . **85.00**
Snow White, hard plastic, c1952,
NMIB **475.00**
15" h
Caroline, all orig **250.00**
McGuffey Ana, composition head
and five piece body, blonde human
hair wig in pigtails, brown sleep
eyes, open mouth, teeth, plaid
dress, c1943 . . . . **115.00**
Patchity Pam, cloth, yellow yarn hair,
blue felt eyes, orig tagged clothes,
c1966 . . . . **100.00**
16½" h, Dionne Quintuplets, Yvonne,
baby, soft body, orig tagged dress . . **300.00**
18" h
Fairy Princess, composition head,
jointed at neck, jointed arms and
legs, orig blonde mohair wig,
brown sleep eyes, real lashes,
closed mouth, white satin gown,
silver slippers, c1950 . . . . **200.00**
Sonja Henie, composition socket
head, five piece jointed composition body, human hair wig, blue
sleep eyes, open mouth, orig outfit,
c1939 . . . . **450.00**
19" h, Princess Elizabeth, minor crazing **225.00**
22" h, Pinkie Baby, composition head
and limbs, cloth body, molded hair,
sleep eyes, rosebud mouth, white organdy christening gown and ruffled
bonnet, clover wrist tag, MIB, c1937 **400.00**

MATTEL, INC.

Mattel, Inc., was started in 1945. The company's most celebrated doll is Barbie, which was
designed by one of the company's founders, Ruth
Handler, in 1958. Barbie dolls were dressed in
bathing suits and sold in boxes. Her many outfits
and accessories were also marketed successfully.
Skipper, Ken, Midge, Skooter, and Francie are
part of Barbie's extended circle of family and
friends. Mattel has sponsored two trade–in programs for Barbie dolls, the first in 1967. The purpose was to introduce the new bendable Barbie.
This trade–in drew more than 1,250,000 dolls. In
1970, Mattel introduced Living Skipper with a
trade–in deal.

6" h
Doug Davis Spaceman, vinyl, posable, dark brown hair, marked
"Mattel Inc/1967/Hong Kong" on
head **10.00**
Major Mat Mason, vinyl, brown crew
cut hair, marked "Mattel Inc/1967/
Hong Kong" **10.00**
Todd and Tutti Sundae Treat Gift Set,
vinyl, MIB, 1965 . . . . **250.00**
9" h, Mork, Robin Williams, voice box,
1979 . . . . **25.00**
10½" h, Buffy and Mrs Beasley, vinyl
head, plastic body, blonde ponytails,
painted blue eyes, pull talk string,
MIB, c1969 . . . . **125.00**
11" h
Baby Walk 'N Play, plastic, vinyl,
rooted yellow hair, painted eyes,
two upper teeth, battery operated,
plays with yo–yo and walks,
marked "1967 Mattel Inc/Hong
Kong" on head **12.00**
Live Action Christie, vinyl, MIB, 1970 **85.00**
11½" h
Barbie
1959, #1, vinyl, blonde hair, MIB **950.00**
1960, #3, vinyl, blonde hair, MIB **375.00**
Barbie's Family and Friends
1961, Ken, flocked hair **75.00**
1966, Francie **50.00**
1972, Skipper, Quick Curl **20.00**
Wayne Gretzky, The Great Gretzky,
vinyl, 1982 . . . . **35.00**
16" h
Bozo The Clown, vinyl head, cloth
body, pull talk string, c1962 . . . . . **65.00**
Talking Baby Tenderlove, one piece,
inset scalp, rooted white hair,
painted eyes, open mouth, nurser,
pull talk string, marked "677K/1969
Mattel Inc/Mexico" on head **12.00**
21" h, Mrs Beasley, cloth body, vinyl
head and hands, blue eyes, rooted
blonde hair, voice box, orig tag **150.00**

30" h, Marie Osmond, hard plastic body, movable vinyl arms and head, pink dress, white shoes, orig box with unused contents **300.00**

MOLLYE DOLLS, INTERNATIONAL DOLL COMPANY

Mollye Dolls, International Doll Co., was founded by Mollye Goldman in the 1930s, starting as a cottage industry in Philadelphia. Mollye also made finely detailed clothes for other dolls. The patent for Raggedy Ann, Andy, and Belinda faces are held by Mollye. Finely executed clothes were a standard of the Mollye Co.

8" h, Martha Washington, hard plastic, hand painted face, white mohair wig   **50.00**
14" h, Judy Garland, Wizard of Oz, composition head and five piece body, dark brown wig in braids, blue tin sleep eyes, white checked skirt and blouse, c1940 . . . . **135.00**
15" h, Ginger Rogers, human hair pageboy style wig, closed mouth **325.00**
17" h, Business Girl, hard plastic, blonde wig, business suit **125.00**
19" h, Princess Elizabeth Rose, hard plastic, vinyl, white wig, orig bridal outfit, marked "X" in circle on head   **275.00**

REMCO

Remco Industries, Inc., was founded by Sol Robbins, and was the first company to advertise its products on television. Part of what made this company unique was that many products were related to television and promotional character dolls. The company closed in January 1974.

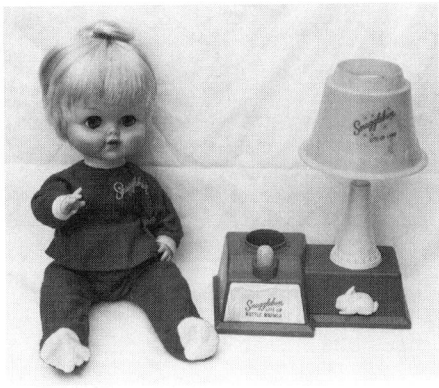

Remco, Snugglebun, plastic, rooted ash blonde hair, closed mouth, orig red flannel pajamas, marked "1/Remco Ind. Inc./1965" on head, red, yellow, and white plastic lamp and bottle warmer, $30.00.

5" h, Morticia, Addams Family, plastic body, vinyl head, rooted black hair, 1964 . . . . **135.00**
6½" h, I Dream of Jeannie, vinyl, fully jointed **25.00**
19" h, Laurie Partridge, vinyl and plastic, 1973 . . . . **100.00**

SUN RUBBER COMPANY

The Sun Rubber Company produced all rubber or lasiloid vinyl dolls. Many have molded features and clothes.

9" h, So Wee, rubber, Ruth Newton designer, good condition **20.00**
10" h
Peter Pan, one piece, molded clothes, marked "Peter Pan/W. Disney Prod./ The Sun Rubber Co./Barberton, O. USA," 1953 . . . . **30.00**
Tod–L–Lee, vinyl, molded hair, closed mouth, painted sunsuit, shoes, and socks, jointed at neck marked "Sun Rubber Co," 1956 . . . . **30.00**
11" h, Betty Bows, rubber, fully jointed, molded hair, blue sleep eyes, drinks and wets, marked "Betty Bows/copyright The Sun Rubber Co/Barberton, OH USA/34A," c1953 . . . . **35.00**
17" h, Sun–Dee, lasiloid vinyl, black, nurser, marked "Sun–Dees/Sun Rubber 1956" **45.00**

VOGUE DOLLS

Vogue Dolls was founded by Mrs. Jennie H. Graves. She began a small doll shop which specialized in well made costumes. The original business of doll clothing led to a cottage industry which employed over 500 home sewers in 1950. This branch of the industry peaked in the late 1950s with over 800 home workers plus several hundred more at the factory. During World War II, the shortages created a market for an American doll source. Mrs. Graves created the Ginny Doll and promoted her heavily. The Ginny Doll was the first doll created with a separate wardrobe and accessories. For many years Vogue issued one hundred new outfits each year for Ginny alone, while continuing to produce its own dolls and clothing for others. Ginny Dolls reached their heyday in the 1950s and are still being made today.

Note: The Ginny Doll was reproduced in 1985.

8" h, Ginny Doll, hard plastic
Bride, 1963, soft vinyl head, rooted hair **55.00**
Catholic Nun, moving eyes, marked "Vogue" on head, "Vogue Doll" on back, 1950–53 . . . . **150.00**

Vogue, Ginny, Mickey Mouse outfit, 8" h, $135.00.

Easter Parade, painted eyes, molded hair, mohair wig, marked "Vogue" on head, "Vogue Doll" on back, 1948–50 .... 100.00
Roller Skater, walking mechanism, marked "Ginny" on back, "Vogue Dolls, Inc., Pat. Pend., Made in USA," 1954 .... 85.00
Southern Belle, bending knees, striped skirt, straw hat, 1957 .... 85.00
10" h, Jill, bride, handpainted, 1958 .. 48.00
12" h, Betty Jane, composition, bent right arm, braided pigtails, red plaid woven cotton dress, white eyelet trim, "Vogue Dolls, Inc" on tag, 1947 .... 85.00
18" h, Brickette, rooted curly strawberry blonde hair, sleep eyes, polka dot dress, straw hat, 1979–80 .... 65.00
22" h, Hug A Bye Baby, pink pajamas, MIB 45.00

DRUGSTORE COLLECTIBLES

Collecting Hints: There are several suggestions to consider when starting a drugstore collection: (1) Buy the best that you can afford (It is wise to pay a bit more for mint/near mint items if at all possible.); (2) Look for excellent graphics on the packaging of items; (3) Do not buy anything that is rusty or damp; (4) Before purchasing an item, ask the dealer to remove price tags or written prices (If this isn't possible, consider how badly you really want the item.); (5) Buy a variety of items (Consider placing several like items together on a shelf for increased visual effect.); and (6) Purchase items from a variety of time periods.

History: The increasing diversity of health related occupations has also encouraged an awareness in collecting pharmaceutical material, items that appeared in old drugstores from the turn of the century through the 1950s. Products manufactured before the Pure Food and Drug Act of 1906 are eagerly sought by collectors. Patent medicines, medicinal tins, items from a specific pharmaceutical company, dental items, and shaving supplies are a few key collecting areas.

The copyright date on a package, graphics, style of lettering, or the popularity of a specific item at a particular period in history are clues to date a product. Other approaches to finding information are talking with a pharmacist who has been in the business for a number of years or checking old manufacturing directories at a regional library.

References: Al Bergevin, *Drugstore Tins & Their Prices*, Wallace–Homestead, 1990; A. Walker Bingham, *The Snake–Oil Syndrome: Patent Medicine Advertising*, Christopher Publishing House, 1994; Douglas Congdon–Martin, *Drugstore & Soda Fountain Antiques*, Schiffer Publishing, 1991; Martin R Lipp, *Medical Museums USA: A Travelguide* McGraw Hill Publishing; Patricia McDaniel, *Drugstore Collectibles*, Wallace–Homestead, 1994.

Periodical: *Siren Soundings*, 1439 Main St., Brewster, MA 02631.

Museums: National Museum of Health & Medicine, Walter Reed Medical Center, Washington, DC; New England Fire & History Museum, Brewster, MA.

Advisor: Patricia McDaniel.

COLD, ALLERGY, HAY FEVER REMEDIES

Bionoid Tablets, Henry K Wampole & Co, Inc, Philadelphia, brown glass bottle, white metal lid, yellow label with black and white letters, unopened, 12 tablets, 2" h 6.50
Dristan Decongestant Tablets, Whitehall Laboratories, Inc, NY, brown glass bottle, white metal lid, white and red label with blue and white letters, unopened, 24 tablets, 2½" h 4.75
Kemp's Balsam, Kemp & Lane, Inc, LeRoy, NY, clear glass bottle, metal lever–open lid, green cardboard box with black letters and adv for Kemp & Lane products, 2 fl oz 12.00
Lee's Crea–Lyptos, Crea–Lyptos Co, NY, Kansas City, clear glass long necked

bottle, brown metal lid, brown label
with black letters, 6⅛" h 9.00
Zerbst's Capsules, Zerbst Pharmacal Co,
St Joseph, MO, white cardboard box
with black and red letters, instruction
sheet, 15 tablets, 1½ x 2 x½" 5.75

DENTAL

Colgate Brisk, Colgate–Palmolive Co,
New York, NY, two 1¾ oz fluoride
toothpaste tubes in orig boxes, held
together with tape offering 15¢ off,
red, white, and blue boxes and letters 9.00
Dent Glo, Fort Orange Chemical Co,
Inc, Albany, NY, dental plate cleanser,
full 8 oz tin, 5¼ x 3 x 1", navy and
white tin and lettering 8.00
Dr Wernet's Powder, Wernet Dental
Mfg Co, Inc, Jersey City 6, NJ, "holds
false teeth tight," full 1.75 oz tan and
red tin, blue and red letters, hands
putting powder on dentures illus on
front, 4¼ x 2¼ x 1¼" 11.00
Great Zeeth's Mighty White, Albert
O–Culver Co, Melrose Park, IL,
sugar–free children's fluoride toothpaste, full 3 oz tube, 6½ x 1¼ x 18"
red and white box, black and white
lettering, chimpanzee, poem, and
Great Zeeth character 6.50

FIRST AID

Band–Aid, Johnson & Johnson, New
Brunswick, NJ, Chicago, IL, assorted
adhesive bandages, mercurochrome
pad, empty 2¼ x 3½ x 1" tan, red,
and black tin with flip top lid, red and
black lettering 3.25
Landford Boric Acid, The George H.
Nowland Co, Cincinnati, OH, powder, can be used with water as an
eyewash, full 2 oz tin, 3 x 2 x¾" navy,
blue, and white tin and lettering . . . 7.00
Tincture of Iodine, The Penslar Co, Inc,
Detroit, MI, empty 1 oz brown glass
bottle with glass applicator, 3 x 1¼ x
1¼", red and white label and lettering 3.00
Unguentine, The Norwich Pharmacal
Co, Norwich, NY, analgesic, anes-
thetic, and antiseptic surgical dressing, relieves pain, promotes healing,
full 1 lb, 3 x 4 x 3" tin, yellow, black,
and red, black lettering 11.00
Uniflex First Aid Unit, Bauer & Black,
Chicago, New York, and Toronto, ammonia inhalant, revives fainted or in-
jured patient, 4 vivo tubes in 4 x 2⅛
x⅝" light blue and red box with dark

blue and white lettering, box illus
with image of lady patient 13.00

FOOT

Dr Scholl's Lastik Metatarsal Pads, The
Scholl Manufacturing Co, Inc,
Chicago, New York, London, Toronto,
and Paris, designed to relieve calluses
and burning, tenderness, or cramps in
ball of foot, 4 x 1 x 2½" box contains
1 pr, size 8, combined bandage and
metatarsal pad, yellow, blue, and tan
box, blue and black lettering, size
chart on bottom, hand, foot, and foot
pad illus on top 8.00
Mexsana Powder, formerly called
Mexican Heat Powder, Plough Inc,
New York, NY, Memphis, TN, and
San Francisco, CA, medicated, relieves itching, stinging, and burning
of skin rashes, insect bites, and sunburn, promotes healing, almost full
2½ oz cardboard cylinder with metal
cap and bottom, red and tan label,
black and red letters 7.00
Naprylate Powder, R J Strasenburgh Co,
Rochester 14, NY, for superficial fun-
gus infections including athlete's foot,
full 1¼ oz round plastic squeeze bottle, tan cap, white lettering, 1⅜ x 3½" 6.75
Sani–Ped Corn Pads, United Drug Co,
Boston and St Louis, zinc oxide corn
pads and medicated discs, relieves
pressure and softens corn for removal, sold only at Rexall Drug
Stores, full box contains 8 medicated
discs and 12 corn pads, 1⅞ x 2¾ x¾"
blue, black, and white box, black and
white lettering 5.50

HOSPITAL, SURGICAL

Bed Pan and Urinal, cov, light gray and
gray porcelain coated metal, 19" l
from end to spout 15.00
Cotton Root Bark, Wm S Merrell Co,
Cincinnati, OH, uterine stimulant, as-
tringent to increase uterine contrac-
tions during pregnancy, empty¼ pint
round brown bottle, 2 x 5¼", tan,
green, and navy label and lettering,
factory illus on front, cork stopper . . 15.00
Glass Urinal, made in USA, clear glass
with handle, able to stand up or lie
down, emb measurements to 32 oz 9.00
Yale Needles, Becton, Dickinson & Co,
Rutherford, NJ, regular point, stainless hypodermic needles, unopened
2¾ x 2⅓ x ½" navy and white box
with navy and red lettering, 1 dozen
needles 6.00

INFANTS AND CHILDREN

Bib–ex, The Bib–ex Corp, St Louis, MO, disposable baby bibs, 45 bibs, 10 x 15 x 1" light blue cardboard box, pink and white horizontal stripes, light blue and white letters, picture of baby boy seated in high chair feeding himself, full 12.00

Binky Teething Toy Rattle, Binky Baby Products Co, New York City, lightweight plastic baby teething rattle with duck in center, 6 x 3¼ x ¾" red, white, and light blue clear cellophane and cardboard box with black and red lettering 6.00

Book, *Story of Our Baby, Baby's First Five Years*, copyright 1938 by Whitman Publishing Co, 20 pgs, hard cov, 5½ x 6⅞", light blue, pink, and white, pink ribbon 12.00

Brother & Sister Bath Set, Cardinal Distributor, New York, NY, two 3 x 1⅞ x ½" bars castile baby soap dec with boy and girl transfers, two 1¼ x 3" cardboard cylinders bubble foam, one blue with boy transfer, other pink with girl transfer, 3½ x 6⅝ x 1⅜" outer box, pink, white, yellow, and brown with dark blue lettering, boys and girls playing illus 17.00

Mennen Borated Powder, The Mennen Co, Newark, NJ and Toronto, Ont, antiseptic powder, 5¼ x 3⅛ x 2" light blue and white vertically striped tin with white and dark blue lettering, 9 oz, empty 8.00

Sanatare Gum Massage, Harris Pharmacal Co, Sikeston, MO, relieves pain of minor mouth irritations, 1 oz round brown bottle, 1⅜ x 3⅜ x 1⅜" red and white box with black and white lettering, almost empty 4.00

Stork Nurser, Nurse–Matic Corp, Chicago, IL, 8 oz clear glass baby bottle, flying stork illus and "Rexall & Duraglas," blue letters and numbers   6.00

Walls' Children's Cod Wafers, Walls' Drugs, Indianapolis, IN, relieves cold discomforts, 1 x 2⅜" glass cylinder, pink, blue, and white inside label with blue and white lettering, 12 wafers, full 6.00

LAXATIVES

Dime Lax, World's Products Co, Spencer, IN, ¼ x 1½ x 2" brown and orange metal box with orange, brown, and white lettering, 6 tablets, full 7.75

Garfield's Seidlitz Powders, laxative, antacid, $10.00.

Lamarine, Lamarine Laboratory, Atlanta, Ga, keeps stomach, liver, and bowels healthy and breath pure and sweet, regulates bowels to perform their duty naturally and easily, a benefit in the treatment of indigestion and dyspepsia arising from inactive bowels and in clearing the skin, 2½ x 1" clear glass bottle with cork stopper top, 3 x 1 x 1" yellow cardboard box with brown letters, instruction sheet, full   8.50

Lydia E Pinkham's Pills for Constipation, Lydia E Pinkham Medicine Co, Lynn, MA, vegetable laxative, ⅝ x 1¼ x 1¾" brown cardboard box with black lettering, empty 9.00

Phenolphtalein Wafers, Brewer and Co, Inc, Pharmaceutical Chemist's, Worcester, MA, 4 x 1½ x 1" brown glass bottle with black metal lid, brown label with black lettering, 100 wafers, ½ full 8.00

2223 Liver Pills, C–2223 Laboratories, Memphis, TN and New York, NY, relieves constipation biliousness, headache, and increases the appetite, ¼ x 1¼ x 1¾" blue metal box with black lettering, full 7.00

Vegets, King Vegets Co, Cincinnati, OH, relieves liver, stomach, and bowel distress caused by constipation, 3 x ¾" wooden bottle with wooden stopper top, 3 x 1 x 1" blue and white cardboard box with blue and white lettering, instruction sheet, full 7.50

MISCELLANEOUS

Davol–Hard Rubber Pile "Pipe," Davol Rubber Co, Providence, RI, 4¼ x 1⅜ x 1⅜" box contains one "pipe" and instruction folder for hemorrhoid ointment, blue, white, and yellow, and orange 7.00

Dill's Nose Drops, The Dill Co, Morristown, PA, for nose and throat irritations, ½ fl oz bottle with stopper, 3⅞ x 1½ x 1½" orange, dark green, and yellow box with orange and black lettering, with folder and sample pack of Dill's cold tablets, full .. **6.00**

Eyecup, tin, unknown manufacturer, 1 x 1⅜″ **3.75**

Penny Royal Leaves, Allaire, Woodward & Co, Peoria, IL, teas for aid to digestion and soothes upset stomachs, 3 x 3 x 1⅜″ green and yellow cardboard box with black lettering, 1 oz, full .. **7.00**

Vick's VA–TRO–NOL, Vick Chemical Co, Greensboro, NC, New York, NY, and Philadelphia, PA, nose drops, relieves cold discomforts, 3½ x 1½″ round blue bottle, stopper **8.00**

REDUCING AIDS

Metrecal, Edward Dalton Co, Division of Mead Johnson & Co, Evansville 12, IN, weight control, liquid, vanilla flavor, gold and white 1 quart tin with brown and white lettering, full **7.75**

Necta Liquid Saccharin, The Norwich Pharmacal Co, Norwich, NY, sweetener, 3½ x 2½″ shaker top re–usable tapered clear bottle, red plastic reversible top, pink and red label with black and red lettering, instructions, 4 fl oz, full **7.00**

Sucaryl, Abbott Laboratories, N. Chicago, IL, for calorie controlled and diabetic diets, tablet dispenser, light blue and clear plastic, triangular, empty **4.75**

REXALL DRUG COMPANY

Gravida Supplement, Los Angeles, Boston, and St Louis, vitamin and mineral dietary supplement for use in pregnancy and lactation, 5¼ x 1¾ x 2¾″ brown glass bottle with white metal lid, 5½ x 3 x 1⅞″ gray and white cardboard box with blue lettering, 100 capsules, almost full **9.00**

Quik Puffs, Los Angeles and Toronto, printed in USA, clean sanitary cotton, full 300 inches of cotton in 6¾ x 3½″ metal can with white metal lid, white and blue label with white letters, snowflakes illus **12.00**

Tiny Tot Aspirin, Los Angeles, St Louis, Boston, and Toronto, helps relieve headache, minor muscular aches and pains, and simple throat irritation accompanying colds in children, 2¾ x 1¼ x¾″ clear glass bottle with white metal lid, 3 x 1⅜ x 1″ white, blue, and pink cardboard box with white and blue lettering, 100 tablets, full .. **5.50**

RUBS, LINIMENTS, OINTMENTS

Chloroform Liniment, Drugmaster Inc, St Louis, MO, relieves muscular aches and pains, 4½ x 2¼ x 1⅛″ brown glass bottle with white metal lid, white and gray label with gray letters, 4 fl oz, empty **5.00**

Frey's Uka–Vita Balm, Omar F Frey & Son Co Laboratories, Toledo, OH, quick relief in treatment of croup, colds, and respiratory tract congestion, 1½ x 2″ cloudy white glass jar with black plastic lid, 1¾ x 2 x 2″ brown and blue striped cardboard box with blue lettering, instruction, 1 oz, full **6.00**

Klonene, Klonene Products Co, Indianapolis, IN, antiseptic, disinfectant, and germicidal, destroys germs, non–injurious to cell tissue, 5¾ x 2″ brown glass bottle with cork stopper top, 6 x 2⅛ x 2⅛″ white box with black and red lettering, instruction, 6 fl oz, full **15.00**

MA–LE–NA, Consolidated Royal Chemical Corp, Chicago, IL, for minor cuts, scratches, and abrasions, minor burn, scalds, sunburn and windburn, insect bites, fever blisters, chafes, chapped and cracked hands, ¾ x 2½″ white and black metal container, 1.5 oz, half full, 2¾ x 2¾ x ⅞″ brown and black cardboard box with black lettering **8.50**

McQueen's Pure Mutton Tallow, Washington 15, DC, family remedy for chapped and rough skin caused by exposure to inclement weather, skin cleanser, foundation for various medical ointments, ⅝ x 1⅞″ green and white metal container with green and white letters, sheep illus, 1 oz .. **7.50**

STOMACH

Al–Caroid Antacid Powder, Subsidiary of Sterling Drug Inc, NY 16, NY, relieves distress from acid indigestion, heartburn, hyperacidity, flatulence, gastritis, morning sickness, and dietary indiscretion, 3 x 2½ x 2½″ white cardboard box with blue and black lettering, instruction sheet, 2 oz, full **7.50**

Diotex, The Knox Co, Los Angeles, CA, relieves acid indigestion, gas in stomach, heartburn, sourness, bloating, bad breath, and nausea due to gastric hyperacidity, 4 x 3 x ½″ cellophane wrapped red and blue checkered cardboard box with blue lettering, 144 tablets, unopened **6.00**

Dr Pierce's Golden Medical Discovery, Pierce's Proprietaries, Inc, New York, NY, relieves gas pains, heartburn, and other symptoms of common indigestion, clear glass bottle with black metal lid, 3 x 1⅞ x 1¼" blue and white cardboard box with black lettering, trademark stamp with Dr. Pierce illus, instruction sheet, 56 tablets, unopened **9.00**

Norwich Milk of Magnesia USP, The Norwich Pharmacal Co, NY, milk laxative, antacid for sour and acid stomach, bad breath, and heartburn due to excess stomach acid, 10 x 3⅜" blue glass bottle with metal lid, black and white label with black and white lettering, 1 quart, almost empty **11.00**

Phillips Milk of Magnesia Tablets, The Chas H Phillips Co, division of Sterling Drug Inc, New York, NY, fast relief from upset stomach indigestion and heartburn, 3⅝ x 1½ x 1" blue glass bottle with blue metal lid, white label with blue and red lettering, 75 tablets, unopened **9.00**

Sedagel, Pharmaceuticals, Inc, Newark, NJ, relieves heartburn, excess acid stomach, diarrhea, gas distress, 4¾ x 2½ x 1" blue glass bottle with black metal lid, blue and white label with blue letters, 4 fl oz, almost full **8.00**

Syntrogel, Sauter Laboratories, Inc, Distributor, Nutley, NJ, symptomatic relief of gastric hyperacidity, 4 x 1½ x 1½" brown glass bottle with white metal lid, blue and white label with blue letters, 100 tablets, unopened . . **6.50**

THROAT

Dr Marker's Mouth Komfort, Oral Prophylactic Assoc, Inc, Duluth, MN, relieves cold sores, fever blisters, and chapped lips, 2¼ x⅞" round green bottle, 3 fl drams, full **4.75**

Nullo Chlorophyll Tablets, The De Pee Co, Holland, MI, controls body odors and bad breath, 1½ x 3½ x 1½" round clear glass bottle, light gray, pink, and white box with green and black lettering, pink floral wreath on top, 45 tablets, full **8.00**

Pen–Mint, The Penslar Co, Inc, New York, NY, chlorophyll mouth wash, 7¼ x 2½" round green bottle, white, dark green, and light green label and lettering, 12 fl oz, full **6.50**

Sucrets, Merck, Sharp & Dohme, division of Merck & Co, Inc, Philadelphia, PA, soothes irritated mouth and throat, 2½ x 3½ x ¾" tan dark blue and white tin with blue and white lettering, empty **7.00**

UNITED STATES DRUG COMPANY

Blue Ointment, Pharmaceutical Chemists, Boston and St Louis, mild mercurial ointment for treatment of pediculosis pubis, 4⅜ x 3¼" brown glass jar with metal lid, red and white label with red and white lettering, 1 lb, full **28.00**

Compressed Tablets, Phenolphthalein, Boston, 2⅞ x 1⅛ x ¾" brown glass bottle with cork stopper, white label with black lettering, 100 tablets **25.00**

Sodium Phosphate, Boston and St Louis, laxative and purgative, 8½ x 3½" blue glass bottle with cork stopper top, brown and white label with brown and white letters, 1 lb, full size **40.00**

Vibopyrine, Boston and St Louis, relieves menstrual pain, 5 x 1⅞" brown glass bottle with cork stopper top, white and brown label with white and brown letters, 4 fl oz, empty . . . **36.00**

UNITED–REXALL DRUG COMPANY

Rexall Bronchial Salve, Boston and St Louis, treats congestion and inflammation of bronchial catarrh, common colds of head, throat, and chest, and neuralgic and rheumatic pains and headache, 5⅛ x 1¾" green and blue tube with silver metal lid, 5¼ x 1⅜ x 1⅜" white and blue cardboard box with white and blue lettering, instruction, full **18.00**

Rexall Mucu–Tone, Boston, St Louis, Liverpool, and Toronto, alternative tonic for promoting the appetite and giving tone and strength to those who are weak and run–down as a result of over–work, mental strain, or exhausting illness, 6¼ x 2 x 1¼" brown glass bottle with cork stopper top, 6¾ x 2⅞ x 2" gray cardboard box with blue letters, 6 fl oz, almost full **20.00**

Puretest Compound Licorice Powder USP, Boston and St Louis, laxative for correction of constipation and bowel disorders, 6½ x 3" cardboard container, white and blue label with white and blue lettering, 1 lb, almost full **23.00**

Puretest Spirit Ammonia Aromatic USP, Boston and St Louis, 4½ x 1½ x ⅞" brown glass bottle with black metal lid, blue and white label with blue and white lettering, 2 fl oz, empty . . **19.00**

ELECTRICAL APPLIANCES

Collecting Hints: Small electric appliances are still readily available and can be found at estate and garage sales, flea markets, auctions, and best of all, Grandma's attic. They generally cost very little, making them attractive to collectors on a limited budget.

Most old toasters, waffle irons, and other appliances still work. Construction was simple with basic, 2-wire connections. If repairs are necessary, it usually is simple to return an appliance to good working order.

Whenever possible ask to plug in the appliance to see if it heats. On "flip–flop" type toasters (the most numerous type), check to see if elements are intact around mica and not broken.

Most appliances used a standard size cord, still available at hardware stores. Some early companies did have strange plugs and their appliances will only accept cords made for that company. In such an instance, buy the appliance only if the cord accompanies it.

Do not buy an appliance that is in non–working order, in poor or rusted condition, or with missing parts unless you plan to strip it for parts. Dirt does not count. With a little care and time, most of the old appliances will clean up to a sparkling appearance. Aluminum mag wheel polish, available at auto parts stores, used with a soft rag will produce wonderful results. Also, a non–abrasive kitchen cleanser can be of great help.

As with most collectibles, the original box or instructions for any item can enhance the value and add up to 25%. Also beware of chrome, silver, and other plated articles stripped to their base metal, usually brass or copper. Devalue these by 50%.

History: The first all–electric kitchen appeared at the 1893 Chicago World's Fair and included a dishwasher, that looked like a torture device and range. Electrical appliances for the home began gaining popularity just after 1900 in the major eastern and western cosmopolitan cities. Appliances were sold door to door by their inventors. Small appliances did not gain favor in the rural areas until the late 1910s and early 1920s. However, the majority of the populace did not trust electricity.

By the 1920s, competition among electrical companies was keen; innovations in electrical appliances were many. Changes were rapid. The electric servants were here to stay. Most small appliance companies were bought by bigger companies. These, in turn, have been swallowed up by the huge conglomerates of today.

Some firsts in electrical appliances are:
1882 Patent for electric iron (H. W. Seeley [Hotpoint])
1903 Detachable cord (G. E. Iron)
1905 G. E. Toaster (Model X–2)
1905 Westinghouse toaster (Toaster Stove)
1909 Travel iron (G. E.)
1911 Electric frying pan (Westinghouse)
1912 Electric waffle iron (Westinghouse)
1917 Table Stove (Armstrong)
1918 Toaster/Percolator (Armstrong "Perc–O–Toaster")
1920 Heat indicator on waffle iron (Armstrong)
1920 Flip–flop toasters appear (everyone)
1920 Mixer on permanent base (Hobart Kitchen Aid)
1920 Electric egg cooker (Hankscraft)
1923 Portable mixer (Air–O–Mix "Whip–All")
1924 Automatic iron (Westinghouse)
1924 Home malt mixer (Hamilton Beach #1)
1926 Automatic pop–up toaster (Toastmaster #1h–A–1)
1926 Steam iron (Eldec)
1937 Home coffee mill (Hobart Kitchen Aid)
1937 Automatic coffee maker (Farberware "Coffee Robot")
1937 Conveyance device toaster ("Toast–O–Lator")

References: Linda Campbell Franklin, *300 Years of Kitchen Collectibles, Third Edition*, Books Americana, 1991; Don Fredgant, *Electrical Collectibles, Relics of the Electrical Age*, Padre Productions, 1981; Howard Hazelcorn, *Hazelcorn's Price Guide To Old Electrical Toasters, 1908–1940*, H. J. H. Publications, no date, 1988–1989 revised price list available; Greg Ivy (compiler), *Early Fans*, Kurt House, 1983; Norman E. Martinus and Harry L. Rinker, *Warman's Paper*, Wallace–Homestead, 1994; Gary Miller and K. M. Scotty Mitchell, *Price Guide To Collectible Kitchen Appliances*, Wallace–Homestead, 1991; Ellen M. Plante, *Kitchen Collectibles: An Illustrated Price Guide*, Wallace–Homestead, 1991; Diane Stoneback, *Kitchen Collectibles: The Essential Buyer's Guide*, Wallace–Homestead, 1994; John M. Witt, *Witt's Field Guide To Electric Desk Fans*, published by author, 1993.

Collectors' Clubs: American Fan Collector Association, PO Box 804, South Bend, IN 46624; Electric Breakfast Club, PO Box 306, White Mills, PA 18473.

Advisors: Gary L. Miller, K. M. Scotty Mitchell.

BLENDERS

Berstead Drink Mixer, Eskimo Kitchen Mechanic, 1930s, Berstead Mfg Co, domed chrome motor, single shaft,

lifts off metal base, receptacle for tapered ribbed glass, 12" h 30.00
Chronmaster Mixall, 1930s, Chronmaster Electric Corp, NY and Chicago, chrome and black motor, single shaft, hinged black base, orig silver stripe glass 30.00
Dorby Whipper, Model E, 1940s, chrome motor, black Bakelite handle, off/on toggle, clear, measured Vidrio glass 25.00
Electromix Whipper, 1930s, Chicago, ivory, offset metal motor housing, push–down break, filler hole in lid, measured glass base, 7½" h 25.00
Gilbert Mixer, Polar Club, 1929, AC Gilbert Co, New Haven, CT, lift off gray painted metal, rear switch, blue wood handle, premium for Wesson–Snowdrift, orig box, 10" h   75.00
Hamilton Beach, Hamilton Beach Malt Machine, 1930s, chrome motor, green cast base, push–up switch, nickel cup, 18½" h 75.00
Kenmore, Sears, Roebuck & Co, Chicago, Kenmore Hand Mixer, 1940s, small, cream colored plastic, single 4½" beater, orig box, booklet, warranty, and hanger plate 25.00
Knapp Monarch Whipper, mid 1930s, Knapp Monarch, St Louis, MO, white metal motor, top red plastic handle, round milk glass base with reeded, fin feet, white plastic beater, 9½" h 25.00
Kwick Way, St Louis, MO, white metal motor top over angular, clear glass base, no switch, decal label, 7½" h 20.00
Silex Blender, 1940s, Silex Corp, NY, sq, white cast base, push button switch, silver foil, Art Deco label, clear glass, four cup top has Silex spelled out vertically on black stripe, plastic lid . . .   15.00

CHAFING DISHES

American Beauty, 1910s, American Electrical Heater Co, Detroit, MI, three part, nickel on copper, sealed element in base, hot water container, separate plugs, marked "fast" and "slow", black painted wood handles and knob 50.00
Manning Bowman, Meriden, CT, 1930s, bright chrome Art Deco design, reeded edges, two part top, hot plate base, black Bakelite knob and handles 45.00
Universal, 1910s, Landers, Frary & Clark, nickel on copper faceted body, three parts, sealed element in base

hot water pan, three prong heat adjustment in base, large black wooden handle and knob 50.00

COFFEE MAKERS AND SETS

Coffee Robot, Farberware, 1937, SW Farber, Brooklyn, NY, #610, round chrome two part body, glass top, chrome lid, walnut handle, Bakelite knob, screw–on cover spout 60.00
Manning Bowman Percolator, Manning Bowman, Meriden, CT
Cat. #32, Ser. #4–30, 1920s, 15" percolator/urn, creamer, open sugar, nickel chrome vertically faceted bodies, short cabriole legs on urn, up–turned black wood handles, glass knob insert 60.00
Ser. #636, mid 1930s, graceful, tall Art Deco design, reeded dec around neck and base, bright chrome, 12" h 40.00
Porcelier Breakfast Set, 1930s, Porcelier Mfg Co, Greensburg, PA, all porcelain bodies, basketweave design accents, floral transfers, silver line dec
Complete set 350.00
Creamer and sugar, cov 30.00
Percolator, #5007 . . . .   65.00
Sandwich Grill, #5004 . . . .   60.00
Toaster, #5002 . . . .   75.00
Rome Electric Percolator, 1910–20s, Rome Mfg Co, Rome, NY, coffee urn #CEU 47, chrome, wide, flared black wooden handles, turned feet, 14" h 25.00
Royal Rochester Corp, Rochester, NY, Model E 610, coffee set, three pcs, lusterware bodies, marked "Fraunfelter China, OH," tall vertically faceted alternating orange luster and white stripes, floral transfers 150.00
Universal, Landers, Frary & Clark, New Britain, CT
Breakfast Set, 1930s, cream porcelain, blue and orange floral transfers
Complete Set, 5 pcs 350.00
Percolator, #E 6927 . . . .   65.00
Waffle Iron, #E 6324, pierced chrome base, porcelain insert, front drop handle 65.00
Coffee Set, #E 9119–1, 1920s, chrome, tall chrome handles, swirl glass insert, octagonal body, handled tray, 4 pcs 125.00
Coffee Urn, #E 9219, late 1910–20s, sq cabriole legs, large wooden ear handles, nickel body, oval tray, 14" h 65.00

EGG COOKERS

Hankscraft Co, Madison, WI, Model #730, Art Deco design, ivory china, silver trim, cooker, four egg cups, and nickel tray, 6 pcs **50.00**

Rochester, 1910s, Rochester Stamping Co, Rochester, NY, egg shaped, four part, chrome, small base, int. fitted with skillet with turned black wooden handle, six egg holder with lift out handle, enclosed heating element .. **40.00**

FOOD COOKERS

EC Junior 10, Everhot, 1920s, Swartz Baugh Mfg Co, Toledo, OH, large chrome and black cylindrical body, aluminum lid, Art Deco design, front emb "Everhot," int. fitted rack, two open semi–circular pans, one circular lidded pan, three prong heating control, 13" h **50.00**

Eureka Portable Oven, 1930s, Eureka Vacuum Cleaner Co, Detroit, MI, Art Deco style, cream painted body, black edges, sides let down and contain hot plates on chrome surfaces, fitted int. wire racks, controls across bottom front, 15 x 13 x 19" **80.00**

Hankscraft, 1920s, Hankscraft, Madison, WI, green enamel pan, chrome, detachable hinge pin lid, green lusterware china knob, chrome base, black wooden flaring handles **50.00**

Nesco Electric Casserole, early 1930s, National Enamel & Stamping Co, Inc, Milwaukee, WI, cream colored body, green enamel lid, high/low control, three prong plug, 9" d **25.00**

Quality Brand, 1920s, Great Northern Mfg Co, Chicago, IL, model #950, cylindrical body, insulated sides and lid, fitted int., aluminum pan lids, brown with red stripe on body, lift out rods, 14" h **40.00**

HOT PLATES

Edison–Hotpoint, 1910s, Edison Electric, New York, Chicago, and Ontario, solid iron surface, clay filled int., very heavy, pierced legs, china feet, copper control, china knob **25.00**

Thermax, 1920s, Universal, Landers, Frary & Clark, iron top, pierced swirl design, nickel tripod base, four prongs to heat outer ring, inner ring or both, special two head cord **25.00**

Westinghouse, 1920s, Westinghouse, Mansfield, OH, round top, green porcelain metal top surrounding element, hollow legs, no control, 7½" d top **25.00**

MISCELLANEOUS

Angelus–Campfire Bar–B–Q Marshmallow Toaster, 1920s, Campfire, Milwaukee, WI, 3" sq, flat topped, pierced pyramid top pc, base stands on loop, wire legs, rubber encased feet, flat wire forks **55.00**

Coffee Grinder, Kitchen Aid, 1936, Hobart, Troy, OH, Model #A–9, first home coffee grinder, heavy cream colored cast base houses motor, course/fine adjustment on neck, clear glass jar container with screw–off top **60.00**

Flour Sifter, Miracle, introduced c1934, Miracle Products, Chicago, IL, electric, cream body, blue wooden handle at base with hold–down button, vibrates flour through wire strainer .. **35.00**

Juicer, Vita–Juicer, 1930s, Kold King Dist Corp, Los Angeles, Hoek Rotor Mfg Co, Reseda, CA, heavy cream painted cast metal, three parts: base motor, container, and fitted lid, lock groove and lock down wire handle, aluminum pusher, 10" h **35.00**

Perc–O–Toaster, Armstrong, toast rack interchangeable with optional waffle iron, 1918, $60.00.

Tea Kettle, Universal, 1910s, Landers, Frary & Clark, Model #E 973, bright nickel squatty body and base in one pc, long spout, high curved black painted wood handle, vertically curved mounts **45.00**

MIXERS

Dominion Modern Mode Mixer, 1932–33, Dominion Electrical Mfg Co, Minneapolis, MN, faceted, angular Art Deco body and base, three speed rear lever control, runs on a.c. or d.c., two custard glass bowls and juicer, mechanism to control beater height **75.00**

General Electric, 1938, GE Corp, Ser. #10–A, upright housed motor, top speed control, three synchronized beaters in row, work light shines in bowl, two white glass bowls, black Bakelite handle **40.00**

Hamilton Beach, 1930s, Hamilton Beach, Racine, WI, Model "G", cream metal, black Bakelite handle, lever off–on control, mix guide in window below handle, bowl control lever, lifts off base to be portable, two white glass bowls **35.00**

Hobart Kitchen Aid, 1939, Model K 4–B, looks like today's models, but quite a bit heavier, cream body trimmed in heavy aluminum, heavy cast aluminum bowl screws to base   **50.00**

Sunbeam Mixmaster, early 1930s, Chicago Flexible Shaft Co Attachments, fit most models

Bean slicer	**20.00**
Cabinet, 60½ x 24"	**175.00**
Can opener	**5.00**
Churn	**25.00**
Coffee grinder	**25.00**
Drink mixer	**15.00**
Grater, slicer shredder, three blades	**25.00**
Grinder/chopper	**8.00**
Juicer, mayonnaise maker	**8.00**
Knife sharpener	**8.00**
Pea sheller	**8.00**
Potato peeler	**20.00**
Power unit	**8.00**
Ricer	**20.00**
Silver polisher and buffer	**2.00**

POPCORN POPPERS

Berstead, 1930s, Berstead Mfg Co, Model #302, sq, chrome, box body with circular int., Fry glass lid, large black knob on top, rod through top for stirring **45.00**

Excel, 1920s, Excel Electric Co, Muncie, IN, one pc cylindrical nickel body, metal handles form legs, lock–down levers, black wooden hand crank knob, top vent holes . . .   **25.00**

Manning Bowman, early 1940s, Manning Bowman Co, Meriden, CT, Model #500, detachable, large aluminum container, chrome hotplate, floral emb glass lid, black Bakelite knob, unused **15.00**

Rapaport, 1920s, Rapaport Bros, Inc, Chicago, IL, sq black base, metal legs, round aluminum upper part, at-

tached lid and red knob, chrome handle squeeze through slot in side to agitate corn, 5½" **25.00**

US Mfg Corp, Decatur, IL, 1930s, #1, all one unit, cylindrical, rounded body, painted aluminum and red, top crank, three red vertical wooden dowel legs **20.00**

White Cross, late 1910s, National Stamping & Electrical Co, Chicago, tin can base with heater and cord, wire basket fits into can, metal top with stirrer mounted through handle, side wooden handle **30.00**

TOASTERS

Dominion, mid 1920s, Dominion Mfg Co, Minneapolis, MN, flip–flop type, bright chrome pierced body, green wooden handles, Bakelite tab door openers, never used **30.00**

Edison, mid to late 1910s, Edison Appliance Co, NY, Cat. #214–T–5, nickel open body, free swinging tab closures at top, single side knob, removable toast warming rack **45.00**

General Electric, 1908, Model D–12, white porcelain base, wire body, removable wire toast rack, porcelain plug with screw in socket cord
Complete, decorated **175.00**
Complete, plain **150.00**

General Mills, early 1940s, General Mills, Minneapolis, MN, Cat #GM 5A, two slice pop–up chrome body, white dec sides, black Bakelite base, a.c. or d.c., red knob, light/dark control **20.00**

Heat Master, 1923–25, sq chrome body, rounded corners, end opening, two slice, manual operation, black Bakelite handle and feet **30.00**

Kenmore, early 1940s, Sears, Roebuck & Co, Chicago, IL, mechanical, two slice, pop–up, chrome body, rounded edges and sides, black Bakelite handles, mechanical clock mechanism, light/dark control **15.00**

Knapp Monarch Reverso, 1930, Cat. #505, light weight rect nickel body, rounded corners, black painted base, flip–flop doors with tab handles, no mica, wires just stretched across . . .   **15.00**

Manning Bowman, early 1920s, Cat. #1225, open nickel body, black Bakelite knobs that open toast cages that turn completely over **55.00**

Miracle, late 1930s, Miracle Electric Co, Chicago, Cat. #210, slightly rounded gray enamel body, black

Bakelite handles, flip–flop type, unused **30.00**
Montgomery Ward, mid 1930s, Montgomery Ward & Co, Chicago, IL, Model #94–KM 2298–B, flip–flop type, solid nickel chrome body, end Bakelite handle, both doors open simultaneously **18.00**
Steel Craft, late 1920s, open, painted green wire construction, flip–flop type, red painted wooden knobs and feet **35.00**
Sunbeam, 1936, Sunbeam Corp, Chicago, IL, Art Deco design, rect, rounded corners, chrome, black Bakelite base, heat indicator light on front, fitted clear "Hostess" tray **65.00**
Toastmaster, Waters–Genter Co, Minneapolis, MN, Model 1–A–3, 1929, third model, Art Deco, chrome body, vertically scalloped sides, mechanical clock mechanism, light/dark knob **35.00**
Universal, Landers, Frary & Clark, late 1920s, mechanical, clock mechanism, circular side design, nickel chrome body, end pops open and out, Model #E 7732, double **75.00**
Westinghouse, Mansfield, OH
Toaster Stove, 1909, first toaster, flat rect body, four flat drip plates, removable cabriole legs, tray, and wire rack, orig box and paper guarantee, never used **125.00**
Turnover Toaster, 1920s, Cat. #TT 3, nickel body, pierced doors and top, flat tab handles, pierced, flat warming top **15.00**

WAFFLE IRONS & SANDWICH GRILLS

Armstrong Waffle Iron, 1920, (Pat. Pend.) Model W, first waffle maker to have heat ready/thermometer light on top, round nickel body, black wooden handles, distinctive prongs, cord, 7" d **45.00**
Berstead Mfg Co, Fostoria, OH and Oaksville, Ontario, Canada
Victorian Sandwich Grill, 1920s, rect nickel body, permanent plates, flared legs, curved mounts, black turned handles, 10" l **20.00**
Waffle Iron, 1930s, low profile, rounded chrome body, little curved Bakelite feet and front drop handle, top head indicator and wheat shaft dec **30.00**
Coleman Waffle Iron, early 1930s, Coleman Lamp & Stove Co, Wichita,

KS, high Art Deco style, chrome, low profile, small black and white porcelain top insert of impala, black Bakelite handles **45.00**
Excelsior Waffle Iron, 1930s, Perfection Electric Co, New Washington, OH, white porcelainized iron body, four little stamped legs, plug in front, turned painted wood handle, 6" round **20.00**
Fitzgerald Star Waffle Iron, 1920s, Fitzgerald Mfg Co, Turrington, CT, solid flared base, unique handle design locks in position for raising or carrying, 7" **35.00**
General Electric Waffle Iron, early 1940s, chrome body, ivory Bakelite handles, heat control/off front lever, top dec of circle of stars surrounding stripes and leaves **35.00**
Hostess Sandwich Grill, 1930s, All Rite Co, Rushville, IN, cast aluminum body, angled at bottom to form feet, screw off wooden handle, orig box and suggestions booklet, 5" sq **40.00**
Hotpoint Waffle Iron, 1920s, Edison, General Electric, Chicago, Ontario, round chrome body, top dec, "Automatic" below front handle, rotating cold/hot in small window on front, ivory Bakelite handles, scalloped base dec **35.00**
Lady Hibbard Sandwich Grill, 1930s, Hibbard, Spencer, Bartlet & Co, Chicago, rect nickel body, cast cabriole legs, black wooden side handles, front handle swivels to form foot for top plate enable use of both plates as grills, drip spout **18.00**
Majestic Waffle Iron/Hot Cake Griddle, 1920s, Majestic Electric Appliance Corp, San Francisco, CA, 8" round reversible plates, little pierced tower on top with Bakelite cap that serves as foot for use as double grill when opened out, nickel body, brown Bakelite front swing handle **45.00**
Manning Bowman, Sandwich Grill/ Waffle Iron/Frying Pan, early 1920s, rect nickel body, drip tube, indented grill plates serve as frying pan, black wooden handles, two sets of plates, 10½ x 6½" **35.00**
Sampson Waffle Iron, 1930s, Sampson United Corp, Rochester, NY, Art Deco design, chrome body, asymmetrical wing–like flared Bakelite side handles, stationary front handle **40.00**
Torrid Waffle Iron, 1920s, Beardsley & Wolcott Mfg Co, Waterbury, CT, good basic design, flared base, 7½" round plate, chrome body, green up–turned

handles, front knob, window on front indicates "too cold," "too hot," and "bake" 35.00
Universal Waffle Iron, 1930s, Universal, Landers, Frary & Clark, part of larger breakfast set, large floral dec porcelain inset into chrome body, pierced round flared pedestal base with up–turned handles, fancy mounted front drop handle, light/dark adjustment 60.00
Westinghouse Waffle Iron, patent date 1905–21, Westinghouse E & M Co, East Pittsburgh, PA, earliest Westinghouse waffle iron, rect chrome body, mechanical front handle, wooden hand hold, removable cabriole legs slip into body slots, off/on switch ... 75.00

ELEPHANTS

Collecting Hints: There is a vast number of elephant shaped or elephant related items. Concentrate on one type of object (toys, vases, bookends, etc.), one substance (china, wood, paper), one chronological period, or one type of elephant—African or Indian. The elephants of Africa and India do differ, a fact not widely recognized by the lay reader.

Perhaps the most popular elephant collectibles center around Jumbo and Dumbo, the Disney character who was a circus outcast and the first flying elephant. The "GOP" material is usually left to the political collector.

Because of the large number of items available, stress quality. Study the market carefully before buying. Elephant collecting is subject to phases of popularity, with its level being modest at the current time.

History: The elephant held a unique fascination to early Americans. Early specimens were shown in barns and moved at night to avoid a free look. The arrival of Jumbo in England, his subsequent purchase by P. T. Barnum, and his removal to America brought elephant mania to new heights.

American zoological parks always have had an elephant as one of their main attractions. The popularity of the circus in the early 20th century also helped draw continual attention to the elephant, through posters, setup, the parade, and center ring.

Hunting elephants was considered "big game" sport; participants included President Theodore Roosevelt. The search always was for the largest known example. It is not unexpected that it is an elephant that dominates the entrance to the Museum of Natural History of the Smithsonian Institution in Washington, D.C.

Television, through shows such as "Wild Kingdom," has destroyed some of the fascination of a first encounter with all real wild animals, the elephant included. The elephant has become so well known that it is, alas, now considered quite commonplace.

Collectors' Club: The National Elephant Collector's Society, 380 Medford St., Somerville, MA 02145.

Periodical: *Jumbo Jargon,* 1002 W. 25th St., Erie, PA 16502.

Advisor: Richard W. Massiglia.

ABC Plate, Wild Animals—The Elephant, ceramic, dark brown transfer, green enameled highlights, alphabet border, Staffordshire, 7½" d 75.00
Ashtray
    Dedham, 3¾" d 330.00
    Occupied Japan 12.00
Automaton
    Jumbo the Bubble Blowing Elephant 100.00
    Mambo the Drumming Elephant ... 130.00
Baby Bottle, glass, emb elephant, wide mouth, 1930s, 8 oz 30.00
Bank
    Cast Iron, mechanical, elephant with howdah, Penny Lane, #173 ..... 770.00
    Ceramic, pink glaze, Rosemeade ... 95.00
    Chalkware, Dumbo, 8¾" h 20.00
    Metal, still, seated elephant 35.00
Blotter, rocker, amethyst glass, figural elephant 85.00
Bottle Opener, cast iron, seated, flat, painted pink 135.00
Brooch, Bakelite, multicolor, movable legs, 1930s, 1¾ x 2½" 25.00

Children's Book, *Kellogg's Funny Jungleland Moving Pictures,* **copyright 1909, Patented Jan. 15, 1907, published by W. K. Kellogg, $17.50.**

Butter Dish, frosted elephant finial   . . .   **350.00**
Calling Card Holder, cast iron, Hubley   **150.00**
Chocolate Mold, standing elephant . . .   **65.00**
Cookie Jar, figural, McCoy **45.00**
Creamer, Shawnee **25.00**
Doily, crocheted, elephant in center,
8½" w **25.00**
Doorstop, cast iron, Bradley Hubbard .   **190.00**
Figure
   Carnival Chalkware **20.00**
   Glass, red **55.00**
   Pottery
      Rookwood, brown, #6490 . . . . . .   **135.00**
      Zsolnay, green **60.00**
Hair Brush, baby's celluloid **15.00**
Incense Burner, bronze, Art Deco ele-
phant, trunk handles, sgd foo dog
finial, French **125.00**
Jar, peanut butter, emb Jumbo, 4 oz . . .   **25.00**
Lamp, ceramic, Dumbo **55.00**
Letter Opener, celluloid, painted de-
tails, elephant head, trunk raised . . .   **30.00**
Mug, Nixon and Agnew, sand white
glaze, Frankoma, 1968 . . . .   **55.00**
Napkin, "Win With Wilkie!," elephant
logo, red, white, and blue **15.00**
Night Lamp, carved ivory, cylindrical,
two elephants circling tree, intricate
openwork flowers at top, India,
1950s **125.00**
Nodder, Alex Ceramics **20.00**
Nutcracker, brass **80.00**
Paper Dolls, Dumbo, mint, uncut **45.00**
Paperweight, Rookwood factory label,
dated 3–5–30, 3¼ x 4¼" **250.00**
Pin, green elephant, rhinestone trim,
Hattie Carnegie, 2" l **50.00**
Pin Tray, elephant holding shell,
Bavarian **18.00**
Planter, blue, Rosemeade, 5" h **60.00**
Plate, "I Like Ike!," elephant **20.00**
Poster, Le Nil Cigarette Papers, trumpet-
ing elephant, litho, linen backing,
French, 47 x 58" **200.00**
Powder Jar, cov, double elephant, green
frosted **35.00**
Razor Blade Bank, figural **15.00**
Rug, three elephants each with blanket
across back lettered "We Bring,"
"You," and "Luck," gray, white, pur-
ple, and shades of gold and blue, 30
x 60" **400.00**
Salt and Pepper Shakers, pr
   Ceramic Arts Studio **35.00**
   Rosemeade **40.00**
Soap, Elmer, Castle Soap **30.00**
Sprinkler Bottle, ceramic, gray and
pink, 6" h **35.00**
Stuffed Toy, Steiff **75.00**
Tape Measure, figural **30.00**
Teapot, figural, orange luster, Nippon . .   **125.00**
Toothpick Holder, glass, amber **15.00**

Toy
   Dumbo Carousel, tin, windup, three
   Dumbo figures, litho Disney char-
   acters, Louis Marx, 5" h **715.00**
   Wood, pull toy **20.00**
Tray, wood, ivory inlay, four elephants
walking up hill, one in foreground,
tree design carved in wood **450.00**
Vase
   Austrian, elephant handles **25.00**
   Satsuma, elephant handles, diapered
   top, Nishikisa, c1920, 16" h **150.00**
Walking Stick, rosewood shaft, carved
ivory elephant head handle, ivory tip   **250.00**
Whiskey Bottle, Jim Beam, 1956 . . . . .   **30.00**

FARM COLLECTIBLES

Collecting Hints: The country look makes farm implements and other items very popular with interior decorators. Often items are varnished or refinished to make them more appealing, but in fact this lowers their value to the serious collector.

Farm items were used heavily; collectors should look for signs of use to add individuality and authenticity to the pieces.

When collecting farm toys, it is best to specialize in a single type of model, e.g., cast iron; models by one specific company; models of one type of farm machinery; or models in one size—1/16 scale being the most popular.

History: Initially farm products were made by local craftsmen—the blacksmith, wheelwright, or the farmer himself. Product designs varied greatly.

The industrial age and the "golden age" of American agriculture go hand in hand. By 1880–1900 manufacturers saw the farm market as an important source of sales. Farmers demanded quality products, capable of withstanding hard use. In the 1940s urban growth began to draw attention away from the rural areas and consolidation of farms took place. Bigger machinery was developed. Farm collectibles after 1940 have not yet achieved great popularity.

The vast majority of farm models date from the early 1920s to the present. Manufacturers of farm equipment such as John Deere, International Harvester, Massey–Ferguson, Ford, and White Motors issued models to correspond to their full–sized products. These firms contracted with America's leading toy manufacturers, such as Arcade Company, Dent, Ertl, Hubley, Killgore, and Vindex, to make the models.

References: Bristol Wagon & Carriage Works, Ltd., *Bristol Wagon & Carriage Illustrated Catalog 1900*, Dover, 1994; Terri Clemens, *American Family Farm Antiques*, Wallace–Homestead,

1994; Raymond E. Crilley and Charles E. Burkholder, *International Directory of Model Farm Tractors,* Schiffer Publishing, 1985; David Erb and Eldon Brumbaugh, *Full Steam Ahead: J. I. Case Tractors & Equipment, 1842–1955,* American Society of Agricultural Engineers, 1993; Carol Belanger Grafton (ed.), *Horses and Horse–Drawn Vehicles: Pictorial Archive,* Dover, 1994; Lar Hothem, *Collecting Farm Antiques: Identification and Values,* Books Americana, 1982; Douglas R. Hurt, *American Farm Tools from Hand–Power to Steam Power,* Sunflower University Press, 1982; Norman E. Martinus and Harry L. Rinker, *Warman's Paper,* Wallace–Homestead, 1994; Jim Moffet, *American Corn Huskers: A Patent History,* Off Beat Books, 1994; Dana Gehman Morykan and Harry L. Rinker, *Warman's Country Antiques & Collectibles, Second Edition* Wallace–Homestead, 1994; Dave Nolt, *Farm Toy Price Guide, 1988 Edition,* published by author, 1988; Richard Sonnek, *Dick's Farm Toy Price Guide & Checklist: Tractors and Machinery, 1886–1990,* published by author, 1990.

Periodicals: *Antique Power,* PO Box 1000, Westerville, OH 43081; *Farm & Horticultural Equipment Collector, Kelsey House, 77 High St., Beckenham Kent BR3 1AN England;* Farm Antiques News 812 N. Third St, Tarkio, MO 64491; *Rusty Iron Monthly,* PO Box 342, Sandwich, IL 60548; *Spec–Tuclar News,* PO Box 324, Dyersville, IA 52040; *The Belt Pulley,* PO Box 83, Nokomis, IL 62075; *The Country Wagon Journal,* PO Box 331, West Milford, NJ 07480; *The Iron–Men Album,* PO Box 328, Lancaster, PA 17603; *The Toy Farmer,* H C 2, Box 5, LaMoure, ND 58458; *The Toy Tractor Times,* PO Box 156, Osage, IA 50461; *Tractor Classics,* PO Box 191, Listowel, Ontario N4H 3HE Canada; *Turtle River Toy News & Oliver Collector's News,* RR1, Box 44, Manvel, ND 58256.

Collectors' Clubs: Antique Engine, Tractor & Toy Club, 5731 Paradise Rd., Slatington, PA 18080; Cast Iron Seat Collectors Assoc., PO Box 14, Ionia, MO 65335; CTM Farm Toy & Collectors Club, PO Box 489, Rocanville, Saskatchewan S0A 3L0 Canada; Early American Steam Engine & Old Equipment Society, PO Box 652, Red Lion, PA 17356; Ertl Replicas Collectors' Club, Highways 136 and 20, Dyersville, IA 52040; Farm Toy Collectors Club, PO Box 38, Boxholm, IA 50040; International Harvester Collectors, RR2 Box 286, Winamac, IN 46996.

Museums: Billings Farm & Museum, Woodstock, VT; Bucks County Historical Society, Doylestown, PA; Carroll County Farm Museum, Westminster, MD; Living History Farms, Urbandale, IA; Makoti Threshes Museum, Makoti, ND; National Agricultural Center & Hall of Fame, Bonner Springs, KS; Never Rest Museum, Mason, MI;

New York State Historical Assoc and The Farmers' Museum, Cooperstown, NY; Pennsylvania Farm Museum, Landis Valley, PA.

Ashtray	
Gehl Farm Equipment	**75.00**
John Deere	**15.00**
Book, *John Deere Model A Tractor Instructions and Parts List,* 1936	**28.00**
Brochure	
International Harvester, 3 x 5½", 1910	**15.00**
Vulcan Plows, multicolored	**5.00**
Cane, Osborne Farm Implements, wood	**28.00**
Catalog	
Improved DeLaval Cream Separators, 1910	**10.00**
Murray Co, horse drawn vehicles, 1912, 160 pgs	**65.00**
Parker & Wood, Boston, 1891, 216 pgs, 6½ x 9"	**75.00**
Change Tray, Bettendorf Axle Co, shows farm wagon	**60.00**
Chick Feeder, tin	**15.00**
Corn Husk Bag, cloth, cross and pointed rect design	**650.00**
Egg Basket, 5 x 8½", splint, wood handle	**65.00**
Egg Box, 12" sq, wood, apple green wire bail	**72.00**
Egg Shipping Crate, Bangor, ME, 14 x 28", cardboard egg holders	**25.00**

Egg Shipping Crate, wood, marked "Gardiner Egg Carrier," made by New England Box Co., Boston, MA, 13¾ x 10¼", $200.00.

Goat Yoke, single, wood, bentwood bow	**50.00**
Grain Scoop, 38" l, wood, hand carved	**75.00**
Hay Fork, 65" l, metal tines	**20.00**
Horse Feeding Box, 13 x 17 x 8", wood	**20.00**
Ledger, pocket, John Deere, machinery illus, 1930	**8.00**

Mirror, Milling and Cattle Feeding, celluloid, black and white grain mill,
c1900 .... **45.00**
Needle Book, Globe Fertilizer **4.00**
Paperweight, Southern Plow Co,
horse–drawn plow decal **100.00**
Pinback Button
Ellwanger & Barry Wire, pink, green
rim, white lettering **25.00**
Minneapolis–Moline Machinery,
multicolored, diamond image, starburst and rainbow motifs **25.00**
Nebraska State Fair, white, multicol-
ored star, black lettering **25.00**
New Idea Manure Spreader, multicol-
ored, horsedrawn vehicle, early
1900s **100.00**
Rumely Oil Pull Tractor, green multi-
colored, steam tractor image, red
rim with white lettering **125.00**
Saginaw Silo, black, white, and red,
silo image **20.00**
Poster, Ferry Seeds, litho **125.00**
Print, Battle of the Chicks, yard long,
Austrian, c1902 .... **135.00**
Seeder, push type **65.00**
Sickle, 21″, wood handle, iron blade .. **18.00**
Sign
Farmer's Union, tin **20.00**
Oliver Plows, Knoxville, TN, plow
scene, flanged **275.00**
Stevens Threshing Machine, people
and thresher, 1880 .... **1,250.00**
Stick Pin
Emerson Farm Implements, brass, cel-
luloid oval of bare foot on green
ground, "Emerson Foot Lift Farm
Implements/Emerson Mfg Co
Rockford, IL" inscribed on foot,
early 1900s **65.00**
P & O Plow Co **25.00**
Tape Measure, John Deere **25.00**
Thermometer, John Deere **85.00**

FAST FOOD MEMORABILIA

Collecting Hints: Premiums, made primarily of cardboard or plastic and of recent vintage, are the mainstay of today's fast food collector. Other items sought are advertising signs and posters, character dolls, promotional glasses and traylin-ers. In fact, anything associated with a restaurant chain is collectible. The most sought after mater-ial is from McDonald's.

Collectors should concentrate only on mint items. Premiums should be unassembled or sealed in an unopened plastic bag.

Collecting fast food memorabilia has grown rapidly during the last half of the 1980s. Efforts are underway for a national convention of fast food collectors. More than ever before, the fast food chains continue to churn out an amazing array of collectibles.

History: During the period just after World War II, the convenience restaurants were the cof-fee shops and diners located along America's highways or in the towns and cities. As suburbia grew, its young families created a demand for a faster and less expensive type of food service.

Ray A. Kroc responded by opening his first McDonald's drive–in restaurant in Des Plaines, Illinois, in 1955. By offering a limited menu of hamburgers, french fries, and drinks, Kroc kept his costs and prices down. This successful con-cept of assembly line food preparation soon was imitated, but never surpassed, by myriad com-petitors.

By the mid–1960s the race was on with fran-chising seen as the new economic frontier. As the competition increased, the need to develop ad-vertising promotions was imperative. A plethora of promotional give–aways entered the scene.

References: Ron Abler, *Happy Meal Pocket Checklist, 1975–1993,* published by author, 1993; Ken Clee and Susan Hufferd, *Tomart's Price Guide To Kid's Meal Collectibles (Non–McDonalds),* Tomart Publications, 1993; Gary Henriques and Audre DuVall, *McDonald's Collecting: The Illustrated Price Guide to McDonald's Collectibles,* Piedmont Publishing, 1992; Terry and Joyce Losonsky, *The Original Illustrated Collector's Guide To McDonald's Happy Meal Boxes, Premiums, and Promotions, 1970–1994, 8th Edition,* SKI Publishing, 1994; Norman E. Martinus and Harry L. Rinker, *Warman's Paper,* Wallace–Homestead, 1994; Jeffrey Tennyson, *Hamburger Heaven,* Hyperion, 1993; Meredith Williams, *Tomart's Price Guide To McDonald's Happy Meal Collectibles, Second Edition,* Tomart Publications, 1995; Michael Karl Witzel, *The American Drive–In,* Motorbooks International, 1994.

Periodicals: *Collecting Tips Newsletter,* PO Box 633, Joplin, MO 64802; *The Fast Food Collectors Express,* PO Box 221, Mayview, MO 64071.

Collectors' Clubs: McD International Pin Club, 3587 Oak Ridge, Slatington, PA 18080; McDonald's Collectors Club, 424 White Rd., Fremont, OH 43420.

Note: Prices are for mint condition items sealed in their original wrappers or packages and unassembled.

BIG BOY

Bank, Big Boy holding hamburger **24.00**

Doll
  10" h, plastic, 1974–78, name across
    front of shirt 2.50
  14", cloth, pillow type, litho, Big Boy,
    name on shirt 5.00
Key Chain, red, white, and black trade-
  mark, plastic 2.00
Nodder, 5" h, papier mache head,
  heavy base, red and white checkered
  overalls 7.50
Tee Shirt, white ground, red, white, and
  black trademark 6.00

BURGER KING

Calendar, Olympic Games, 1980 . . . .   2.50
Car, Burger King Wind Car, plastic,
  1979 75
Doll, Burger King 7.00
Drafting Set, plastic, blue 1.00
Glider, King Glider, styrofoam, 1978 . .   1.50
Pencil Eraser, bust of King, rubber, 1979   .75
Puppet, hand, plastic, King, 1977 . . . .   1.50
Tablet, Burger King characters, 1979 . .   1.00
Whistle, green, plastic, pickle 1.25

DENNY'S

Menu, child's, games and activities,
  1978 . . . .   2.00
Pencil, Deputy Dan 1.50
Puppet, hand, plastic, Deputy Dan,
  1976 . . . .   1.00

HARDEE'S

Doll, cloth, pillow type, litho, Gilbert
  Giddyup, orange cowboy outfit, 1971   8.50
Mug, plastic, Gilbert Giddyup, orange
  and brown 2.00
Tumbler, multicolored illus of Smurf . .   .50

HOWARD JOHNSON'S

Candy Box, salt water taffy, multicol-
  ored 50
Doll, 11½" h, vinyl head and arms, plas-
  tic body, girl, black painted eyes,
  waitress uniform, hounds tooth check
  dress, apron 12.00
Menu, ice cream cov 1.00
Swizzle Stick, plastic, HoJo logo 50

KENTUCKY FRIED CHICKEN

Bank, Colonel Sanders 20.00
Frisbee, plastic, red, white Colonel dec   2.25
Light Globes, 8" h, 8" d, milk glass,
  bucket of chicken shape, red, white,
  and black, orig fitter and wire 125.00
Nodder, 7" h, Colonel, white goatee,

mustache, eyebrows, and hair, white
  double-breasted suit, marked "Kentucky Fried Chicken" on base 12.00
Pinback Button, 1½" d, "Vote for Col
  Sanders," blue and white, c1972 . . .   20.00
Sand Bucket and Shovel, plastic,
  chicken bucket design 4.00

MCDONALD'S

Comb, Ronald McDonald, plastic, 1980   .75
Crayons, 1½ x 4" box, red, white, and
  yellow illus, orig unused crayons,
  c1960 . . . .   1.00
Cup Holder, dark blue, orig pkg 2.50
Doll
  Hamburglar 20.00
  Ronald 7.50

**Doll, Ronald McDonald, printed cloth,
red, yellow, black, and white, 16½" h,
$7.50.**

Game, McDonald's Waste Basket
  Game, 1976 . . . .   2.50
Hat, visor type, cloth, cloth patch on
  front 1.50
Map, Ronald McDonald Map of the
  Moon, 1969 . . . .   5.00
Music Box, restaurant shape, "Good
  Times/Good Taste" theme, plays
  when front door is opened, orig pack-
  age 17.50
Patch, 2¼ x 3½", cloth, red, white,
  blue, and yellow stitching, Ronald
  McDonald illus 1.50
Pin, 1⅞" w, 1984 Olympics, red, yel-
  low, blue, and white, brass, inscribed
  "Ronald and Sam" 3.00
Puppet, hand, plastic, Ronald
  McDonald, red, yellow, and black,
  c1977 . . . .   1.00
Tumbler, Capt Crook 5.00

Wallet, Capt Crook Wrist Wallet, plastic, green, bracelet with compartment to carry coins **1.00**

PIZZA HUT

Bank, 7½" h, Pizza Pete, plastic **6.00**
Menu, Pizza Pete and logo **2.00**
Napkin, paper, logo . . . .   **.50**
Puppet, hand, plastic, Pizza Pete caricature **1.00**

SAMBO

Doll, Sambo
5" h, rubber, oversized head, short legs, marked "Copyright 1972 Kings/Import/Spain" **5.00**
10" h, cloth, standing, crimson shoes, little red jacket, turban, holding closed umbrella in one hand, plate of felt pancakes in other, marked "Dream Doll/R. Dakin & Co/Japan   **12.00**
Menu, Sambo on front . . . .   **.75**
Placemat, paper, tiger . . . .   **.50**
Puppet, hand, plastic, Mother Tiger with spatula in hand **1.00**
Stuffed Toy, Tiger
7" h, sitting on back legs, wearing chef's hat marked "Sambo's," fuzzy beard, felt facial features **10.00**
9" h, knit velvet stretched over firm base, felt facial features, marked "Dream Pets/R. Dakin & Co" **5.00**

STEWARTS DRIVE INN

Mug, glass, diamond shape painted labels, orange and black lettering, 1950–60 . . . .   **15.00**

WENDY'S

Doll, 11½" h, cloth, Wendy **5.00**
Earrings, hamburgers **10.00**
Frisbee, 3½" d, Fun Flyer, plastic **1.00**
Puppet, hand, plastic, Wendy sitting . .   **.50**

FENTON GLASS

Collecting Hints: During the past thirty years Fenton has produced some of the most beautiful glass ever made by this firm. Many pieces duplicate examples made by 19th century glass houses. Since that glass is so difficult to find, the new collector has turned to this reproduction glass.

Carnival glass made by Fenton after 1970 has their logo in the glass. Milk glass made after 1973 and all Fenton glass made after 1974 is marked with their logo.

It is advisable for the beginning collector to understand and study Fenton glass and purchase *Fenton Glass—The Third Twenty–Five Years* so that they can identify what glass was from 1960 to 1980. The last ten identified years, while not covered by this book, can be studied by visiting gift shops and talking to dealers.

Many collectors begin collecting with the most recently made glass, then work their collecting back in time. For example, Fenton first started making Burmese in 1971. They made it almost continuously until 1990. By beginning with pieces in 1990, then 1989, and so on the collector will be lucky enough to put together a collection of all Burmese pieces.

History: The Fenton Art·Glass Company began as a cutting shop in Martins Ferry, Ohio, in 1905. In 1906 Frank L. Fenton started to build a plant in Williamstown, West Virginia, and produced the first piece of glass in 1907. Early production included carnival, chocolate, custard, and pressed plus mold blown opalescent glass. In the 1920s stretch glass, Fenton dolphins, jade green, ruby, and art glass were added.

In the 1930s boudoir lamps, "Dancing Ladies," and various slags were produced. The 1940s saw crests of different colors being added to each piece by hand. Hobnail, opalescent, and two–color overlay pieces were popular items. Handles were added to different shapes, making the baskets they created as popular today as then.

Through the years Fenton has added beauty to their glass by decorating it with hand painting, acid etching, color staining, and copper wheel cutting. Several different paper labels have been used. In 1970 an oval raised trademark also was adopted.

References: Robert E. Eaton, Jr. (comp.), *Fenton Glass: The Second Twenty–Five Years Comprehensive Price Guide 1995*, Antique Publications, 1995; Fenton Art Glass Collectors of America (comp.), *Fenton Glass: The Third Twenty–Five Years Comprehensive Price Guide 1995*, Antique Publications, 1995; Shirley Griffith, *A Pictorial Review Of Fenton White Hobnail Milk Glass*, published by author, 1984; William Heacock, *Fenton Glass: The First Twenty–Five Years*, O–Val Advertising Corp, 1978; William Heacock, *Fenton Glass: The Second Twenty–Five Years*, O–Val Advertising Corp, 1980; William Heacock, *Fenton Glass: The Third Twenty–Five Years*, O–Val Advertising Corp, 1989; Naomi L. Over, *Ruby Glass of the 20th Century*, Antique Publications, 1990, 1993–94 value update; Ferill J. Rice (ed.), *Caught In The Butterfly Net*, Fenton Art Glass Collectors of America, Inc., distributed by Antique Publications, 1991; Ellen Tischbein Schroy, *Warman's Glass, Second Edition* Wallace–Homestead, 1995.

Collectors' Clubs: Fenton Art Glass Collectors Of America, Inc., PO Box 384, Williamstown, WV 26187; National Fenton Glass Society, PO Box 4008, Marietta, OH 45750.

Videotape: Michael Dickensen, *Fenton: Glass Artistry In The Making, Art, Etc.,* Video Prod.

Advisor: Ferill Jeane Rice.

Advertising Sign, Jade Green, 1980 . . .	**95.00**
Animal Dish, cov, hen, Blue Marble, #5182, large	**125.00**
Animal Figurine	
Bunny, Lavender Satin	**25.00**
Donkey and Cart, Crystal Velvet . . .	**100.00**
Swan, Lavender Satin	**25.00**
Ashtray	
Hobnail, Jonquil Yellow, #3878, 1968	**30.00**
Roses, Colonial Pink, #9271, 1966–68	**18.00**
Banana Bowl, Hobnail	
Milk Glass, #3620, 1961–78	**35.00**
Topaz Opalescent, #3720	**35.00**
Basket	
Bluebirds in Winter #4, #7667	**35.00**
Burmese, #7388, hand painted roses, 7"	**55.00**
Cardinals in Winter, #7237, 1977–79, 7"	**55.00**
Hobnail	
Blue Opalescent, #3834, 4½" . . .	**45.00**
Milk Glass, #3637, 7" deep	**50.00**
Plum Opalescent, #3839, 12" oval	**250.00**
Turquoise, #3834, 4½"	**45.00**
Silver Rose, #7237, 7"	**200.00**
Bell	
Five Petal Blue Dogwood, Cameo Satin, #7564, 1980	**55.00**
Jade Green, #7564, 1980	**20.00**
Knobby Bull's Eye, French Opalescent, #9061, 1980	**45.00**
Lily of the Valley, Blue Burmese, #8265	**65.00**

Bell, Lily of the Valley, Blue Burmese, $65.00.

Patriots, Independence Blue, #8467, 1976	**85.00**
Sable Arch, Cameo Opalescent, #9065, 1980	**55.00**
Sunset, Cameo Satin, #7564, 1980 . .	**65.00**
Bonbon	
Hobnail, hand painted bluebells, metal handle, #3706	**45.00**
Silver Crest, hand painted roses, #7225	**24.00**
Silver Rose, #7225	**18.00**
Boot	
Daisy and Button, #1990	
Colonial Pink	**25.00**
Lime Sherbet	**25.00**
Hobnail, Topaz Opalescent, #3992 . .	**40.00**
Jade Green, #3992	**35.00**
Bowl	
Basketweave, Rosalene, #8222	**26.00**
Butterfly and Berry, Blue Burmese, #8422	**120.00**
Curtain, Cameo Opalescent, #8454	**24.00**
Rolled Rim, Peking Blue, #7523, 1980	**26.00**
Waterlily, Blue Satin, #8424, 9" d . .	**30.00**
Candy Box	
Baroque, cov, #9388	**50.00**
Diamond Optic, Colonial Blue, #1680	**60.00**
Little Church in the Vale, Amethyst Carnival	**55.00**
Oval, Colonial Blue, #4486	**22.00**
Waterlily, ftd, Lavender Satin, #8480	**65.00**
Cake Plate	
Apple Blossom Crest, 13" d	**165.00**
Waterlily, Crystal Velvet, #8410, 12½" d	**50.00**
Candlesticks, pr	
Jade Green, #7572, 1980	**45.00**
Lily of the Valley, Topaz Opalescent, #8475, 1980	**45.00**
Thumbprint, Colonial Blue, #4470 . .	**25.00**
Velva Rose, #7572, 1980	**35.00**
Waterlily, Custard Satin, #8473	**60.00**
Comport	
Persian Medallion	
Burmese, 1986–87	**55.00**
Velva Rose, 1980	**65.00**
Roses, Peking Blue, #9222, 1969 . . .	**125.00**
Silver Crest, hand painted decoration	
Apple Blossoms, #7429, 1969 . . .	**115.00**
Yellow Roses, #7329, 1969	**65.00**
Waterlily, Custard Satin, ftd, #8481 . .	**30.00**
Cookie Jar, cov	
Grape and Cable	
Blue Marble	**105.00**
Colonial Orange	**65.00**
Rosalene	**150.00**
Cruet	
Burmese, hand painted decoration, #7468	
Roses	**125.00**
Violets	**225.00**

Hobnail, Cranberry Opalescent, applied clear handle, ground clear stopper **85.00**

Fairy Lamp
Beaded, Crystal Velvet #8405 . . . . . **35.00**
Carnival, Currier & Ives, #8409 . . . . **80.00**
Log Cabin, Custard Satin **45.00**
Owl, Rosalene, #5108 . . . . **50.00**
Strawberry, Crystal Velvet, #9407, two piece **40.00**

Goblet
Empress, Rosalene, #9229 . . . . **325.00**
Fine Cut and Block, Crystal, #9143, 1979 . . . . **10.00**
Hobnail, Turquoise **35.00**
Thumbprint, Colonial Pink, #4445 . . **25.00**

Hat
Green Overlay, #7292, 5″ **55.00**
Hobnail, Blue Opalescent, #3992 . . **30.00**
Violets in the Snow, #7292, 1968–77, 5″ **45.00**

Nut Dish
Five Petal Blue Dogwood, Cameo Satin, #7229, 1980 . . . . **25.00**
Velva Rose, #7629, 1980 . . . . **14.00**

Plate
Anniversary Plate, White Satin **20.00**
Leaf Plate, Rosalene, #5116, 1976 . . **45.00**
Little Brown Church, Carnival, #8270, 1970 . . . . **16.00**
Mission San Xavier Church, Blue Satin, #8281, 1981 . . . . **16.00**

Ring Tree, Turtle, Colonial Blue **20.00**
Syrup Jug, Wild Rose, Hobnail, #3762 **80.00**

Vase
Dogwood, Burmese, Tulip, #7255 . . **95.00**
Hanging Heart, Turquoise, #0008, Robert Barber, 10″ h, 1975 . . . . . . **225.00**
Hobnail
Cranberry Opalescent, #3858, 8″ h **75.00**
Honey amber, #3856, 6″ h **30.00**
Sophisticated Ladies, black, limited edition, 10¼″ h **195.00**
Wheat Vase, Blue Burmese, #5858, 8″ h **40.00**
Yellow Overlay, #186 . . . . **35.00**

FIESTA WARE

Collecting Hints: Buy pieces without any cracks, chips, or scratches whenever possible. Fiesta ware can be identified by bands of concentric circles.

History: Fiesta ware is colorful pottery dinnerware made by the Homer Laughlin China Company. It was designed by Frederick Rhead. Production started in 1936. Fiesta ware was redesigned in 1969 and discontinued in 1972. In 1986 it was reintroduced.

References: Susan and Al Bagdade, *Warman's American Pottery and Porcelain*, Wallace–Homestead, 1994; Linda D. Farmer, *The Farmer's Wife's Fiesta Inventory & Price Guide*, privately printed, 1984; Sharon and Bob Huxford, *The Collectors Encyclopedia of Fiesta with Harlequin and Riviera, Seventh Edition*,Collector Books, 1992 value update.

Collectors' Club: Fiesta Club of America, PO Box 15383, Loves Park, IL 61115.

Periodical: *Fiesta Collectors Quarterly*, 19238 Dorchester Circle, Strongsville, OH 44136.

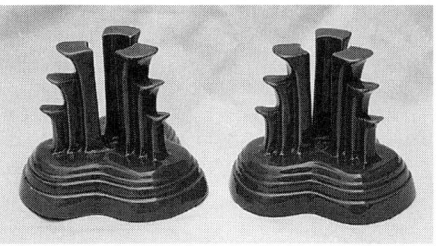

Candleholders, pr, cobalt blue, $125.00.

Ashtray, ivory **40.00**
Candlesticks, pr, tripod, light green . . . **355.00**
Carafe, cov
Light Green **145.00**
Red, flake on lid **130.00**
Yellow **195.00**
Casserole, cov
Forest Green **285.00**
Ivory **185.00**
Rose **285.00**
Yellow **110.00**
Chop Plate
12″ d, cobalt blue **35.00**
13″ d, ivory **25.00**
15″ d, red **50.00**
Coffeepot, large
Turquoise **155.00**
Yellow **135.00**
Compote, 12″ d
Ivory **165.00**
Turquoise **150.00**
Yellow **150.00**
Cream Soup
Forest Green **53.00**
Gray **65.00**
Rose **55.00**
Creamer
Cobalt Blue **16.00**
Red, stick handle **35.00**
Cup and Saucer
Chartreuse **28.00**
Cobalt Blue **30.00**
Dark Green **28.00**

Gray	30.00	7" d	
Turquoise	25.00	Gray	12.00
Yellow	24.00	Yellow	9.00
Demitasse Cup and Saucer		9" d	
Chartreuse	260.00	Chartreuse	12.00
Cobalt Blue	60.00	Dark Green	10.00
Ivory	55.00	Gray	20.00
Light Green	55.00	Ivory	12.00
Red	60.00	Yellow	20.00
Turquoise	35.00	10" d	
Yellow	55.00	Turquoise	14.00
Demitasse Pot, handle on side, light		Yellow	10.00
green	200.00	10½" d, grill, cobalt blue	24.00
Dessert Bowl, 8" d		Platter, oval	
Chartreuse	35.00	Ivory	22.00
Rose	38.00	Yellow	20.00
Fruit Bowl, 11¾" d		Relish Tray, six colors	180.00
Ivory	200.00	Salt and Pepper Shakers, pr, medium	
Light Green	175.00	green	75.00
Yellow	175.00	Sauce Boat	
Gravy, turquoise	30.00	Gray	85.00
Jug, 2 pint, gray	110.00	Medium Green	105.00
Juice Tumbler		Soup, deep	
Rose	36.00	Chartreuse	32.00
Yellow	25.00	Forest Green	34.00
Marmalade, cobalt blue	200.00	Gray	40.00
Mixing Bowl		Ivory	30.00
#3, yellow	95.00	Rose	35.00
#4, yellow	100.00	Turquoise	26.00
#5, yellow	100.00	Sugar, cov, medium green	110.00
#7, ivory	250.00	Syrup	
Mug		Red	260.00
Cobalt Blue	55.00	Turquoise, green top	145.00
Ivory, gold letters	45.00	Teapot, cov, medium	
Light Green	40.00	Chartreuse	250.00
Medium Green	95.00	Forest Green	295.00
Yellow	40.00	Light Green	120.00
Nappy Bowl		Red	120.00
8½" d		Turquoise, pinpoint	100.00
Dark Green	35.00	Yellow	175.00
Gray	38.00	Tom and Jerry Mug	
Rose	38.00	Dark Green	42.00
Yellow	45.00	Light Green	42.00
9½" d, deep, turquoise	60.00	Rose	58.00
Pitcher, water		Yellow	40.00
Disc		Vase, bud, light green	42.00
Chartreuse	180.00		
Cobalt Blue	140.00		
Forest Green	200.00		
Ivory	130.00		
Light Green	85.00		
Rose, hairline on handle	165.00		
Turquoise	90.00		
Yellow	85.00		
Ice Lip			
Cobalt Blue	120.00		
Red	110.00		
Plate			
6" d			
Ivory	7.00		
Red	5.50		
Turquoise	6.00		

FIREHOUSE COLLECTIBLES

Collecting Hints: It was fashionable for a period of time to put a date on the back of a fireman's helmet. This date usually indicates when the fire company was organized, not the date the helmet was made.

Firehouse collectibles is a very broad area of collecting. The older, scarcer collectibles, such as helmets and firemarks, command high prices. The newer collectibles, e.g., cards and badges, are more reasonably priced. This area of collecting is continually growing and expanding.

History: The volunteer fire company has played a vital role in the protection and social growth of many towns and rural areas. Paid professional firemen are usually found in large metropolitan areas. Each fire company has prided itself on equipment and uniforms. Annual conventions and parades give the individual fire companies a chance to show off their equipment. These conventions and parades have produced a wealth of firehouse related collectibles.

References: Chuck Deluca, *Firehouse Memorabilia: A Collectors Reference,* Maritime Antique Auctions, 1989; Andrew G. Gurka, *Hot Stuff!: Firefighting Collectibles,* L–W Book Sales, 1994; Charles V. Hansen, *The History of American Firefighting Toys,* Greenberg Publishing, 1990; Norman E. Martinus and Harry L. Rinker, *Warman's Paper,* Wallace–Homestead, 1994; James Piatti, *Firehouse Memorabilia: Identification & Price Guide,* Avon Books, 1994; Don Stewart, *Bright, Brass & Beautiful: The Hose Nozzle Collections of Thelma Pittenger and Donald Jackson,* Key Collectors International, 1987; Donald F. Wood and Wayne Sorenson, *American Volunteer Fire Trucks,* Krause Publications, 1993.

Collectors' Clubs: Fire Collectors Club, PO Box 992, Milwaukee, WI 53201; The International Fire Buff Associates, Inc., 7509 Chesapeake Ave, Baltimore, MD 21219.

Periodicals: *Fire Apparatus Journal,* PO Box 121205, Staten Island, NY 10314; *The Fire Mark Circle of the Americas,* 2859 Marlin Drive, Chamblee, GA 30341.

Museums: There are many museums devoted to firehouse collectibles. Large collections are housed at: Insurance Company of North America (I.N.A.) Museum, Philadelphia, PA; Oklahoma State Fireman's Association Museum, Inc., Oklahoma City, OK; San Francisco Fire Dept. Pioneer Memorial Museum, San Francisco, CA; and The New York City Fire Museum, New York, NY.

Axe, parade type, brass blade, black
  handle **150.00**
Badge
  Eureka Fire Hose Co, NY, 1¼ x 2",
    metal, bronze finish, "Compliments Of" on top linked piece, illus
    of eagle and fire hoses on pendant,
    early 1900s **30.00**
  Vigilant JFD, 1¾", brass, emb, c1930s **25.00**
Banner, Firemen's Parade, helmet, fire
  axe, and speaking trumpet **125.00**
Bell
  8" h **60.00**
  10" h, Edwards, DC transformer, 1872 **20.00**

Book
  Our Firemen, History of New York Fire Departments, A E Costello,
    1887, first edition **225.00**
  Sheboygan Fire Dept, 1901, leather
    cov **24.00**
Bubble Gum Card, Bowman's
  Firefighters, each 2½ x 3¾", color, series of admonishments such as "Don't
  Play with Matches," "Don't Start
  Fire!"
  No 4, Airport Crash Truck **1.75**
  No 9, Ward LaFrance, three Stage
    Booster **1.50**
Bucket, leather, blue paint, gilt pin striping, iron bail, heart shape attachments **225.00**
Catalog, Darley Municipal–Fire
  Protection–Police Supply, c1928, 35
  pgs **18.00**
Engine Name Plate
  American Locomotive Company,
    Manchester Works, Manchester,
    NY **25.00**
  Mack Trucks, bulldog **18.00**
Fire Extinguisher
  Fyre Fyter, brass **10.00**
  Miller Peerless, pump type, brass, 5
    gal **25.00**
  Presto Fire Extinguisher, 6", MIB,
    c1940 .... **15.00**

Fireman's Helmet, leather, gold painted eagle, Cairns & Brother, NY, $640.00.

Lantern, Dietz
  American LaFrance Dietz King **175.00**
  King Fire Dept, copper bottom **125.00**
Nozzle
  7½" l, Self–Propelling Nozzle Co,
    brass, patent 1922 .... **42.00**
  25½" l, copper, brass fittings, BC Co **90.00**
Parade Helmet
  Columbia Hose No 1, Whitestone,
    NY, high eagle, 1880 .... **150.00**
  Defiance Hook 7 Ladder Co, brass .. **275.00**
  Friendship Co No 1, leather **90.00**

Pin, Pennsylvania State Fireman's Assn, York, 1911	25.00
Pinback Button, 1¾" d, fireman rescuing infant from burning building, multicolored illus, white rim, blue lettering, dated 1898	35.00
Post Card, Sweetwater's Fire Fighters, photo, firefighters and pumper, c1912	35.00
Ribbon	
Convention, "SFE Co", PA, 1895	38.00
Parade	
Somerville, NJ, celluloid medallion	25.00
Syracuse, NY, Second Place	18.00
Toy	
Fire Engine, 12" l, red, white ladders, black rubber wheels, decals, No 301, Buddy L, 1947	35.00
Water Tower Truck, Keystone	325.00

FIRE-KING

Collecting Hints: Anchor Hocking's Fire–King is a contemporary of Pyrex and other "oven–proof" glassware of the 1940s and 1950s. It is only within the past decade that collectors have begun to focus on this range of material. As a result, prices fluctuate. A stable pricing market is several years in the future.

Anchor Hocking introduced a line of children's dishes in 1938. These became part of the Fire–King line. A popular pattern is Little Bo Peep. Like all children's dishes, these objects command strong prices.

Some Fire–King collectors focus on a single color. Jane Ray, a jadite–colored pattern, was introduced in 1945. In 1948 the color was introduced in a series of restaurant wares. It was discontinued in 1963.

Fire–King was sold in sets. Add an additional 25% to 35% to the price of the individual pieces if a set remains intact in its original box.

History: Fire–King is a product of the Anchor Hocking Glass Company. In 1905 Issac J. Collins founded the Hocking Glass Company along the banks of the Hocking River near Lancaster, Ohio. On March 6, 1924, fire completely destroyed the plant, but it was rebuilt in six months. Hocking produced pressed glass dinnerware, many patterns of which have the depression glass designation.

In 1937 Hocking Glass Company merged with the Anchor Cap Company and became Anchor Hocking Glass Corporation. Shortly thereafter the new company began to manufacture glass ovenware that could withstand the high temperatures of a kitchen oven.

Production of oven–proof glass marked "FIRE–KING" began in 1942 and lasted until 1976. Dinnerware patterns include: Alice,

Charm, Fleurette, Game Bird, Honeysuckle, Jane Ray, Laurel, Primrose, Turquoise Blue, Swirl, and Wheat. Utilitarian kitchen items and ovenware patterns also were produced.

Housewives eagerly purchased Fire–King sets and could assemble large sets of matching dinnerware and ovenware patterns. Advertising encouraged consumers to purchase prepackaged sets, starter sets, luncheon sets, and snackware sets, as well as casseroles and baking sets. Oven glassware items included almost everything needed to completely stock the kitchen.

Fire–King patterns are found in azur–ite, forest green, gray, ivory, jade–ite, peach luster, pink, plain white, ruby red, sapphire blue, opaque turquoise, and white with an assortment of rim colors. Decals were applied to increase sales.

Fire–King pieces are found with two types of marks. The first is a mold mark directly on the piece. The second is an oval foil paper label.

References: Gene Florence, *Collectible Glassware From The 40's, 50's, 60's, An Illustrated Value Guide, Second Edition,* Collector Books, 1994; Gene Florence *Kitchen Glassware of the Depression Years, Fifth Edition,* Collector Books, 1995; Gary and Dale Kilgo and Jerry and Gail Wilkins, *A Collectors Guide To Anchor Hocking's Fire–King Glassware,* K & W Collectibles Publisher, 1991; Glyndon Shirley, *The Miracle In Grandmother's Kitchen,* published by author, 1983; April M. Tvorak, *Fire–King '95,* published by author, 1994; April M. Tvorak, *History and Price Guide To Fire–King,* VAL Enterprises, 1992.

Collectors' Club: The Fire–King Collectors Club, 1161 Woodrow St., #3, Redwood City, CA 94061.

Periodicals: *The Fire–King Monthly,* PO Box 70594, Tuscaloosa, AL 35407; *The Fire–King News,* K & W Collectibles, Inc., PO Box 374, Addison, AL 35540.

DINNERWARE

Alice	
Cup	
Jade–ite	3.50
White, blue rim	8.50
White, red rim	12.50
Plate, 9½" d	
Jade–ite	12.50
White, blue rim	18.50
White, red rim	20.00
Saucer	
Jade–ite	2.50
White, blue rim	3.50
White, red rim	5.50
Blue Mosaic	
Berry Bowl	3.00
Creamer	4.50
Cup, stacking	3.50

Plate

7⅜" d, salad	3.50
10" d, dinner	4.50
Salad Bowl	4.00
Saucer	1.00
Snack Set, oval, cup and plate	6.00
Soup Bowl	6.50
Sugar, cov	5.00
Vegetable Bowl	6.00

Bubble

Berry Bowl, blue	15.00

Bowl

4" d, white	4.00
8½" d, white	4.00
Cereal Bowl, blue	14.00
Creamer, white	2.50
Cup and Saucer, blue	5.00
Fruit Bowl, blue	12.00

Plate

7" d, salad, blue	3.00
9¼" d, dinner, blue	6.00
9¼" d, grill, blue	21.00
Platter, blue	18.00
Soup Bowl, blue	15.00
Sugar, white	2.50
Vegetable Bowl, blue	16.00

Charm

Bowl, 4¾" d

Azur–ite	5.00
Green	5.00
Jade–ite	7.00
Red	7.00

Creamer

Azur–ite	6.00
Jade–ite	12.00

Cup and Saucer

Azur–ite	5.00
Jade–ite	8.00
Red	10.00

Plate

6⅝" d, salad

Azur–ite	4.00
Jade–ite	4.50

8⅜" d, luncheon

Azur–ite	5.00
Green	5.00
Jade–ite	7.00
Red	8.00

9¼" d, dinner

Azur–ite	14.00
Jade–ite	24.50

Platter, 11 x 8"

Azur–ite	12.00
Green	24.00
Jade–ite	20.00

Salad Bowl, 7⅜" d

Azur–ite	9.50
Green	12.00

Soup Bowl, 6" d

Azur–ite	12.00
Green	16.00
Jade–ite	15.00

Sugar

Azur–ite	7.00
Jade–ite	12.00
Fleurette, snack tray and cup	4.00

Jade–ite, Restaurant Ware

Batter Bowl	20.00
Berry Bowl, small	4.50
Bowl, 10" d	12.00
Butter Dish, cov	65.00

Cereal Bowl

Flared	15.00
Rimmed	15.00
Chili Bowl	9.00
Cup and Saucer	7.00
Demitasse Cup and Saucer	60.00
Egg Cup, double	18.00
Hot Chocolate Mug	18.00
Milk Pitcher	28.00
Mug	7.00

Plate

Bread and Butter	3.50
Dinner, 9" d	12.00
Grill	12.00
Refrigerator Dish, 4 x 4", clear top	15.00
Relish, 5 part	15.00

Jane Ray, Jade–ite

Berry Bowl	4.00
Cereal Bowl	13.00
Creamer and Sugar, orig labels	18.00
Cup and Saucer	3.50
Demitasse Cup and Saucer	65.00
Dessert	4.00
Mug	6.00

Mug, restaurant ware, jade–ite, 7 oz, $7.00.

Oatmeal Bowl	9.00

Plate

Dinner	6.00
Salad	6.00
Platter	12.50
Soup Plate	13.00
Starter Set, 12 pc, boxed, orig labels	65.00
Vegetable	12.50
Leaf and Blossom, boxed set	15.00

Peach Lustre

Bowl, 4⅞" d	3.50
Creamer and Sugar, ftd	8.50
Cup and Saucer	5.00

Plate

7½" d, salad	2.00

9" d, dinner	6.00
Soup Bowl, 7⅝' d	5.00
Vegetable Bowl, 8¼" d	8.50

Shell
Berry Bowl, Jade–ite	5.00
Cereal Bowl, Jade–ite	12.00
Creamer and Sugar, cov, Jade–ite	15.00
Cup, Jade–ite	4.00
Fruit Bowl, Jade–ite	6.00

Plate
7" d, salad, Jade–ite	6.00

10" d, dinner
Jade–ite	8.00
Luster	8.00
Sauce, Jade–ite	2.00

Serving Bowl
Jade–ite	10.00
Luster	10.00
Soup Plate, flat, Jade–ite	28.00

Sunburst White
Butter, cov, round	15.00
Pitcher, milk	7.50
Sugar, cov	10.00
Tumbler, flat	3.50

Swirl
Berry Bowl, 4⅞" d
Blue	5.00
Golden Shell	3.00
Cereal Bowl, Golden Shell	5.00

Creamer and Sugar
Covered, Golden Shell	10.00
Open, Golden Shell	5.00
Cup, pink	4.00

Cup and Saucer
Blue	6.00
Golden Shell	4.00
Demitasse Cup and Saucer, Golden Shell	10.00

Plate, 9" d, dinner
Blue	7.00
Golden Shell	4.00
Pink	6.00
Platter, Golden Shell	8.00

Soup Bowl, flat
Golden Shell	5.00
Pink	7.00
Vegetable, Golden Shell	7.00

Turquoise
Ashtray, 4⅝" d	9.00
Berry Bowl, 4½" d	6.00
Cereal Bowl, 5" d	12.00
Creamer	6.00
Cup and Saucer	5.00
Deviled Egg Plate, 9¾" d	15.00
Mug, 8 oz	10.00

Plate
7" d	11.00
9" d	8.50
10" d	28.00
Relish	12.00
Soup Bowl, 6⅝" d	15.50
Sugar	5.50

Vegetable	14.00
Wheat, bowl, 4⅝" d	3.00

KITCHENWARE

Batter Bowl
Jade–ite	15.00
Turquoise	45.00
White, hand painted floral	17.50

Butter Dish, clear lid, 2¾ x 6¾"
Clear	4.50
Ivory	8.00
Jade–ite	15.00
Cruet, salt and pepper shakers, price for set, Red Dots	18.00

Mixing Bowl
Apples
3 qt	20.00
4 qt	20.00
Beaded Rim, nested set, 5, 6, 7", price for set of three	45.00

Splash Proof, Jade–ite
8" d	18.00
9" d	22.00
Swirl, white, nested set of five, 5, 6, 7, 8, 9"	85.00
Teardrop, Jade–ite, 8¾" d	22.00
Turquoise, nested set, round, set of 3	45.00

Range Set, grease jar, salt and pepper shakers, price for set
Apples	45.00
Ivory	40.00
Red Dots	55.00
Tulips	55.00

Refrigerator Dish, cov
4 x 4", clear lid
Jade–ite	7.50
White	7.00

4 x 8", clear lid
Jade–ite	15.00
White, hand painted dec	6.50

OVENWARE

Bowl
4⅜" d, Philbe pattern, blue	14.50
5⅜" d, Philbe pattern, blue	12.00
Cake Pan, 8" square, Primrose, white, decal	8.50

Casserole, cov
One pint, Philbe pattern, blue	12.00
One quart, Philbe pattern, blue	12.00

Custard Cup, Philbe pattern, blue
5 oz	2.25
6 oz	3.00
Loaf Pan, 5 x 9", Philbe pattern, blue	20.00

Measuring Bowl, Philbe pattern, blue,
16 oz	22.00
Measuring Cup, Philbe pattern, blue, 1 spout	14.00
Percolator Top, Philbe pattern, blue	3.00

Pie Plate, Philbe pattern, blue
8⅜" d **7.00**
9" d **8.00**
9⅝" d **9.00**
Popcorn Popper, Philbe pattern, blue,
orig box **29.50**
Refrigerator Jar, cov, Philbe pattern,
blue, 5 x 9" **29.00**
Roaster, Philbe pattern, blue
8¾" l **40.00**
10⅝" l **60.00**
Utility Pan, Philbe pattern, blue, 6½ x
10½" **10.00**

FISHING COLLECTIBLES

Collecting Hints: The fishing collectibles category is rapidly expanding as the rare items are becoming more expensive and harder to locate. New categories include landing nets, minnow traps, bait boxes, advertising signs, catalogs, and fish decoys used in ice spearing. Items in original containers and in mint condition command top prices. Lures that have been painted over the original decoration or rods that have been refinished or broken have little collector value.

Early wooden plugs (before 1920), split bamboo fly rods made by the master craftsmen of that era, and reels constructed of German silver with special detail or unique mechanical features are the items most sought by advanced collectors.

The number of serious collectors is steadily increasing as indicated by the membership in the "National Fishing Lure Collectors Club" which has approximately 2,000 active members.

History: Early man caught fish with crude spears and hooks made of bone, horn, and flint. By the middle 1800s metal lures with hooks attached were produced in New York State. Later, the metal was curved and glass beads added for greater attraction. Spinners with wood–painted bodies and glass eyes appeared around 1890. Soon after, wood plugs with glass eyes were being produced by many different makers. A large number of patents were issued in this time period covering developments of hook hangers, body styles, and devices to add movement to the plug as it was drawn through the water. The wood plug era lasted up to the mid–1930s, when plugs constructed of plastic were introduced.

With the development of casting plugs, it became necessary to produce fishing reels capable of accomplishing that task with ease. Reels first appeared as a simple device to hold a fishing line. Improvements included multiplying gears, retrieving line levelers, drags, clicks, and a variety of construction materials. The range of qual-

ity in reel manufacture varied considerably. Collectors are mainly interested in reels made with quality materials and workmanship, or those exhibiting unusual features.

Early fishing rods were made of solid wood which were heavy and prone to break easily. By gluing together strips of tapered pieces of split bamboo, a rod was fashioned which was light in weight and had greatly improved strength. The early split bamboo rods were round with silk wrappings to hold the bamboo strips together. With improvements in glue, fewer wrappings were needed, and rods became slim and lightweight. Rods were built in various lengths and thicknesses depending upon the type of fishing and bait used. Rod makers' names and models can usually be found on the metal parts of the handle or on the rod near the handle.

References: Bruce Boyden, *Fishing Collectibles: Identification and Price Guide*, Avon Books, 1995; Jim Brown, *Fishing Reel Patents of The US, 1838–1940*; published by author; Silvo Calabi, *The Collector's Guide To Antique Fishing Tackle*, Wellfleet Press, 1989; Clyde A Harbin, *James Heddon's Sons Catalogues*, CAH Enterprises, 1977; Art and Scott Kimball, *The Fish Decoy, Volume I*, Aardvark Publications, 1986; Art, Brad, and Scott Kimball, *The Fish Decoy, Volume II* (1987), *Volume III* (1993), Aardvark Publications; Carl F. Luckey, *Old Fishing Lures and Tackle: Identification and Value Guide*, Third Edition, Books Americana, 1991; Norman E. Martinus and Harry L. Rinker, *Warman's Paper*, Wallace–Homestead, 1994; Albert J. Munger, *Those Old Fishing Reels*, published by author, 1982; Dudley Murphy and Rick Edmisten, *Fishing Lure Collectibles: An Identification and Value Guide To the Most Collectible Antique Fishing Lures*, Collector Books, 1995; J. L. Smith, *Antique Rods and Reels*, Gowe Printing, 1986; Bob and Beverly Strauss, *American Sporting Advertising, Volume 2*, L–W Book Sales, 1990, 1992 value update; Richard L. Streater, *Streater's Reference Catalog of Old Fishing Lures, Volume I and II*; Steven K. Vernon, *Antique Fishing Reels*, Stackpole Books, 1984; Karl T. White, *Fishing Tackle Antiques and Collectibles*, Holli Enterprises, 1990.

Periodicals: *Antique Angler Newsletter*, PO Box K, Stockton, NJ 08559; *Fishing Collectibles Magazine*, 2005 Tree House Lane, Plano, TX 75023; *The American Fly Fisher*, PO Box 42, Manchester, VT 05254.

Collectors' Clubs: National Fishing Lure Collectors Club, PO Box 0184, Chicago, IL 60690; Old Reel Collectors Assoc, Inc, 3501 Riverview Dr., PO Box 2540, Weirton, WV 26062.

Museums: American Fishing Tackle Mfg. Assn. Museum, Arlington Heights, IL; American

Museum of Fly Fishing, Manchester, VT; Sayner Museum, Sayner, WI.

REPRODUCTION ALERT: Lures and fish decoys.

EQUIPMENT

Bobber (float)
5", Panfish, hp, black, red, and white stripes **10.00**
6", hand carved, painted, dull green and white **35.00**
Creel
Crushed willow, 14 x 9 x 7", form fit, leather bound **24.00**
Wicker, center hole in lid, early 1900s **55.00**
Decoy
Pike, 12" l, tin fins, carved tail, mouth, and gills, green, white spots **85.00**
Sucker, Randall, 6" l, cast aluminum, painted gold scale **40.00**
Sunfish, 6" l, tin fins and tail, bead eyes, painted gills and scales, carved and painted body, green and yellow spots **45.00**

Decoy, trout, MI, c1940, 7" l, $50.00.

Lure (plug) wooden
Creek Chub Co
Giant Jointed Pike, #800, perch finish, glass eyes **45.00**
Wagtail Chub Deluxe, mullet finish, smooth tail, glass eyes **22.00**
Wiggler, #100, painted perch finish, glass eyes, boxed **20.00**
Heddon Co
Crab Spook, #9900, natural crab color, bead eyes **30.00**
Minnow
#00, white, red and green spots, orig box **95.00**
#150, green crackelback finish, glass eyes **55.00**
Mouse, #4000, white body, red chin, glass eyes **28.00**
Near Surface, #1700, red and white, multiple line tie rig **40.00**
Miscellaneous
Carters Bestever, 3" l, white and red, pressed eyes **8.00**
J T Buel, spinner, 1:0 size, silver plate front, brass back **12.00**
Keeling General Tom, black back, green sides, glass eyes **65.00**

Moonlight, Pikaroom, spotted, red and yellow, glass eyes **45.00**
Paw Paw, underwater minnow, rainbow finish, tack eyes **10.00**
Shakespear Co
Bass–A–Lure Jr, fancy green back and scale finish, glass eyes **18.00**
Slim Jim, 4½" l, pickerel finish, glass eyes **32.00**
Underwater Minnow, #44, rainbow color, glass eyes **35.00**
South Bend Co
Pike Oreno, green scale finish, glass eyes, boxed **25.00**
Underwater Minnow, #903, green back, silver belly, tack eyes ... **32.00**
Minnow Trap
Hand made, 12 x 10 x 10", metal, mesh, hinged door **32.00**
Orvis, clear glass, l gal size, emb name, metal hardware **65.00**
Shakespear, pale green glass, 1 gal size, emb name, metal lid **85.00**
Reel
Hendryx, raised pillar type, multiplying, fancy handle, horn knob, two button back plate, drag, click, nickel over brass **25.00**
Meisselbach Expert, 1¾ x 3", nickel finish, 1886 .... **65.00**
Pflueger Co, Akron model 1893, nickel finish, dual green knobs ... **20.00**
Rochester Ideal No 1, 2⅜" d, German silver, 1910 .... **45.00**
Talbot Star, Kansas City, MO, German silver, ivory handle **275.00**
E Vom Hofe, Salmon, 4:0 size, dial drag, 1879 .... **230.00**
Winona, trolling type, ¾ x 4¾", drag **42.00**
Rod, Split Bamboo Fly
Granger Special, 8' l, 3:2, green wraps, dark colored cane, cork reel seat, featherweight **175.00**
Hardy Deluxe, 9'l, 3:2, brown wraps, aluminum tube, 1949 .... **135.00**
Horrocks & Ibbotson, 9' l, three piece, two tips, maroon wraps ... **40.00**
South Bend, 9'l, three piece, two tips, yellow wraps, orig bag **65.00**

RELATED ITEMS

Advertising Trade Card
Fleischman's Yeast, emb scene of fishermen in boats **25.00**
Gold Medal Cotton Netting, diecut, "Fishes no matter how deeply they've hid Are Caught in the Net of the Gold Medal Kid" **25.00**
Book
Hunting Wildlife with Camera and Flashlight, George Sirjas, c1936, 2 volumes **44.00**

Salt Water Fishing, Van Campen
Heilner, c1946, illus 18.00
The Standard Book of Fishing, Bruce
Tuttle, 1956, orig box, 532 illus pgs 45.00
The Treasury of Angling, Larry Loller,
1963, 251 pgs 16.00
Calendar, 14 x 18", Bristol Steel Rod Co
adv, 1935 . . . . 55.00
Catalog
Edward vom Hofe & Co, blue cov, il-
lus, 1941 . . . . 65.00
Horton & Co, Bristol, CT, 1910, 72
pgs 85.00
South Bend Co, color illus, rods,
reels, and lures, 1931 . . . . 20.00
Label, orange, Golden Trout, trout leap-
ing from water 2.00
Poster, 25 x 40", United Airlines, illus of
fisherman casting rod, c1953 . . . . . . 300.00
Sign, 18 x 24", Heddon & Sons Co,
lures, full color 50.00

FLAG COLLECTIBLES

Collecting Hints: Public Law 829, 77th Congress, approved December 22, 1942, describes a detailed set of rules for flag etiquette. Collectors should become familiar with this law.

The amount of material on which the American flag is portrayed is limitless. Collectors tend to focus on those items on which the flag enjoys a prominent position.

History: The Continental or Grand Union flag, consisting of 13 alternate red and white stripes with a British Union Jack in the upper left corner, was first used on January 1, 1776, on Prospect Hill near Boston. On June 14, 1777, the Continental Congress adopted a flag design similar to the Continental flag, but with the Union Jack replaced by a blue field with thirteen stars. The stars could be arranged in any fashion. Historical documentation to support the claim that Betsy Ross made the first Stars and Stripes is lacking.

On January 13, 1794, Congress voted to add two stars and two stripes to the flag in recognition of Vermont and Kentucky joining the Union. On April 18, 1818, when there were 20 states, Congress adopted a law returning to the original 13 stripes and adding a new star for each state admitted. The star would be added on the July 4th following admission. The 49th star, for Alaska, was added July 4, 1959; the 50th star, for Hawaii, was added July 4, 1960.

Reference: Boleslow and Marie–Louis D'Otrange Mastai, The Stars and Stripes: The American Flag As Art And As History From The Birth Of The Republic To The Present, Alfred Knopf, 1973.

Collectors' Club: North American Vexillological Assoc., Suite 225, 1977 N. Olden Ave., Trenton, NJ 08618.

Museums: State capitals in northern states; Hardisty Flag Museum, Hardisty, Alberta, Canada; Prattaugan Museum, Prattville, AL.

Advisor: Richard Bitterman.

FLAGS

18 star, 33" sq, Navajo hand woven and
carded, natural dyes, c1930 . . . . . . 400.00
29 star, 7 x 10", parade flag, coarse cotton material, Great Star pattern, used
during Mexican–American War, dis-
colored 145.00
36 star
21½ x 36", parade flag, mounted on
stick, five point star design, star
pattern of 6,6,6,6,6,6 . . . . 100.00
25 x 22", parade flag, printed muslin 95.00
Philadelphia Exhibition, "America &
France Union Forever 1776, 1876
Centennial souvenir 250.00
37 star, 16 x 24", parade flag, 1867–77,
muslin, all printed 75.00
38 star
12½ x 22", coarse muslin, mounted
on stick, star pattern of 6,7,6,6,7,6 25.00
20th Reunion, New Hampshire Vol.
Gilmantown Iron Works, NH 1885,
printed on stripes of flag 275.00
42 star, four flags printed on swatch, direct from flag manufacturer, uncut,
were to be 11½ x 16¾" when cut up
and mounted on a stick, flag makers
prepared banners with 42 stars during
the winter of 1889 for adoption on
July 4, 1890; however, a last minute
addition on July 3 of Idaho as a state
made 43 stars necessary, so these
banners never made it 175.00
44 star, 3½ x 2¼", child's parade type,
pattern of 8,7,7,7,7,8 and five point
star 40.00
45 star, 32 x 47", 1896–1908, printed
on silk, bright colors, black heading,
no grommets 125.00
46 star
30½ x 44½", printed coarse cotton,
attached to stick, overall slight fading, no grommets for flying 65.00
4 x 5', 1908–12, stars sewn on,
Oklahoma 95.00
48 star
5¾ x 4½", 1912–59, printed on
heavy canvas type material, D–Day
Infantry Invasion, men wore them
under the camouflage net on their
helmets 65.00

9¼ x 6″, "This flag enthusiastically waved to greet President Herbert Hoover, Nov. 2, 1928," printed on stripes 55.00

Parade Flag, "Victory Day in Milwaukee, Jack & I went out w/Mary & Leo Parkinson in the afternoon for lunch & in the evening for supper w/Harry Scherriffs to Lamb's Nov 11, 1918—Germany signed peace," all printed on stripe   125.00

49 star, 4 x 5¾″, 1959–60, child's parade flag, silk, wood stick, Alaska . .   35.00

FLAG RELATED

Catalog, Detra Flag Company, Catalog #24, 6½ x 9″, 1941, NY and Los Angeles 75.00

China and Glass

Button

1/2″ d, glass dome, flag printed inside, 6 mounted on card 20.00

1¾″ d, horse button, glass dome with eagle and flag 25.00

Magic Lantern Slide, 42 star flag, c1889, hand tinted, mounted in wood 35.00

Magnifying Glass, pocket,¾ x 1¼″, oval, Voorhees Rubber Mfg Co adv, American flag artwork 37.00

Plate

10″ d, Washington's Headquarters, Newburg, NY, 1783–1883, crossed flags under house, brown printing on cream plate   35.00

1904, St Louis World's Fair, Washington, Jefferson, Lafayette, and Napoleon's faces, very colorful 125.00

Fabric

Advertising Button, Leonards Spool Silk, Northampton, MA, silk 30.00

Arm Band, WWII, 48 star flag, worn by paratrooper on D–Day invasion, two safety pins 50.00

Bandanna

16 x 17¾″, silk, Souvenir World's Fair, Chicago, 1893, brown and gray buildings in center against large red, white, and blue flag . .   100.00

22 x 25″, silk, flag inside wreath of 36 stars 145.00

Banner

In Remembrance of My Cruise in China, Japan, and Philippine Waters, dark blue background, sepia eagle resting on life preserver, draped American flags on each side of life preserver, silk embroidery, gold thread, glass

eyes, place for photograph in preserver 400.00

Portrait, against red background, red, white, and blue draped flags, copyrighted 1900 by C. Parker, cotton sail cloth, 22″ sq

William Jennings Bryan 195.00

William McKinley 125.00

Theodore Roosevelt 195.00

Calendar, 8 x 4⅞″, 1905, Betsy Ross making first US flag, woven silk jacquard, Anderson Bros, Paterson, NJ 100.00

Handkerchief, WWI, flags of US and France, embroidered

A Kiss from France 12.00

Souvenir France 1919 . . . .   12.00

To My Dear Sweetheart 12.00

Scarf, 17 x 15″, silk, Chicago 1893 Expo, panorama of Expo overlaying American flag 75.00

Metal

Auto Radiator Cap, tin lithograph, kinetic, patented "Sept 4th 1917" . .   95.00

Badge, Foresters of America, with red, white and blue ribbon 6.00

Clock, God Bless America, mantel, WWII vintage, small American flag waves back and forth as second hand, Howard Miller Mfg 135.00

Match Box, 1½ x 2¾″, Civil War period, emb, picture of Stars and Stripes on one side, Miss Columbia on reverse 80.00

Pinback, Our Flag 4.00

Stickpin

Celluloid, American flag, 48 stars, inscribed "S A Cook for US Senator" 5.00

Metal, ⅜ x ⅝″, 13 stars, c1925, 2″ long pin 8.00

Tray, litho, Francis Scott Key medallion, 1814–1914, Old Glory, flag shield border, compliments of C. D. Kenny Co., $50.00.

Token, 3¾" d, "The Dix Token Coin," Civil War, commemorates the order of General John Adams Dix, Jan 29, 1861, "If anyone attempts to haul down the American flag, shoot him on the spot," copper–colored coin, picture of "The flag of our Union" on one side and quote on the other 20.00

Paper
Advertising Trade Card
Hub Gore, 3½ x 6¼", Uncle Sam holding shoe, saying "Hub Gore Makers of Elastic For Shoes, It Was Honored at the World's Fair of 1893" 15.00

Major's Cement, 3 x 4¼", two American flags decorating display of 125 lb weights holding suspended object, full color, adv "Major's Leather Cement–For Sale By Druggists and Crockery Dealers" 12.00

Merrick's Thread, 2¼ x 4½", two infant children, one beating Civil War type drum, other waving flag, titled "Young America" . . . 8.00

Certificate, Betsy Ross Flag Association, 1917, serial #38181, Series N, 12 x 16", C H Weisgerber painting 50.00

Envelope
Civil War, angry eagle with shield hanging from his mouth and ribbon that reads "Liberty or Death," 34 large stars going around all four edges; each state has its name within its own star 28.00

Printed semblances of Stars and Stripes with 45 stars covering address side 30.00

Fan, 1876 Centennial souvenir, Eagle and Old Glory, 100 years 1776/1876 on one side, "The Horticultural Hall, Made in Japan," on reverse 200.00

Notebook, child's, Yankee Doodle/Uncle Sam striding around world on little pony, published by McLaughlin Bros, NY 30.00

Post Card, printed semblances of Stars and Stripes covering address side, picture of Wm H Taft for President, July 4, 1908, 46 stars, used 30.00

Poster, 14 x 29", lithograph, History of Old Glory, Babbitt soap giveaway 200.00

Print, Currier and Ives, The Star Spangled Banner, #481, 11¼ x 15½" 225.00

Print, Currier & Ives, "The Star Spangled Banner," 11¼ x 15½", $225.00.

Sheet Music
America Forever March, E T Paull Music Co, Columbia draped in flag, shield, and eagle 30.00

Miss America, two step by J Edmund Barnum, lady with stars, red and white striped dress, large flowing flag 20.00

Stars & Stripes Forever March, John Phillip Sousa portrait in upper left hand corner, Old Glory in center, published by John Church Co 20.00

The Triumphant Banner, E T Paull   35.00

Song Sheet, published by Chas Magnus, NY, 5 x 8"
The Female Auctioneer, lady dressed in costume, waving flag   50.00

The Flag With The 34 Stars, six verses and chorus, illus of soldiers marching with hand colored flag 35.00

Thread Box, cov, black lacquer finish, decal, picture of spool of white thread and American flag, marked "Use Merricks Six Cord Thread For Hand and Machine Sewing"
2½ x 1½" 20.00
3 x 1¼" 30.00

FLASHLIGHTS

Collecting Hints: Flashlight collecting is like many other categories; name brands count and flashlights whose manufacturer is unknown have much less value. Check for brand name and/or trademark, patent date, or patent number and any other information that will help identify the manufacturer and the date it was made. Check for overall outside appearance, signs of wear, dents, splits, scratches, discoloration, rust, corrosion, deformation, etc. Carefully look for any cracks in the metal on both ends of tubular flashlights and determine if both ends can be unscrewed easily. End caps and switches play a major role in identifying the date and make. Switches are the most reliable factor as they cannot be changed without some difficulty. The finish as well as the design should be the same on both ends. Check all rivets and make sure they are intact. Brass becomes brittle with age and it is not uncommon to find splits on both the lens ring and end caps. The lens cap should be checked for any visible chips and paint chips. The reflector may be silvered and should be checked for tarnish and scratches. A rusty spring or corrosion damage is a clear sign that the batteries have leaked and may have affected the working mechanism switch. The bulb should be checked to determine if it is original, threaded, flanged, or an unusual shape. The entire flashlight should be checked for completeness, making sure the lens caps and rings all match and all switches work.

Flashlight collectors rely on old catalogs and magazine advertisements to help date and identify their flashlights. They are especially drawn to those with detailed illustrations of switches, finishes, and proper end caps. Many collectors specialize in one type of flashlight, such as pocket watch, vest pocket, pistol, or character flashlights.

History: The flashlight evolved from early bicycle lights. The first bicycle light was invented by Acme Electric Lamp Company of New York City in 1896. A year later, the Ohio Electric Works Company advertised bicycle lights. In 1898, Conrad Hubert, who had been selling electric scarf pins, bought a wood bicycle light patent and began manufacturing them under the name American Electrical Novelty and Mfg Co. This company later became the American Ever Ready Company. Owen T. Bugg patented a tubular bicycle light in 1898. Conrad Hubert worked with an inventor in 1899 who patented the first tubular handheld flashlight which became the basis for the flashlight industry.

Conrad Hubert moved swiftly to take advantage of this unique tubular electrical "novelty." He displayed his products at the first electrical show at Madison Square Garden and again at the Paris Exposition in 1900. He won the only award at the exposition for "Portable Electric Lamps." He had opened offices in London, Berlin, Paris, Chicago, Montreal, and Sydney by 1901.

After the death of Hubert, Joshua Lionel Cowan, founder of Lionel trains, began taking credit for inventing the flashlight. He often gave detailed accounts of his invention, changing details from one account to another. However, his timetable coincided with that of Conrad Hubert and clouds the true history of flashlights.

American Eveready has dominated the flashlight and battery industry since the beginning. National Carbon bought one–half interest in American Eveready in 1906 for $200,000. They purchased the remaining interest in 1914 for $2,000,000. Companies such as Rayovac, Yale, Franco, Bond, Beacon, Delta, Uneedit, Saunders, Winchester, Sharpleigh, and Underwood also made many interesting flashlights.

Collector's Club: Flashlight Collectors of America, PO Box 4095, Tustin, CA 92681.

Periodical: *Flashlight Collectors of America Newsletter*, PO Box 4095, Tustin, CA 92681.

Advisor: Bill Utley.

Aurora	
Pistol, 2 AA batteries, combination lighter and flashlight	**22.00**
Tubular, 2 C batteries, all nickel case	**18.00**
Beacon, tubular, 1919, 2 C batteries, vulcanite case, nickel ends	**14.00**
Bond, tubular, 1930, 2 D batteries, nickel plated brass	**15.00**
Bright Star, pen light, 2 AA batteries . .	**7.00**
British Ever Ready, wood flashlight lantern, all orig	**60.00**
Burgess, vest pocket, No. 2, Art Deco checkerboard pattern, some rust, 1928	**8.00**
Burgess Sub, tubular, 2 D batteries, colorful adv	**22.00**
Chase	
Bomb Light, 2 C batteries, nickel, bail handle, donut shape and size	**28.00**
Vest Pocket, nickel plated, hinged bottom, slide switch, 3/4 x 1 1/2 x 3"	**22.00**
Delta Lantern, Buddy Flashlight Lantern, 1919, 2 D batteries	**10.00**
Embury, railroad, patented Jan 10, 1924	**20.00**
Eveready, tubular	
#2602, 1912, 2 C batteries, vulcanite case, nickel plated ends, small bullseye lens	**15.00**
#2602, 1924, 2 C batteries, black painted case, nickel ends, small bullseye lens	**24.00**
#2604, 1924, 2 D batteries, black painted brass case, nickel ends, small bullseye lens	**17.00**
#2630, 1915, 2 C batteries, nickel plated case and ends, small bullseye lens	**14.00**
#2632, 1915, 3 D batteries, nickel plated case and ends, small bullseye lens	**22.00**

Eveready, Model 2905, Glove-Catch, vulcanite fiber case, 1906, 9¼" l, $20.00.

#2660, 1924, 2 D batteries, black painted case, nickel ends, beveled lens 32.00
Eveready Candle
#1653, 1932, 2 C batteries, cast metal base, candle painted cream color 28.00
#1654, 1932, 2 C batteries, Art Deco, nickel plated, opaque milk glass lens 32.00
Eveready Daylo
Cartridge, #2690, very rare 38.00
Tubular
#2602, 1917, 2 C batteries, vulcanite case, nickel plated ends, small bullseye lens 20.00
#2604, 1917, 2 D batteries, vulcanite case, nickel plated ends, small bullseye lens 13.00
#2616, 1917, 2 D batteries, vulcanite case, nickel ends, large bullseye lens 17.00
#2630, 1917, 2 C batteries, all nickel plated, small bullseye lens 13.00
#2631, 1917, 2 D batteries, all nickel plated, small bullseye lens 15.00
Eveready Lantern
Box
#4706, 1912, nickel plated case, small bullseye lens 28.00
#4707, 1912, nickel plated case, large bullseye lens 22.00

Eveready, Model 4703, lantern, wood, 1914, 5" h, $35.00.

Railroad, #4709, 1915, resembles kerosene lantern 28.00
Round
#4702, 1916, nickel 29.00
#4708, 1915, nickel case, large bullseye lens 42.00
Eveready Masterlite, tubular
#2253, 1935, 2 D batteries 24.00
#2354, 1935, 3 D batteries 24.00
Eveready Pistol Light, #2675, resembles automatic pistol 26.00
Eveready Vest Pocket
#6661, 1904, 2 AA batteries, nickel plated, ruby push button switch, smaller size 18.00
#6662, 1904, 3 AA batteries, nickel plated, ruby push button switch, larger size 20.00
#6900, Dec 1912, 2 AAA batteries, midget, nickel plated, hinged bottom, very small 24.00
#6961, Dec 1912, 2 AA batteries, nickel plated, hinged bottom 14.00
#6982, 1912, 3 AA batteries, silver plated 32.00
#6991, 1914, 2 AA batteries, nickel plated, cigarette case type 18.00
#6992, 1914, 3 AA batteries, nickel plated, cigarette case type 16.00
#6993, 1929, 2 C batteries, nickel plated, cigarette case type 20.00
Eveready Wallite, wall hung, 1931, black hammer tone, oval shape 28.00
Eveready Wood Light, oak flashlight lantern, 1911, black 55.00
Franco
Tubular, 1918, 3 D batteries, vulcanite case, nickel ends 16.00
Vest Pocket, green glass button switch 20.00
Fumalux, #400, combination flashlight and cigarette lighter 15.00
Jack Armstrong Light, 1 D battery, black 22.00
Jenks, railroad, brass, patented July 25, 1911 .... 75.00
Kwik-lite, tubular, 2 C batteries, all nickel, case unscrews in middle of tube 12.00
Liberty Daylo, Eveready, box lantern, #3661, 1919, gun metal finish 25.00
Linemar Toys, Japan, 2 D batteries, resembles half-size kerosene lantern 20.00
Masterlite Table Model, Eveready, #2238, 1935, 2 C batteries, nickel plated, opaque milk glass globe 32.00
Military Right Angle, 2 D batteries, exchangeable lens 14.00
Novelty
Lapel Light
Political, "G.O.P. on the March" 10.00
Santa Claus, bell pull switch 10.00
Winchester, 1 AA battery, resembles 20 gauge shotgun shell, chain ... 68.00

Peerless, vest pocket, push rod switch	**14.00**
Ray–O–Vac, tubular	
Captain Ray–O–Vac, 2 D batteries . .	**28.00**
Miniature, 2 B batteries, all nickel	
Flush bullseye lens	**32.00**
Large bullseye lens	**18.00**
Space Patrol, 2 D batteries	**32.00**
Sportsman, 1960, 2 D batteries, ribbed	**7.00**
Schlitz Flashlight, 2 D batteries, plastic, beer bottle	**9.00**
Seiss, bike, 1 D battery, all nickel	**26.00**
Stewart Browne, 2 D batteries, Bakelite, mine–approved	**24.00**
Tiffany, 1966, 1 AA battery, sterling silver flashlight and chain	**50.00**
USALite Redhead, 2 D batteries, stand, red glass reflector behind lens	**14.00**
Vest Pocket, no brand, nickel plated, hinged bottom, push switch, ¾ x 1½ x 3″	**9.00**
W.B. Mfg, candle, 2 C batteries, bronze, ornate	**32.00**
Yale, tubular, #3302, 3 D batteries, double ended, flood lens one end, spot lens other end	**24.00**
Yale 3–Way, 3 D batteries, three way signal, three bulbs	**24.00**

FLORENCE CERAMICS

Collecting Hints: Florence Ceramics pieces are well marked. Names of figures appear on the bottom of most pieces. A total of six backstamps were used, all containing a variation of the name of the company, location, and/or copyright mark.

Florence Ceramics is in the early stage of collectibility. As a result, stable national pricing has not yet been achieved. It pays to shop around.

Several figures have articulated fingers. In a few instances a figure was issued with both articulated and closed fingers. Figures with articulated fingers command a slight premium.

The company used a rich palette of colors. Look for figures with especially rich colors, elaborate decorations such as bows, flowers, lace, ringlets, and tresses, and gold trim. Aqua, beige, maroon, and gray, occasionally highlighted with green or maroon, are most commonly found on economy line figures. Yellow is a hard–to–find color.

History: In 1939, following the death of a young son, Florence Ward began working with clay as a way of dealing with her grief. Her first pieces were figures of children, individually shaped, decorated, and fired in a workshop in her Pasadena, California, garage. Untrained, she attended a ceramics class in 1942.

She continued to sell her pottery as a means of supplemental income during World War II. Her business grew. In 1946 the Florence Ceramics Company moved to a plant located on the east side of Pasadena. Clifford, Ward's husband, and Clifford, Junior, her son, joined the firm.

With the acquisition of increased production facilities, Florence Ceramics began exhibiting its wares at major Los Angeles gift shows. A worldwide business quickly developed. In 1949 a modern factory featuring a continuous tunnel kiln was opened at 74 South San Gabriel Boulevard in Pasadena. More than one hundred employees worked at the new plant.

Florence Ceramics produced semi=porcelain figurines that featured historic couples in period costumes and ladies and gentlemen outfitted in costumes copied from late 19th century Godey fashions. Fictional characters and movie promotional figurines, e.g., Rhett and Scarlet from *Gone With The Wind*, were made. An inexpensive line of figurines of small children and figural vases also were manufactured.

Florence Ceramics offered a full line of period decorative accessories that included birds, busts, candle holders, clock frames, smoking sets, wall plaques, and wall pockets. Lamps utilizing some of the figural pieces were offered with custom shades.

In 1956 the company employed Betty Davenport Ford, a modeler, to develop a line of bisque–finished animal figures. The series included cats, dogs, doves, rabbits, and squirrels. A minimal airbrush decoration was added. Production lasted only two years.

Florence Ceramics was sold to Scripto Corporation following the death of Clifford Ward in 1964. Scripto retained the Florence Ceramics name but produced primarily advertising specialty wares. The plant closed in 1977.

References: Susan and Al Bagdade, *Warman's American Pottery and Porcelain,* Wallace–Homestead, 1994; Jack Chipman, *Collector's Encyclopedia of California Pottery,* Collector Books, 1992, 1995 value update; Harvey Duke, *The Official Identification and Price Guide to Pottery and Porcelain, Eighth Edition,* House of Collectibles, 1995; Lois Lehner, *Lehner's Encyclopedia of U. S. Marks on Pottery, Porcelain & Clay,* Collector Books, 1988.

Abigail, green, blue, and tan, 8½″ h . .	**140.00**
Adoline, gray, 8¼″ h	**16.00**
Amelia, brown, 9¼″ h	**150.00**
Annette	**190.00**
Belle	**125.00**
Blue Boy and Pinky, 11″ h, pr	**660.00**
Camille, blue, 9″ h	**225.00**
Catherine, on bench, teal	**525.00**
Douglas, white	**230.00**
Edward, gray suit, blue chair	**430.00**

Delia, burgundy dress, gold trim, 7¾" h, $85.00.

Elizabeth, blue dress, gray sofa	430.00
Gary	
Green	230.00
Pink	260.00
Grace, blue	230.00
Haru and Misha, red, 11" h, pr	260.00
Jeannette	160.00
Jennifer, pink, 8½" h	280.00
Joyce, pink	280.00
Karla Ballerina, matte pink	350.00
Lillian, gray	110.00
Louise	155.00
Madonna	190.00
Marie Antoinette	430.00
Mary, gray dress, mauve chair	430.00
Mathilda, tan and blue	125.00
Melanie	125.00
Memories	550.00
Mickey, blue	150.00
Rose Marie, rose	290.00
Sara, gray	105.00
Scarlett and Rhett, green and red, pr	450.00
Shi–Ti and Kiu, white, pr	430.00
Southern Belle, white	240.00
Victoria, burgundy dress, gray sofa	430.00
Wickum Boy and Girl, pr	240.00
Wynken and Blynken, blue, pr	125.00

FOOTBALL CARDS

Collecting Hints: Condition is a key factor. Buy cards that are in very good condition, i.e., free from any creases and damaged corners. When possible strive to acquire cards in excellent to mint condition. Rob Erbe's *The American Premium Guide To Baseball Cards* (Books Americana, 1982) photographically illustrates in the introduction how to determine the condition of a card. What applies to a baseball card is equally true for a football card.

The football card market is just beginning to develop. Prices still are modest. Develop a collecting strategy, such as cards related to one year, one player, Heisman trophy winners, or one team. There are large numbers of cards available; a novice collector can be easily overwhelmed.

History: Football cards have been produced since the 1890s. However, it was not until 1933 that the first bubble gum football card appeared in the Goudey Sport Kings set. In 1935 National Chicle of Cambridge, Massachusetts, produced the first full set of gum cards devoted exclusively to football.

Both Leaf Gum of Chicago and Bowman Gum of Philadelphia produced sets of football cards in 1948. Leaf discontinued production after their 1949 issue. Bowman Gum continued until 1955. Topps Chewing Gum entered the market in 1950 with its college stars set. Topps became a fixture in the football card market with its 1955 All–American set. From 1956 through 1963 Topps printed a card set of National Football League players, combining them with the American Football League players in 1961. Topps produced sets with only American Football League players from 1964 to 1967. The Philadelphia Gum Company made National Football League card sets during this period. Beginning in 1968 and continuing to the present, Topps has produced sets of National Football League cards, the name adopted by the merger of the two leagues. Topps' only competition during this time came in 1970 and 1971 from Kellogg's Cereal, which issued sets of football related cards.

References: James Beckett, *The Official 1995 Price Guide to Football Cards, 14th Edition,* House of Collectibles, 1994; James Beckett, *The Sport Americana Football Card Price Guide, No. 11,* Edgewater Book Co, 1994; Charlton Press, *The Charlton Standard Catalogue of Canadian Baseball & Football Cards, 4th Edition,* Charlton Press, 1995; Jeff Fritsch and Jane Fritsch–Gavin, *The Sport Americana Team Football and Basketball Card Checklist No. 2,* Edgewater Book Co, 1993; Allan Kaye and Michael McKeever, *Football Card Price Guide, 1995,* Avon Books, 1994; Krause Publications, *All Sport Alphabetical Price Guide,* Krause Publications, 1995; Krause Publications, *Sports Collectors Digest Standard Catalog of Football, Basketball & Hockey Cards,* Krause Publications, 1995; Roderick A. Malloy, *Malloy's Guide To Sports Cards Values,* Wallace–Homestead, 1995; Sports Collectors Digest, *Football, Basketball & Hockey Price Guide,* Krause Publications, 1991.

Periodicals: *Beckett Football Card Magazine,* Suite 200, 4887 Alpha Rd., Dallas, TX 75244; *Card Trade,* 700 E. State St., Iola, WI 54990;

Sports Collectors Digest, 700 E. State St., Iola, WI 54990; *Sports Cards,* 700 E. State St., Iola, WI 54990.

BOWMAN GUM COMPANY

1948
Complete Set (108)	**2,800.00**
3 John Lujack	**115.00**
9 Nolan Luhn	**45.00**
22 Sammy Baugh	**170.00**
36 Bulldog Turner	**90.00**
66 Cecil Souders	**45.00**
93 Vic Sears	**45.00**

Bowman Gum, 1950, 2½ x 2¹⁄₁₆″, top: #5, Y. A. Tittle, Jr., $20.00; bottom: #16, Glen Davis, $18.00.

1951
Complete Set (144)	**1,350.00**
Common Player	**6.75**
2 Otto Graham	**60.00**
20 Tom Landry	**230.00**
34 Sammy Baugh	**52.50**
56 Charley Conerly	**18.00**
91 Emlen Tunnell	**36.00**

1952, Large
Complete Set (144)	**5,400.00**
Common Player (1–72)	**11.50**
Common Player (73–144)	**16.00**
4 Steve Owen CO	**23.00**
16 Frank Gifford	**275.00**
36 John Lee Hancock SP	**115.00**
99 Joe Stydahar CO SP	**200.00**

1952, Small
Complete Set (144)	**1,900.00**
Common Player (1–72)	**7.25**
Common Player (73–144)	**9.00**
17 Y. A. Tittle	**38.00**

23 Gino Marchetti	**40.00**
46 Art Donovan	**45.00**
105 Lou Groza	**20.00**
129 Jack Christiansen	**34.00**

1955
Complete Set (160)	**700.00**
Common Player (1–64)	**2.00**
Common Player (65–160)	**2.70**
7 Frank Gifford	**42.50**
32 Norm Van Brocklin	**13.50**
70 Jim Ringo	**18.00**
101 Bob St Clair	**18.00**
152 Tom Landry	**85.00**

FLEER

1960
Complete Set (132)	**300.00**
Common Player (1–132)	**1.15**
7 Sid Gilman CO	**5.75**
20 Sammy Baugh CO	**16.00**
58 George Blanda	**16.00**
116 Hank Stram CO	**8.00**
124 Jack Kemp	**160.00**

1961
Complete Set (220)	**650.00**
Common Player (1–132)	**.90**
Common Player (133–220)	**1.80**
11 Jim Brown	**57.50**
30 John Unitas	**29.00**
41 Don Meredith	**75.00**
89 Jim Taylor	**14.50**
117 Bobby Layne	**10.00**
155 Jack Kemp	**90.00**

1963
Complete Set (88)	**800.00**
Common Player (1–88)	**3.10**
6 Charles Long SP	**115.00**
10 Nick Buoniconti	**29.00**
24 Jack Kemp	**75.00**
47 Len Dawson	**90.00**
72 Lance Alworth	**90.00**

1990
Complete Set (400)	**3.60**
Common Player (1–400)	**.02**
8 Pierce Holt	**.11**
86 Keith Jackson	**.11**
133 Warren Moon	**.09**
209 Derrick Thomas	**.14**
251 Steve Beuerlein	**.14**
311 Anthony Miller	**.11**
382 Deion Sanders UER	**.14**

LEAF

1948
Complete Set (98)	**2,600.00**
Common Player (1–49)	**8.00**
Common Player (1–98)	**34.00**
1 Sid Luckman	**75.00**
6 Bobby Layne	**100.00**
15 Charlie Justice	**25.00**

26 Bob Waterfield	. . . .	57.50
54 Chuck Bednarik	. . . .	115.00
87 Dave Templeton	. . . .	34.00

1949

Complete Set (49)	. . . .	700.00
Common Player (1–49)	. . . .	8.00
13 Tommy Thompson	. . . .	11.50
28 Pete Pihos	. . . .	16.00
49 Charley Conerly	. . . .	34.00
56 John Lujack	. . . .	29.00

PHILADELPHIA

1964

Complete Set (198)	. . . .	400.00
Common Player (1–198)	. . . .	.80
12 John Unitas	. . . .	23.00
30 Jim Brown	. . . .	34.00
51 Don Meredith	. . . .	14.50
79 Bart Starr	. . . .	12.50
91 Merlin Olsen	. . . .	27.00
117 Frank Gifford	. . . .	20.00
161 Jim Johnson	. . . .	2.00

1966

Complete Set (198)	. . . .	400.00
Common Player (1–198)	. . . .	.65
31 Dick Butkus	. . . .	80.00
38 Gale Sayers	. . . .	100.00
41 Jim Brown	. . . .	29.00
69 Alex Karras	. . . .	4.00
88 Bart Starr	. . . .	11.50
114 Fran Tarkenton	. . . .	13.50
194 Charley Taylor UER	. . . .	7.25

SCORE

1989

Complete Set (330)	. . . .	80.00
Complete Fact Set	. . . .	85.00
Common Player (1–330)	. . . .	.05
1 Joe Montana	. . . .	1.55
18 Michael Irvin	. . . .	9.00
43 Christian Okoye	. . . .	.18
72 Cris Carter	. . . .	1.35
105 Mark Rypien	. . . .	3.10
152 Andre Reed	. . . .	.55
211 Thurman Thomas	. . . .	13.50
225 Steve Largent	. . . .	.45
238 John Taylor	. . . .	1.80

1990

Complete Set (660)	. . . .	4.50
Complete Fact Set	. . . .	4.50
Common Player (1–330)	. . . .	.02
Common Player (331–660)	. . . .	.02
Common Player (B1–B5)	. . . .	.05
10 Bo Jackson	. . . .	.23
29 Lorenzo White	. . . .	.14
46 Don Beebe	. . . .	.07
170 Ronnie Lott	. . . .	.05
203 Reggie White	. . . .	.07
245 Sterling Sharpe UER	. . . .	.25
308 Barry Foster	. . . .	.65

506 Haywood Jeffries	. . . .	.45
582 Joe Montana	. . . .	.18

TOPPS CHEWING GUM INC

1956

Complete Set (120)	. . . .	750.00
Common Player (1–120)	. . . .	2.30
11 George Blanda	. . . .	23.00
44 Joe Schmidt	. . . .	20.00
53 Frank Gifford	. . . .	55.00
60 Lenny Moore	. . . .	38.00
78 Elroy Hirsch	. . . .	10.00
86 Y. A. Tittle	. . . .	18.00
110 Joe Perry	. . . .	9.00

1957

Complete Set (154)	. . . .	1,250.00
Common Player (1–88)	. . . .	2.00
Common Player (89–154)	. . . .	3.40
5 Gino Marchetti	. . . .	6.00
22 Norm Van Brocklin	. . . .	11.00
32 Bobby Layne	. . . .	15.00
85 Dick Lane	. . . .	18.00
94 Raymond Berry	. . . .	45.00
119 Bart Starr	. . . .	200.00
138 John Unitas	. . . .	250.00

1959

Complete Set (176)	. . . .	450.00
Common Player (1–88)	. . . .	1.00
Common Player (89–176)	. . . .	.80
10 Jim Brown	. . . .	70.00
23 Bart Starr	. . . .	25.00
51 Sam Huff	. . . .	25.00
60 Lou Groza	. . . .	4.50
82 Paul Hornung	. . . .	27.00
140 Bobby Mitchel	. . . .	18.00

1960

Complete Set (132)	. . . .	300.00
Common Player (1–132)	. . . .	.90
1 John Unitas	. . . .	30.00
23 Jim Brown	. . . .	45.00
56 Forrest Gregg	. . . .	14.50
74 Frank Gifford	. . . .	23.00
113 Y. A. Tittle	. . . .	10.00

1961

Complete Set (198)	. . . .	500.00
Common Player (1–132)	. . . .	.65
Common Player (133–198)	. . . .	.80
35 Alex Karras	. . . .	11.50
59 John Brodie	. . . .	23.00
71 Jim Brown	. . . .	40.00
95 Sonny Jurgensen	. . . .	11.00
145 George Blanda	. . . .	11.50

1964

Complete Set (176)	. . . .	575.00
Common Player (1–176)	. . . .	1.35
1 Tommy Addison SP	. . . .	6.00
30 Jack Kemp SP	. . . .	70.00
31 Daryle Lamonica	. . . .	25.00
96 Len Dawson SP	. . . .	34.00
121 Don Maynard	. . . .	11.50
155 Lance Alworth	. . . .	18.00

1965
Complete Set (176) **1,800.00**
Common Player (1–176) **3.10**
3 Nick Buoniconti SP **11.00**
17 Babe Parilli SP **6.25**
35 Jack Kemp SP **105.00**
46 Willie Brown SP **27.00**
69 George Blanda SP **40.00**
122 Joe Namath SP **700.00**
155 Lance Alworth **25.00**
1968
Complete Set (219) **275.00**
Common Player (1–131) . . . . **.45**
Common Player (132–219) . . . . **.55**
1 Bart Starr **9.50**
65 Joe Namath **36.00**
75 Gale Sayers **27.00**
127 Dick Butkus **16.00**
149 Jack Kemp **20.00**
1970
Complete Set (263) **210.00**
Common Player (91–132) . . . . **.23**
Common Player (133–263) . . . . **.35**
10 Bob Griese **5.50**
25 Jan Stenerud **4.50**
59 Alan Page **13.50**
75 Lem Barney **6.75**
90 O. J. Simpson **60.00**
125 Deacon Jones **1.55**
150 Joe Namath **27.00**
247 Fred Dryer **8.00**
1972
Complete Set (351) **1,100.00**
Common Player (1–132) . . . . **.23**
Common Player (133–263) . . . . **.35**
Common Player (264–351) **8.00**
13 John Riggins **13.50**
35 Willie Lanier **1.80**
55 Archie Manning **7.25**
65 Jim Plunkett **9.00**
106 Lyle Alzado **6.75**
122 Roger Staubach IA **8.00**
150 Terry Bradshaw **16.00**
272 Bob Griese AP **23.00**
331 Mercury Morris **11.50**
343 Joe Namath IA **145.00**
1974
Complete Set (528) **145.00**
Common Player (1–528) . . . . **.16**
40 Joe Greene **2.00**
105 Ahmad Rashad **9.00**
121 Harold Carmichael AP **6.75**
130 O. J. Simpson AP **8.00**
150 John Unitas **7.25**
220 Franco Harris **9.00**
401 Ken Anderson **2.90**
435 Jim Plunkett **1.35**
451 Ken Stabler **3.60**
1977
Complete Set (528) **105.00**
Common Player (1–528) . . . . **.09**
25 Fred Biletnikoff **1.15**

54 Nat Moore **1.35**
75 Terry Bradshaw **3.60**
128 Dan Fouts **11.50**
140 Lynn Swann AP **4.50**
376 Steve Grogan **3.60**
500 Fran Tarkenton AP **3.10**
1979
Complete Set (528) **57.50**
Common Player (1–528) . . . . **.05**
48 Doug Williams . . . . **.80**
77 Steve DeBerg **2.70**
160 Tony Dorsett **3.10**
308 Ozzie Newsome **10.00**
480 Walter Payton AP **4.50**
1981
Complete Set (528) **125.00**
Common Player (1–528) . . . . **.03**
55 Phil Simms **1.15**
150 Kellen Winslow AP **6.25**
194 Art Monk **18.00**
216 Joe Montana **90.00**
1983
Complete Set (396) **20.00**
Common Player (1–396) . . . . **.02**
Common Player DP . . . . **.02**
33 Jim JcMahon **2.70**
38 Mike Singletary **4.50**
133 Lawrence Taylor PB **6.00**
168 Ronnie Lott PB **2.70**
298 Todd Christensen **1.00**
1985
Complete Set (396) **36.00**
Common Player (1–396) . . . . **.02**
111 Carl Banks **2.30**
157 Joe Montana **2.30**
251 Warren Moon **9.00**
314 Dan Marino AP UER **9.00**

FRANCISCAN DINNERWARE

Collecting Hints: The emphasis on Franciscan art pottery and dinnerware has overshadowed the many other collectible lines from Gladding, McBean and Company. Keep your eye open for Tropico Art Ware, made between 1934 and 1937. This company made some very stylistic bird baths, florist vases, flowerpots, garden urns, and hotel cigarette snuffers. Catalina Art Ware (1937–41) also is attracting collector attention.

Most buyers of Franciscan's Big 3 patterns (Apple, Desert Rose, and Ivy) are seeking replacement pieces for sets currently in use. As a result, prices tend to be somewhat inflated, especially for hollow pieces. Keep in mind that these patterns enjoyed strong national popularity.

Early Franciscan lines are in the Bauer and Homer Laughlin Fiesta tradition. Stress shape and color as the principal means of separating them from their more popular counterparts. These pieces are more commonly found on the West Coast than in the East. Current collectible West Coast trendiness compensates for the scarcity in the East.

History: Gladding, McBean and Company, Los Angeles, California, produced the Franciscan dinnerware patterns at their Glendale, California, pottery. The company began in 1875 as a manufacturer of sewer pipe and terra cotta title. In 1922 Gladding, McBean and Company acquired Tropico Pottery in Glendale and the West Coast properties of American Encaustic Tile in 1933.

In 1934 the company began producing dinnerware and art pottery marketed under the name Franciscan Ware. Franciscan dinnerware had talc (magnesium silicate) rather than clay as a base. Early pieces used plain shapes and bright primary colors. Early lines include Coronado, El Patio, Metropolitan, Montecito, Padua, and Rancho. As the line developed, much more graceful shapes were introduced along with pastel colors.

Three patterns are considered Franciscan classics. The Apple pattern with its embossed body, hand decoration, and underglaze staining was introduced in 1940. The Desert Rose pattern (1941) is the most popular dinnerware pattern ever manufactured in the United States. Ivy, the third of the Big 3, was first made in 1948.

Franciscan comes in three distinct lines: (1) masterpiece china, a quality translucent ceramic; (2) earthenware, a cream–colored ware found in a variety of decal– and hand–decorated patterns; and, (3) whitestone or white earthenware.

Gladding, McBean and Company became Interpace Corporation in 1963. In 1979 Josiah Wedgwood and Sons, Ltd., acquired the company. In 1986 the Glendale plant was closed, marking the end of American production.

References: Susan and Al Bagdade, *Warman's American Pottery and Porcelain,* Wallace–Homestead, 1994; Jack Chipman, *Collector's Encyclopedia of California Pottery,* Collector Books, 1992, 1995 value update; Delleen Enge, *Franciscan: Embossed Hand Painted, Made In California Only,* published by author, 1992; Lois Lehner, *Lehner's Encyclopedia of U. S. Marks on Pottery, Porcelain & Clay,* Collector Books, 1988.

Collectors' Club: *Franciscan Collectors Club USA, 8412 5th Ave. NE, Seattle, WA 98115.*

APPLE. Introduced in 1940. Embossed earthenware body, hand decorated and under the glaze stain.

Ashtray	
Apple shape	25.00
Oval	65.00
Baker, 6½" d	125.00

Batter Bowl	225.00
Bowl	
7½" d	28.00
8½" d	32.00
10¼" d	30.00
10¾" d, divided	42.00
Butter Dish, cov	45.00
Candlestick	45.00
Casserole, cov, handled	90.00
Celery	28.00
Child's Plate, 3 part	110.00
Chop Plate	
12½" d	55.00
14" d	75.00
Coaster	28.00
Coffeepot	110.00

Compote, Apple, marked "Franciscan Hand Dec, Oven Safe," large, $90.00.

Comport, large	90.00
Cookie Jar	195.00
Creamer and Sugar	
Individual, open	110.00
Large, cov	60.00
Cup and Saucer	15.00
Demitasse Cup and Saucer	60.00
Eggcup	15.00
Flat Soup	20.00
Gravy with Liner	35.00
Iced Tea Tumbler	35.00
Jumbo Cup and Saucer	65.00
Marmalade, cov	90.00
Mug and Saucer	
7 oz	25.00
10 oz	40.00
Napkin Ring, set of four	150.00
Pepper Mill and Salt Shaker, large	225.00
Pitcher	
Milk, 6¼" h	80.00
Water, ice lip, 8½" h	115.00
Plate	
6" d, bread and butter	8.00
8½" d, salad	14.00
9½" d, luncheon	11.00
10¼" d, dinner	14.00

Platter

12" l	50.00
19" l	220.00
Relish, 3 part	55.00
Salad Bowl	78.00
Salt Shaker and Pepper Mill	175.00
Salt and Pepper Shakers, pr, small	25.00
Sherbet, ftd	25.00
Side Salad, crescent	30.00
Soup Tureen, cov, leaf handles, ftd	395.00
Spoon Holder	25.00
Syrup Pitcher	75.00
Teapot, cov	100.00
Trivet, 6" d	250.00

Tumbler

6 oz	35.00
10 oz	25.00
TV Plate	150.00

Vegetable Bowl

7½" d	20.00
Divided	30.00

CORONADO SWIRL. Dinnerware line produced from 1936 until 1956. Made in fifteen different colors with both satin and glossy glazes.

Bowl, 7½" d, turquoise	15.00

Chop Plate, 12" d

Coral	15.00
Yellow	15.00
Cornucopia, white	40.00
Creamer and Sugar, jumbo, coral	40.00

Cup and Saucer

Coral	7.00
Maroon	18.00
Turquoise	7.00
Demitasse Coffeepot, maroon	75.00
Demitasse Creamer and Sugar, gray	15.00

Demitasse Cup and Saucer

White	35.00
Yellow	15.00

Gravy, attached underplate

Turquoise	18.00
Yellow	20.00
Hostess Plate, coral	35.00
Pitcher, water, coral	40.00

Plate

6" d

Coral	3.50
Turquoise	3.50
7½" d, turquoise	7.00

9¼" d

Coral	6.00
Turquoise	6.00

10½" d

Coral	9.00
Turquoise	7.00
Platter, 13" l, turquoise	21.00
Relish, oval, handled, coral	11.00
Sugar, cov, coral	8.00
Teacup, maroon	10.00

Teapot, white	45.00
Vegetable, oval, yellow	25.00

DESERT ROSE. Introduced in 1941. Embossed earthenware with handpainted under-the-glaze decoration.

Ashtray

Individual	12.00
Oval, large	65.00
Square	75.00

Bakeware

Rectangular

8 x 9½"	155.00
9 x 13½"	195.00
Square	215.00
Bell	60.00

Bowl

9" d	30.00
10½" d, divided	35.00

Box, cov

Heart	150.00
Round	150.00
Butter Dish, cov, quarter lb	30.00
Butter Pat	20.00
Candleholders, pr	55.00
Casserole, cov, 2½ qt	250.00
Celery, oval, 10" l	25.00
Cereal Bowl, 5¾" d	16.00
Chop Plate, paper label, 14" d	85.00
Coffeepot	85.00
Compote	75.00
Cookie Jar, cov	225.00
Coupe Plate, 7½"	45.00
Creamer, individual	35.00
Cup and Saucer	12.50
Demitasse Coffee Server	350.00
Demitasse Cup and Saucer	55.00
Dinner Bell, orig box	90.00
Eggcup, single	25.00
Flat Soup	30.00
Fruit Bowl, 5" d	12.00
Goblet, clear glass, Desert Rose decal	15.00
Gravy Boat	40.00
Grill Plate	125.00
Juice Tumbler, 7 oz	32.00
Jumbo Cup and Saucer	42.00
Mixing Bowl, 6" d	80.00

Mug

7 oz	25.00
12 oz, barrel	30.00
Napkin Ring	35.00

Pitcher

Milk	70.00
Water	95.00

Plate

6½" d, bread and butter	8.00
8½" d, salad	12.00
9½" d, luncheon	15.00
10½" d, dinner	17.00
Divided	85.00
Platter, medium	60.00

Relish, divided 55.00
Salad Bowl, large 95.00
Salt and Pepper Shakers, pr
  Rose bud 23.00
  Short 25.00
  Tall 45.00
Sauce Boat, liner 55.00
Sherbet 25.00
Side Salad, crescent shape 40.00
Soup Bowl, ftd 18.00
Spoon Holder 15.00
Sugar, cov 25.00
Syrup Pitcher 90.00
Tea Canister 145.00
Teacup and Saucer 12.00
Toast Cover 110.00
Trivet 125.00
Turkey Platter 200.00
TV Plate 150.00
Vegetable Bowl
  Oval, two part 50.00
  Round, 8" d 40.00

FORGET–ME–NOT. First produced in 1978. Franciscan's only handpainted dinnerware line with an embossed basket weave design covering the center of the plates.

Butter, cov 45.00
Cereal Bowl 18.00
Creamer 25.00
Cup and Saucer 25.00
Fruit Bowl 16.00
Plate
  Dinner, 10" d 25.00
  Salad 16.00
Platter, 14" l 65.00
Side Salad 20.00
Sugar, cov 35.00
Vegetable 65.00

IVY. Introduced in 1948. Embossed earthenware with handpainted under the glaze decoration.

Butter, cov 65.00
Celery, oval, 10" l 25.00
Cereal Bowl 18.00
Chop Plate, 14" d 75.00
Coffeepot 180.00
Compote, 8" h 110.00
Creamer and Sugar 85.00
Cup and Saucer 30.00
Fruit Bowl 18.00
Gravy, underplate 55.00
Jumbo Cup and Saucer 65.00
Pickle Dish, 10½" l 35.00
Pitcher, water 130.00
Plate
  Bread and Butter, 6½" d 10.00
  Dinner 18.00
  Salad 12.00

Platter
  14" l, oval 65.00
  19" l 275.00
Salt and Pepper Shakers, pr 30.00
Sherbet 14.00
Side Salad, crescent 45.00
Soup Bowl, flat 30.00
Teapot 175.00
Tea Tile 55.00
Tumbler, 10 oz 38.00
TV Plate 195.00
Vegetable Bowl, 7¼" d 38.00

STARBURST. Introduced in 1954.

Bonbon Dish 40.00
Butter, cov 60.00
Canister, 9¼" h 200.00
Casserole, small 35.00
Chop Plate 55.00
Creamer and Sugar, cov 32.00
Cup and Saucer 20.00
Fruit Bowl 15.00
Gravy, attached liner 40.00
Jelly 28.00
Ladle 60.00
Mustard Jar 85.00
Pitcher
  Milk 85.00
  Water 95.00
Plate
  6½" d, bread and butter 8.00
  10" d, dinner 15.00
Platter, oval, 15" l 25.00
Salt and Pepper Shakers, pr, short 30.00
Side Salad, crescent 25.00
Teapot 200.00
Vegetable Bowl
  Divided 45.00
  Oval 38.00

FRANKOMA POTTERY

Collecting Hints: Prior to 1954 all Frankoma pottery was made with a honey–tan colored clay from Ada, Oklahoma. Since 1954 Frankoma has used a brick red clay from Sapulpa. During the early 1970s, the clay became lighter and is now pink in color.

There were a number of early marks. One early, widely sought mark is the leopard pacing on the FRANKOMA name. Since the 1938 fire, all pieces have carried only the name FRANKOMA.

History: John N. Frank founded a ceramic art department at Oklahoma University in Norman and taught there for several years. In 1933 Frank established his own business and began making Oklahoma's first commercial pottery. Frankoma moved from Norman to Sapulpa, Oklahoma, in 1938.

A fire completely destroyed the new plant later the same year, but rebuilding began almost immediately. The company remained in Sapulpa and continued to grow. Frankoma is the only American pottery to be permanently exhibited at the International Ceramic Museum of Italy.

In 1983 Frankoma celebrated its fiftieth anniversary. In September 1983 a disastrous fire struck once again, destroying 97% of Frankoma's facilities. The rebuilt Frankoma Pottery reopened in July 1984. Production has been limited to 1983 production molds only. All other molds were lost in the fire.

References: Susan and Al Bagdade, *Warman's American Pottery and Porcelain,* Wallace–Homestead, 1994; Phyllis and Tom Bess, *Frankoma Treasures,* published by authors, 1983, 1990 value update; Susan N. Cox, *Collectors Guide To Frankoma Pottery, Book I* (1979,) *Book II,* (1982,) published by author.

Periodical: *The Pottery Collectors Express,* PO Box 221, Mayview, MO 64071-0221.

Ashtray, Cocker Spaniel	**20.00**
Bank	
Boot	**10.00**
Owl	**20.00**
Pig	**20.00**
Bell, 7" h	**15.00**
Bookends, pr, charger horse, Ada clay	**200.00**
Bowl, Ada clay, tan	
3½" d	**1.50**
5" d	**2.50**
5½" d	**3.50**
Candlewarmer, Ada clay, tan	
6" h, 3 part	**8.00**
8" h	**6.00**
Cornucopia	
Ada Clay	**35.00**
Blue and Green	**45.00**
Dinner Service, orig box	
Lazybones, Robin's Egg Blue, 45 pcs	**350.00**
Plainsman, Prairie Green, 45 pcs	**250.00**
Westwind, yellow, starter set	**125.00**
Figure, puma	**48.00**
Honey Jar, beehive, Ada clay, tan	**18.00**
Lazy Susan, black	**37.50**
Limited Edition Plate	
Bicentennial, white sand	
1971	**15.00**
1972	**20.00**
1973	**20.00**
1974	**15.00**
1975	**20.00**
1976	**20.00**
Christmas, 1965	**250.00**
50th Anniversary	**25.00**
Teenagers of the Bible, 1973	**30.00**
Mug, large, Ada clay, tan	**5.00**

Pitcher, green and bronze, 8" h, $25.00.

Pitcher, 8" h, ice lip, Ada clay, tan	**12.00**
Plate, Ada clay, tan	
5½" d	**1.50**
6½" d	**2.00**
10" d	**5.00**
Relish Dish, 15" l, leaf, 2 part, Ada clay, tan	**10.00**
Salt and Pepper Shakers, pr, 4" h, Ada clay, tan	**8.00**
Trivet	
Kansas, round, green	**8.00**
Rooster	**25.00**
Vase, flying bird	**22.00**

FRATERNAL ORGANIZATIONS

Collecting Hints: Fraternal items break down into three groups. The first focuses on the literature, pins and badges, and costume paraphernalia which belonged to individual members of each organization. This material can be found easily. The second group is the ornamentation and furniture used in lodge halls for ceremonial purposes. Many of these items were made locally and are highly symbolic. Folk art collectors have latched on to them and have driven prices artificially high.

The third group relates to the regional and national conventions of the fraternal organizations. Each meeting generally produces a number of specialized souvenir items. These conventions are one of the few times when public visibility is drawn to a fraternal group; hence, convention souvenirs are the most commonly found items.

Concentrate on one fraternal group. Since so much emphasis has been placed on Masonic and Shriner material, new collectors are urged to focus on one of the other organizations.

History: Benevolent and secret societies played an important part in American society from the late 18th century to the mid-20th century. Groups ranged from Eagles, Elks, Moose, and Orioles to Odd Fellows, Redmen, and Woodmen. These secret societies had lodges or meeting halls, secret ceremonies, ritualistic materials, and souvenir items from conventions and regional meetings.

Initially the societies were organized to aid members or their families in times of distress or death. They evolved from this purpose into important social clubs by the late 19th century. Women's auxiliaries were organized. In the 1950s, with the arrival of civil rights, the secretiveness and often discriminatory practices of these societies came under attack. Americans had greater outlets for leisure and social life, and less need for the benevolent aspects of the groups. The fraternal movement, with the exception of the Masonic order, suffered serious membership loss. Many local chapters closed and sold their lodge halls. This has resulted in many items arriving in the antiques market.

Note: This category does not include the souvenirs and other items related to the many service clubs of the 20th century, such as the Lions, Rotary, etc., who replaced the focus of many of the fraternal group members. Items from these service groups are not yet viewed as collectible by the general marketplace.

Museums: Iowa Masonic Library & Museum, Cedar Rapids, IA; Knights of Columbus Headquarters Museum, New Haven, CT; Masonic Grand Lodge Library & Museum of Texas, Waco, TX; Museum of Our National Heritage, Lexington, MA; Odd Fellows Historical Society, Payepte, ID.

Benevolent & Protective Order of Elks, BPOE
Badge, 1920 Chicago 56th Annual Reunion **15.00**
Book, *National Memorial*, 1931, color illus **30.00**
Flask, 4" h, elks tooth, opaque white **80.00**
Note Pad and Pencil, Ladies Night, 1916 .... **35.00**
Pinback Button
  Elks Harvest Festival, AERIE 102, Nov–19–08, red, white, and blue, eagle illus **10.00**
  Member Lodge No 481 State Ass'n BPOE, Belleville, 1921, multicolored, elk on hind legs illus .. **5.00**
Pitcher, 6½" h, Louisville, 1911 .... **35.00**
Plate, litho tin, Mt Hood, lodge, and elk by river illus, 1912 .... **75.00**
Tie Rack, tie pin pad, brass finish cast metal, B.P.O.E. embossed on banner **75.00**

Independent Order of Odd Fellows, IOOF
Badge, Rebekah Lodge, 1894 memorial **25.00**
Banner, 33 x 58", felt, red, white, and blue, 1910 .... **25.00**
Booklet, Odd Fellers Pillar Encampment, 1905, 50 pgs, rules, practices, and member information **11.00**
Catalog, IOOF Costumes & Regalia, CE Ward Co, New London, CT, No. 41, c1910, 73 pages, 8 color pages **75.00**
Invitation, Arcancus #102, Lodge Chicken Fry, Elmwood, IL, 1903, 4 x 7" **9.00**
License Tag, multicolored logo, orig package **10.00**
Mug **35.00**
Pamphlet, Odd Fellows Fraternal Accident Association of America, 8 pgs, 1891 .... **4.00**
Pin, Alpha Lodge No 611, hanging oval medal **15.00**
Pinback Button
  Field Day Point of Pines, June 29, 1907, red and white, chain link and eye dec **4.00**
  One Hundredth Anniversary, Independent Order of Odd Fellows, 1818–1919, red, white, and blue, Thomas Widley photo, chain links, eye, and American flag **5.00**
Token, Lexington, KY, 1916 .... **15.00**
Watch Fob, 94th Anniversary April 12, 1913 .... **25.00**
Knights of Pythias
Catalog, Women's Auxiliaries of Knights of Pythias, Rathbone Sisters, Costumes and Supplies, Pettibone Bros Mfg Co, Cincinnati, OH, c1900, 24 pages **45.00**
Pinback Button, Founder of the Order Knights of Pythias, Justus H Rathbone, black and white, Rathbone photo **4.00**
Whirligig, 11⅝" h, carved Pythias .. **450.00**
Knights Templar
Badge, brass link, enameled, 29th Triennial Conclave of Grand Encampment, 1904 .... **25.00**
Book, *Grand Encampment of Knights Templar*, 1895, 160 pgs **40.00**
Pinback Button, Ascalon Commandery No 59, Pittsburgh, PA, 1906, multicolored, chicken standing on sword and branch **12.00**
Plate, 8" d, Pittsburgh Commandery, 1903, china **45.00**
Trade Card, Miss M E Taylor, Knight Templar Plumes a Specialty, black and white, hat illus **10.00**

Tumbler, 4" h, 36th Conclave, glass   **75.00**
Loyal Order of Moose
  Clock, figural, moose **50.00**
  Matchbook Cover **3.25**
  Straight Razor, The Mighty, blade
    with etched crown and two flags,
    moose and LOOM on handle **15.00**
Masonic
  Badge, brass link, 32nd Degree
    Mason, engraved name, dark red
    and blue enameled pendant, early
    1900s **25.00**
  Book
    Encyclopedia of Freemasonry, two
      volumes, 1921 . . . .   **45.00**
    Standard Masonic Monitor, 1899   **40.00**
  Bowl, 5" d, El Riad Temple, 1911,
    brass **30.00**
  Certificate, Third Degree Freemason,
    Penobscot Lodge, dated August 8,
    1863 . . . .   **165.00**
  Cigar Box Label, Tun Tavern, colonial
    view of American Masonic Lodge   **40.00**
  Fez, Mohassen **25.00**
  Ice Cream Mold, 5½" d, pewter, fig-
    ural emblem **15.00**
  Letter Opener, metal, symbols **20.00**
  Medal, Master Mason, purple ribbon,
    man in moon carved moonstone,
    1905 . . . .   **125.00**
  Mug, china, Rising Star Lodge, 1903   **40.00**

Masonic, paperweight, glass, Syria Temple, Pittsburgh, Atlantic City Pilgrimage, 1924, George E. Meyer, Illustrious Potentate, 2½ x 4", $28.00.

Pinback Button
  Bound For Washington, Morocco
    Temple 1900, From the Hot
    Sands of Florida, multicolored,
    man riding alligator **15.00**

Oriental Troy, NY, compliments of
  International Shirts & Collar Co,
  multicolored **12.00**
Pitcher, 12" h, 60th Anniversary,
  Newark, NJ, 1913 . . . .   **95.00**
Plate, 8" d, 64th Annual Conclave,
  Toledo, emblem border, marked "K
  & K," 1906 . . . .   **75.00**
Spoon, SS, Chicago Temple on bowl,
  Masonic emblem on handle **25.00**
Trivet, brass, symbol **35.00**
Watch Fob, J E King, Rockford, IL,
  1919 . . . .   **22.00**
Order of the Eastern Star
  Demitasse Cup and Saucer, porcelain   **18.00**
  Jewelry
    Earrings, pr, 1" d, enamel emblem
      center, two double rows of rhine-
      stones **45.00**
    Pin, 14K gold **35.00**
    Ring, Past Matron, star shape stone,
      diamond center, gold **135.00**
Shrine
  Champagne Glass, 4½" h, New
    Orleans–Syria, alligator dec, 1910   **90.00**
  Cup and Saucer, Los Angeles, 1906,
    glass **70.00**
  Goblet, Pittsburgh, PA, 1908, ruby
    flashed **65.00**
  Medal, St Paul, MN, 1908 . . . .   **12.00**
  Mug, Syria Temple, Pittsburgh, 1895,
    ceramic, gold dec **110.00**
  Pinback Button, Mystic Shrine Day,
    Pan–American, August 31, 1901,
    black, white, and red, buffalo
    wearing hat **15.00**
  Plate, ceramic, man with bandaged
    face **25.00**
  Post Card, A Little Shriner Wearing
    His Frat Pin, child wearing shrine
    hat and diaper, copyright 1908 . . .   **10.00**

FROGS

Collecting Hints: The frog is a popular theme in art work, but often enjoys a secondary rather than a primary position. As with other animal collectibles, the frog collector competes with collectors from other subject areas for the same object.

The frog has lent its name to several items—from flower frog to railroad frog switches to the attachment device holding a sword scabbard to a belt. True collectors usually include an example of these in their collection.

History: A frog is a small, tailless animal with bulging eyes and long back legs. The first frogs appeared about 180 million years ago; today there are more than 2,000 species.

Throughout history frogs have been a source of superstition. One myth says frogs fall from the sky during rain.

The frog in character form has appeared in cartoons, on television and in movies. Flip the Frog is one example. The Buster Brown show featured Froggy the Gremlin. Kermit the Frog is the star of the Muppets, both on television and in the movies.

Collectors' Club: The Frog Pond, PO Box 193, Beech Grove, IN 46107.

Museum: Frog Fantasies Museum, Eureka Springs, AR.

Advertising Trade Card, Lancaster
  Dental Parlors, 4¼ x 3¹⁄₁₆" **6.00**
Bank, Leap Frog, cast iron **145.00**

Candleholders, pr, weightlifters, bronze, painted, green bodies, red eyes, black and white trunks, 4¼" w, 4¾" h, $325.00.

Candy Container, 3⅞" d, frog and chick,
  oval, yellow crepe, cloth animals . . **40.00**
Cane Handle, figural, silvered white
  metal, inset glass eyes, early 1900s **50.00**
Clicker, 3" l, Life of Party Products,
  Kirchhof, Newark, NJ **6.00**
Cookie Jar, figural, marked "2645 USA" **7.00**
Figure
  Frog sitting on leaf, 1", Vienna **25.00**
  Reclining frog wearing jacket **15.00**
Match Holder, 4" l, cast iron, two pcs,
  Pointer Stoves and Ranges adv, match
  striker under mouth **225.00**
Movie Poster, Frogs, Ray Milland, Sam
  Elliot, American International, 1972 **25.00**
Mug, 4½" h, figural frog inside bottom,
  majolica **120.00**
Paperweight, figural, cast iron **30.00**
Planter
  2 x 3 x 3½", Flip the Frog, chased by
    turkey **32.00**
  3 x 3", frog playing instruments near
    water lily **12.00**

Stickpin, figural, bronze, frog wearing
  suit, c1900 . . . . **20.00**
Toothpick Holder, pulling shell
  Glass, amber **40.00**
  Silverplated **55.00**
Stuffed Toy, Froggy, 5", Steiff **45.00**
Toy
  Froggy the Gremlin, 5" h, Sun Rubber **30.00**
  Wind–up, cloth over tin, glass eyes,
    Germany **50.00**

FRUIT JARS

Collecting Hints: Old canning jars can be found at flea markets, household sales, and antiques shows. Interest in fruit jars is stable.

Some collectors base their collections on a specific geographical area, others on one manufacturer or one color. Another possible way to collect fruit jars is by patent date. Over 50 different types bear a patent date of 1858. Note: The patent date does not mean the jar was made in that year.

History: An innovative Philadelphia glass maker, Thomas W. Dyott, began promoting his glass canning jars in 1829. John Landis Mason patented the screw type canning jar on November 30, 1858. The progress of the American glass industry and manufacturing processes can be studied through fruit jars. Early handmade jars show bits of local history.

Many ways were devised to close the jars securely. Lids of fruit jars can be a separate collectible, but most collectors feel it is more desirous to have a complete fruit jar. Closures can be as simple as cork or wax seal. Other closures include zinc lids, glass, wire bails, metal screw bands, and today's rubber sealed metal lids.

References: Douglas M. Leybourne, Jr., *The Collector's Guide To Old Fruit Jars, Red Book No. 7*, published by author, 1993; Dick Roller, *Standard Fruit Jar Reference*, published by author, 1987; Dick Roller, *Supplementary Price Guide to Standard Fruit Jar Reference*, published by author, 1987; Bill Schroeder, *1000 Fruit Jars: Priced And Illustrated*, 5th Edition, Collector Books, 1987, 1995 value update.

Periodical: *Fruit Jar Newsletter*, 364 Gregory Avenue, West Orange, NJ 07052.

Collectors' Clubs: Ball Collectors Club, 22203 Doncaster, Riverview, MI 48192; Midwest Antique Fruit Jar & Bottle Club, PO Box 38, Flat Rock, IN 47234.

Atlas E–Z Seal, quart, blue glass, raised letters, glass lid, wire bail, $10.00.

Hand Made

ARS, ground glass stopper reads "A. Kline Patd Oct. 27, 63"	65.00
Atlas E–Z Seal, aqua, pint, glass lid, wire bail	10.00
Ball, green, pint, zinc lid	2.00
Canton Domestic Fruit Jar, clear, quart, glass lid, wire bail	75.00
Crystal Mason, The, clear, pint, zinc lid	8.00
Dandy, The, Trade Mark, amber, quart, glass lid, wire bail	125.00
EC Flaccus Co, milk glass, pint, threaded lid, elk head and floral design	250.00
Excelsior, aqua, quart, glass lid, screw band	100.00
Federal Fruit Jar, olive, quart, glass lid, wire bail	95.00
Fruit Growers Co, Trade Mark, aqua, pint, wax seal	50.00
Heroine, The, aqua, quart, glass lid, screw band	30.00
Hoosier Jar, aqua, quart, threaded glass lid	325.00
JP Smith & Son Co, Pittsburgh, aqua, quart, wax seal	35.00
Kentucky LG Co, green, quart, wax seal	55.00
Kerr Economy Trade Mark, clear, pint, metal lid, clip	4.00
Kline, blue, quart, glass stopper reads "AR Kline Pat Oct 27 1863"	30.00
Mason's, yellow, quart, zinc lid	25.00
Mason's Improved, aqua, pint, glass lid, screw band	4.00
Pacific SF Glass Works, aqua, quart, glass lid, screw band	30.00
Penn, The, green, quart, wax sealer, footed base	125.00
Red Mason's Patent Nov 30th 1858, aqua, pint, zinc lid	10.00

Security Seal, clear, quart, glass lid, wire bail	6.00
Whitney Mason Pat'd 1858, aqua, quart, zinc lid	20.00
Winslow Improved Valve Jar, The, aqua, quart, glass lid, iron yoke, thumb screw	200.00
Woodbury, aqua, pint, glass lid, metal clip	25.00
Yeoman's Fruit Bottle, aqua, quart, half gallon, cork stopper	50.00

Machine Made

Agee Queen, pint, clear, glass lid, twin toggles	10.00
Amazon Swift Seal, clear, quart, glass lid, wire bail	5.00
Anchor Hocking Mason, clear, square, pint	2.00
Atlas Mason, olive, quart, zinc lid . .	12.00
Atlas Special, blue, pint, zinc lid . . .	25.00
Ball Deluxe Jar, clear, pint, glass lid, wire bail	4.00
Ball Mason, olive, quart, zinc lid, ground lip	25.00
Banner Wide Mouth, aqua, pint, glass lid, wire bail	10.00
Collins & Chapman, Wheeling, WV, aqua, quart, band around mouth	800.00
Double Safety, clear, half pint, glass lid, wire bail	5.00
Durham, green, quart, glass lid, wire bail	15.00
Gem 1908, clear, quart, glass lid, screw band	6.00
King, clear, pint, glass lid, wire bail	15.00
Mansfield Improved Mason, light green, quart, glass lid, screw band	15.00
New Mason Vacuum Fruit Jar, Knowlton Patent June 9th 1908, aqua, quart, glass lid, wire clamp	50.00
Newmark Special Extra Mason Jar, clear, pint, zinc lid	10.00
QG, clear, quart, zinc lid	30.00
Sealtite Wide Mouth Mason, green, quart, metal screw top	10.00
Smalley's Royal Trade Mark Nu–Seal, clear, half pint, glass lid, wire bail	15.00
Veteran, clear, pint, glass lid, wire bail	20.00
Weidman Boy Brand, Cleveland, pint, clear, glass lid, wire bail	6.00

FUNERAL MEMORABILIA

Collecting Hints: Funeral memorabilia should be collected because of love of the items, not strong financial investment. Advertising hand fans and calendars were produced in abundance and therefore are easier to find. Items which predate the decline of the in–home wake will be much rarer, and worth a great deal more.

History: The history of funeral rites is as old as humanity and diverse due to many religions and cultures. Being a funeral director became an acceptable career in the late 19th century. Today's funeral directors' responsibilities encompass everything from the removal of the body through burial. The undertaker of the 1860s was probably a carpenter who also made caskets and was sometimes involved in preserving the body, but not the planning of the funeral. At this time in–home embalming and wakes were by far the dominant form of funeral rites. This tradition carried on in the early 20th century in most cities and more extensively in rural areas. Most of the "Momento Mori" (which translates to "Remember you must die") items to be found are from this period. These items include casket plates, mourning cards, post–mortem photographs, mourning jewelry etc.

Casket plates were mounted to the casket until the procession to the cemetery commenced, at which time they were given to the family. Plates had engraved sayings such as "At Rest," "Mother," "Father," "Rest in Peace," and "Our Darling" or "Our Babe" and sometimes also contained pertinent information about the deceased. Mourning cards were given to friends and relatives and were typically black with gold leaf lettering and designs. They would name the deceased, give birth and death dates, and often had poems or reverent sayings. Post–mortem photographs were popular and many variations can be found. Most of these are of people laid in their coffins, although earlier photographs and tintypes can be found with parents holding their deceased child or members of a family posing around a seated corpse. Examples of post–mortem photograpy can be found as late as the 1950s.

Mourning jewelry is widely collected. Some examples contain locks of hair or may be woven from the hair of the deceased. Hair jewelry can be found in many forms and often has the name or date of the deceased as a memorial. Mourning jewelry can be found in celluloid, jet, and other black materials.

Funeral parlors began to appear more frequently at the beginning of the 20th century. The undertaker of yesterday became the funeral director of today and the person solely responsible for the care of the deceased. The custom of momento mori fell into decline and for the most part disappeared by the beginning of the 1920s.

References: *The American Funeral Director,* Kates–Boylston Publications, 1936; Lawrence G. Frederick, *The Principles and Practice of Embalming, Second Edition,* Frederick and Strub, 1961; Habenstein & Lamers, *The History of*

American Funeral Directing, Revised Edition, Bultin Printers, 1962.

Museum: The American Funeral Home Museum, Houston, TX.

Advisor: Shad John Kvetko.

Bottle, embalming fluid
7½" h, Frigid Fluid, paper label,
   screw top, 1940s **10.00**
9½" h, emb "Undertakers Supply
   Company," c1920 . . . .   **65.00**
Bracelet, woven hair, gold fittings, engraved "In Remembrance," 1870s . .   **250.00**
Brooch, 2 x 2½", celluloid, black, emb
   "In Memoriam," 1870s **100.00**
Brush, wood, Wunderlich & Harris,
   Funeral Directors, 1930s **25.00**
Bumper Flags, blue, white cross, 1940s   **35.00**
Burial Suit, child's, tuxedo, black, white
   shirt, and black pants, 1940s **35.00**

Business Card, Taylor & Hancock Mourning Goods, black and white, c1890, 3⅝ x 2⅛", $6.00.

Calendar
  Crowell Funeral Home, 1947 . . . . .   **25.00**
  Hubbard Casket Company, automatic,
    plastic, brown and cream, 1950s . .   **15.00**
Candle Holder, clip–on style, emb,
   compliments "Toledo Casket Company," c1910 . . . .   **45.00**
Casket Plate, silver finish
  Allice Sheham, Died Sept 3, 1854,
    aged 26 years, emb cross **20.00**
  Our Darling **15.00**
  Rest In Peace IHS, cross shape **25.00**
Clock, wall, lights up, Barre Guild
   Monuments, 1950s **145.00**
Coffee Mug, Ruzich Funeral Home,
   "The last word in fine service," 1950s   **12.00**
Coffin
  Child's, 36½ x 12½", white velour
    ext., white satin int., Bakelite handles, 1940s **295.00**
  Shoulder Casket Style, 60½" l, ornate,
    pin striping, viewing window,
    pewter handles, 1880s **500.00**
Cooling Board, portable, wood, brass
   hardware, BF Gleason, Rochester,
   NY, late 19th C **150.00**

Cup, collapsible, plastic, green, emb "Becks Casket Company," 1950s . . .   10.00
Embalming Kit, 9½" h embalming bottle, 9½" h waste bottle, hand pump, trocars, scissors, tubes, scalpels, and suture, 1930s 150.00
Embalming Table, cast iron base, porcelain top, ornate, early 20th C 300.00
Memorial Sacred Heart, The Crane and Breed Casket Company, brass, box, 1930s 45.00
Mirror, silhouette illus, Wheeler Mortuary, Portales, NM, 1950s 35.00
Mourning Card, 6 x 4", black, gold inscription "In loving remembrance, Fred E. Yoder, Died June 27, 1893, Aged 16 years 2 days" 3.00
Photograph, post mortem, 8 x 10", man lying in coffin, late 19th C 15.00
Pin
    Celluloid, black, hair in locket, 1870s   75.00
    Jet, carved weeping willow mourning scene, 1860s 145.00
Plate, "Made expressly for F. D. Gardener St. Louis Coffin Company," Vienna Art, 1905 . . . .   75.00
Playing Cards, Oehler Funeral Home, 1970s 7.00
Railroad Sign, "Funeral Coach," emb, early 20th C 125.00
Salesman's Samples
    Burial Vault, 12 x 3"
        Ceramic, Christie Vaults, 1950s . .   35.00
        Hammered Metal, felt int., unmarked 30.00
    Coffin, emb
        5 x 2½", Boyertown Famous Bronze, No 2200, bronze finish, 1940s   55.00
        5½ x 2½", Elgin Western Illinois, model #2260, silver finish, 1940s 55.00
Salt and Pepper Shakers, pr, plastic, yellow and white, emb "Wilson Funeral Home," c1960s 10.00
Sign
    D. Brown Joiner and Funeral Director, oak, brass plate, 1880s 150.00
    Funeral No Parking, double sided, emb, 1930s 85.00

GAMBLING COLLECTIBLES

Collecting Hints: All the equipment used in the various banking games such as Chuck-A-Luck, Faro, Hazard, Keno, and Roulette are collected today. Cheating devices used by professional sharpers are highly sought.

Almost all the different types of casino "money" used today are collected. In the gaming industry, "checks" refers to chips with a stated value. "Chips" do not have a stated value. Their value is determined at the time of play.

The best material to store chips, checks, and tokens are the same supplies used by coin collectors.

A well–rounded gambling collectibles display also includes old books, prints, postcards, photographs, and articles relating to the field.

History: American history reveals that gambling always has been a popular pastime for the general public, as well as a sure way to make a "quick buck" for the professional *sharper*.

In the late 18th and early 19th centuries, governmental agencies and other entities used lotteries to supplant taxes as a means to raise funds needed to construct schools, libraries, and other civic developments. Many of the state and city lotteries proved to be crooked and fixed, a fact which adds to the collecting appeal. Lottery tickets, broadsides, ads, and brochures are very ornate and display well when mounted and framed.

Most of the gambling paraphernalia was manufactured by "gambling supply houses" that were located throughout the country. They sold their equipment via catalogs. As the majority of the equipment offered was "gaffed," the catalogs never were meant to be viewed by the general public. The catalogs are sought by collectors for their information and are difficult to find.

References: *Antique Gambling Chips*, Past Pleasures, 1984; Art Anderson, *Casinos And Their Ashtrays: A Collector's Guide With Values & Casino Histories*, published by author, 1994; *Harvey's Guide to Collecting Gaming Checks & Chips*, High Sierra Numismatics, 1984; *Old West Collectibles*, Great American Publishing Co.; Leonard Schneir, *Gambling Collectibles: A Sure Winner*, Schiffer Publishing, 1994; Dale Seymour, *Antique Gambling Chips*, Past Pleasures, 1985.

Collectors' Club: Casino Chips & Gaming Tokens Collector Club, 5410 Banbury Drive, Worthington, OH 43235.

Ashtray, cigar, glass, brass rim, cigar rests, and match holder int. design of hand holding five playing cards, c1900, 5½" d 70.00
Book
    Confessions of a Poker Player, by "King Jack," 1940, New York, I Washburn, Inc, 209 pgs 20.00
    Green, Jonathan Harrington, *Gambler's Tricks with Cards: Exposed and Explained*, 1850, 114 pgs 1,000.00
    How Gamblers Win or The Secrets of Advantage Playing, by "A Retired Professional," 1868, 112 pgs 210.00

Quinn, J P, *Gambling and Gambling Devices*, 1912, 308 pgs **135.00**

Romain, J H, *Gambling*, 1891, 230 pgs **100.00**

Roye, John, *Astrology–The Key to Roulette*, 1908, 114 pgs **120.00**

Booklet, "Gambling to Win," author unknown, 1925, 24 pgs **40.00**

Card Box

Black Lacquer, rect, double deck, four etched silver cards on lid, c1880, 5 x 6½ x 1½" **110.00**

Sterling Silver, rect, single deck, emb, four enameled aces on tortoise shell lid, silver and blue enameled border, c1900, 3 x 6 x 1½" **465.00**

Cigarette Case, silver, rect

Poker, enameled royal flush hand in hearts, c1890 . . . . **925.00**

Roulette, enameled both sides, roulette wheel on obverse, Trente et Quarante layout on reverse, c1880 **875.00**

Cigarette Lighter

Gun shaped, enameled suit signs on grips **50.00**

Sgt Lee, emb, poker chips and enameled aces on sides, c1945 . . . . . . **27.50**

Dice Board, horseshoe shape, poker dice **195.00**

Gaming Box

Bird's Eye Maple, rect, lid inlaid with brass and mother–of–pearl four aces design, metal trim, contains four separate maple boxes each inlaid with metal suit sign, orig key, thin age cracks in lid, c1880, 6 x 10½ x ½" **225.00**

Tin, oblong, depicts roulette wheel, suit signs, crowns and anchors, and sports scenes, 10" d **65.00**

Layout

Chuck–A–Luck **75.00**

Pharo, straight board, oak frame, suit sign of Spades, non–folding, Geo Mason, Denver, CO, c1880 . . . . **1,750.00**

Matchsafe, silver

Poker, enameled poker hand of royal flush in spades, c1890 . . . . **1,000.00**

Roulette, enameled roulette wheel, c1900 . . . . **550.00**

Pharo Casekeeper

Maple Frame, ivory markers, celluloid strips for cards, suit sign of Spades, B C Wills, Detroit, c1910 **650.00**

Oak Frame, clay markers, suit sign of Clubs, Will & Finck, San Francisco, c1880 . . . . **1,150.00**

Pharo Dealing Box, metal, top has cutout to reveal corner index, c1920 **450.00**

Pharo Gaming Box, casino, rosewood, three brass inlays at each corner, brass bound top edge, top is hinged

in two sections, front panel folds down for easy access to 497 individually hand scrimshawed ivory chips, 99 blue border "25" chips, 199 Roman Numeral "V" in red circle with red border chips, and 299 white with eight point web design chips, rear section holds six Samuel Hart Pharo decks, pharo dealing box, and six ivory "coppers," c1865 . . . . . **23,100.00**

Pillow Cover, "What the Bard of Avon Knew About the Game of Draw Poker," litho cotton, poker hands and Shakespearean quotations, c1910, 22" sq **175.00**

Pocket Watch

Crown and Anchor, pointer lands on crown, anchor, or suit sign on painted metal dial, works, c1920 **225.00**

Playing Card, pointer lands on number, card, or color on metal dial, beveled glass, works, c1890 . . . . . **525.00**

Roulette Ideal, center opening shows gear mechanism, enamel dial, beveled crystal, works, c1890 . . . **600.00**

Poker Chip Box

Celluloid, rect, four aces on lid with pearlized centers, red, blue, and black highlights, emb base, sides, and top edges, rose colored satin int. lining, burgundy felt lined compartments, holds two decks and chips, c1900, 7 x 8½ x 2½" **175.00**

Tiger Oak, rect, hinged lid with ridged top, front half of box folds back to sides to allow easy access to chips, 200 ivory chips with individually hand scrimshawed fans in centers, 50 each with blue borders, red borders, white with inscribed circles, and white, orig key **5,050.00**

Wood, rect, woodburned dec, horse head framed by horseshoe and cards, above banner inscribed "Good Luck," fitted int., c1920, 7 x 10 x 2" **30.00**

Poker Chips

Bone, round, square, and rect, red, purple, yellow, and green, designs incised in color sections, fitted hand made mahogany box, c1870, price for set of 160 . . . . **650.00**

Clay

Advertising, Stachelberg Cigars and Silver Age Rye Whiskey, c1900, price for 31 . . . . **165.00**

Etched, playing cards, horses, eagles, and animals designs, c1900, price for 66 . . . . **95.00**

Ivory, scrimshawed floral design, 11 white and 4 white with red border, price for 15 . . . . **465.00**

Poker Dice, leather cup	**35.00**
Punchboard, The National Game, poker	
game scene, c1920, 4½ x 6"	**40.00**
Roulette Wheel	**65.00**
Spinner	
Poker Card Game	**125.00**
Put–N–Take, mechanical	**195.00**
Table Cover, dice, chips, score pad, and	
poker hands, c1920, 30" sq	**130.00**
Watch Fob, gold plated, eight enameled	
suit signs, 6" l	**125.00**

GAMES

Collecting Hints: Make certain a game has all its parts. The box lid or instruction booklet usually contains a full list of all pieces. Collectors tend to specialize by theme, e.g., western, science fiction, Disney, etc. Most television games fall into the ten– to twenty–five dollar range, offering the beginning collector a chance to acquire a large number of games without a big capital outlay. Don't stack game boxes more than five deep or mix sizes. Place a piece of acid–free paper between each game to prevent bleeding from inks and to minimize wear. Keep the games stored in a dry location. Extreme dryness and extreme moisture are both undesirable.

History: A board game dating from 4,000 B.C. was discovered in ruins in Upper Egypt. Board games were used throughout recorded history, but reached popularity during the Victorian era. Most board games combine skill (from chess), luck and ability (from cards), and pure chance (from dice). By 1900 Milton Bradley, Parker Brothers, C. H. Joslin and McLoughlin were the leading manufacturers.

Monopoly was invented in 1933 and first issued by Parker Brothers in 1935. Before the advent of television, the board game was a staple in evening entertainment. Many board games from the 1930s and 1940s focused on radio personalities, e.g., Fibber McGee or The Quiz Kids.

In the late 1940s television became popular. The game industry responded. The golden age of the TV board game was from 1955 to 1968. The movies, e.g., James Bond, also led to the creation of games, but never to the extent of the television programs.

References: Mark Cooper, *Baseball Games: Home Versions of the National Pastime 1860s–1960s,* Schiffer Publishing, 1995; Lee Dennis, *Warman's Antique American Games, 1840–1940, Second Edition,* Wallace–Homestead, 1991; Walter Gibson, *Family Games America Plays,* Doubleday & Co., 1970; Caroline Goodfellow, *A Collector's Guide To Games and Puzzles,* The Apple Press, 1991; Jefferson

Graham, *Come on Down!!!, The TV Game Show Book,* Abbeville Press, 1988; L–W Book Sales, *Board Games of the 50's, 60's, and 70's With Prices,* L–W Book Sales, 1994; L–W Book Sales, *Dexterity Games and Other Hand–Held Puzzles,* L–W Book Sales, 1995; Norman E. Martinus and Harry L. Rinker, *Warman's Paper,* Wallace–Homestead, 1994; Jack Matthews, *Toys Go To War: World War II Military Toys, Games, Puzzles, & Books,* Pictorial Histories Publishing, 1994; Rick Polizzi, *Baby Boomer Games,* Collector Books, 1995; Rick Polizzi and Fred Schaefer, *Spin Again, Board Games from the Fifties and Sixties,* Chronicle Books, 1991; Harry L. Rinker, *Collector's Guide To Toys, Games, and Puzzles,* Wallace–Homestead, 1991; Desi Scarpone, *Board Games,* Schiffer Publishing, 1995; Bruce Whitehill, *Games: American Boxed Games And Their Makers, 1822–1992, With Values,* Wallace–Homestead, 1992.

Collectors' Clubs: American Game Collectors Assoc., 49 Brooks Ave., Lewiston, ME 04240; Gamers Alliance, PO Box 197, East Meadow, NY 11554.

Periodicals: *Toy Shop,* 700 E. State St., Iola, WI 54990; *Toy Trader,* PO Box 1050, Dubuque, IA 52004.

Note: Prices listed below are for games boxed and in mint condition.

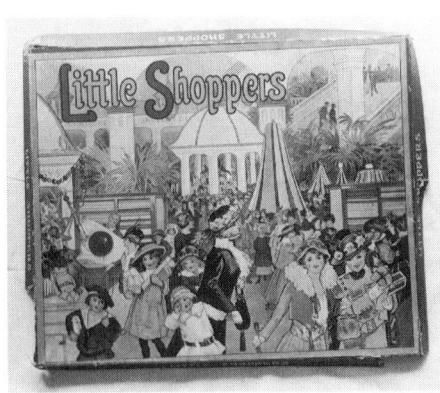

Little Shoppers, $25.00.

Allison, 1961, Car 54	**100.00**
American Publishing Corp, 1977, Gong	
Show	**5.00**
Athletic Products Co, Inc, 1950s, Today	
With Dave Garroway	**45.00**
Frederich H. Beach, 1941, Take It And	
Double, 2nd series	**10.00**
Betty–B	
1955, Break The Bank, 1st ed	**10.00**
1956, Robin Hood	**35.00**
Bilt–Rite, 1956, Wild Bill Hickok	**40.00**

Milton Bradley
c1936, Easy Money, separate board
and pieces box **95.00**
1937, Confucius Say, card game . . .   **55.00**
c1940, Healeah, metal pieces, horse
racing scene on 19 x 12" box **75.00**
1944, Ella Cinders, 4483 . . . .   **35.00**
1950, Howdy Doody's TV Game . . .   **50.00**
c1955, Swayze, based on NBC news
show starring John Cameron
Swayze, 17 x 10" box **40.00**
1956, Chutes and Ladders **28.00**
1956, Li'l Abner: His Game, 4166 . .   **25.00**
1957, Name That Tune **10.00**
1958, Cheyenne **25.00**
1959, Casper the Friendly Ghost, 15
x 8" box **40.00**
1960, Video Village **20.00**
1961, Margie **12.00**
1963, Patty Duke **25.00**
1964, Voyage To The Bottom Of The
Sea **20.00**
1965, 12 O'Clock High, card game,
cards depict WWII aircraft, 8 x 6"
box with German fighter attacking
US bombers **60.00**
1966, Illya Kuryakin, card game,
missing common plastic poker
chips **30.00**
1967, Captain America **15.00**
1968, Road Runner, 19 x 9" box with
Coyote, Road Runner, Tweety, and
Sylvester **45.00**
1969, Official Baseball Game **40.00**
1971, Partridge Family **16.00**
1973, Columbo **16.00**
1974, Apples Way **18.00**
1975, SWAT **2.00**
1976, Baretta, 19 x 8" box, Robert
Blake image **20.00**
1977, Starsky & Hutch **16.00**
1980, Yogi Bear Game, 16 x 8" box
with Yogi and Boo–Boo **16.00**
1982, Fall Guy **2.00**
Cadaco
1966, Basketball **20.00**
1974, The Wizard of Oz, 19 x 9" box
with Dorothy, Scarecrow, Tin Man,
and Lion **50.00**
1982, Sherlock Holmes, 19 x 9" box
with Holmes and crime scene . . .   **50.00**
1984, Alice in Wonderland, 19 x 9"
box with Alice at tea party scene   **40.00**
Cardinal, 1982, General Hospital **2.00**
Club Aluminum Products Co, 1942,
Whirling Words, wood version **30.00**
Corey Game Co, 1941, You're Out,
baseball game **20.00**
CreaTek, 1966, Seduction, no instruc-
tions, 19 x 9" box **22.00**
Embossing Co, 1940s, Jack–Be–Nimble   **8.00**
Ewing, 1955, Davy Crockett **35.00**

Gardner
1956, You'll Never Get Rich, (Sgt
Bilko) **65.00**
Gem, 1965, Gilligan's Island **100.00**
H–G, 1956, Circus Boy **50.00**
Hasbro
c1955, Merry Milkman, orig box . . .   **70.00**
1959, Leave It To Beaver **55.00**
1965, Munsters **150.00**
1968, Laugh–In **25.00**
Highlander, 1955, George Goebel **20.00**
House of Games, 1978, Grizzly Adams   **16.00**
Ideal
1961, Rebel **40.00**
1962, Dr Kildare **20.00**
1963, Combat! Board Game, 10 x
20" box **55.00**
1964, Fugitive **100.00**
1965, Man From UNCLE **20.00**
1966, Mission Impossible **60.00**
1967, Star Trek **125.00**
1970, Quick Shoot, orig box **20.00**
1975, Welcome Back Kotter **2.00**
1978, Fantasy Island **3.00**
1981, Dukes of Hazzard **1.00**
Kenner, 1977, Star Wars: Escape From
The Death Star, missing 1 card, 19 x
9" box with fighter planes illus **16.00**
Leister Game Co, 1945, Autographs . .   **15.00**
Lido Toy Co, 1950s, Air Race Around
The World **8.00**
ES Lowe Co
1940s, Fox Hunt **15.00**
1967, Countdown, rocket launch
scene on 20 x 10" box **65.00**
Lowell
1954, Beat The Clock, 1st ed **10.00**
1956, $64,000 Question **15.00**
1958, Bat Masterson, no instructions,
20 x 10" box with Gene Barry in
gunfight **100.00**
1959, Steve Canyon, one pc broken,
19 x 9" box **55.00**
1960, 77 Sunset Strip, missing set of
diecast figures, 19 x 10" box **26.00**
1961, Charge Account **7.00**
1962, College Bowl **15.00**
1963, Candid Camera **15.00**
Mattel
1963, Word For Word **6.00**
1967, Gentle Ben **10.00**
Memphis Plastic Enterprises, Inc, 1955,
Baseball Game **30.00**
Mutuels, Inc, Los Angeles, 1938,
Mutuels, horse racing game, large
metal pcs, miniature infield, 24 x 12"
box with litho horse racing scene, no
instructions **215.00**
Northern Signal Co, c1958, Tantalizer,
missing 4 pcs, orig box **38.00**
Parker Brothers
1913, Rook, Dixie Rook Edition **22.00**

1936, Monopoly, separate board and
pieces box, box well worn **30.00**
1937, Monopoly, separate board and
pcs box **50.00**
c1940, Quiz Kids Own Game Box,
no instructions **28.00**
1946, Monopoly, Popular Edition,
separate board and pieces box . . .   **25.00**
1950, Baseball, missing 3 common
pegs, 18 x 13″ box with player
chasing fly ball **45.00**
1955, Rich Uncle, 14 x 12″ box . . .   **75.00**
1957, Game of Moon Tag, planets
and smiling moons on board, elves
circling smiling moon on 20 x 10″
box **140.00**
1958, Bird Watcher, robin and other
birds on 19 x 9″ box, bird cards . .   **60.00**
1959, Have Gun Will Travel **40.00**
1960, Park & Shop, 19 x 9″ box . . .   **75.00**
1961, Number Please **9.00**
1962, Long Shot, metal horses, 20 x
14″ box with stylized horses leav-
ing starting gate **90.00**
1966, As The World Turns **15.00**
1968, Undersea World of Jacques
Cousteau, 19 x 9″ box with diver
on coral reef **30.00**
1969, Goodbye Mr Chips, movie . . .   **10.00**
1970, Tiny Tim **20.00**
1975, Bionic Crisis **16.00**
1977, Laverne and Shirley **16.00**
1979, Mork & Mindy **32.00**
1983, Wicket The Ewok **7.00**
1984, The A–Team **16.00**
Play Rite, 1960, Johnny Unitas **50.00**
Pressman, 1954, Groucho TV Quiz
Game **75.00**
Reiss, 1977, Mary Hartmann **15.00**
Remco
1961, Giant Wheel Cowboys 'N
Indians Game, missing one cow-
boy playing pc, 24 x 15″ box **25.00**
1965, Shindig, 19 x 9″ box with four
stylized Rock 'N Roll scenes and
inset of host Jimmy O'Neil **75.00**
1968, Mod Squad **75.00**
RJ McDonald, 1958, Big Board Stock
Market Game, orig box **45.00**
Rosebud Art Co, 1940s, Jungle Hunt . .   **20.00**
Russell Mfg Co, Leicester, MA, 1922,
Game Of Tortoise And The Hare, 10
x 6″ color litho box **135.00**
Samuel Gabriel & Sons
1937, Ching Gong, Chinese checker
type game, no instruction, 22 x 12″
plain box **95.00**
1955, Harpoon Game, 10 x 20″ box   **40.00**
Selchow & Righter
1937, Parcheesi, color snake charmer
on 16 x 8″ box, missing one wood
disc **60.00**

Drive–In, Selchow & Righter, 1949,
$15.00.

1940s, Snake Eyes, Black theme . . .   **25.00**
1948, Huggin' The Rail **30.00**
1953, The Game of Assembly Line,
No. 61 . . . .   **20.00**
1954, Down You Go, early TV quiz
show **20.00**
1961, Straightaway **20.00**
Standard Toycraft
1960, Dennis The Menace **35.00**
1963, Beverly Hillbillies **5.00**
1964, Dick Van Dyke **50.00**
Gidget **30.00**
Teaching Concepts, 1977, Wild
Kingdom, animal board and cards, 19
x 10″ box with Marlin Perkins and
cheetah **32.00**
Teenage Publishing Co, 1957, Elvis
Presley Game Of Love **600.00**
Transogram
1938, Movie Millions, missing 9
cards and some tokens, 16 x 13″
box with movie stars pictures **145.00**
1955, Dragnet **15.00**
1956, Jackie Gleason, Away We Go   **75.00**
1957, Jack & The Beanstalk Adventure Game, 15 x 7″ box with Jack
carrying harp and hen, being
chased by giant **16.00**
1958, Gray Ghost **50.00**
1959, Perry Mason, 19 x 9″ box . . .   **32.00**
1960, Screwball: The Mad Mad Mad
Game, no instructions, 19 x 10″
box with Mad magazine characters   **55.00**
1961, Dino the Dinosaur, Dino on 15
x 8″ box **70.00**
1962, Game Of The Kennedys **10.00**
1963, Mr Novak **20.00**
1966, Hogan's Heroes **50.00**
1967, Gomer Pyle **30.00**
1975, MASH **15.00**
Trivia, Inc, 1984, TV Guide TV Game,
14 x 10″ box with TV Guides collage   **45.00**
Dexter Wayne, 1953, Ramar Of The
Jungle **25.00**
Whiting
1954, Pinky Lee Runaway Frank-
furters **25.00**
1955, Lassie **20.00**
1956, Lone Ranger **60.00**

Throwing The Bull, Wilder Mfg. Co., St. Louis, MO, $30.00.

Whitman Publishing Co
1958, Zorro **25.00**
1960, Hi–Ho! Cherry–O, missing 6
plastic cherries and 1 plastic cup,
12 x 12″ box with children playing
game **45.00**
1968, Dark Shadows **30.00**
1981, Clash Of The Titans **7.00**
1982, Secret of NIMH, 17 x 9″ box   **16.00**

GASOLINE COLLECTIBLES

Collecting Hints: There still is plenty of material in the storage area of old garages; try to find a co-operative owner. If your budget is modest, concentrate on paper ephemera, such as maps. Regionally related items will bring slightly more in their area of origin.

History: The selling of gasoline has come full circle. The general store, livery stable, and blacksmith were the first people to sell gasoline. Today the mini–market is a viable factor in gasoline sales. The gas crisis of 1973 brought the circle to a close. The gas station, whose golden era was from the 1930s to the 1960s, is beginning to disappear. The loss of the independently owned station is doubly felt because it also was the center of automobile repair.

The abolition of credit cards by ARCO marked another shift. Reduction in price for paying cash is a new marketing device. Elimination of free maps, promotional trinkets, and other advertising material already is a fact. As more and more stores in shopping centers sell oil, parts, and other related automobile products, it is doubtful whether the gasoline station will ever recover its past position.

References: Electa, *Gasoline,* Abbeville, 1995; Scott Anderson, *Check The Oil,* Wallace–Homestead, 1986; Mark Anderton and Sherry Mullen *Gas Station Collectibles,* Wallace–Homestead, 1994; Robert W. D. Ball, *Texaco Collectibles,* Schiffer Publishing, 1994; Scott Benjamin and Wayne Henderson, *Gas Pump Globes: Collector's Guide To Over 3,000 American Gas Globes,* Motorbooks International, 1993; Bob Crisler, *License Plate Values: A Guide To Relative Prices of Collectible U.S. Auto License Plates and Their Grading,* King Publishing, 1994; John A. Gunnell (ed.), *A Collector's Guide To Automobilia,* Krause Publications, 1994; Norman E. Martinus and Harry L. Rinker, *Warman's Paper,* Wallace–Homestead, 1994; Rick Pease, *Filling Station Collectibles,* Schiffer Publishing, 1994; Jim and Nancy Schaut, *American Automobilia: An Illustrated History and Price Guide,* Wallace–Homestead, 1994; B. J. Sommers and Wayne Priddy, *Value Guide To Gas Station Memorabilia,* Collector Books, 1995; Sonya Stenzler and Rick Pease, *Gas Station Collectibles,* Schiffer Publishing, 1993; Michael Karl Witzel, *Gas Station Memories,* Motorbooks International, 1994.

Periodical: *Hemmings Motor News,* Box 100, Bennington, VT 05201.

Collectors' Clubs: American Petroleum Collectors/ Iowa Gas, 6555 Colby Ave., Des Moines, IA 50311; International Petroliana Collectors Association, PO Box 1000, Westerville, OH 43081; Spark Plug Collectors of America, 14018 NE 85th St., Elk River, MN 55330; World Oil Can Collector's Organization, 20 Worley Rd., Marshall, NC 28753.

REPRODUCTION ALERT: Small advertising signs and pump globes have been extensively reproduced.

Badge, Amoco Gasoline, Border Patrol   **15.00**
Bank, 3½″ h, Phillips 66 Motor Oil, tin   **15.00**
Blotter, Red Crown Gasoline, 1930s . .   **28.00**
Calendar, White Rose Gasoline, 1933   **10.00**
Clock, 18″ w, Cooper Cordless Tires,
neon, orange, royal blue, and white   **475.00**
Display
Autolite, case, glass front, for spark
plugs **125.00**
Fram Oil Filters, wall mounted **80.00**
Sinclair Opaline Oil, round and flat,
1920 . . . .   **85.00**
Vedoll Oil Guide, wall mounted,
1942–50 . . . .   **50.00**
Employee Badge, Atlantic, White Flash,
Glenn, red, white, and blue, 1930s   **50.00**
Fan, Polarine Oil adv, hot air balloon
shape, small electric fan **850.00**

Pump Globe, Sinclair Dino Supreme, plastic and glass, $100.00.

Gas Globe
  Marathon, glass 375.00
  Standard Gold Crown 235.00
  Vickers, plastic 165.00
Gas Pump, metal case, glass globe
  Mobil Gas 250.00
  Sinclair Power X, Super Fuel 350.00
Gas Pump Sign
  Good Gulf 35.00
  Gulf Kerosene 58.00
  Gulf No–Nox 35.00
  Mobil, Pegasus image 110.00
  Pure Pep 60.00
  Royal 60.00
  Shamrock, 10½ x 12½", porcelain . . 125.00
  Standard Oil, crown, glass globe, one
    piece, good paint 200.00
  Texaco Fire Chief 55.00
  Texaco Supreme 55.00
Glass, 4¾" h, Sinclair, green inscription
  "Drive With Care And Buy Sinclair,"
  dinosaur illus, 1960s 25.00
Lamp, Gastrol GTX 25.00
Lapel Stud, ⅝" d, Fisk Tire, emb silvered
  brass, raised trademark, c1915 . . . . 20.00
License Plate, 1939 World's Fair, CA . . 25.00
Map, Amoco, Space, 1958 giveaway . . 12.00
Mileage Card, Skelly 15.00
Oil Can
  Mother Penn, quart 4.00
  PA Mobilene, motor oil, 5 gallon,
    patent 1925 . . . . 85.00
  Queen, tin, glass insert, patent 12/11/18 45.00
  Sinclair, 1930s 22.00
  Texaco, 1927, orig spout 35.00
Pinback Button
  Goodyear, matte celluloid button,
    bright yellow, blue and white de-
    sign, working thermometer, main-
    tenance record type, c1930 . . . . . 20.00
  Texaco, 1¼" d, celluloid, red and
    green star, black letters, white
    ground, c1930 . . . . 25.00
  Tydol Gasoline, 1" l, oval, red, black,
    and white, winged logo, bright
    gold celluloid ground, c1920 . . . . 17.50

Playing Cards, Mobil, double deck . . . 20.00
Salt and Pepper Shakers, pr, Phillips, fig-
  ural, gas pumps 30.00
Sign
  AAA Service 100.00
  Atlantic Gas, porcelain 50.00
  Dodge Brothers Service Station,
    porcelain, c1930, 15 x 45" 125.00
  Edsel Shock Absorbers 200.00
  Exit, drive–in type 75.00
  Firestone, cream, blue, and orange,
    48 x 16" 65.00
  Gargoyle, 24 x 16", flange 295.00
  Mobil Oil, projecting, gargoyle dec 95.00
  Pennzoil, "Sound Your Z" oval, 32 x
    22" 110.00
  Sinclair Credit Card 75.00
  Standard Oil, red crown with torch 95.00
Thermometer
  Kendall Oil, round 25.00
  Standard Oil, 3" x 12", tin 25.00

GEISHA GIRL PORCELAIN

Collecting Hints: Check for enamel and gold wear as well as porcelain flakes, hairlines, etc. Buy only items in good to mint condition. Become familiar with the type of items produced so you are not fooled by a "pitcher" that actually is a lidless cocoa pot or a lidless sugar bowl which may appear to be a planter.

Check the designs on all items within a set. Be aware that a "set" contains items complementary in size and with the same pattern executed in the same manner on all pieces. Value depends upon condition, quality, pattern, border color, and type of piece. Teapots, cups and saucers, and red bordered items are the most common.

History: Geisha Girl porcelain is a Japanese export ware whose production commenced during the last quarter of the 19th century and continued heavily until WW II. Limited quantities were produced after WW II and are called "modern" Geisha ware.

Geisha Girl porcelain features over 150 different patterns focusing on the flora, fauna, animal life (both real and mythical), and people of pre–modern Japan. The name is derived from the fact that all the wares contain lovely kimono–clad Japanese ladies as part of the pattern. It was manufactured and decorated by over 100 different establishments.

Colors and design methods vary greatly. The most common examples bear a red–orange stencil design over which artists hand–painted enamels. Other examples have a different color stencil, and may be wholly hand painted or decaled.

In the majority of instances, items bear a border color of red, light green, pine green, cobalt blue, greenish blue, turquoise, brown, black, or a lovely combination of several colors. Borders themselves are often further embellished with lacing, flowers, diapering, dots, or stripings of gold or contrastingly colored enamels.

Although Geisha Girl was produced in an Oriental pattern, it was meant for export to the Western market. Therefore, most shapes represent those used in the West during the early days of the twentieth century. These forms include tea items, cocoa sets, luncheon sets, dresser sets, (powder jars, hair receivers, ring trees, etc.), and vases. Examples of children's and doll house size also exist.

Makers' marks found on Geisha Girl porcelain include many of the famous Nippon trademarks, Japanese signatures (including Kutani), and post–Nippon indicators.

Reference: Elyce Litts, *The Collector's Encyclopedia of Geisha Girl Porcelain,* Collector Books, 1988.

REPRODUCTION ALERT: "Modern" Geisha ware was sold in Oriental import shops until the early 1980s. Reproduced forms, all having a red border, include bail handled tea sets, five piece dresser sets, sake sets, toothbrush holders, and ginger jars. Also produced was a children's set of demitasse cups, each having a different border color.

The chief characteristics of reproductions are very white porcelain, minimal background washes, sparse detail coloring, and no gold or occasionally very bright gold enameling. Old gold should show tarnish.

Also watch for Czechoslovakian reproductions made in the 1920s. Some will be marked with the country of origin, but others bear only a faux–Oriental mark. Generally these items are decaled or very simply hand painted. Faces of the geisha will be distinctively different than those on Japanese Geisha ware.

Toy Plate, Pine Green, $15.00.

BAMBOO TREE

Dark green bamboo trees are used to embellish a Processional type pattern. Borders are dark green with yellow or white enamel lines.

Cup and Saucer, tea, Torii, Made in
  Japan **7.00**
Plate, 6" d **5.00**
Tea Set, cov pot, creamer, sugar, six
  cups and saucers, lemon plate, Japan,
  price for sixteen piece set **100.00**

BAMBOO TRELLIS

Three ladies standing and kneeling at water's edge; behind them is a large trellis made of bamboo and overgrown with peonies.

Bowl, 7½" d, light apple green, gold, ftd   **35.00**
Cocoa Set, pot, six cups and saucers,
  fluted, cobalt blue, lattice work backdrop, reserve pattern, Kutani and C O
  N Nippon, price for thirteen piece set   **225.00**
Mug, 4" d, red, gold buds, Japan **18.00**
Mustard Pot, blue, scalloped **25.00**
Plate, 6½" d, blue–green, gold buds,
  sparse decoration **8.00**

BIRD CAGE

Lady and child are featured in a garden. The lady holds a small bird cage.

Cup and Saucer, tea, red–orange, floral
  frame int **12.00**
Plate, 6" d, red–orange, gold **8.00**
Tete–a–tete, pot, two cups and saucers,
  red–orange, floral frame int. **38.00**

IKEBANA IN RICKSHAW

Flower arranger wearing floral headdress is kneeling in presentation of a large ikebana (flower arrangement) in a basket perched atop a rickshaw.

Bowl, 8" d, yellow, ftd **40.00**
Lunch Set, teapot, sugar, creamer, six
  cups and saucers, six scalloped cake
  plates, six scalloped table plates,
  cobalt blue, gold, twenty–seven piece
  set **250.00**
Plate, 7¼" d, cobalt blue, gold, swirl
  fluted scalloped edge **18.00**
Salt and Pepper Shakers, pr, grass green   **15.00**
Teapot, cobalt blue, gold **35.00**

LONG–STEMMED PEONY

The title is a takeoff on the "long–stemmed rose," but aptly describes the unique feature of this pattern. A young boy carries the flower and is accompanied on his walk by two ladies, one with a parasol.

Creamer, slender, fluted, blue and gold, Made in Japan	**9.00**
Eggcup, orange	**5.00**
Hair Receiver, large, wavy, red–orange, lid and side pattern, Japan	**30.00**
Hatpin Holder, hourglass shape, ribbed, cobalt blue and gold, Made in Japan	**35.00**

PORCH

Japanese dwellings were traditionally situated on stilts with walls of sliding doors which, when slid open during the day, created a porch overlooking the gardens. A number of women are depicted against such a backdrop in a scene known to date from the Nippon era but also found on modern productions.

Berry Set, master, five individuals, scalloped edge, red and gold, price for six piece set	**35.00**
Celery set, small rect master, five salts, red–orange and gold, Torii Nippon, price for five piece set	**35.00**
Creamer	
Cobalt blue and gold, Torii Nippon .	**20.00**
Red–orange, modern	**5.00**
Cup and Saucer	
After dinner, dark green, Made in Japan	**10.00**
Tea, cobalt blue, two streams of gold lacing, gold stripe handle	
Red–orange, modern	**8.00**
Dresser Set, rect tray, powder jar, hair receiver, red, modern, price for three piece set	**25.00**
Nut Bowl, master, cobalt blue, Torii Nippon	**25.00**

G.I. JOE COLLECTIBLES

Collecting Hints: It is extremely important to determine the manufacturing date of any G. I. Joe doll or related figure that you have. The ideal method is to discipline yourself to do a check point comparison with the dolls described and dated in the existing reference books. Be alert to subtle variations. You do not have a match until all checking points are identical. Also make a point to learn the proper period costume for each doll variation.

Accessory pieces can be every bit as valuable as the dolls themselves. Whenever possible, accessory pieces should be accompanied by their original packaging and any paper inserts.

G. I. Joe dolls and accessories were produced in the millions. Rarity is not a factor; condition is. When buying dolls or accessories as collectibles, as opposed to acquiring them for play, do not purchase any items in less than fine condition.

History: Hasbro Manufacturing Company produced the first G. I. Joe twelve–inch poseable action figures in 1964. The original line consisted of one male action figure for each branch of the military services. Their outfits were styled after military uniforms from World War II, the Korean Conflict, and the Vietnam Conflict.

In 1965 the first black figure was introduced. The year 1967 saw two additions to the line—a female nurse and Talking G. I. Joe. To keep abreast of changing times, Joe received flocked hair and a beard in 1970.

The creation of the G. I. Joe Adventure Team made Joe the marveled explorer, hunter, deep sea diver, and astronaut, rather than just an American serviceman. Due to the Arab oil embargo in 1976, the figure was reduced in size to eight–inches tall and renamed Super Joe. Production ceased in 1977.

In 1982 G. I. Joe staged his comeback. A few changes were made to the character line and in the way in which G. I. Joe was presented. "The Great American Hero" line now consists of 3¾–inch poseable plastic figures with code names corresponding to their various costumes. The new Joe deals with both current and futuristic villains and issues.

References: Jeff Killian and Charles Griffith, *Tomart's Price Guide to G. I. Joe Collectibles,* Tomart Publications, 1992; Paris and Susan Mano, *Collectible Male Action Figures: Including G. I. Joe Figures, Captain Action Figures and Ken Dolls,* Collector Books, 1990, 1992 value update; Carol Markowski and Bill Sikora, *Tomart's Price Guide to Action Figure Collectibles,* Tomart Publications, 1991; Vincent Santelmo, *The Complete Encyclopedia To GI Joe,* Krause Publications, 1993; Vincent Santelmo, *The Official 30th Anniversary Salute To GI Joe, 1964–1994,* Krause Publications, 1994.

Collectors' Club: GI Joe Collectors Club, 150 S. Glenoaks Blvd, Burbank, CA 91510.

Periodical: *The Barracks: The G. I. Joe Collectors Magazine,* 14 Bostwick Place, New Milford, CT 06776.

Action Figure	
Action Pilot, Scramble Pilot, flight suit, complete, all accessories, painted hair, mint	**495.00**
Action Soldier Sabotage, uniform, boots, life raft, TNT, binoculars,	

wool knit sticking cap, gas mask, signal light, flare gun, radio, submachine gun, oar with yellow tips, mint **475.00**

Adventurer, Negro, #7404, MIB **275.00**

Air Adventurer, #7287, MIB **245.00**

Air Cadet, Parade Dress, #7822, jacket, pants, garrison cap, dress shoes, chest and belt sash, white M–1 rifle, saber, scabbard, complete, all accessories, painted hair, mint **375.00**

Air Force, Dress Uniform, #7803, complete, all accessories, painted hair, mint **295.00**

Astronaut, talking, #7915, near MIB **675.00**

British Commando, #8104, complete, all accessories, mint **395.00**

Demolition, complete, all accessories, mint **175.00**

Eight Ropes of Danger, complete, all accessories, mint **275.00**

French Resistance, #8103, complete, all accessories, mint **350.00**

Frogman, #7602, complete scuba outfit, all accessories, painted hair, mint **395.00**

German Soldier, #8100, complete, all accessories, mint **395.00**

GI Joe, Hasbro, mark 1, 1964, no clothes **52.00**

Green Beret, camouflaged tunic, green jacket and pants, beret with emblem, grenades, pistol, holster, pistol belt, radio, M–16 rifle, bazooka with shells, complete, all accessories, painted hair, mint . . . **375.00**

Heavy Weapons, complete, all accessories, mint **395.00**

High Voltage Escape, complete, all accessories, mint **175.00**

Japanese Imperial Soldier, #8101, complete, all accessories, mint . . . **625.00**

Land Adventurer, #7401, MIB **225.00**

Man of Action, #7284, MIB **225.00**

Marine Jungle Fighter, #7732, complete uniform, campaign hat, field telephone, knife, sheath, flame thrower, pistol belt, holster, canteen and cov, painted hair, mint . . **850.00**

Marine Medic, complete, all accessories, mint **375.00**

Military Police Set, #7512, brown uniform, MP arm band and helmet, duffel bag, red tunic, pistol holder and belt, tall brown boots, dog tag, painted hair, mint **375.00**

Race Car Driver, complete, all accessories, mint **195.00**

Russian Infantry Man, #8102, complete, all accessories, mint **395.00**

Sea Adventurer, #7492, MIB **245.00**

Secret Agent, complete, all accessories, mint **195.00**

Shore Patrol, complete, all accessories, mint **375.00**

Ski Patrol and Mountain Troops, complete, all accessories, painted hair, mint **375.00**

Tanker, complete, leather jacket, helmet with visor, emblem, radio, tripod, machine gun, ammo box, painted hair, mint **650.00**

West Point Cadet, Parade Dress, #7537, complete, all accessories, painted hair, mint **350.00**

Clothing and Accessories

Airvest, orange **8.00**

Ammo Belt, green **12.00**

Astronaut Accessories, mint in orig bag **35.00**

Boots

    Brown, short **20.00**

    Silver **10.00**

Cap, sailor **10.00**

Carbine with sling **7.00**

Dress Outfit, complete outfit

    Medic **135.00**

    Navy, orig tie **75.00**

Helmet, astronaut **25.00**

Medic Bag **15.00**

Netting Set, MOC **15.00**

Pants

    Arctic Explorer **20.00**

    MP, tan **25.00**

Parka, Snow Troops **20.00**

Radio Bag Pack, green **20.00**

Rifle, M1 . . . . **7.00**

Shirt and pants, Sailor, work **15.00**

Tunic

    Green Beret **25.00**

    MP **20.00**

Coloring Book, used **40.00**

Dog Tag, membership **50.00**

GI Joe, Grand Slam, 1982, 3¾" h, $3.50.

Duffel Bag, USN	23.00

Figure, 3¾" h, unpackaged, near mint,
orig file card

Airborne, 1983	15.00
Blowtorch, 1984	9.00
Cobra Commander, 1982, mail pre-mium	50.00
Doc, 1983	15.00
Duke, 1984	9.00
Firefly, 1984	14.00
Flash, 1982	20.00
Grunt, 1982	18.00
Gung Ho, 1983	14.00
Recondo, 1984	9.00
Rock & Roll, 1982	20.00
Scarlett, 1982	35.00
Snake Eyes, 1982	30.00
Snow Job, 1983	15.00
Stalker, 1982	20.00
Zap, 1982	20.00

Game

GI Joe Combat Infantry, MIB	175.00
GI Joe Combat Navy Frogman, MIB	175.00
Playing Cards, mint	95.00

Play Set

GI Joe Training Center, 99% complete	100.00
White Tiger Hunt, MIB	195.00

Puzzle, 221 pcs, Mural

Scene #2, 1985	3.00
Scene #4, 1988	5.00
Table Centerpiece, honeycomb, 1986, sealed	4.00

Vehicle

APC, complete, MIB	30.00
Armadillo,	15.00
Buggy, 1970s	20.00
Cobra Hiss, complete, orig box	60.00
Crew Fire truck	35.00
Desert Patrol Jeep, MIB	900.00
Helicopter, includes orig accessories, 1970s	68.00
Mamba, complete, orig box	30.00
Mobile Command Vehicle, MIB	195.00
Motorcycle, side car	135.00
Night Raven, complete, orig box	45.00
Parasite, complete, MIB	15.00
Rattler, complete, orig box	60.00
Slugger, complete, orig box	35.00
Snow Cat, complete, MIB	20.00
Thunderclap, complete, MIB	25.00
Tomahawk	50.00
Water Moccasin	25.00

GOLF COLLECTIBLES

Collecting Hints: Condition is very important as collectors grow in sophistication and knowledge. The more modern the item, the better the condition should be.

It is extremely rare to find a club or ball made before 1800, and any equipment made before 1850 is scarce. There were few books, with a couple of very rare exceptions, published before 1857. Few pieces of equipment made after 1895 are rare.

Some items, such as scorecards, ball markers, golf pencils, and bag tags are so common that their value is negligible.

Most American clubs and other items manufactured after 1895 are rather common. Some modern equipment, from 1950 to 1965, is in demand, but primarily for actual play rather than collection or display.

The very old material is found in Scotland and England, unless brought to this country early in this century. Christie's, Sotheby's, and Phillips' hold several major auctions of golf collectibles each year in London, Edinburgh, and Chester. Golf collectible sales often coincide with the British Open Championship each July. The English market is more established, but the American market is growing rapidly. Auctions of golf items and memorabilia now are held in the United States.

The prices of golf clubs escalated tremendously in the 1970s, but have stabilized in more recent years. The prices of golf books, which for many years remained static, have risen dramatically in the 1980s. Art prints, drawings, etchings, etc. have remained static, but pottery, china, glass, and other secondary items, especially Royal Doulton, have attracted premium prices.

History: Golf has been played in Scotland since the 15th century. Until 1850 it was a game played by gentry, with a few exceptions. With the introduction of the cheaper and more durable "guttie" ball in 1848, the game became more popular and spread to England and other countries, especially where Scottish emigrants settled.

There are documents indicating golf was played in America before the Revolution. Golf became popular in both England and the United States about 1890.

References: Sarah Fabian Baddiel, *The World of Golf Collectables,* Wellfleet Press, 1992; Henderson & Stark, *Golf In The Making;* Pat Kennedy, *Golf Club Trademarks,* privately printed; Norman E. Martinus and Harry L. Rinker, *Warman's Paper,* Wallace–Homestead, 1994; John M. Olman and Morton W. Olman, *Golf Antiques & Other Treasures of the Game, Expanded Edition,* Market Street Press, 1993; Beverly Robb, *Collectible Golfing Novelties,* Schiffer Publishing, 1992; Janet Seagle, *The Club Makers,* United States Golf Association; Shirley and Jerry Sprung, *Decorative Golf Collectibles: Collector's Information, Current Prices,* Glentiques, 1991; Mark Wilson (ed.), *The Golf Club Identification & Price Guide III,* Ralph Maltby Enterprises, 1993.

Collectors' Clubs: Golf Collectors' Society, PO Box 491, Shawnee Mission, KS 66201; Logo Golf Ball Collector's Assoc., 4552 Barclay Fairway, Lake Worth, FL 33467; The Golf Club Collectors Assoc., 640 E. Liberty St., Girard, OH 44420.

Periodicals: *Golfiana Magazine,* PO Box 688, Edwardsville, IL 62025; *U. S. Golf Classics & Heritage Hickories,* 5407 Pennock Point Rd., Jupiter, FL 33458.

Museums: Ralph Miller Memorial Library, City of Industry, CA; United States Golf Association, "Golf House," Far Hills, NJ; PGA World Golf Hall of Fame, Pinehurst, NC.

BOOKS

Bauchope, C. Robertson (ed.), *The Golfing Annual,* Vol. 1	335.00
Beldam, *Great Golfers at a Glance*	155.00
Braid, James, *Advanced Golf,* 10th ed	14.00
Brown, J. L., *Golf at Glen Falls*	170.00
Christie, A., *The Boomerang Clue*	12.50
Clark, Robert, *Royal and Ancient Game,* 3rd ed, 1899	210.00
Darwin, B., *Green Memories,* 1928	280.00
Duncan, G., *Golf for Women*	25.00
Guldahl, Ralph, *Groove Your Golf*	15.00
Helme, E., *Family Golf,*	25.00
Hones, Ernest, *Swinging into Golf*	10.00
Hunter, Robert, *The Links,* NY, 1926	275.00
Jerome, *The Golf Club Mystery*	10.00
Jones, T. J. Jr., *Down the Fairway*	30.00
Martin, H. B., *What's Wrong with Your Game*	25.00
Rice, G. & C. Briggs, *The Duffers' Handbook of Golf,* NY, 1926	115.00
Snead, Sam, *Quick Way to Better Golf,* 1937	50.00
Steel, C., *The Golf Course Mystery*	10.00
Vaile, P. A., *Modern Golf*	20.00

EQUIPMENT

Bag
Busey Patent Caddy, mahogany, ash pipod, birch handle, canvas and leather ball pocket, club tube	280.00
Osmond Patent Caddy, ashwood, leather handles, straps, canvas club tube and ball pocket	260.00

Ball
  Bramble Ball
Haskell, patent, 1899	45.00
Spring Vale Hawk	22.00
Chemico Bob, yellow dot	35.00
Feather Ball, J. Gourlay, early 19th C, maker's name	1,000.00
Glexite, Phantom, six orig wrappers	45.00
Gutty, hand hammered	180.00
Lynx, rubber core	15.00

Square Dimple
DSO Colonel, 29 weight	60.00
North British, practice, box of 12	110.00

Club (Note: w/s–wood shaft; s/s–steel shaft)

Iron
Burke juvenile mashie, w/s	22.00
Hagen Iron–man sand wedge, w/s	120.00
George Nicol niblic, anti–shank, w/s	40.00
Six smooth face, w/s	25.00
Spalding F–4, c1922, w/s	10.00
Tom Stewart lofter, smooth face, w/s	45.00
Urquehart patent adjustable club, w/s	260.00
Wilson wedge, Staff model, c1959, s/s	36.00

Putter
A. Patrick, long nose, scare head, w/s	140.00
Forgan, scare head, long–nose, shaft stamped	100.00
Mills, "L" model, aluminum head	37.50
R. Simpson, socket head, c1900, w/s	85.00
Schenectady, w/s	50.00
Spalding "Schenectady," aluminum head	100.00
Tommy Armour IMG Ironmaster, s/s	85.00

Wood
Auchterlonie scare head brassie, w/s	30.00
Ben Sayers spoon, scare head, w/s	40.00
C.S. Butchart, scare head driver, shaft stamped	35.00
Davie Anderson scare head driver, w/s	65.00
McGregor Tourney 693W driver, c1953, s/s	115.00
Tom Morris, scare head, bulger and brassie, horn insert, stamped "T. Morris, St. Andrews"	120.00
Willie Dunn, long–nose grassed driver, stained beech head, horn insert	1,700.00

MISCELLANEOUS

Advertising Trade Card, Humphries Witch Hazel Oil, full color, woman golfer	25.00
Box, lady golfer, 1920–30	25.00
Cigarette Box, hammered pewter, surmounted by mesh gutty ball and two clubs	35.00
Cigarette Case, silver, enameled Edwardian golfer scene	280.00
Cookbook, *Golfer's Cookbook,* 91 pgs, 1968	4.00

Cigarette Lighter, Score Totaler, chrome, Japan, 2¾ x 1½", $25.00.

Doorstop, golfer putting, green cap, red
shoes, coat, and knickers, 6½ x 8" . .   **65.00**
Game
Arnold Palmer, Indoor Course, Mary   **35.00**
Spin–Golf, Chad Valley, boxed **45.00**
Greeting Card, "May Every Christmas
Joy Be Yours!," golf scene **50.00**
Magazine, *Golf Digest,* 12 issues, 1963   **12.00**
Mug, Royal Bradwell **15.00**
Plate, 6" d, teddy bear playing golf, bear
caddie, c1920 . . . .   **70.00**
Post Card
Cartoon golf scene **10.00**
Gibson, set of 5, c1905 . . . .   **20.00**
Program, Bob Hope Desert Classic,
1967 . . . .   **15.00**
Punchbowl, "Every dog has his day,"
Crombie–type golfers **700.00**
Sheet Music, 9 x 11¾", *Follow Thru,*
golf balls on cov, De Sylva, Brown,
and Henderson, Inc, 1928 . . . .   **4.00**
Tile, Delft, golfer playing to a stake, pr   **25.00**
Toast Rack, electroplate, four divisions
created by crossed clubs **80.00**
Trophy, silver, three handles, golf club
stem, Bakelite plinth **45.00**
Walking Stick, bronze head in form of
"Jigger" **26.00**
Wristwatch, mesh golf ball shape, Swiss   **110.00**

PRINTS, DRAWINGS, ETC.

Cartoon
"Golf Amenities," A T Smith, orig
Punch, India ink **225.00**
"Spy," Mure Fergusson, *Vanity Fair*   **50.00**
Painting
"The Golfing Lassie," unknown, oil
on board **175.00**
Winter scene showing golfers playing
to the mark, 17th C Dutch School,
oil on relaid canvas **2,750.00**
Photograph, Harry Vardon, sgd, 1929   **200.00**
Print
Aldin, Cecil, "North Berwick:
Perfection and the Redan," sgd by
artist **1,000.00**

Paton, Frank, "Royal and Ancient, St.
Andrews, 1798," etching, vignettes
in margin, sgd by artist **225.00**
Sadler, Dendy, "The First Tee," etch-
ing, colored **30.00**
Sketch, black chalk, Ridgewell
Bobby Jones **40.00**
Gene Sarazen **35.00**

GONDER POTTERY

Collecting Hints: Learn to identify the Gonder
glazes and forms. Once you do, you will have no
trouble identifying the pieces. Since production
is recent, many examples still can be found in
basements and at garage sales. Dealers have
been buying Gonder pieces and placing them in
storage in anticipation of a future rise in prices.

History: Lawton Gonder purchased the Zane
Pottery of Zanesville, Ohio, in 1941. Previously
Gonder had worked for the Ohio Pottery,
American Encaustic Tiling, Cherry Art Tile, and
Florence Pottery. He was a consultant for
Fraunfelter China and Standard Tile. Gonder re-
named the Zane Pottery the Gonder Ceramic
Arts, Inc.
Gonder's pottery was high priced for its time.
Besides a mingled color glaze, the pottery made
a flambe glaze, a gold crackle glaze, and a line
of old Chinese crackle reproduction pottery.
Many shapes followed the Rum Rill patterns from
the Florence Pottery.
Almost all Gonder Pottery is marked. Some
had paper labels, but the majority had one of the
following impressed marks: "GONDER CE-
RAMIC ART," "Gonder/Original" in script,
"Gonder" in script, "GONDER/U.S.A.," "Gonder
(script)/U.S.A.," and "GONDER" in a semicircle.
The company expanded in 1946 and opened
the Elgee Pottery, which made lamp bases. The
plant burned in 1954. A brief expansion occurred
at the main plant, but production ceased in
1957.

References: Susan and Al Bagdade, *Warman's
American Pottery and Porcelain,* Wallace–
Homestead, 1994; Ron Hoopes, *The Collector's
Guide and History of Gonder Pottery,* L–W
Books, 1992.

Collectors' Clubs: American Art Pottery
Association, 125 E. Rose Ave., St. Louis, MO
63119; Gonder Collectors, PO Box 21,
Crooksville, OH 43731.

Basket, twisted handle, brown glaze,
13" w, 9" h, L–19 . . . .   **45.00**
Candleholders, pr
Crescent Moon, white, 6½" h, J–56   **35.00**
Lotus Flower, 5" w, E–14 . . . .   **20.00**

Gonder mark, "H–39, Gonder, U.S.A."

Creamer and Sugar, cov, large, ivory
  ground, brown speckles and drips . . **12.50**
Ewer, shell shape, green and brown
  glaze, 14" h, #508 . . . . **85.00**
Figure
  Oriental Couple, 14" h, price for pair **75.00**
  Panther, 15" l, #217 . . . . **115.00**
  Two Deer, jumping over fronds, Art
  Deco style, brown, 11" h, #690 . . **25.00**
Planter
  Gondola, yellow and pink **25.00**
  Swan, E–44 . . . . **25.00**
Television Lamp
  Seagull, black, flying over yellow
  waves, 12" h **75.00**
  Ship, green and brown speckled
  glaze, 14" h **35.00**
Vase
  Cornucopia, green and brown, 10" h,
  H–14 . . . . **25.00**
  Ewer, brown and yellow glaze, 9" h,
  H–33 . . . . **35.00**
  Rectangular, yellow, 8½" h, H–74 . . **20.00**
  Urn and Leaf shape, pink, 6" h, H–80 **38.00**

GRANITEWARE

Collecting Hints: Old graniteware is heavier than
new graniteware. Pieces with cast iron handles
date from 1870 to 1890; wood handles date from
1900 to 1910. Other dating clues are seams,
wood knobs, and tin lids.

History: Graniteware is the name commonly
given to iron or steel kitchenware covered with
enamel coating.

The first graniteware was made in Germany in
the 1830s. It was not produced in the United
States until the 1860s. At the start of World War
I, when European manufacturers turned to the
making of war weapons, American producers
took over the market.

Colors commonly marketed were white and
gray. Each company made their own special
color, including shades of blue, green, brown, violet, cream, and red. Graniteware still is manu-

factured with the earliest pieces in greatest demand among collectors.

References: Helen Greguire, *The Collector's
Encyclopedia of Graniteware: Colors, Shapes
& Values*, (1990, 1994 value update), Book 2
(1993), Collector Books; Dana Gehman
Morykan and Harry L. Rinker, *Warman's Country
Antiques & Collectibles, Second Edition,* Wallace–
Homestead, 1994; Vernagene Vogelzang and
Evelyn Welch, *Graniteware, Collectors' Guide
With Prices, Volume 1* (1981), and *Volume 2*
(1986), Wallace–Homestead, out–of–print.

Collectors' Club: National Graniteware Society,
PO Box 10013, Cedar Rapids, IA 52410.

Basin, large handled, turquoise swirl . . **85.00**
Bedpan, gray mottled **15.00**
Berry Pail, 7" d, 5" h, tin lid, wood
  knob, wood grip **60.00**
Bowl, deep, gray speckled **70.00**
Bread Box, sq, gray, "Bread" **25.00**
Bundt Pan, gray mottled **25.00**
Cake Pan, 10 x 14", gray **8.50**
Chamberstick, gray speckle **65.00**
Coffee Boiler, 3 gal, speckled **50.00**
Coffee Pot
  Blue and white swirl, 10" h **110.00**
  Gray, gooseneck spout **30.00**
Colander, cobalt **35.00**
Cooking Pot, 2½ gal, gray **48.00**
Cup, blue and white speckled, rust spots **12.00**
Dipper
  Blue and white **35.00**
  Red and white **10.00**
Drain Basket, brown swirl, bail handle **20.00**
Dustpan, miniature, blue, speckled . . . **135.00**
Egg Cup, rooster shape, gray **8.00**
Food Mold, turk's head, turquoise and
  white swirl **200.00**
Foot Tub, 16 x 19", gray mottle, rolled
  edges **56.00**
Fruit Jar Funnel, gray and white, strap
  handle **22.00**

**Lunch Pail, cov, oval, gray, pressed tin
bail handle, 8" l, 5½" w, $110.00.**

Funnel, 8½" h, gray	**18.00**
Grater, 4½" l, gray speckled	**135.00**
Kettle, gray, bulbous, ear handle	**12.00**
Kettle Pan, blue and white swirl	**38.00**
Ladle	
Blue and white swirl	**85.00**
Gray speckled, pierced	**85.00**
Loaf Pan, 7 x 12", gray, mottled	**10.00**
Measure	
Blue and white swirl, pint	**225.00**
Gray, 1 cup	**48.00**
Melon Mold, gray, ribbed, tin bottom	
with ring, marked "Extra Agate," #50	**70.00**
Milk Bowl, small	**8.00**
Milk Pitcher, blue	**40.00**
Mold, fluted, gray speckled	**135.00**
Muffin Pan, gray mottled, eight cavities	**40.00**
Mush Mug, brown and white swirl . . .	**68.00**
Pie Baker, gray	**8.00**
Pie Pan	
Cobalt blue and white swirl	**30.00**
Gray	**10.00**
Pitcher, 7" h, gray	**25.00**
Plate, child's, nursery rhyme	**30.00**
Platter, white, blue edge	**24.00**
Potty, gray, "Poppy Prize, 1935"	**75.00**
Preserving Kettle, green and white mottle	**125.00**
Pudding Pan, cobalt and white swirl . .	**16.00**
Roaster	
Cobalt blue and white swirl, tray in-	
side	**90.00**
Gray	**18.00**
Red, large	**50.00**
Scoop, sq, gray	**78.00**
Skillet	
Blue–green and white swirl	**135.00**
Red	**45.00**
Soap Dish, cobalt blue swirl, hanging	**110.00**
Soap Holder, blue speckled, insert wall	
mount	**30.00**
Stew Pan, red and white swirl, tin lid . .	**40.00**
Tea Set	
Child's size, 7 pcs, gray speckled . . .	**265.00**
Doll size, 12 pcs, blue	**335.00**
Tray, 17¾" l, blue	**45.00**
Tube Pan	
Blue and white swirl	**185.00**
Gray	**20.00**

HALL CHINA

Collecting Hints: Hall China Company named many of their patterns, but some of these pattern names are being gradually changed by dealers to other names. A good example of this is the Silhouette pattern, which is also known as Taverne. Many shapes are also referred to by more than one name, i.e., Radiance aka Sunshine; Terrace aka Stepdown; and, Pert aka Sani–Grid.

Due to their high quality, most Hall China pieces are still in wonderful condition. There is no reason to pay full price for imperfect pieces.

History: Hall China Company was born out of the dissolution of the East Liverpool Potteries Company. Robert Hall, a partner in the merger, died within months of forming the new company. Robert T. Hall, his son, took over.

At first, the company produced the same semi–porcelain dinnerware and toiletware that was being made at the other potteries in East Liverpool, Ohio. Robert T. Hall began to experiment in an attempt to duplicate an ancient Chinese one–fire process that would produce a non–crazing vitrified china, with body and glaze being fired at the same time. He succeeded in 1911. Hall has been made that way ever since.

Hall's basic products are institutional ware (hotel and restaurant) to the trade only. However, they also have produced many retail and premium lines, e.g. Autumn Leaf for Jewel Tea and Blue Bouquet for the Standard Coffee Co. of New Orleans. A popular line is the gold–decorated teapots that were introduced for retail sale in 1920. In 1931 kitchenware was introduced, soon followed by dinnerware. These lines were decorated in both solid colors and decals for retail and premium sales.

Hall is still producing china at its plant in East Liverpool, Ohio.

References: Susan and Al Bagdade, *Warman's American Pottery and Porcelain,* Wallace–Homestead, 1994; Harvey Duke, *Hall: Price Guide Update,* ELO Books, 1992; Harvey Duke, *Superior Quality Hall China,* ELO Books, 1977; Harvey Duke, *Hall 2,* ELO Books, 1985; Harvey Duke, *The Official Price Guide to Pottery and Porcelain, Eighth Edition* House of Collectibles, 1995; C. L. Miller, *The Jewel Tea Company: Its History and Products,* Schiffer Publishing, 1994; Margaret and Kenn Whitmyer, *The Collector's Encyclopedia of Hall China, Second Edition* Collector Books, 1994.

Collectors' Clubs: Autumn Leaf Reissues Assoc., 19238 Dorchester Circle, Strongsville, OH 44136; National Autumn Leaf Collectors Club, 7346 Shamrock Dr., Indianapolis, IN 46217.

Periodical: *Hall China Encore,* 317 N. Pleasant St., Oberlin, OH 44074.

Note: Hall has been reissuing many of its products in its new Americana retail line for several years now. They are all decorated in solid colors. If you are a new collector and are unsure if an item is new or old, you may want to buy only the items with decal or gold decorations, as these pieces have not been reissued and Hall has no intention of doing so. Because of this reissue, prices have dropped slightly on a few solid–colored items.

AUTUMN LEAF Premium for the Jewel Tea Company. Produced 1933 until 1978. Other companies made matching fabric, metal, glass, and plastic accessories.

Baking Dish, 3 part, swirl, 7½" d	18.00
Ball Jug, #3	35.00
Ball Pitcher, icelip, label	50.00
Bean Pot, handled, 1 qt	60.00
Bowl, divided, 10½" d	100.00
Cake Plate, 9" d	20.00
Casserole, cov	
1½ qt	30.00
2 qt, round	45.00
Cereal Bowl, 6¼" d	20.00
Coffeepot, 9 cup	45.00
Coffee Server, 8½" h	35.00
Cookie Jar	145.00
Cream Soup	25.00
Cup and Saucer	12.00
Custard	6.00
Flat Soup, 8½" d	20.00
Fruit Bowl, 5½" d	6.00
Gravy Boat	25.00
Iced Tea Tumbler, frosted, gold trim,	
Libbey Glass	20.00
Irish Coffee Mug	120.00
Jug, ball	30.00
Mayonnaise, cov, underplate	50.00
Milk Pitcher	22.00
Mixing Bowls, nested set of three	50.00
Mug	125.00
Pitcher, utility, 2½ pt	25.00
Platter, 11½" l	20.00
Range Set, pair right handled shakers	
and drip jar	95.00
Salad Bowl, 9" d	32.00
Salt and Pepper Shakers, pr, handled . .	17.00
Stack Dish, 24 oz	25.00
Sugar, open, squatty	12.00
Teapot, cov, Aladdin	70.00
Tidbit, 3 tiers	100.00
Vegetable Dish, cov, 9" d	60.00
Water Pitcher, ice lip	28.00

CAMEO ROSE Pattern made exclusively for the Jewel Tea Company, early 1950s through the early 1970s.

Butter Dish, cov, ¼ lb	30.00
Casserole	30.00
Creamer and Sugar, cov	20.00
Cup and Saucer	8.00
Gravy	15.00
Plate	
6½" d, bread and butter	4.00
8" d, salad	5.00
10" d, dinner	8.00
Relish	12.00
Tidbit Tray	35.00
Vegetable Dish, oval	15.00

COFFEEPOTS

Coffee Queen, red	45.00
Deca Flip, Chinese red and white	55.00
Flamingo Drip Viking	40.00
Flareware, Gold Lace	35.00
Floral Lattice (a.k.a. Flowerpot)	30.00
Imperial, red	50.00
Kadota Pastel Tulips	85.00
Kadota Tulips	100.00
Panel	30.00
Queen, Chinese red	75.00
Rounded Terrace, Rose White pattern .	30.00
Terrace, Gold Label line	38.00

CROCUS Dinnerware pattern produced during the 1930s. This decal with multicolored stylized crocuses and green and black leaves is also found on an endless variety of kitchenware shapes.

Ball Jug, #3	85.00
Butter Dish, cov, 1 lb	500.00
Cake Plate	25.00
Casserole, cov	55.00
Cereal Bowl, 6" d	12.00
Cup and Saucer	15.00
Gravy Boat	30.00
Mixing Bowl	45.00
Plate	
7¼" d, bread and butter	6.00
8¼" d, salad	8.00
9" d, luncheon	12.00
10" d, dinner	35.00
Platter, 13¼" l	30.00
Salt and Pepper Shakers, pr, teardrop	
style	40.00
Teapot, New York shape	165.00
Tidbit, 3 tier	50.00

ORANGE POPPY Premium for the Great American Tea Company. Introduced 1933. Discontinued in the 1950s. Dinnerware made in C–style shape. Metal accessory pieces available, though scarce.

Casserole	55.00
Coffeepot, S lid	40.00
Creamer and Sugar	60.00
Custard	8.00
French Baker	20.00
Metal Accessory, tray, 15" l	38.00
Plate	
6" d, bread and butter	5.00
9" d, luncheon	12.00
Platter, oval, 13¼" l	25.00
Refrigerator Dish, cov, round, small . . .	9.00
Salad Bowl	25.00
Salt and Pepper Shakers, pr	40.00
Saucer	3.50
Teapot, Streamline, lid nick	200.00
Vegetable Bowl, 9¼" d	32.00

PASTEL MORNING GLORY
Dinnerware line produced in the late 1930s and readily found in northern Michigan, Wisconsin, and Minnesota. Design consists of large pink morning glories surrounded by green leaves and small blue flowers on white ground. Pattern also used on kitchenware items.

Ball Jug, #3	75.00
Cereal Bowl, 6" d	16.00
Cup and Saucer	12.00
Custard	10.00
Flat Soup, 8½" d	16.00
Fruit Bowl, 5½" d	5.00
Gravy Boat	25.00
Pie Baker	25.00
Plate	
6" d, bread and butter	4.00
8¼" d, salad	5.00
9" d, luncheon	8.00
10" d, dinner	25.00
Platter, oval	
11¼" l	20.00
13¼" l	25.00
Vegetable Bowl	
Oval	20.00
Round, 9¼" d	25.00

PERT
Streamlined kitchenware shape introduced in 1941. Usually found in Chinese red or cadet with white handles and knobs, sometimes with decal decoration.

Bean Pot, tab handles, Chinese red	45.00
Casserole, cov, tab handles, Chinese red	25.00
Creamer and Sugar, open, Chinese red	20.00
Jug, 7½" h, cadet	28.00
Salt and Pepper Shakers, pr	16.00

RADIANCE
Kitchenware line introduced in 1933. Produced mainly in solid colors, with Chinese red being both the most common and most desirable. May also be found with decal decorations.

Canister	
Coffee, Chinese red	125.00
Flour, Chinese red	125.00
Casserole, cobalt	35.00
Drip Jar, cov	
#3, 4¾", Chinese red	65.00
#5, 6¼", ivory	12.00
Mixing Bowls, stacking set of three, #3, #5, and #6, ivory	25.00
Salt and Pepper Shakers, pr, canister style, yellow	40.00

RED POPPY
Grand Union Tea Company premium, produced from mid 1930s until mid 1950s. Complete line of D–style dinnerware and kitchenware in various forms. Red poppy and black leaves decals on white ground. Glass, metal, wood, and cloth accessories were also marketed.

Bowl, 9¼" d	25.00
Cake Plate	22.00
Cake Server	75.00
Casserole, cov	25.00
Drip Jar	30.00
Jug, large, Radiance	13.50
Metal Accessories	
Cake Safe, tin	30.00
Coffee Dispenser, wall mount	30.00
Match Safe	30.00
Mixing Bowl	
Large	16.00
Stacking, set of three	50.00
Pitcher	24.00
Plate, 9" d, dinner	6.00
Platter, 13" l	17.50
Salt and Pepper Shakers, pr, range	30.00
Teapot, New York shape	95.00

REFRIGERATOR WARE
Items meant specifically for refrigerator storage. Line includes covered casseroles, leftovers, butter dishes, and water servers. Marketed for general retail as well as exclusive designs for companies such as Sears, Westinghouse, General Electric, Hotpoint, and Montgomery Ward.

Butter, Phoenix, delphinium, chips	5.00
Casserole, ridged, canary yellow	40.00
Leftover	
Adonis, daffodil yellow, hairline	20.00
General, sunset orange	30.00
Phoenix, delphinium	15.00
Water Server	
Adonis, blue	45.00
General, garden green	35.00
Nora, daffodil yellow	30.00
Phoenix, delphinium	80.00

ROSE PARADE
Kitchenware line produced in the 1940s. Cadet blue bodies, white handles and knobs decorated with pastel floral decals. Often confused with Royal Rose design. Rose Parade pieces do not have silver trim.

Bean Pot, cov, tab handles	60.00
Bowl, 9" d, straight sides	20.00
Casserole, cov, tab handles	30.00
Creamer and Sugar, open, Pert	28.00
Custard, straight sides	15.00
Drip Jar, cov, tab handles	25.00
French Baker, fluted sides	30.00
Teapot, cov, Pert, 6 cup	40.00

ROSE WHITE
Kitchenware pattern with Hi–white body and pink rose decal. Same shapes as Rose Parade line. Same decal used on Royal Rose pattern.

Bean Pot, cov, tab handles 45.00
Bowl
   6" d, Medallion 15.00
   9" d, straight sides 20.00
Casserole, cov, tab handles 25.00
Custard, straight sides 15.00
Jug, Pert, 7½" 38.00
Salt and Pepper Shakers, pr, Pert 30.00

SPRINGTIME Standard Tea Company premium. Limited Production.

Butter Dish, cov 10.00
Cake Plate 15.00
Creamer and Sugar, cov 15.00
Cup and Saucer 5.00
Fruit Bowl, 5½" d 7.50
Gravy Boat 22.50
Plate
   6½" d, bread and butter 3.00
   9" d, dinner 6.00
Platter 10.00
Starter Set, 16 pcs, service for four,
   plate, fruit bowl, and cup and saucer,
   orig cartons 85.00

TEAPOTS

Aladdin
   Cadet Blue, white morning glory . . .   110.00
   Cobalt, gold dec, oval infusor 110.00
   Yellow, gold dec 60.00
Albany, mahogany, gold dec 40.00
Baltimore, red 350.00
Basket, yellow, small chips on spout . .   135.00
Basketball, red 750.00
Boston
   Delphinium, gold dec 50.00
   Gray 35.00
   Red 225.00
   Sea Spray Green, gold fruit dec 50.00
   Turquoise 45.00
Car, turquoise, platinum dec 750.00
Casual Living, loop handle 125.00
Connie, green 35.00

Teapot, Globe, No Drip, Addison, standard gold dec, 6 cup, $100.00.

Coverlet, yellow 35.00
French, warm yellow, gold dec, 10 cup   40.00
Globe, gray, gold dec, no drip 100.00
Grape, black, gold dec 175.00
Hook Cover, Autumn Leaf, Jewel Tea,
   club 175.00
Kansas, emerald green, lid crack 225.00
Los Angeles
   Celadon, gold dec 50.00
   Cobalt, gold dec 70.00
McCormick, maroon 30.00
Melody
   Ivory, unmarked 165.00
   Red 250.00
Moderne
   Cobalt 175.00
   Marine, gold dec 45.00
   Red 695.00
Murphy, blue 35.00
Nautilus, yellow, gold dec 110.00
New York
   Gamebird, 2 cup 165.00
   Yellow, gold dec, 2 cup 35.00
Parade, Canary yellow, gold dec 28.00
Philadelphia, pink, gold dec 95.00
Regal, white, gold dec 90.00
Star, cobalt, gold dec 125.00
Starlight, lemon 125.00

Teapot, Boston, Dresden blue, standard gold dec, 6 cup, $20.00.

Teapot, Philadelphia, Gold Label Line, pink, gold basket design, 5 cup, $95.00.

Surfside, yellow **90.00**
Twin Spout
  Cobalt, gold dec **140.00**
  Turquoise, lid crack **50.00**
Windshield
  Cobalt, gold dec **150.00**
  Gamebird **275.00**
  Maroon, gold dec **65.00**

WILDFIRE Great American Tea Company premium produced during the 1950s.

Cereal Bowl **8.00**
Cup and Saucer **10.00**
Eggcup **32.00**
Fruit Bowl, 5½" d **6.00**
Gravy Boat **18.00**
Pie Baker **18.00**
Plate, 9" d, dinner **8.00**
Platter, 11" l **12.00**
Salad Bowl, 9" d **16.00**
Salt Shaker, handled **12.00**
Soup **10.00**

HARKER POTTERY

Collecting Hints: In 1965 Harker China had the capacity to produce 25 million pieces of dinnerware each year. Hence, there is a great deal of Harker material available at garage sales and flea markets. Many patterns also were kept in production for decades.

Between 1935 and 1955 the Harker Company organized Columbia Chinaware, a sales organization used to market Harker products in small towns across the country. The line included enamel ware, glass and aluminum products. One pattern of Columbia Chinaware was "Autumn Leaf," eagerly sought by Autumn Leaf collectors.

Collectors should focus on Harker patterns by famous designers. Among these are Russel Wright's White Clover and George Bauer's Cameoware. Many patterns will be found with different color grounds. Other patterns were designed to have mass appeal. Colonial Lady was popular at "dish nites" at the movies or other businesses.

Shapes and forms did change through the decades. An interesting collection might focus on one object, e.g., a sugar or creamer, collected in a variety of patterns from different historical periods. Watch for unusual pieces. The Countryside pattern features a rolling pin, scoop and cake server.

History: The Harker Company began in 1840 when Benjamin Harker, an English slater turned farmer in East Liverpool, Ohio, built a kiln and began making yellow ware products from clay deposits on his land. The business was managed by members of the Harker family until the Civil War when David Boyce, a brother–in–law, took over the operation. Although a Harker resumed management after the war, members of the Boyce family assumed key roles within the firm; David G. Boyce, a grandson of David, served as president.

In 1879 the first whiteware products were introduced. A disastrous flood in 1884 caused severe financial problems which the company overcame. In 1931 the company moved to Chester, West Virginia, to escape the flooding problems. In 1945 Harker introduced Cameoware made by the engobe process. The engobe or layered effect was achieved by placing a copper mask over the bisque and sand blasting to leave the design imprint. The white rose pattern on blue ground was marketed as "White Rose Carv–Kraft" in Montgomery Ward stores.

The Harker Company used a large variety of backstamps and names. Hotoven cookingware featured a scroll, draped over pots, with a kiln design at top. Columbia Chinaware had a circular stamp with the Statue of Liberty.

Harker made a Rockingham ware line in the 1960s. The hound handled pitcher and mugs were included.

The Jeannette Glass Company purchased the Harker Company and the plant was closed in March 1972. Ohio Stoneware, Inc., utilized the plant building until it was destroyed by fire in 1975.

References: Susan and Al Bagdade, *Warman's American Pottery and Porcelain,* Wallace–Homestead, 1994; Neva W. Colbert, *The Collector's Guide To Harker Pottery, U.S.A.: Identification and Values,* Collector Books, 1993; Jo Cunningham, *The Collector's Encyclopedia Of American Dinnerware,* Collector Books, 1982, 1995 value update.

See: Russel Wright

AMY Dinnerware and kitchenware items with floral decal decoration on white ground. Silver trim.

Plate, gray border, 8¼" d, $3.00.

Bean Pot	8.00
Bowl	
5½" d	4.00
6¼" d	5.00
Tab Handles	6.00
Creamer and Sugar	14.00
Cup and Saucer	8.00
Mixing Bowl, 9" d	20.00
Pepper Shaker	10.00
Pie Baker	20.00
Plate	
6¼" d	4.00
7⅜" d	6.00
9⅛" d	8.00
Rolling Pin	100.00
Scoop	28.00
Spoon	28.00

COLONIAL LADY Black silhouette decal of colonial woman in various settings. White ground, silver trim.

Cake Plate	25.00
Cereal Bowl	12.00
Creamer and Sugar	20.00
Cup and Saucer	12.00
Pie Baker	15.00
Plate	
Bread and Butter	4.00
Salad	6.00
Salt and Pepper Shakers, pr, small	18.00
Server	28.00
Vegetable Bowl	22.00

LAURELTON Dinnerware line produced in green and beige, c1958.

Creamer and Sugar, cov	15.00
Cup and Saucer	8.00
Plate	
Dinner	8.00
Luncheon	6.00
Platter, oval	15.00
Soup Bowl	10.00
Vegetable Bowl, round	13.00

MALLOW Decal decoration of pastel pink, blue, and yellow flowers and green leaves on white ground. Black trim.

Bowl	
5" d	15.00
10" d	30.00
Jug, cov	25.00
Plate, 8" d	10.00
Rolling Pin	95.00
Spoon, hairline	10.00

PETIT POINT ROSE Decal decoration of multicolored petit point roses on white ground. Silver trim. There are two variations of this design; most items can be found in both styles.

Batter Bowl	55.00
Bowl, 8¾" d	15.00
Cake Plate	12.00
Cake Server	18.00
Casserole, cov, 7" d	32.00
Coffeepot	40.00
Cup and Saucer	15.00
Pie Baker	12.00
Plate, 8½" d	6.00
Spoon	18.00
Sugar, cov	10.00

HEDI SCHOOP

Collecting Hints: Schoop is best known for creating beautiful figures and figurines executed with exacting details and rich colors. The most difficult pieces to find are the television lamps produced during the mid 1950s. They are highly sought after by collectors.

History: Hedi Schoop Art Creations was incorporated in 1942 in North Hollywood, California. The pottery produced highly detailed figurines, lamps, wall plaques, planters, and other decorative accessories. In the mid 1950s a line of television lamps was introduced, but a fire at the plant in 1958 brought an abrupt end to production. The pottery was not rebuilt, although Ms. Schoop did do some design work for other companies for a short period of time.

Reference: Jack Chipman, *Collector's Encyclopedia of California Pottery,* Collector Books, 1992.

Periodical: *The Pottery Collectors Express,* PO Box 221, Mayview, MO 64071-0221.

Box, cov, boxer	150.00
Cookie Jar, Darner Doll, blue and green	325.00
Double Candleholder, Fantasy series	40.00
Figure	
Art Deco Musicians, white and gold, 13" h	150.00
Claudette Colbert	85.00
Crowing Rooster, 15" h	125.00
Dutch Girl	65.00
French Maid, 10" h	80.00
Greek Couple, 14" h	125.00
Oriental Couple, no lanterns, large size	100.00
Peasant Woman	85.00
Poodle, pink, black, and white, 12" l	125.00
Repose, lime green, 11" h	90.00
Siamese Dancers, 15" h	275.00
Pencil Box, cov, teal and gray, painted feather on cov, 4½ x 7½"	65.00
Planter, lady reading book	60.00
Plate, apple, pr	65.00
Twin Vases, large, pr	125.00

HOLIDAY COLLECTIBLES

Collecting Hints: The most common holiday item is the post card. Collectors tend to specialize in one holiday. Christmas, Halloween, and Easter are the most desirable. New collectors still can find bargains—especially in the Thanksgiving and Valentine's Day collectibles.

Holiday items change annually. Manufacturers constantly must appeal to the same buyer.

History: Holidays are an important part of American life. Many have both religious and secular overtones such as Christmas, St. Patrick's Day, Easter, and Halloween. National holidays such as the Fourth of July and Thanksgiving are part of one's yearly planning. There are regional holidays. Fastnacht day in Pennsylvania–German country is just one example.

Some holidays are the creation of the merchandising industry, e.g., Valentine's Day, Mother's Day, Father's Day, etc. The two leading forces in the perpetuation of holiday gift giving are the card industry and the floral industry. Through slick promotional campaigns they constantly create new occasions to give their products. Other marketing aspects follow quickly.

Holiday collectibles also keep pace with popular trends. Peanuts is now being challenged by Strawberry Shortcake, the Smurfs, and Star Wars.

References: Juanita Burnett, *A Guide To Easter Collectibles*, Collector Books, 1992; Dan and Pauline Campanelli, *Halloween Collectables: A Price Guide*, L–W Books, 1995; *Favors and Novelties: Wholesale Trade List No. 26, 1924–1925*, L–W Book Sales, 1985, 1994–95 value update; Helaine Fendelman and Jeri Schwartz, *The Official Pride Guide to Holiday Collectibles*, House of Collectibles, 1991; Jeanette Lasansky, *Collecting Guide: Holiday Paper Honeycomb, Cards, Garlands, Centerpieces, And Other Tissue–Paper Fantasies Of The 20th C*, published by author, 1993; Dana Gehman Morykan and Harry L. Rinker, *Warman's Country Antiques & Collectibles, Second Edition*, Wallace–Homestead, 1994; Herbert N. Schiffer, *Collectible Rabbits*, Schiffer Publishing, Ltd., 1990; Margaret Schiffer, *Holiday Toys and Decorations*, Schiffer Publishing, 1985; Stuart Schneider, *Halloween In America: A Collector's Guide with Prices*, Schiffer Publishing, 1995; Ellen Stern, *The Very Best From Hallmark: Greeting Cards Through The Years*, Harry N. Abrams, 1988.

Periodical: *Trick or Treat Trader*, PO Box 499, Winchester, NH 03470.

Easter
    Basket, 6" h, reed, pink, handle, Germany **20.00**

Candy Container, papier mache, German, 1950s
    4" h, chick, half egg in front **32.00**
    4¾" h
        Chick with basket **38.00**
        Rabbit with basket **38.00**
    6" h, hen on nest **48.00**
    6½" h
        Chick **42.00**
        Duck with egg shaped body . . . **42.00**
    7" h
        Boy and girl chick, round body, price for pr **80.00**
        Chick, top hat **65.00**
    7¼" h, chick, hat, basket **48.00**
Chick
    4" h, cotton batting wire legs, glass eyes **60.00**
    5½" h, composition, dressed in red coat, marked "Germany" **38.00**
Egg, milk glass, blown out design of hatching chick **85.00**
Eggcup, china, duck, rabbit, chick, marked "Japan," price for 8 pc set **40.00**
Post Card
    "Easter Greetings," two rabbits kissing, children watching, 1910 . . **2.00**
    "Kind Easter Wishes," two boys riding white rabbits **2.00**
    "To Wish You A Happy Easter," chicks pecking out of package, Tuck **2.50**

Ground Hog Day, post card, $20.00.

Rabbit
    Celluloid, 3" h, floppy ears, sitting, radish in mouth, Japan **30.00**
    Composition, 5" h, sitting, Germany **18.00**
    Cotton batting, 2½" h, holding carrot, green tucksheer **85.00**
    Metal, white, marked Germany, set of 4 . . . . **45.00**

Tin, 5½" h, litho, on wheels, USA   25.00
Wind–up, pulling cart with duck
and chick, celluloid and tin,
windup 110.00
Roly Poly, 4½" h, rabbit, celluloid,
dressed in purple, standing on ball,
Japan 25.00
Salt Shaker, egg shaped, Mt
Washington
Blown out rabbit, hen, chicks, sin-
gle 95.00
Columbian Exposition, 1893, price
for pair 245.00
Stuffed Toy
6" h
Duck, novelty 12.00
Rabbit, plush 8.00
8" h, rabbit, plush, squeaker 14.00
9" h, rabbit, straw stuffed, wooden
head 60.00
Fourth of July
Candy Box, 2¼ x 2½", red, white,
and blue, shield shape 10.00
Flag, 10" h, wooden stick, 48 stars . .   2.00
Pencil, lead, red, white, and blue pa-
per 3.00
Pinback Button
⅝" d, "4th of July Middleboro 1936
Contributor," red and white . . .   12.50
1¼" d, red July 4, 1947, blue rim .   10.00
Post Card
"4th of July," spelled out in red fire-
crackers, Germany 2.00
"The Glorious Fourth," large flag,
1911 . . . .   2.00
Halloween
Candy Container, papier mache
Black Cat, 8" h, cut out eyes and
mouth, wire bail, Germany 58.00
Pumpkin, cut–out eyes and mouth,
wire handle
4" h 35.00
5½" h 45.00
7" h 65.00
Clicker, litho tin, orange and black,
frog shape, marked "T. Cohn,
USA" 7.00
Fan
Fold–out, wooden stick, witch rid-
ing broom, black and orange,
1920s, marked "Germany" 10.00
Paper, litho, wooden handle, two
black cats, arched backs, marked
"D.R.G.M. Germany" 15.00
Figure
Black Cat, 9" h, cardboard, flat,
movable legs and tail, Beistle
Co. USA 12.00
Ghost, 9½" h, cardboard,
stand–up, USA 15.00
Pumpkin Head, 3" h, composition,
wearing yellow shirt and pointed
hat, Germany 25.00

Skull, 3½" h, bisque, sitting on
book, marked "Japan" 15.00
Hat
Cardboard and crepe paper, black
and orange, 4" h, Germany 10.00
Crepe paper, orange and black,
gold and black band 15.00
Horn
Cardboard, black and orange, cat,
witch, and moon figures, 9" h,
USA 7.00
Paper, orange and black, wooden
mouthpiece, Germany 5.00
Wooden, black and orange, cat
face, 4" h, marked
"Czecho–Slavakia" 18.00
Lantern, pumpkin, candleholder in
base, papier mache, paper eyes
and mouth, wire handle, 4" h,
1910, Germany 60.00
Mask
Boy, papier mache, painted face,
cloth ties 35.00
Clown, cloth, painted face 7.00
Devil, cloth, red, bells on ears . . .   18.00
Elephant, cloth, black and grey . .   5.00
Face, wire mesh, painted, cloth ties   65.00
Noisemaker, litho tin
Bell, frying pan shape, wooden
clangers, orange and black,
marked "J. Chein" 15.00
Rattle, pumpkins, marked "T Cohn,
USA" . . . .
Post Card
"Halloween," children bobbing for
apples, 1908, Tuck 5.50
Witch reading cards, brew by
table, Germany 5.00
Stand–up, 10" h, witch, cardboard,
USA 15.00
Stickpin, pumpkin head with pointed
hat, composition, Japan 5.00
Tambourine, tin, litho, orange and
black, marked "T Cohn, Inc"

**Halloween, post card, Ellen Clapsaddle,
artist sgd, bright orange pumpkin, $8.00.**

Cat face **10.00**
Witch face **10.00**
Memorial Day
Post Card
"A grateful land remembers all her
promises today," children carry-
ing garlands, Tuck **2.50**
"On Memorial Day," "Hail
Columbia," musical score, angel
flying with flag, 1908 . . . . **4.00**
Print, "On Memorial Day," widow
and children dropping garlands
over father's portrait, Supplement
to *Grit*, May 29, 1904 . . . . **15.00**
President's Day
Axe, 7" h wooden handle, "I cannot
tell a lie" painted on blade **10.00**
Candy Container
Hat, tri–cornered, black, card-
board, cloth cherries **30.00**
Tree stump, papier mache, compo-
sition cherries, 7" h, Germany . . **75.00**
Post Card
"Lincoln Centennial Souvenir,"
Lincoln and slaves, 1909 . . . . . **3.00**
Lincoln statue, surrounded by flags,
Tuck **2.50**
"Three cheers for George
Washington," children waving
flag beneath Washington's por-
trait, 1909 . . . . **1.75**
"Washington, The Father of his
Country," 1912 . . . . **2.00**
Stickpin, bust of George Washington,
diecut hatchet, marked
"Washington's Hatchet, Feb 22,"
gilt finish, red painted highlights . . **65.00**
St. Patrick's Day
Candy Container
3" h, top hat, green, cardboard,
bisque pipe, cloth shamrock,
Germany **25.00**
4" l, potato, papier mache, green
paper shamrock **45.00**
4½" h, Irish girl holding harp,
standing on box, marked
"Germany" **32.00**
Figure, 7" h, Leprechaun, celluloid,
holding pig, Japan **28.00**
Nodder, 3" h, Irish boy, bisque,
marked "Germany" **35.00**
Post Card
"Erin go Bragh," scenes of Ireland
background **3.00**
"St. Patrick was a Gentleman," Irish
boy standing on a chair singing **3.50**
Shamrock, 2½" l, wire wrapped,
green silk floss, small bisque hat at-
tached **5.00**
Sheet Music, *Sing Me A Song of
Ireland,* New York Publishing
House, 1905 . . . . **10.00**

Thanksgiving
Candy Container, turkey
3" h, bisque, standing on card-
board container **35.00**
5" h, papier mache, folded tail,
metal legs and feet, Germany . . **38.00**
5½" h, papier mache, fan tail,
metal legs and feet, glass eyes,
Germany **45.00**
8" h, pale orange, opening in base,
marked "Atco Co., USA" **22.00**
Decoration, 8¾" h, turkey, fold–out,
cardboard, tissue paper base, USA **12.00**
Figure, turkey, composition
2½" h, fan tail, metal legs and feet,
marked "Germany" **15.00**
4½" h, green base, Japan **8.00**
Post Card
"A Joyous Thanksgiving," boy carv-
ing pumpkin, 1913 . . . . **4.00**
"May glad Thanksgiving crown
your days and years," woman
holding turkey, 1912 . . . . **2.50**
"Thanksgiving Greetings," children
playing with white turkeys, 1909 **2.50**
"Wishing You a Happy
Thanksgiving," turkey standing
on a flag, 1910 . . . . **2.00**
Valentine's Day
Greeting Card
"For My Valentine," boy and girl
picking flowers, inside greeting,
4" h, Whitney, USA **1.50**
"Good Wishes For You," two chil-
dren framed, diecut lace, emb
background, inside greeting, 6" h **8.00**
"I'd Make a Bird of a Valentine,"
parrot, stand–up, 5" h, Germany **4.00**
"I'd love to paint you my
Valentine," boy painting a girl's
portrait, fold–out, stand–up, 6" h,
USA **3.00**
"Loving Greetings," diecut girl and
boy sitting on chaise, emb background, fold–out, stand–up, 9" h,
Germany **15.00**
"To My Sweetheart," cupid holding
package, fold–out, red tissue paper, stand–up, 5" h, USA **7.00**
"To My Sweetheart," two cupids,
fold–out, tissue paper, 8" h, USA **7.50**
"To My Valentine," boy and girl
holding flowers, blue diecut
background, fold–out, stand–up,
6" h, Germany **8.00**
"To My Valentine," boy playing a
mandolin, fold–out, stand–up,
diecut background, 6" h,
Germany **8.00**
"To My Valentine," girl holding
flowers, fold–out skirt, tissue paper, stand–up, 6¾", Germany . . **5.00**

"To My Valentine," girl holding envelope, red and pink fold–out,
tissue paper, stand–up, 9" h,
Germany **12.00**
"True to Thee," diecut flowers and
girls, blue windmill background,
fold–out, stand–up, 5¾", Tuck . . **10.00**
Post Card
"Love's Greeting," boy and girl,
1922, sgd "Ellen H. Clapsaddle" **5.00**
"St. Valentine's Greetings," girl and
boy, sgd "Ellen H. Clapsaddle" . **5.00**
"To My Sweet Valentine," woman
greeting three cupids, sepia
tones **1.50**
"To My Valentine with Love," portrait of a young girl, emb background **2.00**

HOME FRONT COLLECTIBLES

Collecting Hints: Home front collectibles
emerged as a separate collecting category approximately three years ago. The fact that it took
so long is surprising. However, many home front
collectibles have been sold for years in crossover
categories, e.g. post cards and magazines.

Some of the most recognizable home front collectibles are posters. These posters are still quite
affordable and range from $50 to $500. A general rule is that the smaller the size, the lower the
price. An identified illustrator adds value.
Graphics and image are everything. Value and
pizazz are closely related.

Propaganda played a major role in home front
material. One of the key propaganda ploys was
to depersonalize the enemy and enemy leaders
by viewing them as ethnic stereotypes, a throw-
back to the image of the Hun in World War I. The
effort was most successful in respect to the Axis
leaders—Hitler, Tojo, and Mussolini—and the
"Jap." Home front collectibles with stereotypical
images command big bucks. They are frequently
among the most expensive of the home front collectibles, a result of their great graphics and the
fact that many of them are three dimensional.

History: World War II was fought on three
fronts—European, Pacific/Asian and Home. The
recognition and honor given the battle waged on
the home front is one of the most surprising aspects of the fiftieth anniversary celebrations of
World War II. Museums across America have
mounted exhibitions focusing on the war effort
made by industry and individuals in their locali-
ties. Home front and battlefront articles share
equal billing in the media from magazines to
television. There seems to be a clear understand-

ing that the war abroad would have been lost if
the war at home was not won.

The home front war effort was total. The civilian population was mobilized as well as the military. All aspects of civilian life were the focus of
propaganda and voluntary, and sometimes invol-
untary, control. The goal was to convince every
individual that they were essential to the war effort—as a worker, volunteer, war bond purchaser,
or young lady willing to use a stocking stick in
lieu of nylons. Civil Defense existed because it
provided an opportunity for its participants to do
their part.

A home front collectible is an object made in
America between 1939 and 1946 with a civilian
orientation that was designed to evoke a spirit of
patriotism or sense of commitment to the war effort. The year 1939 is used instead of 1941 because of America's support for England and
France prior to our entry into the war and to allow inclusion of the anti–war material. The year
1946 serves as the concluding date because
America did not simply end its war efforts on V–J
Day, August 14, 1945. The troops had to come
home and occupation forces had to be put into
place.

Given the totality of the home front effort, virtually every collecting category that covers the
1935 to 1950 period has some form of home
front collectible associated with it. The war effort
also produced new types of collectibles, including Civilian Defense material, ration stamps, sub-
stitutes, victory garden memorabilia, and enemy
stereotype material.

References: Stan Cohen, *V For Victory: America's
Home Front During World War II*, Motorbooks
International, 1991; Robert Heide and John
Gilman, *Home Front America: Popular Culture
of the World War II Era*, Chronicle Books, 1995;
Jack Matthews, *Toys Go To War*, published by
author, 1995.

Arcade Machine, "Civilian Defense–
Remember Pearl Harbor," wooden
case, metal coin slot, clear glass over
vivid colorful scene of city besieged
by enemy bombers while being de-
fended by attacking aircraft and
anti–aircraft guns, winner received 10
cent defense stamp prize, sides with
red, white, and blue Defense Savings
Stamps decal, front with blue fabric
strip lettered in flocked silver
"Remember Pearl Harbor" plus sym-
bols for "Keep 'Em Flying" **2,465.00**
Badge, American Boy Junior Pilot, gold
luster finish metal, wings, center red,
white, and blue paper insert above
metal lettering "Keep 'Em Flying" .. **25.00**
Bank, piggy, painted composition,
bright yellow and glossy black, typi-

Defense Worker ID Badge, photo of worker, Aviation Division of Studebaker Corp., $10.00.

cal pig face, incised inscription "Save For Victory," and "Make Him Squeal," copyrights for Tom Lawson Co, New York City, orig sound mechanism not working, 4½" d, 6½" l ... **250.00**

Banner, loved one in service type, glossy red, white, and blue fabric, gold fringe, wooden dowel rod, gold cord

5½ x 9", single blue star above "V" symbol **35.00**

6 x 8½", gold star indicating deceased loved one **210.00**

Bar Pin, diecut metal

"Husband In Service," cardboard slogan insert, blue letters, white cardboard, tiny red stars, lower diecut with opened letters USA, red, white, and blue accents, gold luster finish **178.50**

"Mother," name in script, small heart shaped suspended pendant accented by gold luster Navy anchor symbol, inscribed "U.S.N.," marked "Sterling" **20.00**

Blackout Kit, Vernon Co, Newton, IA, five rolls of sandpaper textured paper treated for luminosity, another roll with preprinted face mask design, "Official Blackout Test Tube," instructions, 8½ x 11" illustrated 20 page book of Blackout Kutouts, 1942 copyright, unused, 2 x 9½ x 15½" box **200.00**

Blotter, thin cardboard, titled "The Schmidt Family Has Gone To War," text about three of five brothers serving in service, New Bedford, MA, business, full color illus of B–24 Liberator bomber in flight, unused, minor tear, 4 x 9¼" **13.00**

Book

Bowen, R Sidney, *Dave Dawson At Dunkirk,* Saalfield Publishing, 1941, hardcover **15.00**

National Broadcasting Co, *NBC Fourth Chime News Book,* 1944, hardcover, 174 glossy pages, black and white photos, lightly worn covers **70.00**

Snell, Roy J, *Wings For Victory,* 1942, Goldsmith Publishing Co, 252 pages, 27 short stories, hardcover **32.00**

Yoder, Robert M, *There's No Front Like Home,* 1944, 115 pages, orig dust jacket **18.00**

Booklet

"At Ease! You're A Civilian Now," 4¼ x 7", 32 pages, sponsored by American Legion for new members, related cartoon art cover ... **25.00**

"Designed For Wartime Living" 6½ x 8" stiff paper, 40 pages, Gunther Brewing Co, Baltimore, graphic images, recipes, home entertaining games, lunch box suggestions, household hints **22.00**

"What To Eat In Wartime," 5 x 5½" opens to 5½ x 17" sheet printed on both sides, suggested menus, nutritional foods, one panel suggests ways to pacify individual likes and dislikes, sponsored by Ward's Tip–Top Bread **25.00**

Dexterity Puzzle

Trap The Jap In Tokyo, litho paper playing surface, small diecut circular trap recessed marked as Pacific Theater locations, nine glass marbles, solid blue or solid white for forces, one red marble representing Japs, instructions on inner box lid, Modern Novelties, Inc, Cleveland, early 1940s, 1 x 4½ x 4½" **80.00**

"V For Victory," cardboard box frame holding clear plastic over recessed colorful cardboard playing surface, three tiny circular traps and one slot trap, three metal balls, wooden dowel, floral design thin paper, lightly worn edges and corners, 1 x 3¼ x 5" **75.00**

Envelope, "Keep "Em Flying!" red, white, and blue art, titled "The Battle Cry of Freedom!" typewritten addressed name, 1944 postmark, 3¾ x 6½" **12.00**

Figure, painted plaster

"Kilroy Was Here," young sorrowful lass in desolate and pregnant pose, colorful symbolic figure of fleeting Kilroy presence, inscription on

base, few nicks, 10" h, 2½" d base **170.00**
Saluting Soldier, glitter accent on hat
band, necktie, shoulder belt, early
1940s, 14½" h **80.00**
Game, board
Get In The Scrap, Milton Bradley,
1944 copyright, 9½ x 19 x 2" box,
18½" sq playing board, 16 wooden
pawns, some tape to box **60.00**
Salute, Selchow & Righter Co, 9½ x
18 x 2" box, 18" sq playing board,
some tape to box **85.00**
Gas Mask, metal canister jointed to thin
rubber head harness, adjustable cloth
straps, clear plastic–like eye lenses,
instructions for use on canister, 4 x 6"
booklet prepared by US Office of
Civilian Defense in cooperation with
Chemical Warfare Service of US
Army, orig khaki canvas fabric bag,
matching adjustable cloth straps, bag
marked "Non–Combatant Gas
Mask," US Chemical Corps insignia,
medium adult size, unused **70.00**
Gardening Set, "Plant For Victory,"
elaborate colorful set, seed packets
printed for Vaughan's Seed Store,
Chicago/New York, c1944, packets
attached to back side of box insert, illustrated garden book, blueprints for
planting seeds, wooden garden
stakes, row planting tool, name labels
for canning, unused, 16 x 33 x 2" box **200.00**
Glow Button
"Air Raid Warden," red, white, and
blue celluloid pinback badge,
white luminous film, back paper
inscription "Buy War Bonds At
Minnesota Federal Savings & Loan
Association," working condition . . **35.00**
"V For Victory," red, white, and blue,
treated paper background, working
condition, lightly rusted back **75.00**
Magazine, Aircraft Warning Volunteer,
9 x 12", published by I Fighter
Command of Mitchel Field, NY, 16
pages
1943, Oct, Vol 1, #5, aircraft recognition test #4 on back cover **20.00**
1944, Jan, aircraft recognition test #7
on back cover **15.00**
Magazine Tear Sheet
Cartoon, Arthur Szyk, neatly removed
from Esquire magazine, full color
art, 9½ x 14"
"December 7, 1941," western
cowboy figure being attacked by
knife wielding Tojo, inscription
on Tojo's knapsack "Stolen
Goods," Hitler and Mussolini
watch expectantly from back-
ground **40.00**

"Il Duce," Nazi officer Goering
leading Mussolini and Tojo in
chains with Nazi skeleton hold-
ing death scythe, dated 1942 . . **95.00**
"The Map Maker," picturing Hitler
as artist of "Schiklgruber &
Company Fancy Maps," assisted
by Hess and Goering, representatives of nations, including Tojo,
Mussolini, Franco and Arab, line
up to have new Nazi map drawing of their country, caption
"Now that you've joined us, the
Fuhrer will make a special map
for you!" **35.00**
Cover, "Rosie The Riveter," May 29,
1943 Saturday Evening Post, full
color portrait by Norman
Rockwell, 10½ x 13½" **18.00**
Map, "World–Wide News Map,"
Richfield Oil Co, closed 7 x 9½"
folder opens to 21 x 28" sheet, large
colorful map of Europe and North
Africa on one side, smaller red,
white, and blue world map,
Southwest Pacific map, Polar map,
plus listing of major war events from
1931 through early 1943 . . . . **25.00**
Matchbook
Anti–Hitler, slogans "Match
'Em–Bond For Bomb" and "Strike
at the seat of trouble," color car-
toon of Hitler grasping the globe,
gray emery paper match striking
surface inset in trouser seat, flattened, empty, 1½ x 4½" **45.00**
Navy, blue and white cover art re-
lated to slogan "Loose Lips Lose
Ships," opposing panel has "TC
ASF" plus naval transportation insignia and "Los Angeles Port of
Embarkation," flattened, empty, 3 x
4½" **15.00**
Newspaper Supplement, "Home
Defense Guide," March 23, 1942,
Philadelphia Inquirer, 20 pages of
pictorial and text instructions on
home defense procedures, full color
insignias, full page portrait of Gen
MacArthur, small tape repair, 11 x 14" **35.00**
Patch, "American War Mothers," red,
white, and blue stiff felt, graying to
colors, 4" d **25.00**
Pencil Holder, plastic bullet design cartridge, removable tip holding short
pencil stub, yellow, red and blue victory symbol, unused rubber eraser,
3½" l **30.00**
Pillow Cover, glossy fabric, 3" border
hem and fringe, single star service
flag above woven script inscription
"Berlin Or Bust/In God We

Newspaper, Japan Declares War After Attacking U.S., *The Post-Standard*, Syracuse, NY, December 8, 1941, $30.00.

Trust/Serving In US Army," 15½ x 16½" 35.00

Pin

"American Women's Voluntary Services," diecut low relief brass eagle, centered red, white, and blue enameled title shield, single small brass star motif, slightly darkened brass luster 35.00

"AWS," bar link pin, red, white, and blue enameled pendant of official symbol and initials for Air Warning Service, and inscriptions "Army Air Forces" and "FIC" for 1st Fighter Command, blue enamel accents, hanger bar, inscription "For Merit," to center link bars inscribed "500 Hours" of service, marked "sterling silver" 25.00

"Beat Em Down," diecut thick leather, eagle hanger bar, suspended diecut image of drum, blue finish on eagle, red drum with white accents 26.00

"GOC United States Air Force Observer/Asst Chief," wings, blue and white enameled symbol for Ground Observer Corps volunteer worker, marked "sterling silver" .. 12.00

"God Bless America," diecut thick leather bar, three suspended flag outlines, blue finish on upper bar, silver musical notes, each flag different color (red, white, blue) with one word of slogan printed in silver, rusted fastener pin 40.00

"Loose Talk Can Cost Lives," diecut thick brown leather, security slogan lettered in white, image of Uncle Sam with red, white, and blue finished top hat, white hair and beard, blue jacket, slight wear 48.00

"Manhattan Project A Bomb," tiny image of Army Corps of Engineers

under inscription, marked "sterling silver," ¾" d 200.00

Uncle Sam, diecut thin brass, heart shaped, center profile of Uncle Sam in top hat, red, white, and blue enamels, 40% enamel flaked away, worn brass luster 50.00

"U. S. A. Minute Women," red, white, and blue enameled brass, stylized eagle under inscription "Guarding The Land We Love" 30.00

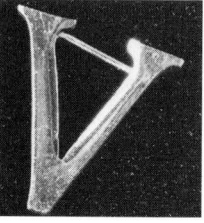

Pin, "V," gold color plating,¾" h, $5.00.

"War Food Administration," insignia symbol of circular wheat stalk and geared wheel centered by letter "A", blue enamel accents, rim inscribed "Achievement Award/Food For Freedom," group title inscription on back 18.00

"Wekearny Garden Club For Victory," diecut plastic, yellow, green, red, and white, rolled back upper edge holds fastener pin on back, slogan in bottom margin "I'm Growing My Own," ⅞" d 35.00

Pinback Button

"Aircraft Warning Service Volunteer Observer," red silhouette image of aircraft, white background, dark blue border, yellow letters 25.00

"Gen Eisenhower," red, white, and blue litho, holding purple fabric ribbon inscribed in gold lettering "Welcome Home Ike," slightly yellowed button, lightly worn ribbon, 1¼" d 35.00

"Help America Stop Waste!," blue, white letters, small damage to celluloid cover 12.00

"I Am Proud To Be An American," blue and white, center red, white, and blue patriotic shield 10.00

"I'm Housing A War Hero," red, white, and blue, illus of "Hospitality House" building with "Welcome" awning 12.00

"Long May It Wave," red, white, and blue, flag against stormy clouds, choppy ocean waters 15.00

"Remember Pearl Harbor," red, white, and blue, tinted full color portrait of unidentified young man in civilian clothing, 2¼" d **85.00**

"Salvage For Victory," white, blue letters, red "V" **25.00**

"The Hero Of Pearl Harbor, Dorie Miller," black and white, Black sailor Miller, mess attendant on the SS Arizona at time of Pearl Harbor attack, awarded Navy Cross, 1¼" d **120.00**

"Vegetable Growers Association of America," full color rim of various vegetables, black and white center victory symbol and inscription ... **90.00**

"Welcome Home Our Heroes!", red, white, and blue, female nurse, soldier, sailor and Marine, ¾" d **20.00**

Pin Cushion, "Hotzy Notzi," painted plaster figure, khaki fabric insert in seat of crouched figure as pin cushion tuft, brown uniform, orange base, black trim, 1941 copyright on base, title card with inscription "It Is Good Luck To Find A Pin, Here's An 'Axis' To Stick It In," reverse with additional inscription and 1942 date, minor damage to paint, reglued after break, 4¾" h, 2½" d rounded base **170.00**

Playbill, "Winged Victory," program from Jan 23, 1944, New York City theater, play presented and sponsored by US Army Air Forces, proceeds designated for Army Emergency Relief, period ads, Air Force related cartoon by Alajalov, back cover sepia ad for Chesterfield cigarettes, 56 pages, 6½ x 9" **30.00**

Post Card, 3½ x 5½"
"Keep 'Em Flying," #1 of US Air Corps series published by Curt Teich & Co, reverse has inked message from serviceman **15.00**

Victory Series, #V1, soldier, civilian worker, sailor, published by Tichnor Bros, copyright 1941, unused **20.00**

Poster
Make Yours A Victory Home, Office of War Information Poster #41, issued 1943, 22 x 28" **80.00**

Office Supplies Conservation, black, white, and khaki, yellow paper, Poster #534708, issued 1943, 20 x 28" **50.00**

Register and Vote, Railway Labor Executives Assoc, c1943, 17 x 22" **75.00**

Third War Loan, large replica image of green and white $100 savings bond above diagonal inscriptions in red, white, and blue, Poster #542950, issued 1943, 20 x 28" .. **55.00**

Portrait Plate, General Arnold, white background, sepia portrait, colorful display of Allied nationality flags, reverse marked "Allied Nations Commemorative Series," Salem China Co, Salem, OH, 11" d **60.00**

Punchboard, "Remember Pearl Harbor," Hula Jackpot, Coconut Jackpot, Hula art, symbols for war bond purchases, unused, 11½ x 8".. **175.00**

Ration Book, "War Ration Book Two," inked name on front cover, 1942, some unused stamps, closed 4¼ x 5½" folder **20.00**

Ruler, wooden, striping and inscriptions on measurement side in red and blue, inscriptions include two "V" letters plus slogan "All Out For Victory," local bank sponsor name on back, 12" l **28.00**

Satchel, child's, "I'm Carrying My Share For Victory," oilcloth carrying bag, front side with illus of young girl carrying teddy bear in one hand and "V" container holding gifts in other, art "Hand painted by Ellen," solid red back panel, 10¼ x 11½" h **65.00**

Sheet Music
"A Yank And A Tank," red, white, and blue cover, symbol of Armored Divisions, Carl Fischer Co, New York City, song by Everett Bentley, 1943 copyright, 9 x 12" **25.00**

"Be A Hero, My Boy," red, white, and blue cover, two page, Patriotic Music Publishing Co, New York City, words by Mark Minkus, music by Henry Kane, 1943 copyright, 9 x 12" **5.00**

"Cheer Up, Uncle Sam!" red, white, and blue cover, two page, Patriotic Music Publishing Co, New York City, words by Mark Minkus, music by Henry Kane, 1943 copyright, 9 x 12" **12.00**

"Marching and Singing!" red, white, and blue cover, two page, Patriotic Music Publishing Co, New York City, words by Mark Minkus, music by Henry Kane, 1943 copyright, 9 x 12" **5.00**

"The Jolly Yanks," red, white, and blue cover, two page, Patriotic Music Publishing Co, New York City, words by Mark Minkus, music by Henry Kane, 1943 copyright, 9 x 12" **5.00**

"When The Lights Go On Again (All Over The World)," black and white cover, Campbell, Loft & Porgie, New York City, 1942 copyright, 9¼ x 12¼" **18.00**

Stamp Album, "Sky Heroes," premium booklet sponsored by Sinclair Oil, 24 pages, 20 pages for mounting single gummed stamp of aircraft of war pilot hero, each page with biography of hero, listing of awarded medals, full color stamps, stamp art from orig paintings by Louis Bonhajo, unused, 4 x 8¾" 110.00

Toy

Model, Victory Series, model airplane, "Allied Sport" aircraft, American Modelcraft, Chicago, mid 1940s, balsa ribs, two preprinted balsa sheets, finish accents, partially assembled, 1 x 3½ x 10¼" red, white, and blue box with "Start 'Em Flying—Keep 'Em Flying" logo, bottom panel includes "For Victory" war bonds symbol plus inscription "Save This Carton—Cardboard Is Needed To Help Win The War" 32.00

Rifle, Daisy Victory, wooden, shoots cork on string, black finish barrel, red front hand grip, khaki web fabric sling, left side with colorful eagle and logo "Keep 'Em Shooting," scattered chips to decal, cork missing, 29" l 100.00

Target, Bombsight, Aluminum Goods Mfg Co, 4 x 4 x 2½" metal bombsight box, 3" metal dart tipped bomb, three 4 x 4½" pressed cardboard targets, top side of targets finished as German and Japan warships, well used toy, lid missing .. 150.00

Valentine

Army Sweetheart, red, white, and blue folder, lightly emb patriotic eagle, flag, and heart design on front cover, inside left panel with red, white, and blue victory symbol and flag, facing panel has sentimental verse to soldier sweetheart, Gibson Greeting Card Co, unsigned, orig unmarked white envelope, 5 x 6" 10.00

Son In Service, full color folder, front with inset red fabric heart bordered in silver foil, inside with patriotic heart symbol, opposite with sentimental valentine verse to son in service, unsigned, orig unmarked white envelope, 5½ x 6¼" 10.00

Window Sign, cardboard, red, white, and blue Navy Dept official symbol at upper left, simulated seal at lower right with individual serial number, stamped facsimile signature of naval commanding officer, wear and damage to cardboard, 8 x 10½" 21.00

Window Sticker, unused
"Garden For Victory," red, white, and blue paper, gummed front, sponsored by National Victory Garden Institute, 4 x 4½" 20.00
"Home of A Marine," diecut paper, gummed front, red and yellow design on white, June 19, 1943 publication date, 4 x 8¼" 15.00

HOMER LAUGHLIN

Collecting Hints: The original trademark from 1871 to 1890 merely identified the products as "Laughlin Brothers." The next trademark featured the American eagle astride the prostrate British lion. The third marking featured a monogram of "HLC" which has appeared, with slight variations, on all dinnerware since about 1900. The 1900 trademark contained a number which identified month, year and plant at which the product was made. Letter codes were used in later periods.

So much attention has been placed on Fiesta that other interesting patterns have not achieved the popularity which they deserve. Prices still are moderate. Some of the patterns from the 1930 to 1940 period have contemporary designs that are highly artistic.

Virginia Rose is a shape, not a pattern name. Several different decals can be found, with delicate pink flowers the most common.

History: Homer Laughlin and his brother, Shakespeare, built two pottery kilns in East Liverpool, Ohio, in 1871. Shakespeare withdrew in 1879, leaving Homer to operate the business alone. Laughlin became one of the first firms to produce American–made whiteware. In 1896, William Wills and a Pittsburgh group led by Marcus Aaron bought the Laughlin firm.

Expansion followed. Two new plants were built in Laughlin Station, Ohio. In 1906, the first plant (#4) was built in Newall, West Virginia. In 1923 plant #6 was built at Newall and featured a continuous tunnel kiln. Similar kilns were added at the other plants. Other advances included spray glazing and mechanical jiggering.

In the 1930 to 1960 period several new dinnerware lines were added, including the Wells Art Glaze line. Ovenserve and Kitchen Kraft were the cooking ware lines. The colored glaze lines of Fiesta, Harlequin and Rhythm captured major market shares. In 1959 a translucent table china line was introduced. Today, the annual manufacturing capacity is over 45 million pieces.

References: Susan and Al Bagdade, *Warman's American Pottery and Porcelain,* Wallace-Homestead, 1994; Jo Cunningham, *The*

Collector's Encyclopedia of American Dinnerware, Collector Books, 1982, 1995 value update; Bob and Sharon Huxford, *The Collector's Encyclopedia of Fiesta With Harlequin and Riviera,* Seventh Edition, Collector Books, 1992; Joanne Jasper, *The Collector's Encyclopedia of Homer Laughlin China: Reference & Value Guide,* Collector Books, 1993, 1995 value update; Leslie Pina, *Pottery: Modern Wares 1920–1960,* Schiffer Publishing, 1994.

Periodicals: *Fiesta Collectors Quarterly,* 19238 Dorchester Circle, Strongsville, OH 44136; *The Laughlin Eagle,* 1270 63rd Terrace South, St. Petersburg, FL 33705.

REPRODUCTION ALERT. Harlequin and Fiesta lines were reissued in 1978 and marked accordingly.

See: Fiesta

BRITTANY Shape produced with a variety of decal decorations from 1930s until 1950s.

Creamer and Sugar	5.00
Cup and Saucer	6.00
Fruit Bowl, Majestic	4.00
Oatmeal, Majestic	6.50
Plate	
Bread and Butter	3.00
Dinner, 10″ d, Majestic	9.00
Platter, 11″ l, Majestic	14.00

CAVALIER Produced from 1950s to 1970s. Eggshell dinnerware decorated in both solid colors and decals.

Casserole, cov, Berkshire	25.00
Fruit Bowl, Springtime	4.00
Plate	
6″ d, bread and butter, Romance	5.00
9″ d, dinner, Romance	8.00
Saucer, Romance	3.00
Soup Bowl	
Jade Rose	8.00
Romance	9.00
Turkey Platter	12.00

DOGWOOD Produced early 1960s. Dogwood decal on white ground. Gold trim.

Bowl, 5¾″ d	3.00
Creamer and Sugar	10.00
Cup	6.50
Gravy	14.00
Plate	
8⅜″ d	7.50
9¼″ d	5.50
Platter, oval, 11¾″ l	14.50
Soup	6.00
Vegetable, oval	9.00

EGGSHELL NAUTILUS Produced from about 1935 to 1955. Eggshell refers to its lighter weight and Nautilus to its shape. Can be found decorated with many different decal designs, including Apple Blossom, Aristocrat, and Priscilla.

Bowl, 5″ d	6.00
Casserole, cov	25.00
Cream Soup	14.00
Fruit Bowl	5.00
Nappy, 10″	15.00
Pickle	8.00
Pie Baker, 10″ d	18.00
Plate	
7″ d	5.00
8″ d	6.00
8″ sq, Aristocrat pattern	9.00
Teacup and Saucer	8.00

EGGSHELL THEME Last Eggshell shape. Designed by Frederick Rhead to commemorate the 1939 World's Fair. Heavily embossed vintage pattern, made with and without decal decorations.

Casserole, cov	35.00
Chop Plate, 14″ d	28.00
Creamer and Sugar, cov	30.00
Cream Soup	15.00
Flat Soup	8.00
Fruit Bowl	4.00
Nappy, 9″ d	18.00
Pie Baker, 9″ d	18.00
Plate	
6″ d	4.00
8″ sq	9.00
10″ d	10.00
Salt and Pepper Shakers, pr	20.00
Teacup and Saucer	8.00
Teapot, cov	50.00

ENGLISH GARDEN Decal design of English garden landscape on ivory ground. Green line trim. Sold by Sears Roebuck, 1930s. Century shape.

Bowl, 5″ d	9.00
Creamer	12.00

Century shape, creamer, ivory, decal dec, platinum trim, $7.00.

Century shape, saucer, ivory, decal dec, 5¾" w, $2.50.

Plate		
6" d	. . . .	**4.50**
9" d	. . . .	**10.00**
Platter		
13" l	. . . .	**25.50**
15" l	. . . .	**37.50**
Saucer	. . . .	**4.00**
Sugar	. . . .	**12.00**

HARLEQUIN Sold by F. W. Woolworth Company. Introduced in the late 1930s in four colors: bright yellow, spruce green, maroon, and mauve blue. Harlequin was eventually produced in all the Fiesta colors except ivory and cobalt blue. The line was discontinued in 1964. It was reissued in 1979 in turquoise, yellow, medium green, and coral. The reissued plates have a Homer Laughlin backstamp.

After Dinner Cup		
Red	. . . .	**75.00**
Rose	. . . .	**65.00**
After Dinner Cup and Saucer		
Rose	. . . .	**115.00**
Spruce Green	. . . .	**195.00**
Ashtray, saucer, spruce green	. . . .	**75.00**
Butter Dish, cov, spruce green	. . . .	**125.00**
Casserole, cov		
Rose	. . . .	**98.00**
Spruce Green	. . . .	**140.00**
Creamer		
Individual, mauve	. . . .	**10.00**
Novelty, spruce green	. . . .	**25.00**
Cup and Saucer, medium green	. . . . .	**18.00**
Eggcup, double, spruce green	. . . .	**25.00**
Flat Soup, rose	. . . .	**20.00**
Jug, 22 oz, rose	. . . .	**40.00**
Marmalade, cov, spruce green	. . . . . .	**240.00**
Mixing Bowl, 10" d, yellow	. . . .	**125.00**
Nut Dish, green	. . . .	**95.00**
Oatmeal Bowl		
Medium Green	. . . .	**45.00**
Rose	. . . .	**15.00**
Spruce Green	. . . .	**65.00**

Pitcher		
Ball		
Dark Green	. . . .	**65.00**
Mauve	. . . .	**55.00**
Red	. . . .	**50.00**
Rose	. . . .	**60.00**
Milk, rose	. . . .	**28.00**
Plate		
7" d, spruce green	. . . .	**10.00**
9" d		
Medium Green	. . . .	**20.00**
Spruce Green	. . . .	**15.00**
10" d		
Mauve	. . . .	**35.00**
Rose	. . . .	**22.00**
Spruce Green	. . . .	**40.00**
Platter		
Large, spruce green	. . . .	**32.00**
Small		
Rose	. . . .	**20.00**
Spruce Green	. . . .	**30.00**
Salad, individual		
Chartreuse	. . . .	**25.00**
Rose	. . . .	**25.00**
Spruce Green	. . . .	**42.00**
Soup		
Light Green	. . . .	**25.00**
Spruce Green	. . . .	**32.00**
Spoon Rest, turquoise	. . . .	**265.00**
Teapot, salmon	. . . .	**110.00**
Vegetable Bowl, oval, spruce green	. . .	**35.00**

KITCHEN KRAFT Kitchenware line with floral decals produced from the early 1930s. Pieces are marked Kitchen Kraft and/or Oven–Serve.

Bowl		
#1, red	. . . .	**195.00**
#2, red	. . . .	**175.00**
#4		
Ivory, marks	. . . .	**100.00**
Yellow	. . . .	**125.00**
Cake Server		
Green	. . . .	**125.00**
Red	. . . .	**150.00**
Drip Jar, cobalt blue	. . . .	**280.00**
Fork, cobalt blue	. . . .	**175.00**
Mixing Bowl, 10" d, Tulip	. . . .	**40.00**
Platter		
Cobalt, holder	. . . .	**45.00**
Green	. . . .	**60.00**
Yellow	. . . .	**65.00**
Salt and Pepper Shakers, pr, red	. . . . .	**75.00**
Spoon		
Cobalt Blue	. . . .	**95.00**
Red	. . . .	**95.00**

RHYTHM Produced from 1950 to 1960 in solid colors of chartreuse, forest green, gray, harlequin yellow, and maroon. The Rhythm shape was also produced with decal decoration on a white ground.

Bowl, 8½" d, yellow	12.00
Creamer, dark green	8.00
Cup and Saucer	18.00
Fruit Bowl	8.00
Plate, 9" d	10.00
Spoon Rest	
Dark Green	310.00
Yellow	195.00

RIVIERA Introduced in 1938, this dinnerware line was sold by the Murphy Company. Though usually unmarked, it is occasionally found with a gold backstamp. Produced in the Century shape in dark blue (rare), light green, ivory, mauve blue, red, and yellow.

Batter Jug Set, ivory syrup, green cov jug, yellow platter	350.00
Butter Dish, cov, ½ lb	
Cobalt Blue	295.00
Ivory	155.00
Cup, green	10.00
Juice Pitcher, mauve	325.00
Mug, ivory	150.00
Starter Set, four cups and saucers, dessert bowls, 9" plates, and 6" plates, ivory, yellow, mauve, and green, orig box	225.00
Sugar, cov, green	15.00
Syrup, cov, red	150.00
Tumbler, juice	
Aqua	45.00
Ivory	60.00

VIRGINIA ROSE This is the name of a shape rather than a decal pattern as the name might imply. It was produced from 1929 until the early 1970s and was decorated with numerous floral decals. Pieces were trimmed with either silver or gold bands.

Baker, oval, 8" l	18.00
Butter, cov, jade	75.00
Creamer and Sugar, cov	32.00
Cup and Saucer, platinum	8.00
Fruit Bowl	4.00
Nappy, 10" d	20.00
Plate	
6" d, bread and butter	3.50
10" d, dinner	11.00
Sauce Boat	20.00
Tray, handles	25.00

HORSE COLLECTIBLES

Collecting Hints: Horses have been a strong influence on most aspects of the American lifestyle. They have been immortalized in nearly every media possible, creating a wide variety of equine–related memorabilia for collectors.

There is almost no category of collecting that does not include some sort of horse collectible. Advertising featuring the horse abounds—from the earliest saddle catalogs to current offerings featuring the Budweiser Clydesdales. Some of the most popular 1990s collectibles are 1950s items such as lamps, china, and blankets decorated with Western themes.

Television cowboy collectibles continue to be very popular. Look for collectibles featuring famous show business horses like Hopalong Cassidy's Topper, Tom Mix's Tony, and Roy Rogers' Trigger. Tack, from the beautifully handcrafted, ornately decorated parade saddles to the simple mochilla carried by the Pony Express rider, is always collectible.

Decorative items, especially figurines, attract the collector. Ceramic figurines and the Breyer and Hartland plastic model horses are enthusiastically collected.

Old rodeo programs, horse show trophies, state fair ribbons, horse racing memorabilia, bridle rosettes, soft plush toys, and advertising signs are a few more examples of collector categories. Equine art has become popular.

Many horse enthusiasts, overwhelmed by the volume and variety of equine collectibles available to them, choose to specialize. A sports fan may collect memorabilia from the Olympic Equestrian Teams, while a racing fan may collect Kentucky Derby glasses. Memorabilia from specific breeds also is popular.

Carousel horses remain a high ticket item, although prices have leveled off for the more common examples. Many smaller horses can be purchased for less than $5,000. The best examples still sell well. In 1992, an outside–row horse carved by the artist Daniel Muller, around 1905, set a new auction record for a Muller figure, selling at $79,500.

Horse related toys, especially horse–drawn cast iron fire trucks, buses, and grocery wagons, continue to be desirable. Buy carefully. Many of these cast iron toys have been reproduced. Reproductions usually have rather gaudy paint schemes, and the pieces fit together poorly.

History: Since the earliest days of our nation's history, the horse has played a vital role in American growth and lifestyle. Even our language reflects our love and respect for the horse. If we make intelligent decisions, we are credited with having "horse sense."

The English colonists brought the horse with them to the New World for transportation, plowing, and even as a food source. A person's social status was determined by the number and quality of his horses. Remember the condescending term "one horse town?"

As the country became more civilized, people could afford an occasional day of rest. It quickly became a day to show off your horses and compete with those of your neighbor. Organized horse races and shows evolved from these casual Sunday afternoon gatherings.

As the motorcar became more affordable, the need for the horse died out. Today's horses are likely to be pampered family pets, living a sheltered life that a hard–working draft animal of the 1800s could only dream about.

References: Dan and Sebie Hutchins, *Old Cowboy Saddles & Spurs: Identifying The Craftsman Who Made Them, Fourth Annual,* Horse Feathers Publishing, n.d.; Jim and Nancy Schaut, *Horsin' Around: A Price Guide To Horse Collectibles,* L–W Books, 1990.

Periodicals: *Hall of Fame Trotters News,* PO Box 590, Goshen, NY 10924; *Just About Horses,* 34 Owens Dr., Wayne, NY 07470.

Museums: Aiken Thoroughbred Racing Hall of Fame & Museum, Aiken, SC; Harness Racing Hall of Fame, Goshen, NY; Gene Autry Western Heritage Museum, Los Angeles, CA; Pony Express Museum, Joplin, MO; The Kentucky Derby Museum, Louisville, KY.

Advisors: Jim and Nancy Schaut.

HORSE EQUIPMENT AND RELATED ITEMS

Bells
  8" l metal strap, four graduated cast
  bells, painted black, probably
  nailed to wagon shaft **125.00**
  84" l, worn leather strap, over forty
  nickel bells, all same size, tug hook **200.00**
Bit, eagle, marked "G.S. Garcia" **700.00**
Bit Emblem, cavalry, brass, marked
  "US," price for pair **15.00**
Blanket, saddle Navajo, early 1900s . . **850.00**
Bridle
  Heiser **225.00**
  Horsehair **200.00**
  Walla Walla Prison made **900.00**
Brush, cavalry, leather back stamped
  "US," patented 1860, Herbert Brush
  Mfg Co **60.00**
Catalog, Chicago, 1929, polo saddles,
  mallets, and equipment **35.00**
Collar, draft horse, leather cov wood,
  brass trim **125.00**
Curry Comb, tin back, leather handle,
  early 1900s **20.00**
Harness Decoration, brass, rearing
  horse in center **35.00**
Hobbles, chain and leather, sideline
  type **75.00**
Hoof Pick, bone handle, Wastenholm,
  Germany, patent date 1855 . . . .   **50.00**

Horse–Drawn Wagon
  Ice Delivery, two horse hitch, some
  wood needs restoring, orig lettering
  on sides **1,800.00**
  Popcorn, Creators, orig condition,
  needs minor cosmetic work **7,500.00**
Horsehide Rug, 4' x 6' **150.00**
Lasso
  Horsehair **50.00**
  Rawhide cov tips, 1890s **250.00**
Mane and Tail Comb, stamped "Oliver
  Slant Tooth," 1940s **20.00**
Riata, braided rawhide **150.00**
Saddle
  FM Sterns, California, tooled leather   **800.00**
  McClelland type, large fenders for leg
  protection, early 1900s **600.00**
Shippley, 16" slick fork, half seat **2,500.00**
Saddle Stand, rough sawn pine, some
  orig paint **45.00**
Sidesaddle, tapestry seat, fair condition,
  pre 1920s **500.00**
Spurs
  Crockett, arrow shank **600.00**
  CSA, brass, very rare **650.00**
Wagon Seat, springs, padded seat, new
  leather upholstery **125.00**
Watering Trough, hollowed–out log, tin
  lining, 2' x 6' **100.00**

HORSE THEME ITEMS

Bank
  Arcade, still, cast iron, horse and
  horseshoe, Buster Brown shoe adv,
  4½" h **250.00**
  Ertl, horse and tank wagon, Texaco,
  #8 in series **35.00**
Blanket, brown wool, Western theme,
  cowboys and horses, twin bed size,
  1950 . . . . **150.00**
Board Game, Derby Day, Parker Bros,
  wood horses, 1959 . . . .   **45.00**
Book, *The Black Stallion,* Walter Farley,
  first edition, dj **15.00**

Ashtray, pink glass base, black horse, Art Deco styling, $35.00.

Calendar, 1907, cardboard, Dousman
  Milling, cowgirl and horse, 10 x 20"   50.00
Carousel Horse, jumper, CW Parker,
  flag on side, American, c1918 . . . . **4,500.00**
Catalog, DF Mangels Co., Carousel
  Works, Coney Island, NY, 1928 edi-
  tion, 28 pgs **200.00**
Cookie Cutter, prancing horse, bobtail,
  flat back, 6½ x 7½" **100.00**
Cookie Jar, sitting horse, American
  Bisque **150.00**
Doorstop,   racehorse,   Virginia
  Metalcrafters, 1949 . . . . **150.00**
Fan, Moxie adv, rocking horse on front,
  1920s 25.00
Figure
  Summit Art Glass, blue horse, short
    legs 25.00
  Vernon Kilns, black unicorn from
    Disney movie *Fantasia*, ceramic . . **250.00**
  Wade, England, miniature pony, ce-
    ramic, Tom Smith artist 25.00
Fruit Crate Label, Loop Loop,
  Washington State Apples, Indian
  chief on Palomino 10.00
Figurine
  Beswick, reclining foal, ceramic, 3" l   50.00
  Breyer, "Secretariat," plastic, gold . .   40.00
  Hagen Renaker, glossy bay quarter
    horse mare, ceramic, small ear
    chip 50.00
  Hartland, gray polo pony, plastic . . .   25.00
  Heisey, Clydesdale, glass, amber . . **2,500.00**
Glass
  Belmont Stakes, 1981 . . . .   90.00
  Kentucky Derby, 1950 . . . . **150.00**
Hobby Horse, Tom Mix, wood,
  wheeled platform **500.00**
Lapel Pin, US Olympic Equestrian
  Team, 1988 . . . .   5.00
Liquor Decanter, Man O' War, Ezra
  Brooks, 1969 . . . .   25.00
Lithograph, Buffalo Bill on horse, 1922 **150.00**
Magazine, *Western Horseman*, Volume
  1, #1, 1935 . . . .   15.00

Mug
  Budweiser   Clydesdales,   holiday,
    1985 . . . .   20.00
  Democratic Party souvenir, ceramic,
    figural donkey, red, Frankoma,
    1976 . . . .   35.00
Nodder, papier mache, donkey wearing
  suit, carrying flag, Democratic party
  symbol, Japan 45.00
Paperweight, donkey, sgd "Louise Able,
  Rockwood," #6241 . . . . **125.00**
Plate
  Syracuse China, Love the Rodeo pat-
    tern 75.00
  Unmarked,   cowboy   on   bucking
    horse, 12½" d 35.00
Post Card
  Three Draft Horses, heads shown,
    Germany, pre 1920 . . . .   8.00
  White Stallion in Moonlight, artist sgd   5.00
Poster, Beery Exhibitions, Dayton, OH
  Fairgrounds,   "Saddle   Horse
  Contests," 1913, framed, under glass **300.00**
Program, Kentucky Derby, 1961 . . . . .   20.00
Rocking Horse, white with black spots,
  horsehair mane and tail, handmade,
  75% orig paint remains, one rocker
  split **275.00**
Salt and Pepper Shakers, pr, donkeys,
  one sitting, one kicking, Japan, 1950s   15.00
Sheet Music, *Dan Patch March*, horse
  photo on cov 60.00
Sign
  Hunter Cigars, tin, fox hunter with
    horse illus, c1915, 19 x 27" **250.00**
  Mobil Oil, porcelain on steel, red
    Pegasus, 6' l **1,200.00**
Snowdome, Budweiser Clydesdales,
  1988 edition, MIB 40.00
Toy
  Hay Cart, Gibbs, paper litho and
    painted wood, c1910, 19" l **300.00**
  Mule, stuffed, collar inscription reads
    "One of the Twenty Mule Team,"
    1980s Boraxo promotion 15.00
Tray, Genessee Twelve Horse Ale, horse
  team illus 75.00
Trophy, metal, horse figure, wood base,
  1964 Oklahoma Horse of the Year . .   15.00
Watch Fob, running horse, ruby eyes,
  gold filled, exceptionally large link
  watch chain **500.00**
Windmill   Weight,   bobtail   horse,
  Dempster, Beatrice, NE, 17" l **750.00**

**Model, Breyer, Percheron, plastic, glossy
finish, $50.00.**

HULL POTTERY

Collecting Hints: Hull Pottery has distinctive
markings on the bottom of its vases that help the
collector identify them immediately. Early

stoneware pottery has an "H." The famous matte pieces, a favorite of most collectors, contain pattern numbers. For example, Camelia pieces are marked with numbers in the 100s, Iris pieces have 400 numbers, and Wildflower items have a W– preceding their number. Most of Hull's vases are also marked with their height in inches, making determining their value much easier. Items made after 1950 are marked with "hull" or "Hull" in large script writing and are usually glossy.

History: In 1905 Addis E. Hull purchased the Acme Pottery Co. in Crooksville, Ohio. In 1917 A. E. Hull Pottery Co. began to make a line of art pottery for florists and gift shops. The company also made novelties, kitchenware, and stoneware. During the Depression, the company's largest production line was tiles.

In 1950 the factory was destroyed by a flood and fire. By 1952 it was back in production, operating with the Hull Pottery Company name. At this time Hull added its newer glossy finish pottery plus developed Regal and Floraline as trade names for pieces sold in flower shops. Hull's brown House 'n Garden line of kitchen and dinnerware achieved great popularity and was the main line of pottery being produced prior to the plant closing its doors in 1986.

Hull's Little Red Riding Hood kitchenware was manufactured between 1943 and 1957 and is a favorite of collectors, including many who do not collect other Hull items.

Hull collectors are beginning to seriously collect the glossy ware and kitchen items. Since the plant has closed, all Hull pieces have become desirable.

References: Susan and Al Bagdade, *Warman's American Pottery and Porcelain,* Wallace–Homestead, 1994; Barbara Loveless Gick–Burke, *Collector's Guide To Hull Pottery, The Dinnerware Lines: Identification and Values,* Collector Books, 1993; Joan Gray Hull, *Hull: The Heavenly Pottery, Fourth Edition,* published by author, 1995; Joan Gray Hull, *Hull: The Heavenly Pottery Shirt Pocket Price Guide,* published by author, 1994; Brenda Roberts, *Roberts Ultimate Encyclopedia Of Hull Pottery,* Walsworth Publishing, 1992; Brenda Roberts, *The Collectors Encyclopedia of Hull Pottery,* Collector Books, 1980, 1995 value update; Brenda Roberts, *The Companion Guide To Roberts' Ultimate Encyclopedia Of Hull Pottery,* Walworth Publishing Co., 1992; Mark E. Supnick, *Collecting Hull Pottery's Little Red Riding Hood,* L–W Book Sales, 1989, 1992 value update.

Periodicals: *Hull Pottery Newsletter,* 11023 Tunnel Hill NE, New Lexington, OH 43764; *The Hull Pottery News,* 466 Foreston Place, St. Louis, MO 63119.

Advisor: Joan Hull.

PRE-1950 PATTERNS

Bow Knot
B 3, 6" vase	165.00
B 7, 8½" vase	275.00
B 13, double cornucopia	275.00
B 28, 10" d, plate	1,200.00

Dogwood (Wildflower)
504, 8½" vase	100.00
507, 5½" teapot	325.00
514, 4" jardiniere	95.00

Iris
405, 4¾" vase	70.00
406, 7" vase	125.00
412, 7" hanging planter	145.00

Jack In The Pulpit/Calla Lily
500/32, 10" bowl	175.00
505, 6" vase	95.00
550, 7" vase	125.00

Magnolia
4, 6¼" vase	55.00
8, 10½" vase	150.00
14, 4¾" pitcher	55.00
22, 12½" vase	250.00

Magnolia (Pink Gloss)
H 5, 6½" vase	30.00
H 17, 12½" vase	200.00

Open Rose (Camelia)
105, 7" pitcher	225.00
114, 8½" jardiniere	350.00
120, 6½" vase	100.00
140, 10½" basket	1,000.00

Orchid
301, 10" vase	325.00
306, 6¾" bud vase	135.00
311, 13" pitcher	650.00

Pinecone, 55, 6" 135.00

Poppy
606, 6½" vase	125.00
607, 8½" vase	165.00
609, 9" wall planter	395.00

Rosella
R 1, 5" vase	35.00
R 8, 6½" vase	75.00
R 15, 8½" vase	85.00

Stoneware
26 H, vase	75.00
536 H, 10" jardiniere	100.00

Thistle, #53, 6" 135.00

Tulip
101–33, 9" vase	195.00
109–33, 8" pitcher	225.00
110–33, 6" vase	125.00

Waterlily
L–8, 8¼" vase	1,325.00
L–18, 6" teapot	185.00
L–19, 5" creamer	50.00
L–20, 5" sugar	50.00

Wildflower
W–3, 5½" vase	55.00
W–8, 7½" vase	85.00
W–18, 12½" vase	250.00
W–54, 6½" vase	135.00

W–66, 10½" basket	1,800.00
W–76, 8½" vase	295.00
Woodland (matte)	
W1, 5½" vase	65.00
W10, 11" cornucopia	145.00
W25, 12½" vase	395.00

POST-1950 PATTERNS (Glossy)

Blossom Flite	
T8, basket	125.00
T10, 16½" console bowl	95.00
T11, candleholders, price for pair	75.00
Butterfly	
B4, 6" bonbon dish	45.00
B13, 8" basket	125.00
B15, 13½" pitcher	185.00
Ebbtide	
E3, 7½" mermaid cornucopia	175.00
E7, 11", fish vase	125.00
Figural Planters	
27, Madonna, standing	30.00
82, clown	50.00
95, twin geese	50.00
Parchment & Pine	
S–5, 10½", scroll planter	85.00
S–15, 8" coffeepot	125.00

Planter, twin geese, large, #95, 1951, 7¼" h, $50.00.

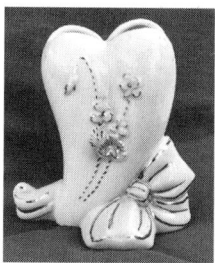

Vase, melon–shaped cornucopia with bow base, white ground, blue tone, gold highlights, high gloss, marked "USA," 5¾" h, $10.00.

Serenade (Birds)	
S7, 8½" vase	55.00
S15, 11½" ftd fruit bowl	110.00
Sunglow	
51, 7½" cov casserole	50.00
80, cup and saucer wall pocket	65.00
95, 8¼" vase	45.00
Tokay (Grapes)	
4, 8¼" vase	95.00
12, 12" vase	125.00
19, large leaf dish	75.00
Tropicana, T53, 8½" vase	500.00
Woodland	
W–6, 6½" pitcher	65.00
W–9, 8¾" basket	110.00
W–13, 7½" shell wall pocket	75.00

HUMMEL ITEMS

Collecting Hints: A key to Hummel figures is the mark. Collectors are advised to get pieces with the early marks whenever possible. Since production runs were large, almost all figurines, no matter what the mark, exist in large numbers.

Prices fluctuate a great deal. Antiques newspapers such as *The Antique Trader* and dealers often run ads showing discounts on the modern pieces. The slightest damage to a piece lowers the value significantly.

Before World War II and for a few years after, the Goebel Company made objects, such as vases, for export. These often had the early mark. Prices are modest for these items because few collectors concentrate on them. The Hummel books do not list them. This aspect of the Goebel Company offers the chance for an excellent research project.

History: Hummel items are the original creations of German artist, Berta Hummel. Born in 1909 in Massing, Bavaria, into a family where the arts were a part of everyday living, her talents were encouraged by her parents and formal educators from early childhood. At the age of 18, she was enrolled in the Academy of Fine Arts in Munich to further her mastery of drawing and the palette.

She entered the Convent of Siessen and became Sister Maria Innocentia in 1934. In this Franciscan cloister, she continued drawing and painting images of her childhood friends.

In 1935, W. Goebel Co. in Rodental, Germany, conceived the idea of reproducing Sister Maria's sketches into three–dimensional bisque figurines. John Schmid discovered the German–made figurines. The Schmid Brothers of Randolph, Massachusetts, introduced the figurines to America and became Goebel's U.S. distributor.

In 1967, Goebel began distributing Hummel items in the U.S. and a controversy developed between the two companies involving the Hummel family and the convent. Lawsuits and countersuits ensued. The German courts finally affected a compromise. The convent held legal rights to all works produced by Sister Maria from 1934 until her death in 1964 and licensed Goebel to reproduce these works. Schmid was to deal directly with the Hummel family for permission to reproduce any pre–convent art work.

All authentic Hummels bear both the signature, M.I. Hummel, and a Goebel trademark. Various trademarks were used to identify the year of production. The Crown Mark (trademark 1) was used in 1935 until 1949; Full Bee (trademark 2) 1950–1959; Stylized Bee (trademark 3) 1957–1972; Three Line Mark (trademark 4) 1964–1972; Last Bee Mark (trademark 5) 1972–1980, Missing Bee Mark (trademark 6) 1979–1990; and the Current Mark or New Crown Mark (trademark 7) from 1991 to the present.

References: Ken Armke, *Hummel: An Illustrated Handbook and Price Guide,* Wallace–Homestead, 1995; Carl F. Luckey, *Luckey's Hummel Figurines & Plates, 10th Edition,* Books Americana, 1994; Robert L. Miller, *The No. 1 Price Guide To M. I. Hummel: Figurines, Plates, More...,* Sixth Edition Portfolio Press, 1995; Wolfgang Schwalto, *M. I. Hummel Collector's Handbook, Part I: Rarities and Collector Pieces,* Schwalto GMBH, 1994; Lawrence L. Wonsch, *Hummel Copycats with Values,* Wallace–Homestead, 1987.

Collectors' Clubs: Hummel Collectors Club, PO Box 257, Yardley, PA 19067; M. I. Hummel Club, Goebel Plaza, PO Box 11, Pennington, NJ 08534.

Museum: Goebel Museum, Tarrytown, NY.

Annual Plate
  1973, Globe Trotter, 266, trademark 5 **200.00**
  1975, Ride Into Christmas, 268, trademark 5 . . . . **115.00**
  1976, Apple Tree Girl, 269, trademark 5 . . . . **90.00**
  1977, Apple Tree Boy, 270, trademark 5 . . . . **125.00**
  1978, Happy Pastime, 271, trademark 5 . . . . **115.00**
  1980, School Girl, 273, trademark 6 **100.00**
Ashtray
  Happy Pastime, 62, trademark 4 . . . **95.00**
  Let's Sing, 114, trademark 5 . . . . **68.00**
  Singing Lesson, 34, trademark 6 . . . **80.00**
Bell
  1979, Farewell, 701, trademark 5 . . **80.00**
  1981, In Tune, 703, trademark 6 . . . **85.00**
  1983, Knit One, 705, trademark 6 . . **90.00**
Bookends
  Apple Tree Girl & Apple Tree Boy, 252 A & B, trademark 5 . . . . **180.00**

Farm Boy & Goose Girl, 60 A & B, trademark 6 . . . . **220.00**
Good Friends & She Loves Me, She Loves Me Not, 251 A & B, trademark 3 . . . . **225.00**
Candleholder
  Begging His Share, 9, trademark 4 . . **115.00**
  Boy With Horse, 117, trademark 3 . . **42.50**
  Girl With Fir Tree, 116, trademark 1 . **125.00**
  Joyous News, 27/1, trademark 2 . . . **325.00**
  Little Band, 388, trademark 6 . . . . . **132.00**
  Silent Night, 54, trademark 5 . . . . . . **105.00**

Doll, Christyl, orig green wrist tag, blue paper label on slipper, marked "1775/M. I. Hummel/copr W Goebel," brown molded hair, red scarf, red, white and blue dress with white dots, orig socks, brown felt slippers, basket of flowers, 12" h, $200.00.

Figurine
  Angel Duet, 261, trademark 6 . . . . . **88.00**
  Angel With Lute, 238/A, trademark 5 **24.00**
  Apple Tree Boy, 142/3/0, trademark 5 **55.00**
  Autumn Harvest, 355, trademark 6 . **88.00**
  Baker, 128, trademark 3 . . . . **95.00**
  Barnyard Hero, 195/2/0, trademark 3 **110.00**
  Bird Duet, 169, trademark 4 . . . . . . **80.00**
  Boy With Accordion, 390, trademark 5 . . . . **34.00**
  Carnival, 328, trademark 5 . . . . **85.00**
  Chick Girl, 57/0, trademark 4 . . . . . **85.00**
  Chicken–Licken, 385, trademark 4 . **300.00**
  Chimney Sweep, 12/2/0, trademark 2 **60.00**
  Close Harmony, 336, trademark 6 . . **125.00**
  Coquettes, 179, trademark 6 . . . . . . **105.00**
  Crossroads, 331, trademark 6 . . . . . **185.00**
  Culprits, 56/A, trademark 5 . . . . **110.00**
  Farm Boy, 66, trademark 3 . . . . **165.00**
  Feeding Time, 199/0, trademark 6 . . **88.00**
  Gay Adventure, 356, trademark 5 . . **80.00**
  Girl with Nosegay, 239/A, trademark 4 . . . . **40.00**

Globe Trotter, 79, trademark 4 . . . . .   85.00
Going to Grandma's, 52/0, trade-
mark 6 . . . .   100.00
Goose Girl, 47/3/0, trademark 2 . . .   140.00
Heavenly Angel, 21/0, trademark 3 .   65.00
Home From Market, 198/12/0, trade-
mark 5 . . . .   58.00
In Tune, 414, trademark 6 . . . .   120.00
Joyful, 53, trademark 3 . . . .   75.00
Just Resting, 112/3/0, trademark 5 . .   68.00
Kiss Me, 311, trademark 5 . . . .   100.00
Latest News, 184, trademark 3 . . . . .   180.00
Letter to Santa Claus, 340, trade-
mark 6 . . . .   137.00
Little Gabriel, 32/0, trademark 1 . . .   275.00
Little Gardener, 74, trademark 3 . . .   85.00
Little Goat Herder, 200/10, trade-
mark 4 . . . .   95.00
Little Helper, 73, trademark 5 . . . . .   60.00
Little Scholar, 80, trademark 2 . . . . .   180.00
Little Sweeper, 171, trademark 6 . . .   55.00
Lost Sheep, 68/2/0, trademark 2 . . . .   135.00
March Winds, 43, trademark 2 . . . .   125.00
Meditation, 13/2/0, trademark 3 . . .   85.00
Merry Wanderer, 11/2/0, trademark 2   135.00
On Holiday, 350, trademark 6 . . . . .   90.00
Out of Danger, 56/B, trademark 2 . .   250.00
Playmates, 58/0, trademark 2 . . . . .   160.00
Postman, 119, trademark 4 . . . .   110.00
She Loves Me, She Loves Me Not,
174, trademark 1 . . . .   350.00
Signs of Spring, 203/2/0, trademark 5   75.00
Singing Lesson, 63, trademark 3 . . .   85.00
Soldier Boy, 332, trademark 4 . . . . .   90.00
Stormy Weather, 71, trademark 6 . . .   200.00
Surprise, 94/3/0, trademark 2 . . . . . .   160.00
Thoughtful, 415, trademark 6 . . . . .   110.00
To Market, 49/3/0, trademark 3 . . . .   130.00
Trumpet Boy, 97, trademark 6 . . . . .   55.00
Village Boy, 51/3/0, trademark 4 . . .   50.00
Volunteers, 50/2,/0, trademark 3 . . .   165.00
Wash Day, 321, trademark 3 . . . . . .   275.00
Wayside Harmony, 111/3/0, trade-
mark 6 . . . .   63.00
Font
Angel Shrine, 147, trademark 2 . . . .   82.00
Child With Flowers, 36/0, trade-
mark 3 . . . .   32.50
Guardian Angel, 248/0, trademark 4   40.00
Holy Family, 246, trademark 3 . . . .   62.00
White Angel, 75, trademark 1 . . . . .   125.00
Worship, 164, trademark 4 . . . .   35.00
Lamp Base
Birthday Serenade, 234, trademark 6   210.00
Culprits, 44/A, trademark 6 . . . .   205.00
Just Resting, 225/1, trademark 6 . . . .   180.00
She Loves Me, She Loves Me Not,
227, trademark 3 . . . .   225.00
To Market, 223, trademark 5 . . . . . .   245.00
Nativity Set Pieces
Angel Serenade, 260/E, trademark 4   80.00
Donkey, standing, 260/L, trademark 6   66.00

Flying Angel, 366, color, trademark 4   68.00
Joseph, 214/B, white, trademark 2 . .   175.00
King, kneeling 260/P, trademark 6 . .   273.00
Lamb, 214/0, color, trademark 3 . . .   14.00
Moorish King, standing, 214/L, white,
trademark 4 . . . .   118.00
Shepherd, kneeling, 214/G, color,
trademark 3 . . . .   78.00
Virgin Mary, 214/A, white, trade-
mark 5 . . . .   55.00
Plaque
Ba–Bee–Ring, 30 A & B, trademark 5   95.00
Flitting Butterfly, 139, trademark 3 . .   125.00
Madonna, 48/0, trademark 4 . . . . . .   65.00
Merry Wanderer, 92, trademark 5 . .   75.00
Standing Boy, 168, trademark 6 . . . .   80.00
The Mail Is Here, 140, trademark 4 .   162.00
Vacation Time, 125, trademark 5 . . . . .   105.00

ICE CREAM COLLECTIBLES

Collecting Hints: The ice cream collector faces a wide range of competitors. One of the most difficult for the generalist ice cream collector is the regional collector, i.e., an individual who exclusively collects ice cream memorabilia related to a specific manufacturer or region. Because of this, highly distorted prices often are reported in trade periodicals.

Many ice cream collectibles are associated with a specific dairy, thus adding dairy collectors into the equation. Since most ice cream was made of milk, milk and milk bottle collectors also hover around the edge of the ice cream collecting scene. Do not forget to factor in the cow collector (ice cream advertising often features cows) and the collecting field becomes very crowded. Advertising, food mold, kitchen, and premium collectors are secondary considerations. The result is fierce competition for ice cream material, often resulting in higher prices.

When buying an ice cream tray, the scene is the most important element. Most trays were stock items with the store or firm's name added later. Condition is critical.

Beware of reproductions. They became part of the ice cream collectibles world in the 1980s. Many reproductions are introduced into the market as "warehouse" finds. Although these items look old, many are poor reproductions or fantasy pieces.

History: During the first century A.D. in ancient Rome, the Emperor Nero had snow and ice brought from the nearby mountains. He then flavored the ice with fruit pulp and honey. This fruit ice was the forerunner of ice cream. The next development occurred in the 13th century. Among the many treasures that Marco Polo brought back from the Orient was a recipe for a frozen milk dessert resembling sherbet.

In the 1530s Catherine de Medici, bride of King Henry II of France, introduced Italian ices to the French court. By the end of the 16th century, ices evolved and became similar to today's modern ice cream. By the middle of the 17th century, ice cream became fashionable at the English court.

Ice cream switched from being a luxury food for kings and their court to a popular commodity in 1670 when the Cafe Procope (rue de l'Ancienne) in Paris introduced ice cream to the general populace. By 1700 the first ice cream recipe book appeared. Ice cream was the rage of eighteenth century Europe.

Ice cream appeared in America by the early 18th century. In 1777 an advertisement by Philip Lenzi, confectioner, appeared in the New York Gazette noting that ice cream was available on a daily basis. George Washington was an ice cream enthusiast, spending over $200 with a New York ice cream merchant in 1790. Thomas Jefferson developed an eighteen step process to make ice cream and is credited with the invention of Baked Alaska.

By the mid–19th century, ice cream "gardens" sprang up in major urban areas. The ice cream street vendor arrived on the scene by the late 1820s. Ice cream remained difficult to prepare with production largely in commercial hands.

In 1846 Nancy Johnson invented the hand–cranked ice cream freezer. Ice cream entered the average American household. By 1850 ice cream was a basic necessity of American life. As the century progressed, the ice cream parlor arrived on the scene. Homemade ice cream competed with commercial products from local, regional, and national dairies.

The arrival of the home refrigerator/freezer and large commercial freezers in grocery stores marked the beginning of the end for the ice cream parlor. A few survived into the post–World War II era. The drug store soda fountain replaced many of them. They in turn passed away in the 1970s when chain drug stores arrived upon the scene.

America manufactures and consumes more ice cream than any other nation in the world. But Americans do not hold a monopoly. Ice cream reigns worldwide as one of the most popular foods known. In France it is called glace, in Germany eis, and in Russia marozhnye. No matter what it is called, ice cream is eaten and enjoyed worldwide.

References: Paul Dickson, The Great American Ice Cream Book, Galahad Books, 1972, out–of–print; Ralph Pomeroy, The Ice Cream Connection, Paddington Press, 1975, out–of–print; Wayne Smith, Ice Cream Dippers, published by author, 1986.

Note: Also check general price guides to advertising and advertising character collectibles for ice cream related material.

Collector's Club: The Ice Screamers, PO Box 465, Warrington, PA 18976.

Museums: Greenfield Village, Dearborn, MI; Museum of Science and Industry, Finigran's Ice Cream Parlor, Chicago, IL; Smithsonian Institution, Washington, D.C.

Advertising Trade Card
Dairylea Ice Cream, diecut, mechanical, boy, eyes roll, Germany	30.00
Semon Ice Cream, diecut, frog, both sides printed	25.00
Ashtray, Breyers, 90th Anniversary, 1866–1956	20.00
Booklet, Eskimo Pie, 2 pgs, premiums, 1952	15.00
Catalog, Ice Cream, Manufacturers' Equipment, 5¾ x 8¾", soft cov, 60 pgs, black and white illus, #31, Thos Mills & Bro, Inc, Philadelphia, early 1900s	65.00
Decal, Mr Softee Ice Cream Safety Club	10.00
Dispenser, Turnball Cones & Cups, tin, cylindrical, orange, side handles, Dairy Queen, OH	130.00
Fan, Hoffman Willis Ice Cream Co, girl eating ice cream	15.00
Ice Cream Container, Hopalong Cassidy, quart, lid	65.00

Ice Cream Scoop
Coronet, metal	20.00
Gilchrist, #31	65.00
Indestructo	
#4	45.00
#16, comet type, black Bakelite handle, marked	25.00
Ice Cream Wrapper, Plamer Cox Brownie illus, unused	5.00
Jiffy Dispenser Co, ice cream sandwich type, curved	300.00
Malt Mixer, Multi–Mixer, five position, three station, working condition . . .	195.00

Mold, pewter
Battle Ship, #1069	48.00
Bull, #223	45.00
Mars, #3251	50.00

Pinback Button
Semon Ice Cream, 1¼" d, red, white, and gold, black lettering, early 1920s	14.00
Skippy Ice Cream, 1⅛" d, litho, red, white, and blue, 1930s	12.00
Popsicle Bag, 1950s	2.00

Post Card
Bodle's Ice Cream Store, diecut	8.00

Telling's Ice Cream 1.50
Sign
  Carrara's, mechanical, papier
    mache, boy in cone, head nods,
    glass eyes **2,600.00**
Crown Quality Ice Cream, 20 x 28",
    tin, buckets of ice cream **125.00**
Golden Rod Ice Cream, little girl eat-
    ing ice cream **90.00**
Lyons Polar Maid, 48" h, figural, ice
    cream cone in stand, metal and
    composition **950.00**
Meadow Gold Ice Cream, porcelain,
    double sided **125.00**
Pretty Lady, serving ice cream, emb
    cardboard, diecut, unlettered,
    c1920 . . . . **40.00**
Seliges Ice Cream, tin, attached ther-
    mometer **35.00**
Sonny, 8 x 19", 5¢ cone, cardboard,
    1920s **18.00**

Scoop, No-Pak 31, Cheater, $100.00.

Tape Measure, Cunningham's Ice
    Cream **15.00**
Thermometer
    Harrington's Ice Cream, 12" h, wood **35.00**
    Puritas Ice Cream, 12½" h, card-
      board, c1923 . . . . **35.00**
Tray
    Banquet Ice Cream, 10½ x 15",
      c1930 . . . . **20.00**
    Hoefler Ice Cream, oval, woman eat-
      ing ice cream **200.00**
    Montrose Dairy, Kewpie eating sun-
      daes **250.00**
    Williams Ice Cream, 13½" d, mother
      and son at table **290.00**
Tumbler, 5¼" h, Sealtest Ice Cream, red
    label **10.00**
Whistle, plastic
    Dairy Queen, cone shape **15.00**
    Purity Ice Cream, trapezoid shape,
      black top with orange name and
      "Penn Dairies, Inc," light blue bot-
      tom, late 1940s **15.00**

INSULATORS

Collecting Hints: Learn the shapes of the insula-
tors and the abbreviations which appear on
them. Some commonly found abbreviations are:
"B" (Brookfield), "B & O" (Baltimore and Ohio),
"EC&M Co SF" (Electrical Construction and
Maintenance Company of San Francisco), "ER"
(Erie Railroad), "WGM Co" (Western Glass
Manufacturing Company), and "WUT Co"
(Western Union Telegraph Company).

The majority of the insulators are priced below
$50.00. However, there are examples of
threaded and threadless insulators which have
exceeded $2,000. There has been little move-
ment in the price of glass insulators for the past
few years. The top insulators in each category
are:
Threaded
    CD 139, Combination Safety/Pat.
      Applied for, aqua **2,500.00**
    CD 180, Liquid Insulator/blank, ice
      aqua **2,500.00**
    CD 138–9, Patent Applied for/blank,
      aqua **2,400.00**
    CD 176, Lower wire ridge, Whitall
      Tatum Co. No. 12 made in
      U.S.A./lower wire ridge, Patent No.
      1708038, straw **2,300.00**
    CD 181, no name and no emboss-
      ing **2,200.00**
Threadless
    CD 731, no name and no embossing,
      white milk glass **3,000.00**
    CD 739, no name and no emboss-
      ing, similar to jade green milk
      glass **3,000.00**
    CD 737, Leffert's/blank, green **2,500.00**
    CD 790, no name and no embossing,
      known as Tea Pot, aqua **2,200.00**
    CD 788, no name and no embossing,
      known as slash top **2,200.00**
The six Fry Glass insulators are not counted in
this survey. They are not common threadless insulators because they were made only between
1844 and 1865.

History: The invention of the telegraph in 1832
created the need for a glass or ceramic insulator.
The first patent was given to Ezra Cornell in
1844. The principal manufacturing era was from
1850 to the mid–1900s. Leading companies include Armstrong (1938–1969), Brookfield
(1865–1922), California (1912–1916), Gayner
(1920–1922), Hemingray (1871–1919), Lynchburg (1923–1925), Maydwell (1935–1940),
McLaughlin (1923–1925), and Whitall Tatum
(1920–1938).

Initially, insulators were threadless. Shortly after the Civil War, L. A. Cauvet received a patent
for a threaded insulator. Drip points prevented

water from laying on the insulator and causing a short. The double skirt kept moisture from the peg or pin.

There are about five hundred different styles of glass insulators. Each different style insulator has been given a "CD" (consolidated design) number which is found in N. R. Woodward's *The Glass Insulator In America*. Colors and names of the makers and all lettering found on the same style insulator have nothing to do with the CD number. Only the style of the insulator is the key to the numbering.

References: Bob Alexander, *Threaded Glass Insulator Price Guide...For The Year 1988*, A. B. Publishing Co., 1988; Gary G. Cranfill and Greg A. Kareofelas, *The Glass Insulator: A Comprehensive Reference*, published by author, 1973, separate price list; Michael G. Guthrie, *A Handbook For The Recognition & Identification Of Fake, Altered, and Repaired Insulators*, published by author, 1988; Paul Keating (ed.), *Milholland's Suggested Insulator Price Guide*, published by author, 1986; John and Carol McDougald, *Insulators: A History And Guide To North American Glass Pintype Insulators, Volume 1* (1990), *Volume 2* (1990), published by authors; John and Carol McDougald, *1995 Price Guide For Insulators: A History And Guide To North American Glass Pintype Insulators*, published by authors, 1995; Marion and Evelyn Milholland, *Glass Insulator Reference Book, 4th Revision*, published by authors, 1976; N. R. Woodward, *The Glass Insulator In America*, published by author, 1973.

Collectors' Clubs: Capital District Insulator Club, 41 Crestwood Dr., Schenectady, NY 12306; Central Florida Insulator Collectors Club, 707 NE 113th St., North Miami, FL 33161; Chesapeake Bay Insulator Club, 10 Ridge Rd., Catonsville, MD 21228; Lone Star Insulator Club, PO Box 1317, Buna, TX 77612; National Insulator Assoc., 5 Brownstone Road, East Granby, CT 06026; Yankee Polecat Insulator Club, 79 New Boltom Rd., Manchester, CT 06040.

Periodicals: *Crown Jewels of the Wire*, PO Box 1003, St. Charles, IL 60174; *The Rainbow Riders' Trading Post*, PO Box 1423, Port Heuneme, CA 93044.

Museums: Big Thicket Museum, Saratoga, TX; Edison Plaza Museum, Beaumont, TX.

THREADED INSULATORS

CD 102
  BGM Co, smooth base, purple **18.00**
CD 112, New England Telegraph & Telephone, aqua **35.00**
CD 122, Lynchburg No 30, light green   **6.00**
CD 145
  Brookfield/New York
    Aqua **5.00**

Medium Green **7.00**
GNW Tel Co, deep purple **25.00**
HG Co, petticoat, cornflower blue . .   **25.00**
KCGW, aqua **10.00**
Postal, light purple **10.00**
CD 155, Armstrong's DPL, smooth base, smoky olive **5.00**
CD 160
Hemingray 14/Made in USA
  Aqua **5.00**
  Clear **6.00**
CD 162, SS & Co, smooth base, lime green **150.00**
CD 168
Hemingray Made in USA/D510
  Clear **4.00**
  Green **7.00**
  Ice Blue **6.00**

Hemingray, #9, aqua, 3¾" h, $3.00.

Whitall Tatum Co No 11/Made in USA
  Ice Blue **15.00**
  Light Green **30.00**
CD 317, Chambers, smooth base, lime green **150.00**
CD 320, Pyrex, smooth base, carnival   **35.00**

THREADLESS INSULATORS

CD 718, no name and no embossing
  Aqua **200.00**
  Black Glass **350.00**
  Emerald Green **300.00**
  Olive Green **300.00**
CD 724, Chester, smooth base, dark cobalt **600.00**
CD 728, Boston Bottle Works, smooth base, light aqua **60.00**
CD 731, McKee, smooth base, aqua . .   **150.00**
CD 735, Mulford & Biddle, UPRR, cobalt blue, repair to skirt **250.00**

IRONS

Collecting Hints: Heavy rusting, pitting, or missing parts detract from an iron's value. As a collector becomes more advanced, he may accept some of these defects on a rare and unusual iron. However, the beginning collector is urged to concentrate on irons in very good to excellent condition.

European, Oriental, and other foreign irons are desirable, since many unusual types come from these areas and some models were prototypes for later American-made irons.

History: Ironing devices have been in use for many centuries, with early references dating from 1100. Irons from the Medieval, Renaissance, and early industrial eras can be found in Europe, but are rare. Fine brass engraved irons and handwrought irons dominated the period prior to 1850.

After 1850 the iron began a series of rapid evolutionary changes. New models were patented monthly. The housewife and tailor sought the latest improvement to keep "up–to–date."

The irons of the 1850 to 1910 period were heated in four ways: (1) A hot metal slug was inserted into the body; (2) A burning solid, such as coal or charcoal, was placed in the body; (3) A liquid or gas, such as alcohol, gasoline, or natural gas, was fed from an external tank and burned in the body; and (4) Conduction heating, usually by drawing heat from a stove top was used.

Irons from the 1850 to 1910 period are plentiful and varied. Many models and novelty irons still have not been documented by collectors.

Electric irons are not being added to older collections. The more sought after are those with special features (temperature indicators, self–contained stands, sets) or those with Deco styling.

References: Esther S. Berney, *A Collectors Guide To Pressing Irons And Trivets*, Crown Publishers, Inc., 1977; A. H. Glissman, *The Evolution Of The Sad Iron*, privately printed, 1970; David Irons, *Irons by Irons*, published by author, 1994; Dave Irons, *Pressing Iron Patents: A Pictorial Presentation of Patent Briefs, 1876–1912*, published by author, 1994; Brian Jewell, *Smoothing Irons: A History And Collectors Guide*, Wallace–Homestead, 1977; Judy (author) and Frank (illustrator) Politzer, *Early Tuesday Morning: More Little Irons and Trivets*, published by author, 1986; Judy and Frank Politzer, *Tuesday's Children*, published by authors, 1977; Ted and V. Swanson, *The Swanson Collection*, published by authors.

Collectors' Clubs: Club of the Friends of Ancient Smoothing Irons, PO Box 215, Carlsbad CA 92008; Midwest Sad Iron Collectors Club, 11940 Lavida Ave., St. Louis, MO 63138.

Museums: Henry Ford Museum, Dearborn, MI; Shelburne Museum, Shelburne, VT; Sturbridge Village, Sturbridge, MA.

Advisors: David and Sue Irons.

REPRODUCTION ALERT: The most often reproduced irons are the miniatures, especially the swan's neck and flat irons. Reproductions of some large European varieties are available, but poor construction, use of thin metals, and the unusually fine condition easily identifies them as new. More and more European styles are being reproduced each year. Construction techniques are better than before and aging processes can fool many knowledgeable persons. Look for heavy pitting on the repros and two or more that are exactly alike. Few American irons have been reproduced at this time, other than the miniatures.

Alcohol
  German
    Feldmeyer, saw grip handle, two
      rows of holes in body, 5" l,
      Berney Fig 144A **175.00**
    Ox tongue style, bullet nose, 8⅜" l,
      Irons 350 (L) **100.00**
    Manning Bowman & Co, 7¼" l, Irons
      348 (L) **150.00**
Charcoal
    Acme, 1910, no chimney, large circu-
      lar damper, Berney Fig 134A **120.00**
    Bless & Drake, 1852, tall chimney,
      vulcan face damper, 6¾" l, Berney
      Fig 128B **110.00**
    Double Spout, "NE Plus Ultra, 1902,"
      7½" l, Irons 83 (M) **150.00**
    Dutch Brass, cut open work on sides,
      hinged top, 7⅝", Irons 65 (M) . . . **300.00**
    Eclipse, may have fluter side plate,
      6½" l, Irons 153 (L) **160.00**
    Indian, massive bronze, cut work
      vent holes, 10½" l, Irons 96 (L) . . . **125.00**
    Junior Carbon Iron 1911, unusual
      damper, no chimney, 6" l, Irons
      89 (L) **170.00**
Children's
    All Wrought, one of a kind, 3½" l,
      Irons 437 . . . . **90.00**
    Brass Goffer, English Queen Anne
      base, 2⅜" barrel, Irons 429 (RR) . . **200.00**

Charcoal, wood handle, #3, $50.00.

Cylinder Grip, all cast, often chromed, 3⅜" l, Irons 457 . . . . . .   **45.00**

Cross Rib, all cast, various sizes, 3⅝" l, Irons 460 . . . .   **40.00**

Dover Sand Iron, 2 pc, metal cover, 4" l, Tuesday's Children Fig 272 . .   **45.00**

Dover USA, wood grip, 3½" l, Irons 472 (RM) **45.00**

English, brass box, 3½" l, Tuesday's Children, Fig 312 . . . .   **170.00**

Enterprise Mfg Co
  Miniature, 2 pcs, advertising piece,⅞" l, Irons 503 (FM) **300.00**
  No. 115, holes in handle, 3⅞" l, Tuesday's Children Fig 170 . . . .   **110.00**

French
  Round back, "F3", 3⅝" l, Irons 448   **75.00**
  Thin cast base, "PG," 4" l, Irons 445 . . . .   **70.00**

Our Pet, wood grip, 3½" l, Irons 470 (RL) **130.00**

Sensible No. O, 2 pc, 4" l, Tuesday's Children, Fig 283 . . . .   **95.00**

Sleeve, "Ober, Chagrin Falls, O," 4½" l, Irons 451 (FL) **250.00**

Swan, all cast, various sizes, Irons 439
  Orig blue, red, or yellow paint . . .   **160.00**
  No paint **75.00**

The Jewel, rainbow wood handle, 3⅞" l, Irons 471 (FR) **150.00**

Tri Bump, three bulbous areas in handle, sizes 1¾ to 3½" l, Tuesday's Children, Fig 58 . . . .   **45.00**

Flat/Sad Iron
  Enterprise, boxed set of five, 2 pc irons, 3 flat, 2 polishers, 3 handles, 2 trivets, Irons 324 . . . .   **300.00**
  French, round back, floral top, 7" l, Irons 303 (M) **130.00**
  HB & Co Reading, all cast, various weights, 5¼" l, Irons 321 (L) **20.00**
  IXL #6, 5¾" l, Irons 315 (L–2) **25.00**
  Ober, 4½" l, Irons 318 (M) **75.00**
  PW Weida's, handle flips back, 7" l, Irons 326 (L) **175.00**
  Soap Stone, Hood's Patent, 3 sizes, 6⅝" l, Irons 331 (RL) **165.00**
  Star Iron, Enterprise #70, cold handle, holes in handle, 6⅛" l, Irons 331 (RR) **75.00**
  Universal Thermo Cell 1911, 2 pc, 6⅜" l, Irons 339 (M) **120.00**

Fluters
  Machine
    Clamp On Companion, 5" roll, Irons 181 (R) **250.00**
    Crown, 5⅞" roll, Irons 158 (L) . . .   **125.00**
    Dudley Fluter, 5¾" roll, Irons 173 (L) **300.00**
    English, fine flutes, 4½" roll, Irons 177 (R) **275.00**
    Royal, 5¾" roll, Irons 157 (R) **150.00**

The Original Knox, with paper picture in oval, 5⅞" roll, Irons 161 (L) **250.00**

Miscellaneous
  Mini cast iron rocker, Irons 428 (L–2) **300.00**
  Wood stack fluter, wood rods in a stack, Irons 200 . . . .   **450.00**
  Young's Improved Plaiter, wire strips, Irons 202 . . . .   **50.00**

Rocker
  Geneva Hand Fluter, 5¾" l, Irons 194 (L) **60.00**
  The Best, 5½" l, Irons 195 (R) **110.00**
  The Erie Fluter, removable handle, 5½" l, Irons 197 (L) **300.00**
  The Star, 5½" l, Irons 196 (M) **140.00**

Roller
  American Machine Co, 7" l, Irons 187 (L) **85.00**
  Clarks, 6¼" l, Irons 185 (R) **140.00**
  CW Whitfield, 5½" l, Irons 186 (L)   **130.00**
  Howell's Wave Fluter, wavy pattern in flutes, Irons 190 (R) **400.00**
  Shephards Hardware 1879, 7¾" l, Irons 189 (R) **130.00**

Gasoline
  Acorn Brass Mfg Co, tank in handle, 6⅞" l, Irons 353 (M) **350.00**
  Coleman, Irons 39
    Black Enamel **140.00**
    Blue Enamel **70.00**
    Green Enamel **175.00**
    Tan Enamel **140.00**
  Diamond, 7⅜" l, Irons 363 (L) **80.00**
  Imperial, 6⅛" l, Irons 360 (R) **65.00**
  Rolier, Argentina, all brass, 7⅜" l, Irons 363 (M) **160.00**

Natural Gas
  Acethylene Stove Mfg Co, 6" l, Irons 378 (M) **60.00**
  Central Flat Iron Mfg Co, 6¼" l, Irons 382 (L) **75.00**
  Fletcher Laurel, gray agate, English, 6⅜" l, Irons 371 (R) **325.00**
  Schreiber & Goldberg, NY, 6" l, Irons 383 (L) **75.00**
  The Uneedit Gas Iron, 6½" l, Irons 372 (L) **120.00**
  Vulcan Gas Iron 764, 6¼" l, Irons 380 (R) **60.00**

Slug/Box
  Belgium, round back, open back, 6⅛" l, Irons 27 (R) **250.00**
  Bless–Drake Salamander Box Iron, 6" l, Irons 53 (L) **350.00**
  Danish, brass, delicate iron posts, small body, 5" l, Irons 33 (L–2) . . .   **175.00**
  European, ox tongue, brass, saw grip handle, 7¼" l, Irons 49 (L) **150.00**
  Scottish, brass "S" style posts, tear drop shape, 6¼" l, Irons 17 (L) . . .   **500.00**
  Sensible, 6½" l, Irons 55 (R) **160.00**

Certain types of unsigned pieces, particularly those made of Bakelite and other plastics, generate collector interest. Because costume jewelry is a wearable collectible, pieces should be chosen with an eye toward suitability to the wearer's personal style and wardrobe.

History: The term costume jewelry was not used until the 1920s, when Coco Chanel made the wearing of frankly *faux* jewels an acceptable part of *haute couture.* Prior to the Jazz Age, manufacturers mass–produced imitation jewelry—exact copies of the real thing. Fine jewelry continued to exert its influence on costume jewelry in the twentieth century, but designers could be more extravagant in producing pieces made of non–precious materials because they were liberated from the costly constraints of valuable gemstones and metals. By the 1930s, when more cost–effective methods were developed, casting superseded die–stamping in mass–production. The Great Depression instigated the use of the first entirely synthesized plastic, trade–named Bakelite, for colorful and inexpensive jewelry. During World War II, restrictions and shortages forced manufacturers to turn to sterling silver as a replacement for base white metals, and to experiment with new materials such as Lucite (DuPont's trade name for acrylic). Today, Lucite and sterling vermeil (gold–plated) animals and other figurals of the period, known as jelly bellies, are highly collectible. Other World War II novelty items were made of make–do materials such as wood, ceramic, textiles, and natural pods and seeds. In the prosperous 1950s, high–fashion rhinestone, faux pearl and colored glass jewelry signed with the names of well–known couturiers and other designers was sold in elegant department stores. A matching suite—necklace, bracelet, earrings, brooch—was the proper complement to the ensemble of a well–groomed 1950s woman.

Smoothing Iron, miniature, 3″ l, $15.00.

Specialty
  Goffering
    Queen Anne base, brass, English
      Double barrel, Irons 121 (M) . . **450.00**
      Single barrel, Irons 117 (L) **225.00**
    "S" style standard, "Clark," English,
      7″ h, Irons 140 (L–4) **75.00**
  Wrought
    Monkey Tail, 9″ h, Irons 110 (M) **450.00**
    Penny feet, European, 9″ h, Irons
      112 (L) **350.00**
  Hat
    Kenrich No. 1, narrow bar, 15″ l,
      Irons 233 (R) **95.00**
    McCoys Pat, arched cut out, 4¾″ l,
      Irons 226 (L) **150.00**
    Shackle, movable side, 3½″ l, Irons
      228 (M) **130.00**
    Wood Tolliker, 5¾″ l, Irons 222 (M) **140.00**
  Polishers
    Enterprise, No. 101, double ptd,
      holes in handle, 4⅞″ l, Irons
      267 (R) **75.00**
    French, gridwork bottom, "Repose"
      with anchor, 6¾″ l, Irons 261 (L) **150.00**
    Keystone (symbol), 4⅞″ l, Irons
      276 (L) **130.00**
    M Mahony, rough ridged bottom,
      5⅜″ l, Irons 290 (L) **70.00**
    Round bottom, Carron, 4⅝″ l, Irons
      273 (L) **90.00**
    Sweeney Iron, 7″ l, Irons 265 (R) . **170.00**

JEWELRY, COSTUME

Collecting Hints: A number of factors influence price. Scarcity and demand drive the market for costume jewelry. Demand is greatest for pieces marked with a recognized and sought–after designer's or manufacturer's name. Name alone, however, does not guarantee high value. Collectors should also consider quality of design and manufacture, size and color. Condition is of primary importance, because costume jewelry is easily damaged and difficult to repair well.

References: Lillian Baker, *Fifty Years Of Collectible Fashion Jewelry: 1925–1975,* Collector Books, 1986, 1992 value update; Lillian Baker, *100 Years of Collectible Jewelry, 1850–1950,* Collector Books, 1978, 1993 value update; Lillian Baker, *Twentieth Century Fashionable Plastic Jewelry,* Collector Books, 1992; Joanne Dubbs Ball, *Costume Jewelers, The Golden Age of Design,* Schiffer Publishing, 1990; Vivienne Becker, *Fabulous Costume Jewelry: History of Fantasy and Fashion In Jewels,* Schiffer Publishing, 1993; Howard L. Bell, Jr., *Cuff Jewelry: A Historical Account For Collectors and Antique Dealers,* published by author, 1994; Jeanenne Bell, *Answers To Questions About Old Jewelry, 1840–1950, Fourth Edition,* Books Americana, 1995; Matthew L. Burkholz and Linda Lictenberg Kaplan, *Copper Art Jewelry: A Different Luster,* Schiffer Publishing, 1992; Deanna Farneti Cera (ed.), *Jewels Of Fantasy: Costume Jewelry Of The 20th Century,* Harry N.

Abrams, 1992; Corinne Davidov and Ginny Redington Dawes, *The Bakelite Jewelry Book,* Abbeville Press, 1988; Maryanne Dolan, *Collecting Rhinestone Jewelry, Third Edition,* Books Americana, 1993; Roseann Ettinger, *Forties & Fifties Popular Jewelry,* Schiffer Publishing, 1994; Roseann Ettinger, *Popular Jewelry: 1840–1940,* Schiffer Publishing, 1990; Gabrielle Greindl, *Gems of Costume Jewelry,* Abbeville Press, 1990; S. Sylvia Henzel, *Collectible Costume Jewelry, Revised Edition,* Wallace–Homestead, 1987, 1990 value update; Sibylle Jargstorf, *Baubles, Buttons and Beads: The Heritage of Bohemia,* Schiffer Publishing, 1991; Sibylle Jargstorf, *Glass in Jewelry: Hidden Artistry in Glass,* Schiffer Publishing, 1991; Susan Jonas and Marilyn Nissenson, *Cuff Links,* Harry N. Abrams, 1991; Lyngerda Kelley and Nancy Schiffer, *Plastic Jewelry,* Schiffer Publishing, 1987, 1995 value update; J. J. Kellner, *The First Complete Reference Guide to Siam Sterling Nielloware,* published by author, 1993; Jack and Elynore "Pet" Kerins, *Collecting Antique Stickpins: Identification & Value Guide,* Collector Books, 1995; J. L. Lynnlee, *All That Glitters,* Schiffer Publishing, Ltd., 1986, 1993 value update; Harrice Simons Miller, *Costume Jewelry: Identification and Price Guide, Second Edition,* Avon Books, 1994; Nancy N. Schiffer, *Costume Jewelry: The Fun of Collecting,* Schiffer Publishing, 1988, 1992 value update; Nancy N. Schiffer, *Rhinestones!,* Schiffer Publishing Ltd., 1993; Nancy N. Schiffer, *Silver Jewelry Treasures,* Schiffer Publishing, 1993; Sheryl Gross Shatz, *What's It Made Of: A Jewelry Materials Identification Guide,* published by author, 1991; Christie Romero, *Warman's Jewelry,* Wallace–Homestead, 1995.

Collectors' Clubs: The National Cuff Link Society, PO Box 346, Prospect Heights, IL 60070; Vintage Fashion & Costume Jewelry Club, PO Box 265, Glen Oaks, NY 11004.

Videotapes: C. Jeanenne Bell, *The Antique and Collectible Jewelry Video Series: Edwardian, Art Nouveau & Art Deco Jewelry, Circa 1887–1930s, Volume II* Antique Images, 1994; C. Jeanenne Bell, *The Antique and Collectible Jewelry Video Series: Victorian Jewelry, Circa 1837–1901, Volume I* Antique Images, 1994; Christie Romero, *Hidden Treasures, A Collector's Guide To Antique and Vintage Jewelry of the 19th and 20th Centuries,* Venture Entertainment Group, 1992, 1995 value update.

Advisor: Christie Romero.

Reproduction Alert: Recasts and knockoffs are a widespread problem. Copies of high–end signed pieces, e.g., Trifari jelly bellies, Eisenberg Originals, Boucher, are common. New Bakelite (sometimes called fakelite) and marriages of old Bakelite parts are also cropping up in many areas.

Beads, unknown maker
  Bakelite, cherry amber–colored, square, uniform size, 40" l **100.00**
  Glass, faceted black, graduated, barrel clasp, 30" l **65.00**
  Mother of Pearl, graduated round, dyed turquoise, 24" l **75.00**
  Plastic, imitation ivory, graduated round, 22" l **25.00**
Bracelet
  Coppola e Toppo, a woven band of faceted black glass beads, 1" wide, large square metal clasp covered in beads, marked "Made in Italy by Coppola e Toppo," c1960 ...... **225.00**
  Haskell, Miriam, faux pearls, brass, hinged brass bangle encircled with a row of applied faux baroque pearls, marked, c1950 .... **125.00**
  Lane, Kenneth J., gold–plated white metal, enamel, rhinestones, hinged bangle in the form of a tiger, black enamel stripes alternating with pavé–set colorless rhinestones, marked "K.J.L." **80.00**
  Napier, sterling vermeil, rose gold plated, looped and scrolled ribbon–like links terminating in a large spring ring clasp marked "Sterling Napier," ¾" w, c1940 ... **150.00**
  Renoir, copper, tapered cuff, 1½" at center, with a row of applied graduated curled copper strips along one edge, marked "C Renoir," c1955 .... **45.00**
  Unknown maker
    Bakelite
      Red bangle with laminated black polka–dots, 1½" w, c1930 ... **275.00**
      Single row of large red hearts suspended from a red celluloid chain, c1940 .... **150.00**
    Celluloid, rhinestones, ivory–colored bangle with alternating rows of yellow and colorless rhinestones, ½" w, c1925 ..... **95.00**
    Wendell August Forge, hammered aluminum, 1½" cuff with rounded ends, raised branch and leaf design, imp "hand made," Wendell August Forge logo, c1950 ...... **25.00**
Brooch/Pin
  Boucher, rhinestones, rhodium–plated white metal, large three–dimensional flower, pierced petals and leaves, pavé–set with colorless round, marquise rhinestones, baguette stamens on wires, 4", c1940 .... **400.00**
  Carnegie, Hattie, gold–plated white metal, plastic, Chinese junk, molded green sail, boat bottom,

and ocean waves, c1960 . . . . **125.00**
Ciner, gold–plated white metal, emerald green glass cabochons, colorless rhinestones, 1½″ d, a cluster of
green cabochons with a raised
gold–plated wave set with colorless
rhinestones **50.00**
Corocraft, sterling vermeil, Lucite,
rhinestones, enamel, jelly belly,
goose in flight, brown, yellow,
green, red enameled details, rhinestones on wings, tail, feet, and
neck, 2¼″ l, c1940 . . . . **350.00**
De Rosa, sterling, rhinestones, glass,
S–scroll and flowerhead suspending two large faceted aquama-
rine–colored drops on chains set
with rhinestones **475.00**
Eisenberg, sterling vermeil, floral
spray with bow at the base set with
rows of colorless rhinestones terminating in cobalt blue pear–shaped
rhinestones, 2¼″, c1940 . . . . **225.00**
HAR, gold–plated white metal, styl-
ized frog with blue enameled body,
large red glass cabochon eyes,
c1950 . . . . **150.00**
Lane, Kenneth J., rhodium–plated
white metal, stylized elephant,
pierced design pavé–set with color-
less rhinestones, 2½″, c1970 . . . . **110.00**
Lisner, gold–plated white metal, large
five–pointed shooting star with five
rays set with blue baguette and
round colorless rhinestones, openwork star with round blue rhinestone center, radiating clusters of
colorless rhinestones, original tag . **70.00**
Matisse/Renoir, copper, "Starburst,"
with inset oval mottled blue/
turquoise enameled plaque, 3 x
1¾″, c1955 . . . . **85.00**
Mazer, gold–plated white metal,
scrolled ribbon with three molded
red glass cherries, interspersed with
small colorless rhinestones, 3½ x
2″, c1940 . . . . **250.00**
Rebajes, copper, cutout stylized fish,
2½″, c1950 . . . . **65.00**
Réja, sterling vermeil, salamander, a
row of square–cut blue rhinestones
down center of back, green rhine-
stone eyes, c1940 . . . . **285.00**
Staret, white metal, large scrolling floral spray set throughout with royal
blue marquise, square, and colorless round rhinestones, imp mark,
3½ x 2½″, c1940 . . . . **225.00**
Stein, Lea, plastic, sleeping cat,
shades of rust and black, 3½″ l,
marked "Lea Stein, Paris" **145.00**
TKF, rhodium–plated white metal,

fruit salad Art Deco design, molded
red, green, and blue glass stones
clustered in center of rounded rec-
tangle set with small colorless
rhinestones, marked "TKF" for
Trifari, Krussman and Fishel, c1930 **250.00**
Trifari
Gold–plated metal
Dragonfly, cast brushed finish,
red glass eyes, c1960 . . . . . . **45.00**
Poodle head, antiqued brushed
gold finish, green glass eyes,
c1955 . . . . **100.00**
Sterling Vermeil
Hummingbird set with faux
moonstones, blue baguette
and colorless round rhine-
stones, c1940 . . . . **300.00**
Skeleton key set with rectangular
green, round and baguette colorless rhinestones, 2½″ l,
c1940 . . . . **80.00**
Sterling Vermeil, Lucite, jelly belly
snail, set with small colorless
rhinestones, red cabochon eyes,
green rhinestone antennae,
c1940 . . . . **350.00**

**Brooch/Pin, sterling vermeil crown, two
large prong–set opalescent glass cabochons, small red and blue cabochons,
blue baguettes, red, blue, and pave colorless rhinestones, marked "Trifari sterling, des. pat. no. 137542," 1944,
$250.00.**

Unknown maker
Apple, red Bakelite with carved
Lucite leaves, c1940 . . . . **75.00**
Baby duck, painted yellow glazed
ceramic, c1940 . . . . **25.00**
Frog, stylized, two–tone, carved
green Bakelite with bulging eyes **150.00**
Hand, carved wood, hold three
gold metal jacks and a red
Bakelite ball **80.00**

Heart
Bakelite, red, with dangling berries on red stems, 2½" w, c1935 .... **265.00**
Rhodium–plated white metal, enclosing two lovebirds and hatching baby bird, pavé–set with colorless rhinestones, red glass cabochon center, marked Déposé (French for registered), 4½" w **350.00**
Horse head, carved colorless Lucite with painted bridle and mane **80.00**
Parrot head, brushed white metal with green glass eye, c1960 ... **45.00**
Pirate skeleton, gold–plated metal and multicolored painted enamel, articulated limbs, rhinestone eyes, c1950 .... **35.00**
Scarecrow, articulated carved wood limbs, Bakelite hands, feet and hat, c1940 .... **175.00**
Seal, stamped brass, balancing colorless Lucite ball on nose **20.00**
Sombrero, carved butterscotch Bakelite, dec with painted stripes and glass beads dangling from brim, c1935 .... **500.00**
Warner, Joseph, gold–plated white metal, Christmas tree set with red, green, blue, and colorless rhinestones, 2" **65.00**
Charm Bracelet
Bakelite, five dark amber–colored carved charms: horse head, horseshoes, boots, suspended from gilded link chain, c1940 .... **250.00**
Silver, cowboy and Indian motifs, fourteen assorted, c1940 .... **100.00**
Sterling, military motifs, twenty assorted, some with moving parts, c1940 .... **150.00**
Clip
Boucher, sterling vermeil, volute with radiating rods set with marquise red rhinestones, pavé faux turquoise, colorless rhinestones, birds head logo, 2½", c1940 .... **225.00**
Eisenberg Original
Sterling, multicolored rhinestones, starburst, c1940 .... **500.00**
White Metal, colorless rhinestones, rectangular openwork leaf design set with four large rhinestones and set throughout with medium and small rhinestones . **175.00**
Trifari
Rhodium–plated white metal
Floral spray, two flowerheads with centers en tremblant, pavé–set with colorless rhinestones, 2", c1940 .... **185.00**

Painted enamel five–petaled flower, small rhinestone accents, c1940 .... **125.00**
Unknown Maker, *pâte de verre* (poured glass), flower bouquet, red petals with rhinestone centers, green leaves, double–pronged hinged clip marked "Made in France Déposé," c1940 .... **150.00**
Cuff Links, pr
Sterling, six–guns with mother–of–pearl handles, revolving barrels, c1945 .... **100.00**
Sterling Vermeil, black enameled playing card motifs, c1955 ...... **50.00**
Double Clip Brooch, Coro Duette
Gold–plated white metal, pair of owls with oval aqua rhinestone eyes, pavé rhinestones on heads, aqua and yellow painted enamel, c1940 **185.00**
Sterling Vermeil, Lucite, pair of fish jelly bellies, set with colorless, blue, and red rhinestones **300.00**
Dress Clips, pr, unknown maker, rhodium–plated white metal, pierced inverted stepped triangles pavé–set with colorless rhinestones, flat–backed hinged clips, c1930 .... **35.00**
Earrings, pr
Jomaz, faux pearl, surrounded by molded green, red, blue, and purple glass stones and colorless rhinestones, clips, c1950 .... **15.00**
KJL, gold–plated white metal, faux pearls and rhinestones, elaborate pendent drops, 4" l, clips, c1965 . **50.00**
Kramer, pendent drops set with square, pear, and round colorless rhinestones, clips, 3¼" l, c1950 .. **30.00**
Matisse/Renoir, copper, disks with enameled mottled green domed centers, clips, 1" d **12.00**
Rosenstein, Nettie, gold–plated white metal, five–petal flowerheads with colorless and green rhinestones, clips **15.00**
Weiss, japanned white metal, strawberries, pavé–set with red rhinestones, clips **15.00**
Necklace
Haskell, Miriam
Black glass, faceted beads, 60" l, c1950 .... **80.00**
Faux pearls, double strand, choker length, oval mark, c1950 ..... **45.00**
Kramer, gold–plated white metal, set with three large round colorless rhinestones encircled by small rhinestones and faux pearls, a fringe of faux pearl and rhinestone pear–shaped drops, and a chain of rhinestones set in gold tone filigree, c1960 .... **400.00**

Necklace, copper, marked "Renoir," $135.00.

Lane, Kenneth J., faux pearls, triple strand choker with a pierced geometric center plaque pavé–set with colorless rhinestones, c1965 .... **75.00**
Unknown Maker
Bakelite
Clusters of red Bakelite cherries with green plastic leaves suspended from a red celluloid chain, c1935 .... **365.00**
Red, yellow and black stars suspended from a double strand ivory–colored celluloid chain, c1940 .... **250.00**
Single row of large red hearts suspended from a red celluloid chain **350.00**
Faceted lead crystal, 15" necklace of prong–set square, baguette, and round colorless stones with a 3¼" geometric pendant and a 3½" back drop, Art Deco, c1925 .... **175.00**
Glass, a linked row of carnelian–colored geometric–cut plaques, prong–set in brass, Czechoslovakia, c1925 .... **95.00**
Glass beads, molded red Egyptian motifs and small round beads, 32" l, Czechoslovakia, c1925 .. **150.00**
Glass, enamel, oval green glass cabochons bezel–set in gilt brass stamped filigree plaques, white and dark green enameled dec, Czechoslovakia, c1930 ...... **125.00**
Rhinestones, bib of graduated rows of marquise and round colorless rhinestones suspending a fringe of pear–shaped turquoise glass beads and faux pearl drops, c1960 .... **365.00**
Pendant
Napier, gold–plated white metal, 14 snake chain suspending two large grape clusters **135.00**

Rebajes, copper, Brazilian Mask, stylized male and female heads mounted on circular disk, original heavy link chain, c1950 .... **65.00**
Unknown Maker
Celluloid, light amber–colored triangular pendant with painted floral motif set with multicolored rhinestones, suspended from a strand of small round yellow glass beads **135.00**
Chrome plated white metal and Bakelite, orange and black half–cylinders set in geometric plaque suspended from tubular bead chain, Germany, c1930 .. **250.00**
Gold–plated metal, large cast brushed textured cross set with multi–colored faceted glass stones, original chain **110.00**
Suite
Boucher, rhodium–plated white metal, link bracelet and necklace, pierced rectangular plaques pavé–set with colorless rhinestones, alternating with large prong–set square red stones, matching clip earrings, c1950 .... **450.00**
Haskell, Miriam, faux pearls, triple strand necklace and clip earrings of one large pearl encircled by rhinestones, c1950 .... **75.00**
Hobé, sterling silver, ribbon bow with a diagonal floral spray set with aqua rhinestones, 4" w, flowerhead screwback earrings with large center stones, c1940 .... **160.00**
Lane, Kenneth J., rhodium–plated white metal, brooch, large bow suspending three large pear–shaped drops, pavé–set with colorless rhinestones, matching pendent earrings, c1965 .... **350.00**
Rosenstein, Nettie, rhodium–plated white metal, flowerhead brooch, 1½" d, pavé–set with colorless round rhinestones, matching spherical clip earrings, c1950 .... **100.00**
Trifari, gold–plated white metal, line bracelet with a center row of blue baguette rhinestones flanked by rows of alternating yellow and colorless square rhinestones, matching pear–shaped clip earrings, necklace suspending rhinestone–set center section and drop from fancy link gold tone chain, c1950 **135.00**
Unknown Maker
Aurora borealis faceted glass beads, bib necklace, a graduated fringe of glass beads and rhinestones suspended from a rhinestone chain, matching flexible

bracelet with glass bead clusters, clip earrings, c1960 . . . . **200.00**
Gilt brass openwork stamped metal brooch/pin in a starburst design set with oval light amber and green faceted glass, matching oval pendant suspended from three gilt chains, and wide flexible bracelet with openwork floral link center joined to seven gilt chains, c1930 . . . . **200.00**
Plastic hinged bangle, off–white, front half pavé–set with black rhinestones, matching hoop earrings, clip backs, c1955 . . . . . . **100.00**
Tie bar and cuff links, gold–plated metal, plain polished rectangles set with circular mother of pearl disks, c1940 . . . . **30.00**

JUKEBOXES

Collecting Hints: Jukebox chronology falls into four distinct periods:

In the pre–1938 period jukeboxes were constructed mainly of wood and resembled a radio or phonograph cabinet. In this period Wurlitzer jukeboxes are the most collectible, but their value usually is under $600.00.

From 1938 to 1948 the addition of plastics and animation units gave the jukebox a more gaudy appearance. These jukeboxes played 78 RPM records. Wurlitzer jukeboxes are king, with Rock–Ola the second most popular. This era contains the most valuable models, e.g., Wurlitzer models 750, 850, 950, 1015, and 1080, plus others.

The 1940–1960 era jukeboxes are collected for the "Happy Days" (named for the TV show) feeling: drive–in food, long skirts, sweater girls, and good times. These jukeboxes play 45 RPM records. They rate in value second to those of the 1938–1948 period. The period is referred to as the Seeburg era. Prices usually are under $1,500.00.

The 1961 and newer jukeboxes often are not considered collectible because the record mechanism is not visible, thus removing one of a box's alluring qualities.

There are exceptions to these generalizations. Collectors should have a price and identification guide to help make choices. Many original and reproduction parts are available for Seeburg and Wurlitzer jukeboxes. In many cases incomplete jukeboxes can be restored. Jukeboxes that are in working order and can be maintained in that condition are the best machines to own.

Wait about three to four months after becoming interested in jukeboxes before buying a machine. Use this time to educate yourself about a

machine's desirability and learn how missing components will affect its value.

History: First came the phonograph; the coin–operated phonograph followed. When electrical amplification became possible, the amplified coin–operated phonograph, known as a jukebox, evolved.

The heyday of the jukebox was the 1940s. Between 1946 and 1947 Wurlitzer produced 56,000 model 1015 jukeboxes, the largest production run of all time. The jukebox was the center of every teenage "hangout" from drug stores and restaurants to pool halls and dance parlors. They even invaded select private homes. Jukeboxes were cheaper than a live band, and, unlike radio, one could hear his or her favorite song when and as often as one wished.

Styles changed in the 1960s. Portable radios coupled with "Top 40" radio stations fulfilled the need for daily repetition of songs. Television changed evening entertainment patterns. The need for the jukebox vanished.

References: Frank Adams, *Wurlitzer Jukeboxes, 1934–1974*, AMR Publishing, 1983; Jerry Ayliffe, *American Premium Guide To Jukeboxes and Slot Machines, Third Edition*, Books Americana, 1991; Rick Botts, *A Complete Identification Guide To The Wurlitzer Jukebox*, privately printed, 1984; Rick Botts, *Jukebox Restoration Guide*, published by author, 1985; Stephan K. Loots, *The Official Victory Glass Price Guide To Antique Jukeboxes 1996*, published by author, 1995; Vincent Lynch, *American Jukebox: The Classic Years*, Chronicle Books, 1990; Christopher Pearce, *Vintage Jukeboxes: The Hall of Fame*, Chartwell Books, 1988; Scott Wood (ed.), *A Blast From The Past, Jukeboxes: A Pictorial Guide*, L–W Book Sales, 1992.

Periodicals: *Always Jukin'* 221 Yesler Way, Seattle, WA 98104; *Antique Amusements, Slot Machine & Jukebox Gazette*, 909 26th St. NW, Washington, DC 20037; *Coin–Op Classica*, 17844 Toiyabe St., Fountain Valley, CA 92708; *Gameroom Magazine*, 1014 Mt. Tabor Rd., New Albany, IN 47150; *Jukebox Collector*, 2545 SE 60th Court, Des Moines, IA 50317; *Loose Change*, 1515 South Commerce St., Las Vegas, NV 89102–2703.

Museums: Jukeboxes have not reached the status of museum pieces. The best places to see approximately 100 or more jukeboxes in one place is at a coin–op show.

Advisor: Rick Botts.

AMI, model
A **1,200.00**
B **800.00**
C **500.00**

D	400.00
E	500.00

Mills, model
Empress	1,400.00
Throne of Music	800.00

Packard, Manhattan 2,500.00

Rock–Ola, model
1422	2,000.00
1426	2,000.00
1428	2,000.00
1432	800.00
1434	900.00
1436	900.00
1438	950.00

Seeburg, model
147	600.00
M100B	850.00
M100C	950.00
HF100G	950.00
HF100R	950.00
V–200	1,300.00

Wurlitzer, model
412	800.00
600	1,000.00
616	600.00
700	3,000.00
750	5,000.00
780	2,500.00
800	4,500.00
850	12,500.00
950	20,000.00
1015	4,500.00

KAY FINCH

Collecting Hints: Collectors should be aware that during the 1980s, Kay Finch's son, George, reportedly resumed production from the original molds containing the original marks.

History: Kay Finch Ceramics began operating a studio in Corona Del Mar, California, in 1935. All pieces were hand decorated and designed by either Kay Finch, or her son, George. The company ceased operations in 1963.

Reference: Jack Chipman, *Collector's Encyclopedia of California Pottery,* Collector Books, 1992.

Periodical: *The Pottery Collectors Express,* PO Box 221, Mayview, MO 64071-0221.

Bank, sassy pig	125.00

Candleholder
4" sq, pink and silver	25.00
14" h, white flower	25.00

Candy Bowl, swan 135.00

Figure
Bird	75.00

Choir Boy
Praying	45.00
Singing	55.00

Court Lady, 10½" h, pink pearl matte
glaze, #401	185.00
Dove	100.00
Jezebel Cat	125.00
Madonna and Child, white	60.00
Mrs Foo, 22" h	395.00
90s Couple	250.00
Owl, small	40.00
Peep and Jeep	85.00
Pigeon, on bright purple bird bath	200.00
Rooster and Hen, brown and gold	85.00
Scandia Girl	30.00
Swan	35.00
Yorkie Puppy	125.00
Mug, Santa, #4950	50.00
Planter, teddy bear	100.00
Wall Plaque, boxer	50.00
Wall Pocket, Santa	75.00

KEWPIES

Collecting Hints: Study the dolls carefully before purchasing. Remember that composition dolls were made until the 1950s; hence, every example is not an early one.

Many collectors concentrate only on Kewpie items. A specialized collection might include other O'Neill designs, such as Scootles, Ragsy, Kewpie–Gal, Kewpie–Kins and Ho–Ho.

The vast majority of Kewpie material is sold in the doll market where prices are relatively stable. Pricing at collectibles shows and malls fluctuates due to seller unfamiliarity with the overall Kewpie market.

History: Rose Cecil O'Neill (1876–1944) was a famous artist, novelist, illustrator, poet, sculptress, and creator of the Kewpie doll. O'Neill's drawing "Temptation" won her a children's art prize at the age of 14 and launched her career as an illustrator.

The Kewpie first appeared in art form in the December, 1909, issue of *Ladies Home Journal* in a piece entitled "Kewpies Christmas Frolic." The first Kewpie doll appeared in 1913. Assisting in the design of the doll was Joseph L. Kallus. Although Geo. Borgfeldt Co. controlled the production and distribution rights to Kewpie material, Kallus continued to assist in design and manufacture through his firm, the Cameo Doll Company.

Kewpie dolls and china decorated items rapidly appeared on the market. Many were manufactured in Germany. Twenty–eight German factories made products during the peak production years. Later other manufacturers joined in the effort.

O'Neill eventually moved to southwest Missouri, settling at Bonniebrook near Bear Creek. She died there in 1944. In 1947 Bonniebrook burned to the ground. Production of

Kewpie items did not stop at O'Neill's death. Today Kewpie material still appears as limited edition collectibles.

References: John Axe, *Kewpies—Dolls and Art Of Rose O'Neill and Joseph L. Kallus,* Hobby House Press, 1987, out–of–print; Janet A. Banneck, *Antique Postcards Of Rose O'Neill,* Greater Chicago Productions, 1992; Lois Holman, *Rose O'Neill Kewpies And Other Works,* published by author, 1983; Maude M. Horine, *Memories of Rose O'Neill,* booklet, published by author; Ralph Alan McCanse, *Titans and Kewpies,* out–of–print; Rowena Godding Ruggles, *The One Rose,* out–of–print; *The Kewpie Kompanion: A Kompendium of Kewpie Knowledge,* Theriault's, 1994.

Collectors' Club: International Rose O'Neill Club, PO Box 668, Branson, MO 65616.

Periodical: *Traveler,* PO Box 4032, Portland, OR 97208.

Museum: Shepherd of the Hills Farm and Memorial Museum, near Branson, MO.

REPRODUCTION ALERT

Bell, brass	**60.00**
Camera, Kewpie Kamera, Sears Roebuck, orig box, instructions, and exposure guide, 1915	**185.00**
Children's Feeding Dish, 10" d, Kewpies and alphabet border	**150.00**
Chocolate Mold, 6" h, pewter	**70.00**
Coloring Book, Christmas	**25.00**
Crumb Tray, brass	**25.00**
Doll, 14" h, vinyl, fully jointed, orig clothes, Cameo Dolls Products, Port Allegheny	**65.00**
Figure	
5" h, Thinker, sgd	**25.00**
6" h, bisque, price for set of three ..	**35.00**

Figure, celluloid, marked "Made In Japan/M" with interlocking reverse "S" import stamp, 5½" h, $17.50.

Letter Opener, 7" l, pewter, Kewpie finial	**40.00**
Magazine Tear Sheet, *Ladies Home Journal* Advertisement, Jello, color, 1917 ...	**15.00**
Article, ten pgs, 1925 through 1928 issues	**100.00**
Pillowcase, 16 x 19", "The Kewpie In The Moon," c1930	**150.00**
Pin Box, cov, 2½" d, Kewpie with foot in air, marked "Goebel"	**450.00**
Pitcher, 3½" h, jasperware, blue ground, white figures	**275.00**
Post Card, Christmas, Gibson, printed color illus, divided back	**20.00**
Powder Shaker, 7" h, jointed arms, heart label on back, French label on feet	**70.00**
Salt and Pepper Shakers, pr, 2½" h, marked "Paye & Baker, Trade Kewpie Mark"	**250.00**
Tin, 5¾" d, 3½" h, round, illus of two on tightrope, two on ground, and five clinging to rope, c1935	**20.00**
Wedding Cake Top, bride and groom ..	**40.00**

KEYS

Collecting Hints: The modern hobby of key collecting began with the publication of *Standard Guide To Key Collecting* which illustrates keys by function and describes keys by style and metal content. Most key collectors focus on a special type of key, e.g., folding keys, railroad keys, car keys, etc.

Very few, if any, American–manufactured keys truly can be called rare, although some may be currently very difficult to find. Little is known as to the quantities that were manufactured, how popular they were when first produced and marketed, and how many survived.

Some keys are abundant in certain areas of the country and scarce in others. Do not spend heavily just because you have never heard or seen an example before. The best advice is to seek out other collectors and join a national organization.

History: The key as a symbol has held a mystical charm since biblical times. The Catholic Church has keys in its coat of arms. During the Middle Ages, noblemen and women carried a large collection of keys hanging from their girdles to denote their status; the more keys, the higher the status.

Many kings and other royal members practiced the art of key making. Presentation keys began during the earliest years when cities were walled enclaves. When a visitor was held in high esteem by the townspeople, he would be presented with a key to the city gate. Thus, we now have the honorary "Key to the City."

When it was popular to go on a Grand Tour of Europe in the 17th to 19th centuries, keys were among the most acquired objects. Unfortunately, many of these keys were fantasies created by the inventive local hustlers. Examples are King Tut's Tomb key, the key to the house where Mary stayed in Egypt, Bastille keys, Newgate Prison keys, and Tower of London keys.

References: Don Stewart, *Antique Classic Marque Car Keys, 2nd Edition,* Key Collectors International, 1993; Don Stewart, *Collectors Guide, Yale Jail/Prison Locks & Keys, 1884–1957,* Key Collectors International, 1982; Don Stewart, *Key Collectors Key Type Identification Guide,* Key Collectors International, 1988; Don Stewart, *Paracentric Guide To Key Collecting, 2nd Edition,* Key Collectors International, 1993; Don Stewart, *Standard Guide To Key Collecting, United States–Canada 1850–1975, Third Edition,* Key Collectors International, 1990; Don Stewart, *Railroad Switch Keys & Padlocks, United States–Canada–World, Second Edition,* Key Collectors International, 1994.

Collectors' Club: Key Collectors International, PO Box 9397, Phoenix, AZ 85068.

Museums: Lock Museum of America, Terryville, CT; Mechanics Institute, New York, NY.

REPRODUCTION ALERT: Railroad keys currently are being reproduced.

Cabinet, Barrel Type
  Brass, decorative bow
    1½" **3.00**
    2½" **5.50**
  Brass, standard bow and bit, 3" **3.50**
  Bronze, gold plated bow
    1½", decorative **8.50**
    2½", dolphin design **12.00**
  Nickel Plated, Art Deco design bow,
    2½" **5.00**
  Steel
    Art Deco design, 2" **6.00**
    Standard bow and bit, 3" . . . .   **.75**
Car
  Basco, early, flat steel **1.50**
  Chrysler "Omega" keys, brass, five
    piece set, 1933, Yale **15.00**
  Dodge
    Brass, reverse "Caskey–Dupree" . .   **1.25**
    Nickel–Silver, reverse "Caskey–
    Dupree" **1.50**
  Edsel, two keys, any maker **5.00**
  Ford, Model "T"
    Any metal, no logo . . . .   **.75**
    Coil Switch Lever Key **2.50**
    Dealers Keys, set of 4 . . . .   **12.50**
    Nickel–Silver, Ford Logo **1.75**
  Nash, Ilco #132 . . . .   **5.00**
  Omega, nickel–silver, 5 piece set,
    1933 or 1934, Yale **6.50**

Packard logo key, gold plated, 50th
  anniversary **9.00**
Studebaker, logo, Eagle Lock Co . . .   **1.50**
Casting Plate, bronze
  3" **18.00**
  6" **29.00**
Door
  Brass, standard bow and bit
    4" **5.00**
    6" **12.00**
  Bronze, Keen Kutter bow, 4" **5.50**
  Steel, standard bow and bit **3.50**
Folding, Jackknife
  Bronze and Steel, bit cuts, maker's
    name, 5" **18.00**
  Steel bit cuts, maker's name, 5½" . .   **8.00**
Gate
  Bronze, bit type, 6" **12.00**
  Iron, bit type, 8" **6.00**
Hotel
  Bronze, bit type, name and room
    number on bow, 3" **4.50**
  Steel, bit type
    Bronze tag **3.00**
    Hotel name and room number on
    bow **3.75**
    Standard Tag, room number,
    bronze **4.00**

Hotel, top: pin tumbler, fiber tag, $1.50; bottom: bit type, building outline tag, $8.00.

Jail
  Bronze
    Bit type with cuts, barrel type, 4½"   **28.00**
    Lever tumbler cut, 4½", Folger–
    Adams, oval bow with "A" **18.00**
    Nickel–Silver, pin tumbler, cut, Yale
    Mogul **15.00**
    Spike Key, 5½"
      Nickel plated steel, open oval bow,
      no maker's name, no serial num-
      ber, bit cuts **30.00**
    Steel, flat, lever tumbler, cut,
    Folger–Adams **18.00**
Pocket Door
  Bronze, "T" bow, knurled nut **9.00**
  Steel, "T" bow, screw **10.00**

Presentation, Keys To The City
  2", iron, brass plated, Master Lock
    Co, 1933 World's Fair **7.50**
  2½", white metal, "Be A Golden Key
    For Happiness" **1.50**
  6 to 10", gold plated, name engraved
    Famous Person **32.00**
    Historical Person **75.00**
  8", copper plated, 1933 Chicago
    World's Fair, Hall of Science **15.00**
  10", Chicago World's Fair, copper,
    thermometer **8.50**
Railroad
  AT&SF Atchison Topeka & Santa Fe   **15.00**
  B&M RR Boston & Maine **20.00**
  CM&ST P SIGNAL Chicago Milwau-
    kee & St Paul **10.00**
  CRI & P RR Chicago Rock Island &
    Pacific **12.50**
  DT RR Detroit Terminal **18.50**
  ESS CO Eastern/Erie Steamship Co . .   **19.00**
  FRISCO St Louis San Francisco **18.00**
  GTW Grand Trunk Western **18.00**
  IC RR Illinois Central **10.00**
  LM RR Little Miami Railroad **55.00**
  MC RR Michigan Central **18.00**
  NP RY Northern Pacific Railway . . .   **18.00**
  O&W RR Oregon & Washington . . .   **35.00**
  SPCO&CS Southern Pacific **9.00**
  TT RR Toledo Terminal Railroad **18.00**
  UPRR Union Pacific **14.00**
  WPRR Western Pacific Railroad **12.50**
Ship
  Bit Type
    Bronze, foreign ship tags **6.00**
    Iron/steel, bronze tags, 3 to 4" . . .   **3.00**
  Pin Tumbler Type
    US Army Ship Tags **8.50**
    USN Tag **2.00**
Watch
  Advertising type
    Brass, shield **10.00**
    Gold Plated, 1" **12.00**
  Art Nouveau, brass, loop bow **9.00**
  Cigar Cutter accessory, gold plated
    and silver, 1" **25.00**
  Jewelers Key
    Brass, 6 point **18.00**
    Steel and Brass, 5 Point **12.00**
  Swivel, brass and steel, 1" **2.00**

KITCHEN COLLECTIBLES

Collecting Hints: Bargains still can be found, especially at flea markets and garage sales. Look to the design of appliances for statements about a given age, e.g., the Art Deco design on toasters and coffee pots of the 1910–1920 period.

The country decorating craze has caused most collectors to concentrate on the 1860–1900 period. Kitchen products of the 1900–1940 period, with their enamel glazes and dependability, are just coming into vogue.

History: The kitchen was a central focal point in a family's environment until frozen food, TV dinners, and microwaves freed the family to concentrate on other parts of the house during meal time. Initially, food preparation involved both the long and short term. Home canning remained popular through the early 1950s.

Many early kitchen utensils were handmade and prized by their owners. Next came a period of utilitarian products of tin and other metals. However, the housewife did not wish to work in a sterile environment, so color was added through enamel and plastic while design began to serve both an aesthetic and functional purpose.

The advent of home electricity changed the type and style of kitchen products. Many products went through fads such as the toaster, electric knife, and now the food processor. The high technology field already has made inroads into the kitchen and another revolution seems at hand.

References: *Collectors Guide To Wagner Ware and Other Companies,* L–W Book Sales, 1994; Linda Campbell Franklin, *300 Years Of Housekeeping Collectibles,* Books Americana, 1992; Linda Campbell Franklin, *300 Years Of Kitchen Collectibles, Third Edition,* Books Americana, 1991; *Griswold Cast Iron: A Price Guide,* L–W Book Sales, 1993; Bill and Denise Harned, *Griswold Cast Collectibles: History & Values,* published by authors, 1988; Jan Lindenberger, *Black Memorabilia For The Kitchen: A Handbook And Price Guide,* Schiffer Publishing, 1992; Jan Lindenberger, *The 50s and 60s Kitchen: A Collector's Handbook & Price Guide,* Schiffer Publishing, 1994; Norman E. Martinus and Harry L. Rinker, *Warman's Paper,* Wallace–Homestead, 1994; Kathryn McNerney, *Kitchen Antiques, 1790–1940,* Collector Books, 1991, 1993 value update; Jim Moffet, *American Corn Huskers: A Patent History,* Off Beat Books, 1994; Dana Gehman Morykan and Harry L. Rinker, *Warman's Country Antiques & Collectibles, Second Edition,* Wallace–Homestead, 1994; Ellen M. Plante, *Kitchen Collectibles: An Illustrated Price Guide,* Wallace–Homestead, 1991; Diane W. Stoneback, *Kitchen Collectibles: The Essential Buyer's Guide,* Wallace–Homestead, 1994; Pat Stott, *The Collectors Book of Egg Cups,* published by author, 1993; Don Thornton, *Beat This: The Eggbeater Chronicles,* Off Beat Books, 1994; Jean Williams Turner, *Collectible Aunt Jemima,* Schiffer Publishing, 1994; April M. Tvorak, *A History And Price Guide To Mothers–In–The–Kitchen,* published by author, 1994.

Periodicals: *Cast Iron Cookware News,* 28 Angela Ave., San Anselmo, CA 94960; *Griswold Cast Iron Collectors' News & Marketplace,* PO Box 521, North East, PA 16428; *Kettles 'n Cookware,* PO Box B, Perrysville, NY 14129; *Kitchen Antiques & Collectibles News,* 4645 Laurel Ridge Dr, Harrisburg, PA 17110.

Collectors' Clubs: Eggcup Collectors' Corner, 67 Stevens Ave., Old Bridge, NJ 08857; Griswold & Cast Iron Cookware Assoc., 54 Macon Ave., Asheville, NC 28801; International Society for Apple Parer Enthusiasts, 3911 Morgan Center Rd., Utica, OH 43080; Jelly Jammers Club, 110 White Oak Dr., Butler, PA 16001; The Corn Items Collectors Assoc., Inc., 613 North Long St., Shelbyville, IL 62565.

Museums and Libraries: Culinary Archives and Museum, Johnson & Wales University, Providence, RI; Culinary Institute of America; H. B. Meek Library, Cornell University; Judith Basin Museum, Stanford, MT; Kern County Museum, Bakersfield, CA; Mandevile Library, University of CA, San Diego, CA; Schlesinger Library, Radcliff College; Strong Museum, Rochester, NY; Wilbur Chocolate Co., Lititz, PA.

See: Advertising, Cookbooks, Kitchen Glassware, Reamers.

Ashtray, skillet shape, Griswold #00	22.00
Asparagus Cutter, wood, Ward's Keen Edge	85.00
Bean Dryer, rect, tin	8.00
Bean Slicer/Pea Huller, green handle, attaches to table	25.00
Beater, Keystone	135.00
Biscuit Cutter, Rumford Baking Powder, tin	14.00
Bread Board, round, maple, matching knife	45.00
Bread Pan, 6½" d, round, stoneware, blue, fireproof	50.00
Broiler Tray, Griswold, aluminum, stylized deer, Aristocraft Ware	30.00
Broom Holder, tin, DeLaval adv	42.00
Butter Cutter, cuts one pound into forty–eight pats, nickel plated brass and wire	40.00
Cabbage Cutter, maple, steel blade	15.00
Cake Decorator, aluminum, tube, six tips	10.00
Cake Mold	
Lamb	
Griswold	85.00
Wagner	85.00
Santa Shape–a–Cake, instructions, MIB	8.00
Can Opener, Peerless, patent 1902	15.00
Carpet Beater, wire, braided	20.00
Catalog	
Kalamazoo Stoves, 1920, 84 pgs	25.00

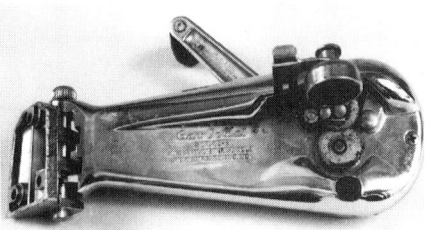

Can Opener, Can–O–Mat, Rival Mfg. Co., wall mount, green metal, plastic crank knob, c1946, 7½" l, $4.50.

Springfield Home Appliances, 1953, 96 pgs	6.00
Cheese Box, cov, Jack Spratt, Marshaltown, IA, rect, wood	10.00
Cheese Grater, tin, hand held	20.00
Cherry Stoner, Enterprise, #16	35.00
Chopper, six sided, iron handle	18.00
Cider Funnel, wood	60.00
Cleanser Shaker, Miss Cutie Pie, small chip	18.00
Coffee Grinder	
Clamp–on, iron, LF & C	45.00
Lap, iron lid sgd "Arcade"	67.50
Table, cast iron and wood, sgd "Imperial"	75.00
Wall Mount, iron and glass, Crystal	57.00
Cookie Cutters, Robin Hood Flour adv, set of 6	25.00
Cookie Peel, 18½" l, iron, closed ring handle, open heart shape, c1800	350.00
Cookie Sheet	
Betty Crocker Bisquick	9.50
Springerle	110.00
Corncob Holders, SS, price for set of 12	95.00
Corn Stick Pan	
Griswold, #273	35.00
Wagner Junior	28.00
Dipper, 25½" l, wrought iron	45.00

Ducks, tin, left: unknown maker, no handle, 4½" h, $15.00; right: Nazareth, PA maker, depression piece for eye, 6" h, $125.00.

Donut Cutter, Rumford Baking Powder adv 15.00
Donut Master, orig box, recipes, 1940s 18.00
Dough Box, cov, 32" l, pine, sliding .. 85.00
Dutch Oven, Wagner, #9 .... 45.00
Egg Basket, wire, folding 15.00
Egg Beater, cast iron
   Dover, 1891 .... 20.00
   Taplin 30.00
Egg Separator, Rumford Baking Powder adv 30.00
Egg Skillet, Griswold, sq 25.00
Egg Timer, tin 30.00
Food Grinder, Russwin, drops open for cleaning, 1902, #1 .... 30.00
Food Mill, tin and steel, Foley 75.00
French Fry Cutter, hand held, red handles 20.00
Garlic Press, wood 28.00
Grapefruit Reamer, yellow, sgd "Red Wing" 150.00
Grater, 4 x 10", tin, Fels Napha adv ... 10.00
Griddle, Griswold, round handle 25.00
Ice Bucket, brass, Pyrex insert 20.00
Ice Cream Scoop
   Gilchrist, wood handle 35.00
   Hamilton Beach, MIB 32.00
   Indestructo, #4 .... 23.00
   Zeroll, #12, Maumee 17.00
Ice Cube Breaker, Lightning, green North Bros catcher 95.00
Ice Pick/Bottle Opener, Conoco 6.00
Jar Opener 12.00
Jello Mold, Phoenix glass, emb, ftd ... 8.00
Juice Dispenser 300.00
Juice Extractor, Handy Andy, green paint, green reamer, green cone 150.00
Kettle, straight sides, bail handle, slant trademark, Griswold #8 .... 60.00
Ladle, mayonnaise, flat bottom, blue .. 18.00
Laundry Sprinkle Bottle, roly poly elephant 150.00
Lemon Reamer, ceramic, 2 pcs, figural 35.00

Juicer, Juice-O-Mat, Rival Mfg. Co., chrome-and-metal top, red metal base, 7⅞" h, $5.00.

Lemon Squeezer, cast iron
   Pearl 35.00
   Williams, glass insert 45.00
Matchsafe, cast iron, wall mounted, ornate 37.50
Measuring Cup, Seller, clear, one cup   20.00
Meat Grinder, Griswold, #2 .... 25.00
Meat Slicer, sterling, cast iron, #10 ... 30.00
Melon Baller, wood handle, Germany   7.00
Mixer, electric, Vidrio, green base 100.00
Mixing Bowl, 10" d, yellow ware, blue bands 55.00
Muffin Pan
   Griswold, #10 .... 40.00
   Kellogg 9.50
Noodle Roller, wood 32.00
Nutmeg Grater, hopper, hand crank .. 35.00
Pan, French roll type 42.00
Pastry Blender, wire and metal, wood handle, dated 1924 .... 5.00
Pastry Crimper
   Aluminum, Just Right Pie Sealer 8.00
   Brass, black globular wood handle   12.00
Pastry Cutter, tow bladed, one wheel, one wedge, red handle 12.00
Patty Mold Set, Griswold, #1, orig box   50.00
Pie Bird, figural
   Dragon, green, horns, spines down back, pottery, imp "England" 50.00
   Duck, blue and yellow 28.00
   Elephant, white elephant standing on back legs, imp "England" 50.00
   Funnel, oval, Blue Willow design on front, two birds and scroll on back   55.00
   Pie, Blackbird's head protruding through center, England 55.00
   Pig, black pig dressed as chef holding pie, England 60.00
Pie Lifter, brass ferule, turned wood handle, Shaker 50.00
Pie Tin
   Bowie Pies 5.00
   Knotts Berry Farm 6.00
Popcorn Popper, wire, green handle .. 28.00
Popover, Erie, cast iron 20.00
Potato Masher, Blue Onion 120.00
Potato Ricer, steel, red trim, 1940s ... 19.00
Pudding Mold
   Acorn, two-part 16.00
   Tin 20.00
Reamer, Sunkist, jadite 60.00
Roaster, cast iron, Mi Pet 35.00
Rolling Pin
   Glass, clear, wood handles 55.00
   Maple, green handles 20.00
   Porcelain, Kelvinator 85.00
   Yellowware 200.00
Sausage Stuffer, cast iron, Enterprise, mounted on wood bench 65.00
Skillet
   Griswold, red enamel, large 20.00
   Martin Stove Co 15.00

Wagner

#4, smoke ring	21.00
#5	19.00
Soap Saver, metal	12.00

Spice Jar Set

| Griffith, red metal rack, ten pcs | 25.00 |
| Hoosier, five pcs | 75.00 |

Spoon Rest, yellowware, incised "Berea, Kentucky" **45.00**

String Holder

Apple, chalk	25.00
Beehive, iron, counter	65.00
Cat, chalk	26.00
Colonial Girl	45.00
Heart, ceramic, "You'll Always Have A Pull With Me"	40.00
Pear, chalk	25.00

Tea Kettle

Griswold, aluminum	15.00
Wagner, 5 qt	24.00
Teapot, Gladding McBean	42.00

Tin

Busy Biddy	45.00
Calumet Baking Powder, paper label	24.00
Davis Baking Powder, sample	65.00
Great American Coffee, key wind–up	18.00
Monarch Cocoa, hinge lid	25.00
Santa Fe Coffee, unopened	45.00
Watkins Pepper	15.00

Vegetable Chopper, crescent blade, wood handle **30.00**

Waffle Iron, Griswold **40.00**

KITCHEN GLASSWARE

Collecting Hints: Kitchen glassware was made in large quantities. Although collectors do tolerate signs of use, they will not accept pieces with heavy damage. Many of the products contain applied decals; these should be in good condition. A collection can be built inexpensively by concentrating on one form, such as canister sets, measuring cups, reamers, etc.

History: The Depression era brought inexpensive kitchen and table products to center stage. Hocking, Hazel Atlas, McKee, U. S. Glass, and Westmoreland were companies which led in the production of these items.

Kitchen glassware complemented Depression glass. Many items were produced in the same color and style. Because the glass was molded, added decorative elements included ribs, fluting, arches and thumbprint patterns. Kitchen glassware was thick for durability. The resulting forms were difficult to handle at times and often awkward aesthetically. After World War II, aluminum products began to replace kitchen glassware.

References: Gene Florence, *Kitchen Glassware of the Depression Years, Fifth Edition*, Collector

Books, 1995; Shirley Glyndon, *The Miracle In Grandmother's Kitchen*, privately printed, 1983; Garry Kilgo and Dale, Jerry, and Gail Wilkins, *A Collectors Guide To Anchor Hocking's Fire–King Glassware*, K & W Collectibles Publisher, 1991; Susan Tobier Rogove and Marcia Buan Steinhauer, *Pyrex by Corning: A Collector's Guide*, Antique Publications, 1993; Diane W. Stoneback, *Kitchen Collectibles: The Essential Buyer's Guide*, Wallace–Homestead, 1994; April M. Tvorak, *Fire–King II*, published by author, 1993; April M. Tvorak, *Fire–King '95*, published by author; April M. Tvorak, *History And Price Guide To Fire–King*, VAL Enterprises, 1992; April M. Tvorak, *Pyrex Price Guide*, published by author, 1992.

Collectors' Club: Glass Knife Collectors Club, PO Box 342, Los Alamitos, CA 90720.

Periodical: *Kitchen Antiques & Collectibles News*, 4645 Laurel Ridge Dr, Harrisburg, PA 17110.

| Batter Bowl, large, handle | 38.00 |

Butter Dish, cov

Criss Cross

Crystal, two pound size	15.00
Green, one pound	45.00
Hocking, green transparent, ribbed	85.00

Canister, 6" h, Hocking, green transparent, smooth, metal lid **33.00**

Cheese Dish, Kraft

| Blue | 22.00 |
| Green | 22.00 |

| Creamer, Criss Cross, crystal | 16.50 |

Cup

Federal Glass Co, Panel Optic, green	5.00
Hocking, green transparent, ribbed	7.00
Ice Cream Dish, Lido, pink	18.00
Iced Tea Tumbler, Louie, 7½" h, Federal Glass Co	5.00

Jar, quart, Hocking, green transparent, smooth **25.00**

Juice Tumbler

| Hocking, pink transparent, ribbed | 12.50 |
| Mission, pink | 35.00 |

Knife, glass

Plain handle, green orig box, 9⅛" l . **35.00**

Three leaf

| Crystal | 15.00 |
| Green, Durex, orig box, 8½" l | 35.00 |

Three star, 9¼" l

Blue	38.00
Blue, orig World's Fair box	45.00
Crystal, orig box	25.00
Pink	38.00
Thumb guard, crystal	30.00

Mayonnaise Ladle

| Amber | 13.00 |

Crystal

| Gold trim | 10.00 |
| Ribbed handle | 7.00 |

Silver trim 10.00
Green 13.00
Pink, deep 16.00
Yellow, fired on 13.00
Measuring Cup
  Federal
    Dry, one cup, crystal 12.00
    Handleless, 3 spouts
      Amber 42.00
      Crystal 6.50
      Green 35.00
    Stick handle, two cup, green 9.00
    Triangular handle, 3 spouts, 1 cup,
      green 40.00
  Jeannette, jadite, one–third cup size .   12.00
  Kelloggs
    Crystal 10.00
    Pink
      Spelled "Kellog" 37.00
      Spelled correctly 28.00
  Unknown Maker, stippled, green, 2
    cup 18.50
Mixing Bowl
  Criss Cross
    5" d, fired-on orange 10.00
    6" d, crystal 8.00
  Hazel Atlas
    7½" d, cobalt blue 45.00
    Nested set, white, ivy dec, price for
      five piece set 50.00
  Jeannette, jadite, 8" d 18.00
  Jennyware, Ultra, 6" d 30.00
  McKee, jade, 7" d 14.00
  US glass, pink, handle, large, small
    under base nick 55.00
Pepper Shaker, McKee, sq, jade 13.00
Pickle Ladle, crystal 20.00
Pitcher
  Jeannette, jadite 35.00
  McKee, jade, small 30.00
Preserve Jar, Hazel Atlas 10.00
Punch Ladle, crystal 25.00
Reamer
  Hocking, green transparent, ribbed . .   15.00

Shaker, blue delphite, 6" h, $9.50.

Sunkist
  Crystal, "Sunkist" embossed in bot-
    tom 40.00
  Jade 45.00
  White 18.00
  US Glass, pink 30.00
Refrigerator Dish, cov
  Rectangular
    Federal, 4 x 8", amber 12.50
    Hocking, green transparent, ribbed   17.00
  Set, fired on color, clear lids, set of
    three 25.00
  Square, 8 x 8"
    Criss Cross, green 50.00
    Federal, amber 18.50
    Hocking, green, slight roughage . .   18.00
    McKee, jade 12.00
Salad Set, light blue and crystal, round   50.00
Salad Spoon and Fork, set
  Blue and crystal 25.40
  Crystal, Art Deco style handle 25.00
  Green and crystal 45.00
  Pink and crystal 45.00
Salt, short, round, Hocking, diamond,
  crystal 22.00
Saucer, Panel Optic, green, Federal
  Glass Co 3.00
Shakers, pr, Hazel Atlas, cobalt blue,
  red tops 30.00
Sherbet, Panel Optic, green, Federal
  Glass Co 4.00
Soap Dish, black, Westite 45.00
Sugar Shaker, Jeannette, jade 50.00
Tumbler, 9 oz, Criss Cross, crystal 35.00
Water Bottle
  Criss Cross, crystal, small 18.00
  Hocking, green transparent, ribbed . .   25.00
  Owens Illinois, dark green 18.00

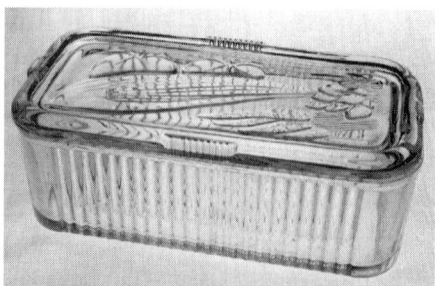

**Refrigerator Dish, rect, clear, raised veg-
etables on lid, ribbed sides, 8⅜" l, 3" h,
$5.00.**

KNOWLES, EDWIN M.

Collecting Hints: Do not confuse Edwin M.
Knowles China Company with Knowles, Taylor,
and Knowles, also a manufacturer of fine dinnerware. They are two separate companies. The
only Edwin M. Knowles China Company mark

that might be confusing is "Knowles" spelled with a large "K."

Knowles dinnerware lines enjoyed modest sales success. No one line dominated. Among the more popular lines with collectors are: Deanna, a solid color line found occasionally with decals introduced in 1938; Esquire, designed by Russel Wright and manufactured between 1956 and 1962; and Yorktown, a modernistic line introduced in 1936 and found in a variety of decal patterns such as Bar Harbor, Golden Wheat, Penthouse, and Water Lily.

When collecting decal pieces, buy only pieces whose decals are complete and still retain their vivid colors. Edwin M. Knowles China Company did make a Utility Ware line that has found some favor with kitchen collectibles collectors. Prices for Utility Ware range between half– and two–thirds of the prices for similar pieces in the dinnerware patterns.

History: In 1900 Edwin M. Knowles established the Edwin M. Knowles China Company in Chester, West Virginia. Company offices were located in East Liverpool, Ohio. The company made semi–porcelain dinnerware, kitchenware, specialties, and toilet wares and was known for its commitment to having the most modern and best equipped plants in the industry.

In 1913 a second plant in Newell, West Virginia, was opened. The company operated its Chester, West Virginia, pottery until 1931, at which time the plant was sold to the Harker Pottery Company. Production continued at the Newell pottery. Edwin M. Knowles China Company ceased operations in 1963.

The Edwin M. Knowles Company name resurfaced in the 1970s when the Bradford Exchange acquired rights to the company's name. The Bradford Exchange uses the Knowles name to front some of its collector plate series, e.g., Gone with the Wind and the Wizard of Oz. The name also has been attached to Rockwell items. Bradford Knowles–marked pieces are made by offshore manufacturers, not in the United States at either of the old Knowles locations.

References: Susan and Al Bagdade, *Warman's American Pottery and Porcelain*, Wallace–Homestead, 1994; Jo Cunningham, *The Collector's Encyclopedia of American Dinnerware*, Collector Books, 1982, 1995 value update; Harvey Duke, *The Official Identification and Price Guide to Pottery and Porcelain, Eighth Edition*, House of Collectibles, 1994; Lois Lehner, *Lehner's Encyclopedia of U. S. Marks on Pottery, Porcelain & Clay*, Collector Books, 1988.

DEANNA Introduced in 1938. This shape was available in both pastel and bright solid colors or designs using stripes, plaids, or decal decoration on white ground. Solid colors included green, light and dark blue, orange–red, bright and pas-

tel yellow, turquoise, peach, burgundy, russet, and pink.

Bowl, 5¼" d, orange–red	**5.00**
Butter dish, open, dark blue	**10.00**
Coffeepot, cov, red and blue stripes	**40.00**
Creamer and Sugar, cov, light blue	**25.00**
Cup and Saucer, yellow	**10.00**
Eggcup, double, turquoise	**12.00**
Plate	
6" d, bread and butter, yellow	**4.00**
8" d, salad, orange–red	**6.00**
10" d, dinner, pink	**8.00**
Platter, 12" d, green	**15.00**
Vegetable Bowl, 8" d, orange–red	**18.00**

ESQUIRE Dinnerware line designed by Russel Wright. Made from 1956 until 1962, it was available in five colors and six designs. Each pattern was produced on a single colored ground: Botanica on beige, Grass on blue, Queen Anne's Lace on white, Seeds on yellow, Snowflower on pink, and Solar on white.

Bowl	
5½" d, fruit, Snowflower	**8.00**
6¼" d, cereal, Queen Anne's Lace	**10.00**
Cup and Saucer, Snowflower	**18.00**
Plate	
6¼" d, bread and butter, Botanica	**6.00**
8¼" d, salad, Seeds	**9.00**
10¾" d, dinner, Grass	**12.00**
Platter, oval	
13" l, Queen Anne's Lace	**20.00**
16" l, Solar	**30.00**
Teapot, Botanica	**95.00**
Vegetable Bowl, divided, Seeds	**65.00**

YORKTOWN Dinnerware line introduced in 1936. Original four colors were burgundy, cadet blue, russet, and yellow. Later produced in Chinese red, green, orange–red, and pink. Also available with decal decoration on white ground.

Plate, Yorktown shape, maroon, 11¾" d, $6.00.

Bowl, 6″ d, cereal, green **6.00**
Casserole, yellow **35.00**
Chop Plate, 10¾″ d, burgundy **15.00**
Creamer and Sugar, cov, yellow **25.00**
Cup and Saucer, orange–red **8.00**
Custard Cup, green **6.00**
Gravy Boat, pink **18.00**
Plate
   6″ d, bread and butter, yellow **5.00**
   8″ d, salad, cadet blue **10.00**
   10″ d, dinner, orange–red **12.00**
Platter, 12″ d, russet **20.00**
Teapot, orange–red **50.00**

LABELS

Collecting Hint: Damaged, trimmed or torn labels are less valuable than labels in mint condition. Collectors prefer labels that can be removed from the product and stored flat in drawers or albums.

History: The first fruit crate art was created by California fruit growers about 1880. The labels became very colorful and covered many subjects. Most depict the type of fruit held in the box. With the advent of cardboard boxes in the 1940s, fruit crate art ended and their labels became collectible.

Over the last decade, label collectors have begun to widen their collecting range. Today can, luggage, and wine labels are sought as well as cigar, fruit crate, and other household type labels.

References: Jerry Chicone, Jr., *Florida's Classic Crates*, privately printed, 1985; David Craig, *Luggage Labels: Mementos from the Golden Age of Travel*, Chronicle Books, 1988; Joe Davidson, *The Art of the Cigar Label,* Wellfleet Press, 1989; Joe Davidson, *Fruit Crate Art,* Wellfleet Press, 1990; Lynn Johnson and Michael O'Leary, *En Route: Label Art from the Golden Age of Air Travel,* Chronicle Books, 1993; Norman E. Martinus and Harry L. Rinker, *Warman's Paper,* Wallace–Homestead, 1994; Gordon T. McClelland and Jay T. Last, *Fruit Box Labels: A Collector's Guide,* Hillcrest Press, 1983; Robert Opie, *The Art of the Label: Designs of the Times,* Chartwell Books, 1987; John Salkin and Laurie Gordon, *Orange Crate Art, The Story of Labels That Launched a Golden Era,* Warner Books, 1976.

Collectors' Clubs: International Seal, Label & Cigar Band Society, 8915 E. Bellevue St., Tucson, AZ 85715; Society of Antique Label Collectors, PO Box 24811, Tampa FL 33623; The Citrus Label Society, 131 Miramonte Dr., Fullerton, CA 92365.

Advisor: Lorie Cairns.

Fruit Crate, Hot Brand California Vegetables, multicolor, cowboys branding steer, 7 x 10″, $1.50.

FRUIT CRATE

Apple
Appleton, apples, ranch scene, and Art Nouveau lady sniffing pink roses **5.00**
Blewett Pass, 1940s auto on mountain pass road **1.00**
Blue Winner, cowboy in arena on horseback, reaching down to pick up apple **2.00**
Dahn–D, top hat, white gloves, and cane, blue ground **1.00**
Diving Girl, girl wearing old fashioned bathing suit diving into lake, friends on pier watching, apples . .   **10.00**
Gosling, fluffy yellow gosling, red ground, Oregon **15.00**
Hesperian, stylized blue Art Deco lady, holding yellow apple, orange ground **3.00**
Merry Christmas, Santa, reindeer, and sleigh high above snowy nighttime scene, 5 x 8″ **1.00**
Mountain Goat, white mountain goat standing on cliff, snow capped mountains and forest, turquoise sky **2.00**
Paradise, bird of paradise, black ground **6.00**
Prices Prize Pack, whole and half apple, navy blue ground **1.00**
Snoboy, happy snowman with red earmuffs holding huge red apple, blue ground, 6½ x 8″ **1.00**
State Seal, George Washington portrait, blue ground, small size . . . .   **.50**
Apricot
Brentwood Acres, three juicy apricots on branch, blue ground . . . .   **.25**
Quail, quail in grass, blue ground . .   **1.00**

Wolfe, silhouette black howling wolf
on peak, blue ground 25
Avocado, Keystone, red keystone, strip
label 25
Cantaloupe, Valley Queen, half can-
taloupe on plate, vase of flowers,
Washington 1.00
Carrot, Doe, doe's head, carrot bunch,
"Doe" on baseball superimposed
over red star and target 1.00
Celery, Moon Lake, moon rising over
palm–lined lake, oval, 7 x 4¼" 75
Cherries
Corvette, warship, three colorful
cherries, blue ground 25
Mountain, snowy Mt Hood, red cher-
ries, red border 50
Citrus
Aunty, smiling black woman holding
citrus blossom branch, Florida, 3½
x 8½" 2.00
Drum Major, strutting majorette, strip
label, Florida 50
Royal Arms, muscle–bound gladiator
with sword and shield, 9" sq 3.00
Valiant, large swordfish, strip label . .   2.00
Zeneda, glass of orange juice, whole
grapefruit, half an orange, and
leaves, Florida, 6¾" sq 1.00
Corn
Hi Up, ear of corn, black ground, 7½
x 4½" 75
Observation, tourist–filled observa-
tion boat, 7¼ x 4¼" 1.00
Topit, ear of corn, blue and yellow
ground, 7½ x 4½" 75
Cranberry
Fenwick, spray of red berries and
green leaves 2.00
Monmouth, Revolutionary War scene   2.00
Fruit, miscellaneous
Air King, evening scene, four–pro-
peller plane coming in for landing   .75
Baby Marie, small girl, yellow and
brown ground 50
Dromedary, two camels and riders,
palms, pyramids, and sphinx, gold
sunset background 25
Giant Tree, fallen redwood tree, three
people, and two old cars, red
ground 50
Golden Trout, hooked trout leaping
from water 1.00
Owl, owl on branch, blue moon in
background 1.50
Peacock, colorful male peacock,
black ground 50
Grapefruit
Beach Lake, grove and lake scene,
6½" sq 1.00
Desert Bloom, desert scene, bloom-
ing yucca, desert greenery, and

mountains, Redlands 4.00
Orchid, two orchids, half sliced
grapefruit in silver bowl, green
ground, Florida, 9" sq 2.00
Snoboy, snowman holding huge
grapefruit, strip label, Florida 50
Grapes
Big Tony, river, hills, orchard, and
purple grapes 75
Black Bear, comical black bear operating wine press, red ground 50
Cal–Ripe, vineyard scene, snowy
mountains, and lady with basket of
grapes on her head, rose–purple
and blue ground 25
L–Z, smiling blond boy holding green
grapes, red and green grapes
nearby 50
Moonlight, moonlit lake scene, cou-
ple in canoe framed by grape clus-
ters 2.00
Small Black, small black child and
grapes, red ground 1.00
Tuxedo Park, young man wearing tux
saying "Grapes are good for you"   .25
Lemon
Basket, golden basket with five
lemons, blue ground, Lemon Cove   1.00
Cambria, brown eagle and two
torches, blue ground, brown bor-
der, Placentia 1.00
Cutter, cutter ship in choppy seas, orange and gold sky, dated 1937,
Oxnard 3.00
Exposition, 1909 Alaska Yukon
Pacific Exposition in Seattle certifi-
cate, shows diploma for lemon exhibit grand prize, black ground,
Santa Barbara 2.00
Fallbrook, rushing mountain stream,
pine trees, lemons, leaves, and
blossoms, black ground, Fallbrook   1.00
Galleon, galleon sailing high seas,
c1937, Oxnard 5.00
Meteor, meteor streaking through
evening sky, San Fernando 2.00
San Marcos, country scene, purple
mountains and homes, blue
ground, Goleta 1.00
Sea Bird, large white flying seagull,
yellow letters, blue ground,
Carpinteria 4.00
Sunkist Californian Lemons, lemon,
yellow letters, black ground, Los
Angeles 1.00
Lettuce, boy and girl twins holding huge
head of lettuce, 7 x 9" 2.00
Melon
Foothigh, girlie, black ground, 9 x 4"   1.00
Levon, snarling green–eyed lion,
green ground, 9 x 11¼", Los Banos,
Blythe, California 3.00

Orange
Athlete, large stadium, three runners
at finish line, Claremont 5.00
Bronco, cowboy on galloping horse,
swinging lariat, western desert
scene background, Redlands 2.00
Cal–Flavor, orange and leaves, black
and woodgrained ground, Lindsay   1.00
California Dream, two peacocks and
castle, gilt trim, Placentia 15.00
Camellia, six red camellias, white
satin ground, Redlands 12.00
Coed, smiling girl graduate, purple
ground, Claremont 2.00
Golden Eagle, fierce eagle guarding
oranges, gilt trim, Fullertown 4.00
Kaweah River Belle, scenic, Spanish
mission, snow capped mountain
peaks in background, oranges,
Lemon Cove 5.00
Lagoon, San Francisco Expo buildings
and lagoon, some moisture rip-
pling, East Highlands 10.00
Legal Tender, $250 currency bundle,
blue and black ground, Fillmore . .   3.00
Metropolitan, big city street scene,
large orange, brown ground,
Orange Cove 1.00
Ponca, large orange in green Art
Deco arch, Porterville 3.00
Redlands Best, four arrows pointing
to large orange, Redlands 7.00
Redlands Choice, shiny blue draped
cloth behind large orange and blos-
soms, 1928, Redlands 8.00
Sierra Vista, groves and snowy moun-
tains, Porterville 8.00
Stalwart, large polar bear, Northern
Lights behind, Santa Paula 28.00
Victoria, ornate lettering and orange,
½ label size 50
Western Queen, Indian woman in
green sunburst, Rialto 10.00
Peach, Crystal, sparkling faceted gem-
stone, orange ground 25
Pear
Big City, skyscrapers, orange ground,
big lug label 50
Buckingham, cowboy riding bucking
pig, blue ground 3.00
Covered Wagon, pioneers, covered
wagon, and ox team, strip label . .   .75
Embarcadero, harbor scene with
gulls, orchard, and pears 2.00
Grand Coulee, dam scene, black
ground, shallow rippling 5.00
Hustler, boy selling newspapers 1.00
Old Gold, ornate yellow letters, red
and blue ground 1.00
Pirate's Cove, lake and country
scene, big lug label 75
Rancheria, Indian village by lake,

Indians and white horse 2.00
Statue, gold and blue Statue of
Liberty, black ground 1.00
Swan, white swan, black ground . . .   4.00
Peas, Kingfish, 5½ x 8¼" oval 1.00
Plum, Valley Home, purple plums, aqua
ground, 7 x 9" 1.00
Tangerine
Desert Glow, no picture, "Desert
Glow" letters shading from red to
yellow, blue ground, lug size,
Highgrove 50
Full Moon, swamp scene, white
heron on branch, full moon, 4¼ x
8" 75
Tomato
Award, farmer holding box of toma-
toes, ranch in background 50
Big Chief, Indian chief and tomatoes,
strip label 75
Bungalow, large tomato, 1920s bun-
galow and grounds, lug size,
Washington 1.50
Green Feather, green feather, black
ground, strip label 25
Tracy, cowboy with tomato head and
lariat, desert background 50
Yams
Coon, raccoon holding large yam . .   3.00
Dove, gray flying dove 1.00
Piney Woods, forest scene, log fence,
three sweet potatoes, Texas, 9" sq   1.00
Treasure, pirate's treasure chest of
jewels, tropical island, four big
yams 1.00
White House, white columned
house, red yams, 4½ x 7" 50

MISCELLANEOUS

Broom
Auto No. 6, speeding race car 50
Dixie, black man sitting on fence
playing banjo, open bolls of cotton
nearby 1.00
Skysweep, single–propeller biplane,
dated 1931 50
Cigar
Lyra, redhead in garden playing harp   2.00
O'San, Egyptian desert scene, pyramids, camels, and people 3.00
Round Up, cowboy smoking by
campfire, faint discoloration on
edge 5.00
Super–5–Cigar, lady in bonnet
smelling pink rose 3.00
Egg Crate, Sleepy Eye, Chief Sleepy Eye
portrait in sunburst, 9¼ x 11¼" 2.00
Tobacco Sack, Big John Cut Plug, blacksmith, Big John, St Louis, MO, 5½ x
3½" 75

TIN CAN

Apple Butter, Mt Vernon, white mansion, Virginia, 7 lbs, 6½ x 8½"	1.00
Applesauce, Miriam, red apples, dishes of applesauce, white ground, New York	1.00
Asparagus, Isaacs, forest, stream, mountains, asparagus on plate	1.00
Baking Powder	
Betty Ann, redhead girl in pink dress skipping rope, gilt border, white ground, Hastings, NE, 6 oz	3.00
Capitol, capitol building, green ground, Nashville, TN, 1 lb	1.50
Clabber Girl, clabber girl carrying plate of biscuits, family scene background, white ground, 4.75 ozs	1.00
Beets, Winsom, bowl of diced beets, gilt	1.00
Clam, Cap'n John Clam Nectar Bouillon, captain, whole clams, and stylized dolphins, Canada	1.00
Corn, Cloth of Gold, Golden Bantam Corn, big red bird, gilt trim	3.00
Evaporated Milk	
Bess, two cow heads, Ohio	2.00
Poplar, three aqua poplar trees on hill, Ohio	1.00
Roseco, light brown cow, milking stool, and bucket, big red rose	2.00
Green Beans	
Maryland Chief, two images of Indian chief	1.00
Mi–Boy, laughing boy and green beans	2.00
Lima Beans	
Dubon, two bowls of lima beans, blue ground, New Orleans, LA	.50
Great A & P, lima bean vines, pods, and yellow flower, gilt ground, New York	1.00
Mackerel, La Conquista, two mackerel on platter, galleon, red ground, 3¼ x 7"	.25
Oysters, Tide Rim, two oysters, waves, Markham, WA	2.00
Peas, June Peas, crystal bowl of peas, red roses, and leaves, Baltimore, MD	2.00
Pumpkin, Norwich, two whole pumpkins, two pieces pie on blue plate, gilt design and borders, light orange and white ground, 1920s	2.00
Salmon	
Dixie, two salmon in ocean, flowers and leaves, red ground, Ilwaco, WA	2.00
Eastpoint, salmon steak on platter, yellow and black ground, gilt highlights, Alaska pink salmon, Ocean Park, WA	1.50
Finast, two leaping salmon, red ground, Sommerville, MA	1.00
Gypsy, dancing gypsy woman, salmon, red ground, Chinook	3.00
Sardines, Patsy, puppy in basket	.25
Skimmed Milk, Country Maid, milk maid in blue and white carrying milk pail, standing beside Bossie, blue and red ground	3.00
Squid, San Xavier, California Squid, California mission and squid, red ground	.25
Succotash	
Butterfly, large butterfly, succotash, bowl of beans, and two ears of corn	1.00
Cloth of Gold, red bird, bowl of succotash	1.00
Rowley's, corn and beans, "Fancy Succotash," white ground	.50

LAMPS

Collecting Hints: Be aware that every lamp has two values—a collectible value and a decorative value. Often the decorative value exceeds the collectible value. Most lamps are purchased as decorative accessories, often as accent pieces in a period room setting.

In the 1980s the hot lamp category was 1950s odd shaped lamps, some abstract and some figural. This craze is documented in Leland and Crystal Payton's *Turned On: Decorative Lamps of the 'Fifties*. While 1950s lamps continue to sell well as part of the 1950s/1960s revival, prices have stabilized due largely to market saturation. A great many 1950s/1960s lamps survived in attics and basements.

Lamp collectors specialize. In the 1970s and 1980s Aladdin was the magic name due in large part to the promotional efforts of J. W. Courter. One man can make a market.

Within the past five years, collector interest is spreading to other manufacturers and into electric lamps. One of biggest drawbacks is the lack of a definitive lamp collecting manual and price guide that shows the full range of the lamp market. Far too many of the lamp books are nothing more than catalog reprints.

Just as post–World War II collectors discovered figural transistor and character radios, so also are they discovering motion lamps, many of which are character related. Look for a growing interest and rise in prices for character lamps once collectors begin to realize what a fertile territory this is for collecting.

The 1990s marks a major transitional period in lamp collecting. The kerosene lamp which dominated lamp collecting through virtually the entire twentieth century is slowly being upstaged by the electric lamp. By the twenty–first century, the electric, not the kerosene lamp, will dominate.

History: The dominant lamp during the nineteenth and first quarter of the twentieth century was the kerosene lamp. However, its death knell was sounded in 1879 when Thomas A. Edison developed a viable electric light bulb.

The success of the electric lamp depended on the availability of electricity. However, what we take for granted did not arrive in many rural areas until the 1930s.

Most electric lamps were designed to serve as silent compliments to period design styles. They were meant to blend, rather than stand out. Pairs were quite common.

Famous industrial designers did lend their talents to lamp design. These are eagerly sought by collectors. Bradley and Hubbard and Handel are two companies whose products have attracted strong collector interest.

References: James Edward Black (ed.), *Electric Lighting of the 20s & 30s, Volume 2 with Price Guide*, L–W Book Sales, 1988, 1993 value update; J. W. Courter, *Aladdin Collectors Manual & Price Guide #15, Kerosene Mantle Lamps*, published by author, 1994; J. W. Courter, *Aladdin Electric Lamps Price Guide #2*, published by author, 1993; J. W. Courter, *Angle Lamps: Collectors Manual & Price Guide*, published by author, 1992; Nadja Maril, *American Lighting: 1840–1940*, Schiffer Publishing, 1989; Richard C. Miller and John F. Solverson, *Student Lamps Of The Victorian Era*, Antique Publications, 1992, 1992–1993 Value Guide; Bill and Linda Montgomery, *Animation Motion Lamps: A Price Guide*, L–W Book Sales, 1991; Leland & Crystal Payton, *Turned On: Decorative Lamps of the 'Fifties*, Abbeville Press, 1989; *Quality Electric Lamps: A Pictorial Price Guide*, L–W Book Sales, 1992.

Collectors' Clubs: Aladdin Knights of the Mystic Light, 3935 Kelley Rd., Kevil, KY 42053; Historical Lighting Society of Canada, 9013 Oxbox Rd., North East, PA 16428.

Figural

Artillery Shell, brass, metal dome shade	**40.00**
Calypso Dancer, plaster, circular red shade, 1950s	**20.00**
Davy Crockett, Davy, tree, and bear ceramic base, Davy, Indians, and fort on shade, 1950s, 16" h	**180.00**
Elephant, ceramic, carousel beaded shade	**195.00**
Fish, jumping over waves, ceramic, brown and ivory paper shade	**25.00**
Football Player, hollow plaster, standing next to football standard, linen over cardboard shade, WK, Japan, Sears, Roebuck, 1978, 14½" h	**20.00**

Fred Flintstone, painted vinyl, black metal base, missing shade, 13¼" h	**45.00**
French Poodle, ceramic, pink, circular base, pink paper shade	**25.00**
Horse Head, ceramic, 12 x 10¾"	**24.00**
Panther, ceramic, black, 8½ x 6½"	**20.00**
Saturn, blue glass, circular stepped base, 1930s	**60.00**
Scottie Dog, with ball, glass, fired–on blue	**125.00**
Ship, ceramic, gold trim, 11 x 10½"	**20.00**
Statue of Liberty, plastic, Econolite, 1957, 11" h	**75.00**
Tara, Southern belle, glass, fired–on pink, matching glass parasol shade	**60.00**
Lava, bottle shaped, Lava Simplex Corp, c1968	**75.00**
Motion, plastic cylinder, metal frame	
Antique Cars, 1957	**35.00**
Forest Fire, LA Goodman, 1956, 11" h	**50.00**
Niagara Falls, Rev–O–Lite, 1930s, 10" h	**85.00**
Roy Rogers Rodeo, rodeo scenes, Pearson, c1950, 17" h	**1,050.00**
Table	
Reverse Painted, glass dome–shaped shade with sailing ships design, gilded white metal vasiform column with painted and emb leaves, flowers, and swags, circular base	**300.00**
Tiffany Type, gilded white metal framework emb with flowers and leaves, domed shade with caramel slag glass panels, tapered cylindrical base with caramel slag glass panels, circular base, double socket lamp with night light in base	**325.00**

LIMITED EDITIONS OR COLLECTOR ITEMS

Collecting Hints: The first edition of a series usually commands a higher price. When buying a limited edition collectible be aware that the original box and/or certificates increase the value of the piece. Be alert to special discounts and sales.

History: Limited edition plate collecting began with the advent of Christmas plates issued by Bing and Grondahl in 1895. Royal Copenhagen soon followed. During the late 1960s and early 1970s, several potteries, glass factories, and mints began to issue plates, bells, eggs, mugs, etc. which commemorated special events, people, places, or holidays. For a period of time these items increased in popularity and value. But in the late 1970s, the market became flooded with many collectibles and the market declined.

There are many new issues of collector items annually. Some of these collectibles can be found listed under specific headings, such as Hummel, Norman Rockwell, etc.

References: Susan K. Elliott and J. Kevin Samara, *The Official Club Directory and Price Guide To Limited Edition Collectibles,* House of Collectibles, 1993; Diane Carnevale Jones, *Collectors' Information Bureau's Collectibles Market Guide & Price Index, 12th Edition,* Collectors' Information Bureau, 1995, distributed by Wallace–Homestead; Diane Carnevale Jones, *Collectors' Information Bureau's Collectibles Price Guide, Fifth Edition,* Collectors' Information Bureau, 1995, distributed by Wallace–Homestead; Diane Carnevale Jones, *Collectors' Information Bureau's Directory To Secondary Market Retailers: Buying and Selling Limited Edition Artwork,* Collectors' Information Bureau, 1992; Rosie Wells (ed.), *Official 1993 Secondary Market Price Guide For Precious Moments Collectibles, Eleventh Edition,* Rosie Wells Enterprises, 1993.

Collectors' Clubs: Club Anri, 55 Parcella Park Dr., Randolph, MA 02368; Del–Mar–Pa Ornament Kollector's Club, 131 S. Tartan Dr., Elkton, MD 21921; Donald Zolan Collectors Society, 133 E. Carillo St., Santa Barbara, CA 93101; Franklin Mint Collectors Society, US Route 1, Franklin Center, PA 19091; Gorham Collectors Club, PO Box 6472, Providence, RI 02940; International Plate Collectors Guild, PO Box 487, Artesia, CA 90702; Lladro Collectors Society, 43 W. 57th St., New York, NY 10019; Lowell Davis Farm Club, 55 Pacella Park Dr., Randolph, MA 02368; Modern Doll Club, 9628 Hidden Oaks Cr., Tampa, FL 33612; Precious Moments Collectors' Club, One Enesco Plaza, PO Box 1466, Elk Grove Village, IL 60009.

Periodicals: *Collector Editions,* 170 Fifth Ave., 12th Floor, New York, NY 10010; *Collector News & The Antique Reporter,* PO Box 156, Grundy Center, IA 50638; *Collectors' Bulletin,* RR#1, Canton, IL 61520; *Collectors Mart Magazine,* PO Box 12830, Wichita, KS 67277; *Contemporary Doll Magazine,* 30595 Eight Mile, Livonia, MI 48152; *Hallmarkers Holiday Happening Collectors Club,* 6151 Main St., Springfield, OR 97478; *Ornament Trader Magazine,* PO Box 7908, Clearwater, FL 34618.

Museum: Bradford Museum, Niles, IL.

BELLS

Anri, J. Ferrandiz, artist, wooden
1976, Christmas, FE	**50.00**
1977, Christmas	**42.00**
1978, Christmas	**40.00**
1979, Christmas	**30.00**
1980, The Christmas King	**15.00**
1981, Lighting the Way	**15.00**
1982, Caring	**15.00**

1983, Behold	**15.00**
1984, With Love	**50.00**
1985, Nature's Dream	**15.00**

Bing & Grondahl, Christmas, annual
1980, Christmas in the Woods	**45.00**
1981, Christmas Peace	**40.00**
1982, Christmas Tree	**40.00**
1983, Christmas in Old Town	**40.00**
1984, Christmas Letter	**40.00**
1985, Christmas Eve at the Farmhouse	**40.00**
1986, Silent Night, Holy Night	**40.00**
1987, Snowman's Christmas Eve	**40.00**
1988, Old Poet's Christmas	**40.00**
1989, Christmas Anchorage	**45.00**
1990, Changing of the Guards	**45.00**
1991, Copenhagen Stock Exchange	**50.00**
1992, Christmas at the Rectory	**55.00**
1993, Father Christmas in Copenhagen	**66.00**

Danbury Mint, Norman Rockwell artist
1975, Doctor and Doll	**50.00**
1976, Saying Grace	**40.00**
1977, Santa's Mail	**40.00**
1979, Friend in Need	**30.00**

Enesco Corp, Precious Moments
1981, Jesus Loves Me	**40.00**
1982, Mother Sew Dear	**35.00**
1983, Surrounded With Joy	**60.00**
1984, Wishing You A Merry Christmas	**45.00**
1985, God Sent His Love	**35.00**
1986, Wishing You A Cozy Christmas	**35.00**
1987, Love Is the Best Gift	**30.00**
1988, Time To Wish You A Merry Christmas	**35.00**
1989, Your Love Is Special To Me	**20.00**
1990, Here Comes The Bride	**25.00**
1991, May Your Christmas Be Merry	**30.00**
1992, But The Greatest Of These Is Love	**25.00**

Gorham
1975, Sweet Song So Young	**50.00**
1976, Snow Sculpture	**30.00**
1977, Chilling Chore	**35.00**
1978, Gay Blades	**20.00**
1979, Beguilling Buttercup	**30.00**
1980, Flying High	**25.00**
1981, Ski Skills	**27.00**
1982, Young Man's Fancy	**25.00**
1983, Christmas Medley	**30.00**
1984, Tiny Tim	**28.00**
1985, Yuletide Reflections	**32.50**
1986, Home For The Holidays	**32.50**
1987, Merry Christmas Grandma	**30.00**
1988, The Homecoming	**37.50**

Hummel, see HUMMEL

Reed and Barton
1980, Noel, musical	**45.00**
1981, Yuletide Holiday	**15.00**
1982, Little Shepherd	**14.00**
1983, Noel, musical	**45.00**

1984, Noel, musical	**45.00**
1985, Caroller	**15.00**
1986, Noel, musical	**25.00**
1987, Jolly St Nick	**15.00**
1988, Christmas Morning	**15.00**
1989, The Bell Ringer	**15.00**
1990, The Wreath Bearer	**15.00**
1991, A Special Gift	**20.00**
1992, My Special Friend	**20.00**
1993, Noel, musical	**30.00**

River Shore

1977, First Day of School	**60.00**
1978, Garden Girl	**35.00**
1979, Allison	**48.00**
1980, Katrina	**45.00**
1981, Spring Flowers	**175.00**
1982, American Gothic	**50.00**

Schmid

Peanuts

1976, Woodstock	**25.00**
1977, Woodstock's Christmas	**18.00**
1978, Mother's Day	**15.00**
1979, A Special Letter	**25.00**
1980, Waiting for Santa	**25.00**
1981, Mission for Mom	**20.00**
1982, Perfect Performance	**18.00**
1983, Peanuts in Concert	**12.00**
1984, Snoopy and the Beagle Scouts	**12.00**

Walt Disney, Christmas

1985, Snow Biz	**15.00**
1986, Tree For Two	**15.00**
1987, Merry Mouse Medley	**17.50**
1988, Warm Winter Ride	**18.00**
1989, Merry Mickey Claus	**24.00**
1990, Holly Jolly Christmas	**25.00**
1991, Mickey & Minnie's Rockin' Christmas	**25.00**

Wedgwood

1979, Penguins, FE	**40.00**
1981, Polar Bears	**45.00**
1982, Moose	**40.00**
1983, Fur Seals	**50.00**
1984, Ibex	**60.00**
1985, Puffin	**60.00**
1986, Ermine	**60.00**

CHRISTMAS ORNAMENTS

Artaffects

1985, Papoose	**60.00**
1986, Christmas Cactus	**45.00**
1987, The Fiddler	**8.00**
1988, Annual	**20.00**
1989, Annual	**20.00**
1990, Annual	**15.00**
1991, Snow Kachina	**15.00**
1992, Sweet Surprise	**15.00**

Department 56

1983, Countryside Church	**125.00**
1984, Crowntree Inn	**40.00**
1985, Golden Swan Baker, lights	**20.00**
1986, Snowbaby, sitting, lights	**35.00**
1987, Weston Train Station	**40.00**
1988, Christmas Carol, Scrooge	**30.00**

Enesco

Precious Moments

1982, Baby's First Christmas	**35.00**
1983, Surround Us With Joy	**60.00**
1984, Peace On Earth	**30.00**
1985, Have A Heavenly Christmas	**20.00**
1986, Rocking Horse	**20.00**
1987, Bear The Good News	**25.00**
1988, Cheers To The Leader	**20.00**
1989, Oh Holy Night	**35.00**
1990, Dashing Through The Snow	**15.00**
1991, Sno–Bunny Falls For You Like I Do	**20.00**
1992, Our First Christmas	**15.00**

Memories of Yesterday

1988, Baby's First Christmas	**35.00**
1989, Christmas Together	**25.00**
1990, Moonstruck	**15.00**
1991, Star Fishing	**12.00**
1992, I'll Fly Along To See You Soon	**15.00**

Goebel, Inc.

1978, Santa, glass	**12.00**
1979, Angel with Tree, glass	**12.00**
1980, Mrs Santa, glass	**12.00**
1981, The Nutcracker, glass	**5.00**
1982, Santa In Chimney, color	**15.00**
1983, Clown, white	**18.00**
1984, Snowman	**15.00**
1985, Angel	**18.00**
1986, Drummer Boy	**10.00**
1987, Rocking Horse	**20.00**
1988, Doll, white	**21.00**
1989, Dove, color	**20.00**
1990, Girl In Sleigh	**30.00**
1991, Baby On Moon	**30.00**

Gorham

1970, snowflake, sterling	**275.00**
1971, snowflake, sterling	**100.00**
1985, crystal	**25.00**
1988, Victorian heart	**50.00**
1990, snowflake, sterling	**50.00**
1992, crystal	**30.00**

Hallmark Keepsake

1973, Manger Scene	**70.00**
1974, Snowman, Yarn series	**20.00**
1975, Locomotive, Handcrafted series	**150.00**
1976, Raggedy Ann	**60.00**
1977, Wreath	**60.00**
1978, Baby's First Christmas	**50.00**
1979, Christmas Angel	**80.00**
1980, Daughter	**25.00**
1981, Mouse, frosted	**20.00**
1982, New Home	**15.00**
1983, Star of Peace	**12.00**
1984, Racoon's Christmas	**40.00**
1985, Holiday Heart	**20.00**
1986, Shirt Tales Parade	**10.00**

1987, Folk Art Santa	25.00		1993, Kitten with ornament	30.00	
1988, Spirit of Christmas	12.00		Ashton–Drake Galleries		
1989, Christmas Kitty	20.00		1985, Jason	650.00	
1990, Billboard Bunny	10.00		1986, Heather	300.00	
1991, Christmas Welcome	15.00		1987, Little Bo Peep	225.00	
1992, For My Grandma	15.00		1988, Amanda	100.00	

Lenox
1984, ball, crystal	50.00
1985, ball, crystal	50.00
1986, annual, china	60.00
1987, partridge bell	45.00
1988, angel bell	40.00
1989, Christmas Tree Top	30.00
1990, Christmas Goose	25.00
1991, Snowman	18.00
1991, Santa in Chimney	25.00
1992, Sweet Shop	35.00

Towle Silversmiths
1971, Partridge in Pear Tree	500.00
1972, Two Turtle Doves	145.00
1973, Three French Horns	125.00
1974, Four Mockingbirds	100.00
1975, Five Golden Rings	60.00
1976, Six Geese	70.00
1977, Seven Swans A Swimming	40.00
1978, Silent Night	55.00
1979, Deck The Halls	45.00
1980, Jingle Bells	50.00
1981, Hark The Hearld Angels Sing	50.00
1982, O Christmas Tree	50.00
1983, Christmas Rose	40.00
1984, Hawthorne	40.00
1985, Chestnuts Roasting	40.00
1986, Laurel Bay	35.00
1987, White Christmas	40.00
1988, Twelve Days of Christmas, goldplated, etched	6.00
1989, Pomander Ball	30.00
1990, Old Master Snowflake	40.00
1991, Partridge in Wreath	40.00
1992, Angel	40.00

DOLLS

Annalee Mobilitee
1971, Choir Girl	385.00
1972, Santa with mushroom	265.00
1973, White Bunny	120.00
1974, Workshop Elf, apron	750.00
1975, Mrs. Claus with plum pudding	300.00
1976, Lass with planter basket	175.00
1978, Pilgrim, boy	300.00
1979, Chimney Sweep Mouse	250.00
1980, C. G. Bunny with basket	115.00
1981, Cat, mouse with mistletoe	125.00
1982, Santa Fox	575.00
1984, Snowman	300.00
1985, Reindeer with bell	50.00
1986, Ballooning Clown	100.00
1987, Victorian Santa	200.00
1988, Easter Parade Pig, pr	165.00
1989, Abe Lincoln	100.00

1989, Goldilocks	90.00
1990, Victorian Lady	110.00
1991, Rosemary	75.00
1992, Daisy	60.00
1993, Laura	75.00

Enesco Imports, Precious Moments
1981, Mikey	225.00
1982, Tammy	650.00
1983, Katie Lynne	185.00
1984, Kristy	160.00
1985, Bethany	145.00
1986, Bong Bong	165.00
1987, Angie, The Angel of Mercy	160.00
1989, Wishing You Cloudless Skies	115.00
1990, The Voice of Spring	150.00
1991, May You Have An Old Fashioned Christmas	110.00

Gorham
1981
Alexandria	550.00
Christina	450.00
Elana	550.00
Melinda	285.00

1982
Alissa	300.00
Jeremy	650.00
Mlle. Monique	275.00
Mlle. Yvonne	375.00

1983
Jennifer, bride	800.00
Meg	650.00

1984
Holly, Christmas	800.00
Merrie	175.00
Nicole	900.00
Sweet Valentine	300.00

1985
Alexander	375.00
Amanda	750.00
Ariel	475.00
Linda	450.00

1986
Emily	350.00
Jessica	350.00
Meredith	375.00
Veronica, 19" h	750.00

1987
Lee Ann	300.00
Rachel, 17" h	800.00
Silver Bell, 17" h	175.00
Valentine Lady, Jane	300.00

1988
Christa	1,000.00
Felicia	375.00
Madeline	350.00
Priscilla	325.00

1989		1982		8.00
Clara	675.00	1983		18.00
Katrina	275.00	Franklin Mint, 1979, porcelain		35.00
Rose	225.00	Goebel		
William	275.00	1978		10.00
1990		1979		8.00
Natalie	375.00	1980		9.00
Peggy	90.00	1981		10.00
Storytime	175.00	1982		8.00
Victoria	375.00	1983		28.00
1991		Noritake		
Baby's First Christmas	125.00	1971, FE		75.00
Jane Eyre	225.00	1972		35.00
Miss January	75.00	1973		18.00
Priscilla	110.00	1974		8.00
1992		1975		10.00
Baby's First Steps	125.00	1976		10.00
Sara's Tea Time	425.00	1977		12.50
Sunday's Child	85.00	1978		14.00
Virginia	350.00	1979		14.00
1993		1980		14.00
Camille	350.00	1981		15.00
Chrissy	140.00	1982		15.00
Melinda, The Tooth Fairy	85.00	1983		28.50
Sitting Pretty	35.00	1984		20.00
Hamilton Collection		Wedgwood		
1981, Hakata, Peony Maiden	150.00	1977		35.00
1985, Heather	125.00	1978		25.00
1986, Nicole	50.00	1979		18.00
1987, Priscilla	50.00	1983		40.00
1988, Mr Spock	75.00			
1989, Scotty	75.00			
1990, Lucy	85.00	**FIGURINES**		
1991, Anastasia	40.00			
1992, Kimberly	125.00	Anri		
1993, Margaret	125.00	1969, Heavenly Quintet		1,900.00
Sarah's Attic, Inc.		1974, Helping Hands		350.00
1987, Molly	30.00	1975, The Gift, 6" h		225.00
1988, Mrs Claus	115.00	1976, Sharing, 3" h		125.00
1989, Spirit of America Santa	125.00	1977, Friendships		500.00
1990, Megan	95.00	1978, Peace Pipe		300.00
1991, Victorian Emma	150.00	1979, Happy Strummer		375.00
Seymour Mann		1980, Melody for Two		300.00
1984, Miss Debutante	180.00	1981, Musical Basket, 3" h		100.00
1985, Wendy	150.00	1982, The Champion, 6" h		200.00
1986, Camelot Fairy	225.00	1983, Morning Chores		475.00
1987, Dawn	175.00	1984, Flowers for You		400.00
1988, Jolie	150.00	1985, Afternoon Tea		325.00
1989, Elizabeth	200.00	1986, Our Puppy		90.00
1990, Ginny	90.00	1987, Little Nanny		180.00
1991, Georgia	90.00	1988, Purrfect Day		400.00
1992, Alice	90.00	1989, Garden Party		195.00
		1990, Season's Greetings		225.00
EGGS		1991, Season's Joy		250.00
		1992, Tulips for Mother, 4" h		275.00
Anri, 1979, Beatrix Potter	5.00	1993, Christmas Time, 5" h		350.00
Cybis Studios, 1983, FE	300.00	Byers' Choice Ltd.		
Ferrandiz		1978, Old World Santa		225.00
1978, FE	15.00	1982, Victorian Caroler, adult		300.00
1979	12.00	1983, Boy on Rocking Horse		1,200.00
1980	9.50	1984, Scrooge		35.00
1981	9.00	1985, Pajama Children		175.00

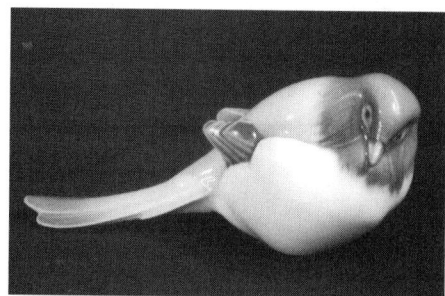

Bing & Grondahl, blue, gray, and white bird, 4½″ l, $70.00.

1986, Victorian Girl with violin 275.00
1988, Singing Cats 15.00
1989, Girl with Hoop 50.00
1990, Holy Family 135.00
1991, Adult Skaters 40.00
1992, Happy Scrooge 60.00
1993, Skating Santa 60.00
Cybis
1959, Hummingbird 850.00
1963, Magnolia 400.00
1964, Rebecca 345.00
1965, Christmas Rose 750.00
1968, Narcissus 500.00
1969, Clematis with house wren . . . 315.00
1970, Dutch Crocus 750.00
1971, Appaloosa Colt 285.00
1972, Pansies 350.00
1973, Goldilocks 325.00
1974, Mary, Mary 750.00
1975, George Washington Bust 300.00
1976, Bunny 125.00
1977, Tiffin 400.00
1978, Edith 300.00
1980, Jogger, female 400.00
1982, Spring Bouquet 750.00
1985, Nativity Lamb 125.00
1986, Dapple Gray Foal 185.00
Department 56
1976, Mountain Lodge 400.00
1977, Mansion 475.00
1978, General Store 425.00
1979, Mission Church 900.00
1980, Ceramic Car 45.00
1981, Corner Store 225.00
1982, Street Car 325.00
1983, Victorian Cottage 325.00
1984, Snow Kids Sledding 40.00
1985, Singing Nuns 80.00
1986, Hold On Tight 12.00
1987, Springfield House 85.00
1988, Tiny Trio 60.00
1989, Icy Igloo 35.00
1990, A Special Delivery 12.00
1991, Just For You 20.00
1992, North Pole Post Office 40.00

Enesco Corp, Precious Moments
1979, Jesus Loves Me 30.00
1980, Come Let Us Adore Him 90.00
1981, But Love Goes On Forever . . . 165.00
1982, I Believe In Miracles 90.00
1983, Sharing Our Season 110.00
1984, Joy To The World 40.00
1985, Baby's First Christmas 35.00
1986, God Bless America 50.00
1987, This Is The Day The Lord Hath
  Made 35.00
1988, Faith Takes The Plunge 30.00
1989, Wishing You Roads of Happi-
  ness 50.00
1990, To My Favorite Fan 15.00
1991, He Loves Me 95.00
1992, Five Years of Memories 50.00
1993, America You're Beautiful 30.00
Goebel
1971, Fritz the Happy Boozer 50.00
1972, Bob the Bookworm 50.00
1973, Maid of the Mist 750.00
1975, With Love 125.00
1979, Birthday
1982, The Garden Fancier 40.00
1983, Gentle Thoughts 40.00
1984, On The Fairway 45.00
1985, Gentle Breezes 45.00
1986, Southern Belle 10.00
1987, Chuck on a Pig 65.00
1988, Bride and Groom 115.00
1989, My First Arrow 70.00
1990, El Burrito 60.00
Hummel, see HUMMEL
Lenox Collections
1984, North American Bighorn Sheep 110.00
1985, Rapunzel 135.00
1986, Grand Tour 85.00
1987, Carousel Horse 150.00
1988, Cinderella 135.00
1989, Angels of Adoration 145.00
1990, Baltimore Oriole 40.00
1991, Rose Grosbeak 40.00
1992, Sheherezade 145.00
1993, Great Orange Wingtip 40.00
River Shore
1978, Akiku, Baby Seal, FE 145.00
1979, Rosecoe, red fox kit 50.00
1980, Lamb 48.00
1981, Zuela, elephant 60.00
1982, Kay's Doll 90.00
1984, Violet Otter 40.00
1985, Reggie Raccoon 40.00
1987, Gilbert, musical 25.00
1988, Katie, musical 25.00
Rockwell, Norman, see NORMAN
  ROCKWELL
Schmid
1979, Country Road 275.00
1980, Two's Company 45.00
1981, Plum Tuckered Out 225.00
1982, Right Church, Wrong Pew . . . 80.00

1983, A Second Chance 600.00
1984, Catnapping Too 72.00
1985, Out of Step 45.00
1986, War Trophy 400.00
1987, Blossom's Gift 325.00
1988, Can't Wait 120.00
1989, Boy's Night Out 200.00
1990, Private Time 35.00
1991, Arrival of Stanley 90.00
1992, Quiet Day at Maple Grove . . 125.00
1993, The Freeloaders 200.00

MUGS

Bing & Grondahl
1978, FE 50.00
1980 . . . . 25.00
Franklin Mint, 1979, Father's Day 40.00
Gorham
1981, Bugs Bunny 8.00
1981, Tom & Jerry, 4 x 4" h 9.00
Lynell Studios, 1983, FE, Gnome Series
Gnomelyweds 8.00
Gnome Sweet Gnome 6.50
Mama Gnome 7.00
Royal Copenhagen
1967, large 200.00
1968, large 24.00
1972, large 24.00
1976, large 25.00
1979, small 28.00
1980
Large 65.00
Small 25.00
1981
Large 70.00
Small 35.00
1983, small 30.00
Royal Doulton, Santa, second edition 75.00
Schmid, Zemsky, musical, 1981, Padding-
ton Bear 25.00
Wedgwood
1971, Christmas 35.00
1972, Christmas 30.00
1973, Christmas 40.00
1974, Christmas 30.00
1975, Christmas 30.00
1976, Christmas 30.00
1977, Father's Day 25.00
1978, Father's Day 25.00
1979, Christmas 25.00
1980, Christmas 25.00
1981, Christmas 35.00
1982, Christmas 40.00

MUSIC BOXES

Anri
Jemima 100.00
Peter Rabbit 100.00
Pigling 100.00

Ferrandiz
Angel 140.00
Chorale 125.00
Drummer 185.00
Flower Girl 150.00
Going Home 275.00
Letter, The 150.00
Proud Mother 140.00
Spring Arrivals 120.00
Wanderlust 110.00
Gorham
Cardinal, double, 6" h, hp, sculp-
tured, porcelain 30.00
Happy Birthday, animals 35.00
Santa & Sleigh, 6" h 20.00
Sesame Street, Big Bird & Snowman,
7" h 24.00
Schmid
Paddington Bear
1981, Christmas 35.00
1982 . . . . 22.00
Peanuts
30th Anniversary 18.00
1981
Christmas 28.00
Mother's Day 18.00
1982
Christmas 30.00
Mother's Day 20.00
Raggedy Ann
1980 . . . . 15.00
1981 . . . . 15.00
1982, Flying High 20.00
Walt Disney
1980, Christmas, FE 42.00
1981, Christmas 30.00
1982, Christmas 25.00

PLATES

Anri (Italy)

Christmas Plates, J Ferrandiz, 12" d
1972, Christ in the Manger 230.00
1973, Christmas 220.00
1974, Holy Night 90.00
1975, Flight Into Egypt 80.00
1976, Tree of Life 60.00
1977, Girl with Flowers 175.00
1978, Leading the Way 165.00
1979, The Drummer 170.00
1980, Rejoice 150.00
1981, Spreading the Word 150.00
1982, The Shepherd Family 150.00
1983, Peace Attend Thee 150.00
Mother's Day Plates, J Ferrandiz
1972, Mother Sewing 200.00
1973, Alpine Mother & Child 150.00
1974, Mother Holding Child 150.00

1975, Dove Girl	**150.00**
1976, Mother Knitting	**200.00**
1977, Alpine Stroll	**125.00**
1978, The Beginning	**150.00**
1979, All Hearts	**165.00**
1980, Spring Arrivals	**160.00**
1981, Harmony	**150.00**
1982, With Love	**150.00**

1984, Christmas in Ramsau	**50.00**
1985, Christmas Eve in Bad Wimpfen	**55.00**
1986, Christmas Eve in Gelnhaus ..	**65.00**
1987, Christmas Eve in Goslar	**70.00**
1988, Christmas Eve in Ruhpolding	**100.00**
1989, Christmas Eve in Freidechsdadt	**80.00**
1990, Christmas Eve in Partenkirchen	**80.00**
1991, Christmas Eve in Allendorf ...	**80.00**

Bareuther (Germany)

Christmas Plates, Hans Mueller artist, 8" d

1967, Stiftskirche, FE	**90.00**
1968, Kapplkirche	**25.00**
1969, Christkindlemarkt	**20.00**
1970, Chapel in Oberndorf	**18.00**
1971, Toys for Sale	**20.00**
1972, Christmas in Munich	**35.00**
1973, Christmas Sleigh Ride	**20.00**
1974, Church In The Black Forest ..	**20.00**
1975, Snowman	**25.00**
1976, Chapel in the Hills	**25.00**
1977, Story Time (Christmas Story) ..	**30.00**
1978, Mittenwald	**30.00**
1979, Winter Day	**40.00**
1980, Miltenberg	**38.00**
1981, Walk in the Forest	**40.00**
1982, Bad Wimpfen	**40.00**
1983, The Night Before Christmas ..	**45.00**
1984, Zeil on the River Main	**42.50**
1985, Winter Wonderland	**42.50**
1986, Christmas in Forchhe	**42.50**
1987, Decorating the Tree	**46.50**
1988, St Coloman Church	**80.00**
1989, Sleigh Ride	**50.00**
1990, The Old Forge in Rothenburg .	**50.00**
1991, Christmas Joy	**55.00**
1992, Marketplace in Heppenheim	**55.00**
1993, Winter Fun	**55.00**

Berlin (Germany)

Christmas Plates, various artists, 7¾" d

1970, Christmas In Bernkastel	**130.00**
1971, Christmas In Rothenburg On Tauber	**30.00**
1972, Christmas In Michelstadt	**50.00**
1973, Christmas In Wendelstein ...	**42.00**
1974, Christmas In Bremen	**25.00**
1975, Christmas In Dortland	**60.00**
1976, Christmas Eve In Augsburg ...	**30.00**
1977, Christmas Eve In Hamburg ...	**32.00**
1978, Christmas Market At The Berlin Cathedral	**55.00**
1979, Christmas Eve In Greetsiel ...	**55.00**
1980, Christmas Eve In Miltenberg ..	**55.00**
1981, Christmas Eve In Hahnenklee	**50.00**
1982, Christmas Eve In Wasserburg	**55.00**
1983, Chapel In Oberndorf	**55.00**

Bing and Grondahl (Denmark)

Christmas Plates, various artists, 7" d

1895, Behind The Frozen Window	**3,400.00**
1896, New Moon Over Snow–covered Trees	**1,975.00**
1897, Christmas Meal Of The Sparrows	**725.00**
1898, Christmas Roses And Christmas Star	**700.00**
1899, The Crows Enjoying Christmas	**900.00**
1900, Church Bells Chiming In Christmas	**800.00**
1901, The Three Wise Men From The East	**450.00**
1902, Interior Of A Gothic Church ..	**285.00**
1903, Happy Expectation of Children	**150.00**
1904, View of Copenhagen From Frederiksberg Hill	**125.00**
1905, Anxiety Of The Coming Christmas Night	**130.00**
1906, Sleighing To Church On Christmas Eve	**95.00**
1907, The Little Match Girl	**125.00**
1908, St. Petri Church of Copenhagen	**85.00**
1909, Happiness Over The Yule Tree	**100.00**
1910, The Old Organist	**90.00**
1911, First It Was Sung By Angels To Shepherds In The Fields	**80.00**
1912, Going To Church On Christmas Eve	**80.00**
1913, Bringing Home The Yule Tree	**85.00**
1914, Royal Castle of Amalienborg, Copenhagen	**75.00**
1915, Chained Dog Getting Double Meal On Christmas Eve	**120.00**
1916, Christmas Prayer Of The Sparrows	**85.00**
1917, Arrival Of The Christmas Boat	**75.00**
1918, Fishing Boat Returning Home For Christmas	**85.00**
1919, Outside The Lighted Window	**80.00**
1920, Hare In The Snow	**70.00**
1921, Pigeons In The Castle Court ..	**55.00**
1922, Star of Bethlehem	**75.00**
1923, Royal Hunting Castle, The Hermitage	**55.00**
1924, Lighthouse In Danish Waters	**65.00**
1925, The Child's Christmas	**70.00**
1926, Churchgoers On Christmas Day	**65.00**
1927, Skating Couple	**80.00**

1928, Eskimo Looking At Village
Church In Greenland **60.00**
1929, Fox Outside Farm **80.00**
1930, Yule Tree In Town Hall Square
Of Copenhagen **85.00**
1931, Town Hall Square **80.00**
1932, Lifeboat At Work **90.00**
1933, The Korsor-Nyborg Ferry **70.00**
1934, Church Bell in Tower **70.00**
1935, Lillebelt Bridge Connecting
Funen With Jutland **65.00**
1936, Royal Guard **80.00**
1937, Arrival Of Christmas Guests . .   **75.00**
1938, Lighting The Candles **110.00**
1939, Ole Lock–Eye, The Sandman . .   **150.00**
1940, Delivering Christmas Letters . .   **170.00**
1941, Horses Enjoying Christmas
Meal In Stable **345.00**
1942, Danish Farm On Christmas
Night **150.00**
1943, The Ribe Cathedral **155.00**
1944, Sorgenfri Castle **120.00**
1945, The Old Water Mill **135.00**
1946, Commemoration Cross In
Honor Of Danish Sailors Who Lost
Their Lives In World War II **85.00**
1947, Dybbol Mill **70.00**
1948, Watchman, Sculpture Of Town
Hall, Copenhagen **80.00**
1949, Landsoldaten, 19th Century
Danish Soldier **70.00**
1950, Kronborg Castle At Elsinore . .   **150.00**
1951, Jens Bang, New Passenger Boat
Running Between Copenhagen
And Aalborg **115.00**
1952, Old Copenhagen Canals At
Wintertime With Thorvaldsen
Museum In Background **85.00**
1953, Royal Boat In Greenland
Waters **95.00**
1954, Birthplace Of Hans Christian
Andersen, With Snowman **100.00**
1955, Kalundborg Church **115.00**
1956, Christmas In Copenhagen . . .   **140.00**
1957, Christmas Candles **155.00**
1958, Santa Claus **100.00**
1959, Christmas Eve **120.00**
1960, Danish Village Church **180.00**
1961, Winter Harmony **115.00**
1962, Winter Night **80.00**
1963, The Christmas Elf **120.00**
1964, The Fir Tree And Hare **50.00**
1965, Bringing Home The Christmas
Tree **65.00**
1966, Home For Christmas **50.00**
1967, Sharing The Joy Of Christmas   **48.00**
1968, Christmas In Church **45.00**
1969, Arrival Of Christmas Guests . .   **30.00**
1970, Pheasants In The Snow At
Christmas **20.00**
1971, Christmas At Home **20.00**
1972, Christmas In Greenland **20.00**

1973, Country Christmas **25.00**
1974, Christmas In The Village **20.00**
1975, The Old Water Mill **24.00**
1976, Christmas Welcome **25.00**
1977, Copenhagen Christmas **25.00**
1978, A Christmas Tale **30.00**
1979, White Christmas **30.00**
1980, Christmas In The Woods **42.50**
1981, Christmas Peace **50.00**
1982, The Christmas Tree **55.00**
1983, Christmas in Old Town **55.00**
1984, Christmas Letter **55.00**
1985, Christmas Eve at the Farm-
house **55.00**
1986, Silent Night, Holy Night **55.00**
1987, The Snowman's Christmas Eve   **60.00**
1988, In The Kings Garden **72.00**
1989, Christmas Anchorage **65.00**
1990, Changing of the Guards **60.00**
1991, Copenhagen Stock Exchange   **70.00**
1992, Christmas at the Rectory **65.00**
1993, Father Christmas in Copen-
hagen **65.00**
Mother's Day Plates, Henry Thelander,
artist, 6″ d
1969, Dog And Puppies **350.00**
1970, Bird And Chicks **35.00**
1971, Cat And Kitten **24.00**
1972, Mare And Foal **20.00**
1973, Duck And Ducklings **20.00**
1974, Bear And Cubs **24.00**
1975, Doe And Fawns **20.00**
1976, Swan Family **22.00**
1977, Squirrel And Young **25.00**
1978, Heron **25.00**
1979, Fox And Cubs **30.00**
1980, Woodpecker And Young **35.00**
1981, Hare And Young **40.00**
1982, Lioness And Cubs **45.00**
1983, Raccoon And Young **45.00**
1984, Stork and Nestlings **40.00**
1985, Bear and Cubs **40.00**
1986, Elephant with Calf **40.00**
1987, Sheep with Lambs **42.50**
1988, Lapwing Mother with Chicks   **48.00**
1989, Cow with Calf **48.00**
1990, Hen with Chicks **50.00**
1991, The Nanny Goat and Her Two
Frisky Kids **70.00**
1992, Panda with Cubs **55.00**
1993, St. Bernard Dog and Puppies   **55.00**

Franklin Mint (United States)

Audubon Society Birds
1972, Goldfinch **115.00**
1972, Wood Duck **110.00**
1973, Cardinal **110.00**
1973, Ruffed Grouse **120.00**
Christmas Plates, Norman Rockwell,
artist, etched sterling silver, 8″ d
1970, Bringing Home The Tree **275.00**

1971, Under The Mistletoe	**125.00**
1972, The Carolers	**125.00**
1973, Trimming The Tree	**100.00**
1974, Hanging The Wreath	**100.00**
1975, Home For Christmas	**125.00**

Goebel (Germany), see Hummel

Haviland (France)

Mother's Day (The French Collection)

1973, Breakfast	**25.00**
1974, The Wash	**30.00**
1975, In The Park	**25.00**
1976, Market	**40.00**
1977, Wash Before Dinner	**35.00**
1978, Evening At Home	**40.00**
1979, Happy Mother's Day	**30.00**
1980, Child & His Animals	**55.00**

1,001 Arabian Nights, Lillian Tellier artist

1979, Cheval Magique, Magic Horse	**60.00**
1980, Aladin et Lampe	**60.00**
1981, Scheherazade	**55.00**

The Twelve Days Of Christmas Series, Remy Hetreau, artist, 8⅜" d

1970, A Partridge In A Pear Tree, FE	**115.00**
1971, Two Turtle Doves	**40.00**
1972, Three French Hens	**35.00**
1973, Four Calling Birds	**35.00**
1974, Five Golden Rings	**30.00**
1975, Six Geese A'Laying	**30.00**
1976, Seven Swans A'Swimming ...	**30.00**
1977, Eight Maids A'Milking	**45.00**
1978, Nine Ladies Dancing	**35.00**
1979, Ten Lords A'Leaping	**40.00**
1980, Eleven Pipers Piping	**50.00**
1981, Twelve Drummers Drumming	**55.00**

Haviland & Parlon (France)

Christmas Series, various artists, 10" d

1972, Madonna And Child, Raphael, FE	**80.00**
1973, Madonnina, Feruzzi	**95.00**
1974, Cowper Madonna And Child, Murillo	**40.00**
1975, Madonna And Child, Murillo	**45.00**
1976, Madonna And Child, Botticelli	**50.00**
1977, Madonna And Child, Bellini	**40.00**
1978, Madonna And Child, Fra Filippo, Lippi	**65.00**
1979, Madonna Of The Eucharist, Botticelli	**150.00**

Lady And The Unicorn Series, artist unknown, 10" d

1977, To My Only Desire, FE	**60.00**
1978, Sight	**40.00**
1979, Sound	**50.00**
1980, Touch	**110.00**

1981, Scent	**60.00**
1982, Taste	**80.00**

Tapestry Series, artist unknown, 10" d

1971, The Unicorn In Captivity	**145.00**
1972, Start Of The Hunt	**70.00**
1973, Chase Of The Unicorn	**120.00**
1974, End Of The Hunt	**120.00**
1975, The Unicorn Surrounded	**75.00**
1976, The Unicorn Is Brought To The Castle	**55.00**

Edwin M. Knowles (United States)

Americana Holidays Series, Don Spaulding, artist, 8½" d

1978, Fourth Of July, FE	**35.00**
1979, Thanksgiving	**35.00**
1980, Easter	**30.00**
1981, Valentine's Day	**25.00**
1982, Father's Day	**35.00**
1983, Christmas	**35.00**
1984, Mother's Day	**20.00**
1986, Grand Finale	**24.00**

Gone With The Wind Series, Raymond Kursar, artist, 8½" d

1978, Scarlett, FE	**300.00**
1979, Ashley	**225.00**
1980, Melanie	**75.00**
1981, Rhett	**50.00**
1982, Mammy Lacing Scarlett	**60.00**
1983, Melanie Gives Birth	**85.00**
1984, Scarlett's Green Dress	**50.00**
1985, Rhett and Bonnie	**35.00**

Lenox (United States)

Boehm Bird Series, Edward Marshall Boehm, artist, 10½" d

1970, Wood Thrush, FE	**135.00**
1971, Goldfinch	**60.00**
1972, Mountain Bluebird	**40.00**
1973, Meadowlark	**50.00**
1974, Rufous Hummingbird	**45.00**
1975, American Redstart	**50.00**
1976, Cardinal	**55.00**
1977, Robins	**55.00**
1978, Mockingbirds	**60.00**
1979, Golden–Crowned Kinglets ...	**65.00**
1980, Black–Throated Blue Warblers	**75.00**
1981, Eastern Phoebes	**90.00**

Boehm Woodland Wildlife Series, Edward Marshall Boehm, artist, 10½" d

1973, Raccoons, FE	**50.00**
1974, Red Foxes	**50.00**
1975, Cottontail Rabbits	**55.00**
1976, Eastern Chipmunks	**60.00**
1977, Beaver	**60.00**
1978, Whitetail Deer	**60.00**
1979, Squirrels	**70.00**
1980, Bobcats	**145.00**
1981, Martens	**100.00**
1982, River Otters	**125.00**

Reco International Corp. (United States)

McClelland's Children's Circus Series, John McClelland, artist, 9" d

1981, Tommy The Clown, FE	45.00
1982, Katie The Tightrope Walker	40.00
1983, Johnny The Strongman	40.00
1984, Maggie The Animal Trainer	30.00

McClelland's Mother Goose Series, John McClelland, artist, 8½" d

1979, Mary, Mary, FE	250.00
1980, Little Boy Blue	100.00
1981, Little Miss Muffet	30.00
1982, Little Jack Horner	30.00
1983, Little Bo Peep	40.00
1984, Diddle, Diddle Dumpling	30.00
1985, Mary Had A Little Lamb	42.00
1986, Jack and Jill	25.00

Reed & Barton (United States)

Christmas Series, Damascene silver, 11" d through 1978, 8" d 1979 to 1981

1970, A Partridge In A Pear Tree, FE	200.00
1971, We Three Kings Of Orient Are	65.00
1972, Hark! The Herald Angels Sing	60.00
1973, Adoration Of The Kings	75.00
1974, The Adoration Of The Magi	60.00
1975, Adoration Of The Kings	65.00
1976, Morning Train	60.00
1977, Decorating The Church	60.00
1978, The General Store At Christmas Time	67.00
1979, Merry Old Santa Claus	65.00
1980, Gathering Christmas Greens	75.00
1981, The Shopkeeper At Christmas	75.00

Rockwell, see Norman Rockwell

Rosenthal (Germany)

Christmas Plates, various artists, 8½" d

1910, Winter Peace	550.00
1911, The Three Wise Men	325.00
1912, Shooting Stars	250.00
1913, Christmas Lights	235.00
1914, Christmas Song	350.00
1915, Walking To Church	180.00
1916, Christmas During War	235.00
1917, Angel Of Peace	210.00
1918, Peace On Earth	210.00
1919, St. Christopher With The Christ Child	225.00
1920, The Manger In Bethlehem	325.00
1921, Christmas In The Mountains	200.00
1922, Advent Branch	200.00
1923, Children In The Winter Wood	200.00
1924, Deer In The Woods	200.00
1925, The Three Wise Men	200.00
1926, Christmas In The Mountains	175.00

1927, Station On The Way	200.00
1928, Chalet Christmas	175.00
1929, Christmas In The Alps	225.00
1930, Group Of Deer Under The Pines	225.00
1931, Path Of The Magi	225.00
1932, Christ Child	195.00
1933, Through The Night To Light	190.00
1934, Christmas Peace	200.00
1935, Christmas By The Sea	185.00
1936, Nürnberg Angel	185.00
1937, Berchtesgaden	195.00
1938, Christmas in the Alps	195.00
1939, Schneekoppe Mountain	195.00
1940, Marien Church in Danzig	250.00
1941, Strassburg Cathedral	250.00
1942, Marianburg Castle	300.00
1943, Winter Idyll	300.00
1944, Wood Scape	275.00
1945, Christmas Peace	375.00
1946, Christmas In An Alpine Valley	250.00
1947, The Dillingen Madonna	975.00
1948, Message To The Shepherds	850.00
1949, The Holy Family	185.00
1950, Christmas In The Forest	175.00
1951, Star Of Bethlehem	450.00
1952, Christmas In The Alps	185.00
1953, The Holy Light	185.00
1954, Christmas Eve	175.00
1955, Christmas In A Village	190.00
1956, Christmas In The Alps	185.00
1957, Christmas By The Sea	195.00
1958, Christmas Eve	185.00
1959, Midnight Mass	195.00
1960, Christmas Eve In A Small Village	185.00
1961, Solitary Christmas	225.00
1962, Christmas Eve	185.00
1963, Silent Night	185.00
1964, Christmas Market In Nurnberg	220.00
1965, Christmas In Munich	185.00
1966, Christmas In Ulm	265.00
1967, Christmas In Regensburg	185.00
1968, Christmas in Bremen	185.00
1969, Christmas In Rothenburg	220.00
1970, Christmas In Cologne	165.00
1971, Christmas In Garmisch	100.00
1972, Christmas In Franconia	90.00
1973, Christmas In Lubeck–Holstein	110.00
1974, Christmas In Wurzburg	90.00

Christmas Plates Series, Bjorn Wiinblad (artist)

1971, Maria & Child	600.00
1972, Caspar	550.00
1973, Melchior	325.00
1974, Balthazar	500.00
1975, The Annunciation	175.00
1976, Angel With Trumpet	200.00
1977, Adoration of Shepherds	200.00
1978, Angel With Harp	275.00
1979, Exodus From Egypt	300.00
1980, Angel With A Glockenspiel	360.00

1981, Christ Child Visits Temple . . . **350.00**
1982, Christening of Christ **375.00**

Royal Copenhagen

Christmas Plates, various artists, 6″ d
1908, 1909, 1910; 7″ d 1911 to present
1908, Madonna And Child **1,750.00**
1909, Danish Landscape **150.00**
1910, The Magi **120.00**
1911, Danish Landscape **135.00**
1912, Elderly Couple By Christmas
Tree **120.00**
1913, Spire Of Frederik's Church,
Copenhagen **125.00**
1914, Sparrows In Tree At Church Of
The Holy Spirit, Copenhagen **100.00**
1915, Danish Landscape **150.00**
1916, Shepherd In The Field On
Christmas Night **85.00**
1917, Tower Of Our Savior's Church,
Copenhagen **90.00**
1918, Sheep and Shepherds **80.00**
1919, In The Park **80.00**
1920, Mary With The Child Jesus . . **75.00**
1921, Aabenraa Marketplace **75.00**
1922, Three Singing Angels **70.00**
1923, Danish Landscape **70.00**
1924, Christmas Star Over The Sea
And Sailing Ship **100.00**
1925, Street Scene From Christianshavn, Copenhagen **85.00**
1926, View of Christmas Canal,
Copenhagen **75.00**
1927, Ship's Boy At The Tiller On
Christmas Night **140.00**
1928, Vicar's Family On Way To
Church **75.00**
1929, Grundtvig Church, Copenhagen **100.00**
1930, Fishing Boats On The Way To
The Harbor **80.00**
1931, Mother And Child **90.00**
1932, Frederiksberg Gardens With
Statue Of Frederik VI **90.00**
1933, The Great Belt Ferry **110.00**
1934, The Hermitage Castle **115.00**
1935, Fishing Boat Off Kronborg
Castle **145.00**
1936, Roskilde Cathedral **130.00**
1937, Christmas Scene In Main
Street, Copenhagen **135.00**
1938, Round Church In Osterlars On
Bornholm **200.00**
1939, Expeditionary Ship In Pack–Ice
Of Greenland **180.00**
1940, The Good Shepherd **300.00**
1941, Danish Village Church **250.00**
1942, Bell Tower of Old Church In
Jutland **300.00**
1943, Flight Of Holy Family To Egypt **425.00**

1944, Typical Danish Winter Scene **160.00**
1945, A Peaceful Motif **325.00**
1946, Zealand Village Church **150.00**
1947, The Good Shepherd **210.00**
1948, Nodebo Church At Christmastime **150.00**
1949, Our Lady's Cathedral, Copenhagen **165.00**
1950, Boeslunde Church, Zealand . . **175.00**
1951, Christmas Angel **300.00**
1952, Christmas In The Forest **120.00**
1953, Frederiksborg Castle **120.00**
1954, Amalienborg Palace, Copenhagen **150.00**
1955, Fano Girl **185.00**
1956, Rosenborg Castle, Copenhagen **160.00**
1957, The Good Shepherd **115.00**
1958, Sunshine Over Greenland . . . **140.00**
1959, Christmas Night **120.00**
1960, The Stag **125.00**
1961, Training Ship Danmark **155.00**
1962, The Little Mermaid **135.00**
1963, Hojsager Mill **80.00**
1964, Fetching The Tree **45.00**
1965, Little Skaters **60.00**
1966, Blackbird **30.00**
1967, The Royal Oak **45.00**
1968, The Last Umiak **20.00**
1969, The Old Farmyard **35.00**
1970, Christmas Rose and Cat **30.00**
1971, Hare In Winter **80.00**
1972, In The Desert **30.00**
1973, Train Homeward Bound For
Christmas **85.00**
1974, Winter Twilight **25.00**
1975, Queen's Palace **85.00**
1976, Danish Watermill **20.00**
1977, Immervad Bridge **45.00**
1978, Greenland Scenery **75.00**
1979, Choosing The Christmas Tree **60.00**
1980, Bringing Home The Tree **45.00**
1981, Admiring The Christmas Tree **55.00**

**Royal Copenhagen, Christmas series,
1981, Admiring Christmas Tree, K. Lange
artist, plate has not appreciated, issue
price $55.00.**

1982, Waiting For Christmas	45.00
1983, Merry Christmas	60.00
1984, Jingle Bells	50.00
1985, Snowman	55.00
1986, Christmas Vacation	55.00
1987, Winter Birds	58.00
1988, Christmas Eve in Copenhagen	70.00
1989, The Old Skating Pond	50.00
1990, Christmas at Tivoli	50.00
1991, The Festival of Santa Lucia	65.00
1992, The Queen's Carriage	65.00
1993, Christmas Guests	65.00

Mother's Day Plates, various artists, 6¼" d

1971, American Mother	125.00
1972, Oriental Mother	60.00
1973, Danish Mother	60.00
1974, Greenland Mother	55.00
1975, Bird In Nest	50.00
1976, Mermaids	50.00
1977, The Twins	50.00
1978, Mother And Child	25.00
1979, A Loving Mother	30.00
1980, An Outing With Mother	35.00
1981, Reunion	40.00
1982, The Children's Hour	45.00

Royal Doulton (Great Britain)

Beswick Christmas Series, various artists, earthenware in hand–cast bas–relief, 8" sq

1972, Christmas In England, FE	40.00
1973, Christmas In Mexico	25.00
1974, Christmas In Bulgaria	40.00
1975, Christmas In Norway	54.00
1976, Christmas In Holland	45.00
1977, Christmas In Poland	100.00
1978, Christmas In America	45.00

Mother And Child Series, Edna Hibel artist, 8" d

1973, Colette And Child, FE	450.00
1974, Sayuri And Child	150.00
1975, Kristina And Child	125.00
1976, Marilyn And Child	120.00
1977, Lucia And Child	100.00
1978, Kathleen And Child	95.00

Valentine's Day Series, artists unknown, 8¼" d

1976, Victorian Boy And Girl	60.00
1977, My Sweetest Friend	40.00
1978, If I Loved You	40.00
1979, My Valentine	40.00
1980, On A Swing	40.00
1981, Sweet Music	35.00
1982, From My Heart	40.00
1983, Cherub's Song	45.00
1984, Love In Bloom	40.00
1985, Accept These Flowers	40.00

Schmid (Japan)

Christmas, J Malfertheiner, artist

1971, St Jakob in Groden, FE	125.00
1972, Pipers at Alberobello	120.00
1973, Alpine Horn	375.00
1974, Young Man and Girl	100.00
1975, Christmas In Ireland	90.00
1976, Alpine Christmas	200.00
1977, Legend of Heligenblut	125.00
1978, Klockler Singers	175.00
1979, Moss Gatherers	130.00
1980, Wintry Churchgoing	165.00
1981, Santa Claus in Tyrol	160.00
1982, The Star Singers	160.00
1983, Unto Us A Child Is Born	150.00
1984, Yuletide in the Valley	150.00
1985, Good Morning, Good Year	160.00
1986, A Groeden Christmas	75.00
1987, Down From The Alps	175.00

Disney Christmas Series, undisclosed artists, 7½" d

1973, Sleigh Ride, FE	400.00
1974, Decorating The Tree	175.00
1975, Caroling	20.00
1976, Building A Snowman	35.00
1977, Down The Chimney	25.00
1978, Night Before Christmas	20.00
1979, Santa's Surprise	20.00
1980, Sleigh Ride	30.00
1981, Happy Holidays	18.00
1982, Winter Games	20.00
1987, Snow White Golden Anniversary	48.00
1988, Mickey Mouse & Minnie Mouse 60th	50.00
1989, Sleeping Beauty 30th Anniversary	75.00
1990, Fantasia Relief	25.00

Disney Mother's Day Series

1974, Flowers For Mother, FE	80.00
1975, Snow White And The Seven Dwarfs	45.00
1976, Minnie Mouse And Friends	20.00
1977, Pluto's Pals	25.00
1978, Flowers For Bambi	20.00
1979, Happy Feet	25.00
1980, Minnie's Surprise	20.00
1981, Playmates	25.00
1982, A Dream Come True	20.00

Peanuts Christmas Series, Charles Schulz, artist, 7½" d

1972, Snoopy Guides The Sleigh, FE	90.00
1973, Christmas Eve At The Doghouse	120.00
1974, Christmas Eve At The Fireplace	65.00
1975, Woodstock, Santa Claus	15.00
1976, Woodstock's Christmas	30.00
1977, Deck The Doghouse	15.00
1978, Filling The Stocking	20.00
1979, Christmas At Hand	20.00
1980, Waiting For Santa	50.00

1981, A Christmas Wish 20.00
1982, Perfect Performance 35.00
Peanuts Mother's Day Series, Charles
Schulz, artist, 7½" d
1972, Linus, FE 50.00
1973, Mom? 45.00
1974, Snoopy And Woodstock On
Parade 40.00
1975, A Kiss For Lucy 38.00
1976, Linus And Snoopy 35.00
1977, Dear Mom 30.00
1978, Thoughts That Count 25.00
1979, A Special Letter 20.00
1980, A Tribute To Mom 20.00
1981, Mission For Mom 20.00
1982, Which Way To Mother? 20.00
Peanuts Valentine's Day Series, Charles
Schulz, artist, 7½" d
1977, Home Is Where The Heart Is,
FE 25.00
1978, Heavenly Bliss 28.00
1979, Love Match 20.00
1980, From Snoopy, With Love 24.00
1981, Hearts–A–Flutter 20.00
1982, Love Patch 18.00
Raggedy Ann Annual Series, undisclosed artist, 7½" d
1980, The Sunshine Wagon 65.00
1981, The Raggedy Shuffle 25.00
1982, Flying High 20.00
1983, Winning Streak 20.00
1984, Rocking Rodeo 22.50

U. S. Historical Society (United States)

Stained Glass Cathedral
1978, Canterbury 175.00
1979, Flight into Egypt 175.00
1980, Washington
Cathedral/Madonna 160.00
1981, The Magi 160.00
1982, Flight Into Egypt 160.00
1983, Shepherds at Bethlehem 150.00
1984, The Navitity 145.00
1985, Good Tidings of Great Joy,
Boston 125.00
1986, The Nativity from Old St.
Mary's Church, Philadelphia 165.00
1987, O Come, Little Children 160.00

Wedgwood (Great Britain)

Calendar Series
1971, Victorian Almanac, FE 20.00
1972, The Carousel 15.00
1973, Bountiful Butterfly 14.00
1974, Camelot 65.00
1975, Children's Games 18.00
1976, Robin 25.00
1977, Tonatiuh 28.00

1978, Samurai 32.00
1979, Sacred Scarab 32.00
1980, Safari 40.00
1981, Horses 42.50
1982, Wild West 50.00
1983, The Age of the Reptiles 50.00
1984, Dogs 55.00
1985, Cats 55.00
1986, British Birds 50.00
1987, Water Birds 50.00
1988, Sea Birds 50.00
Christmas Series, jasper stoneware, 8" d
1969, Windsor Castle, FE 225.00
1970, Christmas In Trafalgar Square   30.00
1971, Piccadilly Circus, London ... 40.00
1972, St. Paul's Cathedral 40.00
1973, The Tower Of London 45.00
1974, The Houses Of Parliament ... 40.00
1975, Tower Bridge 40.00
1976, Hampton Court 46.00
1977, Westminster Abbey 48.00
1978, The Horse Guards 55.00
1979, Buckingham Palace 55.00
1980, St. James Palace 70.00
1981, Marble Arch 75.00
1982, Lambeth Palace 80.00
1983, All Souls, Langham Palace ... 80.00
1984, Constitution Hill 80.00
1985, The Tate Gallery 80.00
1986, The Albert Memorial 80.00
1987, Guildhall 80.00
Mothers Series, jasper stoneware, 6½" d
1971, Sportive Love, FE 25.00
1972, The Sewing Lesson 20.00
1973, The Baptism Of Achilles 20.00
1974, Domestic Employment 30.00
1975, Mother And Child 35.00
1976, The Spinner 35.00
1977, Leisure Time 30.00
1978, Swan And Cygnets 35.00
1979, Deer And Fawn 35.00
1980, Birds 48.00
1981, Mare And Foal 50.00
1982, Cherubs With Swing 55.00
1983, Cupid And Butterfly 55.00
1984, Musical Cupids 55.00
1985, Cupids and Doves 55.00
1986, Anemones 55.00
1987, Tiger Lily 55.00

LITTLE GOLDEN BOOKS

Collecting Hints: Little Golden Books offer something for everybody. Collectors can pursue titles
by favorite author, illustrator, or their favorite
television show, film, or comic strip character.
Disney titles enjoy a special place with nostalgia
buffs. An increasingly popular goal is to own one
copy of each title and number.

Books published in the 1940s, 1950s, and 1960s are in the greatest demand at this time. Books from this period were assigned individual numbers, usually found on the front cover of the book except for the earliest titles where one must check the title against the numbered list on back of the book.

Although the publisher tried to adhere to a policy of one number for each title during the first thirty years, old numbers were assigned to new titles as old titles were eliminated. Also, when an earlier book was re–edited and/or re–illustrated, it was given a new number.

Most of the first thirty–six books had blue paper spines and a dust jacket. Subsequent books were issued with a golden–brown mottled spine. This was replaced in 1950 by a shiny gold spine.

Early books had 42 pages. In the late 1940s the format was gradually changed to 28 pages. Early 42– and 28– page books had no price on the cover. Later the price of 25¢ appeared on the front cover, then 29¢, followed by 39¢. In the mid–1950s the number of pages was changed to 24. In the early 1950s books were produced with two lines that formed a bar across the top of the front cover. This bar was eliminated in the early 1960s.

Little Golden Books can still be found at yard sales and flea markets. Other sources include friends, relatives, and charity book sales, especially if they have a separate children's table. Also attend doll, toy, and book shows. These dealers are sources for books with paper dolls, puzzles, and cutouts. Toy dealers are also a good source for Disney, television, and cowboy titles.

Look for books in good or better condition. Covers should be bright with the spine paper intact. Rubbing, ink and crayon markings, or torn pages lessen the value of the book. Pencil markings are fairly easy to remove, unless extensive. Stroke gently in one direction with an art gum eraser. Do not rub back and forth.

Within the past two years competition has increased dramatically, thus driving up prices for the most unusual and hard–to–find titles. Prices for the majority of titles are still at a reasonable level.

History: Simon & Schuster published the first Little Golden Books in September, 1942. They were conceived and created by the Artists & Writers Guild Inc., which was an arm of the Western Printing and Lithographing Company. The initial 12, forty–two page titles, priced at 25¢ each, sold over 1.5 million books within five months of publication. By the end of WWII thirty–nine million Little Golden Books were sold.

A Disney series was begun in 1944, and Big and Giant Golden Books followed that same year. In 1949 the first Goldencraft editions were introduced. Instead of side–stapled cardboard,

these books had cloth covers and were sewn so that they could hold up under school and library use. In 1958 Giant Little Golden Books were introduced, most combining three previously published titles together in one book.

The year 1958 also marked Simon & Schuster's sale of Little Golden Books to Western Printing and Lithographing Company and Pocket Books. The books then appeared under the Golden Press imprint. Eventually Western bought out Pocket Books' interest in Little Golden Books. Now known as Western Publishing Company, Inc., it is the parent company of Golden Press, Inc.

In 1986 Western celebrated the one–billionth Little Golden Book by issuing special commemorative editions of some of its most popular titles, such as *Poky Little Puppy* and *Cinderella*. In 1992 Golden Press will celebrate the 50th birthday of Little Golden Books.

Note: Prices are based on the first printing of a book in mint condition. Printing is determined by looking at the lower right hand corner of the back page. The letter found there indicates the printing of that particular title and edition. "A" is the first printing and so forth. Occasionally the letter is hidden under the spine or was placed in the upper right hand corner, so look closely. Early titles will have their printings indicated in the front of the book.

Any dust jacket, puzzles, stencils, cutouts, stamps, tissues, tape, or pages should be intact and present as issued. If not, the book suffers a drastic reduction in value—up to 80 percent less than the listed price. Books that are badly worn, incomplete, or badly torn are worth little. Sometimes they are useful as temporary fillers for gaps in a collection.

References: Barbara Bader, *American Picture Books from Noah's Ark to the Beast Within,* Macmillan, 1976; Rebecca Greason, *Tomart's Price Guide To Golden Book Collectibles,* Wallace–Homestead, 1991; Dolores B. Jones, *Bibliography of the Little Golden Book,* Greenwood Press, 1987; Norman E. Martinus and Harry L. Rinker, *Warman's Paper,* Wallace–Homestead, 1994; Steve Santi, *Collecting Little Golden Books, Second Edition* Books Americana, 1994.

Collectors' Club: Golden Book Club, 19626 Ricardo Ave., Hayward, CA 94541.

Advisor: Kathie Diehl.

Airplanes, #180, 1953, 28 pgs, Herbert and Lenora Combes illus, Ruth Mabee Lachman author	**7.00**
Alice in Wonderland Meets the White Rabbit, #D19, 1951, 28 pgs, Al Dempster illus, Jane Werner author	**12.00**
Animals Christmas Eve, The, #154, 1977, 24 pgs, Jim Robison illus, Gale	

Wiersum author **4.00**

Animals of Farmer Jones, The, #211, 1942, 28 pgs, Rudolf Freund illus . . **5.00**

Annie Oakley and the Rustlers, #221, 1955, 28 pgs, Mel Crawford illus, Ann McGovern author, Annie Oakley Enterprises, Inc, copyright **18.00**

Bedtime Stories, #2, 1942, 42 pgs, Gustaf Tenggren illus **20.00**

Brave Cowboy Bill, #93, 1950, 42 pgs, Richard Scarry illus, Kathryn and Byron Jackson authors **15.00**

Bugs Bunny and the Indians, #120, 1951, 28 pgs, Richard Kelsey and Warner Bros illus, Annie North Bedford author, Warner Bros Cartoons, Inc copyright **10.00**

Cats, #150, 1976, 24 pgs, Mel Crawford illus, Laura French author **4.00**

The Chipmunks' Merry Christmas, #375, **David Corwin, Richard Scarry illus, 1959, $6.00.**

Circus Time, wheel book, #A2, 1955, 20 pgs, Tibor Gergely illus, Marion Conger author **15.00**

Color Kittens, The, 1949, 28 pgs, Alice and Martin Provinson illus, Margaret Wise Brown author, puzzle back cov **35.00**

Davy Crockett's Keelboat Race, #D47, 1955, 24 pgs, Mel Crawford illus, Irwin Shapiro author **18.00**

Doctor Dan at the Circus, #399, 1960, 24 pgs, Katherine Sampson illus, Pauline Wilkins author, 2 circus bandaids **25.00**

5 Pennies to Spend, #238, 1955, 28 pgs, Corinne Malvern illus, Miriam Young author **12.00**

Fix It Please, #32, 1947, 42 pgs, Eloise Wilkin illus, Lucy Sprague Mitchell author **20.00**

From Then to Now, #201, 1954, 28 pgs,

Tibor Gergely illus, JP Leventhal author **7.00**

Frosty the Snowman, #142, 1951, 28 pgs, Corinne Malvern illus, Annie North Bedford author **8.00**

Georgie Finds a Grandpa, #196, 1954, 28 pgs, Eloise Wilkin illus, Miriam Young author **18.00**

Ginger Paper Doll, #A14, 1957, 20 pgs, Andriana Mazza Saviozzi illus, Kathleen Daly author **35.00**

Ginghams Backward Picnic, The, #148, 1976, 24 pgs, Jo Ann E Koenig and Creative Studios illus, Joan Chase Bowden author **4.00**

Happy Man and His Dump Truck, The, #77, 1950, 42 pgs, Tibor Gergely illus, Miryam author, puzzle in back cov **30.00**

Heidi, #192, 1954, 28 pgs, Corinne Malvern illus, Johanna Spyri author **6.00**

Heroes of the Bible, #236, 1955, 28 pgs, Rachel Taft Dixon illus, Jane Werner Watson author **8.00**

Hiawatha, #D31, 1953, 28 pgs, Walt Disney Studios illus and author **15.00**

Houses, #229, 1955, 28 pgs, Tibor Gergely illus, Elsa Jane Werner author **7.00**

Jack's Adventure, #308, 1958, 24 pgs, John P Miller illus, Edith Thacher Hurd author **8.00**

J Fred Muggs, #234, 1955, 28 pgs, Edwin Schmidt illus, Irwin Shapiro author, J Fred Muggs Enterprises copyright **12.00**

Little Black Sambo, #57, 1948, 42 pgs, Gustaf Tenggren illus, Helen Bannerman author **75.00**

Little Boy With A Big Horn, #100, 1950, 42 pgs, Aurelius Battaglia illus, Jack Bezchdolt author **10.00**

Little Golden Book of Singing Games, The, #40, 1947, 42 pgs, Corinne Malvern illus, Kathryne Tyler Wessles author **10.00**

Lone Ranger and the Talking Pony, The, #310, 1958, 24 pgs, Frank Bolle illus, Emily Brown author, The Lone Ranger, Inc, copyright **18.00**

Magic Compass, The, #146, 1953, 28 pgs, Gertrude Elliott illus, PL Travers author **15.00**

Merry Shipwreck, The, #170, 1953, 28 pgs, Tibor Gergely illus, Georges Duplaix author **10.00**

Mr Rogers Neighborhood, Henrietta Meets Someone New, #133, 1974, 24 pgs, Jason Art Studios illus, Fred M Rogers author, Small World Enterprises, Inc, copyright **4.00**

My First Book, #10, 1942, 42 pgs, Bob Smith illus and author **18.00**

My First Book Of Sounds, #205–54, 1963, 24 pgs, Trina Schart illus, Melanie Bellah author 1.00

My Teddy Bear, #168, 1953, 28 pgs, Eloise Wilkin illus, Patricia Scarry author 15.00

Night Before Christmas, The, #20, 1949, 28 pgs, Corinne Malvern illus, Clement C Moore author 10.00

Old MacDonald Had A Farm, #200–55, 1975, 24 pgs, Carl & Mary Hauge illus and authors 2.00

Pantaloon, #114, 1951, 28 pgs, Leonard Weisgard illus, Kathryn Jackson author, diecut in cover 15.00

Pat–A–Cake, #54, 1948, 28 pgs, Aurelius Battaglia illus, Mother Goose author 10.00

Pink Panther And Sons Fun At The Picnic, #111–60, 1985, 24 pgs, David Gantz illus, Sandra Baris author 3.00

Poky Little Puppy, The, #8, 1942, 42 pgs, Gustaf Tenggren illus, Janet Sebring Lowrey author 20.00

Pony For Tony, A, #220, 1955, 28 pgs, William P Gottlieb illus and author   9.00

Prayers For Children, #205, 1952, 28 pgs, Eloise Wilkin illus 5.00

Rootie Kazootie Joins the Circus, #226, 1955, 28 pgs, Mel Crawford illus, Steve Carlin author, Steven R Carlin copyright 18.00

Scuffy The Tugboat, #30, 1946, 42 pgs, Tibor Gergely illus, Gertrude Crampton author 18.00

Snow White and The Seven Dwarfs, #D66, 1948, 24 pgs, Ken O'Brien and Al Dempster illus, Brothers Grimm author 8.00

Surprise for Mickey Mouse, #D105, 1971, 24 pgs, Walt Disney Studios author 4.00

Susie's New Stove, #85, 1950, 42 pgs, Corinne Malvern illus, Annie North Bedford author 18.00

Tawny Scrawny Lion and the Clever Monkey, The, #128, 1974, 24 pgs, Milli Jancar illus, Mary Carey author   5.00

Taxi That Hurried, The, #25, 1946, 42 pgs, Tibor Gergely, Irma Black Simington, and Jessie Stanton illus, Lucy Sprague Mitchell author 18.00

Three Bears, The, #47, 1948, 42 pgs, Feodor Rojankovsky illus, second cov   8.00

Thumbelina, #153, 1953, 28 pgs, Gustaf Tenggren illus, Hans Christian Anderson author 10.00

Tiger's Adventure, #208, William P Gottlieb photographer and author . .   8.00

Trim the Christmas Tree, #A15, 1957, 24 pgs, Doris and Marion Henderson illus, Elsa Ruth Nast author 25.00

Walt Disney's Zorro And The Secret Plan, 1958, $10.00.

Twins, The, #227, 1955, 28 pgs, Eloise Wilkin illus, Ruth and Harold Shane authors 25.00

Ugly Dachshund, The, #D118, 1966, 24 pgs, Mel Crawford illus, Carl Memling author 15.00

Uncle Remus, #105–66, 1947, 24 pgs, Walt Disney Studios illus and author   2.00

Very Best Home For Me, The, #204–25, 1953, 24 pgs, Garth Williams illus, Jane Werner Watson author 1.00

What's Next Elephant?, #206–61, 1949, 24 pgs, Feodor Rojankovsky illus, Kathryn & Byron Jackson authors . . .   1.00

Woody Woodpecker Takes A Trip, #445, 1961, 24 pgs, Ben de Nunez and Al White illus, Ann McGovern author, Walter Lantz Productions, Inc, copyright 6.00

LITTLE RED RIDING HOOD

Collecting Hints: Little Red Riding Hood is a "hot" collectible. Prices for many pieces are in the hundreds of dollars. Prices for the advertising plaque and baby dish are in the thousands.

A great unanswered question at this time is how many Little Red Riding Hood pieces have survived. Attempts at determining production levels have been unsuccessful. This category has the potential for an eventual market flooding, especially for the most commonly found pieces. New collectors are advised to proceed with caution.

Undecorated blanks are commonly found. Value them between 25% and 50% less than decorated examples.

History: On June 29, 1943, the United States Patent Office issued design patent #135,889 to Louise Elizabeth Bauer of Zanesville, Ohio, assignor to the A. E. Hull Pottery Company, Incorporated, Crooksville, Ohio, for a "Design for a Cookie Jar." Thus was born Hull's Little Red Riding Hood line. It was produced and distributed between 1943 and 1957.

The traditional story is that A. E. Hull only made the blanks. Decoration of the pieces was done by the Royal China and Novelty Company of Chicago, Illinois. When decoration was complete, the pieces were returned to Hull for distribution. Recent scholarship suggests a somewhat different approach.

Mark Supnick, author of *Collecting Hull Pottery's "Little Red Riding Hood": A Pictorial Reference and Price Guide* feels that A. E. Hull only made the blanks for early cookie jars and the dresser jar with a large bow in the front. They can be identified by their creamy off–white pottery. The majority of pieces have very white pottery, a body Supnick attributes to The Royal China and Novelty Company, a division of Regal China. Given the similarity in form to items in Royal China and Novelty Company's "Old McDonald's Farm" line, Supnick concludes that Hull contracted with Royal China and Novelty for production as well as decoration.

Great hand–painted and decal variations are encountered in pieces, e.g., the wolf jar is found with bases in black, brown, red, or yellow.

References: Harvey Duke, *The Official Identification and Price Guide to Pottery and Porcelain, Eighth Edition,* House of Collectibles, 1995; Mark E. Supnick, *Collecting Hull Pottery's "Little Red Riding Hood": A Pictorial Reference and Price Guide,* L–W Book Sales, 1989, 1992 value update.

REPRODUCTION ALERT: Be alert for a Mexican–produced cookie jar that closely resembles Hull's Little Red Riding Hood piece. The Mexican example is slightly shorter. Hull's examples measure 13 inches high.

Bank, hanging	**3,000.00**
Butter Dish, cov	**350.00**
Canister	
Flour	**650.00**
Salt	**1,000.00**
Cookie Jar	
Open Basket, gold stars on apron	**395.00**
Round Basket, poinsettias on apron	**900.00**
Cracker Jar, cov	**650.00**
Creamer, tab	**350.00**
Lamp, gold trim	**2,000.00**
Match Box	**875.00**
Milk Pitcher, 8" h	**295.00**
Mustard Jar, cov	**285.00**

Salt and Pepper Shakers, pr	
Large, 5½" h	**140.00**
Small, 3¼" h	**60.00**
Sugar, crawling	**350.00**
Teapot, cov	**285.00**

LUNCH KITS

Collecting Hints: The thermos is an intregal part of the lunch kit. The two must be present to have full value. However, there has been a tendency in recent years to remove the thermos from the lunch box and price the two separately. The wise collector will resist this trend.

Prices on lunch kits have increased significantly in the last couple of years, largely due to the publicity generated by the manipulative efforts of Scott Bruce and others. Prices now appear to be stabilizing as the lunch box craze of the 1980s nears its end.

The values listed reflect realistic prices for a kit with thermos, both in near mint condition. Scratches and rust detract from a metal kit's value and lower value by more than fifty percent.

History: Lunch kits date back to the 19th century when tin boxes were used by factory workers and field hands. The modern child's lunch kit, the form most sought by today's collector, began in the 1930s. Gender, Paeschke & Frey Co. of Milwaukee, Wisconsin, issued a No. 9100 Mickey Mouse lunch kit for the 1935 Christmas trade. An oval lunch kit of a streamlined train, marked "Decoware," dates from the same period.

Television brought the decorated lunch box into a golden age. Among the leading manufacturers are: Aladdin Company; Landers, Frary and Clark; Ohio Art (successor to Hibbard, Spencer, Bartlett & Co.) of Bryan, Ohio; Thermos/King Seeley; and Universal.

References: Larry Aikins, *Pictorial Price Guide To Metal Lunch Boxes & Thermoses,* L–W Book Sales, 1992, 1994 value update; Larry Aikins, *Pictorial Price Guide To Vinyl & Plastic Lunch Boxes & Thermoses,* L–W Book Sales, 1992; Scott Bruce, *The Fifties and Sixties Lunch Box,* Chronicle Books, 1988; Scott Bruce, *The Official Price Guide To Lunch Box Collectibles,* House of Collectibles, 1989; Philip R. Norman, *1993 Lunch Box & Thermos Price Guide,* published by author, 1992; Allen Woodall and Sean Brickell, *The Illustrated Encyclopedia of Metal Lunch Boxes,* Schiffer Publishing, 1992.

Collectors' Club: Step Into The Ring, 829 Jackson St. Ext., Sandusky, OH 44870.

Periodical: *Paileontologist's Report* PO Box 3255, Burbank, CA 91508.

Astronaut, dome, King–Seeley Thermos
   Co, 1963 .... **45.00**
Banana Splits, vinyl, King–Seeley
   Thermos Co,1970 .... **65.00**
Barbie and Midge, vinyl, King–Seeley
   Thermos Co,1964 .... **32.00**
Batman and Robin, Aladdin, 1967 ... **24.00**
Beatles
   Air Flite, vinyl, 1965 .... **125.00**
   Aladdin, 1966 .... **85.00**
Beverly Hillbillies, 1963 .... **59.00**
Bonanza, green, 1963 .... **110.00**
Bullwinkle, vinyl, King–Seeley Thermos
   Co, 1963 .... **60.00**
Bullwinkle & Rocky **85.00**
Cabbage Patch Kids **30.00**
Captain Kangaroo, vinyl, King–Seeley
   Thermos Co, 1964 .... **120.00**
Charlie's Angels Brunch Bag, vinyl,
   Aladdin, 1978 .... **35.00**
Daniel Boone, 1955 .... **85.00**
Davy Crockett, Indian Fighter, ADCO
   Liberty,1956 .... **43.00**
Disneyland, castle, Aladdin, 1958 .... **50.00**
Dukes of Hazzard **15.00**
Emergency, dome **100.00**
Fall Guy **22.00**
Flintstones, The, Aladdin, 1964 ...... **41.00**
Flintstones & Dino, The, Aladdin, 1963 **38.00**
Gentle Ben, 1968 .... **40.00**
Gomer Pyle, Aladdin, 1966 .... **53.00**
Green Hornet, The, King–Seeley
   Thermos Co, 1966 .... **75.00**
Grizzly Adams, dome **75.00**
Gunsmoke, Aladdin, 1960 .... **54.00**
Have Gun Will Travel, 1960 .... **60.00**
Hogan's Heroes, dome, Aladdin, 1966 **50.00**
Howdy Doody, ADCO Liberty, 1955 .. **90.00**
Huckleberry Hound and Friends **165.00**
James Bond 007, Aladdin, 1966 ..... **75.00**
Jetsons, dome, Aladdin, 1965 .... **125.00**
Jungle Book, 1966 .... **40.00**
Kiss, 1977 .... **35.00**
Lassie **38.00**
Little House on the Prairie **20.00**
Man From U.N.C.L.E., King–Seeley
   Thermos Co, 1966 .... **60.00**
Mary Poppins Brunch Bag, vinyl,
   Aladdin, 1967 .... **45.00**
Monkees, vinyl, King–Seeley Thermos
   Co,1967 .... **35.00**
Munsters, King–Seeley Thermos Co,
   1966 .... **45.00**
Partridge Family **75.00**
Pebbles & Bamm–Bamm, Aladdin,
   1972 .... **26.00**
Pink Panther, vinyl **75.00**
Porky Pig **150.00**
Road Runner, 1970–73 .... **30.00**
Roy Rogers & Dale Evans, American
   Thermos, 1953–54 .... **115.00**
Scooby Doo, 1973 .... **30.00**

Sleeping Beauty, vinyl, Aladdin, 1970 **75.00**
Snow White vinyl, Aladdin, 1975 .... **55.00**
Star Trek, dome, Aladdin, 1968 ...... **155.00**
Superman, King–Seeley Thermos Co,
   1967 .... **79.00**
Tom Corbett: Space Cadet, Aladdin,
   1952 .... **100.00**
Underdog, Okay Industries, 1974 .... **250.00**
Voyage to the Bottom of the Sea,
   Aladdin, 1967 .... **65.00**
Wild Wild West, Aladdin, 1969 ..... **50.00**
Yellow Submarine, King–Seeley Thermos
   Co, 1969 .... **125.00**
Zorro, Aladdin, 1966 .... **55.00**

MAGAZINE COVERS AND TEAR SHEETS

Collecting Hints: A good cover should show the artist's signature, have no mailing label or have it in a place that does not detract from the design element, and have edges which are crisp, but not trimmed.

When framing vintage paper use acid-free mat board and tape with a water-soluble glue base such as brown paper gum tape or linen tape. The tape should only be affixed to the back side of the illustration. The rule of thumb is don't do anything that can not be easily undone.

Do not hang framed vintage paper in direct sunlight, which causes fading, or in a highly humid area (such as a bathroom or above a kitchen sink), which causes wrinkles in both the mat and art work.

History: Magazine cover design attracted some of America's leading illustrators. Maxfield Parrish, Erte, Leyendecker, and Norman Rockwell were dominate forces in the 20th century. In the mid–1930s photographic covers gradually replaced the illustrated covers. One of the leaders in the industry was *Life*, which emphasized photojournalism.

Magazine covers are frequently collected by artist signed covers, subject matter, or historical events. Artist signed covers feature a commercially printed artist signature on the cover, or the artist is identified inside as "Cover by. . ." Most collected covers are in full color and show significant design elements. Black memorabilia is often reflected in magazine covers and tear sheets. It is frequently collected for the positive affect it has on African–Americans. However, sometimes it is a refl ection of the times in which it was printed and may represent subjects in an unfavorable light.

Many of America's leading artists also illustrated magazine advertising. The ads made advertising characters such as the Campbell Kids, the Dutch Girl, and Snap, Crackle and Pop world famous.

References: Patricia Kery, *Great Magazine Covers of The World,* Abbeyville Press, 1982; Norman E. Martinus and Harry L. Rinker, *Warman's Paper,* Wallace–Homestead, 1994; check local libraries for books about specific illustrators such as Parrish, Rockwell, and Jessie Wilcox Smith.

Periodicals: *PCM (Paper Collectors' Marketplace),* PO Box 128, Scandinavia, WI 54977; *The Illustrator Collector's News,* PO Box 1958, Sequim, WA 98392.

Note: Prices of covers and complete magazines have remained stable during the last few years, but those of tear sheets have declined as more and more magazines have glutted the market. While only a short time ago magazines were thrown away when attics and garages were cleaned, now they are offered for sale. The public has been educated by seeing many magazine tear sheets being offered for sale at flea markets and mall shows. Dealers prefer to purchase complete magazines and glean their profit from the contents.

As more and more magazines are destroyed for the tear sheets, complete magazines rise in value as the supply decreases. If a magazine is in mint condition, it should be left intact. We *do not* encourage removing illustrations from complete magazines. Only the complete magazine can act as a tool to interpret that specific historical time period. Editorial and advertising together define the spirit of the era.

Artist Signed
Armstrong, Rolf	**15.00**
Atkins, Alan	**6.00**
Benito, Edwardo	**20.00**
Cassandre, A M	**20.00**

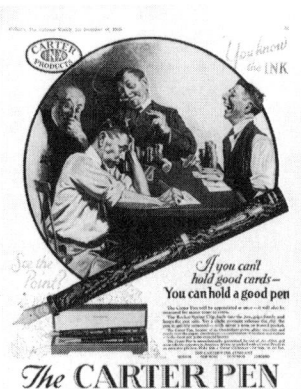

Carter Inx Products, *Collier's,* Dec. 18, 1926, sgd Sam Brown illustration, 10 x 13″, $12.00.

Christy, F Earl	**20.00**
Coffin, Haskell	**15.00**
Crane, S W	**8.00**
Davis, Marguerite	**6.00**
Drayton, Grace, Campbell's Soups, color, small kids	**2.75**
Drayton/Weiderseim, Campbell's Soups	
Black and white	**2.50**
Color, large kids	**6.00**
Eastman, Ruth	**6.00**
Fancher, Louis	**6.00**
Flagg, James Montgomery, black and white illus	**7.50**
Freed, Maurice	**4.00**
Giusti	**4.25**
Gunn, Archie	**8.50**
Hays, Mary A	**6.00**
Hoff, Guy	**9.00**
King, Hamilton	**9.00**
Leyendecker	**6.50**
McClelland, Barclay	**10.00**
O'Neill, Rose	
Illus stories, other than Kewpies	**5.00**
Jello, quarter page	**5.00**
Jello, full page, full color	**10.00**
Kewpie pages	**18.00**
Parrish, Maxfield, Jello	**20.00**
Penfield, Edward	**30.00**
Petruccelli	**8.00**
Sambrook, Russell	**4.25**
Sandberg, Valentine	**8.00**
Smith, Jessie Wilcox	
Early story illus	**10.00**
General	**6.00**
Stanlaws, Penny	**9.00**
Texidor	**4.25**
Willenborg, Lee	**2.00**
Wilson, John F	**5.00**
Wireman, Henry	**6.00**
Automobile	
Prior to 1918	
Black and white	**2.00**
Color	**4.00**
1919–1937	
Black and white	**2.00**
Color	**4.25**
1938–1941	
Black and white	**4.50**
Color	**5.50**
1942–1955	
Black and white	**3.00**
Color	**4.50**
1955–1975	
Black and white	**3.00**
Color	**4.25**
Any outstanding Art Nouveau or Art Deco Auto Ads, e.g. Cadillac produced ads with silver ink	**12.00**
Aviation	
Prior to 1935	
Black and white	**3.50**

Color	5.00
After 1935	
Black and white	3.00
Color	4.25
Named airlines with route maps	4.00
Beverage	
Beer	
Identified brand, color	4.25
No brand	3.00
Coca–Cola	
Prior to 1925	
Black and white	5.00
Color	8.00
1925–1950	
Black and white	3.00
Color	6.00
Featuring vending machine	8.00
Santas	12.00
Santas on National Geographic	6.00
Dr Pepper, early	10.00
Wines and Liquors	3.00
Black Memorabilia	
Cereal, Aunt Jemima	5.00
Stories of black history	4.25
Camera	
Prior to 1918	
Black and white	2.00
Color	4.25
Fashion	
Prior to 1930	
Black and white	2.00
Color	4.00
After 1930	
Black and white	3.00
Color	5.00
Food	
Candy, Lifesavers with children or animals	4.00
Cereal	
Cream of Wheat	8.00
Kelloggs, children by Leyendecker	8.00
Large image of product	2.00
Dairy products, milk, cheese, ice cream	3.00
Gum	
Adams Art Nouveau style	6.00
Other	3.00
Jello	
Animals or children	4.00
General, color	4.25
O'Neill, signed, with Kewpies, color	18.00
Parrish, signed	25.00
Meats	4.25
Soups, Campbell Kids	
Large images	8.00
Small images	4.25
Furniture	
Black and white	3.00
Color	4.25
Household Products	
Bon Ami, children	4.00

Victor Victrola, *The Delineator,* color litho, 9½ x 14½", 1916, $25.00.

Dutch Cleanser, full page, color	5.00
Others	3.00
Jewelry	
Black and white	3.00
Color	4.25
Movie Stars and Famous People	
Beatles	20.00
Bogart, Humphrey	10.00
Chaplin, Charlie	2.00
Fields, W C	7.50
Garbo, Greta	5.00
Kelly, Grace	6.00
Marx Brothers	5.00
Monroe, Marilyn	10.00
Wayne, John	5.00
West, Mae	8.00
Toys	
Bikes	4.25
Dolls	
Shirley Temple	4.00
Unknown	2.00
Erector Sets	4.25
Teddy Bears	6.00
Trains, Lionel and Ives	2.50
Wagons	2.00
Train, major railroad lines	
Black and white	3.00
Color	4.00
Color, route maps and large image trains	5.50

MAGAZINES

Collecting Hints: A rule of thumb for pricing general magazines without popular artist–designed covers is the more you would enjoy displaying a copy on your coffee table, the more elite the publication, and the more the advertising or editorial content relates to today's collectibles, the higher the price. *Life* magazine went into millions of homes each week, *Harper's Bazaar* and *Vogue* did not. Elite families had a greater tendency to discard last month's publication while middle–class families found the art on the *Saturday Evening Post* and *Collier's* irresistible and saved them. The greater the supply, the lower the price.

History: In the early 1700s general magazines were a major means of information for the reader. Literary magazines, such as *Harper's*, became popular in the 19th century. By 1900, the first photo–journal magazines appeared. *Life*, the prime example, was started by Henry Luce in 1932.

Magazines created for women featured "how to" articles about cooking, sewing, decorating, and child care. Many were entirely devoted to fashion and living a fashionable life, such as *Harper's Bazaar* and *Vogue*. Men's magazines were directed at masculine skills of the time, such as hunting, fishing, and woodworking, supplemented with appropriate "girlies" titles.

References: Alan Betrock, *The Illustrated Price Guide To Cult Magazines: 1945–1969,* Shake Books, 1995; Alan Betrock, *Unseen America: The Greatest Cult Exploitation Magazines 1950–1966,* Shake Book, 1990; Jack Bramble, *The Playboy Collectors Guide & Price List, 5th Edition,* Budget Enterprises, 1982; David K. Henkel, *Magazines: Identification and Price Guide,* Avon Books, 1993; Marjorie M. Donald L. Hinds, *Magazine Magic,* The Messenger Book Press, 1972; Denis C. Jackson, *Men's 'Girlie" Magazines: The Only Price Guide: Newstanders, Third Edition,* published by author, 1991; Denis C. Jackson, *The Master's Price & Identification Guide to Old Magazines,* TICN, 1992; Norman E. Martinus and Harry L. Rinker, *Warman's Paper,* Wallace–Homestead, 1994; *1994 Playboy Magazine Price Guide,* Playboy Collectors Assoc., 1994; *Old Magazine Price Guide,* L–W Book Sales, 1994; Lee Server, *Danger Is My Business: An Illustrated History Of The Fabulous Pulp Magazines: 1896–1953,* Chronicle Books, 1993; Gene Utz, *Collecting Paper: A Collector's Identification & Value Guide,* Books Americana, 1993.

Periodicals: *Collecting Cult Magazines,* 449 12th St., #2-R, Brooklyn, NY 11215; *PCM (Paper Collectors' Marketplace),* PO Box 128, Scandinavia, WI 54977; *The Illustrator Collector's News,* PO Box 1958, Sequim, WA 98392.

Note: The prices for general magazines are retail prices. They may be considerably higher than what would be offered for an entire collection filling your basement or garage. Bulk prices for common magazines such as *Life, Collier's,* and *Saturday Evening Post* are generally from fifty cents to one dollar per issue. Dealers have to

sort, protect with plastic covering, discard ones that have items clipped from the interior or have marred covers, and make no money on those which they never sell. The end result is that a lower price is paid for magazines purchased in bulk.

The American Magazine, Dec. 1923, Earl Christy cover illus, 8½ x 11½", $12.00.

American Artist, April, 1960	5.00
American Golfer, Dec, 1932	10.00
American Motorist, 1916	8.50
American Racing Guide, 1940	18.00
American Wool and Cotton Reporter, Boston, MA, 1940	20.00
Antiques, Oct, 1931	7.50
Architectural Record	10.00
Arizona Highways	
1952–55, single issue	5.50
1970s, single issue	2.50
Art and Beauty, 1926	4.00
Atlantic Monthly, Nov, 1907, anniversary edition	18.00
Aviation, 1928	15.00
Ballyhoo, Aug, 1932, 48 pages	20.00
Barnum & Bailey Circus, 1909, 30 pgs	20.00
Better Homes and Gardens, 1930	12.00
Better Photo, 1913	2.50
Black Cat Magazine	10.00
Bonanza, Vol #1, 1965	25.00
Boys' Life, 1916, Rockwell cover	25.00
Breed's Gazette, The, April, 1885	6.50
Building Age National Builder, 1920s	5.00
Carpenter Magazine, 1916, 60 pgs	2.00
Century, 1885	3.50
Children's Play Mate, Sept, 1953	5.00
Child's Life, 1930	3.00
Coast Magazine, Seattle, 1900	10.00
Collier's, June 9, 1938	7.00
Connoisseur, 1907	12.00
Cosmopolitan, 1907	5.00

Children's Play Mate, **April, 1943, Fern Bisel Peat cover, Betty Bunny paper doll, 6" w, 9" h, $5.00.**

Country Gentleman, 1914, Leyendecker cover	20.00
Country Life	.75
Delineator, 1902	20.00
Demorist Fashion, Sept, 1876	10.00
Designer, The, 1900–04, color fashion plates	20.00
Ellery Queen Mystery Magazine, 1950s	5.00
Esquire, Sept, 1934	12.00
Etudes, 1940s	2.00
Farm and Fireside, 1920	4.00
Farmer's Wife Magazine, June, 1936 ..	2.00
Farm Journal, April, 1936	1.50
Farm Mechanics, mid 1920s	8.00
Girl's Companion, 1941	1.00
Golf Illustrated, Sept, 1934	10.00
Good Housekeeping, 1950	2.00
Harvest World, 1931	2.50
Highway Traveler, Greyhound, 1936 ..	2.50
Hobbies, August, 1942	2.00
Hollywood Dream Girl, 1955, 1st issue, 13 pgs of Marilyn Monroe photos ..	30.00
Home Needlework, 1910	12.00
Hounds & Hunting, 1922	4.00
Jack & Jill, 1960, Howdy Doody cover	12.00
Ladies Home Journal, 1917	4.00
Laff, Aug, 1946, Marilyn Monroe on cover, listed as Jean Norman	75.00
Literary Digest, June 24, 1922, Norman Rockwell cover	3.00
Living Church, The, 1924	1.00
London Mystery Magazine, 1950	5.00
Look, Nov 17, 1964, John F Kennedy memorial issue	20.00
Mattel Barbie Magazine, Nov–Dec, 1963	5.00
McCall's, 1925	15.00
Mechanics' Arts, 1989	2.50
Motion Picture Story, 1912	30.00

Motor, Jan, 1927	50.00
Motorcycling & Bicycling, 1920	25.00
Movie Star Parade, Jan, 1947	22.00
National Geographic, June, 1926	3.00
National Observer, Dec, 1968	1.00
Naturo–Post, German, health magazine, 1904	2.50
Needlecraft, 1927	3.00
New England Home, 1898	2.00
New Idea Woman's Magazine, 1902 ..	20.00
New Yorker, 1948	2.50
Outdoor Life, 1932	4.00
Physical Culture, 1917	2.00
Pictorial Review, March, 1915	12.50
Playboy, January 1969, 15th Anniversary Issue, stiff paper covers	100.00
Playmate, 1940s, center uncut paper dolls, Fern Bissel Peat cover	5.00
Popular Mechanics, 1952	1.50
Popular Songs, 1930s	2.00
Prairie Farmer, Feb, 1867	4.00
Radford's American Builder, 1920s ...	6.00
Redbook, April, 1925	5.00
St Nicholas, 1928	7.00
Saturday Evening Post	
1922, New Year's Eve, Leyendecker cover	20.00
1923	
Pearl Harbor	10.00
Rockwell cover	25.00
1936, Springtime, Norman Rockwell	7.50
1938, Christmas, Leyendecker	5.00
1952, Norman Rockwell	4.00
Scientific American, June, 1933	3.50
Screenland, 1939	10.00
Screen Romances, Feb, 1940, Shirley Temple cover	15.00
Spinning Wheel, July, 1960	30.00
Sport, Stan Musial cover, 1950	30.00
Stage, June 1936, WC Fields cover ...	10.00
Stage and Screen, 1926	4.50
Sunbathing for Health, Dec, 1951	2.50
Through The Ages, National Assoc of Marble Dealers, Baltimore, MD, 1929, 70 pages, 8¼ x 11"	10.00
Time	
1939	1.00
1940, Mickey Rooney	10.00
Tip Top Weekly, 1904	9.00
Tobacco World, 1902	8.00
Town and Country, July, 1948, Dali cover, poppy, cornflower, and wheat	35.00
Travel, 1915, Santa cover, Murad	25.00
TV Star Parade, 1961	10.00
Vogue, March, 1935	12.00
Wild West Weekly, 1915	7.00
Woman's Home Companion	
1915	15.00
1916	20.00
1917, Betty Bonnett	25.00
1925	20.00
Woman's World, Feb, 1936	1.50

Working Craftsman, The, winter, 1977   **4.00**
World Today, The, 1909 . . . .   **4.00**
Youth's Companion, bound year, 1908   **125.00**

MARBLES

Collecting Hints: Hand–made glass marbles usually command higher prices than machine–made glass, clay, or mineral marbles. There are a few notable exceptions, e.g., machine–made comic strip marbles were made for a limited time only and are highly prized by collectors. Care must be taken in purchasing this particular type since the comic figure was stenciled on the marble. A layer of glass was to be overlaid on the stencil. However, many examples exist that were not overlaid, and the stencils rub or wear off.

Some of the rarer examples of hand–made marbles are Clambroth, Lutz, Indian Swirls, Peppermint Swirls, and Sulphides. Marble values are normally determined by their type, size, and condition. Usually, the larger the marble, the more valuable it is within each type.

A marble in mint condition is unmarred and has the best possible condition with a clear surface. It may have surface abrasions from rubbing in its original package. A marble in good condition may have a few small surface dings, scratches, and slight surface cloudiness. However, the core must be easily seen, and the marble must be without large chips or fractures.

History: Marbles date back to ancient Greece, Rome, Egypt, and other early civilizations. In England, Good Friday is known as "Marbles Day" because the game was considered a respectable and quiet pastime for the hallowed day.

During the American Civil War, soldiers carried marbles and a small board to play "solitaire," a game whose object was to jump the marbles until only one is left in the center of the board.

In the last few generations, school children have identified marbles as peewees, shooters, commies, and cat's eyes. A National Marbles Tournament has been held each year, beginning in 1922, in June. Wildwood, New Jersey, is its current site.

References: Paul Baumann, *Collecting Antique Marbles, Second Edition* Wallace–Homestead, 1991; Jeff Carskadden and Richard Gartley, *Chinas: Hand–Painted Marbles of the late 19th Century,* Muskingum Valley Archaeological Society, 1990; Everett Grist, *Antique and Collectible Marbles, Identification and Values, Third Edition,* Collector Books, 1992; Everett Grist, *Everett Grist's Big Book of Marbles,* Collector Books, 1993, 1995 value update; Everett Grist, *Everett Grist's Machine Made and Contemporary*

Marbles, Second Edition, Collector Books, 1995; Marble Collectors Society of America, *Identification and Price Guide,* published by author, 1989; Mark E. Randall, *Marbles As Historical Artifacts,* Marble Collectors Society; Dennis Webb, *Greenberg's Guide to Marbles,* Greenberg Publishing, 1994.

Collectors' Clubs: Buckeye Marble Collectors Club, 437 Meadowbrook Dr., Newark, OH 43055; Marble Collectors Unlimited, PO Box 206, Northboro, MA 01532; Marble Collectors Society of America, PO Box 222, Trumbull, CT 06661; National Marble Club of America, 440 Eaton Road, Drexel Hill, PA 19026; Southern California Marble Club, 18361-1 Strathern St., Reseda, CA 91335.

Museums: Corning Museum of Glass, Corning, NY; Sandwich Glass Museum, Sandwich, MA; Smithsonian Institution, Museum of Natural History, Washington, DC; Wheaton Village Museum, Millville, NJ.

Videotape: Elliot Pincus, *Marble World: Video Magazine Issue #1,* Elliot's Marbles, 1994.

Advisors: Stanley A. Block and Robert S. Block.

REPRODUCTION ALERT: Comic marbles are being reproduced.

Note: Prices listed below for handmade marbles are for common examples in mint condition. Unusual examples command prices of 2 to 20 times higher. Prices listed below for machine made marbles are for examples in mint condition, and are $9/16''$ to $11/16''$ diameter unless noted.

HAND MADE MARBLES

End of Day

Onionskin
    3/4'' **35.00**
    1½'' **200.00**
    1¾'' **275.00**
    2'' **300.00**

Lutz

Banded
    5/8'' **100.00**
    3/4'' **150.00**
    1'' **250.00**
    1½'' **300.00**
    1¾'' **450.00**
End of Day Onionskin
    5/8'' **225.00**
    3/4'' **300.00**
    1'' **750.00**
    1½'' **1,750.00**
Ribbon
    5/8'' **300.00**
    3/4'' **400.00**

1″	800.00
1½″	1,500.00

Mica

5/8″	10.00
3/4″	25.00
1″	100.00
1½″	200.00

Other

Benningtons	1.00
Clays	.10
Glazed painted china	10.00
Unglazed painted china	5.00

Sulphide

7/8	200.00
1¼″	125.00
1½″	100.00
2″	125.00

Swirls

Banded
5/8″	10.00
3/4″	15.00
1″	65.00
1½″	140.00

Divided core
3/4″	18.00
1½″	90.00
1¾″	150.00
2″	225.00

Indian
5/8″	75.00
3/4″	125.00
1″	300.00
1½″	1,500.00

Latticinio core
3/4″	15.00
1½″	75.00
1¾″	125.00
2″	200.00

Peppermint
5/8″	65.00
3/4″	125.00

Swirl, core, yellow and white, multicolor core, 1⅝″ d, $48.00.

1″	300.00
1½″	1,500.00

Ribbon core
3/4″	75.00
1½″	200.00
1¾″	300.00
2″	500.00

Solid core
3/4″	25.00
1½″	125.00
1¾″	250.00
2″	300.00

MACHINE MADE MARBLES

Akro Agate Company

Blue oxblood	55.00
Carnelian agate	8.00
Egg Yolk or Carnelian oxblood	80.00
Helmet Patch	2.50
Lemonade corkscrew	10.00
Lemonade oxblood	45.00
Limeade corkscrew	18.00
Limeade oxblood	125.00
Metallic Stripe	12.00
Milky oxblood	12.00
Moonstone	8.00
Patch oxblood	5.00

Popeye corkscrew
Blue/yellow	25.00
Green/yellow	12.00
Purple/yellow	45.00
Red/blue	60.00
Red/green	18.00
Red/yellow	12.00
Silver oxblood	18.00
Slag	1.00
Sparkler	30.00
Swirl oxblood	20.00

Two color
Opaque corkscrew
Color matrix	4.00
White matrix	2.00
Transparent or translucent corkscrew	6.00

Christensen Agate Company

American Agate or Bloodie	35.00
Cobra/Cyclone	750.00
Electric Swirl	50.00

Flame Swirl
Two color	50.00
Three color	150.00
Guinea	350.00
Slag	20.00

Christensen, M. F. & Son Company

Brick, 9¹⁄₁₆ to ¹¹⁄₁₆″	60.00
Oxblood Slag	100.00
Slag	5.00

Marble King Company

Multi color opaque
Color Matrix

Bumblebee/Yellow Jacket (yellow/black)	1.50
Cub Scout (yellow/blue)	5.00
Girl Scout/John Deere (yellow/green)	6.00
Spiderman (blue/red)	150.00
Tiger (orange/black)	12.00
Wasp (red/black)	5.00
Watermelon (red/green)	250.00
White matrix	.25
Two color opaque, white matrix	.10

Master Marble Company

Patch	1.00
Sunburst	
Clear	10.00
Opaque	3.00

Other And Unidentifiable Manufacturers

Bullet mold	15.00
Clearie, Catseye, or Chinese Checker	.01
Common patch or swirl	.25
Ravenswood multicolor	10.00
Wire Pull	
New	5.00
Old	10.00

Peltier Glass Company

Peerless Patch	2.00
Peerless Patch with aventurine	12.00
Slag	10.00
Sunset, Champion Jr, Muddy, Acme Reeler, Rainbo (new type), Tri–color, 7–Up, Banana	1.00
Two color Rainbo, old type	12.00
Two color Rainbo, old type, with aventurine	25.00
Three color Rainbo	
With aventurine	125.00
Xmas Tree, Patriot, Rebel, Ketchup, and Mustard	75.00

Transitional

Creased or pinched pontil transition	10.00
Folded pontil transition	25.00
Melted pontil transition	35.00
Regular, ground, or pinpoint pontil transitional	75.00

Vitro Agate/Gladding-Vitro Company

All–Red	.25
Blackie	.50

Conqueror	1.00
Hybrid catseye	2.00
Oxblood patch	7.50
Patch and Brush Transparent	.10
Patch and Ribbon Transparent	.10
Victory	2.00

MATCHCOVERS

Collecting Hints: Matchcovers generally had large production runs; very few are considered rare. Most collectors remove the matches, flatten the covers, and mount them in albums by category. They prefer the covers to be unused.

Trading is the principal means of exchange among collectors, usually on a one for one basis. At flea markets and shows matchcovers frequently are seen marked for $1.00 to $5.00 for categories such as beer covers or pin–up art (girlies) covers. Actually these purchasers are best advised to join one of the collector clubs and get involved in swapping.

History: The book match was invented by Joshua Pusey, a Philadelphia lawyer, who also was a chemist in his spare time. In 1892 Pusey put 10 cardboard matches into a cover of plain white board. Two hundred were sold to the Mendelson Opera Company who, in turn, hand–printed messages on the front.

The first machine-made matchbook was made by the Binghamton Match Company, Binghamton, New York, for the Piso Company of Warren, Pennsylvania. The only surviving cover is now owned by the Diamond Match Company.

Few covers survive from the late 1890s–1930s period. The modern craze for collecting matchcovers was started by a set of ten covers issued for the Century of Progress exhibit at the 1933 Chicago World's Fair.

The Golden Age of matchcovers was the mid–1940s through the early 1960s, when the covers were a popular advertising medium. Principal manufacturers included Atlas Match, Brown and Bigelow, Crown Match, Diamond Match, Lion Match, Ohio Match and Universal Match.

The arrival of throw–away lighters, such as BiC, brought an end to the matchcover era. Manufacturing costs for a matchbook today can range from below a cent to seven or eight cents for a special die–cut cover. As a result, matchcovers no longer are an attractive "free" give–away item.

Because of this, many of the older, more desirable covers are seeing a marked increase in value. Collectors have also turned to the small pocket type boxes as a way of enhancing and building their collections.

References: Yosh Kashiwabara, *Matchbook Art,* Chronicle Books, 1989; Norman E. Martinus and Harry L. Rinker, *Warman's Paper,* Wallace–Homestead, 1994; Bill Retskin, *The Matchcover Collector's Price Guide,* World Comm, 1993; Bill Retskin, *The Matchcover Collectors Resource Book and Price Guide,* published by author, 1988; H. Thomas Steele, Jim Heimann, Rod Dyer, *Close Cover Before Striking, The Golden Age of Matchbook Art,* Abbeville Press, 1987.

Periodicals: *Matchcover Classified,* 16425 Dam Rd. #3, Clearlake, CA 95422; *The Match Hunter,* 740 Poplar, Boulder, CO 80304.

Collectors' Clubs: Liberty Bell Matchcover Club, 5001 Albridge Way, Mount Laurel, NJ 08054; Long Beach Matchcover Club, 2501 W. Sunflower H–5, Santa Ana, CA 92704; Newmoon Matchbox & Label Club, 425 E. 51st St., New York, NY 10022; Rathkamp Matchcover Society, 1359 Surrey Road, Vandalia, OH 43577; The American Matchcover Collecting Club, 16 Forest View Dr., Asheville, NC 28804; Trans–Canada Matchcover Club, PO Box 219, Caledonia, Ontario, Canada NOA–1A0; Windy City Matchcover Club, 3104 Fargo Ave., Chicago, IL 60645; There are 33 regional clubs throughout the United States and Canada.

Advisor: Wray Martin.

SPECIAL COVERS

Air Force One	**5.00**
Charles Lindbergh, photo on front	**500.00**
Dwight D Eisenhower, 5 Star General	**15.00**
Economy Blue Print, girlies, set of 6, 1950s	**45.00**
General Douglas MacArthur, I Shall Return	
Box	**30.00**
Cover	**100.00**
Joe Louis and Max Schmeling championship fight, giant	**25.00**
President Kennedy, White House cover	**5.00**
Presidential Helicopter, "Marine One"	**10.00**
Pull for Willkie, pull quick match	**28.00**
Stoeckle Select Beer, Stoeckle Brewery, giant	**6.00**
Washington Redskins, pictures on back, set of 20	**40.00**

TOPICS

Americana	.05
American Ace, boxes	.12
Atlas, four color	.05
Banks	.10
Beer and Brewery	.75
Best Western	
Non Stock design	.15
Stock design	.10

French Casino, Chicago, Lion Match Co., Chicago, Giant Feature Match Books, $1.75.

Bowling Alleys	.05
Cameo's, Universal trademark	.10
Canadian, four color	.10
Casinos	.05
CCC Camps	**1.00**
Chinese Restaurants	.05
Christmas	.10
Classiques	.50
Coca–Cola	**1.00**
Colleges	.20
Contours (diecut)	.20
Conventions	.10
Country Clubs	.10
County Seats	.05
Credit Unions	.10
Crown Match	.75
Dated	.10
Diamond Quality	**1.00**
Easel Backs	.20
Elks	.10
Fairs	.10
Features	.50
Federal Match	.75
Foilites, Universal trademark	.05
Foreign	.05
Fraternal	.05
Giants	**1.00**
Girlies	
Non Stock design	.50
Stock design	.15
Group One	
Movies, old	**1.00**
Non–advertising, new	.03
Non–advertising, old	.50
Sports, old	**2.00**
Hillbillies	.05
Hilton Hotels	.15
Holiday Inns	
Non Stock design	.15
Stock design	.10
Indians	.25

Jewelites	.05
Jewels	.05
Knot Holes	.20
Matchorama's, Universal trademark . .	.08
Matchtones, Universal trademark	.10
Midgets	.75
Navy Ships	.30
Odd Strikers	.25
Patriotic	.05
Pearltone	.05
Personalities	1.00
Political	1.50
Pull Quick	1.00
Radio and TV	.05
Railroads	.25
Rainbows, Universal trademark	.10
Restaurants	.05
Savings and Loan	.10
Service	
New	.05
Old	.15
Shiplines	.10
Signets, Universal trademark	.05
Small Towns	.05
Soft Drinks	.75
Souvenir	.20
Sports	
New	.15
Old	1.00
Ten Strikes	.05
Transportation	.15
Travelodges	.05
Truck Lines	.10
Trust Companies	.10
Whiskey	.30

McCOY POTTERY

Collecting Hint: Several marks were used by the McCoy Pottery Co. Take time to learn the marks and the variations. Pieces can often be dated by the mark used.

History: The J. W. McCoy Pottery Co. was established in Roseville, Ohio, in September, 1899. The early McCoy Company produced both stoneware and some art lines, including Rosewood. In October 1911, three potteries in the Roseville area merged, creating the Brush-McCoy Pottery Co. This company continued to produce the original McCoy lines and added several new art lines. Much of the early pottery is not marked.

In 1910, Nelson McCoy and his father, J. W. McCoy, founded the Nelson McCoy Sanitary Stoneware Co. In 1925, the McCoy family sold their interest in the Brush-McCoy Pottery Co. and started to expand and improve the Nelson McCoy Company. The new company produced stoneware, earthenware specialties and artware.

Most of the pottery marked "McCoy" was made by the Nelson McCoy Co.

References: Sharon and Bob Huxford, *The Collectors Encyclopedia of McCoy Pottery*, Collector Books, 1980, 1995 value update; Harold Nichols, *McCoy Cookie Jars: From The First To The Last*, Second Edition, Nichols Publishing, 1991; Martha and Steve Sanford, *The Guide To Brush–McCoy Pottery*, published by authors, 1992.

Periodical: *Our McCoy Matters*, PO Box 14255, Parkville, MO 64152.

REPRODUCTION ALERT: The Nelson McCoy Pottery Co. is currently producing reproductions of their original work. This may add to the confusion about this company's products and will probably affect prices.

Bank	
Clown, TV	25.00
Eagle	35.00
Metz Beer, large	55.00
Pig	40.00
Sailor, "Seaman's Bank for Savings"	38.00
Basket, hanging, white matte glaze . . .	18.00
Bean Pot, cov, brown	8.00
Bookends, pr	
Horse	200.00
Lily	55.00
Bud Vase, lily	40.00
Cookie Jar	
Asparagus	50.00
Bamboo	60.00
Basket of Eggs	65.00
Bobby Baker	45.00
Cabin	50.00
Clown Bust	40.00
Coffee Mug	40.00
Coke Can	155.00
Cookie Kettle	22.00
Covered Wagon	85.00
Crayon Kids	95.00
Cylinder	25.00
Dalmatians in Rocking Chair	400.00
Football Boy	215.00
Forbidden Fruit	65.00
Grandfather's Clock	50.00
Granny	47.00
Keebler Tree	50.00
Kissing Penguins	600.00
Lunch Box	75.00
Mammy	175.00
Milk Can	25.00
Modern Pineapple	155.00
Mr and Mrs Owl	80.00
Oaken Bucket	35.00
Owl, brown	60.00
Panda	45.00
Sad Clown, chipped	65.00
Squirrel	90.00

Tepee, orig price tag	275.00
Winking Pig	325.00
Yosemite Sam	150.00
Cornucopia, Bittersweet, double, 4½ x 11½"	18.00
Creamer, water lily	25.00
Cuspidor, grape, brown glaze	30.00

Decanter

Apollo Missile	30.00
Astronaut	45.00
Jupiter Engine	45.00
Jupiter Train, 4 pcs	200.00
Pierce Arrow Sport Phantom	48.00
Fern Box, blue	14.00

Figure

Dog, face in dish	40.00
Duck with Umbrella	87.00
Lamb, white	20.00
Panther, stalking, black	50.00
Scottie Dog and Cat, pr	40.00

Flower Bowl

Cascade, purple and lavender	45.00
Grapes	35.00

Jardiniere

Blue, 7" h	38.00
Green, Springwood, 6" h, 7" d	15.00
Turquoise, glossy, large	60.00
White, Springwood, 8½" h, 10½" d	20.00
Lamp, cowboy boots, small, orig shade, new wire and socket	100.00

Pitcher

Butterfly pattern, blue, 10" h	95.00
Round, rose colored, large	11.00

Planter

Baby Birds, green	20.00
Bird Dog	125.00
Bittersweet, pedestal, 8" h, 5½" l	15.00

Planter, bust of Uncle Sam, green, 7¼" h, $30.00.

Calypso, boat	110.00
Cowboy Boots, black, decorated	55.00
Mum	72.00
Quail	27.00
Spinning Wheel, dog and cat	22.00
Springwood, white, ftd, 3½" h, 6½" d	12.00
Planting Dish, bud	35.00
Serve–All, El Rancho, orig box	395.00
Sprinkler, turtle	45.00

Strawberry Jar, stoneware, early J.W. McCoy, blue	24.00
Tankard, six matching mugs, grape	200.00

Tea Set

Daisy	55.00
Pine Cone	55.00
Television Lamp, daisy, green	25.00
Urn, Onyx, Nelson McCoy	48.00

Vase

Blue, double footed, 10" h, 1½" hairline	55.00
Butterfly, 6" h	40.00
Cowboy Boots, rustic glaze	37.00
Feather, burgundy	75.00
Grape, #4, 1951	45.00
Onyx, Nelson McCoy	32.00
Orange Swirl Crystalline, 6" h, price for pair	35.00

Springwood

Green, 7½" h, 4½" sq top	15.00
Pink, 10½" h, 6½" d	18.00
Swan, green, #7, 9" h	38.00

Wall Pocket

Apple	28.00
Grape Leaf	32.50
Leaf, pink and blue	30.00
Mailbox	45.00
Orange	28.00
Pear	28.00
Sunflower, rustic orange	18.00
Umbrella, green	45.00

McKEE GLASS

Collecting Hint: McKee Glass was mass produced in most colors. Therefore, a collector should avoid chipped or damaged pieces.

History: The McKee Glass Company was established in 1843 in Pittsburgh, Pennsylvania. In 1852 they opened a factory to produce pressed glass. In 1888, the factory relocated in Jeannette, Pennsylvania, and began to produce many types of kitchenwares. The factory was among several located there to make Depression–era wares. The factory continued until 1951 when it was sold to the Thatcher Manufacturing Co.

The McKee Glass Company produced many types of glass including glass window panes, tumblers, tablewares, Depression glass, milk glass, and bar and utility objects.

McKee named its colors Chalaine Blue, Custard, Seville Yellow, and Skokie Green. They preferred Skokie Green to jadite, which was popular with other manufacturers at the time. McKee also made several patterns on these opaque colors, including dots of red, green, and black and red ships. A few items were decaled. Most of the canisters and shakers were lettered in black to denote their purpose.

References: Gene Florence, *Kitchen Glassware of the Depression Years, Fifth Edition,* Collector Books, 1995; M'Kee and Brothers, *M'Kee Victorian Glass,* Dover Publications, 1871, Reprint 1981; Ellen Tischbein Schroy, *Warman's Glass, Second Edition* Wallace–Homestead, 1995.

KITCHEN WARE

Batter Bowl, 7″ d, Seville Yellow	24.00
Bowl	
4¼″ d, Seville Yellow	14.00
4¾″ d, Art Deco, black, ftd	15.00
7″ d, custard	15.00
Canister, cov	
Cereal, custard, round	50.00
Coffee, Skokie Green, sq	165.00
Sugar, Skokie Green, sq	165.00
Casserole, cov, 10½″ l, pearl finish . . .	50.00
Cheese Dish, cov, Laurel, French Ivory	36.00
Compote, Autumn, oval, ftd, Skokie green	42.00
Custard Cup, Skokie Green	5.00
Drawer Pull, Chalaine blue, medium size, price for pair	25.00
Drip Jar, cov, spout, 3½″ h, custard . . .	18.00
Egg Cup	
French Ivory	5.00
Skokie Green, 4¼″ h, ftd	12.00
Flour Shaker, Skokie Green, sq	32.00
Grease Jar, cov, Vitrock, red, black trim	13.00
Measuring Pitcher	
Four Cup, Skokie Green	60.00
Two Cup, Skokie Green	40.00
Mixing Bowl	
8″ d	
Custard	22.00
White, red ship dec	18.00
9¼″ d, Seville Yellow	35.00
Refrigerator Dish, cov	
3″ sq, fired on blue, clear lid	10.00
4 x 5″	
Custard	20.00
Seville Yellow	18.00
8 x 5″	
Clear	16.00
Skokie Green	22.00
White, red ship dec	18.00
Rolling Pin, custard	275.00
Salt and Pepper Shakers, pr, Roman Arch, black	28.00
Tom and Jerry	
Bowl, custard	50.00
Mug, custard	14.00
Towel Bar, Skokie Green	25.00
Tumbler, ftd, 4¼″ h, Skokie Green	12.00
Water Cooler Set, two bottles, vaseline, orig carton	350.00

STEM WARE

Champagne, Eureka pattern, heavy brilliant flint	85.00

Candy Dish, orange body, gold trim, gold finial, clear base, 7¾″ h, $22.50.

Cordial, Rock Crystal, 1 oz	24.00
Goblet	
French Ivory	30.00
Gothic, flint	37.50
Puritan, pink stem	25.00
Queen, amber	25.00
Rock Crystal	20.00
Iced Tea Tumbler, Rock Crystal, 12 oz, red	65.00
Sherbet	
Flower Band, green	7.00
Laurel, Skokie Green	12.00
Tumbler, Strigil	20.00
Whiskey Tumbler, Rock Crystal	19.00
Wine	
Colonial, green	40.00
Queen	30.00
Rock Crystal	40.00

METLOX POTTERY

Collecting Hints: The choices of patterns and backstamps is overwhelming. Collectors should concentrate on one specific line and pattern. Among the most popular Poppytrail patterns are California Ivy, Homestead Provincial, and Red Rooster.

The recent cookie jar craze has attracted a number of collectors to Metlox's cookie jar line. Most examples sell within a narrow range. The Little Red Riding Hood jar is an exception, often selling at two to three times the price of other cookie jars.

History: In 1921 T. C. Prouty and Willis, his son, founded Proutyline Products, a company designed to develop Prouty's various inventions. In 1922 Prouty built a tile plant in Hermosa Beach, California, to manufacture decorative and standard wall and floor tiles.

Metlox (a contraction of metallic oxide) was established in 1927. Prouty built a modern all-steel factory in Manhattan Beach, California, to manufacture outdoor ceramic signs. The Depression impacted strongly on the sign business. When T. C. Prouty died in 1931, Willis re-organized the company and began to produce a line of solid color dinnerware similar to that produced by Bauer. In 1934 the line was fully developed and sold under the Poppytrail trademark. The poppy is the official state flower for California. Fifteen different colors were produced over an eight-year period.

Other dinnerware lines produced in the 1930s include Mission Bell, sold exclusively by Sears & Roebuck, Pintoria, based on an English Staffordshire line, and Yorkshire, patterned after Gladding–McBean's Coronado line. Most of these lines did not survive World War II.

In the late 1930s Metlox employed the services of Carl Romanelli, a designer whose work appeared as figurines, miniatures, and Zodiac vases. A line called Modern Masterpieces featured bookends, busts, figural vases, figures, and wall pockets.

During World War II Metlox devoted its manufacturing efforts to the production of machine parts and parts for the B–25 bombers. When the war ended, Metlox returned its attention to the production of dinnerware.

In 1947 Evan K. Shaw, whose American Pottery in Los Angeles had been destroyed by fire, purchased Metlox. Dinnerware production with hand-painted patterns accelerated. The California Ivy pattern was introduced in 1946, California Provincial and Homestead Provincial in 1950, Red Rooster in 1955, California Strawberry in 1961, Sculptured Grape in 1963, and Della Robbia in 1965. Bob Allen and Mel Shaw, art directors, introduced a number of new shapes and lines in the 1950s among which are Aztec, California Contempora, California Free Form, California Mobile, and Navajo.

When Vernon Kilns ceased operation in 1958, Metlox bought the trade name and select dinnerware molds. A separate Vernon Ware branch was established. Under the direction of Doug Bothwell, the line soon rivaled the Poppytrail patterns.

Artware continued to flourish in the 1950s and 1960s. Harrison McIntosh was among the key designers. Two popular lines were American Royal Horses and Nostalgia, scale model antique carriages. Between 1946 and 1956 Metlox made a series of ceramic cartoon characters under license from Walt Disney.

A line of planters designed by Helen Slater and Poppets, doll–like stoneware flower holders, were marketed in the 1960s and 1970s. Recent production includes novelty cookie jars and Colorstax, a revival solid color dinnerware pattern.

Management remained in the Shaw family. Evan K. was joined by his two children, Ken and Melinda. Kenneth Avery, Melinda's husband, eventually became plant manager. When Evan K. died in 1980, Kenneth Avery became president. In 1988 Melinda Avery became the guid-ing force. The company ceased operations in 1989.

References: Susan and Al Bagdade, *Warman's American Pottery and Porcelain,* Wallace–Homestead, 1994; Jack Chipman, *Collector's Encyclopedia of California Pottery,* Collector Books, 1992, 1995 value update; Harvey Duke, *The Official Identification and Price Guide to Pottery and Porcelain, Eighth Edition,* House of Collectibles, 1995; Carl Gibbs, Jr., *Collector's Encyclopedia of Metlox Potteries,* Collector Books, 1995; Lois Lehner, *Lehner's Encyclopedia of U. S. Marks on Pottery, Porcelain & Clay,* Collector Books, 1988.

California Aztec	
Berry Bowl	**5.00**
Cereal Bowl	**10.00**
Cup	**15.00**
Gravy Boat	**15.00**
Plate, 6″ d	**8.00**
Vegetable Dish, twin	**45.00**
California Ivy	
Creamer and Sugar, cov	**15.00**
Cup and Saucer	**8.50**
Plate	
10¼″ d, dinner	**11.00**
13″ d	**28.00**
Platter, 13″ l, oval	**24.00**
Sugar, cov	**15.00**
Vegetable Bowl, 9″ d	**24.00**
California Provincial	
Berry Bowl	**12.00**
Bread Tray	**50.00**
Candlesticks, pr	**80.00**
Coaster	**20.00**
Mug	**35.00**
Plate	
6″ d, bread and butter	**4.00**
8″ d, salad	**8.00**
10″ d, dinner	**12.00**
12″ d, chop	**18.00**
Platter, 13½″ l	**25.00**
Salt and Pepper Shakers, pr	**25.00**
Soup	
Flat	**10.00**
Lug	**20.00**
Stein	**50.00**
Teapot	**95.00**
Candy Jar, cov, eggplant	**125.00**
Cookie Jars	
Calf Head, crier	**375.00**
Clown	
Black and White	**245.00**
Yellow	**95.00**
Cow	
Purple, white daisies	**395.00**
Yellow	**250.00**
Drum, underglaze	**225.00**
Francine Duck	**225.00**
Humpty Dumpty	**250.00**
Lamb, lying down	**475.00**
Mammy	**550.00**

Mother Goose	250.00
Noah's Ark	150.00
Panda Bear	95.00
Parrot	295.00
Penguin	95.00
Pinocchio, damaged lid	150.00
Pretty Ann	245.00
Raggedy Andy	150.00
Raggedy Ann	150.00
Santa, black	895.00
Sir Francis Drake	90.00
Topsey, yellow	585.00
Homestead Provincial	
Casserole, hen cov	95.00
Coffeepot	65.00
Creamer and Sugar, cov	25.00
Plate	
10" d, dinner	8.00
12" d, chop	12.00
Wall Pocket	42.00
Planter, carriage	40.00
Poppets	
Girl	
Holding dog	60.00
With ducks	55.00
Man	
With pot, wearing bathing suit	50.00
With wheelbarrow	60.00
Provincial Fruit	
Bowl, 5" d, tab handled	7.00
Butter Dish	45.00
Gravy Boat, handled	20.00
Plate, 6" d, bread and butter	4.00
Platter, 13½" l	25.00
Salt and Pepper Shakers, pr	12.00
Provincial Rooster, casserole	125.00
Red Rooster	
Canister Set, 4 pcs	175.00
Coffeepot	65.00
Creamer and Sugar, open	16.00
Cup and Saucer	10.00
Pipkin Ladle	70.00
Pipkin Strainer	70.00
Plate	
10" d, dinner	12.00
12" d, chop	18.00
Salt and Pepper Shakers, pr, handled	18.00
Sculptured Daisy, dinner service, 56 pcs	280.00
Teapot, Mandy	195.00
Vase	
Poppet Head, girl with blond hair and bow	45.00
Scorpio, Poppytrail Romanelli, 8" h	165.00
Vineyard, dinner service, 42 pcs	135.00

MILITARIA

Collecting Hints: Militaria is any item that was used during or relates to the act of warfare. Tools, clothes, weapons, and items that fulfill that requirement are found in many different places and in varying quantities. Saving militaria may be one of the oldest collecting traditions. Militaria collectors tend to have their own special shows and view themselves outside the normal antiques channels. However, they haunt small indoor shows and flea markets in hopes of finding additional materials.

History: Wars always have been part of history. Until the mid–19th century, soldiers often had to fill their own needs, including weapons. Even in the 20th century, a soldier's uniform and some of his gear is viewed as his personal property, even though issued by a military agency.

Conquering armed forces made a habit of acquiring souvenirs from their vanquished foes. They brought home their own uniforms and accessories as badges of triumph and service.

References: Thomas Berndt, *Standard Catalog of U. S. Military Vehicles: 1940–1965,* Krause Publications, 1993; Ray A. Bows, *Vietnam Military Lore 1959–1973,* Bows & Sons, 1988; Robert Fisch, *Field Equipment of the Infantry 1914–1945,* Greenberg Publishing, 1989; Richard Friz, *The Official Price Guide To Civil War Collectibles,* House of Collectibles, 1995; *North South Trader's Civil War Magazine's Civil War Collectors' Price Guide, 5th Edition,* North South Trader, 1991; Norman E. Martinus and Harry L. Rinker, *Warman's Paper,* Wallace–Homestead, 1994; Jack H. Smith, *Military Postcards 1870– 1945,* Wallace–Homestead Book Company, 1988; Don Stewart, *Collectors Guide: Handcuffs & Restraints,* Key Collectors International, 1993; Sydney B. Vernon, *Vernon's Collector's Guide to Orders, Medals, and Decorations,* published by author, 1986; Windrow & Greene's *Militaria Directory and Sourcebook 1994,* Motorbooks International, 1994.

Periodicals: *Cavalry!,* HC3, Box 378A, Rochella, VA 22738; *Men At Arms,* 222 W. Exchange St., Providence, RI 02903; *Military Collector Magazine,* PO Box 245, Lyon Station, PA, 19536; *Military Collectors' News,* PO Box 702073, Tulsa, OK 74170; *Military History,* 6405 Flank Dr., Harrisburg, PA 17112; *Military Trader,* PO Box 1050, Dubuque, IA 52004; *North South Trader,* PO Drawer 631, Orange, VA 22960; *Wildcat Collectors Journal,* 15158 NE 6 Ave., Miami FL 33162.

Collectors' Clubs: American Society of Military Insignia Collectors, 526 Lafayette Ave., Palmerton, PA 18701; Assoc. of American Military Uniform Collectors, PO Box 1876, Elyria, OH 44036; Company of Military Historians, North Main St., Westbrook, CT 06498; Imperial German Military Collectors Assoc, 82 Atlantic St., Keyport, NJ 07735; Orders and Medals Society of America, PO Box 484, Glassboro, NJ 08028.

Museums: Battlefield Military Museum, Gettysburg, PA; Liberty Memorial Museum, Kansas

City, MO; National Infantry Museum, Fort Benning, GA; Seven Acres Antique Village & Museum, Union, IL; The Parris Island Museum, Parris Island, SC; US Air Force Museum, Wright–Patterson AFB, OH; US Army Transportation Museum, Fort Eustis, VA; US Horse Cavalry Assoc. & Museum, Fort Riley, KS; US Navy Museum, Washington, DC.

Additional Listings: See Home Front Collectibles, World War I, World War II, and *Warman's Antiques And Their Prices* for information about firearms and swords.

CIVIL WAR

Bank Note, Confederate States	35.00
Book	
Beyond the Lines, A Yankee Prisoner Loose In Dixie, Geer, 1863, 1st edition	75.00
Harper's Pictorial History of the Great Rebellion, leather bound, 17 x 12", color litho, price for two volume set	385.00
History of the De Witt Guard 50th Regiment National Guard, 1866	85.00
National Almanac & Annual Records, 1863, day by day record of battles, events	45.00
Private Chapter of the War, Baily, 1st Liet, First Missouri Infantry, 1880s, 1st edition	85.00
Prisoner of War in Virginia, Putnam, 1912, 1st edition	45.00
Red Tape & Pigeon Hole Generals as Seen during a Campaign with the Army of the Potomac, Owen, 1964	75.00
Sketches of the War, Letters to New York's North Moore Street School, 1865	75.00
Three Years in Field Hospitals of the Army of the Potomac, Mrs. H, 1867, 1st edition	100.00
Cartes De Visite, drummer boy, c1860s	140.00
Flag, US, 36 stars, 1864–67, 72 x 98"	500.00
Handkerchief, silk, Farewell Poem	400.00
Hat, slouch, Confederate cavalry	650.00
Jacket, shell, Union cavalry, complete with buttons, lining, and inspector's marks	350.00
Magazine, Saturday Evening Post, 1863, Battle of Gettysburg	125.00
Muster Roll, Ohio Volunteer Infantry, 8th Regiment, 1862, names, condition of soldiers	550.00
Ribbon, 1861–65, Lincoln's head surrounded by "With Malice Toward None, With Charity For All," blue gray	90.00
Saddle, Cavalry, McCullem type	300.00

SPANISH AMERICAN

Belt, officer's, black leather, gilt buckle and hangers	150.00
Cartridge Box, US Army	125.00
Coat, enlisted man's, 1st sergeant stripes	145.00
Hat Badge, infantry, brass, crossed krag rifles, 2" l	60.00
Pinback Button, Remember The Maine, battleship scene, patent 1896	25.00
Spy Glass, pocket, Naval, brass, round holder, brown leather grip, 16"	100.00
Uniform, khaki, tunic and pants	40.00

KOREAN

Book, *Ten Asian Languages,* 1951, unused	70.00
Bush Jacket, tan cotton, dated 1953, British	35.00

VIETNAM

Ammo Box, steel, M5–20A1, dated	10.00
Autograph, card signed, ER Zumwalt, first day cover	12.00
Book, *Frontline—The Commands of Wm Chase,* 1975, autographed 1st edition, 228 pages	38.00
Bracelet, POW, names	25.00
Fatigues, jungle, shirt and trousers, size large, marked "US Navy"	250.00
Helmet, US tanker, dark green fiberglass, intercom system on side	25.00
Leaflet, South Vietnamese Propaganda, 5 x 7", dated April, 1969	5.00
Medal, Air Force Commendation, parade ribbon and lapel bar, case	20.00
Tunic, US Army, sergeant, green, gold stripes, 5th Division red diamonds insignia	25.00

DESERT STORM

Figure, Gen Schwarzkopf, MIB	35.00
Watch, digital	25.00

MISCELLANEOUS

Book, Hungerford, *Transport For War,* 1943, 1st edition, dust jacket	25.00
Christmas Card, Annapolis, sailing ship illus, color, orig mailing envelope, 1920, 8 x 10"	20.00
Ledger Sheet, Bureau of Navigation, payment for services to the *U.S.S. Tuscarora,* 1874	10.00
Medallion, 5½" d, solid cast brass, Bastogne commemorative, American officer saying "Nuts" to German officer	110.00

MILK BOTTLES

Collecting Hints: Many factors influence the price—condition of the bottle, who is selling, the part of the country in which the sale is transacted, and the amount of desire a buyer has for the bottle. Every bottle does not have universal appeal. A sale of a bottle in one area does not mean that it would bring the same amount in another locale. For example, a rare Vermont pyro pint would be looked upon as only another "pint" in Texas.

A general trend indicates the growing popularity of pyroglaze (painted bottles) over embossed bottles. Pyro bottles display better at home or at shows.

History: Hervey Thatcher is recognized as the father of the glass milk bottle. By the early 1880s glass milk bottles appeared in New York and New Jersey. A. V. Whiteman had a milk bottle patent as early as 1880. Patents reveal much about early milk bottle shape and manufacture. Not all patentees were manufacturers. Many individuals engaged others to produce bottles under their patents.

The Golden Age of the glass milk bottle is 1910 to 1950. Leading manufacturers include Lamb Glass Co. (Mt. Vernon, Ohio), Liberty Glass Co. (Sapulpa, Oklahoma), Owens–Illinois Glass Co. (Toledo, Ohio), and Thatcher Glass Co. (New York).

Milk bottles can be found in the following sizes: gill (quarter pint), half pint, 10 ounces (third quart), pint, quart, half gallon (two quart), and gallon.

Paper cartons first appeared in the early 1920s and 1930s and achieved popularity after 1950. The late 1950s witnessed the arrival of the plastic bottle. A few dairies still use glass bottles today, but the era has essentially ended.

References: Don Lord, *California Milks*, published by author; John Tutton, *Udder Delight: A Guide To Collecting Milk Bottles and Related Items*, published by author, 1980.

Periodical: *The Udder Collectibles*, HC73 Box 1, Smithville Flats, NY 13841.

Collectors' Club: National Association of Milk Bottles Collectors, Inc., 4 Ox Bow Road, Westport, CT 06880.

Museums: Billings Farm Museum, Woodstock, VT; Southwest Dairy Museum, Arlington, TX; The New York State Historical Assoc. and The Farmers Museum, Inc., Cooperstown, NY.

Half Pint
  Embossed, round 3
    Frasure–Brown, Logan, OH **24.00**
    Montana Pure Milk Dairy, full
      length fluting **28.00**
    Sibley Farms, Spencer, MA **38.00**

Drink Rutter Bros. Milk, clear glass, pyro glazed, 5½" h, $1.50.

Pyro–glazed, tall, round
  Fairview Farms Jersey Milk, Waterloo, NY, Jersey cow, blue   **28.00**
  Garden Farm Dairy, Denver, CO, rising sun, icebergs, and polar bears, "Polar Bear Ice Cream," made by Garden Farm Dairy, Denver," orange and blue **48.00**
One–Third Quart, 10 oz, pyro–glazed, round
  Diamond Dairy Farms, Salem, NH, child playing with blocks labeled Diamond Dairy, "A bottle of Milk is a Bottle of Health," orange **24.00**
  Evans Bros Dairy, Cumberland, RI, cow's head and "Direct from farm to you" on ribbon, Ashcroft Farms pictured on back, "Bottled on Farm," red **32.00**
Pint
  Embossed, tall, round
    Chestnut Farms Dairy, Washington, DC, emb dairy farm logo, ribbed shoulder and neck **24.00**
    Our Own Dairies, Los Angeles, CA, emb Star of David on front and base **20.00**
    Racy Creamery, Knoxville, TN, full length ribs, bowling pin shape   **28.00**
    Richland Dairy, Reno, NV, script lettering **38.00**
    St Louis Dairy, St Louis, MO, script writing on shoulder, large letter "S" on back **18.00**
  Pyro–glazed, tall, round 6
    A G Dorr Dairy, Watertown, NY, smiling baby, orange **26.00**
    Butler Dairy, Willmantic, CT, milkman with bottle carrier and "Call Butlers for Better Pasteurized Milk and Cream," green **32.00**

Huff Brothers Dairy, Colorado Springs, CO, phone Main 959W, horn of plenty with Huff Brothers' milk, cream, butter-milk, and cottage cheese inside, brown **36.00**

Lueck Dairy, Liverpool, NY, Better quality and service, visit our Ice Cream Bar, happy cow bellow-ing "Good Morning," orange .. **38.00**

Newsoms Pride Dairy, Albany, GA, phone 1729J, Grade A Milk & Cream, boxer and "Milk the champion of drinks," black **38.00**

Ross Corner Dairy, Derry, NJ, cow's head on label, large script "R," orange **32.00**

Stransdale Farms Products, Savanna, IL, "Grade A Pasteurized Milk," black **28.00**

Quart

Embossed, cream–top, round 4

Diamond Creamery Co, Sioux Falls, SD, Riverside Milk **58.00**

Elnog Dairy, Coatesville, PA, "It Whips" on cream top **35.00**

Himes Dairy, Eaton, OH **45.00**

Meadow Gold, Silver Seal **35.00**

Embossed, tall, round 9

Bridgeman–Russell, Hancock, MI, Purity Brand Pasteurized Milk & Cream **38.00**

ERKS, large script lettering, Montgomery, AL **34.00**

Haight's Dairy, Takoma Park, DC **28.00**

Mission Dairy Inc, Phoenix, AZ, phone 3615 .... **58.00**

Sardis Creamery, Sardis, MI, Grade A Pasteurized **35.00**

Terry Dairy Co, Little Rock, AK, Pasteurized Milk & Cream **35.00**

Trifolium Creamery, Kansas City, KS, pasteurized **48.00**

Western Milk & Cream Co, Butte, MT, phone 2–3335 .... **32.00**

Pyro–glazed, tall, round

B & C Dairy, Pasteurized Milk, Phone 166, Havre, MT, black background with little boy pour-ing from giant bottle for little girl, "Those who know choose B & C" **42.00**

Benware Creamery, Malone, NY, dairy farm, cows, barns, and si-los, "Our Milk is Pasteurized Daily, For Mothers Who Care," red **26.00**

Cloverleaf Dairy, Everett, WI, large clover leaf, "You can whip our cream but you can't beat our milk," green **38.00**

Enid Cooperative Creamery Ass'n, Enid, OK, "Gold Spot" pasteur-

ized milk, chain of pictures de-picting milk production from the pasture to your doorstep, "Tested Daily," orange, some fading ... **28.00**

Model Dairy, Huron, SD, Milk, Cream & Chocolate Milk, Guernsey cow's head with ban-ner "Taste the Difference," "A Delicious Drink, A Nutritious Food, Pasteurized," red **78.00**

Mountain Meadow Dairy, Bisbee, AZ, Pasteurized Dairy Foods, yellow and black **68.00**

New England Creamery Co, Livermore Falls, ME, Jersey cow's head, "New England Milk," black **32.00**

Seger–Graham Dairy, Adrian, MI, Pasteurized & Homogenized for Safety & Health, orange **18.00**

Star Dairy, Galveston, TX, large stars, "For health's sake, pasteur-ized," orange **85.00**

Supreme Dairy, Peru, IL, baby in crib with bottle, "Baby's choice," blue **24.00**

Sycamore Farm Dairy, Rockville, MD, large oak tree background, green **65.00**

Topaz Dairy, Hastings, NE, Grade A Pasteurized Milk and Sweet Cream Butter, cottage cheese salad and "Topaz Cottage good with any salad," red **42.00**

War Slogan, pyro–glazed, tall, round

Danville Producer's Dairy, Statue of Liberty, "The United States is a Sound Investment, Buy War Bonds and Stamps," heavy red–orange **75.00**

Freeman's Milk, Best by Test, US map outline with Uncle Sam drinking glass of milk, "A Healthy Nation is a Strong Nation, Milk the Nation Builder," heavy red background **75.00**

Garst Bros. Dairy, cow and bottle in oval logo, registered trade mark, milkman delivering to front porch, "To save our free-dom we must save our materials, America Saves, Save this bottle and return," orange **55.00**

Ridgeview Farms, Finer Dairy Products, Chicago, IL, housewife serving platter of food, "Food Fights Too, use it wisely," "Plan all meals for Victory" in shield, and "Balance your meals with Milk" at bottom, red **65.00**

Valley Gold, "Albuquerque's Fa-vorite Milk," milkman carrying tray of bottles, marching side by side with armed infantrymen, "Both defend your home 'Against all Enemies, Against Ill–Health,'" red **55.00**

MODEL KITS

Collecting Hints: Model kits, assembled or unassembled, are one of the hot collectibles of the 1990s. Even assembled examples, provided they are done well, have value.

In many cases, a kit's value is centered more on the character or object it represents than on the kit itself. The high value of monster-related kits is tied directly to the current monster collecting craze. When kit prices are craze-related, a portion of the value is speculative.

Box art can influence a kit's value. When individual boxes sell in the $40 to $100 range, it becomes clear that they are treated as "objets d'art," a dangerous pricing trend. The value of the box is easily understood when you place an assembled model beside the lid. All too often, it is the box that is more exciting.

History: The plastic scale model kit originated in England in the mid–1930s with the manufacture of 1/72 Frog Penguin kits. The concept caught on during World War II when scale models were used in identification training. After the war companies such as Empire Plastics, Hawk, Lindberg, Renwal, and Varney introduced plastic model kits into the American market. The 1950s witnessed the arrival of Aurora and Monogram in the United States, Airfix in the United Kingdom, Heller in France, and Hasegawa and Marusan in Japan.

The 1960s was the "golden" age of the plastic kit model. Kits featured greater detail and accuracy. Three scale sizes dominated: 1/48, 1/72, and 1/144. The oil crisis in the 1970s caused a temporary setback in the industry.

A revival of interest in plastic scale model kits occurred in the late 1980s. At the same time, collector interest began to develop. The initial collecting focus was on automobile model kits from the 1950s and early 1960s. By the end of the 1980s interest had shifted to character and monster kits.

References: Paul A. Bender, *1990 Model Car Promotional and Kit Guide*, Brasilia Press, 1990; Bill Bruegman, *Aurora: History and Price Guide*, Cap'n Penny Productions, 1992; C & C Collectibles, *Fantasies in Plastic: Directory of Old and New Model Car Kits, Promotionals, and Resin Cast Bodies*, C & C Collectibles, 1991; Gordy Dutt, *Aurora: A Collection of Classic Instruction Sheets, Vol. 1, Figures*, published by author, 1992; Gordon Dutt, *Collectible Figure Kits of the 50's, 60's & 70's: Reference and Price Guide*, Gordy's Kitbuilders Magazine, 1995.

Periodicals: *Kit Builders and Glue Sniffers*, PO Box 201, Sharon Center, OH 44274; *Model and Toy Collector*, PO Box 347240, Cleveland, OH 44134.

Collectors' Clubs: Kit Collectors International, PO Box 38, Stanton, CA 90680; Society for the Preservation and Encouragement of Scale Model Kit Collecting, 3213 Hardy Drive, Edmond, OK 73013.

American Astronaut, Aurora, #409, 1967	**60.00**
American Buffalo, Aurora, #402, 1964	**20.00**
Aston Martin, James Bond, Airfix, #823, 1965	**175.00**
Birthday Bird, Dr Seuss, Revell, 1960	**120.00**
Black Fury, Aurora, #400, 1958	**25.00**
Bride of Frankenstein, Horizon, 1988	**35.00**
Captain Action, Aurora, #480, 1966 . .	**240.00**
Castro, Born Losers, Parks, 1965	**125.00**
Charlie's Angels Van, Revell, 1977 . . .	**15.00**
Chitty Chitty Bang Bang, unassembled, Aurora, 1968	**50.00**
Cro Magnon Man, Aurora, #730, 1971	**20.00**
Daddy the Suburbanite, Weird–Ohs, Hawk, 1963	**65.00**
Dracula, Monsters of the Movies, #656, Aurora, 1975	**150.00**
Drag–u–la, Munsters, AMT, 1965	**200.00**
Dr Jekyll, Aurora, Glow Kit, #482, 1969	**85.00**
Dr Zira, Planet of the Apes, Addar, #105, 1974	**25.00**
Dutch Girl, Aurora, #414, 1957	**20.00**
Flintstones Rock Crusher, AMT, #487, 1974	**50.00**
Flipper and Sandy, Revell, 1968	**80.00**
George Harrison, Revell, 1965	**120.00**
Godzilla, unassembled, MIB, Aurora, 1964	**475.00**
Green Beret, Aurora, #413, 1966	**125.00**
Hulk, Aurora, Comic Scenes, #184, 1974	**75.00**
Indian Warrior, Pyro, 1960	**35.00**
Invisible Man, Horizon, 1988	**25.00**
James Bond, Aurora, #414, 1966	**275.00**
Jesse James, Aurora, #408, 1966	**150.00**
King Arthur of Camelot, Aurora, #825, 1967	**65.00**
King Kong, 9" h, assembled, girl in right hand, Aurora, 1964	**40.00**
Knight Rider, unassembled, orig box, MPC, copyright 1983 Universal Studios, Inc	**25.00**
Mad Barber, Aurora, #455, 1972	**125.00**
Mars Probe Space Station, Lindberg, 1969	**70.00**
McHale's Navy, PT 73, unassembled, Revell, 1965	**85.00**
Monkeemobile, Airfix, 1967	**240.00**
Mr Spock, AMT, #956, large box, 1973	**125.00**
Penguin, Aurora, #416, 1967	**400.00**
Six Million Dollar Man, unassembled, Fundimensions, copyright 1975	**45.00**

Space Taxi, Monogram, 1959 . . . .   **25.00**
Steel Plunkers, Frantics, Hawk, 1965 . .   **30.00**
Susie Whoozis, Aurora, #210, 1966 . .   **65.00**
Tarzan, Comic Series, Aurora, #181,
1974 . . . .   **30.00**
Thunderbird, motorized, unassembled,
1963 . . . .   **25.00**
Tonto, Aurora, #809, 1967 . . . .   **125.00**
Wacky Woodie, Krazy Kar Kustom Kit,
AMT, 1968 . . . .   **70.00**
Willie Mays, Aurora, #860, 1965 . . . .   **250.00**
Wolfman, assembled, painted, Aurora,
1962 . . . .   **50.00**

MONSTERS

Collecting Hints: This is a category rampant with speculative fever. Prices rise and fall rapidly depending on the momentary popularity of a figure or family group. Study the market and its prices carefully before becoming a participant.

Stress condition and completeness. Do not buy any item in less than fine condition. Check carefully to make certain that all parts or elements are present for whatever you buy.

Since the material in this category is of recent origin, no one is certain how much has survived. Hoards are not uncommon. It is possible to find examples at garage sales. It pays to shop around before paying a high price.

While an excellent collection of two-dimensional material, e.g., comic books, magazines, posters, etc., can be assembled, stress three-dimensional material. Several other crazes, e.g., model kit collecting, cross over into monster collecting, thus adding to price confusion.

History: Collecting monster-related material began in the late 1980s as a generation looked back nostalgically on the monster television shows of the 1960s, e.g., Addams Family, Dark Shadows, and the Munsters, and the spectacular monster and horror movies of the 1960s and 1970s. Fueling the fire was a group of Japanese collectors who were raiding the American market for material relating to Japanese monster epics featuring reptile monsters such as Godzilla.

It did not take long for collectors to seek the historic roots for their post–World War II monsters. A collecting revival started for Frankenstein, King Kong, and Mummy material. Contemporary items featuring these characters also appeared.

References: Ted Hake, *Hake's Guide To TV Collectibles*, Wallace–Homestead, 1990; Carol Markowski and Bill Sikora, *Tomart's Price Guide To Action Figure Collectibles*, Revised Edition, Tomart Publications, 1992.

Collectors' Club: Club 13, PO Box 733, Bellefonte, PA 16823.

Periodicals: *Future News,* 5619 Pilgrim Rd., Baltimore, MD 21214; *G–Fan,* Box 3468, Steinbach, Manitoba, Canada ROA 2AO; *Japanese Giants,* 5727 North Oketo, Chicago, IL 60631; *Kaiju Review—The Journal of Japanese Monster Culture,* Suite 5F, 301 E. 64th St., New York, NY 10021; *Monster Attack Team–The Japanese Monster Superhero & Fantasy Fanzine,* PO Box 800875, Houston, TX 77280–0875; *Questnews,* Suite 150, 12440 Moorpark St., Studio City, CA 91604.

ADDAMS FAMILY

Bubble Gum Wrapper, Donruss, 1964   **25.00**
Coloring Book, 8½ x 11", Saalfield,
#4595, 1965 . . . .   **25.00**
Figure, 1964 Filmways copyright
Lurch, 5½" h, hard plastic body, soft
molded vinyl head, Remco **75.00**
Morticia, 5" h, plastic, molded soft
vinyl head, long black glossy gown   **100.00**
Game, The Addams Family, Ideal Toy,
1964, orig box **110.00**
Magazine, *Monster World,* #9, July
1966, Warren Publishing Co, full
color family photo on front cov, 5 pg
article **28.00**
Mechanical Bank, 3¼ x 4½ x 3¼", The
Thing, plastic, black, green hand
grabs coins, orig box, 1964–66 . . . .   **50.00**
Paperback Book, *The Addams Family,*
Pyramid Books, copyright 1965
Filmways TV Productions, Inc, 176
pgs **20.00**
Puppet, 10" h, hand, Gomez, cloth
body, soft molded vinyl head, 1964
copyright Filmways TV Productions   **75.00**
Record, 33 1/3 rpm, RCA Victor label,
six songs, orig cardboard sleeve,
1965 copyright **22.00**

DARK SHADOWS

Comic Book, Gold Key, #5, May 1970   **12.00**
Game
Barnabas Collins/Dark Shadows
Game, Milton Bradley, orig box,
1969 . . . .   **25.00**

Game, Dark Shadows, Barnabus Collins, Milton Bradley, 19 x 9½", $25.00.

Dark Shadows, 30" sq playing board, four cardboard playing pieces, deck of cards, orig box, Whitman, 1968 . . . . **50.00**

Record, 45 rpm, Ranwood label, orig white sleeve, late 1960s **55.00**

DRACULA

Action Figure, 8" h, glow–in–the–dark eyes, removable cape, copyright 1974, Mego **25.00**

Magazine, *Famous Monsters of Filmland*, #92, Sept 1972, Warren Publishing Co, full color cover portrait, 76 pgs **10.00**

Model, Aurora, instruction sheet, 1962 copyright, orig box **75.00**

Paint Set, Dracula Oil Painting By Numbers, 12 x 16" canvas panel, 14 oil paints, one paint brush, orig box, Hasbro, marked "Made In England," copyright 1963 Universal Pictures Corp **100.00**

Promotion Ad, exhibitor's trade magazine, graphic photo **225.00**

Jigsaw Puzzle, full color illus of Dracula holding girl, Frankenstein sleeps in coffin, titled "Vampire's Nest," orig box, Jaymar, copyright 1963 Universal Pictures **28.00**

FRANKENSTEIN

Action Figure, 8" h, glow–in–the–dark eyes and hands, Mego, copyright 1974 . . . . **25.00**

Figure, 7¾" h, flexible rubber, molded, elastic cord mounted in top of head, orig tag "World's Famous Super Monsters," Ahi, 1973 Universal Studio copyright **25.00**

Glass, 6½" h, clear, purple, black, and green illus, purple background, copyright Universal Pictures Co, Inc, late 1960s **40.00**

Inflatable Figure, 36" h, vinyl, Pepsi and Doritos logos, Universal Studios, 1992 copyright **25.00**

Jigsaw Puzzle, Jaymar, 1963 . . . . **130.00**

Magazine, *The Journal of Frankenstein*, first issue, Vol 1, New World Enterprises Syndicated, Inc., copyright 1959, 38 pgs **25.00**

Mold Kit, Mix 'N Mold, sealed box, issued by Catalog Shoppe, West Hartford, CT, 1970s **28.00**

Notebook, 10 x 11", vinyl, three ring binder, black, full color illus on front, late 1960s **50.00**

Robot, 14" h, battery operated, drops pants and blushes, orig box, Galoob,

1960s **140.00**

Soaky Bottle, 10" h, plastic, Colgate–Palmolive Co, 1960s **25.00**

Toy, Frankencycle, glow–in–the–dark, skull on front, includes Frankenstein figure and haunted house, orig box, Ideal, copyright 1978 . . . . **48.00**

Trash Can, 16" h, litho, tin, wrap–around illus, J Chein & Co, 1970s . . **75.00**

View Master Reel, set of 3, booklet, 1976 copyright, hard plastic tray with box **25.00**

GODZILLA

Figure, 18" h, plastic, dark green, yellow claws, teeth, and eyes, wheeled feet, movable arms and legs, copyright 1977, Mattel **100.00**

Game, Godzilla Game, 18½ x 19" playing board, orig box, Ideal, copyright 1963 . . . . **100.00**

Jigsaw Puzzle, 150 pcs, full color illus, HG Toys, copyright 1978 Toho Co . . **15.00**

Pinback Button, 1⅝" d, Godzilla vs Megalon, litho, yellow, dark brown image, red lettering, 1970s **15.00**

View Master Reel, unused, 1970s **8.00**

KING KONG

Bank, 16" h, molded black plastic, red and white accents, A J Renzi Corp . . **30.00**

Bubble Gum Pack, 2½ x 3½", sealed, Donruss, 1965 . . . . **75.00**

Decanter, 10" h, china, dark brown, 1976 Dino de Laurentis Corp copyright, Regal China **30.00**

Game, King Kong Game, 16" sq playing board, playing pieces, orig box, Milton Bradley, copyright 1966 RKO **40.00**

Lunch Box, 7 x 9 x 4", metal, full color illus, copyright 1977 Dino De Laurentis **15.00**

Magazine, *Mid–Week Pictorial*, Vol 36, #25, Feb 4, 1933 . . . . **25.00**

Model, 9" h, assembled, unpainted, girl in right hand, Aurora, 1964 copyright **40.00**

Movie Poster, 24 x 28", stiff paper, 1963, Universal Pictures **50.00**

Pinback Button, Happy Anniversary Kong 1933–1983, black, white, and red **4.00**

Socks, photo illus, unused, orig illus display card, 1977 . . . . **22.00**

Toy, windup, 4¼" h, celluloid and fur, CK, Made in Japan, orig box, 1930s . **300.00**

MISCELLANEOUS

Book, *Monsters*, Wonder Books, Inc., 1965, 48 pgs **15.00**

Bubble Pipe, 9½" l, red plastic, three–dimensional head, Empire, 1960s .. **22.00**

Card Game, Monster Old Maid, 1964, Milton Bradley, 39 cards, instruction card, boxed **50.00**

Doll, Freddy Krueger, 18" h, voicebox, hand with bladed glove, removable hat, orig box, Matchbox copyright 1989 The Fourth New Line–Heron Venture **55.00**

Figure

Cinema Creatures, set of 6, 4½" to 6" h, plastic, orig plastic bag, Marx, 1963 Universal Picture Co, Inc copyright **125.00**

Cyclops, 3" h, plastic, Palmer, 1962 . **52.00**

Kraken, 15" h, hard plastic, green, red mouth, white eyes and teeth, movable arms, copyright 1980 Metro–Goldwyn–Mayer, Inc **50.00**

Game

Green Ghost Game, 11 x 27" glow–in–the–dark playing board, green ghost spinner, twelve playing pieces, instructions sheet, Transogram, copyright 1965 .... **75.00**

Mystic Skull Game of Voodoo, 12½" sq playing board, center spinner, cardboard tokens, voodoo pins, four 5½" h playing pieces, Ideal, copyright 1964 .... **25.00**

Glove, Freddy Krueger, brown cloth, silver blade fingertips, orig blister card, Marty Toy, Inc, 1984 copyright **20.00**

Greeting Card, glossy, includes record, features Universal monsters, unused, set of 3 different cards, Buzza Cardozo, 1963 .... **42.00**

Gum Wrapper, Spook Stories, 6 x 6¼", Leaf Gum, issued 1963–65 .... **50.00**

Jigsaw Puzzle, Weird–Ohs Picture Puzzle, "Davey The Psycho Cyclist," Fairchild copyright 1963, The Hawk Model Co **25.00**

Lunch Box, Universal Movie Monsters, emb metal, color illus, plastic thermos, Aladdin Industries, 1979 Universal City Studios, Inc copyright **125.00**

Magazine

Horror of Party Beach, Warren Publishing Co, 1964, 68 pgs **15.00**

Monster Mania, first issue, Oct, 1966, Renaissance Productions **25.00**

3D Monsters, Vol. 1, #1, Fair Publishing Ltd **30.00**

Mask, Cousin Eerie, soft rubber, Eerie Magazine figure issued by Warren Publications, late 1960s **75.00**

Model, Aurora, instruction sheet, 1964 copyright, orig box **150.00**

Movie Poster

The Lady And The Monster, 27 x 41", Morgan Litho Corp, 1944 .... **75.00**

The Vampire, 14 x 36", full color, John Beal and Coleen Gray, 1957 United Artist Corp **25.00**

Nodder, 6" h, Phantom of the Opera, 1963 .... **79.00**

Pez Container, Creature, includes vending machine box, 1963 .... **90.00**

Pinback Button, 3½" d, The Phantom, full color illus, red background, copyright Universal Pictures Co on rim, 1960s **25.00**

Pressbook, 12 x 16", Creature With The Atom Brain, 1955 Columbia Pictures **25.00**

Soaky Bottle, 10" h, Creature, soft plastic body, hard plastic head, metallic green, 1960s **75.00**

Trading Card, Monster Magic Action Trading Cards, boxed set of 24 cards, full color illus, Abby Finishing Corp, 1960s **25.00**

MUMMY

Action Figure, 8" h, poseable, Remco, Universal City Studios, Inc copyright 1980 .... **22.00**

Film Box, The Mummy's Ghost, 1960s **15.00**

Iron–On Transfer, 9 x 12", blue and red illus, 12 x 18" tee shirt shape retail card, Mani–Yack, copyright 1964 Universal Pictures **50.00**

Jigsaw Puzzle, 8 x 6" box, Jaymar, 1963 **130.00**

Model Kit, unassembled, MIB, Aurora, 1963 .... **275.00**

Pin, 1" d, color photo, 1963 .... **10.00**

Soaky Bottle, 10" h, soft plastic, hard plastic head, 1960s copyright **55.00**

MUNSTERS

Book, *The Munsters and the Great Camera Caper,* 5½ x 8", hard cover, Whitman, 1965, 212 pgs **15.00**

Bubble Gum Wrapper, Leaf, 1966, green, black, and red design, Spook Hand premium **50.00**

Card Game, The Munsters Card Game, 9½ x 14" playing board, 42 cards, two plastic markers, orig box, Milton Bradley, copyright 1964 .... **48.00**

Comic Book, Whitman, #4, Oct 1965 . **15.00**

Doll

Eddie, 8½" h, vinyl plastic, movable head, arms, and legs, orig Ideal Toy tag, 1965 Ideal copyright, homemade clothing **30.00**

Herman, 20" h, stuffed cloth, molded soft vinyl head and hands, disconnected pull cord, orig Mattel tag with 1964 copyright **75.00**

Lily, 8½" h, vinyl plastic, movable head, arms, and legs, orig Ideal Toy tag, 1965 Ideal copyright **40.00**

Game

The Munsters Masquerade Party,
Hasbro 1964, orig box **100.00**
The Munsters Picnic, Hasbro 1964,
orig box with full color illus **125.00**
Paper Doll, cardboard album, with five
cardboard dolls, four pgs uncut cloth-
ing, Whitman, copyright 1966 Kayro–
Vue Productions **75.00**
Puppet, 10½" h, hand, Grandpa,
printed fabric, molded soft vinyl
head, copyright 1966 Kayro–Vue
Productions **75.00**
Ring, set of 4, blue plastic, green, black,
and white image changes when
tilted, Herman, Lily, Grandpa, and
Eddie, c1966 .... **28.50**
Thermos, 6½" h, litho metal, red plastic
cap, King–Seeley, 1965 copyright .. **45.00**

WOLFMAN

Action Figure, 8" h, glow–in–the–dark
hands and eyes, gray suit, orig box,
Mego, copyright 1973 .... **28.00**
Comic Book, Dell, 1963 .... **8.00**
Figure, 4" h, plastic, brown, movable
head, black hair, blue cloth pants,
1960s **18.00**
Glass, 6⅝" h, green, blue, and brown il-
lus, blue background, 1960s copy-
right, Universal Pictures Co, Inc **55.00**
Model, Aurora, instruction sheet, 1962
copyright, orig box
Assembled **50.00**
Unassembled **175.00**
Pinback Button, 3½" d, full color illus,
dark blue background, Universal
Pictures copyright on rim, late 1960s **25.00**
Soaky Bottle, 10" h, plastic, metallic
gold and brown, blue trousers, 1960s **75.00**

MORTON POTTERIES

Collecting Hints: The potteries of Morton,
Illinois, used local clay until 1940. The clay fired
out to a golden ecru color which is quite easy to
recognize. After 1940 southern and eastern clays
were shipped to Morton. These clays fired out
white. Thus, later period wares are sharply distinguished from the earlier wares.

Few pieces were marked by the potteries.
Incised and raised marks for the Morton Pottery
Works, the Cliftwood Art Potteries, Inc., and the
Morton Pottery Company do surface at times.
The Cliftwood, Midwest, Morton Pottery Com-
pany, and American Art Pottery all used paper la-
bels in limited amounts. Some of these have sur-
vived, and collectors do find them.

Glazes from the early period, 1877–1920, usually were Rockingham types, both mottled and
solid. Yellow ware also was standard during the
early period. Occasionally a dark cobalt blue
was produced, but this color is rare. Colorful drip
glazes and solid colors came into use after 1920.

History: Pottery was produced in Morton,
Illinois, for 99 years. In 1877 six Rapp brothers,
who emigrated from Germany, began the first
pottery, Morton Pottery Works. Over the years
sons, cousins, and nephews became involved in
the production of pottery. The other Morton pottery operations were spin-offs from the original
pottery and brothers. When it was taken over in
1915 by second-generation Rapps, Morton
Pottery Works became the Morton Earthenware
Company. Work at that pottery was terminated
by World War I.

The Cliftwood Art Potteries, Inc., operated
from 1920 to 1940. One of the original founders
of the Morton Pottery Works and his four sons organized it. They sold out in 1940, and the operation continued for four more years as the
Midwest Potteries, Inc. A disastrous fire brought
an end to that operation in March 1944. These
two potteries produced figurines, lamps, novelties and vases.

In 1922 the Morton Pottery Company, which
had the longest existence of all of the Morton's
potteries, was organized by the same brothers
who had operated the Morton Earthenware
Company. The Morton Pottery Company specialized in beer steins, kitchenwares, and novelty
items for chain stores and gift shops. They also
produced some of the Vincent Price National
Treasures reproductions for Sears Roebuck and
Company in the mid-1960s. The Morton Pottery
closed in 1976, thus ending the 99 years of pottery production in Morton.

By 1947 the brothers who had operated the
Cliftwood Art Potteries, Inc., came back into the
pottery business. They established the short-lived
American Art Potteries. The American Art
Potteries made flower bowls, lamps, planters,
some unusual flower frogs, and vases. Their
wares were marketed by florists and gift shops.
Production at American Art Potteries was halted
in 1961. Of all the wares of the Morton potteries,
the products of the American Art Potteries are the
most elusive.

References: Doris and Burdell Hall, *Morton's
Potteries: 99 Years,* published by authors, 1982;
Doris and Burdell Hall, *Morton's Potteries: 99
Years, 1877-1976, Volume II* L–W. Book Sales,
1995.

Museum: Illinois State Museum, Springfield, IL;
Morton Public Library (permanent exhibit),
Morton, IL.

Advisors: Doris and Burdell Hall.

MORTON POTTERY WORKS, MORTON EARTHENWARE COMPANY, 1877–1917

Crock, 1 gallon, Rockingham	50.00
Miniature	
Chamber pot, Yellowware	25.00
Jug, Rockingham	45.00
Mug, Yellowware, ½ pint	65.00
Paperweight, buffalo, Rockingham . . .	40.00
Stein, German motto	
Green	80.00
Rockingham	65.00
Teapot, Rebecca, Rockingham, 8½ pint	130.00

CLIFTWOOD ART POTTERIES, INC., 1920–1940

Beer Set, pitcher and six steins, barrel shape, chocolate brown drip glaze, price for set	180.00
Figure	
Bald Eagle, 8½" h, natural colors . . .	95.00
Lion, 16" l, solid cast, natural colors	125.00
Police Dog, 5" h, 8½" l, chocolate brown drip	55.00

Cliftwood Art Potteries, Inc., police dog, 5" h, 8½" l, $55.00.

Match Box Holder, wall mounted, turquoise and pink over white	50.00
Pretzel jar, cov, barrel shape, "Pretzels" embossed on front, green	60.00
Refrigerator Storage Bowl, nested set of three, cov, burgundy, price for set . .	40.00
Sweetmeat Bowl, sq, green lid, yellow drip	50.00
Teapot, Globe, blue–mulberry glaze, 8 cup size, matching ftd trivet	80.00

MIDWEST POTTERIES, INC., 1940–1944

Bust, 8½" h, female, white, platinum dec	75.00

Figure

Afghan Hound, 7" h, white, gold dec	35.00
Deer, 12" h, eight point antlers, white, gold dec	40.00
Irish Setter, 8" l, natural colors	35.00
Pony, 3½" h, yellow, gold dec	18.00
Seagull in Flight, 12" h, solid, 14K gold	40.00
Squirrel, 9" h, brown and white drip	35.00
Planter	
Dog, 5¼" h, wearing bow tie	14.00
Lion, 3¼ x 6½", yellow	12.00
Lioness, 3 x 6½"	12.00

MORTON POTTERY COMPANY, 1922–1976

Bank	
Bulldog, brown	16.00
Log Cabin School, brown	25.00
Pig, wall hanger, blue	25.00
Bookends, pr	
Books, baby shoe planters, white . . .	30.00
Eagles, natural colors	40.00
Figure	
Cat, reclining, white, gray spots	18.00
Horse, colt, wood pump and barrel	40.00
Seeing Eye Dog, marked "Leader Dog," black	20.00
Grass Grower	
Jiggs	30.00
Jolly Jim	20.00
Pig	20.00
Soldier	25.00
Lamp	
Buffalo, TV type	100.00
Davy Crockett	75.00
Irish Setter	70.00
Teddy Bear	25.00
Vase	
Crane in bamboo thicket, white	35.00

Morton Pottery Co., vase, crane, 12½" h, $35.00.

Lady's head, wide brim hat, matte
white **20.00**

AMERICAN ART POTTERIES, 1945–1961

Figure
Hen and Rooster, 8" and 6½", black
spray glaze, price for pair **30.00**
Pig, 5" h, white, gray spots **40.00**
Squirrel, 6" h, brown spray glaze . . .   **20.00**
Wild Horse, 11½" h, brown spray
glaze **35.00**
Lamp
Afghan Hounds, pair, 15" h **70.00**
Driftwood Log, 12" h **25.00**
French Poodle, 15" h **70.00**
Planter
Deer, 6½" l, reclining by log **18.00**
Duck, 5½" h **14.00**
Fish, 5" h **14.00**
Wheel Barrow, 6½" l, parrot shape   **12.00**

American Art Potteries, planter, fish, 4¼"
h, 6½" l, $14.00.

MOVIE MEMORABILIA

Collecting Hints: Collectors tend to focus on the blockbuster hits with *Gone With The Wind* and *Casablanca* among the market leaders. The cartoon image, especially Disney material, also is very popular.

Much of the material is two dimensional. Collectors have just begun to look for three-dimensional objects, although the majority of these are of stars and personalities, rather than movie related.

The market went crazy in the mid–1970s when people sought to speculate in movie memorabilia. A self disciplining has taken place with prices falling in the 1980s. The values correction was compounded further by the large number of reproductions, many made in Europe, which flooded the market.

History: The golden age of movie memorabilia was the 1930s and 1940s. The star system had reached its zenith and studios spent elaborate sums promoting their major stars. Initially, movie

studios and their public relations firms tightly controlled the distribution of material such as press books, scripts, preview flyers, costumes, props, etc. Copyrights have expired on many of these items, and reproductions abound.

The current interest in Hollywood memorabilia can be traced to the pop art craze of the 1960s. Film festivals increased the desire for decorative film–related materials. Collecting movie posters was "hot."

Piracy always has plagued Hollywood and is responsible for the release of many items into the market. Today the home video presents new challenges to the industry.

References: Pauline Bartel, *The Complete Gone With The Wind Sourcebook,* Taylor Publishing, 1993; Tony Fusco, *Posters: Identification and Price Guide, Second Edition* Avon Books, 1994; John Hegenberger, *Collector's Guide To Movie Memorabilia,* Wallace–Homestead Book Company, 1991; Leslie Halliwell, *The Filmgoers's Companion,* Avon, 1978; Ephraim Katz, *The Film Encyclopedia,* Perigee Books, 1979; John Kisch, *Movie Poster Price Database: August–December 1994,* published by author, 1995; Leonard Maltin (ed.), *TV Movies and Videos Guide,* New American Library, 1987; Norman E. Martinus and Harry L. Rinker, *Warman's Paper,* Wallace–Homestead, 1994; Patrick McCarver, *Gone With The Wind Collector's Price Guide,* Collector's Originals, 1990; Robert Osborne, *65 Years of The Oscar: The Official History of The Academy Awards,* Abbeville, 1994; Susan and Steve Raab, *Movie Star Autographs of the Golden Era,* published by authors, 1994; Jay Scarfone and William Stillman, *The Wizard of Oz Collector's Treasury,* Schiffer Publishing, 1992; Jon R. Warren, *Collecting Hollywood: The Movie Poster Price Guide, Third Edition,* American Collectors Exchange, 1994; Dian Zillner, *Hollywood Collectibles,* Schiffer Publishing, 1991; Dian Zillner, *Hollywood Collectibles: The Sequel,* Schiffer Publishing, 1994.

Collectors' Clubs: Emerald City Club, 153 E. Main St., New Albany, IN 47150; Hollywood Studio Collectors Club, Suite 450, 3960 Laurel Canyon Blvd. Studio City, CA 91604; Old Time Western Film Club, PO Box 142, Siler City, NC 27344; The Manuscript Society, 350 N. Niagara St., Burbank, CA 91505; Western Film Appreciation Society, 1914 112 St., Edmonton, Alberta T6J 5P8 Canada; Western Film Preservation Society, Inc., Raleigh Chapter, 1012 Vance St., Raleigh, NC 27608.

Periodicals: *Autograph Times,* 2303 N. 44th St., #225, Phoenix, AZ 85008; *Big Reel,* PO Box 83, Madison, NC 27025; *Celebrity Collector,* PO Box 1115, Boston, MA 02117; *Classic Images,* PO Box 809, Muscatine, IA 52761; *Collecting Hollywood,* 2401 Broad St., Chattanooga, TN

37408; *Gone With The Wind Collector's Newsletter,* 1347 Greenmoss Dr., Richmond, VA 23225; *Hollywood & Vine,* PO Box 717, Madison, NC 27025; *Hollywood Collectibles,* 4099 McEwen Dr., Suite 350, Dallas, TX 75244; *Movie Advertising Collector,* PO Box 28587, Philadelphia, PA 19149; *Movie Collectors' World,* PO Box 309, Fraser, MI 48026; *Poorman's VHS Movie Collectors Newsletter,* 902 E. Country Cables, Phoenix, AZ 85022; *Spielberg Film Society Newsletter,* PO Box 13712, Tucson, AZ 85732; *The Movie Poster Update,* 2401 Broad St., Chattanooga, TN 37408; *The Silent Film Newsletter,* 140 7th Ave., New York, NY 10011; *Under Western Skies,* Route 3, Box 263H, Waynesville, NC 28786.

See: Cartoon Characters, Disneyana, Movie Personalities, and Posters.

Afghan, 46 x 62", Wizard of Oz, poster art image, MIB **110.00**

Book
Film Land Favorites, 1915, 80 pgs, photographs, biographies **65.00**
Gone With The Wind, Motion Picture Edition, 1940, 392 pgs **75.00**
Masters & Masterpieces of the Screen, 1927, 112 pgs, visual history **220.00**
Who's Who at MGM, 1940, 119 pgs, photographs, biographies **60.00**
Comic Book, Little Rascals, 1960 . . . . **15.00**
Cookbook Display, *Gone With The Wind,* Pebeco toothpaste premium, orig unopened package **300.00**
Dixie Cup Dispenser, Wizard of Oz, boxed refill **55.00**
Doll, 14½" h, Wizard of Oz, Largo, MIB, set of 4 . . . . **140.00**
Figure, 6½" h, Stay Puft, *Ghostbusters,* vinyl, movable head and arms **15.00**
Lobby Card, 11 x 14", set of 8
Daughter of Don Q, Republic Pictures, 1946 . . . . **125.00**
Lullaby of Broadway, Warner Bros, 1951 . . . . **75.00**
Operation Pacific, Warner Bros, 1951, full color, John Wayne **150.00**
The Invisible Monster, Republic Pictures, 1950 . . . . **85.00**
The Lemon Drop Kid, Paramount Pictures, 1951, full color **100.00**
The Mating Season, Paramount Picture, 1951 . . . . **75.00**
Magazine
Photoplay, six issues, Nov 1942–Feb 1943, April and June 1943, stars pictured on cov **75.00**
Silver Screen, five issues, Jan, Sept, Dec 1943 and March and July 1944, full color cov photos **55.00**

Magazine Tear Sheet, Wizard of Oz, 1939 . . . . **24.00**
Music Box, Wizard of Oz, Wicked Witch, Enesco, large, orig certificate **195.00**
Photograph
Eagle Squadron, shows movie lobby contest with real airplane **28.00**
Unidentified elegant woman posing with Chaplin mask **28.00**
Pillow, "Souvenir Of Hollywood," 15 x 15", pink glossy fabric, blue brocade border, tourist attractions illus **55.00**
Poster
Alice Doesn't Live Here Anymore, 14 x 36" **45.00**
A Royal Scandal, 41 x 27", Twentieth Century Fox, Tallulah Bankhead and Charles Coburn, 1945 . . . . . . **200.00**
Babes In Toyland, 14 x 36", Annette **110.00**
Brides of Dracula, 14 x 36", Peter Cushing **155.00**
Cat On A Hot Tin Roof, 14 x 36" Elizabeth Taylor **350.00**
Coogan's Bluff, 14 x 36", Clint Eastwood **110.00**
Coquette, 28 x 22", United Artist, Mary Pickford, 1929 . . . . **485.00**
Dangerous When Wet, Esther Williams, pinup art **79.00**
Dr Terror's House Of Horrors, 14 x 36", Christopher Lee, Peter Cushing **60.00**
Five Easy Pieces, 14 x 36", Jack Nicholson **115.00**
Full House, 30 x 40", Twentieth Century Fox, photos of twelve stars, 1952 . . . . **285.00**
Hour Before Dawn, 14 x 36", Veronica Lake **325.00**
Postman Always Rings Twice, 14 x 36", Jack Nicholson and Jessica Lange **90.00**
Proud Rebel, 14 x 36", Alan Ladd and Olivia DeHaviland **225.00**
Splendor In The Grass, 14 x 36", Natalie Wood and Warren Beatty **165.00**
The Actress, 22 x 14", Metro–Goldwyn Mayer, Norma Shearer, red, black, white, and blue, 1928 **230.00**
The Long Voyage Home, 41 x 27", United Artists, John Wayne **315.00**
The Maverick Queen, 14 x 36", Barbara Stanwyck **135.00**
Pressbook
Chandu On The Magic Island, Bela Lugosi **125.00**
Palooka, Lupe Velez and Durante . . **38.00**
Song of the South, 16 pgs, 1950s . . . **75.00**
Program
Gone With The Wind, 16 pgs, full color photo of Vivien Leigh **50.00**
The Grapes of Wrath, 8 pgs **75.00**
What Price Glory, color cov **80.00**

Wizard of Oz, sheet music, *Over The Rainbow,* **E. Y. Harburg lyrics, Harold Arlen music, 1939, $20.00.**

Sheet Music, *Wizard of Oz* 20.00
Song Folio, *Alice In Wonderland,*
  Paramount Films, 1933 . . . . **100.00**
Window Card
  Diary of Anne Frank **29.00**
  Fantasia, 22 x 28", 1940 . . . . **1,430.00**
  Goin' To Town, 14 x 17", Mae West,
    1937 . . . .   **300.00**
  Gypsy **26.00**
  Her Cardboard Lover, 14 x 22", full
    color, MGM, 1942 . . . .   **25.00**
Yearbook, Columbia Pictures, 1940–41,
  48 pgs, film previews **200.00**

MOVIE PERSONALITIES

Collecting Hints: Focus on one star. Today, the four most popular stars are Humphrey Bogart, Clark Gable, Jean Harlow, and Marilyn Monroe. Many of the stars of the silent era are being overlooked by the modern collector. Nostalgia appears to be a key to the star on which a person focuses.

Remember that stars have big support staffs. Not all autograph items were or are signed by the star directly. Signatures should be checked carefully against a known original.

Many stars had fan clubs and the fans tended to hold on to the materials they assembled. The collector should be prepared to hunt and do research. A great deal of material rests in private hands.

History: The star system and Hollywood are synonymous. The studios spent elaborate sums of money promoting their stars. Chaplin, Valentino, and Pickford gave way to Garbo and Gable.

The movie magazine was a key vehicle in promotion. *Motion Picture, Movie Weekly, Motion Picture World,* and *Photoplay* are just a few examples of this genre. *Photoplay* was the most sensational.

Film stars had no private life and individual cults grew up around many of them. By the 1970s the star system of the 1930s and 1940s had lost its luster. The popularity of stars is much shorter lived today.

References: Pauline Bartel, *The Complete Gone With The Wind Sourcebook,* Taylor Publishing, 1993; Leslie Halliwell, *The Filmgoer's Companion,* Avon, 1978; Ephraim Katz, *The Film Encyclopedia,* Perigee Books, 1979; Leonard Maltin (ed.), *TV Movies and Video Guide,* New American Library, 1987; Norman E. Martinus and Harry L. Rinker, *Warman's Paper,* Wallace–Homestead, 1994; Patrick McCarver, *Gone With The Wind Collector's Price Guide,* Collector's Originals, 1990; Robert Osborne, *65 Years of The Oscar: The Official History of The Academy Awards,* Abbeville, 1994; Edward R. Pardella, *Shirley Temple Dolls and Fashions: A Collector's Guide To The World's Darling,* Schiffer Publishing, 1992; Susan and Steve Raab, *Movie Star Autographs of the Golden Era,* published by authors, 1994; Jay Scarfone and William Stillman, *The Wizard of Oz Collector's Treasury,* Schiffer Publishing, 1992; Jon R. Warren, *Collecting Hollywood: The Movie Poster Price Guide, Third Edition,* American Collectors Exchange, 1994; Dian Zillner, *Hollywood Collectibles,* Schiffer Publishing, 1991; Dian Zillner, *Hollywood Collectibles: The Sequel,* Schiffer Publishing, 1994.

Collectors' Clubs: All About Marilyn, PO Box 291176, Hollywood, CA 90029; Emerald City Club, 153 E. Main St., New Albany, IN 47150; Hollywood Studio Collectors Club, Suite 450, 3960 Laurel Canyon Blvd. Studio City, CA 91604; Old Time Western Film Club, PO Box 142, Siler City, NC 27344; The Manuscript Society, 350 N. Niagara St., Burbank, CA 91505; Western Film Appreciation Society, 1914 112 St., Edmonton, Alberta T6J 5P8 Canada; Western Film Preservation Society, Inc., Raleigh Chapter, 1012 Vance St., Raleigh, NC 27608.

Periodicals: *Autograph Times,* 2303 N. 44th St., #225, Phoenix, AZ 85008; *Big Reel,* PO Box 83, Madison, NC 27025; *Celebrity Collector,* PO Box 1115, Boston, MA 02117; *Classic Images,* PO Box 809, Muscatine, IA 52761; *Collecting Hollywood,* 2401 Broad St., Chattanooga, TN 37408; *Gone With The Wind Collector's Newsletter,* 1347 Greenmoss Dr., Richmond, VA 23225; *Hollywood & Vine,* PO Box 717, Madison, NC 27025; *Hollywood Collectibles,*

4099 McEwen Dr., Suite 350, Dallas, TX 75244; *Movie Advertising Collector,* PO Box 28587, Philadelphia, PA 19149; *Movie Collectors' World,* PO Box 309, Fraser, MI 48026; *The Movie Poster Update,* 2401 Broad St., Chattanooga, TN 37408; *The Silent Film Newsletter,* 140 7th Ave., New York, NY 10011; *Under Western Skies,* Route 3, Box 263H, Waynesville, NC 28786.

See: Autographs, Magazines, and Posters.

Bardot, Brigitte, pink, 1" d, litho, silver rim, black and white photo, 1950s .. **12.50**
Bogart, Humphrey, sheet music, *Someday, I'll Meet You Again,* black and white photo with Michelle Morgan, pink montage background **25.00**
Carroll, Nancy, mask, paper, diecut, full color image, Par–T–Mask, 1933 copyright **30.00**
Chaplin, Charlie
  Mirror, pocket, celluloid, black and white photo, 1920s **100.00**
  Puppet, paper, diecut, jointed, full color, marked "Germany," c1920 **35.00**
Clift, Montgomery, photo, 5 x 7¼", black and white glossy, black ink signature, 1940–50 . . . . **400.00**
Coogan, Jackie, tin, 4" d, round, "The Kid," H Clive **45.00**

Bing Crosby, sheet music, *Going My Way,* Johnny Burke lyrics, Jimmy Van Heusen music, 1944, $10.00.

Davis, Bette
  Paper Doll, Merrill, #4816, 40 pcs clothing, 1942 . . . . **35.00**
  Photo, 5 x 7", black and white matte finish, black ink signature "To Dorothy Hall from Bette Davis," 1940s **200.00**
Fairbanks, Douglas, photo, 8 x 10", inscribed and sgd **285.00**

Fields, W. C.
  Cookie Jar, 11" h, ceramic, figural, marked "USA" and "153" **25.00**
  Doll, Effanbee, Centennial, MIB, 1980 . . . . **100.00**
Gable, Clark
  Advertising Display, Boones Farm, 6" h **25.00**
  Cigarette Card, No. 46, Park Drive Cigarettes **25.00**
  Photo, 14 x 17", black and white glossy, white signature, early 1940s **50.00**
Garbo, Greta
  Autograph, letter signed, MGM Studio, 1934 . . . . **40.00**
  Magazine, *Life,* Jan 10, 1955, black and white cov photo **15.00**
  Photo, 14 x 17", black and white glossy, white signature, early 1940s **50.00**
  Tin, litho, Sunshine Biscuits, black and white photo, name on lid, early 1930s **125.00**
Gardner, Ava, pin, 1" d, litho, silver rim, black and white photo, 1950s **15.00**
Garland, Judy, photo, 14 x 17", black and white glossy, white signature, early 1940s **50.00**
Harlow, Jean, photo, 5 x 7", black and white, inscribed "To Dorothy Hall/ Cordially Jean Harlow," c1937 . . . . **55.00**
Hayworth, Rita
  Announcement Folder, 10 x 13", thin cardboard, "After 'Salome,' What?" inscription on front cov, movie title and black and white scene on inside panel **25.00**
  Paper Doll Book, Saalfield, #1529, full color portrait illus, unused . . . **100.00**
Henie, Sonja, program, Howdy Mr Ice, Rockefeller Center, July 5, 1948 . . . . **15.00**
Hepburn, Katharine, playing cards, complete deck, black and white photos of *Little Women* role **30.00**
Hope, Bob
  Coloring Book, 11 x 14", Saalfield, unused **18.00**
  Magazine, *1000 Jokes Magazine,* July–Aug, 1946, color cov, 48 pgs **18.00**
Karloff, Boris
  Photo, 5 x 7", black and white, purple ink signature "For Dorothy Hall, Sincerely Boris Karloff," 1940s . . . **250.00**
Kelly, Grace, magazine, *Life,* two issues, April 26, 1954 with black and white cov photo and April 11, 1955 with color cov photo **25.00**
Lamarr, Hedy, photo, 14 x 17", black and white glossy, early 1940s **55.00**
Laurel and Hardy
  Bank, 7½" h, Stan Laurel, vinyl, 1974 Larry Harmon copyright, Play Pal Plastics **35.00**

Bendee, Knickerbocker, price for pr 45.00
Coloring Book, Saalfield, 96 pgs,
1972 copyright 25.00
Stein, 9½" h, Stan Laurel, figural, ce-
ramic, metal hinge, Japan sticker 75.00
Toy, windup, Oliver Hardy, plastic
and metal, Japan, 1970s 75.00
MacDonald, Jeannette
Coloring Book, 10¼ x 15", Merrill,
1941 . . . . 18.00
Photo, 14 x 17", black and white
glossy, 1940s 55.00
Mansfield, Jayne
Magazine, *Show,* October, 1955, full
color cov photo 25.00
Poster, 62 x 21", wearing red bikini,
c1960 . . . . 315.00
Mitchum, Robert, photo, 5 x 7", black
and white, blue ink signature "To Lila,
Thank You, Bob Mitchum" 50.00
Monroe, Marilyn
Lamp, figural, orig Vandor label 80.00
Paperback Book, *Seven Year Itch,*
1955 . . . . 28.00
Photo, 8 x 10", color glossy, wearing
yellow two piece outfit, A Sheer
copyright, late 1950s 25.00
O'Hara, Maureen, pin, 1" d, litho, sil-
ver rim, black and white photo,
1950s 12.00
Robinson, Edward G., photo, 5 x 7",
black and white glossy, black ink sig-
nature "To Shirley Miller from Edward
G Robinson," 1940s 125.00
Rooney, Mickey
Paint Book, 10 x 15", Merrill, 1940 40.00
Photo, black and white glossy, white
signature, early 1940s 50.00
Scott, George C., lobby card, *The
Hindenberg,* 1975, set of 8 . . . . . . 20.00
Swanson, Gloria
Dress, matching coat, red 48.00
Glove Box, Swanson and Henry Clive 35.00
Souvenir Spoon, price for set of 8 . . 60.00

**Gloria Swanson, tin, head and shoulders
portrait by Henry Clive, marked "Beaute-
box/Canco," 7½" d, $65.00.**

Taylor, Elizabeth, photo, captioned,
1950s, price for set of 7 . . . . 40.00
Taylor, Robert, photo, 14 x 17", black
and white glossy, early 1940s 55.00
Valentino, Rudolph
Figure, metal, jointed, SABA 300.00
Sheet Music, *Respectfully Dedicated
to Rudolph Valentino,* brown and
white cov, 1932 . . . . 22.00
Wayne, John
Magazine, *Look,* October 6, 1942,
color front cov 35.00
Tablet, 5½ l", color photo cov, 1950s 25.00
West, Mae, photo, 9 x 12", black and
white, Lux Soap premium, mid 1930s 25.00

MUSIC BOXES

Collecting Hints: Any figurine or box–shaped object has the potential for insertion of a music box.
The following list of music boxes deals with objects in which the music box is secondary to the
piece. Antique music boxes are covered in
Warman's Antiques And Their Prices.

Collectors often tend to focus on one tune, trying to collect all the variety of ways it is used.
Others concentrate on a musical toy form, such
as dolls or teddy bears. A popular item is the musical jewel box, prevalent during the 1880 to
1930 period.

History: The insertion of a small music box into
toys and other products dates back to the 18th
century. Initially these were limited to the children of the aristocracy; but the mass production
of music boxes in the late 19th century made
them available to everyone.

The music box toy enjoyed greater popularity
in Europe than in America. Some of the finest examples are of European craftsmanship. After
World War II there was an influx of cheap music
box toys from the Far East. The popularity of the
musical toy suffered as people reacted negatively
to these inferior products.

References: Gilbert Bahl, *Music Boxes: The
Collector's Guide To Selecting, Restoring, and
Enjoying New and Vintage Music Boxes,*
Running Press, Courage Books, 1993; H. A. V.
Bulleid, *Cylinder Musical Box Design and
Repair,* Almar Press, 1987; Arthur W. J. G. Ord–
Hume, *The Musical Box: A Guide For Collectors,*
Schiffer Publishing, 1995;

Collectors' Clubs: Musical Box Society
International, 1062 Alber St., Wabash, IN 46992;
Musical Box Society of Great Britain, The
Willows, 102 High St., Landbeach, Cambridge
CB4 4DT England.

Museums: Bellms Cars and Music of Yesterday,
Sarasota, FL; Lockwood Matthews Mansion

Museum, Norwalk, CT; Miles Musical Museum, Eureka Springs, AR; The Musical Museum, Deansboro, NY.

Ballerina, 9", bisque, glass eyes, cylinder base, French	300.00
Bank, plastic, Gorham	
Acrobat, 7½", green	18.00
Cyclist, 7½", red	18.00
Bear, hand carved	65.00
Bird, figural, ceramic	
Cardinal, 6½"	20.00
Dove, 6¼"	15.00
Owl, 6"	20.00
Box	
1¼ x 4¼ x 3½", Thoren's cylinder, grained wood case plays Bicycle Built for Two	45.00
2½", Santa, white, plays Jingle Bells	8.00
2½ x 3½ x 6½", leather, porcelain plaque painting of five mallards on cov	70.00
3 x 3 x 5", Manivelle, three tunes, litho on cov, children feeding swan, tune sheet on bottom, Swiss	80.00
Children on Merry Go Round, 7¾", wood, figures move, plays Around the World in 80 Days	22.00
Children on See Saw, 7", wood, figures move in time to music	20.00
Christmas Tree Stand, revolving, Germany	65.00
Church, 4 x 6", tin, hand crank, Germany	125.00
Cigar Holder, 15", wood and brass	75.00
Clock, Hickory Dickory, Mattel, 1952	28.00
Clown, 5½", plastic, dome, Gorham	18.00
Coffee Grinder shape, 3"	30.00
Dog, 12", Nipper, ceramic	45.00
Doll	
Drum Major, 15", blue uniform, plays Cecile	100.00
Sammy Kay, 11", composition, sways	65.00
Easter Egg, tin	15.00
Kitten with ball, 5½", ceramic	18.00
Lamp, night, 6½", merry–go–round, c1950	30.00
Man, leaning against lamp post, cast iron, plays How Dry I Am, New York City souvenir	18.00
Merry–Go–Round, three horses and riders, 1904	45.00
Phonograph, 5¾ x 3¼ x 3¼", miniature, upright, wind–up, Swiss	78.00
Powder Box	
3½ x 4¼", metal, silver, litho cov, c1940	25.00
4½", enamel, floral, c1950	38.00
Snoopy on doghouse	50.00
Snowball, glass, wood base	
Frosty the Snowman, 5", red base	10.00
Mr and Mrs Santa, 5", green base	10.00

Santa and Rudolph, 5", green base	10.00
Statue, Elvis Presley on music box base, plays "Love Me Tender"	60.00
Stein, 5", porcelain, diamond dec	35.00
Three Little Pigs, Jaymar	48.00
Wizard of Oz, Enesco, large, Scarecrow, orig certificate	195.00

NAPKIN RINGS

Collecting Hints: Concentrate on napkin rings of unusual design or shape. This is one collectible which still can be used on a daily basis. However, check for the proper cleaning and care methods for the type of material you have. Many celluloid items have been ruined by storage in too dry an area or by washing in too hot water.

An engraved initial or other personalizing mark detracts rather than adds value to a napkin ring. Many collectors and dealers have these marks removed professionally if it will not harm the ring.

History: Napkin rings enjoyed a prominent role on the American dinner table during most of the 19th and early 20th centuries. Figural napkin rings were used in the upper class households. However, a vast majority of people used the simple napkin ring.

The shape does not mean that the decorative motif could not be elegant. Engraving, relief designs, and carving turned the simple ring into a work of art. When cast metal and molded plastic became popular, shaped rings, especially for children, were introduced.

The arrival of inexpensive paper products, fast and frozen foods and a quickened pace of American society reduced America's concern for elegant daily dining. The napkin ring almost has disappeared from the dining table.

Bakelite, hexagonal, red, yellow, and green, orig box, set of six	30.00
Bisque, cat, marked "Japan," 2 x 3"	20.00
Brass, emb leaf, dog, and dragon, 1⅛"	15.00
Bronze, bulldog, right paw raised, glass eyes, hammered ring	50.00
Celluloid, Scottie dog	15.00

Bone, floral carving, ⅞" h, 1½" d, $10.00.

Cloisonne, multicolored design, set of
  six **100.00**
Cut Glass
  Harvard pattern **75.00**
  Thistle pattern **45.00**
  Ivory, carved, fish and birds, 2" **45.00**
  Milk Glass, triangular **30.00**
Nippon
  Figural, owl on tree stump, 4" h,
    wreath mark **375.00**
  Multicolored jewels, heavy gold dec,
    turquoise ground, maple leaf mark   **65.00**
Noritake
  Art Deco, orig box, price for pair ... **75.00**
  Butterfly and Flowers **15.00**
Onion Meissen **25.00**
Papier Mache, green **3.00**
Pattern Glass, Hobstar and Fan **35.00**
Pewter, dragon **20.00**
R S Germany, green, pink roses, white
  snowballs **45.00**
Scrimshaw, carved ivory, stalking lion . **50.00**
Shell
  Band, encrusted with tiny shells **12.00**
  Souvenir, Atlantic City, 1895 ...... **28.00**
Silverplate
  Figural, goat pulling wheeled ring .. **195.00**
Round
  Eagle, applied **40.00**
  German scene **35.00**
  Wishbone, applied **30.00**
Sterling Silver
  Art Nouveau, 1½" **30.00**
  Child's, nursery rhyme figures **25.00**

NEW MARTINSVILLE VIKING

Collecting Hints: New Martinsville glass predating 1935 appears in a wide variety of colors. Later glass was only made in crystal, blue, ruby, and pink.

Look for cocktail, beverage, liquor, vanity, smoking and console sets. Amusing figures of barnyard and sea animals, dogs, and bears were produced. Both Rainbow art glass and Viking glass are handmade and have a paper label. Rainbow art glass pieces are beautifully colored and the animal figures are more abstract in design than New Martinsville. Viking makes plain, colored, cut and etched tableware, novelties, and gift items. Viking began making black glass in 1979.

History: The New Martinsville Glass Manufacturing Company, founded in 1901, took its name from its West Virginia location. Early products were opal glass decorative ware and utilitarian items. Later productions were pressed

crystal tableware with flashed-on ruby or gold decorations. In the 1920s innovative color and designs made vanity, liquor, and smoker sets popular. Dinner sets in patterns such as Radiance, Moondrops, and Dancing Girl, as well as new colors, cuttings and etchings were produced. The 1940s brought black glass formed into perfume bottles, bowls with swan handles and flower bowls. In 1944 the company was sold and reorganized as the Viking Glass Company.

The Rainbow Art Glass Company, Huntington, West Virginia, was established in 1942 by Henry Manus, a Dutch immigrant. This company produced small, hand fashioned animals and decorative ware of opal, spatter, cased and crackle glass. Rainbow Art Glass also decorated for other companies. In the early 1970s, Viking acquired Rainbow Art Glass Company and continued the production of the small animals.

References: Lee Garmon and Dick Spencer, *Glass Animals of the Depression Era*, Collector Books, 1993; James Measell, *New Martinsville Glass: 1900–1944*, Antique Publications, 1994; Naomi L. Over, *Ruby Glass of the 20th Century*, Antique Publications, 1990, 1993–94 value update; Ellen Tischbein Schroy, *Warman's Glass, Second Edition*, Wallace–Homestead, 1995; Hazel Marie Weatherman, *Colored Glassware of the Depression Era, Book 2*, Glassworks, 1982.

Animal
  Duck, Epic Line, small
    Amber **20.00**
    Green **20.00**
  Leapy Gazelle **75.00**
  Papa Bear **195.00**
  Swan, deep amber, crystal neck and
    head **15.00**
  Thumper Rabbit, Epic Line, orange . **30.00**
  Woodsman **100.00**
Ashtray, Moondrops, ruby **32.50**
Basket
  6½" h, Janice, crystal, red handle ... **65.00**
  11" h, Janice, black, #4552 .... **195.00**
Bonbon, 6" d, Radiance
  Amber **10.00**
  Crystal **5.00**
  Ice Blue **17.50**
  Red **18.00**
Bookends, pr
  Elephants **95.00**
  Sailboats **48.00**
Bowl, Radiance
  8" d, flower basket etching, handles   **15.00**
  10" d, crimped
    Amber **18.00**
    Crystal **10.00**
    Ice Blue **24.00**
    Red **25.00**
Butter Dish, cov, Radiance
  Amber **185.00**

Crystal	100.00
Ice Blue	400.00
Red	400.00
Cake Stand, Prelude, crystal, 11″ d, ftd	45.00
Candlesticks, pr, 5″ h, Janice, light blue, #4554	42.50
Celery, 11″ l, Janice, light blue	60.00
Cheese and Cracker Set	
#26, crystal	45.00
Radiance	
Amber	25.00
Crystal	16.00
Ice Blue	48.00
Red	48.00
Cocktail, #125, ruby, platinum bands	7.50
Compote	
#26	15.00
Prelude	35.00
Console Set, Florentine Etch, 11½″ #29 bowl, pair #4450/29 double candlesticks, price for set	48.00
Cordial, Moondrops, 1 oz	
Amber	20.00
Red	35.00
Creamer, Radiance	
Amber	14.00
Crystal	6.00
Ice Blue	24.00
Red	22.00
Creamer and Sugar	
Moondrops, individual size, ruby	35.00
Prelude	15.00
Cup and Saucer	
Moondrops, ruby	22.00
Radiance	
Amber	17.50
Crystal	10.00
Ice Blue	25.00
Red	25.00
Goblet	
Georgian, ruby	12.00
Mt Vernon, ruby	9.50
Mustard, cov, Janice, blue	55.00
Pitcher, Radiance, amber	150.00
Plate	
7″ d, Prelude	10.00
8″ d, Radiance	
Amber	10.00
Crystal	5.00
Ice Blue	16.00
Red	16.00
9¼″ d, Moondrops, emerald green	18.00
Punch Bowl, Radiance	
Amber	100.00
Crystal	50.00
Emerald Green	125.00
Ice Blue	175.00
Red	175.00
Punch Bowl Set, Top Prize, punch bowl, metal tray, ladle, 8 cups, price for set	550.00
Punch Cup, Radiance	
Amber	8.00
Crystal	5.00

Ice Blue	17.50
Red	15.00
Relish, 8″ d, 3 part, 3 toes, Moondrops, ruby	35.00
Salt and Pepper Shakers, pr, Radiance	
Amber	50.00
Crystal	25.00
Ice Blue	80.00
Red	80.00
Sherbet	
Georgian, ruby	8.50
Moondrops, ruby	40.00
Mt Vernon, ruby	9.00
Soup Bowl, 7½″ d, Moondrops, ruby	75.00
Sugar	
Moondrops, individual size, emerald green	10.00
Prelude	18.00
Radiance	
Amber	12.00
Crystal	7.50
Ice Blue	20.00
Red	21.00
Torte Plate, 18″ d, Radiance, Prelude etching	75.00
Tumbler, 9 oz	
#34, ftd, amethyst	20.00
Hostmaster, ruby, 4¼″ h	10.00
Moondrops, ruby	20.00
Oscar, amber, platinum rim	7.50
Radiance	
Amber	17.50
Cobalt Blue	28.00
Crystal	8.50
Ice Blue	28.00
Red	26.00
Vanity Set, light blue, two diamond shaped cologne bottles, matching puff box, price for set	65.00
Whiskey, Moondrops, amber, one handle	8.00
Wine, Moondrops, ruby, 4 oz	22.50

NEWSPAPERS, HEADLINE EDITIONS

Collecting Hints: All newspapers must be complete with a minimal amount of chipping and cracking. The post–1880 newsprint is made of wood pulp and deteriorates quickly without proper care. Pre–1880 newsprint was composed of cotton and rag fiber and has survived much better than its wood pulp counterpart.

Front pages only of 20th century newspapers command about 60% of the value for the entire issue, since the primary use for these papers is display. Pre–20th century issues are collectible only if complete, as banner headlines were rarely used. These papers tended to run between four and eight pages.

Major city issues are preferable, although any newspaper providing a dramatic headline is collectible. Banner headlines, those extending completely across the paper, are most desirable. Also desirable are those from the city in which the event happened and command a substantial premium over the prices listed. Complete series collections carry a premium as well, such as all 20th century election reports, etc.

Twentieth century newspapers are easily stored. Issues should be placed flat in polyethylene bags, or acid-free folders that are slightly larger than the paper, and kept from high humidity and direct sunlight.

Although not as commonly found, newspapers from the 17th through the 19th centuries are highly collectible, particularly those from the Revolutionary War, War of 1812, Civil War, and those reporting Indian and "desperado" events. Two of the most commonly reprinted papers are the *Ulster County Gazette,* of January 4, 1800, dealing with Washington's death and the *N.Y. Herald,* of April 15, 1865, dealing with Lincoln's death. If you have either of these papers, chances are you have a reprint.

History: America's first successful newspaper was *The Boston Newsletter,* founded in 1704. The newspaper industry grew rapidly, experiencing its golden age in the early 20th century. Within the last decade many great evening papers have ceased publication, and many local papers have been purchased by the large chains.

Collecting headline edition newspapers has become popular during the last twenty years, largely because of the decorative value of the headlines. Also, individuals like to collect newspapers related to the great events which they have witnessed or which have been romanticized through the movies, television, and other media, especially those reporting events, the Old West, and the gangster era.

References: Harold Evans, *Front Page History,* Salem House, 1984; Robert F. Karolevitz, *From Quill To Computer: The Story of America's Community Newspapers,* National Newspaper Foundation, 1985; Jim Lyons, *Collecting American Newspapers,* published by author, 1989; Norman E. Martinus and Harry L. Rinker, *Warman's Paper,* Wallace–Homestead, 1994; Gene Utz, *Collecting Paper: A Collector's Identification & Value Guide,* Books Americana, 1993.

Periodical: *PCM (Paper Collectors' Marketplace),* PO Box 128, Scandinavia, WI 54977.

Collectors' Club: Newspaper Collectors Society of America, PO Box 19134, Lansing, MI 48901.

Advisor: Tim Hughes.

Note: The listing concentrates on newspapers of the 20th century. The date given is the date of the event itself. The newspaper coverage usually appeared the following day.

1865, April 15, Lincoln's assassination, first report (note: the *New York Herald* for the above date has been reprinted many times and is often the issue being "discovered." The genuine issue should be eight pages and should not have an illus of Lincoln on the front page) **450.00**
1886, September 1, surrender of Geronimo **85.00**
1898, February 15, sinking of the *Maine* **55.00**
1898, August 12, Spanish–American War ends **35.00**
1900, September 19, Butch Cassidy and Kid Curry rob First National Bank in Winnemucca, NV **25.00**
1903, December 17, Wright Brothers' first flight **275.00**
1904, November 8, Teddy Roosevelt elected **20.00**
1908, June 24, President Cleveland dies **20.00**
1912, February 14, Arizona becomes 48th state **15.00**
1912, April 15, *Titanic* sinks **325.00**
1914, July 11, Babe Ruth's first Major League game, Boston **55.00**
1915, May 7, *Lusitania* sinks **275.00**
1917, April 6, World War I, war is declared **30.00**
1918, November 11, Armistice signed, World War I ends **55.00**
1920, January 16, Prohibition goes into effect **25.00**
1920, August 26, Suffrage, women get right to vote **25.00**
1921, March 4, Harding inauguration **20.00**
1923, February 16, King Tut's tomb opened **30.00**
1925, March 4, Coolidge inauguration **23.00**
1926, May 8, Byrd reaches NorthPole . **22.00**
1927, March 2, Babe Ruth gets $210,000 for three years **40.00**
1927, May 20, Lindbergh starts solo flight across Atlantic **44.00**

Lindbergh Does It!, *New York Times,* **May 22, 1927, $45.00.**

1927, November 30, Byrd reaches South Pole 23.00
1928, June 18, Amelia Earhart crosses Atlantic 32.00
1928, October 10, Babe Ruth hits three homeruns in World Series 47.00
1929, May 17, Al Capone gets one year sentence 34.00
1929, October 28, Stock Market Crash 74.00
1920s, generic issues, no historic headlines 3.00
1930, October 13, "Legs Diamond" is shot 22.00
1931, October 17, Thomas Edison death 18.00
1932, March 1, Lindbergh baby kidnaped 24.00
1932, August 5, Bonnie and Clyde kill sheriff Maxwell in Oklahoma 18.00
1933, March 4, Franklin D Roosevelt inauguration 18.00
1933, April 7, Prohibition repealed ... 26.00
1933, September 6, Dillinger robs Indiana bank 22.00
1934, April 23, Baby Face Nelson kills FBI agent 20.00
1935, August 16, Will Rogers and Wiley Post killed in airplane crash 24.00
1937, May 6, *Hindenburg* crashes and burns 57.00
1938, July 17, "Wrong Way" Corrigan flies to Ireland 22.00
1939, May 2, Lou Gehrig's consecutive game streak ends 28.00
1930s, generic issues, no historic headlines 3.00
1941, December 7, Pearl Harbor bombed 35.00
1942, June 5, battle of Midway 18.00
1944, June 6, D–Day 27.00
1945, February 19, battle of Iwo Jima . 17.00

1945, August 14, Japan quits, V–J Day   30.00
1940s, generic issues of World War II with front page war headlines 4.00
1961, January 20, John F Kennedy inauguration 23.00
1962, August 6, Marilyn Monroe dies . 19.00
1963, November 22, John F Kennedy assassination 28.00
1968, April 15, Martin Luther King assassination 20.00
1969, July 21, Man lands on moon ... 23.00
1973, January 26, Vietnam War ends . 16.00
1977, August 17, Elvis Presley dies ... 18.00

NILOAK POTTERY

Collecting Hints: Mission ware pottery is characterized by swirling layers of browns, blues, reds and cream. Very few pieces are glazed on both the outside and inside. Usually only the interior is glazed.

History: Niloak Pottery was made near Benton, Arkansas. Charles Dean Hyten, the founder of this pottery, experimented with the native clay and tried to preserve the natural colors. By 1911 he had perfected a method that produced this effect. The result was the popular Mission ware. The wares were marked Niloak, which is Kaolin, the type of fine porcelain clay used, spelled backwards.

After a devastating fire the pottery was rebuilt and named Eagle Pottery. This factory included the space to add a novelty pottery line which was introduced in 1929. This line continued until 1934 and usually bears the name Hywood–Niloak. After 1934 the name Hywood was dropped from the mark. Mr. Hyten left the pottery in 1941. In 1946 the operation closed.

References: Susan and Al Bagdade, *Warman's American Pottery and Porcelain,* Wallace–Homestead, 1994; David Edwin Gifford, *The Collector's Encyclopedia of Niloak,* Collector Books, 1993; Ralph and Terry Kovel, *Kovels' American Art Pottery: The Collector's Guide To Makers, Marks and Factory Histories,* Crown Publishers, 1993.

Collectors Club: Arkansas Pottery Collectors Society, 12 Normandy Rd., Little Rock, AR 72007.

Ashtray, figural, hat, blue 7.50
Bowl, 8 x 3", chocolate brown, tan, and turquoise swirls, Mission Ware 60.00
Cornucopia
  3", light pink 5.00
  7", light blue 6.50
Creamer and Sugar, rose glaze, Hywood line 24.00
Ewer, eagle, 9½" w 45.00

Roosevelt Dies!, *The Times–Herald,* Newport News, VA, April 12, 1945, $27.00.

Figure
Canoe, 7½", white matte 30.00
Frog 20.00
Polar Bear, white matte 35.00
Squirrel 19.00
Paperweight, rabbit, orig paper label . .   30.00
Pitcher
3¼", yellow 12.00
7", dark green glaze 14.00
Planter
Bear, 3", tan 18.00
Camel, 3" 22.00
Cannon, 3", blue 15.00
Deer, 8", pink and blue, matte 30.00
Duck, 5", pink and blue 18.00
Elephant, 6", white 20.00
Fox, 4", red 20.00
Frog, 4", seated on lily pad 35.00
Kangaroo, 5", white, brown accents .   10.00
Log, 7", white 15.00
Parrot, 5", white, orange accents . . .   12.00
Policeman and Donkey, 5", blue . . .   25.00
Rabbit, 3", green 12.00
Squirrel, 6", light blue shading to tan   25.00
Swallow, 2", green 8.50
Swan, 7" l 35.00
Wishing Well, 7¼", dusty rose 12.00
Salt and Pepper Shakers, pr, Penguin . .   65.00
Vase
6" h, bud, leaf, Hywood line, blue
glaze 18.00
7" h, maroon, handles 15.00
8" h
Aqua–green glaze, Hywood line,
orig paper label 18.00
Gray shaded to pink ground, four
flowers 28.00

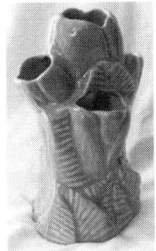

Vase, purple over white ground, center opening surrounded by four additional openings, 6¾" h, $18.00.

NIPPON CHINA, 1891–1921

Collecting Hints: Examine each item carefully. Try not to purchase items with chips, cracks, hairlines, spiderwebs, or that have been restored. The condition of each item, in relation-

ship to selling price, should be taken into consideration.

Also try to avoid buying sets which are incomplete. No matter what people say, you do not easily find the lid which is missing from your humidor, the cup and saucer to complete your chocolate set or the creamer to match your sugar bowl. Know what constitutes a complete set.

Beginning collectors should try to purchase only Nippon marked items. Learn the difference between the authentic marks and the reproduction marks. There are unmarked pieces from the Nippon era, but the purchase of these items should be put off until the collector has a commanding knowledge of Nippon.

History: Nippon, Japanese hand–painted porcelain, was made for export between the years of 1891 and 1921.

In October 1891, the McKinley Tariff Act was passed by Congress, proclaiming that "All articles of foreign manufacture, be stamped, branded, or labeled, and all packages containing such or their imported articles, shall, respectively, be marked, stamped, branded, or labeled in legible English words, so as to indicate the country of their origin; and unless so marked, stamped, branded, or labeled they shall not be admitted to entry."

The Japanese chose to use "Nippon," which is the English equivalent of Japan, as their marking. The McKinley Tariff Act also set rules and regulations on the marking system, stating that "all articles of foreign manufacture which are capable of being marked without injury shall be marked with the country of origin in legible English words and marking shall be nearly indelible and permanent as the nature of the article will permit." Paper labels were accepted. In the case of small articles shipped together, only the inside and outside packages were marked with the country of origin.

In 1921 the government reversed its position and decided that "Nippon" was no longer in compliance with the law. "After examination into the history and derivation of the word `Nippon' and its treatment by lexicographers of recognized standing, the department is constrained to the conclusion that `Nippon' is a Japanese word, the English equivalent of which is `Japan,' and the weight of authority does not support the earlier view that the word has become incorporated into the English language." All Japanese items now had to be marked "Japan," thus ending the Nippon era.

Nippon marks were applied by two methods— an under-the-glaze decal sticker or direct imprinting.

There are over 221 recorded Nippon backstamps or marks known to collectors today. The three most readily found and widely recognized are the "M" in Wreath, Maple Leaf and Rising Sun marks.

The majority of all marks are found in three color variations: green, blue, and magenta. The color of the mark indicates the quality of the porcelain used: green denotes first grade quality of porcelain; blue denotes second grade; and magenta denotes third grade.

References: Gene Loendorf, *Nippon Hand Painted China*, McGrew Color Graphics, 1975; Joan Van Patten, *The Collector's Encyclopedia Of Nippon Porcelain, Series One*, (1979, 1994 value update), *Series Two* (1982, 1995 value update), *Series Three* (1985, 1994 value update), Collector Books; Kathy Wojciechowski, *The Wonderful World of Nippon Porcelain: 1891–1921*, Schiffer Publishing, 1992.

Collectors' Clubs: ARK–LA–TEX Nippon Club, 6800 Arapaho Rd., #1057, Dallas, TX 75248; Buckeye Chapter, 700 E. High St., Hicksville, OH 43526; Dixieland Nippon Club, PO Box 1712, Centerville, VA 22020; International Nippon Collectors Club, PO Box 230, Peotone, IL 60468; Long Island Nippon Collectors Club, 145 Andover Place, W. Hempstead, NY 11552; MD–PA Collectors' Club, 2026 Erwin Dr., Jappa, MD 21085; New England Nippon Collectors Club, 64 Burt Rd., Springfield, MA 01118; Sunshine State Nippon Collectors' Club, 2410 NE 48th St., Lighthouse Pt., FL 33064; The Lakes & Plains Nippon Collectors Society, PO Box 230, Peotone, IL 60468; Upstate New York, 122 Laurel Ave., E. Herkimer, NY 11350.

Advisor: Kathy Wojciechowski.

REPRODUCTION ALERT: Most so-called Nippon reproductions do not even resemble the Nippon era wares; but, there is a "Nippon" backstamp found on them, thus fooling many collectors and dealers.

The pattern often found and on the biggest variety of pieces is "Wildflower." These items have a bisque finish, outside edges are highlighted with gold, and pink to lavender flower blossoms are used as the decoration. All wares in this pattern are marked with a bogus hourglass in a Wreath mark.

The "Green Mist" pattern items are reminiscent of Limoges pieces in shape, have a bisque finish, a light to medium green background, pink flowers, and gold trim. The mark found on these pieces is similar to the familiar Nippon Rising Sun mark except that the rays are connected rather than open as in the genuine mark.

The "Antique Rose" pattern is one of the newest patterns being reproduced. This can be found in a variety of shapes and bears the bogus Maple Leaf mark, which is almost a duplicate of the genuine mark except that it is much larger in size.

Most reproduction Nippon wares are manufactured in Japan and have a "Nippon" mark of some type under the glaze and a small paper label on the bottom saying "Made in Japan." Dealers buy wholesale from the importing firms. First, they discard the shipping boxes, then the paper label, resulting in a genuine marked "Nippon" item for the market.

Ashtray
4½" l
　Phoenix bird in blue, gold trim,
　　Wreath . . . .　90.00
　Scenic lake and trees, shiny finish,
　　Wreath . . . .　65.00
5", colorful playing cards, brown
　ground, Wreath . . . .　135.00
5¼"
　Moriage dragon design, gray
　　ground, Royal Moriage . . . .　175.00
　Scenic, sailboat, beaded trim . . . .　125.00
6" w, triangular, moose decal, Wreath　135.00
7" w, Wedgwood white on blue,
　Maple leaf . . . .　225.00
Asparagus Set, 12 x 7½" master tray, hp
　asparagus, six matching 7½" plates,
　Wreath mark, price for set . . . .　225.00
Basket
3½" h, white ground, blue scenic . .　45.00
4" h, white ground, garlands of tiny
　flowers, Sun . . . .　95.00
5¼" h, heavy all over moriage, un-
　marked . . . .　300.00
7½" h
　Cobalt blue, center portrait medal-
　　lion, loop handle, Maple leaf . .　850.00
　Gray ground, large moriage sea
　　gulls . . . .　350.00
8" h, bisque center of bridge over
　lake, blues and oranges, fancy mo-
　riage handle, Maple leaf . . . .　325.00
Berry Bowl, pierced, underplate
8¼" d round, heavy pink and dark
　pink roses with gold, fancy scroll
　feet, band of gold, Maple leaf . . .　175.00
8¾" d round, scalloped edge, wide
　top band of bright green, heavy
　gold overlay designs, Maple leaf　175.00
Berry Set, master bowl and 6 small
　bowls, price for set
10" d master, 5¼" d small, cobalt blue
　ground, swans on lake medallions,
　heavy gold beading, Wreath mark　425.00
10¼" d master, 5" d small, white
　ground, yellow and blue roses
　bands, Rising Sun mark . . . .　165.00
10½" d master, 5" d small, allover
　geometric design, red, black, and
　gold, gold beading on rims, Maple
　leaf . . . .　225.00
11" d master, 5¼" small, scalloped
　edge, large red and white roses,
　heavy gold dec . . . .　295.00
Blotter, rocking, 6", pink, yellow, and
　blue flowers, gold handle, orig brass

insert, paper label inside reads "Compliments of the Morimura Bros, 1903" **225.00**
Boullion Cup, two handled cup, lid, underplate
4" h, bands of pink roses, red ground, Maple leaf **145.00**
5" h
  Cobalt blue, white, and gold, Wreath **120.00**
  White ground, allover gold design **85.00**
Bowl
5½" d, bisque scenic, lake, windmill, and trees **55.00**
5¾" l, ftd, pierced handles, gold outlined berries and leaves, RC mark **50.00**
7½" d, pink flowers, green garlands, Cherry Blossom **25.00**
7¾" d, geometric designs **65.00**
9¾" d, bisque scenic, house and trees, Wreath **90.00**
10" d, dark green ground, yellow daisies, Kinran mark **165.00**
10¾" h, ftd, white ground, wide band of colorful fruit, gold handles, Wreath mark **125.00**
12" d, RS Prussia mold, blown out sides, heavy red and white roses traced with gold, Wreath mark . . . **285.00**
Box, 2½ x 6", figural, baby grand piano, tall thin gold legs, pink bands with multicolored jewels, scenic lid **450.00**
Butter Tub, lid, insert, and underplate
7¼" d, bisque scenic, TEOH mark . . **85.00**
7½" d
  Cream ground, orange and green floral, Wreath **125.00**
  Red ground, heavy red roses, Maple leaf **210.00**
Cake Plate, pierced handles
10" d, yellow roses, gold outlined garlands, Wreath **115.00**
11" d, bisque scenic, barn on country road, Wreath **85.00**
12" d, band of fruit, Kinran mark . . . **150.00**
Cake Set, master and six small plates
Floral
  Cobalt blue, heavy gold overlay, Wreath **450.00**
  Cream ground, Wreath mark **95.00**
Scenic
  Birds on lake, TEOH mark **75.00**
  Windmill, lake, house **165.00**
Candle Lamp, 15" h, robin's egg blue ground, white doves on base and shade, Wreath mark **1,600.00**
Candlestick
5½" h, child's, bunnies dec, Wreath . **100.00**
6¼" h, Nile scene, ship and moriage flowers **185.00**
7" h, Gouda type dec **95.00**
8" h, triangular base, tiny gold han-

dle, bisque scenic, camel and rider at camp fire, price for pair **550.00**
10" h, triangular base, Galle scene, moriage floral trim and trees in the forest, Maple leaf **275.00**
Celery Set, master and four or six individual salts
11" l master, six 3¾" salts, white ground, heavy cobalt blue and gold bands, heavy gold, Wreath . . **145.00**

Celery Set, white ground, pink and blue flowers, green leaves in tan band, gold scroll, purple stamp "M" in wreath mark, 12½" handled master dish, six 4" l matching salts, price for set, $75.00.

13½" l master, four salts, pastel Geisha girls, red trim, mountains in background, Royal Kaga Nippon mark **115.00**
Child's Feeding Dish, 8" d round
Children playing with dog, Rising sun mark **165.00**
Girl with book, Rising sun mark . . . **150.00**
Children's Tea Set, 3¼" teapot, creamer, sugar, three cups and saucers, two geese with blue top and bottom bands, Sun mark, price for set **250.00**
Chocolate Pot
9" h, pastoral scene, TEOH **85.00**
10" h, graceful shape and handle, gold ground, heavy turquoise beading, central floral medallion, Maple leaf mark **450.00**
Chocolate Set, 12½" h chocolate pot, RS Prussia mold, fancy handle, cream ground, allover gold design and beading, center medallions of lavender and pink violets, six cups and saucers, Maple leaf mark **1,600.00**
Cigarette Box
4¾", earthtone background, brown side profile of Moriage Indian, Wreath mark **200.00**
5½", Japanese pagoda scene, bright blue, green, and gold, Wreath mark **195.00**

Ferner

4½" h, ftd, ruffled top, large moriage
leaves, unmarked **325.00**

5½" w, triangular, earthtone colors,
sailing ships in front, windmill in
background, Wreath **200.00**

8" h, gold handles and feet, large pink
and yellow roses and foliage,
Wreath **250.00**

Hatpin Holder, 4¾" h

Attached rocking bottom, closed top,
cobalt blue, gold, and white,
Maple Leaf **285.00**

White ground, top and bottom dec
bands, RC **85.00**

Woodland scene, closed top, Maple
leaf **235.00**

Humidor, cov

4½" h, rust ground, playing cards,
Wreath **295.00**

5" h, colorful geometric designs,
Wreath **325.00**

5½" h, bisque windmill scene,
Wreath **275.00**

6" h, three gold handles, bisque
windmill scene, person walking in
lane, moon in sky, Wreath **725.00**

7" h, jockey on race horse, Wreath   **450.00**

7½" h, desert scene, palm trees, people, Deco top and bottom band,
Wreath **400.00**

9" h, hexagon shape, four ball feet,
brown moriage Indian on front,
pipe with smoke on back, Wreath   **650.00**

Inkwell, 4 x 4", triangular, Indian in canoe scene, Wreath **325.00**

Mug

4½" h, white ground, pink floral de-
sign, Wreath **135.00**

5" h

Moriage dragon, gray ground,
Wreath **245.00**

Sailing ships, full sails, Wreath . . .   **250.00**

Mustard, cov, 3½" h

Floral, matching underplate and
spoon, Wreath **65.00**

Shiny, scenic, orig spoon, Wreath . .   **35.00**

Napkin Ring

Scenic, Wreath **55.00**

Triangular, forest green ground, magenta and pink roses, gold trim, un-
marked **60.00**

Nut Set, 5½" w master, six cups, ftd,
melon ribbed, cream ground, gold
overlay designs, Leaf **95.00**

Plaque

8½", wide moriage trim border, cen-
ter dog profile **395.00**

9", bisque barnyard scene, ducks in
lane, Wreath **275.00**

10"

Camel and rider desert scene, palm
trees, Wreath **325.00**

Sailing ships, shades of orange,
Wreath **225.00**

10¼", handkerchief center medallion
of horse and two dogs, marbleized
ground, Wreath **300.00**

12", still leaf with lobster, Wreath . .   **275.00**

Plate

6½" d, bisque, scenic, Wreath **45.00**

6¾" d, blown out child's face, Rising
Sun **75.00**

7½" d

Floral border, Wreath **65.00**

Heavy geometric designs, Wreath .   **65.00**

9" d, souvenir of Washington DC,
gold trim, Wreath **145.00**

Powder Box, 8" d, pale green ground,
gold outlined large pink flower and
buds, Maple leaf **300.00**

Punch Set, banquet size punch bowl,
ftd pedestal base, 6 pedestal base
punch cups, scenic, shades of blue,
Leaf **1,600.00**

Salt and Pepper Shakers, pr

Bisque, scenic, Wreath **25.00**

Cobalt blue, gold, and roses, Leaf . .   **95.00**

White ground, bands of orange flow-
ers, Sun **55.00**

Stamp Box

2¼", shiny windmill scenic, Wreath   **85.00**

2¾", black and white geometric de-
signs **110.00**

Sugar Shaker, 5" h

Heavy pink floral, gold, no handle,
Wreath **95.00**

Hexagon, bands of florals, gold han-
dle, Wreath **95.00**

Pale green ground, floral, cobalt blue
trim, gold handle **95.00**

Stein, 7" h

Allover floral design, Wreath **375.00**

Enameled Oriental design, blue and
reds, Wreath **325.00**

Marbleized ground, dancing pheas-
ants, Wreath **525.00**

Monk with beer stein, enameled
flowers, Wreath **525.00**

Scenic, top and bottom bands of
owls, Wreath **425.00**

Tankard

10¼" h, tapestry, pink and yellow
roses, Leaf **750.00**

12" h, forest scene, matte finish,
Wreath **175.00**

13" h, moriage flowers and trim, un-
marked **395.00**

13¾" h, dark green ground, heavy
floral and gold, Leaf **450.00**

14" h, cobalt blue, gold, and roses,
full figure portrait of lady with
doves, rare, Leaf **1,400.00**

Toothpick

Bisque, sailing ship scene, three han-
dles, Wreath **165.00**

Pink roses, white ground, gold bead-
ing, Wreath **120.00**
Souvenir of Washington DC, ftd, two
handles **135.00**
Trinket Box
3", pedestal base, orange flowers, RC
mark **45.00**
3½", pale blue ground, pastel shades
of moriage surrounding center por-
trait, Wreath **285.00**
6½", figural, butterfly, dark magenta,
light pink roses, gold, Wreath **250.00**
Urn, cov, 12½" h, white ground, heavy
gold overlay designs, center medal-
lion of Queen Louise, Leaf **950.00**
Vase
5" h, yellow, blue floral, Rising sun   **65.00**
6½" h, Art Deco design, Wreath . . .   **75.00**
7¼" h, barnyard, chickens, Wreath   **195.00**
8" h, bisque, scenic, sailing ships,
Wreath **235.00**
8½" h, scenic, tapestry, man, lady,
and boat, Leaf **800.00**
9" h, sailing ships, cobalt blue and
gold, Wreath **350.00**
9½" h, molded in relief Apollo and
rearing dogs, Wreath **950.00**
10" h, white orchids, gold outlines,
Wreath **225.00**
11½" h, chrysanthemums and gold
overlay, Wreath **325.00**
13" h, bisque, scenic, fisherman and
cart at waterfront **1,000.00**

NORITAKE AZALEA CHINA

Collecting Hints: There are several backstamps on the Azalea pattern of Noritake China. The approximate dates are:

Prior to 1921: Blue rising sun, printed "Hand painted NIPPON"
1921–1923: Green wreath with M, printed "Noritake, Hand painted, Made in Japan"
1923–1930s: Green wreath with M, printed "Noritake, Hand painted, Made in Japan 19322"
1925–1930s: Red wreath with M, printed "Noritake, Hand painted, Made in Japan 19322"
1935–1940: Red azalea sprig, printed "Noritake Azalea Patt., Hand painted, Japan No. 19322/252622"

Most of the saucers and underplates do not have a backstamp, except those stamped "Azalea 19322/252622."

Most collectors assemble sets and are not concerned with specific marks. Those concentrating on specific marks, particularly the NIPPON one, may pay more. There presently are individuals who offer replacement service.

History: The Azalea pattern of Noritake China, made of fine china, was produced first in the early 1900s. Each piece was hand painted. The individuality of each artist makes it almost impossible to find two pieces with identical painting.

In the early 1900s the Larkin Company of Buffalo, New York, sold many household items to the American public through their catalog (similar to the Sears, Roebuck catalog). In the 1924 Larkin catalog a basic Azalea pattern serving set was advertised. The set included the larger coffee cups with the blue Rising Sun backstamp.

Two forces came together in the 1920s to make the Azalea pattern of Noritake China one of the most popular household patterns in this century. First, the Larkin Company initiated their "Larkin Plan," in which housewives could sign up to become "Larkin Secretaries." Each Larkin Secretary formed a small neighborhood group of five or more women who would buy Larkin products for their homes. The Larkin Secretary earned premiums based on the volume of sales she obtained. Household items, including Azalea china, could then be purchased either for cash or premiums.

Second, many households in the 1920s could not afford a complete set of fine china in a single purchase. The Larkin Club Plan enabled them to obtain items in the Azalea pattern one or a few at a time.

Over the years, and to provide more enticements, additional pieces, such as the nut/fruit shell-shaped bowl, candy jar, and child's tea set were added. Glassware, originally classified as crystal, was introduced in the 1930s but was not well received.

It became somewhat of a status symbol to "own a set of Azalea." The Azalea pattern china advertisement in the 1931 Larkin catalog claimed, "Our Most Popular China."

Some Azalea pieces were advertised for sale in the Larkin catalogs for 19 consecutive years, while others were advertised for only 4 or 5 years. These latter pieces are more scarce, and more sought after by collectors, resulting in a faster appreciation in value.

The ultimate goals of most serious collectors are the child's tea set, which we believe was advertised in only two Larkin Fall catalogs, and the so-called salesmen's samples, which were never advertised for sale.

The Larkin Company ceased operations as a distributor in 1945. Due to the quality and popularity of the Azalea pattern, this beautiful china remains cherished and highly collectible.

References: Larkin catalogs from 1916 through 1941.

Note: The Larkin catalog numbers are given in parentheses behind each listing. If arranged numerically, you will notice gaps in the numbering. For example, numbers 41 through 53 are missing. The "Scenic" pattern, presently called "Tree in the Meadow," also was popular during this same time period. Many of the missing Azalea numbers were assigned to the Scenic pattern.

CHINA

#2, cup and saucer	**15.00**
#4, plate, tea, 7½"	**12.50**
#7, creamer and sugar, cov	**30.00**
#8, plate, bread and butter, 6¼"	**10.00**
#9, sauce dish	**8.00**
#10, cake plate, 9¾"	**45.00**
#12, salad bowl, round, 10"	**28.00**
#13, plate, dinner, 9¾"	**24.00**
#14, condiment set, 5 pcs	**35.00**
#15, teapot, regular	**85.00**
#16, casserole, cov, regular	**60.00**
#17, platter, 14"	**40.00**
#18, relish, oval, 8½"	**18.50**
#39, refreshment set, 2 pcs	**35.00**
#40, gravy boat	**28.00**
#54, butter tub, insert	**25.00**
#56, platter, 12"	**40.00**
#97, syrup pitcher, underplate	**70.00**
#98, plate, breakfast, 8½"	**18.00**
#99, bread tray, 12"	**35.00**
#100, milk jug	**150.00**
#101, vegetable bowl, oval, 10½"	**30.00**
#119, relish, four sections, 10"	**100.00**
#120, egg cup	**32.00**
#121, lemon plate	**12.00**
#123, creamer and sugar, open	**65.00**

Creamer, #123, $35.00.

#124, bouillon cup and saucer, 5¼"	**15.00**
#125, jam jar set, 3 pcs	**115.00**
#126, salt and pepper shakers, pr, 2½"	**10.00**
#169, tile, 6"	**35.00**
#170, compote	**60.00**
#172, vegetable bowl, oval, 9½ x 6¾"	**35.00**
#182, coffeepot	**475.00**
#183, demitasse cup and saucer	**125.00**
#184, bonbon dish, 6¼"	**45.00**
#185, grapefruit bowl, 4½"	**115.00**
#186, platter, 16"	**375.00**
#187, vase, fan, ftd	**125.00**
#189, spoon holder, 8"	**65.00**
#190, cruet bottle	**170.00**
#191, mustard jar	**45.00**
#192, toothpick holder	**75.00**
#193, basket	**145.00**
#194, relish, oval, 7¼"	**45.00**
#310, bowl, deep	**42.00**
#311, platter, 10¼"	**150.00**
#312, butter chip, 3¼"	**65.00**
#313, tobacco jar, cov	**500.00**
#314, cheese dish, cov, 6¼"	**85.00**
#315, plate, sq, 7⅝"	**40.00**
#338, plate, grill, 10¼"	**120.00**
#372, casserole, cov, gold finial	**525.00**
#400, teapot, gold finial	**425.00**
#401, creamer and sugar, lid, gold finial	**100.00**
#439, bowl, divided	**225.00**
#444, celery dish, 10"	**240.00**
#453, mayonnaise set, scalloped, 3 pcs	**400.00**

GLASSWARE, HAND PAINTED

#11, fruit bowl, 8½"	**50.00**
#111, cheese and cracker set, 2 pcs	**60.00**
#112, tray, 10"	**45.00**
#113, compote, 10"	**58.00**
#114, candlesticks, pr	**35.00**
#124, cake plate, 10½"	**40.00**

NUTCRACKERS

Collecting Hints: The most popular modern nutcrackers are the military and civilian figures made in East Germany. These are collected primarily for show and not for practical use.

Nutcracker design responded to each decorating phase through the 1950s. The figural nutcrackers of the Art Deco and Art Nouveau periods are much in demand. Concentrating on 19th century models results in a display of cast iron ingenuity. These nutcrackers were largely utilitarian and meant to be used.

Several cast iron animal models have been reproduced. Looking for signs of heavy use is one method of spotting an older model.

History: Nuts keep well for long periods, up to two years, and have served as a dessert or additive to cakes, pies, bread, etc., since the colonial period. Americans' favorite nuts are walnuts, chestnuts, pecans, and almonds.

The first nutcrackers were crude hammers or a club device. The challenge was to find a cracker that would crack the shell but leave the nut intact. By the mid–19th century cast iron nutcrackers in animal shapes appeared. Usually the nut was placed in the jaw section of the animal and the tail pressed as the lever to crack the nut.

The 19th and early 20th century patent records

abound with nutcracker inventions. In 1916 a lever–operated cracker which could be clamped to the table was patented as the Home Nut Cracker, St. Louis, Missouri. Perhaps one of the most durable designs was patented on January 28, 1889, and sold as the Quakenbush plated model. This hand model was plain at the top where the grip teeth were located and had twist–style handles on the lower half of each arm with the arms ending in an acorn finial.

Reference: Judith A. Rittenhouse, *Ornamental and Figural Nutcrackers: An Identification and Value Guide,* Collector Books, 1993.

Alligator, cast iron, 6" l	**25.00**
Bear, wood, figural, glass eyes	**100.00**
Bird, wood, figural, curved neck, long tail, worn finish	**100.00**
Cat, brass, figural, 4½"	**40.00**
Chicken, head, wood, glass eyes, 1850s, 7"	**90.00**
Dickens, brass, figural	**40.00**
Dog, cast iron, figural, bronzed	**45.00**

Dog, nickel–plated iron, marked "L. A. Althoff Co.," $72.00.

Dragon, brass, figural	**50.00**
Elephant, cast iron, figural, painted . . .	**145.00**
Fish, brass, figural, 5"	**35.00**
Home, cast iron, table top, screw mechanism, long lever, 1915 patent	**25.00**
Jester, brass, figural	**75.00**
Lady's legs, brass, figural	**35.00**
Lion, brass, figural head	**35.00**
Man's head, wood, figural, carved mustache	**115.00**
Monkey, wood, figural, painted eyes . .	**80.00**
Parrot, cast iron, figural	**30.00**
Perfection	**45.00**
Pliers type, silver plate, orig picks, c1909	**35.00**
Rooster, brass, figural	**40.00**
Squirrel, cast iron, figural	**48.00**
Toy Soldier, wood, figural, red, black, and white paint, furry beard, German	**75.00**
Twist and screw type, cast iron, nickel plated, palm size, 5"	**15.00**
Wolf, cast metal, 1920 patent	**60.00**

OCCUPIED JAPAN

Collecting Hints: Buyers should be aware that a rubber stamp can be used to mark "Occupied Japan" on the base of objects. Fingernail polish remover can be used to test a mark. An original mark will remain since it is under the glaze; fake marks will disappear. This procedure should not be used on unglazed pieces; use your eye to identify a bad mark on an unglazed item.

Damaged pieces have little value unless the piece is extremely rare. Focus on quality pieces which are made well and nicely decorated. There are many inferior examples.

History: At the end of World War II, the Japanese economy was devastated. To secure needed hard currency, the Japanese pottery industry produced thousands of figurines and other knickknacks for export. From the beginning of American occupation until April 28, 1952, these objects were marked "Japan," "Made in Japan," "Occupied Japan," and "Made in Occupied Japan." Only pieces marked with the last two designations are of strong interest to Occupied Japan collectors. The first two marks also were used during other time periods.

The variety of products is endless—ashtrays, dinnerware, lamps, planters, souvenir items, toys, vases, etc. Initially figurines attracted the largest number of collectors; today many collectors focus on non–figurine material.

References: Florence Archambault, *Occupied Japan For Collectors,* Schiffer Publishing, 1992; Gene Florence, *The Collector's Encyclopedia Of Occupied Japan Collectibles, 1st Series* (1976, 1992 value update), *2nd Series* (1979, 1995 value update), *3rd Series* (1987), *4th Series* (1993), and *5th Series,* (1994), Collector Books; David C. Gould and Donna Crevar–Donaldson, *Occupied Japan Toys With Prices,* L–W Book Sales, 1993; Carole Bess White, *Collector's Guide To Made In Japan Ceramics: Identification & Values,* Collector Books, 1994.

Collectors' Clubs: Occupied Japan Collectors Club, 18309 Faysmith Ave., Torrance, CA 90504; The Occupied Japan Club, 29 Freeborn St., Newport, RI 02840.

Ashtray, metal, playing card suits	**17.50**
Bell, Dutch girl, 4½" h	**10.00**
Bookends, colonial couple, pr	**15.00**
Box, heart shape, floral design, gold trim, 2¼" w	**10.00**
Candlesticks, pr, colonial man and woman	**28.00**
Cane, bamboo	**20.00**
Celery Tray, rect, fan shaped handles, 8½" l	**8.00**
Child's Dishes, Blue Willow, two place settings	**35.00**

Christmas Tree Ornament, star	**10.00**
Cigarette Box, floral, blue and white . .	**10.00**
Cigarette Dispenser, silverplate, Oriental house shape, pull lever to dispense cigarette	**80.00**
Cologne Bottle, glass, pink	**18.00**
Demitasse Cup and Saucer	
Flamingos, pink	**24.00**
Swirl pattern, cobalt blue and white .	**10.00**
Doll, celluloid, kewpie–type, blue suit	**25.00**
Fan, paper, folding, striped, red, white, and blue	**5.00**
Figure	
Bird, ceramic, 2" h	**10.00**
Boy and Dog, ceramic, 2¾" h	**12.00**
Bunny, pulling cart, celluloid	**28.00**
Cartoon Pig and Duck Girls, ceramic, 4" h, pr	**45.00**
Chinese Man, ceramic	**15.00**
Cowgirl, ceramic, 6" h	**65.00**
Girl, Scottie dog, ceramic	**30.00**
Man and Woman, pr, ceramic	
4½" h	**25.00**
6" h	**35.00**
Man, with pipe, ceramic, 4¼" h . . .	**15.00**
Swan, celluloid	**10.00**

Plate, maple leaf, white and gold	**8.00**
Platter, Blue Willow, oval, 14" l	**18.00**
Reamer, 2 pcs, strawberry shape, red, green leaves and handle, 3¾" h	**65.00**
Rice Bowl, porcelain, emb dragon, 6" d	**25.00**
Salt and Pepper Shakers, pr	
Angelfish	**15.00**
Tomatoes	**6.00**
Shelf Sitter, cowgirl and cowboy, price for pair	**48.00**
Tape Measure, pink pig, celluloid	**15.00**
Teapot, cov, brown ground, gold trim	**15.00**
Tea Set, hp, teapot, two handled sugar, and creamer	**60.00**
Toby Mug, Uncle Sam	**25.00**
Toothpick Holder, donkey pulling cart .	**4.00**
Toy	
Convertible Car, driver	**95.00**
Ice Cream Vendor, windup, litho tin cart, celluloid boy, 1930s, 4" h . . .	**100.00**
Playing Dog, windup, celluloid dog, tin shoe, MIB	**250.00**

OCEAN LINER COLLECTIBLES

Figure, puppies in basket, tan and gray, brown basket, 2⅞" w, 2⅝" h, $10.00.

Halloween Mask, paper	**12.00**
Ice Bucket, tongs, black, floral pattern	**25.00**
Incense Burner, cov, blue floral design, gold trim, 3 pcs	**35.00**
Jewelry Box, metal, twelve drawers . . .	**12.00**
Lamp, colonial couple, bisque, 11" h . .	**55.00**
Lobster Dish, cov	**18.00**
Mug, purple grapes, brown ground, 4" h	**10.00**
Nut Dish, metal, floral border, 6" w . . .	**5.00**
Pencil Holder, cat shape	**4.00**
Pin Cushion, tin, red velvet top, int. mirror	**20.00**
Pin Tray, souvenir NY City, metal	**4.00**
Planter, ceramic	
Donkey, pulling wagon, 4¾" l	**10.00**
Zebra	**6.00**

Collecting Hints: Don't concentrate only on ships of American registry. Many collectors favor material from only one liner or ship line. Objects associated with ships involved in disasters, such as the *Titanic*, often command higher prices.

History: Transoceanic travel falls into two distinct periods: the era of the great Clipper ships and the era of the diesel-powered ocean liners. The latter craft reached their "Golden Age" in the period between 1900 and 1940.

An ocean liner was a city unto itself. Many had their own printing rooms to produce a wealth of daily memorabilia. Companies such as Cunard, Holland–America, and others encouraged passengers to acquire souvenirs with the company logo and ship name. Word–of–mouth was a principal form of advertising.

Certain ships acquired a unique mystique. The *Queen Elizabeth, Queen Mary,* and *United States* became symbols of elegance and style. Today the cruise ship dominates the world of the ocean liner.

References: John Adams, *Ocean Steamers: The History of Ocean Going Steam Ships,* New Cavendish Books, 1992; Norman E. Martinus and Harry L. Rinker, *Warman's Paper,* Wallace–Homestead, 1994; Karl D. Spence, *How To Identify and Price Ocean Liner Collectibles,* published by author, 1991; Karl D. Spence, *Oceanliner Collectibles,* published by author, 1992; James Steele, *Queen Mary,* Phaidon, 1995.

Collectors' Clubs: Oceanic Navigation Research Society, Inc., PO Box 8005, Studio City, CA 91608; Steamship Historical Society of America, Inc., Suite #4, 300 Ray Drive, Providence, RI 02906; Titanic Historical Society, PO Box 51053, Indian Orchard, MA 01151.

Museums: Mystic Seaport, Mystic, CT; The South Street Seaport Museum, New York, NY; University of Baltimore, Steamship Historical Society Collection, Baltimore, MD.

Advertising Display, *Mediterrano Americhe,* 1927, easel back, artwork by Riccobaldi **150.00**
Ashtray
   Holland Lines, hammered aluminum   **7.00**
   Matson Lines, plastic, flag shape, green, center circle with red "M" on white ground **25.00**
   Princess, glass, Swedish **10.00**
Baggage Tag, *Canadian Pacific,* engraved vessel, c1930 . . . .   **3.00**
Bill of Lading, *SS Illinois,* Philadelphia, 1874 . . . .   **22.00**
Book
   Rigby's Book of Model Ships, punch–out, 1953 copyright, unused **50.00**
   Sinking of the Titanic, 1912 memorial edition, cover photo, 288 pages . .   **105.00**
   White Star Line, 1921, illus **50.00**
Booklet, White Star Line, sailing list, 1933 . . . .   **38.00**
Bottle Opener, *R.M.S. Queen Mary,* ship floats in handle **28.00**
Brochure, *Empress of Japan,* Transatlantic sailings, 1930–31 . . . .   **8.00**
Card, White Star Line, *Georgic* ship illus and log abstract on reverse, 1933 . .   **20.00**
Creamer, New England Steamship Co   **35.00**

Cup and Saucer, *Porsgrund,* Norway, $8.50.

Flask, ship's life preserver shape, "When Sinking Take Hold, Compliments of the Season, 1912–13, Oakland, CA," porcelain, marked "Germany" **125.00**
Key Chain, *Carnival,* lucite case, ship photo **2.50**

Letter Opener, *H.M.S. Liverpool,* silver, enamel dec, 1921 . . . .   **65.00**
Life Preserver, *USNS Dutton* **40.00**
Magazine, *Canadian Pacific Princess,* travel type, 16 pgs **3.50**
Letterhead, *Empress of Australia I,* Round the World Cruise, 1929–30 . .   **2.00**
Log, Lykes Bros 1938 *SS Ripley,* New Orleans to Calcutta **8.00**
Matchbook Cover, Holland American Lines **1.75**
Menu
   Europa, 1931, bright colors **22.00**
   Holland–American, 1963 . . . .   **5.00**
   Johnson Line **10.00**
   Matson Line **7.00**
   SS City of Omaha, Christmas 1940   **5.00**
   SS France, final voyage **10.00**
   SS Oakwood, American Export Lines, Christmas, 1939 . . . .   **5.00**
   SS United States, 8½ x 11", Aug 25, 1952, full color cov illus, red, white, and blue cord binding **8.00**
   USS Maryland, 5½ x 8½", Christmas day, 1927 . . . .   **10.00**
Mirror
   American Line, celluloid, ship illus .   **25.00**
   Steamship *Augustus,* pocket, emb . .   **52.00**
Passenger List
   Aquitania, 1937 . . . .   **15.00**
   SS Leviathan, 1924 . . . .   **15.00**
   Transylvania II, Anchor Line, June 22, 1938 . . . .   **18.00**
Pennant, 27" l, *Caribe,* felt, blue, white ship **3.00**
Photogravues, *R.M.P. Aquatania,* 1910, 30 pages **85.00**
Pictorial Layout, *Mauritania,* 33 x 32", cruise ship, diagrams and pictures **30.00**
Plate
   Pacific Steamship Co, china **70.00**
   Prudential Lines, oval, glass **12.00**
Playing Cards
   Carnival Line **5.00**
   Companhia Colonial **10.00**
Post Card, Palladium Lounge of the *R. M. P. Aquatania,* 1910 . . . .   **25.00**
Poster
   Queen Elizabeth II, 24 x 36", ship leaving skyline for Europe titled "For Once In Your Life, Live," post war gray hull **25.00**
   SS Washington, 25 x 30", 1933 . . . .   **150.00**
Radio Message Form, Cunard White Star Line, transmits to and from *R.M.S. Queen Mary,* 8½ x 9½" folder, unused **7.50**
Sign, *Costa Line,* plastic, "Please do not Disturb" **2.00**
Stamp Holder, *R.M.S. Queen Mary,* Art Deco style, metal **38.00**

Stein, *T.S. Bremen,* Caribbean cruise,
1950s, cobalt blue china, hinged top   **20.00**
Stereo Card, ship *Texas,* 1898 . . . .   **20.00**
Stock Certificate, Cunard Steam Ship
Co, Ltd **7.50**
Ticket Folio, Cunard Line, c1928 . . . .   **50.00**
Tin
  Candy, full color *R.M.S. Queen Mary*
  illus on lid, 1930s **40.00**
  Coffee, *T.S. Bremen* at sea on front
  panel, 1930s **50.00**

OWL COLLECTIBLES

Collecting Hints: If you collect the "creature of the night" or the "wise old owl," any page of this book might conceivably contain an owl–related object since the owl theme can be found in hundreds of collectible categories. A sampling of these categories includes advertising trade cards, books, buttons, postcards, etc. Don't confine yourself to these categories. Let your imagination be your guide.

Don't focus solely on old or antique owls. Owl figurines, owl themes on limited edition collectors' plates, and handcrafted items from modern artisans are plentiful. There are many examples available in every price range.

History: Owls have existed on earth for over sixty million years. They have been used as a decorative motif since before Christ. An owl was used with Athena on an ancient Greek coin.

Every culture has superstitions surrounding the owl. Some believe the owl represents good luck, others view it as an evil omen. The owl has remained a popular theme in Halloween material.

Of course, the owl's wisdom is often attached to scholarly pursuits. Expanding this theme, the National Park Service uses "Woodsey" to "Give A Hoot, Don't Pollute."

References: Allan W. Eckert and Karl E. Karalus, *The Owls Of North America,* Doubleday & Company, Inc. 1974; Faith Medlin, *Centuries Of Owls In Art And The Written Word,* Silvermine Publishers, 1967; Heimo Mikkola, *Owls Of Europe,* Buteo Books, 1983; Jozefa Stuart, *The Magic Of Owls,* Walker Publishing, 1977; Krystyna Weinstein, *Owls, Owls: Fantastical Fowls,* Buteo Books, 1985.

REPRODUCTION ALERT: Recently reproduction fruit crate labels with an owl motif have been seen at several antiques and collectibles dealers who wholesale to dealers. These labels are appearing at flea markets and in shops where they are being passed as originals.

Westmoreland Glass molds have been sold to several different manufacturers. The owl sitting on two books is being reissued with the original

"W" still on top of the books. The three-owl plate mold also was sold. Imperial Glass owl molds have also found new owners.

Bank, brass, glass eyes **65.00**
Book, *An Owl Came To Stay,* Clair
Rome, Crown Pub, NY, 1980 . . . . . .   **3.25**
Bookends, pr, brass, Frankart **35.00**
Calendar Plate, owl on open book,
1912, Berlin, NE **25.00**
Calling Card Tray, 8½ x 7", quadruple
plate, emb music staff and "Should
Owl's Acquaintance Be Forgot," two
owls sitting on back of tray **85.00**
Candy Container, glass, owl on branch   **50.00**
Clock
  Metal, 2" dial, 1–day, Bentley,
  German **25.00**
  Wood, 6½" h, hand carved **110.00**
Cookie Jar, 11" h, cream, one winking
eye, Shawnee **45.00**
Fairy Lamp, 4⅛" h, double faced figure,
pyramid size, frosted cranberry glass,
lavender enameled eyes, Clarke base   **200.00**
Figure
  4" h, carnival glass, Mosser **18.00**
  5½" h, milk glass, glass eyes, souvenir
  of Hot Springs, SD **100.00**
  11" h, soapstone, horned owl,
  red–brown, Italian **24.00**
Inkwell, 8 x 4", brass, glass inset, hinged
lid, pen tray, 2" owl figure **75.00**
Jelly Jar, cov, milk glass **95.00**
Mask, papier mache, c1915 . . . .   **90.00**
Match Holder
  2½" h, dark green, Wetzel Glass Co   **5.00**
  8" h, 3" w, metal, hanging type **18.00**
Mustard Jar, 5" h, milk glass, screw top,
glass insert, Atterbury, orig lid **150.00**
Napkin Ring, owl sitting on stump,
Nippon **225.00**
Paperweight, cast iron, owl family, two
babies, plus baby in papa's arms . . .   **35.00**
Pin, blue, green, and gold enamel, amber eyes with rhinestone eye discs,
pearl tail feathers **12.50**
Pitcher
  8" h, pressed glass, figural **110.00**
  9½" h, cov, china, Edwin M Knowles
  China Co **37.50**
Plate, milk glass
  6" d, three owl heads, fluted openwork edge, gold paint **50.00**
  7½" d, Owl Lovers **40.00**
Ring Tree, 3¼" d, 4" h, shallow brown
dish, blue lining, brown and tan owl
perched on back, marked "Doulton
Stoneware" **325.00**
Salt and Pepper Shakers, pr, Shawnee .   **17.00**
Sheet Music, *The Pansy and the Owl*   **4.50**
Shot Glass, clear, Owl Drug Co, one
wing **15.00**

Soda Bottle, blob top, 9½" h, Owl Drug
    Co, teal green, two wing, San
    Francisco **48.00**
Spillholder, wood, hand carved, owl on
    tree branch, red glass eyes **32.50**
Thermometer, 6" h, plaster body **75.00**

**Tape Measure, brass, glass eyes, marked
"Germany," 1⅜" d, $35.00.**

Tin
    Owl Brand Shoe Polish, owl illus . . .   **35.00**
    Theatrical Cold Cream, Owl Drug
        Co, 4¼" d, orange ground, black
        print **24.50**
Tobacco Jar, 6¾" h, octagonal, Nippon,
    green mark **375.00**
Toothpick Holder **22.00**
Vase
    8¼" h, Knifewood, Weller **145.00**
    12½" h, ruffled rim, two handles, 4
        feet, marked on bottom "Royal
        Nishiki Nippon Hand Painted" . . .   **350.00**

PADEN CITY

Collecting Hints: All Paden City glass was handmade and unmarked. The early glassware was of
nondescript quality, but in the early 1930s quality improved dramatically. The cuttings were un-
polished "gray cuttings," sometimes mistaken for
etchings.

Paden City is noted for its colors: opal (opaque
white), ebony, mulberry, Cheriglo (delicate pink),
yellow, dark green (forest), crystal, amber, primrose (reddish–amber), blue, rose, and the ever
popular red. No free–blown or opalescent glass
was produced. Quantities of blanks were sold to
decorating companies for gold and silver overlay
and for etching.

History: Paden City Glass Manufacturing Co.
was founded in 1916 in Paden City, West
Virginia. David Fisher, formerly of the New
Martinsville Glass Manufacturing Co., operated
the company until his death in 1933 when his
son, Samuel, became president. The additional

financial burden placed on the company by the
acquisition of American Glass Co. in 1949 forced
Paden City to close in 1951.

References: Jerry Barnett, *Paden City, The Color
Company,* published by author, 1978; Lee
Garmon and Dick Spencer, *Glass Animals Of
The Depression Era,* Collector Books, 1993;
Naomi L. Over, *Ruby Glass of the 20th Century,*
Antique Publications, 1990, 1993–1994 value
update; Ellen Tischbein Schroy, *Warman's Glass,
Second Edition* Wallace–Homestead, 1995.

Animal
    Chinese Pheasant, blue **145.00**
    Pony **65.00**
Berry Bowl, 5¼" sq, Crows Foot, amber   **7.50**
Bowl, 9" d, ftd
    Black Forest, pink, minor use **95.00**
    Gothic Garden, pink **95.00**
Bud Vase, Peacock Reverse, amber . . .   **195.00**
Cake Plate, ftd
    Ardith Cherry etch, topaz, low, ftd . .   **50.00**
    Peacock & Rose, gold **185.00**
Candlesticks, pr
    Black Forest, mushroom shape **70.00**
    Crystal, double **40.00**
Candy Dish, cov, Gazebo, three part di-
    vided int.   **45.00**
Cheese and Cracker Dish, cov, Gazebo,
    blue **210.00**
Cocktail Shaker, Utopia/Gazebo, 3 pc,
    crystal **155.00**
Compote
    Ardith Cherry etch, topaz **55.00**
    Party Line, #191, ftd, 11" d, pink . . .   **35.00**
    Peacock & Rose, 7" d, green **72.00**
Console Bowl, 11" d, Black Forest,
    black **50.00**
Console Set, bowl, pr #531 candle-
    sticks, black **225.00**
Creamer, Black Forest, black **55.00**
Cream Soup, Crows Foot, amber **8.50**
Cup and Saucer, Crows Foot, amber . .   **8.00**
Goblet
    Cupid **15.00**
    Penny Line, green **12.00**
Ice Bucket, Party Line, amber **25.00**
Iced Tea Tumbler, Popeye & Olive, ruby   **12.00**
Mayonnaise Set, #300 Line, green, orig
    ladle, price for three piece set **35.00**
Pitcher
    Lazy Daisy, pink **60.00**
    Popeye & Olive, green **25.00**
Plate
    7½" d, Penny Line, amethyst **6.50**
    8" d, Chavalier Line 90, ruby **15.00**
    10½" d, indent, Peacock & Rose, pink   **55.00**
    11" d, handle, Black Forest, pink . . .   **6.00**
Relish, Sunset pattern, divided, amber   **20.00**
Salt and Pepper Shakers, pr, Penny Line,
    cobalt blue, flat base **45.00**

Sandwich Tray, Lela Bird, center handle
.... **95.00**
Sherbet, Peacock Reverse **25.00**
Sugar, cov, Wotta Line, ruby **10.00**
Tumbler, Penny Line, amethyst **8.50**
Vase
  6" h, Black Forest, black, Peacock
    Reverse, green **145.00**
  6½" h, Black Forest, black **85.00**
  9" h, Peacock Reverse, black **129.00**
  10" h, Peacock & Rose, pink **130.00**
  10½" h, Peacock & Rose, pink **140.00**
  12" h
    California Poppy, green **150.00**
    Lela Bird, black **285.00**
    Peacock & Rose, pink **195.00**

PADLOCKS

Collecting Hints: A wide range of padlocks can interest a collector. Many collectors specialize in one category, but buy others that appeal to them. Just being old and scarce is not always enough; locks must have some kind of appeal. They must be in a category of special interest, have an interesting design, or have historical significance. Desirable padlocks are embossed with the name or initials of a defunct company or railroad, a logo, an event (such as an exposition), a scroll or a figural design. Other desirable types have unique construction, unusual size, trick or intricate mechanisms. The more recent and inexpensive logo locks, stamped or incised with the names or initials of petroleum, automobile, and other companies, have increased in popularity. The most competitive and expensive collecting areas are the embossed brass locks from the old defunct short line railroads and the very early locks from the larger railroads.

The name or initials of the manufacturer was usually stamped on the lock. If marked with the name of a small company from the 1850s, a lock can be worth many times more than a similar one made by a large, prolific manufacturer. There are always exceptions. For example, Smokies do not have much value no matter how old or scarce.

Locks made by certain manufacturers can be more valuable than similar and even more scarce, locks made by others. The round lever push key locks can be several times more valuable than other types with the same embossments. Locks classified as "Story" are worth many times more than similar locks classified as "Warded." The reason for the differences in value is often inexplicable.

Identifying many of the old padlocks is possible with either markings on the lock or from old catalogs, but for some of the padlocks this is difficult or impossible. They are not marked, and the manufacturer evidently did not publish catalogs. Identical locks can be marked by different manufacturers as a result of one company acquiring another. Dating can also be a problem. Some of the manufacturers made almost identical locks for over fifty years, and there are Yale models that were made for almost 100 years. A lock can be made the same year as the patent date, or the date can be marked on the padlock long after the patent expired. The definitive book on United States lock companies, their padlocks, and padlock construction has not been published.

Original keys can increase the value of locks, but other keys have no value to most collectors. Having a key made can cost more than the value of the lock, and locksmiths who are not familiar with the antique value of old padlocks can do irreparable damage. If you have repairs or a key made, make sure that the locksmith is an expert on old locks. Repairs, cracks, holes, internal damage, or appreciable dents reduce drastically the value of locks.

History: In the 1830s Elijah Rickard was making screw key padlocks. He stamped some of them "B & O RR" for the Baltimore & Ohio Railroad. These were the first marked railroad locks. In the 1840s safe lock manufacturers were adapting their lever tumbler safe lock designs to padlocks. Also in the 1840s the first pin tumbler padlocks were made in the Yale Lock Shop. In the 1850s a few companies were making lever tumbler padlocks simpler than the safe lock designs. The United States Post Office was ordering padlocks with various postal markings, and Linus Yale, Junior, patented the pin tumbler lock. In 1860 Wilson Bohannan returned from the California gold fields, patented a simple, reliable, brass lever padlock and started his lock manufacturing company. The brass lever and the similiar iron lever padlocks were subsequently manufactured in large quantities by many companies. Wilson Bohannan is still an independent company, and the pin tumbler lock is the worldwide standard medium-security lock.

Padlocks of all shapes and sizes have been made in Europe and Asia since the 1600s. Asian locks can be distinguished from European locks, but it is usually difficult to determine which European country made a lock. American collectors generally prefer American manufactured locks.

Over 240 United States padlock manufacturers have been identified. Eight prolific companies were:

Adams & Westlake, 1857– , "Adlake"
    trademark started c1900, made railroad locks.
Eagle Lock Co., 1833–1976, a general line of padlocks from 1880, with padlock patent dates from 1867.
Mallory, Wheeler & Co., 1865–1910,

partnership history started in 1834, predominant manufacturer of wrought iron lever (Smokies) padlocks.

Miller Lock Co. (D.K. Miller from 1870 to c1880, Miller Lock Co. to 1930), a general line of padlocks.

Slaymaker Lock Co. 1888–1985, dates include name changes, partnership changes, mergers. A general line of padlocks.

Star Lock Works, 1836–1926, largest manufacturer of Scandinavian padlocks.

Yale & Towne Mfg. Co., 1884– , Yale Lock Mfg. Co. from 1868 to 1884, started c1840 by Linus Yale, Sr., as the "Yale Lock Shop," started producing padlocks c1875.

Wilson Bohannan, 1860– , made mostly brass lever padlocks to the early 1900s, then changed to the pin tumbler type.

Padlock Types: Padlocks are categorized primarily according to tradition or use: Story, Railroad, etc. The secondary classification is according to the type of construction. For example: If a brass lever lock is marked with a railroad name, it is called a "Railroad" lock. Scandinavian locks have always been called "Scandinavians." "Story" locks became a common usage term in the 1970s, in the 1880s they were listed in various ways.

Railroad, express, and logo locks are identified with the names of the companies that bought and used them. Story locks are a series of odd- and heart-shaped cast iron padlocks with various decorative or figural embossments made from about 1880 to 1900.

Governmental agencies and thousands of companies had locks custom-made with their names to create logo locks. Logo locks are not to be confused with locks that are embossed with the names of jobbers. This applies particularly to the round six-lever push key locks. If "6–Lever" is included in the name, it is not a logo lock. Since 1827 more than 10,000 railroad companies have crisscrossed the United States. Most of these companies used at least two types of locks; some used dozens of types.

References: Franklin M. Arnall, *The Padlock Collector, Illustrations and Prices of 1,800 Padlocks of the Last 100 Years, Fifth Edition*, The Collector, 1988; Jack P. Wood, *Town–Country Old Tools and Locks, Keys, and Closures*, L–W Promotions, 1990.

Collectors' Clubs: American Lock Collectors Association, 36076 Grennada, Livonia, MI 48154; West Coast Lock Collectors, 1427 Lincoln Blvd., Santa Monica, CA 90401.

Museum: Lock Museum of America, Terryville, CT.

Advisor: Franklin M. Arnall

REPRODUCTION ALERT: Beware of bargains and know your locks. Beware of brass story locks, locks from the Middle East, railroad switch locks made in Taiwan and the U.S., and switch lock keys made in the U.S. Story locks should be embossed cast iron; however, there are excellent iron reproductions of the Skull and Crossbones lock.

Screw key, trick, iron lever, and brass lever padlocks are being imported from the Middle East. The Taiwan switch locks are rougher and lighter in color than the old brass ones. The crudely cast new switch keys are obvious. The high quality counterfeits are expertly stamped with various railroad initials, tumbled to simulate wear, and aged with acid. They can be detected only by an expert.

Authentic railroad, express, and logo locks will have only one user name. The size and shape will be like other locks that were in common use at the time, except for a few modified locks made for the U.S. government. All components of an old lock must have exactly the same color and finish. The front, back, or drop of an old lock can be expertly replaced with a reproduced part embossed with the name or initials of a railroad, express company, or other user.

Note: The prices shown are for padlocks in original conditon and without keys.

Brass Lever
Browns Patent, July 4, 1891, 3¼" h	**25.00**
E. Cotterill & Co., 5⅛" h	**500.00**
J.L. Howard & Co., Pat'd Aug. 23, 1858, 3⅜" h	**30.00**
New Champion 6 Lever, 2⅞" h	**2.00**
Ritchie & Boyden, 1¾" h	**12.00**
Safe, 3⅝" h	**20.00**
T. Slaight, Patd Oct. 14, 1851, 2¼" h	**30.00**
W. Bohannan, 1¾" h	**8.00**
Winchester, emb raised letters	**140.00**
Yale, Y & T, rect, keyhole in bottom, emb.	
1½ to 2" w	**3.00**
3" w	**60.00**

Combination
5 brass lettered dials, 2¼" w	**80.00**
J.B. Miller Keyless Lock Co., zinc case	**5.00**
J.B.M.K.L. Co., steel	**5.00**
Miller Keyless Lock Co., iron, 3¼" h	**75.00**
Permutation Lock Co., Denver, CO, 3⅝" w	**550.00**
Sesamee	
Brass or zinc case, 2½" h	**15.00**
Corbin, brass case, 2½" h	**1.00**
Steel case & brass dial, 2½" h	**4.00**

The Edwards Mfg. Co., No-Key, 2¾" h   **25.00**
W.A. Harrison Insurance Lock, brass
case **55.00**
"Your Own" Keyless, brass, 3⅞" h . .   **275.00**
Commemorative
C Q D, Simmons Wireless, (Titanic
SOS) **125.00**
Igloo and rising sun embossed on
front (Adm. Byrd's Expedition),
2⅞" h **135.00**
Louisiana Purchase, 1803, 2½" h . . .   **200.00**
PAX, Universal Exposition, St. Louis
1904 . . . .   **450.00**
Express
AM RY EX, stamped on shackle &
back, steel, iron lever type **30.00**
Pacific Ex Co., emb on back, brass,
lever push key type, 2⅜" dia. **975.00**
RY EX AGY, stamped on back, steel,
iron lever type **30.00**
W F & Co., emb on drop, iron, iron
lever type **400.00**
Iron Lever (includes steel locks)
Browns Patent, iron, July 4, 1871,
3" h **25.00**
Bruno, steel, 2¾" h **15.00**
Dragons embossed, steel, 2¾" h . . .   **15.00**
E T F, iron with brass drop, 3½" h . .   **12.00**
Miller, iron with brass drop, 4½" h . .   **30.00**
The U. L. Co. of N Y, iron, 3⅜" h . . .   **250.00**
Lever Push Key
Baffler Six Lever, Yale, 2⅞" h **8.00**
Champion 6-Lever, 2¼" dia. **5.00**
Columbia 6-Lever, 2¼" dia. **20.00**
Keystone 6-Lever, 2¼" dia. **15.00**
Smith & Egge Mfg. Co., Giant, 2¾" h   **30.00**
Logo
Okla. State Pen., Best **40.00**
Ordnance Dept., embossed cannons   **5.00**
Pauly Jail Bldg. Co., pin tumbler type   **150.00**
76, Best **20.00**
Texaco, T, Best **20.00**
University of Colorado, Yale **75.00**
University of Oklahoma, Yale **40.00**
U P S, Best **15.00**
U.S.B.I.A., brass lever seal lock **50.00**
U S N, several manufacturers **10.00**
Western Union Tel Co., brass lever
type **30.00**
Western Union Telegraph, lever push
key type, 2¼" dia. **290.00**
Zoo, Best **20.00**
Pin Tumbler
Corbin, brass
1¼" to 2" w, keyhole in bottom . .   **2.00**
3" w
Keyhole in bottom **50.00**
Keyhole in front **25.00**
Corbin, steel case **5.00**
Embossed eagle, 3" h **12.00**
R. E. Co., Pat July 30 1878 . . . .   **125.00**
Segal, iron, 3¾" h **25.00**

Simmons, 2" h **15.00**
Yale
Brass case, embossed **2.00**
Iron case, with round brass panels   **5.00**
Nickel plated, with dust cover . . .   **25.00**
Railroad
General Purpose & Signal
B & O RR, Yale, emb, pin tumbler
type **15.00**
Illinois Central Signal, emb, brass
lever **18.00**
K C S Ry, emb, lever push key type   **250.00**
M K & T, Yale, emb, pin tumbler
type **35.00**
N & W Ry, emb, lever push key
type **150.00**
P & R Signal Service, emb, brass
lever **20.00**
Santa Fe, Keen Cotter, emb **300.00**
SO Pacific Co. CS 24, Roadway &
Bridge Dept **35.00**
S P Co.
Ames Sword, brass lever type . .   **20.00**
Steel, iron lever type **10.00**
Switch
Brass
C M & St P RR, emb in panel . .   **95.00**
C R I & P RR, stamped on
shackle **35.00**
Frisco, stamped on shackle,
National Brass **45.00**
G N R'Y, emb across back,
Slaymaker **350.00**
I & G N RR, emb in panel **200.00**
L & N RR, emb in panel **110.00**
L V RR, stamped on back, G.W.
Nock **100.00**
N Y C RR, stamped on back, T.
Slaight **40.00**
P RR, emb across back, A & W or
Fraim **125.00**
SO PAC Co., emb in panel & on
drop **80.00**
Union Pacific, emb in panel,
Adlake **60.00**
U S Y of O, stamped on back,
Adlake **15.00**
W O Ry Co., emb in panel **190.00**
Steel
AT & SF Ry, other common rail-
roads **5.00**
P RR, brass drop **15.00**
St L & S W, Yale **20.00**
Scandinavian
Brass, 2½" h **20.00**
Iron, 2½" h **12.00**
J.H.W. Climax, iron, 3" h **20.00**
99, emb, brass, 1¾" h **60.00**
999, emb, brass, 2½" h **35.00**
Star emb on bottom
1½" h, iron **15.00**
3½" h, brass **90.00**

3¾" h, iron 35.00
Six Lever & Eight Lever
  Eagle Six Lever, steel 5.00
  Mastodon Eight Lever, steel 12.00
  Samson Eight Lever, brass 15.00
  S B H Co. Six Lever, steel 8.00
  Winchester Six Lever, steel 80.00

Favorite 6, Eagle, lever push key, brass, 2¼", $25.00.

Keen Kutter, E.C. Simmons, brass, lever, tumbler, $75.00.

Story, emb cast iron
  Eagle emb, 2½" h 250.00
  Floral and scroll, shield shape
    2⅜" h 80.00
    3⅜" h 150.00
  Mail Pouch, Russell & Erwin 200.00
  N H Co. & scrolls, heart shape 175.00
Warded
  Corbin, emb, brass, 1½" h 10.00
  Floral and scroll, deeply emb, rect
    case, cast iron, 2½" h 15.00
  Motor, emb, brass case, 2½" h 4.00
  Navy, round iron case, 2½" h 10.00
  1902, emb, brass case, 2⅛" h 4.00
  Red Cross, emb, brass, 2" h 8.00
  St. Louis, emb, brass, 2" h 12.00
  Tire shaped iron case, 2⅞" h 15.00
  Winchester, incised, iron case, brass
    panels, 2¾" h 115.00
  Yale Junior, brass case 4.00
Wrought Iron (Smokies, Smoke House,
  Shield), with brass drop
  A. Thompson, VR, 4¾" h 30.00

Improved Tumbler Lock, 5¾" h 35.00
M. W. & Co., 3½" h 10.00
S. & Co., 3½" h 8.00
W & Co., 3¼" h 10.00

PAPERBACK BOOKS

Collecting Hints: For collecting or investment purposes, books should be in fine or better condition because many titles are common in lesser condition (and hence are less desirable). Unique items, such as paperbacks in dust jackets or in boxes, often are more valuable and desirable.

Most collections are assembled around one or more unifying themes. Some common themes are: author (Edgar Rice Burroughs, Dashiell Hammett, Louis L'Amour, Raymond Chandler, Zane Grey, William Irish, Cornell Woolrich, etc.); fictional genre (mysteries, science fiction, westerns, etc.); publisher (early Avon, Dell and Popular Library are most popular); cover artist (Frank Frazetta, R. C. M. Heade, Rudolph Belarski, Roy Krenkel, Vaughn Bode, etc.); and books with uniquely appealing graphic design (Dell mapbacks and Ace double novels).

Because quantity lots of paperbacks still turn up, many collectors are cautious as they assemble their collections. Books in the highest condition grades remain uncommon. Many current dealers try to charge upper level prices for books in lesser condition, arguing that top condition is just too scarce. This argument is not valid, just self-serving.

History: Paperback volumes have existed since the 15th century. Mass–market paperback books, most popular with collectors, date from the post 1938 period. The number of mass market publishers in the 1938–1950 period was much greater than today. These books exist in a variety of formats, from the standard size paperback and its shorter predecessor to odd sizes like 64–page short novels for 10¢ and 5¼" x 7½" volumes known as digests. Some books came in a dust jacket; some were boxed.

The "golden" period for paperback books was from 1939 to the late 1950s, a period generally characterized by a lurid and colorful graphic style of cover art and title lettering not unlike that of the pulp magazines. A lot of early paperback publishers had been or were publishers of pulps and merely moved their graphic style and many of their authors to paperbacks.

References: Kenneth Davis, *Two–Bit Culture: The Paperbacking of America,* Houghton Mifflin, 1984; Kevin Hancer, *The Paperback Price Guide, Third Edition,* Wallace–Homestead, 1989; Bob and Sharon Huxford, *Huxford's Paperback Value Guide,* Collector Books, 1994; Norman E. Martinus and Harry L. Rinker, *Warman's Paper,* Wallace–Homestead, 1994; Dawn E. Reno,

Collecting Romance Novels, Alliance Publishers, 1995; Piet Schreuders, *Paperbacks USA, A Graphic History, 1939–1959,* Blue Dolphin, 1981; Lee Server, *Over My Dead Body: The Sensational Age of the American Paperback: 1945–1955,* Chronicle Books, 1994; Jon Warren, *The Official Price Guide To Paperbacks,* House of Collectibles, 1991.

Periodicals: *Books Are Everything,* 302 Martin Dr., Richmond, KY 40475; *Paperback Parade,* PO Box 209, Brooklyn, NY 11228; *Pulp and Paperback Market Newsletter,* 5813 York Ave., Edina, MN 55410.

Museum: University of Minnesota's Hess Collection of Popular Literature, Minneapolis, MN.

Note: The prices given are for books in fine condition. Divide by 3 to get the price for books in good condition; increase price by 50% for books in near mint condition.

Adventure
Adams, Clifton, *Grabhorn Bounty,* Ace F404	6.00
Burroughs, Edgar Rice, *Tarzan and the Lost Empire,* Ace F–169	3.60
Fox, Gardner F., *Kothar, Barbarian Swordsman,* Belmont, 1969	12.00
Hubbell, Ned, *Adventures of Creighton Holmes,* Poplar	8.00
Siegel, Jerry, *High Camp Super heroes,* Belmont, B50–695, comic book reprints from the co–creator of Superman	3.50

Biography
Gifford, D. *Karloff: Man, Monster, Movies,* Curtis	7.50
Juneau, James, *Judy Garland,* Pyramid, 1974	15.00
Kramer, Freda, *Glen Campbell Story,* Pyramid, 1970	10.00
Martin and Miller, *The Story of Walt Disney,* Dell, D–266	3.00
Thomas, T. T., *I, James Dean,* Popular Library, W–400	2.40
Wright, W., *Life and Loves of Lana Turner,* Wisdom House, 104	1.50

Combat
Boyington, Gregory, *Baa Baa Black Sheep,* Dell, F–88	1.50
Grove, Walt, *The Wings of Eagles,* Gold Medal, 649, tie–in with John Wayne movie	3.60
Tiempo, E. K., *Cry Slaughter,* Avon, T–179	1.75
Uris, Leon, *Battle Cry,* Bantam, F–1996	1.50

Erotica/Esoterica
Adams, Bill, *Bedroom Tramp,* Playtime, 603	10.00

Allison, Clyde, *Money Bed,* Nightstand, 1963	5.00
Farmer, Philip Jose, *Fire and the Night,* Regency, 118	4.00
Holliday, Don, *Lust Lodge,* Sundown Reader	4.00
Low, Glenn, *Perverted Passions,* Novel Book	4.00
Swados, Felice, *House of Fury,* Avon, 298	12.00
Van Vechten, Harold, *Nigger Heaven,* Avon, 314	10.00
Whitney, Hallam, *Backwoods Shack,* Carnival, 943, Whitney is a pseudonym for Harry Whittington	2.40

Horror
Bradbury, Ray, *The Autumn People,* Ballantine, EC, comic reprints with Frazetta cov	4.00
Dear, Ian, *Village of Blood,* New English, 1975	7.50
Hitchcock, Alfred, *12 Stories for Late at Night,* Dell	4.00
Stoker, Bram, *Dracula,* Perma Book, M–4088, tie–in with Christopher Lee movie	4.00

Humor
Addams, Charles, *Drawn & Quartered,* Pocket Book, 1964 . . .	8.00
Cavanaugh and Weir, *Dell Book of Jokes,* Dell, 89	21.00
Gaines, William (ed.), *The Brothers Mad,* Ballantine, 267K	4.00
Kurtzman, Harvey, *Help!,* Gold Medal, K–1485	1.75

Mystery
Abbot, Anthony, *Murder of the Circus Queen,* Popular	7.50
Blochman, Lawrence G. *Recipe for Homicide,* Dell	3.00
Boucher, Anthony, *Case of the Crumpled Knave,* Pyramid, 1967	4.00
Carr, J. D., *The Four False Weapons,* Berkley, G–91	2.40
Hunter, J. *Case of the Stolen Ransom,* Sexton Blake	5.00
Irish, William, *Bluebeard's Seventh Wife,* Popular Library, 473	6.00
Lyon, Dana, *I'll Be Glad When You're Dead,* Quick Reader, 132	2.00

Non–fiction
Disney, Walt, *Our Friend the Atom,* Dell, LB–117	1.50
Galus, Henry, *Unwed Mothers,* Monarch, 524, Robert Maguire cov	2.00
Hynd, Alan, *We Are the Public Enemies,* Gold Medal, 101	4.00
Mager, Slivia K. *Complete Guide To Home Sewing,* Pocket 890	4.00
Sinclair, Gordon, *Bright Path to Adventure,* Harlequin, 288	3.60

Romance
Bronte, Emily, *Wuthering Heights*,
Quick Reader, 122 . . . . **4.50**
Edmonds, Walter, *The Wedding
Journey*, Dell, 10¢, 6 . . . . **3.60**
Gaddis, Peggy, *Dr. Prescott's Secret,
Beacon*, B–302 . . . . **1.50**
Science Fiction
Adler, Allen, *Terror on Planet Ionus*,
PB Library, 1966 . . . . **1.50**
Black, Pansy E, *Men From the
Meteor*, Stellar **20.00**
Garrett, Randall, *Earth Invader,
Leisure* **4.50**
Heinlein, Robert A., *Beyond This
Horizon*, Signet, 1891 . . . . **3.25**
Kline, Otis Adelbert, *Maza of the
Moon*, Ace, F–321, Frazetta cov . . **3.60**
Long, Frank Belknap, *Woman From
Another Planet*, Chariot **15.00**
Orwell, George, *Animal Farm*, Signet,
1289 . . . . **4.00**
Lovecraft, H. P., *Weird Shadow over
Innmouth*, Bart House, 4 . . . . **18.00**
Sports
DiMaggio, Joe, *Lucky to Be a Yankee*,
Bantam, 506 . . . . **2.40**
Jacobs, Bruce, *Baseball Stars of 1957*,
Lion Library **115.00**
Mann, Arthur, *Jackie Robinson Story*,
FJ Low Co **40.00**
Meany, Tom, *Baseball's Greatest
Players*, Dell **6.00**
Robinson, Ray (ed.), *Baseball Stars of
1961*, Pyramid, G–605 . . . . **1.50**
Scholz, Jackson, *Fighting Coach*,
Comet, 25 . . . . **1.50**
Stern, Bill, *Bill Stern's Favorite Boxing
Stories*, Pocket Books, 416 . . . . . . **2.40**
Western
Fisher, Clay, *War Bonnet*, Ballantine,
11 . . . . **2.00**
Haycox, Ernest, *Return of a Fighter,
Corgi*, 1956 . . . . **12.00**
Lehman, Paul Evan, *Valley of Hunted
Men*, Belmont **4.50**
Robertson, Frank C., *Powder Burner,
Belmont* **3.50**

PAPER DOLLS

Collecting Hints: Most paper dolls are collected in uncut books, sheets, or boxed sets. Cut sets are priced at 50% of an uncut set providing all dolls, clothing, and accessories are present.

Many paper doll books have been reprinted. An identical reprint is just slightly lower in value. If the dolls have been redrawn, the price is reduced significantly.

Barbara Ferguson's *The Paper Doll* has an ex-

cellent section on the care and storage of paper dolls.

History: The origin of the paper doll rests with the jumping jacks (pantins) of Europe. By the 19th century famous dancers, opera stars, Jenny Lind, and many general subjects were available in boxed or die–cut sheet form. Raphael Tuck in England began to produce ornate dolls in series form in the 1880s.

The advertising industry turned to paper dolls to sell products. Early magazines, such as *Ladies's Home Journal, Good Housekeeping,* and *McCall's,* used paper doll inserts. Children's publications, like *Jack and Jill,* picked up the practice.

The paper doll books first appeared in the 1920s. The cardboard–covered books made paper dolls available to the mass market. Leading companies were Lowe, Merrill, Saalfield, and Whitman. The 1940s saw the advent of the celebrity paper doll books. Celebrities were drawn from screen and radio, followed later by television personalities. A few comic characters, such as Brenda Starr, also made it to paper doll fame.

The growth of television in the 1950s saw a reduction in the number of paper doll books produced. The modern books are either politically or celebrity oriented.

References: Marian B. Howard, *Those Fascinating Paper Dolls: An Illustrated Handbook For Collectors,* Dover, 1981; Martha K. Krebs, *Advertising Paper Dolls: A Guide For Collectors,* two volumes, privately printed, 1975; Norman E. Martinus and Harry L. Rinker, *Warman's Paper,* Wallace–Homestead, 1994; Mary Young, *A Collector's Guide To Magazine Paper Dolls: An Identification & Value Guide,* Collector Books, 1990; Mary Young, *Tomart's Price Guide To Lowe and Whitman Paper Dolls,* Tomart Publications, 1993.

Collectors' Clubs: Original Paper Doll Artist Guild, PO Box 176, Skandia, MI 49885; United Federation of Doll Clubs, 10920 N. Ambassador, Kansas City, MO 64153.

Periodicals: *Celebrity Doll Journal,* 5 Court Place, Puyallup, WA 98372; *Loretta's Place Paper Doll Newsletter,* 808 Lee Ave., Tifton, GA 31794; *Midwest Paper Dolls & Toys Quarterly,* PO Box 131, Galesburg, KS 66740; *Northern Lights Paperdoll News,* PO Box 871189, Wasilla, AK 99687; *Paper Doll Gazette,* Route #2, Box 52, Princeton, IN 47670; *Paper Doll News,* PO Box 807, Vivian, LA 71082; *Paperdoll Review,* PO Box 584, Princeton, IN 47670; *P.D. Pal,* 5341 Gawain #883, San Antonio, TX 78218.

Museums: Children's Museum, Indianapolis, IN; Detroit Children's Museum, Detroit, MI; Kent State University Library, Kent, OH; Museum of the City of New York, New York, NY; Newark Museum, Newark, NJ; The Margaret Woodbury Strong Museum, Rochester, NY.

Notes: Prices are based on uncut, mint, original paper dolls in book or uncut sheet form. It is not unusual for two different titles to have the same number in a single company.

Ava Gardner, book, one of two 9" dolls, some neatly cut clothing, rest uncut, Whitman	15.00
Baby Sandy, book, Merrill, 1941	40.00
Baby Sister and Baby Brother Dolls, book, Merrill	5.00
Baby Sparkle Plenty, book, Saalfield, 1948	50.00
Betsy McCall and Sandy McCall, uncut sheet, 1958–1960 issues	15.00
Carol Linley, book, autographed, Whitman, 1960	55.00
Children Of America, book, Saalfield, 1941	10.00
Cinderella Steps Out, book, Lowe, 1948	10.00
Debbie Reynolds, c1950	50.00
Dionne Quintuplets, cut	80.00
Donald Duck's Farm, English, color cardboard, 1939	60.00
Doris Day, book, Whitman, 1956	50.00
Eve Arden, book, Saalfield, 1953	25.00

Esther Williams, #2553:25, Merrill Co., 1953, $25.00.

Girl Scouts, Brownies, dolls of 39 nations, c1950, MIGB	65.00
Grace Kelly, book, 9¼" cut dolls, 8 pgs uncut clothing, Whitman	30.00
Happy Bride, book, Whitman, 1967	15.00
Harry The Soldier, book, Lowe 1941	8.00
Henry & Henrietta Paper Dolls for Tiny Tots, book, Saalfield, 1938, unused	50.00
Jane Powell, 1952, uncut	75.00
Janet Leigh, book, Abbott, 1958	50.00

Johnny Funny Bunny And The Tadpole Baby, uncut sheet, *Ladies Home Journal,* February 1921, drawn by Harrison Cady	10.00
Lennon Sisters, book, Whitman, 1957	45.00
Lydia, book, Whitman, 1977	25.00
Kewpie–Kin Paper Dolls, book, Artcraft, 1967	40.00
King Of Swing And Queen Of Song, book, Lowe 1942	12.00
Lindy–Lou 'N' Cindy–Sue, book, Merrill, 1954	8.00
Little Miss America, unused, Saalfield	50.00
Magic Mary, magnetic, c1950, MIGB	45.00
Magic Stay On Dresses, c1950	45.00
Majorette Paper Dolls, book, Saalfield, 1957	6.00
Mary Martin, book, Saalfield, 1942	45.00
Movie Starlets, book, five punchout dolls, 6 pgs clothing, Whitman	100.00
Mrs. Beasley, Family Affair, 1970	40.00
Nanny And The Professor, book, Artcraft, 1970–71	10.00
Nanny And The Professor, book, Saalfield, 1970	5.00
Pat Boone, c1950	50.00
Patti Page, book, Abbott, 1958	35.00
Playhouse Dolls, book, Stephens Co., 1949	15.00
Queen Holden's Nursery School Dolls, book, Whitman, 1953	40.00
Ranchland, 1952, box, complete	35.00
Rosemary Clooney, Bonnie Book, 1958	55.00
Sabrina and the Archies, book, unused, Whitman, 1971 copyright Archie Music Corp	25.00
Sandy and Sue, 1963, complete	20.00
Shari Lewis, book, Saalfield, 1958	15.00
Shirley Temple	
Gabriel, snap on, c1950, MIGB	85.00
Saalfield, four dolls, 1934, uncut	1,050.00
Sonja Henie, book, Merrill, 1940	75.00
Sports Time, book, Whitman, 1952	15.00
The Little Family And Their Little House, book, Merrill, 1949	12.00
The Princess Paper Doll Book, Saalfield, 1939	55.00
Thumbelina, book, Whitman, 1969	25.00
Tuesday Weld, book, orig box, unused, Saalfield, 1960	50.00
Vera Miles, book, Whitman, 1957	75.00
Wedding Party, book, Saalfield, 1951	10.00
Wiggie, Mod Fashions, 1960s	35.00

PATRIOTIC COLLECTIBLES

Collecting Hints: Concentrate on one symbol, e.g., the eagle, flag, Statue of Liberty, Uncle Sam, etc. Remember that the symbol is not always the principal character on items. Don't miss examples with the symbol in a secondary role.

Colored material is more desirable than non–colored material. Much of the material is two dimensional, e.g., posters and signs. Seek three–dimensional objects to add balance to a collection.

Much of the patriotic material focuses on our national holidays, especially the Fourth of July. Other critical holidays include Flag Day, Labor Day, Memorial Day, and Veterans' Day.

Finally, look to the foreign market. Our symbols are used abroad, both positively and negatively. One novel collection would be how Uncle Sam is portrayed on the posters and other materials from communist countries.

History: Patriotic symbols developed along with the American nation. The American eagle, among the greatest of our nation's symbols, was chosen for the American seal. As a result, the eagle has appeared on countless objects since that time.

Uncle Sam arrived on the American scene in the mid–19th century. He was firmly established by the Civil War. Uncle Sam did have female counterparts—Columbia and the Goddess of Liberty. He often appeared together with one or both of them on advertising trade cards, buttons, posters, textiles, etc.

Uncle Sam achieved his modern appearance largely through the drawings of Thomas Nast in *Harper's Weekly* and James Montgomery Flagg's famous World War I recruiting poster, "I Want You." Perhaps the leading promoter of the Uncle Sam image was the American toy industry. The American Centennial in 1876 and Bicentennial in 1976 also helped. A surge of Uncle Sam–related toys occurred in the 1930s, led by American Flyer's cheap version of an earlier lithographed tin, flatsided Uncle Sam bicycle string toy.

Reference: Gerald Czulewicz, *The Foremost Guide To Uncle Sam Collectibles,* Collector Books, 1995.

Collectors' Club: Statue of Liberty Collectors' Club, PO Box 535, Chautauqua, NY 14722.

Periodical: *Pyrofax Magazine,* PO Box 2010, Sartoga, CA 95070.

Museum: 4th of July Americana & Fireworks Museum, New Castle, PA.

See: Flag Collectibles.

Eagle
  Badge, 1½ x 3½", brass, links, eagle sitting on miner's pan, lower part with miner's burro, Fraternal Order of Eagles, Denver, 1905 . . . .   **12.00**
  Banner, 17 x 123", United We Stand, red, white, and blue eagle and shield, Charles Coiner, 1941 . . . .   **300.00**

Calendar, New York City Chapter, DAR, Louis Prang, 1896, red, white, and blue ribbon, color litho, $85.00.

Charm, black and white porcelain, brass hanger, "Barnes White Flier Club," c1890 . . . .   **50.00**
Lapel Stud,⅞" d, multicolored, metal stud back, enrollment type, "US Boys Working Reserve" and "Enrolled" **3.50**
Medal, 1½" d, bronze pendant, "Chicago Daily News Patriotism Medal," spread eagle in center holding shield, crossed flags on bar engraved with name, red, white, and blue ribbon, orig velvet lined box, 1900 . . . .   **25.00**
Pinback Button
  1¼" d, "Now Will You Be Good," multicolored, cartoon type, eagle carrying Spaniard in beak . .   **40.00**
  1¾" d, "Victory Celebration/Official Souvenir," black and white, 88th Division, WWI **18.00**
Poster
  11 x 14", NRA Code, Motor Vehicle Maintenance Trade, red, white, and blue, eagle symbol, Coiner, c1934 . . . .   **100.00**
  29 x 40", America Calling—Take Your Place In Civilian Defense, red, white, and blue, screaming eagle, Herbert Matter, 1941 . . .   **450.00**
  34 x 43", Pledge of the Soldier of Supply, eagle and flag, Zarv, 1943 . . . .   **175.00**
Program
  Democratic National Convention, 1948, 80 pgs, eagle on cov . . .   **45.00**
  Inauguration, Jan 20, 1961, 64 pgs, flag and eagle on cov **50.00**
Ribbon, 7" l, silk, "Our Nation Mourns A Hero Gone," 1841 . . . .   **85.00**

Sticker, jugate, Roosevelt and Garner, red, white, and blue 35.00
Tape Measure, red, white, and blue, eagle in circle, Alreco Fabrics adv 45.00
Flags and Shields
Flag, 46 stars, red, white, and blue silk, issued when Oklahoma became a state, 7 x 9" 15.00
Lapel Stud, 2" d, metal, shield center with photo of Boise Penrose, flag background, two red, white, and blue ribbons, 1896 . . . . 55.00
Mirror, 2" d, red, white, and blue stars and stripes ground, letters in shield shape, The Peoples Store, Stylish Clothes, Kingston, NY adv 25.00
Paper Clip, 1½" l, red, white, and blue celluloid, steel spring clip, center inscription in shield "The Grand Rapids Furniture Record," 1922 . . . . 10.00
Paperweight, 6" d, Flor De Moss, Kraus & Co., Inc Successors, litho, monogram with shield in center, black letters, gold trim 30.00
Pin, Our Country's Flag, 1930s 15.00
Pinback Button
7/8" d, Trolley Union, red, white, blue, and green, Boston Carmen's Union Division 589, March 1918 . . . . 3.50
1¼" d, Stars and Stripes Forever! red, white, and blue, WWII . . . 10.00
Poster
Let's All Pull Together, 29 x 40", full color, 1943 . . . . 125.00
Long May It Wave, 41 x 31", 1942 . . . . 150.00
Patriotic League, 20 x 28", girl

Magazine, The Home Magazine, July 1932, cover illus by Charles Twelvetrees, 8⅝ x 11⅝", $12.00.

holding flag behind her, Howard Chandler Christy, 1918 . . . . 275.00
Your War Bonds Are A Stake In The Future, 20 x 28", Allen Saalburg, 1943 . . . . 75.00
Liberty Bell
Badge, 4½" l, Liberty Bell with FDR and Garner, red fabric ribbon, 1936 . . . . 60.00
Jar, 6 x 6½", clear glass, emb "Liberty Cherries Jar 1776–1976," metal lid with flag and black letters 8.00
Mirror, 4" d, celluloid, full color illus of headquarters, founder, and Liberty Bell, Wm F Murphy's Sons Company Blank Book and Loose Leaf Manufacturers adv 35.00
Pin
1/4 x ⅜", blue enameled brass, diecut, "Local and Long Distance Telephone," Bell Telephone, c1920 . . . . 7.50
1¾", brass plated white metal, red, white, and blue accents on eagle, movable bell 20.00
Poster, What So Proudly We Hailed, 16 x 20", full color, Liberty Bell, and tourists, quote on bottom, c1943 . . . . 75.00
Program, Republican National Convention, 1948, 92 pgs, Liberty Bell on cov 30.00
Sign, 29½ x 34", litho tin, yellow and black, Dr Bell's Pine Tar Honey adv 35.00
Tape Measure, The Sesqui–Centennial International Exposition, Philadelphia, 1776–1926, full color Independence Hall, flags, and Liberty Bell 80.00
Statue of Liberty
Broadside, All About Liberty Bonds, 18 x 24", red, white, and blue, Liberty in center, Adolph Treidler, 1917 . . . . 50.00
Figure, American committee model   2,300.00
Pinback Button
1" d, red, white, and blue, "Liberty Button," Sept, 1918 . . . . 10.00
1¼" d, aqua–yellow, "Welcome Home 77th Division," WWI . . . 8.00
Poster
Before Sunset To–Day, Buy A Liberty Bond, 22 x 11", Statue of Liberty, harbor, and skyline, 1917 . . . . 70.00
Have You Bought Your Bond?, 21 x 25", brown Statue of Liberty, blue background, 1917 . . . . . . 150.00
That Liberty Shall Not Perish, 20 x 30", Statue of Liberty and New York in flames, Joseph Pennell, 1918 . . . . 275.00

Reverse Painting on Glass, oval,
metal frame **95.00**
Watch, commemorative, 1986,
quartz, orig box and papers **50.00**
Uncle Sam
Advertising Trade Card
Emmert Proprietary Co., Uncle
Sam Harness Oil **5.00**
Frank Millers Blacking, Uncle Sam
shaving with straight razor, using
polished boot as mirror, eagle
looking at reflection on other
boot **25.00**
Bank, 6¼" h, sheet metal, "Uncle
Sam's Register Bank," red enamel,
gold and black labels **40.00**
Dish, cov, 6⅝" l, milk glass, Uncle
Sam on battleship, c1900 . . . .   **50.00**
Paper Doll, Uncle Sam's Little
Helpers Paper Dolls, Ann Kovach,
1943 . . . .   **15.00**
Pinback Button, 1¼" d, multicolored,
cartoon, "The Yanko Spanko War,"
Uncle Sam using a paddle on
Spaniard **45.00**
Post Card, Uncle Sam sporting pair of
Taft campaign buttons on lapels,
1908 copyright . . . .'. **35.00**
Poster
Buy War Bonds, 22 x 28", Uncle
Sam leading battle, NC Wyeth,
1942 . . . .'. . .   **250.00**
Cost Of Living In Two Wars, 20 x
28", Uncle Sam pointing to
graph, 1944 . . . .   **110.00**
Jap. . .You're Next! Buy Extra
Bonds, 13 x 20", Uncle Sam
rolling up sleeves, James
Montgomery Flagg, 1945 . . . . .   **225.00**
Sign, 4½" w, 8" h, Uncle Sam leaning
on fence, jackknife in hand, whit-
tling on stick, easel back, Jaxon
Soap adv **50.00**
Stickpin, ¼ x½", brass, emb, profile,
1¾" l brass stickpin **18.00**
Watch Fob, Always A Winner, Uncle
Sam standing by globe **35.00**
Washington, George
Card, celluloid, ribbon tied, engraved
portrait **30.00**
Plate, 8" d, clear, Washington
Bicentennial, star border, stippled
ground, bust of Washington,
1732–1932, No. 258 . . . .   **50.00**
Poster, Think American–Remember
You Are Free Men, 20 x 27", red,
white, blue, and black, silhouette
of Washington, 1943 . . . .   **90.00**
Stickpin, bust of George, diecut
hatchet, marked "Washington's
Hatchet, Feb 22," gilt finish, red
painted highlights **65.00**

PENNSBURY POTTERY

Collecting Hints: Concentrate on one pattern or
type. Since the pieces were hand carved, aesthetic quality differs from piece to piece. Look for
pieces with a strong design sense and a high
quality of execution.

Buy only clearly marked pieces. Look for decorator and designer initials that can be easily
identified.

Pennsbury collectors are concentrated in the
Middle Atlantic states. Many of the company's
commemorative and novelty pieces relate to
businesses and events in this region, thus commanding their highest price within that region.

History: Henry and Lee Below established
Pennsbury Pottery, named for its close proximity
to William Penn's estate "Pennsbury," three miles
west of Morrisville, Pennsylvania, in 1950.
Henry, a ceramic engineer and mold maker, and
Lee, a designer and modeler, had previously
worked for Stangl Pottery in Trenton, New Jersey.
Many of Pennsbury's forms, motifs, and manufacturing techniques have Stangl roots. A line of
birds similar to those produced by Stangl were
among the earliest Pennsbury products. The
carved design technique is also Stangl in origin,
high bas–relief molds were not.

Pennsbury products are easily identified by
their brown wash background. The company
also made pieces featuring other background
colors. Do not make the mistake of assuming that
a piece is not Pennsbury because it does not
have a brown wash.

Pennsbury motifs are heavily nostalgic, farm,
and Pennsylvania German related. Among the
most popular lines were Amish, Black Rooster,
Delft Toleware, Eagle, Family, Folkart, Gay
Ninety, Harvest, Hex, Quartet, Red Barn, Red
Rooster, Slick–Chick, and Christmas plates
(1960–1970). The pottery made a large number
of commemorative, novelty, and special order
pieces.

In the late 1950s the company had 16 employees, mostly local housewives and young
girls. In 1963 employees numbered 46, the company's peak. By the late 1960s, the company had
just over 20 employees. Cheap foreign imports
cut deeply into the pottery's profits.

Marks differ from piece to piece depending on
the person who signed the piece or the artist who
sculptured the mold. The identity for some initials has still not been determined.

Henry Below died on December 21, 1959,
leaving the pottery in trust for his wife and three
children with instructions that it be sold upon the
death of his wife. Lee Below died on December
12, 1968. In October 1970 the Pennsbury Pottery
filed for bankruptcy. The contents of the company were auctioned on December 18, 1970.

On May 18, 1971, a fire destroyed the pottery and support buildings.

References: Susan and Al Bagdade, *Warman's American Pottery and Porcelain,* Wallace–Homestead, 1994; Lucile Henzke, *Pennsbury Pottery,* Schiffer Publishing, 1990; Dana Gehman Morykan and Harry L. Rinker, *Warman's Country Antiques & Collectibles, Second Edition* Wallace–Homestead, 1993; Mike Schneider, *Stangl and Pennsbury Birds: Identification and Price Guide,* Schiffer Publishing, 1994.

Look–Alike Alert: The Lewis Brothers Pottery, Trenton, New Jersey, purchased fifty of the lesser Pennsbury molds. Although they were supposed to remove the Pennsbury name from the molds, some molds were overlooked. Further, two Pennsbury employees moved to Lewis Brothers when Pennsbury closed. Many pieces similar in feel and design to Pennsbury were produced. Many of Pennsbury's major lines, including the Harvest and Rooster patterns, plaques, birds, and highly unusual molds, were not reproduced.

Glen View in Langhorne, Pennsylvania, continued marketing the 1970s Angel Christmas plate with Pennsbury markings. The company continued the Christmas plate line into the 1970s utilizing the Pennsbury brown wash background. In 1975 Lenape Products, a division of Pennington, bought Glen View and continued making products with a Pennsbury feel.

Ashtray
Amish man and woman	**18.00**
Fairless Works, gray	**30.00**
Such Schmootzers	**20.00**
Baker, Mother Serving Pie	**75.00**
Bank, pig, Stuff Me, 7" h	**100.00**
Bread Tray, Wheat	**30.00**
Cake Stand, Amish	**75.00**
Candleholders, pr, roosters, 4" h	**75.00**
Canister Set, cov, Black Rooster, flour, sugar, coffee, and tea	**400.00**

Coaster
Shultz	**15.00**
Sweet Adeline	**12.00**
Creamer, Red Rooster, 4" h	**32.00**
Cruet Set, oil and vinegar, Amish, figural head stoppers, pr	**120.00**
Cup and Saucer, Red Rooster	**15.00**

Mug
Farmer	**28.00**
Red Barn, 4½" h	**40.00**
Red Rooster	**28.00**

Pitcher
Hex, 6½" h	**40.00**
Rooster, 6¼" h	**70.00**
Plaque, paddlewheel riverboat, Nat'l Newark & Essex Banking Co. 1804–1954	**35.00**

Plaque, Central R.R. of New Jersey, Star, imp "Pennsbury Pottery, Morrisville, PA" on bottom, 7⅞" l, 5⅞" w, $30.00.

Plate
1972, Countryside	**35.00**
1974, Mother's Day	**35.00**
Dinner, 10" d, Red Rooster	**18.00**
Salt and Pepper Shakers, pr, Amish heads	**60.00**
Snack Set, Black Rooster	**20.00**

Tile
Outen the Light, 4" sq	**25.00**
Skunk, 4" sq	**18.00**
Vinegar Bottle, Amish	**70.00**

PENS AND PENCILS

Collecting Hints: Any defects seriously reduce the value. Defects include scratches, cracks, dents, warping, missing parts, bent levers, sprung clips, nib damage, and mechanical damage. Engraved initials or names do not detract seriously from the price.

History: The steel pen point or nib was invented by Samuel Harrison in 1780. It was not commercially produced in quantity until the 1880s when Richard Esterbrook entered the field. The holders became increasingly elaborate. Mother–of–pearl, gold, Sterling silver, and other fine materials were used to fashion holders of distinction. Many of these pens can be found intact with their velvet–lined presentation cases.

Lewis Waterman invented the fountain pen in the 1880s. Three other leading pioneers in the field were Parker, Sheaffer (first lever filling action, 1913), and Wahl–Eversharp.

The mechanical pencil was patented in 1822 by Sampson Mordan. The original slide–type action developed into the spiral mechanical pencil. Wahl–Eversharp was responsible for the automatic "clic" or repeater-type pencil which is used on ball points today.

The flexible nib that enabled the writer to individualize his penmanship came to an end when Reynolds introduced the ball point pen in October, 1945.

References: Glen Bowen, *Collectible Fountain Pens,* L–W Book Sales, 1992, 1994 value update; George Fischler and Stuart Schneider, *Fountain Pens and Pencils,* Schiffer Publishing, 1990; Cliff Lawrence, *Fountain Pens: History, Repair & Current Values, Second Edition,* Pen Fancier's Club, 1985; Cliff and Judy Lawrence, *The 1992 Official P. F. C. Pen Guide,* Pen Fancier's Club, 1991; Stuart Schneider and George Fischler, *The Illustrated Guide To Antique Writing Instruments,* Schiffer Publishing, 1994; Jonathan Steinburg, *Fountain Pens,* Running Press, Courage Press, 1993.

Collectors' Clubs: American Pencil Collectors Society, 2222 S. Milwood, Wichita, KS 67213; Pen Collectors of American, PO Box 821449, Houston, TX 77282; Pen Fancier's Club, 1169 Overcash Drive, Dunedin, FL 34698.

Periodicals: *Pens,* PO Box 64, Teaneck, NJ 07666; *Pen World Magazine,* PO Box, 6007, Kingwood, TX 77325.

Advisor: Dick Bitterman.

Conklin
1903, pen, Model 30, black hard rubber **80.00**
1918, pen, Model 20, 5⁵⁄₁₆″ l, #2 Conklin point–nib, black crescent filler #20, gold clip, narrow gold band on cap, patent date May 28, 1918 stamped on clip **85.00**
1923, pen, Model 25P, lady's filigree cap ribbon, black, crescent filler **60.00**
1925, desk set, black marble base, two pens, 7¼″ l Endura model, side lever fill, double narrow gold color bands, marked "Patent Nov 17, 1925" on pen barrel, black–brown overlay color **155.00**
1945, pen, Cushion Point, silver–pink stripes, gold filled trim, NOZAK filler **75.00**
Dunn, 1920, pen, black, red barrel, gold plated trim **50.00**

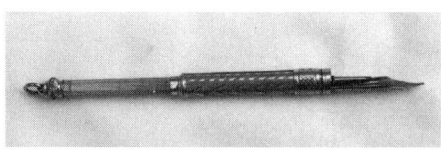

E. J. Johnson & Co., New York, No. 4, combination, one unit, pencil turns out, pen turns out, gold plated, point marked, 4⁷⁄₈″ l fully extended, $65.00.

Epenco, pen, black case, gold plated trim **40.00**
Eversharp
1920, pencil, silver plated **22.00**
1931, pen, lady's, Doric, Eversharp Gold Seal, gold marble color, 14 carat point, twelve sided cap and barrel **150.00**
1935, desk pen, Doric, gold seal, green marble cov, lever fill, large adjustable nib **200.00**
1936, pencil, green marbleized base, upper half gold color metal cap, first of the repeater pencil **100.00**
1946, ball point pen, CA model, black, gold filled cap **40.00**
Laughlin, 1905, pen, silver overlay case, eyedropper filled **200.00**
Marvel, 1906, black chased hard rubber, eyedropper **100.00**
Moore
Desk Set, gray and black marble base, black pen, 12 carat nib, side lever fill **125.00**
Pen, rose color, fancy band around cap, warranted nib, side lever filler **100.00**
Ribbon Pen, lady's, black, three narrow gold bands on cap, lever filler, patent nib #2 . . . . **100.00**
Onoto, 1924, Ink Pencil Stylographic pen, black chased hard rubber, eyedropper **55.00**
Parker
1915, pen, Model 48, ring top, gold filled barrel and cap, button filled **275.00**
1917, pen, Lucky Curve, push button filler **195.00**
1921, ring pen, Lucky Curve, black hard rubber, gold filled trim **150.00**
1923
Pen, Duofold Senior, Flashing Black **200.00**
Pen, Duofold Senior, red hard rubber, single gold color band cap . **225.00**
Pen, No. 42, gold filled metal mounted **120.00**
Pencil, Duofold, Model 78M, lady's, fuchsia color, gold color cap and tip, originally sold for $3 . . . . **145.00**
1928, Duofold Jr, lapis blue **275.00**
1929, pen and pencil set, Duofold Deluxe, black and pearl, three narrow gold color bands on cap, push button fill **450.00**
1932
Duofold Streamline, burgundy and black, double narrow band on cap **150.00**
Vacumatic, gray–black, arrow clip, arrow design engraved on nib,

silver color clip and band on cap, oversized model **140.00**
1942, pen, Blue–Diamond–51, black, gold plated cap, button filled **100.00**
1944, pen, Blue–Diamond–Vacumatic, blue and black, gold plated trim, button filled **100.00**
1950, pen, Model 51, maroon, stainless steel cap, chrome plated trim, aerometric filler **95.00**
1956, pen, Model 61, first edition . . **100.00**
Independence Hall, #900 of limited edition of 10,000 . . . . **450.00**
Set, lady's, Deluxe Duofold, pale green, pearl, orig box **190.00**
Pick, 1922, Exceptional pen, black chased hard rubber, gold filled trim, lever filled **140.00**
Reynolds, pen, orig ball point, Model 2 (1945–46) **110.00**
Security, 1923, pen, check protector, red hard rubber, gold filled trim **125.00**
Sheaffer
1923, pen, White Dot, green jade, gold plated trim, lever filled **140.00**
1930, pen, White Dot Lifetime, classic torpedo design cap and body, lever filler on side **125.00**
1938, pen, White Dot, pearl inlay, full size **110.00**
1940s, desk set, Triumph Lifetime, green marble base, two black snorkel design pens **140.00**
1946, pencil, Fineline 4000, novel point, platinum plating **40.00**
1948, pen, ballpoint, Strato writer, gold filled metal mounted **65.00**
1953, pen, White Dot, snorkel, black, 14 carat gold cap and band, plunger filled **50.00**
Lifetime, jade green, oversize **150.00**
Swan, made by Mabie, Todd & Co., NY and London
Pen, Eternal Model, black, gold filled trim, marked "44 E.T.N., Model 4," nib marked 14 carat **70.00**
Pen, hard rubber, red marbleized, lever fill, double gold band on cap, marked "Eternal" **80.00**
Pen, red ripple, band at top and bottom of cap, marked "model 54 Eternal" on barrel, nib marked 14 carat **95.00**
Wahl
1918, pen, silver overlay case, eyedropper filled **245.00**
1919, pen, Tempoint No. 305A, gold filled metal mounted, eyedropper **180.00**
1928, ribbon pen, lady's double narrow band on cap, 14 carat #2 nib, lever fill **100.00**

Wahl–Eversharp
1919, pencil, gold filled metal mounted **60.00**
1923, pencil, ring top, gold filled case **50.00**
1924, pencil, sterling silver, engraved case **175.00**
1930, pen, gold seal, black, gold filled trim, lever filled **190.00**
Waterman
1886, pen, Model #12 Black chased hard rubber, star imprint nib, eyedropper **275.00**
Mottled brown, 14 carat gold bands **250.00**
1906, Safety Pen, Model 42½V, gold filigree, retractable screw action nib, 3½" l **200.00**
1925, pen, Model #71, red ripple, hard rubber case, gold plated trim, wide clip, lever filled **225.00**
1936, pen, Lady Patricia, gray mottled finish, lever fill **75.00**
1944, pen, 100 Year Model, black, gold color clip, nib marked "100 Year Pen, 1944" **150.00**
1949, pen, Taperite, black, gold filled metal mounted cap, gold filled trim, lever filler **100.00**
Model #42, red ripple safety, #2 18 karat nib, French type clip **235.00**
Model #94, set, olive ripple color . . **395.00**

PEPSI

Collecting Hints: Advertising items from Pepsi, Hires, and a number of other soft drink companies became hot collectibles in the 1980s, fueled in part by the pricey nature of Coca–Cola items. The Pepsi market is still young; some price fluctuations occur.

Pepsi–Cola enjoys a much stronger market position in many foreign countries than it does in the United States. As a result, the best sales market for Pepsi items may be outside the United States. Look for major developments in this area in the decade ahead.

Reproductions, copycats, and fantasy items are part of the Pepsi collecting scene. Be on the alert for the Pepsi and Pete pillow issued in the 1970s, a 12" high ceramic statue of a woman holding a glass of Pepsi, a Pepsi glass–front clock, a Pepsi double bed quilt, and a set of four Pepsi glasses. These are just a few of the suspect items, some of which were done under license from Pepsi–Cola.

History: Pepsi–Cola was developed by Caleb D. Bradham, a pharmacist and drugstore owner, in New Bern, North Carolina. Like many drugstore owners of his time, Bradham provided "soda" mixes for his customers and friends. His favorite was "Brad's Drink."

In 1898, Bradham named "Brad's Drink" Pepsi–Cola. Its popularity spread. In 1902 Bradham turned the operation of his drugstore over to an assistant and devoted his full time energies to perfecting and promoting Pepsi–Cola. He sold 2,008 gallons of Pepsi–Cola syrup in his first three months of production. By 1904 Bradham was bottling Pepsi–Cola for mass consumption. Within a short time, he sold his first franchise.

By the end of the twentieth century's first decade, Bradham had organized a network of over 250 bottlers in twenty–four states. The company's fortunes sank shortly after World War I when it suffered large losses in the sugar market. Bankruptcy and reorganization followed. Roy Megargel, whose Wall Street firm advised Bradham, helped keep the name alive. A second bankruptcy occurred in 1931, but the company survived.

In 1933 Pepsi–Cola doubled its bottle size, but still held to its nickel price. Sales soared. Under the direction of Walter Mack (from 1938–1951), Pepsi challenged Coca–Cola for market dominance. In the 1950s Pepsi advertising became slogan oriented: "Pepsi Cola Hits The Spot, Twelve Full Ounces That's A Lot."

PepsiCo is currently a division of Beatrice. It has a worldwide reputation and actually is the number one soft drink in many foreign countries.

References: Ted Hake, *Hake's Guide To Advertising Collectibles: 100 Years of Advertising from 100 Famous Companies*, Wallace–Homestead, 1992; Everette and Mary Lloyd, *Pepsi–Cola Collectibles*, Schiffer Publishing, 1993; Norman E. Martinus and Harry L. Rinker, *Warman's Paper*, Wallace–Homestead, 1994; Bill Vehling and Michael Hunt, *Pepsi–Cola Collectibles*, Vol. 1 (1990, 1993 value update), Vol. 2 (1990, 1992 value update), and Vol. 3 (1993, 1995 value update), L–W Book Sales.

Collectors' Club: Pepsi–Cola Collectors Club, PO Box 1275, Covina, CA 91722.

Museum: Pepsi–Cola Company Archives, Purchase, NY.

Bottle Carrier, six pack size, 1960s, 8 x 9 x 5", $25.00.

Ashtray, 4" sq, glass, "Pepsi Beats The Others Cold!," 1960s **25.00**
Bottle, 32 oz, applied color label, c1960 . . . .   **25.00**
Bottle Carrier, cardboard, six bottle, c1960 . . . .   **25.00**
Cake Pan **25.00**
Calendar, 1955, cardstock, 12 x 20" . .   **400.00**
Cigarette Lighter, 4" l, metal, bottle cap illus on side, 1950s **150.00**
Clock, light up, MIB, 1967 . . . .   **185.00**
Cooler, aluminum **200.00**

Drinking Glass, Robin **15.00**
Fan, 10" sq, cardboard, wood handle, c1940 . . . .   **75.00**
Indian Headdress, 6 x 24" **15.00**
Letterhead, 8½ x 11", Pepsi–Cola Bottling Works, Greensboro, NC, 1916 . . . .   **100.00**
Napkin, 19" sq, cloth, c1940 . . . .   **25.00**
Patch, 2 x 2", cloth, c1960 . . . .   **10.00**
Pinback Button, 2" d, "I Drank A Pepsi, Did You?," tin, 1970s **10.00**
Poster
  Counter Spy, 8 x 19", radio thriller, 1940s **24.00**
  Indiana Jones, 18 x 32", premiums . .   **16.00**
Program, 6 x 12", 1947 Everess Convention, Atlantic City, November 12–15, Pepsi adv **75.00**
Radio, can shape **40.00**
Ruler, 12" l, tin, c1950s **20.00**
Sign
  9" d, "Ice Cold Pepsi–Cola Sold Here," celluloid and tin, 1930s . .   **275.00**
  12 x 8", "Take Home Pepsi," plastic, light–up, bottle cap illus, 1950s . .   **150.00**
  13 x 15½", "Pepsi," steel, double sided, red, white, blue, and gray bottle cap, yellow ground, c1950   **450.00**
  18 x 27", "Pepsi–Cola, The Big Picnic Drink," family enjoying picnic, easel back, 1940s **450.00**
  22 x 7", "Have A Pepsi," paper, man, woman, and bottle cap illus, 1950s   **25.00**
  24 x 28", "Drink Pepsi–Cola," tin, bottle cap illus, 1950s **50.00**
Snowdome, soda can form **25.00**
Syrup Tin, ten gallon, lid **350.00**
Thermometer, 27" d, emb cap **75.00**
Toy, truck
  7½" l, metal, Pepsi adv, Tonka, 1978   **65.00**

15" l, plastic, delivery van, 1970s .. **55.00**
Tray, 13" d, "Have A Pepsi," 1950s ... **75.00**
Umbrella, 1960s **25.00**

PEZ

Collecting Hints: PEZ developed as a hot collectible in the late 1980s. Its rise was due in part to PEZ's use of licensed cartoon characters as heads on their dispensers. Initially PEZ containers were extremely affordable. Generic subjects often sold for less than $5.00, character containers for less than $10.00. This changed when PEZ developed its own collecting category. It is one of the 1990s' "hot" collectibles.

Before investing large amounts of money in PEZ containers, it is important to recognize that: (1) PEZ containers are produced in the millions; (2) PEZ containers have a high saveability potential; and (3) no collecting category stays hot forever. PEZ prices fluctuate. Advertised and field prices for the same container can differ by as much as fifty percent depending on who is selling.

Starting a PEZ collection is simple. Go to a local store that sells PEZ and purchase the current group of products. Your initial cost will be less than $3.00 a unit.

History: Vienna, Austria, is the birthplace of PEZ. In 1927 Eduard Haas, an Austrian food mogul, invented PEZ and marketed it as a cigarette substitute, i.e., an adult mint. He added peppermint oil to a candy formula, compressed it in small rectangular bricks, and named it PEZ, an abbreviation for the German word *Pfefferminz*. Production of PEZ was halted by World War II. When the product appeared again after the war, it was packaged in a dispenser that resembled a BiC lighter. These early 1950s dispensers had no heads.

PEZ arrived in the United States in 1952. PEZ–HAAS received U.S. Patent #2,620,061 for its "table dispensing receptacle." The public response was less than overwhelming. Rather than withdraw from the market, Haas repositioned his product for the children's market. First, fruit flavors were added. Second, novelty dispensers, e.g., a space gun, and the addition of heads to the top of the standard rectangular containers combined the dual elements of a candy and a toy in one product. PEZ's success was assured.

PEZ carefully guards its design and production information. As a result, collectors differ on important questions such as dating and variation. Further complicating the issue is PEZ production outside the United States. A company in Linz, Austria, with PEZ rights to the rest of the world, including Canada, frequently issues PEZ containers with heads not issued by PEZ Candy, Inc., an independent, privately owned company which by agreement manufactures and markets PEZ only in the United States. PEZ Candy, Inc., is located in Connecticut.

There is a communication link between the American and Austrian companies producing PEZ. Both use a common agent to manage the production of dispensers. The result is that occasionally the same container is issued by both companies. However, when this occurs, the packaging may be entirely different.

PEZ Candy, Inc., issues generic, seasonal, and character licensed containers. Container design is continually evaluated and upgraded. The Mickey Mouse container has been changed more than a dozen times.

Today PEZ candy is manufactured at plants in Austria, Hungary, Yugoslavia, and the United States. Previously, plants had been located in Czechoslovakia, Germany, and Mexico. Dispensers are produced at plants in Austria, China, Hong Kong, Hungary, and Slovenia.

References: Richard Geary, *PEZ Collectibles,* Schiffer Publishing, 1994; David Welch, *A Pictorial Guide to Plastic Candy Dispensers Featuring PEZ,* Bubba Scrubba Publications, 1991; David Welch, *Collecting Pez,* Bubba Scrubba Publications, 1994.

Periodical: *Positively PEZ,* 3851 Gable Lane Drive, #513, Indianapolis, IN 46208.

Annie, 1970s **20.00**
Baseball Glove, 1960s **100.00**
Batgirl, soft head, 1970s **40.00**
Betsy Ross, 1976 .... **35.00**
Boy, Pez Pal, 1960–70 .... **5.00**
Bozo, 4" h, Bozo and Butch image on
    stem **75.00**
Brutus, 1960s **100.00**
Bugs Bunny, 4½" h, yellow base, gray
    and white head, 1978 .... **25.00**
Bullwinkle, 1960s **150.00**
Captain Hook, 4¼" h, copyright Walt
    Disney Productions **30.00**
Casper, 4" h, orig unopened package .. **75.00**
Chick In Egg, 1960s **1.00**
Chip, 1980s **8.00**
Creature, 1960s **75.00**
Crocodile, 1970s **30.00**
Daffy Duck, 1970–80 .... **2.00**
Daniel Boone, 1976 .... **100.00**
Donald Duck **12.50**
Donky Kong, Jr, premium, 1980 ..... **200.00**
Droopy Dog, 1980s **10.00**
Dumbo, 1960s **5.00**
Fozzie Bear, 1991 .... **1.00**
Garfield, 1980s **2.00**
Goofy, 1960s **1.00**
Gorilla, 1970s **10.00**
Green Hornet **100.00**
Incredible Hulk, 1970s **5.00**

Indian Squaw, 1976 .... 50.00
Jerry, 1980s 10.00
Jiminy Cricket, 4½" h, copyright Walt
  Disney Productions, Inc 30.00
Joker, 4¼" h, copyright 1978 DC
  Comics, Inc 25.00
Kermit the Frog, 1991 .... 1.00
Knight, Pez Pal, 1960–70 .... 75.00
Lion, 1970s 10.00
Mexican Boy, orig unopened package 75.00
Mickey Mouse, 1950s 50.00
Miss Piggy, 1991 .... 1.00
Nurse, Pez Pal, 1960–70 .... 10.00
Olive Oyl, 4" h 75.00
Penguin, 4½" h, copyright 1978 DC
  Comics, Inc 25.00
Peter Pan, 4" h, green base, copyright
  Walt Disney Productions 25.00
Pluto, 1960s 1.00
Pony, 4½" h, blue base, 1952–68 .... 22.00

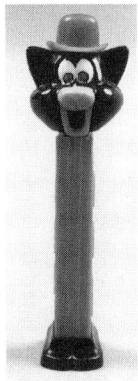

Puzzy Cat, black head, marked "Made in Austria," 4½" h, $10.00.

Pumpkin, 1960s 1.00
Road Runner, 1970–80 .... 10.00
Rooster, 4½" h, orig unopened package 50.00
Sailor, Pez Pal, 1960–70 .... 50.00
Santa Claus, 1950s 1.00
Scare Wolf, 1960s 50.00
Scrooge McDuck, 1970s 10.00
Sheriff, Pez Pal, 1960–70 .... 10.00
Skeleton 9.50
Smurf, 1980s 2.00
Spaceman, 4" h, metallic blue stem ... 75.00
Speedy Gonzales, 1970–80 .... 10.00
Spiderman 15.00
Spike, Tom and Jerry dog, 1980s 10.00
Tinkerbell, 1960s 75.00
Truck, 4" h, orange base, dark brown
  cab top, c1976 .... 20.00
Wile E Coyote, 1970–80 .... 5.00
Witch, 1960s 1.00

PHOENIX BIRD CHINA

Collecting Hints: The Phoenix Bird pattern has over 450 different shapes and sizes. The quality found in the execution of design, shades of blue, and shape of the ware itself also varies. All these factors must be considered in pricing. The maker's mark tends to add value; over 100 marks have been cataloged.

The more one studies Phoenix Bird china, the more one recognizes the variances. Collectors are urged to travel with a notebook in which is listed the shape, pattern, backstamp, dimensions, and conditions of the pieces owned. If the head of the phoenix is on a forward slant and its head feathers point upwards, also on somewhat of a slant, the rest of the motif will be well executed. If this is combined with a piece having an oversized border, the collector has found a "superior piece." Generally these superior pieces are marked with a flower with a "T" inside, but not always. The one rule about Phoenix Bird is that there always is an exception to the rule.

Don't buy Phoenix Bird unseen. Insist on a drawing of the piece, but most preferably a photograph. Photographs can be deceiving so ask for the dimensions as well. Xeroxing a plate is helpful for a buyer's identification of Phoenix Bird China or any of the similar Phoenix patterns.

History: The manufacture of Phoenix Bird pattern china began in the late 19th century. The ware was heavily imported into the United States during the 1920s to the 1940s. The Phoenix Bird pattern shows a bird facing back over its left wing, spots on its chest and wings that spread upward. The vast majority of the ware was of the transfer print variety. Blue and white was the dominant color scheme. Pieces also can be found in green (celadon), but are quite rare. Coveted are the few hand–painted pieces in blue which are signed with six Japanese characters on the underside and which always have the heart border. Some of the transfer pieces also have a heart-like border and are referred to as HO–O for identification. Many of these early pieces are not marked. The majority of Phoenix Bird has the traditional border called the cloud and mountain (c/m) and sometimes has "Nippon" backstamped when of the 1891–1921 era.

Phoenix Bird pattern china primarily was sold through Woolworth's 5 & 10 Cent stores. It could also be ordered from the wholesale catalogs of Butler Brothers and the Charles William stores, the latter also retailing it at its New York city store. All the pieces offered were only the most basic shapes. Phoenix Bird also was carried by A. A. Vantine Co., NY, exported by Morimura Brothers, Japan.

A Phoenix Bird breakfast set could be acquired by selling a certain number of subscriptions to *Needlecraft* magazine. Ward's Grocery Catalog and A. J. Kasper Importers, Chicago, offered a Phoenix Bird cup and saucer as a premium for purchasing a particular brand of tea or coffee.

Once known as "Blue Howo Bird China," the Phoenix Bird pattern is the most sought after of several variations of the HO–O bird series. Other variations are:

Firebird—one of several less common patterns, flowing tail dragging downward; majority is hand painted, marked with six Oriental characters.

Flying Dragon—all over pattern comes in blue and white as well as green and white; always has six characters underneath; bird's wings are fatter and rounder; in place of flower there is a pinwheel like design.

Flying Turkey—blue and white with heart border, head always facing forward; no spots on chest; and left wing, as one faces design, only half showing; majority is transfer printed; a larger minority than Phoenix Bird is hand painted; mark is six Oriental characters.

Howo—in some cases the pattern's name is on the underside along with "Noritake," other times it is not; phoenix shows no feet; flower is more peony-like.

Twin Phoenix—made by Noritake, but not always marked; pattern is only on outer–edge, rest is white; two birds face one another in pairs.

During the 1920s and 1930s an overwhelming number of potteries put their trademarks on the pieces. A majority have "Made in Japan," an M/wreath (concave M), crossed stems with a convex "M," or a flower with a "T" inside and "Japan" underneath. The last mark shows up on some of the more uniquely shaped pieces and pieces of highest quality. Most Japanese potteries were destroyed during WWII, making it difficult to trace production records. The Phoenix Bird pattern was copied by an English firm, Myott & Son, in the mid–1930s. The English examples are earthenware and not porcelain as are the Japanese pieces.

References: Joan Collett Oates, *Phoenix Bird Chinaware, Book I* (1984), *Book II* (1985), *Book III* (1986), *Book 4* (1989), published by author.

Collectors' Club: Phoenix Bird Collectors of America, 685 S. Washington, Constantine, MI 49042.

Museums: Historic Cherry Hill, Albany, NY; Huntingdon County Historical Society, Huntingdon, PA; Charles A. Lindbergh Home, Little Falls, MN; Eleanor Roosevelt's Vall–Kill Cottage, Hyde Park, NY.

Advisor: Joan Collett Oates.

REPRODUCTION ALERT. Reproductions of later shapes have been around since 1970. The repro-

ductions are more modern in shape, have more precise designs and more brilliant blue, have a milk–white ground, and rarely are backstamped, with the exception of a covered jam jar and a butter pat dish. The reproductions generally had paper stickers on them at one time. Diagonal lines within the various designs are prevalent. The all–over design is more sparse on the post 1970 pieces and does not always reach the bottom of an item as it does on earlier Phoenix Bird; the majority of newer pieces do not have a backstamp.

A new type of Phoenix is on the market in various forms and also is a dark blue design. It is called "T–Bird" for identification. At least one maker, Takahashi, has been identified. Sometimes it is found with a group of Oriental markings within a blue square.

Note: The numbering system used to identify pieces is from the four–volume set of *Phoenix Bird Chinaware* by Joan Collett Oates.

Cereal Bowl, 6" d	**15.00**
Creamer, #9	**15.00**
Cup and Saucer, 3⅞" d, 2" h, common	**9.00**
Custard Cup, "A"	**15.00**
Fruit Bowl, 5½"	**9.00**

Hot Water Pot #4, Mark #17, 5¾" h, $45.00.

Plate	
6" d, bread and butter, quality design	**8.00**
7" d, dessert, quality design	**12.00**
8½" d, luncheon, quality design	**20.00**
9¾" d, dinner	**45.00**
Platter, oval	
9¾" l	**35.00**
12" l	**55.00**
17" l	**165.00**
Rice Bowl #1, 4¾" d, 1⅞" h, pattern inside	**12.00**
Soup Dish, 7¼" d	**35.00**
Sugar Bowl, cov, #3	**25.00**
Teapot, #5, medium	**45.00**

Tile, 6" d, round **38.00**
Vegetable Dish, large, oval, 10" l **45.00**

PHOTOGRAPHS

Collecting Hints: The first and most important thing to remember is that most personal photographs, no matter how old, are virtually worthless. This is especially true of unidentified family views.

Value rests in content and artistry. Photographs of towns, occupations, and other special interest categories do have value to collectors. Pictures of children sledding down a snow bank or standard soldiers in uniform usually do not.

Take a few minutes during your next visit to your local library and review the books dealing with twentieth century photographers. Memorize their names and work. Examples of their work turn up in unexpected places. However, before paying a premium, double check to make certain that the example is not one from a mass–produced folio. These usually have very limited value.

History: Next to the Bible, the most important book a family owned in the second half of the nineteenth and first half of the twentieth centuries was the nucleated family photo album. Filled primarily with individual head and shoulder photographs in the early period to numerous christening, graduation, wedding, and vacation photographs in the later period, it provided a visual chronicle of the family's history. Also accompanying the album are usually dozens of envelopes with pictures and negatives that were meant to be added "some day."

The chief problem is that most photographs are unidentified. The individuals who took or received the pictures knew who everyone was. Information was passed orally from generation to generation. Most information was lost by the third and fourth generations.

In late nineteenth and early twentieth century albums, principal photographs are cartes de visite and cabinet cards. It is common to find memorial cards and mass–produced photographs of important military and historical figures. Pictures that show a person in a working environment, identifiable building or street scene, or a special holiday, e.g., Christmas, are eagerly sought. Most studio shots have little value.

Many of the albums were ornately decorated in velvet and applied ormolu. Some covers contained celluloid pictures, ranging in theme from a beautiful young woman to the battleship *Maine.* The Victorian decorating craze drew attention to these albums in the late 1980s. Prices have risen significantly over the last several years.

Carte de visite, or calling card, photographs

were patented in France in 1854, flourished from 1857 to 1910, and survived into the 1920s. The most common cartes de visite were 2¼ x 3¾" head and shoulder portraits printed on albumen paper and mounted on 2½ x 4" cards. Multi–lens cameras were used by the photographer to produce four to eight exposures on a single glass negative plate. A contact print was made from this which would yield four to eight identical photographs on one piece of photographic paper. The photographs would be cut apart and mounted on cards. These cards were put in albums or simply handed out when visiting, similar to today's business cards.

In 1866 the cabinet card was introduced in England and shortly thereafter in the United States. It was produced similarly to cartes de visite, but could utilize several styles of photographic processes. A cabinet card measured 4 x 5" and was mounted on a 4½ x 6½" card. Portraits in cabinet size were more appealing because of the large facial detail and the fact that the images could be retouched. By the 1880s the cabinet card was as popular as the carte de visite and by the 1890s was produced almost exclusively. Cabinet cards flourished until shortly after the turn of the century.

George Eastman revolutionized the photography industry in 1888 when his simple box camera was introduced. It was small—3¼ x 3¾ x 6½". The camera had a magazine and could take 100 pictures without being reloaded. The pictures were 2½" in diameter. Many later models built upon the success of Kodak No. 1. Kodak's first folding camera was Model No. 4; the Brownie arrived in 1900.

Americans loved photographs. Everyone took pictures. A family's photographic treasures grew exponentially. Professional "art" photographers arrived on the scene. Folios were mass produced and sold in quantities.

Two developments in the post–1945 era changed the impact level of photographs in everyday life. The 35mm slide diminished the importance of the print. Home movie cameras and later the video camera made amateur moving pictures possible. Many modern families no longer maintain a photograph album or family photograph archives. They simply do not have the desire or time.

References: Stuart Bennett, *How To Buy Photographs,* Salem House, 1987; William C. Darrah, *Cartes de Visite in Nineteenth Century Photography,* William C. Darrah, 1981; B. E. C. Howarth–Loomes, *Victorian Photography: An Introduction for Collectors and Connoisseurs,* St. Martin's Press, 1974; O. Henry Mace, *Collector's Guide to Early Photographs,* Wallace–Homestead, 1990; Norman E. Martinus and Harry L. Rinker, *Warman's Paper,* Wallace–Homestead, 1994; Lou W. McCullough, *Card Photographs: A Guide To Their History and*

Value, Schiffer Publishing, Ltd., 1981; Floyd and Marion Rinhart, *American Miniature Case Art,* A. S. Barnes and Co., 1969; Susan Theran, *Leonard's Annual Price Index of Prints, Posters and Photographs, 1993–1994 Auction Season,* Auction Index, Inc., 1995; Susan Theran, *Prints, Posters and Photographs: Identification and Price Guide,* Avon Books, 1993; John Waldsmith, *Stereoviews: An Illustrated History and Price Guide,* Wallace–Homestead, 1991.

Periodicals: *Autograph Times,* 2303 N. 44th St., #225, Phoenix, AZ 85008; *Camera Shopper,* 313 N. Quaker Lane, PO Box 370279, W. Hartford, CT 06137; *The Photograph Collector,* The Photographic Arts Center, 163 Amsterdam Ave. #201, New York, NY 10023.

Collectors' Clubs: American Photographical Historical Society, 1150 Avenue of the Americas, New York, NY 10036; Photographic Historical Society of Canada, PO Box 54620, Toronto, Ontario M5M 4N5 Canada; Photographic Historical Society of New England, Inc., PO Box 189, West Newton Station, Boston, MA 02165; Photographic Society of America, 1305 Foxglove Dr., Batava, IL 60510; The Daguerrian Society, PO Box 2129, Green Bay, WI 54306; The Photographic Historical Society, PO Box 39563, Rochester, NY 14604; Western Photographic Collectors Association, PO Box 4294, Whittier, CA 90607.

Museums: Center for Creative Photography, Tucson, AZ; International Center of Photography, New York, NY; International Museum of Photography at George Eastman House, Rochester, NY; International Photographic Historical Association, San Francisco, CA; Smithsonian Institution, Washington, DC; University of Texas at Austin, Austin, TX.

REPRODUCTION ALERT: Excellent reproductions of Lincoln as well as other Civil War era figures on cartes de visite and cabinet cards have been made.

Note: Prices listed are for black and white photographs in excellent condition. Photographs with soiling, staining, tears, and copy photographs are worth less than half prices listed.

Album
    Embossed Leather, presented to Gracie by Mrs Roger, 1882, 44 tintypes of Gracie with her family, friends, dolls, and pet chicken ... **750.00**
    Views of China, Philippines, and Japan, c1900 .... **150.00**
Albumen on Cardboard, steamer *Judelle,* pen and ink calligraphy inscription "Compliments of Steamer, L.F. Bergenroth, Master, W.A. Marshall, Clerk," c1885, framed, 12¼ x 10¼" **225.00**

Cabinet Card
    Advertising, Howe Sewing Machines, large porcelain doll sitting at small sewing machine, text on back, edges and corners rough, some soiling **60.00**
    Basketball Team **82.00**
    Fort Monroe, VA, 1870s **25.00**
    Mob Scene **38.00**
    Occupational, John F Cahill, seated, holding newspaper, publisher of El Commerico Del Valle, autographed, dated 1878 .... **95.00**
    Young Girl, studio pose, meadow flowers, doll hanging from fence, Gibson, Norwalk, OH, tiny spots on image **34.00**

Cabinet Card, young girl wearing First Holy Communion dress, photo by Sol Young, NY, oval mat, 5 x 8″, 1909, $12.00.

Carte De Visite
    Children, two boys and two girls at tea party, girls holding dolls, older boy reading book, small stove at right, Merz, NY, c1865 .... **105.00**
    Pool Player, holding cue stick, outside, standing before studio backdrop hung on wall **55.00**
Daguerreotype, 6th plate
    Elderly Woman, seated at table with book, wearing white bonnet and capelet collar, faint tarnish lower edge, split leather case **30.00**
    Girl, wearing gold highlighted jewelry, portrait by A Boisseau, Cleveland, mat stamped "1856," emb velvet pad, repaired split case, minor tarnish **105.00**
    Man, wearing eye patch, early mat form, split leather case, pad missing, tarnish halo **385.00**
    Man and Woman **65.00**

Photograph
Circus, Ringling Brothers Barnum &
Bailey Combined Circus group
shot, sepia tone, 12 x 20" 45.00
Coastal Artillery, soldiers, pre WWI,
set of four large views 85.00
Mexican Army Troops, lot of 75 activ-
ity photos 95.00
Minstrel Group, black face, 1920s,
Chicago, 8 x 14" 140.00
Picture Case, hinged, emb cov design
Ballerina, brown, contains two am-
brotypes of man and woman,
2½ x 3" 165.00
Catching Butterflies, oval, no pic-
tures, small rim chip, chips by
clasp, 2¼ x 2½" 72.00
Geometric, contains tintype of young
man, 2½ x 3" 45.00
Tin Type
Five Young Men, school letters and
diplomas, outdoor setting, 6th plate 40.00
Little Girl, sitting on chair, holding
dark–haired porcelain doll, album
size 35.00
Two Firemen, wearing dress uni-
forms, parade ribbons, and hats, "I"
on hats and belt buckles, posed
with draped US flag, album size . . 185.00

PIG COLLECTIBLES

Collecting Hints: Bisque and porcelain pig items
from the late 19th century European potters are
most widely sought by collectors. Souvenir items
should have the decals in good shape; occasionally the gilding wears off from rubbing or washing.

History: Historically the pig has been an important food source in the rural economies of Europe
and America. It was one of the first animals imported into the American colonies. A fatted sow
was the standard gift to a rural preacher on his
birthday or holiday.

As a decorative motif the pig gained prominence with the figurines and planters made in the
late 19th century by English, German, and
Austrian potters. These "pink" porcelain pigs
with green decoration were popular souvenir or
prize items at fairs or carnivals or could be purchased at five–and–dime stores.

Many pig figurines were banks. "Piggy Bank"
became a standard term for the coin bank by the
early 20th century. When tourist attractions began along America's sea coasts and in the mountain areas, many of the pig designs showed up as
souvenir items with the name of the area applied
in gilded decal form.

The pig motif appeared on the advertising
items associated with farm products and life. The

era of the movie cartoon introduced "Porky Pig"
and Walt Disney's "Three Little Pigs."

In the late 1970s pig collectibles caught fire
again. Specialty shops selling nothing but pig–related items were found in the New England area.
Time magazine devoted a page and one–half to
the pig phenomena in one of its 1981 issues.

Advisor: Mary Hamburg.

See: Cartoon Characters and Disneyana

REPRODUCTION ALERT: Reproductions of
three German–style, painted bisque figurines
have been spotted in the market. They are pig by
outhouse, pig playing piano, and pig poking out
of large purse. The porcelain is much rougher
and the green is a darker shade.

Ashtray
Artist pig painting, pig sketch on
tablet 95.00
Bowling, one pig bowling, one
watching, pink with green, 5" w . . 95.00
Camera, two pigs looking into old
fashioned camera, 4½" w 75.00
Hugging, two pigs hugging, sitting in
dish, bisque, stamped "Made In
Germany" 80.00
Victrola, two pigs looking into old
fashioned victrola, 4½" w 75.00
Bank, 3½" h
Saving His Pennies To Make Pounds,
pink pig along side band 95.00
Souvenir of Danville, IL, front pink
pig sticking out of bank, back end
sticking out other end, gold pig,
yellow pouch 50.00
Carnival Chalkware, 7" h, 1950s 45.00
Figure
Automobile, two pigs riding 55.00
Barbershop scene, caption "Little Bit
Off The Top," incised "Made In
Germany," 2¾" h 80.00
Canoe, pink pig sitting in canoe . . . 75.00
Cart
Pig pushing cart, caption "Porker
Sausage Maker Are The Best
Value," 2½" 65.00

**Figure, A Present from Southend on Sea,
5½" l, $150.00.**

Pink pig wheeling cart with three piglets in it, caption "The More The Merrier" **75.00**
Chef pig standing by barrel, blue hat and jacket **95.00**
Cradle, pig in cradle **60.00**
Dutch Shoe, pig sitting in shoe **35.00**
Gazebo, orange roof, two pink pigs sitting on bench, 5½" h **100.00**
Heidsieck Dry Champagne Cork, two pigs in front, 3" h **85.00**
Jar, orange seal, pig along side, 2¾" h **60.00**
Mama pig looking over baby piglet in crib, caption "Hush A Bye Baby Don't You Cry You'll Be A Sausage Bye and Bye," incised "Made in Germany" **90.00**
Money Bag, pink pig poking out, "5,000,000" on front **85.00**
Organ, one pig playing organ, other along side playing banjo, caption "Home Sweet Home" **85.00**
Outhouse, pig looking in, caption "Engaged," 4" h, 2½" w **78.00**
Pig in small washtub **60.00**
Table Tennis, two pigs playing, caption "Patience" **90.00**
Train
    Caboose, two pigs **80.00**
    Engine, pig, 4¼" l **90.00**
Two pigs sitting on bench in front of large money pouch, orange seal, 4½" h **88.00**
Windmill, pink pig sitting, orange roof **80.00**
Grease Jar, figural, Old MacDonald pattern **195.00**
Inkwell, 3" h pink pig sitting on top of inkwell **100.00**
Liquor Tote, figural, Hull **145.00**
Matchsafe
    4½" w, pink pig poking head through fence **65.00**
    5" h, bisque, pink pig, one captioned "Scratch My Back," other reads "Me Too" **100.00**
Pinback Button
    Blue Ribbon For Hogs Meat Meal, blue and white, crowned pig sitting upright on rear haunches, c1920 .   **20.00**
    The Yankee Pig, pig dancing on island of Cuba, multicolored, Spanish–American war era, c1898   **85.00**
Pin Dish
    4¾" w, 3½" h, pink pig bride (yellow bonnet and bow) and groom (top hat, green bow tie, umbrella) **125.00**
    5" w, yellow and green Good Luck horseshoe, pink pig, stamped "Made in Germany" **80.00**
Salt

Post Card, child riding pig, German greetings, $30.00.

2½" h, three little pigs around water trough **50.00**
3½" h, two pigs along side bucket, stamped "Made in Germany" **50.00**
Toothpick Holder
    2½" h, one small and one large pig in front of open mushroom **54.00**
    2¾" h, two little pigs in front of egg .   **50.00**
    3" h, pig with mug in hand leaning on fence **60.00**
    3" w, Souvenir of Watertown, NY, stamped "Made in Germany" **54.00**
    3¼" l, pink pig pushing wheelbarrow, worn **65.00**
    3¾" h, single pig with racquet, caption "Lawn Tennis" **75.00**
    4" h, three large pigs in front of water trough **60.00**
    4½" h, three pigs sitting on large water trough, two orange mushrooms in front **65.00**
Vase
    Red Devil's arm around pink pig, sitting on log, 7¼" l **110.00**
    Two pigs looking out of large shoe, Germany **60.00**

PINBALL MACHINES

Collecting Hints: Cosmetic condition is paramount. Graphics are complex and difficult to impossible to repair. Graphics are unique to a specific model, especially backglass and playfield plastics, making replacements scarce. Prices are given for cosmetics in good shape, 95% or more of backglass decoration present, games in good working condition.

Some wear is expected in pinballs as a sign that the game was a good one, but bare wood detracts from overall condition. Watch for signs of loose ink on the rear of the glass. Unrestorable games with good cosmetics are valuable for restoration of other games. Discount 30 to 40% of the price for a nonworking game.

Add 10% if the paper items such as score card, instruction card, and schematic are present and in good condition. It is fair to suggest that regardless of mechanical condition, a game in good cosmetic condition is worth roughly twice what the same game is worth in poor cosmetic condition.

Pinball collecting is a new hobby which is still developing. It can be started inexpensively, but requires space to maintain. The tremendous diversity of models made has prevented the market from becoming well developed. There are relatively few people restoring antique pinball machines for sale. Expect to buy games in nonworking condition and learn to repair them yourself.

History: Pinball machines can trace their heritage back to the mid–1700s. However, it was not until 1931 when Gottlieb introduced "Baffle Ball" that pinball machines caught on and became a popular and commercial success. It was the Depression, and people were hungry for something novel and the opportunity to make money. Pinball machines had both. The first games were entirely mechanical, cost about twenty dollars and were produced in large numbers—25,000 to 50,000 were not uncommon.

Pinball developments include:
1932—addition of legs
1933—electric, at first using batteries
1936—addition of bumpers
1947—advent of flippers
1950—kicking rubbers
1953—score totalizers
1954—multiple players
1977—solid state electronics

The size also underwent change. The early countertops were 16 x 32 inches. Later models were free standing with the base 21 x 52 inches and the backbox 24 x 30 inches.

The total number of pinball models that have been manufactured has not yet been determined. Some suggest over 10,000 different models from more than 200 makers. After 1940 most models were produced in quantities of 500 to 2,000; occasionally games had production figures as high as 10,000. Pinball machines have always enjoyed a high attrition rate. New models made the most money and were introduced by several of the major manufacturers at the rate of one entirely new model every three weeks during the mid–1940s and 1950s. Today the rate of new model introduction has slowed to an average of four to six new games per year.

Most operators of pinballs used the older games for spare parts to repair newer models.

The earning life of a machine was less than three years in most markets. Many games were warehoused or destroyed to keep them from becoming competition for the operator's newest games; they did not want older pinball machines winding up in the wrong hands. At the very least, the coin mechanisms were removed before the game was sold. Most machines that have survived have come from home basements or from operators' storage.

Most pinballs were made in Chicago. Major manufacturers were Gottlieb, Williams, and Bally. Pinballs by D. Gottlieb & Co. are the most sought after due to generally superior play and graphics. Games from the 1947 to mid–1970s period are especially popular.

Pinball art is part of the popular culture and kinetic art. The strength of the pinball playfield design carried Gottlieb as the predominant maker through the 1950s and into the 1970s. During the 1960s Gottlieb's fame grew due to the animated backglasses, intended to both amuse and attract players, which featured movable units as part of the artwork. The combination of animation and availability make the 1960s machines a key target period for collectors.

The advent of solid state games in 1977, coupled with the video game boom, dramatically changed the pinball machine market. The late electromechanical games became obsolete from a commercial point of view. Initially Bally was the predominant maker, but Williams has since attained this position. Solid state game production was high as manufacturers attempted to replace all obsolete electromechanical games. A severe dent in pinball machine production was caused by the video games of the 1980s. Collectors, who are rediscovering the silver ball, are helping the pinball machine recover some of its popularity.

References: Richard Bueschel, *Pinball I: Illustrated Historical Guide To Pinball Machines, Volume 1,* Hoflin Publishing, 1988; Richard Bueschel, *Collector's Guide To Vintage Coin Machines,* Schiffer Publishing, 1995; Heirbert Eiden and Jurgen Lukas, *Pinball Machines,* Schiffer Publishing, 1992; Gary Flower and Bill Kurtz, *Pinball: The Lure of the Silver Ball,* published by authors; Bill Kurtz, *Arcade Treasures,* Schiffer Publishing, 1994; Bill Kurtz, *Slot Machines and Coin–Op Games,* Chartwell Books, 1991; Donald Mueting and Robert Hawkins, *The Pinball Reference Guide,* Mead Co.

Periodicals: *Coin Drop International,* 5815 W. 52nd Ave., Denver, CO 80212; *Coin–Op Classics,* 17844 Toiyabe St., Fountain Valley, CA 92708; *Gameroom Magazine,* 1014 Mt. Tabor Rd., New Albany, IN 47150; *Pin Game Journal,* 31937 Olde Franklin Dr., Farmington Hills, MI 48334; *Pinball Trader,* PO Box 1795, Campbell,

CA 95009; *The Coin Slot,* 4401 Zephyr St., Wheat Ridge, CO 80033.

Note: Pinballs are listed by machine name and fall into various classifications: novelty with no awards, replay which awards free games, add–a–ball which awards extra balls instead of games, and bingo where players add additional coins to increase the odds of winning bingo cards played. Some payout games were made in the mid to late 1930s which paid out coins for achieving scoring objectives. After the first add–a–ball games in 1960, many game designs were issued as both replay and add–a–ball with different game names and slight play rules modifications but similar art work.

Bally
   1933, Airway, first mechanical scoring **325.00**
   1951, Coney Island, bingo **350.00**
   1963, Moon Shot, replay **275.00**
   1964, Mad World, captive ball **250.00**
   1968, Rock Makers, replay, unusual playfield **250.00**
   1968, Safari, replay **275.00**
   1973, Nip–It, ball grabber **225.00**
   1975, Bon Voyage, replay **275.00**
   1978, Lost World, electronic **350.00**
   1979, Harlem Globetrotters, electronic **300.00**
   1980, Xenon, electronic **425.00**
Chicago Coin
   1948, Spinball, spinner action **175.00**
   1974, Gin, replay **175.00**
Exhibit
   1941, Big Parade, patriotic theme, classic art **450.00**
   1947, Mam'selle, replay **400.00**
Genco
   1937, Cargo **375.00**
   1949, Black Gold, replay **325.00**
Gottlieb
   1936, Daily Races, one–ball **375.00**
   1948, Buccaneer, replay, mirrored graphics **350.00**
   1950, Just 21, turret shooter **325.00**
   1955, Duette, replay, first 2–player **325.00**
   1956, Auto Race, replay **350.00**
   1961, Big Casino, replay **250.00**
   1965, Cow Poke, animation classic **475.00**
   1966, Hurdy Gurdy, add–a–ball version of Central Park **375.00**
   1967, King of Dinosaurs, replay, roto **375.00**
   1968, Royal Guard, replay, snap target **300.00**
   1969, Spin–A–Card, replay **300.00**
   1970, Aquarius, replay **325.00**
   1971, Roller Coaster, replay, multi–level **325.00**
   1975, Atlantis, replay **350.00**
   1977, Target Alpha, multi–player ... **350.00**

   1981, Black Hole, electronic, multi–level **475.00**
Mills Novelty Co., 1932, Official, push button ball lift **350.00**
Pacific Amusement, 1934, Lite–A–Line, first light up backboard **325.00**
Rock–Ola
   1932, Juggle Ball, countertop, rod ball manipulator **295.00**
   1935, Flash, early free play **315.00**
United
   1948, Caribbean, replay **225.00**
   1951, ABC, first bingo **400.00**
Williams
   1948, Yanks, baseball theme, animated **300.00**
   1953, Army–Navy, replay, reel scoring **300.00**
   1958, Gusher, disappearing bumper **375.00**
   1961, Metro, replay **225.00**
   1964, Palooka, add–a–ball **275.00**
   1967, Touchdown, animation **250.00**
   1972, Olympic Hockey, replay **275.00**
   1973, Travel Time, timed play **225.00**
   1975, Triple Strike, replay **300.00**
   1977, Grand Prix, replay **350.00**
   1980, Firepower, electronic **450.00**

PIN–UP ART

Collecting Hints: Try to collect calendars intact. There is a growing practice among dealers to separate calendar pages, cut off the date information, and sell the individual sheets in hopes of making more money. Buyers are urged not to succumb to supporting this practice.

Concentrate on the work of one artist. Little research has been done on the pin–up artists so it is a wide open field. The original works of art, whether in oils or pastels, on which calendar sheets and magazine covers are based have begun to appear on the market. High prices are being asked, but the market is not yet stabilized— beware!

Pin–up material can be found in many other collectible categories. Usually the items are referred to as "girlies" on the list. Many secondary pin–up items are not signed, but a collector can easily identify an artist's style.

History: Charles Dana Gibson created the first true pin–up girl with his creation of the Gibson Girl in the early 1900s. Other artists, such as Howard Chandler Christy, Coles Phillips and Charles Sheldon, followed. The film magazines of the 1920s, such as *Film Fun* and *Real Screen Fun,* developed the concept further. Their front covers featured the minimally clad beauties to attract a male readership.

The 1930s featured the work of cover artists Charles Sheldon, Cardwell Higgins and George

Petty. Sheldon did calendar art for Brown & Bigelow as well as covers. *Esquire* began in 1933; its first Petty gatefold appeared in 1939.

The golden age of pin–up art was 1935 to 1955. The 1940s brought Alberto Vargas (the "s" was dropped at *Esquire's* request), Gillete Elvgren, Billy DeVorss, Joyce Ballantyne and Earl Moran into the picture. Pin–up girl art appeared everywhere—magazine covers, blotters, souvenir items, posters, punchboards, etc. Many other artists adopted the style.

Photographic advertising and changing American tastes ended the pin–up reign by the early 1960s.

References: Denis C. Jackson, *The Price And Identification Guide To Alberto Vargas And George Petty, Second Edition,* published by author, 1987; Denis C. Jackson, *The Price And Identification Guide To Coles Philips,* published by author, 1986; *Pin–Up Poster Book: The Elvgren Collection,* Collectors Press, 1995.

Periodicals: *Glamour Girls: Then and Now,* PO Box 34501, Washington, DC 20043; *The Illustrator Collector's News,* PO Box 1958, Sequim, WA 98382.

Advisor: Dick Bitterman.

Calendar
1938, sample, DeVorss, "Do I Attract Your Attention?" caption, 31 x 47" **250.00**
1940, Blue Nude, E Moran **40.00**
1942
A Good Number, Petty, 14 x 21½" **95.00**
Lovely Lady, DeVorss, 11 x 23" . . **95.00**
1943
For You A Rose, Mozert, 11 x 23" **95.00**
Hello Skipper, Moran, 11 x 23" . . **95.00**
Hold Everything, Armstrong, Brown & Bigelow, 11 x 23" **125.00**
It's Your Dance, Erbit, 11 x 23" . . . **95.00**
1944, *Esquire,* Vargas **85.00**

Calendar, The Esquire Girl Calendar, 1947, 12 pages, Alberto Vargas, artist, $75.00.

1949, Nursery Nifties, spiral bound, Brown & Bigelow, 8½ x 14½" . . . **75.00**
1950, Irresistible, Armstrong, Brown & Bigelow, 11 x 23" **95.00**
1954, artist sketch pad, Dr Ted Withers **25.00**
1955, Studio Sketches, spiral bound, TN Thompson, orig envelope, 8¼ x 11¼" **85.00**
1956, *Esquire* girl, George Petty, spiral bound, full color, 8¼ x 11" . . . **55.00**
Cigarette Lighter, metal, chrome finish, two different poses, Omega, 1950s **30.00**
Folder
Petty Girl Revue, *Esquire,* Dec 1941, double sided, verses, different girl in each drawing, four 3¾ x 8½" drawings, six 5 x 7⅝" drawings, one 6½ x 5½" drawing **65.00**
Sally of Hollywood & Vine, cardboard, sliding insert undresses model **40.00**
Jigsaw Puzzle, Playboy, Vargas art, full color, 1971 Playboy copyright **50.00**
Magazine
Esquire, Sept, 1951, Marilyn Monroe fold–out, 148 pgs **50.00**
Marilyn Monroe Pin–Ups, 1953, 8½ x 11", 32 pgs, black and white and full color photos **70.00**
Movieland Pin–Ups, Anita Ekberg cov, 1955 . . . . **16.00**
Match Book Cover, Petty girl, "It's In The Bag," Martins Tavern, Chicago, late 1940s **3.00**
Mirror
Rectangular, 2 x 3", DeVorss, full color, red haired woman holding gown tugged by puppy, 1940s . . . **75.00**
Round, standing nude, wooded background, multicolored, early 1900s **55.00**
Photo, 8 x 10"
Fanne Foxe, black and white glossy, blue ink signature **125.00**
Marilyn Chambers, full color, blue marker signature, 1970s **50.00**
Playing Cards
Elvgren, complete deck, blonde seated on couch wearing black negligee, unused **55.00**
Esquire, blonde model, double deck, brown textured leatherette case, 1940s **75.00**
Vargas, 53 Vargas Girls, complete deck, orig box, 1950s **250.00**
Poster
17 x 33", full color, woman in shorts walking wire hair terrier, Walt Otto, c1951 . . . . **50.00**
22 x 40", Martin Senour Paint adv, woman removing robe to reveal sheer underwear **100.00**

Print

Armstrong, Rolf, brunette in overall shorts, yellow blouse, 11 x 14", matted and framed 30.00

Elvgren, Thar She Blows, 8 x 10", framed 25.00

Seeman, The Enchanted Pool, 15 x 20", 1930s 100.00

Vargas, from *Esquire*, Phil Stack verse, WWII, 11 x 14", matted, framed . . 65.00

Record Album, The Cars, Vargas art, red haired model with gray bodysuit on hood of car, 1979 . . . . 45.00

Stationery, six 6¼ x 9½" sheets, full color art top left corner, three poses, unused, 1940–50 . . . . 25.00

Tray, 10½ x 14", litho tin, model posed in martini glass, art by Henry Clive, tray made by Beautebox, 1920s 150.00

PLANTERS PEANUTS

Collecting Hints: Planters Peanuts memorabilia is easily identified by the famous Mr. Peanut trademark. Items from the 1906 to 1916 period have the "Planters Nut And Chocolate Company" logo.

Papier mache, diecut, and ceramic pieces must be in very good condition. Cast iron and tin pieces should be free of rust and dents and have good graphics and color.

History: Amedeo Obici and Mario Peruzzi organized the Planters Nut And Chocolate Company in Wilkes–Barre, Pennsylvania, in 1906. Obici had conducted a small peanut business for several years and was known locally as the "Peanut Specialist."

Early peanut sales were the Spanish salted red skins which sold for 10¢ per pound. Soon after Obici developed the whole, white, blanched peanut, his product became the consumer's favorite.

In 1916 a young Italian boy submitted a rough version of the now famous monocled and distinguished Mr. Peanut as an entry in a contest held by Planters to develop a trademark. A wide variety of premium and promotional items were issued shortly thereafter.

Planters eventually was purchased by Standard Brands, which itself later became a division of Nabisco.

References: Norman E. Martinus and Harry L. Rinker, *Warman's Paper*, Wallace–Homestead, 1994; Richard D. and Barbara Reddock, *Planters Peanuts Advertising And Collectibles*, Wallace–Homestead Book Company, 1978, out-of-print.

Collectors' Club: Peanut Pals, 804 Hickory Grande Rd., Bridgeville, PA 15017.

REPRODUCTION ALERT

Ashtray, gold painted metal, Mr Peanut in center, orig box 75.00

Bank, 10" h, figural Mr Peanut, blue . . 38.00

Bookmark, 7" l, figural Mr Peanut, three color 12.00

Clock, alarm 40.00

Dish, 5½" d, divided, plastic, green, center figural handle, slotted spoon, 6" l, figural handle 25.00

Glass, yellow Mr Peanut illus, old logo 45.00

Jar

Round, red printing 150.00

Square, emb four sides, peanut finial 100.00

Kazoo, blue and yellow, 1970s 12.00

Keychain Figure, 2¼" l, figural, plastic, day glow, molded keychain loop, 1940s 25.00

Letter Opener, figural Mr Peanut, brass 75.00

Marbles, mesh bag, 1950s giveaway . . 15.00

Mug, yellow Mr Peanut, old logo 65.00

Nodder, orig box 125.00

Peanut Box, Mr Peanut and other graphics 10.00

Pencil, mechanical, Mr Peanut floating in oil 38.00

Pinback Button, 1⅛" d, Vote for Mr Peanut, black and white figure, white ground, white lettering on red rim, 1930s 25.00

Punchboard, Mr Peanut, 1940s, chances to win tin of Planter's Cocktail Peanuts, 2 cents a try, unused, orig tissue wrapping paper . . . 125.00

Ring, metal, adjustable, figural Mr Peanut, enameled, yellow and black, 1960s 30.00

Scale, figural, Mr. Peanut, 20 x 45 x 22", $18,150.00. Photograph courtesy of James D. Julia.

Salt and Pepper Shakers, pr, celluloid,
figural Mr Peanut, made in USA . . . **24.00**
Serving Spoon, Mr Peanut **17.50**
Swizzle Stick **5.00**
Tab, figural Mr Peanut, 2″ h, white plas-
tic day glow, WWII Victory wings at
top, red, white, and blue litho metal
tab **30.00**
Thermometer, 16″ h, tin, blue and yel-
low **40.00**
Tin, Novola, 5 gal, peanut oil, Mr
Peanut logo, light green and yellow
Mr Peanut on orig box **95.00**
Whistle, 2½″, Mr Peanut **7.50**

PLASTICS

Collecting Hints: The key point to remember
about plastic items is that they were mass–produced, often in numbers in the high hundreds of
thousands or millions. The concept of *rare* does
not apply. Because of these large production runs,
it is wise to stress condition as a major value consideration. Period surface appearance is also important.

The price difference between pieces that are in
the collecting market versus those in the process
of surfacing, e.g., at garage sales, is often large.
You can save considerable money if you are willing to devote time to the hunt. Likewise, shop
and compare. Prices vary within the trade.

There are few collectors of celluloid per se.
Most celluloid is sought because it relates to another collecting field. It was possible to place a
printed message on a celluloid surface. For this
reason celluloid was a popular medium for the
advertising giveaways of the 1880 to 1900 period. Old celluloid is quite brittle and can be easily broken. It must be handled carefully.
Collectors should be aware of celluloid's flammable tendencies.

Bakelite often is confused with acrylic and
other types of plastic. There are three key questions to help identify Bakelite: (1) Is it thick and
in a bright, primary color [black, green, red, or
yellow]?; (2) Is the object from the 1920 to 1940
period?; and, (3) Is the object normally associated with a synthetic material?

History: Plastic is derived from the Greek word
plasticos that translated as "able to be molded."
A dictionary definition states "any of numerous
organic synthetic or processed materials that are
mostly thermoplastic or thermosetting polymers
of high molecular weight and that can be
molded, cast, extruded, drawn, or laminated into
objects, films, or filaments."

Hundreds of different types of plastics—natural, semisynthetic, and synthetic—are known.
With the exception of celluloid and Bakelite, it

makes little difference to collectors the type of
plastic from which the object is manufactured.

Celluloid is the trade name for a thin, tough,
flammable material made of cellulose nitrate and
camphor. It was invented just prior to 1870 and
used mainly in making toilet articles. It also was
an inexpensive material for jewelry, figurines,
vases, etc. Celluloid frequently was made to simulate more expensive materials, e.g., amber,
bone, ivory, and tortoise shell. Celluloid became
a popular medium for the toy industry of the
1920s and 1930s. Character toys included
Charlie Chaplin and Charlie McCarthy. The advent of Bakelite and acrylic plastic brought an
end to celluloid items.

Bakelite, a substitute for hard rubber, celluloid,
and similar materials, is a synthetic resinous material made from formaldehyde and phenol. It
was invented by L. H. Baekeland in 1913.
Bakelite was easily dyed and molded into many
brightly colored objects during the Art Deco period. Bakelite has been used as the secondary element in many household and kitchen items (especially handles), as ornamentation on clothing,
and in jewelry of the Art Deco and Modernism
periods.

Acrylic, also known as Lucite (DuPont's tradename) or Plexiglas (Rohm and Haas Company
tradename), was developed in 1927. This lightweight, petrochemical plastic is valued for its
transparent and translucent qualities. It is highly
versatile, having a surface that can range from
dull to glossy and a body that can be cast, cut,
drilled, extruded, faceted, molded, or shaped. Its
major drawbacks are that it scratches easily,
tends to yellow (older examples), and does not
resist heat well.

References: Lillian Baker, *Twentieth Century
Fashionable Plastic Jewelry*, Collector Books,
1992; Corinne Davidov and Ginny Redington
Dawes, *The Bakelite Jewelry Book*, Abbeville
Press, 1988; Bill Hanlon, *Plastic Toys: Dimestore
Dreams of the '40s & '50s*, Schiffer Publishing,
1993; Lyngerda Kelley and Nancy Schiffer,
Plastic Jewelry, Schiffer Publishing, 1987, 1994
value update; Jan Lindenberger, *Collecting
Plastics: A Handbook and Price Guide*, Schiffer
Publishing, 1991; Lyndi Stewart McNulty,
*Wallace–Homestead Price Guide To Plastic
Collectibles*, Wallace–Homestead, 1987, 1992
value update; Holly Wahlberg, *Everyday
Elegance: 1950s Plastic Design*, Schiffer
Publishing, 1994.

BAKELITE

Bar Utensil Set, green handles, five
piece set **40.00**
Bracelet
Black and clear, on elastic, 1⅜″ w . . **70.00**

Red, uncarved **65.00**
Buckle, hat ornament type, red, 3" ... **12.50**
Clock, Telechron, black, octagon **85.00**
Corn Cob Holders, orig box **30.00**
Desk Light, stepped base, revolving tin globe, stem, pen and paper clip holders **45.00**
Lighter, table, Dunhill, standing nude, 3 x 5" h **125.00**
Pencil Sharpener
  Joe Carioca, figural **55.00**
  Donald Duck, figural **65.00**
  Mickey Mouse decal, green **50.00**
Poker Chip Caddy, round, brown **15.50**
Poker Set, 500 poker chips, six Bakelite trays with center copper ashtray, red, green, gold, bright green, light green, turquoise, orig fitted carrying case **220.00**
Ring, carved, red **75.00**
Shaving Brush, Klenzo, two part handle **8.50**
Viewer, Tru–Vue, fifteen "Tru–Vue" cards **35.00**

CELLULOID

Bill Hook, 2¼" d, round, illus of Buster Brown and Tige, slogan "Buster Brown Vacation Days Carnival," 1946 copyright **40.00**

Brooch, celluloid, basket of flowers, green leaves, pink basket, $40.00.

Card Holder, black base, two Mickey Mouse figures, paper stick reads "Walt Disney Enterprises Ltd/Japan," 1930s **90.00**
Charm, pig in green overalls, pink cap, holding gray trowel, brass loop, Japan, early 1930s **30.00**
Doll, 7" h, dressed in Welsh costume, 1950 .... **20.00**
Fan, painted flowers, dated 1914, replaced ribbon **25.00**
Ink Blotter Pad, 3¼ x 7¾", adv for India–Down Bedding, cardboard pad, celluloid cov, c1910 .... **75.00**
Memo Book, Spirit of St Louis **18.00**

Counter, Compliments of Kennedy Furniture Co., Chicago, IL, two openings, scores "Games" and "Points," list of merchandise on back, 3 x 1⅜", $9.50.

Nail File, folding, figural, lady's leg, painted high heel and garter **35.00**
Purse, beaded, celluloid frame, sunburst style, butterfly motif **35.00**
Ruler, 7½" l, diecut, Western Union, silver and blue logo, telegraph and cable rates on back, 1905 patent **25.00**
Stamp Case, 1½ x 2½", Aetna Life Insurance Co., Hartford, CT, red and white, 1907 calendar **18.00**
Tape Measure, black man ....\ **150.00**
Toy
  Airship, 1½ x 2¼ x 5½", hollow, red and blue, wood wheels, pull string, US Star Co logo on tail fin, 1930s **100.00**
  Felix The Cat, 2" h, jointed **85.00**
  Hula Dancer, windup, metal legs and feet **85.00**
  Santa, tin windup cycle **75.00**

PLASTIC

Bar Pin, brown, five hanging yellow bananas **55.00**
Bowl, gray, multicolored speckles, marked "Texas Ware" **15.00**
Canister Set, red sq container, white name, white lid, price for set of four **15.00**
Dispenser, bowling ball shape, Catalin **100.00**
Dominoes, red Catalin, extra thick, orig instructions, damage to orig box, 1940s **28.00**
Dresser Set, hand mirror and matching button hook, orange, green rhinestones, butterfly motif, price for two piece set **35.00**
Match Holder, wall type, red **7.50**
Powder Shaker, Kewpie, 6½" h, marked "Irwin Toys," price for pair **37.00**
Sewing Box, round, pink, clear lid, divided int. **10.00**
Spice Shelf, pink, cut–out letters, repaired crack **25.00**
Spoon Rest, chef holding two pans, white, black trim **7.50**
Thimble, adv, NuMaid Margarine **2.50**
Tray, 13 x 7" **15.00**

PLAYING CARDS

Collecting Hints: Always purchase complete decks in very good condition. Do research to identify the exact number of cards needed. An American straight deck has 52 cards and usually a joker; pinochle requires 48 cards; tarot decks use 78. In addition to decks, uncut sheets and single cards, if very early, are sought by collectors.

Many collectors focus on topics. Examples are politics, trains, World's Fairs, animals, airlines, advertising, etc. Most collectors of travel–souvenir cards prefer a photographic scene on the face.

The most valuable playing card decks are unusual either in respect to publisher, size, shape, or subject. Prices for decks of late 19th- and 20th-century cards remain modest.

History: The first use of playing cards dates to 12th-century China. By 1400 playing cards were in use throughout Europe. French cards were known specifically for their ornate designs. The first American cards were published by Jazaniah Ford of Milton, Massachusetts, in the late 1700s. United States innovations include upper corner indexes, classic joker, standard size, and slick finish for shuffling. Bicycle Brand was introduced in 1885 by the U.S. Playing Card Company of Cincinnati.

Card designs have been drawn or printed in every conceivable size and on a variety of surfaces. Miniature playing cards appealed to children. Novelty decks came in round, crooked, and diecut shapes. Numerous card games, besides the standard four–suit deck, were created for adults and children.

References: Phil Bollhagen (comp.), *The Great Book of Railroad Playing Cards,* published by author, 1991; Everett Grist, *Advertising Playing Cards: An Identification and Value Guide,* Collector Books, 1992; Gene Hochman, *Encyclopedia of American Playing Cards,* published by author, 1976 to 1982, six parts, out–of–print; Sylvia Mann, *Collecting Playing Cards,* Crown, 1966; Norman E. Martinus and Harry L. Rinker, *Warman's Paper,* Wallace–Homestead, 1994; Roger Tilley, *Playing Cards,* Octopus, London, 1973.

Collectors' Clubs: American Game Collectors Assoc., 49 Brooks Ave., Lewiston, ME 04240; Chicago Playing Card Collectors, Inc., 1559 West Platt Blvd., Chicago, IL 60626; 52 Plus Joker, 204 Gorham Ave., Hamden, CT 06514; International Playing Card Society, 3570 Delaware Common, Indianapolis, IN 46220; Playing Card Collectors Assoc., 337 Avelon St, #4, Roundlake, IL 60073; The American Antique Deck Collectors Club, 204 Gorham Ave., Hamden, CT 06514.

Museum: Playing Card Museum, Cincinnati Art Museum, Cincinnati, OH.

Note: We have organized our list by both topic and country. Although concentrating heavily on cards by American manufacturers, some foreign makers are included.

COUNTRY

England, Prince of Wales National Relief Fund, WWI, De La Rue, 1914, MIB	30.00
France, Bataille De Nancy, 500th Anniversary, Grimaud, 1977, 54 cards	12.00
Italy, World Bridge, Modiano, 1953, 54 cards	28.00
Japan, Fujitsu, Nintendo, 1973, 2½ x 3¹⁵⁄₁₆", orig box	30.00
United States	
Chicago, Sears Tower, skyline	7.50
Dorney Park, Allentown, PA, Alfundo the clown illus	5.00
Kennedy Space Center, FL, Space Shuttle, lift off photo	6.50
Mount Rushmore, SD, photo	12.50
Santa Clausland, Santa Claus, IN, Santa photo	7.50

TOPIC

Advertising	
Blue Bonnet, margarine, Blue Bonnet girl on both ends	10.00
Briner Electric Company, motor	3.50
Capital Bakers, "the Aristocrat of Breads," bread loaf	5.00
Clifford's Rexall Pharmacy, "The Drug Store That Cares," black and white old time auto	7.50
Drehmann–Harral, "One of St. Louis' Finest Funeral Homes," black and white funeral home photo, gold and red borders	15.00
IGA Food Store, line drawing of store	5.00
Keebler Zesta Saltine Crackers, cracker box	10.00
Kellogg's Frosties, cereal box with Tony the Tiger	5.00
Life Savers, rolls of Life Savers candy	5.00
Mader's Famous Restaurant, Schnitzelbank song words and illustrations	7.50
Monarch, "Better Outdoor Garments,"clothing tag with lion logo	5.00
Pepperidge Farm Mixed Suits Snack Crackers, playing card joker and face cards	5.00
Robbins Potato Co., sailboat on ocean, rope and anchor border	7.50
Superior Dairy, National Pro Football	

Hall of Fame building, "Superior
Dairy Products Build Champions"   **6.50**
Tommy Borders Wholesale Meats,
sepia tone photo of Borders **17.50**
West Coast Mushroom, mushroom
drawing, black and white **3.50**
Animals, kitten heads, light blue
ground, boxed set **6.00**
Automotive
Champion, repeating logo **5.00**
Ford GT, race car **10.00**
Michelin, repeating pattern, black
tires, yellow ground **6.00**
Aviation
Delta Air Lines, New York, traffic cop **10.00**
Overseas National Airways, logo,
blue and white **6.50**
TWA, Douglas DC–4, 1946 ....   **15.00**
United, "fly the friendly skies of
United" **5.00**
Brewery
Arrow Beer, gold arrows, lettering,
and border, red ground **10.00**
Budweiser Beer, top view of open
case of bottled beer **7.50**
Carling Black Label Beer, beer can .. **17.50**
Old Tavern Lager Beer, black and
white factory scene **15.00**
Schlitz Malt Liquor, black bull, white
letters and border, blue ground ...   **7.50**
Casinos
Caesars Palace, Las Vegas, Nevada,
gold logos, dark blue ground **5.00**
Flamingo Capri, red and white,
crosshatched design, bullet hole
center **5.00**
Golden Nugget Gambling Hall, mir-
ror image of white lettering sur-
rounded by gold scrollwork and
nugget **5.00**
Schiaparelli, outdoor cafe table and
chairs, red, white, and black **7.50**
Nautical
Caribbean Cruise Lines, flag and
bongo drummer **15.00**
Great White Fleet, map of US and
Central America **7.50**
S S Milwaukee Clipper, sailing vessel **12.50**
States Marine Lines, life preserver,
rope border, black ground **10.00**
Oil Companies
Schmuckal Oil Co., truck fleet color
photo **6.50**
Sinclair Oils, red oil well logo, white
ground, gold and red borders **5.00**
Sohio, small red and white logo,
black and white flying eagle **10.00**
Railroad
C & O RR, Peake, Chessie's "Old
Man" **5.00**
Chicago, Milwaukee & St Paul, 53
scenic views, 1919, orig box **40.00**

New York, New Haven & Hartford
RR, orig box and wrapper **65.00**
Tobacco
Ace Cigarette Service Co., black and
white vending machine **10.00**
Camel, black silhouette camel sur-
rounded by gold silhouette camels,
red ground **10.00**
Kent, two cigarette packs on chess
board **6.50**
Kool, cigarette pack **7.50**
World's Fair and Exposition
Century of Progress, 1933, Sky Ride,
multicolored, bridge deck, orig box   **20.00**

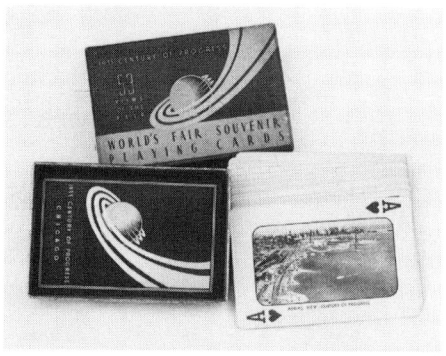

**World's Fair, 1933 Century of Progress,
$20.00.**

Columbian Exposition, 1892–93,
landing scene on back, fair buildings on faces, multicolored, 52
cards, 3½ x 2½" **100.00**
Louisiana Purchase Exposition, black
and white scenes of buildings and
exhibits, leaf and Fair logo design
on backs, copyright 1904 Samuel
Cupples Envelope Co., St Louis and
New York **165.00**
Pan–American Exposition, 1901,
Buffalo, NY, building scenes, logo
on back, gilt edges, orig box **45.00**
Panama–Pacific and Panama–Cali-
fornia Exposition, 1915, Bal-boa
Park, San Diego, multicolored,
bridge deck, orig box **20.00**

POCKET KNIVES

Collecting Hints: The pocket knife collector has
to compete with other collectors such as advertising collectors, character collectors, and period
collectors.
    The pocket knife with a celluloid handle and
advertising underneath dates back to the 1880s.

Celluloid–handled knives are considered much more desirable than the plastic–handled models. Collectors also tend to shy away from purely souvenir–related knives.

History: Pocket knife collecting falls into two major categories. There are collectors who concentrate on the utilitarian and functional knives from firms such as Alcas, Case, Colonial, Ka–Bar, Queen, Remington, Schrade, and Winchester. The second group deals with advertising, character, and other knives, which, while meant to be used, were sold with a secondary function in mind. These knives were made by companies such as Aerial Cutlery Co., Canton Cutlery Co., Golden Rule Cutlery Co., Imperial Knife Company, and Novelty Cutlery Co.

The larger manufacturing firms also made advertising, character, and figural knives. Some knives were giveaways or sold for a small premium, but most were sold in general stores and souvenir shops.

References: Jerry and Elaine Heuring, *Keen Kutter Collectibles, 2nd Edition,* Collector Books, 1990, 1993 value update; Jacob N. Jarrett, *Price Guide To Pocket Knives: 1890–1970,* L–W Book Sales, 1993, 1995 value update; Bernard Levine, *Levine's Guide To Knives And Their Values, Third Edition,* DBI Books, 1993; Bernard Levine, *Pocket Knives: The Collector's Guide To Identifying, Buying, and Enjoying Vintage Pocketknives,* Apple Press, 1993; L–W Book Sales, *A Price Guide To Keen Kutter Tools,* L–W Book Sales, n.d., 1993–94 value update; C. Houston Price, *The Official Price Guide To Collector Knives, Tenth Edition,* House of Collectibles, 1991; Jim Sargent, *Sargent American Premium Guide To Knives and Razors: Identification and Values, Fourth Edition* Books Americana, 1995; Roy Ritchie and Ron Stewart, *The Standard Knife Collector's Guide: Identification and Values, Second Edition,* Collector Books, 1993, 1995 value update; J. Bruce Voyles, *The American Blade Collectors Association Price Guide To Antique Knives,* Krause Publications, 1995.

Collectors' Clubs: American Blade Collectors, PO Box 22007, Chattanooga, TN 37422; Canadian Knife Collectors Club, 3141 Jessuca Court, Mississauga, ON L5C 1X7 Canada; Ka–Bar Knife Collectors Club, PO Box 406, Olean, NY 14760; National Knife Collectors Association, PO Box 21070, Chattanooga, TN 37421.

Periodicals: *Blade,* 700 E. State St., Iola, WI 54990; *Edges,* PO Box 22007, Chattanooga, TN 37422; *Knife World,* PO Box 3395, Knoxville, TN 37927.

Museum: National Knife Museum, Chattanooga, TN.

REPRODUCTION ALERT: Advertising knives, especially Coca–Cola, have been heavily reproduced.

Note: See *Warman's Antiques And Their Prices* for a list of knife prices for major manufacturers.

Advertising
Anheuser–Busch	**45.00**
Champion Spark Plugs	**30.00**
Columbia Clay Co., SC, 2⅞″	**70.00**
Fernet Branka, Italian wine company	**35.00**
House Hasson Hardware Co., 3⅛″	**22.00**
Purina, 3⅜″, checkerboard	**200.00**
Say It With Flowers, 5¼″, white celluloid	**45.00**
Schrade Cutlery Co., NY, marine pearl	**60.00**
Swift's Canned Foods, 5″, ivory celluloid	**145.00**
The Franklin Fire, Philadelphia 1829–1929, 3″, metal	**75.00**
Art Nouveau, 6″, sterling silver, ferrule MOP blade	**22.00**
Bartender's, 3″, marine pearl	**22.00**
Case Bros, #6253, bone	**65.00**

Character
Dick Tracy, red and white, celluloid	**40.00**
Hopalong Cassidy	
Black, white, name engraved on back, miniature	**50.00**
Blue, riding Topper, belt loop	**40.00**
Jimmy Allen, silver wings	**65.00**
Roy Rogers, 3¼″, chain, black and white	**32.00**
Tom Mix and Tony, blue and white	**40.00**
Dog Grooming, 3¾″, Airedale head	**200.00**

Figural
Fish, 2¾″, silver, W.B. Kero Co., maker, Curby Pat. 1885	**100.00**
Letter Opener, 4″ mother of pearl handle	**300.00**
Keen Kutter, two blade jack	**45.00**
Zippo, orig box	**30.00**

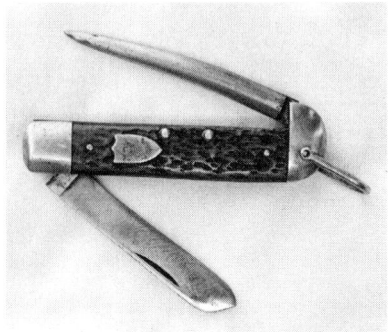

Union Cutlery, Boy Scout, rigger, $50.00.

POLICE COLLECTIBLES

Collecting Hints: Police collectibles are primarily collected by people employed in law enforcement areas. Collectors often base their collection on badges or material from a specific locality. As a result, prices are regionalized, e.g., a California collector is more interested in California material than items from another state.

Condition is critical. Badges were worn every day so a minimum of wear is expected.

The emphasis on police shows on television has attracted many non–law enforcement people to the field of police collectibles.

History: The first American colonists appointed someone from among their midst to maintain and enforce the laws of the land. The local sheriff had an important social and political position.

The mid–nineteenth century witnessed the development of two important trends: the growth of the professional police force in cities and the romanticizing of the western lawman. Arthur Conan Doyle's Sherlock Holmes novels popularized the modernization of police methods. Magazines, such as the *Police Gazette,* kept the public's attention focused on the sensationalism of police work.

The gangster era of the 1920s and 1930s and the arrival of the "G–Men," glamorized by Hollywood movies, kept police work in the limelight. Finally, television capitalized on the public enthusiasm for police drama through shows such as *Dragnet, The Untouchables, Starsky and Hutch, Hill Street Blues,* and *NYPD Blue.*

References: Monty McCord, *Police Cars: A Photographic History,* Krause Publications, 1991; Don Stewart, *Collectors Guide: Handcuffs & Restraints,* Key Collectors International, 1993; Don Stewart, *Collectors Guide: The Yale & Towne Mfg Co., Yale Trade Mark Prison Jail Locks and Keys 1884–1957,* Key Collectors International, 1982; George E. Virgines, *Badges of Law and Order,* Cochran Publishing Co., 1987.

Periodical: *Police Collectors News,* RR1 Box 14, Baldwin, WI 54002.

Museums: American Police Center & Museum, Chicago, IL; American Police Hall of Fame & Museum, Miami, FL; New York City Police Academy Museum, New York, NY; Suffolk County Police Dept. Museum, Yaphank, NY.

REPRODUCTION ALERT: Be especially wary of police badges.

Automobile Emblem, "Prison," Nigerian	**35.00**
Badge	
Birmingham, cloth, English	**8.00**
Illinois State Police, Corporal	**60.00**
Lincolnshire, cloth, English	**8.00**

New Mexico, Deputy Sheriff, made from US silver dollar, hand carved, c1967	**150.00**
Staffordshire, cloth, English	**8.00**
Uganda	**22.00**
West Yorkshire, metal, English	**22.00**
Belt Buckle, NYC, brass	**75.00**
Button, coat	
Lincolnshire	**5.00**
Nigerian	**3.00**
Call Box, Chicago Police, cast aluminum, c1920	**120.00**
Club, San Francisco Police, mahogany, carved handle, cord and tassel, c1900	**75.00**
Handcuffs, key, c1900	**70.00**
Helmet	
Bobby's, English	**120.00**
Policewoman's, English	**90.00**
Magazine Cover	
Harper's Weekly, March 27, 1897 . .	**40.00**
Saturday Evening Post, Norman Rockwell painting, Nov 4, 1939 . .	**8.00**

Magazine Tear Sheet, Conoco Germ Processed Oil, illus Police Motorcycle Stunt Team, Lieut. Gainer in Command, *The Saturday Evening Post,* red, white, and blue, 10½ x 13¾", August 3, 1940, $12.00.

Medal, George VI, Military Police	**45.00**
Nodder, policeman, marked "Japan" . .	**18.00**
Painting, 22 x 11", wood board, old time policeman	**100.00**
Paperweight, plastic, souvenir of Los Angeles	**8.00**
Patch, Baltimore Police, cloth	**3.00**
Plate, Texas Ranger Anniversary, 1973, SS	**120.00**
Pocket Watch, Boston Police, engraved badge, silver, Waltham, c1800	**485.00**

Post Card, policeman on horse, The
Texas Ranger **4.00**
Shaving Mug, blue uniform, badge, and
nightstick **675.00**
Sheet Music, *Police Parade March*,
c1917 . . . .   **22.00**
Statue
Old Time Policeman, 8", ceramic,
color **48.00**
Present Day Policeman, 12" **38.00**
Sheriff, 5½", pewter sculpture, c1975   **100.00**
Suspenders, slide adjusters marked
"Police," club engraving **22.00**
Toy
Motorcycle, policeman on top, rub-
ber **8.00**
Patrol Car, Number 79, litho tin,
spring mechanism, red and yellow,
Cragston, c1950 . . . .   **25.00**

POLITICAL AND CAMPAIGN ITEMS

Collecting Hints: Items selling below $100 move
frequently enough to establish firm prices. Items
above that price fluctuate according to supply
and demand. Many individuals now recognize
the value of political items, and acquire them
and hold them for future sale. As a result, modern material has a relatively low market value.

The pioneering work in the identification of
political materials has been done by Theodore L.
Hake, whose books are listed below. Two books
have greatly assisted in the identification and cat-
aloging of campaign materials, especially for the
earlier period: Herbert R. Collins's *Threads of
History* and Edmund B. Sullivan's *American
Political Badges and Medalets 1789–1892*.

History: Since 1800 the American presidency always has been a contest between two or more
candidates. Initially, souvenirs were issued to
celebrate victories. Items issued during a campaign to show support for a candidate were actively distributed in the William Henry Harrison
election of 1840.

Campaign items cover a wide variety of materials—buttons, bandannas, tokens, license plates,
etc. The only limiting factor has been the promoter's imagination. The advent of television
campaigning has reduced the emphasis on individual items. Modern campaigns do not seem to
have the variety of materials which were issued
earlier.

Modern collectors should be aware of
Kennedy material. Much has been reproduced
and many items were issued after his death.
Knowledgeable collectors also keep in touch
with presidential libraries to find out what type of
souvenir items they are offering for sale. The collector should concentrate on the items from the
time of the actual campaigns.

References: Herbert R. Collins, *Threads of
History,* Smithsonian Institute Press, 1979;
Theodore L. Hake, *Encyclopedia of Political
Buttons, United States, 1896–1972,* Americana &
Collectibles Press, 1985; Theodore L. Hake,
Political Buttons, Book II, 1920–1976,
Americana & Collectibles Press, 1977; Theodore
L. Hake, *Political Buttons, Book III, 1789–1916,*
Americana & Collectibles Press, 1978; Theodore
L. Hake, *1991 Revised Prices For The
Encyclopedia Of Political Buttons,* Americana &
Collectibles Press, 1991; Norman E. Martinus
and Harry L. Rinker, *Warman's Paper,*
Wallace–Homestead, 1994; Keith Melder, *Hail
To The Candidate: Presidential Campaigns From
Banners To Broadcasts,* Smithsonian Institution
Press, 1992; Edmund B. Sullivan, *American
Political Badges and Medalets, 1789–1892,*
Quarterman Publications, 1981; Edmund B.
Sullivan, *Collecting Political Americana,*
Christopher Publishing House, 1991.

Collectors' Clubs: American Political Items
Collectors, PO Box 134, Monmouth Junction, NJ
08852; Indiana Political Collectors Club, PO Box
11141, Indianapolis, IN 46201.

Periodicals: *Autograph Times,* 2303 N. 44th St.,
#225, Phoenix, AZ 85008; *The Political
Bandwagon,* PO Box 348, Leola, PA 17540; *The
Political Collector Newspaper,* PO Box 5171,
York, PA 17405.

Museums: Museum of American Political Life,
Hartford, CT; Smithsonian Museum, Washington,
DC; Western Reserve Historical Society,
Cleveland, OH.

Advisor: Ted Hake.

Abraham Lincoln, 1860, 1864
Cigar Box, 6 x 8½ x 2½", Old Abe
Cigars, Honest/True/Merit/Quality,
wood, tan, black and white paper
edge strips, black, white, gold, and
gray label, c1900 . . . .   **20.00**
Medal,⅜" d, white metal, 1864 . . . .   **125.00**
Print, 12 x 16", photographic portrait,
color tinting, green–gold background, name, birth and death
dates, caption "Art Supplement to
The Philadelphia Press, Feb 9,
1896," wood frame **65.00**
Vase, 5" h, pottery, dark brown, raised
black designs and Lincoln image,
c1864 . . . .   **600.00**
Ulysses S. Grant, 1868, 1872
Electoral Ticket, 6 x 12½", Grant and
Colfax, paper, black and white
print, 1868 . . . .   **40.00**

Lantern, 12" h, paper and cardboard, dark blue and light purple, tin candle holder int., 1872 . . . . **300.00**

Portrait Plate, 8½" d, glazed china, black and white portrait, brown border of foliage, flags, and eagle, inscription "1869/1877 Ulysses S Grant/General," marked "Made in Germany" **40.00**

James A. Garfield, 1880

Bandanna, 20 x 21", Garfield/Arthur portraits, black and white, 1880 . . **275.00**

Collar Box, 5 x 5 x 3", wood, brown thermo–plastic lid with raised portrait, 1880 . . . . **200.00**

Plate, 11½" d, center portrait, floral border, inscription "We Mourn Our Nation's Loss," 1881 . . . . **35.00**

James G. Blaine, 1884

Bandanna, 17½ x 19", Blaine/Logan portraits, black and white, 1994 . . **200.00**

Cigar Box, 5½ x 9 x 3", "James G Blaine/The Greatest Statesman of Them All," red, green, black, and white edge trim, full color end labels, early 1900s **35.00**

Medal, 1½" d, white metal, 1884 . . . **50.00**

Poster, 22½ x 28", The Republican Candidate For 1884, black and white **300.00**

Grover Cleveland, 1884, 1888, 1892

Bandanna, 16½" sq, black and white center portrait, red, white, and blue striped border, minor fading and damage **60.00**

Lapel Stud, red, white and blue, fabric covered, American flag center, 1884 . . . . **20.00**

Plate, 8" d, china, brown image, gold band rim, 1888 . . . . **50.00**

Ribbon, 2¼ x 4", black and white portrait, bright red, white, and blue flag, gold eagle design, facsimile signature at bottom **80.00**

Benjamin Harrison, 1888, 1892

Bandanna, 19" sq, Harrison and Reid portraits, black and white **125.00**

Bar Pin, 2½" l, brass, horn shape with banner, 1888 . . . . **100.00**

Lapel Stud, ivory colored celluloid disk, black portrait, c1892 . . . . . . **35.00**

Plate, 8" d, china, brown image, gold band, 1888 . . . . **50.00**

William McKinley, 1896 and 1900

Glass, 4" h, clear, white frosted portrait, 1896 . . . . **50.00**

Lapel Stud, ⅞" l, McKinley—Protection '96, brass, diecut, Napoleon's hat shape **25.00**

Ribbon, 2½ x 5½", McKinley and Hobart, Sound Money and Protection, black letters and portrait, bright yellow, 1896, ... **25.00**

Tile, 3" sq, ceramic, blue glaze, 1896 **40.00**

Tray, 13 x 16", litho tin, oval, color portrait, green ground, facsimile signature, minor wear and paint nicks, c1900 . . . . **100.00**

William Jennings Bryan, 1896, 1900, and 1908

Glass, 3½" h, clear, Sixteen To One, white frosted portraits **80.00**

Medal, 1¼" brass, Taft's portrait on one side with 1908 and slogan "I'll Toss You," other side with Bryan and "I'll Match You" **20.00**

Pinback Button, ⅝" d, WB's OK, blue and white, 1908 . . . . **50.00**

Watch Fob, Bryan and Kern, enamel, eagles and flags center, orig strap . **35.00**

Theodore Roosevelt, 1904 and 1912

Bandanna, 21 x 24", portrait center, red, white, and brown **150.00**

Campaign Book, 1¾ x 2¾", yellow fabric cov, 1904 . . . . **30.00**

Lapel Stud, ¾", brass, on back of rearing horse, small red, white, and blue fraternal enamel symbol and letters "P.O.S. of A." **30.00**

Post Card, 3½ x 5½", Teddy in Africa, caricature illus, 1909 copyright, unused **35.00**

Token, 1¼" d, aluminum, portrait on front, reverse "26th President/New York/Republican," birth and death dates, c1930 . . . . **5.00**

Alton B. Parker, 1904

Bandanna, 20" sq, black and white portrait center, blue stripe border . **150.00**

Pinback Button, 1¼" d, Parker And Davis League, red, white, and blue **85.00**

William Howard Taft, 1908 and 1912

Mirror, 2¹⁄₁₆" d, color portrait, inscribed "Oh My! the Souvenir Popcorn, Made By National Candy Co," c1908 . . . . **300.00**

Pinback Button, ⅝" d, For President Wm H Taft, gray and white **15.00**

Plate, 6" d, china, For President William H Taft, brown photo image, 1908 . . . . **25.00**

Platter, 11½" l, Taft/Sherman, oval, china, color portraits, 1908 . . . . . **40.00**

Woodrow Wilson, 1912 and 1916

Necktie, 47" l, Wilson/Marshall, black fabric, white embroidered names, red, white, and blue flag . **50.00**

Pennant, 17" l, dark purple, tin support bar, Wilson portrait and inscription "March 4th Inauguration/1913 Washingt'n D.C." . . . **40.00**

Spoon, 6" l, Wilson, In God We Trust, silver plate, portrait handle with eagle, c1916 . . . . **20.00**

Charles Evans Hughes, 1916
Blotter, Hughes, Washington, and Lincoln pictures with slogans **45.00**
Pinback Button, "For President Charles E Hughes," black and white **15.00**
Warren G. Harding, 1920
Pinback Button, "Harding & Coolidge," red, white, and blue litho **10.00**
Poster, 16 x 21", Harding/Coolidge, paper, sepia portraits, 1920 . . . . .   **65.00**
James M. Cox, 1920
Pinback Button, "Cox/Roosevelt," red, white, and blue, dark blue ground **45.00**
Poster, 11 x 17", paper, portrait, 1920   **200.00**
Calvin Coolidge, 1924
Bell, brass, Ring for Coolidge **25.00**
Fan, 9 x 15", cardboard, wood handle, black letters "We Will Help To Keep Cool–idge," imprinted "Mifflin County Women's Coolidge Club Lewistown, Pennsylvania 1924" **40.00**
Pitcher, 4½ x 6 x 6", dark blue and white, illus of Coolidge's home, marked "The Adams Souvenir Series/Made In England" **35.00**
Post Card, Coolidge/Dawes, black and white photo, c1924 . . . .   **20.00**
Poster, 9 x 12", paper, sepia portrait, 1924 . . . .   **35.00**
Herbert Hoover, 1928 and 1932
Bandanna, 17 x 18", red, white, and blue, 1932 . . . .   **50.00**
Flue Cover, "Hoover For President," litho tin, white portrait, dark blue ground, 8" d **35.00**
License Plate, 5 x 12", cast aluminum, silver finish, c1928 . . . .   **100.00**
Mirror, 2⅛" d, Hoover/Keene/Larson, black and white, 1928 . . . .   **350.00**
Pinback Button, Hoover and Curtis, celluloid, red, white, and blue, PA keystone symbol, GOP elephant . .   **12.00**
Alfred E. Smith, 1928
Banner, 3 x 4½", canvas, red, white, and blue, black and white illus, 1928 . . . .   **400.00**
Flue Cover, 8" d, For President Al Smith, litho tin, portrait, name, light blue and cream **40.00**
Key Chain, silvered brass ring, black enamel donkey's head **35.00**
Franklin D. Roosevelt, 1932, 1936, 1940, and 1944
Bank, 5" h, bust form, white metal, dark bronze finish, c1940 . . . . . .   **40.00**
Cigar Band, 3" l, black, white, red, and gold, "Franklin D Roosevelt Hand Made," c1933 . . . .   **10.00**

Clock, FDR, The Man of the Hour, United Clock Co **150.00**
Fan, cardboard, full color picture, coffee adv on back, 1940 . . . . . .   **25.00**
Mug, FDR New Deal **15.00**
Pinback Button, 3½" d, Re–Elect Our President Franklin D Roosevelt, black and white, c1940 . . . .   **30.00**
Sheet Music, 9½ x 12½", Nation's Prayer For The President/Dedicated To Franklin D Roosevelt, black and white, 1933 copyright **15.00**
Thermometer, 4 x 6", plaque, bright gold ground, black NRA symbol, portrait, and inscription "Together We Cannot Fail," brass frame, chain at top for hanging **35.00**
Token, Lucky Tillicum/Re–Build With Roosevelt, brass, portrait on front, airship flying over US Capitol on back **8.00**
Alfred Landon, 1936
Pinback Button, Landon/Knox/G.O.P., bright yellow, dark brown ground, celluloid **10.00**
Poster, 11 x 16", Landon For President, paper, brown and white, 1936 . . . .   **25.00**
Wendell L. Willkie, 1940
Banner, 9 x 11½", God Bless America/Wendell Willkie, fabric, red, white, and blue, 1940 . . . . . .   **25.00**
License Plate, 4 x 13½", orange, gold letters outlined in dark blue, blue edge **20.00**
Pin, 2 x 3½", red, white, and blue enameled metal, ribbon like design, ten inset rhinestones and center Willkie button **35.00**
Pinback Button, Willkie Square Deal, red, white, and blue litho **15.00**
Sticker, 3½ x 6", diecut foil, silver, blue, and red, inscribed "Willkie/The Hope of America" **10.00**
Thomas E. Dewey, 1944 and 1948
Campaign Booklet, 2½ x 4", portrait on cov, black and white photos and information about Dewey, Bricker, and PA candidates, 24 pgs **6.00**
Pennant, 11" l, Thomas Dewey For President, white letters, bright red felt, yellow felt streamers **15.00**
Post Card, The Way Ahead/Dewey–Warren, black and white, 1948 . .   **12.00**
Ribbon, 6" l, Elect Dewey and Warren/Vote Republican, black letters, silvery white fabric ribbon . .   **20.00**
Tie, 8" l, Dewey In '48, dark brown fabric, white image, orig tags inscribed "Rembrandt Paints Another Crosley Creation" **35.00**

Harry S Truman, 1948
Autograph, 5 x 8" magazine photo, black ink signature "Kind regards from Harry Truman 7/11/64" **175.00**
Fan, *Philadelphia Evening Bulletin* Newspaper, Democratic National Convention, Decker cartoon on one side, "Welcome Delegates" on other, 1948 . . . . **28.00**
Magazine, *Time,* Man Of The Year issue, Dec 31, 1945, Artzybasheff cover artist **20.00**
Pinback Button, 3½" d, gold wreath surrounding black and white portrait, dark blue eagle, crossed red, white, and blue flags **75.00**
Program, 8½ x 11", Inaugural Ball, Jan 20, 1949, National Guard Armory, portraits of Pres and Mrs Truman, Margaret, and Barkley, gold cov, blue binding cord **35.00**
Dwight D. Eisenhower, 1952 and 1956
Bandanna, 26" sq, Win With Ike For President, blue and white image, bright red ground **60.00**
Cigarettes, Eisenhower & Stevenson, unopened pack, price for pr **60.00**
Matchbook, Inaugural, portraits, unused, 1953 . . . . **10.00**
Necktie, rust, bright yellow lightning bolt leading into US Capitol building, orig label **35.00**
Pennant, 29" l, dark brown felt, white illus and lettering "Eisenhower–Nixon Inauguration," white Capitol building with blue, yellow, and green shading, 1953 . . . . **20.00**
Pinback Button, Make The White House The Dwight House, blue letters, yellow ground **8.00**
Post Card, Eisenhower/Nixon, Vote for Your Future/Vote Republican, multicolor, 1956 . . . . **10.00**

Pinback Button, Eisenhower/Nixon, red, white, and blue, Vote Republican, Pull 1st Lever, 3" d, $7.50.

Plate, 1956 National Convention, San Francisco, CA, Eisenhower/Nixon, marked "Vernon Kilns," 12¾" d, $65.00.

Adlai E. Stevenson, 1952 and 1956
Brochure, 5 x 7", *A Man Named Stevenson,* The Democratic National Committee, 16 pgs, 1952 . . **8.00**
Pinback Button, Stevenson 1960, hopeful button, blue star, gold lettering **10.00**
Poster, 8½ x 22", cardboard, red, white, and purple, 1956 . . . . . . **75.00**
Sheet Music, 9 x 12", *Believe In Stevenson,* blue and white cov, 1956 . . . . **15.00**
John F. Kennedy, 1960
Bandanna, 31" sq, color portrait, white ground, red, white, and blue flag border, 1965 copyright tag . . . **15.00**
Campaign Hat, 11 x 13 x 4", white plastic, red, white, and blue striped paper strip with black lettering "Kennedy for President," stars with state abbreviations, 1960 . . . . **25.00**
Cigar, 10" l, Kennedy and Johnson 1960, cellophane wrapper, multicolored band **55.00**
Coloring Book, 10 x 13", JFK Coloring Book, 24 pgs, unused **20.00**
Folder, JFK A Time For Greatness, black and white photos, 1960 . . . **20.00**
Magazine, *Time,* Election Extra, 1960, 16 pgs, photos and summary of election **12.00**
Pinback Button, Kennedy/Johnson, red, white, and blue celluloid . . . **20.00**
Pitcher, 2¾" h, Mrs John F Kennedy, white china, full color photo, gold accents **20.00**
Plate, 7" d, President and Mrs John F Kennedy, china, full color portraits, gold edge band **15.00**
Salt and Pepper Shakers, pr, President and Mrs. John F. Kennedy, ceramic, color portraits, c1961 . . . . **30.00**

Richard M. Nixon, 1960, 1968, and 1972

Bank, 2½" h, cast iron, elephant shape, painted silver, raised "Nixon Agnew 68" on side, 1968 . . . . 30.00

Christmas Card, 4 x 6", full color photo of family, orig envelope postmarked 1967, New York return address 30.00

Coloring Book, 8 x 11", Watergate Coloring Book/Join The Fun/Color The Facts, 48 pgs, 1973 . . . . 15.00

First Day Cover, autographed by Nixon and Ford 195.00

Nodder, Nixon for President, elephant head, orig box 125.00

Pinback Button

Dick Nixon For President, red, white, and blue litho, 1960 . . . 10.00

Nixon/Nunn, white and orange . . 10.00

Plate, 9" d, Richard Nixon 37th President, china, full color portrait, 1969 . . . . 15.00

Lyndon B. Johnson, 1964

Bottle Stopper, 4" h, three dimensional, composition 35.00

Magazine, *Time,* Election Extra, 1964, 16 pgs, photos and summary of election 8.00

Pinback Button, 6" d, Inauguration, full color portrait, red, white, and blue rim 10.00

Barry M. Goldwater, 1964

Bolo Tie, green plastic slide, gold elephant and lettering, 1964 . . . . 8.00

Fan, cardboard, Goldwater Fan Club, portrait image, wood handle, 1964 . . . . 30.00

License Plate, 4 x 12", metal, yellow, blue raised letters 20.00

Pen, 5" l, brass, black inscriptions, 1964 . . . . 10.00

Pinback Button, Goldwater Miller GOP Party 1964, red, white, and blue 5.00

Poster, 14 x 21", "A Choice...Not An Echo," red, white, and blue 15.00

Soda Can, 5" h, "Gold Water," metallic green, gold, and white, caption "The Right Drink For The Conservative Taste," unopened, orig contents, 1964 . . . . 35.00

Hubert H. Humphrey, 1968

Bank, 1½ x 4½ x 4", raised "Humphrey Muskie 68," cast iron, figural, donkey, 1968 . . . . 30.00

Pinback Button

Humphrey, blue and white, 1972 hopeful campaign 5.00

Justice For All/Humphrey–Muskie in 1968, red, white, and blue . . 8.00

Poster, 21 x 28", cardboard, We're Coming Back!, Student Coalition for Humphrey/Muskie, blue, white, and orange, 1968 . . . . 15.00

George McGovern, 1972

Bandanna, 31" sq, McGovern For President/Come Home America, silk-like fabric, red and blue US image, campaign slogans, white ground, 1972, 31" sq 35.00

Bank, 4" h, Liberty Bell shape, white metal, bronzed finish, raised lettering, 1972 . . . . 25.00

Jugate, McGovern/Shriver, black, white, and blue, 1972 . . . . 8.00

Pinback Button, North Carolina's One Of A Million/McGovern, white letters, dark pink ground . . . 3.00

Gerald R. Ford, 1976

First Day Cover, autographed 55.00

Mirror, 2" d, Ford/Dole, black, white, and blue 8.00

Pinback Button, For President 1976 Ford, black and white, bright red, white, and blue rim 8.00

James E. Carter, 1976

Bandanna, 28" sq, Carter–Mondale, white and green, 1980 . . . . 25.00

Bank, 11½" h, figural, smiling peanut, beige vinyl, c1976 . . . . 15.00

Pen, 5¼" l, Carter–Mondale, plastic, green and white, 1976 . . . . 4.00

Pencil, 7" l, wood, green inscription "Carter/Mondale '76" 3.00

Pinback Button, Carter–Mondale 76, black and white, green slogan . . . 3.00

Sheet Music, 9 x 12", *Hello Jimmy,* red, white, and blue cov, 1976 . . . 5.00

Walter Mondale, 1976

Brochure, *Why Women in the AFT Should Support Walter Mondale,* 1984 . . . . 20.00

Pinback Button, "Mondale/Ferraro," red, white, and blue litho 5.00

Tile, 6" sq, white ceramic, "Thanks For All Your Help In Making This Possible, Fritz & Joan," orig box . . 15.00

Ronald Reagan, 1980 and 1984

Menu, White House, navy blue stiff cardboard folder, full color presidential seal, blue fabric cord, light blue menu sheet 10.00

Mug, 5" h, white ceramic, blue portraits of Reagan and Bush, red letters, inscribed "Republican National Convention August 20–23, 1984" 12.00

Pinback Button, Vote Reagan For President In 1980, black and white ground, red and blue slogans 5.00

Plate, 10½" d, Reagan/Bush, full

color portraits, waving flag back-
ground, 1981 . . . .   **35.00**
Poster, 16 x 22″, Reagan–Bush '84,
paper, multicolored **12.00**
George Bush, 1980, 1984, 1988
Box, bubble gum cigars, "Bush/
Dukakis Presidential Favorites,"
red, white, and blue, unopened
box of 24, Philadelphia Chewing
Gum Corp, c1988 . . . .   **10.00**
Bumper Sticker, 3½ x 9½″,
Bush/Quayle 88, red, white, and
blue **2.00**
Golf Ball, white, full color vice presi-
dential seal, orig blue box with
gold signature, Wilson **35.00**
Program, 8½ x 11″, Republican
National Convention, New
Orleans, Bush on cov, 92 pgs, 1988   **15.00**

POST CARDS

Collecting Hints: Concentrate on one subject
area, publisher, or illustrator. Collect cards in
mint condition when possible.

The more common the holiday, the larger the
city, the more popular the tourist attraction, the
easier it will be to find post cards about these
subjects because of the millions of cards that still
remain in these categories. The smaller runs of
"real" photo post cards are the most desirable of
the scenic cards. Photographic cards of families
and individuals, unless they show occupations,
unusual toys, dolls, or teddy bears have little
value.

Stamps and cancellation marks may affect the
value of cards, but rarely. Consult a philatelic
guide.

Post cards fall into two main categories: view
cards and topics. View cards are easiest to sell in
their local geographic region. European view
cards, while very interesting, are difficult to sell
in America.

It must be stressed that age alone does not determine price. A birthday post card from 1918
may sell for only ten cents, while a political campaign card from the 1950s may bring ten dollars.
Every collectible is governed by supply and demand.

Although the most popular collecting period is
1898–1918, the increasing costs of post cards
from this era have turned collectors' interest to
post cards from the 1920s, 1930s, and 1940s.
The main interest in the 1920–1930 period is
cards with an Art Deco motif. The cards collected from the 1940s are "linens" which feature
a textured "linen–like" paper surface.

Cards from the 1950–1970 period are called
"chromes" because of their shiny surface paper.
Advertising post cards from this chrome era are
rapidly gaining popularity while still selling for
under $3.00.

History: The golden age of post cards dates from
1898 to 1918. While there are cards printed earlier, they are collected for their postal history.
Post cards prior to 1898 are called "pioneer"
cards.

European publishers, especially in England
and Germany, produced the vast majority of
cards during the golden age. The major post card
publishers are Raphael Tuck (England), Paul
Finkenrath of Berlin (PFB–German), and
Whitney, Detroit Publishing Co., and John
Winsch (United States). However, many
American publishers had their stock produced in
Europe, hence, "Made in Bavaria" imprints.
While some Tuck cards are high priced, many
are still available in the "ten cent" boxes.

Styles changed rapidly, and manufacturers responded to every need. The linen post card
which gained popularity in the 1940s was
quickly replaced by the chrome cards of the
post–1950 period.

References: Many of the best books are
out–of–print. However, they are available
through libraries. Ask your library to utilize the
inter–library loan system.

Postcard Collector Annual, published annually
by Jones Publishing; Diane Allmen, *The Official
Price Guide to Postcards,* House of Collectibles,
1990; Janet A. Banneck, *The Antique Postcards
of Rose O'Neill,* Greater Chicago Productions,
1992; Norman E. Martinus and Harry L. Rinker,
Warman's Paper, Wallace–Homestead, 1994; J.
L. Mashburn, *The Artist–Signed Postcard Price
Guide: A Comprehensive Reference,* Colonial
House, 1993; J. L. Mashburn, *The Postcard Price
Guide: A Comprehensive Listing, Second Edition*
Colonial House, 1995; Joseph Lee Mashburn,
The Super Rare Postcards of Harrison Fisher,
Colonial House, 1992; Frederic and Mary
Megson, *American Advertising Postcards—Set
and Series: 1890–1920,* published by authors,
1985; Mary and Frederick Megson, *American
Exposition Postcards, 1870–1920: A Catalog And
Price Guide,* The Postcard Lovers, 1992; Susan
Brown Nicholson, *Antique Postcard Sets and
Series Price Guide,* Greater Chicago Productions,
1993; Susan Brown Nicholson, *The Encyclo-
pedia of Antique Postcards,* Wallace–Home-
stead, 1994; Cynthia Rubin and Morgan
Williams, *Larger Than Life; The American
Tall–Tale Postcard, 1905–1915,* Abbeville Press,
1990; Dorothy B. Ryan, *Picture Postcards In The
United States, 1893–1918,* Clarkson N. Potter,
1982; Nouhad A. Saleh, *Guide To Artist's
Signatures and Monograms on Postcards,*
Minerva Press, 1993; Jack H. Smith, *Postcard
Companion: The Collector's Reference,* Wallace–Homestead, 1989; Robert Ward, *Investment Guide To North American Real Photo*

Postcards, Antique Paper Guild, 1991; Jane Wood, *The Collector's Guide To Post Cards,* L–W Promotions, 1984, 1995 value update.

Periodicals: *Barr's Post Card News,* 70 S. 6th Street, Lansing, IA 52151; *Gloria's Corner,* PO Box 507, Denison, TX 75021; *Postcard Collector,* 121 N. Main St., Iola, WI 54945.

Collectors' Clubs: *Barr's Post Card News* and the *Post Card Collector* publish lists of over fifty regional clubs in the United States and Canada.

Advisor: Susan Brown Nicholson

Note: The following prices are for cards in excellent to mint condition—no sign of edgewear, no creases, no trimming, no writing on the picture side of the card, no tears, and no dirt. Each defect would reduce the price given by 10%.

ADVERTISING

Bell Telephone	15.00
Bull Durham	30.00
Buster Brown	12.00
Campbell Soup	
Horizontal format	35.00
Vertical format	85.00
Chief Sleepy Eye	150.00
Coca–Cola, Duster Girl	450.00
Cracker Jack Bears	25.00
DuPont Gun, dogs	100.00
Frog–in–the–Throat	
Oversized	50.00
Small Size	45.00
Gold Dust Twins	50.00
Job Cigarettes	
Mucha	300.00
Other artist	100.00
Kornelia Kinks	10.00
McDonald's	6.00
Quaddy	20.00
Studebaker Wagon	65.00
Swifts Pride	15.00
Tupperware	3.00
Vin Fiz	100.00
Zeno Gum	6.00

ARTIST SIGNED

Atwell, Mabel Lucie	
Early by Tuck	20.00
Regular, comic	15.00
Basch, Arpad, Art Nouveau	150.00
Bertiglia, children	15.00
Bompard, art dec	15.00
Boulanger, Maurice, cats	20.00
Brill, Ginks	10.00
Browne, Tom	
American Baseball series	15.00
English comic series	3.50
Brundage, Frances	
Children	10.00

Early chromolithographic	30.00
Brunelleschi, Art Nouveau	150.00
Caldecott	
Early	5.00
1974 reprints	.25
Carmichael, comic	3.00
Carr, Gene, comic	8.00
Chiostri, Art Deco	40.00
Christy, Howard Chandler	10.00
Clapsaddle, Ellen	
Children	9.00
Floral, sleds, crosses	3.00
Halloween, mechanical	150.00
Suffrage	55.00
Corbella, Art Deco	15.00
Corbett, Bertha, sunbonnets	12.00
Curtis, E, children	3.00
Daniell, Eva, Art Nouveau	100.00
Drayton/Weiderseim, Grace, children	30.00
Dwig	10.00
Fidler, Alice Luella, women	10.00
Fisher, Harrison	15.00
Gassaway, K, children	6.00
Gibson, Charles Dana	5.00·
Golay, Mary, flowers	2.00
Greiner, M	
Blacks	8.00
Children	3.50
Molly and Her Teddy	15.00
Griggs, HB	9.00
Gunn, Archie	3.50
Gutmann, Bessie Pease	25.00
Humphrey, Maud, sgd	75.00
Innes, John	5.00
Johnson, J, children	6.00
Kirchner, Raphael	
First period	125.00
Second period	65.00
Third period	45.00
Klein, Catherine	
Alphabet	15.00
Alphabet, letters X, Y, Z	25.00
Floral	3.00
Koehler, Mela, early	100.00
Mauzan, Art Deco	15.00
May, Phil, British	6.00
McCay, Winsor, Little Nemo	30.00
Mucha, Alphonse	
Art Nouveau, months of the year	125.00
Women, full card design	500.00
O'Neill, Rose	
Kewpies	40.00
Pickings from Puck, Blacks	150.00
Suffrage	200.00
Opper, Frederick, comic	6.00
Outcault	
Buster Brown calendars	12.00
Yellow Kid calendars	75.00
Parkinson, Ethel, children	6.00
Payne, Harry	22.00
Phillips, Cole	30.00
Price, Mary Evans	5.00

AN' YOU KNOW WHAT MEN ARE!
Et tu sais ce que les hommes valent !

Artist Signed, Mabel Lucie Attwell, $6.00.

Remington, Frederic	25.00
Robinson, Robert	25.00
Rockwell, Norman, after 1918	35.00
Russell, Charles	9.00
Shinn, Cobb	4.00
Smith, Jessie Wilcox	15.00
Tam, Jean	15.00
Thiele, Arthur	
Blacks	
Large faces	35.00
On bikes	35.00
Cats	
In action	30.00
Large heads	30.00
Twelvetrees, Charles, comic, children	5.00
Underwood, Clarence	8.00
Upton, Florence, Golliwoggs, Tuck	35.00
Wain, Louis	
Cat	45.00
Dog	25.00
Paper dolls	300.00
Wall, Bernhardt, sunbonnets	15.00
Wood, Lawson	6.00

EXPOSITION

Alaska–Yukon–Pacific	6.00
California Midwinter	200.00
Cotton States Exposition	125.00
Hudson–Fulton	10.00
Jamestown Bears, mechanical, 144 designs on one card	500.00
Lewis and Clark	10.00
Pan American	
Black and white	5.00
Color	10.00
Panama–Pacific	
General	8.00
Mitchell Publishing	2.00
Portland Rose Festival	3.50

Portola Festival	
Poster style	15.00
Views	1.50
Priest of Pallas	10.00
St Louis, 1904	
Eggshell paper	6.00
Hold to light type	35.00
Silver background	7.50
Trans–Mississippi	
Advertising	100.00
Officials	55.00
World Columbian, 1893	
Officials	15.00
Pre–Officials, without seals	100.00

GREETINGS

April Fools	
American comic	1.50
French litho with fish	5.00
Birthday	
Children	.50
Floral	.10
Christmas, no Santa	.25
Christmas, Santa	
German, highly embossed	30.00
Installment, unused	150.00
Red Suits	8.00
Suits other than red	15.00

Greetings, Christmas, Ellen Clapsaddle, $20.00.

Easter	
Animals, dressed	6.00
Chicks or rabbits	2.00
Children dressed as animals	4.50
Crosses	.50
Fourth of July	
Children	6.00
Uncle Sam	6.00
Others	1.50
Ground Hog Day	
Early large image	200.00
After 1930	25.00
Halloween	
Children	6.00

Children, extremely colorful or artist
sgd 10.00
Plain 2.00
Labor Day
Lounsbury Publishing 200.00
Nash Publishing 85.00
Leap Year 4.50
Mother's Day, early 5.00
New Year
Bells .... .50
Children or Father time 2.50
St Patrick's Day
Children 4.50
No children 1.50
Thanksgiving
Children 3.50
No children 1.00
Valentines
Children, women 3.50
Hearts, comic 1.00

PATRIOTIC

Decoration Day 7.50
Lincoln 4.50
Patriotic Songs 3.00
Uncle Sam 7.50
Washington 3.50
World War II, linen 1.00

PHOTOGRAPHIC

Children under Christmas trees 3.50
Children with animals or toys 4.50
Christmas trees 2.00
Circus Performer, close–up 8.00
Exaggerations
Conrad Publishing, after 1935 ..... 6.00
Martin Publishing 8.50
Martin Publishing, US Coin 75.00
Family, unidentified .... .50
Main Streets
Large cities 4.00
Small towns 9.00
Unidentified .... .50
With trains or trolleys 20.00
People on Paper Moons 3.00
Railroad Depots, with trains, identified 20.00
Shop Exteriors, identified 6.00
Shop Interiors
Clear images or products 15.00
Workers, barbers, blacksmiths, etc. . 20.00

POLITICAL AND SOCIAL HISTORY

Billy Possum 15.00
Blacks 12.00
Campaign
1900 .... 75.00
1904 .... 45.00
Indians, named 8.00
Jewish, comic 8.00

McKinley's death 6.00
Prohibition 6.00
Roosevelt's African Tour 3.00
Russo–Japanese War 25.00
Suffrage
Cargill publisher
Number 111 only 150.00
General 30.00
Parades 20.00
Taft, cartoons 15.00
Wilson 8.00

PUBLISHERS

Detroit
Indians 10.00
Views 1.50
Paul Finkenrath/Berlin (PFB)
Children 8.00
Comic 6.00
Greetings 1.50
Punch and Judy, mechanical 100.00
Santas 30.00
Tuck Publishing
Children, unsigned 4.50
Greetings 1.00
Views 1.00
Whitney
Children 4.50
Nibble Picks, Santas 12.00
Winsch Publishing
Greetings 1.50
Halloween, SL Schmucker 100.00
Santas 30.00
Valentines, SL Schmucker 35.00

RARE AND UNUSUAL

Boileau, Tuck 150.00
Coke Advertising, Hamilton King 400.00
DuPont Dirigible 125.00
Greenaway, Kate, sgd 200.00
Hold–To–Lights, other than buildings . . 40.00
Installment, Uncle Sam 150.00

HELLERTOWN VIEWS.   Photo by Calvin Bergstresser.
Hellertown, Pa.

Scenic, Saucon Furnace, Hellertown
Views, Calvin Bergstresser photographer,
dated 1911, $3.50.

Kewpies
  Gross Publishing Co **125.00**
  Ice Cream advertising, spell "Victory" **200.00**
  Mechanicals **85.00**
  Paper Dolls, Tuck **100.00**
Santa Claus
  Black Faced **150.00**
  Hold–To–Light **200.00**
Silks
  Applied, Santas and state bells **45.00**
  Woven **100.00**
Tuck Scouts, Harry Payne **125.00**
Warner Corset, Mucha **300.00**
Waverly Cycle, Mucha **13,500.00**
Wiener Werkstatte, Kokoschka **3,000.00**

POSTERS

Collecting Hints: Posters are collected either for their subject and historical value, e.g. movie, railroad, minstrel, etc., or for their aesthetic appeal. Modern art historians have recognized the poster as one of the most creative art forms of our times.

Often a popular film would be re–released several times over a period of years. Most re–releases can be identified by looking at the lower right corner in the white border area. A re–release will usually be indicated with an "R" and a diagonal slash mark with the year of the newest release. Therefore, a "R/47" would indicate a 1947 issue.

History: The poster was an extremely effective and critical means of mass communication, especially in the period before 1920. Enormous quantities were produced, helped in part by the propaganda role played by posters in World War I.

Print runs of two million were not unknown. Posters were not meant to be saved. Once they served their purpose, they tended to be destroyed. The paradox of high production and low survival is one of the fascinating aspects of poster history.

The posters of the late 19th century and early 20th century represent the pinnacle of American lithography printing. The advertising posters of firms such as Strobridge and Courier are true classics. Philadelphia was one center for the poster industry.

Europe pioneered in posters with high artistic and aesthetic content. Many major artists of the 20th century designed posters. Poster art still plays a key role throughout Europe today.

References: John Barnicoat, *A Concise History of Posters*, Harry Abrams, Inc., 1976; *Pin–Up Poster Book: The Elvgren Collection*, Collectors Press, 1995; Tony Fusco, *Posters: Identification and Price Guide, Second Edition* Avon Books, 1994; John Kisch, *Movie Poster Price Database:*

August–December 1994, published by author, 1995; Norman E. Martinus and Harry L. Rinker, *Warman's Paper*, Wallace–Homestead, 1994; Walton Rawls, *Wake Up, America!: World War I And The American Poster*, Abbeville Press, 1988; Stephen Rebello and Richard Allen, *Reel Art: Great Posters From The Golden Age of the Silver Screen*, Abbeville Press, 1988; George Theofiles, *American Posters of World War I: A Price and Collector's Guide*, Dafram House Publishers; Susan Theran, *Leonard's Annual Price Index of Prints, Posters and Photographs, 1993–1994 Auction Season*, Auction Index, 1995; Susan Theran, *Prints, Posters, and Posters: Identification and Price Guide*, Avon Books, 1993; Jon R. Warren, *Collecting Hollywood: The Movie Poster Price Guide, Third Edition*, American Collector's Exchange, 1994; Bruce Lanier Wright, *Yesterday's Tomorrows: The Golden Age of Science Fiction Posters, 1950–1964*, Taylor Publishing, 1993.

Periodicals: *Collecting Hollywood*, 2401 Broad St., Chattanooga, TN 37408; *The Movie Poster Update*, 2401 Broad St., Chattanooga, TN 37408.

Advisor: George Theofiles.

REPRODUCTION ALERT:

ADVERTISING

Buckwheat Flour, 19 x 10", flour bag
  shape **25.00**
Ceresota Flour, 20 x 24", mother and
  son illus **50.00**
Chase & Sanborn Coffee, 23 x 20", grocery store, framed **200.00**
Diamond Gloss Starch, 17 x 22", baby
  illus **55.00**
Fatima Turkish Cigarettes, 14 x 17", harem girl's face, yellow, red, and green ground, c1910 . . . . **125.00**
Henry Clay Haban, 19 x 25", Clay, plant, banded cigars, and boxes **425.00**
Holsum Bread, 12 x 20" **8.00**
Independent Brewing Co., 21 x 11", Maynard Williamson, 1910 . . . . **85.00**
International Stock Food, 17½ x 28½", sitting pig, horse and cow, framed . . **200.00**
Pacific Paints, 47 x 62", sailors rowing out to steamship, c1900 . . . . **135.00**
Swing With Sinclair, 44 x 28", red car, blue ground, c1938 . . . . **85.00**
Take Some Home—Independent Brewing Co of Pittsburgh, 21 x 11", Maynard Williamson, 1910 . . . . **85.00**
Van Heusen Century Shirts, 23 x 17", Ronald Reagan modeling shirt, 1953 **45.00**
Wrigley's Gum—Pioneer Women Helped Build Our Great Country, 28 x 11", Otis Shepard, 1943 . . . . **115.00**

CAUSES

American Field Service, Nuyttens, 20 x 30", 1917, man in French helmet leads way for transport under flare lit sky, light and dark blues 275.00

Be Ready! Keep Him Smiling, United War Work, 21 x 11", smiling Doughboy 95.00

Cleveland—Many Peoples One Language, Board of Education, JH Donahey, 11 x 18", 1917, appeal in six languages, gives locations where classes are held 175.00

Hey Fellows! Your Money Brings The Book We Need, JE Sheridan, 20 x 30", 1918, Doughboy holds book high while sailor reads at his side, vivid orange background 75.00

1919 War Chest—Minneapolis, J Almars, 54 x 40", lists agencies to be financed by campaign 175.00

The Comforter, Gordon Grant, 18 x 24", Red Cross nurse comforts refugee, pinks, blue, red, and brown 125.00

MOVIES

One Sheet, 27 x 41"

Adventures of Robin Hood, 1950s reissue, Errol Flynn 330.00

Beast From 20,000 Fathoms, 1953 .. 360.00

Crazy Knights, Monogram, 1944, Three Stooges, Shemp Howard, Billy Gilbert, Maxie Rosenbloom 125.00

Frankenstein Meets The Wolfman, 1949 re–release, Lon Chaney and Bela Lugosi, framed 220.00

Great Plane Robbery, Columbia, 1940, Jack Holt 75.00

Movie, All Hands On Deck, Pat Boone, Buddy Hackett, Barbara Eden, 20th Century Fox, 1961, $20.00.

Haunted House, Monogram, 1940, Jackie Moran, Marcia Mae Jones   75.00

Laurel & Hardy In The Big Noise, Fox, 1944, Tooker litho 300.00

Midnight Cowboy, 1969, foreign ... 100.00

One New York Night, MGM, 1935, Franchot Tone, Una Merkel 110.00

Paleface, Paramount, 1948, Bob Hope, Jane Russell 100.00

Rookie Cop, RKO, 1939, Ace the Wonder Dog, Tim Holt 100.00

Song of Love, MGM, 1947, Katharine Hepburn, Paul Henreid 75.00

Sweet Rosie O'Grady, Fox, 1943, Betty Grable, Robert Young, Adolphe Menjou 150.00

Thunderball, 1965, Sean Connery .. 125.00

Up The River, Fox, 1938, Preston Foster, Tony Martin 100.00

You'll Never Get Rich, Columbia, 1942, Fred Astaire and Rita Hayworth 690.00

Three Sheets, 41 x 81"

An Affair to Remember, 20th Century Fox, 1957, Cary Grant and Deborah Kerr, linen back 1,495.00

Courtship of Andy Hardy, MGM, 1942, Mickey Rooney, Tooker litho 110.00

Guilty, Monogram, 1944, Bonita Granville, Don Castle 125.00

Phantom of 42nd Street, PRC, 1945, Dave O'Brien, Kay Aldridge 100.00

The Three Caballeros, 1945, Disney 575.00

SPORTS

British Empire & Commonwealth Games, Perth, Western Australia, 25 x 40", panorama of city, 1962 ...... 150.00

Fidass Sporting Goods, 29 x 52", F Romoli, Italian soccer player, 1946 300.00

Grays of Cambridge, 24 x 39", Affiches Marci, large tennis racket bounces "The Light Blue Tennis Ball" toward viewer, c1947 .... 225.00

High Diver, 27 x 29", Arthur Albrecht & Co., swimming exhibition, c1910 .. 325.00

Let's Go Skiing—Use The New Haven RR Snow Trains, 14 x 22", Sascha Maurer, c1937 .... 125.00

Munich Olympics 1972—Fencing, 33 x 46", Gaebele, posted at Olympics .. 125.00

Ninth International Students' Games Paris 1947, 30 x 46", P Colin 350.00

Philadelphia Sunday Press, 16 x 22", red haired female tennis player, c1896 .... 125.00

Radio Returns of the Louis–Schmeling Fight, 14 x 22", Martin's Scotch Whiskey adv, O Soglow illus 100.00

Samson Kina, 20 x 30", Goffart,

Brussels, chromolithograph of two boxers, c1910 .... **275.00**

The Saturday Evening Post 100th Year of Baseball, 22 x 28", Norman Rockwell, 1939 .... **175.00**

Wrestling, 14 x 22", York Beach Casino, Mon. July 8, Pat "Crusher" O'Hara vs Luke Graham and Diamond Jim Brady vs Vincent Garabaldi, cardboard, black and white **25.00**

THEATER

A Royal Rogue Starring Jefferson De Angelis & Company, 40 x 80", Metropolitan Printing, c1900 ...... **175.00**

Blue Jeans, 40 x 30," Enquirer Co., c1905 .... **200.00**

Charles A Gardner In His New Comedy—The Prize Winner, 42 x 80", Greve Litho Co., Milwaukee, c1900 .... **175.00**

Child Slaves of New York, 20 x 30", Strobridge Litho, 1903 .... **165.00**

La Glu, 26 x 35", Robert DuPont, 1910 **175.00**

Lena Horne: The Lady and Her Music, 14 x 22", c1980 .... **35.00**

Life's Shop Window, 40 x 80", Ritchey Litho, c1900 .... **210.00**

Madame Butterfly—A Grand Opera by Giacomo Puccini, 28 x 42", Enquirer Litho Co., c1900 .... **175.00**

Nip and Tuck, Detectives Out Of The Window Into The Water, 28 x 21", J M Jones Co., Chicago, c1880 .... **225.00**

Patterson's New York Opera Co—In The Queen's Handkerchief, 13 x 28", Currier Co., Buffalo, c1885 .... **250.00**

Penelope, 27 x 35½", George Rochegross **150.00**

Rosemarie, 40 x 90", English, c1948 .. **200.00**

Salisbury's Troubadours—Nelly McHenry, 20 x 30", Strobridge, c1880 .... **225.00**

TRANSPORTATION

Automobile Club Show Old Deer Park, London, 20 x 30", c1905 .... **600.00**

Buick, 25 x 38", Kansas City, black and white, 1921–22 .... **85.00**

Chicago, Milwaukee And St Paul Railway, 24 x 34", c1870 .... **250.00**

Favor Cycles, 62 x 47", c1925, linen backing **350.00**

Mercedes Benz, 23 x 33", showroom, brown, blue, black, red, and yellow . **975.00**

National Flying Day, 15 x 23", 1937 .. **100.00**

Nice Auto Races—12 June 1949, 25 x 39", J Ramel, 1949 .... **350.00**

Speed To Winter Playgrounds In Pullman Safety and Comfort, 19 x 27", William Welsh, 1935 .... **300.00**

SS France, A New Concept In Luxury For All, launching, 34 x 45", Bob Peak Litho, 1962 .... **225.00**

SwissAir, 27 x 39", Herbert Leupin, c1955 .... **250.00**

Veritable Vieux Systems, 17 x 23", chromolithograph, drinkers in hot air balloon gondola, 1890 .... **175.00**

TRAVEL

American Airlines, 40 x 30", Arizona, c1955 .... **50.00**

Berwick Upon Tweed—It's Quicker By Rail–liner, 25 x 40", Frank Mason, 1935 .... **275.00**

Britain In Winter, 29 x 19", Terence Cuneo **50.00**

Come to Britain for Racing, 20 x 30", Lionel Edwards, litho, c1948 ...... **65.00**

Genoa and the Italian Riviera, 27 x 39", Graffonara, 1931 .... **325.00**

Montage De France, 24 x 39", Nathan, c1947 .... **125.00**

Panama Pacific, New York–California, 27 x 23", white liner passing through Panama Canal, framed **250.00**

Sunny Ryhl—The Children's Paradise, 25 x 40", Mays, c1946 .... **300.00**

TWA, Las Vegas—Fly TWA, 25 x 40", showgirl, casino items, and airliner in background, c1960 .... **225.00**

WORLD WAR I

Americans! Join And Fight, 28 x 42", blue, red, tan, brown, fighting doughboys, American flag, and biplanes, 1918 .... **975.00**

Be a Sea Soldier, 20 x 40", Marine sitting on dock **200.00**

Call To Duty Join The Army For Home And Country, 30 x 40", Army bugler and unfurled banner, 1917 .... **250.00**

Columbia Calls—Enlist In The Army, Francis A Halstead, 28 x 40", chromolithograph, Columbia with banner and sword atop globe, sky blue ground **200.00**

Do Your Duty, Join The Marines, 20 x 30", gun crew loading on deck, c1917 .... **135.00**

Earn While You Learn, 19 x 24", machinist illus, purple and white, 1919 **95.00**

Follow The Flag For Freedom The Navy Strikes Now, James Daugherty, 14 x 22", stylized Columbia points sword to multicolored horizon as sailor looks on, vivid colors **125.00**

He Is Getting Our Country's Signal Are You? Join The Navy, 20 x 30", Navy signalman waving flag, 1917 ...... **300.00**

It Protected You, Will You Defend It?, 25 x 35", artillery crew silhouette **225.00**

Join The Quartermaster Corps, John W. Sheeres, 18 x 26", 1919, smiling Uncle Sam in doughboy outfit, purple starry heavens **150.00**

Keep The American Flag On The Seas, 14 x 22", battleship in rough seas, 1917 .... **175.00**

Men Wanted For The Army, 30 x 40", cavalryman on horse blowing bugle, Rocky Mountain background, c1908 .... **975.00**

Over There—US Navy, 38 x 56", sailor holding banner, 1917 .... **750.00**

Register! Tuesday, June 5th, 14 x 22", State of Massachusetts draft, 1917 .. **75.00**

Tell That To The Marines, 20 x 40", man taking off suit coat, James Montgomery Flagg, 1918 .... **375.00**

US Marines, Active Service On Land And Sea, 30 x 40", marine marching on pier **275.00**

WORLD WAR II

All Soldiers Can't Be In The Infantry, 17 x 25", charging soldier holding bayonet, 1944 .... **125.00**

Be A Marine—Free A Marine To Fight, 28 x 40", woman Marine in uniform, 1943 .... **125.00**

Build And Fight In The Navy Seabees, 28 x 42", recruiting image, 1943 ... **300.00**

Defend Your Country, 21 x 11", Uncle Sam rolling up sleeves, 1940 ...... **125.00**

Dish It Out With The Navy, 28 x 42", gun crew in battle, 1942 .... **135.00**

Enlist Now, US Marine Corps, 28 x 40", full color island setting, 1942 ..... **200.00**

Join The WAC, 22 x 28", WAC sitting on bunk typing letter, c1942 .... **100.00**

Let's Hit 'Em With Everything We've Got!, 28 x 41", Naval deck gunner firing, raging battle, 1942 .... **150.00**

Marines Have Landed, 30 x 40", Marines wade ashore, James Montgomery Flagg, 1941 .... **350.00**

Now Is The Time, 25 x 38", army war jobs, red, mauve, blue, and white, 1942 .... **125.00**

Proud I'll Say—Join The Waves, 14 x 20", father showing picture of Wave daughter, 1943 .... **100.00**

Put The Squeeze On Food Waste, 7 x 10", cartoon image of Navy kitchens, 1945 .... **45.00**

Soldier—Take Care Of Your G.I., 25 x 36", soldier pointing to poster, 1943 **300.00**

Speed Up The Process, 19 x 27", endless line of Marines with man at desk, J Hearne, 1945 .... **250.00**

Take Your Place In The Ranks, 25 x 38", recruiting image, 1942 .... **175.00**

Want Action?—Join US Marine Corps!, 28 x 41", Marine holding out right hand, rifle in left hand, James Montgomery Flagg, 1942 .... **350.00**

We're In The Fight Too!, 14 x 20", farm woman, blue, red, black, and white, 1942 .... **150.00**

You Can Build and Fight, 19 x 25", trooper with jack hammer, 1943 ... **135.00**

ELVIS PRESLEY

Collecting Hints: Official Elvis Presley items are usually copyrighted and many are dated.

Learn to differentiate between items licensed during Elvis's lifetime and the wealth of "fantasy" items issued after his death. The latter are collectibles, but have nowhere near the value of the pre–1977 material.

Also accept the fact that many of the modern limited edition issues are purely speculative investments. It is best to buy them because you like them and plan to live with them for an extended period of time.

History: When Elvis Presley became a rock 'n' roll star, he became one of the first singers to have a promotion aimed at teenagers. The first Elvis merchandise appeared in 1956. During the following years new merchandise was added both in America and foreign countries. After his death in 1977, a vast number of new Elvis collectibles appeared.

References: Pauline Bartel, *Everything Elvis,* Taylor Publishing, 1995; Rosalind Cranor, *Elvis Collectibles,* Collector Books, 1983, out–of–print; Norman E. Martinus and Harry L. Rinker, *Warman's Paper,* Wallace–Homestead, 1993; Jerry Osborne, *The Official Price Guide To Elvis Presley Records and Memorabilia,* House of Collectibles, 1994; Jerry Osborne, Perry Cox, and Joe Lindsay, *The Official Price Guide To Memorabilia of Elvis Presley and The Beatles,* House of Collectibles, 1988; Richard Peters, *Elvis: The Golden Anniversary Tribute,* Salem House, 1984.

Clubs: Elvis Forever TCB Fan Club, PO Box 1066, Pinellas Park, FL 34665; Graceland News Fan Club, PO Box 452, Rutherford, NJ 07070.

Museums: Jimmy Velvet's Elvis Presley Museum, Franklin, TN; Graceland, Memphis, TN.

Autograph, 8 x 10" glossy photo, blue ball point pen signature, 1959 .... **1,200.00**

Book, *The Elvis Presley Story,* Hillman Books, 1960, 160 pgs, 32 black and white photo pgs **25.00**

Bracelet, 3", silver metal, stretch band,

cover flips up, reveals black and white photo, marked "Hong Kong," 1960 .... **100.00**
Catalog, Elvis RCA Victor Records, list of albums and 45 rpm singles, 3½ x 7" **18.00**
Charm Bracelet, metal link band, gold finish, 1956 Elvis Presley Enterprises **120.00**
Christmas Ornament, Hallmark, figural, 1992, orig box **25.00**
Doll, 21" h, hard vinyl body, soft molded vinyl head, Celebrity Collection, white leather jumpsuit with gold trim, red scarf, white vinyl boots, jewelry accessories, microphone in one hand, authenticity certificate and magazine, orig box, World Doll, copyright 1984 Elvis Presley Enterprises, Inc **125.00**
Guitar, 31" l, hard plastic, brown marble body, white plastic top, braided strap, marked "Emenee Official Elvis Presley Guitar" **400.00**
Lamp, 36" h, figural, bust **110.00**
Lobby Card, 11 x 14"
  Flaming Star, color illus, copyright 1960 20th Century Fox **12.50**
  Love Me Tender, 20th Century Fox, 1956 .... **22.00**
Magazine, *Country and Western Music Stars*, 8 x 11", issue #1, 2 pg article, Fawcett Publications, copyright 1958 **25.00**
Menu, Sahara Tahoe, large program type, 1970s **45.00**
Mug, plastic, multicolored, marked "Elvis the King Lives On, 1935–1977" **5.00**
Newspaper, Memphis, reporting death **45.00**
Pen Knife, minor wear **20.00**
Pennant, 18" l, felt, red and green, center photo **12.00**

Perfume Bottle, 3½" h, glass, Teddy Bear, white plastic cap, black and white photo sticker, orig box, 1957 copyright by Elvis Presley Enterprises, Inc **150.00**
Pillow, 10" sq, cotton stuffed, blue piped trim, blue printed picture, Love Me Tender, and signature, orig tag marked "Personality Products Co Decorative Autographed Pillow" and 1956 Elvis Presley Enterprises copyright **250.00**
Pinback Button
  3", color photo portrait, blue signature, 1956 Elvis Presley Enterprises copyright **50.00**
  3½" d, full color photo, "Sincerely Elvis," 1970s **12.00**
Pocket Watch **45.00**
Post Card, 3¼ x 5", two full color photos, Army uniform, marked "Holiday Greetings to You All From Elvis And The Colonel" in red **30.00**
Poster, 27 x 41", *Blue Hawaii*, Paramount, 1961 .... **50.00**
Record
  Hard Headed Woman/Don't Ask Me Why, 45 rpm, RCA Victor label, 1958 .... **25.00**
  King Creole, RCA Victor, black label, long play **15.00**
  Love Me Tender/Any Way You Want Me, RCA Victor label, 1956 ..... **50.00**
  Loving You, 45 rpm, includes Lonesome Cowboy, Hotdog, Mean Woman Blues, and Got A Lot O' Livin To Do, orig sleeve, 1957 ... **20.00**
Salt and Pepper Shakers, pr, figural television, Elvis on screen **15.00**
Scarf, 32" sq, 1956 .... **325.00**
Serving Tray, late 1970s **20.00**
Sheet Music, *Love Me Tender* **25.00**
Tab
  2" d, litho, tin, blue and gold lettering, "I Love Elvis," metallic gold background, 1970s **10.00**
  2¼", litho, tin, yellow, red name with blue inscription, c1970 .... **15.00**
Trash Can, metal, several pictures of Elvis, c1977 .... **50.00**
Tumbler, early 1970s **50.00**
Wrist Watch **40.00**

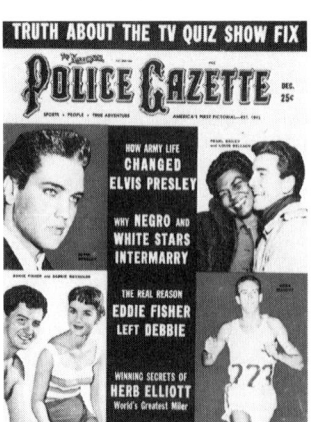

Magazine, *National Police Gazette*, December, 1958, 10½ x 13¼, $35.00.

PSYCHEDELIC COLLECTIBLES

Collecting Hints: Look for psychedelic material in a wide range of areas, e.g., books, magazines, and newspapers, clothing, jewelry, home decorations, music and music festivals, and television.

Include as many three–dimensional items as possible.

When displaying your collection, keep it concentrated in one location. The psychedelic era emphasized a wild intermingling of color and design.

An excellent collection can be built focusing solely on pieces associated with the social protest movement. Collect over a wide range. A collection of just anti–war material is too limited.

History: Psychedelic collectibles are defined by period (1960s and 1970s) and by the highly innovative use of colors and design. The roots of psychedelic art and color are many, e.g., late nineteenth century graphics, paisley fabrics, quilts and coverlets, the color reversal techniques of Joseph Alberts, American Indian art, and dancer Loie Fuller's diaphanous material which produced a light show as she moved and swirled.

It was a period without limits on design. As a result, the period was marked by eclecticism rather than unity. Among its features was the incorporation of new technological advances, e.g., vinyl, polyester, metallic fabrics, non–woven fabric (paper), into its products. Inflatable plastic furniture was made. Everywhere the look was "far out" and informal.

Peter Max was the leading designer of the period. Few items in the late 1960s escaped his art. Although mass produced, many items fall into the scarce category.

References: Alison Fox, *Rock & Pop—Phillips Collector's Guide*, Dunestyle Publishing/Boxtree, 1988; Paul D. Grushkin, *The Art of Rock: Posters from Presley to Punk*, Abbeville Press, 1987; Joel Lobenthal, *Radial Rags: Fashions of the Sixties*, Abbeville Press, 1990; Susanne White, *Psychedelic Collectibles of the 1960s & 1970s: An Illustrated Price Guide*, Wallace–Homestead, 1990, out–of–print.

Belt, cloth, leather fringed ends, green, light green, orange, and gold design, c1968 . . . . **10.00**
Book
   American Psalms, Hallmark copyright 1971, Peter Max illus **25.00**
   Peter Max/Love, Hallmark copyright 1971, 32 pgs **28.00**
   Peter Max Paper Airplane Book, Pyramid Books, copyright 1971 Peter Max Enterprises, 92 pgs **30.00**
Book Cover, Peter Max design, paper, multicolored design, orange background, 21 x 14", unused, 1969–70 . **20.00**
Comic Book, The Forty Year Old Hippie, No. 2, 1979, The Rip Off Press, Inc **5.00**
Dress, Flower Fantasy, paper, pink, yel-

low, green, and white, Hallmark, Kansas City, MO, c1969 . . . . **18.00**
Game, The Peter Max Chesset, orig box, unused parts, Kontrell, late 1960s . . **250.00**
Greeting Card, 8 x 14½", Laugh=In, 1969 . . . . **15.00**
Headband, cloth, elastic band, blue and white, peace signs and birds, c1970 **10.00**
Ice Bucket, 5½" d, 7" h, litho tin, white plastic int., plastic and metal lid, sunglasses handle, one side with female facial features, other with male facial features **125.00**
Jacket, Granny Takes A Trip, black, pink and green sequins, c1970 . . . . **50.00**
Jell–O Shaker, 7" h, plastic, yellow, black and red Peter Max illus, copyright 1972 Peter Max Enterprises, Inc **55.00**
Lava Lamp, 15" h, red **50.00**
Magazine
   Avant Garde, 1960s **18.00**
   Freak Out USA, February, 1967 . . . . **15.00**
Mini Dress, cotton, blue, orange, pink, yellow, and green print, 1969–70 . . **35.00**
Necktie, Peter Max, orange, yellow, and blue design **50.00**
Pinback Button, 2½" d, Woodstock, blue, white, and orange, 1969 . . . . . **25.00**
Playing Cards, complete deck, Stancraft Products, Inc, late 1960s **18.00**
Poster, concert
   Family Dog
      14 x 20½", July 1–3, 1966 concert, pink and purple design, Wes Wilson art **40.00**
      14 x 21", July 26–28, 1968, Avalon Ballroom, Casey Simpson art . . **35.00**
      14 x 22", June 21–23, 1968, Avalon Ballroom, Victor Moscoso art **35.00**
   Moby Grape/The Charlatans, Victor Moscoso artist, February 24–25, 1967, orange, blue, and bright pink, 14 x 20" **40.00**
   The Doors/Jim Kweskin Jug Band, Bonnie MacLean artist, June 9–10, 1967, ocher, pink, and black, 14 x 23" **85.00**
Purse, vinyl, bold black and white design, c1969 . . . . **30.00**
Puzzle, Zodiac, #5, orig box, 1970 copyright, issued by *Life* magazine **40.00**
Shirt, dacron polyester and cotton, brown and white design, Majesty label, c1970 . . . . **25.00**
Stationery, 8½ x 11", typed letter, Oct 1, 1968, colorful design **25.00**
Table, side, 16¼" h, fiberboard, black, purple, light blue, and dark blue silkscreen print, Joyce Miller, Manufactured by William Products, York, PA, 1967 . . . . **150.00**

Teapot, 8½" h, enameled metal, red, Peter Max illus, 1960–70 . . . . **150.00**
Thermos, 6½" h, plastic, Aladdin, copyright 1968 George Schlatter–Ed Friendly Productions and Romart, Inc **25.00**
Toy, Yellow Submarine, orig box, Corgi, 1968 . . . . **325.00**
Tray
  Happy **75.00**
  Love, Peter Max artwork, 1960s **75.00**
Umbrella, 26½" h, vinyl, Peter Max design, yellow, purple, green, gray, black, and white, "Made In USA," 1968–69 . . . . **350.00**
Waste Can, 13" h, Laugh–In, litho tin, Cheinco copyright 1968 George Schlatter–Ed Friendly Productions and Romart, Inc **55.00**

PUNCHBOARDS

Collecting Hints: Punchboards which are unpunched are collectible. A punched board has little value unless it is an extremely rare design. Like most advertising items, price is determined by graphics and subject matter.

The majority of punchboards sell in the $8.00 to $30.00 range. The high end of the range is represented by boards such as Golden Gate Bridge at $85.00 and Baseball Classic at $100.00.

History: Punchboards are self–contained games of chance made of pressed paper containing holes with coded tickets inside each hole. For an agreed amount the player uses a "punch" to extract the ticket of his or her choice. Prizes are awarded to the winning ticket. Punch prices can be 1¢, 2¢, 3¢, 5¢, 10¢, 20¢, 50¢, $1.00 or more.

Not all tickets were numbered. Fruit symbols were used extensively as well as animals. Some punchboards had no printing at all, just colored tickets. Other ticket themes included dice, cards, dominoes, words, etc. One early board had Mack Sennet bathing beauties.

Punchboards come in an endless variety of styles. Names reflected the themes of the boards. Barrel of Winners, Break the Bank, Baseball, More Smokes, Lucky Lulu and Take It Off were just a few.

At first punchboards were used to award cash. As legal attempts to outlaw gambling arose, prizes were switched to candy, cigars, cigarettes, jewelry, radios, clocks, cameras, sporting goods, toys, beer, chocolate, etc.

The golden age of punchboards was the 1920s to the 1950s. Attention was focused on the keyed punchboard in the film *The Flim Flam Man.* This negative publicity hurt the punchboard industry.

Reference: Norman E. Martinus and Harry L. Rinker, *Warman's Paper*, Wallace–Homestead, 1994.

Museum: Amusement Sales, 127 North Main, Midvale, UT 84047.

Advisor: Clark Phelps.

Bell Pots, slot symbols, $1.00 punch . . **30.00**
Big Bills, 25¢ punch **18.00**
Block Buster, 5¢ punch, double jackpot, cash pay **18.00**
Canasta, 5¢ punch, removable score card **50.00**
Cross Country Winner, seals, cash pay **20.00**
Dime Joe, cash pay, 10¢ punch **15.00**
Full of Tens, 25¢ punch, cash pay **15.00**
Good As Gold, colorful, seals **20.00**
Hi Yo Silver, 25¢ punch, cash pay with jackpot **15.00**
Joe's Special Prize, 25¢ punch, cash board **18.00**
Johnson's Chocolates, Elvgren girl, 8½ x 8½" **25.00**
Junior Kitty, kitten picture, cash pay . . **30.00**
Man of War, race horse **20.00**
Mr. Peanut, 1940s, chances to win tin of Planter's Cocktail Peanuts, 2¢ punch, unused, orig tissue wrapping paper **125.00**
National Winner **20.00**
Nickel Fins, 1,000 holes with seals . . . **15.00**
Odd Pennies, candy bars, 2¢ or 3¢ punch, girl illus, 11 x 6¾" **18.00**
Pass–Hit & Crap, dice tickets, 50¢ punch **25.00**
Pick a Cherry, cherry seals, cash pay . . **20.00**
Prize Pots, red head girl, 50¢ punch . . **65.00**
Sports Push Cards, baseball, football, basketball **5.00**
Take It Easy, colorful, nude **50.00**
Ten Big Sawbucks, 20¢ cash board . . . **20.00**

Off We Go!, 5¢, 10 x 12½", $20.00.

Tiny, 7, 11, book cover, fold over to
conceal, Blacks shooting dice, 19 x
6" open **50.00**
Worth Going For, 50¢ punch, girlie
board **20.00**
Yankee Trader **20.00**
Your Pick, 10¢ punch, money seals ... **30.00**

PURINTON POTTERY

Collecting Hints: The most popular patterns
among collectors are Apple, Intaglio (brown),
Normandy Plaid (red), Maywood, and
Pennsylvania Dutch. Variations, e.g., a green
ground Intaglio, are known for many of these
patterns.

Purinton also made a number of kitchenware
and specialty pieces. These should not be overlooked. Among the harder to find items are animal figurines, tea tiles, and a Tom and Jerry bowl
and mug set.

History: Bernard Purinton founded Purinton
Pottery in 1936 in Wellsville, Ohio. This pilot
plant produced decorative dinnerware as well as
some special order pieces. In 1940 Roy
Underwood, President of Knox Glass Company,
approached Purinton about moving his operation
to Knox's community, Shippenville.

In 1941 the pottery relocated to a newly built
plant in Shippenville, Pennsylvania. The company's first product at the new plant, a two–cup
premium teapot for McCormick Tea Company,
rolled off the line on December 7, 1941.

Dorothy Purinton and William H. Blair, her
brother, were the chief designers for the company. Maywood, Plaid, and several Pennsylvania
German designs were among the patterns attributed to Dorothy Purinton. William Blair, a graduate of the Cleveland School of Art, designed the
Apple and Intaglio patterns.

Initially slipware was cast. Later it was pressed
using a Ram Press process. Clays came from
Florida, Kentucky, North Carolina, and
Tennessee.

Purinton Pottery did not use decals as did
many of its competitors. Greenware was hand
painted by locally trained decorators who then
dipped the decorated pieces into glaze. This demanded a specially formulated body and a more
expensive manufacturing process. Hand painting
also allowed for some of the variations in technique and colors found on Purinton ware today.

Purinton made a complete dinnerware line for
each pattern plus a host of accessory pieces ranging from candleholders to vases. Dinnerware patterns were open stock. Purinton's ware received
national distribution. Select lines were exported.

The plant ceased operations in 1958, reopened briefly, and finally closed for good in
1959. Cheap foreign imports were cited as the
cause of the company's decline.

References: Pat Dole, *Purinton Pottery,* pub-
lished by author, 1984; Pat Dole, *Purinton
Pottery: Book II,* Denton Publishing, 1990;
Harvey Duke, *The Official Identification and
Price Guide To Pottery and Porcelain, Eighth
Edition,* House of Collectibles, 1995; Lois
Lehner, *Lehner's Encyclopedia of U. S. Marks on
Pottery, Porcelain & Clay,* Collector Books, 1988;
Susan Morris, *Purinton Pottery: An Identification
& Value Guide,* Collector Books, 1994.

Periodical: *Purinton Pastimes,* 20401 Ivybridge
Court, Gaithersburg, MD 20879.

Apple
  Casserole, cov, oval **24.00**
  Coffeepot, cov **25.00**
  Creamer, high lip **10.00**
  Cups, set of four **60.00**
  Kent Jug **25.00**
  Plate, 9" d, luncheon **15.00**
  Salt and Pepper Shakers, pr, range
    size **25.00**
  Tea Canister, no lid **45.00**
  Vegetable Dish, oval **20.00**
Fruit
  Canister Set, wood lazy susan, flour,
    sugar, coffee, and tea canisters,
    straight sides **125.00**
  Chop Plate **35.00**
  Pitcher, water **30.00**
  Plate, 9¼" d, dinner **12.00**
  Relish, 3 part, handled **15.00**
  Teapot, cov
    4 cup **25.00**
    6 cup **55.00**
Heather Plaid, pour and shake salt and
  pepper set **50.00**
Ivy
  Pitcher, small loop handle **45.00**
  Teapot
    4 cup **25.00**
    6 cup **35.00**
Mountain Rose
  Planter, basket **38.00**
  Teapot, individual **25.00**
Normandy Plaid
  Canister Set, sq **100.00**
  Coffee Mug, 8 oz **15.00**
  Cup **10.00**
  Dessert Bowl **10.00**
  Grease Jar, cov **20.00**
  Plate, 9¾" d, dinner **12.00**
  Salt and Pepper Set, pour and shake **65.00**
  Saucer **3.00**
  Vegetable, open **20.00**
  Oriental, teapot **35.00**
  Shooting Star, honey jug **35.00**

RACING COLLECTIBLES

Collecting Hints: This is a field of heroes and also fans. Collectors love the winners. A household name counts. Losers are important only when major races are involved. Pre–1945 material is especially desirable because few individuals were into collecting prior to that time.

The field does have problems with reproductions and copycats. Check every item carefully. Beware of paying premium prices for items made within the last twenty years.

Auto racing collectibles is one of the hot collectible markets of the 1990s. Although interest in Indy 500 collectibles remains strong, the market is dominated by NASCAR collectibles. In fact, the market is so strong that racing collectibles have their own separate show circuit and supporting literature.

Because racing collecting is in its infancy, price speculation is rampant. Market manipulators abound. In addition, copycat, fantasy, and contemporary limited edition items are being introduced into the market as fast as they can be absorbed. A shakeout appears years in the future. In the interim, check your engine and gear up for fast action.

There are so many horse racing collectibles that one needs to specialize from the beginning. Collector focuses include a particular horse racing type or a specific horse race, a breed or specific horse, or racing prints and images. Each year there are a number of specialized auctions devoted to horse racing, ranging from sporting prints sales at the major New York auction houses to benefit auctions for the Thoroughbred Retirement Foundation.

History: Man's quest for speed is as old as time. Although this category focuses primarily on automobile and horse racing, other types of racing memorabilia are included. If it moves, it will and can be raced.

Automobile racing dates before the turn of the century. Many of the earliest races took place in Europe. By the first decade of the twentieth century, automobile racing was part of the American scene.

The Indianapolis 500 began in 1911 and was interrupted only by World War II. In addition to Formula 1 racing, the NASCAR circuit has achieved tremendous popularity with American racing fans. Cult heroes such as Richard Petty have become household names.

The history of horse racing dates back to the domestication of the horse itself. Prehistoric cave drawings show horse racing. The Greeks engaged in chariot racing as early as 600 B.C. As civilization spread, so did the racing of horses.

Each ethnic group and culture added its own unique slant.

The British developed the concept of the Thoroughbreds, a group of horses that are descendants of three great Arabian stallions— Carley Arabian, Byerley Turk, and Goldolphin Arabian. Receiving royal sponsorship, horse racing became the Sport of Kings.

Horse racing reached America during the colonial period. By the 1800s four–mile match races between regional champions were common. In 1863 Saratoga Race Track was built. The first Belmont Stakes was run at Jerome Park in 1867. As the nineteenth century ended over 300 race tracks operated a seasonal card. By 1908, society's strong reaction against gambling reduced the number of American race tracks to twenty–five.

Of course, the premier American horse race is the Kentucky Derby. Programs date from 1924 and glasses, a favorite with collectors, from the late 1930s.

References: Willis Ackerman, *Dan Patch: Mass Merchandiser*, published by author, 1981; William Boddy, *The History of Motor Racing*, G. P. Putnam's Sons, 1977; Roderick A. Malloy, *Malloy's Sports Collectibles Value Guide: Up–To–Date Prices for Noncard Sports Memorabilia*, Attic Books, Wallace–Homestead, 1993.

Periodicals: *Collector's World*, PO Box 562029, Charlotte, NC 28256; *Racing Collectibles Price Guide*, PO Box 608114, Orlando, FL 32860.

Collectors' Clubs: National Indy 500 Collectors Club, 10505 N. Delaware Street, Indianapolis, IN 46280; Sport of Kings Society, 1406 Annen Lane, Madison, WI 53711.

Museums: Aiken Thoroughbred Racing Hall of Fame & Museum, Aiken, SC; Indianapolis Motor Speedway Hall of Fame Museum, Speedway, IN; International Motor Sports Hall of Fame, Talladega, AL; Harness Racing Hall of Fame, Goshen, NY; The Kentucky Derby Museum, Louisville, KY; National Museum of Racing & Hall of Fame, Saratoga Springs, NY.

AUTO RACING

Catalog, 501 Fiat and Winners 1925 Autodromo, color Mingossi lithos, illus, photogravures	**185.00**
Cigarette Lighter, 2¼" l, Mickey Thompson Speed Equipment, metal, chrome finish, mid 1960s	**20.00**
Cracker Jack Prize, spinner disk, cardboard, five racing cars illus, 1940s	**22.00**
Game, Auto Race Game, multicolored playing board, four metal race cars, four spinners, instructions on back box cov, orig box, Milton Bradley, c1925	**95.00**

500 MILE RACE WINNERS

1920 **Gaston Chevrolet** CAR NO. 4
MONROE • AVG. SPEED 88.62 MPH.

Card, SW, 500 Mile Race Winners, Car No. 4, Gaston Chevrolet, 1920 Monroe, full color image, 3¾ x 2½", $1.00.

Glass, 5¼" h, Indianapolis Motor Speedway, white frosted, red race car, 1950s 25.00
Golf Badge, 1966 Indianapolis Speedway, 500 Festival Golf 28.00
Magazine, *Racing Pictorial*, 8½ x 11", late 1963, 48 pgs 10.00
Pinback Button
  George Vanderbilt Cup Race, multicolored 12.00
  Indianapolis The Speedway City, yellow, red, and black, 1930s 75.00
  Roosevelt Raceway, red, white, and blue, race car image, 1930s 30.00
Post Card, 3½ x 5½", black and white photo, race car 25.00
Toy, Formula–1, Texaco, Marlboro, tin and plastic, orig box 95.00
Tray, 3½ x 4½", Indianapolis Motor Speedway, metal, bronze finish, 1950–60 . . . .   40.00

HORSE RACING

Ashtray, 5¼", china, full color thoroughbred racehorse portrait, Kentucky Derby and Belmont Stakes winner . .   15.00
Badge, 3" d, Budweiser Million, Second Running, August 29, 1982, full color illus 8.00
Glass, 5¼" h
  1964, Kentucky Derby/Churchill Downs, frosted, horse head illus, gold inscription, white lettering on back 12.00
  1964, Kentucky Derby, frosted, brown illus, gold lettering 25.00
  1975, Kentucky Derby, frosted, yellow, black, red, and white accents   12.50
  1977, clear, brown and ivory illus, dark pink roses and green leaves   25.00
  1986, Kentucky Derby, clear, frosted white panel, red roses and green

leaf accents, red and green inscriptions 10.00
Label, 10¼ x 10¼", The Derby Tobacco, framed 150.00
Needle Book, 4½ x 4¾", Steeple Chase, cardboard, full color art, 1930s 25.00
Pass, Florida Jockey Club, 1926 . . . . .   25.00
Pennant, 18" l, Derby Day, felt, red, white lettering, red and white design with pink accents, 1939 . . . .   15.00
Pin, Triple Crown, 1", metal, gold colored, red and white enamel accents, crown and thoroughbred illus, winners' names 8.00
Pinback Button
  Him, Race Horse Special Event, New York Racing Assn, 1975 . . . .   12.00
  Pimlico Preakness, 1¾" d, multicolored, horse head illus, white ground, blue lettering, 1960s 15.00
Print, 20½ x 16", The American Quarter Horse Racing, Randy Steffen, 1972   10.00
Program, 4 x 9", Kentucky Derby, May 4, 1963 . . . .   18.00
Stickpin, brass, jockey cap over entwined initials, green and white enamel accents, dated 1906 . . . . . .   25.00
Ticket
  Kentucky Derby, Saturday, May 2, 1936 . . . .   8.00
  State Fair of Texas, Jockey Club, 1937   35.00
Tray, 13¼ x 21½", 100th Running Kentucky Derby, litho tin, full color illus black rim, gold rose design rim   55.00

MISCELLANEOUS

Game
  Speed Boat Race, Milton Bradley, 1930s 25.00
  The New World To World Airship Race, orig box, The Chicago Game Co 95.00
Medal, 1½" d, American Motorcycle Association National Competition, silvered brass, emb, motorcycle race illus, applied enameled symbol, maroon fabric ribbon, engraved back 200.00
Pinback Button
  Cleveland National Air Races, silver, red, white, and blue, 1932 . . . . . .   50.00
  Linton vs Elkes Bicycle Race, May 30, 1898, Charles River Park, Cambridge, MA, six cyclists image . . .   30.00
  Los Angeles National Air Races, red and white, 1928 . . . .   75.00
  Reno Regatta, multicolored, 1959 . .   25.00
  Spalding Bicycle, Souvenir Cycle Show 1896, purple and white, two racing cyclists 25.00

RADIO CHARACTERS AND PERSONALITIES

Collecting Hints: Many items associated with radio characters and personalities were offered as premiums. This category focuses mostly on the non–premium items. Radio premiums have their own separate listing elsewhere in this book.

Don't overlook the vast amount of material related to the radio shows themselves. This can include scripts, props, and a wealth of publicity material. Collecting autographed photographs was popular, and many appear on the market. Books, especially Big Little Books and similar types, featured many radio–related characters and stories.

Radio characters and personalities found their way into movies and television. Serious collectors do differentiate the products which spun off from these other two areas.

History: The radio show was a dominant force in American life from the 1920s to the early 1950s. Amos and Andy began in 1929, The Shadow in 1930, and Chandu the Magician in 1932. Although many of the characters were fictional, the individuals who portrayed them became public idols. A number of figures achieved fame on their own—Eddie Cantor, Don McNeill of The Breakfast Club, George Burns and Gracie Allen, Arthur Godfrey, and Jack Benny.

Sponsors and manufacturers were quick to capitalize on the fame of the radio characters and personalities. Premiums were offered as part of the shows' themes. However, merchandising did not stop with premiums. Many non–premium materials such as bubble gum cards, figurines, games, publicity photographs, dolls, etc., were issued. Magazine advertisements often featured radio personalities.

References: Norman E. Martinus and Harry L. Rinker, *Warman's Paper,* Wallace–Homestead, 1994; Jon D. Swartz and Robert C. Reinehr, *Handwood of Old–Time Radio: A Comprehensive Guide to Golden Age Radio Listening and Collecting,* Scarecrow Press, 1993; Tom Tumbusch, *Tomart's Price Guide To Radio Premium and Cereal Box Collectibles,* Wallace–Homestead, 1991.

Periodicals: *Friends of Old Time Radio,* PO Box 4321, Hamden, CT 06514; *Old Time Radio Digest,* 4114 Montgomery Rd., Cincinnati, OH 45212.

Collectors' Clubs: Friends of Vic & Sade, 7232 N. Keystone Ave., Lincolnwood, IL 60646-2025; Golden Radio Buffs of Maryland, Inc., 301 Jeanwood Ct., Baltimore, MD 21222; Illinois Old Radio Shows Society, 10 S. 540 County Line Rd., Hinsdale, IL 60521; National Lum & Abner Society, #81 Sharon Blvd., Dora, IL 35062; North America Radio Archives, 134 Vincewood Dr., Nicholasville, KY 40356; Old Time Radio Club, 56 Christen Ct., Lancaster, NY 14086; Old Time Radio Collectors Traders Society, 725 Cardigan Ct., Naperville, IL 60565; Oldtime Radio Show Collectors Association, 45 Barry St., Sudbury, Ontario P3B 3H6 Canada; Pow–Wow, 301 E. Buena Vista Ave., North Augusta, SC 29841; Radio Collectors of America, Ardsley Circle, Brockton, MA 02402; Society To Preserve & Encourage Radio Drama, Variety & Comedy, PO Box 7177, Van Nuys, CA 91409-9712; The Manuscript Society, 350 N. Niagara St., Burbank, CA 91505.

Museum: The Museum of Broadcasting, New York, NY.

See: Big Little Books, Comic Books, Radio Premiums, Super Heroes.

Allen, Jimmie
  Bag, 4 x 6", cloth, drawstring, white, red printing both sides, Cleo Cola logo, bottle cap, and "Listen To The Air Adventures of Jimmie Allen Every Broadcast For Bulletins About Premiums," c1934 . . . . . . **150.00**
  Model, airplane, 19" l, Thunderbolt, 19" l, 24" wingspan, orig box, 1930s **100.00**
Amos 'n Andy
  Booklet, *All About Amos 'n Andy,* photos, scripts, 128 pgs, 1929 . . . **50.00**
  Doll, 5¾" h, wood, jointed, yellow pants, green jacket, black tie, orange hat, 1930s **200.00**
  Game, Card Party, M Davis Co, two score pads, eight tallies, orig box, 1938 . . . . **70.00**
  Get Well Card, 4½ x 5½", black and white photo, Hall Brothers, 1931 **30.00**
  Photo, 5 x 7", browntone, matte finish, Pepsodent Co, 1929 . . . . . . **25.00**
  Puzzle, color scene, Pepsodent Co, copyright 1932 . . . . **75.00**
  Record, two of four, color illus on cov of sleeve, issued by Top Ten, copyright 1947 Gosden & Correll **30.00**
  Sheet Music, 9 x 12", *The Perfect Song/Musical Theme Of The Pepsodent Hour,* copyright 1937, 8 pgs **25.00**
Armstrong, Jack, reel, magnetic tape, The All American Boy Radio Shows, 15 minute episodes, 1940–41, 7 pcs **70.00**
Benny, Jack
  Photo, 8 x 10", black and white glossy, sgd "Jello Again, Jack Benny," 1930s **45.00**
  Program, 9 x 12", Jack Benny Show, black and white photos, Phil Harris signature, 12 pgs, late 1930s **24.00**

Record Set, four 78 rpm records, comedy sketches, Top Ten Records, orig cov, 1947 . . . . **45.00**

Bergen, Edgar and Charlie McCarthy
Bubble Gum Wrapper, Bergen's Better Bubble Gum **6.00**
Get Well Card, talking **20.00**
Pencil Sharpener, figural, diecut plastic, color decal, 1930s **70.00**
Photo, Bergen and Charlie McCarthy **8.00**
Radio, 6" h, plastic, ivory colored, figural, electric, Majestic, c1940 . . . **800.00**
Soap, 4" h, figural, orig box, Kerk Gild, 1930–40 . . . . **75.00**
Ventriloquist Dummy **125.00**

Burns & Allen, coffee server, 1950s, price for complete set **120.00**

Cantor, Eddie
Book, *Eddie Cantor in Laughland,* Goldsmith Publishing Co, 1934 . . **25.00**
Booklet, 4¾ x 6¾", *Cantor's Comics,* issued by Pebeco toothpaste, copyright 1936 Lehn & Fink, Inc, 28 pgs **30.00**
Poster, 11½ x 19", paper, movie and radio show adv, New Pebeco Tooth Paste, 1935–36 . . . . **70.00**

Dragonette, Jessica, photo, 8 x 10", black and white glossy, white ink bold signature "For: S. H Sweiber Your Appreciation Is Very Inspiring–Gratefully Yours, Jessica Dragonette," 1934 . . . . **35.00**

Edwards, Ralph, book, *Radio's Truth or Consequences Party Book,* 1940 . . . **8.00**

Fibber McGee and Molly
Fan Card, 8 x 10", black and white, one large photo and six small photos below **50.00**
Photo, 8 x 10", black and white

Folder, Meet The Radio Folks, Keystone Barn Dance program, black-and-white photos, 12 pages, 1930s, $8.00.

glossy, eleven cast members, Kolynos Dental Cream, copyright 1933 . . . . **55.00**
Record Album, 10¼ x 12", four 78 RPM records, live broadcasts, colorful Fibber design on cover, 1947 **50.00**

Little Orphan Annie
Book, *The Little Orphan Annie Book,* James Whitcomb Riley, color illus by Ethel Betts, 1908 . . . . **25.00**
Glass, 5½" h, The Sunday Funnies, clear, continuous Annie, Sandy, Daddy Warbucks, Asp, and Punjab illus, 1976 . . . . **12.50**
Mug, 5" h, 50 Year Anniversary, plastic, white, red lid, 1932 and 1983 Annie and Sandy illus, Ovaltine premium, 1982 . . . . **15.00**
Salt Shaker, composition **15.00**

Lyman, Abe, photo, 8 x 10", black and white glossy, "The World's Biggest 15 Minute Show" text **30.00**

Major Bowes, clock, 5½" h, metal, brass luster, raised numerals, Ingersol, 1930s **125.00**

Merman, Ethel, sign, 8½ x 12", cardboard, Radio Star Magazine adv . . . **15.00**

Paul, Les, song folio, 1951 . . . . **3.00**

Pearson, Drew, game, Drew Pearson's Predict–A–Word, Deejay Products, copyright 1949 . . . . **50.00**

Penner, Joe
Sheet Music, 9 x 12", *Don't Never Do–o–o That,* black and yellow cov, copyright 1934 T B Harms Co **20.00**
Valentine, 4½ x 7", mechanical, diecut, Penner holding duck on shoulder, eyeballs and mouth move back and forth, "I'll Gladly Buy A Duck," 1930–40 . . . . **20.00**

Quiz Kids, game, electric, Rapaport Bros, orig box and instructions **18.00**

Seckatary Hawkins, record brush, The Ink Spots adv, Decca **15.00**

Sgt Preston
Book, *Sgt Preston and Yukon King,* Rand McNally & Co, copyright 1955, 28 pgs **30.00**
Coloring Book, 8½ x 11½", Whitman, 32 pgs, unused, 1943 . . . . **20.00**
Coloring Set, orig box **50.00**
Goggles, Sgt Preston Trail Goggles, cardboard, red, yellow name, color illus, cut from Quaker cereal box . **50.00**
Poster, 16½ x 22", Quaker Puffed Wheat and Puffed Rice cereal adv, Mounted Police Whistle offer, c1950 . . . . **200.00**
Whistle, brass, gold finish **50.00**

Skippy
Figurine, bisque, jointed arms, Japan, 1930s **60.00**

Playing Cards, 36 numbered cards, Poll parrot shoe sticker on lid, mid 1930s **60.00**

Smith, Kate
Autograph, stationery, 7 x 10″, Office of Kate Smith, A & P Coffee Service, bold signature, 1936 . . . .   **30.00**
Pinback Button, 2¼″ d, photo illus, black and red lettering "Kate Smith's Philadelphia A & P Party, Nov 4, 1935, Hello Everybody" . .   **25.00**

The Shadow
Blotter, 4 x 9″, black, white, red, yellow, and blue, Shadow illus, Lancaster, PA coal company, 1940s   **25.00**
Book, *The Living Shadow,* Maxwell Grant, c1931 . . . .   **8.00**
Figure, 7″ h, china, glossy black cloak and hat, c1930 . . . .   **250.00**
Game, The Shadow, 20″ sq board, one wood token, play money, colored discs, four wood black cap dice, dice shaker, Toy Creations, 1940 . . . .   **250.00**

White, John, Death Valley Days, song folio, *Cowboy Songs in Death Valley,* 1934 . . . .   **8.00**

Winslow, Don, bank, 2¼″ h, Uncle Don's Earnest Saver Club, oval, paper label, photo and cartoon illus, Greenwich Savings Bank, New York City, 1930s **35.00**

RADIO PREMIUMS

Collecting Hints: Most collections are centered around one or two specific personalities or radio programs.

History: Radio premiums are nostalgic reminders of childhood memories of radio shows. Sponsors of shows frequently used their products to promote the collection of premiums, such as saving box tops to exchange for gifts tied in with the program or personality.

References: Norman E. Martinus and Harry L. Rinker, *Warman's Paper,* Wallace–Homestead, 1994; Robert M. Overstreet, *Overstreet Premium Ring Price Guide,* Gemstone Publishing, 1995; Tom Tumbusch, *Tomart's Price Guide To Radio Premium and Cereal Box Collectibles,* Wallace–Homestead, 1991.

Periodical: *Box Top Bonanza,* 3403 46th Ave., Moline, IL 61265.

REPRODUCTION ALERT

See: Radio Characters and Personalities.

Amos 'n' Andy
Book, 6 x 8″, 128 pgs, Rand McNally & Co, copyright 1929, hard cover, autographed **250.00**
Map, 15 x 20″, Webber City, cartoon illus, orig cover letter and mailing envelope, Pepsodent Toothpaste, 1935 . . . .   **60.00**

Benny, Jack, promotional booklet, Zenith Radios, Burns & Allen, Boswells, 1930s **40.00**

Buck Rogers
Helmet, child's, stiff paper, multicolored, Cocomalt, c1933 . . . .   **175.00**
Photo, 7½ x 10″, glossy, Buck and Wilma, cov letter, facsimile signatures, Cocomalt, c1934 . . . .   **80.00**

Captain Midnight
Iron–On Transfer, 4″ d, Captain Midnight's Secret Squadron, orig envelope, Ovaltine, c1948 . . . . .   **110.00**
Photo, 6 x 7½″, Chuck Ramsey, black and white, matte, white facsimile signature, Captain Midnight's ward, Skelly Oil, c1939 . . . .   **65.00**
Shake–Up Mug, 5″ h, plastic, orange, blue lid, raised portrait, "Remember Your Secret Squadron Pledge," Ovaltine, c1947 . . . .   **90.00**

Counter–Spy, Certificate, 6 x 8½″, Counter–Spy Junior Agents Club, paper, Pepsi–Cola, c1950 . . . .   **25.00**

Fibber McGee & Molly, menu, 9½ x 12¼″, stiff paper, Brown Derby Restaurant, autographed **100.00**

Little Orphan Annie
Handbook, 3¾ x 8½″, Secret Guard,

Just Plain Bill, Kolynos Dental Cream giveaway, 150 pcs, orig envelope, 12 x 9″, $30.00.

paper sheet, decoder, clicker, orig mailing envelope, Quaker Puffed Wheat Sparkies and Rice Sparkies, 1941 . . . .   **90.00**

Manual, Secret Society, 8 pgs, password, signs, and signals, Ovaltine, 1938 . . . .   **60.00**

Mug, 3″ h, white ceramic, Annie and Sandy illus, Ovaltine, 1932 . . . . .   **65.00**

Puzzle, 9 x 12½″, Tucker County Horse Race, orig instruction sheet and mailing box, Ovaltine, c1933   **70.00**

Shake–Up Mug, 5″ h, Beetleware, brown, orange lid, decal, Ovaltine, 1937 . . . .   **60.00**

Sheet Music, 8¾ x 11¼″, *Little Orphan Annie's Song*, 4 pgs, black and white, Harold Gray illus cov, Ovaltine, 1931 . . . .   **24.00**

Lone Ranger

Badge, star shape, two–tone brass, "A Republic Serial/The Lone Ranger," 1938 . . . .   **70.00**

Ring, brass bands, plastic six–gun, sparking, 1947 . . . .   **75.00**

Lum And Abner, family almanac, 6 x 9″, 34 pgs, orig mailing envelope, Horlick's Malted Milk, 1936 . . . . . .   **40.00**

McCarthy, Charlie, game, Radio Party, orig mailing envelope, complete, 1938 . . . .   **35.00**

Mix, Tom

Arrowhead, 2½ x 3½″, lucite, clear, whistle, siren, and magnifying lens, Ralston, 1949 . . . .   **70.00**

Catalog, 8¼ x 10¼″, premiums, folder, paper **25.00**

Decoder, brass, revolving six–guns, 1941 . . . .   **85.00**

ID Bracelet, silvered brass chain, disc, two six–guns, letter "J," Ralston address and serial number, 1947 . . . .   **50.00**

Purvis, Melvin

Badge, 1½″ h, two–toned brass, black and red enamel, "Roving Operative Melvin Purvis Junior G–Man Corps," 1936 . . . .   **25.00**

Ring, adjustable, brass, eagle and shield design, 1936 . . . .   **30.00**

Sgt Preston

Flashlight, 3″ l, plastic, black, red and green color discs, facsimile signature, "Challenge of the Yukon" copyright 1949 . . . .   **25.00**

Photo **35.00**

The Shadow

Blotter, 4 x 9″, red, white, and blue, Shadow silhouette, Lancaster, PA coal company, 1940s **50.00**

Matchbook Cover, 1½ x 4″ open size,

black and red silhouette illus, skeleton holding dagger, diecut portrait flap inside, Pawtucket, RI sponsor, 1940s **30.00**

Ring, alligator, plastic, white day glow, black plastic insert, Carey Salt, 1947 . . . .   **575.00**

Sky King

Figure, set of 6, 2½″ h, plastic, Sky King, Clipper, Penny, Sheriff, Songbird, and Yellow Fury, 1950s   **150.00**

Newspaper Advertisement, 11½ x 15½″, Name–A–Plane Contest, 1950s **25.00**

Superman, ring, Superman Crusader, silvered brass, 1938–40 . . . .   **160.00**

Tracy, Dick, ring, litho tin, Post Raisin Brand, copyright 1948 . . . .   **25.00**

RADIOS

Collecting Hints: Radio collectors divide into three groups: those who collect because of nostalgia, those interested in history and/or acquiring radios that represent periods prior to or after World War II, and collectors of personality and figural radios. Most collectors find broadcasting, and therefore broadcast receivers, their primary interest.

The significant divisions of broadcast receivers that are represented in a small collection are:

—Crystal sets and battery powered receivers of the early 1920s
—Rectangular electric table models of the late 1920s
—Cathedrals, tombstones, and consoles of the 1930s
—Midget plastic portables and wood cabinet table models built before and after World War II
—Shaped Bakelite and other plastic cased radios
—Personality and figural radios beginning in the 1930s and extending into the 1960s.

Because the emphasis for nostalgia seems to fall on the decade of the 1930s, the cathedral–style, socket–powered radios, e.g., the Philco series, have become sought after items. Recently the younger set has exhibited a very strong nostalgia interest in the plastic cabinet radios built between 1945 and 1960.

The underlying force that values a radio to a traditional collector, and consequently sets the price in the market, is rarity. Very rare radios usually go directly to major collectors, seldom appearing in the general market. Wireless equipment and radios used commercially before

World War I are considered rare and are not listed here.

With the newer radio collector, the controlling force is novelty with the outside appearance the primary feature. The radio must play; but, shape, color, decoration, and condition of the case far outweigh the internal workings of the set in determining desirability and consequently the price. Enclosures that represent things or figures e.g., Mickey Mouse, command premium prices.

The prices of 1920s radio sets have been stabilized by collectors' demands. Typical prices are listed. The values of 1930s radios fall into two ranges. Cathedrals bring an average of $100 to $150, with Philco and Atwater Kent on the high end and names like Airline and Stewart Warner on the low end. Consoles bring substantially lower prices, seldom reaching $100 except for very ornate models, such as the Victrola Hyperion or Orchestrion and the Atwater Kent Model 812.

The squarish table models of the later 1930s and the midget sets of the late 1930s and 1940s recently have attracted the attention of nostalgia buffs and new collectors. Generally their demand in the face of supply keeps their price low, holding below $75. An exception to this rule is based on decoration. Columns, figurework, and dramatic changes in texture add interest and raise the potential prices. A radio with columns outlining the dial or the speaker opening can command $150. Another exception to this is the novelty radio. Treasure chest barrels, mirrored cases, and specialty items bring prices as high as $500.

The value of a radio is directly related to its condition. The critical factors are appearance and operability. The prices listed are for sets of average to good condition and based on an electrically complete receiver that operates when powered.

Minor scratches are to be expected as is alligatoring of the surface finish. Gouges, cracks, and delaminated surfaces will cut the price by 50%. However, the penalty for a crack or broken place for plastic closures is severe. A Catalin radio with a blue case might bring $400–$600 in good condition, but with a visible crack the price drops to $30.

If parts, tubes, or components are missing or if major repairs must be made in order for the set to work, the price again must be reduced by as much as 50%. A particular radio that is unrestored, in excellent or mint condition, and playing satisfactorily can command an increase of 30 to 50% over the prices listed below.

In addition to radios, many collectors specialize in a facet of the general radio art such as loudspeakers, tubes, microphones, memorabilia, or brand names. As a result, auxiliary and related radio items are becoming collectibles along with radios themselves.

History: The art and science of radio as a communication medium is barely ninety years old. Marconi was the first to assemble and employ the transmission and reception instruments that permitted electric message-sending without the use of direct connections. The early name for radio was "Wireless," and the first application was in 1898 as a means of controlling ships. Early wireless equipment is not generally considered a collectible since its historic value makes it important for museum display.

Between 1905 and the end of World War I many technical advances, including the invention of the vacuum tube by DeForest, resulted in an extensive communication art and a very strong amateur interest in the strange new technology. The receiving equipment from that period is considered highly desirable by collectors and historians but is rarely available outside the main body of early radio and wireless collectors.

By 1920, radio technology offered the means to talk to large numbers of people simultaneously and bring music from concert halls directly into living rooms. The result was the development of a new art that changed the American way of life during the 1920s. The world became familiar in the average listener's home.

Radio receivers changed substantially in the decade of the 1920s. They progressed from black boxes with many knobs and dials powered by expensive and messy batteries, to styled furniture pieces that were simple to use and operated from the house current that had become the standard source of energy for service in the home. During the 1920s radios grew more complicated and powerful as well as more ornate. Consoles appeared, loudspeakers were incorporated into them, and sound fidelity joined distance as criteria for quality.

In the early 1930s demand changed. The large expensive console gave way to small but effective table models. The era of the "cathedral" and the "tombstone" began. By the end of the 1930s, the midget radio had become popular. Quality of sound was replaced by reduction of price and most homes had more than one radio.

Shortly after World War II the miniature tubes developed for the military were applied to domestic radios. The result was further reduction in size with a substantial improvement in quality. The advent of FM also speeded the development. Plastic technology made possible the production of attractive cases in many styles and colors.

The other development that drastically changed the radio receiver was the invention of the transistor in 1927. A whole new family of radio sets that could be carried in the shirt pocket became popular. As they became less and less expensive, their popularity grew rapidly. Consequently, they were throwaways when they stopped working. Today they are not easy to find in good condition and are quite collectible.

References: Robert F. Breed, *Collecting Transistor Novelty Radios: A Value Guide*, L–W Books, 1990; John H. Bryant and Harold N. Cones, *The Zenith Trans–Oceanic: The Royalty of Radios*, Schiffer Publishing, 1995; Marty and Sue Bunis, *Collector's Guide To Antique Radios, Third Edition* Collector Books, 1995; Marty and Sue Bunis, *Collector's Guide To Transistor Radios*, Collector Books, 1994; Marty Bunis and Robert F. Breed, *Collector's Guide To Novelty Radios*, Collector Books, 1995; Philip Collins, *Radio Redux: Listening In Style*, Chronicle Books, 1992; Philip Collins, *Radios: The Golden Age*, Chronicle Books, 1987; Alan Douglas, *Radio Manufacturers of the 1920's, Volume I* (1988), *Volume 2* (1989), and *Volume 3* (1991), The Vestal Press; Robert Grinder and George Fathauer, *Radio Collector's Directory and Price Guide,*, Ironwood Press, 1986; Roger Handy, Maureen Erbe, and Aileen Farnan Antonier, *Made In Japan: Transistor Radios of the 1950s and 1960s*, Chronicle Books, 1993; David Johnson, *Antique Radio Restoration Guide, Second Edition*, Wallace–Homestead, 1992; David R. Lane and Robert A. Lane, *Transistor Radios: A Collector's Encyclopedia and Price Guide*, Wallace–Homestead, 1994; Michael Lawlor, *Lawlor's Radio Values: Catalin, Character Mirrored, Novelty, Plastic*, Bare Bones Press, 1991; Harry Poster, *Poster's Radio & Television Price Guide: 1920–1990, Second Edition* Wallace–Homestead, 1994; Harry Poster, *The Illustrated Price Guide To Vintage Televisions and Deco Radios*, published by author, 1991; Ron Ramirez, *Philco Radio: 1928–1942*, Schiffer Publishing, 1993; John Sideli, *Classic Plastic Radios of the 1930s and 1940s: A Collector's Guide To Catalin Radios*, E. P. Dutton, 1990; Scott Wood (ed.), *Evolution Of The Radio*, Vol I (1991, 1994 value update), Vol II (1993), L–W Book Sales.

Periodicals: *Antique Radio Classified*, PO Box 2, Carlisle, MA 01746; *Radio Age*, 636 Cambridge Road, Augusta, GA 30909; *The Horn Speaker*, PO Box 1193, Mabank, TX 75147; *Transistor Network*, RR1, Box 36, Bradford, NH 03221.

Collectors' Clubs: Antique Radio Club of America, 300 Washington Trails, Washington, PA 15301; Antique Wireless Association, 59 Main St., Bloomfield, NY 14469; New England Antique Radio Club, RR1 Box 36, Bradford, NH 03221; Vintage Radio & Phonograph Society, Inc., PO Box 165345, Irving, TX 75016.

Museums: Antique Wireless Association's Electronic Communication Museum, Bloomfield, NY; Caperton's Radio Museum, Louisville, KY; Muchow's Historical Radio Museum, Elgin, IL; Museum of Broadcast Communications, Chicago, IL; Museum of Wonderful Wireless, Minneapolis, MN; New England Museum of

Wireless and Steam, East Greenwich, RI; Voice of the Twenties, Orient, NY.

Advisor: Lewis S. Walters.

Admiral
#33, #35, #37, portable, 1940s	**25.00**
#218, portable, leatherette, 1958 . . .	**40.00**
#909, All World, portable, 1960 . . .	**85.00**

Air King, #1946, tombstone, Art Deco,
plastic, 1935	**3,000.00**

Arvin
Character, Hopalong Cassidy, lariatenna	**475.00**
#522A, table, metal, ivory, 1941 . . .	**60.00**
#617, Rhythm Maid, tombstone, 1936	**215.00**

Atwater Kent
#9A, breadboard	**550.00**
#10, breadboard	**1,000.00**
#10C	**825.00**
#55, table, Keil	**225.00**
#80, cathedral, 1931	**380.00**

Bulova
#100, clock, 1957	**40.00**
#120, clock, 1958	**40.00**

Crosley
#1–N, Litfella, cathedral	**175.00**
#122, Super Buddy Boy, 1930	**325.00**
#601, Bandbox, 1927	**75.00**
#609, Gemchest, 1928	**410.00**
#706, Showbox, 1928	**100.00**
Pup, box	**560.00**
Sheraton Cathedral, 1933	**290.00**
X Table Radio, 1922	**175.00**

Dumont, #RA–346, table model, scroll
work, 1956	**110.00**

Emerson
#400
Aristocrat, catalin, 1940	**600.00**
Patriot, 1940	**750.00**
#409, Mickey Mouse, wood, black and red metal trim, 1933	**1,300.00**
#411, Mickey Mouse, pressed wood, Mickey playing instrument, 1933	**1,400.00**
#570, Memento, picture holder, 1945	**110.00**
#640, portable, plastic, flip–up front, battery set, 1950	**30.00**
#AU–190, tombstone, catalin, 1938	**1,000.00**
#BT–245, tombstone, catalin, scalloped dial, darker grill	**1,000.00**

FADA
#43, cathedral, pressed wood	**240.00**
#60W, table, plastic	**75.00**
#136, table, catalin, 1941	**1,000.00**
#252, Temple, table, catalin, 1941 . .	**575.00**

Federal
#58DX, table, 1922	**500.00**
#110, table, 1924	**425.00**

General Electric
Clock Radios #515, #517, 1950s . .	**30.00**
Console, #K–126, wood, 1933	**150.00**

Fada, 1930–1940, $40.00.

Table Radios, #400, #410, #411,
#414, all plastic 30.00
Grebe
#CR–12, table, 1923 . . . . 600.00
#MU–1, table, with chain, 1925 . . . 200.00
Hallicrafters
TW–200, World Wide 110.00
TW–600, portable, with map and
whip antenna, AC/DC/battery,
1954 . . . . 100.00
Majestic
Charlie McCarthy, 1938 . . . . 1,000.00
Console, #92, 1929 . . . . 125.00
Treasure Chest, #381, 1934 . . . . 225.00
Motorola
Jet Plane Transistor, #7X23E 55.00
Jewel Box, #5J1 . . . .   80.00
M Logo, transistor, 1960 . . . .   25.00
Pixie Transistor 45.00
Ranger
#700, 1957 . . . .   45.00
Portable, leatherette trim 40.00
Table, plastic, 1950s 35.00
Olympic, wood, with phonograph, lift
top 40.00
Paragon
#DA–2, table, 1921 . . . . 450.00
#RD–5, table, 1922 . . . . 600.00
Philco
#17–20–38, cathedral 250.00
#37–602, table, Art Deco grill 90.00
#46–132, table 35.00
#40–180, console, wood 130.00
#49–506, Transitone 35.00
#T–7–126, transistor, plastic 65.00
#T1000, table, clock 80.00
Radiobar, complete console, glasses
and decanter 1,200.00
Radio Corporation of America, RCA
#6X7, table, plastic, 1956 . . . .   25.00
#40X56, 1939 World's Fair 975.00

#8BT–7LE, portable transistor, 1957   **35.00**
Radiola
#18 . . . .   **55.00**
#24 . . . . **160.00**
#28, console, highboy **200.00**
#33 . . . .   **40.00**
La Siesta, 1939 . . . . **300.00**
Silvertone, Sears
#1, table, 1950 . . . .   **75.00**
#1582, cathedral, wood **225.00**
Sony
#TFM–151, transistor, 1960 . . . .   **50.00**
#TR–63, transistor, 1958 . . . . **140.00**
Sparton, #506, Bluebird, table, round
blue or peach mirror **3,600.00**
Stewart–Warner, table, slant, 1938 . . . **175.00**
Zenith
#6D2615, table, boomerang dial,
1942 . . . .   **95.00**
Royal, transistor, 1959
#500, owl eye **75.00**
#500D, plastic **55.00**
#750L, leather case **40.00**
Trans–Oceanic **100.00**

RAILROAD ITEMS

Collecting Hints: Most collectors concentrate on
one railroad as opposed to one type of object.
Railroad material always brings a higher price in
the area from which it originated. Local collectors tend to concentrate on local railroads.
Material from railroads which operated for only a
short time realizes the highest prices. Nostalgia
also influences the collector.

There are many local railroad clubs. Railroad
buffs tend to have their own specialized swap
meets and exhibitions. A large one is held in
Gaithersburg, Maryland, in the fall each year.

History: It was a canal company, the Delaware
and Hudson, which used the first steam locomotive in America. The Stourbridge Lion moved
coal from the mines to the canal wharfs. Just as
America was entering its great canal era in 1825,
the railroad was gaining a foothold. William
Strickland recommended to the Commonwealth
of Pennsylvania that they not build canals, but
concentrate on the railroad. His advice went un-
heeded.

By the 1840s the railroad was established.
Numerous private companies, many in business
for only a short time, were organized.

The Civil War demonstrated the effectiveness
of the railroad. Immediately following the war
the Transcontinental Railroad was completed,
and entrepreneurs such as Gould and Vanderbilt
constructed financial empires built on railroads.
Mergers created huge systems. The golden age of
the railroad extended from the 1880s to the
1940s.

After 1950 the railroads suffered from poor management, a bloated labor force, lack of maintenance, and competition from other forms of transportation. The 1970s saw the federal government enter the picture through Conrail and Amtrak. Thousands of miles of track were abandoned. Many railroads failed or were merged. Today the system still is fighting for survival.

References: Susan and Al Bagdade, *Warman's American Pottery and Porcelain,* Wallace–Homestead, 1994; Stanley L. Baker, *Railroad Collectibles: An Illustrated Value Guide, Fourth Edition,* Collector Books, 1990, 1993 value update; Richard C. Barrett, *The Illustrated Encyclopedia of Railroad Lighting, Volume 1: The Railroad Lantern,* Railroad Research Publications, 1994; Phil Bollhagen, (comp.), *The Great Book Of Railroad Playing Cards,* published by author, 1991; Arthur Dominy and Rudolph A. Morgenfruh, *Silver At Your Service,* published by authors, 1987; Richard Luckin, *Dining On Rails,* RK Publishing, 1994; Richard Luckin, *Mimbres to Mimbreno: A Study of Sante Fe's Famous China Pattern,* RK Publishing, 1992; Richard Luckin, *Teapot Treasury and Related Items,* RK Publishing, 1987; Everett L. Maffett, *Silver Banquet II,* Silver Press, 1990; Norman E. Martinus and Harry L. Rinker, *Warman's Paper,* Wallace–Homestead, 1994; Douglas McIntyre, *The Official Guide To Railroad Dining Car China,* Walsworth Press, 1990; Larry R. Paul, *Sparkling Crystal: A Collector's Guide To Railroad Glassware,* Railroadiana Collectors Assoc., Inc., 1990; Don Stewart, *Railroad Switch Keys & Padlocks, 2nd Edition,* Key Collectors International, 1993.

Periodicals: *Key, Lock and Lantern,* PO Box 65, Demarest, NJ 07627; *U. S. Rail News,* PO Box 7007, Huntingdon Woods, MI 48070.

Collectors' Clubs: Chesapeake & Ohio Historical Society, Inc., PO Box 79, Clifton Forge, VA 24422; Illinois Central Railroad Historical Society, 14818 Cliron Park, Midlothian, IL 60445; Railroad Enthusiasts, 102 Dean Rd., Brookline, MA 02146; Railroadiana Collectors Association, 795 Aspen Drive, Buffalo Grove, IL 60089; Railway and Locomotive Historical Society, PO Box 1418, Westford, MA 01886; The Twentieth Century Railroad Club, 329W. 18th St., Ste 902, Chicago, IL 60616.

Museums: Baltimore and Ohio Railroad, Baltimore, MD; Museum of Transportation, Brookline, MA; New York Museum of Transportation, West Henrietta, NY; California State Railroad Museum, Sacramento, CA.

Almanac, "Every Man's Almanac," presented by MO Pacific Lines, 1927 ..	**22.50**
Annual Report	
Atchison, Topeka & SF, 1929, 17 x 28" map	**25.00**

Boston Elevated Railway, 1924	**8.00**
Fitchburg, Mass, 1873	**12.00**
Ashtray, porcelain, VP, shield logo	**20.00**
Atlas, Atlas of Railway Traffic Maps, Wymond, LaSalle University, Interstate Commerce Course, 1919, folio, 29 foldout maps	**35.00**
Badge, VP, conductor's hat type, gold plated	**75.00**
Baggage Sticker	
Milwaukee Road, "Hiawatha," 3½" d, streamlined Hiawatha steam locomotive, multicolored	**5.00**
Santa Fe, "El Capitan," 3" d, Santa Fe logo, red, yellow, black, and white	**4.50**
Better Little Book, *Union Pacific,* Cecil B DeMille	**25.00**
Blotter, Soo Line, unused, 1920s	**1.75**
Book	
Hollenback, *Pikes Peak by Rail,* 1962, 1st edition, soft cover	**18.00**
Miller, *The Golden Spike,* Utah State, 1973, 1st edition	**25.00**
Starr, *Lincoln and the Railroads,* 1927, 1st edition	**35.00**
Booklets and Brochures	
Canadian Pacific, "Montreal Viewbook," 1915	**8.00**
Erie, "The Erie Limited," 8½ x 11", June, 1929, three large panels, nine int. views, four ext. views of equipment, blue and white cov	**15.00**
Lehigh Valley, "Claremont—The Great Terminal of the World's Great Port," 7 x 10", c1920, data and bird's eye view of Jersey City facility	**18.00**
Northern Pacific RR, 1913	**30.00**
Oregon and Idaho Railroad, locomotive on cov	**20.00**
Pacific RR, "Wayside Notes on Sunset Route"	**8.00**
Salt Lake Route, "Southern California Mid–Winter Excursion," four panels, Feb, 1913	**8.00**
Boxcar Seal, lead, set of 4	**15.00**
Calendar	
1934, GN RR, Reiss painting	**50.00**
1940, Santa Fe RR, End Of The Trail	**75.00**
1949, CNW RR	**35.00**
1953, PRR, illus only	**60.00**
1956, PRR, illus only	**60.00**
1960, UP RR	**10.00**
Catalog, Pullman Coach Co, 1920 . . .	**16.00**
China	
Bouillon Cup	
CM St P	**30.00**
Pennsylvania Railway	**35.00**
Butter Pat	
B & O, Centenary, Shenango backstamp	**45.00**
Santa Fe RR, blue and white	**35.00**

Hat, conductor's, Milwaukee RR, Carlson
& Company, Chicago, IL, $35.00.

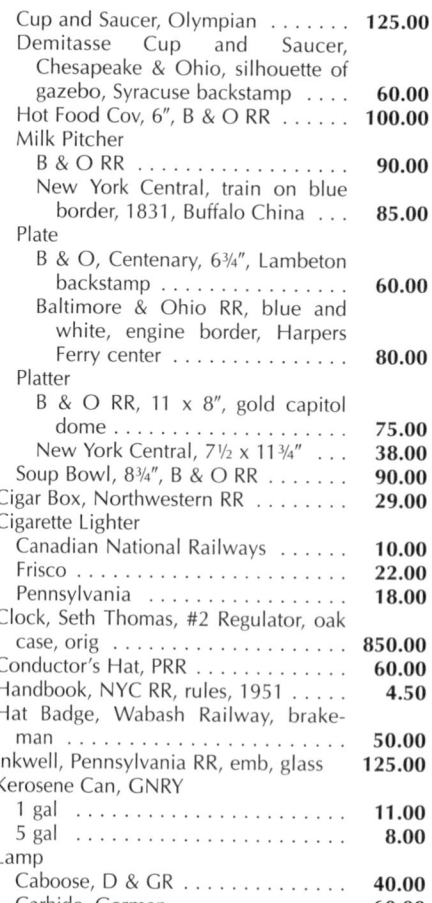

Calendar, C & O Railroad, Chessie,
Charles E. Bracker artist, 1947, 15 x 24",
$24.00.

Cup and Saucer, Olympian 125.00
Demitasse   Cup   and   Saucer,
 Chesapeake & Ohio, silhouette of
 gazebo, Syracuse backstamp 60.00
Hot Food Cov, 6", B & O RR 100.00
Milk Pitcher
 B & O RR 90.00
 New York Central, train on blue
  border, 1831, Buffalo China . . . 85.00
Plate
 B & O, Centenary, 6¾", Lambeton
  backstamp 60.00
 Baltimore & Ohio RR, blue and
  white, engine border, Harpers
  Ferry center 80.00
Platter
 B & O RR, 11 x 8", gold capitol
  dome 75.00
 New York Central, 7½ x 11¾" . . . 38.00
Soup Bowl, 8¾", B & O RR 90.00
Cigar Box, Northwestern RR 29.00
Cigarette Lighter
 Canadian National Railways 10.00
 Frisco 22.00
 Pennsylvania 18.00
Clock, Seth Thomas, #2 Regulator, oak
 case, orig 850.00
Conductor's Hat, PRR 60.00
Handbook, NYC RR, rules, 1951 . . . . . 4.50
Hat Badge, Wabash Railway, brake-
 man 50.00
Inkwell, Pennsylvania RR, emb, glass 125.00
Kerosene Can, GNRY
 1 gal 11.00
 5 gal 8.00
Lamp
 Caboose, D & GR 40.00
 Carbide, German 60.00

Lantern
 B & O, Adams & Westlake, hand,
  clear cast 5⅜" globe 65.00
 Belt Railroad, hand type 45.00
 C M St P & P, red globe, unfired . . . 65.00
 Chicago, Milwaukee, & St Paul,
  switch, emb metal, 5½" globe . . . 60.00
 D & H RR, Adlake Kero, red 3¼"
  globe 25.00
 D SS & A, amber globe 90.00
 GNRY, Adams & Westlake, Adlake
  Reliable, 5⅜" clear globe, "Safety
  Always" 175.00
 Missouri Kansas Texas, amber globe,
  etching 60.00
 MK & T RR, bell bottom, etched
  globe 120.00
 PRR, Keystone Casey, hand, 1903,
  clear cast 5⅜" globe, cleaned to
  metal, keystone logo 35.00
 Rock Island, clear globe 50.00
 Southern, Armspear Manufacturing,
  hand, clear cast 5⅜" globe 75.00
Letter Opener, Pacific Railroad, brass 40.00
Linens
 Headrest Cover
  Norfolk & Western, tan, red name 10.00
  Seaboard Coast Lines, gold, light
   blue letters, train illus 10.00
 Napkin
  Pennsylvania Railroad 12.00
  Rock Island Lines, logo in center 10.00
  Seaboard Railway, linen, pr 50.00
 Tablecloth
  B & O, 40" sq, train in center,
   "Linking the Great Train with the
   Nation" 40.00
  Frisco Railway, 36" sq, white,
   Frisco emblem, white on white 30.00
  Union Pacific, pink, bridge table
   size 25.00
 Towel
  Illinois Central, dated "64," white,
   red letters 10.00

Penn Central 4.50
Pullman, white and blue 8.00
Lock, steel, emb "CR RR" 125.00
Magazine, Saturday Evening Post, May
8, 1943, "A Night on Troop Train,"
Norman Rockwell illus, 2 pgs of
sketches 50.00
Map
United States, Canada, Indian territo-
ries, 1855, tinted, 21½ x 31½" . . .   175.00
Wisconsin, linen, routes of 41 rail-
roads, 1898 . . . .   135.00
Match Holder, Burlington Zephyr, stain-
less steel 22.00
Matchbook, gift pack
Delaware/Hudson 10.00
Soo Line 12.00
Union Pacific 15.00
Matchsafe, Union Pacific, aluminum,
emb 56.00
Meal Ticket, Santa Fe, 1920 . . . .   4.00
Menu
Canadian Pacific Railroad, 1928 . . .   6.00
Frisco, dinner, 6 x 9¼", color cov . .   6.50
Great Northern, 1944 . . . .   12.50
Lehigh Valley, A la Carte Breakfast,
c1950, logo in lower corner 3.75
Santa Fe, Super Chief, luncheon,
folder, 1971, unused 4.25
Meter, Chicago trolley, brass, orig bell   200.00
Milk Bottle, Missouri Pacific, half pint   10.00
Model, steam engine and tender,
inscribed "Model of the Hudson
type locomotive used in the 20th
Century—service built by American
Locomotive Co for New York Central
Lines," sgd Van Gytenbeck Sales Co
Inc, New York, 1928 . . . .   185.00
Notebook, Missouri Pacific 16.00
Paperweight, Missouri Pacific RR 55.00
Pass
Atchison, Topeka & Santa Fe 3.50
Erie RR 8.00
Erie RR Veteran Assoc 12.00
Pennsylvania RR 10.00
Pin, 25 Year Rutland Service 16.00
Playing Cards
C & O RR, Peake Chessie's "Old
Man" 5.00
Chicago, Milwaukee & St Paul, 53
scenic views, orig box, 1919 . . . .   40.00
New York, New Haven & Hartford
RR, orig wrapper and box 65.00
Southern Pacific 20.00
Postcard
Depot, interior view 1.50
Freedom Train, 6¼ x 8", full color
"Spirit of 1776" streamliner engine,
General Electric logo, American
Heritage Foundation, 1949 copy-
right, unused 10.00
Train Wreck, c1900 . . . .   1.50

Posters and Signs
Chicago Aurora & Elgin RR, "Bad
Order" placard, 3½ x 8", stiff card   1.50
New York Central, poster/handbill,
"State Fair–Syracuse–Sept 7 to Sept
12, 1931," includes fare chart from
numerous stations on upstate
branch lines, old NYC oval herald
with speeding locomotive at bot-
tom 6.00
Old Colony Line to Cottage City,
Oak Bluffs, Martha's Vineyard &
Nantucket, wall poster, map of
line and connections, c1880, 18 x
28" 30.00
Railway Express Agency, depot ext.,
yellow letters, black porcelainized
steel, 11½ x 72" 150.00
Schedule, Southern Pacific RR, 1927 . .   7.50
Service Pin, Pennsylvania, locomotive
illus 18.00
Silver Flatware and Holloware
Caster Set, Chicago, Burlington, and
Quincy, three bottles, California
Zephyr route, SP frame 150.00
Coffeepot
PRR, individual, International Sil-
ver Co, 10 oz 85.00
Union Pacific, hinged cov, wing
finial, Challenger pattern,
marked "International Silver Co,
32 oz" 250.00
Creamer, Wabash, 2 oz, backstamped
International Silver 45.00
Creamer and Sugar, Atchison, Topeka
& Santa Fe, SP, bottom stamped
"Fred Harvey, Gorham Mfg Co" . .   60.00
Crumb Scraper, Louisville/Nashville
RR 45.00
Dish Cover, Rock Island Lines, SP,
1927 . . . .   120.00
Fork
Dinner, Southern Pacific,
Broadway pattern 8.50
Oyster, NYC, Century pattern, un-
derside marked "NYC" 10.00
Pickle, Rock Island Lines, 5¼" . . .   5.00
Knife
Bread and Butter, ACL, Zephyr pat-
tern, handle marked "ACL" 8.00
Dinner, New York Central 10.00
Spoon
Iced Tea, MP Lines, Century pattern   18.00
Soup, Frisco, Art Nouveau style . .   25.00
Sugar Bowl, cov, Burlington Railroad,
silver, double handles, Reed &
Barton 75.00
Sugar Tongs, Southern RR 26.00
Teapot, Union Pacific, SP, marked
"Reed & Barton" 40.00
Tray, oval, 8", International 1936,
backstamped 25.00

Vase, GM & O, bud, 7", backstamped
  International Silver **75.00**
Stocks and Bonds
  Buffalo and Susquehanna Railroad,
    100 shares preferred, engraved
    borders in orange–rust, vignette of
    steam locomotive hauling coal
    train, issued and canceled **20.00**
  Erie RR Co, stock certificate, 1950s   **8.00**
  Erie–Lackawanna Railroad Co, stock
    certificate, 1960s **6.00**
  Gulf Mobile & Northern, stock certifi-
    cate, train vignette, issued **7.50**
  New Haven & Northampton, $5,000
    bond, engraved vignette of speed-
    ing steam locomotive pulling pas-
    senger train, unissued **12.00**
Survey Lithograph, Pacific RR, 1855 . . **17.50**
Switch Key
  Chicago & Northwestern **13.00**
  Illinois Valley & Northern **55.00**
  Michigan Central **25.00**
  Monon **12.00**
  Pere Marquette **30.00**
  San Antonio & Arkansas Pass **24.00**
Tape Measure, N. &W. RR, 50 ft **23.00**
Ticket Puncher, conductor's **18.00**
Timetable
  Chesapeake & Ohio, 1957 . . . . **5.00**
  Great Northern RR, 1896 . . . . **40.00**
  Illinois Central, 1961 . . . . **5.00**
  New York Central, 1959 . . . . **6.00**
  Rutland, 1957 . . . . **5.00**
  Santa Fe, 1962 . . . . **5.00**
  Southern Pacific, 1948 . . . . **10.00**
  Union Pacific, 1963 . . . . **6.00**
Token
  B & O, brass, 1927 . . . . **20.00**
  C & O, "Good for Sanitary Cup,"
    brass **14.00**
  Union Pacific, 1934 . . . . **5.00**
Tool, raises coach window, hinged . . . **75.00**
Uniform, brakeman's, C & O, coat,
  pants, vest, and hat **450.00**
Wax Seal, mushroom shape top,
  marked "S Jackson, Conductor" **45.00**
Whistle
  Peanut, C & O RR, brass **40.00**
  Steam, brass
    3" **110.00**
    10" I valve **100.00**

RAZORS

Collecting Hints: A major revolution occurred in razor collecting in the 1980s. At the beginning of the decade almost all collectors focused on the straight razor. By the late 1980s the collecting of safety razors and their related material as well as electric shavers had achieved a popularity that should equal or exceed that of straight razor collecting in the 1990s.

Many straight razor collectors focus on the products of a single manufacturer. Value is increased by certain names, e.g., H. Boker, Case, M. Price, Joseph Rogers, Simmons Hardware, Will & Finck, Winchester, and George Wostenholm. The ornateness of the handle and blade pattern also influences value. The fancier the handle or more intricately etched the blade, the higher the price. Rarest handle materials are pearl, stag, Sterling silver, pressed horn, and carved ivory. Rarest blades are those with scenes etched across the entire front.

Initially safety razor collectors focused on those razors that were packaged in elaborately lithographed tins during the 1890 to 1915 period. Since a safety razor involves several items, i.e., razor, blades, case or tin, instructions, etc., completeness is a critical factor. Support items such as blade banks, boxes, and sharpeners also attract collectors. Many safety razors from the early period already exceed $50. As a result, new collectors are seeking safety razors from the 1920s through the 1950s because a comprehensive collection can still be assembled at a modest price.

When buying an electric shaver, make certain that it is complete and in working order. Many were sold originally with cleaning kits, most of which have been lost.

History: Razors date back several thousand years. Early man used sharpened stones. The Egyptians, Greeks, and Romans had metal razors.

Straight razors made prior to 1800 generally were crudely stamped WARRENTED or CAST STEEL with the maker's mark on the tang. Until 1870 almost all razors for the American market were manufactured in Sheffield, England. Most blades were wedge shaped; many were etched with slogans or scenes. Handles were made of natural materials—various horns, tortoise shell, bone, ivory, stag, silver and pearl. All razors were handmade.

After 1870 most straight razors were machine made with hollow ground blades and synthetic handle materials. Razors of this period usually were manufactured in Germany (Solingen) or in American cutlery factories. Hundreds of molded celluloid handle patterns were produced, such as nude women, eagles, deer, boats, windmill scenes, etc.

By 1900 the safety razor was challenging the straight razor for popularity among the shaving community. A wealth of safety razor patents were issued in the first decade of the 20th century. World War I insured the dominance of the safety razor as American troops abroad made it their preferred shaving method.

By the 1930s the first electric shavers appeared. However, electric shavers did not achieve universal acceptance until the 1950s.

References: Robert A. Doyle, *Straight Razor Collecting,* Collector Books, 1980, out–of–print; Phillip L. Krumholz, *Value Guide For Barberiana & Shaving Collectibles,* Ad Libs Publishing, 1988; Roy Ritchie and Ron Stewart, *The Standard Guide To Razors,* Collector Books, 1995; Jim Sargent, *Sargent American Premium Guide To Knives & Razors: Identification And Values, Fourth Edition,* Books Americana, 1995.

Collectors' Club: Safety Razor Collectors' Guild, PO Box 885, Crescent City, CA 95531.

Christy Safety Razor, black case, 4½ x 2 x 1" **15.00**
Curfit, The Woman's Razor, patent date 1945, gold plated, orig box, 2⅜ x 3½ x 1" **15.00**
Devine Caretaker, Chicago, ivory handle, double edge, blade guard, leather cov wood box, adv sharpener   **75.00**
Enders Speed Razor Travel Set, gold plated razor, strop, orig Stropper & Williams Glider shaving cream, black fabric case, snap lid, 6⅞ x 5 x 2" . . .   **35.00**
Eveready, cardboard **22.00**
Eversharp Schick Injector, 1940s, blades missing
  Aqua handle, gold plated, cardboard box, 2⅜ x 4⅝ x 1" **15.00**
  Black handle, gold plated, black and clear plastic case, 4½ x 2½ x 1⅛"   **12.00**
  White and tan handle, gold plated, black and clear plastic case, 4½ x 2½ x 1⅛" **12.00**
  White handle, red plastic case, 4⅞ x 2½ x 1⅛" **6.00**
Gem Feather Weight Deluxe Model Gift Set, No 198, 6¾ x 5⅜ x 1½", MIB, price for set **30.00**
Gem Safety Razor, gold plated, white handle, plastic case, 1940s, 5⅛ x 2¼ x 1¼" **10.00**
Gillette Big Fellow, metal black box, wood dovetailed box, 1920s, 4½ x 2⅞ x 1⅜" **40.00**
Hoffritz, angle head razor, chrome metal case, two black boxes, 3½ x 2⅛ x 2" **25.00**
Keen Kutter, black case, 1920s, 4¼ x 1⅝ x⅞" **25.00**
Kewtie, lady's, 2⅝ x 3½ x 1", price for set **15.00**
Pacific Safety Razor, large hollow handle, 4¾ x 2½ x 1½", MIB **12.00**
Schermack, lady's, round shaving head, octagonal, tan marbleized celluloid case, 2¾ x 1⅛" **25.00**

Schermach, lady's underarm, mother-of-pearl handle, 2½" l, $35.00.

Schick
  Repeating, gold plated, cardboard box, 6½ x 1¼ x 1" **35.00**
  Super Classic II, International Silver Co, lady's, raised flowered handle and lady's ring, pink leather cov box, 7½ x 2¾ x 1⅝", MIB **125.00**
Simplex Military Safety Razor, Stock No 29–R–1035, 1940s, 4⅛ x 2¼ x¾", MIB **15.00**
Stahley Line, windup, black pigskin case, orig box, 5⅜ x 3 x 1⅝" **35.00**
Star, sq tin **55.00**
The "4 S" Razor, transition type, c1920, 6 x 1⅜ x 1½", MIB **20.00**
Valot Auto Strop Safety Razor, Model C, adv "The Community Weekly of Character," 1920s, 4⅛ x 1⅞ x 1⅜", price for razor and strop set **15.00**
Wilkinson Sword Company, plated, seven day set, razor fitted in holder over leather strop, day of week engraved on blades, blue velvet satin lined chrome case **50.00**

REAMERS

Collecting Hints: Reamers seldom are found in mint condition. Cone and rim nicks are usually acceptable, but cracked pieces bring considerably less. Ceramic figurals and U. S. made glass are collected more than any other category.

Reamer collecting first became popular with the advent of the Depression Glass collector in the mid–1960s. Reamer collecting can be an endless hobby. It may be impossible to assemble one of every example made. One–of–a–kind samples do exist; they never were put into mass production.

History: Devices for getting the juice from citrus fruit have been around almost as long as the fruit itself. These devices range in materials from wood to glass and from nickel plated and Sterling silver to fine china.

Many different kinds of mechanical reamers were devised before the first glass one was pressed around 1885. Very few reamers have been designed since 1940, when frozen juice entered the market. Modern–day ceramists are making clown- and teapot–shaped reamers.

References: Gene Florence, *Kitchen Glassware of the Depression Years, Fifth Edition,* Collector Books, 1995; Mary Walker, *Reamers—200 Years,* Muski Publishers, 1980, separate price guide; Mary Walker, *The Second Book, More Reamers—200 Years,* Muski Publishers, 1983.

Collectors' Club: National Reamer Collectors Association, 405 Benson Rd. N., Frederic, WI 54837.

REPRODUCTION ALERT: Reproduced reamers include:

An old 5" Imperial Glass Co. reamer, originally made in clear glass, was reproduced for Edna Barnes in dark amethyst. 1,500 were made. The reproduction is marked "IG" and "81."

Mrs. Barnes has reproduced several old 4½" Jenkins Glass Co. reamers in limited editions. The reproductions are also made in a 2¼" size. All Jenkins copies are marked with a "B" in a circle.

Note: The first book on reamers, now out–of–print, was written by Ken and Linda Ricketts in 1974. Their numbering system was continued by Mary Walker in *Reamers—200 Years.* The Ricketts–Walker numbers will be found in the china and metal sections. The numbers in parentheses in the glass section are from Gene Florence's *Kitchen Glassware of the Depression Years.*

CHINA AND CERAMIC

Bavaria, 4" h, orange shape, yellow, green leaves and handle, white top, 2 pc (L–7) **18.00**
Czechoslovakia, 3¾" h, orange luster, pink flowers, green leaves, 2 pc (E–48) **30.00**
Japan
2¾" h, duck, various color combinations, 2 pc (F–12) **30.00**
4½", Baby's Orange, blue on white (B–4) **28.00**
4½ x 5", pear, yellow and orange, green leaves, 3 pc (L–39) **32.00**
7½" h, clown, pale green and white, orange hands and feet (C–40) **40.00**

Ceramic, cottage, beige, green grass, blue windows, Japan, 2 pieces, $70.00.

Nippon, 3¼" h, hp, white, floral, 2 pc   **75.00**
United States
Hall China, large, flat, lettuce green, marked "Hall," 1 pc **155.00**
Red Wing, 6¾" h, pedestal type, yellow, 1 pc (A–7) **75.00**

GLASS

Cambridge, Seville yellow, grapefruit (145–4–1) **275.00**
Federal, green transparent, pointed cone, tab handle (135–3–4) **28.00**
Fenton, clear, elephant dec, two handles (131–7–5) **95.00**
Fry
Canary Vaseline, tab handle (133–3–2) **60.00**
Pearl Opalescent (133–3–1) **22.00**
Hazel Atlas
Cobalt Blue, tab handle, small (138–4–3) **225.00**
Pink, tab handle, large (138–4–4) . .   **27.50**
Hocking, green
Circle Pitcher, reamer top (139–1–1)   **55.00**
Clambroth, tab handle (193–3–3) . . .   **88.00**
Indiana, amber, handle opposite spout (135–4–1) **200.00**
Jeannette
Jadite, dark, small (143–3–1) **40.00**
Pink, Hex Optic, bucket reamer (143–1–1) **55.00**
MacBeth–Evans, clambroth (142–3–2)   **375.00**
McKee
Chalaine Blue, emb Sunkist (146–3–3) **185.00**
Delphite, small (147–5–4) **345.00**
Vaseline Green, emb Sunkist (146–5–4) **38.00**
US Glass
Green, four cup pitcher set (151–1–2)   **75.00**
Light Pink, two cup pitcher set (151–2–1) **35.00**
Westmoreland, baby
Crystal, 2 pc (131–1–2) **95.00**
Pink, 2 pc (131–1–1) **195.00**

METAL

Gem Squeezer, aluminum, crank handle, table model, 2 pc (M–100)	**10.00**
Knapps Orange Juicer, aluminum, hinged, crank handle, hand held (M–86)	**10.00**
Kwicky Juicer, aluminum, pan style, Quam–Nichols Co (M–97)	**8.00**
Lemon–Lime Roto Squeezer, scissor type (M–73)	**5.00**
Pearl, cast iron, wood insert, long handled (M–27)	**18.00**
Presto Juicer, porcelain, metal stand (M–112)	**60.00**
Sealed Sweet, mechanical, clamps to table, tilt model (M–120)	**40.00**
Yankee–Lidon, iron, cast aluminum parts, long handled (M–62)	**24.00**

RECORDS

Collecting Hints: Collectors tend to focus on one particular area of the music field, e.g., jazz, the big bands, or rock 'n' roll, or on one artist. Purchase records with original dust jackets and covers whenever possible.

Also check the records carefully for scratches. If the record cannot be played, it is worthless.

Proper storage of records is critical to maintaining their value. Keep stacks small. It is best to store them vertically. Place acid–free paper between the albums to prevent bleeding of ink from one cover to the next.

History: The first records were cylinders produced by Thomas Edison in 1877 and played on a phonograph of his design. Edison received a patent in 1878, but soon dropped the project in order to perfect the light bulb.

Alexander Graham Bell, Edison's friend, was excited about the phonograph and developed the graphaphone, which was marketed successfully by 1889. Early phonographs and graphaphones had hand cranks which wound the mechanism which keep the cylinders moving.

About 1900 Emile Berliner developed a phonograph which used a flat disc, similar to today's records. The United States Gramophone Company marketed his design in 1901. The company eventually became RCA Victor. By 1910 discs were more popular than cylinders.

The record industry continued to develop as progress was made in the preservation of sound and the increased quality of sound. The initial size of 78 rpm records was replaced by 45 rpm, then 33 1/3 rpm, and finally, compact discs.

References: Steven C. Barr, *The Almost Complete 78 RPM Record Dating Guide (II),* Yesterday

Once Again, 1992; Les R. Docks, *American Premium Record Guide, 1900–1965,* Fourth Edition, Books Americana, 1992; Steve Gelfand, *Television Theme Recordings: An Illustrated Discography, 1951–1991,* Popular Culture, 1993; Anthony J. Gribin and Matthew M. Schiff, *Doo–Wop: The Forgotten Third Of Rock 'n Roll,* Krause Publications, 1992; Joe Lindsay (comp.), *Picture Discs of the World Price Guide: International Reference Book for Picture Records: 1923–1989,* BIOdisc, 1990; Ron Lofman, *Goldmine's Celebrity Vocals,* Krause Publications, 1994; Vito R. Marino and Anthony C. Furfero, *The Official Price Guide To Frank Sinatra Collectibles, Records and CDs,* House of Collectibles, 1993; Bonni J. Miller (ed.), *Goldmine's 1995 Annual: The Standard Reference For Music Collectors,* Krause Publications, 1994; William M. Miller, *How To Buy & Sell Used Record Albums,* Loran Publishing, 1994; Jerry Osborne, *The Official Price Guide, Movie/TV Soundtracks and Original Cast Albums,* House of Collectibles, 1991; Jerry Osborne, *The Official Price Guide To Records,* Tenth Edition, House of Collectibles, 1993; Jerry Osborne and Pat Brown, *Rockin Records: Buyers-Sellers Reference Book and Price Guide,* 16th Edition, Jellyroll Publications, 1994; Neal Umphred, *Goldmine's Price Guide To Collectible Jazz Albums, 1949–1969,* Krause Publications, 1992; Neal Umphred, *Goldmine's Price Guide To Collectible Record Albums,* Fourth Edition Krause Publications, 1994; Neal Umphred, *Goldmine's Rock 'n Roll 45 RPM Record Price Guide,* Third Edition, Krause Publications, 1994.

Collectors' Clubs: Collectors Record Club, 1206 Decatur St., New Orleans, LA 70116; International Association of Jazz Record Collectors, PO Box 75155, Tampa, FL 33605.

Periodicals: *Cadence,* Cadence Building, Redwood, NY 13679; *DISCoveries Magazine,* PO Box 309, Fraser, MI 48026; *Goldmine,* 700 E. State St., Iola, WI 54990; *Joslin's Jazz Journal,* PO Box 213, Parsons, KS 67357; *Record Collectors Monthly,* PO Box 75, Mendham, NJ 07945; *Record Finder,* PO Box 1047, Glen Allen, VA 23060; *The New Amberola Graphic,* 37 Caledonia St., St Johnsbury, VT 05819.

Note: Prices are for first pressings in original dust jackets or albums.

Additional Listings: Elvis Presley and Rock 'N' Roll.

Big Bands

Gus Arnheim & His Orchestra, Love In The Moonlight, Victor, 24235 . .	**7.00**
Les Brown, Decca, Swamp Fire, Decca, 1231	**10.00**

Benny Carter, Everybody Shuffle,
Vocalion, 2870 .... 12.50
Count Basie & His Orchestra
Louisiana, Columbia, 35448 .... 5.00
The Blues I Like To Hear, Decca,
2284 .... 8.00
Bob Crosby & His Orchestra, Decca
On Treasure Island, 614 .... 6.00
What's The Name Of That Song?,
727 .... 8.00
Tommy Dorsey, Okeh, It's Right Here
For You, 41178 .... 12.00
Duke Ellington
Cotton Club Stomp, Victor, 38079 25.00
Got Everything But You, Victor,
21703 .... 18.00
Sam And Delilah, Victor, 23036 .. 15.00
Benny Goodman
King Porter, Victor, 25090 ...... 6.00
Overnight, Melotone, 12024 .... 15.00
We Can Live On Love, Melotone,
12120 .... 20.00
Glen Miller, Sweet Stranger, Bruns-
wick, 8041 .... 10.00
Mills Brothers, Brunswick
Doin' The New Low–Down, 6517 12.00
Smoke Rings, 6225 .... 8.00
Rudy Vallee
Nasty Man, Victor, 24581 ...... 8.00
Right Out Of Heaven, Harmony,
724–H 10.00
Thomas "Fats" Waller
Birmingham Blues, Okeh, 4757 .. 25.00
Stompin' The Bug, Victor, 20655 24.50
Country/Western
Aiken Country String Band, Okeh,
Charleston Rag, 45219 .... 12.00
Allen Brothers
It Can't Be Done, Bluebird, 5533 15.00
Salty Dog Blues, Columbia,
15175–D 25.00
Triple Blues, Bluebird, 5104 ..... 12.00
Gene Autry
Cowboy Yodel, Gennett, 7243 ... 75.00
That's How I Got My Start,
Superior, 2681 .... 50.00
Carter Family
Broken Hearted Lover, Vocalion,
02990 .... 18.00
Keep On The Sunny Side, Bluebird,
5006 .... 6.00
Delmore Brothers, Bluebird, Big Ball
In Texas, 7560 .... 8.00
East Texas Serenaders
Combination Rag, Columbia,
15229–D 5.00
Ozark Rag, Brunswick, 538 ..... 10.00
Johnny Horton, Abbott
Candy Jones, 100 .... 8.00
Smokey Joe's Barbeque, 106 .... 12.00
Kessinger Brothers, Brunswick,
Arkansas Traveler, 247 .... 8.50

Hopalong Cassidy, Square Dance Hold-
up, Capitol, 1950, 78 rpm, 2 records,
story, illus text, $24.00.

Bradley Kincaid
Old Coon Dog, Brunswick, 485 .. 10.00
The Old Wooden Bucket, Bluebird,
5201 .... 5.00
Lone Star Rangers
Farm Relief Song, Paramount, 3202 8.00
The Train That Never Arrived,
Broadway, 8142 .... 10.00
Movie and TV Soundtracks
Advance To The Rear, Columbia,
1964 .... 25.00
Auntie Mame, Warner Bros, 1958 .. 50.00
Avengers, 1966 .... 45.00
Barbarella, Dyno Voice, 1968 ..... 22.00
Big Chill, Motown, 1983 .... 8.50
Blue Hawaii, RCA Victor, 1961 .... 35.00
Bye Bye Birdie, Columbia, 1960 ... 25.00
Cactus Flower, Bell, 1970 .... 12.00
Camelot, orig cast, Columbia, 1960 22.00
Car Wash, MCA, 1978 .... 8.00
Cocoon, Polydor, 1985 .... 8.00
Damn Yankees, orig cast, RCA Victor,
1955 .... 25.00
Dragnet, RCA Victor, 1953 .... 55.00
East Of Eden, Columbia, 1957 ..... 30.00
Footloose, Columbia, 1983 .... 8.00
Fun In Acapulco, RCA Victor, 1963 45.00
Gypsy, orig cast, Columbia, 1959 .. 12.00
Hamlet, orig cast, Columbia, 1964 18.00
Hawaii Five–O, Capitol, 1969 ..... 15.00
Ivanhoe, MGM, 1952 .... 26.00
Jamaica, RCA Victor, 1957 .... 25.00
Lady Sings The Blues, Motown, 1972 10.00
Lawrence Of Arabia, Colpix, 1962 .. 38.00
Let's Make Love, Columbia, 1960 .. 20.00
Macbeth, studio cast, RCA Victor,
1953 .... 45.00
Magnificent Seven, United Artists,
1960 .... 18.00
Mary Poppins, Sidewalk, 1968 .... 10.00
Night Shift, Warner Bros, 1982 .... 10.00

No Way To Treat A Lady, Dot, 1968   **8.00**
Oklahoma, orig cast, Decca, 1943 . .   **12.50**
Patton, 20th Century Fox, 1970 . . . .   **10.00**
Pennies From Heaven, Warner Bros,
  1981 . . . .   **12.50**
Psycho II, MCA, 1983 . . . .   **8.00**
Ragtime, Electra, 1981 . . . .   **8.50**
Rocky, United Artists, 1976 . . . .   **10.00**
Rosemary's Baby, Dot, 1968 . . . . . .   **25.00**
Scarface, MCA, 1984 . . . .   **10.00**
Some Like It Hot, United Artists,
  1959 . . . .   **25.00**
Taste Of Honey, studio cast, Atlantic,
  1960 . . . .   **20.00**
Three Days of the Condor, Capitol,
  1975 . . . .   **22.00**
To Kill A Mockingbird, Ava, 1962 . .   **30.00**
What's New Pussycat?, United Artists,
  1965 . . . .   **15.00**
Rock N' Roll
Paul Anka, My Heart Sings, ABC
  Paramount, 296 . . . .   **12.00**
Beach Boys
  Surfin', Candix, 301 . . . .   **50.00**
  The Beach Boys Today, DU, 2269   **25.00**
Beatles, All You Need Is Love,
  Capitol, 5964 . . . .   **18.00**
Chubby Checker, The Class, Parkway,
  804 . . . .   **55.00**
Bobby Darin, Splish Splash, Atco,
  6117 . . . .   **24.00**
Bo Diddley
  Have Guitar Will Travel, Chess,
  2974 . . . .   **18.00**
  Say! (Boss Man), Checker, 878 . . .   **8.00**
The Drifters
  Bip Bam, Atlantic, 1043 . . . .   **5.00**
  The World Is Changing, Crown,
  108 . . . .   **45.00**
Duprees, Have You Heard, Coed,
  906 . . . .   **40.00**
The Everly Brothers, Cadence
  Bird Dog, 1350 . . . .   **25.00**
  Wake Up Little Susie, 1337 . . . . .   **18.00**
Bill Haley and The Comets
  Crazy Man Crazy, Essex, 321 . . . .   **15.00**
  Green Tree Boogie, Holiday, 108   **80.00**
  Rock The Joint, Essex, 303 . . . . .   **12.00**
  Shake, Rattle And Roll, Decca,
  2168 . . . .   **10.00**
Buddy Holly, Coral
  Listen To Me, 81169 . . . .   **20.00**
  Peggy Sue Got Married, 81191 . . .   **15.00**
Jerry Lee Lewis, Sun, Great Balls Of
  Fire, 281 . . . .   **20.00**
Muddy Waters, Loving Man, Chess,
  1585 . . . .   **10.00**
Platters, I'll Cry When You're Gone,
  Federal, 12164 . . . .   **30.00**
Supremes
  Just For You And I, Ace, 534 . . . .   **12.00**
  Meet The Supremes, Motown, 606   **30.00**

Wanderers, Everybody's Somebody's
  Fool, Kent, 356 . . . .   **12.00**
Slim Whitman, Imperial, My Love Is
  Growing Stale, 8134 . . . .   **12.00**

RED WING POTTERY

Collecting Hints: Red Wing Pottery can be found with various marks and paper labels. Some of the marks include a red wing which is stamped on, a raised "Red Wing U.S.A. #___", and an impressed "Red Wing U.S.A. #___". Paper labels were used as early as 1930. Pieces with paper labels easily lost their only mark.

Many manufacturers used the same mold patterns. Study the references to become familiar with the Red Wing forms.

History: The category of Red Wing Pottery covers several potteries which started in Red Wing, Minnesota. The first pottery, named Red Wing Stoneware Company, was started in 1868 by David Hallem. The primary product of this company was stoneware. The mark used by this company was a red wing stamped under the glaze. The Minnesota Stoneware Company was started in 1883. The North Star Stoneware Company opened a factory in the same area in 1892 and went out of business in 1896. The mark used by this company included a raised star and the words "Red Wing."

The Red Wing Stoneware Company and the Minnesota Stoneware Company merged in 1892. The new company was called the Red Wing Union Stoneware Company. The new company made stoneware until 1920 when it introduced a line of pottery.

In 1936 the name of the company was changed to Red Wing Potteries Incorporated. They continued to make pottery until the 1940s. During the 1930s they introduced several lines of dinnerware. These patterns were all hand painted, very popular, and sold through department stores, Sears, and gift stamp centers. The production of dinnerware declined in the 1950s. The company began producing hotel and restaurant china in the early 1960s. The plant was closed in 1967.

References: Susan and Al Bagdade, *Warman's American Pottery and Porcelain*, Wallace–Homestead, 1994; Dan and Gail DePasquale and Larry Peterson, *Red Wing Collectibles*, Collector Books, 1983, 1994 value update; Gary and Bonnie Tefft, *Red Wing Potters and Their Wares*, Second Edition Locust Enterprises, 1987, 1995 value update; Lyndon C. Viel, *The Clay Giants: The Stoneware of Red Wing, Goodhue County, Minnesota, Book 2* (1980), *Book 3* (1987), Wallace–Homestead, out–of–print.

Collectors' Club: Red Wing Collectors Society, PO Box 124, Neosho, WI 53059.

BOB WHITE Casual shape, 1956–1967.

Butter Warmer	30.00
Casserole, cov	42.00
Creamer	12.50
Cup and Saucer	18.00
Gravy, cov	30.00
Hors d'oeuvre Bird	40.00
Mug	75.00
Plate	
6" d, bread and butter	5.00
7" d, salad	6.00
10½" d, dinner	10.00
Platter, 13" l	15.00
Relish, 3 part	28.00
Salad Bowl	40.00
Salt and Pepper Shakers, pr, tall	25.00
Vegetable Bowl, divided	28.00

COUNTRY GARDEN Anniversary shape, 1953.

Gravy	25.00
Nappy	18.00
Plate	
8" d, salad	10.00
10½" d, dinner	15.00
Sauce Dish	12.00
Vegetable Bowl, divided	20.00

LUTE SONG Casual shape, true china, 1960.

Beverage Server	45.00
Bowl, 8" d	15.00
Bread Tray, 19" l	20.00
Butter Dish	20.00
Casserole	25.00
Celery, 16" l	15.00
Creamer	10.00
Platter, 13" l	15.00
Vegetable Bowl, divided	20.00

MAGNOLIA Concord shape, 1947.

Bowl, 5" d	5.00
Cup and Saucer	6.00
Dinner Service, 30 pcs	125.00
Pitcher, #1028	35.00
Plate	
6" d, bread and butter	4.00
7" d, salad	5.00
10" d, dinner	10.00
12" d, chop	18.00

SMART SET Casual shape, 1955.

Casserole, cov, 1 quart, wire base	95.00
Cruet	50.00
Gravy, cov, stand	35.00
Relish	30.00
Salt and Pepper Shakers, pr, tall	65.00
Sugar, cov	30.00
Teapot	275.00
Vegetable Bowl, 9" d	32.00

TAMPICO Futura shape, 1955.

Berry Bowl, 5½" d	6.00
Bowl	
8" d	25.00
12" d	40.00
Cereal Bowl, 6½" d	10.00
Coffee Mug	40.00
Creamer and Sugar, cov	30.00
Cup and Saucer	12.00
Gravy, stand	32.00
Pitcher, water	25.00
Plate	
6" d, bread and butter	5.00
7" d, salad	5.00
10½" d, dinner	10.00
Platter, 13" l	20.00
Relish, divided	25.00
Shaker	4.00
Tidbit Tray, 2 tiers	30.00

MISCELLANEOUS

Ash Receiver, brown donkey	90.00
Beater Jar, spongeware, adv, cracked	400.00
Clock, Mammy	395.00
Cookie Jar, King of Tarts, multicolored	875.00
Crock	
1 Gallon	295.00
8 Gallon, handles, no lid	150.00

Vase, green–blue, marked "Red Wing USA 1563," 10" h, $25.00.

Figure	
Deer, #1126	**75.00**
Flamenco Dancer	**195.00**
Fruit Jar, stone mason	**200.00**
Jug, 1 gallon	**175.00**
Koverwate, 5 gallon	**185.00**
Mug, white, "Happy Days Are Here Again"	**65.00**
Umbrella Stand, cylindrical, emb stag and doe in forest and mountain landscape, tan matte glaze, 15" h, 12" d	**1,500.00**
Vase	
#803, terra cotta, orig paper label	**110.00**
#1143, deer and woman's face	**55.00**
Water Cooler, St Paul Book adv	**595.00**

ROBOTS

Collecting Hints: The name for a robot comes from markings on the robot or box and from the trade. Hence, some robots have more than one name. Do research to know exactly what robot you have. A leading auctioneer of robots is Lloyd Ralston Toys, Fairfield, Connecticut.

Condition is critical. Damaged lithographed tin is almost impossible to repair and repaint. Toys in mint condition in the original box are the most desirable. The price difference between a mint robot and one in very good condition may be as high as 200%.

Working condition is important, but not critical. Many robots never worked well, and larger robots stripped their gearing quickly. The rarer the robot, the less important is the question of working condition.

Finally, if you play with your robot, do not leave the batteries in the toy. If they leak or rust, the damage may destroy the value of the toy.

History: Atomic Robot Man, made in Japan between 1948 and 1949, is the grandfather of all robot toys. He is an all metal wind-up toy, less than 5" high and rather crudely made. Japanese robots of the early 1950s tended to be the friction or wind-up variety, patterned in brightly lithographed tin and made from recycled materials.

By the late 1950s robots had entered the battery-powered age. Limited quantities of early models were produced; parts from one model were used in later models with slight or no variations. The robot craze was enhanced by Hollywood's production of movies such as *Destination Moon* (1950) and *Forbidden Planet* (1956). Roby the Robot came from this latter movie.

Many Japanese manufacturers were small and lasted only a few years. Leading firms include Horikawa Toys, Nomura Toys, and Yonezawa Toys. Cragstan was an American importer who sold Japanese-made toys under its own label.

Marx and Ideal entered the picture in the 1970s. Modern robots are being imported from China and Taiwan.

The TV program *Lost in Space* (1965–1968) inspired copies of its robot character. However, the quality of the late 1960s toys began to suffer as more and more plastic was added; robots were redesigned to reduce sharp edges as required by the United States government.

Modern robots include R2D2 and C3PO from the Star Wars epics, Twiki from NBC's Buck Rogers, and V.I.N.CENT from Disney's *The Black Hole*. Robots are firmly established in American science fiction and among collectors.

References: Teruhisa Kitahara, *Tin Toy Dreams: Robots*, Chronicle Books, 1985; Teruhisa Kitahara, *Yesterday's Toys, & Robots, Spaceships, and Monsters*, Chronicle Books, 1988; Robert Maline, *The Robot Book*, Push Pin Press/ Harcourt Brace, 1978; Crystal and Leland Payton, *Space Toys*, Collectors Compass, 1982; Stephen J. Sansweet, *Science Fiction Toys and Models*, Vol. 1, Starlog Press, 1980.

Periodical: *Robot World & Price Guide*, PO Box 184, Lenox Hill Station, New York, NY 10021.

Note: The following abbreviations are used:
SH = Horikawa Toys
TM = K. K. Masutoku Toy Factory
TN = Nomura Toys
Y = Yonezawa Toys

Acrobat Robot, Yonezawa, Japan, plastic body, litho tin chestplate, battery operated, orig box, 1960s, 9¾" h	**285.00**
Atomic Robot Man, Japan, litho tin, pressed tin arms, windup, orig box, 5" h	**1,700.00**
Chief Robotman, KO, Japan, tin, battery operated, 12" h	
Silver, orig box	**1,800.00**
White	**1,200.00**
Cone Head Robot, Yonezawa, Japan, tin, plastic eyes, rubber antennae, windup, 8¾" h	**2,800.00**
Cragstan Astronaut, Japan, litho tin, clear plastic helmet, battery operated, orig box, 14" h	**1,075.00**
Dino the Robot, SH, Japan, litho tin and plastic, battery operated, orig box, 11" h	**1,025.00**
Dux Astroman, Dux, Germany, tin and plastic, battery operated, orig box, 12" h	**1,400.00**
Earth Man, Kitahara #144, TN, Japan, litho tin, battery operated, remote control, needs bulb, 9¼" h	**550.00**
Electric Robot and Son, Marx, plastic, battery operated, orig box and cardboard insert, motor sluggish, 15" h	**600.00**

Mechanical Moon Robot, Kitahara #6, Yonezawa, Japan, tin, windup, orig box, 10¾" h **3,300.00**
Mechanical Robot, Linemar, Japan, litho tin, plastic claw hands, windup, orig box, 6" h **800.00**
Mechanical Walking Spaceman, Tomiyama, Japan, tin and hard plastic, windup, orig box and cardboard inserts, 5½" h **1,200.00**
Mr Atom, Advance Toy, West Haven, CT, plastic, battery operated, orig box, 18" h **700.00**
Mr Mercury, Marx, litho tin, battery operated, remote control, 13" h **600.00**
Mr Robot The Mechanical Brain, Alps, Japan, tin, windup, orig box and instruction sheet, 8¼" h **900.00**
Nando Robot, Italy, tin, air powered, gray unpainted finish, decal facial features, 1950s, orig box, not working, 5" h **465.00**
Planet Robot, KO, Japan, tin and plastic, windup, orig box, 9" h **300.00**
Radar Robot, Kitahara #8, Japan, tin, battery operated, primitive style, walking mechanism not working, orig box bottom and insert, 9" h **450.00**
Red Rosko Astronaut, Japan, litho tin and plastic, battery operated, 13" h **1,100.00**
Robot, Linemar, Japan, litho tin, battery operated, remote control, orig box, 6" h **4,100.00**
Robot, Yonezawa, Japan, tin and litho tin, battery operated, orig box, 11" h **1,600.00**
Robot Lilliput, KT, Japan, litho tin, key wind, laser copy of orig box, 6½" h **4,600.00**
Robot ST1, West Germany, silvered tin, key wind, orig box, 7½" h **500.00**
Smoking Spaceman, tin, plastic dome, battery operated, 12" h **1,900.00**
Space Man, Sonsco, TN, Japan, litho

Marvelous Mike, litho tin, plastic, rubber, and wire, robot on tractor, battery operated, Saunders, Aurora, IL, 1954, $245.00.

tin, battery operated, blue version, orig box, 9" h **3,850.00**
Television Spaceman, Alps, Japan, tin, battery operated, orig box, 11" h ... **725.00**
Video Robot and Dinosaur, SH, Japan, tin and plastic, battery operated, orig box, 11" h **675.00**

ROCK 'N' ROLL

Collecting Hints: Many rock 'n' roll collections are centered around one artist. Flea markets and thrift shops are good places to look for rock 'n' roll items. Prices range according to the singer or group. The stars who have died usually command a higher price.

Glossy 8 x 10s of singers, unautographed, are generally worth $1.00.

History: Rock music can be traced back to early rhythm and blues music. It progressed and reached its golden age in the 1950s. The current nostalgia craze for the 1950s has produced some modern rock 'n' roll which is well received. Rock 'n' roll memorabilia exists in large quantities, each singer or group having many promotional pieces made.

References: Pauline Bartel, *Everything Elvis,* Taylor Publishing, 1995; Les R. Docks, *American Premium Record Guide, 1900–1965, Fourth Edition,* Books Americana, 1992; Alison Fox, *Rock & Pop,* Boxtree Ltd. (London); 1988; Anthony J. Gribin and Matthew M. Schiff, *Doo–Wop: The Forgotten Third Of Rock 'n Roll,* Krause Publications, 1992; Paul Grushkin, *The Art of Rock—Posters From Presley To Punk,* Abbeville Press, 1986; David K. Henkel, *The Official Price Guide To Rock And Roll,* House of Collectibles, 1992; Karen and John Lesniweski, *Kiss Collectibles: Identification And Value Guide,* Avon Books, 1993; Norman E. Martinus and Harry L. Rinker, *Warman's Paper,* Wallace–Homestead, 1994; Stephen Maycock, *Miller's Rock & Pop Memorabilia,* Millers Publications, 1995; Bonni J. Miller (ed.), *1995 Goldmine Annual,* Krause Publications, 1994; Greg Moore, *A Price Guide To Rock & Roll Collectibles, Second Edition,* published by author, 1993; Jerry Osborne, *The Official Price Guide To Elvis Presley Records and Memorabilia,* House of Collectibles, 1994; Michael Stern, Barbara Crawford, and Hollis Lamon, *The Beatles: A Reference & Value Guide,* Collector Books, 1994; Paul Trynka (ed.), *The Electric Guitar: An Illustrated History,* Chronicle Books, 1993; Neal Umphred, *Goldmine's Price Guide To Collectible Record Albums, 1949–1989, 4th Edition,* Krause Publications, 1994; Neal Umphred, *Goldmine's Rock 'n Roll 45 RPM Record Price Guide, Third Edition,* Krause Publications, 1994.

Periodicals: *Kissaholics Magazine,* PO Box 22334, Nashville, TN 37202; *The New England KISS Collector's Network,* 168 Oakland Ave., Providence, RI 02908; *Tune Talk,* PO Box 851, Marshalltown, IA 50158.

Collectors' Club: American Bandstand 1950's Fan Club, PO Box 131, Adamstown, PA 19501.

See: Beatles and Presley, Elvis.

Book, *James Dean,* Ballantine Books, 150 pgs, biography by William Bast, paperback, 1956	15.00
Box, bubble gum, Monkees, 4 x 8 x 1½″, held 24 packs, Donruss, 1966 series, full color picture, yellow background, red design, diecut lid	25.00
Bracelet, gold chain link, burnished gold disc with raised Monkees guitar symbol, orig retail card, 1967 copyright	25.00
Contract	
Buddy Holly, Elks Hall concert, August 3, 1957, 2 pg letter and envelope	500.00
Frank Zappa, Today Show appearance, glossy finish, 1990	750.00
Rolling Stones, Savoy Ballroom concert, September 6, 1963	350.00
Yes, Marquee Club concert, January, 1969, early logo	250.00
Cuff Links, pr, Dick Clark, MIB	30.00
Doll	
Boy George, 12″ h, hard plastic, soft vinyl head, hat, microphone and posing stand, orig box, made in China for LJN of New York	25.00
Diana Ross, 19″ h, molded hard plastic body, vinyl face and arms, gold glitter dress, orig box with The Supremes picture, Ideal, copyright 1969 Motown, Inc	100.00
Dick Clark, 25″ h, soft plush stuffed body, hard molded vinyl head and hands, marked "Juro," 1950s	150.00
Michael Jackson, 12″ h, hard plastic, soft molded vinyl head, poseable, Grammy Awards outfit, LJN, copyright 1984 MJJ Productions, Inc, orig box	45.00
Folder, 4½ x 6″, "Swap Notes," beige vinyl cov with emb image, note pad, reply cards	45.00
Handbill	
Jimi Hendrix, Newport '69, Devonshire Downs	250.00
Rolling Stones, May 19, 1964 concert	350.00
Handkerchief, Buddy Holly, silk, red and gold paisley, authenticity card	400.00
Jigsaw Puzzle, 11 x 17″ assembled, 200 pcs, Love Gun album scene, orig box, American Publishing Corp, 1977 copyright	15.00

Nodder, 4½″ h, man, gold base with "Let's Twist" decal, Japan sticker, c1960	75.00
Pinback Button	
Freddy and the Dreamers, 3½″ d, black and white photos, red and white "I Love Freddy and the Dreamers," copyright Premier Talent Associates, Inc., 1960s	22.00
Herman's Hermits, 3½″ d, five black and white photos, red and white "I Love Herman's Hermits," copyright Premier Talent Associates, Inc., late 1960s	15.00
James Dean, 2½″ d, color photo	58.00
Pat Boone, 3½″ d, blue "Swoon With Pat Boone" inscription, white background, red rim	5.00
Rock–Ola, 3″ d, red, white, and blue illus, black "Rock–Ola Leads Again," c1950	15.00
Post Card, Rolling Stones, 4½ x 6½″, two, perforated, "The Rolling Stones Exile On Main Street" in red, marked "Scene 1" and "Scene 2," c1972	15.00
Poster	
Alice Cooper, Cowtown Ballroom, red and yellow, 1970s	200.00
Billy J Kramer, concert, English, 1963	300.00
Buddy Holly, 17¼ x 24¾″, Buddy Holly and the Crickets, Thursday March 20th, 1958, Liverpool Philharmonic Hall	5,500.00
Doors, 36 x 24″, promotional, Elektra stereo tapes, group photo, blue, black and white lettering	200.00
Rolling Stones, concert, English, 1963	2,200.00
Program	
Rock And Rollorama #1, Jan 27–29, 1956, 8½ x 11″, 14 pgs	40.00
The Biggest Show Of Stars For '58, 9 x 12″, 24 pgs	125.00
Record	
Buddy Holly, 78 rpm, *Peggy Sue/Every Day,* Coral label, 1957	25.00
Fabian, Hound Dog Man, 45 rpm, Chancellor label, orig cardboard sleeve, 1950s	20.00
Record Case, 7½ x 9″, red vinyl covered cardboard, emb design, Ponytail, 1950s	50.00
Sheet Music	
Bill Haley and The Comets, *Green Tree Boogie,* greentone photo on front, copyright 1955 Myers Music, 9 x 11″	20.00
The Who, *Substitute,* bluetone group photo on cov, copyright 1966 Fabulous Music Ltd, 8½ x 11″	12.50
Sign, Brenda Lee, black and white photo, small inset color "This Is Brenda" record album photo, top	

Sheet Music, *(We're Gonna) Rock Around The Clock,* Bill Haley and the Comets, $5.00.

marked "The Exciting Brenda Lee/America's Newest Singing Sensation," pop–out easel **75.00**
Song Album, souvenir, 8½ x 11", More of the Monkees, 64 pgs, 1967 Raybert Productions copyright **45.00**
Thermos, Monkees, 6½" h, metal, full color illus, copyright 1967 Raybert Productions, Inc **25.00**
Tour Book, Bob Dylan, 10 x 14", 28 pgs, c1977 .... **25.00**
Toy
  Guitar, Monkees, 20" l, plastic, full color diecut litho paper label, 1966 copyright **75.00**
  Saxophone, Spike Jones Sax–O–Fun, 7" l, hard plastic, marked "A Trophy Product," c1950 .... **25.00**
Window Card
  Beatles, 22 x 13", *A Hard Day's Night,* yellow, orange, and green, black lettering **175.00**
  Rolling Stones, 22 x 14", *Gimme Shelter,* blue, yellow, and white, movie scenes **150.00**
Yearbook, Dick Clark Official American Bandstand Yearbook, 9 x 12", 40 pgs, color and black and white photos, c1950 .... **25.00**

NORMAN ROCKWELL

Collecting Hints: Learn all you can about Norman Rockwell if you plan to collect his many artworks. His original artworks and illustrations have been transferred onto various types of objects by clubs and manufacturers.

History: Norman Rockwell, the famous American artist, was born on February 3, 1894. His first professional illustrations were for a children's book, *Tell Me Why Stories,* at age 18. Next he worked for *Boy's Life* magazine (the Boy Scouts' publication) and other magazines. By his death in November 1978, he had created more than 2,000 paintings.

Many of his paintings were done in oil and reproduced as magazine covers, advertisements, illustrations, calendars, and book sketches. Over 320 of these paintings became covers for the *Saturday Evening Post.*

Norman Rockwell painted everyday people in everyday situations with a little humor mixed in with the sentiment. His paintings and illustrations are well loved because of this sensitive nature. He painted people he knew and places with which he was familiar. New England landscapes are found in many of his illustrations.

Because his works are so well liked, they have been reproduced on many objects. These new collectibles should not be confused with the original artwork and illustrations. The new collectibles, however, offer Norman Rockwell illustrations to the average pocketbook and serve to keep his work alive.

References: Denis C. Jackson, *The Norman Rockwell Identification and Value Guide,* published by author, 1985; Mary Moline, *Norman Rockwell Collectibles Value Guide, Sixth Edition,* Green Valley World, 1988.

Collectors' Club: Rockwell Society of America, 597 Saw Mill River Road, Ardsley, NY 10502.

Museums: Museum of Norman Rockwell Art, Reedsburg, WI; Norman Rockwell Museum, Philadelphia, PA; The Norman Rockwell Museum at Stockbridge, Stockbridge, MA; Norman Rockwell Museum, Northbrook, IL.

Bell
  Gorham, 1982, Lovers **30.00**
  Grossman, Dave
    1975, Christmas, first edition **30.00**
    1976, Ben Franklin Bicentennial . **28.00**
Figurine
  Gorham
    1976, Saying Grace **150.00**
    1980, Four Seasons, A Helping Hand, price for set of 4 ...... **450.00**
    1982, Jolly Coachman **50.00**
    1983, Christmas Dancers **75.00**
  Dave Grossman Designs, Inc.
    1973, No Swimming **45.00**
    1978, At The Doctors **125.00**
    1980, Exasperated Nanny **125.00**
    1982, Doctor and the Doll **125.00**
    1983, The Graduate **32.00**
  Lynell Studios
    1979, Snow Queen **85.00**

1980, Cradle of Love	**85.00**
Rockwell Museum	
1978, Bedtime	**50.00**
1979, Bride & Groom	**90.00**
1980, Wrapping Christmas Presents	**120.00**
1981, Music Maker	**90.00**
1982, Giving Thanks	**160.00**
1983, Painter	**90.00**

Ingot
Franklin Mint
1972, Spirit of Scouting, price for
set of 12 . . . . **275.00**
1974, Tribute to Robert Frost, price
for set of 12 . . . . **285.00**
Hamilton Mint
1975, Saturday Evening Post
Covers, price for set of 12 . . . . . **210.00**
1977, Charles Dickens **50.00**
Magazine
American Artist, July, 1976, Self
Portrait and article **18.00**
Country Gentleman, 1979, memorial
issue **20.00**
Saturday Evening Post, August, 1977,
250th Edition, Rockwell cov, illus,
and portfolio **25.00**
Magazine Cover
American Boy
1916, Dec **30.00**
1920, April **27.50**
American Legion, 1978, July **5.00**
Boys Life
1915, Aug **50.00**
1947, Feb **45.00**
1957, June **42.50**
Colliers, 1919
March 1 . . . . **25.00**
April 19 . . . . **20.00**
Country Gentleman
1920, May 8 . . . . **48.50**
1922, March 18 . . . . **45.00**
Family Circle, 1967, Dec, Santa
Claus **10.00**
Fisk Club News, 1917, May **18.00**
Jack and Jill, 1974, Dec **5.00**
Literary Digest
1918, Dec 14 . . . . **30.00**
1922, April 15 . . . . **18.00**
Look, 1964, July 14 . . . . **10.00**
McCall's, 1964, Dec **12.00**
Parents
1939, Jan **10.00**
1951, May **9.00**
Red Cross, April, 1918 . . . . **25.00**
Saturday Evening Post
1916, Oct 14 . . . . **100.00**
1918, Jan 26 . . . . **90.00**
1922, Feb 18 . . . . **85.00**
1945, March 21 . . . . **70.00**
1946, Nov 16 . . . . **25.00**
1950, April 29 . . . . **80.00**
1952, Aug 30 . . . . **40.00**

1955, March 12 . . . . **20.00**
1957, Sept 7 . . . . **21.50**
1960, Feb 13 . . . . **60.00**
1962, Jan 13 . . . . **12.00**
Scouting
1934, Feb **10.00**
1944, Dec **12.00**
1953, Oct **8.50**
TV Guide, 1970, May 16 . . . . **5.00**
Yankee, 1972, Aug **9.50**
Paperweight, River Shore **100.00**
Plate
Franklin Mint
1971, Under The Mistletoe **175.00**
1972, The Carolers **165.00**
1973, Trimming The Tree **165.00**
1974, Hanging The Wreath **180.00**
1975, Home For Christmas **190.00**
Gorham
Boy Scout, 1975, Our Heritage . . **60.00**
Christmas Series
1975, Good Deeds **64.00**
1976, Christmas Trio **60.00**
1977, Yuletide Reckoning **45.00**
1978, Planning Christmas Visits **25.00**
1979, Santa's Helpers **20.00**
1980, Letter to Santa **25.00**
1981, Santa Plans His Visit **30.00**
1982, The Jolly Coachman **30.00**
1983, Christmas Dancers **30.00**
Four Seasons, price for set of 4
1971, A Boy & His Dog **400.00**
1972, Young Love **200.00**
1973, Ages of Love **300.00**
1974, Grandpa & Me **175.00**
1975, Me & My Pal **200.00**
1976, Grand Pals **200.00**
1978, The Tender Years **115.00**
1979, A Helping Hand **100.00**
1980, Dad's Boy **130.00**
1982, Life With Father **100.00**
1983, Old Buddies **115.00**
1984, Traveling Salesman **115.00**
Dave Grossman Designs
Annual Series, bas–relief
1979, Leapfrog **50.00**
1980, Lovers **60.00**
1981, Dreams of Long Ago **60.00**
Christmas Series, bas–relief
1981, Santa's Good Boys **75.00**
1982, Faces of Christmas **75.00**
Huckleberry Finn Series
1979, The Secret **49.00**
1980, Listening **40.00**
1981, No Kings Nor Dukes **40.00**
Tom Sawyer Series
1976, Whitewashing Fence . . . **75.00**
1977, Take Your Medicine **50.00**
Lynell Studios
Christmas
1979, Snow Queen **30.00**
1980, Surprises For All **30.00**

Mother's Day
1980, Cradle of Love	40.00
1981, Mother's Blessing	30.00
1983, Dear Mother	26.00

River Shore
| 1979, Spring Flowers | 120.00 |
| 1980, Looking Out To Sea | 110.00 |

Rockwell Museum
American Family Series
| 1978, Baby's First Step | 80.00 |
| 1979, First Prom | 30.00 |

American Family II Series
| 1980, New Arrival | 40.00 |
| 1981, At The Circus | 96.00 |

Rockwell Society
Christmas Series
1975, Angel With Black Eye	100.00
1976, Golden Christmas	55.00
1977, Toy Shop Window	50.00
1978, Christmas Dream	50.00
1979, Somebody's Up There	30.00
1980, Scotty Plays Santa	32.00
1981, Wrapped Up In Christmas	30.00
1982, Christmas Courtship	30.00
1983, Santa on the Subway	30.00

Heritage Series
1977, Toy Maker	260.00
1978, The Cobbler	155.00
1979, Lighthouse Keeper's Daughter	80.00
1980, Ship Builder	60.00
1981, Music Maker	30.00
1982, The Tycoon	20.00
1983, Painter	25.00
1984, Story Teller	25.00

Mother's Day Series
| 1976, A Mother's Love | 120.00 |
| 1977, Faith | 75.00 |

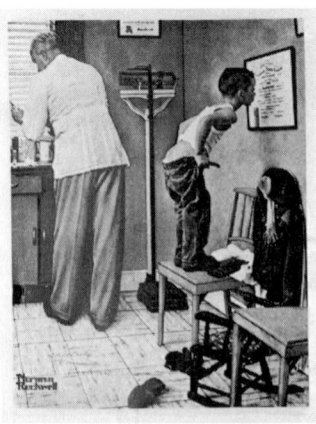

Print, Before The Shot, *Saturday Evening Post* **cover, March 15, 1958, 11 x 14",** **$40.00.**

1978, Bedtime	100.00
1979, Reflections	38.00
1980, A Mother's Pride	30.00
1981, After The Party	25.00
1982, Cooking Lesson	25.00
1983, Add Two Cups	24.00
1984, Grandma's Courting Dress	25.00

Royal Devon
Christmas Series
1975, Downhill Daring	50.00
1976, The Christmas Gift	90.00
1977, The Big Moment	80.00
1978, Puppets For Christmas	45.00
1979, One Present Too Many	35.00
1980, Gramps Meets Gramps	35.00

Mother's Day Series
1975, Doctor And The Doll	85.00
1976, Puppy Love	80.00
1977, The Family	90.00
1978, Mother's Day Off	72.00
1979, Mother's Evening Out	35.00
1980, Mother's Treat	35.00

| Playing Cards, Four Seasons, unopened, orig box | 12.00 |

Stein
| Gorham, Pensive Pals | 37.50 |

Rockwell Museum
Fishin' Pals	75.00
For A Good Boy	95.00
The Music Lesson	90.00

ROSEVILLE POTTERY

Collecting Hints: Because of the availability of pieces in Roseville's later commercial ware, the prices for this type of ware are stable and unlikely to rise rapidly.

For the popular middle period patterns, which were made during the Depression and had limited production and sale, the prices are strong. Among the most popular patterns from this middle period are Blackberry, Cherry Blossom, Falline, Ferella, Jonquil, Morning Glory, Sunflower, and Windsor. The Art Deco craze has focused on Futura, especially the more angular–shaped pieces.

Pine Cone in blue or brown glaze continues to have a strong following as do the earlier lines of Juvenile and Donatello.

Desirable shapes include baskets, bookends, cookie jars, ewers, tea sets, and wall pockets.

Most pieces are marked. However, during the middle period paper stickers were used. These often were removed, leaving the piece unmarked.

Roseville made over one hundred and fifty different lines or patterns. Novice collectors would benefit from reading one of the several books about Roseville and viewing the offerings of dealers who specialize in art pottery. Collections generally are organized around a specific pattern or shape.

History: In the late 1880s a group of investors purchased the J. B. Owens Pottery in Roseville, Ohio, and made utilitarian stoneware items. In 1892 the firm was incorporated and joined by George F. Young, who became general manager. Four generations of Youngs controlled Roseville until the early 1950s.

A series of acquisitions began: Midland Pottery of Roseville in 1898, Clark Stoneware Plant in Zanesville (formerly used by Peters and Reed), and Muskingum Stoneware (Mosaic Tile Company) in Zanesville. The year 1898 also saw offices move from Roseville to Zanesville.

In 1900 Roseville developed Rozane, its art pottery line. Ross Purdy designed this line to compete with Weller's Louwelsa. Rozane became a trade name to cover a large series of lines by designers such as Christian Neilson, John J. Herold, and Gazo Fudji. The art lines of hand-decorated underglaze pottery were made in limited quantities after 1919.

The success of Roseville depended on its commercial lines, first developed by John J. Herald and Frederick Rhead in the first decade of the 1900s. Decorating techniques included transfers, pouncing (a method producing a pattern on the ware which could be followed), and air brush work or sponging following embossed motifs. Among the lines from this early period are Dutch, Juvenile, Cameo, and Holland.

George Young retired in 1918. Frank Ferrell replaced Harry Rhead, who had replaced Frederick Rhead, as art director. Ferrell developed over 80 lines, the first being Sylvan. The economic depression of the 1930s caused Roseville to look for new product lines. Pine Cone was introduced in 1935, made for 15 years, and issued in over 75 shapes.

In the 1940s a series of high gloss glazes were tried to revive certain lines. Other changes were made to respond to the fluctuating contemporary markets. Mayfair and Wincraft date from this period. In 1952 Raymor dinnerware was produced. None of these changes brought economic success back to Roseville. In November, 1954, Roseville was bought by the Mosaic Tile Company.

References: Susan and Al Bagdade, *Warman's American Pottery and Porcelain,* Wallace–Homestead, 1994; John W. Humphries, *A Price Guide To Roseville Pottery By The Numbers,* published by author, 1993; Sharon and Bob Huxford, *The Collectors Encyclopedia of Roseville Pottery, First Series (1976, 1995 value update); Second Series (1980, 1995 value update),* Collector Books; Ralph and Terry Kovel, *Kovels' American Art Pottery: The Collector's Guide To Makers, Marks and Factory Histories,* Crown Publishers, 1993; Dana Gehman Morykan and Harry L. Rinker, *Warman's Country Antiques & Collectibles, Second Edition* Wallace–Homestead, 1994; Leslie Pina, *Pottery: Modern Wares, 1920–1960,* Schiffer Publishing, 1994.

Collectors' Clubs: American Art Pottery Association, 125 E. Rose Ave., St. Louis, MO 63119; Roseville's of the Past Pottery Club, PO Box 681117, Orlando, FL 32868.

Ashtray, Imperial II, blue	**245.00**
Basket	
Bittersweet, 810–10	**180.00**
Freesia, green, 392–10	**225.00**
Montacello, brown, 632	**550.00**
Pine Cone, brown	**350.00**
Poppy, pink, 347–10	**395.00**
Basket, hanging	
Bushberry, green	**225.00**
Dahlrose	**175.00**
Silhouette	**135.00**
Zephyr Lily, green	**175.00**
Bookends, pr	
Gardenia	**165.00**
Pine Cone, brown	**195.00**
Thorn Apple	**190.00**
Zephyr Lily, green	**195.00**
Bowl	
Apple Blossom, green, 326–6	**120.00**
Baneda	**165.00**
Clematis, green, 667–5	**80.00**
Ferella, 12" d	**695.00**
Florentine, 7" d	**75.00**
Fuchsia, 348–3	**165.00**
Lombardy, dark teal	**75.00**
Pine Cone	
Brown, 278–4	**225.00**
Green	**100.00**
Candleholder	
Clematis, brown, 1154–2	**50.00**
Cosmos, pink, 113–6	**40.00**
Tourmaline, dark pink and turquoise	**100.00**
White Rose, pr	**75.00**
Candlesticks, pr, Pine Cone, green, 5" h	**140.00**
Console Bowl	
Freesia, brown, 468–12	**100.00**
Pine Cone, brown, 11" d	**295.00**
Console Set, bowl and pr candleholders	
Calla Lily, 7" d bowl	**100.00**
Columbine, blue, 10" bowl, 2½" h candleholders	**175.00**
Tuscany, 12" d bowl, 4" h candleholders	**170.00**
Cornucopia	
Bleeding Heart, green, 141–6	**85.00**
Clematis, green	**65.00**
Peony, tan, 171–8	**120.00**
Creamer and Sugar, Zephyr Lily, blue	**105.00**

Ewer
Chloron, 5" h 150.00
Clematis, 18–15 .... 295.00
Freesia, blue, 19–6 .... 120.00
Flower Pot, matching underplate
Poppy, green 245.00
Thorn Apple, blue 210.00
Jardiniere
Normandy, 7" h 180.00
Snowberry, green, 8" h 950.00
Jardiniere and Pedestal, Dahlrose 500.00
Pedestal, Freesia, green, 17" h 215.00
Pitcher
Colonial, cream gloss, blue stripes,
8¼" h 40.00
Holland, 6½" h 225.00
Planter
Magnolia, 388–6 .... 110.00
Pine Cone, 12 1/2 x 4½", repair 115.00
Poppy, blue 40.00
Urn, Florentine, brown, 463–5 ...... 85.00
Vase
Baneda, green, 7½" h 495.00
Cherry Blossom
5" h, two handled 225.00
7½" h, brown 280.00
Clematis
Blue, 193–6 .... 80.00
Tan, 111–10 .... 120.00
Dahlrose, 6" h 120.00
Foxglove
Blue, 116–7 .... 75.00
Pink, 54–15 .... 350.00
Freesia, two handles, brown, 124–9 120.00
Fudji, Rozane, 6" h 1,250.00
Fuschia
Brown, two handles, 8½" h 165.00
Green, 895–7 .... 285.00
Futura, green, 389–0 .... 475.00
Iris, brown, 917–6 .... 95.00
Ixia, 855–7 .... 75.00
Jonquil, squatty, 4" h 110.00
Laurel, green, 7 x 6" 185.00
Magnolia
Blue, 185–8 .... 135.00
Green, 96–12 .... 225.00
Peony, tan, 171–19 .... 90.00

Vase, white magnolia flowers, apricot ground, two handles, #446-4, 4¼" h, $45.00.

Pine Cone
Blue, 840–7 .... 185.00
Brown, 913–18 .... 1,000.00
Poppy, pink, 873–9 .... 245.00
Primrose, 760–6 .... 90.00
Rosecraft, black, 5½" h 40.00
Rozane, pansies, 5" h 150.00
Snowberry, green, 1V1–12 .... 225.00
Tourmaline, blue 75.00
White Rose, 994–18 .... 695.00
Windsor, blue, green design, 5½" h 175.00
Wisteria, brown, 8" h 425.00
Zephyr Lily, green, 141–15 .... 575.00
Wall Pocket
Bittersweet, green 295.00
Carnelian 1, pink and blue 175.00
Clematis, green 175.00
Cosmos, blue 375.00
Florentine, 12½" h 275.00
Gardenia, green 250.00
Lotus, burgundy 145.00
Snowberry 125.00
White Rose, pink, 8" h 325.00

ROYAL CHINA

Collecting Hints: Collectors tend to concentrate on specific patterns. Among the most favored are Bluebell (1940s), Currier and Ives (1949–1950), Colonial Homestead (ca. 1951–1952), Old Curiosity Shop (early 1950s), Regal (1937), Royalty (1936), blue and pink willow ware (1940s), and Windsor.

Royal China patterns were widely distributed. Colonial Homestead was sold by Sears through the 1960s. The result is that pieces are relatively common and prices moderate.

Because of the ease of accessibility, only purchase pieces in fine to excellent condition. Do not buy pieces whose surface is marked or marred in any way.

History The Royal China Company, located in Sebring, Ohio, utilized remodeled facilities that originally housed the Oliver China Company and later the E. H. Sebring Company. Royal China began operations in 1934.

The company produced an enormous number of dinnerware patterns. The backs of pieces usually contain the names of the shape, line, and decoration. In addition to many variations of company backstamps, Royal China also produced objects with private backstamps. All records of these markings were lost in a fire in 1970.

The company's Currier and Ives pattern, designed by Gordon Parker, was introduced in 1949–1950. Early marks were date–coded. Other early 1950s patterns include Colonial Homestead and Old Curiosity Shop.

In 1964 Royal China purchased the French–

Saxon China Company, Sebring, which it operated as a wholly owned subsidiary. On December 31, 1969, Royal China was acquired by the Jeannette Corporation. When fire struck the Royal China Sebring plant in 1970, Royal moved its operations to the French–Saxon plant. The company changed hands several times, being owned briefly by the Coca–Cola Company, the J. Corporation from Boston, and Nordic Capitol of New York, New York. Production continued until August 1986 when operations ceased.

References: Susan and Al Bagdade, *Warman's American Pottery and Porcelain*, Wallace–Homestead, 1994; Jo Cunningham, *The Collector's Encyclopedia of American Dinnerware*, Collector Books, 1982, 1995 value update; Harvey Duke, *The Official Identification And Price Guide To Pottery And Porcelain, Eighth Edition*, House of Collectibles, 1995; Lois Lehner, *Lehner's Encyclopedia of U. S. Marks on Pottery, Porcelain & Clay*, Collector Books, 1988.

COLONIAL HOMESTEAD Heritage Series, introduced 1950–1952. Sold by Sears.

Bowl, 5½" d	3.00
Cake Plate, tab handles	12.00
Creamer and Sugar, cov	15.00
Plate	
Bread and Butter	1.50
7" d	2.50
Dinner	3.50
Salt and Pepper Shakers, pr	12.00

CURRIER & IVES Blue and White scenic design, Cavalier Ironstone, introduced 1949–1950. Part of the Heritage Series.

Ashtray	10.00
Berry Bowl, 5½" d	3.00
Butter Dish	18.00
Cake Plate, handled	12.00
Casserole, cov	62.00
Creamer and Sugar, cov	17.00
Cup and Saucer	4.50
Gravy Boat, underplate	22.50
Pie Plate, 10" d	15.00
Plate	
6" d, bread and butter	2.50
10¼" d	4.50
Platter, oval	22.00
Sandwich Plate, tab handles	13.00
Soup, flat	7.50
Vegetable Bowl	
9" d	13.00
10" d	14.00

Currier & Ives, cup and saucer, blue and white, $4.50.

MEMORY LANE Pink and White.

Berry Bowl	3.00
Cake Plate, handled, round	12.00
Chop Plate	25.00
Creamer and Sugar	15.00
Cup and Saucer	4.00
Gravy, underplate	20.00
Plate	
6" d	2.50
7" d, salad	6.00
9" d, lunch	6.00
Dinner	4.00
Platter, large	30.00
Soup, flat	6.00
Vegetable Bowl	
9" d	18.00
10" d	20.00
Willow Ware	
Bowl, 5½" d	4.00
Casserole, cov, 8" d	18.00
Cup and Saucer	5.00
Plate, 6" d	2.00
Sugar, cov	7.50

OLD CURIOSITY SHOP Cavalier shape, 1950s.

Berry Bowl, 5" d	3.00
Bowl, 9¼"	18.00
Cake Plate, handled	15.00
Cereal Bowl, tab handles	8.00
Creamer and Sugar, cov	17.00
Cup and Saucer	4.00
Plate	
6" d, bread and butter	2.50
Dinner	4.00
Platter, handled, 10" l	13.00
Soup, flat	6.00
Vegetable Bowl	15.00

SALOON COLLECTIBLES

Collecting Hints: Collectors concentrate on materials from the pre–Prohibition (1918) era, with many recreating the decor of an old–time saloon in one room of their house. This material also is extremely popular with decorators. The field still is in its infancy with little information available. Many bargains can be found by the knowledgeable collector.

History: The American saloon throughout history has been a refuge and playground for off-duty males. Women and children often were forbidden to enter this masculine turf. Gambling, cursing, drinking, smoking, and fighting were the primary forms of entertainment at the saloon. Today the illusion exists that life was much more exciting in a yesteryear saloon than a modern bar.

The saloon consisted of many units—the back bar, the front bar, and the room itself. All types of materials existed to fill needs, from bottles to spittoons.

References: Roger Baker, *Old West Antiques & Collectibles Illustrated Price Guide*; George J. Baley, *Back Bar Breweriana: A Guide To Advertising, Beer Statues, and Beer Shelf Signs*, L–W Book Sales, 1992.

Back Bar, carved wood
  94″ l, mahogany, leaded windows
    and mirrors **8,000.00**
  190″ l, stained glass columns, marble
    top, dated 1910 . . . . **9,000.00**
Bottle
  Burke's Union Club, 8″ h, clear **35.00**
  Westminster Rye, 11″ h, cut letters
    emb in gold **100.00**
Cash Register, National, brass, wood
  base, two drawers **1,000.00**
Counter Display, 11½″ h, 12″ l, Cognac
  Brandy, Hennessy dog with bag **85.00**
Decanter
  Belle of Kentucky, clear, ribbed, gold
    cut letters, stopper **100.00**
  Maryland Club, 8½″ h, cut, fluted
    neck, cut stopper **45.00**
Figure, Teachers Scotch Whiskey **35.00**
Ice Chopper, cast steel, wood handle,
  Gilchrist **25.00**
Match Dispenser, 3¾ x 2½ x 12″, metal
  and cast iron, dark blue, black base,
  "1¢ Match Dispenser" **125.00**
Photograph, interior scene with mustached bar keeper, fixtures, bar, 8 x
  6″, c1900 . . . . **115.00**
Player Piano, coin–operated, rebuilt
  case, stained glass section lights up,
  includes rolls **4,000.00**
Salt and Pepper Shakers, Cuckenheimer
  Whiskey, glass bottles **15.00**
Shot Glass, etched, "Ruby Saloon" . . . **20.00**
Sign
  Ginger Cordial, Clayton and Russel,
    reverse painting on glass, 15 x 8″ **380.00**
  Old Overholt Pennsylvania Rye,
    gold, silver leaf, reverse painting

    on glass, orig ornate wood frame **400.00**
  Schmidt City Club, tin litho, 9″ d . . . **60.00**
  Sherwood Pure Rye, leaf lettering outlined in red and green, reverse
    painting on glass, orig ornate wood
    frame **375.00**
Spittoon
  7½″ d, 4″ h, pottery, brown, glazed,
    ribbed flared bowl, beaded rim,
    white mouth **75.00**
  8½″ d, 5½″ h, cast iron, white porcelain int., c1850 . . . . **45.00**
  24″ d, 5½″ h, porcelain, green, white
    int. **35.00**
Token, brass, Deer Lodge, Montana . . . **12.00**
Tray, 12″ d, Straus, Gunst & Co, Full
  Dress Maryland Rye, tip, 1907 . . . . . **100.00**
Whiskey Dispenser, 15½″ h, glass,
  etched, "Ask for Sanderson's
  Whiskey" **475.00**

SALT AND PEPPER SHAKERS

Collecting Hints: Collect only sets in very good condition. Make certain the set has the proper two pieces, and base if applicable. China shakers should show no signs of cracking. Original paint and decoration should be intact on all china and metal figures. All parts should be present, including the closure if important.

A collector will have to compete with collectors in other areas, e.g., advertising, animal groups, Blacks, and holiday collectibles. Many shakers will have souvenir labels which may have been added later to stock items. The form, not the label, is the important element.

Black figural shakers are rising in price. The same is true for advertising sets and comic and cartoon characters.

History: The Victorian era saw the advent of the elaborate glass and fine china salt and pepper shaker. The pioneering research work by Arthur Goodwin Peterson in books such as *Glass Salt Shakers: 1,000 Patterns* attracted collectors to this area. Figural and souvenir shakers, most dating from the mid–20th century and later, were looked down upon by this group.

This attitude is slowly changing. More and more people are collecting the figural and souvenir shakers, especially since prices are lower. Many of these patterns were made by Japanese firms and imported heavily after World War II.

Production of a form might continue for decades; hence, it is difficult to tell an early example from a modern one. This is one factor in keeping prices low.

References: Gideon Bosker, *Great Shakes: Salt and Pepper For All Tastes*, Abbeville Press, 1986;

Gideon Bosker and Lena Lencer, *Salt and Pepper Shakers: Identification And Price Guide*, Avon Books, 1994; Larry Carey and Sylvia Tompkins, *Salt and Pepper: Over 1001 Shakers With Prices*, Schiffer Publishing, 1994; Melva Davern, *Collectors' Encyclopedia of Figural and Novelty Salt & Pepper Shakers*, First Series (1985, 1991 value update), *Second Series* (1990, 1993 value update), Collector Books, Helene Guarnaccia, *Salt & Pepper Shakers: Identification and Values*, Vol. I (1985, 1993 value update), Vol II (1989, 1993 value update), Vol III, (1991, 1995 value update), Vol IV, (1993, 1995 value update), Collector Books; Mildred and Ralph Lechner, *The World Of Salt Shakers, Second Edition*, Collector Books, 1992; Arthur G. Peterson, *Glass Salt Shakers*, Wallace–Homestead, 1970, out–of–print; Mike Schneider, *The Complete Salt And Pepper Shaker Book*, Schiffer Publishing, 1993.

Collectors' Clubs: Antique and Art Glass Salt Shaker Collector's Society, 2832 Rapidan Trail, Maitland, FL 32751; Novelty Salt and Pepper Shakers Club, 581 Joy Road, Battle Creek, MI 49017.

Museum: Judith Basin Museum, Stanford, MT.

Ceramic
Babies in basket	75.00
Barber Shaves Pig	48.00
Black head, white gloves	195.00
Boy and Dog, huggies, Van Telligen	85.00
Boy Davy Crockett	75.00
Cereal Sisters, Disney	85.00
Chef Garfield	125.00
Dick Tracy and Junior	35.00
Elephant, Rosemeade	50.00
Elsie and Elmer, Borden adv, cows, 4" h, holding bowl, c1940	50.00
Friar Tuck, Goebel	35.00
Goldilocks, Regal	150.00
Greyhound Dogs, Rosemeade	20.00
Jam and Rolls	35.00
Kate Greenaway Children	110.00
King Cole and Fiddler	35.00

Ceramic, birds, white, gold trim, marked "Made in Japan," 3" h, $4.50.

Laurel and Hardy, figural, tray base, Dresden, 1930s	100.00
Lawn Mower, moving wheels and pistons, c1950s	25.00
Little Red Riding Hood, Regal	60.00
Milk Cans, Shawnee	10.00
Mugsey, Shawnee, 3" h	58.00
Nipper, adv, dog, 3" h, black and white, "His Master's Voice" and "RCA Victor" base inscriptions, Lenox, 1930s	48.00
Owls, Shawnee	17.00
Peekaboos, Regal, small	185.00
Pennsylvania Dutch, Shawnee	60.00
Pinocchio, Disney	165.00
Princess of Thumb	55.00
Rockabye Baby	60.00
Thermos and Lunch Pail	32.00
Thread and Thimble	30.00
Trylon and Perisphere, 3" h, white, gold trim, orange and white serving tray, 1939 New York World's Fair, Japan	55.00
Valentine Kids, black hair	235.00
Winnie and Smiley, no gold trim, Shawnee, 3" h	58.00

Glass
Art Glass, each
Blossomtime, amethyst colored, hp, two piece top	145.00
Christmas Pearl, yellow ground, hp leaves, earthy colors, dated and sgd agitator	115.00
Tomato, yellow ground, hp pink and white rosebuds, Mt Washington	85.00
Wavecrest, hp, green tint, orange flowers, Kelva	235.00

Depression Glass, pr
American Sweetheart, Monax	265.00
Delphite, round, Jeannette	45.00
Floragold	40.00
Florentine #2, yellow	38.00
Madrid, amber, flat	60.00
Moderntone, blue	35.00
Royal Lace, clear	30.00
Sharon, pink	42.00
Thistle, green, tray	50.00
Transparent Green, sq, Owens Illinois	20.00
Vitrock, red tulip, range, Hocking	15.00

Pattern Glass, each
Aster, blue opaque, sq, pedestal, tinplate top	55.00
Banded Fleur–De–Lis, clear, large, US Glass Co	32.00
Curlique, clear, small pedestal, pewter top	38.00
Daisy and Button, sapphire blue, small pedestal, moon and stars pewter top	36.00
Dewey, green, pewter top	95.00

Earlybird, clear, bird shape, pewter
top **55.00**
Shrine, clear, domed tinplate top,
US Glass **68.00**
Willow Oak, amber, tinplate top,
US Glass **45.00**
Plastic
Budweiser, 1976 . . . .   **165.00**
Mammy, Luzianne, green **225.00**
TV set, 3″ h, brown, gold accents and
legs, white viewing screen, on/off
switch raises shakers, orig box,
1950s **65.00**
Washer and Dryer, Westinghouse adv   **15.00**
Wood, natives, pr **15.00**

SANTA CLAUS

Collecting Hints: The number of Santa Claus–related items is endless. Collectors are advised to concentrate on one form (postcards, toys, etc.) or a brief time period. New collectors will find the hard plastic 1950s Santas easily accessible and generally at a reasonable price.

History: The idea for Santa Claus developed from stories about St. Nicholas, who lived about 300 A.D. By the 1500s, "Father Christmas" in England, "Pere Noel" in France, and "Weihnachtsmann" in Germany were well established.

Until the 1800s Santa Claus was pictured as a tall, thin, stately man wearing bishop's robes and riding a white horse. Washington Irving in *Knickerbocker's History of New York* (1809), made him a stout, jolly man who wore a broad–rimmed hat and huge breeches and smoked a long pipe. The traditional Santa Claus image came from Clement C. Moore's poem "An Account of a Visit from St. Nicholas" (*Troy Sentinel,* NY, 1823) and the cartoon characterizations by Thomas Nast which appeared in *Harper's Weekly* between 1863 and 1886.

References: Ann Bahar, *Santa Dolls: Historical To Contemporary,* Hobby House Press, 1992; E. Willis Jones, *The Santa Claus Book,* Walker, 1976; Polly and Pam Judd, *Santa Dolls and Figurines Price Guide: Antique To Contemporary,* Revised, Hobby House Press, 1994; Mary Morrison, *Snow Babies, Santas and Elves: Collecting Christmas Bisque Figures,* Schiffer Publishing, 1993; Maggie Rogers and Peter R. Hallinan, *The Santa Claus Picture Book: An Appraisal Guide,* E. P. Dutton, 1984.

Additional Listings: Christmas Items.

Advertising Trade Card
Dundee Smart Clothes, Allentown,
PA, Santa with pack on back **4.00**
Greenpoint Savings Bank, Brooklyn,
NY, Santa with pack on back **4.00**

Santa Claus Soap, Santa carrying tree
on shoulder, child and doll at feet,
1899 . . . .   **15.00**
Woolson Spice Co, Father Christmas,
Santa, and reindeer **12.00**
Bank
2″ h, Japan, bisque, Father Christmas,
green base **12.00**
3¼″ h, Japan, bisque **20.00**
6½″ h, metal, Santa sleeping in chair   **30.00**
11″ h, chalkware, Santa in chimney,
pack on back, 1950s **25.00**
11½″ h, Noel Decorations, Inc, Santa
sitting on litho tin house, shakes
presents and bell when coin is deposited, battery operated, wearing
felt costume, orig box **175.00**
Book
Around the World with Santa Claus,
McLoughlin Bros, NY, 1900 . . . . .   **25.00**
How Santa Filled the Christmas
Stockings, Stecher Litho Co,
Rochester, NY, 1916 . . . .   **12.00**
Watching for Santa Claus, Hurst &
Co, NY, 1912 . . . .   **15.00**
Booklet, children's, Snellenberg's Dept
Store, Philadelphia, PA, Santa and
children cov, 1930s **10.00**
Calendar Plate, 9¾″ d, Santa on sleigh,
whip in hand, four reindeer, 1909 . .   **50.00**
Candy Box, cardboard, rect, Santa face
on all sides, 1950s **7.50**
Candy Container
5½″ h, Victory Candy Co, glass,
Father Christmas in chimney, metal
base **75.00**
8½″ h, Germany, Belsnickle, papier
mache, white mica coat, holding
feather tree, early 1900s **450.00**
9″ h, USA, papier mache, waving,
large belly, red coat, 1940s **50.00**
10″ h, USA, candy cane holder,
molded cardboard, holding open
sack over chimney, late 1940s . . .   **50.00**
Candy Dispenser, 4″ h, Pez type, plastic,
red and white **10.00**
Card Holder, Hallmark, paper, fold–up
Santa and reindeer, 1940s **18.00**
Chocolate Mold, 9″ h, Santa carrying
basket, tin, double hinged, c1930 . .   **125.00**
Cigar Store Figure, 60½″ h, carved
wood, worn and flaked polychrome
paint, deep age cracks **650.00**
Clicker, litho tin, Santa at fireplace,
1930s **40.00**
Diecut, Germany, paper costume and
boots, 1920 . . . .   **75.00**
Display
42″ h, Santa head, papier mache, hollow, Westinghouse **35.00**
60″ h, Pepsi–Cola Santa, cardboard,
one leg raised, bottle in hand **75.00**

Figure

 2½" h, Japan, cotton, plaster face, papier mache reindeer, cardboard sled, 1930s **40.00**

 3" h

  Japan, composition face, red chenille body **40.00**

  USA, Santa face, open at top, 1940s **8.00**

 4" h, cardboard, Santa holding tree, black platform, ¼" thick **7.00**

 4½" h, USA, hard plastic, holding green tree, wearing white snowshoes, c1950 .... **6.50**

 5" h, Japan, celluloid, holding fruit basket **75.00**

 6½" h, Japan, skier, red cloth coat, tan pants, wood skis and poles **60.00**

 8" h, Germany, Father Christmas, blue pants, red flannel jacket, rabbit fur beard, basket on back, holding feather tree, 1920s **200.00**

 8½" h, Irwin, USA, Father Christmas, red and white, pack over shoulder **48.00**

 10" h, Germany, cotton flannel suit, rabbit fur beard, carrying goose feather tree, c1910 .... **500.00**

 12" h, papier mache, Father Christmas, yellow coat, 1910 .... **750.00**

 17" h, hard plastic, light bulb inserted in back **35.00**

Game, 10" h, Santa Claus Ring Toss, First National Bank, Berwick, PA premium, "Season's Greetings" **8.00**

Greeting Card

 5" h, "Christmas Greeting In My House," house shape, Santa with tree, 1930s **3.00**

 7" h, "Christmas Greetings," Santa cutout, poem inside, 1930s **3.50**

Jigsaw Puzzle, Santa Claus Puzzle Box, Milton Bradley, 3 dimensional multicolored litho puzzles, orig box, c1924 .... **95.00**

Lamp

 8½" h, Glo–Light Corp, Chicago, IL, Santa figure, molded plastic front with red flocked suit, tin back with hole for light bulb, 1950s **10.00**

 10½" h, US Glass Co, Santa in chimney, glass, c1925 .... **925.00**

Lantern, Japan, Santa face, battery operated, green metal base, 1950s **25.00**

Light Bulb, 3" h, Japan, milk glass, painted, one leg in chimney **35.00**

Mask, painted cloth, cotton batting beard, 1930s **15.00**

Music Box, Japan, plays *Jingle Bells*, wood sleigh, composition Santa face, flannel body, two 10" h celluloid deer **100.00**

Nodder, 7" h, Japan, celluloid, 2–di-

mensional, tin base, marked with "K" inside bell **350.00**

Ornament

 3¾" h, glass, holding tree, 1930s ... **25.00**

 6" h

  Cotton Batting, scrap face, carrying goose feather tree **75.00**

  Glass, holding sack, attached to metal clip, 1920s **135.00**

 7" h, Japan, cotton, plaster face **40.00**

Pin, wood, diecut, shellacked finish, c1940 .... **8.00**

Pinback Button

 1³⁄₁₆" d, Wiebolt's, Santa greeting young girl at Christmas tree, white ground, blue lettering, light blue rim, c1935 .... **22.00**

 ⅞" d, National Tuberculosis Assn, Santa with boy and girl at top of chimney, "Merry Christmas, Healthy New Year," issued 1921 **20.00**

 1¼" d, department store Santa image, rim inscription, 1920s **18.00**

Planter, stoneware, painted **28.00**

Post Card, Germany, Father Christmas handing toys through window, "Christmas Greetings" **7.00**

Post Card, Ellen H. Clapsaddle, artist, International Art Publ. Co, red outfit, $8.50.

Stereoview, Keystone View Co, children and Santa peeking at each other through keyhole, 1899 .... **10.00**

Stuffed Toy, 16" h, Coca–Cola Santa, plush, plastic face, holding miniature Coke bottle, 1950 .... **75.00**

Teapot, 7½" h, England, figural Santa, backstamped "Lucky Santa Claus Teapot, Made in England, Reg. No. 835362" **95.00**

Tin, Blue Bird Toffee, Henry Vincent, Ltd, Worcestershire, England, litho Santa's face and toys, octagonal **40.00**

Token, 1" d, copper colored emb coin, detailed portrait, "Merry Christmas, Santa Claus' Xmas Gift Store, Dive, Pomeroy & Stewart," c1920 ...... **8.50**

Toy, cloth, straw filled, papier-mâché face, composition boots, 9" h, $72.00.

Toy
Bell Ringing Santa, 7" h, Alps, Japan, windup, vinyl face, cloth costume, orig box 70.00
Roly Poly Santa, 6" h, composition, wearing red suit, green belt 250.00
Santa Claus Waddler, 4½" h, Great Britain, windup, litho tin 100.00
Santa on Tricycle, 4" l, Japan, windup, litho tin tricycle, celluloid Santa 45.00
Walking Santa Claus, 6¼" h, Occupied Japan, windup, celluloid, metal feet, holding sack and flower, orig box 475.00

SASCHA BRASTOFF

Collecting Hints: When collecting items made by Brastoff, take special note of the signature. Pieces made exclusively by Brastoff are marked with his full name. A "Sascha B" signature indicates he only supervised the production.

History: Internationally known designer, artist, sculptor, and ceramist Sascha Brastoff began producing ceramic artware in 1953. His hand–painted china originally commanded prices ranging from $25.00 to thousands of dollars for a single item. He also designed a full line of dinnerware.

References: Jack Chipman, *Colector's Encyclopedia of California Pottery,* Collector Books, 1992; Lois Lehner, *Lehner's Encyclopedia of U.S. Marks on Pottery, Porcelain & Clay,* Collector Books, 1988.

Ashtray
Eskimo, 7" d 60.00
House, kidney shaped, 8" l 35.00

Poodle, 7" d 40.00
White, raised gold floral dec 30.00
Basket, 17" h 150.00
Candleholder, walrus, 8" h 70.00
Charger, 17" d 145.00
Compote, striped white, 12" h 85.00
Cuspidor, lion 60.00
Fruit Bowl
Striped 75.00
Surf Ballet, gold dec, emerald green ground, ftd 35.00
Mug, eskimo and walrus, 6" h 75.00
Pipe, 4" l, white, birds wearing crown 45.00
Pitcher, cov, green, stylized flowers design, 15" h 250.00
Plate
4" sq, pink roses, purple berries 30.00
8¼" d, Surf Ballet, luncheon, gold dec, emerald green ground 35.00
12" d, pagoda design, curled lip ... 85.00
Platter
15" d, round, rose, blue, and white leaves, gold highlights, deep teal ground, glossy finish, piecrust fluted edge 250.00
17¾" l, 14" w, rect, wavy rim with one large green and white leaf, shaded deep green ground, glossy finish 250.00
Vase
9½" h, rearing stallion 95.00
12" h, white ground, silver and gold flowers 85.00
12" h, Alaskan 225.00

SCOUTING

Collecting Hints: Nostalgia is one of the principal reasons for collecting scouting memorabilia; individuals often focus on the period when they were in the scouting movement. Other collectors select themes, e.g., handbooks, jamborees, writings by scout movement leaders, Eagle Scout material, etc. Jamboree ephemera is especially desirable.

Scouting scholars have produced a wealth of well–researched material on the scouting movement. Many of these pamphlets are privately printed and can be located by contacting dealers specializing in scouting items.

Scout material enjoys popularity among collectors. The greatest price fluctuation occurs in modern material and as collectors define new specialized collecting areas.

Girl Scout material is about five to ten years behind Boy Scout material in respect to collecting interest. A collection can still be assembled for a modest investment. While Boy Scout uniforms have remained constant in design throughout time, the Girl Scout uniform changed almost every decade. This increases the number of desirable collectibles.

History: The Boy Scout movement began in America under the direction of William D. Boyce, inspired by a helping hand he received from one of Baden–Powell's English scouts when he was lost in a London fog in 1910. Other American boy organizations, such as the one organized by Dan Beard, were quickly brought into the Boy Scout movement. In 1916 the Boy Scouts received a charter from the United States Congress. Key leaders in the movement were Ernest Thompson–Seton, Dan Beard, W. D. Boyce, and James West.

A young illustrator, Norman Rockwell, received his first job as editor of *Boys' Life* in 1913, which began a lifelong association with the Boy Scouts.

The first international jamboree was held in England in 1920. America's first jamboree was held in 1937 in Washington, D.C. Manufacturers, quick to recognize the potential for profits, issued a wealth of Boy Scout material. Local councils and Order of the Arrow lodges have added significantly to this base, especially in the area of patches.

The Girl Scout movement began on March 12, 1912, under the direction of Juliette Gordon Low of Savannah, Georgia. The movement grew rapidly and in 1928 the Girl Scout manual suggested selling cookies as a way of raising funds. The Girl Scout movement also received wide recognition for its activities during World War II, selling over $3 million of bonds in the fourth Liberty Loan drive.

Boy Scout patch trading started around the time of the 1950 National Jamboree, where everything from patches to lizards was traded.

References: Mary Degenhardt and Judy Kirsch, *Girl Scout Collector's Guide*, Wallace–Homestead, 1987; Rudy Dioszegi, *Scouting Exonumia*, privately printed, 1985; Fred Duersch, Jr., *Green Khaki Crimped–Edge Merit Badges*, Downs Printing, 1993; Franck, Hook, Ellis & Jones, *An Aid To Collecting Selected Council Shoulder Patches,* privately printed, 1994; Patrick Geary, *National Scout Jamboree Memorabilia*, privately printed, 1988; William Hillcourt, *Norman Rockwell's World of Scouting*, Harry Abrams, 1977; Alburtus Hoogeveen, *Arapaho I, Council Shoulder Patches, Red & Whites, Council Patches, Jamboree Patches, Council Histories,* privately printed; Alburtus Hoogeveen, *Arapaho II, Order of the Arrow, Complete Guide To Order Of Arrow Insignia*, privately printed; Alburtus Hoogeveen, *Arapaho II, Update*, privately printed; Rick Hubbard, *Merit Badge Chronicle*, privately printed, 1986; Norman E. Martinus and Harry L. Rinker, *Warman's Paper*, Wallace–Homestead, 1994; J. Bryan Putman, ed., *Official Price Guide To*

Scouting Collectibles, House of Collectibles, 1982, 1984, 1985; R. J. Sayers, *Identification & Value Guide To Scouting Collectibles*, Books Americana, 1984; R. J. Sayers, *A Guide To Boy Scout Collectibles*, published by author, 1992; Richard Shields, *Patrol Yell, The History of the Patrol Medallions of the B.S.A.*, The Carolina Trader, 1989; Harry D. Thorsen, *Scouts On Stamps Of The World*, privately printed.

Collectors' Clubs: American Scouting Traders Assoc., PO Box 92, Kentfield, CA 94914–0092; International Badgers Club, 7760 NW 50th St., Lander Hill, FL 33351; National Scouting Collectors Society, 806 E. Scott St., Tuscola, IL 61953; Scouts On Stamps Society International, 7406 Park Dr., Tampa, FL 33610.

Periodicals: *Fleur–de–Lis*, 5 Dawes Ct., Novato, CA 94947; Scout Memorabilia Magazine, c/o The Lawrence L. Lee Scouting Museum, PO Box 1121, Manchester, NH 03105.

Museums: Girl Scout National Headquarters, New York, NY; Juliette Gordon Low Girl Scout National Center, Savannah, GA; Lone Scout Memory Lodge, Camp John J. Barnhardt, New London, NC; Murray State University National Museum of the Boy Scouts Of America, Murray, KY; The Lawrence L. Lee Scouting Museum and Max J. Silber Scouting Library, Manchester, NH; Western Scout Museum, Los Angeles; Zitelman Scout Museum, Rockford, IL.

Advisor: Richard Shields.

REPRODUCTION ALERT: Be wary especially of Boy Scout jamboree patches, rare Council Shoulder patches, and rare Order of the Arrow patches.

BOY SCOUTS

Equipment
First Aid Kit, Johnson and Johnson, green cov, New York City, orig contents **15.00**
Flint and Steel Kit, orange box **30.00**
Official BSA Firebuilding Kit **50.00**
Sewing Kit, plastic cover, orig contents **4.00**
Silva Compass, clear plastic base . . . **10.00**
Toilet Kit, canvas cov, orig contents . **15.00**
Yucca Backpack, canvas **20.00**
Handbook
Boy Scout Handbook, 6th edition, 1st printing **5.00**
Handbook for Patrol Leaders, 1929 **20.00**
Handbook for Boys, 1930 . . . . **30.00**
Official Boy Scout Handbook, 9th edition **3.00**
Insignia
Eagle, oval, Boy Scouts of America, silver border **15.00**

First Class
Gold hat pin, safety pin clasp 20.00
Oval 1.00
Life, heart shaped 12.00
Scoutmaster, round, green back-
ground 3.00
Second Class, khaki, cut edge with
border 1.00
Star, dark blue, felt 40.00
Tenderfoot, tan background, folded
under 20.00
Medal
Activity, bronze, 1st class emblem . .   5.00
God and Country, blue ribbon 20.00
Pinewood Derby, car on medallion   1.00
Presidents Trail, Washington, DC . . .   6.00
Mugs Camps, Order of the Arrow
Camporees, Cub Scout activities,
Scout shows 4.00
Jamborees, NOAC, national activities
and bases 7.50
National Jamboree
1950 canvas pocket patch 50.00
1950 embroidered pocket patch . . .   50.00
1953 neckerchief 30.00
1957 leather patch 45.00
1960 pocket patch 20.00
1964 Atlantic Refining Co. map of
Valley Forge 6.00
1964 pocket patch 7.00
1969 jacket patch 5.00
1973 pocket patch 3.00
1977 fishing pass, State of PA 3.00
1981 mug 5.00
1985 leather patch 6.00
1993 hat 3.00
Patrol Medallions, red and black
Embroidered
Colored background 50

**Magazine Tear Sheet, Shredded Krum-
bles, *The Delineator,* 1920, sgd Andrew
Loomis illustration, 14½ x 19½", $30.00.**

**Neckerchief, 1935 Jamboree, blue
ground, white lettering, $90.00.**

Red and black, white glue back . .   .50
Felt, black and white threads on back   2.00
Patches
Go Roundup 1.00
50th Anniversary Achievement Strip   5.00
1960 camp patch, most 2.00
1964–5 NY World's Fair, jacket patch   25.00
Northeast Region, rect 4.00
Schiff Scout Reservation, shield shape   6.00
Scouting Rounds A Guy Out 1.00
State stripe red and white, any of the
50 US 1.00
Philmont
Arrowhead, gauze back 25.00
Belt buckle, rect, Tooth of Time
(mountain), heavy metal 10.00
Neckerchief slide, ceramic, Tooth of
Time (mountain) 3.00
Patch, round, white background, bull   3.00

GIRL SCOUTS

Beret, green, patch 3.00
Book, *Juliette Lowe and The Girl
Scouts,* Choate & Ferris, 1928 . . . . .   10.00
Calendar
1953, full color cov photo, unused .   20.00
1954, 8½ x 10", full color photo, pen-
ciled notes 15.00
Certificate, guardian, 8½ x 15", wood
grain paper, brown construction pa-
per backing, numbered 8816 . . . . . .   25.00
Charter, 9 x 14¾", tan textured paper,
dated Jan 1921, dark brown inscrip-
tion and design, inked signatures . . .   22.00
Coin, 1962 50th Anniversary, gold . . .   5.00
Comic Book, Daisy Lowe of the Girl
Scouts, 6½ x 10", 16 pgs, history text,
full color, 1954 copyright 15.00
Compass, green, six sided 10.00
Cup, collapsible, Eagle in trefoil 10.00
Figure, Girl Scout, small 18.00
Handbook, Intermediate, 1959 . . . . . .   3.00
Magazine, *The American Girl,* June,
1934, 8½ x 12", 52 pgs 10.00

Pin, ¹¹⁄₁₆″, Fiftieth Anniversary **12.00**
Sewing Kit, Brownies, red case, 1940s   **10.00**
Thermos, 6½″ h, metal, red, green, and
  white, stripes and logos, white plastic
  cup, Aladdin, 1960s **37.50**

SEWING ITEMS

Collecting Hints: Collectors tend to favor Sterling silver items. However, don't overlook the material in metals, ivory, celluloid, plastic, and wood. Some metals were plated; the plating should be in very good condition before you buy a piece.

Advertising and souvenir items are part of sewing history. Focusing on one of these aspects will develop a fascinating collection. Another focus is on a certain instrument, with tape measures among the most common. Finally, figural items have a high value because of their strong popularity.

Most collectors concentrate on material from the Victorian era. A novice collector might look to the 20th century, especially the Art Deco and Art Nouveau periods, to build a collection.

History: Sewing was considered an essential skill of a young woman of the 19th century. The wealth of early American samplers attests to the talents of many of these young seamstresses.

During the Victorian era a vast assortment of practical as well as whimsical sewing devices appeared on the market. Among the forms were tape measures, pincushions, stilettos for punchwork, and crochet hooks. The sewing birds attached to table tops were a standard fixture in the parlor.

Many early sewing tools, e.g., needleholders, emery holders and sewing boxes, were made of wood. However, the Sterling silver tool was considered the height of elegance. Thimbles were the most popular. Sterling silver–handled items included darning eggs, stilettos, and thread holders.

In the 20th century needlecases and sewing kits were an important advertising giveaway. Plastic sewing materials are available, but they have not attracted much collector interest.

References: Carter Bays, *The Encyclopedia of Early American Sewing Machines,* published by author, 1993; Pamela Clabburn, *The Needlework Dictionary,* William Morrow & Co., 1976; Joyce Clement, *The Official Price Guide To Sewing Collectibles,* House of Collectibles, 1987, out–of–print; *Advertising & Figural Tape Measures,* L–W Book Sales, 1995; Wayne Muller, *Darn It! The History and Romance of Darners,* L–W Book Sales, 1995; Gay Ann Rogers, *American Silver Thimbles,* Haggerston Press, 1989; Gay Ann Rogers, *An Illustrated History Of Needlework Tools,* Needlework Unlimited,

1983, 1989 price guide; Gay Ann Rogers, *Price Guide Keyed To American Silver Thimbles,* Needlework Unlimited, 1989; James W. Slaten, *Antique American Sewing Machines: A Value Guide,* Singer Dealer Museum, 1992; Glenda Thomas, *Toy and Miniature Sewing Machines: An Identification & Value Guide,* Collector Books, 1995; Estelle Zalkin, *Zalkin's Handbook of Thimbles and Sewing Implements,* Warman Publishing, 1988.

Collectors' Clubs: International Sewing Machine Collectors Society, 1000 E. Charleston Blvd., Las Vegas, NV 89104; Toy Stitchers, 623 Santa Florita Ave., Millbrae, CA 94030.

Museums: Fabric Hall, Historic Deerfield, Deerfield, MA; Museum of American History, Smithsonian Institution, Washington, DC; Sewing Machine Museum, Oakland, CA; Shelburne Museum, Shelburne, VT.

See: Thimbles.

Basket, wicker, round, beaded lid **22.00**
Booklet, Singer, *How to Make
  Children's Clothes,* illus, 1930 . . . . .   **8.00**
Button Box, round, wood shoe, boot label **22.50**
Catalog
  Domestic Sewing Machine, 11½ x
    12″, 16 pages, c1900 . . . .   **18.00**
  Home Needlework Co, Chicago, IL,
    Catalog No. 15, 9 x 11¼″, 40
    pages, c1915 . . . .   **21.00**
  Nonotuck Silk Co, Florence, MA,
    Corticelli Home Needlework, 5½ x
    7¾″, 96 pages, 1898 . . . .   **20.00**
  O. R. Ingersoll, Universal Underfeed
    Sewing Machines, 3 x 5½″, 12
    pages, 1878 . . . .   **15.00**
  Wilcox and Gibbs Sewing Machines,
    New York, 5 x 8″, 38 pages, 1921   **15.00**
Clamp, wood
  Painted, pin cushion, cupid decal . .   **95.00**
  Sycamore, pin cushion, horn embroidery hoops **85.00**
Crochet Hook, metal, capped **15.00**
Darner, egg, scissors inside **42.00**
Emery, cat head, black **18.00**
Lingerie Straps, orig Art Nouveau card,
  woman at dressing table with poem,
  straps attached to card with pink ribbon, 1900s, unused **22.00**
Machine, Singer, Featherweight 221,
  orig case **400.00**
Mending Kit
  Art Deco, "Handy Pack" **10.00**
Bakelite
  Purple, German **14.00**
  Red, thimble cap **16.00**
Birchwood, hp flowers, French souvenir **26.00**

Bullet Shape, Mt Royale **18.00**
Eastern Star **22.50**
Leather Box, "Needles & Cotton/
   Should Not Be Forgotten," scissors   **25.00**
Plastic, bee with scissors **16.00**
Suede Envelope **18.00**
Needle Book, Army–Navy, German . . .   **7.00**
Needle Case
  Advertising
    Bengal Range **8.00**
    Crystal Baking Powder **10.00**
    Lydia Pinkham **15.00**
  Brass, apricot colored enamel and
    handpainted floral design, Ger-
    many **95.00**
  Felt, basket shape **12.00**
  Ivory, scrimshaw, sgd **145.00**
  Leather, "Needles to say . . ." **12.00**
  Wood, beaded, Victorian **165.00**

Needle Case, Linco, Medium Motor Oil, white ground, blue-and-red lettering, Lincoln Oil Refining Co., Robinson, IL, $4.00.

Needle Gripper, Nimble Thimble, orig
  pkg **20.00**
Needle Sharpener
  Cat **48.00**
  Strawberry **6.00**
Needle Threader, adv, Prudential **8.00**
Pin Cushion
  Advertising, Success Horse Drawn
    Manure Spreader **60.00**
  Apple, figural
    Satin, 2½ x 3", red and yellow,
     green leaves and stem **60.00**
  Silk, hp, celluloid baby head in
    bonnet on top, green fabric
    leaves **55.00**
  Camel, figural **15.00**
  Disc, velvet, embroidered **12.00**
  Doll
    China, holding mirror, German . .   **90.00**
    Cloth, Black, holding pin cushion   **28.00**

    Composition **25.00**
    Indian–made **26.00**
  Doll face, bisque, blue glass eyes,
    blonde hair, open mouth with
    teeth, mounted on purple orchid,
    5" h, 5½" w, orig box, German . . .   **85.00**
  Dutch Boy, figural **10.00**
  Flower, plump **12.00**
  Heart, Indian beadwork **48.00**
  Hitler, dated 1941 . . . .   **45.00**
  Horse and Wagon **10.00**
  Orange, figural **25.00**
  Reindeer Hoof, fur and velvet shoe,
    1908 . . . .   **23.00**
  Revolving, tape measure in base,
    thimble **30.00**
  Shoe, figural, metal, Dutch boy and
    girl dec **45.00**
  Silk, blue, hair filled **6.00**
  Strawberry, 3 x 5", red velvet, green
    felt leaves, c1870 . . . .   **85.00**
  Turtle, cast iron body **22.00**
Pin Disc, adv, Prudential **4.00**
Pin Holder, adv
  Cube, German **12.00**
  Prudential **7.00**
Punch, gauge, Sterling silver, pat 1909   **60.00**
Scissors, chicken **24.00**
Sewing Bird, hand held, sgd "Turner"   **75.00**
Sewing Box, red leather, silverplated
  panel on lid **45.00**
Shuttle, wood **60.00**
Skirt Lifter, brass, Art Nouveau, lady's
  profile **95.00**
Spool Cabinet, JP Coats, metal, black,
  glass slant front **95.00**
Spool Holder, souvenir, Indian head de-
  cal **18.00**
Tape Measure
  Advertising
    Hoover Vacuum **25.00**
    Lydia Pinkham, celluloid, portrait
     front, adv back **79.00**
    Zippo **40.00**
  Chrome, brass owl front, German . .   **55.00**
  Figural
    Apple, hard plastic, red, leaf pull   **18.00**
    Clock, metal, pull tab and hands
     turn, marked "Germany" **120.00**
    Dress form **45.00**
    Fish, celluloid **25.00**
    Indian Boy Head, celluloid **30.00**
    Little Boy, wearing clown hat, 4¼"
     h, German **18.00**
    Ivory **60.00**
Tatting Shuttle, adv, Lydia Pinkham, cel-
  luloid, portrait top, adv bottom **99.00**
Thimble Case
  Brass, walnut **20.00**
  Crocheted **5.00**
  Sweet Grass **25.00**
Thread Caddy, metal, 2 tiers **25.00**

Thread Winder, figural fish, mother–
of–pearl 12.00
Tin, Dr Moon's Sewing Machine Oil,
4⅛" 5.00
Toy Sewing Machine
Betsy Clark, 1973 .... 25.00
Kaynee 45.00
Sew Master, Model #550, orig box . . 45.00
Singer
Model 24–7 .... 145.00
Model #50, MIB 60.00

SHAWNEE POTTERY

Collecting Hints: Many Shawnee pieces came in several color variations. Some pieces also contained both painted and decal decorations. The available literature will indicate some but not all of the variations.

Not a great deal of interest is being shown in the Shawnee art and dinnerware lines. Among the lines are Cameo, Cheria (Petit Point), Diora, and Touche (Liana). New collectors may wish to concentrate in these areas.

History: The Shawnee Pottery Co. was founded in 1937 in Zanesville, Ohio. The company acquired a 650,000 square foot plant that formerly housed the American Encaustic Tiling Company. There it produced as many as 100,000 pieces of pottery per day. In 1961 the plant closed.

Shawnee limited its chief production to kitchenware, decorative art pottery, and dinnerware. Distribution was primarily through jobbers and chain stores.

Shawnee can be marked "Shawnee," "Shawnee U.S.A.," "USA #———," "Kenwood," or with character names, e.g., "Pat. Smiley," "Pat. Winnie," etc.

References: Susan and Al Bagdade, *Warman's American Pottery and Porcelain,* Wallace–Homestead, 1994; Jim and Bev Mangus, *Shawnee Pottery: An Identification and Value Guide,* Collector Books, 1994; Mark Supnick, *Collecting Shawnee Pottery,* L–W Books, 1989, 1992 value update; Duane and Janice Vanderbilt, *The Collector's Guide To Shawnee Pottery,* Collector Books, 1992, 1994 value update.

Collectors' Club: Shawnee Pottery Collectors Club, PO Box 713, New Smyrna Beach, FL 32170.

Bank
Smiley, brown 500.00
Winnie
Brown 500.00
Butterscotch 500.00
Bookends, pr, cattails and ducks 65.00

Casserole, Corn King, large 65.00
Cookie Jar
Basketweave, gold 95.00
Carousel 110.00
Corn King 225.00
Dutch Boy
Flowers, gold dec 275.00
Stripes 195.00
Farmer Pig, blue scarf 265.00
Hamm's Bear 175.00
Mugsey 425.00
Owl, gold 300.00
Panda, with swirl 195.00
Smiley Pig, shamrock 295.00
Winking Pig 265.00
Creamer
Elephant 35.00
Puss 'N Boots, gold 175.00
Smiley Pig, gold 225.00
Creamer and Sugar
Blue Flower and Fern 35.00
Puss 'N Boots 48.00
Cup and Saucer, Corn King 65.00
Figurine
Pekingese 60.00
Squirrel 60.00
Flower Bowl, Medallion 15.00
Grease Jar
Fruit 40.00
Lobster 45.00
White Corn, gold 150.00
Ice Bucket, Elephant, pink 195.00
Incense Burner 85.00
Lamp Bracket, blue 110.00
Mug, Toby, maroon 25.00
Pitcher
Bo Peep
Gold Trim 225.00
No Gold 125.00
Pink, blue, and yellow, marked #47 85.00
Chanticleer 120.00
Fern and Flower 45.00
Smiley Pig
Clover Blossom, pink scarf 295.00
Peach Flowers 165.00
Red feet, gold trim 350.00

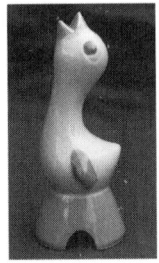

Pie Bird, white, green eyes and wings, pink beak and base, glossy, 5" h, $35.00.

Planter
Elephant, pink and black **60.00**
Fawn, large **38.00**
Mexican Boy and Girl **24.00**
Salt and Pepper Shakers, pr
Chanticleer, small **45.00**
Chefs **18.00**
Dutch Boy and Girl
Gold Trim **100.00**
No Gold **45.00**
Farmer Pigs **25.00**
Flower Pots
Gold Trim **55.00**
No Gold **18.00**
Fruit
Large **30.00**
Small, gold **40.00**
Lobster, upright **45.00**
Milk Cans
Gold Trim, lightly worn **50.00**
No Gold **16.00**
Mugsey, small **75.00**
Owl
Gold Trim **50.00**
No Gold **18.00**
Pennsylvania Dutch **85.00**
Puss 'N Boots **125.00**
Sailor Boy and Girl **25.00**
Smiley Pig
Blue, small **65.00**
Green
Large **110.00**
Small **55.00**
Red, large **125.00**
Smiley Pig and Winnie Pig
Cloverbud, small **65.00**
Green, small **55.00**
Swiss Children
Gold Trim **85.00**
No Gold **40.00**
Watering Cans **25.00**
Wheelbarrows **25.00**
White Corn, large
Gold Trim **150.00**
No Gold **40.00**
Sugar Shaker, White Corn, gold **150.00**
Teapot
Blue, 18 oz **50.00**

Sugar Bowl, King Corn, 5¼" x 4¼", $18.00.

Corn King, individual **225.00**
Elephant **250.00**
Granny Anne **175.00**
Heart Flower **65.00**
Tom the Piper's Son **105.00**
Yellow, 10 oz **55.00**
Vase
Burlap, green, 9" h **10.00**
Donkey with basket, #722 . . . . **22.00**
Dove, yellow, large, #829 . . . . **30.00**
Wall Pocket, wheat **35.00**

SHEET MUSIC

Collecting Hints: Center your collection around a theme—show tunes, songs of World War I, Sousa marches, Black material, songs of a certain lyricist or composer—the list is endless.

Be careful about stacking your sheets on top of one another. The ink on the covers tends to bleed. The most ideal solution is to place acid free paper between each cover and sheet.

Unfortunately, people used tape to repair tears in old sheet music. This discolors and detracts from value. Seek professional help in removing tape from rarer sheets.

During the late 1980s, mid–nineteenth century sheet music rose rapidly in value. World War I covers and covers featuring Blacks currently enjoy great popularity among collectors.

History: Sheet music, especially piano scores, dates to the early 19th century. The early music contains some of the finest examples of lithography. Much of this music was bound in volumes and accompanied a young lady when she was married.

Sheet music covers chronicle the social and political climate and trends of any historical period. The golden age of the hand–illustrated cover dates from 1885. Leading artists, such as James Montgomery Flagg, used their talents in the sheet music area. Cover artwork was critical to helping the song sell.

Once radio and talking pictures became popular, covers featured the stars. A song sheet might be issued in dozens of different cover versions depending on who was featured. By the 1950s piano playing was no longer as popular and song sheets failed to maintain their high quality of design.

References: Debbie Dillon, *Collectors Guide To Sheet Music*, L–W Promotions, 1988, 1993 value update; Anna Marie Guiheen and Marie–Reine A. Pafik, *The Sheet Music Reference and Price Guide, Second Edition* Collector Books, 1995; Norman E. Martinus and Harry L. Rinker, *Warman's Paper*, Wallace–Homestead, 1994; Daniel B. Priest, *American Sheet Music With Prices*, Wallace–Homestead, 1978, out–of–print.

Collectors' Clubs: City of Roses Sheet Music Collectors Club, 13447 Bush St., SE, Portland, OR 97236; National Sheet Music Society, 1597 Fair Park Ave., Los Angeles, CA 90041; New York Sheet Music Society, P.O. Box 1214, Great Neck, NY 11023; Remember That Song, 5623 N. 64th St., Glendale, AZ 85301; The Sheet Music Exchange, 1202 12th St., Key West, FL 33040.

Doctor Brown, Fred Irwin, 1914	**5.00**
Does It Pay?, Zittel and Sutton, 1907 ..	**15.00**
Doin' The Raccoon, Raymond Klages and J Fred Coots, 1929	**10.00**
Five Minutes More, Sammy Cahn and Jule Styne, 1946, George Olsen photo	**3.00**
For The First Time, I've Fallen In Love, Charles Tobias and David Kapp, 1943, Kay Kyser photo	**5.00**
He, Richard Mullan and Jack Richards, 1954, Maguire Sisters photo	**2.00**
Hello, Baby, Edward Harrigan and David Braham, 1884	**15.00**
He's Got The Whole World In His Hands, Geoff Love, 1957, Laurie London photo	**2.00**
I Enjoy Being A Girl, Richard Rodgers and Oscar Hammerstein II, 1961, from movie *Flower Drum Song*	**5.00**
If I Had My Life To Live Over, Henry Tobias, Moe Jaffe, and Larry Vincent, 1948, Kate Smith photo	**5.00**
I'm Getting Corns For My Country, Jean Barry and Dick Charles, 1944, from movie *Hollywood Canteen,* Andrews Sister, Jack Benny and other stars' photos	**5.00**
I'm Going Home To Mobile On The Morgan Line, Leap, 1914	**20.00**
I Never Slept A Wink Last Night, Andy Razof and Nat Simon, 1934	**3.00**
Keep Your Sunny Side Up, B G DeSylva, Lew Brown, and Ray Henderson, 1929	**20.00**
Kentucky Home, Abe Brashen and Harold Weeks, 1921	**5.00**
La Boheme, G Puccini, 1898	**15.00**
La Bomba, Leo Robin and Ralph Rainger, 1936, from movie *The Big Broadcast Of 1937,* Jack Benny and other stars' photos	**8.00**
Little Love Will Go A Long, Long Way, A Carmen Lombardo and John Jacob Loeb, 1938	**3.00**
Little White Church In The Niche, The, Rose Estelle Oliver, 1934, sgd Tito Guizar photo	**5.00**
Mammy's Shufflin' Dance, L Wolfe Gilbert and Melville J Gideon, 1911, Courtney Sisters photo	**15.00**
Mandy Lou, Paul Laurence Dunbar and Frederick Hall, 1926	**3.00**

Love Walked In, Goldwyn Follies, Chappel & Co., real photo cover, tan wash, c1938, $25.00.

Memories Of Mother And Home, Simpson and Maxwell	**10.00**
Molly–O, I Love You, James C Emery and Norman McNeil, 1921	**10.00**
Myopia Fox Trot, Brennan, 1915, Maurice and Florence Walton photo	**15.00**
My Sweet Italian Man, Irving Berlin, 1911	**1.500**
Nothing Can Stop Me Now, Walter Bullock and Harold Spina, 1937, from movie *52nd St.*	**5.00**
Piano Concerto In B flat Minor, Peter I Tschaikowsky, 1941	**2.00**
Pickin' On De Ole Banjo, Widmer, 1915	**10.00**
Remember When, Buck Ram and Mickey Addy, 1945	**2.00**

Will You Tell Me Fair Young Lady, words and music by Suzanne Jonet Gill, autographed on moon, $5.50.

Silhouette One Step, Harold Bien, 1914	**50.00**
Speed Kings, The, Losey, 1912	**15.00**
Take Me Out To The Ball Game, Jack Norworth and Albert Von Tilzer, 1908	**20.00**
That's What The Rose Said To Me, B F Barnett and Leo Edwards, 1906, Bessie Wynn photo	**10.00**
U S Field Artillery March, The Lieutenant John Philip Sousa, 1917, dedicated to "Officers and Men Of The 306th Field Artillery, National Army, U.S.A."	**25.00**
Where The Black Eyed Susans Grow, Dave Radford and Richard A Whiting, 1917, Al Jolson photo	**10.00**
You Never Miss The Water Till The Well Runs Dry, Paul Secon and Arthur Kent, 1946	**3.00**

SHELLEY CHINA

Collecting Hints: The familiar Shelley script signature in a shield mark was used as early as 1910, even though the firm's name was still Wileman & Co. Dainty White was one of the company's most popular shapes, and is therefore relatively easy to acquire.

History: While the Shelley family has been producing pottery since the mid 1880s, it wasn't until 1925 that the company bore their family name. Joseph Shelley and James Wileman became partners in 1872. Their pottery operated under the name Wileman & Company. Joseph's son, Percy, joined the company in 1881 and assumed full control after his father's death in 1896. It was under Percy's direction that the company introduced its most popular shapes, i.e. Dainty White, Intarsio, Queen Anne, and Vogue.

Percy's three sons became involved in the business following World War I. During the 1920s and 1930s the pottery produced miniatures, heraldic and souvenir china, Parian busts of military figures, teawares, and nursery items, in addition to its fine dinnerware lines. Percy retired in 1932. After World War II the company concentrated solely on its dinnerware lines. In 1965 the firm's name was changed to Shelley China Ltd. The Shelley family ties to the company were severed in 1966, when Allied English Potteries took control. Allied merged with the Doulton Group in 1971.

Reference: Susan and Al Bagdade, *Warman's English & Continental Pottery & Porcelain, 2nd Edition,* Wallace–Homestead, 1991.

Begonia	
Creamer and Sugar	**40.00**
Cup and Saucer	**50.00**
Demitasse Cup and Saucer, sixteen flutes	**50.00**

Nappy, six flutes	**35.00**
Plate	
6" d	**28.00**
8" d, Westminster Abbey	**32.00**
10¾" d	**75.00**
Blue Rock	
Cereal Bowl, 6¼" d	**35.00**
Coffeepot, 6½" h	**200.00**
Creamer and Sugar, six flutes	**50.00**
Cup and Saucer	**42.00**
Hostess Set, cup and 8" plate with cup ring	**55.00**
Bridal Rose	
Cup and Saucer, six flutes	**50.00**
Plate, 6" d	**22.00**
Campanula	
Creamer and Sugar Set, undertray . .	**98.00**
Hostess Set, cup and 8" plate with cup ring	**55.00**
Charm 5	
Cake Set, two handled plate and six serving plates	**240.00**
Creamer and Sugar	**58.00**
Colonial Bouquet, coffeepot	**360.00**
Crochet	
Cake Plate, handled, yellow	**105.00**
Cake Serving Plates, set of six, various colors	**170.00**
Candy Dish, white, blue trim, 4½" d	**32.00**
Creamer and Sugar, yellow	**110.00**
Plate, 8" d	**28.00**
Dainty White	
Coffeepot, large, gold	**190.00**
Cup and Saucer, oversized, gold . . .	**48.00**
Eggcup, gold	**35.00**
Hostess Set, cup and 8" plate with cup ring, gold	**45.00**
Mug and Saucer	**40.00**
Plate, 6" d	**30.00**
Forget–Me–Nots	
Candy Dish, 4" l	**38.00**
Creamer and Sugar	**115.00**
Plate, 5" d	**33.00**
Georgian, creamer and sugar	**99.00**
Lily of the Valley	
Cup and Saucer, fourteen flutes	**45.00**
Demitasse Cup and Saucer	**45.00**
Sugar, individual	**25.00**
Pansy	
Candy Dish, 4" l	**38.00**
Coffeepot	**350.00**
Creamer and Sugar	**115.00**
Demitasse Cup and Saucer	**63.00**
Plate, 5" d	**33.00**
Pink Charm	
Cup and Saucer	**42.00**
Primrose	
Creamer and Sugar, six flutes	**45.00**
Cup and Saucer, miniature	**125.00**
Eggcup, six flutes	**60.00**
Plate, 6" d, six flutes	**30.00**
Rock Garden, creamer and sugar	**70.00**

Rose
Candy Dish, 4" l	**38.00**
Coffeepot	**350.00**
Creamer and Sugar	**115.00**
Demitasse Cup and Saucer	**63.00**
Plate, 5" d	**33.00**
Violets	
Demitasse Cup and Saucer, sixteen	
flutes	**60.00**
Wildflower	
Coffeepot	**370.00**
Creamer and Sugar	**115.00**
Cup and Saucer	**60.00**
Demitasse Cup and Saucer	**68.00**
Plate, 7" d	**35.00**
Vegetable Dish, oval	**200.00**

SILVER FLATWARE

Collecting Hints: Focus on one pattern by one maker. Several makers used the same pattern name and a similar pattern design. Always check the backmarks carefully; several thousand patterns were manufactured. Popularity of pattern, not necessarily age, is the key to pricing.

A monogram on a piece will reduce its value substantially, at least by 50%. On Sterling, monograms occasionally can be removed. This, however, is not the case with silver plate. A worn piece of silver plate virtually has no market value.

Silver flatware sold in sets often brings less than pieces sold individually. The reason is that many buyers are looking to replace pieces or add place settings to a pattern they already own. Sterling silver sets certainly retain their value better than silver plate sets. A number of dealers specializing in replacement services have evolved in past years. Many advertise in *The Antique Trader Weekly*.

Flatware marked as Alaska Silver, German Silver, Lashar Silver, and Nickel Silver is not silver plated. These materials are alloys designed to imitate silver plate.

Doris Snell's *American Silverplated Flatware Patterns* contains a section on the care and cleaning of flatware. Individuals must keep in mind that plated wares have only a very thin surface over the base metal. Once removed, it cannot be easily replaced.

Finally, there is one form of silver flatware that has value with a monogram. It is the flatware used by American railroads, for which there exists a strong market among railroad buffs.

History: The silver table service became a hallmark of elegance during the Victorian era. The homes of the wealthy had Sterling silver services made by Gorham, Kirk, Tiffany, and Towle. Silver place settings became part of a young girl's hope chest and a staple wedding gift. Sterling silver

consists of 925 parts silver and 75 parts copper per 1,000 parts Sterling.

When electroplating became popular, silver plated flatware gave the common man a chance to imitate the wealthy. Silver plated flatware has a thin layer of silver plated by a chemical process, known as electrolysis, onto a base metal, usually britannia (an alloy of tin, antimony and copper) or white metal (an alloy of tin, copper and lead or bismuth). Leading silver plate manufacturers are Alvin, Gorham, International Silver Co. (a modern company which merged many older companies such as Holmes & Edwards, Rogers, etc.), Oneida, Reed & Barton, Wm. Rogers, and Wallace.

References: Fredna Harris Davis and Kenneth K. Deibel, *Silver Plated Flatware Patterns*, Bluebonnet Press, 1981; Maryanne Dolan, *1830's–1990's American Sterling Silver Flatware: A Collector's Identification And Value Guide*, Books Americana, 1993; Tere Hagan, *Silverplated Flatware: An Identification & Value Guide*, Revised Fourth Edition, Collector Books, 1990, 1995 value update; *Jewelers' Circular Keystone Sterling Flatware Pattern Index*, Second Edition, Wallace–Homestead, 1989; Joel Langford, *Silver: A Practical Guide To Collecting Silverware And Identifying Hallmarks*, Chartwell Books, 1991; Everett L. Maffet, *Silver Banquet II: A Compendium On Railroad Dining Car Silver Serving Pieces*, Silver Press, 1990; Richard Osterberg, *Sterling Silver Flatware for Dining Elegance*, Schiffer Publishing, 1994; Benton Seymour Rabinovitch, *Antique Silver Servers For The Dining Table*, Joslin Hall, 1991; Dorothy T. and H. Ivan Rainwater, *American Silverplate*, Schiffer Publishing, 1988; Jeri Schwartz, *The Official Identification and Price Guide To Silver and Silverplate*, Sixth Edition House of Collectibles, 1989.

Periodical: *Silver*, PO Box 1243, Whitter, CA 90609.

Adam, Whiting
Cream Soup Spoon	**25.00**
Gumbo Spoon	**25.00**
Ice Cream Fork, monogram, set of six	**270.00**
Salad Fork, monogram, set of six . . .	**180.00**
Angelo, Wood and Hughes	
Demitasse Spoon, set of four	**100.00**
Gravy Ladle, ruffled edge, monogram	**175.00**
Pie Server, monogram	**180.00**
Serving Spoon, gilt bowl	**90.00**
Tablespoon	**95.00**
Antique Engraved #10, Gorham	
Fork, 7½" l	**18.00**
Teaspoon	**10.00**
Beekman, Tiffany, sugar shifter, 7" l . . .	**250.00**
Bridal Bouquet, Alvin	
Butter Pick	**55.00**
Luncheon Fork, monogram	**25.00**

Luncheon Knife, monogram	**25.00**
Teaspoon	**20.00**
Cambridge, Gorham	
Cake Fork, price for set of twelve ...	**190.00**
Salad Set, 8½″ l, 2 pcs	**150.00**
Canterbury, Towle	
Bonbon Scoop, monogram	**75.00**
Butter Spreader, filled handle	**20.00**
Demitasse Spoon, monogram	**15.00**
Gravy Ladle	**50.00**
Luncheon Fork, monogram	**30.00**
Olive Fork	**55.00**
Seafood Fork, monogram, set of eight	**160.00**
Century, Tiffany	
Butter Spreader, filled handle, set of six	**240.00**
Cake Fork, set of six	**275.00**
Luncheon Fork	**60.00**
Luncheon Knife, serrated blade, 8½″ l	**60.00**
Salad Fork	**65.00**
Teaspoon	**40.00**
Chantilly, Gorham, luncheon forks, 7″l	**16.00**
Chrysanthemum, Durgin	
Egg Spoon, set of six	**360.00**
Fish Fork, monogram, set of seven ..	**525.00**
Ice Cream Fork, monogram, set of twelve	**1,020.00**
Lobster Pick, monogram, set of twelve	**1,500.00**
Colonial, Tiffany, salad set, 10″	**500.00**
Contour, Towle	
Cold Meat Fork	**51.00**
Dinner Fork	**25.00**
Soup Spoon, oval	**20.00**
Teaspoon	**17.00**
Corinthian, Gorham	
Cheese Knife, comb top, monogram	**150.00**
Pie Server	**135.00**
Serving Spoon	**135.00**
Youth Fork, monogram	**20.00**
Essex, Durgin, salad fork, monogram ..	**18.00**
Etruscan, Gorham, cake fork	**12.00**
Fairfax, Durgin	
Ice Cream Fork	**35.00**
Salad Fork, monogram	**25.00**
Florentine, Gorham, salad set, monogram, 10½″ l	**575.00**
Fontainbleau, Gorham	
Gravy Ladle	**140.00**
Salt Spoon, master, monogram	**40.00**
Francis I, Reed & Barton, citrus spoon, set of twelve	**300.00**
Frontenac, International	
Cake Fork, monogram	**22.00**
Salad Fork, monogram	**45.00**
Georgian Maid, International, dessert fork, monogram	**10.00**
Grande Baroque, Wallace	
Cream Soup Spoon	**28.00**
Dinner Fork	**40.00**
Luncheon Fork	**28.00**
Luncheon Knife	**25.00**
Place Setting, dinner	**100.00**

Hannah Hull, Tuttle	
Demitasse Spoon	**17.00**
Dessert Spoon	**35.00**
Gravy Ladle	**75.00**
Iced Tea Spoon	**28.00**
Luncheon Fork	**30.00**
Luncheon Knife	**30.00**
Salad Set	**25.00**
Sugar Spoon	**32.00**
Tablespoon	**60.00**
Hepplewhite, Reed & Barton, fruit spoon	**15.00**
Hizen, Gorham, sugar tongs	**185.00**
Hyperion, Whiting, berry spoon	**150.00**
Irian, Wallace	
Butter Pick	**120.00**
Dinner and luncheon service for 12, 169 pieces **10,140.00**	
Iris, Durgin, sugar spoon	**75.00**
Irving, Wallace	
Dessert Spoon	**28.00**
Gravy Ladle	**65.00**
Luncheon Fork	**22.00**
Luncheon Knife	**22.00**
Salad Fork	**28.00**
Sauce Ladle	**45.00**
Tablespoon	**42.00**
Teaspoon	**15.00**
Italian, Tiffany, soup ladle, 12¾″ l, monogram	**450.00**
Ivy, Gorham	
Beef Fork, monogram	**50.00**
Fish Knife, individual, monogram ..	**50.00**
Mustard Ladle, monogram	**75.00**
Japanese, Gorham, tablespoon, monogram	**65.00**
King George, Gorham	
Fish Set, monogram, 12⅛″ slice, 8¾″ l fork, price for set	**750.00**
Ice Cream Slice, replaced blade	**150.00**
Stuffing Spoon, monogram, 10¾″ l ..	**375.00**
Tablespoon, monogram, set of six ..	**300.00**
Kings, Reed & Barton, dessert spoon, monogram, 7⅛″ l	**30.00**
Kings, Wallace	
Butter, flat handle, monogram	**20.00**
Dinner Fork	**48.00**
Dinner Knife	**48.00**
Tablespoon	**38.00**
Lancaster, Gorham	
Baked Potato Serving Fork, monogram	**21.00**
Beef Fork, large	**35.00**
Cake Saw	**225.00**
Dessert Spoon, monogram	**15.00**
Dinner Fork, monogram	**35.00**
Dinner Knife, 9½″	**60.00**
Lettuce Fork, monogram	**55.00**
Pie Server	**125.00**
Sardine Fork, monogram	**60.00**
Sugar Spoon, monogram	**10.00**
Teaspoon	**9.00**
Tomato Server, monogram	**125.00**

Lancaster Rose, Gorham
Bouillon **15.00**
Butter, filled handle
Individual **15.00**
Master **35.00**
Luncheon forks, 7" l **16.00**
Tablespoon, monogram **14.00**
Teaspoon, monogram **7.00**
La Parisienne, Reed & Barton, demi-
tasse spoons, monogram, set of
twelve **240.00**
Les Cinque Fleurs, Reed & Barton
Beef Fork, monogram **95.00**
Cake Fork, monogram, set of six ... **125.00**
Dinner Fork **45.00**
Dinner Knife **30.00**
Soup Spoon, monogram **28.00**
Sugar Tongs **40.00**
Teaspoon, monogram **15.00**
Lexington, Knowles
Caviar Spoon **50.00**
Cheese Knife, comb top, monogram **98.00**
Jelly Knife, gilt blade **75.00**
Sugar Spoon, gilt bowl, monogram **45.00**
Louis XV, Durgin
Butter Spreader, filled handle, mono-
gram **12.00**
Demitasse, monogram **10.00**
Louis XV, Whiting
Bouillon Spoon, monogram, set of
six **80.00**
Cheese Knife, comb top, monogram **110.00**
Chocolate Spoon, set of six **150.00**
Fruit Spoon, monogram, set of six .. **270.00**
Lettuce Fork, monogram **75.00**
Oyster Fork, monogram, set of six .. **108.00**
Oyster Ladle, monogram **210.00**
Pickle Fork, monogram **45.00**
Sugar Sifter, monogram **65.00**
Tea Caddy Spoon, monogram **95.00**
Tongs, small, 3¾" l **48.00**
Luxembourg, Gorham, soup ladle,
10½" l, monogram **195.00**
Madam Morris, Whiting
Almond Scoop, large **90.00**
Berry Spoon, monogram **70.00**
Ice Tongs **175.00**
Salad Fork, monogram **25.00**
Sugar Sifter **80.00**
May Melody, International
Butter Spreader, filled handle **14.00**
Cream Soup Spoon **16.00**
Luncheon Fork **15.00**
Luncheon Knife **14.00**
Salad Fork **16.00**
Teaspoon **8.00**
Meadow Song, Towle, place setting,
four piece **64.00**
Medallion, Duhme, dessert spoon **75.00**
Medallion, Wood and Hughes, pie
server **350.00**
Morning Glory, Alvin
Dinner Fork, monogram **22.00**

Luncheon Fork **20.00**
Luncheon Knife, set of twelve, new
blades **350.00**
Tablespoon **32.00**
Teaspoon **13.00**
Mythologique, Gorham, ice cream fork,
monogram **60.00**
Old Baronial, Gorham
Butter Spreader **25.00**
Chocolate Muddler **80.00**
Salad Fork **30.00**
Old Brocade, Towle
Blush Brush **15.00**
Cosmetic Brush **14.00**
Old Colonial, Towle
Bonbon Spoon **55.00**
Chocolate Spoon, 4¾" l **45.00**
Cold Meat Fork **57.00**
Gravy Ladle **62.00**
Luncheon Fork **25.00**
Luncheon Knife **25.00**
Olive Fork **35.00**
Salt Spoon **11.00**
Steak Knife **32.00**
Strawberry Fork **20.00**
Old Lace, Towle
Bonbon Spoon **19.00**
Butter, filled handle
Individual **13.00**
Master **14.00**
Letter Opener **18.00**
Salt Spoon **10.00**
Sugar Spoon **15.00**
Teaspoon **12.00**
Youth Set, 3 piece set **63.00**
Old Master, Towle
Iced Tea Spoon **27.00**
Pasta Scoop **25.00**
Place Setting, 4 piece **104.00**
Salt Spoon **11.00**
Soup Spoon, oval **28.00**
Steak Knife **30.00**
Teaspoon **14.00**
Old Orange, Alvin, bouillon spoon,
monogram, set of six **250.00**
Palm, Gorham, chocolate ladle, mono-
gram **135.00**
Paris, Gorham
Citrus Spoon, set of seven **245.00**
Oyster Fork, set of ten **280.00**
Pompadour, Whiting
Cake Fork **20.00**
Cream Ladle **55.00**
Poppy, Gorham, cream ladle, mono-
gram **50.00**
Primrose, Wood and Hughes
Butter Knife **35.00**
Cream Ladle **50.00**
Gravy Ladle **65.00**
Luncheon Service, knife, fork, salad
fork, teaspoon, price for service for
four **350.00**
Meat Fork **65.00**

Sugar Spoon 35.00
Princess, Gorham, salt and pepper
shakers, pr, monogram, 11 oz,
4¾" h 485.00
Queen Elizabeth I, Towle
Cake Server 31.00
Carving Set, 2 piece 65.00
Lasagna Server 30.00
Pie Server 31.00
Raphael, Gorham
Dinner Fork, monogram 60.00
Gravy Ladle, monogram 135.00
Rambler Rose, Towle
Butter, filled handle, individual 12.00
Cream Soup Spoon 15.00
Dinner Fork 23.00
Lunch Fork 21.00
Salad Fork 20.00
Salt Spoon 10.00
Sugar Spoon 14.00
Teaspoon 11.00
Renaissance, Tiffany, luncheon service
for 12, price for 93 pieces 6,045.00
Repousse, James Armiger, pancake
server, monogram 160.00
Rose, Jensen
Dinner Fork, 8" l, c1920, set of six .. 250.00
Serving Spoon, 7½" l 120.00
Tablespoon, 8¼" l 85.00
Rose, Stieff
Butter Knife 12.00
Iced Tea Spoon 22.00
Luncheon Fork 26.00
Luncheon Knife 22.00
Orange Spoon 28.00
Teaspoon 15.00
Tray, oval 550.00
Rose Point, Wallace
Butter Knife 15.00
Dinner Fork 20.00
Dinner Knife 18.00
Gravy Ladle 65.00
Pie Server 30.00
Salt and Pepper Shakers, 5¾" h, 6
troy oz 145.00
Sugar Spoon 55.00
Tablespoon 40.00
Teaspoon 15.00
Sculptured Rose, Towle
Butter, hollow handle, individual ... 12.00
Cosmetic Brush 14.00
Luncheon Fork 18.00
Sugar Spoon 13.00
Teaspoon 11.00
Silver Plumes, Towle
Butter, master, hollow handle 31.00
Cream Soup Spoon 24.00
Iced Tea Spoon 22.00
Nut Spoon 25.00
Place Setting, 4 piece 120.00
Salad Fork 21.00

Sugar Spoon 32.00
Tablespoon 46.00
Silver Spray, Towle
Butter, hollow handle
Individual 13.00
Master 14.00
Six Fleurs, Reed & Barton, berry spoon,
9¾" l, 6.4 oz 3400.00
Trilogy, Gorham
Dinner Fork 28.00
Dinner Knife 26.00
Place Setting 81.00
Teaspoon 18.00
Twilight, Oneida
Place Setting 54.00
Teaspoon 15.00
Vienna, Reed & Barton
Butter Knife, hollow handle 18.00
Cream Soup Spoon 26.00
Luncheon Service, 12 place settings,
modern 77.00
Pie Server 34.00
Sugar Shell 26.00
Virginia Sterling, Weidlich
Baby Spoon 21.00
Butter
Individual, flat handle 14.00
Master, flat handle 20.00
Cold Meat Fork 41.00
Gravy Ladle 41.00
Luncheon Place Setting 61.00
Salad Fork 20.00
Soup Spoon, oval 24.00
Steak Carving Set, three piece set ... 71.00
Sugar Spoon 18.00
Tablespoon 37.00
Teaspoon 11.00
Virginian, Oneida
Butter Knife, filled handle 14.00
Demitasse Spoon 18.00
Luncheon Knife, modern 24.00
Luncheon Place Setting 61.00
Salad Fork 24.00
Vivant, Oneida
Butter, master, hollow handle 26.00
Cold Meat Fork 44.00
Lemon Fork 17.00
Pickle Fork 18.00
Pie Server 34.00
Place Setting 58.00
Tablespoon, pierced 44.00
Wadefield, Kirk
Butter, filled handle 20.00
Cheese Server 28.00
Cocktail Fork 20.00
Cold Meat Fork, large 67.00
Fish Knife, hollow handle 38.00
Lemon Fork 26.00
Pickle Fork 26.00
Pie Server 50.00
Sugar Shell 30.00

Teaspoon	**18.00**
Vegetable Spoon, oval	**67.00**
Watteau, Durgin, preserve spoon	**60.00**

Wave Edge, Tiffany

Dessert Spoon, monogram, set of six	**360.00**
Dinner Fork, monogram, set of six . .	**450.00**
Ice Cream Fork, monogram, set of ten	**650.00**
Salad Set, monogram, 10" l, 2 pieces	**625.00**
Stuffing Spoon, monogram, 11¼" . . .	**550.00**
Tablespoon, monogram, set of six . .	**570.00**

Winchester, International, cream soup

spoon, set of six	**80.00**

SLOT MACHINES

Collecting Hints: Check the laws in your state. Some states permit the collecting of slot machines manufactured prior to 1941, while others permit the collecting of all machines 25 years old or older provided that they are not used for gambling. A few states prohibit the ownership of any gambling machine.

A complete slot machine is one that is in working order, has no wood missing on the case, and no cracked castings. All that is needed to restore the machine is some work on appearance. Restoration costs range from $100 to more than $1,000. The average restoration includes plating of all castings, refinishing the cabinet, repainting the castings to the original colors, rebuilding the mechanism, tuning up the operation of the mechanism, new reel strips, and a new award card. A quality restoration will add between $400 to $800 to the value of a machine. If buying a restored machine from a dealer, a guarantee usually is given.

Most collectors stay away from foreign machines; foreign coins are hard to find. If the machine has been converted to accept American coins, it frequently may jam or not pay off the proper amount on a winner.

Condition, rarity, and desirability are all very important in determining the value of a machine. Try to find one that is in as close to new condition as possible, as "mint original" machines are bringing the same or more money than restored machines.

History: The first three–reel slot machine was invented in 1905 by Charles Fey in San Francisco. The machine was called the Liberty Bell. One of the three known survivors can be seen at the Liberty Bell Saloon, his grandson's restaurant, in Reno, Nevada.

In 1910 the classic fruit symbols were copyrighted by Mills Novelty Company. They were immediately copied by other manufacturers. The first symbols still are popular on contemporary casino machines. The wood cabinet was re-

placed by cast iron in 1916. By 1922 aluminum fronts were the norm for most machines. In 1928 the jackpot was added.

The 1930s innovations included more reliable and improved mechanisms with more sophisticated coin entry and advance and slug detection systems. In the 1940s drill–proof and cheat–resistant devices were added. The 1950s brought electronic lighting and electronics.

Although the goosenecks of the 1920s and 1930s often are more intricate and rarer than the models of the 1930s and 1940s, the gimmick and more beautiful machines of this later period, such as Rolatop, Treasury, Kitty or Triplex, bring more money.

References: Jerry Ayliffe, *American Premium Guide To Jukeboxes and Slot Machines, Third Edition,* Books Americana, 1991; Richard M. Bueschel, *Collector's Guide To Vintage Coin Machines,* Schiffer Publishing, 1995; Richard Bueschel, *Illustrated Guide To 100 Collectible Slot Machines, Volume 1,* Hoflin Publishing, 1978, 1989 value update; Marshall Fey, *Slot Machines: A Pictorial History of the First 100 Years,* published by author, 1983; Bill Kurtz, *Slot Machines And Coin–Op Games: A Collector's Guide To One Armed Bandits And Amusement Machines,* Chartwell Books, 1991; Daniel R. Mead, *Loose Change Blue Book Slot Machine Price Guide, 1986–87 Edition,* published by author, 1987.

Periodicals: *Antique Amusements, Slot Machines & Jukebox,* 909 26th St. NW, Washington, DC 20037; *Chicago Land Slot Machine & Jukebox Gazette,* 909 26th St., NW, Washington, DC 20037; *Coin Drop International* 5815 W. 52nd Ave., Denver, CO 80212; *Coin–Op Classics,* 17844 Toiyabe St., Fountain Valley, CA 92708; *Coin–Op Newsletter* 909 26th St., NW, Washington, DC 20037; *The Coin Slot,* 4401 Zephyr St., Wheatridge, CO 80033; *Loose Change,* 1515 South Commerce Street, Las Vegas, NV 89102.

Note: All machines listed are priced as if they were in "good" condition, meaning the machine is complete and working. An incomplete or non–working machine is worth only 30% to 70% of the listed price.

Machines listed are for 5¢ and 10¢. Quarter and 50¢ machines can run several hundred dollars higher. A silver dollar machine, if you are lucky enough to find one, can add $400 to $800 to the price.

Advisor: Bob Levy.

Buckley

Bones, countertop, spinning disks roll dice for craps, similar to Bally's Reliance, ca1937	**3,500-5,000.00**

Criss Cross, revamp of Mills machine, escalator coin entry, fancy casting around escalator and jackpot, usually has guaranteed jackpot, c1948 . . . . **900-1,000.00**

Caille

Cadet, circular jackpot, escalator moves from bottom up, c1938 . . . . **700-1,100.00**

Detroit Floor Wheel, upright one reeler, six way play action, bettors pick color wheel will land on, c1899 . . . . **7,000-9,500.00**

Superior, nude woman on front, scroll–work lower casting, coin entry in center above award card, c1928 . . . . **1,500-2,000.00**

Victory Mint, center pull handle, ladies pictured on both sides of handle, c1924 . . . . **2,500-3,000.00**

Groetchen, Columbia, the size of normal slot machine, club handle, small reels, coins go around in circle behind coin head, 1934 . . **200-300.00**

Jennings

Challenger Console, 4' h, vertical glass and horizontal glass with silkscreen design, reels seen from top of lower glass, plays two coin denominations, usually 5¢ and 25¢, c1946 . . . . **1,200-1,500.00**

Duchess, three reel, front vendor with mints or candy displayed behind windows flanking jackpot, orig decal, c1934 . . . . **1,600-2,500.00**

Four Star Chief, Indian carrying deer on front, large Indian chief above jackpot, four stars on top, 1936 . . . . **1,000-1,300.00**

Governor, tic tac toe theme, Indian head above jackpot, 1948 **800-1,000.00**

Little Duke, large coin headcasting on top of machine, classic Art Deco design, reels spin concentrically, 1932 . . . . **1,100-1,500.00**

Silver Moon, moon above jackpot, stars on side of jackpot, 1941 . . . . **900-1,100.00**

Sportsman, golf ball vendor, pay card placed at angle, 1937 . . . **2,500-3,000.00**

Standard Chief, chrome finish, teardrop design on both sides of jackpot, flat Indian above jackpot, 1948 . . . . **800-1,100.00**

Sun Chief, Indian bust, illuminated side panels, c1948 . . . . . . **1,500-1,800.00**

Victoria, three reel, two jackpots, fortune strips, c1932 . . . . . . **1,500-2,500.00**

Victory Chief, wood front, eagle above jackpot, minutemen soldiers to right and left of eagle, 1945 . . . . **900-1,200.00**

Mills

Black Cherry, escalator, painted silver with black case, four applied cherries, bib award card front, 1947 . . . . **850-1,100.00**

Diamond Front, escalator, ten raised diamonds around large "bib" award card, 1940 . . . . . . **900-1,200.00**

Eagle, gold coins, c1936 . . . **2,200-2,800.00**

Futurity Bell, three reel, 5¢, 1936 . . . .**1,800-2,200.00**

High Top, light colors, strong player, 1946–62 . . . . **900-1,200.00**

Lion Front, gooseneck coin entry, large lion with mouth open around jackpot, three rows of six circles below reels, 1929 . . . . . . **1,300-1,800.00**

Melon Bell, three reel, high top, melon on front, 1948 . . . . **1,200-1,500.00**

Mystery Front, three reels, 26" h, c1932 . . . . **1,500-2,500.00**

Operator Bell, 23½", 5¢, three reel, c1926 . . . . **800-1,000.00**

Owl, oak cast, upright floor model, color wheel, c1905 . . . . . **5,000-6,000.00**

Poinsettia, gooseneck coin entry, flowers on lower casting, Liberty bell under coin entry c1930 . . . . **1,000-1,200.00**

Silent Golden, three reel, Roman's head on front, 1932 . . . . . **1,900-2,800.00**

Vest Pocket, three reel, box shape, plain design, 1938 . . . . **350-550.00**

Pace

All Star Comet, rotary escalator, stars and vertical pointed stripes on front, 1936 . . . . **850-1,150.00**

Bantam, three reel, jackpot vendor front, appealing design, 1932 . . . . **1,200-1,800.00**

Watling

Blue Seal, gooseneck, twin jackpot, fancy front, 1930 . . . . **900-1,100.00**

Exchange, one wheel, countertop model, five way coin head, oak case, c1910 . . . . **2,000-3,000.00**

Gumball Vendor, gooseneck, ornate casting around reels, gumball vendors on each side of twin jackpot, 1¢ only, c1921 . . . . **1,500-2,000.00**

Rolatop, rotary escalator, twin jackpot with eagle above, checkerboard **1,300-1,700.00**

L. E. SMITH GLASS COMPANY

Collecting Hints: L.E. Smith glass is hand made and usually unmarked. Some older pieces bear a "C" in a circle with a tiny "S." Current glass has a paper label. The collector of older items should especially study black and Depression pieces. The Moon and Star pattern has been reproduced for many years. Smith glass of recent manufacture is found in house sales, flea markets, and gift and antiques shops.

History: L. E. Smith Glass Company was founded in 1907 in Mount Pleasant, Pennsylvania, by Lewis E. Smith. Although Smith left the company shortly after its establishment, it still bears his name. Early products were cooking articles and utilitarian objects such as glass percolator tops, fruit jars, sanitary sugar bowls, and reamers.

In the 1920s, green, amber, canary, amethyst, and blue colors were introduced along with an extensive line of soda fountain wares. The company also made milk glass, console and dresser sets, and the always popular fish–shaped aquariums. During the 1930s, Smith became the largest producer of black glass. Popular dinner set lines were Homestead, Melba, Do–Si–Do, By Cracky, Romanesque, and Mount Pleasant.

L. E. Smith presently manufactures colored re-production glass and interesting decorative objects. A factory outlet is available as well as factory tours. Contact the factory for specific times.

References: Lee Garmon and Dick Spencer, *Glass Animals Of The Depression Era,* Collector Books, 1993; Hazel Marie Weatherman, *Colored Glassware of the Depression Era 2,* Glassbooks, 1982.

Candlestick, Moon and Star Heritage Collection, yellow shading to red, 4¾″ h, $6.00.

Animal	
Cow, black, c1930	**18.00**
Dog, Scottie, frosted	**50.00**
Rooster, black, c1930	**15.00**
Swan, small, white opaque	**15.00**
Aquarium, 10″ h, 15″ l, green, King–Fish, c1920	**250.00**
Ashtray, elephant, black	**30.00**
Bookends, pr	
Horse Head, clear	**45.00**
Rearing Horse, emerald green	**100.00**
Bowl, #77, amethyst	**8.00**
Cake Plate, Do–Si–Do, handles	**12.00**
Candlesticks, pr	
By Cracky, green	**12.00**
Romanesque, pink	**10.00**
Candy Dish, turkey shape, blue	**40.00**
Casserole, Melba, 9½″ l, oval	**15.00**
Cologne Bottle, Colonial, black	**30.00**
Compote, cov, Moon n'Star, amberina	**35.00**
Cookie Jar, cov, Amy, black	**95.00**
Cordial Tray, #381, black	**9.50**
Creamer	
Homestead, pink	**5.00**
Moon n' Star, amberina	**10.00**
Cruet, Moon n' Star, ruby	**30.00**
Cup and Saucer	
Do–Si–Do, pink, gold trim	**6.50**

Melba, pink	**4.50**
Fairy Lamp, Moon n' Star, ruby	**30.00**
Fern Dish, 3 ftd, 1930s	
Greek Key, white, opaque	**8.00**
Kent	**8.50**
Flower Block, By Cracky, 3″ h	**3.75**
Flower Pot, 4″ h, black, silver floral dec	**8.00**
Goblet, water, Moon 'n Star, amberina	**15.00**
Ladle, crystal	**20.00**
Mayonnaise, Kent	**6.00**
Mug, crystal, 12 oz	**5.00**
Parfait	
Homestead	**5.00**
Soda Shop	**5.00**
Planter, black amethyst, nude dancers on sides, marked "L. E. Smith"	**45.00**
Plate	
6″ d, Melba, amethyst	**4.50**
8″ d, Mt Pleasant, pink, scalloped edge	**6.00**
9″ d, Homestead, grill	**5.00**
Rose Bowl, Mt Pleasant, cobalt blue, rolled edges	**18.00**
Salt and Pepper Shakers, pr	
Dresden, white	**18.00**
Mt Pleasant, cobalt blue	**24.00**
Sherbet, Romanesque, black	**10.00**
Slipper, 2½″ h, Daisy and Button, amber	**4.00**
Soda Glass	
Jumbo, crystal, ribbed	**6.50**
Soda Shop	**6.00**
Sugar, cov	
Homestead	**5.50**
Kent	**6.50**
Moon n' Star, amberina	**12.00**
Tray, 15 x 6″, crystal, oval	**10.00**
Urn, 8½″ h, black, emb, two handles, ftd	**40.00**
Vase	
6½″ h, #102–4, black	**10.00**
7″ h, #433, dancing girls, black	**18.00**
7½″ h, Romanesque, fan shape, black	**12.00**
Violet Bowl, Hobnail, white opaque	**7.50**

Window Box, F W Woolworth **25.00**
Wine, Moon 'n Star, amberina **12.00**

SNOWDOMES

Collecting Hints: Snowdomes are water–filled paperweights with figurines and/or panels inside a globe or dome, which are magnified by the water. The water contains loose particles (white snow, metallic or colored flecks, etc.) which swirl when the globe is turned upside down.

There are two distinctly different types of snowdomes. The first have round, leaded glass balls set on a base of ceramic, Bakelite or other plastic, wood or "marble." These are older and generally 3–4" high. The second have plastic objects, in dozens of shapes ranging from simple designs, such as drums, cubes, and bottles, to elaborate figurals. Production of this second type, which average 2½" high, started in the 1950s.

Within both categories (especially the plastic examples), there are many sub–groups and themes which appeal to collectors, e.g., Christmas (probably the most familiar), tourist souvenirs, biblical scenes, Disney and other cartoon characters, commercial advertisements, fairy tales, scenic railroads, famous buildings, sailing ships, geographic regions, and ones representing each state.

There is great variety not only in the subject of the inner image of snowdomes, but in the outer shapes as well. Collectors find it challenging to find as many of the dozens of shapes as possible.

Figurals are divided into two categories: first, the entire object is a figural, such as a house, apple, bear, or seated cartoon character with the water ball incorporated into the design at different places; and second, a plastic figurine is placed on top of the dome. Christmas figurals alone constitute a large category. Dozens of different figurines of a standing Santa are known, to say nothing of the dozens of other elaborate designs. Other novelty features include battery powered flashing lights which illuminate the inner scene; salt and pepper snowdomes, perpetual calendars and banks designed in the base, and water/ring toss games.

Many snowdomes have parts that move—a seesaw, bobbing objects attached to strings, and small objects that move back and forth on a groove in the bottom of the dome. Objects range from a ferry or bus to Elvis Presley.

The value of a particular snowdome depends on several factors, starting with the physical condition of the object itself. In dealing with glass domes it is important that the water is clear enough to see the object or is at a level which does not distort the image. Although it is possible to open and refill many of the older glass and ceramic or Bakelite base styles, it is a risky procedure. Examine, also, whether the ceramic base is cracked, the condition of the label (if there is one), the condition of the figurine, and whether the paint has chipped or the colors seem faded. The water level is not a factor in any plastic snowdome that has a plug either on the bottom of the base or at the top of the dome. Bottle–on–its–side shapes cannot be refilled, and the domes designed by the Marx Company in the 1960s have safety plugs that cannot be removed. Safety caps on the plugs of snowdomes made for "Walt Disney Production" can be pried off with a knife point. Murky water can be drained and replaced. Clumped, dirty snow can be caught in a handkerchief, washed, and put back. Distilled water must be used to fill plastic domes made in Germany and France, but tap water may be used in Hong Kong and China made domes.

Of great importance is whether the front of the dome is free of streaking that obscures the scene inside. Any cracks or holes would prevent refilling with water.

While long–time collectors recognize common snowdomes, even new collectors can make an educated guess at scarcity by remembering a few key points. Snowdomes with a glass, ceramic, or Bakelite base, single figurine, and no specific label on the base were the most common. The same figurine with a decal on the base saying "Souvenir of . . ." is more valuable as a smaller number were sold of that figurine with that particular decal. The same figurine was sold in innumerable places, hence there is often no connection between the object and the place. An incongruous match–up may have value to a particular collector, but would not necessarily affect its market value. Of greater value are those snowdomes which were obviously made for a specific place or event and for which the object and the decal match, e. g., the ceramic base snowdome with a bisque Trylon and Perisphere in the globe with a decal "1939 World's Fair."

Plastic snowdomes are also subject to the same principle of logic—"generic" ones, without a name plaque, had the widest possible distribution.

Souvenirs of states and popular tourist attractions had a wide distribution. Since many more were made and sold, their prices are lower than commemoratives or souvenirs of smaller places. *Scarcity,* which can be determined by the size or popularity of a city or tourist attraction, is very important in pricing snowdomes and is a factor in the desirability of particular domes.

While mismatched figurines and decals of the glass/ceramic style should not be priced higher than logical match–ups, there are many examples of obvious mistakes in the plastic variety which are worth more than a perfect one, e. g., a dome with "Milano" printed upside down or a souvenir of a religious shrine with a "Kings Island" plaque.

The age of a plastic snowdome affects its value and can usually be determined by examining stylistic differences. It is often the style associated with a certain era that bears on its value, rather than the actual age itself. Generally, early snowdomes (1950s and 1960s) have greater detail and more sophisticated colors. Later snowdomes are less rich in detail and have a harsh, mass–produced appearance. Many early mass–produced snowdomes look as if they were hand painted. Characters often have a "folk" quality to them. Most important, earlier snowdomes have much more specific detail. State souvenirs from the 1950s and 1960s have many panels inside, depicting noted tourist attractions, famous citizens, and the state slogan. Later versions use only one feature. The newest mass–produced state souvenirs consisted of a rainbow with a pot of gold and a glittery outline of the state's shape on a clear panel. There was no individuality.

The effects of time on snowdomes vary. A dome's physical deterioration, i. e., fading, chipping paint, even "bleaching" of the words on the plaque, must be constantly evaluated by the collector. The plastic snowdomes that were introduced in the 1950s were fragile objects, easily broken, and often discarded. It is indeed a challenge to find unusual "survivors."

History: Snowdomes originated in mid–19th–century Europe, particularly in France, where they evolved from the round, solid glass paperweights. By 1878 there were seven French manufacturers of snowdomes. They also were produced in what is now Germany, Austria, Poland, and Czechoslovakia, often in "cottage industries."

Snowdomes were widely popular during the Victorian era as paperweights, souvenirs, and toys. Early domes featured religious scenes and saints, tourist sites, and children and animals associated with winter or water. A variety of materials were used to create the "snow," ranging from ground porcelain and bone to rice. The figurines inside were made of carved bone, wax, porcelain, china, metal, or stone. The bases were made in a variety of shapes in many materials, including marble, wood, glass, and metal.

German companies exported their snowdomes to North American in the 1920s. The bases were blue cobalt glass and were occasionally etched with the name of a town or tourist attraction.

The first American patent was granted in 1927 to a design of a fish floating on a string among seaweed. The Novelty Pond Company of Pittsburgh was the manufacturer. Japanese companies soon copied the idea. Novelty and other American manufacturers used a black plastic base, either smooth or tiered; Japanese companies used a glazed brown ceramic base.

In addition to an enormous number of figurine designs, either painted or unpainted bisque domes also featured Art Deco buildings, saints, and snow babies. Another design form consisted of a flat, rubberized insert showing a photograph of a tourist attraction, such as Niagara Falls or the Skyline Drive.

The Atlas Crystal Works was founded in the early 1940s to fill the void created by the unavailability of the popular glazed style which had been made in Japan. Atlas became the giant in the snowdome field, creating hundreds of different designs. Popular series included U.S. servicemen, servicewomen, and generals. Decals were added by towns and tourist attractions, creating some unusual matches, e.g., a skier from Atlantic City.

Snowdomes also were manufactured in Italy in the late 1940s using a distinctive scallop–shaped base covered with seashells and pebbles. The glass globe contains a flat rubberized panel with the name of the tourist attraction or saint shown inside written on a shell on the base.

In the 1950s the Driss Company, Chicago, Illinois, made four designs of popular characters—"Frosty the Snowman," "Rudolph the Red Nosed Reindeer in the Snow," "Davy Crockett," and "The Lone Ranger: The Last Round Up" with the decals on the base. The Davy Crockett and Lone Ranger used identical figurines in identical poses with different clothes and accessories. The Lone Ranger also was a ring toss game. You looped his lasso over the calf's head. The Driss Company made many other "novelty" designs, such as an American flag with red, white, and blue "snow."

Progressive Products of Union, New Jersey, created a variation of the classic snowdome in the 1940s and 1950s. They filled their glass ball with an oily liquid, either clear or yellow, and used a glittery "snow." They squared the base and widened it at the bottom, giving it a more angular, Art Deco look. In addition to their "generic" snowdomes with a single object inside, they made souvenirs with the name of a place written on the front of the base.

Their specialties, however, were awards and commercial advertisements. Many of the awards used a royal blue or red base with white trim around the bottom. One image could be adapted to many uses: A golden crown suspended in the liquid was used for a Winter Sports King, an ad for "Crown Termite Control," and a Baltimore newspaper. The same was true for a specific backdrop panel. There were three basic designs—an Art Deco city skyline, country landscape, and a Southwest Indian scene. A wide range of objects and images were placed inside the ball: trucks, ships, a Masonic symbol, a faucet, a fishing boat used for seafood restaurants, and even a two–sided photo of a publishing house owner.

In the early 1950s three West German companies, using plastic, created small cubed or domed snowdomes. Koziol and Walter & Prediger, two of these companies, remain in business today manufacturing hand–painted domes with blizzards of white snow. Herr Koziol claims it was the "domed" view of a winter snow scene as seen through the rear window of a VW that inspired the shape. As a result of court action, Walter & Prediger gained the right to the dome shape and Koziol was restricted to the round ball shape.

The Erwin Perzy Company of Vienna, Austria, founded in 1900, creates glass snowdomes with traditional themes such as Christmas and other holidays, snowmen, skiers, mountain chalets, clowns, bears, and sailboats. These have smooth black (or white) plastic bases and a red sticker that reads "Made in Austria" on the glass ball.

The majority of plastic and glass snowdomes in the 1990s are made in the Orient, a few are produced in France and Italy. There are no American manufacturers, but rather dozens of large gift companies who design and import an array of styles, shapes, and themes. Enesco Corporation of Elk Grove Village, Illinois, is one of the largest.

References: Helen Guarnaccia, *Collector's Guide To Snow Domes: Identification and Values,* Collector Books, 1994; Nancy McMichael, *Snowdomes,* Abbeville Press, 1990; Connie A. Moore and Harry L. Rinker, *Snow Globes: The Collector's Guide To Selecting, Displaying, and Restoring Snow Globes,* Running Press, Courage Books, 1993.

Collectors' Club: Snowdome Collectors Club, PO Box 53262, Washington, DC 20009.

Advisor: Nancy McMichael.

Advertising
Heinz Ketchup, bottle, black lettered words "The Sign Of Good Eating" on front of white plastic dome, 2½" flat sides, "H & R Tomato Products" printed on side of truck, oily liquid, 1950s **60.00**
News Post and American, printed gold letters on front, 5" l black plastic desk pen set, 2½" glass globe with figure of paperboy, oily liquid, 1950s **70.00**
Newsweek, "No one covers the world like Newsweek" printed on red plastic base, large dome, 3½" l, 2½" w, 2¾" h, globe inside with floating plastic bars printed with "Newsweek" **25.00**
Nikon, camera company logo, small plastic dome **20.00**
Snow Tech/Larchmont Engineering,

telephone number, man and snow-blowing machine, small plastic dome **20.00**
Amusement Park
Carowinds, 3" h, plastic dome, ski lift swinging from top, park scene ... **8.00**
Coney Island, glass globe, beach scene, shell encrusted scalloped shape base, marked "Made in Italy," 1940s **30.00**
Great Adventure, 1½" plastic cube, three animals inside **8.00**
Heidi Park Soltau, Switzerland, small plastic dome, stage coach scene .. **10.00**
Kings Dominion
Large dome, figural lion on top .. **20.00**
Small plastic dome, Scooby Doo inside **8.00**
Sea World, 5½" l, large bottle, dolphin jumping through hoop on a see–saw **6.00**
The Enchanted Forest, 3" l, bottle, round sides, forest scene **6.00**
Wildworld, plastic ball, red base, park scene, perpetual calendar ... **10.00**
Animal Shape Figurals
Brown Bear, 5½" h, Canada plaque inside **20.00**
Owl, 5½" h, figural, brown, outstretched wing, scarecrow in 2¼" ball, orange ground **30.00**
Panda Bear, souvenir of Washington, DC **25.00**
Ashtray, Empire State Building, black Bakelite, 2¾" d glass ball, bisque figure, tiered base, early 1940s **50.00**
Award, title printed on front of flat, black 2½" base, 2½" glass globe, oily liquid
Jiminy Cricket Award for Outstanding Community Chest Service–1958, figure of Jiminy with his award ... **70.00**
Winter Sports King, Brookfield Sausage Promotion January–1954, golden crown inside **60.00**
Bank, coin slot on back
Florida, beach scene, plastic ball, red base, flat sides, perpetual calendar **5.00**
Paris, pale blue plastic **8.00**
Black, Watermelon Boy Down In New Orleans, gold decal on front of black ceramic base, heavy glass globe, painted figure of black boy eating watermelon, marked "Atlas Crystal Works, Covington, Tenn," 1940s .. **80.00**
Bottle Shape
Lying on side
Flat side, Rhode Island, The Ocean State, plaque in neck, three other plaques and scenes **15.00**

Round, Atlanta Stadium, Atlanta, Georgia, two sportsmen on see-saw 10.00
Upright Flat sides, Jamaica in neck, policeman inside, 5" h 9.00
Round shape, Wales on plaque, woman in native costume inside, 3" h 7.00
Boxed Set, "Wild West Snow Scenes, 6 Assorted by Marx," boxed set, small plastic domes, c1960, cowboy and Indian characters
Sold individually 10.00
Sold as set 100.00
Breweriana, Guinness, label on beer bottle and beer stein, 5" h blue plastic dome, int. plaque reads "Ireland," 1970s 20.00
Cartoon Character
Dogpatch USA, 2⅝ x 2½ x ¾", TV shape, plastic, brown, shows Mammy and Pappy Yokum, 1960s   18.00
Flintstones, on plaque, Hanna Barbera Productions on other plaque, three characters in front of cave 15.00
Kermit the Frog, 3½ x 3", sitting on brown trunk, clear dome, round base, marked "Koziol" on bottom, 1980s 20.00
Little Orphan Annie, 3⅝ x 2⅞ x 2¾", plastic dome, Annie and Sandy, 1970s 18.00
Popeye, figural, seated, plastic, holds water ball between hands, Olive Oyl, Sweetpea, and Wimpy in row boat that moves, King Features Syndicate, 1950s 40.00
Snoopy, 3¾ x 2½ x 2¾", lying on doghouse, clear sides, yellow, green, and orange base 5.00
Ziggy, 3¾ x 3 x 4", raised letters, fuchsia base, hearts instead of snow 4.00
Cats
Figural, dressed in Christmas suit, playing drum, 5½" h 20.00
Large plastic dome 6.00
Salt and Pepper Shakers, pr, glazed black ceramic, 1950s, water bowl with fish next to cat 50.00
Character
Davy Crockett, glass ball, decal and profile on base, marked "The Driss Co, Chicago, IL, Made in USA," late 1950s 60.00
Elvis, singing into mike, rect shape, moves back and forth in front of Graceland mansion panel, Graceland plaque, 1970s 15.00

Lone Ranger, round glass ball, Bakelite base, green, yellow, and red, decal "Lone Ranger: The Last Round-Up" 40.00
Marilyn Monroe, small red plastic dome, marked "Koziol" 30.00
Christmas
Bell, clear, red church and pine trees, 1970s 10.00
Elf, figural, red suit, green jester collar, ball in tummy, snowman, trees, and house scene, 1960s 25.00
Fireplace, 3½ x 3¼ x 2¼", child sleeping in pajamas in hearth, Santa in sled on see-saw in dome, marked "CSA Inc, Curt S. Adler, Inc., NY, NY 10010," 1970s 20.00
Frosty the Snowman, figural, 5½" h, standing black boots and top hat, removable broomstick, angel and deer in ball, 1960s 12.00
Nativity Scene, 4½ x 3¼ x 3", round dome, eight panels, three dimensional figures, late 1950s 8.00
Rudolph the Red Nosed Reindeer, green plastic base, "Rudolph the Red Nosed Reindeer in the Snow, copyright RLM" on decal, 1950s   30.00
Santa
Figural, 5¾ x 3½ x 1", driving sleigh, two reindeer, rect dome with elf sitting under a mushroom, 1960s 20.00
Pivot, plastic, round dome, holding boy and girl, yellow bag of toys, marked "MCMLXVI" and "Louis Marx" 7.00
Workshop, figural, red brick design, Mr and Mrs Claus work at workbench, rocking horse, marked "SANTA'S WORKSHOP" on top 15.00
Sled, 2¼ x 1¼ x 1", Santa, tree with candles, and reindeer, green, brown, and orange, arch dome, orange snowflake plug, beige base, marked "Made in West Germany," 1950s 12.00
Three snowmen, slanted eyes, red plastic base, seaweed trees, marked "Made in Japan," 1960s . .   10.00
Disney
Bambi, plaque, television shape, marked "WDP," 1959 . . . .   25.00
Disneyland, 2¾ x 2¼ x 2", plastic dome, Tinkerbell and castle, 1970s   12.00
Mickey Mouse, figural, plastic, 5" h, holds 2" d ball in lap, castle scene, 1960s 40.00
Pirates of the Caribbean, bottle shape, sq sides, three panels,

Figural, left: Old Salts, plastic, 5½″ h, 2¾″ d water ball, 1970s, $10.00; right: Mickey Mouse, 5½″ h, Disneyland in 2¾″ d water ball, 1970s, $12.00.

"Disneyland copyright Walt Disney Productions" plaque 20.00

Figural

Alligator, 5″ h, ball is between hands and bent legs, two gators on see–saw, dark green, Florida plaque, 1970s 8.00

Angel, golden wings, all plastic, 5½″ h 40.00

Apple, red, green leaves, round white base, New York City plaque, 1980s 20.00

Bird, on side of plastic ball, elongated base 15.00

Church, steeple, 2¼ x 2¾ x 2½″, plastic, altar, bride, and groom, marked "W Germany" on bottom, 1980s 15.00

Clown, all plastic, 5½″ h 40.00

Dolphin, 4 x 2½ x 4½″ dome, dolphin draped over dome, wave covered elongated base, Florida plaque, two dolphins on see–saw, 1970s 7.00

Fish, 4 x 7″, plastic, bright orange, green movable plastic fins, Florida plaque, 1970s 15.00

Heart, red, gold letters, I Love NY, city skyline, 1980s 7.00

Lantern, 4 x 2″, movable handle on top, red frame, clear plastic on four sides, girl pulling sled, trees, 1980s 6.00

Mermaid, 4 x 2½ x 4½″ dome, mermaid draped over dome, wave covered elongated base, Weeki Wachi Spring, Florida plaque, water–skiers and boat in dome, 1970s 10.00

Sea Captain, standing, 5½″ h, 2½″ d ball in middle, white beard, blue cap, orange shirt, movable pipe, Ocean City, Maryland plaque, sailing ships against clouds, 1970s 20.00

Tiger, 3½″ , two tigers in dome,

"Southwick's Wild Animal Farm, Mendon, MA," 1970s 14.00

Game, ring toss

Dolphin, 2½″ h clear plastic dome, colored rings

Cape Hatteras plaque 7.00

Florida plaque 5.00

Without plaque 3.00

Halloween

Cat, 6½″ h, figural, black, 2¾″ d orange plastic ball, witch riding broomstick 30.00

Grim Reaper, figural, black, 5½″, crossed bones as base, all plastic 40.00

Jack 'O Lantern, black cat, 3¾″ d clear glass ball, wood base 8.00

Hotel

Hyatt at Palmetto Dunes Hilton Head, SC, 1½″ plastic cube 10.00

Kuwait International Hotel, phone and fax numbers also printed on ext. of white plastic base, 3″ l, 1½″ w, 2½″ h 50.00

Regency Hyatt House Atlanta Georgia, 3″ h, plastic 12.00

Moving Parts

Balloons on string, 3½ x 2¾ x 3″, monkey swings on hook, four animals in cage, "Philadelphia Zoo," 1970s 10.00

Champagne, shot, and martini glass on strings, 3¾ x 2¾ x 2¼″, naked lady, painted "The Bar is Open" bar scene backdrop, "This one is on me" plaque, "Las Vegas" on outside, 1960s 15.00

Dice, 2⅝ x 2 x 2¼″, red, float in water, blue ground, main strip in Vegas scene, 1970s 7.00

Rocking Horse on glider, 3⅛ x 1¼ x 2⅝″, toy soldier on his back, arched dome, black base, 1970s 8.00

Wagon, horse drawn, bottle shape, moves in and out of covered barn, large dome, "New Hampshire," 1970s 9.00

Museum

Roy Rogers and Dale Evans Museum, Victorville, CA, plastic dome, barn scene and Trigger moves on slide, 1960s 15.00

Salem Witch Museum, 1692, 2¾ x 2¼ x 2″, small plastic dome, house and witch on broomstick, 1970s 10.00

The American Museum of Natural History, Hayden Planetarium, NY," 2¾ x 2¼ x 2″, plastic dome, printing on back, camera and city skyline scene, 1980s 6.00

Native Americans

Family, Winchester, VA, in front of large tee pee, large plastic dome 9.00

Indian Chief, figural, all plastic, 5½"
h, green headdress **50.00**
Two Indians on see–saw, small plastic
dome **8.00**
Village, American, painted scene,
brown Bakelite base, oily liquid,
late 1940s **20.00**
Ocean Liner, glass ball, sq white base,
SS Independence, blue lettering, ship
in globe, Art Deco city skyline
ground, oily liquid, 1940s **50.00**
Pencil Sharpener
Niagara Falls, large plastic dome,
Maid of Mist moves in groove,
standard pencil sharpener attached
to bottom **6.00**
UFO shape, figural, pink plastic, pen-
cil sharpener hole in side of space
ship, domed top with space crea-
tures floating in water, marked
"Koziol" on bottom **10.00**
Regional
California Redwoods, large plastic
dome with orange trees and deer   **10.00**
Cape Cod, MA, bottle shape, three
sea captains in front of clouds,
1970s **8.00**
Florida, small plastic dome, fisher-
man and fish on see–saw **4.00**
Massachusetts, small dome with his-
toric sites, 1960s **8.00**
Ohio, red bird in tree, yellow flowers,
state outline on front, 1970s
Bottle shape **8.00**
Small dome **6.00**
Skyline Drive, VA, small plastic
dome, two deer on see–saw **8.00**
West Virginia, large plastic dome,
three dimensional bear figurine,
1960s **8.00**
Religious
Bethlehem, small plastic dome, Holy
Family **10.00**
Crucifixion, 3⅝ x 2⅞ x 2¾", plastic
dome, Jesus on cross, battery oper-
ated, 1960s **15.00**
Holy Family and Atlantic City decals,
black ceramic base, glass globe,
three figures, 1940s **60.00**
Nativity Scene, small plastic dome,
1980s **3.00**
Noah's Ark, small plastic dome,
1970s **10.00**
The Resurrection, rounded dome,
Christ flanked by two sleeping soldiers, red ground, cut–out starburst
lights up, 1970s **20.00**
Salesman's sample, "Sample Sno–Globe
Tell–A–Story No. 2166–GLT" printed
in gold lettering on front, sq black
Bakelite base, 2½" sides, 2½" glass
globe, office scene, clients looking at

snowdome with company name, oily
liquid, 1950s **70.00**
Salt and Pepper Shakers, pr
Civil War, 3¼ x 1¼ x 2", plastic, pink
"P" with American flag, blue "S"
with Rebel flag, soldiers and cannon scene, back compartments,
1960s **20.00**
Florida's Silver Springs, 3 x 2¼ x 1",
TV shape, plastic, blue "P," pink
"S," boat on see–saw, side com-
partments, 1970s **15.00**
Mickey Mouse, inverted cone, clear,
cylinder in center **15.00**
Sea Shell Covered Base, glass ball sits
on scalloped shape base, cov with
pebbles and sea shells, St Anthony
figure inside, marked "Made in Italy"
on bottom **30.00**
Souvenir
Chinatown, NY, small plastic dome,
Oriental scene, 1960s **15.00**
Hearst Castle, large dome, two zebras
on see–saw in front of castle **10.00**
Hoover Dam, small plastic dome,
dice in water **10.00**
Story Land, plastic club, fairy tale
characters, 1960s **9.00**
Wisconsin Dells decal, glass globe,
tiered black plastic base, seaweed
and fish on strings inside, 1930s . .   **40.00**
Winter Sports
Boy pulling girl on sled, small plastic
dome **5.00**
Skier, white bisque, glass globe, black
Bakelite base **40.00**
Winter Olympics, Albertville, France,
Olympic symbol, small plastic
dome **25.00**
World's Fair
1939, New York World's Fair
Administration Building, white
bisque figure of building **85.00**
Trylon and Perisphere bisque fig-
urine, brown ceramic base
With decal **70.00**
Without decal **60.00**
1964–65, New York World's Fair
Unisphere, plastic, round ball, red
sq base, perpetual calendar,
"Unisphere presented by USS
United States Steel, 1964
NYWF" **18.00**
1982, 3½ x 2 x 1¼", tall dome,
Sunsphere **11.00**
1984, plastic dome, fair archway,
ferry moves back and forth on
groove, plaque **9.00**
World War II
Douglas MacArthur, America's Hero,
glass ball, black ceramic base,
bisque bust **50.00**

Souvenir, World's Fair, left: 1939 New York, Trylon and Perisphere, bisque figurine, brown ceramic base, no decal, $60.00; right: 1982, Sunsphere, $11.00.

General Eisenhower, glass ball, black ceramic base, bisque bust, "General Dwight D Eisenhower, Commander in Chief, Allied Invasion Forces" decal, marked "Atlas Crystal Works, Covington, TN, US Patents 231423/4/5," 1940s **70.00**

Plane, painted bisque figurine, red star on wings, tail and nose markings, glass ball, black ceramic base, marked "Atlas Crystal Works, Trenton, NJ, Patents Pending, Made in USA," 1940s **55.00**

Sailor, white uniform, black ceramic base, glass globe **30.00**

SODA BOTTLES

History: Soda bottles were made to contain soda water and soft drinks. A beverage manufacturer usually made his own bottles and sold them within a limited area. Coddball stoppers and a stopper perfected by Hutchinson were popular with early manufacturers before the advent of metal or screw top caps.

References: Paul and Karen Bates, *Commemorative Soda Bottles*, Soda Mart, 1988; Paul and Karen Bates, *Embossed Soda Bottles*, Soda Mart, 1988; Paul and Karen Bates, *Painted Label Soda Bottles*, Soda Mart, 1988; Ralph and Terry Kovel, *The Kovels' Bottle Price List, Ninth Edition*, Crown Publishers, 1992; Peck and Audie Markota, *Western Blob Top Soda and Mineral Bottles, Second Edition*, published by authors, 1994; Jim Megura, *The Official Identification and Price Guide To Bottles, Eleventh Edition*, House of Collectibles, 1991; Tom Morrison, *Root Beer: Advertising and Collectibles*, Schiffer Publishing,

1992; Michael Polak, *Bottles: Identification and Price Guide*, Avon Books, 1994; Carlo and Dot Sellari, *The Standard Old Bottle Price Guide*, Collector Books, 1989.

Collectors Club: Painted Soda Bottle Collectors Assoc., 9418 Hilmer Dr., La Mesa, CA 91942.

Periodical: *Antique Bottle And Glass Collector*, PO Box 187, East Greenville, PA 18041.

See: Coca–Cola, Pepsi and Soft Drink Collectibles.

Abilena National Cathartic Water, amber, 10" h	**6.00**
Alter & Wilson Manuf, light green, applied top, 7" h	**17.50**
Bacon's Soda Works, light green, blob top, 7" h	**8.00**
Bryant's Root Beer, This Bottle Makes Five Gallons, amber, applied top, 4½" h	**4.00**
Cape Arco Soda Works, Marshfield, OR, round, light green applied top, 7" h	**8.00**
Coke, 24" h	**25.00**
Deadwood, SD, blob top	**125.00**
Deamer Grass Valley, aqua, blob top, 7¼" h	**5.00**
Dr Pepper, Colorado	**17.50**
English Soda, light green, applied top, 8" h	**4.00**
Fizz, Southern State Siphon Bottling Co, golden amber, 11" h	**15.00**
Golden West Soda Works, light green, 7" h	**10.00**
Hawaiian Soda Works, aqua, emb, 7½" h	**8.00**
Hippo Size Soda Water, clear, crown top, 10" h	**5.00**
Jackson's Napa Soda, crown cap, 7¼" h	**5.00**
Kolshorn, Chas & Bros, Savannah, GA, aqua, blob top, 8" h	**15.00**
Long Distance, green, emb	**25.00**
Mason's Root Beer, painted label	**12.00**
Mendocin Bottling Works, A L Reynolds, light green, 7" h	**7.00**
Mission Dry Sparkling, black, 9¾" h ..	**3.00**
Nevada City Soda Works, ETR Powell, aqua, applied top, 7" h	**8.00**
Orange Crush Co, Pat'd July 20, 1926, light green, 9" h	**3.50**
Perrier, clear, bowling pin shape, paper label, 8½" h	**2.00**
Phenis Nerve Beverage Co, Boston, clear, crown cap, 9½" h	**4.00**
Rapid City Bottling Works, light green, crown cap, 8" h	**5.00**
Ross's Royal Belfast Ginger Ale, green, diamond shape paper label, 10" h ..	**5.00**
Rummy, painted label	**12.00**
Sandahl Beverages, clear, 8" h	**4.00**

American Ice Cream Book, Galahad Books, 1972; Ray Klug, Antique Advertising Encyclopedia, Vol I (1978, 1993 value update), Vol II, (1985, 1990 value update), L–W Promotions; Tom Morrison, Root Beer: Advertising and Collectibles, Schiffer Publishing, 1992; Ralph Pomeroy, The Ice Cream Connection, Paddington Press, 1975.

Collectors' Clubs: National Association of Soda Jerks, PO Box 115, Omaha, NE 68101; The Ice Screamer, PO Box 465, Warrington, PA 18976.

Bon-Ton, Harold Teen Highball, Chicago, IL, printed label, 7⅞" h, $25.00.

Museums: Greenfield Village, Dearborn, MI; Museum of Science and Industry, Finigan's Ice Cream Parlor, Chicago, IL; Smithsonian Institution, Washington, DC.

REPRODUCTION ALERT

Scott & Gilbert Co, San Francisco, brown, crown top, 10" h	5.00
Sequoia Soda Works, aqua, 7½" h	5.00
Solano Soda Works, aqua, 8" h	5.00
Squeeze, painted label	12.00
Tahoe Soda Springs Natural Mineral Water, light green, 7½" h	9.00
Union Glass Works, dark blue, blob top, 7⅓" h	20.00
Williams Bros, San Jose, CA	7.00
XLCR Soda Works, light green, 7¼"	5.00

SODA FOUNTAIN COLLECTIBLES

Collecting Hints: The ice cream collector competes with collectors in many other categories—advertising, glassware, postcards, food molds, tools, etc. Material still ranges in the twenty–five cent to $200 range.

When buying a tray, the scene is the most important element. Most trays were stock items with the store or firm's name added later. Always look for items in excellent condition.

History: From the late 1880s through the end of the 1960s, the local soda fountain was the social center of small town America, especially for teenagers. The soda fountain provided a center for conversation and gossip, a haven to satisfy the mid–afternoon munchies, and a source for the most current popular magazines.

Ice cream items began to appear about 1870 and extend to the present. The oldest items are the cone–shaped ice cream scoops. Beginning in the 1920s, manufacturers of ice cream began to issue premiums. These items are among those most eagerly sought by collectors.

References: Douglas Congdon–Martin, Drugstore and Soda Fountain Antiques, Schiffer Publishing, 1991; Paul Dickson, The Great

Ashtray, Breyers, 90th Anniversary, 1866–1956	20.00
Bin, counter, Quaker Brand Salted Peanuts, 9 x 13¾ x 4¼"	40.00
Blackboard, Squirt, 15 x 30"	18.00
Clock, Seven–Up, "You Like It, It Likes You," wood frame	75.00
Dish, ice cream	
Amber, banana split	12.50
Elsie	15.00
Display Case, counter top, Popcorn, wood and glass, hinged lid, 11 x 11"	45.00
Display Rack	
Beech–Nut Chewing Gum, 1920s	300.00
Lance Candy, four shelves	15.00
Door Pull, Drink Hire's, tin	50.00
Fan	
Goold's Orangeade, cardboard, wooden handle	15.00
Hoffman Willis Ice Cream Co, girl eating ice cream	15.00
Hat, soda jerk style	3.00
Hot Plate, commercial, Nestle's Hot Chocolate, 8" x 12" standing metal sign, red and white snowman graphics, late 1940s–early 1950s	95.00
Ice Chipper, Gilchrist, #50	8.00
Ice Cream Cone Holder	
Heisey, individual	50.00
Vortex, patented 1916	6.50
Ice Cream Scoop	
Dover, brass	68.50
Erie, round, size 8, aluminum	180.00
Gilchrist, #30, size 8, polished	65.00
No–Pak 31, size 5	75.00
Scoop Rite	15.00
Jar, Borden's Malted Milk, glass label	175.00
Magazine Cover, Saturday Evening Post, young soda jerk talking to girls at counter, Norman Rockwell, Aug 22, 1953	12.00
Malt Mixer, Dairy Bar, metal, white Bakelite canister, logo	110.00

Milk Shake Machine
  Gilchrist, orig cup, c1926 . . . . **65.00**
  Hamilton Beach, push down type . . **135.00**
Mirror
  Angelus Marshmallows, multicolored
  symbolic angel figure, dark green
  ground, premium offer printed on
  rim curl **80.00**
  Horlicks Malted Milk, maid with cow **30.00**
Pencil Clip, Kramer's Beverages, red
  and white, celluloid, c1930 . . . . **7.50**
Pinback Button
  Bemis Bags, multicolored, brown cat
  emerging from paper bag inscribed
  "Bemis Bros, St Louis," c1896 . . . **20.00**
  Harry Hood, multicolored, HP Hood
  Dairy, c1970s **6.00**
  Hi–Hat Ice Cream Soda 10¢, 2¼" d,
  McCrory's, c1940 . . . . **15.00**
  Sanderson's Drug Store, 1" d, blue
  and white, soda fountain glass il-
  lus, "Ice Cream Soda/Choice
  Cigars/Fine Candies," 1901–12 . . **24.00**
Post Card
  Bodle's Ice Cream Store, diecut **8.00**
  Gunther's Soda Fountain, Chicago . . **12.00**
Puppet, Teddy Snow Crop, 9" h, white
  plush, thin vinyl applied face, red and
  silver fabric name sticker on chest,
  c1950 . . . . **40.00**
Sign
  Bowey's Hot Chocolate, black logo **150.00**
  Coca–Cola Fountain Service, porce-
  lain, diecut, shield shape **425.00**
  Golden Rod Ice Cream, diecut, girl
  with ice cream **85.00**
  Nehi, diecut, woman at marble soda
  fountain, sitting on wire stool, sip-
  ping through two straws, giant bottle on floor, Columbus, GA, 1920 **1,250.00**
  Orange County Fountain, 24 x 18",
  porcelain on steel, yellow oval
  center, blue and white lettering,
  dark blue ground **100.00**
  True Fruit, J Hungerford Smith
  Fountain Syrups, 24 x 34", self
  framed tin **295.00**
Soda Holder, metal, blue **5.00**
Spoon, Borden's, silver plated **1.50**
Straw Jar, glass
  Frosted Panel **225.00**
  Green Panel **410.00**
  Illinois, lid **450.00**
  Red, metal lid, 1950s **175.00**
Syrup Dispenser Pump
  Hires **135.00**
  Wards Lemon Crush **950.00**
Tin, Schrafft's Marshmallow Topping, 25
  lbs **35.00**
Tray
  Chero–Cola **65.00**
  Pepsi Cola, Hits the Spot, 1940s . . . **15.00**

Tip Tray, Everybody's Favorite, Bingham-ton Ice Cream Co., young lady, red ker-chief, red border, 6⅛ x 4⅜", $35.00.

  Schuller's Ice Cream, 13 x 11", ice
  cream sodas and cones **200.00**
Tumbler
  Grapette **8.00**
  Lemonette **8.00**
  Orange Crush, 5" h, clear, etched de-
  sign **95.00**
  Orangette **8.00**
Wafer Holder
  Reliance **165.00**
  Tin, polished **100.00**

SOFT DRINK COLLECTIBLES

Collecting Hints: Coca–Cola items have dominated the field. Only recently have collectors begun concentrating on other soft drink manufacturing companies. Soft drink collectors must
compete with collectors of advertising, bottles
and premiums for the same material.

National brands such as Canada Dry, Dr.
Pepper, and Pepsi–Cola are best known.
However, regional soft drink bottling plants do
exist, and their products are fertile ground for the
novice collector.

History: Sarsaparilla, a name associated with soft
drinks, began as a medicinal product. When carbonated water was added, it became a soft drink
and was consumed for pleasure rather than medical purposes. However, sarsaparilla was only
one type of ingredient added to carbonated water to produce soft drinks.

Each company had its special formula.
Although Coca–Cola has a large market share,
other companies provided challenges in different
historical periods. Moxie was followed by Hire's
which in turn gave way to Pepsi–Cola and 7–Up.

The 1950s brought soft drinks to the forefront
of everyday life. Large advertising campaigns and
promotional products provided a wealth of ma-

terial. Regional bottling plants were strong and produced local specialties such as "Birch Beer" in eastern Pennsylvania. By 1970 most of these local plants had closed.

Many large companies had operations outside of the United States, which also produced a wealth of advertising and promotional materials. Today, the diet soda is a response to the current American lifestyle.

References: Q. David Bowers, *The Moxie Encyclopedia,* Vestal Press, 1985; Norman E. Martinus and Harry L. Rinker, *Warman's Paper,* Wallace–Homestead, 1994; Tom Morrison, *Root Beer: Advertising and Collectibles,* Schiffer Publishing, 1992; Frank N. Potter, *The Book of Moxie,* Collector Books, 1987; Frank N. Potter, *The Moxie Mystique—The Word, The Drink, The Collectible,* published by author, 1981.

Collectors' Clubs: Dr. Pepper 10–2–4 Collectors Club, 1529 John Smith, Irving, TX 75061; Moxie Enthusiasts Collectors Club of America, Route 375, Box 164, Woodstock, NY 12498; National Pop Can Collectors, PO Box 7862, Rockford, IL 61126; New England Moxie Congress, 445 Wyoming Ave., Millburn, NJ 07041.

Museums: Clark's Trading Post, North Woodstock, NH; Matthews Museum of Maine Heritage, Union, ME.

See: Coca–Cola, Pepsi, Soda Bottles, and Soda Fountain Collectibles.

Advertising Trade Card, Hire's Root
  Beer, late 1800s **10.00**
Badge, Dad's Root Beer, "Fastest Draw
  in the West" **30.00**
Blackboard
  Frostie Root Beer, tin, 1950s **65.00**
  Grapette, 1971 . . . .   **150.00**

Nehi, tin **75.00**
Blotter, Pete & Pepsi, #709, 1930 . . . .   **100.00**
Book, adv
  Hire's Root Beer, *1940 Football Book,*
    schedules and rules, 40 pgs **28.00**
  Hood's Sarsaparilla, palette shape,
    1894 . . . .   **30.00**
Booklet, adv, Hire's Root Beer, fantasy,
  The Legend of the Golden Chair, 3½
  x 5", 16 pgs, black and white illus,
  c1894 . . . .   **6.00**
Bottle Carrier, 7–Up, aluminum, twelve
  bottles **50.00**
Bottle Opener, 7–Up, cast iron **15.00**
Calendar
  Nehi, 1927, woman leaning on boat
    at beach **125.00**
  Nu–Grape **45.00**
Carrier, Spur Cola, unused, 1940s **8.00**
Carrying Case, Uncle Joe's Soda, 1929   **75.00**
Catalog, Nehi premiums, baseball,
  pocket knives, watches, 1920s **22.00**
Clock
  Dr Pepper, bottle cap **60.00**
  Royal Crown Cola **90.00**
  Sun Crest Orange **35.00**
Coupon, Hire's Root Beer, Good For
  One Stein or Glass, St Louis Fair . . .   **28.00**
Dispenser, child's, 7=Up Uncola **20.00**
Door Decal, Mission Orange, 1940s . .   **15.00**
Door Plate
  Canada Dry, bottle shape **45.00**
  Hires **85.00**
Figure, 9" h, Fresh Up Freddie, soft vinyl
  rooster, tan body, red head and tail
  feathers, white shirt, dark green
  trousers, replica bottle in hand, copy-
  right 1959 . . . .   **195.00**
Match Holder, Dr Pepper **5.00**
Miniature Bottle, Canada Dry, 3½",
  c1950 . . . .   **5.00**
Mirror, Hire's Root Beer, oval, Victorian
  lady with roses **80.00**

Advertising Stringer, Cheer Up, green bottle, red label, double sided cardboard hanger, unused, 2½ x 8½", $15.00.

Fan, Moxie Man, "Frank Archer says. . .," copyright 1922, back with girl in pigtails, 7 x 8", $35.00.

Mug

A & W Root Beer, child's **15.00**

Hires Root Beer, barrel shape, marked "Mettlac, Germany," 1906 . . . . . .   **200.00**

K W Rootbeer **15.00**

Pencil Clip, Orange Crush, black and white, orange ground, c1940 . . . . . .   **18.00**

Pin Tray, Dr Pepper, 3", oval, black boy eating watermelon illus **275.00**

Pinback Button, Fresh Up Freddie, 7–Up adv, 1⅜" d, litho, multicolor, cartoon bird illus, 1950s **15.00**

Pitcher, Orange Crush, glass **28.00**

Post Card, RC and Nehi, price for 3 pc set **10.00**

Poster

Grapette, 9 x 23", 1972 . . . .   **8.00**

Orange Crush, 12 x 18", cardboard, woman wearing swimsuit, beach **32.00**

7–Up, 5 x 15", store window type, 1960s **12.00**

Puzzle, Hood's Sarsaparilla Rainy Day Puzzle **35.00**

Radio, Royal Crown, can shape, late 1970s **35.00**

Ruler, Fresh Up Freddie, 2 x 6¼", clear plastic, yellow strip, full color illus of Freddie, black, white, and red 7–Up logo, bicycle riding safety rules text, late 1950s **20.00**

Salt and Pepper Shakers, 7–Up, orig box, pr **4.00**

Sheet Music, *Moxie Song,* one–step, 1921 . . . .   **12.00**

Shirt Patch, Grapette

5 x 2" **5.00**

10 x 6" **9.00**

Shirt Pin, Grapette, metal, 5 x 3" **6.00**

Sign

Canada Dry, 10 x 47", tin **40.00**

Capital Club Soda, 6 x 9", cardboard, 1940s **10.00**

Dad's Root Beer **85.00**

Dr Pepper

Cardboard, girl in convertible, 1940 . . . .   **350.00**

Porcelain, Good For Life **160.00**

Dr Swift's Root Beer, diecut, girl holding drinks, asking for ride, boy in pedal car, tongue hanging out . . .   **375.00**

Hire's Root Beer, tin **175.00**

Nehi, paper, woman's legs, bottle, 1920s **35.00**

Orange Crush

3 x 27", Ask For A Crush **145.00**

9" d, round, reverse painted on glass, illus of Crushy **225.00**

7–Up, diecut, grocer with bottles . . .   **85.00**

Squirt, tin, yellow, flange **110.00**

Wonder Orange, tin, colorful **150.00**

Stuffed Toy, Grapette, label and cap

Bear **50.00**

Clown **25.00**

Elephant **35.00**

Thermometer

Bierley's Orange **50.00**

Dr Pepper, round **80.00**

Frosty Root Beer, Frosty illus **75.00**

Hire's, bottle shape, diecut **78.00**

Sun Drop Cola **65.00**

Ya Gotta Have Moxie, yellow, kid boxer **35.00**

Token, Moxie, 1¼", aluminum, Good For One Drink, c1900 . . . .   **15.00**

Toy Truck, Canada Dry–Special Sparkle, 4" l **25.00**

Tray, Hire's Root Beer

Boy, Just What the Doctor Ordered, 1914 . . . .   **385.00**

Coffin Girl, Haskell **145.00**

Tumbler, Drink Fry's, Colfax Ginger Ale, Noticeably Better **20.00**

SOLDIERS, DIMESTORE

Collecting Hints: Soldier figures are preferred over civilian figures. The most valuable figures are the ones which had short production runs, usually because they were less popular with the youthful collectors of the period.

O'Brien and Pielin use numbering systems to identify figures in their books. Newcomers should study these books, taking note of the numerous variations in style and color.

Condition, desirability and scarcity establish the price of a figure. Repainting or rust severely reduces the value.

Auction prices often mislead the beginning collector. While some rare figures have sold in the $150 to $300 range, most sell between $10 and $25.

History: Three–dimensional lead, iron, and rubber soldier and civilian figures were produced in the United States by the millions before and after World War II. These figures were called "dimestore soldiers" because they were sold in "five and dime" stores of the era, the figures usually costing a nickel or dime. Although American toy soldiers can be traced back to the early 20th century, the golden age of the dimestore soldier was 1935 until 1942.

Four companies—Barclay, Manoil, Grey Iron and Auburn Rubber—mass produced the three–inch figures. Barclay and Manoil dominated the market, probably because their lead castings lent themselves to more realistic and imaginative poses than iron and rubber.

Barclay's early pre–war figures are identifiable by their separate glued–on and later clipped–on tin hats. When these are lost, the hole in the top of the head always identifies a Barclay.

The Manoil Company first produced soldiers, sailors, cowboys, and Indians. However, the younger buyers of the period strongly preferred military figures, perhaps emulating the newspaper headlines as World War II approached. Manoil's civilian figures were made in response to pacifist pressure and boycotts mounted before the war began.

Figures also were produced by such companies as All–Nu, American Alloy, American Soldier Co., Beton, Ideal, Jones, Lincoln Log, Miller, Playwood Plastics, Soljertoys, Tommy Toy, Tootsietoy, and Warren. Because of the short–lived nature of these companies, numerous limited production figures command high prices, especially those of All–Nu, Jones, Tommy Toy, and Warren.

From 1942 through 1945 the wartime "scrap drives" devoured tons of the dimestore figures and the molds that produced them.

In late 1945 Barclay and Manoil introduced modernized military figures, but they never enjoyed their pre–war popularity. "Military operations" generally were phased out by the early 1950s. Similarly, the civilian figures could not compete with escalating labor costs and the competition of plastic.

References: Bertel Bruun, *Toy Soldiers: Identification and Price Guide*, Avon Books, 1994; Norman Joplin, *The Great Book Of Hollow–Cast Figures*, New Cavendish Books, 1992; Norman Joplin, *Toy Soldiers*, Running Press, Courage Books, 1994; Richard O'Brien, *Collecting Toy Soldiers: An Identification and Value Guide, No. 2*, Books Americana, 1992; Don Pielin, *American Dimestore Soldier Book*, published by author, 1983.

Periodicals: *Old Toy Soldier*, 209 N. Lombard, Oak Park, IL 60302; *Plastic Warrior*, 905 Harrison St., Allentown, PA 18103; *Toy Soldier Review*, 127 74th Street, North Bergen, NJ 07047.

REPRODUCTION ALERT: Some manufacturers identify the newer products; many do not.

Notes: Prices listed are for figures in original condition with at least 95% of the paint remaining. Unless otherwise noted, uniform colors are brown.

CIVILIAN FIGURE

Auburn Rubber
Baseball	**28.00**
Football	**28.00**

Barclay
Civilian Figures
Girl Skater	**8.00**
Mailman	**9.00**
Newsboy	**10.00**
Pirate	**8.00**
Policeman with raised arm	**8.00**
Redcap with bag	**15.00**
Santa Claus on skis	**55.00**
Woman Passenger with dog	**9.00**

Barclay, walking boy in jacket, knickers, holding toy car in one hand, $9.00.

Cowboy
Mounted, firing pistol	**12.00**
With lasso	**15.00**

Indian
Standing, bow and arrow	**8.00**
Tomahawk and shield	**9.00**

Grey Iron
American Family Series, 2¼" h	**5.00-25.00**

Western
Bandit, hands up	**4.00**

Cowboy
Hold–up man	**15.00**
Standing	**9.00**

Manoil
Happy Farm Series
Blacksmith
Making horseshoes	**20.00**
With wheel	**20.00**
Farmer, sowing grain	**18.00**

Lady
Sweeping	**20.00**
With pie	**25.00**

Man
Chopping wood	**18.00**
Juggling barrel	**30.00**
Man and woman on bench	**18.00**
Watchman blowing out lantern	**25.00**

Western
Cowboy
Arm raised	**17.00**
One gun raised, flat base	**14.00**

Cowgirl riding horse **25.00**
Indian with knives **18.00**

MILITARY FIGURE

Auburn Rubber
Charging with Tommy gun **8.00**
Grenade Thrower **15.00**
Machine Gunner, kneeling **11.00**
Marching with rifle **7.00**
Motorcycle with sidecar **55.00**
Motorcyclist **30.00**
Soldier
Kneeling with binoculars **12.00**
Searchlight **28.00**
Barclay, pod foot series
Post War, pot helmet
Flag Bearer **15.00**
Machine Gunner, prone **15.00**
Officer with sword **15.00**
Rifleman, standing **15.00**
Pre World War II
Anti–Aircraft Gunner, standing . . . **15.00**
Bugler, tin helmet **15.00**
Cameraman, kneeling, tin hat . . . **20.00**
Cook in white, holding roast **12.00**
Dispatcher with dog **35.00**
Doctor, white coat, carrying bag **12.00**
Flag Bearer, tin helmet **18.00**
Machine Gunner, kneeling, tin hat **10.00**
Marching with rifle, tin hat **12.00**
Marine Officer, marching, sword,
blue uniform, tin hat **22.00**
Nurse, kneeling with cup, white . . **15.00**
Parachutist, landing **25.00**
Pilot, standing **18.00**
Sailor
Carrying flag, white **20.00**
Marching, white **20.00**
Signal flags, white **20.00**
Sharpshooter
Prone **15.00**
Standing **11.00**
Signalman with flags **20.00**
Soldier
Crawling, tin hat **18.00**
Lying wounded, tin hat **12.00**
Peeling potatoes **20.00**
Prone with binoculars **15.00**
Releasing pigeons, tin hat **18.00**
Running with rifle **18.00**
Searchlight **20.00**
Standing at attention, tin hat . . . **14.00**
Stretcher Bearer **15.00**
Telephone Operator, tin hat **15.00**
Two man rocket team **20.00**
Wireless Operator, antenna, tin hat **28.00**
Wounded
On crutches **15.00**
Sitting, arm in sling **15.00**
Podfoot Series, 2¾" h
Bugler **7.00**

Flag Bearer **10.00**
Machine Gunner
Charging **6.00**
Prone **8.00**
Nurse, white **18.00**
Officer **6.00**
Pilot, standing **9.00**
Sailor, blue **8.00**
Soldier
Charging **6.00**
Marching with rifle **7.00**
Grey Iron
Cavalryman **25.00**
Colonial Soldier **15.00**
Doctor, white, bag **12.00**
Doughboy
Crawling **15.00**
Marching **10.00**
Rifle, kneeling **15.00**
Sentry **10.00**
Drum Major **17.00**
Drummer **15.00**
Ethiopian
Charging **35.00**
Marching **28.00**
Flag Bearer **15.00**
Machine Gunner
Kneeling **10.00**
Prone **15.00**
Nurse, white and blue **12.00**
Radio Operator **45.00**
Sailor, marching
Blue **12.00**
White **14.00**
Manoil
Post War
Marching with rifle **16.00**
Soldier
Bazooka **20.00**
Mine Detector **30.00**
Tommy Gunner, standing **22.00**
Post War, 2½" size, marked "USA"
Aircraft Spotter **25.00**
Aviator, holding bomb **24.00**
Flag Bearer **26.00**
Grenade Thrower **24.00**
Machine Gunner, seated **20.00**
Observer with binoculars **27.00**
Soldier with bazooka **18.00**
Pre World War II
Bicycle Rider **30.00**
Bomb Thrower, three grenades . . . **14.00**
Boxer **65.00**
Cameraman, flash overhead **35.00**
Cannon Loader **14.00**
Cooks helper with ladle **24.00**
Deep Sea Diver, silver **15.00**
Doctor, white **12.00**
Firefighter, "Hot Papa," gray **65.00**
Flag Bearer **18.00**
Hostess, green **45.00**
Machine Gunner, prone **15.00**

Marching	**16.00**
Navy Gunner, white, firing deck	
gun	**32.00**
Nurse, white, red dish	**16.00**
Observer with periscope	**20.00**
Radio Operator, standing	**33.00**
Rifleman, standing	**15.00**
Sailor, white	**18.00**
Sharpshooter, camouflage, prone .	**20.00**
Signalman, white, two flags	**24.00**
Soldier	
At searchlight	**18.00**
Charging with bayonet	**28.00**
Gas mask and flare gun	**18.00**
Running with cannon	**28.00**
Sitting, eating	**26.00**
Wounded	**15.00**
Writing letter	**50.00**
Stretcher carrier, medical kit	**17.00**

SOLDIERS, TOY

Collecting Hints: Consider three key factors: condition of the figures and the box, the age of the figures and the box, and the completeness of the set.

Toy soldiers were meant to be playthings. However, collectors consider them an art form and pay premium prices only for excellent to mint examples. They want figures with complete paint, all moving parts, and additional parts.

The box is very important, controlling 10 to 20% of the price of a set. The style of the box is a clue to the date of the set. The same set may have been made for several decades. The older the manufacture date, the more valuable the set.

Sets have a specific number of pieces or parts. They must all be present to have full value. The number of pieces in each set, when known, is indicated in the listings that follow.

Beware of repainted older examples and modern reproductions. Toy soldiers still are being manufactured, both by large companies and private individuals. A contemporary collection may prove a worthwhile long–term investment, at least for the next generation.

History: The manufacture of toy soldiers began in the late 18th century by individuals such as the Hilperts of Nuremberg, Germany. The early figures were tin, pewter or composition. By the late 19th century companies in Britain (Britain, Courtenay), France (Blondel, Gerbeau and Mignot), and Switzerland (Gottschalk, Wehrli) were firmly established. Britain and Mignot dominated the market into the 20th century.

Mignot established its French stronghold by purchasing Cuperly, Blondel and Gerbeau, who had united to take over Lucotte. By 1950 Mignot had 20,000 models representing soldiers from around the world.

Britain developed the hollow–cast soldiers in 1893. Movable arms were another landmark. Eventually bases were made of plastic, followed finally by the whole figure in plastic. Production ceased within the last decade.

The English toy soldier was challenged in America in the 1930 to 1950 period by the dime-store soldiers of Barclay, Manoil, and others. Nevertheless, the Britains retained a share of the market because of their high quality. The collecting of toy soldiers remains very strong in the United States.

References: Bertel Bruun, *Toy Soldiers: Identification and Price Guide,* Avon Books, 1994; Cynthia Gaskill, (ed.), *Elastolin: More Miniature Figures And Groups From The Hausser Firm Of Germany, Including Select Figures From The Houses of Lineol, Tipple–topple, Durso, and Chailu, Volume 2,* Theriault's, 1991; Peter Johnson, *Toy Armies,* Forbes Museum, 1984; Norman Joplin, *The Great Book Of Hollow–Cast Figures,* New Cavendish Books, 1992; Norman Joplin, *Toy Soldiers,* Running Press, Courage Books, 1994; Henry I. Kurtz & Burtt R. Ehrlich, *The Art Of The Toy Soldier,* Abbeville Press, 1987; Richard O'Brien, *Collecting Toy Soldiers: An Identification and Value Guide, No. 2,* Books Americana, 1992; James Opie, *Collecting Toy Soldiers,* Pincushion Press, 1992; Art Presslaff, *Hitler's Army of Toy Soldiers Featuring Elastolin, Lineol, & Tipco, 1928–40: A Price Guide,* published by author, 1987; James Opie, *Britain's Toy Soldiers, 1893–1932,* Harper & Row, 1986; John Ruddle, *Collectors Guide To Britains Model Soldiers,* Argus Books, 1980; Theriault's (comp.), *Elastolin, Miniature Figures And Groups From The Hausser Firm Of Germany, 1900–1950,* Theriault's, 1990; Joe Wallis, *Armies of the World, Britains Ltd. Lead Soldiers 1925–1941,* published by author, 1993.

Periodicals: *Old Toy Soldier,* 209 North Lombard, Oak Park, IL 60302; *Plastic Warrior,* 905 Harrison St., Allentown, PA 18103; *Toy Soldier Review,* 127 74th Street, North Bergen, NJ 07047.

Collectors' Clubs: American Model Soldier Society, 1528 El Camino Real, San Carlos, CA 94070; Military Miniature Society of Illinois, PO Box 394, Skokie, IL 60077; Northeast Toy Soldier Society, 12 Beach Rd., Gloucester, MA 09130; Toy Soldier Collectors Of America, 6924 Stone's Throw Circle, #8202, St. Petersburg, FL 33710.

REPRODUCTION ALERT

Authenticast, Russian Infantry, advancing with rifles at the ready, two officers carrying pistols and swords, no box	**65.00**
Blenheim	
B2, Coldstream Guards Colors, 1812, two color bearers, escort of four	

privates, orig box, mint, box excellent **115.00**

B17, Royal Marines, 1923, marching at the slope, officer, sword at carry, orig box, mint, box excellent **75.00**

B63, Royal Company of Archers Colors, two color bearers, escort of four privates, orig box, mint, box excellent **90.00**

C13, 17th Lancers, 1879, foreign service order, officer, bugler, and trooper with lance, orig box, mint, box excellent **150.00**

U.S. Naval Academy Color Guard, four standard bearers, escort of two midshipmen, orig box, mint, box excellent **100.00**

Britain, sets only

28, Mountain Gun of the Royal Artillery, with gun, gunners, mules, and mounted officer, orig box, excellent, box good **250.00**

33, 16th/5th Lancers, mounted at the halt in review order with officer turned–in–the–saddle, orig illus box, excellent **170.00**

44, 2nd Dragoon Guards, The Queen's Bays, mounted at the gallop with lances and trumpeter, one trooper missing, c1940, orig Whisstock box, excellent, box good ... **100.00**

48, Egyptian Camel Corps, mounted on camels, detachable riders, tied in orig box, mint, box excellent .. **80.00**

117, Egyptian Infantry, at attention in review order, c1935, orig Whisstock box, good **180.00**

122, The Black Watch, standing firing in tropical service dress with officer holding binoculars, c1940, orig Whisstock box, good **300.00**

136, Russian Cossacks, mounted at the gallop with officer, orig box, excellent **170.00**

138, French Cuirassiers, mounted at the walk in review order with officer, orig box, excellent **140.00**

Britains, African Warriors, Zulus, Set No. 147, $125.00.

167, Turkish Infantry, standing on guard in review order, c1935, orig Whisstock box, good/fine **130.00**

190, Belgian 2nd Regiment Chasseurs a Cheval, mounted in review order with officer, orig box, good **130.00**

201, Officers of the General Staff, comprising Field Marshal, General Officer, and two Aides–de–Camp, good **120.00**

216, Argentine Infantry, marching at the slope in review order, c1940, orig "Types of the Argentine Army" box, excellent, box good **325.00**

217, Argentine Cavalry, mounted in review order with lances and officer, orig box, excellent **250.00**

1323, The Royal Fusiliers, The Royal Sussex Regiment, and The Seaforth Highlanders, marching at the slope with mounted and foot officers, orig box, excellent, box good **300.00**

1339, The Royal Horse Artillery Khaki Service Order, with six–horse team, limber, gun, drivers with whips, four mounted outriders on trotting horses, and officer on galloping horse, orig "Types of the British Army" box with gold and black label, excellent, box good **1,700.00**

1343, The Royal Horse Guards, mounted in winter cloaks with officer, c1940, orig "Armies of the World" box, good **130.00**

1631, The Governor General's Horse Guards of Canada, mounted in review order with officer on prancing horse, orig box, mint, box excellent **110.00**

1632, The Royal Canadian Regiment, marching at the slope with officer, c1940, orig "Soldiers of the British Empire" box, good, box fine ... **1,100.00**

1835, Argentine Naval Cadets, marching at the slope in review order with officer, 1948–49, orig box, excellent, box good **1,800.00**

1836, Argentine Military Cadets, marching at the slope in review order with officer, c1940, orig "Armies of the World" box, excellent **3,250.00**

2009, Belgian Grenadier Regiment, marching in review order with officer, orig box, excellent **120.00**

2028, Red Army Cavalry, mounted at the halt in parade uniform with officer, orig box, excellent **200.00**

2035, Swedish Life Guard, marching at the slope in review order with officer, tied in orig box, mint, box excellent **200.00**

2059, Union Infantry, action poses, with officer holding sword and pistol, bugler, and standard bearer, orig box, excellent **90.00**

9217, 12th Royal Lancers, mounted in review order with officer, orig window box, mint, box good **80.00**

9291, Arabs of the Desert on Horses, with jezails and scimitars, orig window box, excellent, box good . . .   **80.00**

9402, State Open Road Landau, drawn by six Windsor Greys, with three detachable positions, attendants, and Queen Elizabeth and prince Philip as passengers, tied in orig box, mint, box excellent **325.00**

9407, British Regiments on Parade, comprising General Officer, Royal Horse Artillery at the walk, 17th Lancers in review order on trotting and cantering horses with officer, Life Guards with trumpeter and officer, Royal Norfolk Regiment at the slope with officer, Scots Greys on trotting and walking horses with officer, The Black Watch marching at the slope with piper and officer, and a Band of the Line, orig two–tray display box, excellent **2,500.00**

Elastolin/Lineol

Flak Gunner, blue and gray uniform, kneeling with shell, very good . . .   **40.00**

Medic, walking, helmet, big pack with red cross **35.00**

Nurse, attending wounded, kneeling, holds foot of soldier sitting on keg, excellent **40.00**

Staff Officer, pointing, field glasses, aristocratic pose **35.00**

Heyde

Chicago Police, 1890s, on foot with billy clubs, including policeman with dog, standard bearer, and mounted policeman, very good . .   **225.00**

French Ambulance Unit, horse drawn ambulance, two–horse team, rider with whip, stretcher bearers, stretchers and casualties, mounted and foot medical officers, and medical orderly, orig box, very good, box fair **275.00**

German Infantry, WW I, attacking with fixed bayonets, officer with extended sword, no box, very good **90.00**

Hessian Infantry, 1777, marching at the slope, officers, standard bearer, four mounted dragoons, movable reins on horses, no box, good . . .   **375.00**

U.S. Army World War I Pontoon Train, four horse drawn pontoon

wagons, pontoon boats, engineer detail on foot with mounted officer, orig display box, very good, box poor **475.00**

Mignot

Ancient Gaul Cavalry, mounted with swords, spears, and shields, orig box, excellent **275.00**

Ancient Greek Cavalry, mounted with swords, spears, and shields, orig box, excellent **250.00**

Austrian Cavalry, 1814, mounted in review order, with officer, trumpeter, and standard bearer, orig box, mint, box excellent **200.00**

Austrian Infantry, 1805, standing at attention at shoulder arms with officer, drummer, and standard bearer, limited issue, tied in orig box, mint, box excellent **225.00**

Band of Napoleon's Imperial Guard, 1812, marching with full instrumentation and band director with baton, excellent **350.00**

Bavarian Infantry, 1812, marching at the slope in blue and white uniforms with yellow facings and plumed light infantry caps, with standard bearer and bugler, eight piece set in orig box, excellent . . .   **250.00**

Drum Majors of the Empire, drum majors of French Napoleonic regiments including Orphans of the Guard, Marines of the Guard, St Cyr Academy, and various line infantry regiments, special limited edition, all in orig boxes, mint, boxes excellent **475.00**

French Musketeers Period of King Louis XIII, marching with muskets at shoulder arms, with officer and standard bearer, c1960, orig box, excellent **275.00**

French Napoleonic Skirmishers of the 17th Line Regiment, 1809, marching in blue and white uniforms faced in red with tall plumed shakos, gloss paint, c1965, four piece set in orig window box and outer cardboard box, mint, boxes excellent **80.00**

Infantry of King Louis XIV, marching at the slope with officer, standard bearer, and drummer, c1950, orig box, excellent **400.00**

Italian Light Infantry, Regiment de Beauharnais, 1810, marching at the slope in green uniforms with pale blue facings and plumed shakos, with drummer and officer, eight piece set in orig box, excellent **275.00**

Spanish Hussars, 1805, mounted in green uniforms with red facings and tall plumed shakos, with officer, trumpeter, and standard bearer, orig box, mint condition, box in excellent condition 275.00

Militia Models

Gatling Gun Team of 3rd London Rifles, Gatling gun and gunner, two ammunition carriers, officer holding binoculars, orig box, mint condition, box in excellent condition   90.00

The Pipes and Drums of 1st Battalion Royal Irish Rangers, pipe major and four pipers, two snare and two tenor drummers, drum major, limited edition, orig box, mint condition, box in excellent condition . . 125.00

Nostalgia

1st Gurkha Light Infantry, 1800, red and blue uniforms, marching with slung rifles, officer with sword at the carry, orig box, excellent condition 80.00

Kaffrarian Rifles, 1910, gray uniforms, plumed pith helmets, marching at the trail, officer with sword at the carry, orig box, mint condition, box in excellent condition 125.00

New South Wales Irish Rifles, 1900, marching at the trail, officer holding sword at the carry, orig box, mint condition, box in excellent condition 95.00

New South Wales Lancers, 1900, marching carrying lances on the shoulder, khaki uniforms, trimmed in red and plumed campaign hats, officer holding swagger stick, orig box, mint condition, box in excellent condition 85.00

S. A. E.

1358, Royal Horse Guards, 1945, mounted at the halt with officer, orig box, mint condition, box in excellent condition 50.00

1761, French Cuirassiers, mounted at the walk, orig box, mint condition, box in excellent condition

3310, 1st Bengal Lancers, at the halt, orig box, mint, box excellent 115.00

SOUVENIR AND COMMEMORATIVE ITEMS

Collecting Hints: Most collectors of souvenir and commemorative china and glass collect items from a region which is particularly interesting to

them—a hometown, birthplaces or place of special interest such as a president's home. This results in regional variations in price, because a piece is more likely to be in demand in the area it represents.

When collecting souvenir spoons be aware of several things: condition, material, subject, and any markings, dates, etc. Damaged spoons should be avoided unless they are very rare and needed to complete a collection. Some spoons have enamel crests and other decoration. This enameling should be in mint condition.

History: Souvenir and commemorative china and glass date to the early fairs and carnivals when a small trinket was purchased to take back home as a gift or remembrance of the event. Other types of commemorative glass include pattern and milk glass made to celebrate a particular event. Many types of souvenir glass and china originated at the world's fairs and expositions.

The peak of souvenir spoon collecting was reached in the late 1800s. During that time two important patents were issued. The first patent was issued on December 4, 1884, to Michael Gibney, a silversmith in New York who patented the first design for flatware. The other important patent was the first spoon design which commemorated a place. That patent was given to Myron H. Kinsley in 1881 for his spoon of Niagara Falls. The spoon showed the suspension bridge and was the first of many spoons to be made showing Niagara Falls.

Spoons depicting famous people soon followed with the issue of May, 1889, showing George Washington. That was followed by the issuance of a Martha Washington spoon in October of 1889. These spoons, made by M. W. Galt of Washington, D.C., were not patented, but were trademarked in 1890.

During the 1900s it became popular to have souvenir plates made for churches and local events such as centennials, homecomings, etc. These plates were well received because of their local interest. Collectors search for them today because they were made in a limited number. Many show how the area changed architecturally and culturally.

References: Bessie M. Lindsey, *American Historical Glass,* Charles E. Tuttle, 1967; Norman E. Martinus and Harry L. Rinker, *Warman's Paper,* Wallace–Homestead, 1994; Dorothy T. Rainwater and Donna H. Felger, *American Spoons, Souvenir and Historical,* Everybodys Press, 1977; Dorothy T. Rainwater and Donna H. Felger, *Spoons From Around The World,* Schiffer Publishing, 1992; Frank Stefano, Jr., *Wedgwood Old Blue Historical Plates and Other Views of the United States Produced for Jones, McDuffe & Stratton Co., Boston, Importer, A Check–List With Illustrations,* published by author, 1975; *Sterling*

Silver, Silverplate, and Souvenir Spoons With Prices, L–W Books, 1988, 1994 value update.

Collectors' Clubs: American Spoon Collectors, 4922 State Line, Westwood Hills, KS 66205; Antique Souvenir Collectors News, Box 562, Great Barrington, MA 01230; Northeastern Spoon Collectors Guild, 52 Hillcrest Ave., Morristown, NJ 07960; The Scoop Club, 84 Oak Avenue, Shelton, CT 06484.

Periodical: *Souvenir Building Collector,* 25 Falls Rd., Roxbury, CT 06783.

Salt and Pepper Shakers, pr, egg shape, yellow and orange florals, green leaves, St Paul in gold lettering, 2¾″ h, 2″ w, pr, $165.00.

Ashtray, brass, Florida, shaped like state, emb attractions	**12.00**
Axe, 4″, "Cut Out the Whiskey, Laurel Stove Detroit," Carrie Nation, 1901	**25.00**
Booklet, Yosemite Visitor's Guide, 32 color photos	**8.00**
Bottle	
Deadwood, SD	**95.00**
Dodge City	**25.00**
Bowl, Centenary M E. Church, South Bonne, Terre, MO, scalloped edge, blue tint	**12.00**
Card Folder, Yellowstone Park, 1928 . .	**5.00**
Comb, hair bun, pictures Golden Gate Bridge, wood	**6.00**
Compact, Empire State Building, Art Deco	**35.00**
Creamer	
St James, MN	**25.00**
The Flume, Franconia Notch, NH, left handed	**25.00**
Dish, 4¼″ l, 3½″ w, Atlanta, state capitol embossed in center, floral border, monogram, Watson	**55.00**
Fur Clip, Beckman Bros, Great Falls, MT	**25.00**
Goblet, Minocqua, WI, Inverted Thumbprint pattern, ruby stained . . .	**35.00**
Ink Blotter, Yellowstone Park, metal . . .	**35.00**
Loving Cup, 3½″ h, Oneonta, NY, ruby stained shading to clear, gold trim, two handles	**45.00**
Match Box, Niagara Falls, sterling silver	**100.00**
Memo Pad, Aberdeen, SD, 1909, aluminum	**17.50**
Mug	
Elkport, IA, Punty Band pattern, green opaque glass	**20.00**
Joilet High School, Joilet, IL, china . .	**17.50**
Ottawa, IL, Star & Punty Band pattern, custard glass, gold trim	**35.00**
Paperweight, Old South Church, Boston, MA, 4 x 2½″, glass, brown tone photo scene	**18.00**
Pencil Box, Alaska, snap closure, pyrography of Eskimo totem pole	**13.00**
Pin, New York City, enamel dec	**20.00**
Pinback Button	
Detroit, multicolored, lighthouse scene, red slogan "Where Life Is	

Worth Living"	**45.00**
Grand Island Fair, multicolored, laughing devil	**60.00**
Long Beach Festival of the Sea, 1908, 2⅛″ d, multicolored scene of mermaid, small boats floating in sea	**500.00**
Niagara County Pioneers Association, multicolored Indian portrait, white ground, 1918	**100.00**
Red Wing Street Fair, multicolored, masked jester, 1899	**65.00**
Pipe and Match Holder, Hot Springs, AR, cobalt blue glass	**22.50**
Plate	
City Meat Market, Leonardsville, KS, sheep	**35.00**
Clark House, Lexington, MA, four sided	**12.00**
Fort Duquesne, Pittsburgh, PA, La Francaise Porcelain, 1764	**28.00**
Ocean Pier & Fun Chase, Wildwood, NJ, pierced border	**8.00**
Perry Centennial, 1913, Cauldon . . .	**30.00**
Ring, Yellowstone Park, brass, enameled bear	**15.00**
Salt and Pepper Shakers, pr, Alcasar de Segovia emblem, Limoges	**30.00**
Spoon	
Algiers, sterling	**20.00**
Bangor, ME, sterling	**12.00**
Birthday, 1913, sterling	**40.00**
Brooklyn Bridge, "New York" on handle, sterling	**35.00**

Spoon, Atlantic City, skyline on handle, ocean scenes on back, push cart in bowl, sterling, 6″ l, $42.00.

Butte, MT, Anaconda Mine	30.00
Canton, MS, sterling	12.00
Capri, Italy, embossed bowl, enameled classical urn at top, 5½" l, sterling	45.00
Checolah, OK, three figures on handle, sterling	20.00
Chief Omaha, demitasse, Gorham ..	75.00
Collingwood, sterling	20.00
Colorado, sterling	10.00
Cuba, Havana, "Yumuri Valley" embossed on bowl, embossed wagon on handle, 5½" l, sterling	75.00
Detroit, cutout handle, sterling	18.00
Grand Rapids, cut handle, sterling, 4¾" l	27.50
Hawaii, Waikiki, embossed bowl, figural nude woman handle, 5½" l, sterling	75.00
Helen, silver plated	20.00
Indianola, MS, sterling	18.00
Mackinac Lake, sterling	30.00
New Orleans, enameled bowl "New Orleans Levee," 6" l, teaspoon, sterling	175.00
New Year's, sterling	35.00
Pike's Peak, Manitou, CO, cut out handle, sterling	18.00
San Francisco, sterling	18.00
St Augustine, sterling	18.00
St Just, sterling	12.00
Toronto, sterling	15.00
Uruguay, sterling	18.00
Washington, DC, sterling	15.00
Tea Set, Niagara Falls, hp scenic transfers, Stadler	120.00
Tray, metal	
Alabama	28.00
Florida	28.00
Fort William Henry	7.00
Georgia	28.00
Grand Canyon National Park	28.00
Illinois	28.00
Indiana	28.00
Lake George, NY	7.00
Luray Caverns, VA	28.00
Mexico	28.00
Mississippi	28.00
Missouri	28.00
New York	7.00
North Carolina	7.00
Pennsylvania	28.00
Plymouth, MA	28.00
South Carolina	28.00
Texas	28.00
Washington DC	28.00
Williamsburg, VA	28.00
Tumbler	
Pearl Harbor	10.00
Saratoga Springs, 1901, pewter	8.00
Vase, Camp Lake View, Lake City, MN	12.00

SOUVENIR BUILDINGS

Collecting Hints: Collectors look for rarity, architectural detail, and quality of material, casting, and finishing. As in real estate, location affects price: European and East Coast buildings are more expensive on the West Coast and vice versa.

History: Small metal replicas of famous buildings and monuments first became popular souvenirs among Victorian travelers returning from the Grand Tour of Europe. In the 1920s and 1930s, metal replicas of banks and insurance companies were made as promotional give-aways to new depositors and clients. In the 1950s and 1960s, Japanese manufactured metal souvenir buildings were the rage for motorists visiting attractions across America.

Souvenir buildings are still being manufactured and sold today in cities and capitals around the world. They include churches, cathedrals, skyscrapers, office buildings, capitols, and towers.

Most souvenir buildings are made of white (or pot) metal with a finish of brass, copper, gold, silver, or bronze. Souvenir buildings are also made of Sterling silver, brass, silvered lead, plastic, resin composition, and ceramic.

References: Dort Fratzke Brown, *Souvenir Buildings: A Collection of Identified Miniatures,* Volumes I and II, published by author, 1977.

Periodical: *The Souvenir Building Collector,* 25 Falls Rd., Roxbury, CT 06783.

Advisor: Dixie Trainer.

Additional Listings: See Banks, Still.

Alamo, San Antonio, TX, 2 x 4 x 3½", copper finish	15.00
Alder Planetarium, Chicago, IL, incense burner, 3 x 4" d, copper finish	40.00
Arc de Triomphe, Paris, 1¾ x 1½ x 1", copper finish	5.00
Brandenberg Gate, Berlin, 4 x 3¾ x 2", antique bronze, wooden base	35.00
Bunker Hill Monument, Boston, MA, copper finish	12.00
Capitol, Washington, DC	
Jewelry Box, 4¼ x 5 x 3½", gold, marked "JB" on bottom	50.00
Souvenir, 2¼ x 3½ x 2"	5.00
Coit Tower, San Francisco, 6½" h, 2¼" sq base, antique bronze finish	75.00
Cologne Cathedral, Germany, 4⅛ x 3¾ x 1½", antique pewter or silver finish	12.00
Colosseum, Rome, 1½ x 2¼ x 2", copper finish	15.00
Dollar Savings Bank, Pittsburgh, PA, 3⅛ x 4 x 3", silvered lead bank	85.00

Capitol, Washington, DC, 2¼ x 3½ x 2", $5.00.

Easton National Bank, Easton, PA, 4½ x 3¾ x 2½", bank, copper finish **65.00**

Eiffel Tower, Paris
3 x 1 x 1", copper, antique brass or silver finish **7.00**
6 x 2½ x 2½", copper, antique brass or silver finish **12.00**
11 x 5 x 5", copper, antique brass . .   **35.00**

Empire State Building, New York City
Prewar, no spire
3½ x 1½ x 1", antique brass finish   **25.00**
5¾ x 2½ x 2", silver finish **60.00**
Postwar, with radio antenna spire
3½ x 1¼ x ¾", gold platic **3.00**
5 x 1¾ x 1¼", antique brass finish   **7.00**
7½ x 2¾ x 1¼", copper finish . . .   **13.00**

Field Museum of Natural History, Chicago, IL, 1 x 4¼ x 3", silver or copper finish **30.00**

Flatiron Building, New York City, 5½" h, cast iron bank, silvery finish **150.00**

Ft Dearborn, Chicago, IL, 4 x 3⅛ x 2", green or tan paint, souvenir of 1933 Chicago World's Fair **35.00**

General Motors Building, Detroit, MI, 3¾ x 6¼ x 4", antique bronze finish   **110.00**

La Giralda, Seville, Spain, 7½" h, antique brass, 2¼" black marble base   **45.00**

Empire State Building, New York City, postwar, radio antenna spire, antique brass finish, 5 x 1¾ x 1¼", $7.00.

Havoline Tower, thermometer, souvenir of 1933 Chicago World's Fair, 4⅝" h
Cast iron, ivory paint **35.00**
Plastic, marble base **20.00**

Immaculate Conception National Shrine, Washington, DC
3 x 3 x 2", antique copper finish . . .   **15.00**
5 x 5 x 4", antique copper finish . . .   **35.00**

Ivan's Bell Tower, Moscow, 3½ x 2 x 1¼", solid brass, marble base **85.00**

Jefferson Memorial, Washington, DC, 1½ x 2 x 2", copper finish **15.00**

Kraft International Headquarters, Chicago, IL, 3⅛ x 2¾ x 3¼", silvered lead paperweight, cast by A. C. Rehberger **75.00**

Lamar Life Building, Jackson, MS, 4½ x 2½ x 3½", silvered lead paperweight   **75.00**

Leaning Tower of Pisa, Italy
3½", silver finish, metal ashtray **32.00**
5 x 1¾" d, white alabaster **25.00**

Lincoln Memorial, Washington, DC, 1½ x 3 x 2, copper finish **8.00**

Louisiana State Capitol, Baton Rouge, LA, 7 x 5½ x 2¾", antique copper finish   **85.00**

Metropolitan Life Insurance Co, New York City, 5¼ x 3¾ x 2¼", silver or gold finish **110.00**

Miami Beach Federal Saving, Miami, FL, 5½ x 3½ x 3¼", brass finish, Banthrico Bank **65.00**

Mormon Temple, Salt Lake City, UT, 4 x 2¼ x 3⅜", copper finish **27.00**

Notre Dame, Paris, 2 x 3 x 1½", bronze finish **15.00**

Parthenon, Athens, Greece, 3¼ x 6 x 3½", copper, marble base **95.00**

Pilgrim Memorial Monument, Provinceton, MA, 4¾" h, 2¼" d base **20.00**

Rockefeller Center (RCA Building) New York City
2⅝ x 2 x 1", copper finish **25.00**
4¼ x 3 x 1⅜", silver finish **85.00**

Sacre Coeur, Paris, 4½ x 4¼ x 2½", antique brass **30.00**

Singing Tower, Bok Tower, Lake Wales FL, 5" h, 1¾" d base **20.00**

Space Needle, Seattle, WA, 6" h, revolving turret on top, silver or copper finish **20.00**

Statue of Liberty, New York City
2" h **3.00**
4½" h **5.00**
6" h **7.00**

St Basil's Cathedral, Moscow, 4 x 3½ x 3½", solid brass, marble base **285.00**

St Mary's Cathedral, Florence, Italy, 2½ x 3½ x 2½", silver finish **25.00**

St Peter's Cathedral, Rome, 3½ x 3½ x 2½", silver finish **26.00**

Syracuse Savings Bank, Syracuse, NY, 5½ x 4 x 3", copper finish **65.00**

Taj Mahal, Agra, India, 8 x 7 x 7", white
marble, nightlight **60.00**
United Nations Building, New York
City, 3 x 4 x 2½", antique brass **20.00**
US Fidelity & Guaranty Co, 5¾ x 7¼ x
6", building as combination cigar humidor, inkwell, and clock, cast by Art
Metal Works, NJ, antique bronze fin-
ish **175.00**
Washington Monument, Washington,
DC
3¼" h, silver, salt and pepper set . . . **25.00**
6" h, copper, thermometer **8.00**
Woolworth Building, New York City, 4 x
1¾ x 1¼", gold finish **25.00**
Zembo Museum, Harrisburg, PA, 2½ x
4½ x 1¾", antique copper finish . . . **60.00**

SPACE ADVENTURERS AND EXPLORATION

Collecting Hints: There are four distinct eras of fictional space adventurers—Buck Rogers, Flash Gordon, the radio and television characters of the late 1940s and 1950s, and the Star Trek and Star Wars phenomena. Condition is not as major a factor in Buck Rogers material, because of its rarity, as it is in the other three groups. Beware of dealers who break apart items and sell parts separately, especially game items.

In the early 1950s a wealth of tin, battery operated, friction, and wind–up toys, not associated with a specific space adventurer, were marketed in the shape of robots, space ships, and space guns. They are rapidly gaining in popularity.

The "Trekkies" began holding conventions in the early 1970s. They issued many fantasy items, which must not be confused with items issued during the duration of the TV show. The fantasy items are numerous and have little value beyond the initial selling price.

The American and Russian space programs produced a wealth of souvenir and related material. Beware of astronaut–signed material that may contain printed or autopen signatures.

History: In January, 1929, "Buck Rogers 2429 A.D." began its comic strip run. Buck, Wilma Deering, Dr. Huer, and Killer Kane, a villain, were the creations of Phillip Francis Nowlan and John F. Dille. The heyday of Buck Rogers material was 1933 to 1937, when products such as Cream of Wheat and Cocomalt issued Buck Rogers items as premiums.

Flash Gordon followed in the mid–1930s. Buster Crabbe gave life to the character in movie serials. Books, comics, premiums, and other merchandise enhanced the image during the 1940s.

The use of rockets at the end of World War II and the beginning of the space research program gave reality to future space travel. Television quickly capitalized on this in the early 1950s with programs such as *Captain Video* and *Space Patrol*. Many other space heroes, such as Rocky Jones, had short–lived popularity.

Star Trek enjoyed a brief television run and became a cult fad in the early 1970s. *Star Trek: The Next Generation* has an established corp of watchers. *Star Wars* (Parts IV, V, and VI) and *ET* produced a wealth of merchandise which already is collectible.

In the 1950s, real–life space pioneers and explorers replaced the fictional characters as the center of the public's attention. The entire world watched on July 12, 1969, as man first walked on the moon. Although space exploration has suffered occasional setbacks, the public remains fascinated with its findings and potential.

References: Sue Cornwell and Mike Kott, *The Official Price Guide To Star Trek and Star Wars Collectibles, Third Edition,* House of Collectibles, 1991; Christine Gibson and Sally Gibson–Downs, *Greenberg's Guide To Star Trek Collectibles, Volumes I–III,* Greenberg Publishing, 1992; Norman E. Martinus and Harry L. Rinker, *Warman's Paper,* Wallace–Homestead, 1993; Stephen J. Sansweet, *Star Wars: From Concept To Screen To Collectible,* Chronicle Books, 1992; Stuart Schneider, *Collecting The Space Race,* Schiffer Publishing, 1993; Don and Maggie Thompson, *The Official Price Guide To Science Fiction and Fantasy Collectibles, Third Edition,* House of Collectibles, 1989; Stephen Sansweet and T. N. Tumbusch, *Tomart's Price Guide To Star Wars Collectibles Worldwide,* Tomart Publications, 1994; T. N. Tumbusch, *Space Adventure Collectibles,* Wallace–Homestead, 1990; Bruce Lanier Wright, *Yesterday's Tomorrows: The Golden Age of Science Fiction Movie Posters, 1950–1964,* Taylor Publishing, 1993.

Collectors' Clubs: Galaxy Patrol, 22 Colton St., Worcester, MA 01610; International Federation of Trekkers, PO Box 3123, Lorain, OH 44052; Lost In Space Fan Club, 550 Trinity, Westfield, NJ 07090; Society for the Advancement of Space Activities, PO Box 192, Kent Hills, ME 04349; Starfleet, PO Box 430, Burnsville, NC 28714; Starfleet Command, PO Box 26076, Indianapolis, IN 46226; Star Trek: The Official Fan Club, PO Box 111000, Aurora, CO 80011.

Periodicals: *Starlog Magazine,* 475 Park Ave. S, New York, NY 10016; *Strange New Worlds,* PO Box 223, Tallevast, FL 34270; *The Star Wars Collection Trading Post,* 6030 Magnolia, PO Box 29396, St Louis, MO 63139; *Trek Collector,* 1324 Palm Blvd., Dept. 17, Los Angeles, CA 90291.

Museums: Alabama Space & Rocket Center, Huntsville, AL; International Space Hall of Fame, The Space Center, Alamogordo, NM.

See: Robots and Space Toys.

CHARACTERS

Battlestar Galactica
Game, game board, spinner, cards, playing pieces, Parker Brothers, copyright 1978 Universal City Studios, Inc 20.00
Trading Cards, set of 36, Wonder Bread, copyright 1978 Universal City Studios Inc 15.00
Buck Rogers
Big Little Book, *Buck Rogers and the Depth Men of Jupiter,* Whitman, #1169, 1935 .... 65.00
Communications Outfit, 25th Century, Remco 250.00
Gun
  Atomic Pistol, 10" l, blued metal barrel, gold finish, sparking, Daisy Mfg Co, c1946 .... 100.00
  Rocket Pistol, 9½" l, 25th Century, metal, blued and silvered, Daisy Mfg Co, late 1934 .... 125.00
  Sonic Ray Gun, 7½" l, plastic, black, yellow, and red, orig box, Norton–Honer, 1952 .... 180.00
Jigsaw Puzzle, Marauder, #3 of series, Milton Bradley, orig sealed box, Universal City Studios copyright 1979 .... 15.00
Kite, orig pkg 40.00
Pencil Box, 10½" l, cardboard, action illus on dark green ground, mid 1930s 95.00
Pin, brass 50.00

Toy, **Buck Rogers Super Sonic Ray Gun,** plastic, Norton-Honer Mfg. Co., copyright 1955, $50.00.

Pinback Button, 1" d, club member, "Buck Rogers in the 25th Century," c1935 .... 50.00
Toy
  Attack Ship, #1033, 5" l, cast metal, orig box, Tootsietoy, 1930s 420.00
  Battlecruiser, #1031, 5" l, cast metal, orig box, Tootsietoy, 1937 367.00
  Flash Blast Attack Ship, Tootsietoy, 1930s 135.00
  Space Ship, Morton's Salt premium, umbrella girl on bomb sight, orig pkg 75.00
Captain Video
Card, 3 x 4", Luma–Glo, black and white, Rite–O–Lite premium, 1950s 25.00
Movie Poster 325.00
Playset, Superior Space Port, litho tin building, nine litho tin wall sections, gateway, space cannon, 14 plastic figures, nine ships, plastic pcs marked "Captain Video," complete 225.00
Pressbook, 7½ x 10½", 4 pgs, glossy, black and white, "Captain Video/ Hero of Outer Space" promotion, Columbia Pictures, 1958 .... 50.00
Secret Ray Gun, 3½" l, Power House candy bar premium, orig instructions 65.00
Tom Corbett
Belt, child's, leather, black and silver, repeated "Space Cadet" and illus, leather slide attachment, mint on card, 1950s 75.00
Binoculars, 2 x 4½ x 5", white metal, red plastic eye piece, yellow lenses, blue plastic strap, 1950s .. 125.00
Book, *Tom Corbett Stand By For Mars,* Grosset & Dunlap, copyright 1952 Rockhill Radio, 216 pgs, dj 20.00
Lunch Box, thermos 125.00
Patch, 4" l, fabric, stitched Space Cadet name and symbol, Kellogg's premium 45.00
Playset, Space Academy, Marx 250.00
Record, Rescue in Space, 78 rpm, RCA Victor label, Little Nipper series, orig album cov, Rockhill Productions copyright 1952 ..... 20.00
Ring, "Space Cadet Dress Uniform" 15.00
View Master Reel, set of 3, story booklet, orig envelope, copyright 1954 Rockhill Radio 30.00
Watch, Tom Corbett Space Cadet, 1" d dial, Corbett and rocket illus, black, white, red, and yellow, red lightning bolt hands, orig illus straps, 1950s 200.00
Wrist Compass 70.00

E.T.

Child's Dishes, four cups, saucers, plates, and spoons, pitcher, tray, sugar and creamer, plastic, orig unopened box, Chilton–Globe, Inc 50.00

Ring, gold metal band, enamel painted image, orig blister card, Star Power copyright 1982 Universal City Studios, Inc 8.00

Flash Gordon

Arm Patch 8.00

Movie Poster, *Flash Gordon Conquers the Universe*, chapter 11, Stark Treachery, 27 x 41", black, white, and red, 1973 .... 50.00

Record, 78 rpm, *City of Sea Caves*, cardboard, sleeve with color illus, Record Guild of America, copyright 1948 .... 35.00

Spaceship, 3" l, metal, diecast, blue, white accents, LJN Toys, orig pkg, copyright 1975 .... 12.00

Wrist Compass, 1950s, mint on card 40.00

Space Patrol

Coin, 1¼" d, plastic, metallic blue, "Terra/Interplanetary Space Patrol Credits" 12.00

Emergency Kit, 7 x 7 x 2" plastic case, gray and white, raised lettering and illus, two slide out trays, bandages, tape, space emergency rations, space sickness pills, cosmic ray pills, complete, Regis Space Toys, early 1950s 800.00

Gun

Cosmic Smoke Ray Gun, 6" l, plastic, metallic green, fires smoke puffs, early 1950s 175.00

Dart Gun, 9½" l, plastic, red, black and white trim, logo, 1950s ... 85.00

Super Beam Signal Ray Gun, 8" l, plastic, red, white, and blue, marked "Official Space Patrol," Marx, 1950s 175.00

Handbook, 4½ x 6", *Space Patrol Handbook*, 16 pgs, black and white illus, 1950s 90.00

Helmet, 9 x 10 x 12", cardboard, diecut, six–sided, yellow, red, green, and black, 1950s 100.00

Party Plates, 8½" sq, paper, spaceships and planets illus, sealed, 1950s, set of 6 .... 28.00

Projector, 5½" h, Space Patrol Terra V, rocket shape, hard plastic, blue and yellow, 1950s 200.00

Ring, siren, silvered white metal, Japan, 1950s 150.00

Script, 8½ x 11", television program #544, April 10, 1952 .... 90.00

Sheet Music 35.00

Slides, set of 6, Stori–View, cast por-

traits, color, copyright Space Patrol Enterprises, 1950s 98.00

Wristwatch, silvered chrome, black lettering, military time, orig band, US Time, early 1950s 175.00

Star Trek

Bank, 11" h, Captain Kirk, hard vinyl, Play Pal, Inc, copyright 1975 Paramount Pictures Corp 75.00

Carrying Case, 10½ x 16 x 10", vinyl, USS Enterprise flight deck, Mego Corp, copyright 1975 .... 85.00

Cereal Set, bowl and mug, plastic, "The Motion Picture," 1979 ..... 20.00

Costume, Mr Spock, mask, Paramount Pictures, 1975 .... 55.00

Doll, Klingon 18.00

Game, Star Trek Game, Milton Bradley, 27" sq playing board, plastic pawns, and cardboard Space Sector cards, orig box 50.00

Helmet, 7 x 8½ x 9", plastic, battery operated, white, adjustable tinted solar visor, adjustable chin strap, orig box, Enco Industries, Inc 75.00

Mobile, Enterprise, paper, orig envelope 35.00

Photo, 8 x 10", television series cast, autographed, glossy, black and white 100.00

Program, International Convention, 1973 .... 55.00

Starship, inflatable 25.00

Trading Cards, set of 88, complete, 1979 .... 35.00

TV Tray, 12½ x 17", metal, collapsible legs, color photo, copyright 1979 Paramount Pictures Corp and Marsh Allan Products, Inc, orig sealed plastic bag 75.00

Star Wars

Belt, Darth Vader, boxed 20.00

Cookie Jar, R2D2 .... 65.00

Game, Escape from Death Star, Kenner, 20th Century Fox Film Corp copyright 1977, complete .. 15.00

Frame, 5¼ x 7¼", ceramic, glazed and painted, orig cardboard tag and shipping box, Sigma, 1980s copyright Lucasfilm Ltd 25.00

Game, Yoda The Jedi Master Game, orig sealed box, Kenner, copyright 1981 Lucasfilm Ltd 25.00

Helmet, Darth Vader, Don Post, orig box, 1977 .... 90.00

Lunch Box, 7 x 9 x 4", metal, thermos with color decal, King–Seeley, 1977 20th Century Fox Corp 40.00

Movie Poster 90.00

Pop–Up Book 12.50

Radio, R2–D2 .... 75.00

Roller Skates, Return of the Jedi/Darth Vader, child's size 3, black, red trim, laces, and wheels, Darth Vader and royal guard illus, orig box, Brookfield Athletic Shoe Co, Lucasfilm Ltd copyright 1983 .... **25.00**

Shampoo Bottle, 9" h, Star Wars Luke Skywalker Shampoo, soft plastic body, hard plastic head, orig contents, sealed, story booklet, Omni Cosmetics Corp, Lucasfilm Ltd copyright 1981 .... **12.00**

Sneakers, child's size 5½, Star Wars shoelaces, Darth Vader illus, orig illus box and punch–out sheet, Stride Rite, Lucasfilm Ltd copyright 1982 .... **12.00**

Trading Card, 2½ x 3½", set of 66, color photo front, text and puzzle piece back, Topps, 20th Century Fox Film Corp copyright 1977 ... **15.00**

Wallet, Return Of The Jedi, vinyl, color Yoda illus, orig blister card, Adam Joseph Industries **25.00**

EXPLORATION

Badge, 3½" d, John Glenn, black and white portrait, red inscription **25.00**

Bank, 4¾" h, space project program, clear plastic, launcher base, red space capsule cap
Gemini Dime Bank, c1965 .... **35.00**
Mercury Space Saver, 1961–63 .... **50.00**

Book, We Came In Peace, Gulf Oil Co premium, hard cov, 78 pgs **15.00**

Coloring Book, 8½ x 11", Apollo/Man on the Moon, Saalfield, July 20, 1969 moon landing illus, unused **15.00**

Commemorative Spoon
Friendship 7, 6" l, silverplated, capsule bowl illus, raised John F Kennedy handle illus, vertical lettering, Wm Rogers, c1963 ...... **25.00**
Moon Landing, 6¼" l, silverplated, names Armstrong, Aldrin, and Collins engraved in bowl, geometric floral design and moon landing illus handle, inscribed "Apollo 11/July 20, 1969/Man on the Moon," orig box, Holland **20.00**

Figure, John Glenn, 16½" h, stiff paper, jointed **23.00**

Glass, 5½" h, Mercury Spacecraft/Cape Canaveral, clear weighted bottom, frosted light blue top, silver and orange spacecraft and galaxy illus, souvenir, early 1960s **35.00**

Jigsaw Puzzle, Journey to the Moon, Life puzzle series, magazine cover photo illus, orig box and 29 x 40" poster, copyright 1969 .... **20.00**

Lunch Box, Space Shuttle Challenger, vinyl, copyright 1982 .... **65.00**

Magazine, *Time*, July 25, 1969, Man On The Moon, $5.00.

Magazine
Life, 10½ x 13½", 136 pgs, recovery photo cov, 10 pg article, Alan Shepard first US space flight, black and white photos, May 12, 1961 issue **14.00**
Time, Feb 2, 1962, Astronaut John Glenn on cov **15.00**

Model Kit, Edwin "Buzz" Aldrin's space walk, Aurora Plastics Corp, #409–100, orig box and instructions, complete, unassembled, c1966 .... **60.00**

Paperweight, 2" h, John Glenn Flight Commemorative, solid aluminum, Friendship 7 replica, engraved "John Glenn Jr Feb 20, 1962" **50.00**

Patch, 3½ x 4", Teacher in Space, woven fabric, official Challenger Space Shuttle insignia symbol **13.00**

Pennant, 17½" l, felt, white, red and blue illus and lettering, 3" black and white Glenn photo, commemorates Feb 20, 1962 first US orbital space flight **40.00**

Plaque, 15" d, Apollo 11, plaster, raised moon landing illus, "Small Step, Giant Leap" inscription, dated July 1969 .... **40.00**

Plate, 8" d, glass, raised images of astronauts Lovell, Swigert, and Haise, inscribed "Lucky 13" and "Farewell Aquarius" **18.00**

Record, 33⅓ rpm, radio presentation, The Space Story, Monaural **12.00**

Thermos, 7¼" h, litho metal, ivory plastic cap, rocket scene illus, commemorates John Glenn flight **28.00**

Tie Bar, Freedom 7, metal, gold colored, space capsule illus, unmarked, early 1960s **20.00**

Tray, 5 x 6¾", moon landing, dark clear glass, gold and white design and inscriptions **15.00**

View Master Reel, set of 3, US Spaceport, NASA JFK Space Center, orig envelope and catalog sheet **12.00**

SPACE RELATED

Alarm Clock, animated, steel case, glossy black enamel, orbiting spacecraft illus, digital numerals, Westclox of Scotland, 1960s **180.00**

Book
   Andy Astronaut, 6½ x 16", hard cov, Golden Press, 24 pgs, copyright 1968 . . . .   **12.00**
   Into Space With the Astronauts, 8 x 11", soft cov, Wonder Book, 48 pgs, 1965 . . . .   **15.00**
   Man in Flight, 8 x 11", soft cov, Saalfield, 48 pgs, 1962 . . . .   **17.00**

Candy Container, 6" d, Riley's Toffee, litho tin, Riley Bros, Halifax, England, two children in space outfits, moonscape, c1950 . . . .   **25.00**

Card Game, complete deck of 40, rule card, and adv card, orig box, Arrco Playing Card Co, 1950s **15.00**

Cigarette Lighter, 5½" l, space rocket shape, chrome colored, red, and black plastic, tabletop model, "Miners National Bank," 1950–60s   **28.00**

Coloring Book, UFO/Seeing Is Believing, 8 x 11", Whitman, copyright 1978 . . . .   **15.00**

Comic Book, *The Outer Limits*, Dell, April 1963 . . . .   **2.50**

Crayon Box, spaceship shape, cylinder, stiff litho cardboard, enameled wood nosecone, diecut porthole openings reveal multiplication tables **20.00**

Flashlight, 8" l, "Captain Ray–O–Vac Rocket Ship," bright red, chrome ends, decal of spaceman with battery body soaring through space, colorful box, MIB **38.00**

Game, Trip To The Moon Game, orig bag with header card, unopened, Makatoy Co, 1950s **25.00**

Glass, 6¼" h, rocketships, planets, stars, and skyline illus, 1950s **25.00**

Key Chain, 2¼" l, multicolored plastic rocket, puzzle type, c1950 . . . .   **18.00**

Mug, 6½" h, ceramic, white, green *New York Times* illus of July 21, 1969 "Men Walk on Moon" edition, ESB Brands Inc **20.00**

Needle Case, 3½ x 6", Rocket, diecut cardboard, full color illus of giant needle flying through space, starry ground, planet Saturn in distance,

marked "Made in Occupied Japan," orig needles, unused **15.00**

Pencil, 3" l, mechanical, red, plastic, rocketship, brass nosecone, brass key chain, c1950 . . . .   **8.00**

Planter, 5½" d, 5" h, china, figural, toddler wearing space uniform, white, pink and blue accents, late 1960s . .   **24.00**

Pocket Knife, 3½" l, bright yellow plastic knife, rocketship shape, working siren whistle in nosecone, brass key chain loop, c1950 . . . .   **35.00**

Record, 33⅓ rpm, *The Space Story*, NASA Radio Presentation, 1976 . . . .   **12.50**

Water Gun, 6" l, hard plastic, futuristic design, 1950s **18.00**

SPACE TOYS

Collecting Hints: The original box is an important element in pricing, perhaps controlling 15 to 20% of the price. The artwork on the box may differ slightly from the toy inside; this is to be expected. The box also may provide the only clues to the correct name of the toy.

The early lithographed tin toys are more valuable than the later toys made of plastic. There is a great deal of speculation in modern toys, e.g., Star Wars material. Hence, the market shows great price fluctuation. Lloyd Ralston Toys, Fairfield, Connecticut, is a good barometer of the auction market.

Collect toys in very good to mint condition. Damaged and rusted lithographed tin is hard to repair. Check the battery box for damage. Don't ever leave batteries in a toy after you have played with it.

History: The Hollywood movies of the early 1950s drew attention to space travel. The launching of Sputnik and American satellites in the late 1950s and early 1960s enhanced this fascination. The advent of man in space, culminating with the landing on the moon, made the decade of the 1960s the golden age of space toys.

The toy industries of Japan and America responded to this interest. Lithographed tin and plastic models of astronauts, flying saucers, spacecraft and space vehicles followed quickly. Some were copies of original counterparts; most were the figments of the toy designer's imagination.

The 1970s saw a shift in emphasis from the space program and a decline in the production of science fiction–related toys. The earlier Japanese– and American–made products gave way to cheaper models from China and Taiwan.

References: Teruhisa Kitahara, *Yesterday's Toys, Robots, Spaceships, and Monsters,* Chronicle

Books, 1988; Crystal and Leland Payton, *Space Toys,* Collectors Compass, 1982; Stephen J. Sansweet, *Science Fiction Toys and Models,* Vol. 1, Starlog Press, 1980; Leslie Singer, *Zap! Ray Gun Classics,* Chronicle Books, 1991.

Periodical: *Robot World & Price Guide,* PO Box 184, Lenox Hill Station, New York, NY 10021.

See: Robots and Space Adventurers and Explorations.

REPRODUCTION ALERT

Astronauts and Spacemen
    Astro–Scout, Yonezawa, Japan, litho tin, astronaut, advances using crank friction lever, separate litho tin chest plate with #3, clear plastic helmet visor over litho tin face, 9½" h **2,300.00**
    Captain Astro Spaceman, Mego, Japan, windup, litho tin, orig box   **195.00**
    Cragstan Astronaut, Daiya, Japan, battery operated, red, walks, stops, raises firing gun with illuminated barrel, realistic oxygen tanks hold batteries, orig box, 14" h **4,400.00**
    Earth Man, TN, Nomura Toys, Japan, battery operated, remote control, litho tin astronaut, walks, stops, raises gun, and fires through illuminated barrel, telescoping antenna, separate oxygen tanks, 9¼" h **550.00**
    Man in Space, Alps, Japan, battery operated, litho tin and plastic space man, litho tin space illus battery box, spaceman floats, hand position controls directions, orig box, 8" l **900.00**
    Mark Apollo Astronaut, Marx, plastic, jointed, orange space suit, white helmet, plastic accessories, orig instructions and box, 7½" h **125.00**
    Martie the Martian, Donal Lee Cyr, Pasadena, CA, 1950s, hard rubber figure with spring arms and legs ending in suction cups, orig box, 6½" h **250.00**
    Moon Astronaut, Daiya, Japan, windup, litho tin, blue helmet, red space suit, walks, raises space rifle, gun noise, 9" h **550.00**
    Space Man, Sonsco, TN, Nomura Toys, Japan, battery operated, litho tin, blue version, walking astronaut, flashlight and helmet lights, arms swing, telescoping antenna, orig box, 9" h **3,850.00**
    X–27 Space Explorer, Yonezawa, Japan, friction, tin astronaut, advances using crank friction lever, separate litho tin chest plate, plas-

tic visor covers litho tin face, twin helmet antennae, 9" h, orig box **2,300.00**
Gun
    Atomic Disintegrator, Hubley, cap pistol, metal and plastic, silvered metal, red grips, orig box, 7½" l .. **175.00**
    Cosmic Ray Gun, Ranger Steel Products Corp, 1950s, plastic, red, blue, and amber, transparent barrel, sparking, orig box, 8" l **35.00**
    Electronic Space Gun, Remco, plastic, see–through dual telescopic sights, color rays, high speed atom smasher twirls, atomic sound waves, orig box, 9" l **120.00**
    Mars Gun, friction, litho tin, clear red plastic insert windows, sparking, siren noise, orig box, 9" l, not working **100.00**
    Master Gun, Interplanetary War Flying Saucer Gun, Spain, plastic, two satellite launchers, orig box .. **60.00**
    Space Gun, #8, tin, sparking action, gray, red lettering, 7¾" l, 5" h **28.00**
    Space Outlaw Atomic Pistol, England, cap pistol, silvered metal, rocket, planet, and stars on grips, red tinted plastic side pieces, telescopic rear sight, sonic ray selector, smoking and flashing action, recoil barrel, orig box, 10" l **275.00**
    Space Pilot X–Ray Gun, KO, Japan, friction, plastic, gold, simulated satellite openings, two sounds emitted simultaneously as trigger is pressed, barrel flashes, orig box, 8½" l **85.00**
    Space Super Jet Gun, KO, Japan, litho tin, see–through green barrel, sparking light, sound, orig box, 9½" l **65.00**
Miscellaneous
    Astro Base, Ideal Toy Co, motorized plastic, orig box, 10" h, 8" d **75.00**
    Electric Rainbow Top, Haji, Japan, battery operated, litho tin, outer space images of planets and stars, top lights, orig box, not working, 7½" d **110.00**
    Flashlight, rocket shape **75.00**
    Palm Puzzle, Ked's shoe premium, 1950s, cardboard disc, plastic cov, two metal balls, planet and rocketship graphics, 1¼" d **12.00**
    Project Mercury Recovery Set, Marx, c1961, helicopter, space capsule, and astronaut, orig box **75.00**
    Rocket Darts, American Toy Works, 1950s, diecut space target board, wooden shooter with diecut cardboard spaceships attached, rubber

band propulsion, orig instructions
and box **75.00**

Space Faces, Create Your Own Vegetable People, Pressman, 1950s, plastic pieces, orig box, few pieces missing **50.00**

Space Helmet with Radar Goggles, Banner Plastics, 1950s, copper metallic swirled plastic with day–glow orange trim, helmet top shaped as rocketship, yellow and green goggles, orig box with inserts forming child's face **600.00**

Space Patrol Walkie Talkie, J & L Randall, England, battery operated, plastic microphones, orig 6 x 9½" box with space graphics, copyright 1955 .... **135.00**

Space Port Planetary Cruiser Patrol, Pyro, 1950s, litho tin hangar with spaceships, spacemen, lightning bolts, and control panels graphics, 10½" l plastic space ship fits in spring loaded slot, fired by release mechanism in back, six hard plastic spacemen, plastic 3" h "boiler plate" type robot **400.00**

Space Trip, MT, Japan, litho tin, cars navigate track as space station spins, missile, planets, and stars graphics, orig box **175.00**

Space Whale, KO, Japan, windup, litho tin, marked "Pioneer" on tailfin, advances, mouth opens and closes, eyeballs roll in clear plastic shells, ears flap, red clear plastic insert window on body, 9½" l ... **500.00**

Steve Scott Crayons and Stencil Set, Transogram, 1952, litho cardboard box with Steve on alien planet and rocket ships in background, two rows of crayons with outer space wrapping, punchout space cards, coloring pages, unused **225.00**

Superior Space Port, T Cohn, litho tin, two levels, marked "Space Drome," plastic figures, orig box, 11 x 16" **550.00**

Spacecraft (Rockets, Capsules, Satellites, and Flying Saucers)

Docking Rocket, Daiya, Japan, battery operated, tin and plastic docking rocket and capsule, revolving radar, lights, orig box and inserts, 16" l **50.00**

Flying Saucer, Haji, Japan, friction, litho tin, sparking action behind red clear plastic window inserts, siren sound, clear cockpit dome with two litho tin pilots at controls, orig box, 7" d **145.00**

Flying Saucer with Space Pilot, KO,

Japan, battery operated, tin capsule, non–stop mystery action, space noise, revolving antenna, swivel lighted engine, litho tin astronaut at controls, orig box, 7½" d **125.00**

Flying Spaceman Motorcycle, Bandai, Japan, friction, litho tin motorcycle, unauthorized Superman rubber figure, 12 x 5¾" ... **8,000.00**

Interplanetary Spaceship Atom Rocket–15, Yone, Japan, early 1970s, battery operated, litho tin and plastic, orig instructions and box, 13" h **125.00**

King Flying Saucer, KO, Japan, battery operated, litho tin and plastic, marked "Space Patroler," flashing lights, space sound, turning action simulates space flight, orig box, 7½" d **110.00**

Lunar–1 Two–Stage Moon Rocket, Scientific Products Co, 1960s, plastic rocket and launch pad, fuel, oxidizer, measuring tank, pivot pin, release cord, manual, orig box ... **75.00**

Man Made Satellite, Yonezawa, Japan, friction, litho tin, spring antennae, red, dog head image at each window, orig box, 7" l **225.00**

Marsman Space Car, MT, Japan, friction, litho tin car and driver, erratic motion, 1950s colors with parachutist, spacecraft, planet, missile, and stars images, 5½" l **425.00**

Mechanical Jumping Rocket, SY, Japan, windup, litho tin, three dimensional robot in cockpit, advances on feet with hopping and bucking motions, orig box, 6" l .. **175.00**

Mercury ME–56 Space Rocket, Daiya, Japan, friction, litho tin, four rear fins, sparking action, needs new flint, 10" l **385.00**

Mini–Martians Jet Car, Ideal, 1967, plastic, spacecraft with clear bubble dome similar to Jetson vehicles, orig box, 8½" l **85.00**

Moon Rocket, MT, Japan, friction, litho tin, marked "3," astronaut at controls, orig box, 7" l **485.00**

NASA Columbia Space Ship, Spain, battery operated, tin and plastic space vehicle, rolls forward, bump–and–go action, stops, canopy opens, tin astronaut "floats" through space, space noise, lights up, orig box, 14 x 9½" **110.00**

NASA Space Shuttle Challenger and Flying Jet Plane, Taiwan, battery operated, tin and plastic shuttle, 1/175 scale, taxies, takes off, flies, and lands, toy removed from market following Challenger crash, orig box, 16" wing span **195.00**

New Space Capsule, SH, Horikawa Toys, Japan, battery operated, tin and plastic Apollo capsule with graphic interior and NASA markings, mystery action, stop–and–go action, opening hatch, tin astronaut, orig box and inserts, 9½" l, hatch mechanism not working . . . **85.00**

NR562 Space Satellite, Western Germany, friction, litho tin, three astronauts wearing square helmets, one with telescope, one with flashlight, one with spear–like weapon, satellite advances, inner circle with three antennae spins, orig box, 4" d **150.00**

Planet Explorer, MT, Japan, battery operated, litho tin, advances with non–fall action, clear plastic dome over litho tin astronaut with moving right arm working controls, red and green flashing lights, spinning plastic antenna, orig box, 9" l **200.00**

Planet–Y Space Station, TN, Nomura Toys, Japan, battery operated, litho tin, circular station with two antennae and plastic astronaut under clear plastic dome, lower half spins with bump–and–go action as upper half turns with light and space sound, orig box, 8½" d **125.00**

Rocket Fighter, Marx, windup, litho tin, rocketship and pilot, sparking action, space noise, rolls forward, 12" l, needs flint **225.00**

Sonar Space Patrol, Yonezawa, Japan, battery operated, litho tin, clear plastic dome, ship changes direction when plastic whistle is blown, orig box, 14" l **600.00**

Space Patrol Fire Bird, MT, Japan, battery operated, litho tin rocket advances with mystery action, blinking light, clear plastic dome over litho tin astronaut, orig box, 14" l **585.00**

Space Patrol Round Rocket, Asahitoy, Japan, windup, litho tin, raised pilot's helmet in cockpit, attached key, orig box, 5½" l **150.00**

Space Ships, The Space Fleet of the Future, Pyro, 1950s, plastic, four ships include 5" l X–100 Space Scout, 7" l X–200 Space Ranger, 10" l X–300 Space Cruiser with pilot, and 7 x 8" X–400 Satellite Explorer with two pilots, orig box with litho graphics **350.00**

Space Station, SH, Horikawa Toys, Japan, battery operated, earlier tin version, red, mystery action, blinking lights, space noise, revolving

Super Space Capsule, SH, Japan, battery operated, litho tin and plastic, stop-and-go and circular motion, two doors open, astronaut comes out, lights up, orig box, $225.00.

plastic antenna, three dimensional tin figures and furniture in five visible rooms, SANA markings, orig box, 9¼" h, 11½" d **1,500.00**

Sputnik, late 1950s, hemisphere in center, two 6" wires protrude from either side, tin replica attached to one, red, white, blue, and yellow spaceship attached to other, globe spins, rubber disc on base **110.00**

Super Sonic Speedster Rocket Racer, Modern Toys, Japan, friction, litho tin, sparking, orig box and cardboard insert, 6½" l, sparking action not working **325.00**

XZ–7 Space Ship, ST, Japan, friction, litho tin, spinning overhead rotor, orig box, 6½" l **60.00**

Tanks and Vehicles

Flying Jeep, Asahitoy, Japan, friction, litho tin and plastic, orig box, 8½" l **100.00**

Gama A–9 Exploration Vehicle, Western Germany, c1969, battery operated, remote control, plastic, orig box marked "Monsieur Tap–Tap," 10" l

Magic Color Moon Express, Daysran, Taiwan, battery operated, tin and plastic, spaceship resembles train engine, non–stop action, space noise, light display, orig box, 14" l **55.00**

Mars Patrol Space Tank, #17, MY, Japan, friction, litho tin, metal antenna, tin astronaut at controls, half–circle cockpit ball spins as tank advances, astronaut appears and disappears, orig box, 6" l **225.00**

Moon City, Cragstan, Japan, battery operated, plastic Apollo moon shuttle travels around Lunar Command Posts, blinking lights, orig 15 x 17½" box **55.00**

Moon Explorer
MT, Japan, battery operated, litho tin, figural astronaut under clear cockpit dome, bump–and–go action, flashing red and green tail lights, orig box, 14" l **650.00**

Yonezawa, Japan, battery operated, remote control, litho tin, astronaut beneath clear plastic dome, revolving rear lights, moon motor noise, rotating antenna, advances on suction type legs, hatch opens to reveal plastic astronaut taking photos, plastic remote control box shaped as missile, orig box, 9" l, 7" h **1,150.00**

Moon Orbiter, Yonezawa, Japan, battery operated, plastic and tin space vehicle moves along Magnet Rail track, orig 9 x 11" box **325.00**

Robby Space Patrol, TN, Nomura Toys, Japan, battery operated, litho tin, unauthorized copy of vehicle from movie *Forbidden Planet*, rolls forward, stop–and–go action, revolving illuminated gold Robby body, 12½" l, 9¾" h, missing battery cover, minor split on side of Robby's dome, green and red passenger lights not working **6,325.00**

Robert the Robot and his Remote Control Bulldozer, Ideal, plastic, crank wind, battery operated light, seated robot works gears, trigger gun with crank control for forward/reverse action and left/right directions, blue and yellow bulldozer with red treads, red and silver robot, orig box, 9" l **1,900.00**

Rocket Fighter, Marx, windup, litho tin, sparking, rolls forward, space noise, 12" l **225.00**

Space Bus, Usagayi, Japan, friction, litho tin, astronauts, capsules, planets, rockets, and comets illus, destination plate reads "Space," Robbie robot image on roof, clear plastic window inserts, orig box, 14½" l **1,500.00**

Space Patrol Super Cycle, Bandai, Japan, friction, litho tin motorcycle, sparking action, rotating radar, working compass, green rubber figure with bubble helmet, orig box, 14" l, figure missing one forearm from elbow to wrist **3,750.00**

Space Patrol Tank, Yonezawa, Japan, battery operated, litho tin, ad-

vances with non–fall action, flashing light, moving antenna, space noise, flashing lighted cockpit appears and disappears into turret, 8" l, orig box **400.00**

SPARK PLUGS

Collecting Hints: There is no right or wrong way to collect spark plugs. Some people collect a certain style of plug, while others grab any plug they can find.

Finding plugs can be as easy as looking in the machine shed of an old farm. Check out local garages. Many service stations never discarded old plugs. You may get lucky and find new old stock plugs still on the shelf. Other good places to find plugs are at auto parts swap meets and steam and gas engine shows.

Spark plugs are classified into six different types. First are name plugs, most of which have unusual names but no special features. The second type are gadget plugs, which have an interesting style. Examples include plugs with a little fan on the electrode to blow the carbon off or a breather on the side to allow more air in the combustion chamber to help dry out an oily cylinder. The third type are primer plugs, those plugs with priming cocks built either into the side of the plug or into the insulator, which aided in faster and easier engine starting. The fourth type are visible plugs. These plugs were built so the motorist could observe the spark and make necessary adjustments. This style of plug has holes in the insulator for viewing the spark. Some plug manufacturers made the entire insulator out of glass, allowing the explosion in the cylinder to be observed. The fifth type are coil plugs, which had the spark coil built into the plug. Less voltage would be lost as the spark did not have to travel through the plug wire, thus giving a hotter spark. Coil plugs are very large, some weighing four pounds. Coil plugs did not work well in automobiles as engine heat melted the coil's insulation and rendered it useless. Coil plugs did find a niche with the boating set. Water splashed on the plug of marine duty engines and kept them cool. Another plus was for the operator of the boat. His chance of getting shocked by a wet plug wire was greatly diminished. Last of all are quick detachable or QD plugs. These plugs were designed with a built–in wrench. With a turn of the handle, the insulator may be taken out, cleaned, and replaced in only a few seconds. Many of these plugs were sold with an air pump that would be installed, in place of the insulator, thus enabling the driver to pump a flat tire along the road.

Most plugs in collections are in used condition. Plugs may be cleaned without lowering their value. The choice to restore plugs—re–blue or re–plate the bases—is up to the owner of the collection. The debate rages both ways. There are valid arguments on both sides of the issue.

New collectors should be especially careful when handling plugs. While most logos or names are fired onto the insulator's glaze, some have either fragile paper labels or names inked on them. Mishandling can ruin the logo, making the plug worthless.

History: Spark plugs date back to the early 1800s. The first internal combustion engines were equipped with a mechanical sparking device known as an igniter. The igniter was very troublesome, had many moving parts, and fouled out very easily. It was during this period, in Europe, that the spark plug was invented. It has an insulator made of mica and sparked off a grounded lug on the base of the plug. By the late 1800s and early 1900s, the internal combustion engine was found to be a viable and better source of power than steam. With the introduction of the horseless carriage, people saw the opportunity to cash in by building a better spark plug. Many different materials were used for the insulators: mica, glass, Bakelite, and even pipestone. However, porcelain was the most preferred material. Various gadgets were invented, either to be attached to or built into spark plugs, to increase their performance. While some of these ideas were no better than snake oil, many did have merit.

Today, common names of spark plugs include Champion, AC, and Autolite. Collectors have identified over 4,000 different plug names. Today's spark plugs are almost identical to their early counterparts.

References: Cornelius Bergbower, *Sparkling Plug Collectors Guide, Vol. 1 (1986) and Vol. 2*, published by author; Jack Martells, *Antique Automotive Collectibles,* Contemporary Books; A. M. Parker, *Spark Plugs, Vol. 1 and Vol. 2,* published by author; The Spark Plug Collectors of America, *The Spark Plug Masterlist,* published by authors.

Collectors' Club: The Spark Plug Collectors of America, 14018 NE 85th St., Elk River, MN 55330.

Museums: Antique Auto Sales Car & Engine Museum, Monroe, MI; Ellingson Car Museum, Rogers, MN.

Advisor: Jeff Bartheld.

Agway	3.00
Albrite	25.00
Aldor Automatic	8.00
All In One Primer	45.00
Allstate	3.00
Anderson, flat glass insulator	45.00
Asko, brass	35.00
Autoking	2.00

Barney Google, Breather Plug, $200.00.

Barney Goodle, breather plug	200.00
Bathurst	25.00
Beacon Light, glass insulator	5.00
Benfords Golden Giant, gold plated	55.00
Bergie National	10.00
B. F. Goodrich	3.00
Bitter Root	15.00
Blue Crown, Indy 500 winner	8.00
Blue Ribbon, large breather plug	175.00
Bond Bread	8.00
Breech Block, quick detachable	100.00
Chain–O–Spark	65.00
Champion	
Harley Davidson, air cooled	10.00
Primer	45.00
X	1.00
C–R	3.00
Confidence	40.00
Cross Country	3.00
Curtis, monoplane on insulator	20.00
Dandy 999	10.00
Derf	15.00
Diamond Z	17.00
Dr. Coyls Wonder	30.00
Dur–A–Ball, caged ball on bottom	50.00
Dynam Visible, with hole in insulator	160.00
E. C. Simmons, paper decal	25.00
Edison	2.00
Fan Flame, fan on bottom	20.00
Fire–A–Ford	100.00
Fisk	4.00
Fitzgo	10.00
Fleetwing Air Spark	30.00
Flint Aero	3.00
For–A–Ford	150.00
Fyrac	10.00
Goodyear	3.00
Heli Fi, paper decal	15.00
Herz	20.00
HMS Bulldog, bulldog logo	15.00
Horseshoe	3.00
Impaco	3.00
Janesville	7.00
J. D.	
Jeffery Dewit	5.00
Visible, with hole in insulator	100.00

Kant Break	20.00
King Bee	25.00
KLG, made in England	2.00
Kopper King	20.00
Lesota	6.00
Liberty, brass	30.00
Little Giant	3.00
Lyndon Lynamite	5.00
MS Morespark	15.00
Nabon	10.00
PAF Non Foul	5.00
Pep	40.00
Perfex Coil Plug	250.00
Phillips 66	3.00
Porters Keepskleen	20.00
Power Mower	3.00
Quikfyr	10.00
Red Head	
Big Boy	20.00
Primer	60.00
Rentz Deluxe	20.00
Rex	5.00
Rulisons Red Devil	6.00
Shurhit	5.00
Sootless, brass	15.00
Splitdorf, green hex insulator	5.00
Sterling	7.00
Storms Special	20.00
Sudig Series Plug	150.00
TNT	20.00
Trojan	3.00
Tungsten, blue insulator	10.00
Twin, plug reverses	100.00
Twin Fire	5.00
U. S. Rubber Co.	30.00
V–D	10.00
Viz Spark	100.00
Wards Standard Quality	3.00
Warren, all glass insulator	45.00
Watters All Spark	30.00
Wearever Sapphire	3.00
Wellman Turn Clean	50.00
White	3.00
Wingfoot	4.00
Winstock Quick Detachable, brass	200.00
Wnax Yankton SD	15.00
Worthmore Supreme	1.00
Zip	25.00
ZWP, fires off top of piston	200.00

SPORTS COLLECTIBLES

Collecting Hints: The amount of material is unlimited. Pick a favorite sport and concentrate on it. Within the sport, narrow collecting emphasis to items associated with one league, team, or individual, equipment, or chronological era. Include as much three–dimensional material as possible.

Each sport has a "hall of fame." Make a point to visit it and get to know its staff—an excellent source of leads for material that the museum does not want. Induction ceremonies provide an excellent opportunity to make contact with heroes of the sport as well as with other collectors.

History: Individuals have been saving sports–related equipment since the inception of sports. Some was passed down from generation to generation for reuse. The balance occupied dark spaces in closets, attics, and basements.

In the 1980s two key trends brought collectors' attention to sports collectibles. First, decorators began using old sports items, especially in restaurant decor. Second, card collectors began to discover the thrill of owning the "real" thing. Although the principal thrust was on baseball memorabilia, by the beginning of the 1990s all sport categories were collectible, with automobile racing, boxing, football, and horse racing especially strong.

References: Mark Allen Baker, *All Sport Autograph Guide,* Krause Publications, 1994; Mark Allen Baker, *Complete Guide To Boxing Collectibles,* Krause Publications, 1995; David Bushing, *Sports Equipment Price Guide,* Krause Publications, 1995; Ted Hake and Roger Steckler, *An Illustrated Price Guide to Non–Paper Sports Collectibles,* Hake's Americana & Collectibles Press, 1986; Roderick A. Malloy, *Malloy's Guide To Sports Cards Values,* Wallace–Homestead, 1995; Roderick A. Malloy, *Malloy's Sports Collectibles Value Guide, Up–To–Date Prices For Noncard Sports Memorabilia,* Wallace–Homestead, 1994; Norman E. Martinus and Harry L. Rinker, *Warman's Paper,* Wallace–Homestead, 1993.

Collectors' Clubs: Boxiana & Pugilistica Collectors International, PO Box 83135, Portland, OR 97203; The Glove Collectors Club, 14057 Rolling Hills Lane, Dallas, TX 75240.

Periodicals: *Boxing Collectors Newsletter,* 59 Bosson St., Revere, MA 02151; *Kovels on Sports Collectibles,* PO Box 22200, Beachwood, OH 44122; *Sports Collectors Digest,* 700 E. State St., Iola, WI 54990; *The Olympic Collectors Newsletter,* PO Box 41630, Tucson, AZ 85717.

See: Baseball Collectibles and Golf Collectibles.

BASKETBALL

Cereal Box, Larry Bird, Wheaties, unopened, sample size from fan kit	25.00
Jammer, Michael Jordan Jr	25.00
Miniature Basketball Rim and Backboard, University of Missouri	25.00
Nodder, 7" h, composition, player holding basketball, rounded gold base, sticker inscribed "Millersville," 1960s	22.00

Program
  Harlem Globetrotters, 1953 . . . .   15.00
  Magicians of Basketball, Harlem
  Globetrotters, 8 x 10½", 30 pgs,
  1965 . . . .   15.00
Ticket, 4½ x 9", Larry Bird Night, retire-
  ment ceremony, full color illus 18.00

BOATING

Pinback Button
  Annual International Yacht Competi-
  tion, ⅞" d, white background
  Puritan 1885 . . . .   10.00
  Volunteer 1887 . . . .   7.50
  Devil's Lake Regatta, 1¼" d, blue and
  white, speedboat races, July, 1934   12.00
  Outboard Regatta, 2⅛" d, tan, cellu-
  loid, black lettering, 1930s 12.00

BOWLING

Dispenser, marbleized plastic bowling
  ball, chrome push top, six glasses, figural bowler handle 60.00
Medal, 1¾ x 4½", brass, International
  Bowling Association, Minneapolis
  1915, raised relief image of male
  bowler, red, white, and blue ribbon   15.00
Nodder, 6" h, composition, yellow shirt
  and shoes, blue trousers, holding
  bowling ball, mounted on wood
  block base, inscribed "You're Right
  Down My Alley" 45.00
Pinback Button, American Bowling
  Congress, 35th Annual Tournament,
  Syracuse, NY, 1935 . . . .   15.00
Salt and Pepper Shakers, pr, souvenir,
  American Bowling Congress Tournament, irid, gold trim, bowling ball
  on pepper, bowling pin on salt 25.00

BOXING

Badge, 3½" d, George Foreman, full
  color photo 25.00
Book, *Jack Dempsey/The Idol of
  Histiana*, 1936 revised edition, Nat
  Fleischer, 158 pgs, inked autograph
  "To Bob/Best Wishes/Nat Fleischer"   25.00
Boxing Gloves, Larry Holmes, Everlast   100.00
Boxing Shorts, Muhammad Ali, Everlast   100.00
Bust, John Sullivan, Red Top Beer 240.00
Catalog, Draper & Maynard Boxing
  Gloves, Striking Bags, Ashland, NH,
  1895, 20 pages 50.00
Exercise Club, graduated and re-
  tractable handle, patented 1897 . . .   175.00
Flask, John Sullivan 225.00
Game, Muhammad Ali's Boxing Ring,
  mechanical, Mego Corp, 1976 copy-
  right Herbert Muhammad Enterprise

Inc, orig box 50.00
Handbill, Roar of the Crowd, Joe Louis   20.00
Magazine
  Life, Oct 23, 1970, 6 pg article on
  Muhammad Ali titled "No More
  Boasting, Just The Fight" 15.00
  The Ring, Sept, 1951, 64 pgs, full
  color Joe Louis and Ezzard Charles
  on cov 18.00
Pennant, 26½" l, blue felt, white letters,
  March 24, 1975 heavyweight cham-
  pionship, Ali and Wepner 28.00
Pin, Joe Louis, attached ribbon and
  plastic gloves 35.00
Poster, 28 x 22", Joe Louis Story, 1953   225.00
Print Portfolio, Art Folio Of Muscular
  Marvels, illus of Sandow, Dempsey,
  Tunney, 1926, 72 pages 45.00
Puppet, Joe Louis, Zimmerman, orig
  box 225.00
Puzzle, Sugar Ray Leonard, 1980, un-
  opened, MIB 30.00
Ring, Gene Tunney, plastic, yellow, in-
  sert illus, issued by Kellogg's cereals,
  1950s 12.50
Statue, Louis Golden, Hollywood
  Studios, 1947 . . . .   350.00

FOOTBALL

Badge, 3" d, cardboard, Brooklyn Ball
  Club, 1891 . . . .   20.00
Bank, 6" h, Pittsburgh Steelers, helmet
  shape, plastic, 1970s 23.00
Football, Joe Montana 120.00
Glass, 5¼" h, Notre Dame University,
  blue and gold, Victory March on
  back, 1950s 12.50
Hartland Figure, 7½" h, Jon Arnett, in-
  scription on base, 1950–60 . . . .   100.00
Nodder
  6½" h, Philadelphia Eagles, composi-
  tion, sq green base 55.00
  7½" h, vinyl, blue and gold outfit,
  green base, "Made in Hong Kong"   25.00
Paperback
  *O. J. Simpson, Football's Record
  Rusher* 15.00
  Spaulding's *Official Intercollegiate
  Football Guide*, edited by Walter
  Camp, 1922 . . . .   18.00
  Super Joe, The Joe Namath Story . . .   12.00
Pennant, 28" l, Boston Yanks, felt,
  green, football player illus, yellow
  lettering, c1950 . . . .   20.00
Program
  Hall of Fame
    1969, Packers vs Falcons 10.00
    1970, Vikings vs Saints 10.00
  Super Bowl IV 125.00
  Super Bowl V 250.00
Radio, transistor, player shaped, MIB . .   25.00

Football, ticket, Blue & Gray Championship Football Game, Montgomery, AL, 5¼ x 2⅛", December 16, 1964, $8.00.

Stadium Cushion, 11 x 16", vinyl, stuffed, red, NFL team names and mascot illus, orig tag, unused, 1950s ... **18.00**
Ticket, 2¾ x 6½", Army–Navy Game, Nov 26, 1938 .... **12.00**
Tray, tin, 1976 Cotton Bowl Champs, Coca–Cola **25.00**

HOCKEY

Nodder, 4½" h, MIB, 1960s
Boston Bruins **45.00**
Chicago Blackhawks **45.00**
Detroit Redwings **45.00**
Montreal Canadiens **45.00**

OLYMPICS

Cigarette Lighter, 2¾" h, 1984 Winter Olympics, red plastic, silvered metal, Olympic ring symbol, insignia, and "Sarajevo, Yugoslavia" in black on one side, black cartoon snowman illus other side **10.00**
Coin, 1½" l, 1980 Winter, oval, rolled, stamped "Lake Placid, NY," pine tree,

Olympics XXII, Moscow, stickpin, 1980, $12.00.

Olympic rings **8.50**
Ewer, 12" h, ceramic, nude man stringing bow, Olympic logo **33.00**
Fan, folding, paper, hp, balsa sticks, Tenth Olympic Games/1932/Los Angeles, chapel building illus, Olympic symbol, Japan **34.00**
Flask, 5½" h, white china, issued by Lufthansa Airlines, Olympic logo, "XVII Olympiade Rom 1960" inscription **15.00**
Glass, 5½" h, 1932 Olympics, clear, frosted white picture **50.00**
Jigsaw Puzzle, 1932 Olympic Games, 10 x 13¼", Toddy, Inc, 1932 copyright **30.00**
Magazine, *Sports Illustrated*, Nov 19, 1956 issue, Summer Olympic articles **15.00**
Manual, 3¼ x 6¼", Olympic Edition, 48 pgs, issued by Shell Petroleum, 1936 **15.00**
Patch, 6½" d, felt, bluish–purple background, blue, yellow, black, green, and red symbol **48.00**
Pinback Button
Olympic Team Support, 1¼" d, red, white, and blue, 1970s **8.00**
US Ski Team, 1" d, red, white, and blue, enamel, diecut, brass, 1960s **15.00**
Winter Olympics, 1⅛" d, diecut brass, red, blue, green, black, and white, 1980 Winter Olympics, Lake Placid **8.00**
Post Card, Olympic Stadium, 1939, real photo **30.00**
Program
1948 Summer Olympic Trials, 8 x 10½", weight lifting trials, 20 pgs **15.00**
1952 Olympic Tryouts, July 3–5, 1952, rowing tryouts, 72 pgs **20.00**
Stadium Cushion, 11 x 13½", 1956 Summer, red vinyl, yellow, white, and blue Olympics logo **45.00**

SWIMMING

Autograph, Gertrude Ederly, 6½ x 8" sheet, printed black and white drawing, blue ink inscription "Hold Strongly To 'Faith' in All You Do!/Best Always/Swimmingly Yours/Gertrude Trudy Ederly/New York/Successful Channel Swim/August 6, 1926/35 miles In 40½ Hrs/Cape Gris Nez to Kingdown," inked 1969 date **22.00**
Bathing Suit, man's, Spaulding, woolen, c1920, Art Deco style **65.00**

TENNIS

Pin, enameled brass, white tennis racquet outline and tennis ball, dark red background, inscribed "Lazar/Koli–Basse," 1920s **25.00**

Tennis, napkin ring, $145.00.

Pinback Button, US Open Tennis
Championship, 2⅛" d, celluloid,
1975 championships **10.00**
Racket
    Chris Evert **40.00**
    Jack Kramer
      Kramer Cup **75.00**
      Speed Flo **95.00**
    Maureen Connolly **75.00**
    Pancho Gonzales **125.00**
    Wilson, Tony Trabert **40.00**

STANGL POTTERY

Collecting Hints: Stangl Pottery produced several
lines of highly collectible dinnerware and decorative accessories, including the famed Stangl
birds. The red–bodied dinnerware was produced
in distinctive shapes and patterns. Shapes were
designated by numbers. Pattern names include
Country Garden, Fruit, Tulip, Thistle, and Wild
Rose. Special Christmas, advertising, and commemorative wares also were produced.

Bright colors and bold simplistic patterns make
Stangl pottery a favorite with Country collectors.
Stangl's factory sold seconds from its factory store
long before outlet malls became popular. Large
sets of Stangl dinnerware currently command
high prices at auctions, flea markets, and even
antiques shops.

Stangl's ceramic birds were produced from
1940 until 1972. The birds were produced in
Stangl's Trenton plant, then shipped to the
Flemington plant for hand painting. During
World War II the demand for these birds and
Stangl pottery was so great that 40 to 60 decorators could not keep up with the demand. Orders
were contracted out to private homes. These
pieces were then returned for firing and finishing.
Colors used to decorate these birds varied according to the artist. Several birds were reissued
between 1972 and 1977. These reissues are
dated on the bottom and worth approximately
one half the value of the older birds.

As many as ten different trademarks were used.
Dinnerware was marked and often signed by the
decorator. Most birds are numbered; many are
artist signed. However, signatures are useful for
dating purposes only and add little to values.

History: The origins of Fulper Pottery, the predecessor to Stangl, are clouded. The company
claimed a date of 1805. Paul Evans, a major
American art pottery researcher, suggests an
1814 date. Regardless of which date is right, by
the middle of the nineteenth century an active
pottery was located in Flemington, New Jersey.

When Samuel Hill, the pottery's founder, died
in 1858, the pottery was acquired by Abraham
Fulper, a nephew. Abraham died in 1881, and
the business continued under the direction of
Edward, George W., and William, Fulper's sons.

In 1910 Johann Martin Stangl began working
at Fulper as a chemist and plant superintendent.
He left Fulper in 1914 to work briefly for Haeger
Potteries. By 1920 Stangl was serving as general
manager at Fulper. In 1926 Fulper acquired the
Anchor Pottery in Trenton, New Jersey, where a
line of solid color dinnerware in the California
patio style was produced.

William Fulper died in 1928 at which time
Stangl became president of the firm. In 1920
Johann Martin Stangl purchased Fulper and
Stangl Pottery was born. During the 1920s pro-
duction emphasis shifted from art pottery to din-
ner and utilitarian wares.

In 1929 fire destroyed the Flemington pottery.
Rather than rebuild, a former ice cream factory
was converted to a showroom and production fa-
cility. By the end of the 1930s production was
concentrated in Trenton with the Flemington kiln
used primarily for demonstration purposes.

On August 25, 1965, fire struck the Trenton
plant. The damaged portion of the plant was rebuilt by May 1966. On February 13, 1972,
Johann Martin Stangl died. Frank Wheaton, Jr., of
Wheaton Industries, Millville, N.J., purchased
the plant in June 1972 and continued Stangl production. In 1978 the Pfaltzgraff Company purchased the company's assets from Wheaton.
Production ceased. The Flemington factory became a Pfaltzgraff factory outlet. One of the original kilns remains intact to exemplify the hard
work and high temperatures involved in the production of pottery.

References: Susan and Al Bagdade, *Warman's
American Pottery and Porcelain,* Wallace–
Homestead, 1994; Harvey Duke, *Stangl Pottery,*
Wallace–Homestead, 1993; Joan Dworkin and
Martha Horman, *A Guide To Stangl Pottery Birds,*
Willow Pond Books, 1973, out–of–print; Norma
Rehl, *The Collectors Handbook of Stangl Pottery,*
Democrat Press, 1982; Mike Schneider, *Stangl
and Pennsbury Pottery Birds: Identification and
Price Guide,* Schiffer Publishing, 1994.

Collectors' Club: Stangl/Fulper Collectors Club,
PO Box 64–A, Changewater, NJ 07831.

BIRDS

#3250C, White Duck	70.00
#3275, Turkey	55.00
#3276D, Bluebirds	190.00
#3276S, Bluebird	100.00
#3401, Wren	55.00
#3401S, Wren	200.00
#3405D, Cockatoos	195.00
#3407, Owl	350.00
#3432, Running Duck	425.00
#3445 and #3446, Gray Hen and Rooster, price for pair	430.00
#3447, Prothonotary Warbler	65.00
#3454, Key West Quail Dove	325.00
#3456, Cerulean Warbler	65.00
#3490D, Redstarts	165.00
#3582, Parakeet, blue	165.00
#3599, Hummingbirds	300.00
#3715, Blue Jay with peanut	550.00
#3722, European Finch	650.00
#3751, Red Headed Woodpecker	160.00
#3756F, Audubon Warbler	350.00
#3812, Chestnut Sided Warbler	85.00
#3814, Black Throated Warbler	85.00
#3844, Goldfinch	145.00
#3848, Kinglet	65.00
#3853, Kinglets	650.00
#3868, Summer Tanager	450.00

DINNERWARE

Amber Glo
Plate	
Chop, 12½" d	20.00
Dinner	12.00
Luncheon	10.00
Vegetable Bowl	
Divided	30.00
Round	22.00
Apple Delight, #5161	
Bowl, 8" d	25.00
Cereal Bowl	12.00
Chop Plate, 12½" d	25.00
Plate	
6" d	5.00
10" d	15.00
Snack Plate, 8¼" d	3.50
Sugar, cov	20.00
Bella Rosa	
Butter Dish, ¼ lb	35.00
Casserole, individual, stick handle	15.00
Cup and Saucer	12.50
Fruit Dish, 5½" d	10.00
Pitcher, ½ pint	20.00
Plate, 6" d, bread and butter	5.00
Blueberry	
Plate	
6" d	7.00
10" d	16.50
Soup	15.00

Country Garden	
Creamer and Sugar	25.00
Cup and Saucer	15.00
Gravy Boat, stand	35.00
Relish	20.00
Soup, lug	15.00
Tidbit	12.00
Fruit and Flowers	
Gravy Boat, stand	30.00
Soup, lug, 5¼" d	7.50
Garden Flower, teapot	45.00
Golden Blossom	
Bowl, 8" d	30.00
Deviled Egg Server	40.00
Vegetable Bowl, divided	35.00
Golden Harvest, #3887	
Chop Plate, 14¼" d	35.00
Coffee Warmer	12.00
Cup	5.00
Fruit Bowl, 12" d	40.00
Plate, 10" d	12.00
Salad Bowl	35.00
Vegetable Bowl, divided	35.00
Magnolia, #3870	
Chop Plate, 12" d	20.00
Plate, 10" d	12.00
Orchard Song, #5110	
Bread Tray	25.00
Cereal Bowl, 5½" d	12.00
Chop Plate, 12" d	25.00
Cup	10.00
Server, handle	14.00
Starflower, cake set	90.00
Thistle, #3847	
Eggcup, double	12.00
Fruit Bowl, 5½" d	12.00
Mixing Bowl, 5½" d	20.00
Plate, 9" d	10.00
Sauce Boat	18.00
Town and Country, blue	
Candlesticks, pr	75.00
Coffeepot	75.00
Pitcher, small	50.00
Sugar Bowl	40.00
Teapot, chip under spout	75.00

Colonial Rose, plate, pink rose, 10½" d, $4.50.

GIFTWARE

Ashtray, oval
Deer **70.00**
Pheasant **35.00**
Basket, Terra Rose, #3251, 11 x 9"   . . .   **75.00**
Bowl, Antique Gold, #4061, 8" d **25.00**
Cigar Box, Oriole **100.00**
Pitcher, Antique Gold, #4052, 14½" h   **35.00**
Planter, Platina, swan, #5033, 6¾" h . .   **20.00**
Vase, Tropical Ware, #2027, 8" h **100.00**

STEREOGRAPHS

Collecting Hints: Value is determined by condition, subject, photographer (if famous), rarity, and age—prior to 1870 or after 1935. A revenue stamp on the back indicates an age of 1864–1866, when a federal war tax was imposed. Litho printed cards have very little value.

Collect images that are of good grade or above, except for extremely rare images. Very good condition means some wear on the mount and a little dirt on the photo. Folds, marks on the photo, or badly worn mounts reduce values by at least 50%. Faded or light photos also reduce value.

Don't try to clean cards or straighten them. Cards were made curved to heighten the stereo effect, an improvement made in 1880.

With common cards it pays to shop around to get the best price. With rarer cards it pays to buy them when you see them since values are increasing annually. Dealers who are members of the National Stereoscopic Association are very protective of their reputation and offer a good starting point for the novice collector.

Use your public library to study thoroughly the subject matter you are collecting; it is a key element to assembling a meaningful collection.

History: Stereographs, also known as stereo views, stereo view cards, or stereoscope cards, were first issued in the United States on glass and paper in 1854. From the late 1850s through the 1930s, the stereograph was an important visual record of every major event, famous person, comic situation, and natural scene. It was the popular news and entertainment medium until replaced by movies, picture magazines, and radio.

The major early publishers were Anthony (1859–1873), Kilburn (1865–1907), Langeheim (1854–1861), and Weller (1861–1875). By the 1880–1910 period the market was controlled by large firms among which were Davis (Kilburn), Griffith & Griffith, International View Company, Keystone, Stereo Travel, Underwood & Underwood, Universal Photo Art, and H.C. White.

References: William C. Darrah, *Stereo Views, A History Of Stereographs in America And Their Collection,* published by author, 1964, out–of–print; William C. Darrah, *The World of Stereographs,* published by author, 1977, out–of–print; Norman E. Martinus and Harry L. Rinker, *Warman's Paper,* Wallace–Homestead, 1994; John S. Waldsmith, *Stereo Views: An Illustrated History and Price Guide,* Wallace–Homestead, 1991.

Collectors' Clubs: National Stereoscopic Association, Box 14801, Columbus, OH 43214; Stereo Club of Southern California, PO Box 2368, Culver City, CA 90231.

Note: Prices given are for very good condition, i.e., some wear and slight soiling. For excellent condition add 25%, and for mint perfect image and mount, double the price. Reverse the process for fair, i.e., moderate soiling, some damage to mount, minor glue marks, some foxing (brown spots) and poor folded mount, very dirty and damage to tone or both images. Where applicable, a price range is given.

Animal
Birds, Hurst's 2nd series, #7, birds in
tree **4.00**
Cat
Keystone #2314, average cat view . .   **4-5.00**
Keystone #9651, man and cat **4.00**
Soule, The Pickwickian Ride, highly
collectible **20.00**
Dog
Kilburn #1644, "Home Protection,"
dog close up **6.00**
U & U, the puppies singing school . .   **4.00**
Universal #3231, average dog view   **4-5.00**
Farm Yard, Kilburn #739, sheep and
cows, 1870s **4.00**
Horses, Schreiber & Sons, Jarvis and
sulky, early **18.00**
Walrus, Keystone #V21232, Bronx Zoo   **3.00**
Zoo, London Stereo Company, animals
in London Zoo, each **8-10.00**

Astronomy
Comet, Keystone #16645, Morehouse's   **9.50**
Mars, Keystone #16767T, the planet . .   **6.00**
Moon
Beer Bros. 1866, photo by Rutherford   **15.00**
Kilburn #2630, full moon **6.00**
Soule #602, last quarter **8.00**
Planetarium, Keystone #32688, Adler's
Chicago **10.00**

Aviation
Air Mail Plane
Keystone #29446, at Cleveland **30.00**
Keystone #32372, Inaugural, Ford Tri-
motor, air-rail serivece NY to LA,
7/2/29 . . . .   **20.00**
Aviators, Keystone #26408t, 6 men who
first circled earth **25.00**
Balloon, Anthony #4114, Prof. Lowe's
flight from 6th Ave. in NYC **100.00**

Aviation, Keystone View Co., #775 8632, The Graf Zeppelin's rendezvous with the Eternal Desert and the Ancient Pyramids of Giza, Egypt, information on back includes facts about desert and zeppelin, $25.00.

Dirigibles and Zeppelins, Keystone
#17397, Los Angeles at Lakehurst   **45-50.00**
#17398, The Los Angeles **45.00**
#18000, flying over German town . .   **6.00**
#32277, Graf Zeppelin in hanger at
    Lakehurst **35.00**
#32740, framework of ZRS-4, Akron **55-65.00**
#V19216, 1918, R-34 at Mineola,
    from WWI set, common view . . .   **15.00**
Doolittle, Keystone #28031, Major
    Doolittle, 1931 . . . .   **65.00**
General View, Keystone #32785, five
    biplanes fly over Chicago's field mu-
    seum **20.00**
Lindbergh, Keystone
#28029, in plane with wife **55.00**
#30262T, next to Spirit of St. Louis   **30.00**
Plane, Keystone
#18920, Michelin bomber **20.00**
#19049, Nieuport **9.00**
#V18921, twin seat fighter **9.00**
Wright Bros., Keystone #V96103, in
    flight at Ft. Meyers **85.00**

Black
Keystone #9506, "we done all dis a'
    morning," picking cotton **6.00**
Kilburn #14317, boy and mule, typical,
    common **3.00**
Singley
#10209, "one never came up," swim-
    mers **12.00**
#10217, "one got an upper cut," fighting   **10.00**
U & U, "Cotton is King," picking **5.00**
U & U, "Keystone, Kilburn, Whiting,
    etc., cheating at cards, stealing mil-
    lions, infidelity, etc **10-15.00**
Whiting
#960, "there's a watermelon smiling
    on the vine" **10.00**
#961, "Happiest Coon" **8.00**

Cave
Keystone
#9586, man in front of Great Oregon
    Caves **6.00**

#33516, int. of Crystal Springs Cave,
    Carlsbad **4.50**
U & U, Luray Caverns, typical **8.00**
Waldack, 1866, Mammoth Cave, typi-
    cal early magnesium light view **15.00**

Christmas
Brownies & Santa, Universal #4679,
    Graves, sleigh in foreground **20.00**
Children with Tree
Griffith #16833, children's Christmas
    dinner **17.00**
Keystone, 1895, #987, Santa in front
    of fireplace **15.00**
Santa coming down chimney, Keystone
    #11434, Santa with toys **25.00**
Santa with Toys, Keystone 1898, #9445,
    Santa loaded with toys **14.00**

Comics
Bicycle   Bum,   Graves   #4551–58,
    "Weary Willie," 4 card set **20.00**
Drinking
Kilburn 1892, #7348, "Brown just in
    from the club" **3.00**
R. Y. Young 1901, Woman drinking,
    two cards, unusual subject **16.00**
U & U, 1897, man sneaks in after
    drinking, 2 card set **7.50**
English, boy carves roast, "The Attack,"
    ivory mount, hand tinted **4.00**
Humor
Keystone #2346-7, before (cuddling)
    and after (reading) marriage **7.00**
U & U, 1904, "Four queens and a
    jack," 4 girls and a jackass **6.00**
Infidelity
Foolin–around, 1910, husband fools
    around with his secretary, 12
    cards **48.00**
Keystone #12312–22, The French
    Cook–Communist version **50.00**
U & U
    Sneaking–in, 1897, caught by wife
    after nite on the town **8.00**
    The French Cook, 10 card set   . . .   **50.00**
Romance
U & U, "Going with Stream," hugging
    couple **6.00**
Weller #353, "Unexpected," neck-
    ing **4.00**
Rumors, H. C. White, 5576-5578,
    quickest way to spread news: "Tell a
    graph, tell a phone, tell a woman," 3
    card set **20.00**
Sentimental, American Stereo, #2001-
    2012, He goes to war; wounded; re-
    turns; reunited, etc., 12 card set **60.00**
Wedding Set, White #5510–19, getting
    ready, wedding, reception, alone in
    bedroom **40.00**

Disaster

Boston Fire, 1872, Soule, ruins	8.00
Chicago Fire, 1871, Lovejoy & Foster, ruins	8.00
Galveston Flood, 1900, Graves, ruins	9.00
Johnstown Flood, ruins	
Barker	9.00
U & U	7.00
Mill Creek Flood, 1874, popular series, house	4.00
Portland Fire, 1866, Soule #469, ruins	8.00
St. Pierre Eruption, Kilburn #14941, ruins	3.00
San Francisco Earthquake Scenes	
Keystone #13264, Market St	9.00
U & U #8180, California St	16.00
White #8713, wrecked houses	20.00
Train Wreck, Dole	50.00
Worcester, MA, Flood, 1876, Lawrence, damage	5.00

Doll

Graves #4362, Sunday School Class ..	20.00
Kilburn	
#15, tired of play	15.00
When will Santa come?	12.00
U & U	
#6922, playing doctor	15.00
#6952, girl asleep with cat and doll	9.00
Webster & Albee #160, doll's maypole	20.00

Entertainer

Actress, J. Gurney & Son, 1870s, Mrs. Scott or Mrs. Roland, etc.	10.00
Dancers, Keystone #33959, Bali, Dutch Indies	2.00
Natives, Keystone #16423, Java, good costumes	3.00
Singer	
J. Gurney & Son, Annie Cary	15.00
James Cremer, opera, studio pose in costume	12.00

Exposition

NY Sanitary Fair, Anthony #1689-2864, fair view of fountain (for better view, double value)	15.00
1872, World Peace Jubilee, Boston Pollock, interior view	8.00

World's Peace Jubilee, 1872, Coliseum exterior, yellow ground, Wm. G. Preston, $9.00.

1876, U.S. Close Up Centennial, Centennial Photo Co.	
Common view of grounds and buildings	4.00-10.00
Corliss Engine	12.00
Monorail	65.00
Statue of Liberty Hand	85.00
1894	
California Mid-Winter, Kilburn #9474-2894, urns, etc. (for better subject, double value)	12.00
Columbian Chicago, Kilburn	
Most views	4-7.00
Ferris Wheel	7-10.00
1901, Pan American Buffalo, Kilburn	
Most views	4-6.00
President McKinley	7-9.00
1904, Louisiana Purchase Exposition, St. Louis	
Graves for Universal Photo or U & U, most views	4-8.00
White #8491, Education & Manufacturing buildings	8.00
Whiting #620, Missouri Fruit Exhibit	12.00
1905, Lewis & Clark Centennial, Portland, Watson Fine Art #34, building	9.00
1907, Jamestown Exposition, Keystone #14219, life saving demonstration ..	7.00
1908, West Michigan State Fair, Keystone #21507	12.00
1933, Century of Progress, Chicago, Keystone #32993, Lief Ericksen Dr.	12-20.00

Hunting & Fishing

Bass, Ingersoll #3159, string of bass ..	7.00
Deer, Keystone #26396, hunters and kill, typical	5.00
Halibut, Keystone #22520, commercial fishing	5.00
Moose, Keystone #9452, 1899, typical big game kill	6.00
Trout, Kilburn, #115, 1870, a day's catch	5.00
Wildcat, Keystone #12264, man shoots sleeping wildcat	6.00

Indian

Burge, J. C., Apaches bathing	75-125.00
Continental Stereo Co., Pueblo eating bread	50-65.00
Griffith #11873, Esquimau at St. Louis Fair	8.00
Hayes, F. J.	
#865, Crow burial ground	17-25.00
#1742, Sioux	20-30.00
Ingersoll #496, lithograph of Gray Eagle, typical printed Indian	2.00
Jackson, Wm. H., #202, Otoe, with bow, rare	80-100.00
Keystone	
#23095, Chief Black Hawk	10.00

#23118, Indian girl, common view   **4-5.00**
#V23181, Blackfeet **8.00**
Montgomery Ward, squaws **6.00**
Soule #1312, Piute squaw **40-60.00**
U & U
  Hopi **9.00**
  Wolpi **8.00**
White #12279, pueblo **12.00**

Mining
Alaska Gold Rush
  Keystone
  #9191, men with supplies getting
    ready to climb the "golden
    stairs" at Chilkoot Pass **9.00**
  #9195, preparing to climb the
    "golden stairs," common **9.00**
  #21100, panning for gold **12.00**
  U & U #10655, looking into glory
    hole **15.00**
Universal, Graves, 1902, man work-
  ing a sluice, scarce card by scarce
  publisher **40.00**
Easter, Anthony #474, working a gold
  chute **45.00**
Gold Hill, Houseworth #743, city
  overview **65-95.00**
Hydraulic, Houseworth #799, typical
  water spraying **60-80.00**
Virginia City
  Houseworth #713, street view **65-95.00**
Watkins
  Opera House **75-95.00**
  Panorama, new series **85-125.00**

Miscellaneous
Auto
  Keystone #22143, employees leaving
    Ford **8.00**
  U & U, early auto in Los Angeles,
    1903 . . . .   **17-20.00**
Beach scenes, H.C. White, #476,
  bathers, Atlantic City **5.00**
Bicycles
  Kilburn #11924, women and bike . .   **6.00**
  Thorne, big two wheeler, early
    1870s **35-50.00**
Circus
  U & U, Chicago **20.00**
  Windsor & Whipple, Olean, NY, peo-
    ple with elephant **35-40.00**
  Crystal Palace, yellow mount, outside,
    general view **25.00**
Firefighting
  Early 1870s, unknown maker, close
    view of pumpers **40.00**
  Keystone #11684, action view of
    pumpers **25.00**
Glass Stereos
  Foreign Scenes, e.g., Fifth, etc. . . .   **60-80.00**
  United States Scenes, e.g., Niagara
    Falls **50-100.00**

Groups, various, Rogers statuaries such
  as "Taking the Oath," or "Courtship in
  Sleepy Hollow" **7-9.00**
Gypsies, unknown maker, in front of
  tent **15-20.00**
Hawaii, Keystone
  #10156, hula girls **9.00**
  #10162, Waikiki Beach **9.00**
Lighthouses
  Keystone #29207, common view . . .   **4.00**
  Williams, Minot Ledge Light **15-17.00**
New York City, Anthony #3938, typical
  street view **15-25.00**
Opium Dens
  X82, 1900 . . . .   **25.00**
  Unknown Maker, two tier bed, pipe
    for smoking opium **60.00**
Prisons, Pach, view of cabinets of rifles   **15.00**
Tinted Views
  Foreign **4-6.00**
  United States **5-10.00**
Tunnel, ward #808 Hoosac Tunnel, just
  completed **15.00**
Toy train, Keystone P-21329, boy play-
  ing with Lionel trains **25.00**

National Park
Death Valley, Keystone #32666, pool   **9.00**
Garden of the Gods, Rodeo McKenney,
  Pike's Peak **5.00**
Grand Teton, Wm. H. Jackson, #503,
  average for this prized photographer   **20.00**
Yellowstone
  Jackson, Wm. H., #422, average for
    this prized photographer **15.00**
  Universal, nice, average peak view   **4.00**
Yosemite
  Keystone #4001, Nevada Falls **4.00**
  Kilburn #9284, Bridal Veil Falls **4.00**
  Reilly, tourists at Yosemite Falls **8.00**
  U & U, Glacier Point **5.00**

Niagara Falls
Anthony #3731, falls **4.00**
Barker, ice bridge **2.00**
U & U
  Tourists, common **2.00**
  Whirlpool rapids **1.00**
White #7, tourists, 1903 . . . .   **5.00**

Occupational
Blacksmith, Keystone #18206, many
  tools in picture **5.00**
Cowboys, Keystone
  #12465, Kansas **7.00**
  #13641, Yellowstone, Montana **7.00**
Farming, Kilburn #1796, hay, 1870s . .   **7.00**
Fireman
  G. K. Proctor, Mid-distance hooklad-
    der, horse drawn **35.00**
  1870s, good view of steam pumper   **45.00**
Milkman, Keystone #P-26392, horse-
  drawn wagon **10.00**

Mill, U & U, linen factory, typical industrial view 2-3.00
Store, Keystone #18209, grocery store int. 15.00

Oil
Pennsylvania
  Detlor & Waddell, #76, burning tanks 15.00
  Robbins #32, Triumph Hill 13.00
  Keystone #20352T, shooting a well 5.00
  Robbins, #88, gas well 8.00
  Wilt Brothers, Allegheny area 8.00
Texas, Keystone #34864, tanks near Kilgore, common 6.00

Person, Famous
Barton, Clara, Keystone #28002, founder of American Red Cross . . 50-60.00
Buffalo Bill, American Scenery #1399, on horseback in New York City, most common view 50.00
Buntline, Ned, J. Gurney, portrait 150.00
Burbank, Luther, Keystone #16746, with a cactus 8.00
Bryan, W. J., Keystone #15539, on way to hotel in NYC 30.00
Coolidge, President, Keystone #26303, President and Cabinet, scarce view 50.00
  #26303 . . . . 30.00
  #28004, at desk, typical 12.00
Custer, General
  Lovejoy & Foster, with bear he killed 300-450.00
  Taylor #2438, with his dog in camp 500-600.00
Czar of Russia, U & U, with President of France 10.00
Edison, Thomas
  Keystone, #V28007, in lab 100.00
  U & U, in lab 100-150.00
Edison, Ford and Firestone, Keystone
  #18551 . . . . 75-125.00
  #45612 . . . . 75-125.00
Eisenhower, President, Keystone, at table with microphones, about 1954, rare 150-250.00
Faraqutt, Admiral, Anthony, from Prominent Portrait Series 40.00
Ford, Henry, Keystone #28023 . . . . . . 60.00
Gandhi, Mahatma, Keystone #33852, portrait 25-35.00
Gehrig, Lou, Keystone #32597, baseball player 150-200.00
Grant, President, Bierstadt Bros., on Mount Washington 75.00
Hayes, B., president, party at Hastings 75-100.00
Harding, W., president, addressing boy scouts 15-20.00
Hoover, President, Keystone #28012, close portrait 35.00

Kettering, C. F., Keystone, inventor of auto self starter 60.00
Kingman, Seth, no maker, famous California Trapper 95-120.00
Lincoln, Abraham, Anthony
  Funeral, #4596 . . . . 50-65.00
  President, #2969, scarce, highly prized view 800-1,200.00
Marconi, Keystone #V11969, radio inventor 45.00
McKinley, President, Keystone, Kilburn, U & U, most views 5-15.00
Morse, Samuel, J. Gurney 175-225.00
Queen Victoria, U & U 1897, having breakfast with Princesses 35.00
Rockefeller, J.D., Keystone #V11961, world's richest man 25.00
Rogers, Will, Keystone #32796, at 1932 Chicago Democratic Convention . . . 75.00
Roosevelt, Franklin D., president, Keystone #33535, at his desk 75.00
Roosevelt, Theodore, president
  Keystone, Kilburn, U & U, most views [at Panama Canal, Glacier Pt., Yosemite, etc.] 8-30.00
  U & U, on horseback, typical view 12-20.00
Ruth, Babe, Keystone #32590, baseball player 200-250.00
Sarazen, Gene, Keystone #32436, golfer 35.00
Schmeling, Max, Keystone #28028, boxer 75.00
Shaw, Dr. Anna, Keystone #V26151, suffrage leader 25.00
Shaw, George Bernard, Keystone #34505, on a ship 50-60.00
Strauss, Johann, Gurney, typical of a Gurney well-known person such as Bret Harte, Horace Greeley, etc 90.00
Taft, President, U & U #10062, at desk 20.00
Thomas, Lowell, Keystone #32812, world travel expert and newsman . . 50.00
Twain, Mark
  Evans & Soule 350.00
  U & U #8010 or White #13055, in bed writing 250.00
Washington, Booker T., Keystone #V11960, with Andrew Carnegie . . 50-70.00
Wirewalkers, Barker
  Belleni on wire 10.00
  Blondin on rope 15.00
Young, Brigham, C. W. Carter, bust portrait 20.00

Photographer, Famous
Brady, Anthony
  1863, Tom Thumb Wedding, famous 100-125.00
  #428, Captain Custer with Confederate prisoner 900.00
  #3376, Jeff Davis Mansion 50.00

Houseworth, San Francisco, e.g.,
#150, show photo studio **100-150.00**
#429, Golden Gate **35-45.00**
Langenheim, 1856, Trenton Falls, typi-
cal view, but scarce, on glass **135.00**
Muybridge
#318, The Golden Gate **80.00**
#880, Geyer Springs **35-45.00**
#1623, Indian scouts **250.00**
O'Sullivan, T.H., Anthony #826, Men's
Quarters **60.00**
Pond, C. L., #786, Mirror Lake **30.00**
Watkins, C. E.
Panoramic, #1338, from Telegraph
Hill **45-55.00**
San Francisco street scene, e.g.,
#767, panorama from Russian Hill   **55.00**
Trains, any **75-140.00**
Virginia City, NV, Panorama, new se-
ries **90.00**
Yosemite series, #1066, Yosemite
Falls **25-30.00**

Photographica
Camera, Houseworth #1107, wet plate
camera in Yosemite **75.00**
Comic, Keystone #423, many viewers
and cards in this comic "mouse" rou-
tine **15.00**
Gallery, American scenery, street with
gallery sign visible **50.00**
Photo Wagon, Weitfle's Photograph
Van, close view with sign on
wagon **75-1500.00**
Photography with stereo camera above
street, Keystone #8283, classic col-
lectible **65.00**
Viewing, Keystone #11917, looking
through viewer **10.00**

Railroad
American stereo, view in Penn Station   **15.00**
Centennial, 1876 Monorail, World's
Fair, scarce **65.00**
Keystone
#2367, loop at Georgetown, com-
mon **5.00**
#7090, interior of Baldwin Works . . **8.00**
#37509, The Chief, 1930s **75.00**
Kilburn
#135, pushing car up Jacob's Ladder   **7.00**
#432, large side view of locomotive   **35.00**
#779, train with engineer posed,
1870 . . . . **55.00**
#2941, silver ore train **5.00**
U & U
#52, train going through Pillars of
Hercules, common **7.00**
#6218, Royal Gorge, common **5.00**
Universal Photo Art #2876, Columbian
Express **20.00**

Unknown Maker, dramatic close-up of
a 1870 locomotive **75.00**

Religious
Bates, open *Bible*, St. Luke **3.00**
Keystone, Billy Sunday, evangelist **20.00**
Keystone, Kilburn, U & U, Holy Land,
Palestine, etc **1-2.00**
Pope, any **4-7.50**
Life of Christ, unmarked, usually set of
photos of drawings or lithographed
set, per set of 10-12 . . . . **7.00**
Shakers, Irving, view of people **50-75.00**

Risque
1820s, unmarked, typical "peek-a-
boo" **10-20.00**
Griffith #2427, two girls, arms around
each other, lightly clad **20.00**
Keystone, #9489, school girls retiring,
in nightgowns **7.00**
Nude, early, bare breast **45.00**
Nude, 1920s or 1930s **40.00**

Sets
Boxer Rebellion, U & U 1901, 72 cards,
rare **200.00**
Bullfight, U & U, set of 15 . . . . **100.00**
China, Stereo Travel, set of 100, unusual
subject **400.00**
Egypt, U & U set of 100, better subject,
typical **310.00**
France
Stereo Travel, set of 30, typical for this
publisher, popular country **70.00**
U & U, set of 100 . . . . **250.00**
Glacier Park, Forsyth, set of 30 . . . . **125-150.00**
India, U & U, set of 100 . . . . **250.00**
Italy, U & U, set of 100 . . . . **200.00**
Jerusalem, U & U, set of 30, poor sub-
ject **30-40.00**
Switzerland, U & U, set of 100, guide-
book and maps **200.00**
United States, U & U, set of 100, good
U. S. tour **350.00**
Wild Flowers, Keystone, 100, hand
tinted **400.00**
World Tour, Keystone
Set of 200, trip from U.S. around world
and back **350.00**
Set of 400 . . . .**500-700.00**
Set of 600, trip from U.S. around
world and back, oak cabinet **900-1,000.00**
Yellowstone, U & U, set of 30 . . . . .**90-100.00**
Yosemite, U & U, set of 30 . . . .**100-125.00**

Ship
Battleships
Griffith #2535, 1902, USS *Brooklyn*   **8.00**
Universal Photo Art, USS *Raleigh*,
common **7-9.00**

Cruiser, White #7422, 1901, USS *New York* 10.00

Deck View, American Stereo, 1899, USS *Iowa* 8.00

Foreign, Keystone #16090, HMS *Albemarie* 6.00

Riverboat, Anthony #7567, sternwheeler at Cincinnati 25.00

Sailboat, Anthony #22 or #5179, early view 15-20.00

Steamers
Pettit, Wilson, 1880 .... 15-20.00
Yukon, Keystone #24704, sternwheeler being loaded in Alaska 330-35.00

Steamships
Anthony #8691, *Bristol*, good average early view 15.00
London Stereo, *Great Eastern*, early view 75.00
Submarine, Keystone #16667, at San Diego 8.00

Survey
Amundsen, Keystone #13327, at Antoretie Glacier, 1911 .... 7.00
Gerlache, Keystone #13328, hunting seals at South Pole 6.00
Hayden, Jackson #796, people view, typical 22-25.00
Lloyd, Grand Canyon, U & U, at work on mountain, 1903 .... 25.00
Perry, Greenland, Keystone #13325, ships 6.00
Powell, #13, the wall, typical 10-20.00
Wheeler, William Bell
#14, Canon de Chelle, wall, 1873 .. 40.00
#15, Canon de Chelle, wall, 1872 .. 25.00

Tissue, French
Balloon, close view 60-70.00
Diablo, 1870s, devils, skeletons, etc., good shape with lots of "evil" 30.00
Interior scene, 1870s, minor damage, viewable 7.50
Interior scene, 1870s, nice stereo, pinpricked, no tears 20.00
Wedding, Young #7, typical US, wedding vows 10.00

War
Boer, U & U, artillery firing, typical view 7.00
Boxer Rebellion, U & U, 1901, typical view 4-7.00

Civil War
Anthony
#3031, Dunlop Home 20.00
#3365, Brady, Libby Prison, yellow mount 25.00
#3406, chair in which Lincoln was shot 60.00

Gardner #237, home of Rebel sharpshooter 45-50.00
Taylor & Huntington
#458, Conferdate fortifications ... 25.00
#2557, pontoon boats 25.00
#6705, powder magazine 35.00
Russo-Japanese, U & U #4380, general view of Port Arthur, typical view ... 5.00
Spanish American, U & U, typical view 5-12.00
World War I
Set of 100 .... 175.00
Set of 200 .... 300.00
Set of 300 .... 400.00

Whaling
Freeman, beached whales 50.00
Keystone
#14768T, floating whale station, common 10.00
#V27198T, whalers cruising, common 8.00
Nickerson, beached whales, rare 70.00
Unknown maker, beached whale .. 18-30.00

STEREO VIEWERS

Collecting Hints: Condition is the key in determining price. Undamaged wooden hood models are scarce and demand a premium price if made of bird's–eye maple. All original parts increases the value. Lots of engraving adds 20 to 30%.

Longer lenses are better than short ones. Lenses held in place by metal are better than those shimmed in by wood.

Because aluminum was the same price as silver in the late 19th century, aluminum viewers often are the more collectible.

History: There are many different types of stereo viewers. The familiar table viewer with an aluminum or wooden hood was the joint invention in 1860 of Oliver Wendell Holmes and Joseph Bates, a Boston photographer. This type of viewer also was made in a much scarcer pedestal model.

In hand viewers, three companies—Keystone, Griffith & Griffith, and Underwood & Underwood—produced viewers between 1899 and 1905 in the hundreds of thousands.

In the mid–1850s a combination stereo viewer and picture magnifier was developed in France and eventually made in England and the United States. The instrument was called a Graphascope. It usually consisted of three pieces and folded for storage. When set up, it had two round lenses for stereo viewing, a large round magnifying lens to view cabinet photographs and a slide, often with opaque glass, for viewing stereo glass slides. The height was adjustable.

A rotary or cabinet viewer was made from the late 1850s to about 1870. Becker is the best known maker. The standing floor models hold several hundred slides, the table models hold 50 to 100.

From the late 1860s to 1880s there were hundreds of different viewer designs. Models had folding wires, collapsible cases (Cortascope), pivoting lens to view postcards (Sears' Graphascope) and telescoping card holders. The cases also became ornate with silver, nickel and pearl trimmed in velvets and rosewood.

Reference: John Waldsmith, *Stereo Views: An Illustrated History and Price Guide,* Wallace–Homestead, 1991.

Collectors' Clubs: National Stereoscopic Association, PO Box 14801, Columbus, OH 43214; Stereo Club of Southern California, PO Box 2368, Culver City, CA 90231.

Binocular Style, Telebinocular, black
crinkle metal finish, excellent optics,
came with "book" box **45.00**
Counter Top Style, Sculptoscope,
Whiting, penny operated **600.00**
Hand, wood
   Folding handle, focusing slide, wire
   prong holder fold inward, c1890   **90.00**
   Keystone, wide dark brown metal
   hood, metal clip handle **75.00**
   Rectangular hood, tongue and groove
   edges, fancy edge trim, screw–on
   handle **100.00**
   Scissor device to focus, groove and
   wire device to hold card **125.00**
Pedestal, French or English, nickel
plated with velvet hood **450.00**
Stand, Bates–Holmes, paper or wood
hood **175.00**
Stereographascope, Sears Best, rotating
lens for photos or post cards **100.00**

STOCK AND BOND CERTIFICATES

Collecting Hints: Some of the factors that affect price are (1) date [with pre–1900 more popular and pre–1850 most desirable], (2) autographs of important persons [Vanderbilt, Rockefeller, J. P. Morgan, Wells and Fargo, etc.], (3) number issued [most bonds have number issued in text], and (4) attractiveness of the vignette.

Stocks and bonds are collected for a variety of reasons, among which are the graphic illustrations and the history of romantic times in America, including gold and silver mining, railroad history, and early automobile pioneers.

History: The use of stock to raise capital and spread the risk in a business venture dates back to England. Several American colonies were founded as joint venture stock companies. The New York Stock Exchange on Wall Street in New York City traces its roots to the late eighteenth century.

Stock certificates with attractive vignettes date to the beginning of the nineteenth century. As engraving and printing techniques developed, so did the elaborateness of the stock and bond certificates. Important engraving houses emerged among which were the American Bank Note Company and Rawdon, Wright & Hatch.

References: Norman E. Martinus and Harry L. Rinker, *Warman's Paper,* Wallace–Homestead, 1994; Gene Utz, *Collecting Paper: A Collector's Identification & Value Guide,* Books Americana, 1993; Bill Yatchman, *The Stock & Bond Collectors Price Guide,* published by author, 1985.

Periodical: *Bank Note Reporter,* 700 E. State St., Iola, WI 54990.

Collectors' Club: Bond and Share Society, 26 Broadway, New York, NY 10004.

BOND

Arlington Gas Co, $1000, state seal vi-
gnette, coupons, New Jersey, 1880,
issued **20.00**
Atchison, Topeka & Santa Fe RR, blue
$1000, two vignettes of railroad sta-
tion int., issued **18.00**
Baltimore & Annapolis Short Line RR,
$1000, engraved, two women and
street and trolley scene, 1906, issued   **48.00**
Broadway Surface RR, gray $1000, ea-
gle and flag vignette, New York City,
1885, issued **35.00**
Central New York & Western RR,
$1000, green and gold, engraved, old
train vignette, very decorative border,
pages of coupons, 1892, issued but
not canceled **85.00**
Columbus & Ninth Ave RR, $5000, en-
graved, fancy company name,
coupons, New York City, 1893, is-
sued **35.00**
Consolidated Edison Co of New York,
blue $1000, vignette of tower with
light on top with Brooklyn Bridge and
New York city in background, 1949,
thirty year, issued **7.50**
Constant Refining Co, $1000, orange,
large vignette, 1929 . . . .   **12.00**
Denver & Rio Grande Western RR,
$1000, engraved, two trains and sta-
tions, issued **125.00**

Ford International Capital Corporation,
1968, $1000, blue, black, and white   **12.00**
General Motors Corp, green $1000, vi-
gnette of streamlined car, truck, locomotive, three heads, and factory
building, coupons, 1954, issued ...   **15.00**
Lehigh Valley RR, different colors, vignette of steam locomotive in switch
yard with tower and workers, issued   **25.00**
Socony Mobil Oil Co, $1000, engraved
goddess and two hemispheres, issued   **12.00**
Southern Bell Telephone & Telegraph,
$1000, top vignette of person speak-
ing on phone with city and rural landscapes in background flanked by
seated goddesses, center vignette of
large bell, coupons, 1947, issued ...   **15.00**
Wisconsin Interurban System, green, orange, gold, state seal vignette,
coupons, 1917, issued but not can-
celed **45.00**

STOCK

American Antimony Company, Utah
Territory, 1883, vignette of eagle atop
beehive, flanked by Indian village
and locomotive passing through
town, second vignette of young girl   **75.00**
Ben–Hur Motor Car, 1917, issued but
not canceled
    Brown certificate, car and chariot vi-
    gnette **75.00**
    Green certificate, globe vignette ...   **75.00**
California Street Cable RR Co, cable car
vignette, punch canceled **125.00**
Chicago Cotton Manufacturing Co, or-
nate design in brown in center of certificate, place for revenue stamp, fac-
tory vignette, 1870, unissued **10.00**
Cincinnati, New Orleans & Texas
Pacific RR, gray and white certificate,
steam train vignette, issued
    1910s **18.00**
    1930s **13.00**
Continental Motors Corp, vignette of
car engine, issued, orange certificate   **15.00**
Egypt Silver Mining Company, Franklin,
ME, vignette of miners working with
pick and shovel, 1880s, unissued . .   **10.00**
Fairmount Park Transportation Co,
green certificate, Philadelphia, PA,
1900–02, issued **12.00**
Fairview Golden Boulder Mining Co,
brown certificate, gold nugget vi-
gnette, Nevada, 1900, unissued **12.00**
Fruit of the Loom, Inc, script certificate
for fractional share of common stock,
1938, green, black, and white **5.00**
Gambrinus Brewing Co, vignette of king
savoring a glass of beer, Columbus,
OH, 1909–13, issued **25.00**

**Mt. Tamalpais and Muir Woods Railway,
common stock, 1914, litho by H. S.
Crocker Co., 7⅜ x 10⅛", $185.00.**

General Public Utilities Corp (owner of
Three Mile Island), green certificate,
vignette of man and generator wheel,
issued **3.00**
Jantzen Knitting Mills, engraved, vi-
gnette of woman in early swim suit
diving into water, 1930s, issued **35.00**
Kaiser–Frazer Corp, blue or brown cer-
tificate, 1940s, issued **6.00**
Nashville, Chattanooga & St Louis RR,
bright pink certificate, railroad station
vignette, issued **10.00**
New York Central RR, brown certificate,
vignette of Commodore Vanderbuilt,
1940s, issued **10.00**
Northampton Brewery Corp, orange
certificate, engraved, vignette featuring woman, ship, and city skyline,
Pennsylvania, 1930s, issued **15.00**
Oakland Traction Co, orange certificate,
engraved, two vignettes of old trolley
cars, California, 1910s, issued **25.00**
Ottaquechee Woolen Co, Vermont,
1870s, unissued **4.50**
Pabst Brewing Co, green certificate, vi-
gnette of brewery, Milwaukee, WI,
1900s
    Issued and signed by Pabst as presi-
    dent **95.00**
    Unissued **25.00**
Pacific Railroad of Missouri, green cer-
tificate, vignette of train and mountains, 1875, issued but not canceled   **75.00**
Penn National Bank & Trust Co of
Reading, gray certificate, vignette of
colonial man, Pennsylvania, 1930, is-
sued but not canceled **15.00**
Pepsi–Cola United Bottlers, orange or
green certificate, vignette of goddess
holding world globe and Pepsi bottle
in oval medallion to left of her feet, is-
sued **10.00**
Piggly Wiggly Western States Co, or-
ange certificate, photo vignette of

early Piggly Wiggly food store, 1920s, issued 7.50
Plymouth Rock Mining Co, gray and white certificate, vignette of four miners working underground, Territory of New Mexico, 1880, issued 35.00
Rio Grande Southern RR, rust certificate, engraved, vignette of train coming out of mountain pass, signature of Otto Mears as president, Colorado, 1890s
Issued 250.00
Unissued 95.00
Santa Clara Valley Mill & Lumber Co, vignette of early lumber mill, California, 1873, unissued 15.00
Sentinel Radio Corp, green or brown certificate, vignette of goddess and two radio towers, 1956, issued 5.00
Submarine Signal Co, green certificate, vignette of ship on ocean, 1940, issued 15.00
Thomas B Jeffery Co of California, eagle vignette, c1910
Issued and canceled 125.00
Unissued 10.00
Tide Water and Southern RR Co, olive certificate, engraved, vignette of river boat at dock, Stockton, CA, 1910, unissued 28.00
Tuolumne County Water Co, California gold rush 1854–62 certificate, vignette of mining methods in use at time 75.00
Utica & Mohawk Valley Railway, engraved, street car vignette, c1900, unissued 25.00
Vallejo City Water Co, vignette of early Vallejo city area, California, 1868, unissued 15.00
Waldorf System, Inc, purple certificate, engraved, vignette of apple with motto in circle flanked by goddesses, issued 5.00
Wee–Wee Antic Gold, Silver, and Copper Mining Company, Stockton, CA, 1863, black and white, no cancellation marks, affixed revenue stamp 250.00

STUFFED TOYS

Collecting Hints: The collector tends to focus on one type of animal and collects material spanning a long time period. The company with the strongest collector following is Steiff.

Collectors stress very good to mint condition. Often stuffed toys had ribbons or clothing. All accessories must be intact to command full value.

History: The stuffed toy may have originated in Germany. Margarete Steiff GmbH of Germany began making stuffed toys for export beginning in 1880. By 1903 the teddy bear had joined Steiff's line and quickly worked its way to America. The first American teddy bears were made by the Ideal Toy Corporation. Not much is known about earlier manufacturers since companies were short lived and many toys have lost their labels.

The stuffed toy has enjoyed a favorite position in the American market. Some have music boxes inserted to enhance their appeal. Carnivals used stuffed toys as prizes. Since the 1960s America has been subjected to a wealth of stuffed toys imported from Japan, Taiwan, and China. These animals often are poorly made and are not popular among serious collectors.

References: Dottie Ayers and Donna Harrison, *Advertising Art of Steiff: Teddy Bears and Playthings,* Hobby House Press, 1990; Peggy and Alan Bialosky, *The Teddy Bear Catalog,* Workman Publishing, Revised Edition, 1984; Kim Brewer and Carol–Lynn Rössel Waugh, *The Official Price Guide To Antique & Modern Teddy Bears,* House of Collectibles, 1990; Pam Hebbs, *Collecting Teddy Bears,* Pincushion Press, 1992; Dee Hockenberry, *Collectible German Animals Value Guide: 1948–1968,* Hobby House Press, 1988; Dee Hockenberry, *Enchanting Friends: Collectible Poohs, Raggedies, Golliwoggs & Roosevelt Bears,* Schiffer Publishing, 1995; Margaret Fox Mandel, *Teddy Bears And Steiff Animals, First Series* (1984, 1993 value update), *Second Series* (1987, 1992 value update), and *Third Series* (1990), Collector Books; Terry and Doris Michaud, *Contemporary Teddy Bear Price Guide: Artists To Manufacturers,* Hobby House Press, 1992; Linda Mullins, *American Teddy Bear Encyclopedia,* Hobby House Press, 1995; Linda Mullins, *4th Teddy Bear And Friends Price Guide,* Hobby House Press, 1993; Linda Mullins, *Teddy Bears Past and Present, Volume II,* Hobby House Press, 1992; Christel and Rolf Pistorius, *Steiff: Sensational Teddy Bears, Animals, and Dolls,* Hobby House Press, 1991; Cynthia Powell, *Collector's Guide To Miniature Teddy Bears: Identification & Values,* Collector Books, 1994; Gustav Severin, *Teddy Bear: A Loving History of the Classic Childhood Companion,* Running Press, Courage Books, 1995; Carol J. Smith, *Identification & Price Guide To Winnie The Pooh Collectibles,* Hobby House Press, 1994; Jean Wilson, *Steiff Toys Revised,* Wallace–Homestead, 1989.

Periodicals: *National Doll & Teddy Bear Collector,* PO Box 4032, Portland, OR 97208; *Teddy Bear and Friends,* 6405 Flank Dr., Harrisburg, PA 17112; *Teddy Bear Review,* 170 Fifth Ave., New York, NY 10010.

Collectors' Clubs: Collectors Club for Classic Winnie The Pooh, 468 W. Alpine #10, Upland,

CA 91786; Good Bears Of The World, PO Box 13097, Toledo, OH 43613; Steiff Collectors Club, PO Box 798, Holland, OH 43528; Teddy Bear Boosters Club, 19750 SW Peavine Mtn. Rd., McMinnville, OR 97128.

Bear
Bellhop, 11", mohair, German	275.00
Cosy Orsi, 8" h	95.00
Eden, rattle, orig tags, 1970s	25.00
Ideal, 17", plush, brown, cream paws, plastic eyes, molded nose and mouth, tail squeaks, orig label	40.00
Knickerbocker, 21", mohair, brown, fully jointed	250.00
Roddy, 22", mohair, jointed limbs, mechanical tail moves head, English	400.00

Steiff
American Bear, Ralph Lauren	350.00
Chocolate Brown, 3½" h	225.00
Circus Dolly, 1987, gold, green, and purple	175.00
Bunny, Dakin, bean bag, glass eyes, 1977	25.00

Camel
| 8", tan plush, single hump, glass eyes, c1950 . . . . | 65.00 |
| 13½", Cosy, orig tags . . . . | 90.00 |

Cat
| Kliban . . . . | 35.00 |
| Siamese, 9", mohair, sitting, c1950 | 100.00 |

Siamese Cat, R. Dakin Co., San Francisco, 14" l, $10.00.

Tabby, Steiff	65.00
Tom, 5", black velvet body, mohair tail, glass eyes, sewn nose and mouth, c1960	85.00
Chick, Steiff	55.00

Deer
9", straw stuffed, mohair	28.00
15", Bambi, plush, Gund, 1953	60.00
Dinosaur, 14", multi–mohair, glass eyes, felt fins, 1960	100.00

Dog
Beagle
| 4", Steiff . . . . | 40.00 |
| 9", plush, glass eyes . . . . | 25.00 |

Collie, long and short mohair, glass eyes, sewn nose, felt mouth	125.00
Dalmatian, 5½", jeweled crown, red taffeta cape, Steiff, c1950	175.00
Laika, Steiff	292.00

Poodle
10", plush, c1960	125.00
12", curly, gray, standing, 1960 . .	15.00
Schnauzer, 11", mohair, gray, 1950s	100.00
Scottie, 18"	39.00

Duck
| 7", yellow and green, felt beak . . . . | 60.00 |
| 8", pull toy, felt and velvet, metal wheels . . . . | 275.00 |

Elephant
8", acrylic, gray and pink, Steiff, c1950	60.00
14½", musical, sitting, gray and white, 1960	30.00
Elf, 10", felt body, mohair beard, glass eyes, 1930s	100.00

Frog
4", felt, orig neck tag	45.00
9", green, velvet top, white satin bottom, c1960	12.00
Giraffe, 11", gold and orange mohair, felt ears, glass eyes, 1950s	70.00
Grasshopper, 18", mohair, felt clothes, glass eyes, 1950s	100.00
Hamster, 5", mohair, gold, jointed head, glass eyes, felt paws and mouth	48.00
Kangaroo, 20", baby in pouch, Steiff . .	475.00
Lamb, 10", black, curly, glass eyes, embroidered features, ribbon at neck . .	110.00
Leopard Cub, 18", plush, green glass eyes, paper	150.00
Lion, 45", Leo, mohair, reclining, orig tag, c1955	600.00
Lobster, 7", felt, orange, glass eyes . . .	45.00

Monkey
Dakin, Astronaut, mohair, glass eyes, elaborate velvet uniform, rocket, 1961	100.00
Mango, Steiff	120.00
Mohair, 8", jointed, glass eyes, felt clothes, 1953	90.00
Plush, 18", brown, curly, swivel neck and bent arms, felt paws, glass inset eyes, paper label, Steiff	75.00
Straw stuffed, rubber face	40.00
Mouse, Annalee, Christmas Caroler, elaborate dress, orig tags	70.00
Ocelot, 6½ x 13", gold and black mohair, sewn nose and mouth, 1955 . .	95.00
Owl, Wittie, small, Steiff	165.00
Penguin, Steiff, 5" h, orig tag	55.00
Pig, 6½", mohair, pink, felt mouth and tail, cord on neck	85.00
Polar Bear, 16", champagne plush, straw fill, movable arms and legs, long snout, black button eyes, stitch face, leather collar, c1920	300.00

Porcupine, mohair, brown, felt ears and
feet, jointed head	**48.00**
Rabbit, 19", "Ruth the Rabbit", gold
plush, standing, jointed, purple bead
eyes, long lashes, sheer organdy over
flowered print costume, cloth tag,
c1934	**525.00**
Ram, 7½" h, woolly coat, black velvet
trim, glass eyes	**35.00**
Reindeer, mohair, Steiff	**70.00**
Seal
5½", mohair, Steiff	**45.00**
6", Floppy Robby, soft stuffing, sewn
eyes, c1950	**65.00**
10", black fur, black glass eyes	**85.00**
Tiger
13", Shere Kahn, Disney character,
Steiff	**140.00**
16", mohair, reclining, orig button,
Steiff	**400.00**
Troll, two headed	**75.00**
Turtle, 5", mohair body, vinyl shell, glass
eyes, Steiff	**65.00**
Walrus, 4", mohair, plastic tusks, 1950s	**50.00**
Wild Boar, 8" l, Steiff	**210.00**
Wittie, Steiff	**165.00**
Zebra, 8", mohair, black and white,
1950s	**70.00**

SUPER HEROES

Collecting Hints: Concentrate on a single super
hero. Because Superman, Batman, and Wonder
Woman are the most popular, new collectors are
advised to focus on other characters or one of the
modern super heroes. Nostalgia is a principal
motivation for many collectors; hence, they pay
prices based on sentiment rather than true market value for some items.

Comics are a fine collectible but require careful handling and storage. An attractive display requires a three–dimensional object. Novice collectors are advised to concentrate on these first
before acquiring too much of the flat paper material.

History: The super hero and comic books go
hand in hand. Superman made his debut in 1939
in the first issue of *Action Comics*, six years after
Jerry Siegel and Joe Shuster conceived the idea of
a man who flew. A newspaper strip, radio show,
and movies followed. The Superman era produced a wealth of super heroes, among them
Batman, Captain Marvel, Captain Midnight, The
Green Hornet, The Green Lantern, The Shadow,
and Wonder Woman.

These early heroes had extraordinary strength
and/or cunning and lived normal lives as private
citizens. A wealth of merchandising products sur-

round these early super heroes. Their careers
were enchanced further when television chose
them as heroes for Saturday morning viewing as
well as in prime time.

The Fantastic Four—Mr. Fantastic, The Human
Torch, The Invisible Girl, and The Thing—introduced a new type of super hero, the mutant.
Among the most famous of this later period are
Captain America, Spiderman and The Hulk.
Although these characters appear in comic form,
the number of secondary items generated is
small. Television has helped to promote a few of
the characters, but the list of mutant super heroes
is close to a hundred.

References: Joe Desris, *The Golden Age of
Batman: The Greatest Covers of Detective
Comics From The '30s To The '50s*, Artabras,
1994; Steven H. Kimball, *Greenberg's Guide To
Super Hero Toys, Volume I*, Greenberg
Publishing, 1988; Alex G. Malloy and Stuart W.
Wells, III, *Comic Collectibles & Their Values*,
Wallace–Homestead, 1995; Jeff Rovin, *The
Encyclopedia of Super Heroes*, Facts on File
Publications, 1985.

Collectors Clubs: Air Heroes Fan Club, 19205
Seneca Ridge Club, Gaithersburg, MD 20879;
Batman TV Series Fan Club, PO Box 107, Venice,
CA 90291.

See: Comic Books, Radio Characters, and
Personalities.

Aquaman
Costume, Ben Cooper, orig box,
1967	**198.00**
Game, Justice League of America,
Hasbro, 1967	**180.00**
Jigsaw Puzzle, Whitman, 1967	**40.00**
Batman and Robin
Bank, porcelain, figural, mint	**45.00**
Batmobile, 11½" 1, metal, blue body,
red accents, yellow interior, seated
Batman and Robin figures, bump–
and–go action, battery operated,
ASC, Japan, c1966	**200.00**
Batplane, 10½" 1, plastic, battery op-
erated, orig box, Azrak–Hamway,
copyright National Periodical
Publications 1975	**75.00**
Colorforms, diecut vinyl, Batmobile
and skyline illus, orig box and in-
structions, Colorforms Toys, copy-
right 1976	**10.00**
Costume, molded plastic full face
mask, blue and yellow fabric cape,
Ben Cooper, orig box, National
Periodical copyrights 1965 and
1966	**35.00**
Figure, 4" h, Robin, jumping, soft rub-
ber, string attached to neck, Fun
Things, unopened, copyright

Coloring Book, Batman, Whitman Publishing, unused, 8 x 11", 1974, $17.50.

National Periodical Publications 1966 .... **28.00**
Grenade Gun, plastic, 17" 1, green, gold trim, blue plastic grenade, orig display card, Lincoln International, copyright National Periodical Publications, 1966 .... **95.00**
Jokermobile, 3" 1, diecast metal, Mettoy Co, unopened, Corgi, copyright DC Comics, Inc 1978 ..... **23.00**
Lamp, figural, Bat Cave **75.00**
Marionette, 14" h, Robin, plastic head, fabric body, marked "Batman Characters," National Periodical Publications copyright, 1966 .... **100.00**
Model, Batmobile, #486–98, Aurora Plastics Corp, complete, unassembled, copyright 1966 .... **115.00**
Night Light, 2½ x 2½", figural, plastic, Snapit, copyright National Periodical Publications 1966 .... **25.00**
Pencil Box, gun shape, orig contents **20.00**
Pennant, 29" l, felt, black, white lettering, full color illus, copyright 1966 .... **25.00**
Pinball Game, 10 x 21½ x 1", plastic and litho metal, orig box, Marx, National Periodical copyright 1966 **100.00**
Shooting Arcade, metal and plastic, black gun, Marx, 1966 .... **25.00**
Soaky Bottle, 10" h, Batman, soft plastic, copyright 1966 National Periodical Publications, Inc **75.00**
Sponge, 5" d, blue Batman illus, yellow ground, orig pkg, copyright National Periodical Publications 1966 .... **20.00**
Stationery, 7¼ x 10½", bond paper, purple bat symbol and trim, yellow ground, purple "Bat Mail" symbol

on envelopes, five sheets and envelopes, c1966 .... **18.00**
Trash Can, 1966 .... **35.00**
Captain America
Badge, Sentinels of Liberty **330.00**
Coloring Book, Whitman, unused, 1966 .... **32.00**
Figure, 12" h, plastic, flying Trans–Ogram, orig display card, 1966 .. **52.00**
Hand Puppet, molded soft vinyl head, Imperial Toy Corp, Marvel Comics Group copyright 1978 ... **15.00**
Iron–On Transfer, Kirby art, unused, 1960s **10.00**
Jigsaw Puzzle, 14 x 18", attacking zombies illus, boxed Whitman Marvel Comics Group copyright 1976 .... **18.00**
Captain Marvel
Book, *Captain Marvel and the Return of the Scorpion*, 4 x 5½", soft cov, 192 pgs, black and white illus, Fawcett Publications, Inc copyright 1941 .... **65.00**
Cereal Bowl, plastic, white, "Captain Marvel/Shazam," 1973 .... **30.00**
Iron–On Transfer, tissue paper sheets, orig black, white, and red envelope, set of 6, c1940 .... **28.00**
Pencil Clip, silvered brass, cream color ground, red and blue portrait illus, "Captain Marvel/Shazam," 1940s **75.00**
Pennant **95.00**
Puzzle, Picture Puzzle #1 ...... **35.00**
Rocket Raider, punch–out figures, Captain Marvel and missile, stand–up, cardboard, Reed, 1940 **98.00**
Ski Toy, punch out, mint in package **8.50**
Captain Midnight
Better Little Book, *Captain Midnight and the Secret Squadron vs the Terror of the Orient*, Whitman, #1458, 1942 .... **50.00**
Decoder, 1¾" d, disc, plastic, silvered, "SQ," 1955–56 .... **175.00**
Ring, Flight Commander, eagle and shield design brass bands, wing and propeller design top, marked "Captain Midnight Super Code 3," 1940–41 .... **185.00**
Shoulder Patch, orig wrapper **40.00**
Whistle, plastic, dark blue, logo, code wheel, "Captain Midnight's SS 1947" **75.00**
The Flash
Figure, 3" h, plastic, hp, Ideal, 1967 **160.00**
Game, Justice League of America, Hasbro, 1967 .... **300.00**
Glass, Pepsi premium, 1973 ...... **29.00**
Jigsaw Puzzle, battle scene illus, Whitman, 1967 .... **59.00**

Ring, flasher, Flash running/Flash punching villain, 1960s **20.00**

Green Hornet

Book, *The Case Of The Disappearing Doctor,* Whitman, 212 pgs **20.00**

Car, Green Hornet Black Beauty, diecast black metal, orig box, Corgi **400.00**

Fork and Spoon, silvered metal, vertical lettering and Hornet illus on handle, Imperial, c1966 .... **25.00**

Glass, 4¾" h, Green Hornet and Kato, copyright 1966 Greenway Productions, Inc **150.00**

Lunch Box, King–Seely Thermos Co, Greenway Productions, Inc copyright 1967 .... **100.00**

Magic Rub–Off Set, eight 8½ x 11" glossy cardboard pictures, crayons, tissues, orig box, Whitman, copyright National Periodical Publications 1966 .... **100.00**

Mug, white, color illus, 1966 ...... **35.00**

Record, *The Horn Meets The Hornet,* Al Hirt, orig jacket **20.00**

Tee Shirt, Hornet logo, 1966 ...... **39.00**

The Phantom

Coloring Book, Ottenheimer, unused, 1965 .... **42.00**

Costume, Collegeville, purple silk, orig box, 1956 .... **200.00**

Game, Trans O gram, Phantom Skull ring, diecut cardboard figures, sealed, 1965 .... **240.00**

Model Kit, Revell, unassembled, 1965 .... **190.00**

Superman

Air Freshener, color illus, orig unopened display card, Car–Freshener Corp, copyright 1978 DC Comics, Inc **15.00**

Bank, dime register, 2½" sq, metal, blue and red lettering, yellow ground, Superman illus, 1940s ... **80.00**

Bedspread **35.00**

Button, Superman Club of America **50.00**

Candy Box, 6 x 2", multicolor, 1966 **12.00**

Cap, nautical, cotton twill, glossy black vinyl visor, 1960s **60.00**

Centerpiece, 10" h, stiff cardboard, diecut, red tissue paper honeycomb base, Hallmark, c1996 .... **25.00**

Disc, 2" d, plastic, blue, Clark Kent/Superman flasher portrait center, "Happy Birthday 50 Years," DC Comics, Inc copyright 1982 ..... **8.00**

Figure, eyes light up, orig card **28.00**

Fork **20.00**

Glass, 4¼" h, Superman Finds the Spaceship, light blue continuous illus, pink lettering, National Periodical Publications copyright 1964 .... **50.00**

Hand Puppet, Ideal, 1965 .... **30.00**

Magic Slate, 8½ x 14", stiff cardboard, color illus, Whitman copyright 1965 .... **50.00**

Mug, 4" h, plastic, insulated, red and yellow Superman symbol, blue ground, white trim, Nestles' premium, DC Comics copyright 1944, c1980 .... **10.00**

Patch, 2 x 2½", Supermen of America, premium, 1940s **300.00**

Pillow Case, Superman flying, saving Lois Lane illus, 1966 .... **40.00**

Poster, 27 x 41", Superman at Bay, 1948 .... **100.00**

Record Player **25.00**

Scrapbook, 10½ x 14½", spiral bound, black and white movie star pictures, Superman, Inc copyright 1940 .... **100.00**

Wonder Woman

Action Figure, 12½" h, orig unopened blister card, Mego, copyright 1979 Marvel Comics Group **75.00**

Costume, Ben Cooper, orig box, 1976 **15.00**

Doll, 12" h, Steve Trevor, pilot uniform, orig box, Mego **70.00**

Model Kit, Aurora, unassembled, 1965 .... **400.00**

Planter, ceramic, 1978 .... **15.00**

Tattoo, unused, 1966 .... **50.00**

SWANKYSWIGS

Collecting Hints: Ideally select glasses whose pattern is clear and brightly colored. Rarer patterns include Carnival, Checkerboard, and Texas Centennial. Look–alike patterns from other manufacturers include the Rooster's Head, Cherry, Diamond over Triangle, and Circus patterns. The look–alike patterns date from the 1930s to the 1950s–1960s.

History: Swankyswigs are decorated glass containers that were filled with Kraft Cheese Spreads. The first Swankyswigs date from the early 1930s. Production was discontinued during the last days of World War II because the paints were needed for the war effort. Production was resumed after the war ended. Several new patterns were introduced including Posy or Cornflower No. 2 (1947), Forget–Me–Not (1948), and Tulip No. 3 (1950). The last colored pattern was Bi–Centennial Tulip (1975).

In the mid–1970s, several copycat patterns emerged including: Wildlife Series (1975) and Sportsman Series (1976), most likely Canadian varieties; Rooster's Head, Cherry; Diamond over Triangle; and Circus. Kraft Cheese Spread is still available today, but in crystal–type glass.

Swankyswigs were very popular with economy–minded ladies of the Depression era and used as tumblers and juice containers. They served as perfect companions to Depression glass table services and also helped to chase away the Depression blues.

The first designs were hand applied. When the popularity of Swankyswigs increased, more new and intricate machine–made patterns were introduced. Designs were test marketed. As a result of limited distribution, designs that failed are hard to identify and find.

The lack of adequate records about Swankyswigs makes it very difficult to completely identify all patterns. Since 1979, quite a few look–alikes have appeared. Although these glasses were similar, only Kraft glasses are considered Swankyswigs.

References: Gene Florence, *Collectible Glassware From The 40's, 50's, 60's: An Illustrated Value Guide, Second Edition,* Collector Books, 1994; M. D. Fountain, *Swankyswigs, Price Guide,* published by author, 1979; Ian Warner, *Swankyswigs, A Pattern Guide Checklist, Revised,* Depression Glass Daze, 1988, 1992 value update.

Collectors' Club: Swankyswig Club, 201 Alvena, Wichita, KS 67203.

Advisor: M. D. Fountain.

Pricing Note: If a Swankyswig retains its original label, add $4.00 to the value of the glass. Glasses with labels or original lids are scarcer than the checkerboards.

Antique
Black, coffeepot and trivets	4.25
Brown, coal bucket and clock	4.00
Orange, crib and butter churn	2.25
Bands, black and red	3.00
Bicentennial, 1938 type tulip, red, yellow or green, coin dot design, 1975	10.00
Bustlin Betsy	2.25
Carnival, Fired on Fiesta colors, dark blue, orange, yellow, and light green	7.50
Checkerboard, green, red, and dark blue	25.00
Daisies, red daisies on top row, white in middle, green leaves	3.00
Dots & Circles, black, blue, green, or red	4.50

Kiddie Cup or Animal
Black, pony and duck	2.25
Blue, pig and bear	2.00
Brown, deer and squirrel	2.00
Dark Blue, pig and bear	2.25
Green, kitten and bunny	2.00
Orange, puppy and rooster	2.00
Red, bird and elephant	2.00

Modern Flowers, dark and light blue, red, or yellow
Cornflower	3.00
Forget–me–not	3.00
Jonquil, yellow, green leaves	3.00
Posy	3.00

Kiddie Kup, chipmunk, brown, white trim, $1.75.

Tulip, dark and light blue, red, or yellow flowers, green leaves	
No. 1, 1937, white leaves	6.00
No. 2, 1938, six mold bands around top	20.00
No. 3, four molded bands around top	3.00
Violets, blue flowers, green leaves . .	2.00
Sailboat, red, green, or dark blue, racing or sailing	20.00
Star, black, dark blue, green, or red . . .	5.00
Texas Centennial, cowboy, riding bucking horse on one side, Texas State Seal on other, black, dark blue, green, and red	9.00

SWAROVSKI CRYSTAL

Collecting Hints: Swarovski crystal figurines from Austria have sophisticated designs skillfully manufactured in high–quality lead crystal. The first mark was a block–style SC. In 1989 the mark was changed to a swan, augmented with the letters SCS. Marks on larger items also include the name Swarovski. SCS figurines are further identified with the SCS logo, the year, and the designer's initials. The first SCS logo featured an eidelweiss flower above the SCS monogram. With rare exceptions, Swarovski crystal figurines are not individually numbered, but sometimes have been autographed by the artist with an engraved signature, usually accompanied by the date. Generally, an artist's signature will enhance the desirability of a figurine, but is not reflected in a significantly higher value.

Some designs were distributed regionally, making pursuit of retired items an interesting challenge that spans the globe. While some items were produced in a European version and a US version, many items were offered only in one area. Animal figures have been the most popular among collectors, and the US market has seen several of these crystal critters that were not offered in other countries. These are among the most sought after items among collectors worldwide. Many Swarovski crystal items are members of a larger family grouping, and some collectors pursue their collection by families. Figurines sold in a set do not command higher prices than individual transactions. Many items featuring metal trim were first available in both rhodium (white metal) and then in a gold version.

Condition is of the utmost importance. Broken, chipped, or scratched crystal is almost impossible to sell to collectors. Edges of some pieces, particularly the fins of the dolphins and whales, are not crisply polished where the original molding process leaves these edges a bit uneven. Occasionally the glue joints will contain small bubbles. Neither wavy edges from molding or bubbles in the glue joint should be considered flaws.

Swarovski collectors are particularly keen to obtain the correct original box when purchasing a figurine on the secondary market. Most Swarovski silver crystal items were sold in a cylinder box with plastic ends. In order to be considered correct and complete, the original product identification sticker must still be present on the box. For items in the Swarovski Collectors Society limited edition series, the certificate of authenticity should also be present. All Swarovski silver crystal items are packed inside the carton within a fitted foam insert that is designed to cushion the article. While there is a market for items that do not have the complete original packaging, prices are compromised.

History: The Swarovski family has been perfecting the glassmaker's art in Wattens, Austria, since 1895. The company has produced high quality crystal stones for the costume jewelry industry for decades, manufactures premium quality optics, and also is one of the world's leading producers of abrasives. The company also produces costume jewelry, ranging from the inexpensive Savvy line to the Daniel Swarovski boutique collection which includes haute couture accessories such as purses and gloves.

Collectible figurines and desk items were introduced in 1977, when a crystal mouse was the original design and a spiny crystal hedgehog followed shortly thereafter. Featuring lead content of 30%+, (with some older packaging stating 32% PbO), these "silver crystal" decorative accessories have attracted a following of over 200,000 dedicated collectors worldwide and the line has expanded to include many different animals and other crystal objects.

The Swarovski Collectors Society (SCS) was created in 1987. SCS members are offered the opportunity to purchase an annual limited edition figurine. To date, the annual SCS items have been designed in series of three figurines that share a common theme. The first theme was

"Caring and Sharing" and all figurines in the series show a pair of birds. The second theme was "Mother and Child," and the figurines in that series show a mother sea mammal and her offspring. The most recent theme has been "Inspiration Africa," which started with an elephant and ends with a lion. In 1995, an eagle was produced in an edition of 10,000 pieces, each serially numbered.

References: Swarovski, *Swarovski, The Magic of Crystal*, Harry N. Abrams, 1995; Tom and Jane Warner, *Warner's Blue Ribbon Book on Swarovski Silver Crystal*, published by authors, 1994, revised 1995.

Collectors' Club: Swarovski Collectors Society, 2 Slater Rd., Cranston, RI 02920.

Periodicals: *Swan Seekers Marketplace*, 4118 E. Vernon Ave., Phoenix, AZ 85008; *Swan Seekers News*, 4118 E. Vernon Ave., Phoenix, AZ 85008; *Swarovski Collector*, General Wille Strasse 88, SH-8706 Feldmeilen, Switzerland.

Advisor: Maret Webb.

Reproduction Alert: As far as collectors know, there are no counterfeit articles being passed off as Swarovski. There are, however, several imitators. Another company's figurines are made of 24% lead crystal parts which are available from Swarovski's Strass chandelier catalog. The telltale sign of this type of figurine will be the presence of small holes in the crystal pieces, lack of the Swarovski logo, and often unrefined design and craftsmanship of assembly.

Versions of a particular design which might incorporate a different element or be assembled differently than the widely acknowledged form of a figurine are an interesting pursuit, but harbor the risk of fraudulent items being offered by unscrupulous dealers who manipulate parts to create fantasy items. Recently, the Swarovski company has introduced replicas of several early designs. The replica designs are sufficiently different from the originals to be readily identifiable. Among other differences, original designs will always have the SC mark while replica designs will bear the swan trademark.

Note: Prices listed below are for items in perfect condition, presence of complete original packaging, and enclosures, without which prices are compromised 10% to 35%.

ACCESSORIES

Apple, photo, apple hinged at side,
  when top is tilted back, it reveals a
  photograph
  King Size, 60mm d, SC logo
    #7504nr060, gold **300.00**
    #7504nr060R, rhodium **350.00**

Large Size, 50mm d
#7504nr050, gold, SC or swan logo **180.00**
#7504nr050, rhodium, SC logo . . **225.00**
Small Size, 30mm d
#7504nr030, gold, SC or swan
logo **180.00**
#7504nr030R, rhodium, SC logo **225.00**
Ashtray, #7461nr100, sculpted crystal,
3⅜″ d, SC or swan logo **225.00**
Bell, large, #7467nr071000, 5¾″ h, SC
or swan logo **125.00**
Blush Brush, prototype item, black bris-
tles, row of rhinestones around fer-
rule, crystal ball handle, large SC logo
on end **885.00**
Candleholder
#7600nr116, for 5 candles, found
with sockets or pickets, SC logo **1,200.00**
#7600nr130, for 4 candles, found
with sockets or pickets, SC logo **1,050.00**
#7600nr131, small, prickets, set of
six, ¹⁵⁄₁₆″ h, SC logo **350.00**
#7600nr136001, gold metal foliage,
pineapple, SC logo **425.00**
#7600nr136002, rhodium metal fo-
liage, pineapple, SC logo **475.00**
Christmas Ornament
1981, not dated, crystal snowflake,
hexagonal metal trim ring and neck
chain, hexagonal ring is stamped
"SC" at top on back side, orig blue
velour pouch, silver logo box,
called the "First Annual Edition,"
only ornament produced in the
Silver Crystal line **350.00**
1987, dated, Giftware Suite, etched
baroque teardrop shape, first in
"Holiday Etching" series, no mark **150.00**
Cigarette Holder, #7463nr062, sculpted
crystal, 2⅜″ h, SC or swan logo **110.00**
Grapes, large, #7550nr30015, cluster of
thirty 1⅛″ d clear grapes, clear stem,
SC logo, USA only **1,000.00**
Lighter, #7462nr062, 3½″ h, chrome
lighter in crystal base, SC or swan
logo **275.00**
Paperweight
Atomic, 2¾″ h, hexagonal facets, SC
logo, often found without logo,
sometimes paper label on felted
bottom
Bermuda Blue, #7454nr600, color
shades from dark to light blue . . **950.00**
Clear, #7454nr60095 . . . . **700.00**
Barrel, 2⅝″ h, rect facets that line up
vertically, SC logo, often found
without logo, sometimes paper label on felted bottom
Bermuda Blue, #7453nr60088,
color shades from dark to light
blue **400.00**
Clear, #7453nr60095 . . . . **240.00**

Carousel, 2¾″ h, flared sides, vertical
facets, SC logo, often found without logo, sometimes paper label on
felted bottom
Clear, #7451nr60095 . . . . **800.00**
Vitrail, medium color, color
strongest when viewed from top,
shades from lime green to
fuschia **1,000.00**
Cone, 3⅛″ h, facets that spiral around
cone, SC or swan logo
Bermuda Blue, #7452nr600, color
shades from dark to light blue . . **275.00**
Clear, #7452nr600878 . . . . **175.00**
Vitrail, medium color, color
strongest when viewed from top,
shades from lime green to
fuschia **175.00**
SCS dealer, 50mm d, SCS eidelweiss
logo in blue **225.00**
SCS member gift, 40mm d, SCS eidel-
weiss logo in blue **65.00**
Picture Frame
Oval, #7505nr75G, 3″ h, gold trim,
SC or swan logo **275.00**
Square, #7506nr60, gold or rhodium
trim, SC or swan logo **225.00**
Pineapple, rhodium metal foliage
Large, #7507nr105002, 4⅛″ h, SC
logo **400.00**
Small, #7507nr060002, 2½″ h **130.00**
Salt and Pepper Shakers, pr,
#7508nr068034, 2⅜″ h, rhodium
screw off tops, SC logo **300.00**
Schnapps Glass, #7468nr039000, ap-
prox 2″ h, SC or swan logo
Europe, set of 3 . . . . **180.00**
USA, set of 6 . . . . **275.00**
Treasure Box, cov
Butterfly on removable lid
Heart shape, #7465nr52/100, SC
or swan logo **175.00**
Oval shape, #7466nr063100, SC
logo **300.00**
Round shape, #7464nr50/100, SC
logo **200.00**
Flowers on removable lid
Heart shape, #7465nr52, SC logo **175.00**
Oval shape, #7466nr063000, SC
or swan logo **225.00**
Round shape, #7464nr50, SC or
swan logo **150.00**
Vase, #7511nr70, 2⅞″ h, sculpted crys-
tal, three frosted crystal flowers, SC or
swan logo **140.00**

FIGURINES

Bear
Giant, #7636nr112, 4½″ h, SC mark
only, USA only, SC logo **1,300.00**

King Size, #7637nr92, 3¾" h, USA
only, SC logo **1,100.00**
Mini, #7670nr32, 1⅛" h, SC logo . . **130.00**
Bee, crystal and metal bee feeding on
crystal lotus flower, 4" w, SC logo
#7553nr100, gold metal bee **1,500.00**
#7553nr200, silver metal bee **1,500.00**
Butterfly
1" h, mini, #7671nr30, crystal, metal
antennae, no base, USA only, SC
logo **85.00**
4" w, crystal and metal butterfly feeding on crystal lotus flower, SC
logo
#7551nr100, gold metal butterfly **650.00**
#7551nr200, silver metal butterfly **1,500.00**
Cat
Large, #7634nr70, 2⅞" h, SC or swan
logo **100.00**
Medium, #7634nr52, 2" h, flexible
metal tail, SC logo **375.00**
Mini, #7659nr31, 1¼" h, flexible
metal tail, SC or swan logo **65.00**
Chicken, mini, #7651nr20, ⅞" h, coni-
cal metal beak and metal feet, SC
logo **80.00**
Dachshund, metal tail
Large, #7641nr75, 3" l, rigid, limp, or
gently arched, SC or swan logo . . **90.00**
Mini, #7672nr42, 1¼" l, SC logo ... **150.00**
Dog, Pluto (name on European list), SC
or swan logo **90.00**
Duck
Large, #7653nr75, 3" l, crystal beak,
USA only, SC logo **240.00**
Medium, #7653nr55, 2⅛" l, silver
beak, USA only, SC logo **100.00**
Mini, #7653nr45, 1⅞" l, silver beak,
SC logo **80.00**
Elephant
Dumbo
#7640nr100, 1990, black eyes,
clear hat, only 3,000 made, most
have swan logo, few unmarked **1,000.00**
#7640nr100001, 1993, blue eyes,
frosted hat, swan logo and
Disney copyright symbol **240.00**
Large
#7640nr40, 2" h, frosted tail, swan
logo **100.00**
#7640nr55, 2½" h, flexible metal
tail, SC logo **165.00**
Falcon Head
Large, #7645nr100, 4" h, SC or swan
logo **1,200.00**
Small, #7645nr45, 1¾" h, SC or swan
logo **130.00**
Frog, #7642nr48
Black eyes and clear crown, SC or
swan logo **90.00**
Clear eyes and clear crown, usually
found with SC logo **225.00**

Hedgehog, silver whiskers
King, #7630nr60, 2⅜" h including
spines, 60mm body, SC logo, USA
only **400.00**
Large, #7630nr50, 2" h including
spines, 50mm body, SC logo,
worldwide distribution **130.00**
Medium, #7630nr40, 1¾" h includ-
ing spines, 40mm body, found only
with SC mark, worldwide distribution **110.00**
Small, #7630nr30, 1¼" h including
spines, 30mm body, SC logo, USA
only **360.00**
Hummingbird, crystal and metal hummingbird feeding in crystal lotus
flower, 4" w, SC logo
#7552nr100, gold metal humming-
bird, green stones on wings **900.00**
#7552nr200, silver metal humming-
bird, red stones on wings **2,000.00**
Mallard, #7647nr80, 3½" l, frosted
beak, SC or swan logo **135.00**
Mouse, silver whiskers, metal coil tail
King, #763nr60, 3¾" h to top of ears,
60mm body, square base, USA
only, SC logo **700.00**
Large, #763nr50, 2⅞" h to top of ears,
50mm body, square base, USA
only, SC mark **250.00**
Mini, #7655nr23, 1³⁄₁₆" h, SC logo . . **90.00**
Small, #763nr30, 1¾" h to top of
ears, 30mm body, octagonal base,
SC or swan logo **125.00**
Pig, large, #7638nr65, 1¾" l, crystal "J"
shaped tail, SC logo **200.00**
Rabbit, ears lay flat on top of head, SC
logo
Large, #7652nr45, 1½" h **180.00**
Mini, #7652nr20, 1" h **85.00**
Sparrow, silver metal open beak
Large, #7650nr32, 1¼" h, SC logo . . **140.00**
Mini, #7650nr20, ¾" h, SC or swan
logo **65.00**
Swan, mini, #7658nr27, 1" h, delicate
crystal neck connected to body, two
wings, tail, SC logo **125.00**
Turtle, king size, #7632nr75, 3" l, green
eyes, SC logo **250.00**

SWAROVSKI COLLECTORS SOCIETY ITEMS

Anniversary Figurine, 1991, Birthday
Cake for SCS 5th anniversary,
#003–0168678, cake on pedestal,
one candle in center, SCS swan logo **125.00**
Limited Edition Figurine
1987, Togetherness, Lovebirds,
#do1x861, two lovebirds on tree
stump, cantilevered branch, SCS
eidelweiss mark on bottom of tree **3,500.00**

1988, Partnership, Woodpeckers, #do1x881, two woodpeckers on tree trunk, orig hexagonal 3½" w beveled edge mirror, first SCS logo on top surface in white, SCS eidel-weiss mark **1,200.00**
1989, Amour, Turtledoves, #d01x891, two doves on tree branch shaped like arch, SCS swan mark **700.00**
1990, Lead Me, Dolphins, #d01x901, mother and baby dolphins riding crest of wave, SCS swan mark . . **1,000.00**
1991, Care For Me, Seals, #d01x911, mother and baby harp seal on ice floe, no whiskers, SCS swan mark   **360.00**
1992, Save Me, Whales, #d01x921, mother and baby whales breaching the surf, noses in air, SCS swan mark **330.00**
1993, Inspiration Africa, Elephant, #d01x931, single bull elephant, frosted tusks, optional wood display pedestal, SCS swan mark . . . **700.00**
Renewal Gift
1988, Cactus, almost 1" h, three flowers, SCS eidelweiss mark **200.00**
1989, keychain, 15mm crystal ball, SCS swan logo on rhodium chain   **50.00**
1990, Chaton, large diamond, 1" d, swan logo **80.00**

TAYLOR, SMITH, AND TAYLOR

Collecting Hints: Collector interest focuses primarily on the LuRay line, introduced in 1938 and named after Virginia's Luray Caverns. The line actually utilized forms from the Empire and Laurel lines. Pieces from the Coral–Craft line are very similar in appearance to pink LuRay. Do not confuse the two.

Vistosa, introduced in 1938, is another example of the California patio dinnerware movement that featured bright, solid color pieces. Unfortunately, the number of forms was restricted. As a result, many collectors shy away from it.

Pebbleford, a plain colored ware with sand–like specks, was the company's third most popular line. It is found in gray, dark blue green, light blue green, light tan, and yellow. The pattern is only moderately popular among collectors.

A dating system was used on some dinnerware lines. The three number code included month, year, and crew number. It was discontinued in the 1950s.

History: W. L. Smith, John N. Taylor, W. L. Taylor, Homer J. Taylor, and Joseph G. Lee founded Taylor, Smith, and Taylor in Chester, West Virginia, in 1899. In 1903 the firm reorganized and the Taylors bought Lee's interest. In 1906 Smith bought out the Taylors. The firm remained in the family's control until it was purchased by Anchor Hocking in 1973. The tableware division closed in 1981.

Taylor, Smith, and Taylor started production with a nine–kiln pottery. Local clays were used initially. Later only southern clays were used. Both earthenware and fine china bodies were produced. Several underglaze print patterns, e.g., Dogwood and Spring Bouquet, were made. These prints, made from the copper engravings of ceramic artist J. Palin Thorley, were designed exclusively for the company.

Taylor, Smith, and Taylor also made LuRay, produced from the 1930s through the early 1950s. Available in Windsor Blue, Persian Cream, Sharon Pink, Surf Green, and Chatham Gray, their coordinating colors encourage collectors to mix and match sets.

Competition for a portion of the dinnerware market of the 1930s through the 1950s was intense. LuRay was designed to compete with Russel Wright's American Modern. Vistosa was Taylor, Smith, and Taylor's answer to Homer Laughlin's Fiesta.

Taylor, Smith, and Taylor used several different backstamps and marks. Many contain the company name as well as the pattern and shape names.

References: Susan and Al Bagdade, *Warman's American Pottery and Porcelain,* Wallace–Homestead, 1994; Jo Cunningham, *The Collector's Encyclopedia of American Dinnerware,* Collector Books, 1982, 1995 value update; Harvey Duke, *The Official Identification and Price Guide to Pottery and Porcelain, Eighth Edition,* House of Collectibles, 1995; Lois Lehner, *Lehner's Encyclopedia of U. S. Marks On Pottery, Porcelain and Clay,* Collector Books, 1988; Kathy and Bill Meehan, *Collector's Guide To Lu-Ray Pastels: Identification and Values,* Collector Books, 1995.

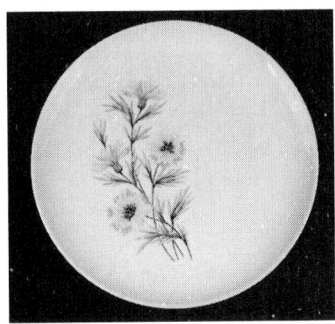

Golden Button, Ever Young shape, dinner plate, 10¼" d, $3.50.

LU-RAY Produced from the late 1930s until the early 1950s. Available in five pastel colors: Chatham Gray, Persian Cream, Sharon Pink, Surf Green, and Windsor Blue.

Berry Bowl, Sharon Pink	12.00
Bud Vase, Surf Green	150.00
Cream Soup, Sharon Pink	60.00
Cup and Saucer, Windsor blue	18.00
Demitasse Cup and Saucer, Chatham Gray	16.00
Eggcup	
Persian Cream	18.00
Surf Green	18.00
Windsor Blue	18.00
Fruit Bowl, Persian Cream	6.00
Pitcher, Sharon Pink	60.00
Plate	
6" d, bread and butter, Windsor Blue	5.00
8½" d	
Sharon Pink	20.00
Windsor Blue	20.00
10" d, dinner	
Persian Cream	18.00
Sharon Pink	18.00
Surf Green	18.00
Windsor Blue	18.00
14" d, chop, Sharon Pink	30.00
Platter	
12" l, Surf Green	20.00
13" l, Windsor Blue	28.00
Salad Bowl, Sharon Pink	45.00
Salt and Pepper Shakers, pr, Persian Cream	15.00
Sauceboat, underplate, Persian Cream	25.00
Soup, flat, Persian Cream	15.00
Teapot, Sharon Pink	50.00
Tidbit Tray, Chatham Gray	80.00
Tumbler, juice	
Sharon Pink	40.00
Windsor Blue	40.00
Vegetable	
Oval, Sharon Pink	20.00
Round, 8½" d, Windsor Blue	15.00

VISTOSA Solid-colored dinnerware similar to Homer Laughlin's Fiesta, Vistosa pieces have piecrust edges and were produced from 1938 until early 1940s. Vistosa pieces are available in four colors: Cobalt Blue, Deep Yellow, Light Green, and Mango Red.

Bowl	
8" d	
Cobalt Blue	65.00
Mango Red	65.00
12" d, ftd, Mango Red, small chip	95.00
Creamer and Sugar, cov, Light Green	35.00
Gravy Boat, Cobalt Blue	150.00
Jug, Mango Red	50.00
Plate, 11" d, chop, Mango Red	18.00

Salt and Pepper Shakers, pr, Cobalt Blue	20.00
Soup, flat	
Deep Yellow	20.00
Mango Red	20.00
Teacup, Cobalt Blue	8.00

TEAPOTS

Collecting Hints: Most collectors focus on ceramic examples. Do not overlook teapots made in other materials ranging from silver and silver plate to wood.

The approach to collecting teapots is almost as unlimited as the number of teapot forms and designs. Some common approaches are country, color, design motif, and manufacturing material. One approach, albeit expensive, is to collect teapots designed by famous industrial designers.

History: The origin of the teapot has been traced back to the Chinese village of Vi–Hsing in the late sixteenth century. The teapots, similar to ones still being produced today, were no bigger than the tiny cups previously used for drinking tea.

By the seventeenth century, the drinking of tea had spread throughout the world. Every pottery and porcelain manufacturer from the Orient to Europe to the Americas produced teapots. The number and variety are unlimited. Forms range from functional to ornately decorative and whimsical. The vast majority of teapots available in today's market date from 1870 to the present.

References: Tina M. Carter, *Teapots: The Collector's Guide to Selecting, Identifying and Displaying New and Vintage Teapots,* Running Press, Courage Books, 1995; Garth Clark, *The Eccentric Teapot: 400 Years of Invention,* Abbeville Press, 1989; Richard Luckin, *Teapot Treasury And Related Items,* RK Publishing, 1987.

Periodicals: *Tea Talk,* 419 North Larchmont Blvd., #225, Los Angeles, CA 90004; *Mary Mac's Tea Times Newsletter,* PO Box 841, Langley, WA 98260.

Museum: Greater Gibson County Area Chamber of Commerce, PO Box 464, Trenton, TN 38382, sponsors an annual Teapot Festival.

Advisor: Tina M. Carter.

Reproduction Alert: Watch out for figural teapots mimicking older ones, e.g., Granny Anne, Cottage Ware, small beckoning cat, and a blue and white duck. There are several modern Blue Willow patterns.

Buff Sharkskin, bisque, unmarked, c1910, Japan	28.00
Clock Pattern, Sessions	45.00

Mason's Ironstone, Vista pattern, square, blue transfer, white body, marked "Mason's Patent Ironstone China, Vista, England, Guaranteed Permanent & Acid Resisting Colours," incised "24," 6¾" h, 9½" w, $25.00.

Cottage Ware, house, lid is roof, marked "Price Kensington, Made in England, Ye Olde Cottage" 32.00
Dragonware, 6 cup, raised dragon and coralene dec, gold trim, marked "Made in Occupied Japan" 30.00
Earthenware
  Brown, "Simple Yet Perfect", c1905   95.00
  Double spout, slip dec, c1890 ..... 80.00
Figural
  Bluebird, 6 cup, bright blue, Lefton China, Japan 30.00
  Bunny, Treasurecraft, USA, 1990s .. 25.00
  Cat, 6 cup, beckoning pose, black and white, green eyes and ribbon, paper label, Cortendorf, Germany   48.00
  Scottie Man, spout is nose, lid is cap, brown, yellow or green, Wade, England 40.00
  Snow White, 6" h, lid is Snow White, body is her dress, dwarfs in relief, musical, marked "Walt Disney Productions" 55.00
  Whimsical man, spout is nose, pastel pink, blue, and yellow, marked "Japan," c1930 .... 25.00
Ironstone, 2 cup, floral, Ellgreave, Wood & Sons, England 35.00
Jasperware, 2 cup, blue and white, Wedgwood, c1784 .... 350.00
Miniature
  Tea Set, teapot, creamer and sugar, cov casserole, salt and pepper, six plates, cups and saucers, Moss Rose, Japan 85.00
  White Glass, gold trim, rough seams, Made in Japan
    Teapot 7.00
    Tea Set, teapot, creamer, and sugar   12.00
Musical, 6 cup, oval, Japan 10.00

Pearl Luster, 6 cup, oval, gold trim, Poland 45.00
Pottery, brown glaze, hp flowers, imp "Royal Canadian Art Pottery, Royal Dripless, Hamilton Canada" 30.00
Silver Lustre, 6 cup, hexagonal, Sutherland, England 60.00
Souvenir
  2" h, tea set, teapot, cup and saucer, hp, California Redwoods, Chandelier Drive–Thru Tree, Victoria Ceramics, Japan, c1940 .... 18.00
  3¼" h, cobalt, scene, Lewis & Clark, Portland, OR, no mark, 1905 .... 20.00
  4½" h, sq, gold trim, scene, US Capitol, Washington DC, Germany   20.00
  5⅞" h, tepee shape, spout is Indian, handle is totem pole, "Greetings from Canada," made by Clarice Cliff, Britain, c1950 .... 150.00

TV PERSONALITIES & MEMORABILIA

Collecting Hints: Collectors of television memorabilia fall into two categories. One is those who specialize in acquiring items from a single television series. Among these, Star Trek, Hopalong Cassidy, Howdy Doody, Roy Rogers, and Leave It To Beaver are the most popular series. The other category specializes in TV memorabilia of one type such as TV guides, model kits, films, and cards.

There have been over 3,750 series on television since 1948. Therefore, the number of artifacts and memorabilia relating to television is large. Especially rich in TV collectibles are the early space shows and cowboy adventure series. The premiums from these shows are beginning to appear at auctions and commanding high prices; they are eagerly sought by the pop culture collectors.

Systematic scheduling of television programs developed into a new type of publication called *TV Guide.* The early guides are sought avidly. The first schedules were regional such as *TV Today* in Philadelphia, *TV Press* in Louisville, *Radio–Television Life* in Los Angeles. The first national *TV Guide* was published on April 3, 1953. Collectors enjoy these older magazines because they are often good sources for early stories about stars and their lives.

History: The late 1940s and early 1950s was the golden age of television. The first programming began in 1948. Experimentation with programming, vast expansion, and rapid growth marked the period. Prime time live drama series were very successful. Many popular stars of today first appeared on these live dramas, such as Paul

Newman, Steve McQueen, Rod Steiger, Jack Lemmon, and Grace Kelly. The stars signed autographs and photographs to promote the dramas. These items, plus scripts and other types of articles, have become very collectible.

After the period of live drama came to an end, the Western assault began. In 1959 there were 26 "Western" series. Many of them were movie and radio heroes adapted to life on television. The Western era continued until the early 1960s when it was replaced by the space adventure series and science fiction.

The 1970s brought the era of situation comedies, including All In The Family and M*A*S*H*. The collectibles resulting from these series are numerous. Only time can tell what values they will have.

References: Jefferson Graham, *Come On Down!!!—The TV Game Show Book,* Abbeville Press, 1988; Ted Hake, *Hake's Guide To TV Collectibles,* Wallace–Homestead, 1990; David Inman, *The TV Encyclopedia,* Perigee Book, 1991; Norman E. Martinus and Harry L. Rinker, *Warman's Paper,* Wallace–Homestead, 1994; Brian Paquette and Paul Howley, *The Toys From U.N.C.L.E.: Memorabilia And Collectors Guide,* Entertainment Publishing, 1990; Neil Summers, *The Official TV Western Book, Volume 4,* The Old West Shop Publishing, 1992; Vincent Terrace, *Encyclopedia Of Television—Series, Pilots, And Specials, 1937–1973,* 3 volumes, Zoetrope, 1986; Ric Wyman, *For The Love Of Lucy: The Complete Guide For Collectors and Fans,* Chronicle Books, 1995; Alan Young, *Mister Ed and Me,* St. Martin's Press, 1994.

Collectors' Club: TV Western Collectors Fan Club, PO Box 1361, Boyes Hot Springs, CA 95416.

Periodicals: *Autograph Times, 2303 N. 44th St., #225,* Phoenix, AZ 85008; Big Reel, PO Box 83, Madison, NC 27025; Celebrity Collector, PO Box 1115, Boston, MA, 02117; Collecting Hollywood, 2401 Broad St., Chattanooga, TN 37408; Norm's Serial News, 1726 Maux Dr., Houston, TX 70043; Television History Magazine, 700 E. Macoupia St., Staunton, IL 62088; The TV Collector, PO Box 1088, Easton, MA 02334.

Museum: Smithsonian Institution, Washington, DC.

Addams Family
  Card Game, complete, 1965 ...... **30.00**
  Coloring Book, 8½ x 11", Saalfield, #4595, 1965 .... **32.00**
  Light Bulb, Uncle Fester, lights when placed in mouth, orig box, unused, 1965 .... **148.00**
  Plate, ceramic, artist Chas Addams, Wednesday, miniature family man-

sion bird house, occupied by vulture, 1960s **40.00**
All in the Family
  Game, Archie Bunker Card Game, 1972 .... **25.00**
  Pinback Button, 3½" d, America's Foist Family/The Bunkers, red, white, and blue, black and white photo, N G Slater Corp, copyright 1972 Tandem Productions, Inc ... **15.00**
Ben Casey, MD, game, unused **45.00**
Bewitched
  Book, *Bewitched,* Grosset & Dunlap, copyright 1965 Screen Gems, Inc, 48 pgs **20.00**
  Magazine, *TV Guide,* June 18, 1966, Vol 14, #25, 4 pg article **25.00**
Bonanza
  Cup, tin, Ponderosa, pictures of ranch and cast of show **15.00**
  Play Set, Ponderosa Ranch Weapons, 31" l rifle, 9" l revolver, 9½" l knife, plastic and metal, vinyl cartridge belt and holster, plastic knife sheath and bullets, orig unopened pkg, Marx, late 1960s **180.00**
Brady Bunch
  Banjo, 12" l, hard plastic, blue and yellow, orig unopened package, Larami Corp, copyright 1973 Paramount Pictures Corp **45.00**
  Paper Doll, 10 x 13", Whitman, copyright 1973 Paramount Pictures Corp, two cardboard pgs with punch out dolls, six pgs uncut clothing **150.00**
Buffalo Bill Jr, belt buckle **5.00**
Cheyenne, puzzle, set of three, orig box **15.00**
Columbo, game **25.00**
Death Valley Days, premium, 20 mule team model, unassembled, sealed in orig mailer **25.00**
Dragnet
  Cap Gun, Detective Special, MIB .. **65.00**
  Coloring Book, 8¼ x 10¾", Jack Webb's Safety Squad Coloring Book, Samuel Lowe Co, 1956 Sherry TV, Inc copyright, unused **25.00**
  Sheet Music, 9 x 12", theme song, 4 pgs, Schumann Music Co copyright 1953 .... **22.00**
Dr Kildare
  Book, *Golden Funtime,* punch–out, 1962 .... **20.00**
  Stethoscope, Thumpy the Heart Beat Stethoscope, picture of Richard Chamberlain on pkg **35.00**
Family Affair
  Doll, 10" h, Buffy, holding 4¼" h Mrs. Beasley doll, orig box, Mattel, copyright 1968 Family Affair Co .. **300.00**

Lunch Box, 7 x 9 x 4", metal, color illus, King–Seeley copyright 1969 Family Affair Co **65.00**

Thermos, 6½" h, metal, color illus, King–Seeley **30.00**

Flipper, Colorform set, Standard Toykraft, orig box, 1966 . . . .   **52.00**

Gidget
Comic Book, 6¾ x 10¼", #2, Dec, 1966, Dell, copyright Frederick Kohner **12.50**

Game, orig box, Standard Toykraft, copyright Screen Gems, Inc, c1965   **50.00**

Groucho Marx, cocktail napkin set, 36 napkins, series #1, "That's Me, Groucho," paper, cartoon illus, orig box, monogram of California, copyright 1954 . . . .   **45.00**

Gunsmoke
Big Little Book, 1958 . . . .   **14.00**

Gun and Holster Set, black vinyl, silver trim, 8" l gray plastic six–shooter, black vinyl belt, orig unopened pkg **45.00**

Puzzle, frame tray **10.00**

Vest, cowboy, orig pkg, 1959 . . . . .   **35.00**

Happy Days
Jigsaw Puzzle, 1976 . . . .   **15.00**

Lunch Box **18.00**

Have Gun Will Travel, figure, Paladin and horse, Hartland, mint on card . .   **135.00**

Hee Haw, thermos, 6½" h, metal, color illus, King–Seeley **55.00**

Howdy Doody
Doll, Goldberger, MIB **35.00**

Figure
Clarabell, Bend–Me Toy, 12" h, foam rubber over wire, orig unopened bag, Ben–Her Industries, Kagran copyright, 1951–56 . . . .   **20.00**

Howdy Doody, wood, jointed, push–up, NBC microphone . . .   **145.00**

Ice Cream Spoon **40.00**

Ice Cream Wrapper, Howdy Doody Fudge Bar, 1950s **3.00**

Toy, Howdy Doody, Airplane Squeeze Toy, orig box, $38.50.

Lamp, Howdy Doody with Santa, wall light **110.00**

Mittens, pr, 8" h, wool, red, Howdy and Clarabell portrait illus **25.00**

Place Mat, set of 8 . . . .   **45.00**

Puzzle, frame tray, 11½ x 15", amusement park airplane ride illus, Whitman, Kagran copyright 1953   **24.00**

Shade, 11½" sq, glass, four character portraits, Kagran copyright, 1951–56   **175.00**

I Dream Of Jeannie, doll, 20" h, orig box, Libby copyright 1966 Sidney Sheldon Productions, Inc **450.00**

I Love Lucy
Coloring Book, 11¼ x 13¾", Whitman, copyright 1954 Lucille Ball and Desi Arnaz **75.00**

Comic Book, I Love Lucy, 1956 . . . .   **3.00**

Doll
Lucy, 27" h, stuffed, molded plastic face with painted features, shirt and pants, removable apron, 1950s **400.00**

Ricky Jr, 1950s **250.00**

Jackie Gleason
Coloring Book, 11 x 12¼", Abbott copyright 1956 VIP Corp, 16 pgs, unused **75.00**

Toy, Aw–a–a–ay We Go Climbing Toy, Reggie Van Gleason III, MOC, 1950s **95.00**

Uniform, bus driver, includes cap, coin changer, coins, bus tickets, and ticket puncher, VIP, orig box, 1956 . . . .   **395.00**

Kit Carson
Coloring Set, saddlebag **75.00**

Record, 78 rpm, western songs, orig picture sleeve **9.00**

Kukla, Fran & Ollie, game **25.00**

Land of the Giants
Book, 5¼ x 8", *Flight of Fear,* Carl Henry Rathjen, hard cov, Whitman, #1516, 212 pgs, 1969 . . . . .   **17.50**

Coloring Book, 8 x 10", Whitman, #1138, unused, 1969 . . . .   **25.00**

Lassie, wallet, photo front, membership card, Campbell Soup premium, orig envelope, 1958 . . . .   **40.00**

Laugh–In
Drawing Set, orig box, unused, Lakeside, 1968 . . . .   **60.00**

Notebook Binder, 1969 . . . .   **20.00**

Waste Can, character illus **55.00**

Laverne and Shirley, purse, red vinyl, gold metal closure and carrying chain, orig unopened package, Continental Plastics Corp **15.00**

Liberace, sheet music, 9 x 12", *I'll Be Seeing You,* bluetone photo portrait on cov, 6 pgs, copyright 1938, re–released c1953 . . . .   **15.00**

Man From U.N.C.L.E.
Game **25.00**
Gum Cards, complete set, 1960s . . .   **60.00**
Ring, Solo and Kuryakin portraits,
plastic, dark blue, 1960s **12.00**
M.A.S.H.
Game, orig box, Transogram, copy-
right 1975 20th Century Fox Film
Corp **40.00**
Vodka Bottle, 9″ h, wire frame,
"Bottled By Hawkeye Distilling Co,
Cleveland, OH" **55.00**
Maverick
Cap Gun, 10½″ l, silvered metal,
white plastic grips, crossed horse-
shoes inset, c1960 . . . .   **40.00**
Paint By Number Set, oil, unused,
photo of Garner on box **125.00**
Puzzle, frame tray, 11½ x 14½″,
Whitman, gunfight illus, 1959 . . .   **22.00**
McHale's Navy
Game, McHale's Navy Game, orig
box, Transogram, copyright 1962
Sto–Rev Co **55.00**
Model Kit, PT 73, Revell, complete,
unassembled, orig instructions and
box, Sto–Rev Co copyright 1965   **85.00**
Merv Griffin, game, Merv Griffin's Word
For Word Game, Mattel, Inc, copy-
right 1963 NBC, orig box **35.00**
Miami Vice, game, orig box, Pepper
Lane Industries, copyright 1984
Universal City Studios, Inc **25.00**
Mr Ed, doll, talking, Mattel **65.00**
Mr T, The A Team
Air Freshener, 4½″ h, diecut, orig un-
opened package, TR-3 Products,
1980s **15.00**
Alarm Clock, 5″ h, metal, blue, sil-
vered metal bells, color illus, Zeon
copyright 1983 Ruby–Spears
Enterprises, Inc **25.00**
Munsters
Bubble Gum Wrapper, 6″ sq, waxed
paper, Leaf, 1966 . . . .   **50.00**
Doll, Herman Munster **20.00**
Flasher Ring, set of four, plastic, blue,
Herman, Lily, Grandpa, and Eddie,
c1966 . . . .   **28.50**
Lunch Box **75.00**
Ozzie and Harriet
Candy Box, Mounds, Nelson family
cartoon illus, 1957 . . . .   **98.00**
Coloring Book, 8¼ x 10¾″, Saalfield,
copyright 1973 Filmways Televi-
sion Corp, 32 pgs, unused **30.00**
Partridge Family, lunch box, metal ther-
mos **40.00**
Perry Mason, game, Missing Suspect,
1959 . . . .   **39.00**
Police Woman, doll, Angie Dickinson,
orig box **22.50**

Rat Patrol, book, *The Rat Patrol,* Whit-
man, copyright 1968 Mirisch–Rich
Television Productions, 212 pgs   **12.00**
Sea Hunt, magic slate, 1960 . . . .   **59.00**
Starsky & Hutch, jigsaw puzzle, 1976   **15.00**
Tales of Wells Fargo
Game, complete, orig box **40.00**
TV Projector, complete with film, orig
unused batteries, MIB **135.00**
Trouble With Father, coloring book, 11 x
14″, June and Stu Erwin, Whitman, 16
pgs, unused, 1954 . . . .   **35.00**
Wagon Train, coloring book, Whitman,
unused, 1959 . . . .   **30.00**
Wanted: Dead or Alive, rifle, Mares Laig
replica, plastic and metal, orig card   **75.00**
Welcome Back Kotter
Colorforms, orig box, copyright 1976
The Wolper Organization **25.00**
Paper Doll, 14″ h diecut figure,
rub–on clothes and accessories,
orig box, The Toy Factory, copyright 1976 The Wolper Organiza-
tion, Inc **40.00**
Waste Can, 13″ h, litho tin, color il-
lus, Cheinco, marked "The Wolper
Organization, Inc," c1976 . . . . . .   **35.00**

TELEVISIONS

Collecting Hints: There are two distinct types of
early television sets: mechanical and electronic.
Mechanical televisions, the earliest, look nothing
like their modern counterparts. Mechanical sets
from the 1920s typically have a motorized 12″
diameter metal disc with a "glow tube" in back
and a magnifier in front. Starting in 1938 sets
used picture tubes as they do today. Generally
the earlier the set, the smaller the screen. The
easiest way to gauge the age of a television set is
by the numbers found on the channel selector.
Pre–1946 television sets will tune a maximum of
five stations, usually channels 1–5. In 1946 channels 7–13 were added, thus sets made between
1946 and 1948 will show channels 1–13 on the
station selector.

In 1949, channel 1 was dropped, leaving all
1949 and newer sets with V.H.F. channels 2–13,
as we have them today. The U.H.F. band was
added in 1953, thus any set with U.H.F. capabil-
ity is less than 40 years old.

Brand and model number are essential to determining a set's worth. However, physical condition of the cabinet is much more important
than the operating condition of the set.

History: There are three distinct eras of early television. The first, the "mechanical" era, was from
1925–1932. Sets often were known as "radiovi-
sors," since they were visual attachments to ra-

dios. Many mechanical television sets did not have cabinets and resembled an electric fan with a round metal disk in place of the blades. These units were most prevalent in the New York City and Chicago areas.

Any complete mechanical set is valued in the several thousand dollar range. Manufacturers included Jenkins, Baird, Western Television, Insuline Corp. of America, Short–Wave and Television Corp., Daven, See–All, Rawls, Pioneer, Travler Radio & Television Corp., and others.

The second era was the pre–World War II era, which spanned 1938–1941. These were the first all–electronic sets and usually were combined with a multi–band radio in fancy cabinets. A favorite design of the era was the "mirror in the lid" arrangement, whereby a mirror in the underside of a lift–lid reflected the picture tube, which was pointed straight up. No more than 2,000 sets were produced during the three years. They were concentrated in those areas with prewar television stations: New York City, Albany/Schenectady/Troy, Philadelphia, Chicago, and Los Angeles. Depending on model and condition, these sets usually start at $1,000 and can range to $5,000 or more.

The final era of television started in 1946 with the resumption of post–war television production. Production rose rapidly. Few sets after 1949 have collectible value. There are some notable exceptions, e.g., the first "color wheel" sets [1951], the giant Dumont 30" screen sets [1953], and limited production or "oddball" sets.

References: Morgan E. McMahon, *A Flick of The Switch,* Vintage Radio, 1975; Harry Poster, *Poster's Guide To Collectible Radios and Televisions, 1920–1990,* Wallace–Homestead, 1993; Scott Wood (ed.), *Classic TVs With Price Guide: Pre–War thru 1950s,* L–W Book Sales, 1992.

Collectors' Club: Antique Wireless Association, 59 Main St., Bloomfield, NY 14469.

Periodical: *Radio Age, 636 Cambridge Rd., Augusta, GA 30909.*

Caution: Do not plug in a set that has been in storage for more than 30 years without an inspection by a serviceman. Components can go bad and short–circuit, causing a fire. Many early sets had no fuses for protection.

1925–1932, MECHANICAL

Daven, parts kit **500.00**
Insuline Corp of American (ICA)
  Bakelite cabinet model **3,000.00**
  Oak box kit **1,000.00**
Jenkins, Model 202 . . . . **4,000.00**
See–All, open frame **1,500.00**

Short–Wave and Television Corporation,
  drum scanner **3,000.00**
Western Television Corp, "Ship's wheel,"
  cabinet type **2,000.00**

1938–1941, ELECTRONIC

Andrea
  1–F–5 . . . . **4,000.00**
  KTE–5 . . . . **2,500.00**
Dumont
  180 . . . . **2,000.00**
  181 . . . . **3,000.00**
General Electric
  HM–171 . . . . **2,500.00**
  HM–225 . . . . **5,000.00**
  HM–226 . . . . **3,000.00**
RCA
  RR–359 . . . . **5,000.00**
  TRK–5, television "Attachment" . . . **4,000.00**
  TRK–9 . . . . **3,000.00**
  TRK–12 . . . . **2,500.00**
  TRK–120 . . . . **4,000.00**
  TT–5 . . . . **3,500.00**
Stromberg–Carlson, 112 . . . . **5,000.00**

1946 AND LATER

Admiral
  19A11, table top, dark brown Bakelite,
    7" screen, 1948 . . . . **125.00**
  20X122, console, Bakelite, 10"
    screen, 1950 . . . . **350.00**
  24A12, console, Bakelite, 12" screen,
    1948 . . . . **350.00**
Airline
  84GSE–3011A, portable, leatherette,
    7" screen, 1949 . . . . **150.00**
  94GSE–3015, portable, Telephoto
    Control button, 7" screen, 1948 . . **175.00**

Magazine Tear Sheet, Sparton TV!, *Collier's,* **March 31, 1951, full color, 10½ x 13½", $9.00.**

CBS/Columbia, 12CC2, color wheel set	5,000.00
Hallicrafters, T–54	200.00
Motorola, VT–71	150.00
Philco Predicta	
Pole Model	500.00
Table Model	250.00
Two Piece Model	200.00
Safari	350.00
Pilot, TV–37	
Carry case	100.00
Magnifier	100.00
Set	250.00
RCA	
621TS	500.00
630TS	250.00
648PTK	250.00
721TS	200.00
8TS30	150.00
CT–100, 1st RCA Color Set	500.00
Stromberg Carlson, TC 10H, Manhattan Porthole, table top, wood, 10" d screen, 1958	125.00
Zenith, 24H21, console, wood, 19" d screen, 1950	175.00

SHIRLEY TEMPLE

Collecting Hints: Dolls are made out of many materials—composition, cloth, chalk, papier mache, rubber, and vinyl. Composition dolls are the earliest. Shirley Temple's popularity received a renewed boost through television, resulting in a new series of Shirley Temple products being issued in the 1950s.

History: Shirley Jane Temple was born April 23, 1928, in Santa Monica, California. A movie scout discovered her at a dancing school. "Pie Covered Wagon" in 1932 was her screen test. During the 1930s she made twenty movies, earning as much as $75,000 per film.

Her mother supervised the licensing of over fifteen firms to make Shirley Temple products. These included dolls, glassware, china, jewelry, and soap. The first Shirley Temple dolls were made in 1934 by The Ideal Toy Company. They varied in height from 11 to 27 inches and were composition (pressed wood). Ideal made the first vinyl dolls in 1957.

References: John Axe, *The Encyclopedia of Celebrity Dolls*, Hobby House Press, 1983; Norman E. Martinus and Harry L. Rinker, *Warman's Paper*, Wallace–Homestead, 1994; Edward R. Pardella, *Shirley Temple Dolls And Fashion: A Collector's Guide To The World's Darling*, Schiffer Publishing, 1992; Patricia R. Smith, *Shirley Temple Dolls And Collectibles*, Volume I (1977, 1992 value update), Volume II (1979, 1992 value update,) Collector Books.

Videotape: *Shirley Temple Dolls & Memorabilia,* Sirocco Productions, 1994.

REPRODUCTION ALERT

Barrette, bow, Temple cameo	85.00
Book	
Dimples, 9½ x 10", 1936	20.00
Heidi, 1937	22.00
My Life & Time by Shirley Temple, 1936	25.00
Shirley Temple at Play, 1935	45.00
Shirley Temple Through the Day, 1935	45.00
Suzanna of the Mounties, 9½ x 10", 1939	22.00
Bowl, 6½", glass, blue	35.00
Bracelet, child's, charm, 1930s	45.00
Button, c1936	50.00
Cake Topper, Happy Birthday	75.00
Christmas Card, 4 x 5", Hallmark, 1935	12.00
Cigar Band, Spanish, 1930s	22.00
Clothes Hanger, cardboard, blue, 1930s	10.00
Clothing Tag, 3 x 5", black and white photo, endorsed by Shirley Temple, orig string cord, 1930s	12.00
Doll	
12", orig clothes, 1957	95.00
13", composition, 1935	450.00
16", red polka dot dress, 1972	120.00
19", vinyl, 1959	250.00
22", composition, marked "Curly Top," 1934	600.00
23", composition, orig clothes, pin, wig, Ideal	750.00
Figure	
5"	45.00
6½", bisque, movable arms and legs, marked "Made in Japan"	90.00
Gloves, leather, blue, 1930s	38.00
Handkerchief, 9 x 9", "Little Colonel"	20.00

Magazine, *Life,* March 30, 1942, 132 pages, 10½ x 14", $25.00.

Headband, pink, cameo and name in center 85.00
Lobby Card, "Adventure in Baltimore," RKO, 1949 .... 12.00
Magnetic TV Theater, MIB 125.00
Mirror, purse size 15.00
Movie Still
"Captain January," 8 x 10", 1936 ... 15.00
"Poor Little Rich Girl," 8 x 10", 1936 15.00
Paper Doll, clothes, orig box, Gabriel Co, 1958 .... 25.00
Party Invitations, packet of ten, 1973 .. 4.00
Paperweight 40.00
Pen, blue, name on body and clip 85.00
Pencil, pink 85.00
Pin
Everybody Loves Me, Miss Charming, oval, black and white, doll pictured 85.00
Everybody Loves Me, Little Miss Movie, oval, blue and white, doll pictured 85.00
Sunday Referee, Shirley Temple League, round, porcelain, finger to face, copper back marked "Roden London" 85.00
Playing Cards, Temple in duck dress, complete deck, 1930s 45.00
Portrait, 8 x 10", sepia 10.00
Purse, 2⅞ x 4", 1958 .... 32.00
Sewing Machine, Little Miss 125.00
Sheet Music
Stowaway 12.00
That's What I Want For Christmas, 6 pgs, sung in Stowaway film, greentone photo on cov, 1935 copyright 25.00
Sign, 11 x 14", cardboard, c1930 .... 60.00
Soap, 5", figural, two in orig box 85.00
Statue, 14½", plaster, painted, rosy accents, late 1930s 110.00
Store Display Sign, 19 x 30", cardboard, "Shirley Temple Loves Quaker Puffed Wheat" 90.00
Tablecloth, 1930s 18.00
Tablet, writing, 5½ x 9", 1935 .... 20.00
Tea Set, glass, pink 85.00
Treasure Board, wipe–off back 65.00

THIMBLES

Collecting Hints: There are many ways to approach thimble collecting. You can collect by material (metal or porcelain), by design (cupids or commemorative), by types (advertising or political), or limited editions (modern collectibles). However, in reality, there is only one philosophy that should determine what you collect. Collect what you like.

There are thousands of thimbles. The wise collector narrows her approach. This saves money

and enables her to assemble a meaningful collection.

The wonderful thing about thimble collecting is that there is something for everybody's budget. Collectors with unlimited funds can focus on gold thimbles. The person on a limited budget might look at advertising or modern collectible thimbles.

History: Silver thimbles were imported from England during the colonial period, and only the wealthy could afford to buy them. By the late 18th century advertisements appeared in the *New York Weekly Post,* the *New York Gazette,* and the *Philadelphia Directory,* offering American made thimbles. These were gold, silver, or pinchbeck thimbles, some with steel caps.

The Industrial Revolution during the 19th century brought the "Golden Age" of thimble production. Machinery was created that could produce fine working thimbles. By the end of the 19th century, world production of thimbles was about eighty million per year.

Long before the sewing machine became a permanent member of the household, all sewing and mending was done by hand. Needlework can be divided into two kinds: plain and fancy. Plain sewing required a utilitarian thimble made of steel, brass, or celluloid. A process for making celluloid thimbles was patented by William Halsey in 1880. Eugene Villiers patented a thimble molding process in the same year. Aluminum was a costly metal during the 19th century. Aluminum thimbles did not appear on the market until the 20th century, when it became cheaper and practical to make thimbles.

The frontier homemaker guarded her thimble. If it was lost, it was difficult to replace. Her source was in a general store, often miles away, or she had to wait until a traveling peddler came along. City ladies had no problem replacing a lost thimble. A selection was always available at the local dry goods store. The name "dry goods" assured a lady that no "wet goods," or alcoholic beverages, were sold in that store, and it was perfectly proper for her to shop there.

Fancy sewing was considered a parlor or social activity. Ornate thimbles made of precious metals were saved for this purpose. Many gold and silver thimbles were received as gifts. In years past proper etiquette did not permit a young man to give his lady any gift that was personal, such as jewelry or clothing. Flowers, books, or sweets were considered proper gifts. The thimble somehow bridged this rule of etiquette. A fancy gold or silver thimble was a welcomed gift. Many of these do not show signs of wear from constant use. This may result from the poor fit of the thimble or from it simply being too elegant for mundane work.

Advertising thimbles cover an extensive area of goods and services. These little advertising ploys helped a salesman to open a door. Tradesmen knew that these tokens would constantly remind the customer of their product. Many collectors specialize in collecting only advertising thimbles because they are easy to find and inexpensive to buy. Advertising thimbles made of celluloid or metal are older than the modern plastic examples. There was no standard method of distributing advertising thimbles. Most were handed to a potential customer by a salesman. Others were packaged with a product, such as flour or bread. Most were used for sewing, but others were not. In either case, advertising thimbles found a home in the family sewing basket.

The history of political campaign advertising thimbles began with the amendment giving the vote to women, ratified on August 20, 1920, just in time for the 1920 political campaign. The first presidential candidate to use the advertising thimble was Warren Harding. Political thimbles are priced higher than other advertising thimbles. Thimble collectors find they have to compete with political memorabilia collectors for these.

References: Edwin Holmes, *A History of Thimbles,* Cornwall Books, 1985; Eleanor Johnson, *Thimbles,* Shires Publications, Aylesbury, Bucks, England, 1982; Myrtle Lundquist, *The Book of a Thousand Thimbles,* Wallace Homestead, 1970, out–of–print; Myrtle Lundquist, *Thimble Treasury,* Wallace Homestead, 1975, out–of–print; Myrtle Lundquist, *Thimbles Americana,* Wallace Homestead, 1981, out–of–print; Averil Mathis, *Antique and Collectible Thimbles,* Collector Books, 1986, 1989 value update, out–of–print; Bridget McConnell, *A Collector's Guide To Thimbles,* Wellfleet Books, 1990; Gay Ann Rogers, *American Silver Thimbles,* John Murray, 1989; Gay Ann Rogers, *Price Guide Keyed To American Silver Thimbles,* Needlework Unlimited, 1989; John von Holle, *Thimble Collectors Encyclopedia,* Wallace Homestead, 1986, out–of–print; Estelle Zalkin, *Zalkin's Handbook of Thimbles and Sewing Implements,* Wallace Homestead, 1988.

Collectors' Clubs: Empire State Thimble Collectors, 8289 Northgate Dr., Rome, NY 13440; The Thimble Guild, PO Box 381807, Duncanville, TX 75138; Thimble Collectors International, 6411 Montego Bay Rd., Louisville, KY 40228.

Periodical: *Thimbletter,* 93 Walnut Hill Rd., Newtown Highlands, MA 02161.

Advisor: Estelle Zalkin

REPRODUCTION ALERT: As soon as thimble collecting became popular, recast reproductions appeared in the market. The cast reproduction of a pre–revolution Russian enamel surfaced in antiques shows and shops across the country. The "84" Russian silver mark is clear, but the maker's mark is deliberately smeared. The rim of the re-

production is thick and the inside of the thimble is rough.

American thimbles have been reproduced. An artisan is casting many of the popular patterns, including the cottage scene, harbor scene with lighthouse, anchors, and chains, cupid and garlands, the teddy bear, two birds on a branch and other popular collectible thimbles. No maker's mark appears inside the cap and the "Sterling" mark is stamped on the band. This is the first clue that these are recast reproductions. It is illegal to use the word "Sterling" on any silver piece without the manufacturer's name or trademark. These cast thimbles are thick and rough inside. The cast thimbles are much heavier than the genuine machine–drawn antique thimbles. The casting process does not duplicate the fine engraved designs that the originals have.

Gadget or Patented
M.T. (Magic Thimble), thread cutter
  and needle threader **25.00**
Thread Cutter, lip on band **15.00**
Gold, 1900–40
  Plain band **75.00**
  Scenic band **100.00**
  Semi precious stones on band **300.00**
Ivory
  Modern scrimshaw **25.00**
  Vegetable ivory **75.00**
Metal, common
  Brass
    Ornate band **20.00**
    Plain band **3.00**
  Cast pot metal, "For a Good Girl" . . **5.00**
  Cloisonne on brass, modern, China **15.00**
  Diragold **125.00**
Silver, 1900–1940
  Atlantic Cable **150.00**
  Birds **50.00**
  French Fables, 1970 issue **150.00**
  Raised Grape **150.00**
  Toledo, Spain, damascene **35.00**
Porcelain
  Meissen, German, modern, hand
    painted **125.00**
  Modern collectible, transfer print design **15.00**

Royal Worcester, England, modern, fruit, flowers, and bird dec, price each, $25.00.

Royal Worcester, England, hand
painted
Signed 50.00
Signed by Powell, birds 300.00
Souvenir and Commemorative, silver
Columbian Exposition, 1892
Buildings in relief 500.00
Words only 400.00
Liberty Bell, 1976 issue 75.00
Statue of Liberty, French 50.00
St Louis Fair, 1904, Golden Spike . . 600.00
Thimble Holder
Glass Slipper 150.00
Silver, round, filigree 150.00

TINSEL ART

Collecting Hints: Look for those pieces which are
elaborate in design and contain different colored
foil. Signed pictures often are viewed as folk art
and may be priced higher.

Nineteenth century material is preferred over
the nondescript 20th century examples. However, Art Deco and Art Nouveau designs of quality are sought by collectors from these fields.

History: Tinsel pictures (or paintings) were both a
"cottage art" and a commercial product which
enjoyed popularity from the late 19th century
through the 20th century. The "painting" took
two forms. The first was similar to a reverse
painting on glass. A design was placed on the
glass and colored foil was placed behind to accent the piece. The second form consisted of a
silhouette or cutting, separate from the glass,
placed over a layer of crumpled foil.

The reverse painting type was highly personalized; a mother and her children could work on
tinsel pictures as a family project. This handi-
work often contained presentation remarks and
was artist signed and dated. The silhouette type
appears to be related to the Art Deco and Art
Nouveau periods and may have been a form of
souvenir at carnival games and the seashore. The
sameness of many designs, e.g., flamingos in a
swamp–like setting, denotes its commercial production.

Reference: Shirley Mace, *Encyclopedia Of
Silhouette Collectibles On Glass*, Shadow
Enterprises, 1992.

Birds, drinking from stylized fountain,
trees in background, 19th C, 23 x 27"   **225.00**
Flamingos, pink flamingos, palm tree,
reeds, yellow sun, black ground, 10¾
x 8¾" **90.00**
Flowers, multicolored flowers arranged
in basket, black ground, 17¾ x 13½" **150.00**
Fountain, surrounded by garland of
flowers, multicolored, 15¾ x 15½"   **120.00**

Storks, 10¾ x 8¾", $15.00.

Lilacs, black ground, gilt frame, 10½ x
7½", 19th C **165.00**
Motto, Home Sweet Home, houses and
trees, reverse painted, 12¼ x 18" . . .   **75.00**
Peacock, silver peacock, gold mar-
bleized fence, black ground, authentic peacock feather tail, mounted as
tray, 19 x 13" **65.00**
Silhouettes, girl and boy, facing pr,
framed **50.00**
Statue of Liberty, multicolored, reverse
painting on glass highlights, ornate
oval wooden frame **85.00**

TOOTHPICK
HOLDERS

Collecting Hints: Toothpick holders have been
confused with many forms—from match holders,
shot glasses, miniature spoon holders to toy table
settings, mustard pots without lids, rose or violet
bowls, individual open sugars, and vases. Use
toothpicks to test what you have. The toothpicks
should rest well in the holder with an ample extension to allow an individual toothpick to be selected easily. Match holders often are figural in
nature and have a striking surface on them.

The biggest danger to the collector is a salt
shaker with a ground top or a wine glass with the
stem removed. Knowing the forms of salt shakers
and wine glasses will avoid any confusion.

Among the forms, perhaps the silverplated figural toothpicks are least appreciated. They offer
the beginner a reasonable area upon which to
build an inexpensive collection.

History: Toothpick holders are small containers
used to hold toothpicks. They were an important
table accessory during the Victorian period.

Toothpick holders were made in a wide range
of material—Art glass, colored pattern glass, col-

ored glass novelties, milk glass, china, bisque and porcelain, crystal pressed glass, cut glass, and silverplated figurals. Makers include both American and European firms.

Toothpick holders were used as souvenir items by applying decals or transfers. The same blank may contain several different location labels.

References: Neila and Tom Bredehoft, *Findlay Toothpick Holders,* Cherry Hill Publications, 1995; William Heacock, *Encyclopedia of Victorian Colored Pattern Glass, Book I, Toothpick Holders from A to Z, Second Edition,* Antique Publications, 1976, 1992 value update; William Heacock, *1000 Toothpick Holders: A Collector's Guide,* Antique Publications, 1977; William Heacock, *Rare & Unlisted Toothpick Holders,* Antique Publications, 1984; National Toothpick Holder Collectors Society, *Toothpick Holders: China, Glass, and Metal,* Antique Publications, 1992.

Collectors' Club: National Toothpick Holder Collectors Society, 1224 Spring Valley Lane, West Chester, PA 19380.

Additional Listings: See *Warman's Antiques And Their Prices.*

Agata, tri–corner, peachblow base, New
  England Co. **1,150.00**
Amberina
  Diamond Quilt, square top, Fuscia   **350.00**
  Venetian Diamond, urn shape **465.00**
Bisque, boy with bottle **25.00**
Brass, "I'm From Missouri" **25.00**
Burmese, square top, dec, slight blush   **535.00**
China
  Bavarian, hp florals **40.00**
  German, Baby Pierrette, imp "Germany 3315," 3" h **40.00**
  Majolica, sunflower **90.00**
  Nippon, windmill scene, gold dec and beading, 3" h **20.00**
  Occupied Japan, boot, floral dec, 2¾" h **10.00**
  R S Prussia, lily of the valley dec, three handles, white ground, blue rim shading **250.00**
  Royal Bayreuth, elk's head, figural . . **85.00**
Custard
  Argonaut Shell **375.00**
  Inverted Fan & Feather **695.00**
  Ring Band, flower bud **165.00**
Glass, figural
  Anvil, Windsor, amber **35.00**
  Cat on Cushion **45.00**
  Gattling Gun, blue **35.00**
  Horse, pulling cart, amber **75.00**
Milk Glass
  Button & Bulge, hp florals **35.00**
  Owl **45.00**
  Tramp's Shoe **30.00**

Opalescent Glass
  Reverse Swirl
    Blue **85.00**
    Cranberry **395.00**
  Ribbed Lattice
    Blue **165.00**
    Cranberry **240.00**
Pattern Glass
  Beatty Honeycomb, blue **50.00**
  Bohemian, green, gold dec **265.00**
  Box in Box, green, gold dec **80.00**
  Croesus, amethyst, gold dec **150.00**
  Daisy & Button, blue, V ornament . . **50.00**

Pattern glass, Daisy and Button, bucket, amber, Heacock #211, $35.00.

Delaware, rose stain, gold dec **150.00**
Elephant Toe, rose stain **80.00**
Empress, green, gold dec **275.00**
Fancy Loop, green, gold dec, Heisey   **165.00**
Forget–Me–Not, pink **60.00**
Gonterman Swirl, blue **225.00**
Grecian Column, blue **115.00**
Hobnail, Frances Ware **50.00**
Klondike, clear **175.00**
Leaf Umbrella, mauve, cased **365.00**
Nestor, amethyst **110.00**
Petticoat, vaseline, gold dec **125.00**
Pineapple & Fan, green **185.00**
Priscilla, clear, Fostoria **125.00**
Punty & Diamond Point, Heisey . . . **260.00**
Ribbed Pillar, pink **85.00**
Royal Ivy
  Clear **160.00**
  Frosted Rubina **165.00**
  Rainbow Spatter **325.00**
  Texas Star, clear **130.00**
Vermont
  Blue, flower dec **150.00**
  Opaque Ivory **125.00**
Ruby Stained
  Diamond Peg **25.00**
  New York, (U.S. Rib) **70.00**
  Zipper Slash **25.00**
Silver Plate
  Chick, half egg and wishbone **30.00**
  Dog, seated with bone, ornate border, Tufts **115.00**
  Owl, seated on branch, 2" h **75.00**
  Rabbit, beside egg **25.00**

TOYS

Collecting Hints: Condition is a very critical factor. Most collectors like to have examples in very fine to mint condition. The original box and any instructional sheets add to the value.

Sophisticated collectors concentrate on the tin and cast iron toys of the late 19th and early 20th centuries. However, more and more collectors are concentrating on the 1940 to 1970 period, including products from firms such as Fisher–Price.

Many toys were characterizations of cartoon, radio, and television figures. A large number of collectible fields have some form of toy spinoff. The result is that the toy collector constantly is competing with the specialized collector.

History: In America the first cast iron toys began to appear shortly after the Civil War. Leading 19th century manufacturers included Hubley, Dent, Kenton, and Schoenhut. In the first decades of the 20th century Arcade, Buddy L, Marx, and Tootsietoy joined the earlier firms. The picture became complete with the addition of firms such as Built Rite, Ideal, and Fisher–Price.

In Europe, Nuremberg, Germany, was the center for the toy industry from the late 18th through the mid–20th centuries. In England the Britain and Lesney companies challenged the German supremacy. Lesney originated the famous Matchbox toys. German manufacturers were especially skilled in the areas of toy trains and stuffed toys.

References: Linda Baker, *Modern Toys, American Toys, 1930–1980,* Collector Books, 1985, 1993 value update; William M. Bean and Al M. Sternagle, *Greenberg's Guide To Gilbert Erector Sets Volume One, 1913–1932,* Greenberg Publishing, 1993; Raymond V. Brandes, *Big Bang Cannons,* Ray-Vin Publishing, 1993; Bill Bruegman, *Toys Of The Sixties: A Pictorial Guide,* Cap'n Penny Productions, 1991; Steve Butler and Clarence Young, *Autoquotes, The Complete Reference For: Promotions, Pot Metal & Plastic with Prices,* Autohobby Publications, 1993; Roger Case and Tom Hammel (eds.), *1995 Toys & Prices, 2nd Edition,* Krause Publications, 1994; Robert Carter and Eddy Rubinstein, *Yesterday's Yesteryears: Lesney "Matchbox" Models,* Haynes Publishing Group (London), 1986; Wallace M. Chrouch, *Mego Toys: An Illustrated Value Guide,* Collector Books, 1995; Jurgen and Marianne Cieslik, *Lehmann Toys,* New Cavendish Books, 1982; John A. Clark, *HO Slot Car Identification and Price Guide,* L–W Book Sales, 1995; Don Cranmer, *Collectors Encyclopedia, Toys–Banks,* L–W Books, 1986, 1993 value update; Gael de Courtivron, *Collectible Coca–Cola Toy Trucks: An Identification and Value Guide,* Collector Books, 1995; Elmer Duellman, *Elmer's Price*

Guide To Toys, L–W Book Sales, 1995; Edward Force, *Classic Miniature Vehicles: Made In Italy,* Schiffer Publishing, 1992; Edward Force, *Corgi Toys,* Schiffer Publishing, 1984, 1991 value update; Edward Force, *Dinky Toys,* Schiffer Publishing, 1988, 1992 value update; Edward Force, *Matchbox and Lledo Toys,* Schiffer Publishing, 1988; Edward Force, *Miniature Emergency Vehicles,* Schiffer Publishing, 1985; Edward Force, *Solido Toys,* Schiffer Publishing, 1993; Tom Frey, *Toy Bop: Kid Classics of the 50's & 60's,* Fuzzy Dice Productions, 1994; Richard Friz, *The Official Price Guide to Collectible Toys, 5th Edition,* House of Collectibles, 1990; Gordon Gardiner and Alistar Morris, *Illustrated Encyclopedia of Metal Toys,* Harmony House, 1984; Sally Gibson–Brown and Christine Gentry, *Motorcycle Toys, Antique and Contemporary: Identification and Values,* Collector Books, 1995; David C. Gould and Donna Crevar–Donaldson, *Occupied Japan Toys With Prices,* L–W Book Sales, 1993; Lillian Gottschalk, *American Toy Cars & Trucks,* Abbeville Press, 1985; Jeffrey C. Gurski, *Greenberg's Guide To Cadillac Models And Toys,* Greenberg Publishing, 1992; Bill Hanlon, *Plastic Toys: Dimestore Dreams of the '40s & '50s,* Schiffer Publishing, 1993; Michael V. Harwood, *The Hess Toy Collector,* F.S.B.O. Books, 1991; Jay Horowitz, *Marx Western Playsets: The Authorized Guide,* Greenberg Publishing, 1992; Don Hultzman, *Collecting Battery Toys: A Reference, Rarity and Value Guide,* Books Americana, 1994; Sharon and Bob Huxford (eds.), *Schroeder's Collectible Toys: Antique to Modern Price Guide,* Collector Books, 1995; Dana Johnson, *Matchbox Toys 1948 to 1993: Identification and Value Guide,* Collector Books, 1994; Joe Johnson and Dana McGuinn, *Toys That Talk: Over 300 Pullstring Dolls & Toys—1960s To Today,* Firefly Publishing, 1992; Dale Kelley, *Collecting The Tin Toy Car, 1950–1970,* Schiffer Publishing, Ltd, 1984; Constance King, *Metal Toys & Automata,* Chartwell Books, 1989; Raymond R. Klein, *Greenberg's Guide To Tootsietoys 1945–1969,* Greenberg Publishing, 1993; Sharon Korbeck (ed.), *Toy Shop 1995 Annual Directory,* Krause Publications, 1995; Samuel H. Logan and Charles H. Best, *Cast Iron Toy Guns And Capshooters,* published by authors, 1990; Ernest & Ida Long, *Dictionary Of Toys Sold In America,* published by author, two volumes; David Longest, *Antique & Collectible Toys, 1870–1950: Identification & Values,* Collector Books, 1994; David Longest, *Character Toys and Collectibles, First Series* (1984, 1992 value update,) and *Second Series* (1987), Collector Books; David Longest, *Toys: Antique & Collectible,* Collector Books, 1990, 1995 value update; L–W BookSales, *Cartoon & Character Toys of the 50s, 60s, & 70s: Plastic & Vinyl,* L–W Book Sales, 1995; L–W Book Sales, *Riding Toys,* L–W Book

Sales, 1992; Charlie Mack, *Lesney's Matchbox Toys: Regular Wheel Years, 1947–1969,* Schiffer Publishing, 1992; Charlie Mack, *Lesney's Matchbox Toys: The Superfast Years, 1969–1982,* Schiffer Publishing, 1993; Charlie Mack, *Matchbox Toys: The Universal Years, 1982–1992,* Schiffer Publishing, 1993; Jack Matthews, *Toys Go To War: World War II Military Toys, Games, Puzzles & Books,* Pictorial Histories Publishing, 1994; Albert W. McCollough, *The New Book Of Buddy L Toys, Volume I,* (1991), and *Volume II,* (1991), Greenberg Publishing; Neil McElwee, *McElwee's Collector's Guide #1: Smith–Miller, 1944–1955,* published by author, 1994; Neil McElwee, *McElwee's Collector's Guide #3: Tonka Toys, 1947–1961,* published by author, 1992; Neil McElwee, *McElwee's Collector's Guide #5: Postwar Buddy "L," 1945–1970,* published by author, 1992; Neil McElwee, *McElwee's Collector's Guide #6: Ny–Lint, 1946–1970,* published by author, 1993; Neil McElwee, *McElwee's Collector's Guide #7: Big Ertl, Cast Commercial Trucks & Construction Vehicles, 1950's–1990,* published by author, 1993; Neil McElwee, *McElwee's Collector's Guide #8: Gasoline Company Toys . . . Trucks & Automotive, 1930's–1990's,* published by author, 1994; Neil McElwee, *McElwee's Collector's Guide #9: Structo, 1912–1976,* published by author, 1993; Neil McElwee, *McElwee's Collector's Guide #10: Postwar Big Metal Classics,* published by author, 1994; Neil McElwee, *McElwee's Small Motor News Annual 1995,* published by author, 1994; Brian Moran, *Battery Toys: The Modern Automata,* Schiffer Publishing, Ltd, 1984; John J. Murray and Bruce Fox, *Fisher–Price, 1931–1963: A Historical, Rarity, Value Guide, Second Edition* Books Americana, 1991; Nigel Mynheer, *Tin Toys,* Boxtree (London), 1988; Richard O'Brien, *Collecting Toy Cars & Trucks: Identification and Value Guide,* Books Americana, 1994; Richard O'Brien, *Collecting Toys: A Collectors Identification and Value Guide, Seventh Edition,* Books Americana, 1995; Bob Parker, *Hot Wheels: A Collector's Guide,* Schiffer Publishing, 1993; Maxine A. Pinsky, *Greenberg's Guide To Marx Toys, Volume I* (1988) and *Volume II* (1990), Greenberg Publishing; David Richter, *Collectors Guide to Tootsietoys,* Collector Books, 1990, 1993 value update; Harry L. Rinker, *Collector's Guide To Toys, Games, and Puzzles,* Wallace–Homestead, 1991; Nancy Schiffer, (comp.), *Matchbox Toys, Revised,* Schiffer Publishing, 1995; Ron Smith, *Collecting Toy Airplanes: An Identification and Value Guide,* Books Americana, 1995; Robin Langley Sommer, *I Had One Of Those: Toys Of Our Generation,* Crescent Books, 1992; Bruce and Diane Stoneback, *Matchbox Toys: A Guide To Selecting, Collecting, and Enjoying New and Vintage Models,* Chartwell Books, 1993; Jack Tempest, *Post–War Tin Toys: A Collector's Guide,*

Wallace–Homestead, 1991; Glenda Thomas, *Toy and Miniature Sewing Machines: An Identification and Value Guide,* Collector Books, 1995; Tom Tumbusch, *Tomart's Price Guide To Hot Wheels,* Tomart Publications, 1993; Carol Turpen, *Baby Boomer Toys And Collectibles,* Schiffer Publishing, 1993; Peter Viemeister, *Micro Cars,* Hamilton's, 1982; Gerhard C. Walter, *Metal Toys From Nuremberg: hanical Toys Of The Firm Of Georg Kellerman & Co. Of Nuremberg 1910–1979,* Schiffer Publishing, 1992; James Weiland and Dr. Edward Force, *Tootsie Toys, World's First Die Cast Models,* Motorbooks Inteternational, 1980.

Collectors' Clubs: A. C. Gilbert Heritage Society, 594 Front St., Marion, MA 02738; American Game Collectors Assoc., 49 Brooks Ave., Lewiston, ME 04240; American International Matchbox Collectors & Exchange Club, 532 Chestnut St., Lynn, MA 01904; Anchor Block Foundation, 980 Plymouth St., Pelham, NY 10803; Antique Engine, Tractor & Toy Club, 5731 Paradise Rd., Slatington, PA 18080; Antique Toy Collectors of America, Two Wall Street, 13th Floor, New York, NY 10005; Capitol Miniature Auto Collectors Club, 10207 Greenacres Dr., Silver Spring, MD 20903; Diecast Exchange Club, PO Box 1066, Pineallas Park, FL 34665; Ertl Collectors Club, Highways 186 & 120, Dyersville, IA 52040; Farm Toy Collectors Club, PO Box 38, Boxholm, IA 50040; Girder and Panel Collectors Club, PO Box 494, Bolton, MA, 01740; H.O. Slot Car Collecting & Racing Club, 284 Willets Lane, West Islip, NY 14795; Majorette Diecast Toy Collectors Association, 1347 NW Albany Ave., Bend, OR 97701; Matchbox Collectors Club, PO Box 278, Durham, CT 06422; Matchbox Collectors Club, 62 Saw Mill Rd., Durham, CT 06422; Matchbox International Collectors Association, 574 Canewood Crescent, Waterloo, Ontario N2L 5P6 Canada; San Francisco Bay Broolin Club, PO Box 61018, Palo Alto, CA 94306; Schoenhut Collectors Club, 45 Louis Ave., West Seneca, NY 14224; Schoenhut Toy Collectors, 1916 Cleveland St., Evanston, IL 60202; Southern California Meccano & Erector Club, 9661 Sabre Ave., Garden Grove, CA 92644; Southern California Toy Collectors Club, Suite 300, 1760 Termino, Long Beach, CA 90804.

Periodicals: *Action Toys Newsletter,* PO Box 31551, Billings, MT 59107; *Antique Toy World,* PO Box 34509, Chicago, IL 60634; *Canadian Toy Mania,* PO Box 489, Rocanville, Saskatchewan SOA 3LO Canada, *Collectible Toys and Values,* Attic Books, 15 Danbury Road, Ridgefield, CT 06877; *Collecting Toys,* PO Box 1989, Milwaukee, WI 53201; *Die Cast Digest,* PO Box 12510, Knoxville, TN 37912; *Die Cast & Tin Toy Report,* PO Box 501, Williamsburg, VA

23187; Matchbox USA Newsletter, 62 Saw Mill Rd., Durham, CT 06422; *Model and Toy Collector*, 137 Casterton Ave., Akron, OH, 44303; *Plastic Figure & Playset Collector*, Box 1355, La Crosse, WI 54602; *Spec–Tacular News*, PO Box 324, Dyersville, IA 52040; *The Plane News*, PO Box 845, Greenwich, CT 06836; *Toy Cannon News*, PO Box 2052-N, Norcross, GA, 30071; *Toy Collector Marketplace*, 1550 Territorial Rd., Benton Harbor, MI 49022; *Toy Collector and Price Guide*, 700 E. State St., Iola, WI 54990; *Toy Farmer*, HC 2, Box 5, LaMoure, ND 58458; *Toy Gun Collectors of America Newsletter*, 312 Starling Way, Anaheim, CA 92807; *Toy Shop*, 700 E. State St., Iola, WI 54990; *Toy Tractor Times*, PO Box 156, Osage, IA 50461-0156; *Toy Trader*, PO Box 1050, Dubuque, IA 52004; *Tractor Classics*, PO Box 191, Listowel, Ontario N4H 3HE Canada; *Turtle River Toy News & Oliver Collector's News*, RR1, Box 44, Manvel, ND 58256-9763; *Wheel Goods Trader*, PO Box 435, Fraser, MI 48026; *U.S. Toy Collector Magazine*, PO Box 4244, Missoula, MT 59806; *Yo–Yo Times*, PO Box 1519, Herndon, VA 22070.

Museums: American Museum of Automobile Miniatures, Andover, MA; Museum of the City of New York, New York, NY; Matchbox & Lesney Toy Museum, Durham, CT; Matchbox Road Museum, Newfield, NJ; Smithsonian Institution, Washington, DC; Margaret Woodbury Strong Museum, Rochester, NY; Toy Museum of Atlanta, Atlanta, GA.

See: Battery Operated, Cartoon Characters, Disneyana, Dolls, Games, Paper Dolls, Radio Characters, Dimestore Soldiers, Toy Soldiers, Toy Trains and many other categories.

ALPS

Alps Shoji Ltd., located in Tokyo, Japan, was founded in 1948. The company manufactured windup and battery powered toys made from tin and plastic. Toys are marked "ALPS."

Daredevil–Acrobatic Stunt–Motorcycle, friction, litho tin, figural driver wearing helmet and goggles, orig box, 5½" l **150.00**
Hot Rod Custom 'T' Ford, battery operated, litho tin and plastic, stop–and–go action, lighted engine, orig box, 10½" l **190.00**
Merry Go–Round, windup, litho tin, four cars and celluloid balls rotate above base, child rider in each car, orig box, 10" l **250.00**
School Bus, battery operated, doors open and close, flashing headlights, MIB **120.00**

ARCADE

The Arcade Manufacturing Company first produced toys in 1893. In 1919, the firm began to make the yellow cabs for the Yellow Cab Company of Chicago. The exclusive advertising rights were sold to the cab company with Arcade holding the right to make toy replicas of the cabs. This idea was popular and soon was used with Buick, Ford, etc., and McCormack and International Harvester farm equipment. The company continued until 1946 when it was sold to Rockwell Manufacturing Company of Pittsburgh.

Arcade, Greyhound Bus, A Century of Progress, Chicago, 1933, painted cast iron, rubber tires, orig label, 11½" l, $375.00.

Model A, cast iron, nickel plated wheels, 1930s, 4" l **125.00**
Model T Four Door Sedan, cast iron, nickel plated spoke wheels, 6½" l . . **550.00**
Railplane **175.00**
Road Roller, cast iron, wood roller, 5½" l **300.00**
Roadster, cast iron, white rubber tires, 1930s, 4½" l **150.00**
Stake Truck **175.00**
Trailer, two wheels, 3½" l **100.00**

BANDAI, Japan

Bandai Co., one of the many toy manufacturers which began production in Japan after World War II, started with tin toys and later changed to plastic and steel. Bandai Toys are found with friction action and battery operation. They are often marked "Bandai Toys, Japan." Bandai still produces toys and is a major Japanese exporter to the US and other foreign countries.

Chrysler Valiant Sedan, #736, tin, detailed litho tin int., rear mounted spare, "Valiant" plate, orig box, 8¼" l   **95.00**
Citreon DS–19, friction, tin, detailed litho tin int., "DS" litho tin hubs, 8¼" l **100.00**
Ford Falcon Licensed Plated Model Car, tin, detailed litho tin int., black rub-

ber tires, windshields, orig box, 1961,
8¼" l **90.00**

Ford Falcon Sedan, #812, friction, tin,
detailed litho tin int., raised "Ford"
emblem on hood, orig box, 8¼" l . . **85.00**

Ford GT, battery operated, tin, black
plastic tires, mystery bump–and–go
action, motor sound, flashing red
light in rear window, doors fly open
when car stops, orig box, 10" l **95.00**

Isetta, #588, friction, tin, two–tone
green, tin steering wheel, door opens,
orig box, 6½" l **400.00**

Ocean Boat, litho tin, crank handle, driver wearing goggles, orig box, 12" l **150.00**

Plymouth Valiant, friction, tin, litho tin
int., plastic windshield and steering
wheel, engine noise, 1961 . . . . **115.00**

Rambler Classic Station Wagon
Licensed Plated Model Car, friction,
tin, detailed litho tin int., roof rack,
black rubber tires with "R" hubs,
windshields, orig box, 1961, 8¼" l **90.00**

Sparkling Rocket Car, friction, tin and
plastic, black rubber tires, orig box,
1950s, 7½" l **225.00**

Vespa Scooter, friction, tin, Vespa li-
cense plates, 9" l **275.00**

Volkswagen Beetle, friction, tin, plastic
steering wheel and windshield, 8" l **115.00**

X–3 Racer, friction, litho tin, driver
wearing helmet and goggles, full
windshield, black rubber tires, no
hubs, orig box, 7½" l **135.00**

CHEIN

The Chein Company was in business from the
1930s through the 1950s. Most of these lithographed tin toys were sold in dimestores. Chein
toys are clearly marked.

Chein, World War I Lorry, $65.00.

Alligator, windup, native on back **300.00**
Busy Mike Sand Toy, tin **200.00**
Circus Roller Coaster, windup, litho tin,
red, white, and blue tin cars, yellow
metal ramps, bell rings, circus scenes
around sides, built–in key, 1950s, 8 x
19½ x 9" **350.00**

Disney Top, litho tin, Walt Disney
Productions, c1950, 5½" d **100.00**

Duck, windup, litho tin **45.00**

Ferris Wheel, Hercules, 1930s **390.00**

Hopping Rabbit, windup, litho tin,
wearing tuxedo and bowtie, 1930,
5" l **135.00**

Mechanical Drummer, #109, windup,
litho tin, orig box, 9" h **235.00**

Motorboat, windup, litho tin, 8" l **50.00**

Pig Waddler, windup, litho tin, 4½" h **95.00**

Rocket Ride, windup, litho tin, four
rockets, 18", 11" d base **650.00**

Sand Pail, nursery rhyme characters,
4" h **50.00**

Seaplane, windup, pilot, spinning propellers, orig box, 1930s, 8½" l **290.00**

Three Little Pigs Wringer Washer, crank,
litho tin tub, wood and tin ringer attachment, 1930s, 8" h **215.00**

Windmill Sand Toy **75.00**

Yellow Taxi, litho tin, marked "Yellow
Taxi Main 7570," early mark, 6" l . . **100.00**

CORGI

Playcraft Toys introduced Corgi miniature vehicles in 1956. This popular line soon became
Corgi Toys. The first cars were made on a 1:45 to
1:48 scale. Corgi cars were the first miniature
cars to have clear plastic windows. Other design
features included opening doors and interiors. In
1972, the scale of 1:36 was introduced. This
scale was more durable for play but less desirable to collectors. Finally, the company added
other types of cars and trucks, including character representations.

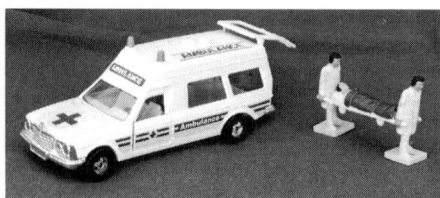

**Corgi, Ambulance, Bonna 2500, red
blanket, red stripes and cross, $35.00.**

Army Field Kitchen, #359 . . . . **195.00**

Avengers Gift Set #40, diecast metal
vintage Bentley and Lotus Elan S2 au-
tos, John Steed and Emma Peel figures, Bentley needs steering wheel,
orig box, 1966 . . . . **160.00**

Chevrolet SS 350 Camaro, #338,
diecast, scale model, opening doors,
sliding headlight covers, tilting seats,
detachable hardtop, spring suspen-
sion, orig box, 4" l **55.00**

Ford Cortina Estate Golf, #440, MIB . . **160.00**

Ford T.T. Express Service, #1137 . . . . . **165.00**
Greyhound Bus, #2008 . . . . **75.00**
Hardy Boys Rolls Royce, #805 . . . . . . **250.00**
Karrier Bantam Mobile Butcher, #413 **195.00**
London Bus, #468, MIB **40.00**
Lotus Elan Coupe, #319 . . . . **95.00**
Mack Trans Continental, #1100 . . . . . . **95.00**
Maserati Form 1, #155 . . . . **70.00**
Massey Fergueson Combine, #1111 . . . **200.00**
Popeye's Tugboat, metal and plastic . . **26.00**
Shelvoke Trash Truck, #1116 . . . . **45.00**
VW Breakdown Truck, #490, orig box **150.00**
Wrecker Truck, #1144, red, white, and
blue **95.00**

DINKY

Dinky Toys, made by the Meccano Toy Company of England, were first created by Frank Hornby in 1933. The Dinky series of diecast cars and trucks continued until World War II precluded the use of metal for toys. In 1945, production of diecast metal toys began with the introduction of a military line, as well as new cars and trucks. Production continued in factories in England and France until competition from Corgi, Tootsietoy, and Matchbox caused a decline in sales. The Dinky line was discontinued in 1979.

Alpha Romeo 1900M, #527–A **65.00**
AMX Bridgelaying Tank, #883–A, MIB **300.00**
Bell Police Helicopter, #732–A, MIB . . **65.00**
Cement Mixer, #960–A, MIB **150.00**
Coast Guard Missile Launcher, #674–B,
MIB **65.00**
DUKW Amphibian, #681=A, MIB **45.00**
Ford D800 Tipper Truck, #438–A, MIB **95.00**
Land Rover Wrecker, #442–A, MIB . . . **55.00**
Leopard Tank, #692–B, MIB **125.00**
Michigan Tractor Dozer, #976–A, MIB **95.00**
Missile Servicing Platform, #667–A, MIB **275.00**
Studebaker Commander M, #540–A . . **150.00**
USS Enterprise, #803–B, MBP **45.00**

ERTL

Fred Ertl, Senior, founded Ertl in 1945. Blueprints obtained from companies such as John Deere and International Harvester were used as patterns, thus insuring a high level of similarity when comparing the toy with the original. Ertl produces a full line of wheeled vehicles and is recognized as the world's largest manufacturer of toy farm equipment.

Caterpillar D25D Dump Truck, 1/64
scale **7.00**
Chevy Bel Air, 1/18 scale, 1957, hard-
top, green and ivory **25.00**
Coke Beverage Truck, 1/64 scale **13.00**
Ford Big Farm Pickup Truck, 1/32 scale **10.00**
Ford F150 Pickup Truck, 1/16 scale . . . **20.00**

Ford #846 4 Wheel Drive Tractor, 1/32
scale **23.00**
Hemi Roadrunner, '69, 1/18 scale, blue **23.00**
Hesston SL–30 Skid Steer Loader, 1/64
scale **4.50**
John Deere, Ford R–250 Pickup Truck,
1/64 scale **3.00**
Rumley #6 Tractor, 1/16 scale **50.00**
Thunderbird, 1957, 1/43 scale, black
and white **6.00**

FISHER–PRICE

Fisher–Price Toys was founded in East Aurora, NY, in 1930. The original company consisted of Irving L. Price, retired from F. W. Woolworth Co., Herman G. Fisher, who was associated with the Alderman–Fairchild Toy Co. in Churchville, NY, and Helen M. Schelle, a former toy store owner. Margaret Evans Price, wife of the company president, was the company's first artist and designer. She was formerly a writer and illustrator of children's books. The company began with sixteen designs. Herman Fisher resigned as president in 1966. In 1969 the company was acquired by the Quaker Oats Company.

Black and white rectangular logos appeared on all toys prior to 1962. The first plastic part was used after 1949.

Chatter Telephone, #H747, MIB **65.00**
Circus Wagon, #900 . . . . **75.00**
Dr Doodle, #132, 1940, 10" h **75.00**
Farm, #1005 . . . . **50.00**
Hickory Dickory Dock, radio and clock **25.00**
Huffy Puffy Train, 1955, MIB **250.00**
Kris Kricket, #678, 9" l **75.00**
Little Snoopy, wood, plastic wheels and
shoe **15.00**
Magic Key Mansion, six rooms, furnish-
ings, price for 125 piece set **230.00**
Merry Mousewife, #662 . . . . **65.00**
Mickey Drummer, missing drum **100.00**
Mighty Tractor, #629 . . . . **25.00**
Musical Duck, #795, orig box, 1952,
6½" h **100.00**
Pony Express, #733 . . . . **75.00**
Pop–Up Kritter, Pluto, wood, Walt
Disney Enterprises copyright **40.00**
Quackie Family, #799 . . . . **85.00**
Running Bunny, #722 . . . . **45.00**
Snoopy Sniffer, No. 180 . . . . **175.00**
Talking Donald Duck, #765, pull toy,
wood, Donald on wheeled cart,
voice mechanism, arms swing, feet
pedal, orig box, 1955 . . . . **275.00**

HUBLEY

The Hubley Manufacturing Company was founded in 1894 in Lancaster, Pennsylvania, by John Hubley. The first toys were cast iron. In

1940 cast iron was phased out and replaced with lesser metals and plastic. The production of cap pistols was increased at this time. By 1952, Hubley made more cap pistols than toys. Gabriel Industries bought Hubley in 1965.

American Eagle Plane, diecast metal, retractable wheels, folding wings, opening cockpit, orig display box, unused, 1971, 11" l **100.00**
Bell Telephone Truck, pot metal, hoist and tools, 9" l **175.00**
Boat Tail Racer, cast iron, 6½" l **200.00**
Corvette, diecast metal, marked "Hubley Corvette," 1954 . . . .   **85.00**
Dump Truck, plastic, green and yellow, silver accents, black rubber wheels, spring loaded bed, 1950s, 6" l **30.00**
Earth Mover, #354, plastic, automatic dumping action, spare tire, orig box, 14" l **90.00**
Kiddie Toy Race Car, metal, nickel plated driver, red, black rubber tires, 1950s, 7" l **25.00**
Racer #6, cast iron, nickel plated driver, white rubber tires, red, 1930s, 4¾" l   **95.00**
Surf 'n Sand, metal, jeep and boat with trailer, blue and white, orig window box, 15" l **75.00**

IDEAL

The Ideal Toy Company was owned by Lewis David Christie. It was located in Bridgeport, Connecticut. Among the toys it produced were dolls, cars, trucks, and even a line of toy soldiers produced c1920 until 1929.

Car, plastic, resembles Jaguar, blue, hood opens, silver plastic engine, 1950s **15.00**
Evel Knievel Precision Miniature, Formula 5000 race car replica, diecast metal, white, orig box, 1977 . . .   **20.00**
Fix–It Truck, plastic, tools, flat tire, spare, jack, 1950s **35.00**
Flintstone Cave House, 1964 . . . .   **60.00**
Hickory Dickory Clock, talking, red, yellow, blue, and black, 1950s, MIB   **50.00**
Jeep, plastic, brown, star sticker, 1950s, 4" l **20.00**
Mr Machine, 1970s **30.00**
Washing Machine, windup, MIB **40.00**

JAPANESE, POST WAR

Following World War II, a huge variety of tin toys produced in Osaka and the Koto District of Japan flooded the American market. The vast majority of these toys are marked only with the country of origin and a trademark, usually consisting of a two– or three–letter monogram. It is virtually impossible to trace these trademarks to a specific manufacturer. Also, many toys were assembled from parts made by several different factories. To make matters even more confusing, names found on boxes are often those of the agent or distributor, rather than the manufacturer.

The following toys are listed by their trademarks. When possible, the toy's manufacturer and/or distributor are also identified. Also see specific listings for other Japanese toy companies.

Japanese Postwar, AHI, KO Combat Jeep, #5907, battery operated, remote control, litho tin, orig box, 4¾" l, 2¾" h, $85.00.

Asahi, Volvo 164, battery operated, tin, silver, orig box, 8" l **100.00**
ATC
Air Carrousel, windup, litho tin tower, base, and canopy, three celluloid prop airplanes with litho tin riders, 6" h **120.00**
Ferrari Berlinetta 250/Lemans, battery operated, litho tin racer, marked "24 Heures Le Mans," bump–and–go action, engine sound, orig box, 11" l **110.00**
Cragstan
Crap Shooter, battery operated, vinyl face, MIB **145.00**
Pet Shop Truck, friction, litho tin, swivel bed doors, black rubber tires, orig box, 11" l **115.00**
Star of the Circus Clown, friction, litho tin, clown driving red and yellow car, clown tips hat, turns head, and waves, car advances, 6½" l . .   **180.00**
Poodle, battery operated, white **40.00**
Daito, Pleasure Goose, friction, litho tin, advances with flapping wings, beak opens and shuts, clicking sounds, orig box, 1950s, 6" h **125.00**
Daiya, Cradle Bus, friction, litho tin bonnet bus marked "Cradle Bus" on sides, black rubber tires, siren sound, orig box, 7½" l **415.00**
Ichida, Ford Gyron, Mystery Car of the Future, battery operated, tin, litho tin int., black rubber tires, two rear an-

tennae, non–stop action, cockpit opens and closes, orig box, 11″ l ... **425.00**

Indian Head Logo

Flying Jeep, friction, litho tin, Navy watercraft with pilot and gunner, clear plastic windscreen, spinning disc engine, orig box, 6½″ l **175.00**

Ford Station Wagon, friction, litho tin, marked "Country Squire" and "Ford," siren sound, black rubber tires, orig box, 9¾″ l **90.00**

K, Circus Trailer, friction, tin cab, two litho tin trailer cages hold swaying elephant and tiger, orig box, 18″ l .. **625.00**

KA, Circus Elephant, windup, litho tin, rolls plastic ball, twirls litho tin umbrella, orig box, 5½″ h **95.00**

KO, Kanto Toys, Circus Boat, crank friction, litho tin, boat with clown driver, vinyl head, mystery action, clown rocks back and forth, orig box, 7½″ l **140.00**

KSK, Monkey–Dean, windup, plush monkey with celluloid face, dressed as professor with cap, glasses, and cane, walks, orig box, 6″ h **110.00**

M, San Francisco Cable Car, #514, friction, litho tin, roof plates marked "Powell & Mason Sts," black passengers and conductor, orig box marked "An exact replica of Andrew Hollidies famous cable car," 8″ l **140.00**

Marusan, Main Street Bakery, litho tin van, black rubber tires, orig box ... **325.00**

MM

Drummer Clown with Horn, windup, litho tin, cloth outfit and hat, walks, beats drum, head sways, 10″ h ... **175.00**

Yo Yo Playing Bunny, windup, plush rabbit, litho tin face, head moves, rolls yo yo, orig box, 7½″ h **75.00**

S & E

Playing Family Dach's Hund, windup, litho tin, mother dachshund carrying puppies on her back, rubber tail, erratic motion, orig box, 11″ l **120.00**

Snapping Alligator, windup, litho tin, bee suspended in front of alligator's jaws, alligator twists head and snaps jaws, orig box, 12″ l **95.00**

Showa, Walking Cadet, windup, litho tin, hp celluloid face, fabric hat with feather, head turns, orig box, 6½″ h **125.00**

SSS, Old Timer Delivery Truck, battery operated, tin, orig box, 10½″ l ... **130.00**

TKR, Bingo the Clown, battery operated, plastic and cloth, hp facial features, as clown advances his body collapses like an accordion, then returns to full height, squeaks, orig window box, 14″ h **385.00**

TTT, Mechanical Jolly Drummer, windup, hp papier mache face, cloth

costume, rubber drumsticks, litho tin snare drum, plays drum and sways head as he marches, orig box, 7″ h **135.00**

Usagayi, Camouflage Soldier Cycle, friction, litho tin, cycle marked "C–7" and "Combat," telescoping antenna, rifle, siren sound, 8″ l **225.00**

Yone

Amusement Park Rocket Ride, windup, litho tin, two rockets suspended from tower, vinyl head boy riders, bell rings as rockets circle, orig box **215.00**

Flying Elephant, windup, litho tin, gyro attached to trunk, orig box, 1950s, 6″ l **100.00**

Spin Turn Racer, windup, tin, plastic tires, orig box, 5″ l **65.00**

Super Rocket Ride, windup, litho tin base and two rockets, vinyl head riders, orig box, 9″ h **235.00**

Yonezawa, "Y" in flower mark

Amphibious Nautilus Y–10 Submarine, friction, litho tin, crank lever advances wheeled sub, mounted machine gun, orig box, 15″ l **200.00**

Boxing Dog, windup, plush and litho tin, sign around neck reads "Next 4th Round," orig box, 6″ h **95.00**

Old Timer, battery operated, litho tin, man driving jalopy, bump–and–go action, orig box, 9″ l **180.00**

Sight Seeing Bus, battery operated, tin, lift–up windows, cutout individual seats, tin driver, bump–and–go action, orig box, early 1950s, 9″ l **225.00**

LEHMANN

The Ernst Paul Lehmann Company was located in Brandenburg, Germany. The company began in 1881 and continues to the present. Lehmann toys are known for attractive lithography and patina. The use of clockwork and mechanical friction action was prevalent. Export to the United States was sporadic after 1933. Most Lehmann toys were sold in America through jobbers, such as Butler Bros., George Broadway Rouss, and Montgomery Ward. Many popular toys, such as the Balky Mule, were offered for over 25 years. Lehmann toys are marked "E.P.L." and/or "Lehmann."

Africa **725.00**

Gaudi Yoyo, #800, US Zone Germany, c1952 .... **75.00**

Quack Quack, windup, litho tin, mother mallard pulling basket of three ducklings, 1903, 8″ l **350.00**

Rigi Cable Car, #900, crank, tin, West Germany, 8″ h **125.00**

Tam Tam, #677, spinning top, spiral drive rod, spring, hand grasp mechanism, litho tin, orig box, 1920 . . . . .   **425.00**

Torpedo Boat Taku, #671, windup, litho tin, 1907, 10″ l **675.00**

LINEMAR

Linemar is a subsidiary of Marx. Linemar toys are manufactured in Japan.

Linemar, Service Station, #J1199, battery operated, litho tin, orig box, 10¼″ l, 3½″ h, $225.00.

Disney Donald Duck Flivver, friction, litho tin convertible, press down on Donald's head to activate motor, 5½″ l **250.00**

Hauler and Trailer, friction, litho tin, marked "Pacific Intermountain Express," orig box, 1950s, 6″ l **100.00**

Livestock Trailer, tin, 14″ l **95.00**

Mechanical Cat, windup, litho tin, cat with vacuum, ribbon collar, vibrating motion, twirling rubber tail, 1950s, orig box, 3½″ h **150.00**

Mickey Driver, windup, litho tin, convertible and Mickey Mouse driver, non–fall action, Mickey waves and nods head, orig box, 6½″ h **865.00**

Patsy the Pig, windup, litho tin, pink, blue, and yellow, orig box, 1960s, 4″ h **60.00**

Playtime Airlines, friction, tin, four metal propellers, 7½″ l wingspan . . .   **150.00**

Pluto the Drum Major, litho tin, rubber ears and tail, rocks while tooting horn and shaking bell and baton, orig box, 6″ h **550.00**

Pull Back Donald Duck with Huey & Voice, litho tin, Huey attached to Donald by rope, orig box, 5½″ h . . .   **865.00**

MARX

Louis Marx founded the Marx Toy Company in 1921, stressing quality at the lowest possible price. His popular line of toys included every type of toy except dolls. The company was sold to Quaker Oats Company, who sold it in 1976 to the European company of Dunbee–Combex–Marx.

American Trucking Company, litho tin truck marked "Moving–Shipping–Storing" on sides and "Padded Van" on doors, three stars on roof, rear door opens, 1930s, 5″ l **300.00**

Army Fort **35.00**

Bengal Tiger on Wheels, hard plastic, movable mouth **35.00**

Big–3 Aerial Acrobats, windup, metal frame, litho tin acrobats, two 5½″ h boy acrobats, 4″ girl acrobat, orig box, 1930s **300.00**

Chris Craft Cruiser, windup, plastic, white, brown deck, red keel, 1950s, 18″ l **85.00**

City Sanitation Truck **175.00**

Climbing Fireman, Howdy Doody look alike face on box, MIB **350.00**

Coal Dump Truck, battery operated, tin, automatic dumping, forward, and reverse, MIB **150.00**

Combat Airplane, pressed steel, four propellers, separate litho tin nose cone and side plates with gunman and airman each side, 10″ l **450.00**

Construction Camp, tin building, construction equipment, and accessories, orig box **125.00**

Convertible, Fix–All, plastic, hard top, blue and yellow, small tools in trunk, orig box, 1950s, 10″ l **90.00**

Corn Planter, 5″ l **115.00**

Disney Parade Roadster, windup, litho tin convertible, plastic Donald, Goofy, Minnie, and one nephew riders, orig box, 11″ l **650.00**

Donald the Driver, windup, litho tin convertible, hp plastic Donald Duck driver, Donald waves and nods head, orig box, 6½″ l **650.00**

Doughboy Tank, windup, guns move back and forth, soldier pops out, flag appears, gun noise, orig box, 1930s, 9″ l **375.00**

Drumming Major, windup, litho tin . . .   **175.00**

Dump Truck, 1930–40s, 4½″ l **75.00**

Easter Bunny Delivery **95.00**

Farm Mower, 10″ l **125.00**

Flintstone Pals on Dino, windup, litho tin, vinyl headed Barney rider, advances, sound, orig box and instruction sheet for removing Barney's head, 8½″ l **535.00**

Flintstones Playset, tin, 1962 . . . .   **265.00**

Flippo Dog **60.00**

Freight Station Playset, tin, three plastic trucks, several hand carts, complete   **275.00**

GI Joe and His Jouncing Jeep 250.00
Go–Kart Racer, friction, plastic, full figure driver, rear raised engine, 1960s,
orig box, 5½″ l 65.00
Gold Star Transfer Company Truck,
company name on trailer, rear doors
open, 1950s, 22″ l 60.00
Hess Tank Trailer, battery operated
lights, hard plastic, rubber hose, orig
box, c1972, 13½″ l 95.00
Huckleberry Car, friction, MIB 375.00
International Agent Car, friction, litho
tin, marked "UEA, United Espionage
Agency," copyright 1966, 4″ l 85.00
Jaguar Coupe, E Type, battery operated,
remote control, plastic, red, silver accents, orig box, 1960s, 8″ l 100.00
Joy Rider Eccentric Car, windup, litho
tin, driver in graffiti decorated car
with suitcase and rear trunk, rocking
and tipping motions, drives in circles,
1928, 8″ l 300.00
M–16 Assault Rifle, plastic, 1966, 32″ l   35.00
Marxie Mustard, friction, litho tin, soft
vinyl caricature mustard bottle driver,
1969, 4″ l 40.00
Midget Climbing Tractor, windup, litho
tin, red, black and yellow trim, orig
box, c1950, 5″ l 85.00
Nutty Mad Car, friction, litho tin, red,
soft molded vinyl head, 1960s 60.00
Press Lever Top Set, plunger and two
litho tin globes, one with map of
world, other with faces, pump plunger
to spin globes, orig box 175.00
Racer, litho tin race car and driver, oversized wheels, 5″ l
#3 . . . .   260.00
#4 . . . .   150.00
#5 . . . .   120.00
Sam The Gardener, figure pushing
wheelbarrow, garden tools, MIB   . . .   350.00
Sports Car, #2, friction, plastic, visible
Straight Eight engine, black rubber
tires, sparking action, needs new flint,
orig box, 1950s, 7½″ l 175.00
Walking Pinocchio 525.00
Watch Me Roll Over Pluto 225.00

MATCHBOX

Matchbox cars were first manufactured by
Lesney Products, an English company founded in
1947 by Leslie Smith and Rodney Smith. Their
first diecast cars were made in 1953 on a scale of
1:75. The trademark "Matchbox" was registered
in 1953. In 1979, Lesney Products Corp. made
over 5.5 million toys a week. The company was
sold to Universal International in 1982.

Bus, London to Glasgow 25.00
Caterpillar DW20 Earth Scraper,

Matchbox, #8, Morris Cowley, light tan
body, brown fender, $70.00.

M–A–A, Major Pack Series, 1957,
4½″ l 45.00
Commer Lyons Maid Ice Cream Truck,
47–B, 1–75 Series, blue body, white
plastic vendor, 1963, 2½″ l 35.00
Daimler, Lesney Yesteryears, Y13 . . . .   15.00
Double Decker London Bus, 5–A, 1–75
Series, gold radiator, 1954, 2″ l 60.00
Fire Station Gift Set, G–10–A, orig box,
1964 . . . .   140.00
Flyabout, Lesney Yesteryears, Y12 . . . .   15.00
Ford Galaxy Police Car, 55–C, 1–75
Series, white body, red bubble light,
driver, 1966, 2⅞″ l 30.00
Ford Thames Singer Van, 59–A, 1–75
Series, regular wheels, plastic wind-
shields, two–tone flesh and cream
body, 1959, 2⅝″ l 45.00
Horse–drawn Bus, Y–12–A, Models of
Yesteryear 75.00
Jaguar MK 10 . . . .   25.00
Leyland Site Office Truck, 60–C, 1–75
Series, superfast wheels, 1970, 2½″ l   15.00
Massey Harris Tractor, 4–A, 1–75 Series,
attached driver, with fenders, 1⅝″ l   60.00
Mercedes 500 SL Convertible, Series III,
World Class Series, Goodyear rubber
tires, mirrored windows, 1991 . . . . .   5.00
Pontiac Convertible 25.00

MISCELLANEOUS COMPANIES

American Flyer, race car set 75.00
Biller, West Germany, Atom–Gun, litho
tin gun resting on platform, lever action controls elevation and directions,
spring action firing, orig ammo pel-
lets and box with bullseye target,
1950s, 9″ l 135.00
Borgfeldt
Donald Duck Carousel, windup, celluloid, hp, figural long billed
Donald, spinning umbrella with
sixteen hanging balls balanced on
forehead, pressed steel wheeled
base, orig box, 4½″ h Donald . .   6,800.00

Buddy L, steam shovel, $265.00.

Pluto the Pup Fun E Flex, wood, fabric
ears, decal on neck, orig box, 6" l   **885.00**
Buddy L
Air Force Missile Interceptor, #5547,
pressed steel truck with side decals, plastic launcher and two mis-
siles, orig box and instruction
sheet, 15" l **300.00**
Emergency Auto Wrecker, #3317,
pressed steel, black rubber tires,
side decal, orig box, 12½" l **325.00**
Buffalo, Aero Speeders, tin carousel
with planes, 1920s, 10" h **390.00**
Courtland, Ice Cream Truck, windup,
litho tin, marked "Ice Cream 5¢,"
bell, driver, built-in key, 1950s, 6" l   **95.00**
Doepke
Adams Motor Grader, orange **250.00**
Bull Dozer, orig box **400.00**
Gilbert
Erector Set
No. 8½, ferris wheel **90.00**
No. 10052, rocket launcher, c1950   **100.00**
Microscope Set, orig box, 1940s ...   **25.00**
Mysto-Magic Exhibition Set, 11
tricks, instruction booklet, orig box,
1938 ....   **95.00**
Joustra, France, International Transport,
windup, tin tractor and trailer, orig
box, 18½" l **275.00**
Kalon Radio Corp, FAS, Dick Tracy
Washing Machine, crank handle,
litho tin, Dick Tracy and Sparkle
Plenty and family images all around,
words to song "This is the way we
wash our clothes" printed around
rim, 13" h **150.00**
Kamar, JFK & Rocking Chair, windup,
cloth and vinyl JFK sitting on wood
rocking chair, reading newspaper
with Kennedy family articles, chair
rocks while music plays, orig Kamar
tag and box, 1963, 11" h **315.00**
Kilgore
Eagle Six Shooter Cap Gun, disc cap
type, metal, plastic grips, raised eagle illus, orig box, 8" l **80.00**
Firecracker Cannon **50.00**
Mountie Pistol, MIB **75.00**

Rebel Scatter Gun, metal and plastic,
orig box, 1960, 14" l **95.00**
Lincoln Logs, orig box, 1923 ....   **45.00**
Lindstrom
Dancing Katrinka, windup, litho tin,
vibrating, 1930s, 8" h **150.00**
Sweeping Betty, windup, litho tin, vi-
brating, 1930s, 8" h **200.00**
Martin, France, Le Pompier a L'Echelle,
climbing fireman, windup, tin, hp de-
tails, fireman climbs ladder, orig box,
8" h **1,250.00**
Mattel
Agent Zero-M Radio Rifle, orig box,
1964 ....   **135.00**
Egg, windup, tin, plays "Here Comes
Peter Cottontail," 1953, 7" h **28.00**
Mickey Mouse pull string talker **20.00**
Musical Man on Flying Trapeze, plas-
tic clown, litho tin base, crank,
plays "Man on the Flying Trapeze,"
orig box, 1953 ....   **115.00**
V-Room! Dump Truck, plastic, 1964   **30.00**
Mego, amazing Spider-Car, orig box ..   **120.00**
Metalcraft, truck, pressed steel, tin tires,
c1930, 11" l
CW Brand Coffee **475.00**
St Louis **375.00**
Metal Masters Co, bus, blue, black plas-
tic wheels, 1930s, 7" l **225.00**
Mettoy, England, Mechanical Carousel
Ride, windup, litho tin carousel, plastic riders, two boys on airplanes, two
girls on horses, 9" h **100.00**
Modern Toys
Engine, friction, litho tin, multicolor,
engineer's cap activates friction
mechanism, 1950s **45.00**
Patrol 95 Helicopter, litho tin and
plastic, detachable propellers,
three-dimensional litho tin pilot,
marked "made in Japan," 1960s ..   **45.00**
Police Car, litho tin, black and white
body, red, beige, blue, and yellow
detailing, orig box marked "Press
Action Car," 1950s, 5½" l **35.00**
Multiple Products, fire engine, steamer,
detachable ladders, four horses and
harness unit, five firemen, accessory
pcs, 1960s, 8" l **35.00**
Ny-Lint
Deliverall, #1000, windup, full figure
driver, plastic windshield, orig box,
10" l **285.00**
Ford Camper with Radio **250.00**
Horse Van **150.00**
Jungle Wagon **125.00**
U-Haul Set, orig box **200.00**
PN, West Germany, Thunderbird, litho
tin convertible, hp composition driver, working horn and windshield
wipers, orig box, 13" l **150.00**

Remco
Long Range Bazooka, shells, orig box, 1961 .... 60.00
Marine Raider Long Range Mortar, metal and plastic, shells, tripod legs, meter gauge, orig box, 1960   130.00
Mighty Magee, aircraft carrier, hard plastic, gray and blue, twelve plastic planes, one truck, manually operated elevator, orig instruction sheet, 1960s, 4 x 18 x 4½" 50.00
Rosco Plastics, fire truck, hard plastic, green, three firemen, metal bell, 1950s, 10" l 40.00
Saunders, Super Motor Bus, plastic, reverso–gyro motor, orig box, 1950s, 13" l 150.00
Schuco, West Germany
Aral Gas Pump, #5506, orig box, 4" h   375.00
Boy holding girl in air, litho tin windup, 5" h 225.00
Elektro Fernlenk Mercedes 230 SL, #5307, battery operated, tin body, plastic int., hood and trunk open, ignition key starts and stops engine, steering controlled by remote control or steering wheel, orig box with pylons and steering cable, 10" l 2,000.00
Examico 4001, windup, tin, working gear shift, stop and start lever, black rubber tires, needs windshield, orig box and instruction sheet, 5½" l .. 135.00
Frog 195.00
Porsche Formel II Micro Racer, #1037, tin racer marked "#1," rubber tip, lever controls wheel direction, wrap around windshield, orig box, 4¼" l 110.00
Strauss
Butterfly, windup, litho tin, flapping wings, c1925, 7" wingspan 85.00
Jenny the Balking Mule, windup, tin, mule cart, clown driver, c1920, 9" l 250.00
Structo
American Airlines Sky Chief Lift Truck 195.00
Dump Truck, yellow and green, 1964   95.00
Emergency Van, blue and white, 1962 .... 175.00
Sanitation Truck, #178, pressed steel, lever action dumping, rubber tires, plastic windows, side decals, orig window box, 11½" l 110.00
Suburban Toy Company, PA
Bus, streamlined, 1938, 4¼" l 45.00
Donald Duck Car, 6½" l 75.00
Mickey Mouse Doll, rubber, orig window box, 10" h 145.00
Racer, white rubber tires, 7" l 165.00
Sutcliffe, England, Valiant Battleship, windup, metal, orig box, 12" l 280.00

Technofix, US Zone, Germany, Gebrüder Einfalt
Clown Cyclist, windup, litho tin, pedals cycle as his head nods, 5½" h   860.00
Traffic Control, windup, tin, three vehicles, orig box 225.00
Triang, England
Dump Truck, pressed steel, 18" l ... 150.00
Timber Lorry, Minic, windup, tin, green and red, lumber cargo, orig box 195.00
Transogram, Ben Casey Doctor Outfit, plastic, doctor's bag, stethoscope, and other instruments, orig display package 100.00
US Metal Toy Mfg Co, Brooklyn, US Champion Derby Racer, #8, litho tin parts, brown plastic wheels, flat wood chassis, orig box 30.00
Woodhaven Metal Stamping Co, Mysterious Twin–Train Set, battery operated, litho tin, layout of town, rail yard, power station, and Woodhaven RR building, six litho tin vehicles navigate track, 1950s, orig box 150.00

NOMURA TOYS

Nomura Toys, located in Tokyo, was one of the many Japanese suppliers of post war tin toys. Identified by the trademark "TN," the firm produced a large assortment of novelty toys ranging from friction police cars to windup animals to the battery–operated Charlie Weaver Bartender.

Circus Boy, windup, litho tin, turns head, rings bell, waves circus sign, orig box, 6" h 200.00
Circus Truck with Four Animals and Voice, friction, litho tin, two animals on each side peek out windows, orig box, 10" l 400.00
Dozo the Steaming Clown, battery operated, orig box, 14" h 300.00
Farm Truck, battery operated, litho tin, farmer John driver, exposed engine with lighted cylinders, bump–an–go action, bouncing basket of chicks in truck bed, orig box, 9" l 350.00
Ferris Wheel Truck, friction, litho tin and tin, children ride on spinning ferris wheel mounted in truck's bed, bell rings, orig box, 8½" l 415.00
Flag Fire Engine, friction, litho tin, No. 4 engine, siren, spinning extension ladder, two figural firemen hang on sides, one raises and lowers flag, orig box, 6" l 150.00
Jet Plane, friction, tin, marked "NAVY" on sides, orig box, 7" wingspan 135.00
Knitting Cat, windup, plush over tin,

wearing tin glasses, litho tin base, moving arms knit, orig box, 6" h ... **125.00**

Ko–Ko the Sandwich Man, windup, tin, vinyl, and cloth, orig box, 8" h **175.00**

Musical Clown
Battery Operated, cloth over tin, vinyl head, plays "London Bridge" on litho tin xylophone, orig box, 9" l   **750.00**

Windup, cloth over tin, vinyl face, plays drum, orig box, 7" h **100.00**

Pilot Electro Boat, battery operated, litho tin, spinning rudder, orig box, 9½" l **100.00**

Police Car, friction, litho tin, swiveling gun mounted on hood, engine noise, orig box, 7" l **125.00**

Skipping Puppy, windup, litho tin, dog dressed as young boy, jumps rope, nods head, orig box, 6" h **110.00**

OHIO ART

The Ohio Art Company was started in 1908 by Henry S. Winzeler, in Archbold, OH. The company produced metal picture frames. Toy production began in 1912. In 1969, Ohio Art purchased Emenee Industries. Ohio Art is noted for colorful lithographed tin toys.

Dancin' Dan Jr, orig box **275.00**

Disney Sand Sifter, litho tin, wire mesh bottom, tin handle, Disney character around sides, 8" d **75.00**

Donald Duck Watering Can, litho tin, Donald being hit by brick image, 1938, 3" h **70.00**

Drum, tin, marching band illus **18.00**

Giant Ride Ferris Wheel, windup, litho tin, carnival midway scenes, six plastic gondolas, plastic children, bell noise, box, 17" h **375.00**

Mickey Mouse Washer **200.00**

Mickey Mouse Watering Can, narrow spout **150.00**

Sunnie Miss Ironing Board **25.00**

Tea Set, tin
Circus motif, 30 pcs **70.00**
Squirrel motif, 1932, 24 pcs **60.00**

TONKA

In 1946 Mound Metal Crafts Inc., Mound, Minnesota, manufactured the first Tonka Toys. *Tonka* was derived from the firm's proximity to the banks of Lake Minnetonka. The company introduced a full line of trucks in 1949. In 1956 it changed its name to Tonka Toys.

AAA Wrecker **75.00**

Car Hauler **50.00**

Fire Truck, 1953, mint **350.00**

Livestock Trailer, 8½" l **45.00**

Pepsi Truck, 8" l, MIB **55.00**

Pickup Truck, sign on door reads "Gambles, Need Help," 1950s, 12½" l   **60.00**

Sand Loader and Dump Truck, 1958 .. **195.00**

Turbine Fire Pumper Truck **95.00**

TOOTSIETOY

The first Tootsietoys were made in 1911, although the name was not registered until 1924, and it was not until after 1930 that the name appeared on the toys. Tootsie was an early manufacturer of prizes for Cracker Jack. Tootsie produced copies of real vehicles beginning in 1914 and continued until World War II. After the war, cars were made as toys rather than models.

Automobile, resembles MG, dark red, silver grille and headlights, 3" l **25.00**

Blimp, USN Los Angeles, 1930s **175.00**

Bluebird 1 Daytona Racer, white rubber wheels, 1930s, 3¾" l **45.00**

Cadillac Four–Door Sedan, gray and silver, black rubber wheels, c1954, 6" l **20.00**

Car Carrier, International, 1940s **85.00**

Chevrolet, Corvette, metallic copper color, black plastic wheels, 1955 style **30.00**

Civil War Figures, wagon, caisson, two horses, orig card, 1950s **18.00**

Fire Department Set, 6" l 1947 Mack pumper, ladder and hose attachments, 9" l 1947 Mack fire trailer, 4" l 1950 Pontiac fire chief sedan, 4" l 1950 Chevy panel truck ambulance, fire hat and shovel, orig box, 1950s **200.00**

Ford Thunderbird, dark blue, black rubber wheels, c1955 .... **20.00**

Greyhound Bus, silver and blue, Greyhound Lines logo, 1950s, 6" l .. **75.00**

Interchangeable Truck Set, #4900, diecast metal, two 1947 Mack tractor trucks, van trailer, utility trailer, and machinery trailer, orig box, c1958 .. **300.00**

Oil Tanker, red, silver detailing, orig box, 1950s, 9" l **65.00**

Shell Truck **35.00**

Sohio–Giro Plane, light green, yellow propeller, 12 pg instruction booklet, issued by Standard Oil Co, 1931 copyright **100.00**

Venus Duo–Destroyer, Buck Rogers 25th Century, diecast rocket ship travels along string, orig box, 4½" l **250.00**

TOPLAY, LTD.

Identified by the "TPS" trademark, this Japanese company was founded in 1956 and is well known for its litho tin windup toys.

Champ on Ice Bear Skater Trio, windup,
litho tin, orig box, 9" l 900.00
Circus Seal, windup, plush seal, tin feet,
cloth collar, waddles, balances ball
on nose, orig box, 6½" h 80.00
Climbo the Climbing Clown, litho tin,
climbs string, orig box, 6" h 285.00
Fishing Monkey on Whales, windup,
litho tin, monkey seated on whale's
back, holding fishing rod attached to
two fish, advances with rocking mo-
tion, fish fins flap, orig box, 9" l 335.00
Giraffe, windup, litho tin, bounces
beach ball, 9" h 135.00
Girl Skipping Rope, windup, litho tin,
boy and girl spin rope, smaller girl
jumps, girls with vinyl faces, orig box,
12" l, 6" h 300.00
Joe the Acrobat, windup, litho tin, cloth
pants, clown doing handstand on
ball, ball rolls forward, legs move up
and down, orig box, 6" h 800.00
Jolly Wiggling Snake, windup, litho tin,
metal tongue, body wiggles as head
turns, orig box, 7½" l 165.00
Monkey Basketball Player, windup,
litho tin, shoots underhanded foul
shots, orig box, 8" l 350.00
Monkey Golfer, windup, litho tin, mon-
key hits ball across bridge into net,
orig box, 7" l 300.00
Mounted Cavalryman with Cannon,
windup, litho tin, soldier on horse,
dragging cannon, orig box, 6" l 500.00
Mustang Swinger, battery operated,
litho tin, orig box, 10" l 80.00
Skippy the Tricky Cyclist, windup, litho
tin, cloth outfit, animated leg action,
orig box, 6" h 280.00

UNIQUE ART COMPANY

Little is known of the exact origins of the
Unique Art Manufacturing Company. Located in
Newark, New Jersey, the firm was in business as
early as 1916, the period in which it introduced
its Merry Juggler and Charlie Chaplin toys.
Unique was still operating as late as 1952.

GI Joe and His K–9 Pups, windup, litho
tin, carrying pups in dog cages, orig
box, 9" h 300.00
Hee–Haw, windup, litho tin, farmer dri-
ving wagon loaded with milk cans,
mule, orig box, c1930, 10" l 375.00
Kiddy Cyclist, windup, litho tin, boy on
tricycle, jointed legs, ringing bell,
orig box, 9" h 300.00
Lincoln Tunnel 325.00
Musical Kiddie–Go–Round, windup,
litho tin, two–dimensional litho tin

Unique Art, Lil' Abner Band, windup,
litho tin, $525.00.

boy riders in plastic boats, plastic
horses with riders, musical, orig box,
11" h 325.00

UNKNOWN MAKERS

England, Drumming Clown, windup,
litho tin, 1950s, 5" h 185.00
Germany, Clown Walking Dog,
windup, litho tin, clown holds umbrella in one hand, leash in other,
4½" h 625.00
Japan
Musical Merry–Go–Round, windup,
litho tin, four cars and celluloid
balls rotate above base, child rider
in each car, orig box marked
"Foreign," 9" l 235.00
Walking Bear with Grasscutter,
windup, litho tin, cloth overalls,
walks, turns head, orig box, 7" h   275.00
US Zone, Germany, Speedboat, #2050,
windup, litho tin, figural driver wearing helmet and goggles, 9" l 95.00
West Germany
Airplane Carousel, windup, litho tin,
four airplanes with celluloid props,
orig box, 9" h 375.00
Mechanical Carnival Ride, #104,
windup, litho tin, 9 x 12" track, car
travels down sloping track, rotating
metal rod picks up car at bottom
and deposits it at top, orig box . . .   175.00
Space–Satellite, windup, tin, orig
box, 13" l 190.00

WOLVERINE

The Wolverine Supply & Mfg Co. was founded
in 1903 and incorporated by Benjamin F. Bain in
1906. The first type of toys they produced were
lithographed tin sand toys. They began to make
girls' housekeeping toys and action games by the
1920s. Production of toys continued and ex-

panded in 1959 to include children's appliances, known as "Rite–Hite." The name was changed to Wolverine Toy Company in 1962. The company was originally located in Pittsburgh, PA, but relocated to Booneville, AK, in 1970 after being acquired by Spang and Company.

Carnival Platform Toy, pull toy, litho tin
  platform, wood wheels, full figure
  clown rings bell, three small revolving horses and riders, 1930s, 10" l
  platform **200.00**
Express Bus **300.00**
Farm Wagon, windup, plastic, horse
  pulls wagon, orig box, 10" l **100.00**
Iron, red handle **10.00**
Jet Roller Coaster, one car, orig box ... **130.00**
Loop the Loop, #30, windup, tin, 2¼" l
  car, orig box, 19" l, 4" w **300.00**
Merry Masons, automatic sand toy, litho
  tin, building shape, three litho tin masons, orig box, 1950s, 16" h **115.00**
Snow White Ironing Board, tin, white
  ground, Snow White and Seven
  Dwarfs top, 8 x 27" top, 21" h **125.00**
Snow White Kitchen Appliance Set, tin,
  refrigerator, sink, and range, unused,
  orig display box, 30 x 16" **195.00**

WYANDOTTE

All Metal Products Company, located in Wyandotte, Michigan, has been in operation since the early 1920s. The company, better known as Wyandotte Toys, originally produced wood and steel toy weapons. In 1935 it introduced an innovative line of streamlined wheeled vehicles. The firm ceased operations in 1956.

China Clipper, airplane, pressed steel,
  four propellers, no decals, 1930s, 9" l **425.00**
Coast to Coast Bus **295.00**
Fire Engine Truck, pressed steel and tin,
  wood tires, two metal ladders,
  marked "Engine Co No 4," 1939,
  12" l **195.00**
Giant Construction Dump, 1950s **175.00**
Highway Freight Truck, pressed steel,
  red trailer, blue and yellow cab, early
  1950s, 16" l **25.00**
Medical Corps Truck, pressed steel,
  wood tires, c1939, 12" l **140.00**
Nationwide Air Rail Service Truck, litho
  tin, marked "Wyandotte" on doors,
  black rubber tires, 12" l **200.00**
Pickway Pasture Truck **70.00**
Racer, white tires, 5" l **90.00**
Spur Set, western, mint on orig card .. **25.00**
Steam Shovel, pressed steel **125.00**
Tipper Truck, 1950s **175.00**
Trailer, semi, stainless steel **195.00**

TRAINS, TOY

Collecting Hints: Prices do fluctuate. Prices from mail order houses and stores generally are higher than those found at train swap meets. A large train swap meet is held in York, Pennsylvania, each year. Condition is critical. Items in fair condition (scratched, chipped, dented, rusted or warped) and below generally have little value to the collector.

Restoration is accepted, provided it is done accurately. It does enhance the price one or two grades. Spare parts are actively traded and sold among collectors to assist in restoration efforts.

Exterior condition often is more important than operating condition. If you require a piece to operate, you should test it before you buy it.

Toy trains is a very specialized field. Collectors tend to have their own meets. A wealth of literature is available, but only from specialized book, railroad or toy train dealers. Novice collectors should read extensively before beginning to buy.

History: Railroading was an important part of many boys' childhoods, largely because of the romance associated with the railroad and the emphasis on toy trains. Almost everyone had a train layout; basements, back rooms, or attics allowed the layout to remain up year–round.

The first toy trains were cast iron and tin; the wind–up motor added movement. The golden age of toy trains was 1920–1955 when electric powered units were available, and Ives, American Flyer and Lionel were household names. Construction of the rolling stock was of high quality. The advent of plastic in the late 1950s lessened this quality considerably.

Toy trains are designated by a model scale or gauge. The most popular are HO, N, O, and S. Narrow gauge was a response to the modern capacity to miniaturize. Its popularity has lessened in the last few years.

References: Paul V. Ambrose, *Greenberg's Guide to Lionel Trains, 1945–1969, Volume III, Sets*, Greenberg Publishing, 1990; Paul V. Ambrose and Joseph P. Algozzini, *Greenberg's Guide to Lionel Trains 1945–1969, Vol IV: Uncatalogued Sets*, (1992), *Vol V: Rare and Unusual*, (1993), Greenberg Publishing; Susan and Al Bagdade, *Collector's Guide To American Toy Trains*, Wallace–Homestead, 1990; John O. Bradshaw, *Greenberg's Guide to Kusan Trains*, Greenberg Publishing, 1987; W. Graham Claytor, Jr., Paul A. Doyle and Carlton Norris McKenney, *Greenberg's Guide To Early American Toy Trains*, Greenberg Publishing, 1993; Joe Deger (ed.), *Greenberg's Guide To American Flyer S Gauge, Fourth Edition, Volume I* Greenberg Publishing, 1991; Joe Deger (ed.), *Greenberg's Guide To American Flyer S Gauge, Volume I, 4th ed.*,

(1991), *Volume II,* (1991), *Volume III,* (1992), Greenberg Publishing; Cindy Lee Floyd (comp.), *Greenberg's Marx Train Catalogues, circa 1938–1975,* Greenberg Publishing, 1993; Richard Friz, *The Official Identification and Price Guide To Toy Trains,* House of Collectibles, 1990; Bruce C. Greenberg, *Greenberg's Guide To Ives Trains, 1901–1932, Volume II,* Greenberg Publishing, 1992; Bruce Greenberg (edited by Frank Reichenbach), *Greenberg's Guide To Ives Trains, 1901–1932, Volume I* 1991, *Volume II,* 1992, Greenberg Publishing; Bruce Greenberg, *Greenberg's Guide To Lionel 1901–1942, Pre War Vol. I: Standard and 2⅞"* Gauge, Greenberg Books, 1994; Bruce Greenberg, (edited by Christian F. Rohlfing), *Greenberg's Guide To Lionel Trains: 1901–1942, Volume 1* 1988, *Volume 2* 1988, Greenberg Publishing Co.; Bruce Greenberg (edited by Paul V. Ambrose), *Greenberg's Guide To Lionel Trains:1945–1969, Volume 1* (1993), *Volume 2* (1993), Greenberg Publishing; Greenberg Publishing, *Greenberg's Lionel Catalogues, Volume V: 1955–1960,* Greenberg Publishing, 1992; George J. Horan, *Greenberg's Guide To Lionel HO Volume II, 1974–1977,* Greenberg Publishing, 1993; George J. Horan and Vincent Rosa, *Greenberg's Guide To Lionel HO Volume I, 1957–1966,* Second Edition, Greenberg Publishing, 1993; John Hubbard, *The Story of Williams Electric Trains,* Greenberg Publishing, 1987; Steven H. Kimball, *Greenberg's Guide To American Flyer Prewar O Gauge,* Greenberg Publishing, 1987; Roland La Voie, *Greenberg's Guide To Lionel Trains, 1970–1991, Volume I,* 1991, *Volume II,* 1992, Greenberg Publishing, 1989; Roland E. La Voie, Michael A. Solly, and Louis A. Bohn, *Greenberg's Guide To Lionel Trains, 1970–1991, Volume II,* Greenberg Publishing, 1992; Lionel Book Committee Train Collectors Association, *Lionel Trains: Standard of the World, 1900–1943,* Train Collectors Association, 1989; Dallas J. Mallerich III, *Greenberg's American Toy Trains From 1900 with Current Prices,* Greenberg Publishing, 1990; Dallas J. Mallerich, III, *Greenberg's Guide to Athearn Trains,* Greenberg Publishing, 1987; Eric J. Matzke, *Greenberg's Guide To Marx Trains, Volume I,* 1989, *Volume II,* 1990, Greenberg Publishing; Tom McComas and James Tuohy, *Lionel: A Collector's Guide & History,* 6 volumes, Chilton Books, 1993; Robert P. Monaghan, *Greenberg's Guide to Marklin OO/HO,* Greenberg Publishing, 1989; Richard O'Brien, *Collecting Toy Trains: An Identification and Value Guide, No. 3,* Books Americana, 1991; John R. Ottley, *Greenberg's Guide To LGB Trains,* Greenberg Publishing, 1989; Rick Ralston, *Cast Iron Floor Trains: An Encyclopedia With Rarity & Price Guide,* Ralston Publishing, 1994; Vincent Rosa and George J. Horan, *Greenberg Guide To HO Trains,* Greenberg Publishing, 1986; Alan R. Schuweiler, *Greenberg's Guide to American*

Flyer, Wide Gauge, Greenberg Publishing, 1089; John David Spangel, *Greenberg's Guide To Varney Trains,* Greenberg Publishing, 1991; Alan Stewart, *Greenberg's Guide To Lionel Trains 1945–1969, Vol. VI: Accessories,* Greenberg Books, 1994; Robert C. Whitacre, *Greenberg's Guide To Marx Train Sets, Volume III,* Greenberg Publishing, 1992.

Note: Greenberg Book Division, Kalmbach Publishing Co., 21027 Crossroads Circle, Waukesha, WI 53187, is the leading publisher of toy train literature. Anyone interested in the subject should write for their catalog and ask to be put on their mailing list.

Collectors' Clubs: American Flyer Collectors Club, PO Box 13269, Pittsburgh, PA 15243; Lionel Collector's Club of America, PO Box 479, La Salle, IL 61301; Lionel Operating Train Society, 18 Eland St., Fairfield, OH 45014; Marklin Club–North America, PO Box 51559, New Berlin, WI 53151; Marklin Digital Special Interest Group, PO Box 51319, New Berlin, WI 53151; The National Model Railroad Association, 4121 Cromwell Road, Chattanooga, TN 37421; The Toy Train Operating Society, Inc., 25 W. Walnut St., Suite 308, Pasadena, CA 91103; The Train Collector's Association, PO Box 248, Strasburg, PA 17579.

Periodicals: *Classic Toy Trains,* PO Box 1612, Waukesha, WI 53187; *Lionel Collector Series Marketmaker,* PO Box 1499, Gainesville, FL 32602; *O Scale Railroading,* PO Box 239, Nazareth, PA 18064; *S Gaugian,* 7236 Madison Ave., Forest Park, IL 60130.

Note: All prices given are for items in very good condition, meaning that the piece shows some signs of use but all parts are present and damage from use is minor.

AMERICAN FLYER N GAUGE

Locomotive
1093, 7", two tone green **155.00**
3198, black, brass trim **225.00**
Rolling stock
1106, log car, 6½" **12.00**
1114, caboose, 6½" **15.00**
3102, automobile car **18.00**
3141, pullman, brass trim **15.00**
Set
Major Leaguer 1329, locomotive and tender 3193, tank car 3018, sand car 3016, automobile car 3015, caboose 3017 . . . . **400.00**
The Explorer 1333, locomotive 3110, baggage car 1204, pullman 1203, observation 1209 . . . . **275.00**
Vanguard 1312, locomotive 3100, pullman 3141, observation 3142, 88" track **200.00**

AMERICAN FLYER S GAUGE

Accessories

Bridge, trestle, 750, 1946–56	12.50
Cartridge, smoke, 25, 1947–56	3.00
Crossing gate, 592, 1949–50	12.00
Flasher signal, 23764, 1969–64	4.50
Tunnel, 249, 1947–56, orig box	5.50

Engines, Diesel, Electric, and Steam
Diesel and Electric

290, electric	80.00
360A, diesel, tender	125.00
21234, Chesapeake and Ohio, GP–7, 1961–62	110.00
21573, New Hampshire diesel, GE Electric	250.00
21918/21918–1, Seaboard, Baldwin, 1958	175.00
Motorized Unit, 741, handcar and shed	50.00

Rolling stock
Box car

639, light yellow	25.00
923, Illinois Central	10.00
994, Union Pacific	25.00
24052, United Fruit Growers Express	8.00

Caboose

630	4.50
806	12.00
24634	12.00

Flat Car

627, American Flyer Lines	8.00
928, New Haven	6.50
969, rocket launcher	18.00
24556, Rock Island	20.00

Gondola

631, T&P, green	12.00
24120, T&P	15.00

Hopper and Dump Car

640, Wabash, black	30.00
24219, Western Maryland	20.00
9200, B & O, Fundimensions Production	10.00

Passenger Car

502, American Flyer Lines, Vista Dome	70.00
649, circus coach	30.00
732, operating baggage car, unpainted red plastic shell, 1951–54	18.00
953, baggage and club car, 1953–56	32.50
24739, Niagara Falls	165.00
24868, American Flyer Lines, observation	40.00

Steam Locomotive

320, 4–6–4, Hudson, 1946–47	60.00
332, 4–8–4, 1946–49	100.00
343, 0–8–0, 1953–54	80.00
21130, 4–6–4, 62–63, 1959–60	110.00

Tank Car

625G, Gulf	8.00
958, Mobilgas, 1957	10.00
9101, Union, 1980	12.00

IVES

Accessories

Bridge, arch base, two sections, 21" l	275.00
Passenger station, 113, 1906–28	200.00
Scenery, 80, pastoral, six 20 x 15" sections	250.00
Semaphore, double arm, 107D, 1908–30	80.00
Tunnel, 105, mountain style, 11" l	120.00

Locomotive

5, Steam, 0–4–0, mechanical, 1911–28	180.00
10, Electric, standard gauge, 1931–32	260.00
20, Steam, 4–4–0, mechanical, 1908–14	175.00
258, Steam, 2–4–0, O gauge, 1931–32	255.00
1760, Steam, 4–4–2, standard gauge, 1931–32	700.00

Passenger Car

50, baggage car, O gauge, 1901–30	75.00
186, observation car, standard gauge, 1922–30	65.00
339, pullman, standard gauge, 1931–32	95.00
1812, observation, O gauge, 1931–32	120.00

Rolling stock

65, stock car, O gauge, 1908–30	35.00
70, caboose, O gauge, 1929–30	4.00
123, lumber car, O gauge, 1911–30	75.00
190, tank car, standard gauge, 1921–30	130.00
559, lumber car, O gauge, 1930	40.00
1677, gondola, O gauge, 1931–32	50.00
1774, box car, standard gauge, 1931–32	225.00
1775, tank car, standard gauge, 1931–32	65.00

LIONEL, O GAUGE

Accessories

Beacon, 394, swivel action, blue	5.00
Billboard, 310, "B. P."	4.00
Bridge, single span, 270, standard gauge	150.00
Coal loader, 97, scoop and drawer, shoot action	150.00
Diner, 442, aluminum style, simulated windows	350.00
Left hand switch, 5021	15.00
Log loader, 364, crane and hook	90.00
Oil derrick, 455, movable arms	110.00
Station, 122, chimney lighted, benches, dome	160.00

Engines, Diesel, Electric and Steam
  Diesel and electric
    153, Electric, 0–4–0, 1917–27 . . .   **50.00**
    204, Santa Fe, Alco AA units, 1957   **60.00**
    706, Electric, 0–4–0, 1913–1916   **240.00**
    1700E, Diesel, 1935–37 . . . .   **110.00**
    2023, Erie, Alco AA units, 1952–54   **115.00**
    2344, New York Central, F–3,
      1950–52 . . . .   **160.00**
    3927, Lionel Lines, 1956–60 . . . .   **60.00**
    Handcar, 1100, Mickey Mouse,
      1935–37 . . . .   **600.00**
  Steam Locomotive
    203, 0–6–0, 1940–42 . . . .   **325.00**
    233, 0–6–0, 1940–42 . . . .   **800.00**
    665, 4–6–4, 1954–59 . . . .   **75.00**
Rolling stock
  Box car
    514, Union Pacific **75.00**
    1514, Baby Ruth **30.00**
    2954, 1940–42 . . . .   **145.00**
    3366, circus car, 1959–62 . . . . . .   **65.00**
    3428, United States Mail, 1959 . .   **20.00**
    6014, Campbell Soup, 1969 . . . .   **28.00**
    6454, Erie, 1949–53 . . . .   **16.00**
    6464–735, New Haven, 1969 . . .   **15.00**
  Caboose
    657 . . . .   **12.00**
    801, 1915–26 . . . .   **15.00**
    1007, Lionel Lines, 1948–52, SP
      Die 3 . . . .   **1.50**
    2357, silver and blue **18.00**
    4457, Pennsylvania, 1946–47, N5   **40.00**
    6417–50, Lehigh Valley, 1954,
      N5C, gray **32.00**
    6517–75, Erie, 1966, bay window   **200.00**
  Flat car
    811, 1926–40 . . . .   **40.00**
    831, 1927–34 . . . .   **28.00**
    2461, transformer car, 1947–48 . .   **20.00**
    3364, log dump, 1965–69 . . . . . .   **15.00**
    3519, satellite car, 1961–64 . . . .   **18.00**
    6361, flat, timber, 1960–61, 1964–
      69 . . . .   **20.00**
    6413, Mercury Project, 1962–63   **18.00**
    6819, flat, helicopter, 1959–60 . .   **25.00**
  Gondola
    812, 1926–41 . . . .   **35.00**
    2812, 1938–42 . . . .   **30.00**
    3444, Erie, 1957–59 . . . .   **30.00**
    4452, Pennsylvania, 1946–48 . . .   **48.00**
    6462, NYC, red **4.50**
  Hopper and Dump Car
    816, 1927–42 . . . .   **55.00**
    2816, 1935–42 . . . .   **48.00**
    3456, N&W, 951–55 . . . .   **20.00**
  Passenger Car
    530, observation, 1926–32 . . . . .   **16.00**
    604, observation, 1920–25 . . . . .   **20.00**
    605, pullman, 1925–32 . . . .   **65.00**
    607, pullman, 1926–27 . . . .   **30.00**
    637, coach, 1936–39 . . . .   **55.00**

Lionel, No. 233, "O" gauge, #262 engine,
#803 hopper, #902 gondola, #806 cattle
car, #802 caboose, $125.00.

    783, coach, 1935–41 . . . .   **240.00**
    1687, observation **145.00**
    1813, baggage **18.00**
    2400, Maplewood, green and gray   **25.00**
    2442, brown, gray trim **35.00**
    2445, Elizabeth, pullman, 1955–56   **35.00**
    2522, President Harrison, 1962–66   **60.00**
    2533, Silver Cloud, pullman,
      1952–60 . . . .   **45.00**
    2615, baggage, 1928–42 . . . .   **175.00**
    2631, observation, 1938–42 . . . .   **25.00**
  Tank Car
    815, 1926–42 . . . .   **48.00**
    1515, 1933–37 . . . .   **25.00**
    2555, Sunoco, 1946–48 . . . .   **30.00**
    2955, 1940–42 . . . .   **165.00**
    6463, rocket fuel, 1962–63 . . . . .   **12.00**
    6465, Lionel Lines, 1958–59 . . . .   **5.00**

N GAUGE

Bachmann
  Locomotive
    EMF GP40 diesel, Union Pacific . .   **15.00**
    GE U36B diesel, Seaboard Coast
      Line, Bicentennial **18.00**
    4–4–0, steam, Central Pacific **25.00**
  Rolling stock
    Hopper, 5523, Reading **2.25**
    Passenger coach, Pennsylvania,
      lighted **4.00**
    Reefer, 5181, Gerber's **1.50**
Con–Cor
  Locomotive
    Alco PA–PB diesel, Pennsylvania,
      PA, powered **35.00**
    4–6–4, J3A Hudson, Union Pacific   **50.00**

Rolling stock
  Box car, wood, New York Central,
    1021F **4.00**
  Caboose, bay window, Illinois
    Central, 1251N **4.00**
  Flat car, US Steel, 1201E **4.50**
  Passenger cars, smooth sides **6.50**
  Tank car, Cities Services, 1601A . . **5.00**
Revell/Rapido
  Locomotive
    EMD FP9 Diesel, Santa Fe, set . . . **18.00**
    Steam, medium, Baltimore and
      Ohio, yellow lettering **60.00**
  Rolling stock
    Hopper, Boston and Maine, 2543 **7.75**
    Tank car, Sinclair, 0484R **6.50**

TYPEWRITERS

Collecting Hints: Patent dates marked on frames are not accurate indicators of age, as these only indicate the date of the mechanical innovation's patent. A machine with a 1890s patent date may have been made as long as twenty–five or more years later. The serial number is a far more useful tool in dating a machine. However, there are many different manufacturers' numbering systems that are unknown, extremely confusing, or illogical.

In quite a number of cases, the only way to date a particular machine is through the use of old advertisements and catalogs. These references can also reveal particular models, colors, and unusual features produced.

Most manual typewriters produced after 1920 have little value, albeit some later models with unusual features have attracted collector interest. Some electro–mechanical (or electric) typewriters manufactured before 1933 are scarce and hence, valuable.

Domestic typewriter collectors are a small but steadily growing group. There is a well–established and active international typewriter collecting community, especially in Europe where mechanical objects and typewriters are eagerly sought. American collectors have generally swapped and traded among themselves, thus keeping prices reduced. This is changing as a result of increased attention and interest in American machines by international collectors.

History: The first commercially produced American typewriter was the Sholes & Glidden Typewriter, manufactured by E. Remington & Sons in 1874. This typewriter produced a row of tiny, uneven capital letters. In 1876 Remington exhibited an example of the Sholes & Glidden at the Philadelphia United States Centennial Exhibition. For twenty–five cents people watched souvenir messages being typed, letters that are highly collectible today. Mark Twain was one of the first to purchase a Sholes & Glidden. Although his review of it was rather mixed, his *Life on the Mississippi* is thought to be the first typewritten manuscript.

In 1878 Remington produced the Perfected Type Writer #2, later named the "Standard Remington Typewriter #2." This machine was far more reliable and useful than its predecessor. Both of these typewriters typed on paper wound on a platen suspended over a circular typebasket. To view the typing performed, the carriage had to be lifted away from the basket. This was known as a blind typewriter and was the most common machine style for the next thirty years.

Like so many other manufacturers of the time, five major typewriter companies joined together in 1893 to form the Union Typewriter Company, in essence a trust formed to limit competition and fix prices. Members of the trust produced thick, squat, blind writing office machines exclusively, with little impetus for innovation. Two companies formed in competition to the Union Typewriter trust. Underwood Typewriter Company (1895) and L. C. Smith & Brothers Typewriter Company (1903) manufactured machines with a visible writing surface. These companies became the powerhouses of the typewriter industry for the next thirty years.

The first American–made electric machines appeared and quickly disappeared just after the turn of the century. The famous Blickenderfer Electric and little–known Cahill Electric are two of the earliest examples. The first successful electric typewriter was the IBM Model 01, introduced in the early 1930s.

Early typewriters generally have a glossy black finish, sometimes decorated with colored pinstripes or, less frequently, highly detailed painted designs and inlays. This was the general trend until the 1920s when various bright colors were used, generally on portable machines. Many examples had a wood grain finish. Black typewriters with a two–tone finish of glass and crackle panels were exclusively produced during the 1930s. Starting in the 1940s, typewriters and other office equipment was manufactured in "designer" colors to match office interiors.

The electronic typewriter, the newest advance in typewriting technology, is light, has few moving parts, and many additional features. The growth in personal computers and related printers is fast making the typewriter obsolete.

References: Michael H. Adler, *The Writing Machine*, George Allen & Unwin Ltd., 1973; Wilfred A. Beeching, *Century of the Typewriters*, William Heinemann, 1974; Richard N. Current, *The Typewriter and the Men Who Made It*, University of Illinois Press, 1954; Darryl Matter, *Simplex Typewriters from the Early Twentieth Century*, Green Gate Books, 1984; Dan R. Post,

Collector's Guide to Antique Typewriters, Post–Era Books, 1981.

Collectors' Clubs: Internationales Forum Historische Burowelt, Postfach 50 11 68, D–5000 Koln–50, Germany; Early Typewriter Collectors Association, 2591 Military Ave., Los Angeles, CA 90064.

Periodical: Typewriter Times, 1216 Garden St., Hoboken, NJ 07030.

Museums: Henry Ford Museum, Dearborn, MI; Milwaukee Public Museum, Milwaukee, WI; Onandaga Historical Society, Syracuse, NY; Smithsonian Institution, National Museum of American History, Washington, DC.

Advisor: Todd Holmes.

Underwood Standard #5, $25.00.

American/Globe	425.00
Barlock No 7–14	225.00
Bennett	325.00
Bing	130.00
Blickensderfer No 5–9	200.00
Boston	17,000.00
Caligraph	600.00
Chicago	800.00
Columbia No 2	3,400.00
Corona Folding	60.00
Demountable	80.00
Densmore No 2–5	600.00
Emerson No 3	700.00
Fox	
No 2–4	350.00
No 23–24	140.00
Franklin No 7–10	700.00
Hall	750.00
Hammond	
Multiplex	225.00
No 1	1,200.00
No 2–12	275.00
Harris Visible No 4	90.00
Junior	350.00
Lambert	800.00
LC Smith No 2–8	25.00
Merritt	1,000.00
Mignon No 4	150.00
Molle No 3	275.00
National No 2–5	100.00
New American No 5	1,600.00
Noiseless	175.00
Odell No 2–4	1,000.00
Oliver	
No 2	200.00
No 3–11	100.00
Pittsburgh Visible No 11–12	800.00
Postal	750.00
Rem–Sho	250.00
Remington	
No 2	700.00
No 4	2,800.00
No 7	100.00
No 10–12	50.00

Royal	
No 1	75.00
No 5	25.00
No 10	25.00
Sholes & Glidden	4,000-12,000.00
Simplex	25-200.00
Smith Premier	
No 1	650.00
No 2–10	50.00
Standard Folding	250.00
Sun No 3	250.00
Underwood	
No 5	25.00
Portable	25.00
Varityper	150.00
Wellington	150.00
Williams No 2–6	600.00
Woodstock No 5	25.00
World	700.00

UNIVERSAL POTTERY

Collecting Hints: Not all Universal pottery carried the Universal name as part of the backstamp. Wares marked "Harmony House," "Sweet William/Sears Roebuck and Co.," and "Wheelock, Peoria" are part of the Universal production. Wheelock was a department store in Peoria, Illinois, that controlled the Cattail pattern on the Old Holland shape.

Like many pottery companies Universal had many shapes or styles of blanks, the most popular being Camwood, Old Holland, and Laurella. The same decal might be found on several different shapes.

The Cattail pattern had many accessory pieces. The 1940 and 1941 Sears catalogs listed an oval wastebasket, breakfast set, kitchen scale, linens, and bread box. Calico Fruits is another pattern with accessory pieces.

The Calico Fruits decal has not held up well

over time. Collectors may have to settle for less than perfect pieces.

History: Universal Potteries of Cambridge, Ohio, was organized in 1934 by The Oxford Pottery Company. It purchased the Atlas–Globe plant properties. The Atlas–Globe operation was a merger of the Atlas China Company (formerly Crescent China Co. in 1921, Tritt in 1912 and Bradshaw in 1902) and the Globe China Company.

Even after the purchase, Universal retained the Oxford ware, made in Oxford, Ohio, as part of their dinnerware line. Another Oxford plant was used to manufacture tiles. The plant at Niles, Ohio, was dismantled.

The most popular lines of Universal were "Ballerina" and "Ballerina Mist." The company developed a detergent–resistant decal known as permacel, a key element in keeping a pattern bright. Production continued until 1960, when all plants were closed.

References: Susan and Al Bagdade, *Warman's American Pottery and Porcelain*, Wallace–Homestead, 1994; Jo Cunningham, *The Collector's Encyclopedia of American Dinnerware*, Collector Books, 1982, 1995 value update; Harvey Duke, *The Official Identification and Price Guide To Pottery and Porcelain, Eighth Edition*, House of Collectibles, 1995.

CALICO FRUIT

Custard Cup, 5 oz	5.00
Milk Jug, 3 quart	25.00
Plate, 6" d, bread and butter	3.50
Refrigerator Set, three jars, 4", 5", and 6" d	50.00
Salt and Pepper Shakers, pr, utility	18.00
Soup, tab handle	6.00
Utility Pitcher, cov	40.00
Utility Plate, 11½" d	20.00

CATTAIL

Butter dish, cov, 1 lb	40.00
Cake Lifter	18.00
Casserole, cov, 8¼" d	15.00
Cookie Jar, cov	50.00
Fork	20.00
Gravy Boat	20.00
Milk Pitcher, 1 quart	20.00
Platter, oval	20.00
Range Set, 5 pcs	40.00
Spoon	20.00
Tea Set, 4 pcs	25.00
Utility Jug, cork stopper	35.00

LARGO

Creamer and Sugar	15.00
Pie Baker	10.00

Plate	
Dessert, 6" d	3.50
Luncheon, square	5.00
Salt and Pepper Shakers, pr	8.00
Utility Bowl, cov	6.00

RAMBLER ROSE

Gravy Boat	8.00
Milk Pitcher	18.00
Plate, 9" d	6.00
Salt and Pepper Shakers, pr, range	15.00
Soup, flat	5.00

THREE RED ROSES

Bowl, 9¾" d	12.00
Casserole, cov, tab handles	
4¼" d	15.00
5¼" d	18.00
6" d	20.00
8½" d	22.50
Pie Plate, 9¼" d	10.00
Soup, 8" d	10.00

VALENTINES

Collecting Hints: Valentine collectors tend to focus on cards made before 1930, with special emphasis on the nineteenth century. Cards made before 1800 are known, but most are in the hands of museums.

At present collectors tend to specialize in one type of card, e.g., transportation theme cards, lacey, honeycomb, etc. Comic sheets, Art Nouveau, and Art Deco cards are gaining in popularity. Valentine collectors now face heavy competition from other theme collectors who want valentines as supplements to their collections.

Condition of the card is more important than age in most cases. Collectors like clean cards in very good repair.

Early German mechanical cards open and close from the middle; later examples and reproductions pull down. Early mechanicals used more delicate pastel shades. Bright red is found on later cards.

Keep cards out of the light to prevent fading and brittleness. Store cards in layers in a drawer with acid–free paper between them.

History: Early cards were handmade, often containing both handwritten verses and hand–drawn pictures. Many cards also were hand colored and contained cutwork.

Mass production of machine–made cards featuring chromolithography began after 1840. In 1847 Esther Howland of Worcester, Massachusetts, established a company to make valentines which were hand decorated with paper lace and other materials imported from England. They had a small "H" stamped in red in the top left corner. Howland's company eventually became the New England Valentine Company [N.E.V. Co.].

George C. Whitney and his brother founded a company after the Civil War which dominated the market from the 1870s through the first decades of the twentieth century. They bought out several competitors, one of which was the New England Valentine Company.

Lace paper was invented in 1834. The 1835 to 1860 period is known as the "golden age" of lacey cards.

Embossed paper was used in England after 1800. Embossed lithographs and woodcuts developed between 1825–40, with early examples being hand colored.

References: Ruth Webb Lee, *A History of Valentines, Fifth Edition,* Lee Publications, 1952; Norman E. Martinus and Harry L. Rinker, *Warman's Paper,* Wallace–Homestead, 1994; National Valentine Collectors Association, *Bulletins;* Frank Staff, *The Valentine And Its Origins,* out of print.

Collectors' Club: National Valentine Collectors Association, PO Box 1404, Santa Ana, CA 92702.

Advisor: Evalene Pulati.

Diecut, Dutch girl and windmill scene, 4⅜ x 7⅜", $12.00.

Animated, child	
1918, artist sgd	12.00
1923, 6" h	4.00
Art Deco	
Folder	
Child's, Whitney, 3 x 5"	3.00
Fancy, orig lined envelope	14.00
Standup, flapper, 8"	8.00
Art Nouveau	
Booklet, fancy, emb, cupids, vines, 5 x 7"	8.00
Diecuts, boxed, emb, pretty girls, flowers	12.00
Folder, fancy, cutwork, butterfly, cherubs	10.00
Standup, layered	
5 x 8", parchment	8.00
10 x 14", silk inserts	18.00
Standup, pasteboard, easel back, 4 x 6"	6.00
Comic	
McLoughlin	
4 x 6", 1898	6.00
8 x 12", sheet, sgd "CJH"	15.00
8 x 14", sheet, sgd "H"	10.00
Unknown, sheet, 8 x 10", 1925	5.00
Heart Shape	
Clapsaddle design, 6 x 9"	10.00
Diecut, F. Brundage, 3 x 3"	8.00

Folder	
McLoughlin, cupids, 1915	4.00
Whitney, children, 5 x 5", 1925	3.00
Honeycomb, pull out to open	
Beistle	
1926, red, 6" h	5.00
1927, light red, 10" h	8.00
German	
5 x 6", umbrella	25.00
7 x 12", blue and white scale	35.00
Lacy	
Handwritten, poem on front, emb lace, 5 x 7", 1855	30.00
McLoughlin, three dimensional folder, lace and ribbons, 5 x 8", 1885	10.00
N.E.V. Co, folder, lace attached, 3 x 5", 1875	20.00
Mechanical, pull down	
American	
Automobile, 8 x 12", 1923	35.00
Cupids and flowers, 5 x 8", 1925	10.00
Seaplane, 8 x 12", 1930	35.00
German, pre–WWI	
Coronation Coach, 8 x 10"	30.00
Ship, 8 x 10"	45.00
German, small children, 3 x 5", 1915	7.50
Post card, Victorian, silk fringe	
Prang	
3 x 5"	7.50
5 x 7"	12.00
Tuck, R	
3 x 5"	4.50
5 x 7"	8.00
Unknown, folder	
2 x 4", cameo style, lace front, c1850	8.00
5 x 8", fancy, pasted–on cupids and flowers, 1930	2.50
Whitney	
Folder, lace front, 3 x 4", 1865	10.00

Three dimensional folder
    7 x 10", 1895 . . . .   **15.00**
    8 x 10", applied ribbon and lace,
    1920 . . . .   **15.00**

VENDING MACHINES

Collecting Hints: Since individual manufacturers offered such a wide range of models, some collectors choose to specialize in a particular brand of machine. Variations are important. Certain accessories, porcelain finish, colors or special mechanical features on an otherwise common machine can add much to its value.

Original paint adds value. But numerous machines, especially peanut vendors with salt damaged paint, have been repainted. Most vendors were in service for ten to twenty years or more. Repainting normally was done by the operator as part of the repair and maintenance of his route. Repaints, recent or otherwise, if nicely done, do not necessarily lessen the value of a desirable machine. Original paint should be retained if at all possible.

Decals add much to the appearance of a vendor and often are the only means of identifying it. Original decals, again, are the most desirable. Reproductions of many popular styles have been made and are a viable alternative if originals are not available.

Some reproduction parts also are available. In some cases, entire machines have been reproduced using new glass and castings. Using one or two new parts as a means of restoring an otherwise incomplete machine is generally accepted by collectors.

Collecting vending machines is a relatively new hobby. It has increased in popularity with other advertising collectibles. New machines constantly are being discovered, thus maintaining the fascination for the collector.

History: Most of us still remember the penny gumball or peanut machine of our childhood. Many still survive on location after thirty years or more of service, due in part to the strength and simplicity of their construction.

The years 1910 to 1940 were the heyday of the most collectible style of vendor, the globe–type peanut or gumball machine. Machine manufacturers invested a great deal of money throughout this period in the form of advertising and research. Many new designs were patented.

The simple rugged designs proved the most popular with the operator who had an established route of vendors as a means of making a living. Many operators made their fortunes "a penny at a time," especially during the Depression when dollars were hard to come by. Fifty years later, the same vendor that originally

cost four to fifteen dollars commands a much higher price.

In addition to the globe–style variety of vendor is the cabinet–style machine. These usually incorporate a clockwork mechanism and occasionally mechanical figurines to deliver the merchandise. The earliest examples of these were produced in the 1890s.

References: Richard M. Bueschel, *Collector's Guide To Vintage Coin Machines*, Schiffer Publishing, 1995; Nic Costa, *Automatic Pleasures: The History of the Coin Machine*, Kevin Frances Publishing, 1988; Bill Enes, *Silent Salesmen: An Encyclopedia of Collectible Gum, Candy & Nut Machines*, published by author, 1987; Roger Pribbenow and Jimm Lehmann, *Gumball Guide*, privately printed.

Periodicals: *Around The Vending Wheel*, 5417 Costana Ave., Lakewood, CA 90712; *Coin Machine Trader*, 569 Kansas SE, PO Box 602, Huron, SD 57350; *Coin–Op Newsletter*, 909 26th St., NW, Washington, DC, 20037.

Advisor: Bob Levy.

Aspirin, Winthrop Metal Products, 10¢,
    c1940 . . . .   **40.00**
Cigar, Malkin Phillies, steel metal, 10¢,
    c1930 . . . .   **75.00**
Cigarette, Rowe Mfg Co, six column,
    glass and metal 15¢ package,
    c1935 . . . .   **250.00**
Collar Button, Zeno Machine, metal
    and glass, with marquee, c1905 . . .   **375.00**
Combs, Advance machine, Model #4,
    10¢, c1950 . . . .   **40.00**
Condoms, Harmon Mfg, 25¢ package,
    c1962 . . . .   **75.00**
Food, Horn & Hardart Automat, metal
    and marble, glass doors, four unit
    complete, c1902 . . . .   **1,500.00**
Gum
    Adams, stick gum, tutti–frutti, wood
        upright case, 1¢, c1890 . . . .   **700.00**
    Advance, stick gum, metal upright
        case, c1925 . . . .   **75.00**
    Atlas, ball gum, aluminum with tray,
        c1950 . . . .   **85.00**
    Becker, ball gum, "Ring Ding
        Clown," plastic vendor, c1950 . . .   **45.00**
    Caille Bros, ball gum, cast iron, claw
        feet, etched globe, c1909 . . . . . .   **2,000.00**
    Columbus, ball gum, cast iron and
        round globe, Model "A", c1915 . .   **200.00**
    Dugreiner, 4 column tab gum, stainless case, Adams decal, c1934 . . .   **75.00**
    Ford, gum ball, 1¢, chrome, c1947   **45.00**
    Kayum, stick or pack gum, metal
        case, Adams or Beechnut decal,
        c1947 . . . .   **195.00**
    Masters, gum ball, aluminum with
        porcelain base and lid, #2, c1925   **200.00**

Penny King, ball gum, Art Deco chrome design, four sections, c1935 .... **550.00**
Pulver, stick gum, Too Choos and Joy Mint, red porcelain case with policeman, c1930 .... **400.00**
Victor, gum ball, plastic top, "Topper," c1950 .... **40.00**
Zeno, stick gum, yellow porcelain case, black lettering, 1908 ...... **300.00**
Hot Nuts, Cebco Products, cast aluminum, c1930 .... **175.00**
Lotion, National Dispenser, 1¢ Jergens, c1938 .... **50.00**
Matches, Kelley Mfg, boxes, 1¢, c1920 **200.00**
Peanut, Oak Mfg, Acorn, c1947 ..... **35.00**
Pens, Victor Vending, revolving, 25¢, c1962 .... **55.00**
Perfume, Mercury Tool, "Perfumatic," c1950 .... **225.00**
Post Card, Exhibit Supply, 1¢ novelty, c1930 .... **125.00**
Stamps, Postage Stamp Machine Co, metal, 5¢ and 10¢, c1948 .... **40.00**

VERNON KILNS

Collecting Hints: Vernon Kilns used 48 different marks during its period of operation. Collect examples which are in very good condition and concentrate on the specialty items rather than dinnerware.

History: During the Depression, many small potteries flourished in southern California. One of these, Poxon China, was founded in Vernon, California, in 1912. This pottery was sold to Faye G. Bennison in 1931. It was renamed Vernon Kilns and also was known as Vernon Potteries, Ltd. Under Bennison's direction, the company became a leader in the pottery industry.

The high quality and versatility of its wares made it very popular. Besides a varied dinnerware line, Vernon Kilns also produced Walt Disney figurines, advertising, political, and fraternal items. One popular line was historical and commemorative plates, which included several plate series, featuring scenes from England, California missions, and the West.

Vernon Kilns survived the Depression, fires, earthquakes, and wars. However, it could not compete with the influx of imports. In January, 1958, the factory was closed. Metlox Potteries of Manhattan Beach, California, bought the trade name and molds along with the remaining stock.

References: Susan and Al Bagdade, *Warman's American Pottery and Porcelain*, Wallace–Homestead, 1994; Maxine Feek Nelson, *Collectible Vernon Kilns*, Collector Books, 1994.

Periodical: *Vernon View*, PO Box 945, Scottsdale, AZ 85252.

Bark
    Bowl, 9" d **18.00**
    Gravy **18.00**
    Salt and Pepper Shakers, pr **20.00**
Brown Eyed Susan, demitasse cup and saucer **18.00**
Casual, teapot, dark green, large **40.00**
Cosmos, salt and pepper shakers, pr .. **25.00**
Disney
    Bowl
        #120, Fantasia, mushroom, aqua **180.00**
        #125, pink **245.00**
Early California
    Creamer, demitasse, orange **20.00**
    Cup and Saucer, demitasse, dark blue **25.00**
    Eggcup, ivory **10.00**
    Salt and Pepper Shakers, pr
        Dark Blue **25.00**
        Orange **25.00**
Gingham
    Carafe **30.00**
    Casserole, handled **25.00**
    Cup and Saucer **8.00**
    Pitcher, 11½" h, ice lip **48.00**
    Plate
        6½" d, bread and butter **7.00**
        10½" d, dinner **10.00**
    Salt and Pepper Shakers, pr, large .. **35.00**
    Soup, 8½" d **12.00**
    Syrup **60.00**
    Vegetable Bowl, 9" d **18.00**
Hawaiian Flowers
    Chop Plate, 12" d **150.00**
    Coffeepot **125.00**
    Creamer **30.00**
    Cup and Saucer **25.00**
    Plate
        6" d, bread and butter **8.00**
        8" d, luncheon **18.00**
        9" d, dinner **25.00**
    Salt and Pepper Shakers, pr **25.00**
    Sugar **35.00**

Child's Feeding Dish, Golliwogg decal, white ground, marked "Vernon China, Vernon, Cal," $48.00.

Homespun

Casserole, cov, round, 2 handles . . .	45.00
Creamer, individual	17.50
Cup and Saucer	10.00
Gravy	18.00
Mixing Bowls, nesting, set of five . . .	175.00
Mug	25.00
Plate	
6½" d, bread and butter	5.00
7½" d, salad	8.00
10" d, dinner	12.00
Platter, 12½" l	17.50
Salad Bowl, individual, 5½" d	15.00
Salt and Pepper Shakers, pr, large . .	25.00
Sauce Boat, 6½" l	15.00
Soup, flat, 8½" d	12.00
Sugar, cov, individual	25.00
Teacup	7.50

Lei Lani

Chop Plate, 12" d	165.00
Creamer	30.00
Cup and Saucer	25.00
Plate, 9" d	25.00
Sugar	35.00

Mayflower

Cup and Saucer	14.00
Plate, 14" d	40.00

Mission, chop plate . . . . | 85.00

Moby Dick

Chop Plate, 12" d	150.00
Creamer and Sugar	70.00
Cup and Saucer	25.00
Plate	
9" d	25.00
12" d, brown	75.00
Salt and Pepper Shakers, pr	50.00
Sauce Boat	30.00
Soup	24.00

Organdie

Coaster	15.00
Creamer and Sugar, cov	15.00
Custard	25.00
Eggcup	25.00
Mixing bowls, nesting, set of five . . .	125.00
Mug, 9 oz	18.00
Plate	
6½" d, bread and butter	3.00
10½" d, dinner	12.00
Platter, 12¾" l	10.00
Salt and Pepper Shakers, pr	18.00
Soup, lug	20.00
Spoon Holder	25.00

Tam O'Shanter

Bowl, 1 pint	22.00
Eggcup	30.00
Pitcher, 2 quart, ice lip	35.00
Platter, oval, 12" l	18.00
Tidbit Tray, 3 tiers, wood handle . . .	40.00

Ultra California

Dinner Service, 47 pcs	135.00
Plate, 12" d, green	25.00

VIEW–MASTER PRODUCTS

Collecting Hints: Condition is the key in determining price. In most cases because of relative newness of this collecting category and quantities of material made, viewers and reels in mint or near new condition may still be found.

Original packaging is sought by collectors. Many viewers and reels were removed from boxes and envelopes and became subject to damage and excessive wear.

History: The first View–Master viewers and reels were made available in 1939. Invented by William Gruber, View–Master products were manufactured and sold by Sawyer's, Inc., of Portland, Oregon. The sudden growth of View–Master was cut short by World War II. Shortages of film, plastic, and paper would have crippled the operation and possibly ended the existence of View–Master had not the Army and Navy recognized the visual training potential of this product. Between 1942 and the war's end, about 100,000 viewers and 5 to 6 million reels were ordered by the military.

After the war, public demand for View–Master products soared. Production barely satisfied the needs of the original 1,000 dealer network. The year 1946 saw the introduction of the Model C viewer which was practically indestructible, thus making it the most common viewer found by collectors today.

In October 1966, General Aniline & Film Corporation (GAF) bought Sawyer's and revamped the View–Master line. GAF introduced new 2–D projectors and 3–D Talking View–Master.

In late 1980 GAF sold the View–Master portion of their company to a limited partnership headed by businessman Arnold Thaler. Further acquisition resulted in the purchase of Ideal Toys. Today the 3–D viewers and reels are manufactured by View–Master Ideal, Inc.

References: Roger T. Nazeley's *View–Master Single Reels, Volume I*, published by author, 1987; John Waldsmith, *Stereo Views: An Illustrated History And Price Guide*, Wallace–Homestead, 1991.

Collectors' Club: Many View–Master collectors are members of the National Stereoscopic Association, PO Box 14801, Columbus, OH 43214.

VIEWER

Model C, black Bakelite, insert in top, light attachment, batteries, no corrosion, 1946–56 . . . . **25.00**

Model D, focuses, orig box **85.00**
Model F, lighted, dark brown plastic, pressure bar on top **20.00**
Model H, lighted, round bottom, GAF logo on front, 1967–81 . . . . **15.00**
Modern Viewers **1.50**

PROJECTOR

S–1, metal, brown, single lens, carrying case **48.00**
Sawyer's, plastic, single lens **10.00**
Stereomatic 500, 3–D, two lens, carrying case **250.00**

CAMERA

Personal 3–D, custom film cutter **175.00**
Mark II, film cutter, made in Europe . . **200.00**

REEL, SINGLE

Early hand–lettered, white reel, blue and white envelopes
58, Golden Gate Exposition, Flowers and Landscaping **15.00**
62, Hawaiian Hula Dancers **3.00**
76, Mount Vernon, VA **10.00**
92, Oregon Caves National Monument **2.00**
101, Rocky Mountain National Park, CO **2.00**
137, Washington, DC **3.00**
145, Sanctuary of Our Sorrowful Mother, Portland, OR **10.00**
152, Water Falls along Columbia Highway **5.00**
167, Marine Studios, St Augustine . . **5.00**
181, Colonial Williamsburg, VA . . . **10.00**
203, The Black Hills, SD **2.00**
236, The Million Dollar Highway . . **5.00**
253, Carlsbad Caverns National Park **5.00**
267, Cranmore Mt Skimobile Tramway, White Mountains **8.00**
284, Death Valley National Monument **5.00**
339, Mammoth Cave National Park **6.00**
348, Gettysburg National Military Monument, PA, II **10.00**
501, Mexico City and Vicinity **3.00**
510, Lake Patzcuaro and Paricutin Volcano **6.50**
623, Ruins of Pachacamac, near Lima, Peru **21.00**
667, La Plata, Argentina **5.00**
C–1, Morphology of Succulents **8.00**
Standard white reels, printed titles, blue and white envelopes
14, Reno, "Biggest Little City in the World" **8.00**
51, Garden of the Gods, Colorado . . **1.00**
72, Island of Kuai, HI **6.00**

86, Franklin D Roosevelt's Home, Hyde Park, New York, 1950 . . . . . **2.00**
118, Kings Canyon National Park, CA **2.00**
151, Columbia River Highway, OR **1.00**
196, Grand Coulee Dam, Washington, 1949 . . . . **2.00**
198, San Francisco, CA, 1948 . . . . . **1.00**
222, Tournament of Roses, Pasadena, CA, 1953 . . . . **10.00**
253, Carlsbad Caverns National Park, NM, III **1.00**
299, Hot Springs National Park, AR **1.00**
332, The Mardi Gras, New Orleans, LA, 1949 . . . . **3.00**
342, Race Horses of the Bluegrass Country, KY, 1952 . . . . **3.00**
343, Roosevelt's Little White House, Warm Springs, GA, 1949 . . . . **1.00**
349, Amish Country, PA, 1951 . . . . . **1.00**
360, Historic Charleston, SC, 1950 **1.00**
400, The Inauguration of President Dwight D Eisenhower, 1953 . . . . **10.00**
641, Santiago, Chile, 1946 . . . . **2.00**
742, Movie Stars, Hollywood III . . . **15.00**
810, Tom and Jerry in The Cat Trapper, 1951 . . . . **2.00**
820, Woody Woodpecker in the Pony Express Ride, 1951 . . . . **2.00**
942, Life with the Cowboys, 1951 . . **2.00**
1075, Scarborough, Yorkshire, England **15.00**
1705, The Alhambra Palace, Granada, Spain, 1953 . . . . **2.00**
2014, Lucerne, Switzerland, 1948 . . **1.00**
3100, Victoria Falls, Southern Rhodesia, Africa, 1948 . . . . **2.00**
3308, People of the Nile Valley, Egypt, 1950 . . . . **3.00**
4017, Wilderness of Judea, Palestine, 1949 . . . . **2.00**
4820, Buddhist Temples of Bangkok, Siam, 1949 . . . . **2.00**
5261, The Maoris, Natives of New Zealand, 1950 . . . . **2.00**
9055, Prehistoric Cliff Dwellers of Mesa Verde, CO, 1950 . . . . **5.00**
C–18, Euphorbiacease, 1945 . . . . . . **8.00**
FT–3, Jack and The Beanstalk, 1951 **1.00**
SAM–1, Adventures of Sam Sawyer, Sam Flies to the Moon, booklet . . **5.00**
SP–305, Sitka, AK, 1950 . . . . **8.00**
SP–9034, Sea Lion Caves, Florence, OR, 1948 . . . . **1.00**
SP–9039, San Diego, CA, 1949 . . . . **1.00**
SP–9062, Boys Town, NE, 1951 . . . . **1.00**

3–REEL PACKETS

Values are for complete, nearly new packets. In most cases the 3–reel packets came with story booklets. Sawyer issues (SAW) 1953–1966, GAF issues (GAF) 1967–1981, and View–Master International (VMI) 1981–1982.

Arabian Nights, FT–50 A, B, and C, SAW **11.00**
Christmas Carol, FT–31A, B and C ... **3.00**
Cowboy Star Adventures, 946, 951, and 956 .... **10.00**
Dale Evans, Queen of the West, 944–A, B, and C **25.00**
Easter Story, EA–1, 2, and 3 .... **5.00**
Garden Flowers, 980, 981, and 982 .. **10.00**
A–102, Eskimos of Alaska **8.00**
A–163, Yosemite National Park, Packet No 2 .... **9.00**
A–181, Los Angeles, CA, edition B ... **6.00**
A–219, San Francisco, Tour No 3 .... **6.00**
A–321, Pikes Peak, Garden of the Gods, Cave of the Winds, CO **6.00**
A–376, Carlsbad Caverns National Park **6.00**
A–635, Historic Philadelphia, edition A **12.00**
A–798, The Restored Ford's Theatre and Lincoln Museum, edition A **12.00**
A–818, Arlington National Cemetery, edition A **6.00**
A–949, Walt Disney World, Adventureland **6.00**
B–215, Grand Tour of Asia **15.00**
B–343, Mark Twain's Huckleberry Finn **30.00**
B–406, Raggedy Ann and Andy **6.00**
B–444, Tarzan of the Apes, edition A .. **30.00**
B–503, Dark Shadows, edition A, 1968 **20.00**
B–576, Barbie's Great American Photo Race **10.00**
B–750, Royal Canadian Mounted Police **12.00**
B–811, Forging A Nation, America's Bicentennial Celebration **8.00**
BB–432, Treasure Island **6.00**
BB–452, The Rookies **10.00**
H–19, Disney World, Tomorrowland, VMI **5.00**
J–32, Thailand, GAF **6.00**

WATCH FOBS

Collecting Hints: The most popular fobs are those relating to old machinery—either farm, construction or industrial. Advertising fobs are the next most popular group.

The back of a fob is helpful in identifying a genuine fob from a reproduction or restrike. Genuine fobs frequently have advertising or a union trademark on the back. Some genuine fobs do have blank backs; but a blank back should be a warning to be cautious.

History: A watch fob is a useful and decorative item attached to a man's pocket watch by a strap. It assists him in removing the watch from his pocket. Fobs became popular during the last quarter of the 19th century. Companies such as The Greenduck Co. in Chicago, Schwabb in Milwaukee, and Metal Arts in Rochester produced

fobs for companies who wished to advertise their products or to commemorate an event, individual, or group.

Most fobs are made of metal and are struck from a steel die. Enamel fobs are scarce and sought after by collectors. If a fob was popular, a company would order restrikes. As a result, some fobs were issued for a period of twenty–five years or more. Watch fobs still are used today in promoting heavy industrial equipment.

Reference: John M. Kaduck, *Collecting Watch Fobs,* Wallace–Homestead, 1973, 1995 value update.

Collectors' Clubs: Canadian Association of Watch Fob Collectors, PO Box 787, Caledonia, Ontario, N0A IAO Canada; International Watch Fob Association, Inc., RR5, PO Box 210, Burlington, IA 52601; Midwest Watch Fob Collectors, Inc., 6401 W. Girard Ave., Milwaukee, WI 53210.

REPRODUCTION ALERT

Altman–Taylor **90.00**
Arrowhead, saddle, Texas souvenir ... **35.00**
Atlantic City, city seal, 1854 .... **20.00**
Avery Tractor Co **85.00**
Baseball Bat and Glove, sterling silver, 1920s **75.00**
Buffalo Bill Pawnee Bill **125.00**
Bull Durham **75.00**
Case Plow **60.00**
Caterpillar Diesel Engines, brass **45.00**
Champlain Oils, enamel, red, white, and blue **75.00**
Cincinnati Horseshoe Company **85.00**
Covered Wagon and Team **47.50**
De Laval Separator, 1¾" l, oval, silvered brass, blue, white, pink, and cherry red porcelain accents, back inscribed "De Laval Cream Separators/World's Standard/Over 2,500,000 In Use," early 1900s **85.00**
Diamond Edge **32.00**
Fireman **35.00**
Flint Wagon Works **40.00**
French Auto Oil **45.00**
Galion Tandem Rollers, Galion, OH, 1950s **12.00**
Grand Island Horse and Mule Co, 1916 **50.00**
Heinz 57 .... **55.00**
Horseshoe and Horse, gold filled, chain **110.00**
Human Hair **165.00**
Hutchinson, KS, sunflower, button and ribbon **48.00**
Indian Motorcycles, 1¼ x 2", brass, bronze–like finish, diecut arrowhead, Indian head logo center, early 1900s **75.00**
International Harvester **65.00**

Laddie Athlete, white metal, leather strap, $27.50.

Western Live Stock Insurance Co, sterling silver **15.00**
Woodrow Wilson, emb brass, black ribbon **50.00**

WATT POTTERY

Collecting Hints: Since Watt pottery was hand painted, there is a great deal of variation in patterns. Look for pieces whose design is aesthetically pleasing. Also focus on pieces whose designs remain bright and cheerful.

Watt had strong regional sales in New England and New York, over 50% of its product. Little made its way west. Beware of placing too much emphasis on availability as a price consideration when buying outside the New England and New York area.

Watt made experimental and specialty advertising pieces. These are eagerly sought by collectors. In addition, Watt made pieces to be sold exclusively by other distributors, e.g., Ravarino & Freschi Company's "R–F Spaghetti" mark.

History: Watt Pottery traces its roots back to W. J. Watt, who founded the Brilliant Stoneware Company in 1886 in Rose Farm, Ohio. Watt sold his stoneware company in 1897. Between 1903 and 1921 W. J. Watt worked at the Ransbottom Brothers Pottery owned by his brothers–in–law.

In 1921 W. J. Watt purchased the Globe Stoneware Company, known briefly as the Zane W. Burley Pottery between 1919 and 1921, in Crooksville, Ohio, and renamed it Watt Pottery Company. Watt was assisted by Harry and Thomas, his sons; C. L. Dawson, his son–in–law; Marion Watt, his daughter; and numerous other relatives.

Between 1922 and 1935 the company produced a line of stoneware products manufactured from clay in the Crooksville area. The company prospered, exporting some of its wares to Canada.

In the mid–1930s Watt introduced a kitchenware line. The background color consisted of earth tones of off–white and light tan. The overall feel of this new ware was similar to dinnerware patterns made by Pennsbury, Pfaltzgraff, and Purinton. English Torquay is another possible comparison.

Most Watt dinnerware featured an underglaze decoration. Prior to 1950 decoration was relatively simple, e.g., blue and white banding. Starting in 1950 patterns were introduced. A pansy motif was the first. Red Apple began in 1952 and Rooster in 1955. Floral series such as Starflower and Tulip variations were made. New patterns were introduced yearly.

Watt sold its pottery through large chain stores such as Kroger's, Safeway, and Woolworth, and

James & Meyer Buggy Co, Lawrenceburg, IN	70.00
John Deere, mother–of–pearl	125.00
Kansas Livestock Co, horse and shoe . .	45.00
Keystone Lumber, elephant	40.00
Kress Corp, Brimfield, IL, cement truck	10.00
Mack Trucks, bulldog	35.00
MacLarens Imperial Cheese, multicolored enamel	75.00
Mayflower, calf skin, German	12.50
McFarland, Connersville, IN, carriage shape	95.00
Mexican Border Service, 1916	145.00
Nash Hardware, Panther Cutlery & Tools, Ft Worth	75.00
National Guard, Nevada, MO, 1913 . .	75.00
New Mexico, 1908 Territorial Fair	37.50
Novary Pure Foods, silvered brass	12.00
Peace Bridge, Toronto, 1930	12.00
P & H Qualila Service	27.50
Plymouth Division, military meet, best regimental parade, Nov 1918	25.00
Race Horse	37.50
Red Man Tobacco	30.00
Roosevelt and Fairbanks, 1¼" sq, brass, bronze color finish, diecut elephant	85.00
Roundup Saddle, Pendleton, OR	125.00
Sam Houston, 1½" white metal, raised portrait, reverse "Compliments of F W Heitmann Co/Hardware/Houston, TX," early 1900s	40.00
Shawmut Rubbers, Boston, celluloid . .	25.00
Stirrup, brass	22.00
Traveler's Protective Ass'n, diecut, state of IL shape, small enclosed compass, 1917	25.00
United States Revolvers Assoc Championships, 3rd place, 1927 . . .	37.50
Vandium–Alloys Steel Co Red Cut Cobalt High Speed Steel, brass, red devil on machinery	64.00
Wards Tip Top Bread	50.00

grocery, hardware, and other retail merchants. The greatest amount of their products were sold in New England and New York. The balance was sold in the Midwest, Northwest, and South.

In the early 1960s Watt was grossing over three–quarters of a million dollars annually. Future prospects were promising. On October 4, 1965, fire destroyed the factory and warehouse. The company never recovered; the pottery was never rebuilt.

References: Susan and Al Bagdade, *Warman's American Pottery and Porcelain,* Wallace–Homestead, 1994; Harvey Duke, *The Official Identification and Price Guide to Pottery and Porcelain, Eighth Edition,* House of Collectibles, 1995; Sue and Dave Morris, *Watt Pottery: An Identification and Value Guide,* Collector Books, 1993; Dennis Thompson and W. Bryce Watt, *Watt Pottery: A Collector's Reference with Price Guide,* Schiffer Publishing, 1994.

Collectors' Club: Watt Pottery Collectors USA, Box 26067, Fairview Park, OH 44126.

Periodical: *Watt's News,* PO Box 708, Mason City, IA 50401.

Reproduction Alert: A Japanese copy of a large spaghetti bowl marked simply "U.S.A." is known. The Watt example bears "Peeddeeco" and "U.S.A." marks.

Apple
  Bean Cup, #75 . . . . 500.00
  Bean Pot, #76, three leaf 295.00
  Bowl
    #6 . . . . 55.00
    #7 . . . . 75.00
    #8 . . . . 60.00
  Casserole, cov, #18
    French handle 270.00
    Tab handle 325.00
  Creamer, #62 . . . . 170.00
  Grease Jar, #01, three leaf 495.00
  Ice Bucket, two leaf, #59 . . . . 265.00
  Mug, #121, three leaf 295.00
  Pitcher
    #16 . . . . 125.00
    Advertising, Fowler, CO grocery . . 125.00
    Commemorative, 1994 . . . . 300.00
  Platter, #49 . . . . 395.00
  Refrigerator Pitcher, two leaf, #69 . . 395.00
  Salt and Pepper Shakers, pr, hour
    glass, adv 275.00
  Shaker, barrel 205.00
  Sugar, open, #98
    Advertising 225.00
    Three leaf 355.00
Banded
  Bowl
    #8 . . . . 30.00
    #9, pink and blue, ribbed 65.00
    #12, brown 85.00

Cookie Jar, blue and white 135.00
Cherry
  Berry Bowl, #4 . . . . 25.00
  Bowl, #52 . . . . 40.00
  Pitcher, #15 . . . . 55.00
  Platter 150.00
  Salt Shaker 50.00
  Spaghetti Bowl, #39 . . . . 100.00
Double Tulip, mixing bowl, #63 . . . . . 125.00
Dutch Tulip
  Creamer, #62, flake 275.00
  Mixing Bowl, #64 . . . . 135.00
Nassau, salad set, vinegar and oil, salt and
  pepper shakers, and #106 salad bowl 275.00
Pansy
  Berry Bowl, #22 . . . . 35.00
  Pie Plate, #33, adv 60.00
  Pizza Plate 275.00
  Platter, #31 . . . . 70.00
  Spaghetti Bowl
    #11 . . . . 125.00
    #39 . . . . 100.00
Rooster
  Bowl, adv 50.00
  Creamer, #62 . . . . 95.00
  Ice Bucket 125.00
  Pitcher, #15 . . . . 115.00
  Refrigerator Pitcher, #69 . . . . 595.00
  Salt Shaker, adv 50.00
  Sugar, open, 398 . . . . 375.00
  Vegetable Bowl, adv 50.00
Starflower
  Bowl
    #8 . . . . 80.00
    #24 . . . . 85.00
  Casserole, cov
    #18 . . . . 120.00
    #67 . . . . 100.00
  Creamer, #62, 4 petal 500.00
  Mixing Bowls, nesting, set of four, #4,
    #5, #6, and #7 . . . . 175.00
  Mug, #501 . . . . 85.00
  Pitcher
    #15, four petal starflower, chip on
      spout 75.00

Pitcher, Rooster, 6¼" w, 7" h, $95.00.

#17	125.00
Salt and Pepper Shakers, pr, barrel	250.00
Spaghetti Bowl, #39	125.00

Teardrop

Bean Cup	40.00
Casserole, cov, 8" sq	275.00
Pitcher, #15	95.00
Salt Shaker, barrel	175.00

Tulip, bowl

#64, hairline	40.00
#65	95.00

WELLER POTTERY

Collecting Hints: Because of the availability of large numbers of pieces in Weller's commercial ware, prices are stable and unlikely to rise rapidly. Forest, Glendale, and Woodcraft are the popular patterns in the middle price range. The Novelty Line is most popular in the lower–priced items.

Novice collectors are advised to look to figurals as a starting point. There are over fifty variations of frogs in the figural area. Many other animal shapes also are available.

Pieces in the middle range tend to be marked with an impressed "Weller" in block letters or a half circle ink stamp with the words "Weller Pottery." Late pieces are marked with a script "Weller" or "Weller Pottery." Many new collectors see this dated mark and incorrectly think the piece is old.

There are well over a hundred Weller patterns. New collectors should visit other collectors, talk with dealers, and look at a large range of pieces to determine which patterns they like and want to collect. It is pattern, not shape or type, by which most collections are organized.

History: In 1872 Samuel A. Weller opened a small factory in Fultonham, near Zanesville, Ohio, to produce utilitarian stoneware, such as milk pans and sewer tile. In 1882 he moved his facilities to Zanesville. In 1890 Weller built a new plant in the Putnam section of Zanesville along the tracks of the Cincinnati and Muskingum Railway. Additions followed in 1892 and 1894.

In 1894 Weller entered into an agreement with William A. Long to purchase the Lonhuda Faience Company, which had developed an art pottery line under the guidance of Laura A. Fry, formerly of Rookwood. Long left in 1895 but Weller continued to produce Lonhuda under a new name, Louwelsa. This shaded brown pottery with hand decoration under glaze was produced in over 500 different shapes. Replacing Long as art director was Charles Babcock Upjohn. He, along with Jacques Sicard, Frederick Hurten

Rhead and Gazo Fudji, developed Weller's art pottery lines.

At the end of World War I, many prestige lines were discontinued and Weller concentrated on commercial wares. Rudolph Lorber joined the staff and designed lines such as Roma, Forest and Knifewood. In 1920 Weller purchased the plant of the Zanesville Art Pottery. Weller claimed to be the largest pottery in the country.

Art pottery enjoyed a revival when the Hudson Line was introduced in the early 1920s. The 1930s saw Coppertone and Graystone Garden ware added. However, the Depression forced the closing of a Putnam plant and one on Marietta Street in Zanesville. After World War II inexpensive Japanese imports took over Weller's market. In 1947 Essex Wire Company of Detroit bought the controlling stock. Early in 1948 operations ceased.

References: Susan and Al Bagdade, *Warman's American Pottery and Porcelain*, Wallace–Homestead, 1994; Sharon and Bob Huxford, *The Collectors Encyclopedia of Weller Pottery*, Collector Books, 1979, 1994 value update; Ralph and Terry Kovel, *Kovels' American Art Pottery: The Collector's Guide To Makers, Marks, and Factory Histories*, Crown Publishers, 1993; Ann Gilbert McDonald, *All About Weller: A History and Collectors Guide To Weller Pottery, Zanesville, OH*, Antique Publications, 1989.

Collectors' Club: American Art Pottery Association, 125 E. Rose Ave., St. Louis, MO 63119.

Note: For pieces in the middle and upper price range see *Warman's Antiques And Their Prices*.

Ashtray, dog, white	135.00
Basket, Wild Rose, shaded brown, 6" h, 5" d	60.00

Bowl

Marbleized, 7" d	125.00
Scandia, 6½" d	75.00
Squirrel on rim	95.00

Bud Vase

Eocean, berries, 10" h	195.00
Roma, double	65.00
Rowa Flora	55.00
Candleholders, pr, Silvertone	175.00
Chalice, iridescent lemon, stamp mark, 8" h, 6" d	90.00
Cigarette Holder, Coppertone, figural frog	200.00
Console Set, Warwick	165.00
Cornucopia, pastel, raised florals, price for pair	60.00

Ewer

Eocean, gooseberries, 12½" h	495.00
Etna, 9" h	150.00
Forest, 8" h	165.00
Knifewood, green, 9" h	450.00

Louwelsa, sgd "McLaughlin," 9½" h   750.00
Wild Rose, green, 6¾" h, price for
pair 75.00
Woodcraft, 13" h 395.00
Mug
Floretta, grapes, 5½" h 155.00
Souevo, #30 . . . .   140.00
Pedestal Base, Dickensware, daffodil
dec, artist sgd "Hattie Mitchell," 22" h   465.00
Pitcher, Kingfisher, green 130.00
Planter
Dog, two noses 75.00
Duck and Rabbit 55.00
Klyro, die stamped, 4" sq 60.00
Plate, Anton Lang, turquoise orange 8" d   75.00
Urn
Double handles, high gloss, blue
shaded glaze, unmarked 90.00
Sculpted handles, matte blue, un-
marked, 5½" h 50.00
Vase
Art Nouveau, floral dec, 5½" h 145.00
Chase, 9" h 345.00
Coppertone, frog on lily pad 175.00
Eocean, floral, 7½" h 195.00
Etna, 8½" h 275.00
Fleron, 8" h 130.00
Floretta, 17" h 395.00
Greora 90.00
Hudson, 11" h, sgd Leffler 895.00
Ivory, peacocks, 11" h 80.00
Juneau, 6" h 90.0
Louwelsa
Cornflowers, squatty 150.00
Mums, cylindrical, sgd Butterworth   285.00
Orange Flowers, brown luster,
8¼" h 195.00
Panella, green, 10½" h 60.00
Perfecto, floral, sgd, 10" h 795.00
Stellar, 7" h 695.00
Turquoise, round, low, handled 30.00
Voila, fan shape 65.00
Wild Rose, 9½" h 80.00
Zona, bird 300.00

**Wall Pocket, owl, green, brown, 11" h,
5¾" d, $145.00.**

Wall Pocket
Hobart Girl, blue **350.00**
Squirrel **375.00**

WESTERN AMERICANA

Collecting Hints: Western Americana is a relatively new field. The initial emphasis has been on books, prints, and paper products. The barbed wire craze of the early 1970s drew attention to three–dimensional objects.

Texas material is the most sought after. All collectors tend to focus on the 19th century, rather than modern material. Within the last decade, Indian materials have moved into the level of sophisticated antique collecting.

Collectors should pick a theme or subject. The military West, exploration accounts and maps, and early photography are a few of the more popular focal points. The collecting field now has progressed to the point where there are more than a half–dozen dealers specializing solely in western materials.

History: From the Great Plains to the Golden West, the American West was viewed as the land of opportunity by settlers from the mid–19th century to the early 20th century. Key events caused cataclysmic changes—the 1848 Gold Rush, the opening of the Transcontinental railroad, the silver strikes in Nevada, the Indian massacres, and the Oklahoma land rush. By 1890 the West of the cowboy and cattle was dead; Indians had been relocated onto reservations.

The romance did not die. Novels, movies and television, whether through the Ponderosa or Southfork, keep the romance of the West alive. Oil may have replaced cattle, but the legend remains.

References: Warren R. Anderson, *Owning Western History: A Guide To Collecting Rare Documents, Historical Letters And Valuable Autographs From The Old West,* Mountain Press Publishing, 1993; Robert W. D. Ball, *Western Memorabilia and Collectibles,* Schiffer Publishing, 1993; Robert W. D. Ball and Edward Vebell, *Cowboy Collectibles And Western Memorabilia,* Schiffer Publishing, 1991, 1993 value update; James Lynn Bartz, *Company Property of Wells, Fargo & Co's Express 1852–1918,* The Westbound Stage Co, 1993; Robert T. Clifton, *Barbs, Prongs, Points, Prickers & Stickers: A Complete and Illustrated Catalogue of Antique Barb Wire,* University of Oklahoma Press, 1970; Judy Crandall, *Cowgirls: Early Images and Collectibles,* Schiffer Publishing, 1994; *Cowboy Clothing and Gear: The Complete Hamley Catalog of 1942,* Dover Publications,

1942, 1995 reprint; Michael Friedman, *Cowboy Culture: The Last Frontier Of American Antiques,* Schiffer Publishing, 1992; R. C. House, *The Official Price Guide To Old West Collectibles,* House of Collectibles, 1994; Dan and Sebie Hutchins, *Old Cowboy Saddles & Spurs: Identifying The Craftsmen Who Made Them, Fourth Annual,* Horse Feathers Publishing; William C. Ketchum, Jr., *Collecting The West,* Crown Publishing Group, 1993; William C. Ketchum, *Western Memorabilia: Identification and Price Guide,* Avon Books, 1993; Bill Macklin, *Cowboy and Gunfighter Collectibles,* Mountain Press Publishing, 1989; Norman E. Martinus and Harry L. Rinker, *Warman's Paper,* Wallace–Homestead, 1994; Richard C. Rattenbury, *Packing Iron: Gunleather of the Frontier West,* Zon International Publishing, 1993.

Collectors' Clubs: National Bit, Spur & Saddle Collectors Association, PO Box 3098, Colorado Springs, CO 80934; Western American Collectors Society, PO Box 620417, Woodside, CA 94062.

Periodicals: *American Cowboy,* PO Box 12830, Wichita, KS 67277; *Boots,* Lone Pine Rd., PO Box 766, Challis, ID 83226; *Cowboy Guide,* PO Box 47, Millwood, NY 10546; *Southwest Art,* Suite 1440, Houston, TX 77056; *Texas Monthly,* PO Box 7088, Red Oak, IA 51591; *The Westerner,* PO Box 5253, Vienna, WV, 26105; *Yippy Yi Yea Magazine,* 8393 E. Holly Rd., Holly, MI 48442; *Wild West,* 6405 Flank Dr., Harrisburg, PA 17112.

Museums: Cowboy & Gunfighter Museum, Craig, CO; Gene Autry Western Heritage Museum, Los Angeles, CA; National Cowgirl Hall of Fame & Western Heritage Center, Hereford, TX; Pony Express Museum, St. Joseph, MO; Round Up Hall of Fame & Museum, Pendleton, OR 97801; Seven Acres Antique Village & Museum, Union, IL; Texas Ranger Hall of Fame & Museum, Waco, TX; The Rockwell Museum, Corning, NY; Wells Fargo History Museum, Los Angeles, CA.

Advertising Counter Display, Barn Dance, Alka Seltzer	**40.00**
Barbed Wire, 18" l, lot of fifty different types	**25.00**
Belt Buckle, brass, emb, Stetson	**17.50**
Bit	
Half breed, "S" shank	**85.00**
Star, steel and silver	**100.00**
Book	
Apache Gold And Yanqui Silver, Frank J Dobie, New York, 1939, 384 pgs, illus by Tom Lea	**25.00**
2–Gun Montana, Better Little Book, 1939	**9.00**

The Overland Trail, Jay Monaghan, Indianapolis, 1947, 432 pgs, plates, maps, 1st ed	**40.00**
Bookends, pr, cast iron, End of the Trail	**27.50**
Bootjack	
Metal, Superior Foundry, Cleveland	**42.50**
Wood, Lee Rivers	**42.50**
Boots, Hudson Bay Indian	**86.00**
Brand Certificate, Montana, 1917	**12.00**
Cabinet Card, 5 x 8", Hop Pickers, Puyallup, WA, group with rakes and other equipment standing in front of their crops and horses	**12.00**
Catalog	
H T Daniel, Dardanelle, AR, Catalogue of Indian Relics, c1929, 5¾ x 8¾", 16 pages	**28.00**
Ottawa Log and Tree Saws, Ottawa Mfg Co, Ottawa, KS, 9 x 12", orig mailing envelope, 16 pages	**30.00**
Chaps	**60.00**
Check	
Gould and Curry Silver Mining Company, Virginia City, NV, 8 x 3", Nov 1876, IRS stamp and Nevada State Revenue stamp	**25.00**
Wells Fargo, 7¾ x 3", San Francisco, 1972, ornate	**65.00**
Clothing, Mexican outfit, child's	**30.00**
Cowboy Hat, Texas 1836–1936 Centennial	**295.00**
Document	
Indian Territory, sgd by chief	**125.00**
Land Certificate, Creek Nation, 1899	**65.00**
Engravings, Indian Chiefs, reproduced in 1965 from 1840 McKenny & Hall engravings, price for set of eight	**185.00**
Gauntlets, US Cavalry, pre 1900	**135.00**
Handcuffs, Marlin Firearms Co, c1880s	**375.00**
Jug, imprinted cobalt blue airplane, marked "Love Field, Dallas, Texas"	**45.00**
Knife, buffalo horn, brass cap, skinning blade	**110.00**
Lamp, ceramic, cactus and hitching post	**60.00**
Letterhead, Montana, longhorn steer, 1911	**15.00**
Magazine Article, *TV Guide,* Paladin, May 10, 1958, cov with full color photo of Richard Boone	**10.00**
Magazine Cover, *Harper's Weekly,* Jan 1849, Elk Hunting in The Bandlands of the Upper Missouri, W M Cary, artist, 11 x 16"	**20.00**
Map	
Cherokee Nation, Indian Territory, Dept of Interior, Commission to the Five Civilized Tribes, 1900, issued folded, 37 x 27"	**75.00**
Nevada Pony Express Map, 1860–1960, published by the	

Nevada Pony Express Centennial Committee, chromolithograph, 23 x 17", framed **250.00**
Texas, Mitchell, 1860, 12 x 15" **45.00**
Mitts, bearskin gauntlet type **125.00**
Moccasins, Sioux, fully beaded, c1880 **1,100.00**
Photograph, cowboy riding horse, wearing wooly chaps **7.50**
Pin
  Enameled, rope circled horse rider, 1920s **32.50**
  Sterling Silver, horse, Richardo **37.50**
Pinback Button
  Enid, Oklahoma Stock Show, 1909 **45.00**
  Wilson Brothers Jewelers, black, white, brown, and red, Indian riding unicycle **7.50**
Pipe Holder, bronze, double, cowboy riding horse **75.00**
Pocket Watch Chain, Silver Gents, horses slide **157.00**
Poster
  14 x 36", Outlaws Of Texas, 1950 Monogram Pictures, Whip Wilson and Andy Clyde, minor creasing **15.00**
  27 x 41", Along The Rio Grande, 1941 RKO Radio Film, Tim Holt **50.00**
  30 x 40", Rodeo Parade In The Montana=Wyoming Dude Ranch Country, Edward P Brewer, c1935, Northern Pacific Railway adv, full color litho, Indian chief leading parade of cowboys **275.00**
Pouch, canvas, 101 Ranch & Wild West Show **250.00**

Pulp, *Buffalo Bill's Spy Shadower*, from the Buffalo Bill Stories, Gold Star Books, $20.00.

Print Portfolio, set of six unframed prints
  Catlin, George, North American Indian and Cowboy color plates .. **160.00**
  Russell, Charles M, dated 1958 .... **150.00**
Radio Premium Kit, "Wild West Rodeo," General Electric, 15 x 16", red, white, and blue envelope, punchout sheets, 1952 .... **25.00**
Ribbon
  Fredonia Texas Rodeo, bucking horse, 1929 .... **42.50**
  Salt Lake City Cattlemen's Convention, 1901 .... **85.00**
  Texas Cowboy Reunion, Stamford, 1938, attached fob **75.00**
Roach, Chippewa **165.00**
Rug, Navajo, early, 40 x 68" **695.00**
Saddle Bags
  Doctor's, c1870 .... **695.00**
  Pommel, Main & Winchester, built in holder **1,950.00**
Salt and Pepper Shakers, pr, man and horse head, Ceramic Arts Studio ... **38.00**
Scabbard
  Carbine **65.00**
  US Spr mod, 1887 .... **185.00**
Scale, buffalo hide type **95.00**
Sign, Wells Fargo & Co Express, metal, blue and white, 15 x 10" **900.00**
Spurs, pr
  Anchor Brand **295.00**
  Chilean, fine silver inlay, 1800s, 9" l, 5" d rowel, orig leathers **425.00**
  North & Judd, bronze **295.00**
Tablecloth, Colorado, Western figs and branding marks **35.00**
Tie Bar, Life Time Gate Mineral Wells, TX **32.50**

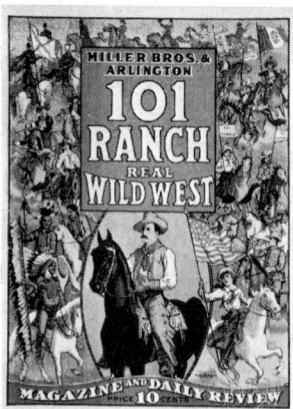

Program, Miller Bros. & Arlington 101 Ranch, Real Wild West Magazine and Daily Review, 40 pages, color litho covers, black-and-white photos and illus, 7¼ x 9¾", 1915, $60.00.

Timetable, Nevada Pony Express, 1960
Centennial Re–Run, offset litho, 22 x
14″, framed **75.00**
Tintype, Jessie James, framed **200.00**
Trade Card, 9½ x 5″, Never Rip
Nonpariel, blue jeans, San Francisco
dry goods store, c1890 . . . .   **8.50**
Trade Token, Pearce, AZ **75.00**
Tom Tom, Little Chief, Blue G Coffee . .   **30.00**
Watch Fob
Grand Island Horse & Mule Co,
Nebraska, 1916 . . . .   **45.00**
Kansas Livestock Co, horse and shoe   **45.00**
New Mexico Territorial Fair, 1908 . .   **37.50**
Nobby Harness Co, Fort Worth, TX   **75.00**
Weaver
Comb **35.00**
Pouch, Navajo **250.00**

WESTMORELAND GLASS COMPANY

Collecting Hints: The collector should become
familiar with the many lines of tableware produced. English Hobnail made from the 1920s to
1960s is popular. Colonial designs were reproduced frequently, and accessories with dolphin
pedestals are distinctive.

The trademark, an intertwined "W" and "G,"
was imprinted on glass since 1949. After January,
1983, the full name "Westmoreland" is on all
glass. Early molds were reintroduced. Numbered,
signed, dated "Limited Editions" were offered.

History: The Westmoreland Glass Company was
founded in October, 1899, at Grapeville, Pennsylvania. From the beginning, Westmoreland
made handcrafted high quality glassware. In
early years the company processed mustard, baking powder, and condiments to fill its containers.
During World War I candy–filled glass novelties
were popular.

Although Westmoreland is famous for its milk
glass, large amounts of other glass were produced. During the 1920s, Westmoreland made
reproductions and decorated wares. Color and
tableware appeared in the 1930s; but, as with
other companies, 1935 saw the return to mainly
crystal productions. In the 1940s to 1960s, black,
ruby, and amber colors were made.

In May 1982 the factory closed. Reorganization brought a reopening in July, 1982. The
Grapeville plant closed again in 1984.

References: Lorraine Kovar, *Westmoreland
Glass, 1950–1984*, Antique Publications, 1991;
Lorraine Kovar, *Westmoreland Glass, 1950–
1984, Volume II*, Antique Publications, 1991;
Ellen Tischbein Schroy, *Warman's Glass, Second*

Edition, Wallace–Homestead, 1995; Hazel Marie
Weatherman, *Colored Glassware of the
Depression Era, Book 2*, Glassbooks, Inc., 1982.

Collectors' Clubs: National Westmoreland Glass
Collectors Club, PO Box 372, Westmoreland
City, PA 15692; Westmoreland Glass Collectors
Club, 2712 Glenwood, Independence, MO
64052; Westmoreland Glass Society, Inc., 513
Fifth Ave., Coralville, IA 51141.

Museum: Westmoreland Glass Museum, Port
Vue, PA.

Almond Heart Plate, pink dogwood dec   **25.00**
Appetizer, Paneled Grape, Pattern
#1881, white milk glass, spoon miss-
ing **30.00**
Basket, English Hobnail, ruby **50.00**
Basket, Paneled Grape, Pattern #1881,
white milk glass, oval **12.00**

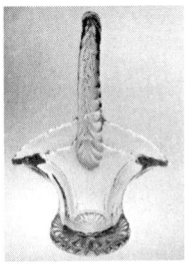

Basket, vaseline, 7″ h, $20.00.

Bonbon, cov, Irish Waterford
Crystal **45.00**
Ruby Stained **55.00**
Bowl, cov, Beaded Grape, 9″ d, ftd,
white milk glass **25.00**
Bowl, open, lipped, Paneled Grape,
Pattern #1881, white milk glass
9½″ d, pedestal **95.00**
12″ d, oval, ftd **100.00**
Butter Dish, cov, 1/4 lb size
Old Quilt, Pattern #500, white milk
glass **20.00**
Paneled Grape, Pattern #1881, white
milk glass **27.00**
Cake Salver
Beaded Grape, skirt, ftd, white milk
glass **65.00**
Paneled Grape, Pattern #1881, white
milk glass, 11″ d **65.00**
Candelabra, English Hobnail, two light,
white milk glass **18.00**
Candlesticks, pr
Beaded Grape, white milk glass **20.00**
English Hobnail, white milk glass . .   **65.00**
Old Quilt, Pattern #500, white milk
glass, 4″ h **20.00**

Paneled Grape, Pattern #1881, white milk glass, 4″ h	22.00	
Candy Dish, Paneled Grape, Pattern #1881, white milk glass, 7½″ d, 3 toes, crimped edge	32.00	
Celery Vase		
Old Quilt, Pattern #500, white milk glass, ftd	15.00	
Paneled Grape, Pattern #1881, white milk glass	40.00	
Champagne, Princess Feather, green	22.50	
Cheese Dish, cov, Old Quilt, Pattern #500, white milk glass	55.00	
Compote, cov		
Beaded Grape, white milk glass, blue grapes dec, gold trim, low standard	50.00	
Della Robia, amethyst stain	24.00	
Paneled Grape, Pattern #1881, white milk glass, 7″ h	22.00	
Compote, open, Old Quilt, Pattern #500, white milk glass, 8″ d	29.00	
Creamer and Sugar		
American Hobnail, blue opal	50.00	
Beaded Grape, white milk glass	27.50	
Della Robia, white milk glass	16.00	
Old Quilt, Pattern #500, white milk glass, large size	25.00	
Paneled Grape, Pattern #1881, white milk glass		
Lacy Edge	55.00	
Large size	30.00	
Cruet, orig stopper		
Old Quilt, Pattern #500, white milk glass, orig label	30.00	
Paneled Grape, Pattern #1881, white milk glass	20.00	
Cup and Saucer, Paneled Grape, Pattern #1881, white milk glass	22.00	
Epergne Set, Paneled Grape, Pattern #1881, white milk glass, 12″ h, 3 pc set	300.00	
Fruit Cocktail, Paneled Grape, Pattern #1881, white milk glass	12.00	
Goblet		
Della Robia		
Red stain	25.00	
White milk glass	18.00	
Paneled Grape, Pattern #1881, white milk glass, 8 oz, ftd	12.00	
Gravy and Liner, Paneled Grape, Pattern #1881, white milk glass	55.00	
Honey, cov, Beaded Grape, white milk glass	25.00	
Iced Tea Tumbler, Della Robia, white milk glass	20.00	
Ivy Ball, Paneled Grape, Pattern #1881, white milk glass	30.00	
Jardiniere, Paneled Grape, Pattern #1881, white milk glass		
5″ h	15.00	
6½″ h	20.00	

6¾″ h	38.00	
Jug, Paneled Grape, Pattern #1881, white milk glass		
Three Pint	40.00	
Two Pint	42.00	
Loving Cup, English Hobnail, 8″ h, hex foot, ruby	85.00	
Mayonnaise Set, Paneled Grape, Pattern #1881, white milk glass	20.00	
Mint Compote, Irish Waterford, 5½″ d, ruby stained	24.00	
Pansy Basket, white milk glass	15.00	
Pistol, solid, black milk glass	65.00	
Pitcher, Paneled Grape, Pattern #1881, white milk glass		
16 oz	25.00	
32 oz	20.00	
Planter, Paneled Grape, Pattern #1881, white milk glass, 5 x 9″	40.00	
Plate		
7½″ d, white milk glass, beaded edge		
Apple dec	12.50	
Cherries dec	12.50	
Grapes dec	12.50	
Peaches dec	12.50	
Plum dec	12.50	
8″ d, black milk glass, Mary Gregory dec, forget me not border		
Boy with dog and rake	45.00	
Girl with dog	45.00	
10½″ d, Beaded Edge	15.00	
Platter Zodiac, 15″ l, milk glass	90.00	
Punch Bowl, Old Quilt, Pattern #500, white milk glass	175.00	
Punch Bowl Set, Paneled Grape, Pattern #1881, white milk glass, 15 pcs	795.00	
Relish, Old Quilt, Pattern #500, white milk glass, 9″ l, 3 part	40.00	
Rose Bowl, English Hobnail, 4″ h, cupped, pink milk glass	35.00	
Salt and Pepper Shakers, pr		
Della Robia, red stain, ftd	55.00	
English Hobnail, white milk glass	20.00	
Old Quilt, Pattern #500, white milk glass	25.00	
Paneled Grape, Pattern #1881, white milk glass		
Flat	55.00	
Footed	25.00	
Sandwich Plate, 14″ d, Della Robia, red stain	65.00	
Sherbet		
English Hobnail, high, round foot	9.00	
Paneled Grape, Pattern #1881, white milk glass, amethyst	20.00	
Soap Dish, Paneled Grape, Pattern #1881, white milk glass	77.50	
Spooner, Paneled Grape, Pattern #1881, white milk glass, 6″ h	40.00	
Tidbit Tray, 7½″ and 11″ d tiers, white milk glass, Forget me not border	35.00	

Tumbler, Paneled Grape, Pattern #1881, white milk glass
9 oz, flat	**25.00**
12 oz	**20.00**

Vase
Old Quilt, Pattern #500, white milk glass, 9" h, fan **20.00**
Paneled Grape, Pattern #1881, white milk glass
6" h, bell shape	**10.00**
8½" h, bell shape	**15.00**
9" h, bell shape	**15.00**
13¾" h, swung, flared, 4½" base, 4½" scalloped top	**145.00**
15" h, flat	**95.00**

Wall Pocket, Paneled Grape, Pattern #1881, white milk glass, 8" h **325.00**
Wine, Paneled Grape, Pattern #1881, white milk glass, 2 oz **24.00**

WHISKEY BOTTLES, COLLECTORS' SPECIAL EDITIONS

Collecting Hints: Beginning collectors are advised to focus on bottles of a single manufacturer or collect around a central theme, e.g., birds, trains, western, etc. Make certain to buy bottles whose finish is very good (almost no sign of wear), with no chips, and with the original labels intact.

A major collection still can be built for a modest investment, although some bottles now command over $1,000, such as the Beam Red Coat Fox. Don't overlook miniatures if you are on a restricted budget.

Finally, it is common practice to find bottles empty. In many states it is against the law to sell liquor without a license; hence, collectors tend to focus on the empty bottle.

History: The Jim Beam Distillery began the practice of issuing novelty (collectors' special edition) bottles for the 1953 Christmas trade. By the late 1960s over one hundred other distillers and wine manufacturers followed suit.

The Jim Beam Distillery remains the most prolific of the bottle issuers. Lionstone, McCormick and Ski Country are the other principal suppliers today. One dealer, Jon–Sol, Inc., has distributed his own line of collector bottles.

The "golden age" of the special edition bottle was the early 1970s. Interest waned in the late 1970s and early 1980s as the market was saturated by companies trying to join the craze. Prices fell from record highs. Many manufacturers dropped special edition bottle production altogether.

A number of serious collectors, clubs, and dealers have brought stability to the market. Realizing that instant antiques cannot be created by demand alone, they have begun to study and classify their bottles. H. F. Montague deserves special recognition for his classification work. Most importantly, collectors have focused on those special edition bottles which show quality of workmanship and design and which have true limited editions.

References: Hugh Cleveland, *Bottle Pricing Guide, Third Edition*, 1988, 1993 value update; Ralph and Terry Kovel, *The Kovels' Bottle Price List, Ninth Edition*, Crown Publishers, 1992; Jim Megura, *The Official Price Guide to Bottles*, House of Collectibles, 1991; H. F. Montague, *Montague's Modern Bottle Identification and Price Guide, Third Edition*, H. F. Montague Enterprises, 1984; Michael Polak, *Bottles: Identification and Price Guide*, Avon Books, 1994.

Collectors' Clubs: Cape Codders Jim Beam Bottle & Specialty Club, 80 Lincoln Rd., Rockland, MA 02370; Hoffman National Collectors Club, PO Box 37341, Cincinnati, OH 45222; International Association of Jim Beam Bottle & Specialties Clubs, 5013 Chase Ave., Downers Grove, IL 60515; National Ski Country Bottle Club, 1224 Washington Ave., Golden, CO 80401; Space Coast Jim Beam Bottle & Specialties Club, 2280 Cox Rd., Cocoa, FL 32926.

Museum: American Outpost, James B. Beam Distillery, Clermont, KY.

JIM BEAM

Beam Clubs and Conventions
Akron—Rubber Capital, 1973	**22.50**
Blue Hen Club, 1982	**25.00**

Convention
First, Denver, 1971	**15.00**
Third, Detroit, 1973	**25.00**
Fourth, Lancaster, 1974	**100.00**
Ninth, Houston, Cowboy, antique, 1979	**150.00**
Eleventh, Las Vegas, Dealer Fox, 1981	**35.00**
Twelfth, New Orleans, 1982, King Rex	**35.00**

Fox
Red coats, 1973	**2,000.00**
Uncle Sam, 1971	**12.00**
White, 1969	**45.00**
Monterey Club, 1977	**15.00**
Twin Bridge Club, 1971	**55.00**

Beam on Wheels
Cable Car, 1968	**5.00**
Circus Wagon	**15.00**
Model A	**22.00**
Model T	**22.00**

Train
Baggage Car	50.00
Dining Car	55.00
Passenger Car	55.00

Centennial Series, First Issued, 1960
Alaska Purchase, 1966	8.00
Anitoch, 1967, arrow	7.00
Civil War, North, 1961	25.00
Key West, 1972	6.00
St. Louis Arch, 1966	18.00
Washington Bicentennial, 1976	15.00

Clubs and Organizations
Ahepa, 1972	5.00
Bald Eagle	35.00
Blue Goose, 1971	5.00
Ducks Unlimited, #1, 1974	40.00
Fleet Reserves 1974	5.00
Marine Corps, 1975	40.00
Shriner, Rajah Temple, 1977	20.00
VFW, 1971	10.00

Customer Specialties
Antique Trader	30.00

Armanetti
Bacchus, 1970	8.00
Fun Shopper, 1971	7.00
First National Bank, Chicago, 1964	3,000.00
Hyatt House, Chicago, 1971	15.00
Travel Lodge, 1972	8.00

Executive Series, First Issue, 1955
1957, Royal DiMonte	75.00
1959, Tavern Scene	70.00
1969, Sovereign	12.00

Foreign Countries
Australia
Kangaroo, 1978	15.00
Sydney Opera, 1978	20.00

Germany
Germany, 1970	5.00
Weisbaden, 1973	6.00

People Series
Buffalo Bill, 1971	7.00
Emmett Kelly, 1973, Kansas autograph	65.00
Indian Chief, 1980	17.50
Mortimer Snerd, 1976	30.00
Sea Captain & Mate, 1980	15.00

Political Series
Football, 1972
Donkey	12.50
Elephant	12.50

Regal China Series
A–C Spark Plug, 1977	10.00
Bellringer #2, Afore Ye Go, 1970	12.00
Franklin Mint, 1970	8.00
Jug, 1982, 1.75 liters	25.00
Ohio State Fair, 1972	7.50
Seattle World's Fair, 1962	15.00
Truth or Consequences, 1974	10.00

Sport Series
Bing Crosby National Pro–Am
33rd, 1974	27.50
37th, 1978	25.00

Jim Beam Bottle, The Broadmoor, Royal China, 1968, $7.50.

Bob Hope Desert Classic, 15th, 1974, case	12.50
Football Hall of Fame, 1972	8.00
Kentucky Derby, 95th, 1969, pink roses	7.50
Louisville Downs, 1978	8.50
Red Mile Race, 1975	8.00
U.S. Open, 1972	15.00

State Series
Alaska, Star, 1958–64–65	60.00
Florida, Shell, 1968, pearl	4.50
Michigan, 1972	8.50
New Jersey, 1963, blue	65.00
Ohio, 1966	12.00
South Dakota, Mt. Rushmore, 1969	6.00

Trophy Series, First Issue, 1957
Bird
Cardinal, male, 1968	40.00
Goose, Blue, 1979	10.00

Fish
Bass, smallmouth, 1973	10.00
Muskie, 1971	16.00
Sturgeon, 1980	24.00
Horse Series, rearing, 1967–68	15.00
Owl	20.00
Pheasant	20.00
Sailfish	75.00
Tiffany Poodle in Bag	15.00

EZRA BROOKS

Animal Series
Bear, 1968	6.00
Bull Elephant	20.00
Clown	20.00
Elk, 1972	20.00
Leopard, Snow, 1980	40.00
Tiger with football	15.00

Automotive/Transportation Series
Corvette, 1962, Mako Shark, 1979	25.00
Motorcycle, 1971	12.00
Pontiac Indy Pace Car, 1980	30.00
Stagecoach, Overland Express, 1969	10.00
Train, Casey Jones #1, 1980	45.00

Bird Series
Duck, Canadian Loon, 1979 . . . . . .   **32.50**
Owl, Old Ez #1, 1977 . . . .   **60.00**
Turkey, white, 1971 . . . .   **20.00**
Heritage China Series
Cannon, Antique, 1969 . . . .   **8.00**
C B Convoy, 1976 . . . .   **8.00**
EZ Jug #2, 1980, 1.75 liters **25.00**
Telephone, 1971 . . . .   **12.00**
Truckin an Vannin, 1976 . . . .   **14.00**
Institutional Series
American Legion
1973, Hawaii **15.00**
1982, Chicago **75.00**
Drum & Bugle, Conquistadors, 1971   **9.00**
F.O.E., 1980 . . . .   **30.00**
Foremost, Astronaut, 1970, gallon . .   **55.00**
Indian, Ceremonial, 1970 . . . .   **20.00**
Kachina
#1, Morning Singer, 1971 . . . . . .   **165.00**
#3, Antelope, 1974 . . . .   **50.00**
#7, Mud Head, 1978 . . . .   **40.00**
Political, 1972, Donkey or Elephant   **12.00**
Shrine, Fez, 1976 . . . .   **9.00**
Walgreen Drugs, 1973 . . . .   **25.00**
People Series
Court Jester, 1971 . . . .   **9.00**
Dakota Cowboy, 1975 . . . .   **40.00**
Dakota Cowgirl, 1976 . . . .   **30.00**
Groucho Marx, 1977 . . . .   **40.00**
Mr. Merchant, 1970 . . . .   **10.00**
West Virginia Mountain Man, 1970   **90.00**
Sport Series
Auburn War Eagle, 1982 . . . .   **35.00**
Casey at Bat, 1973 . . . .   **15.00**
Gator #1, passing, 1972 . . . .   **15.00**
Greater Greensboro Open, 1977 . . .   **35.00**
Jayhawk–ansas, 1969 . . . .   **10.00**
Ski Boot, 1972 . . . .   **10.00**
Vermont Skier, 1972 . . . .   **14.00**

CABIN STILL

Anniversary, 1960 . . . .   **10.00**
Deer Browsing, 1967 . . . .   **7.00**
Hillbilly, fishing, quart **90.00**
Mallard, 1966 . . . .   **10.00**

CYRUS NOBLE

Animal Series
Bear & Cub, 1978, miniature **15.00**
Buffalo Cow & Calf, 1977, Second
Edition **80.00**
Moose & Calf, First Edition **100.00**
Mountain Lion & Cubs, 1979, minia-
ture **15.00**
Mine Series
Assayer, 1972 . . . .   **175.00**
Landlady, 1977 . . . .   **30.00**
Mine, 1979, miniature **20.00**
Whiskey Drummer, 1975 . . . .   **40.00**

Miscellaneous
Dancers, South of the Border, 1978   **35.00**
Delta Saloon Suicide Table, 1971,
miniatures, 4 units **300.00**
Sea Animal
Harp Seal, 1979 . . . .   **50.00**
Penguin Family, 1980, miniature . . .   **18.00**

J. W. DANT

American Legion, 1969 . . . .   **6.00**
Boeing 747 . . . .   **10.00**
Ft. Sill, 1969 . . . .   **10.00**
Stove, Pot Belly, 1966 . . . .   **8.00**

DOUBLE SPRINGS

Bicentennial Series, Washington Monu-
ment
California **45.00**
Iowa **50.00**
Washington, DC **12.00**
Car Series
Cale Yarborough, 1974 . . . .   **25.00**
Ford, Model T, 1970 . . . .   **40.00**
Miscellaneous
Milwaukee Buck, 1971 . . . .   **12.00**
Water Tower **15.00**

FAMOUS FIRSTS

Airplane Series
Lockheed C–130 Hercules, 1979 . . .   **50.00**
Spirit of St. Louis, 1969, large **100.00**
Winnie Mae, 1972, miniature, 1972   **30.00**
Animal Series
Butterfly, miniatures, series of 4, each   **15.00**
Panda, baby, 1980 . . . .   **50.00**
Tiger, Circus, 1980 . . . .   **25.00**
Car–Transportation Series
Bugatti Royale, 1974 . . . .   **200.00**
Cable Car, miniature, 1973 . . . .   **20.00**
Corvette 1963 Stingray, 1977, white   **45.00**
Duesenberg, 1980 . . . .   **225.00**
Marmon Wasp #32, type 1, 1968 . .   **70.00**
Porsche Targa, 1979 . . . .   **50.00**
Miscellaneous
Coffee Mill, 1971, orange or blue . .   **50.00**
Hurdy Gurdy, miniature, 1979 . . . . .   **14.00**
Roulette Wheel, miniature, 1980 . . .   **20.00**
Swiss Chalet, 1974 . . . .   **35.00**

GRENADIER

American Revolution Series
Baylor's 3rd Continental, 1969 . . . .   **30.00**
Third New York, 1970 . . . .   **20.00**
Bicentennial Series, 1976, 10ths, 13
types, each **20.00**
British Army Series
Fusileer Guards, Scots, Officer, 1971   **20.00**

Guard Regiment, 3rd, Officer, 1971   **20.00**
Civil War Series
   Captain, Union, 1970 . . . .   **20.00**
   General Robert E. Lee, 1976,½ gal   **120.00**
Miscellaneous
   Fire Chief, 1973 . . . .   **85.00**
   Moose Lodge, 1970 . . . .   **14.00**
   San Fernando Electric Mfg Co, 1976   **60.00**
Napoleonic Series
   Eugene, 1970 . . . .   **20.00**
   Murat, 1970 . . . .   **20.00**

HOFFMAN

Band Series, Street Swingers #1, 1978,
   miniature music, six types, each . . .   **15.00**
Bird Series
   Dove, Closed Wing, 1979,½ pint . . .   **25.00**
   Eagle, 1977, music **45.00**
   Love Birds, 1979,½ pint **20.00**
Cheerleader
   Dallas, 1979, nude,½ pint **150.00**
   Rams, 1980, miniature **20.00**
Children of the World Series, 1979,
   miniature, music, six types, each . . .   **30.00**
Horse Series, 1979, miniature, six types,
   each **12.00**
Mr. Lucky Series, music
   Dentist, 1980 . . . .   **35.00**
   Mr. Lucky, 1973 . . . .   **40.00**
   Policeman, 1975 . . . .   **25.00**
Rodeo Belt Buckle Series, 1979, six
   types, each **25.00**
Rodeo Series, 1978, six types, each . . .   **35.00**
School Series
   Kentucky Wildcats, basketball **30.00**
   Nevada Wolfpack **40.00**
   Tennessee Volunteers **27.50**
Wildlife Series
   Falcon & Rabbit, 1978, miniature . .   **10.00**
   Panda, 1976 . . . .   **50.00**
Wildlife bottles were designed by Lucas
   Miguer(LM), Bill Ohrman (BO), and
   Jack Richardson (JR)
   Bear, 1978, BO **40.00**
   Fighting Rams, set, 1977, JR **250.00**
   Stranger, This Is My Land, 1979, LM   **425.00**

LIONSTONE

Bicentennial Series
   Betsy Ross, 1975 . . . .   **25.00**
   Valley Forge, 1975 . . . .   **22.50**
Bird Series
   Blue Bird, Eastern, 1972 . . . .   **20.00**
   Capistrano Swallow, 1972, gold bell   **25.00**
   Meadowlark, 1969 . . . .   **22.50**
   Woodpecker, 1975 . . . .   **35.00**
Car–Transportation Series, Turbo Car
   STP, 1972, red **25.00**
Clown Series
   #2, Sad Sam, 1978 . . . .   **40.00**

   #6, Lampy, 1979 . . . .   **35.00**
European Workers Series, 1974, six
   types, each **25.00**
Firefighter Series
   Fireman #1, 1972, yellow hat **125.00**
   Fireman #4, 1978, emblem **30.00**
Old West Series
   Bar Scene, nude, 1970 . . . .   **600.00**
   Cowboy, 1969 . . . .   **10.00**
   Highway Robber, 1969 . . . .   **12.50**
   Indian Squawman, 1969 . . . .   **25.00**
   Lucky Buck, 1975, miniature **12.00**
   Molly Brown, 1973 . . . .   **25.00**
   Sheepherder, 1969 . . . .   **50.00**
   Telegrapher, 1969 . . . .   **18.50**
Oriental Workers Series, 1974, six
   types, each **32.50**

LUXARDO

Apple, figural **15.00**
Cellini **32.50**
Coffee Carafe **20.00**
Duck, green **30.00**
Gondola **7.50**
Owl, onyx **35.00**
Pheasant, black **125.00**
Puppy, base **25.00**
Squirrel **30.00**
Zodiac **22.50**

MC CORMICK

Bicentennial Series
   Betsy Ross **25.00**
   John Hancock, miniature **20.00**
   Paul Revere **45.00**
Bird Series
   Eagle, 1983, white **140.00**
   Wood Duck, 1980 . . . .   **30.00**
Bull Series, Hereford, 1972 . . . .   **45.00**
Elvis Series, #3, 1980, black **50.00**
   Aloha, 1981 . . . .   **80.00**
   Bust, 1978 . . . .   **25.00**
   Gold, 1979 . . . .   **225.00**
   Silver, 1980 . . . .   **110.00**
Entertainment Series
   Jimmy Durante, 1981 . . . .   **50.00**
   Tom T. Hall, 1980 . . . .   **25.00**
Great American Series
   Stephen Austin, 1977 . . . .   **20.00**
   William Clark, 1978 . . . .   **22.50**
   Henry Ford, 1977, miniature **12.00**
   Charles Lindbergh, 1977 . . . .   **30.00**
   Mark Twain, 1978, miniature **15.00**
Miscellaneous
   Airplane—Spirit of St. Louis, 1969 . .   **125.00**
   Clock, Queen Anne, 1970 . . . .   **25.00**
   Globe, Angelica, 1971 . . . .   **25.00**
   Mikado, 1980 . . . .   **200.00**
   Paul Bunyan, 1979 . . . .   **25.00**

Thelma Lu	35.00
Yacht America, 1970	35.00

Pirate Series, 1972, miniature, twelve types

#1 to #9, each	8.00
#10 to #12, each	17.50
Train Series, Engine, Jupiter, 1969	25.00

MICHTER'S

Barn, Daniel Boone Homestead, 1977	45.00
Conestoga Wagon, 1976	200.00
Halloween Witch, 1979	50.00
Jug, 1957, adv, pint	20.00
Pennsylvania Dutch Hex, 1977	15.00
Volunteer Fireman, 1979	85.00

MISCELLANEOUS

Aesthetic Specialties, Inc

Bing Crosby National Pro–Am, 39th, 1979	30.00
Cadillac, 1903, gold, white trim, 1980	1,500.00
Model T, Telephone Truck, 1980 ...	45.00
World's Greatest Golfer, 1979	40.00

Anniversary

Atlanta, GA, 1972	15.00
Happy Birthday, 1974, blue	20.00
Ohio Presidents, 1972	18.00

Beneagle

Burns Cottage, miniature, green	6.00
Eagle, 1969, golden	35.00
Pheasant, miniature	5.00

Bischoff

Cat, black	12.00
Fish, ashtray	10.00
Pirate	15.00

Collector's Art

Charolais Bull, 1974	30.00
Goldfinch, miniature	15.00
Irish Setter, miniature	15.00
Meadowlark, miniature	25.00
Rabbit, miniature	25.00
Texas Longhorn, 1974	32.50

George Dickel

Jug	8.00
Powder Horn, gal	150.00

Dugs Nevada Brothels, miniature

#2, Shamrock Ranch	40.00
#6, Fran's Ranch	20.00
#10, Barbara's My Place	20.00
Eagle Rare, Eagle #4, 1982	50.00

Garnier (France)

Alladin's Lamp	18.00
Coffeepot	15.00
Ford, 1913	30.00
Maharajah	32.50
Violin	10.00

Gemini, miniature

David, 1980	10.00
Okinawain, pr	18.00

I. W. Harper

Croquet Players	20.00
Guitar	10.00
Harper Man, 1955, white	45.00

Inca Pisco, miniature

#1, black	5.00
#7, black	10.00
#10, gold	15.00

Jon–Sol, Inc, miniature

Blue Jay	10.00
Warner Bros, set #2	25.00
Lord Calvert, Eider Duck	15.00

OBR

Hockey Players Series, 1971, each ..	15.00

Transportation Series

Balloon, 1969	15.00
Titanic, 1970	40.00

Old Bardstown

Bulldog, 1980, 1.75 liter	200.00
Foster Brooks, 1978	35.00
Kentucky Colonel, #1, 1978	25.00
Wildcat #1, 1978	70.00

Old Crow

Bugatti Royale, 1974	250.00
Chess Series, pawn, each	20.00

OLD COMMONWEALTH

Apothecary Series

Alabama University, 1980	27.50
Thomas Jefferson/University of Virginia, 1979	20.00
Coal Miner, #1, 1975	90.00

Fireman, Modern, Series

#2, Nozzleman, 1983, miniature ...	25.00
#4, Fallen Comrade, 1983	65.00
#5, Harmony, 1984	65.00

Miscellaneous

Golden Retriever, 1979	25.00
Indian Chief Illini, University of Illinois, 1979	60.00
Lumberjack, Oldtime, 1979	20.00

OLD FITZGERALD

America's Cup, 1970	25.00
Blarney (Irish Toast), 1970	14.00
Classic, 1972	6.00
Executive, 1960	7.00
Geese, 1970	6.00
Irish Patriots, 1971	17.50
Ohio State, 1970	20.00
Ram Bighorn, 1971	5.00
Rip Van Winkle, 1971, blue	35.00
Triangle Bond, 1977	4.00

OLD MR. BOSTON

Assayrian Convention, 1975	15.00
Black Hills Motor Classic, 1976	25.00

Dan Patch, 1970	10.00
Fire Engine, 1974	35.00
Lincoln on Horseback, 1972	10.00
Nebraska #1, gold, 1970	15.00
Ships Lantern, 1974	15.00
Town Crier, 1976	16.00

PACESETTER

Camaro Z28, 1982, gold, edition limited to 500	125.00
Corvette	
1975, red	40.00
1980, silver	75.00
Olsonite Eagle #8, 1974	32.00
Vokovich #2, 1974, Sugarripe	50.00

SKI COUNTRY

Christmas Series	
Ebenezer Scrooge, 1979	40.00
Mrs. Cratchit, 1978	42.00
Circus Series	
Circus Wagon, 1977, giraffe	30.00
Elephant on Drum, 1973, miniature	35.00
Jenny Lind, yellow	75.00
Customer Specialties	
Burro–Colorado School of Mines, 1973	50.00
Oregon Cave Man, 1974	17.00
Skier, 1975, gold plated	100.00
Domestic Animal Series	
Bassett, 1978, miniature	20.00
Labrador Dog, 1977, mallard	100.00
Indian Series	
Arizona Eagle Dancer, 1979	200.00
Dancers of Southwest Series, miniature	25.00
Warrior #1, 1975, hatchet	110.00
Waterfowl Series	
Duck	
King Eider, 1977	45.00
Pintail, 1979, ½ gal	175.00
Widgeon, 1979	32.50
Pelican, 1976, brown	40.00
Swan, Australian, 1974, black	30.00
Wildlife Series	
Bear, 1974, brown	25.00
Eagle, Majestic, 1972	300.00
Elk, 1979	80.00
Fox Family, 1979	50.00
Hawk, Red Shoulder, 1972	65.00
Kangaroo, 1974	25.00
Owl	
Baby Snow, miniature	40.00
Northern Snowy, 1972	100.00
Peace Dove, 1973	100.00
Skunk Family, 1978	40.00

WILD TURKEY

Series #1	
#1, Male, 1972	300.00
#4, With Poult, 1974	80.00

Lore Series	
#2	20.00
#3	20.00
#7, Taking Off	20.00
#8, Strutting	20.00

WORLD'S FAIRS AND EXPOSITIONS

Collecting Hints: Familiarize yourself with the main buildings and features of the early World's Fairs and Expositions. Many of the choicest china and textiles pictured an identified building, assuming the buyer was aware of the significance. Many exposition buildings remained standing long after the fair was over, and souvenirs proliferated. Prices almost always are higher in the city or area where an exposition was held.

There have been hundreds of local fairs, state fairs, etc., in the last one hundred years. These events generally produced items of little value except to local collectors.

History: The Great Exhibition of 1851 in London marked the beginning of the World's Fair and Exposition movement. The fairs generally feature exhibitions from nations around the world displaying the best of their industrial and scientific achievements.

Many important technological advances have been introduced at world's fairs. Examples include the airplane, telephone, and electric light. The ice cream cone, hot dog, and iced tea were products of vendors at fairs. Art movements often were closely connected to fairs, with the Paris Exhibition of 1900 generally considered to have assembled the best of the works of the Art Nouveau artists.

References: *American Art, New York World's Fair, 1939,* Apollo Books, 1987; Carl Abbott, *The Great Extravaganza: Portland and the Lewis and Clark Exposition,* Oregon Historical Society, 1981; S. Applebaum, *The New York World's Fair 1939–40,* Dover Pub., 1977; Patricia F. Carpenter and Paul Totah, *The San Francisco Fair, Treasure Island, 1939–40,* Scottwall Associates, 1989; Richard Friz, *World's Fair Memorabilia,* Collector Books, 1989; Robert L. Hendershott, *1904 St. Louis World's Fair Mementos and Memorabilia,* Kurt R. Krueger Publishing, 1994; Kurt Krueger, *Meet Me In St. Louis—The Exonumia of the 1904 World's Fair,* Krause Publications, 1979; Howard Rossen and John Kaduck, *Columbia World's Fair Collectibles,* Wallace–Homestead, 1976, revised price list 1982; Norman E. Martinus and Harry L. Rinker, *Warman's Paper,* Wallace–Homestead, 1994; Frederick and Mary Megson, *American Exposition Postcards, 1870–1920: A Catalog And*

Price Guide, The Postcard Lovers, 1992; Larry Zim, Mel Lerner, and Herbert Rolfes, *The World Of Tomorrow: The 1939 New York World's Fair,* Main Street Press Book, Harper & Row, 1988.

Collectors' Clubs: 1904 World's Fair Society, 529 Barcia Dr., St Louis, MO 63119; World's Fair Collectors' Society, Inc., PO Box 20806, Sarasota, FL 34276.

Periodical: *World's Fair,* PO Box 339, Corte Madera, CA 94976.

Museums: Atwater Kent Museum, History Museum of Philadelphia, Philadelphia, PA; Buffalo & Erie County Historical Society, Buffalo, NY; California State University, Madden Library, Fresno, CA; 1893 Chicago World's Columbian Exposition Museum, Columbus, WI; Museum of Science & Industry, Chicago, IL; Presido Art Museum, San Francisco, CA; The Queens Museum, Flushing, NY.

1876, PHILADELPHIA, Centennial Exposition
Booklet, *Centennial Book,* 2½ x 3", 16 pgs, issued by Orange Judd Company **15.00**
Inkwell, glass, Memorial Hall **100.00**
Ticket, admission **20.00**
Trade Card, Rockhill & Wilson Tailors, exhibition building **20.00**
1893, CHICAGO, The Columbian Exposition
Advertising Trade Card, Traveler's Insurance Co, color **22.00**
Bell, etched glass, frosted handle ... **65.00**
Change Tray **30.00**
Fan, hand, large **50.00**
Glass, 3½" h, clear, frosted white inscription "World's Fair Agricultural Building" and building illus **10.00**
Matchsafe, Columbus head **125.00**
Medal, brass, two piece, "Wisconsin–Columbian Exposition 1893" **20.00**
Medallion, 1½" d, brass, emb **16.00**
Paperweight, Liberty Bell, fused glass, "Made at World's Fair by Libbey Glass Co" **82.00**
Print, set of 12, 15¾ x 11½", architecture, color, "Book of Builders," 1894 .... **100.00**
Puzzle, egg shape, silvered brass, Christopher Columbus portrait on one end, inscribed 1492–1892 ... **50.00**
Sugar Spoon **25.00**
Ticket, admission, Manhattan Day, NY, Oct 21, 1893 .... **38.00**
Token, ferris wheel **25.00**
1898, OMAHA, Trans–Mississippi Exposition
Handkerchief, embroidered **6.50**
Souvenir Cup, ruby flashed **58.00**

1901, BUFFALO, Pan American Exposition
Letter Opener, buffalo **30.00**
Stickpin, frying pan shape, emb buffalo head **36.00**
Whiskey Glass, etched, "Pan American Exposition 1901," orig round box .. **60.00**
1904, ST LOUIS, Louisiana Purchase Exposition
Card, 3 x 5", litho, tin, full color aerial panorama illus, company text and logo on reverse, issued by American Can Company **45.00**
Corset, orig box **30.00**
Matchsafe, plated, relief scenes **55.00**
Shaker, ruby flashed, two in one, inside glass bladder holds pepper, salt on outside **99.00**
Spooner, custard, enamel flowers ... **65.00**
Tray, 3¼ x 5", litho, tin, issued by American Can Company **50.00**
1915, SAN FRANCISCO, Panama–Pacific International Exposition
Book, hand colored **15.00**
Pin, 2¼" l, 1915 Pan–Pac Closing Day, brass hanger bar with attached silk ribbon **35.00**
Watch Fob, leather, black, holds diecut brass poinsettia **75.00**
1926, PHILADELPHIA, Sesquicentennial Exposition
Pin, blue Liberty Bell, "Crane's Ice Cream Served Everywhere—Keep Cool During The Fair" adv **12.50**
Pinback Button, 1¼" d, multiple designs **25.00**
Ring, metal, silvered, diecut Liberty Bell underneath seated eagle, patriotic motifs, inscribed "1776 Sesquicentennial 1926" **35.00**
1933, CHICAGO, Century of Progress
Booklet, 5¼ x 8", *Ford At The Fair,* 24 pgs, issued by Ford Motor Co **25.00**
Card Set, building and exhibit ext. views, self–mailer design packet folder with snap fastener, set of 20 cards, unused **18.00**
Change Tray, 4½" d, round, bronzed, twelve relief buildings and fountain, box **22.00**
Cigarette Case, 2½ x 3½ x 2", wood, black, hinged brass lid with symbol in center, unfinished int. **28.50**
Compact, chrome, emb **12.00**
Cookbook, *The Wonder Book of Good Meals* **20.00**
Film Package, Cine Vue **22.50**
Glass, 5½" h, clear, black and red inscriptions, silvered illus of Fort Dearborn building **22.00**
Guide Book, *1933 Century of Progress,* Art Deco cov **24.00**

Hotpad, set of 3, emb silver foil covering, orig clear cellophane wrap attached with purple ribbon, orig box 32.00

Key, 8½" l, metal, "Key to Chicago World's Fair 1933" 20.00

Map, Milwaukee Road Railway, price for set of 5 .... 55.00

Needle Book, Durkee 5.00

Paperweight, metal, painted gold, Fort Dearborn exhibit shape, inscribed "1833 Fort Dearborn Chicago 1933," orig box 30.00

1933 Century of Progress, Chicago, paperweight, glass globe, flattened base, Tailors' Building in center, "John A. Griffith & Co., Incorporated, 1893–1921, Tailors' Trimmings" adv, 3" d, $40.00.

Pillow Cover, 20½" w, leather, tan, stitched fringe border, hand colored scenes, W A L Co, 1934 copyright 75.00

Plate, 7½" d, china, white, blue illus of Carillon Tower and buildings, "Chicago 1934" title, stamped "Pickard" 25.00

Playing Cards, "54 Different Views" 14.00

Poster, 13 x 19½", globe image, color, "World's Brightest Spot" 27.00

Salt, master 20.00

Teaspoon, gold 10.00

View Cards, set of 16, full color, linen–textured paper, orig mailing envelope, unused 15.00

Watch Fob, 1893–1933 .... 25.00

1939, NEW YORK, New York World's Fair

Ashtray

Bronze, 6½" d Trylon, 2" d Perisphere 150.00

Glass 25.00

Metal, white, diving figure, raised Trylon and Perisphere, inscription 50.00

Bag, suitcase shape, contains pictures to color 175.00

Bank, 5" h, wood, horseshoe shape, orange and blue tinted Trylon and

Perisphere, brown inscription and horseshoe markings, pull–out drawer 50.00

Banner, 26½ x 8½", "World of Tomorrow 1939," felt 15.00

Bookends, pr, figural, Trylon and Perisphere, marble, licensed for Italian exhibit 125.00

Booklet, 7 x 8¼", Futurama, 20 pgs, General Motors Building 25.00

Bottle, 9" h, milk glass 30.00

Cane, baseball type 69.00

Charm Bracelet, brass, seven scenic charms 15.00

Chocolate Tin, 4½ x 6½ x 3", colorful, building illus 75.00

Compact, plastic, red, marbleized, tricolor brass fair image inset, "1939 World's Fair New York" ... 45.00

Cup, 3" h, china, yellow, Trylon and Perisphere imprinted around side 24.50

Flipbook, hula girl 15.00

Glass, 4½" h, clear, colorful design, inscribed "Twentieth Century Transportation" and "Exhibits Of Railroads And Railroad Equipment Display—The Transportation Bldg" 38.00

Guide Book 25.00

Jack Knife, large 35.00

Letter Opener 15.00

Matches, sealed display package, color illus of exhibits, orig mailing envelope, official seals 55.00

Nappy, 6" d, multicolored, handled 20.00

Nut Set, Mr Peanut, four small and one large bowls 45.00

Pencil, 10½" l, mechanical, eagle, MIB 41.00

Puzzle, Trylon and Perisphere, orange trylon, five blue pcs form perisphere, includes instruction sheet, orig box 48.00

Salt and Pepper Shakers, pr, plastic, Trylon and Perisphere, cream, black base 20.00

Scarf, 19 x 20½", printed design, dark blue, light blue, lime green, red, and white 30.00

Snowdome, Trylon and Perisphere .. 95.00

Souvenir Book, Official Souvenir Book, 10 x 14", spiral bound, orange and blue cov with Trylon and Perisphere illus 50.00

Spoon

Agriculture 20.00

Trylon and Perisphere on handle, "New York World's Fair" and stars in bowl, 6" l 23.00

Tapestry, 21½ x 40½", woven, Trylon, Perisphere, and Lagoon, sky background, rust colored fringe 110.00

Tray, 12" l, metal, silvered, engraved illus, "World's Fair New York

1939" inscription, Made in
England on bottom **52.50**
1962, SEATTLE, Century 21 Exposition
Cigarette Lighter, space **12.00**
Creamer and Sugar, miniature **20.00**
Shoehorn, 5½" l, metal, gilt, crown
design on handle **18.00**
Tray, 11" d, litho, tin, full color illus of
Space Needle **18.00**
1964, NEW YORK, New York World's
Fair
Book, pop–up **17.00**
Booklet, Progressland, Disney exhibit   **18.00**
Bookmark, 5¾" l, woven, silvery
white, Unisphere illus, Alkahn Silk
Label Co, orig clear cellophane
packet **22.00**
Butter Dish **20.00**
Camera, Kodak World's Fair Flash
Camera, plastic and metal, black
and gray, foil sticker with Unisphere
on front lens, black fabric strap . . .   **25.00**
Game, World's Fair Game, Milton
Bradley, vinyl plastic playing sheet,
orig box **25.00**
Glass, 4¼" h, clear, orange and white
Unisphere illus **12.00**
Hard Hat, white plastic, crown front
with full color sticker, Arlington
Hat maker **30.00**
License Plate, colorful **35.00**
Magazine, *Newsweek,* Jan 13, 1964,
5 pg article with six black and
white photos **12.00**
Mug, marked "New York World's
Fair" **17.50**
Pennant, 27" l, felt, dark blue,
day–glo orange and white design
and lettering **18.00**
Pin, diecut, Unisphere shape, red and
blue enamel accents, brass finish,

**1948–1949 Chicago Railroad Fair, Guide
Book, 16 pages, 1949 edition, $9.50.**

**New York World's Fair, 1964–65, plate,
Unisphere center, blue on white, 10¼" d,
$37.50.**

orig retail card **12.50**
Poster, Progressland, Disney exhibit .   **40.00**
Salt and Pepper Shakers, pr, glazed
ceramic, Unisphere illus, plastic
stopper on bottom **25.00**
Souvenir Book, *Official Souvenir
Book,* 7 x 10", 24 pgs **20.00**
Stein, 6" h, raised scene of Unisphere,
tan and black striping around top
and bottom **25.00**
Tile, 6" sq, ceramic, full color Uni-
sphere, Statue of Liberty, and skyline illus, gold accented border,
copyright sticker and hanging loop
on back **18.00**
Tray, round, Unisphere **25.00**
1967, MONTREAL, Montreal Expo
Cup, 3" h, china, white, full color aerial illus, Montreal background, bottom marked "Royal Darwood/Expo
67/Bone China/England" **18.00**
Lapel Pin, brass, repeated motif
around edge, threaded post fas-
tener on back **10.00**
Stickpin, brass, diecut, maple leaf
shape, dark red enamel accents . .   **8.00**
Tab, 1½" d, litho tin, blue and white,
US Pavilion, "Compliments of Avis
Car Rental" on reverse **5.00**
1982, KNOXVILLE, World's Fair
Badge, 2½" d, set of 4, official energy
symbol, three with animal symbols,
fourth with closing day inscription   **50.00**
Cap, sailor type, black and red in-
scription on brim **5.00**
Glass, 5½" h, clear, tapered, illus and
"Energy Turns The World" theme,
McDonald's and Coca–Cola Co
trademarks **8.00**
Pennant, 25" l, felt, red scene and en-
ergy symbol, white background . .   **6.00**
Plate, oval, clipper ships, Galerie
Barbizon limited edition **15.00**

1984, LOUISIANA, Exposition, snowdome, 3¼" h, hard plastic, pelican in
blue outfit, exhibit buildings background, white oval base, made in
Hong Kong **55.00**

WORLD WAR I COLLECTIBLES

Collecting Hints: Be careful. Uniforms and
equipment from World War I were stockpiled at
the end of the war and reissued in the early years
of World War II. Know the source of the items
that you have received or buy. Scrutinize all unknown materials. Some research and investiga-
tion might be necessary to correctly identify an
item as an actual war artifact.

Collector clubs and re–enactment groups are
one of the best sources for information and identification due to their quest for authenticity.
These groups also are very knowledgeable about
reproductions, copycats, and fantasy items.

History: Power struggles between European
countries raged for hundreds of years. As the
twentieth century dawned, leading European
countries became entangled in a series of complex alliances, many sealed by royal marriages,
and a massive arms race. All that was needed to
set off the powder keg was a fire. The assassination of Austrian Archduke Franz Ferdinand by a
Serbian national, on June 28, 1914, ignited the
fuse. Germany invaded Belgium and moved into
France. Russia, England, and Turkey joined the
war. Italy and the United States were involved by
mid–1917.

In 1918 Germany sued for peace. A settlement
was achieved at the Versailles Conference,
January–June 1919. The United States remained
in the background. President Wilson's concept of
a League of Nations failed to gain acceptance in
his own country, opening the door to the events
leading up to World War II.

References: W. K. Cross, *The Charlton Price
Guide to First World War Canadian Infantry
Badges*, The Charlton Press, 1995; Robert Fisch,
Field Equipment of the Infantry 1914–1945,
Greenberg Publishing, 1989; Norman E.
Martinus and Harry L. Rinker, *Warman's Paper*,
Wallace–Homestead, 1994; Jack H. Smith,
Military Postcards 1870–1945, Wallace–
Homestead Book Company, 1988; Sydney B.
Vernon, *Vernon's Collector's Guide to Orders,
Medals, and Decorations*, published by author,
1986; Windrow & Greene's *Militaria Directory
and Sourcebook 1994*, Motorbooks Inter-
national, 1994.

Periodicals: *Men At Arms*, 222 W. Exchange St.,
Providence, RI 02903; *Military Collector*

Magazine, PO Box 245, Lyon Station, PA, 19536;
Military Collectors' News, PO Box 702073,
Tulsa, OK 74170; *Military History*, 6405 Flank
Dr., Harrisburg, PA 17112; *Military Trader*, PO
Box 1050, Dubuque, IA 52004; *Wildcat
Collectors Journal*, 15158 NE 6 Ave., Miami FL
33162.

Collectors' Clubs: American Society of Military
Insignia Collectors, 526 Lafayette Ave., Palmer-
ton, PA 18701; Assoc. of American Military
Uniform Collectors, PO Box 1876, Elyria, OH
44036; Company of Military Historians, North
Main St., Westbrook, CT 06498; Orders and
Medals Society of America, PO Box 484,
Glassboro, NJ 08028.

Museums: Liberty Memorial Museum, Kansas
City, MO; National Infantry Museum, Fort
Benning, GA; Seven Acres Antique Village &
Museum, Union, IL; The Parris Island Museum,
Parris Island, SC; US Air Force Museum,
Wright–Patterson AFB, OH; US Army Transporta-
tion Museum, Fort Eustis, VA; US Navy Museum,
Washington, DC.

Book
  Hoyt, Edwin P, *The Army Without A
    Country*, Macmillan, 1967, first
    edition, 243 pages, dust jacket . . .   **15.00**
  Pershing, John J, *My Experiences In
    The World War*, two volumes,
    Frederick Stokes, 1931, illus, maps,
    price for set **25.00**
Canteen, aluminum, brown felt cover,
  German, expanding rubber stopper,
  worn leather straps **30.00**
Cartridge Belt, canteen, two medical
  packs **35.00**
Cartridge Pouch, leather, triple pocket,
  "D" rings **30.00**
Catalog, The Warnock Uniform Co,
  New York, NY, illus of uniforms and
  equipment for US Army and National
  Guard, 1910, 64 pages, 5½ x 7¾" . .   **45.00**
Clothing, uniform, Doughboy **85.00**
Cup, German, porcelainized steel,
  gray–green, fixed handle, slightly
  dented, marked "B & F16" **20.00**
Field Shoes, US, brown leather, marked
  "Kennedy, St Louis Depot 9A" on
  soles, heels marked "U. S. Army 9A"   **90.00**
Gas Mask, bag, Doughboy
  "307 M. G. Battalion" **33.00**
  "S.R.O.U.S.A.–AEF Cavalry" **33.00**
Helmet, German
  Spiked, gray plate, two lions, crown,
    left rosette missing **110.00**
  Steel, orig liner, no chin strap **55.00**
Knapsack
  Austrian, hair, complete, blanket
    straps, marked "Ott Romer & Co,
    Wein, 1916" **180.00**

United States, canvas, model 1910, khaki colored, marked "P.B & Co. 4–18" 20.00
Lapel Stud, enamel, US Naval Reserve   13.00
Magazine
Army Pictorial Section of the Homeback, published for soldier patients at Walter Reed Hospital, 1912, 9 x 12", black and white . .   10.00
To The Homeward Bound Americans, B Von Vorst, published in France, 32 pages, black and white 6.00

Magazine, *The Delineator,* July, 1918, Doughboy cover, $24.00.

Map, Official War Map Western Battle Front, bank advertisement on back   10.00
Medal, Victory
Italian 45.00
United States, with ribbon 45.00
Mess Kit, US, Model 1910, aluminum, steel knife, fork, and spoon, marked "U.S.J.W.B.A. 1918" 20.00
Pennant, 27th Division 24.00
Photograph, 37 x 22", mounted on wood, enlarged news type photo, German biplane, Lt Gerhart Bessenge, Lt Kempf, and Lt Dr Herman Vallenor in foreground 225.00
Pin, World War Veteran 10.00
Poncho, US, dual layer canvas, steel buttons, marked "Hodgman Rubber Co, Contract 47, Philadelphia, PA," slightly worn, small holes, 69 x 53"   65.00
Print, Lt Werner Ross' Plane, Mylogar, multicolor 125.00
Sea Bag, Navy, American issue, unit marked 15.00
Sheet Music, patriotic pictorial cov
Break The News To Mother 7.50
For Your Boy & My Boy 5.00
In The Navy 5.00

The Girls We Leave Behind 5.00
The Red, White & Blue Is Calling You   5.00
Stickpin, Over There, cloisonne, flag . .   15.00
Tunic, Canadian, moth damage 57.00
Watch Fob, Hickok, holds manicure kit   20.00

WORLD WAR II COLLECTIBLES

Collecting Hints: To the victors go the spoils—or so WWII collectors would like to think. Now that the Soviet Bloc has disintegrated, a large number of dealers are making efforts to import Soviet Bloc WWII collectibles into the United States. Be careful when buying anything that has a new or unused appearance. Many Soviet countries continued to use stockpiled WWII equipment and still manufacture new goods based on WWII designs.

The Korean Conflict occurred shortly after WWII. The United States and other armed forces in the conflict used equipment and uniforms similar to those manufactured during WWII. Familiarize yourself with model styles, dates of manufacture, and your buying sources.

If you locate a WWII item, make certain to record all personal history associated with the item. This is extremely important. Collectors demands this documentation. If possible, secure additional information on the history of the unit and the battles in which it was engaged. Also make certain to obtain any extras such as insignia or a second set of buttons.

History: With the rise of the German Third Reich, European nations once again engaged in a massive arms race. The 1930s Depression compounded the situation.

After numerous compromises to German expansionism, war was declared in 1939 following German's Blitzkrieg invasion of Poland. Allied and Axis alliances were formed.

America was heavily supportive of the Allied cause. The December 7, 1941, Japanese attack on the US Naval Station at Pearl Harbor, Hawaii, forced America into the war. It immediately adopted a two–front strategy.

During 1942 to 1945 the entire world was directly or indirectly involved in the war. Virtually all industrial activity was war related. The technological advances guaranteed that life after the war would be far different than before the war.

Germany surrendered on May 7, 1945. Japan surrendered on August 14, 1945, after the atomic bombing of Hiroshima on August 6, 1945, and Nagasaki on August 9, 1945.

References: Thomas Berndt, *Standard Catalog of U. S. Military Vehicles: 1940–1965,* Krause Publications, 1993; Stan Cohen, *V For Victory:*

America's Home Front During World War II, Pictorial Histories Publishing, 1991; Robert Fisch, *Field Equipment of the Infantry 1914–1945,* Greenberg Publishing; Robin Lumsden, *A Collector's Guide To Third Reich Militaria,* Hippocrene Books, 1987; Robin Lumsden, *A Collector's Guide To Third Reich Militaria: Detecting The Fakes,* Hippocrene Books, 1989; Jon A. Maguire, *Silver Wings, Pinks & Greens: Uniforms, Wings, & Insignia of USAAF Airmen in World War II,* Schiffer Publishing, 1994; Norman E. Martinus and Harry L. Rinker, *Warman's Paper,* Wallace–Homestead, 1994; Jack Matthews, *Toys Go To War: World War II Military Toys, Games, Puzzles & Books,* Pictorial Histories Publishing, 1994; Walton Rawls, *Disney Dons Dogtags: The Best of Disney Military Insignia from World War II,* Abbeville Publishing, 1992; Jack H. Smith, *Military Postcards 1870–1945,* Wallace–Homestead Book Company, 1988; Sydney B. Vernon, *Vernon's Collector's Guide to Orders, Medals, and Decorations,* published by author, 1986; Richard Windrow and Tim Hawkins, *The World War II GI: US Army Uniforms 1941–45,* Motorbooks International, 1993; Windrow & Greene *Militaria Directory and Sourcebook 1994,* Motorbooks International, 1994.

Periodicals: *Men At Arms,* 222 W. Exchange St., Providence, RI 02903; *Military Collector Magazine,* PO Box 245, Lyon Station, PA, 19536; *Military Collectors' News,* PO Box 702073, Tulsa, OK 74170; *Military History,* 6405 Flank Dr., Harrisburg, PA 17112; *Military Trader,* PO Box 1050, Dubuque, IA 52004; *Wildcat Collectors Journal,* 15158 NE 6 Ave., Miami FL 33162.

Collectors' Clubs: American Society of Military Insignia Collectors, 526 Lafayette Ave., Palmerton, PA 18701; Assoc. of American Military Uniform Collectors, PO Box 1876, Elyria, OH 44036; Company of Military Historians, North Main St., Westbrook, CT 06498; Imperial German Military Collectors Assoc., 82 Atlantic St., Keyport, NJ 07735; Orders and Medals Society of America, PO Box 484, Glassboro, NJ 08028.

Museums: Liberty Memorial Museum, Kansas City, MO; National Infantry Museum, Fort Benning, GA; Seven Acres Antique Village & Museum, Union, IL; The Parris Island Museum, Parris Island, SC; US Air Force Museum, Wright–Patterson AFB, OH; US Army Transportation Museum, Fort Eustis, VA; US Navy Museum, Washington, DC.

Advisor: Harry L. Rinker, Jr.

Armband, 4 x 17½", glossy white oil-cloth, crisply inked red and blue stenciled insignia for Christian Chaplain, unused **20.00**

Auto Attachment, 4 x 6", red, white, and blue litho tin, license plate attachment, slogan "Keep Us Out Of War," late 1930s **65.00**
Bank
 3½" d, 5" l, glossy white ceramic, piggy shape, white, red and black trim, front pig shedding tears, rear image of Hitler face, protruding tail forming nose, coin slot inscribed "Cents 4 Defense," four blunted hoof feet, made by Botay, Kansas City, MO **200.00**
 4½" h, 3½" w, composition eagle figure, solid blue glossy enamel, 1½" d cardboard trap with inscription urging purchase of war bonds and stamps **75.00**
Banner, 11½ x 18", Welcome Home, red, white, and blue linen fabric, gold fringe, hanging rod, cord at top edge **60.00**
Belt Buckle, Nazi **25.00**
Blotter, 3½ x 6", Welcome Home, cardboard, gold Badge of Honor emblem of Honorable Discharge from Armed Forces, congratulatory text sponsored by Massachusetts Life Insurance Co, unused **20.00**
Booklet
 4 x 5¼", The WAC, 32 pages, photos and text related to Women's Army Corps in European Theater of Operations, centerfold art of WAC symbol and ETC map **20.00**
 5¼ x 7¾", Know Your War Planes, early 1940s, sponsored by Coca–Cola, 26 full color illus of American fighting planes in action, 96 warplane silhouettes for US, British, Russian, German, Italian, and Japanese aircraft, full page Coca–Cola ads, full color illus of aviators of various nations drinking bottled Coke **70.00**
Certificate, Worker Award, 8 x 10½", Army–Navy, "E" Worker, stiff white paper, to employee of Davison Chemical Corp, Curtis Bay Works, Baltimore, pre–printed award date, July 5, 1944, name inked in blue . . . **12.00**
Cigarette Case, 3 x 5¼", British War Relief Society, hinged metal case, white enamel, red, white, blue, and gold official symbol on lid, burnished swirl pattern bright gold luster int. . . **35.00**
Clothing
 Cap, overseas, unused **35.00**
 Deck Pants, wool, lined, Navy Dept, contract carrier **30.00**
 Jacket
  British, RAF, green wool, officer's insignia **45.00**

Vest, C-1 Survival, $35.00.

US, Army, bomber type, wool ...	25.00
Pants, US Army, wool, olive	15.00

Shirt, wool, olive, T–3 rank, three hash, mint **15.00**

Decal, 3½ x 4¾", Golden Eagle V–Gas For Victory, full color water transfer, fleshtone hand in victory gesture, dark blue circular background, white letters **30.00**

Entrenching Tool and Carrier, US, painted olive green, stamped "U. S. Ames 1945" **25.00**

Flag, 46" x 8', Army–Navy, "E" Factory, canvas, swallow tailed banner, award for production excellence, tag "Manufactured By Philadelphia Quartermaster Depot/U. S. War Department," three metal grommets, minor wear **700.00**

Greeting Card, 5 x 6", diecut, stiff paper folder, full color patriotic aviation art on front cover, patriotic greeting verse on both panels, references to bond buying, scrap salvage, rationing, Thomas Jefferson quote, unused ... **15.00**

Handkerchief, 9" sq, sheer white fabric, victory symbols and border striping in red and blue **35.00**

Identification Tag (Dog Tag), US, stainless steel, rect, rounded end, bead chain **10.00**

Insignia Guide, 5 x 6½", full color cardboard mechanical dial, shows sleeve chevrons or shoulder insignias of Army and Navy personnel, reverse with full color display of Army, Navy, Coast Guard and Marines as well as medal decorations, used condition **35.00**

Jewelry

 Charm Bracelet, 6½" l, enameled miniature flags of Soviet Union, US, Great Britain, and China, red, white, and blue enameled charm in image of window flag for loved one in service, marked "sterling" **65.00**

Pin, Worker Award, 2½ x 4½" presentation card, individual employee, S. Morgan Smith Co, ⅞" w red, white, blue, and silver luster metal pin, inscribed on reverse "Army Navy Production Award," card reverse with congratulatory form message from President Roosevelt **35.00**

Newspaper, 17 x 23½", May 8, 1945, *Philadelphia Inquirer* Late City Edition, Nazi surrender, V–E announcement, complete 20 page first section, 8 page second section, numerous war news and surrender articles, folded **35.00**

Pin, mechanical, 1⅝" d, "Let's Pull Together," full color litho, lever at left raises and lowers diecut figure of Hitler on hanging noose held by Uncle Sam, orig thin red pull string attached, made by Evans Novelty Co, Chicago **75.00**

Pinback Button

 5/8" d, "Halt Hitler," Jewish sentiment, blue and white, inscription under Star of David **25.00**

 1" d, "V For Victory," full color stylized circular image of flags of US, Great Britain, Greece, and Russia on gold background **20.00**

 1⅛" d, "Psychiana, Spiritual Blitzkrieg," black and white litho tin, illus of Hitler above inscription "Believing That Right Is Superior To Brute Force, I Am Helping To Bring Hitler's Defeat By Repeating Hourly. The Power of Right (God) Will Bring Your Speedy Downfall," copyright 1940 by Psychiana Inc, Moscow, Idaho **75.00**

 1½" d, "Welcome To St Louis USO," red, white, and blue celluloid, added inscription slogan "Friendship and Hospitality" **25.00**

Poster, 19 x 25½", America Calling, Civilian Defense recruitment, red,

Post Card, Curtis Hawk P-40, details on back, one of series of ten, $2.50.

Dexterity Puzzle, Keep 'Em Rolling For Victory, 1 x 3¼ x 5", $75.00.

white, and blue, Poster #423671, issued in 1941 by U. S. Division of Information, Office for Emergency Management **65.00**
Scrapbook, 13½ x 20½", rigid scrapbook, special printed "World War II" cover inscription, printed name of collector, 35 stiff paper album sheets holding over 30 newspaper front pages from Dec 1941 through V–E Day, other mounted clippings, comic strips, etc., lightly browned, good condition **120.00**
Toy, 3½" w, 4" h, 8" l Victory Tank, wood, dark olive green, black cannon barrels, red, white, and blue insignia star decal on turret top and tank front, 4 x 4 x 8" box, made by Richard Appel, New York City **150.00**

WRIGHT, RUSSEL

Collecting Hints: Russel Wright worked for many different companies in addition to creating material under his own label, American Way. Wright's contracts with firms often called for the redesign of pieces which did not produce or sell well. As a result, several lines have the same item in more than one shape.

Wright was totally involved in design. Most collectors focus on his dinnerware; however, he also designed glassware, plastic items, textiles, furniture, and metal objects. Bleached and blonde furniture were part of his contributions. His early work in spun aluminum often is overlooked as is his later work in plastic for the Northern Industrial Chemical Company.

History: Russel Wright was an American industrial engineer with a design passion for domestic efficiency through simple lines. His streamlined influence is found in all aspects of living. Wright and his wife, Mary Small Einstein, wrote *A Guide To Easier Living* to explain the concepts.

Russel Wright was born in 1904 in Lebanon, Ohio. His first jobs included set designer and stage manager under the direction of Norman Bel Geddes. He later used this theatrical flair for his industrial designs, stressing simple clean lines. Some of his earliest designs were executed in polished spun aluminum. These pieces, designed in the mid–1930s, included trays, vases, teapots, and other items. Wright received awards from the Museum of Modern Art in 1950 and 1953. His designs garnered many other awards.

Among the companies for which Russel Wright did design work are Chase Brass and Copper, General Electric, Imperial Glass, National Silver Co., Shenango, and Steubenville Pottery Company. In 1983 a major exhibition of Wright's designs was held at the Hudson River Museum in Yonkers, New York, and at the Smithsonian's Renwick Gallery in Washington, D.C.

References: Susan and Al Bagdade, *Warman's American Pottery and Porcelain*, Wallace–Homestead, 1994; Ann Kerr, *The Collector's Encyclopedia of Russel Wright Designs*, Collector Books, 1990, 1993 value update; Dana Gehman Morykan and Harry L. Rinker, *Warman's Country Antiques & Collectibles, Second Edition* Wallace–Homestead, 1994; Leslie Pina, *Pottery: Modern Wares 1920–1960*, Schiffer Publishing, 1994.

AMERICAN MODERN Made by the Steubenville Pottery Company, 1939–1959. Originally issued in Bean Brown, Chartreuse Curry, Coral, Granite Grey, Seafoam Blue, and White. Later color additions were Black Chutney, Cedar Green, Cantaloupe, Glacier Blue, and Steubenville Blue. The Ideal Toy Company made a set of miniature dishes, which was distributed by Sears, Roebuck.

Baker, small, Cantaloupe	**65.00**
Butter, cov	
Black Chutney	**285.00**
Chartreuse Curry	**285.00**
Coral	**285.00**
Carafe, Granite Grey	**175.00**
Child's Dish, Granite Grey	**50.00**
Coaster, White	**24.00**
Coffeepot, after dinner	
Coral	**65.00**
Granite Grey	**75.00**
Seafoam Blue	**145.00**
Creamer, Granite Grey	**10.00**
Cup and Saucer, Granite Grey	**12.00**
Cup and Saucer, after dinner	
Chartreuse Curry	**20.00**

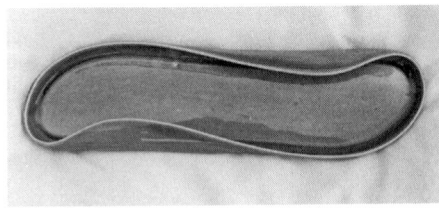

American Modern, celery tray, chartreuse, $12.00.

Coral	20.00
Granite Grey	20.00
Seafoam Blue	20.00
Dinner Service, Seafoam Blue, 74 pcs	600.00
Fruit Bowl, lug handle, Granite Grey	15.00
Hostess Plate	
Chartreuse Curry	75.00
Granite Grey	85.00
Pitcher, Coral, missing lid	65.00
Plate	
6" d, bread and butter, Granite Grey	5.00
8" d, salad, Granite Grey	12.00
10" d, dinner, Granite Grey	10.00
Refrigerator Dish, cov	
Coral	225.00
Granite Grey	165.00
Relish	
Rosette	
Chartreuse Curry	150.00
Granite Grey	165.00
Raffia, Seafoam Blue	185.00
Salad Bowl	
Black Chutney	95.00
Cedar Green	95.00
Soup Bowl, lug handle, Granite Grey	15.00
Stack Server, Cedar Green	245.00
Sugar, Granite Grey	14.00
Teapot, Granite Grey	75.00
Tumbler	
Black Chutney	60.00
Cedar Green	70.00
Chartreuse Curry	55.00
Coral	60.00
Granite Grey	60.00
Vegetable Bowl	
Cedar Green, divided	135.00
Chartreuse Curry, divided	125.00
Granite Grey	22.00
Water Pitcher	
Black Chutney	50.00
Seafoam Blue	100.00

IROQUOIS CASUAL Made by the Iroquois China Company and distributed by Garrison Products, 1946–1960s. Initially issued in Ice Blue, Lemon Yellow, and Sugar White. Later colors produced were Aqua, Avocado Yellow, Brick Red, Cantaloupe, Charcoal, Lettuce Green,

Oyster, Nutmeg Brown, Parsley Green (later called Forest Green), Pink Sherbet, and Ripe Apricot.

Butter, cov	
Avocado Yellow	60.00
Ice Blue	85.00
Lemon Yellow	65.00
Pink Sherbet	75.00
Ripe Apricot	85.00
Sugar White	85.00
Carafe	
Avocado Yellow	175.00
Charcoal	285.00
Ice Blue	125.00
Ripe Apricot	175.00
Casserole, cov, 2 qt	
Avocado Yellow	35.00
Oyster	20.00
Ripe Apricot	20.00
Cereal Bowl, 5" d	
Avocado Yellow	5.00
Cantaloupe	15.00
Oyster	6.00
Cereal Bowl, cov, 5" d	
Avocado Yellow	12.00
Oyster	16.00
Chop Plate, 13" d	
Ripe Apricot	22.00
Sugar White	32.00
Coffeepot, cov	
Ice Blue	135.00
Nutmeg Brown	125.00
Coffeepot, after dinner, cov	
Avocado Yellow	60.00
Nutmeg Brown	75.00
Coffee Service, Nutmeg Brown, 10 pcs	130.00
Creamer and Sugar, cov, stacking	
Avocado Yellow	12.00
Ice Blue	14.00
Sugar White	30.00
Cup and Saucer	
Avocado Yellow	5.00
Charcoal	10.00
Ice Blue	6.00
Lemon Yellow	6.00
Pink Sherbet	6.00
Ripe Apricot	6.00
Sugar White	10.00
Cup and Saucer, after dinner	
Avocado Yellow	150.00
Ice Blue	150.00
Fruit Bowl, 5½" d	
Avocado Yellow	3.50
Ice Blue	3.50
Oyster	7.00
Gumbo	
Ice Blue	35.00
Pink Sherbet	30.00
Mug	
Avocado Yellow	55.00
Ripe Apricot	75.00

Party Plate, 14″ d, Avocado Yellow . . .   **45.00**
Plate
  6½″ d, bread and butter
    Avocado Yellow **2.50**
    Charcoal **5.00**
    Ice Blue **3.50**
    Oyster **4.00**
    Pink Sherbet **3.50**
    Ripe Apricot **3.00**
    Sugar White **6.00**
  7½″ d, salad
    Avocado Yellow **6.00**
    Lemon Yellow **7.00**
    Oyster **8.00**
    Sugar White **10.00**
  9″ d, luncheon
    Avocado Yellow **5.00**
    Ice Blue **6.00**
    Oyster **8.00**
  10″ d, dinner
    Avocado Yellow **6.00**
    Charcoal **10.00**
    Ice Blue **7.00**
    Lemon Yellow **8.00**
    Lettuce Green **8.00**
    Oyster **10.00**
    Sugar White **12.00**
Platter, oval
  12½″ l
    Avocado Yellow **10.00**
    Ice Blue **12.00**
    Nutmeg Brown **12.00**
  14″ l
    Avocado Yellow **45.00**
    Ice Blue **16.00**
    Pink Sherbet **16.00**

Salt and Pepper Shakers, pr, stacking
  Avocado Yellow **8.00**
  Oyster **14.00**
  Sugar White **15.00**
Vegetable Bowl
  8″ d, open
    Avocado Yellow **12.00**
    Ice Blue **14.00**
    Nutmeg Brown **14.00**
    Oyster **15.00**
    Pink Sherbet **14.00**
    Ripe Apricot **14.00**
  10″ d, cov, divided
    Avocado Yellow **16.00**
    Lemon Yellow **18.00**
    Ripe Apricot **16.00**
  10″ d, open
    Avocado Yellow **14.00**
    Nutmeg Brown **16.00**
    Oyster **20.00**

IROQUOIS CASUAL, REDESIGNED In
1959 Iroquois Casual dinnerware was produced in patterns and offered in 45 piece sets, Cookware was another later addition in the re-designed style.

Gravy, Ice Blue **220.00**
Mug
  Apricot Yellow **75.00**
  Ice Blue **65.00**
  Lemon Yellow **70.00**
  Pink Sherbet **65.00**
  Ripe Apricot **65.00**
  Sugar White, Christmas dec **70.00**

INDEX